The Troubling History of Women's Rights in AMERICA

The BOUNDARIES of HER BODY

The Troubling History of
Women's Rights in AMERICA

Debran Rowland

Attorney at Law

SPHINX® PUBLISHING
AN IMPRINT OF SOURCEBOOKS, INC.®
NAPERVILLE, ILLINOIS
www.SphinxLegal.com

First Edition, 2004
Second Printing: November, 2004

Published by: **Sphinx® Publishing, An Imprint of Sourcebooks, Inc.®**

<u>Naperville Office</u>
P.O. Box 4410
Naperville, Illinois 60567-4410
630-961-3900
Fax: 630-961-2168
www.sourcebooks.com
www.SphinxLegal.com

This publication is designed to provide accurate and authoritative information in regard to the subject matter covered. It is sold with the understanding that the publisher is not engaged in rendering legal, accounting, or other professional service. If legal advice or other expert assistance is required, the services of a competent professional person should be sought.
From a Declaration of Principles Jointly Adopted by a Committee of the American Bar Association and a Committee of Publishers and Associations

This product is not a substitute for legal advice.
Disclaimer required by Texas statutes.

Library of Congress Cataloging-in-Publication Data
Rowland, Debran.
  The boundaries of her body : the troubling history of women's rights in america / by Debran Rowland.-- 1st ed.
    p. cm.
  Includes index.
  ISBN 1-57248-368-7 (alk. paper)
  1. Women--Legal status, laws, etc.--United States--History. I. Title.

KF478.R69 2004
342.7308'78--dc22
                                                      2004004012

Printed and bound in the United States of America.

LB 10 9 8 7 6 5 4 3 2

DEDICATION

This book is dedicated to the three men in my life:
Luke, Demetrius, and Maximus.
May they all grow up to be "feminists."

PERSONAL ACKNOWLEDGEMENTS

After working so long on this book, it is impossible for me to convey the gratefulness and the enormous thanks I feel for all of those people who helped me along the way. On a personal level, I thank my family and friends for standing by me and for supporting me during all of the months—and years—it took to get this book done and (finally!!!) get it into print. Specifically, I thank my husband, Luke, and my brother, Demetrius; his wife, Amy; and my two amazing nephews, Little D and Max. I thank my two greatest friends in Chicago who bought me lunch and kept me going—Judge Diane Larsen and Special Assistant Corporation Counsel Dawn Bode. I also thank my two oldest friends and their families—Kim, Vincent, and Solange van Doorn and Kathleen H. Dickerson and Carlos, Gail, and Julian Figueroa.

Thanks must also be given to the people involved in the actual "making" of this book. A heartfelt thanks goes to Mark Warda, who originally recruited me for this project, and to Deb Werksman, who was so interested in seeing this book come about, there was a time when she would call me every week. Further, I would like to acknowledge the efforts of all of the folks in editorial and marketing at Sourcebooks, Inc., who shepherded this book through the editing process and on to bookstore shelves. Many of them I don't know by name. But some of them I do. Thanks to Todd Stocke, Jill Amack, and Michelle Schoob in editorial; Mike Bowen who swam the sea of endnotes; to Kelly Barrales-Saylor, who put the scattered pieces together in a comprehensible, readable way; to Megan Dempster for a cover I love; to Dianne Wheeler, who heads Sphinx Publishing (an imprint of Sourcebooks, Inc.); to Dominique Raccah for wanting to see this book published; and, to Christine Lock Garcia, whose job in getting the word out, has just begun.

But most of all, I would like to thank Ray Bennett, who read and reread, and worked and reworked this book with me until it was finished. By the end, it was a far better book than it might have been otherwise. My most profound thanks to Ray for all of his help.

Debran Rowland

PROFESSIONAL ACKNOWLEDGEMENTS

I would like to thank all of the publishers and authors who were kind enough to permit me to use excerpts from their publications. Where these excerpts were used, specific notation is made in the endnote in the citation form used, which is usually as offered by the publishers and included as per their specific reference.

Debran Rowland

CONTENTS

INTRODUCTION

The Politics of Biology—
The Essence of Control

"PBS's *NOW with Bill Moyers* tonight will examine claims that recent government policies, regulations, and executive orders are part of an 'organized campaign aimed at rolling back women's reproductive rights'" said the email forwarded to me by my publisher. "The segment, titled, 'Politics of Choice,' will explore federal actions, including the legislation that would ban so-called 'partial-birth' abortion[;] bill (HR 760); the Unborn Victims of Violence Act, a bill introduced in both the House (HR 1997) and the Senate (S 1019) that would make harming a fetus while committing a federal criminal act [,] a separate crime; the White House's so-called 'Mexico City' policy, which prohibits federal aid from going to groups that fund or counsel on abortion; and the Bush administrator's final regulation allowing states to define fetuses as 'unborn children' eligible for health coverage under the State Children's Health Insurance Program," the email continued.

I marked my calendar and went back to work. Since 1999, I had been working on a women's rights book. And by the time of the email, I was on intimate terms with the cycle of advances and digressions characterizing women's rights in America, historically and today. More specifically, I had come to know the arguments, accusations, ideologies and pervasive extremes offered as evidence of the various claims by the various interests in an emotional, and often polarized, debate. A debate over what a woman *is*; what a woman *ought* to be; and what a woman should, therefore, be *allowed to do*.

It is a long-lived debate, peppered in the last two centuries by a handful of hard-won victories occasionally granting women rights and privileges deemed "naturally" held by men. Far more numerous during this period, however, were hard-fought defeats foreclosing those rights to women, especially in the early days of the American nation. The reason often advanced for these denials was that women were *women*.

Biological differences between men and women have historically been read to mean that women were "dumber" and "weaker" and, thus, in need of the paternal protection of fathers, husbands, and sometimes even sons. But the construction of women as wards has always been multifaceted in the way that a house of cards is multifaceted. Because women bore children, it has often been argued—indeed, *understood*—that by God and nature women had been assigned the "divine mission" of motherhood.

To men—and to many of the women—of this time, motherhood was a godly thing, blissful in its achievement (especially when the children were male), and of utilitarian benefit to mankind. It also happened to be one of the few areas of human life where the abilities of women were recognized as superior to those of men. But as with all swords, there was a double edge. The notion of women as mothers soon turned towards the broader understanding that a woman's place was solely within the home. The "addled" minds and "weaker constitutions" of women added further to this understanding.

In light of the contemporary debate, ancient "understandings" of this kind are easily labeled misogynist or oppressive. But in terms of history, some scholars suggest that the woman-as-subordinate construct served as useful a purpose in the new world as it had in England by establishing the hierarchical framework "necessary" for the formation of a well-ordered society. State and territory leaders—like the American Founding Fathers later—were grounding states, territories, and eventually a nation. There had to be rules.

By limiting the roles of women to wives and mothers in the burgeoning United States, women became helpers to husbands, caretakers of the home; appendixes to men, their civil identities literally "absorbed" into those of their husbands upon marriage. As such, they remained the subordinates of spouses and fathers. Married women, like children, were the wards of men.

Is it really a surprise, then, that the Founding Fathers would decide—either by conscious deliberation or unconscious acceptance—that women need not be mentioned in the grounding documents of our nation? Men saw women the way parents saw children. But this absence would eventually raise questions. As subordinates with no expressed mention of rights in the United States Constitution, leaders and lawmakers reasoned and assumed that women were deserving of, and, indeed, could only be granted, a lesser array of rights and privileges. If this were not so, women would be equal and the hierarchy would crumble.

This may have worked for men. But by the mid-nineteenth century, women were asking for a clarification of their status in court. Were they "citizens" entitled to the protection of the Privileges and Immunities Clause of the United States Constitution? According to the Justices of the United States Supreme Court, they were not. Were women free to choose professions? Not unless the state they lived in permitted it, the Justices held. Could they vote? Not until 1920, when the Nineteenth Amendment was ratified, overruling a Supreme Court decision.[1]

The status of women in America remained unsettled in many areas well into the mid-twentieth century, with the exception of a few distinct areas. Among them was the interracial, "inter-status" marriage to slaves. In that case, women *foolish enough* to enter so "shameful" a union assumed the status of their husbands.[2] Again, in the context of history, this made sense to the leaders of a scrappy new nation struggling into being.

Whatever their beliefs in "natural law" and "greater superiority," to the Founding Fathers, landed-gentry, and plantation owners of the times, free labor was a necessary component to building a nation and an undeniable asset to building wealth. Slaves and indentured servants were that labor, though they were of distinctively separate classes. Indentured servants, overwhelmingly of European descent, were "whole," but "bound" men, while slaves, overwhelmingly of African descent, were "part" men mentioned in the United States Constitution only for purposes of taxation.[3]

But even that stood in contrast to women. Though slaves had no rights in early America, the fact that they were mentioned, even as "three fifths" men for purposes of taxation, offers a point of comparison for women. Like slaves, rights for women were never expressly enumerated in the original articles of the Constitution. Unlike slaves, absent was any "measure" of women.

For women, there was neither express inclusion, nor exclusion. Rather, there was silence, raising the emerging question during the nineteenth century of what rights women were to have in their new land. British common law tradition suggested that women were to have no independent or individual rights. Instead, they would derive rights, once married. And it was the goal of every woman to be married.

Many early American states adopted similar laws, and thus entered similarly hierarchical relationships with women. As a result, women in the early United States were often not allowed to own land or other real property. Further, the question of whether a woman's private property could still be called "hers" after marriage remained open in many states, with some lawmakers concluding that upon marriage, even a woman's dresses became the possession of her husband. Women could not enter into contracts or file lawsuits without the permission or assistance of husbands, which tended to foreclose participation in white-collar professions.

But women—or perhaps more precisely, husbands on behalf of their wives—would eventually bring suit, challenging these and other laws. Still, it wasn't until the mid-twentieth century that things began to change for women. For example, not until the 1960s did the United States Supreme Court recognize certain "zones of privacy" for women, which would later form the basis for many of the landmark decisions of this period. By contrast, as far back as the 1600s, certain "zones of privacy" were deemed legally to exist for men.[4]

A seventeenth century Massachusetts law that would set the tone for the laws of other New England colonies provided, for example, that male magistrates, jurors, and other various "officers" were not "bound to inform, present, or reveal any private crime or offence, wherein there is no peril or danger to this plantation or any member thereof, when any necessary tie of conscience binds him to secrecy grounded upon the word of god, unless it be in case of testimony lawfully required."[5]

Secrecy laws of this kind were justified by the lawmakers of the time as protective of "family privacy." They tended in reality most often, however, to protect the privacy of men. The private acts and conversations of women were not similarly protected, historian Mary Beth Norton suggests, noting, for example, that in 1646, New Haven authorities "did not hesitate to prosecute a group of three women—the mistress of the household, her mother, and a friend—for speaking contemptuously of the colony's political and religious leaders." A male servant apparently reported the content of the conversation to a nosy neighbor.[6]

With no protection for personal conversations taking place within the space of their own homes, it should come as no surprise that it wasn't until the early 1960s that American courts began advancing these kinds of "family" privacy protections to women. But why the three-century wait? And why such clear difficulty defining the rights and status of women in a land whose Founding Fathers evidently believed in the unequivocal enumeration of rights?

Because the rights of women are—and always have been—hopelessly tangled in that political and cultural imbroglio of religion, "natural law," arguments purporting to assert the *common good*, and ancient themes of female subordination and procreative obligation. Untangling this tapestry of conflict is what this book is about. And we will take it step by step, starting with the most ancient of structural elements: religion.

From the many faces of Mary to her most enduring contrast, Eve, religion has always played a role in the lives of women. Church "fathers" extolled the virtues of chastity, obedience, and female subordination.[7] Social leaders—also often the religious and the wealthy (few others had the status to be admitted)— became the *de facto* lawmakers of the young states, finding frequent rationale and resolve in the passages of the Bible. Adding to the mix was a fledgling Supreme Court whose justices praised the godly gift of procreation and the women who would do the nation proud in honoring it. These are the narratives of American history that will be covered in *Chapter One*.

But there has always been more to the equation than religion. There has also been sex. Women have long derived value from their ability to bear children: heirs in feudal times,[8] extra hands in agricultural times,[9] "mothers of the nation" in the eighteenth and nineteenth century;[10] or just plain obligated— unfairly or not—to carry an "unborn child" to term, antichoice advocates argue today. Arguments of this sort led prosecutors to assert in 1914 that Margaret Sanger's efforts in distributing information on birth control was equivalent to disseminating "...articles advocating bomb throwing and assassination."[11] And that is where "sex" comes in.

Until recently, a woman could not become pregnant without sex. And, thus, sex has always been a problem for women. Or more precisely, the possibility that a woman might have sex for reasons other than procreation has always been a problem for women. Sexual conduct and female reproduction has been intertwined historically around notions of identity and proper social roles: women bore children and took care of the family *they* had invented. But what if a woman did not intend to bear children? Could she still have sex?

An independent female sexual identity, one devoid of maternal instincts or disinclined to have heirs, has been perceived throughout history as nothing less than dangerous. Dangerous to families suffering the taint of a daughter's less-than-virtuous conduct. Dangerous to women, who were "more prone" to spread and suffer disease than men. Dangerous to men, who might "catch" these diseases and/or suffer the stain of "bastardy" proceedings.

But most of all, "unchaste" women were dangerous to society, capable of unraveling the delicate fibers and disconnecting the threads of their new community with a single tug of their corset strings. Or so it was argued by prosecutors as the men of the time moved with swift determination to suppress any and all discussion of birth control. Thus, Margaret Sanger became a "bomb thrower" and rules regarding "quickening"—the predecessors of modern abortion laws—began to take shape.

To be sure, women fought back in favor of birth control, though generally in smaller numbers and with little clear success. Contraceptives would save lives, early advocates argued. No, no, it would take lives, opponents argued. Of course, the "lives" involved were different. Women were arguing on behalf of women, who were dying in childbirth or as a result of botched or self-induced abortions. Men were arguing on behalf of the "unborn children" and "families denied," given the selfish, "unsacrificing" attitude of women.

Though the perspectives were clearly different, central to both sides of the debate was the "coming apart" of the relationship between sexual activity and reproduction and all that has come to mean. Which was, in fact, the problem: the widespread use of birth control had the potential to render inconsequential an act that was meant by God and nature to lead to children. Discussion of these issues can be found in *Chapter Two*.

In early America, the ability of women to conceive and carry children also foreclosed their rights to choose professions and sometimes to work at all. Seventeenth century scholars spoke glowingly of a woman's "desire...to bee [*sic*] married."[12] With marriage came conception, pregnancy, child birth and motherhood—all of which seemed to trouble judges and lawmakers of the time. State officials sought to "protect" women from unscrupulous employers and perhaps themselves by limiting the hours they could work. This, they argued, was for the good of mankind.

Judges in the nation's courts—among them the Justices of the United States Supreme Court—agreed, holding in case after case (with rare exception during the first half of the twentieth century) that the mission of motherhood and orderly function of the home were enough to justify limiting working hours for women. With the exception of pornography, in industries across the board, women have always earned less than men. Thus, limiting the working hours of women literally meant limiting the lives of women.

For "properly married" women, this mattered less, of course, than for women who had married less well or women who had not married at all. Tossing a monkey wrench in all of the works, however, were "well married" women who chose not only to work, but also to attempt to enter the ranks of the higher professions. They failed. So did politicians and lawmakers seeking to set a "protective" minimum wage for women. As it happens, this measure was challenged by women on both sides, setting the stage for the modern-day debate over "protective" legislation versus discriminatory legislation. *Chapter Three* will cover these issues.

Women have always worked in America, despite the hurdles; their traditional presence apparent in the "womanly" professions. Despite public objections and limited work hours, by the turn of the twentieth century women crowded factory floors, sewing shirts or handling laundry. Women were nurses like Sanger. And bakers. They cleaned houses and cared for children. Occasionally they became teachers. Even more occasionally, lawyers and doctors, their numbers growing steadily, but slowly, each year until the Second World War.

World War II marked a turning point in American history for women. With the assertive propaganda of Rosie the Riveter to encourage them, women entered the workforce in record numbers, filling jobs that would ordinarily have been held by men. Following the war's end, women were pushed out of the labor force as men reclaimed jobs and the "baby boom" generation was conceived. But the extraordinary absence of men seemed to open a door for women, who began to slip quietly back into the workforce almost as soon as they were ousted. And would continue to do so steadily for the next two decades.

With the presence of women firmly established, the workplace was due for a few changes. But these changes were about battle and an uncomfortable ground shift. Women were claiming space in once all-male offices and later all-male professions, putting men with families to support out of work. This angered a great many men, and the debate spawned by that anger resembled modern antiaffirmative action arguments. Women, opponents said, were not as "strong" or as "smart" as men. And they certainly did not have a head for business. Thus, they had no business doing the jobs *of men*. Women should be home taking care of the children. Not competing with men.

Informing every aspect of the debate, of course, was procreation and the fact that women could—and did—get pregnant and have babies. But there were also the changing times to be considered. During the 1940s and early 1950s, working women tended overwhelmingly to be lower-class women, at times desperate, often in need of cash for survival. But by the 1960s, women were turning work into professions and they were looking for careers that would allow them greater freedoms and choices.

In other words, women intended to work and to have jobs to return to should they decide to have children (and at this point, there was, in fact, still very little choice). The only problem was that without laws to protect them, women were routinely fired for doing "what comes naturally," further proving to some that women had no business in the work place. That had to change. *Chapter Four* will provide an overview of this period in history and the changes that would begin to shape the modern workplace.

Of course, real change never takes place in a vacuum. And by the late 1950s and early 60s, a chain reaction of events had been set into motion that would change the course of American history. Laws separating facilities along racial lines were called into question as civil and women's rights movements gained momentum. Driven by protests and headline-grabbing sit-ins, response to these events was a reverse domino-effect of new laws and legislature.

A watered-down Civil Rights Act was passed in the late 1950s, for example, by representatives still bristling at the thought of widespread change, only to be revised by Congress—giving it back "its teeth"—and repassed in 1964. During this same period, the United States Supreme Court was making new law as well. Whether in recognition of the place women now held in the workforce, the women's movement, or simply because it was time, the Justices began to separate the identity of "woman" from that of "wife" and "mother," and to concede that there could be one without the others.

Reviving the earlier notion of familial "zones of privacy," the Justices ruled in 1963 that husbands and wives were entitled to make the decision of whether or not to have children privately. Decisions permitting single women to similarly choose birth control and later abortion followed with a majority of the Justices extending the "right of privacy" to women, a right allowing them to "choose" whether or not they would become mothers. Though this decision has been challenged nearly every day since it was handed down and has led to more than twenty decisions by the United States Supreme Court, so far it has stood. An overview of these decisions and the background of the time frame can be found in *Chapter Five*.

Of course, "the state" has always had a greater interest in women choosing "motherhood" than not. Citizens and society were at stake, it was historically argued. But by the 1960s, women were part of the workforce and they had finally emerged as a full-blown political constituency in their own right. And the coupling of these realities allowed for a different kind of choice: the choice to have children and to continue to work. Legislation was passed to make that possible.

The Civil Rights Act of 1964 prohibited discrimination based upon race and gender. Though "gender discrimination" was not formally defined until 1978, challenges were immediately brought under the Act, as well under the Due Process and Equal Protection Clauses of the United States Constitution. The cases of the 1960s and '70s form the spine of *Chapter Six*.

But sorting out the ultimate meaning of a new law takes time, and for the next two decades immediately following the passage of Title VII of the Civil Rights Acts of 1964, courts argued back and forth over whether the protections it offered were meant to be a "sword" or a "shield." Congress did attempt to clarify the meaning of the Act in 1977, by amending Title VII to include the Pregnancy Discrimination Act.

Between 1978, when then-President Jimmy Carter signed the bill into law and the late 1990s, when the law would take a quantum leap in the direction women's rights advocates had always hoped to move it, nearly every manner of challenge was brought under the Pregnancy Discrimination Act, beginning with an initial challenge brought by a man seeking benefits coverage, to a bank receptionist whose attempts to reclaim her job would steer the debate towards the dangerous eddy of "protectionism."

Feminists would join conservatives on both sides of the aisle in the battle over the "proper" reach of the Pregnancy Discrimination Act and the meaning of Title VII overall, given the inclusion of language prohibiting discrimination based upon "gender." The language of Title VII has been read to prohibit discrimination based upon gender. The measure, along with the Pregnancy Discrimination Act, was used initially to challenge discriminatory policies and practices associated with pregnancy or a related condition. But Title VII would eventually emerge, specially during the late 1990s, as a formidable tool against "sexual harassment" (*i.e.*, harassment based solely upon gender). Cases involving an overview of this area of the law can be found in *Chapter Seven*.

Though sexual harassment issues create a fervor all their own, the area of the law that remains the most emotionally and politically contentious is reproductive rights. The debate over procreation, sexual choice, and pleasure have always been linked. In the historic context, these issues were exclusively part of the debate of what conduct should be regulated by the state. But in the last two decades, issues of sexual intimacy have turned on the question of *natural* procreation.

Despite the monumental changes that have taken place across the nation in the last two decades, the United States Supreme Court was still debating "sodomy" as it related to homosexuality in 2003. It was a debate, however, that until recently didn't get any better on the state level. Alabama authorities moved in 1998, for example, to prevent the purchase and sale of sexual stimulation devices as violative of state law.

The American Civil Liberties Union filed suit against the state on behalf of six women, alleging that the Alabama law placed an undue burden on their right to privacy.[13] Central to both the Alabama and Supreme Court sodomy cases (and their corresponding high-profile challenges) was the question of what sexual acts a person *should* be allowed to engage in when those acts have no clear relationship to traditional notions of "family" and will never "naturally" lead to children.

The use of words like "naturally" or "should" has never been accidental with regard to this debate. Rather, authoritative words of this sort have long been used to connote what some deem the "essence" of the issue: the "natural" biology of mankind and the gifts God has allowed. And that seems to be where some people would like to see reproductive issues remain—chained to procreation—despite the legal and scientific advances and social changes of the past three decades. Thus, they have done all they can in recent years to keep "God" in the picture.

In that sense, women today are living through one of the most politically provocative and historically significant periods since the 1960s and early 70s, when most of the landmark reproductive rights decisions were handed down. Those decisions changed the course of American history, and that is what makes the current times so extraordinary. Nearly every year since 1973, when the United States Supreme Court issued the decision in *Roe v. Wade*—considered by many to be the most seminal of the reproductive rights cases—that ruling has been challenged with a mind towards overturning it.

So far, those efforts have failed. But even so, they have resulted in more than twenty "follow-up" decisions by the United States Supreme Court, more than in any other single area of the law during that same period. And these challenges have not diminished. They have merely changed or taken new form. In that regard, the next threat, scholars and feminists argue, may come from the United States Supreme Court itself.

Speculation ran wild during the summer of 2003 that at least one, but perhaps as many as three, of the aging Justices on the Court could retire in the next two years, opening the door to the appointment of that many new, and almost certainly, conservative Justices opposed to abortion. President George W. Bush, the man whose administration would likely do the appointing, staunchly opposes abortion and is known to be a zealously religious man. His administration has already attempted to pedal an antiabortion, anticivil rights slate of jurists on the lower federal level.

Adopting the view that life begins at "conception," members of the George W. Bush administration have: moved to extend medical benefits to "unborn children" and authored legislation that would recognize "unborn children" as the victims of federal crimes. These measures are contrary, of course, to the law established by the United States Supreme Court decision in *Roe v. Wade*. They also stand in defiance of long-standing public policy that did not recognize *fetuses*—as opposed to the "unborn"—until they were born alive, acknowledging, of course, that even under the best of circumstances, not every "child" is born alive.

The Bush administration has also: pushed initiatives prohibiting certain late-term abortion procedures; reversed the Clinton-era policy of providing financial support to international family planning groups; and announced its intentions to "revisit" the Food and Drug Administration's approval of medical abortion protocol RU 486, citing "safety concerns." And if appointments in and of themselves are any indication of the administration's intent to finally get the job done, during the first few months in office, the Bush administration announced the appointment of John Ashcroft as attorney general.[14] Ashcroft, a conservative Christian and staunch antiabortion opponent, presided over challenges to *Roe v. Wade* while attorney general of Missouri.[15]

And yet, these are among the more obvious attempts at change. In recent years, a war of words that has always involved turning one man's "facts" into another man's "polemics," has escalated and gone underground, emerging into the public eye only occasionally in an abrasive campaign of guerrilla tactics as questionable in their legality, some scholars say, as in their dishonesty.

In the spring of 2003, for example, charges flew after the National Cancer Institute published research findings in a fact sheet. The findings showed no evidence of a scientific link between an increased risk of breast cancer and abortion. Research literature does suggest that women who have no children may face a slightly elevated risk of breast cancer. But there appears to be no similar link for women who have had abortions, NCI researchers reported.

Antiabortion activists have long argued, however, that there is such a link. And some twenty-eight of them—who also happened to be members of Congress—demanded removal of the information from the agency's website, challenging the sheet as "scientifically inaccurate and misleading." The information was removed, a measure that infuriated pro-choice politicians, who then charged in response that scientific information posted on an official government website had been changed to reflect the antichoice agenda of the current White House.

These and other similar efforts resulted in the summer of 2003 in the publication of a 40-page report by the minority staff of the House Committee on Government Reform, which found that "[t]he administration's political interference with science has led to misleading statements by the president, inaccurate responses to Congress, altered websites, suppressed agency reports, erroneous international communications and the gagging of scientists."[16]

These are aggressive moves, concerted efforts in the politics of disassembly by an administration and like-minded supporters willing to use every conceivable back door to undermine public policy and the law because they simply do not agree with it. An overview of these issues will be covered in *Chapter Eight* of this book.

Of course, issues of reproductive rights fold into the larger context of American society. In the last three decades, sweeping change was apparent in many areas of American society. For women, change was perhaps most apparent in the gains made in the education arena. The rate of college enrollment rose for women between 1980 and 1990, until it finally began to approach that of men.[17] At the same time, the percentage of women entering traditionally "male" fields also rose—from one percent in 1980 for women graduating with majors in engineering to 14 percent by 1990.[18]

Gains were also made on the graduate level, where in 1970, only 9 percent of all business degrees earned went to women. But by 1997, that number had risen to 47 percent of all degrees earned.[19] There was also progress in the field of law. In 1970, only 10 percent of the students entering law school were women. But by 2001, 49.4 percent of the 43,518 first-year students entering laws schools across the country were women.[20] Women entering medical school had also neared the 50 percent range by 2003, up from 25 percent in 1975.[21]

But these gains have not automatically translated into gains in the working world. Although women made up nearly half of all law school students, the opportunities appear to be fewer once women leave school.[22] The challenge of monetary equality also remains an issue. Although experts reported that by the mid-1990s there were more than 100,000 decamillionaires—people with a personal worth of $10 million or more—in the country, a relative few were women.

In addition, though women narrowed the wage gap some during the 1980s,[23] scholars note that for many women, the lion's share of these gains was consumed by the day-to-day necessities of life.[24] At the same time, the number of female-headed households increased, suggesting that while wealth seemed to grow, women with children remained among the poorest Americans.[25]

Specifically, single-wage, single-headed households accounted for nearly half of all poor families.[26] This remained true despite "the New Economy" of the 1990s, when many Americans appeared to ride the technology bubble to greater wealth. Today, despite more advanced degrees, more education, and more women in the workforce women still earn roughly 76 cents for every dollar a man earns. These issues of inequity will be discussed in *Chapter Nine*.

In addition to progress on the work front, there was progress in the area of assisted reproduction, which has reportedly grown in the last two decades into a billion-dollar a year industry.[27] Among the modes of reproduction available to women today are *in vitro* fertilization, embryo storage, egg and sperm donors, the retrieval of semen from dead "fathers," and the fast-approaching possibility of human cloning.

Pleasure, procreation, and sexual choice have always been linked. As a result, there have always been questions of how far women (and others "outside of the mainstream") should be allowed to go. Throughout the 1960s and 1970s, privacy issues turned the tables of state-regulated permissibility, and the advances—scientific as well as legal—pushed issues of intimate "choice" even further. Today, that "choice" involves scientifically advanced methods of overcoming "nature's failing." Those methods, along with an overview of the social and legal implications of science in the womb will be discussed in *Chapter Ten*.

Of course, the vast majority of children are still "made" the old-fashioned way. But *natural* reproduction still requires sex, or something like it. Indeed, one of the biological truths about procreation is that whenever there is a pregnancy, there has been unprotected sex. And sex of all varieties has shown itself to be the more frequent practice of women on college campuses, according to a 2001 survey published by the Independent Women's Forum.[28]

Increasingly casual sexual practices have led, however, to the increased spread of sexually transmitted diseases, some argue. In 1999, for example, the national rates of gonorrhea, syphilis, and HPV—the virus responsible for several other infections, including genital warts and cervical cancer—rose after a long period of decline.[29] Though men have traditionally comprised the majority of people living with HIV in the United States and continue to do so today, the rate of infection among heterosexual women rose steadily throughout the 1990s, with thousands of new infections the direct result of unprotected sex with an infected male partner.[30]

But the spread of sexually transmitted disease—be it deliberate or negligent—has opened the door to litigation.[31] Suits grounded in assertions of "sexual deception" or involving allegations of "sexual fraud" or "fraudulent coupling" are increasingly common today. These and other related issues will be covered in *Chapter Eleven*.

By contrast, there are the lives and "couplings" of girls. For every hurdle an adult woman faces, there are at least two for girls. Adolescence is a time of confounding realities, when peers, the media, popular culture, and even a young woman's body may dictate who she is or is thought to be. The contradiction of these years is most apparent, of course, where an adolescent *looks* the part of an "adult woman." And girls more and more often *look* like women.

A young woman may be "sexualized" long before she is able legally, in most states, to consent to sex. Her contemporary male peers and often adult men as well, may take a sexual interest in her. And yet, regardless of how she dresses and/or of how boys and men respond to her, the adolescent girl remains in most states and by most legal definitions "a minor child" legally incapable prior to a certain age of consenting to those acts generally thought to make a girl a "woman."[32] So who is the adolescent girl today? These and other questions and issues will be discussed in *Chapter Twelve*.

Issues of violence comprise the final three chapters of this book. Every day across America, women are battered, beaten, raped, and killed. In 1994 for example, women survived[33] five million violent "victimizations."[34] In more specific terms, "women age 12 or older" survived more than 400,000 rapes or sexual assaults, nearly half a million robberies, close to a million aggravated assaults, and more than 3 million simple assaults.

In 1999, three out of every 1,000 women in the United States was raped or sexually assaulted,[35] and nearly 5,000 women 12 or older were murdered.[36] A million women are stalked each year,[37] and when they are attacked, women are "more likely than [men][38] to sustain an injury."[39] About a quarter of the time, weapons are used against women.[40] Women are most likely to be victimized at a private home (their own or that of a neighbor, friend, or relative).[41]

And yet, as often as there are crimes against women, there are attempted defenses, some as degrading as the violence itself. And where there are charges of rape, there are often suggestions of "consensual" sex.[42] To a charge of "date rape,"[43] there may be talk of an "obsessed" woman crying-wolf or falsely accusing as a form of revenge, for example.[44] Newer to the mix are "date rape drugs."[45] An overview of these and other issues will be discussed in *Chapters Thirteen, Fourteen*, and *Fifteen*.

ENDNOTES FOR INTRODUCTION

1   The Nineteenth Amendment was ratified in August of 1920. The ratification overruled the United States Supreme Court's decision in *Minor v. Happersett*, 88 U.S. (21 Wall.) 162 (1875). But even that was not without controversy. Some suggested that as the abolition of slavery movement grew, "[t]he argument for suffrage...became more expedient: white women's votes would balance those of newly enfranchised black males and immigrants. The majority that ratified the 19th Amendment in 1920 was built on these racist grounds." *See* Natalie Zemon Davis & Jill Ker Conway, *The Rest of the Story*, N.Y. TIMES MAG., May 16, 1999, Sec. 6, at p. 84.

2   *See* Mary Beth Norton, FOUNDING MOTHERS & FATHERS: GENDERED POWER AND THE FORMING OF AMERICAN SOCIETY (New York: Alfred A. Knopf, 1996), at p. 72. (Norton notes that during discussion of the state's first slave code, members of the Maryland assembly held, given the "shame" of

such matches, that "'whatsoever free borne woman shall intermarry with any slave from and after the Last day of this present Assembly shall Serve the master of such slave during the life of her husband And that all the Issue of such freeborne women soe marryed shall be Slaves as their fathers were.'" In addition, "[c]hildren already born from such unions were ordered to serve their father's master until they reached the age of thirty" (citing MARYLAND ARCHIVES I, 527, 533–534).)

3   The Founding Fathers set forth in Article I, Section 2, paragraph 3 of the United States Constitution that "[R]epresentatives and direct Taxes shall be apportioned among the several States which may be included within this Union, according to their respective Numbers, which shall be determined by adding to the whole Number of free Persons, including those bound to Service for a Term of Years, and excluding Indians not taxed, **three fifths of all other Persons.**" That language was later relied upon by Justice Taney in the *Dred Scott* decision in reaching the conclusion that slaves and their descents were only "three-fifths" of men. Section 2 of the Fourteenth Amendment, adopted after the Civil War—which some scholars argued was brought on by the *Dred Scott* decision— effectively rendered this language meaningless.

4   *See* Norton, *supra* note 2, at pp. 43–45.

5   *Id.* at 44 (citing Massachusetts Bay General Court approved BODY OF LIBERTIES, 226 (1641) and the LAWS AND LIBERTIES, 47). (The language of the text has been edited to reflect modern spellings and abbreviations. The actual language and context of this quote is as follows: "In the province's first comprehensive legal code, the Body of Liberties (1641), using language that was also later incorporated into the Laws and Liberties (1648), the General Court provided that '[n]o Maestrate, Juror, Officer or other man shall be bound to inform[e], present, or reveal[e] any private crim[e] or offence, wherein there is no perill or danger to this plantation or any member thereof, when any necessarie tye of conscience binds him to secresie grounded upon the word of god, unlesse it be in case of testimony lawfully required.'")

6   *Id.*

7   *See* Cullen Murphy, THE WORD ACCORDING TO EVE: WOMEN AND THE BIBLE IN AN ANCIENT TIMES AND OUR OWN (London: Allen Lane, The Penguin Press, 1998), at pp. 15–16. ("In the New Testament, the duties and the proper place of women are delineated by what are known as household codes, rules governing private behavior in and outside the home. In the Hebrew Bible, the book of Leviticus by its nature is concerned with rules—it is, in essence, a book of instructions and laws, for the use of priests—and among its many strictures are those governing personal behavior as it relates to cultic purity and impurity and hence governing menstruation, sexual relations, and childbearing. Women, in the view of these codes, represent a very real threat to purity. A palpable sense of threat ('Give not your strength to women') emerges too even from the accessible poetry of Proverbs, a more congenial and kindred book than Leviticus to a modern reader. The famous 'woman of worth' passage at the very end of the book (PROVERBS 31:10-31), which defines the qualities of an ideal wife, is noteworthy for expressing this ideal exclusively from the point of view of the husband and the household:

The heart of her husband trusts in her,
and he will have no lack of gain.
She does him good, and not harm,
all the days of her life.
She seeks wool and flax,
and works with willing hands.
She is like the ships of the merchant,
she brings her food from afar.

The Bible is the best-selling book in the world. It has been and still is presumed by hundreds of millions of people to speak with authority, both explicitly through precept and implicitly through what it holds up by way of example. That authority, though it falls along a broad spectrum of fastidiousness, has helped to enforce what it prescribes.")

8   *See* Laura M. Otten, WOMEN'S RIGHTS AND THE LAW, (Westport, Connecticut: Praeger 1993), at p. 36. (America began as a British colony, and England turned to feudalism in the thirteenth century. Thus, it should come as no surprise that those fingerprints have always been felt on American life.) ("With the introduction of feudalism in the thirteenth century, and the fief's replacement of the family as the important legal and economic unit, women were no longer valued for their economic productivity," says Otten. "Instead, with this loss of status, women became valued solely for their procreative abilities—namely the ability, as wives, to produce legitimate heirs, thereby enhancing men's status, since a man's status was directly proportionate to his property and number of heirs. As part of this valuation process that established a woman's worth only as a wife and mother, laws were passed defining single women as 'surplus labor.' These laws were accompanied by additional legislation setting women's wages lower than those of males. Even when such laws were not on the books, it became practice to pay women lower wages. Thus, women were either forced to exist at a marginal level of subsistence or to engaged in one of the three traditional arenas for single women to enter: domestic service, prostitution, or marriage.")

9   For discussion, *see* Mary P. Ryan, WOMANHOOD IN AMERICA FROM COLONIAL TIMES TO THE PRESENT (New York: Franklin Watts, Inc., 1975), at p. 162.

10   *See, e.g.,* Ann Ferguson, BLOOD AT THE ROOT: MOTHERHOOD, SEXUALITY & MALE DOMINANCE (London, England: Pandora Press, 1989), at pp. 102–103. (According to Ferguson, several kinds of patriarchies have existed and served to control women's lives. Among them was the "father patriarchy," prevalent in feudal Europe and colonial America, in which "fathers exercise[d] coercive control over the resources of the family economy (itself the only available source of income other than the army or the church) available to their children. Households are usually not nuclear but extended in two senses: first, they may contain the older generation relatives and unmarried relatives; second, they may contain servants and apprentices, usually young relatives 'put out' from their family of origin to learn a trade. [¶] In such extended family households, some class relations were often internal to the household: the father was the master not only of his own children and wife but of indentured servants and young apprentices. In the South under slavery, his situation was even more despotic, since he had slaves over whom he had complete sexual and reproductive control. [¶] The father in the father-patriarchal household owned the family property and dispensed it at will to his children, the land to sons and a lesser dowry to daughters. The father was the religious/moral head of the household. Children needed their father's permission to marry and were completely dependent on his largesse in inheritance. A woman's sexuality was controlled first by her father, then by her husband or male relatives if she remained single.")

11   *See* Margaret Sanger, AN AUTOBIOGRAPHY (New York: W.W. Norton, 1938), at p. 115. (Wrote Sanger in recounting the experience, "August twenty-fifth I was arraigned in the old Post Office way downtown. Judge Hazel, himself a father of eight or nine children, was kindly, and I suspected the two Federal agents who had summoned me had spoken a good word on my behalf. But Assistant District Attorney Harold A. Content seemed a ferocious young fellow. When the Judge asked, "What sort of things is Mrs. Sanger doing to violate the law?" he answered, "She's printing articles advocating bomb throwing and assassination." [¶] "Mrs. Sanger doesn't look like a bomb thrower or an assassin," [the judge said.] [¶] Mr. Content murmured something about not all being gold that glittered; I was doing a great deal of harm. He intimated he knew of my attempts to get *Family Limitations* in print when he said, "She is not satisfied merely to violate the law, but is planning to do it on a very large scale.")

12   *See* Norton, *supra* note 2, at p. 57 (citing T.E., *The Lawes Resolutions of Women's Rights; or, The Lawes Provision for Woemen* (London: John Moore, 1632), at p. 6).

13   *See Williams, et. al v. Pryor et. al.,* 220 F. Supp. 2d 1257 (N.D. Ala. 2002).

14   Ashcroft was nominated after losing his seat in the Senate to then-deceased Governor of Missouri, Mel Carnahan. Ashcroft faced a long list of critics opposing his appointment as the top law enforcement official in the country. Among them was the National Abortion Rights Action League, which noted in a fact sheet that "[t]he landmark of John Ashcroft's long public career has been his dedication to taking away women's constitutional rights. He has pressed litigation and legislation seeking to curtail women's reproductive rights. He goes beyond the antichoice beliefs of many of his antichoice peers: he opposed abortion even in cases of rape and incest. He even opposes common forms of contraception, including the birth control pill. If John Ashcroft's world view becomes embodied in law, the clock would be turned back to the days of common illegal abortion and women would be disempowered socially and legally as a result of losing control over their reproductive lives." (*See* NARAL: FACT SHEETS. The Department of Justice and Reproductive Freedom.) Ashcroft was confirmed by the Senate Judiciary Committee by a 58 to 42 vote. As Attorney General, Ashcroft still is charged with shaping legal policy, which has almost certainly included some efforts to restrict access to abortion and birth control. Ashcroft will also likely assist in the selection of judicial candidates, which may include Supreme Court Justices, should there be retirements.

15   *See Planned Parenthood v. Ashcroft,* 462 U.S. 476 (1983). Three years earlier, Ashcroft filed an *amici curiae* brief in *Williams v. Zbaraz,* 448 U.S. 358 (1980).

16   *See* Christopher Marquis, *Bush Misuses Science Data, Report Says,* N.Y. TIMES, August 8, 2003, at p. A14.

17   *See* David Leonhardt, *Wage Gap Between Men and Women Closes to Narrowest,* N.Y. TIMES, Feb. 17, 2003, A1, at A15.

18   *See* Rachel Sobel, *The Doctor Wore a Dive Mask,* U.S.NEWS & WORLD REPORT, March 10, 2003, at p. 59; Natalie Angier, *Pay Gap Remains for Women in Life Sciences,* N.Y. TIMES, Oct. 16, 2001, at D3.

19   *See* Ann Scott Tyson, *Another Day, Another 75 Cents,* CHRISTIAN SCIENCE MONITOR, July 17, 1998, at pp. 7–9; Julie Flaherty, *Beyond the Glass Ceiling,* N.Y. TIMES, Aug. 30, 2000, at C1.

20   *See* Jonathan D. Glater, *Women Are Close to Being Majority of Law Students,* N.Y. TIMES, March 26, 2001, at A1.

21   *See* Sobel, *supra* note 18, at p. 59.

22   *See* Hope Viner Samborn, *Higher Hurdles for Women,* A.B.A. J., Sept. 2000, at pp. 30–42; Kristin Choo, *Moving into the Driver's Seat,* A.B.A. J. June 2001, at pp. 84–85.

23   *See* Kevin Phillips, POLITICS OF RICH AND POOR: WEALTH AND THE AMERICAN ELECTORATE IN THE REAGAN AFTERMATH (New York: HarperPerennial, 1989), at p. 202.

24   *Id.* at 202–203 (citing *People Patterns,* WALL ST. J., Sept. 7, 1988).

25   *Id.* at 9.

26   *Id.*

27   For an overview of the debate, *see, e.g.*, JANE BARTLETT, WILL YOU BE A MOTHER?: WOMEN WHO CHOOSE TO SAY NO (New York: New York University Press, 1995) (uncorrected proof); Mary Gaitskill, *A Woman's Prerogative: Can a Woman Be Complete Without Becoming a Mother?*, ELLE, Sept, 1999, at pp. 282–291; Lisa Belkin, *The Backlash Against Children*, N.Y. TIMES MAG., July 23, 2000, Section Six, at pp. 30–64; *The Biological Clock*, 60 MINUTES (Leslie Stahl reporting), CBS-TV, airing April 7, 2002, at pp. 15–21 (transcript); Elizabeth Hayt, *Admitting to Mixed Feelings About Motherhood*, N.Y. TIMES, May 12, 2002, Sect. 9, at p. 1; Regan Cameron, *Rescue Me from Motherhood*, VOGUE, May 2002, at pp. 116–118; Deborah L. Rhode, *Having it All, or Not?*, NAT'L L.J., June 10, 2002, at A21; Madelyn Cain, *The Childless Revolution*; UTNE READER, July-Aug. 2002, at pp. 71–72; Christopher Clausen, *To Have…Or Not to Have*, UTNE READER, July-Aug. 2002, at pp. 67–70; Kristin Rowe-Finkbeiner, *Oops, I Forgot to Have Kids*, BUST, Summer 2002, at pp. 44–49; CHAPTER TEN, *infra*.

28   *See Hooking Up, Hanging Out, and Hoping for Mr. Right: College Women on Mating and Dating Today*, commissioned by the Independent Women's Forum (2001). (The report is described by its authors as an 18-month study of "attitudes and values of today's college women regarding sexuality, dating, courtship, and marriage—involving in-depth interviews with a diverse group of 62 college women on 11 campuses, supplemented by 20-minute telephone interviews with a nationally representative sample of 1,000 college women.")

29   *See* Lawrence K. Altman, *Rates of Gonorrhea Rise After a Long Decline*, N.Y. TIMES, Dec. 6, 2000, at A-28. (According to Altman, "[a]fter falling steadily for more than 20 years, the rate of gonorrhea increased 9 percent from 1997 to 1999, officials at the [Centers for Disease Control and Prevention in Atlanta] said. The rate peaked at 467.7 cases per 100,000 people in 1975, then fell steadily in all regions by 72 percent until stabilizing at rates of 123.2 in 1996 and 122.0 in 1997. The rate is now 133.2, with a total of 360,078 cases." In addition, the CDC "also releases findings from the first national survey on human papilloma virus, or HPV. It is believed to be the most common sexually transmitted infection among young, sexually active people, but the agency did not specify the age range. The 30 types of the virus have been linked to several diseases like genital warts and cancer of the cervix, penis, and anus. Papilloma virus accounts for 93 percent of cervical cancer, and one type, HPV-16, accounts for half of all such cases."

30   *The Second 100,000 Cases of Acquired Immunodeficiency Syndrome – United States, June 1981-December 1991*, 41 MORBIDITY AND MORTALITY WEEKLY REPORT (1992); *Mortality Attributable to HIV. Infection/AIDS–United States, 1981-1990*, 40 MORBIDITY AND MORTALITY WEEKLY REPORT 41 (1991). *See also* Chu et al., *Impact of the Human Immunodeficiency Virus Epidemic on Morality in Women of Reproductive Age, United States*, 264 JAMA 225 (1990).

31   *See, e.g.*, Lynn Darling, *Sweet Chastity*, BAZAAR, August 1999, at pp. 168–170; Phoebe Hoban, *Single Girls: Sex But Still No Respect*, N.Y. TIMES, Oct. 12, 2002, at A19.

32   *See* D. Kilpatrick, B. Saunders, *et al.*, *Criminal Victimization: Lifetime Prevalence, Reporting to Police, and Psychological Impact*, 33 CRIME AND DELINQUENCY 479, 488 (1987). ("'Children' is something a term of legal classification, but it is more common to find the categories of 'infancy' or 'minority' describing people under twenty-one, or under eighteen for some purposes. The status of infancy or minority, largely determines the rights and duties of a child before the law regardless of his or her actual age or particular circumstances. Justification for such a broad, chronologically determined classification rely on the physical and intellectual differences between adults and children.")

33   "Experienced" is the word used by Justice Department officials in their report. It is not the choice of the author. The author notes that the Department of Justice defines "women" as females as young as 12.

34   *See* Diane Craven, *Special Report: Sex Differences in Violent Victimization, 1994*, U.S. DEPARTMENT OF JUSTICE, OFFICE OF JUSTICE PROGRAMS, BUREAU OF JUSTICE STATISTICS, Sept. 1997, at p. 1. (By comparison, men experienced "almost 6.6 million violent victimizations," Craven writes. But women were more likely in 1994—and are more likely today—to be victimized by men they knew, or know, than strangers. Writes Craven, "for every 5 violent victimizations of a female by an intimate, there was 1 of a male." Men, by contrast, are more often victimized by strangers, according to Justice Department research. "Victimizations" as a category include murders, rapes, sexual assaults, robberies, aggravated assaults, and simple assaults. According to Craven, "[w]omen age 12 or older experienced 5 million violent victimizations: about 432,000 rapes and sexual assaults, 472,000 robberies, over 940,000 aggravated assaults, and over 3 million simple assaults. In addition, 4,489 females age 12 or older were victims of homicide." *Id.* at 2-3.)

35   *See* Warren E. Leary, *Violent Crime Continues to Decline, Survey Finds*, N.Y. TIMES, Aug. 28, 2000, at A10.

36   *See* Craven, *supra* note 34, at p. 3.

37   *See* Patricia Tjaden & Nancy Thoennes, *Prevalence, Incidence, and Consequences of Violence Against Women: Findings From the National Violence Survey*, U.S. DEPARTMENT OF JUSTICE, OFFICE OF JUSTICE PROGRAMS, NATIONAL INSTITUTES OF JUSTICE, Nov. 1998, at p. 4. (By contrast, an estimated "371,000 men are stalked annually in the United States.")

38   The word used by the authors but substituted by the author of this book was "males."

39   *See* Craven, *supra* note 34, at p. 1.

40   *Id.* (According to Craven, "[o]ffenders were armed in 34% of victimizations of males (2,047,502) and in 24% of victimizations of females (1,128,100)." But "[m]ost violent victimizations did not involve the use of weapons.")

41   *Id* at p. 2. (By contrast, "[m]ales were most likely to be victimized in public places such as businesses, parking lots, and open areas," Craven writes.)

42   Judges and juries across the country continue to grapple with what the requirement of a clear lack of consent means. *See, e.g., U.S. v. Norrquay,* 987 F.2d 475 (8th Cir. 1993), *app. after rem.; U.S. v. Schoenborn,* 19 F.3d 1438, *cert. den.,* 115 S. Ct. 284 (holding that a defendant's need to employ force generally will indicate a lack of consent); *State v. Jackson,* 620 A.2d 168 (Conn. 1993) (holding that the victim of a potential rape need not resist to the point of physical injury in order to establish that she did not consent to the acts); *State v. Mezriouri,* 602 A.2d 29 (Conn. App. 1992) (holding that a woman need not say no or physically resist); *State v. Sedia,* 614 So.2d 533 (Fla. App. 4 Dist. 1993) (holding that a where a physical therapy patient had no opportunity to communicate her unwillingness to have sex, she was "physically helpless to resist" the encounter within the meaning of Florida sexual abuse law); *State v. Simmons,* 621 So.2d 1135 (La. App. 4 Cir. 1993), *amended on rehearing* (holding that as defined by law, the act of forcible rape occurs upon a victim "without consent; upon a victim who was prevented from resisting by force or threat of physical violence; and who reasonably believed that resistance would not prevent rape"); *State v. Gallen,* 613 So.2d 1145 (La. App. 5 Cir. 1993) (defining that the difference between aggravated and forcible rape is the degree of force used by the defendant and the amount of resistance attempted by the victim); *Commonwealth v. Price,* 616 A.2d 681 (Pa. Super. 1992) (clarifying that the subsection of the Pennsylvania criminal statutes proscribing intercourse with "unconscious" people was intended to protect persons not able to give or refuse consent to intercourse due to their unconscious state); *Commonwealth v. Berkowitz,* 641 A.2d 1161 (Pa. 1994) (holding that where there is a lack of consent, but no showing of either a threat or physical force, "forcible compulsion" requirement of the rape statute was not met); *State v. Jackson,* 679 A.2d 572 (N.H. 1996) (holding that "consent" issue involves objective manifestation of unwillingness).

43   *See, e.g., State v. Thompson,* 861 P.2d 492 (Wash. App. Div. 2 1993); *Commonwealth v. Odell,* 607 N.E.2d 423 (Mass. App. Ct. 1993), *rev. den.,* 617 N.E.2d 639.

44   For beginning overview of the issue, *see, e.g.,* Helen Benedict, VIRGIN OR VAMP: HOW THE PRESS COVERS SEX CRIMES (New York: Oxford, 1993), at pp. 13–24. (In the introduction to this chapter, Benedict notes that "[i]n spite of the attempts by feminists and psychologists to explain away rape myths over the last two decades, studies have found that those myths are still alive and well. In his 1982 book, MEN ON RAPE, Timothy Beneke interviewed a large sample of men and found that many not only blamed female victims for having been raped, but also admitted to being tempted to commit rape themselves. Other studies conducted in 1987 found that victims are still widely blamed for inviting rape, while perpetrators are seen as lustful men driven beyond endurance. In 1991, *The New York Times* featured an article about rape victims who blame themselves. A telephone survey of 500 American adults taken for *Time* magazine in May 1991, found that 53 percent of adults age fifty and 31 percent of adults between thirty-five and forty believe that a woman is to be blamed for her rape if she dressed provocatively. And at the end of 1991, Newsweek pointed out that the public's disinclination to believe either Anita Hill during the Justice Clarence Thomas hearings on sexual harassment or [the woman], who said she was raped by William Kennedy Smith, 'show the lengths skeptics will go to deny the possibility of sexual offense.' Because rape myths continue to hold such sway, and because they lie at the root of my discussion in this book, they must be explained again.")

45   *See, e.g.,* Cam Simpson, *Man Pleads Guilty in "Date-Rape Drug" Case,* CHI. SUN-TIMES, July 14, 2000, at p. 21. *See also People v. Mack,* 15 Cal. Rptr. 2d 193 (Cal. App. 3 Dist. 1992) (holding that where resistance is thwarted by administration of "intoxicating or anesthetic substance" by the accused via force or trick, rape conviction may still occur); *People v. Cortez,* 35 Cal. Rptr. 2d 500 (Cal. App. 5 Dist. 1994); *Stadler v. State,* 919 P.2d 439 (Okla. Crim. App. 1996), *cert. den.,* 117 S. Ct. 369.

The
BOUNDARIES
of HER
BODY

The 1600s—Early 1900s

CHAPTER ONE

Women and the
Hierarchy of Gender

EARLY AMERICA:
A New World of European Ideals and Godly Influence

While journeying across the American West, famed explorer Meriwether Lewis disapprovingly declared that the Shoshone Indians "treat their women…with little rispect [sic], and compel them to perform every species of drudgery. [The women] collect the wild fruits and roots, attend to the horses or assist in that duty, cook, dreess [sic] the skins and make all their apparel, collect wood and make their fires, arrange and form their lodges, and when they travel pack the horses and take charge of all the baggage; in short the man dose [sic] little else except attend his horses, hunt, and fish."[1]

Lewis may have furrowed his brow at the treatment of Native American women at the hands of Native American men. But European women didn't always fair better at the hands of European men in the fledgling American colonies. A leader among men in a "nursery of explorers," Lewis was born into a distinguished Virginia family on the eve of a "world of conflict between Americans and the British," historian Stephen Ambrose notes.[2] His great-grandfather had come to America in 1635 to take possession of a 33,000-acre land grant made by the King of England for service in the British army.

And his wealth only grew, so much so that by the time of his death, the elder Lewis was able to leave "substantial plantations" to his nine children, including a behest to Lewis's father of a 1,900-acre farm "within sight of Monticello,"[3] replete with a field of slaves.[4] This was the life that Meriwether Lewis came into in 1774, and it was typical in many ways of the lives of wealthy, educated Anglo-American men in the nascent United States.

But the story was often quite different for women.

The birth of the American nation was tumultuous. In a distant and unsettled land, Native Americans led raids, slaves attempted revolts, and pioneers pushed westward in a land grab. In the chaos of the time, it may have been easy for the privileged men of Lewis's class to overlook the clear inequities facing *their own women* as they mapped out the rules for their brave new world, even as they criticized the treatment of women by others (usually non-Europeans). At other times, it may simply have been that European history and an exalted way of life made it impossible for even the most educated and "fair-minded" of men to admit what was clearly true: that women weren't part of the political debate.

Long before Lewis was born—indeed, even before the first boatload of pilgrims set scarred boot to cold Massachusetts soil—women were being devised out of the burgeoning power structure and, thus, away from the potential for equality in their new land. With the signing of the Mayflower Compact off the shores of Cape Cod in November of 1620, a "civil body politick" [*sic*] was born, with the goals of "order[ing]" and "preserv[ing]" society by framing "such just and equal laws…as shall be thought most meet and convenient for the general good of the colony."[5]

A "general good" determined by men and expressly inclusive only of men.

The signing of the Mayflower Compact set the stage for the Constitutional Convention of 1787, with "[t]he men in both contexts…engaged in the same enterprise—mutual consent to the creation of elected governments," argues Cornell University Professor of American History, Mary Beth Norton.[6] But these were governments by men, for men. Though the Founding Fathers of the 1780s were "children of the Enlightenment," their ultimate "ideology" was respectful of "men's equality, rationality, and individuality."[7]

And though the meeting of the minds off the coast of Cape Cod and the Constitutional Convention were separated by 167 years, these events mirrored each other in two important ways: "All of those who signed both documents were white male heads of households, men of substance and standing in their respective communities. In both 1620 and 1787, women rarely played a role of independent actors in the political arena. Instead, society conceptualized them as dependents whose menfolk would speak and act for them in economic, political, and legal affairs," Norton notes.[8]

The smaller bones of the female skeleton and the narrowness of her shoulders were offered historically to explain why women and young girls should be steered away from exercise. Concern for healthy heirs—especially among the upper classes—was offered to explain why women should be protected by *limiting legislation* from the rigors of common labor.

"For women, certainly, anatomy is destiny," argues writer Mary Lekfowitz. "Not so much because of what they lack as because of what they possess, which is to say wombs, vaginas, breasts: the female reproductive system is a weakness of both the body and the mind."[9]

Women were thought incapable of profound reasoning, because—in the words of William Shakespeare—they were "ruled by the moon."[10] In addition, an "addled" brain and a "child-like" disposition explained why women should not study math or science. Women of the upper class *should* learn to write, of course, because good penmanship was a sign of good breeding. And to read, so that she might pepper her conversation with swift quips and clever quotes. A young lady should learn to paint to amuse herself and to play a musical instrument so that she might amuse others.

But a woman shouldn't sully herself with higher thoughts, the quest of higher aspirations, the strain of daily work, or the sordid scurry of politics. Women were simply not built for involvement in these things, it was thought. What women were built for was bearing children. Thus, the determinative factor in the lives of women in early America and even before was (and still is for some) that women have the ability to bear children.

"Every known human society has rules and customs concerning gender," argues Stanford Professor Emerita Eleanor Maccoby in *The Two Sexes: Growing Up Apart, Coming Together*. "Members of every society have expectations and beliefs—sometimes explicit, sometimes unspoken—concerning what boys and girls, or men and women, are supposed to do or not do. Some of these expectations are clearly grounded in the different roles of the two sexes in human reproduction, and relate to their different physical characteristics."[11]

Through the eyes of America's early lawmakers, women were meant—by God, Darwinian invention, or man-made interpretation—to *serve* mankind. "In a relatively primitive society based mainly on agriculture and animal husbandry, security and wealth do not depend primarily on technical and rational factors," notes essayist Erich Fromm. "It is nature's productive force—that is, the fertility of the soil, the effects of water and sunlight—that plays the decisive role in human life and death. The crux of the economy is the mysterious power of nature giving birth out of itself to ever new products essential for human life. Who possesses this mysterious power of natural productiveness? Only woman."[12]

Women had—and have—the mysterious power to give birth to "themselves"—and to men—which has been held through time immemorial to be their societal mission. Therefore, although the stated goals of the Mayflower Compact and the Constitutional Convention were "justice" and "equality," the rule of law laid down during this time would limit the rights and choices of women in every aspect of life for the next three centuries. Indeed, it was not until the 1960s, for instance, that the notion of personal privacy was extended to women, allowing women to make certain choices regarding their bodies.

Prior to that, female reproduction and a body that could nurture life was largely deemed public property, certainly public enough that the state would have a say in a woman's decisions regarding reproduction. Women, lawmakers argued well into the twentieth century, were obligated to reproduce. It was an obligation long justified by talk of God and His "remarkable providences."

IMPOSSIBLE WOMEN:
"Remarkable Providences" and God in a History of Details

"God has no place in politics," declared a dashing Antonio Banderas in the 2001 religious mystery, *The Body*. Perhaps never before has so naïve a statement been uttered by such a pretty male mouth. In the real world, some form of God has always had a hand in politics and a starring role in the passions of the Church. God is apparent in the law, and in the lexicon of modern thought, where He is said to live in the details. And God has always had a presence in the bedroom, though the side of His face most often shown with regard to women there has been one of their own: a very young woman called Mary.

Despite a near millennium of praise as the yardstick by which women should be measured, Biblical scholars note that relatively little is actually known about Mary. Though she is mentioned in the books of Matthew[13] and Luke,[14] "[y]ou could copy on an eight-and-a-half-by-eleven sheet everything there is about Mary in the New Testament," argues Jaroslav Pelikan, author of *Mary Through the Centuries* and the former president of the American Academy of Arts and Sciences.[15]

There is conjecture, of course. But much of it introduces aspects of Mary unfamiliar to most Westerners. Given the time in which she is supposed to have lived, for example, Mary was probably "a Semitic woman" at home in "a hot Mediterranean environment, [where] custom would have demanded that she be veiled," some scholars suggest.[16] Self-possessed, we are to understand, yet barely beyond childhood and so innocent that she would exclaim with wide-eyed wonder in response to the news from the angel Gabriel that she would bear a child, "How shall this be, seeing I know not a man?"[17]

"Mary was probably twelve or thirteen when she and Joseph were committed to one another," author and Stanford research scholar Marilyn Yalom suggests. But she had already been "impregnated by the Holy Ghost." Luckily for Mary, "given the death sentence that could be inflicted on Jewish brides who were not virgins, 'Joseph was a just man, and not willing to make her a public example.'"[18]

Of course, the purity of the connection between Mary and Joseph is integral to the ultimate construct of Mary. While it has long been argued that consummation of the marriage between Mary and Joseph did not take place until after the baby Jesus was born,[19] some Biblical scholars suggest that Mary remained a virgin—and, thus, pure—her entire life.[20] The significance of the story of Mary for women in medieval Europe and later in early America was that "Christians could look to the supreme model of the Virgin Mary for virtues that were touted above all others: obedience and chastity," says Yalom.[21]

"The Mary of today started not with Christ's birth, nor with the Gospels, but with a second century document called The Book of James," Robert Sullivan argues in *The Mystery of Mary*.[22] "The text filled in details of Mary's birth, marriage, the Annunciation. It was not then—and never has been—accorded canonical authority, but that didn't prevent it from inspiring the tradition of devotion to Our Lady."[23]

But there were bumps on the way to the current construct of Mary. The concept of a virgin birth was fiercely debated by religious leaders during the Second Century, with the notion that Mary would remain a virgin her entire life never "on the table."[24] But during the next two centuries, metaphysics entered the picture. In 431 A.D., over protests the Council of Ephesus accorded Mary, "the title of Mother of God." And by the close of the Fifth Century, "Mary's perpetual virginity was part of who she was," says Sullivan.[25]

The change was fundamental for Mary. And for women. Though the Immaculate Conception is often "confused with the virgin birth of Jesus," the idealized notion of a pure birth is a medieval construct devised by theologians to free Mary of "Original Sin from her first moment in the womb of her mother, rendering her saintly even before birth," Sullivan argues.[26] This fundamental change made Mary a "major celebrity," divinity scholar Karen Armstrong suggests.[27]

Mary has proved a powerful religious and political force ever since. During the next ten centuries, reinventing Mary became part of the religious, political, and social continuum.[28] She was a child, naïve and guileless. But a submissive and obedient woman as well, who would conceive God's child without sin.[29] She was the Mother of Jesus, and—during the Crusades—even an idolized "military figure." According to Pelikan, "[s]he is a warrior against the devil. In Constantinople they went to war with the Virgin on the sails of their warships. *Onward Christian soldiers!*"[30]

"The Bible offers no other human so useful in this way, extremely significant to the Christ story, yet so inscrutable that she can be known—and used—in various ways through subtle amendment," Sullivan argues.[31]

Of course, "good" plays best when stood in direct contrast to "bad." And for every Mary—or Sarah, Rebekah, Rachel, and Leah— the "virtuous women" of the Old Testament, "who brought nothing but blessings to [their husbands]," says Yalom[32]—there are examples of women of the less virtuous sort. Perhaps the greatest contrast to Mary is Eve: where Mary is chaste and without sin, Eve is naked, tempting,[33] and possessed of an appetite so greedy that—as Milton sets forth—the world would feel the wound of her bite.[34]

The story of Eve is the story of the deceitful, treacherous nature of woman.[35] It was Eve's "wiles," after all, that led Adam (and mankind) astray. And yet, in a bit of contrast, Milton offers a slightly kinder interpretation: Adam is "overcome" not by deceit or treachery, but *fondly* by Eve's "female charm."[36] Still, to men, this "fondness" was just as dangerous, suggested Fromm in *Love, Sexuality and Matriarchy*.

Patriarchal interpretations of the Bible held that "[t]he woman is dangerous; she is the evil principle, and the man stands in fear of her," argues Fromm.[37] "The woman lacks self-restraint, is sensual and reckless; she seduces the man with her desire, which he cannot resist. As a result, he meets with disaster. There is probably no document that expresses more clearly and dramatically man's fear of women and his accusation that she is a seductress who brings ruin then does this myth embodying the male, patriarchal worldview."

But in addition to Eve, there is Jezebel, who marries, then tricks King Ahab into doing "evil in the sight of the Lord...."[38] But Jezebel pays for her sins: she is cast from a window and her body is eaten by dogs.[39] Elizabeth Wurtzel, author of the provocative *Bitch: In Praise of Difficult Women*, offers another example of the "treachery of women" in the "scandal sheet approach" historians—predominantly male, Wurtzel argues—have traditionally taken in interpreting the story of Samson and Delilah.

The adolescent Delilah, Wurtzel contends, represents "...the first episode of the *femme fatale*—of a woman whose mere existence is a contagious, airborne virus for that certain susceptible sucker of a man...."[40] Wurtzel's remarks may seem overblown. But the notion of women as fatal, "viral," the literal bearers of *contagions* has a history and it remains a valid charge to some today.[41]

"Early attitudes toward women were poisonous," writes Daniel Maguire, professor of ethics in the theology department at Marquette University. "The Mosaic law assumed male ownership of women. Early church writers said women lacked reason and only possessed the image of God through their connection to men. Luther saw women as being nails in a wall, prohibited by their nature from moving outside their domestic situation. And Aquinas said that females are produced from male embryos damaged though some accident of the womb."[42]

Without *natural* reason or the guidance of God—men in His stead—women would *naturally* wallow in sin, it was argued. And a *sinful* woman would lead others—men—toward evil, injuring society in the process. "Since all women were the daughters of Eve, they were, according to both Jewish and Christian lore, capable of leading men astray," says Yalom.[43] And men would not be able to do a thing about it.

The problem with this view of women, however, was that "[a] culture that looks on women, like Pandora and Eve, as sources of evil is going to have trouble justifying having sex with them," Maguire notes. In an effort to resolve the tension between what Yalom calls "Mary's miraculous purity and their own carnality,"[44] men—the founders of society—decreed that "only reproduction can justify sexual collusion with women. That is exactly what happened in Christianity. Augustine said that if [sex] were not for reproduction there would be no use for women at all," says Maguire.[45]

"It is often said Mary enhances the dignity of women," argues Northwestern University history professor Garry Wills in *Papal Sin: Structures of Deceit*. And yet, "for misogynists an idealized mother is both safe in herself and an alternative to lesser women."[46] Of course, with Mary setting the standard, all (mortal) women were "lesser," a position that served the men of the time well.

THE CATHARS AND THE ALBIGENSIAN CRUSADE

But this view of Mary and the universe of female subjugation constructed around her were not without challengers. During the twelfth century, a regional movement of rebel Christians began openly opposing traditional Catholic doctrine, defying Church directives, scoffing at the pageantry of its ceremonies, and refusing to pay Church-levied taxes. The Cathars—or the Albigenses—as the people of this movement were known, lived in contempt of papal authority and proclaimed the Church the "mother of fornication and abomination."[47]

The seat of the Cathar faith rested in and around Languedoc, a region that became known during the twelfth century for its religious tolerance. As Cathar missionaries walked rural pathways, for example, "…the Jews of Languedoc were inventing and exploring the mystical implications of the Kabbalah, proving that spiritual ferment was by no means confined to the Christian majority," argues author and historian Stephen O'Shea in *The Perfect Heresy: The Revolutionary Life and Death of the Medieval Cathars.*[48]

Grounding their village lives in traditional vocations—often as weavers— the Cathars cultivated a reputation as hard workers. But "[w]hen the time came, they would talk—first, in the moonlight beyond the walls, then out in the open, before the fireplaces of noble and burgher, in the houses of tradespeople, near the stalls of the marketplace. They asked for nothing, no alms, no obeisance; just a hearing. Within a generation, these Cathar missionaries had converted thousands [and] Languedoc had become host to what would be called the Great Heresy."[49]

Central to Christian Catharist beliefs was the dualist notion that while evil is visible, good is invisible, offers O'Shea. "For the Cathars, the world was not the handiwork of a good god. It was wholly the creation of a force of darkness, immanent in all things. Matter was corrupt, therefore irrelevant to salvation." Thus, the Church, with its decorative vestments and enduring quest for wealth and worldly power was a "hoax." Its agents—the Pope among them—were at best "merely unenlightened; at worst…active agents of the evil creator."[50]

The relevance of the Cathars to women was simple: they offered an inclusive alternative. By the start of the thirteenth century, the Roman Catholic Church had turned its back on women, excluding them from all public and authoritative roles. Integral to this exclusion was that "[i]n the latter stages of the Middle Ages, the Virgin Mary would be tapped as a body double for all banished women of influence, her stature of semidivinity, arguably, a bone thrown to the metaphysically dispossessed. For many women, shut out of the sacristy and shut in the cloister, this was hardly enough," O'Shea explains.[51]

By contrast, the Cathars embraced two ideas that might have made a world of difference for women had history worked out differently: in direct opposition to the teachings of the Church, the Cathars placed no value on female virginity and they did not oppose premarital sex. They also thought of women as equals. Cathar women were allowed to preach and head assemblies—something the Roman Catholic Church does not even permit today—though it reportedly riled conservative monks at the time.[52]

And though female Cathars didn't wander from village to village proselytizing, they set up group homes for the daughters, widows, and dowagers of the artisan and petty nobility classes. Young girls were raised in the faith in these homes and would, in turn, raise their children in the faith. Thus, "[t]he number of credentes (followers of the Cathar faith) grew accordingly with each generation, as did the number of females opting for the rigors of life as a Perfect (Cathar elect)."[53]

Of course, the "medieval sexual status quo" would have been undermined "…if everybody had believed, as the Cathars did, that a nobleman in one life might be a milkmaid in the next, or that women were fit to be spiritual leaders," O'Shea notes. The elevation of women to positions of power within the Church would also have challenged the mandate of Mary. Not surprisingly, Church leaders saw the Cathar movement for the threat it was and set about to do something about it.

In 1200, Pope Innocent III issued a decree calling for the forfeiture of all assets belonging to "heretics."[54] This, some scholars note, was a medieval template for modern drug forfeiture laws. Pope Innocent III also sought to stamp out tolerance by declaring that the property of Catholics who refused to hunt down Cathars would be confiscated.[55] A threatening proposition to be sure. But it had little effect on the people of Languedoc. Pope Innocent III struggled to up the ante.

In letters written between 1204 and 1207, Innocent pushed King Philip Augustus of France to crack down on the Cathars. King Philip declined. But then, finally in 1209, after one of his representatives was killed, Innocent hired mercenaries to do what King Philip had been reluctant to. And in sending them on their way, the Pontiff is reported to have said: "Forward soldiers of Christ! Forward, volunteers of the army of God! Go forth with the church's cry of anguish ringing in your ears. Fill your souls with godly rage to avenge the insult done to the Lord."[56] The words launched the Albigensian Crusade.[57]

By the mid-summer of 1209, Béziers had been attacked. It fell within three hours.[58] Hundreds were killed in a slaughter so indiscriminate that historians tend to repeat the often-quoted remarks of a German monk said to have witnessed the events. According to the monk, when asked during the battle "how the [C]atholics could be distinguished from the heretics," the Church-hired crusader is said to have replied, "Kill them all; God will recognize his own."[59]

Carcassonne took longer, but it too fell in the initial rampage.[60] Northern Languedoc, Moissac, and Montauban resisted Church forces longer. But they too eventually fell.[61] The campaign would continue for the next four decades. Those Cathars lucky enough to survive the strikes were driven underground only to later face an inquisition. Some historians suggest that the violence of the Albigensian Crusade was indicative of the Church's approach to dissidents. And though the Cathars may be viewed as little more than a minor footnote in history today, the destruction of their culture in the name of religion was part of a larger trend, scholars argue.

"[T]he Cathar wars arose because Western civilization had reached a crossroads." [H]istorian R. I. Moore has provocatively seen the years around 1200 as a watershed that led to 'the formation of a persecuting society,'" O'Shea notes.[62] "The Albigensian Crusade…was a cataclysm of the Middle Ages, a ferocious campaign of siege, battle, and bonfire during which supporters of the Catholic Church sought to eliminate…the Cathars. That thirteenth-century crusade, directed not against Muslims in distant Palestine but against dissident Christians in the heart of Europe, was followed by the founding of the Inquisition, an implacable machine expressly created to destroy the Cathar survivors of the war."[63]

This too was a template: two centuries later Spanish officials would recommend "the establishment in Castile of an inquisition to root out the 'Judaic heresy'—an inquisition of the kind that functioned in Languedoc and virtually destroyed the [Cathars]. It was to be an institution subject to Rome, and thus immune to the influence of the converso bishops and the corruption of other Spanish prelates. All that was needed to establish such an institution was the consent of the King," renowned religious scholar B. Netanyahu notes.[64]

RELIGIOUS NOTIONS OF CHASTITY AND OBEDIENCE

From the perspective of history, "[c]hoices were made [during the Middle Ages] that would take centuries to undo," O'Shea notes.[65] Among those choices was the elevation of a 13-year-old girl, capable of conceiving without sex, as the supreme model for women. Since then, conservative clerics worldwide have remained unmoved on issues of chastity, reproduction, and status. In terms of the spread of this ideal, "[b]y about 1600 the Catholic Church had become the first religious body—indeed, the first institution of any sort—to operate on a global scale," argues historian Philip Jenkins. "Even in the Protestant heartlands of Northern and Western Europe—England, Sweden, and the German lands—the heirs of the Reformation had to spend many years discouraging their people from succumbing to the attractions of Catholicism."[66]

Religious notions of chastity and obedience made their way to early America as well where they remained a social force well into modern times. And though traditionalists may be in the minority in America today in continuing to urge a literal interpretation of the stories of the Bible, the shadow of Mary continues to reach into these areas. Roman Catholic authorities, for example—always stringent in their interpretation—have continued to preach in this vein.

Pope John Paul II declared in his 1994 international bestseller, *Crossing the Threshold of Hope*, for instance, that "[a] remarkable expression of [faith and the living tradition of the Church] is found in Marian devotion and in Mariology: 'He was conceived by the Holy Spirit and born of the Virgin Mary.'[67] *A Marian dimension and Mariology in the Church are simply another aspect of the Christological focus.*"[68]

The Vatican continues to oppose birth control, abortion, and women in the priesthood: all issues that would despoil Mary were "concessions" of this sort made. Given this kind of activism, Mary—once the mere instrument of the

Holy Ghost—continues to hold center stage. In the last 150 years, the Vatican has issued only three new dogmas: two have directly involved Mary. One of the two was issued in 1854, and it mandated unequivocal belief in the Immaculate Conception (*i.e.*, that Mary was without "Original Sin"). The other, issued in 1950, dealt with the Assumption and Mary's rise to Heaven.

In addition, as unrealistic as it may seem, Mary's popularity has spiked in the last century. In 1917, the Virgin Mary reportedly appeared before a group of peasant children in Portugal. To these children she is said to have entrusted three prophecies, the third of which reportedly predicted the assassination attempt on Pope John Paul II in 1981. The 1917 vision is one of the few Mary sightings officially sanctioned by the Vatican until 1969, when Pope Paul VI reportedly lifted "a canonical requirement that religious books, including one on apparitions, be preapproved."[69] After that, Mary seemed to be everywhere.

Hardened New Yorkers were said to have glimpsed her in Bayside, Queens, in 1970, and then promptly issued a pamphlet, replete with an 800 number.[70] And there were tears of exultation in Medjugorje in 1981, when six peasants told of a visitation.[71] More than 11 million people have visited since the sighting.[72] Many have reported miracles.

Mary was next seen in the American Midwest, where in January of 1993, a 58-year-old retired bread truck driver from Renault, Illinois, reported "a very beautiful lady, very young and regal" dressed "all in white," who confessed that she had chosen to appear before him because he was "the least apt instrument. Therefore, people that know you will know this is not your word."[73] And in Italy, between 1994 and 1996, Italians reported some fifty weeping Madonnas.[74]

But does Mary still matter today?

Roughly 56 percent of Americans identify themselves as Protestants, compared to roughly 28 percent who identify themselves as Catholic and 2 percent who identify themselves as Jewish.[75] Given these numbers, it might be argued that God, the Pope, and the lingering image of Mary have little or no influence in the modern United States. But the Roman Catholic Church has always been a formidable political force, determined to shape international law and society, and powerful enough to do it.

"[T]he Catholic Church is the only world religion with a seat in the United Nations," writes Marquette's Maguire. From this "unduly privileged perch" Vatican officials have blocked family planning and contraception programs and "impeded any reasonable discussion of abortion."[76]

The reach of religion into the formative politics of early America was at least as profound. Religion has shaped almost every society in the world. The nascent American states were no different. Though there was more than an element of commerce to the mission, the Mayflower's journey was also about exodus. And among the settlers making America their new home during the 1600s were hundreds of Christians fleeing Europe to escape religious persecution.

These were the people who planted America's religious roots, and while the leaders among these migrants may not have adopted a literal interpretation to Catholic doctrine, many of its conservative themes regarding women—subordination, subservience, the obligation of virtue—made their way into emerging America law. In this sense, the "creators" of the new country to be known as America would find their inspiration in history.

INVENTING AMERICA:
The European Tradition,
Obedient Women, and American Common Law

Women are 10 to 15 percent smaller than men on average and the bones of a woman's skeleton tend to be thinner and shorter than a man's. A woman's joints tend to be looser than a man's. Her neck longer and slimmer. She is more likely to be right-handed than a man, but less likely to be color-blind. Women also bear children, and throughout history this along with other minor physical differences have hindered and disqualified women from all but life in the home.

And yet, "[b]y most measures of performance," these differences make little actual difference, author Dianne Hales argues. "The abilities of the sexes, physical and mental, often overlap. And the variability within each sex can be greater than that between them.... Nonetheless, for centuries, biological differences, alleged or actual, were used to justify discrimination."[77]

Since the Middle Ages, when fief authority began replacing the family "as the important legal and economic unit" and serf labor pushed women out of the workforce, a catalog of "disabilities" has been assigned women.[78] "With this loss of status, women became valued solely for their procreative abilities—namely the ability, as wives, to produce legitimate heirs, thereby enhancing men's status, since a man's status was directly proportionate to his property and number of heirs," argues Laura M. Otten in *Women's Rights and the Law*.[79]

And then, the fiction began.

To explain the absence of women from all but the "domestic realm," assertions of "disabilities" and/or the physical and mental failings of women became part of the collective consciousness and, thus, British common law, which "evolved in England over many centuries, because judges originally had no statutes to guide them in deciding cases," author Agnes Thorton Bird notes in *Women's Rights and State Constitutions*.[80] So instead, "they relied upon a combination of church law, general attitudes in the community, and, of course, their own innate feelings of right and wrong."[81]

But neither general attitudes nor church law have ever done much to further the interests of women. By the mid-seventeenth century, a series of political and social hierarchies structured British society. Central to every one was the hierarchy of husband and wife as "the locus of production and reproduction."[82] In the thinking of the time, a well-ordered society was grounded in a well-ordered family, whose members understood the importance of staying in their proper place. Men [certainly those of the upper class] were expected to marry so they might have *legitimate* heirs and women were expected to obey their husbands. These themes were widely reflected in the literature and philosophy of the time.

In 1632, for example, an anonymous—but often-relied upon—attorney wrote in England's first legal treatise on the status of women that "[a]ll of them [women] are understood either married or to bee [sic] married and their desires ar[e] subject to their husband."[83] The passage is believed by scholars to allude to Genesis 3:16, "a Biblical passage that would have been familiar to any literate English person of his day."[84] In Genesis, God curses Eve with the pain of childbirth as punishment for her defiance. It was here, the anonymous lawyer concluded, that "[t]he common...Law shaketh hand with Divinitie [sic]."[85]

A few decades later, Sir Robert Filmer argued similarly in edicts published between 1648 and 1652 that God "gave the sovereignty to the man over the woman, as being nobler and principal agent in generation."[86] Filmer reasoned that "...the subordination of wife to husband was the foundation of political as well as familial power."[87] The noted philosopher John Locke offers two divergent theories on the "natural subordination" of women as well in the *Two Treatises of Government.* In the First Treatise, Locke suggests that Eve was "accidentally" placed below Adam, though the declaration by God of childbirth as punishment was directed as Eve as the "representative to all... [w]omen," Locke argues.[88]

In the *Second Treatise*, Locke outlined the "voluntary compact" between "man and wife" with the goal of "procreation," though this compact also involved "mutual Support, and Assistance, and a Communion of Interest too."[89] Even so, because "the Husband and Wife, though they have but one common [c]oncern, yet having different understandings, will unavoidably sometimes have different will too; it therefore being necessary, that the last [d]etermination, *i.e.*, the Rule, should be placed somewhere, it naturally falls to the Man's share, as the abler and the stronger," Locke concluded.[90]

The role of the proper wife in society, then, it was agreed, was to submit to the will of her husband. This was *the* foundation of society. Tory writer Mary Astell concurred with this view, writing in 1700 that God had "'[a]llotted...[m]an to [g]overn' his family because he was 'best [q]ualify'd.'"[91] As "inferiors," wives should "respect their Governours as plac'd in God's stead and contribute what they can to ease them of their real Cares." Finally, husbands were "the [r]epresentatives of God whom they ought to imitate in the Justice and Equity of their Laws," Astell concluded.[92]

The sum of this gathering consensus was a general acceptance of the idea that "women could rarely, if ever, be considered independent beings in law or in society at large," Norton argues. The reasoning underlying this notion went something like this, "[i]f all women were 'either married or to bee [sic] married,' and all wives were necessarily subject to their husbands, then a woman's fundamental calling, in the words of the English Puritan cleric William Perkins, was located 'in their subjection and obedience to their owne [sic] husband,'" Norton explains.[93]

"Whether they focused primarily on politics or chiefly on the family, early modern Anglo-American theorists concurred on three key points: hierarchy was necessary to the operations of the household; the proper director of the family's activities was its husband/father/master; and the subordination of wife to husband was the foundation of the family unit and thus of society itself," writes Norton.

It was in this way that the submission of women became the nucleus of European society. It would also become the nucleus of early American society. The "symbiotic" relationship between family and the state was "naturally" understood by leaders of a young America, historians argue. Thus, as the new American Founding Fathers began laying the ground work for a "successful society" of their own, they did so by adopting the kind of hierarchical rules that had worked so well in Europe, (*i.e.*, the submission of women to the will of husbands, fathers, and masters).[94] But what that meant to women in America was the formal codification of their lack of an individual civil identity upon marriage.

IDENTITY CRISIS:
Women and the Constitution: What Went Without Saying

Early America marked the formation of a new country, made of immigrants breaking ground on the shores of a land with no exclusively American laws. Thus, colonies, territories, states, and later a new federal government had a choice to make: Would they rely upon British common law? Or would they start anew? For the leaders of many early territories, British common law was good enough. But British common law reflected the hierarchy that offered women few rights and no civil identity separate from that of her husband's,[95] a fact that eventually raised questions regarding the status of women.

The United States would become a "break-away republic." But at its conception, it was a British colony. With British common law and theories of hierarchy as its foundation, the biological ability of women to bear children and the societal "need" for their submission held sway, foreclosing the rights of women to own property, to work outside of the home in many professions, to bring suit in court without her husband's or father's permission and assistance, or to vote.

But from the start, America was different. A land in flux; politically unstable; peopled by enemies, the emerging United States was harsh in its accommodations and unforgiving of mistakes. And yet, for women, these rugged realities offered some measure of opportunity. Life on the frontier wore away traditional male-female roles as women struggled alongside men to build a new land.[96] And the outbreak of the American Revolution brought even greater change. Military service led to the disappearance of men from communities, requiring that women assume financial and management responsibility for home and property. The necessity of the situation took women outside of work in the "domestic sphere."[97]

This, some scholars suggest, gave women a taste of what they had been missing and may have spurred on the gentle, but growing, movement towards equality. A 19-year-old Abigail Smith, the young bride of John Adams, reportedly ran the family farm during her husband's service in Philadelphia at the Second Continental Congress, for example, and is said that she counseled her husband to "[r]emember the Ladies, and be more generous and favourable [*sic*] to them than your ancestors" as the Founding Fathers attempted to draft national documents.[98]

Necessity, rebellion and court challenge, more than "kindness" would lead to eventual advances for women. "As the English colonists in America attempted to implement the ideal of marital subjection in their families, their laws, their communities, and their courtrooms, they encountered a wide range of practical difficulties with the concept," Norton notes. "In a multitude of ways the unequal status of husbands and wives manifested itself in the daily life of the colonies, thus allowing a sustained analysis of the concrete results for women and men of the subordinate relationship enshrined in the marital ideal."[99]

There was also sustained debate—if not analysis—regarding the role women should be allowed to play in American society. According to historian Marjorie Wall Bingham, from 1775 to 1777—as the Founding Fathers grappled with the creation of constitutional rights and privileges—the "language in American documents moved from the term 'subject' to 'inhabitant' to 'member' and finally, 'citizen.' That shift in language is symbolic of the entire era in which Americans took up arms, proclaimed their independence, and fought against England to prove themselves 'citizens' of a new state. American women were part of that struggle, but not, at the end, part of the new definition of 'citizen.'"[100]

In the end, the language of many of the nation's early documents spoke of "persons," "citizens," or "man." But women were not expressly mentioned. It has long been argued that the word "man" inherently includes women. And yet, for decades scholars have debated the meaning of these words with regard to women, because that is not how the language has been traditionally applied. Instead, because the Founding Fathers were "silent" on specific issues regarding women, the law was often deemed to be "silent" and it was left open to the states to determine what to do with women. Often they did what had previously been done.

Specifically, some scholars suggest that because the Founding Fathers "did not challenge English common law traditions" in unequivocal language within the United States Constitution, their silence "left family law [and, thus, 'women's law'] to the states" to define. In short, "[t]he absence of a clear statement on women's rights, critics charge, meant that Amendment X of the Constitution went into effect," Bingham argues. "This Amendment said that 'powers not delegated to the United States, nor prohibited by it to the States,' were reserved to the states or the people. Since the federal government did not specifically mention women, state laws regarding family and women prevailed."[101]

And that meant legal invisibility for women. At least in the civil context.

"Since most of the laws in these states were built on English common law, it meant that the ideas of *feme sole* and *feme covert* were often applied to American women," Bingham notes.[102]

British common law tradition held that a woman and a man became "one person in law" upon marriage, with the man emerging as the dominant and singular identity. The effect was the complete "absorption" or "incorporation," some have argued, of women into men, their legal existence—in the civil context—"suspended" during marriage. Once married, a woman was deemed to be under the "protection and cover" of her husband's wing, a *feme covert*, as the French would say. It is from this covered perch that "she performs everything...under the protection and influence of her husband, her baron or lord; and her condition during her marriage is called her *coverture*."[103]

This was the view of women under British common law as it was often also applied to women in the fledgling states. "American legislators and judges, like their English counterparts, assumed an '*identitie* of person' between spouses after marriage," Norton notes.[104] As a result, a woman's "moveable property" owned before marriage, became her husband's to "sell, keep, or bequeath if he dies."[105] Without a husband, a married women could not "do much at home, and even less abroad," it was often said.[106]

But there was hardly uniformity. While some states relied heavily upon British common law in drafting their own codes and laws, others did not. The effect for women was a checkerboard of inequity and uncertainty throughout the eighteenth and nineteenth centuries.[107] For example, married women could not vote, become attorneys, or buy land in their own names in most states. These things were understood for all of the reasons set forth above. But there were also questions about "smaller things," such as whether a woman could own personal property (*i.e.*, clothes and jewelry) after marriage.

British common law seemed to imply that this too became the property of husbands, given its "mobility." But some early states declined to adopt such an oppressive measure. Thus, while husbands in New York,[108] Maryland, and Mississippi[109] could not sell off their wives' personal property without her consent if that personal property were brought into the marriage, husbands in Pennsylvania and many other states could.[110] And yet, a universal certainty for women, even in such a time of uncertainty, was that even though women "died" a civil death upon marriage with their independent civil identities tossed aside upon consummation, they were still recognized independently for purposes of crime.[111]

But America was evolving with industrialization, with it came the possibility of jobs for women in mills and factories.[112] There was progress on the educational front as well. In 1833, Oberlin College became the first college in the nation to admit women. Four years later, Mount Holyoke Seminary was founded as the first college for women in the United States. The constant change of the times led women and minorities to seek change for themselves.

In an effort to set a national agenda, American women gathered in Seneca Falls, New York, in 1848 for what would become the annual Woman's Rights Convention.[113] Though hardly the first meeting of its kind, historians note that the 1848 convention was significant because it marked the "first time a woman's rights meeting led to a sustained movement for reform."[114] For the next decade, beginning in 1850, a national women's convention was held every year, except 1857.[115]

And yet, moving beyond the orbit of the "domestic sphere" to the world of working women would prove a hundred-year struggle amid continued religious, social, and legal efforts to pull women "back into the fold." "[A] new ideology of motherhood and sexuality came into existence in American history during the 1840s: the 'moral motherhood' and 'cult of domesticity' paradigm," offers author Ann Ferguson.[116] "In this ideology, which…did not refer to all women, women were no longer conceived as inferior helpmates to men. Rather, women were 'moral mothers.' The domestic world was now conceived as a separate sphere and motherhood as a chosen vocation, one that required specilised [sic] skills: moral perception, intuition, and emotional connection."

But there was another hierarchy at work in early America as well that would prove significant to women. It was the racial hierarchy that justified slavery, and in the 1850s, that hierarchy would be tested before the United States Supreme Court. The Court's decision would divide the nation, setting the stage for sweeping changes in the law, including several amendments to the United States Constitution. These amendments—among the most notable and well-used today—have proved crucial tools in the struggle for equality for women, as well as minorities.

THE *DRED SCOTT* DECISION:
Carving Women's Rights Out of "Human Rights"

Many Americans believe that "the law" offers absolute protection against mistreatment and discrimination and that because of these laws, "going to court" means swift justice. But the process is far slower in reality, and for women hoping for equality and change, the wait proved painfully long. As set forth above, God's will, a "divine mission," gender, or socio-legal hierarchy has long justified discriminatory, selective, or unjust treatment toward women.

It was not until 1971, for example, with the United States Supreme Court's decision in *Reed v. Reed*,[117] that gender-preference statutes were struck down as unconstitutional. *Reed v. Reed* involved an Idaho probate statute declaring a preference for men to serve as executors of estates.[118] Statutes of this sort date back to the beginning of the United States, and in early America, neither the Bill of Rights nor the individual amendments to the United States Constitution— as they were then—had much force where women and minorities were concerned. Thus, it may be *divine* in its own right, as some have suggested, that one of the strongest constructs to gain a toehold in the battle for women's rights in America can be found, not in a pivotal case centered on traditional "women's issue." But rather in the historic *Dred Scott v. Sandford*[119] decision and the question of what makes a man.

In terms of background, the first ten amendments to the United States Constitution and the Preamble were collectively ratified on December 15, 1791.

These amendments, commonly known as the Bill of Rights, are often thought to have granted equal rights for everyone all at once. But what we know today is that "We the People,"—the oft-quoted language of the Preamble—did not include everyone. Descendants of African slaves and women were not initially thought to be part of the "we." Neither group was held to be comprised of equal "citizens" entitled to the equal protection of—and/or equal privileges under— the law.

Thus, women were relegated to the kitchen and "[s]laves had little protection…from a master's excessive cruelty."[120] Less protection even than children for whom "colonial legislators adopted policies designed to prevent heads of households from defrauding and cheating," Norton notes.[121] The deciding factor in both the case of slaves and women was biology, which established places for them in the social hierarchy—somewhere lower than men. Then came the *Dred Scott*[122] decision, and everything changed.

The year was 1857, and scholars admit today that the Justices of the United States Supreme Court were caught between the proverbial rock and a hard place as they faced the question of whether one's "property" had the right to freedom and equal rights under the United States Constitution. The descendants of slaves were human beings. But in early America, they were also "property"— *valuable property*—that labored, free of charge, in the sun-soaked fields of the agricultural South. Entire economies rested on their backs; the wealth of garden plantations the product of their labor.

Commerce was clearly in the mix. Did the Justices dare disturb this universe? Though that may have been on the Justices's minds as they considered the decision and all of the possible implications, the question before the Court was whether slaves and their descendants were "property" or equal men and women? Chief Justice Taney apparently drew the task of detailing the Court's effort to make sense of the apparent contradiction.

It is a decision that began and ended with a bang. According to Chief Justice Taney, he and his brethren were of the mind that neither slaves nor free blacks were "citizens" under the Constitution. Once that had been established, the Justices moved directly to the task of striking down a federal statute that forbid slavery in the new territories. In voiding the law, the Justices held that slaves were property. Therefore, the release of slaves would serve as a confiscation of property, and that "could hardly be dignified with the name of due process,"[123] the Justices reasoned.

It was a bad decision by most accounts, one that scholars say accelerated the Civil War,[124] and the subject of comment far and wide. Abraham Lincoln is reported to have remarked during his first inaugural address, for example, that "[t]here is always, of course, the chance that the decision may be overruled and never become a precedent for other cases."[125] It never did. The nation went to war instead. Afterwards, post-Civil War amendments to the United States Constitution effectively overruled the Court's decision in the *Dred Scott* case.

Women were always involved in the abolition movement, and following the Civil War, they stepped into high gear again. Legal scholars note that "[i]mmediately after Lincoln issued the Proclamation, abolitionists started to push for a constitutional amendment banning slavery. Elizabeth Cady Stanton and Susan B. Anthony organized the National Loyal Women's League, which collected 400,000 signatures in just fifteen months in support of the proposed Thirteenth Amendment. The league received substantial credit for the Amendment's passage, and disbanded once this goal was reached in February 1865."[126]

And though the *Dred Scott* case did not directly involve "women's issues," the decision would prove crucial to women for several reasons, chief among them that it sparked immediate and heated outrage. And outrage, more than a few conservative scholars note with some chagrin, popped the top on a "Pandora's box of substantive due process."[127] In an effort to make a relatively complex legal construct accessible, scholars have taken to describing "substantive due process" as the practice of "breathing life into" and/or giving "substance" to such previously undefined constitutional notions as "liberty" and "personhood," among others. [128]

The importance of substantive due process for women and minorities is that it provided the framework under which the Justices of the United States Supreme Court began to "uncover" and define fundamental constitutional rights. The substantive due process approach would lay the groundwork for many of the landmark cases of the 1960s and '70s, granting greater reproductive freedoms for women and female minors. But for nine decades between the *Dred Scott* decision and the landmark cases of the 1960s, America wrestled with the question of what rights and freedoms women should have and whether they were truly equal "citizens" with equal rights and privileges.

BRADWELL v. ILLINOIS:
Why Women Couldn't and Shouldn't Practice Law

In 1872, a young women from Illinois named Myra Bradwell raised the question. And she looked to the newly enacted Fourteenth Amendment—one of the post-Civil War amendments—for help. Scholars note that in many ways, Myra Bradwell was an ideal plaintiff for a test case. By all accounts, Bradwell was a "well-respected legal scholar, who served as editor of *The Chicago Legal News*."[129] And that might have been enough for other people.

But Myra Bradwell wanted to be an attorney. So, she began studying for the bar exam with the help of her husband, an attorney, and soon applied for admission to practice law before the Illinois bar. But that is where the problems began. The Supreme Court of Illinois refused to grant her a law license. The reason for this denial was that Myra Bradwell was *Myra* Bradwell. But there is a bit of historic controversy here.

Historians and legal scholars generally agree that "the Illinois Supreme Court ultimately denied Myra Bradwell membership in the bar because she was a woman." There are those who note, however, as a matter of proper historic context, that the state's rejection of her application was "based upon the fact that she was a wife."[130] But it is a distinction that may be technical at best. In Myra Bradwell's time, Illinois subscribed to the notion of *feme covert*.[131]

What this meant was that under Illinois law, because she was a married woman, Myra Bradwell could not enter into contracts. And, therefore, she could not practice law, the Illinois Supreme Court held.[132] Undaunted and with the help of her husband,[133] Myra Bradwell took her suit to the United States Supreme Court. The year was 1872, and Myra Bradwell looked to two recent events to offer justice. The first was that Iowa had admitted a married woman to its state bar. Belle A. Mansfield became the first female attorney in the United States in 1869.[134]

The second inspiration was the newly-amended United States Constitution, which now included the Fourteenth Amendment. Myra Bradwell's attorney argued that the Illinois Supreme Court's refusal to grant her a law license violated the Fourteenth Amendment, which sets forth the Equal Protection and Privileges and Immunities Clauses.[135] *Bradwell v. State*[136] offered one of the Fourteenth Amendment's first tests,[137] and although Myra Bradwell would probably prevail in a suit brought under either the Equal Protection or Due Process Clauses of that amendment today, it is a good thing she didn't hold her breath back then.

Amid considerable anticipation, the United States Supreme Court promptly declared that Myra Bradwell was *not* protected by the newly enacted Fourteenth Amendment's Privileges and Immunities Clause.[138] According to the Justices, the Illinois Supreme Court could deny Myra Bradwell the right to practice law, even if the decision rested solely on the fact that Myra Bradwell was a woman. In writing for the Court, Justice Miller reasoned that "admission to practice in the courts of the State is not [one of the protected federal privileges and immunities] which a State is forbidden to abridge."[139] In other words, the "federal" Supreme Court would not get involved.

Legal scholars note that *Bradwell v. Illinois*[140] was the first case argued under the newly enacted Fourteenth Amendment, though the United States Supreme Court's decision in the *Slaughter-House Cases*[141] was actually delivered first to the express defeat of the arguments made in *Bradwell v. Illinois*.[142] The *Slaughter-House Cases* involved challenge to a Louisiana statute prohibiting livestock yards and slaughterhouses in New Orleans and the surrounding area. Though the statute generally prohibited these institutions, a special exception was included for the Crescent City Company, allowing it to operate in the city. Butchers and others adversely affected by the statute brought suit, seeking to have it declared void. But the Louisiana Supreme Court upheld the statute.

The butchers appealed to the United States Supreme Court, arguing that the Louisiana statute violated the Thirteenth and Fourteenth Amendments. The Justices held, however, that all arguments regarding the Thirteenth Amendment were misplaced, because the sole purpose of that amendment was to abolish slavery. The Justices also rejected the Fourteenth Amendment arguments. The butchers alleged specifically that the statute violated the

Privileges and Immunities, Due Process, and Equal Protection Clauses of the Fourteenth Amendment.

In a decision that would defeat challenges of this sort for a century to come,[143] the Justices held that the Privileges and Immunities Clause of the Fourteenth Amendment effectively creates two kinds of citizenship: state citizenship and federal—or national—citizenship. The Justice held further that the language of the Privileges and Immunities Clause prohibited states from enacting laws infringing upon the privileges and immunities only of national citizens (*i.e.*, citizens outside of the state). The Justices also held that the Due Process Clause of the Fourteenth Amendment only required procedural due process where the enactment of a law was at issue and that the drafters only intended the Equal Protection Clause to apply to African Americans.

That was the historic context facing Bradwell's challenge of Illinois law before the United States Supreme Court, and it was apparently as noteworthy to the Justices as it would later become for historians. In issuing the decision for the Court in *Bradwell v. Illinois*, Justice Miller noted that the decision in *Slaughter-House Cases* rendered unnecessary the "elaborate" arguments offered in *Bradwell v. Illinois*.[144] Justice Miller also wrote the majority opinion in the *Slaughter-House Cases*.

Absent discussion of these "elaborate" arguments, the Court held that Myra Bradwell was entitled to no relief under the Fourteenth Amendment's Privileges and Immunities Clause,[145] because "the right to control and regulate the granting of license to practice law in the courts of a State is one of those powers which are not transferred for its protection to the Federal Government, and its exercise is in no manner governed or controlled by citizenship in the United States in the party seeking such license."[146]

In other words, the State of Illinois could deny women the right to practice law without violating the Privileges and Immunities Clause of the Fourteenth Amendment, which dealt with "federal citizenship," because that was an "internal" controversy. And that is where the law stood for nearly a century. Scholars have argued in recent years that the force of the Court's ruling in *Slaughter-House Cases* appears to have waned in the last century.[147]

And yet, the question remains as to whether something else might have been at work. Though Justice Miller chose, in writing the Court opinion, to answer this question in strictest legal form, Justice Joseph Bradley apparently felt compelled, in concurring, to offer his view of the nature of things. "The claim...under the [F]ourteenth [A]mendment of the Constitution" that it is one of "the privileges and immunities of women as citizens to engage in any and every profession, occupation, or employment in civil life" could not be affirmed,[148] Justice Bradley wrote.

And why not?

Because "[t]he natural and proper timidity and delicacy which belongs to the female sex evidently unfits it for many of the occupations of civil life. The constitution of the family organization, which is founded in the *divine* ordinance, as well as the nature of things, indicates the domestic sphere as that which properly belongs to the domain and functions of womanhood. The harmony, not to say identity, of interests and views which belong, or should belong, to the family institution is repugnant to the idea of a woman adopting a distinct and independent career from that of her husband."[149]

For the grand finale, Justice Bradley reasoned "[t]he paramount destiny and mission of woman is to fulfill the noble and benign offices of wife and mother. This is the law of the Creator." His ideas were hardly unique. What review of American caselaw shows instead is that in the early United States, not only did biology render women unfit for most things, it also allowed the states to treat them as less than equal "citizens."

THE AUTHORITY OF UNITED STATES SUPREME COURT DECISIONS

There are fifty-two separate court systems at work on a daily basis across the United States. Every state has its own state-run court system, handling state crimes, offenses, or civil claims arising under state law. The District of Columbia has a similar district-run system. In addition to the state court system, there is a parallel federal court system, straddling the states and District of Columbia, where cases involving federal crimes, federal offenses, and civil claims arising under federal statute or law are heard.

Most states have three-tier court systems. The lower courts, often called trial or superior courts, have jurisdiction over general matters where second-tier courts, often known as appellate courts, hold jurisdiction over the appeals of lower court decisions. The third tier of state courts—often called Supreme Courts—have the jurisdiction and authority to review appeals from the appellate as well as the lower courts. But these are state supreme courts, which are different from the United States Supreme Court.

The federal system has a similarly three-tiered structure. But the division of the lower federal trial courts within the states runs along federal "district" lines. Depending on the size and population, a state may be divided into anywhere from one to four federal judicial districts. There are some ninety-one federal districts across the United States. The federal system also has a second tier of appellate circuit courts, eleven in all, which are generally referred to in the legal context by their circuit number, (*i.e.*, the First Circuit Court of Appeals; the Second Circuit Court of Appeals, etc.). There is also a federal appellate court for the District of Columbia.

The final tier in the federal system is the United States Supreme Court, which is unique in its authority to review not only appeals of decisions by the lower federal courts as well as the federal appellate circuit courts, but also decisions issued by state supreme courts. Thus, United States Supreme Court decisions represent the final decision on the law, and that is why decisions by the United States Supreme Court have long been held to establish "the law of the land." It should be noted, however, that where a decision is not appealed, a lower federal circuit court or state supreme court ruling has been held to establish the law in either that circuit or that state.

The federal appellate courts hear nearly 30,000 cases a year compared to roughly 75 to 80 heard by the United States Supreme Court.

MINOR v. HAPPERSETT:
When is a Citizen Not a Citizen?

Two years after Justice Bradley's eloquent concurrence in *Bradwell v. Illinois*, the United States Supreme Court took up another case involving the question of "citizenship" and its meaning to women in light of the Constitution in the case of *Minor v. Happersett.*[150]

Virginia Minor was "a native born, free, white citizen of the United States, and of the State of Missouri,"[151] which were good things to be in the 1870s. But Virginia Minor wanted "to vote for electors for president and vice-president of the United States, and for a representative in Congress, and for other officers, at the general election held in November, 1872."[152] So she became a member of the National Woman Suffrage Association and attempted, along with dozens of other women, to register to vote in defiance of a Missouri law permitting only "male inhabitants" of the state to exercise that right.

As the "gentler sex," women were urged "not to wrinkle their foreheads with politics."[153] Women should be "content," instead "to soothe and calm the minds of their husbands returning ruffled from political debates," it was argued.[154] Most states had laws denying women the right to vote. Missouri was one of those states. But instead of giving up, when Virginia Minor was turned away from the polls she obtained permission from her husband to file suit, and the case eventually made its way to the United States Supreme Court.

The basis for Minor's claim was also the Fourteenth Amendment's Privileges and Immunities Clause. But this time, attorneys for Minor argued that as a United States "citizen," she was entitled to vote.[155] Again the Justices of the United States Supreme Court held that discrimination against women was a privilege of the states.

"There is no doubt that women may be citizens," the Court held. But the Constitution "has not added the right of suffrage to the privileges and immunities of citizenship as they existed at the time it was adopted." Thus, the question before the Court in the eyes of the Justices was whether the right of suffrage "was coexistent with the citizenship of States." After considered analysis, the Justices held that the "Constitution of the United States does not confer the right of suffrage upon anyone, and...the constitutions and laws of the several States which commit that important trust to men alone are not necessarily void."

What this construct means in practical terms was that the Justices were willing to accept a double standard in upholding the Missouri law. "The same laws precisely apply to both [sexes]," the Justices wrote. And, thus, Virginia Minor's rights under the Fourteenth Amendment had not been violated. Since birth, she had been a citizen, entitled to all the privileges and immunities of citizenship.[156] But the right to vote was not a federal privilege, the Justices held. It was a privilege to be granted by the states, and "all the citizens of the States were not invested with the right of suffrage."[157]

"No new state has ever been admitted to the Union which has conferred the right of suffrage upon women," according to the Court. "For nearly ninety years the people have acted upon the idea that the Constitution, when it conferred citizenship, did not necessarily confer the right of suffrage. If uniform practice long continued can settle the construction of so important an instrument as the Constitution of the United States confessedly is, most certainly it has been done here. Our province is to decide what the law is, not to declare what it should be."

How could it be that women could be denied the right to vote while with nearly the same stroke of the pen, the Justices of the United States Supreme Court would also declare that women are citizens and that the "same laws precisely apply to both sexes?" In upholding the Missouri law, the Justices essentially held that "[t]he same laws precisely apply to both [sexes]," and that Virginia Minor was a (federal) citizen from her birth, entitled to all the privileges and immunities of federal citizenship.[158] But as the Justices saw it, the right to vote was a "state privilege."

Women were finally granted the right to vote following the ratification of the Nineteenth Amendment on August 18, 1920,[159] and statutes that prescribe activities solely for reasons of gender are generally illegal today. But as legal scholars note, and as the examples of *Bradwell v. State* and *Minor v. Happersett* suggest, from "the beginning" defining the rights of women in America has been *complicated.*[160]

In that sense, the denial of the right to vote was simply symptomatic of a larger reality for women: arguments founded in biology, a social hierarchy that made feminine submission necessary, or simply because it "worked best" have been used throughout history to justify the treatment and cultural rank of women. Since the medieval period, when religion and politics went hand in hand, women have been trying to fend off demands that they embrace the virtue and perfection of Mary in a world of men, whose desires reflect the needs of a temporal life.

Women were good or bad. Often "dumb," but rarely smart. Childlike and foolish. Submissive by godly mandate. And always the tool of men. These were the early themes that shaped the lives of women, eventually making their way into the law in Europe and later into the young United States. For most of the twentieth century, women tried to undo many of these laws.

ENDNOTES FOR CHAPTER ONE

1   From the *Meriwether Lewis Anderson Papers* (manuscript on file with the Missouri State Historical Society), quoted by Stephen Ambrose in UNDAUNTED COURAGE (New York: Touchstone Books, 1996), at p. 285.
2   *Id.* at 20.

3   *Id.* (citing Rochonne Abrams, *The Colonial Childhood of Meriwether Lewis,* BULLETIN OF THE MISSOURI HISTORICAL SOCIETY, VOL. XXXIV, NO. 4, PT. 1 (July 1978), at p. 218).

4   *Id.* at 21.

5   *See* Norton, supra note 2, ENDNOTES FOR INTRODUCTION, at p. 3.

6   *Id.*

7   *Id.,* at p. 4 (citing, as reference and support: Peter Gay, THE ENLIGHTENMENT: AN INTERPRETATION, 2 VOLS. (New York: Alfred A. Knopf, 1966, 1996); Richard Godbeer, THE DEVIL'S DOMINION: MAGIC AND RELIGION IN EARLY NEW ENGLAND (New York: Cambridge University Press, 1992)).

8   *Id.* at 3–4.

9   *See* Mary Lefkowitz, *The Wandering Womb,* THE NEW YORKER, February 26 and March 4, 1996.

10   William Shakespeare, AS YOU LIKE IT, Act 3, Scene 2. (Shakespeare grants Rosalind all of the schizophrenic "qualities" belonging to "a woman in love." Says Rosalind: "Yes, one; and in this manner. He was to imagine me his love, his mistress; and I set him everyday to woo me; at which time would I, being but a *moonish* youth, grieve, be effeminate, changeable, longing and liking, proud, fantastical, apish, shallow, inconstant, full of tears, full of smiles, for every passion something and for no passion truly anything, as boys and women are for the most part cattle of this colour; would now like him, now loathe him; then entertain him, then forswear him; now weep for him, then spit at him; that I drave my suitor from his bad humour of love to a living humour of madness; which was, to forswear the full steam of the world and to live in a nook merely monastic. And thus I cur'd him; and this way will take upon me to wash your liver as clean as a sound sheep's heart, that there shall not be one spot of love in't.")

11   Reprinted by permission of publisher of THE TWO SEXES: GROWING UP APART, COMING TOGETHER, by Eleanor E. Maccoby, (Cambridge, Mass.: The Belknap Press of Harvard University Press, ©1988, by the President and Fellows of Harvard College), at p. 2.

12   *See* Erich Fromm, LOVE, SEXUALITY, AND MATRIARCHY (New York: Fromm International Publishing Corp., 1997), at p. 49.

13   In varying passages of the Bible, Mary is described in the following way: "And Jacob begat Joseph the husband of Mary, of whom was born Jesus, who is called Christ." MATTHEW 1:16. "Now the birth of Jesus Christ was on this wise: When as his mother Mary was espoused to Joseph, before they came together, she was found with child of the Holy Ghost. [¶] Then Joseph her husband, being just a man, and not willing to make her a public example, was minded to put her away privily. [¶] But while he thought on these things, behold, the angel of the Lord appeared unto him in a dream, saying, Joseph, thou son of David, fear not to take unto thee Mary thy wife; for that which is conceived in her is of the Holy Ghost." MATTHEW 1:18-20. And "[b]ehold, a virgin shall be with child, and shall bring forth a son, and they shall call his name Emmanuel, which being interpreted is, God with us." MATTHEW 1:23.

14   The GOSPEL ACCORDING TO LUKE includes that "[a]nd the angel came unto her, and said, Hail, thou that art highly favoured, [sic] the Lord is with thee; blessed art thou among women. [¶] And when she saw him, she was troubled at his saying, and cast in her mind what manner of salutation this should be. [¶] And the angel said unto her, Fear not, Mary; for thou hast found favour with God. [¶] And, behold, thou shalt conceive in thy womb, and bring forth a son, and shalt call his name JESUS. [¶] He shall be great, and shall be called the Son of the Highest: and the Lord God shall give unto him the throne of his father David: [¶] And he shall reign over the house of Jacob for ever; and of his kingdom there shall be no end. [¶] Then said Mary unto the angel, How shall this be, seeing I know not a man?" LUKE 1: 28–34.

15   *See, e.g.,* Robert Sullivan (with reporting by Cynthia Fox), *The Mystery of Mary,* LIFE, December 1996, at p. 45.

16   *See Who Was Mary?,* 20/20, ABC-TV, airing December 15, 2000, at 8 (transcript) (quoting Virginia Kimble, then a member of the Board of Directors of the Mariological Society of America). *See* ABCNEWS.com for actual transcript.

17   *See* The GOSPEL ACCORDING TO LUKE, *supra* note 14, at 1:34.

18   *See* Marilyn Yalom, A HISTORY OF THE WIFE (New York: HarperCollins, 2001), at p. 11 (citing MATTHEW 1:18-25)).

19   *Id.*

20   *See* Sullivan, *supra* note 15, at p. 45.

21   *See* Yalom, *supra* note 18, at p. 16.

22   *See* Sullivan, *supra* note 15, at p. 46.

23   *Id.*

24   *Id.*

25   *Id.*

26   *See* Sullivan, *supra* note 15, at pp. 46–48. Former priest-turned-writer Thomas Keneally explains this elevation in more political terms. According to Keneally, "[t]he rule of celibacy has meant that, as with the relationship between Christ and Mary, a priest's safest relationship with an earthly female is with his mother….(The linen bands that bind a priest's hands during his ordination ceremony are customarily put in his mother's casket after her death.) [¶] In keeping with the presumption that a priest's mother has no sexual meaning for her son, the Church has generated

doctrines of the Virgin Mary as a woman from whom all sexuality has been leached. According to the Gospels, Mary conceived Christ as a virgin, without intervention by a man. For centuries, the Church glorified the divine conception in art, music, and literature as one of its most alluring aspects. But, for Pius IX, whose papacy lasted from 1846 to 1878, it was not alluring enough. Worried by the spread of Freemasonry in Europe and by the forces of the Italian Risorgimento which meant to subsume the Papal States, he looked for special help from the Virgin, and, in 1854, declared her to have been immaculately conceived without the human stain of original sin." *See* Thomas Keneally, *Cold Sanctuary,* THE NEW YORKER, June 17 and 24, 2002, at pp. 58, 65.

27   *Id.* (citing Karen Armstrong, author of A HISTORY OF GOD: "Mary is continually reinvented. In each age, people have changed their definition of her to fit their own circumstances").

28   *Id.*

29   LUKE 1:31.

30   Pelikan is quoted by Sullivan, *supra* note 15, at p. 48.

31   *Id.*

32   *See* Yalom, *supra* note 18, at p. 16.

33   *See* GENESIS 3:6–7.

34   *See* JOHN MILTON, PARADISE LOST: AN AUTHORITATIVE TEXT BACKGROUNDS AND SOURCES CRITICISM (New York: W.W. Norton & Co., 1975), at p. 202.

35   From Elizabeth Cady Stanton, THE WOMAN'S BIBLE (Amherst, N.Y.: Prometheus Books, 1999), at p. 7. (Reprinted by permission of the publisher.) (Stanton writes that "[t]he Bible teaches that woman brought sin and death into the world, that she precipitated the fall of the race, that she was arraigned before the judgment seat of Heaven, tried, condemned, and sentenced. Marriage for her was to be a condition of bondage, maternity a period of suffering and anguish, and in silence and subjection, she was to play the role of a dependent on man's bounty for all her material wants, and for all the information she might desire on the vital questions of the hour, she was commanded to ask her husband at home"). *See also* Cullen Murphy, THE WORD ACCORDING TO EVE: WOMEN AND THE BIBLE IN ANCIENT TIMES AND OUR OWN (New York: Houghton Mifflin Company, 1998).

36   *See* Milton, *supra* note 34, at p. 207.

37   *See* Fromm, *supra* note 12, at pp. 55–56 (citing GENESIS 3:6).

38   *See* Cullen Murphy, *Is the Bible Bad News for Women?* THE WILSON QUARTERLY 14 (Summer 1998), at pp. 19–20.

39   *Id.*

40   *See* Elizabeth Wurtzel, BITCH: IN PRAISE OF DIFFICULT WOMEN (New York: Doubleday, 1998), at pp. 40–41 (Wurtzel argues that Delilah was not sixteen at the time of the infamous betrayal of Sampson).

41   *See, e.g.,* Angela Davis in *Racism and Reproductive Rights* (reprinted in FROM ABORTION TO REPRODUCTIVE FREEDOM: TRANSFORMING A MOVEMENT (Marlene Gerber Fried, ed. 1990) (Boston: South End Press, 1990), at pp. 19–20); Reay Tannahill, SEX IN HISTORY (New York: Stein and Day, 1982), at pp. 364–65 (Tannahill explains that during the Victorian Age, indiscriminate sexual activity led to a near epidemic of disease, which women bore much of the societal blame for, due in some measure to the biological fact that women could be infected and continue to spread disease without knowing it. By contrast, early symptoms of infection were often apparent to men, who could then seek treatment); Linda Gordon, WOMAN'S BODY, WOMAN'S RIGHT: A SOCIAL HISTORY OF BIRTH CONTROL IN AMERICA (Toronto, Canada: Woman's Educational Press, 1977), at p. 20.

42   *See* Daniel Maguire, SACRED CHOICES: THE RIGHT TO CONTRACEPTION AND ABORTION IN TEN WORLD RELIGIONS (Minneapolis, Minnesota: Fortress Press, 2001), at p. 39.

43   *See* Yalom, *supra* note 18, at p. 16.

44   *Id.*

45   *See* Maguire, *supra* note 42, at p. 39.

46   *See* Garry Wills, PAPAL SINS: STRUCTURES OF DECEIT (New York: Doubleday, 2000), at p. 204.

47   *See* Stephen O'Shea, THE PERFECT HERESY: THE REVOLUTIONARY LIFE AND DEATH OF THE MEDIEVAL CATHARS (New York: Walker & Co., 2000), at p. 56.

48   *Id.* at 20.

49   *Id.*

50   *Id.* at 10–12.

51   *Id.* at 40–41.

52   *Id.* (According to O'Shea, "[i]n a debate of 1207, when a female Perfect rose to rebut a point of discussion, a monk snapped at her, 'Go back to your spinning, Madame, it's not your place to speak to such an assembly.'" *Id.* at 56.)

53   *Id.* at 41.

54   *Id.* at 12, 57, at 106–107.

55   *Id.*

56   *See* Jonathan Sumption, THE ALBIGENSIAN CRUSADE (New York: Faber & Faber, 1999, paperback edition), at pp. 77–81. (In offering this and other points surrounding these events, Sumption notes that "[t]he chronology of these events is highly conjectural.")

57   Some historians note that there was a far larger backdrop to the these events. Specifically, although the defiance of the Cathars had always been a problem, only after a papal representative was mur-

dered is the Pontiff said to have "sunk his head into his hands and retired to pray at the shrine of St. Peter below the high altar of the Vatican basilica." In the next few weeks, the Pope began inviting French knights to hunt down the Count of Toulouse, the man believed responsible for the murdered legate's death. Once the Count was dead, the knights were free to lay claim to his property. *See* Sumption, *supra* note 56, at p. 77.

58   *Id.* at p. 93.

59   *Id.* (Sumption notes that "this motto has passed into history as the epitome of the spirit which had brought the crusaders to the south." But accounts of the crusading army's mass as well as the number killed in Béziers vary. Though one writer suggests that "about twenty thousand men, women, and children, including Catholic priests, [were killed] in the space of the morning." Sumption reports simply that "[t]he legate reported the massacre without comment to [Pope] Innocent III, remarking only that 'neither age, nor sex, nor status had been spared.'")

60   *See* O'Shea, *supra* note 47, at pp. 88–92.

61   *See* Sumption, *supra* note 56, at p. 149.

62   *See* O'Shea *supra* note 47, at p. 13.

63   *Id.* at 2.

64   *See* B. Netanyahu, THE ORIGINS OF THE INQUISITION IN FIFTEENTH CENTURY SPAIN (New York: Random House, 1995), at p. 734.

65   *See* O'Shea, *supra* note 47, at p. 13.

66   *See* Philip Jenkins, *The Next Christianity*, THE ATLANTIC MONTHLY, October 2002, pp. 53–68, at p. 55.

67   *See* His Holiness John Paul II, CROSSING THE THRESHOLD OF HOPE (New York: Alfred A. Knopf, 1994), at p. 45 (citing the Apostles' Creed).

68   *Id.*

69   *See* Sullivan *supra* note 15, at pp. 48, 50. (Writes Sullivan, "[i]n 1974 [Pope Paul VI] sought, in the words of feminist theologian Marina Warner, 'to represent [Mary] as the steely champion of the oppressed and a woman of action and resolve.' This sounded good to many modernist women in the Church, who wondered if a new day was dawning for them. *Inside the Vatican*, commenting on the 'remarkable and completely unexpected rebirth of attention,' to Mary, said the aims of Vatican II had been foiled 'by events themselves, as if a "highest authority" has decreed that Mary receive great honor despite all the hesitations of "reasonable" theologians.'")

70   *Id.* at 54. ("In Bayside, Queens, where there was a Mary appearance in 1970, a brochure of her wisdom can be obtained by calling a toll-free number: 800-345-MARY," Sullivan writes.)

71   *Id.*

72   *Id.*

73   *Id.*

74   *Id.*

75   *See* Maguire, *supra* note 42, at p. 121.

76   *Id.* at 31. (In a telling note Maguire adds that "[w]ith more than a bit of irony, the then Prime Minister Brundtland of Norway said of the Rio conference: 'States that do not have any population problem—in one particular case, even no births at all [Vatican City]—are doing their best, their utmost, to prevent the world from making sensible decisions regarding family planning.'")

77   *See* Dianne Hales, JUST LIKE A WOMAN: HOW GENDER SCIENCE IS REDEFINING WHAT MAKES US FEMALE (New York: Bantam Book, 1999), at p. 9.

78   *See, e.g.,* Otten, *supra* note 8, ENDNOTES FOR INTRODUCTION, at p. 36.

79   *Id.*

80   *See* Agnes Thorton Bird, quoted in Keith Curry and Elizabeth M. Almquist, *Winning the Vote: The Battle at the State Level*, in WOMEN AND THE CONSTITUTION: SYMPOSIUM PAPERS (Joyce M. Pair, ed. 1990) (Atlanta, Georgia: The Carter Center of Emory University, 1990), at p. 75.

81   *Id.*

82   *See* Norton, *supra* note 5, at p. 57.

83   *Id.* (citing T.E., *The Lawes Resolutions of Women's Rights; or, The Lawes Provision for Woemen* [sic] (London: John Moore, 1632), at p. 6).

84   *Id.*

85   *Id.*

86   *See* Peter Laslet (ed.), PATRIARCHA AND OTHER POLITICAL WORKS OF SIR ROBERT FILMER (Oxford: Basil Blackwell, 1949), at pp. 245, 283, 57. *See also* Gordon J. Schochet, PATRIARCHALISM IN POLITICAL THOUGHT: THE AUTHORITARIAN FAMILY AND POLITICAL SPECULATION AND ATTITUDES ESPECIALLY IN SEVENTEENTH-CENTURY ENGLAND (New York: Basic Books, 1975), at pp. 110–113.

87   *Id.* at 59–60.

88   *See* John Locke, TWO TREATISES (Laslett, ed.), I Sec. 44-47 (pp. 172–73).

89   *See* Norton, *supra* note 5, at pp. 61–62.

90   *See* Locke, *supra* note 88, at pp. 319–321.

91   *See* Norton, *supra* note 5, at p. 59.

92   *Id.* (citing Mary Astell, SOME REFLECTIONS UPON MARRIAGE (2d ed., London: R. Wilkin, 1703), pp. 47–48). (Norton notes that "[s]ix years later, in the preface to the third edition, Astell adopted a more secular approach, arguing that the need for a final authority in the family and women's phys-

ical weakness had combined to give men their superior position. *See* Bridget Hill ed., THE FIRST ENGLISH FEMINIST: REFLECTIONS UPON MARRIAGE AND OTHER WRITINGS BY MARY ASTELL (New York, St. Martin's Press, 1986), at p. 75).

93   *Id*. at 58.

94   *Id*. at 59.

95   *See* Sir William Blackstone, *Commentaries on the Laws of England*, in MALE AUTHORITY IN MARRIAGE, WOMEN, THE FAMILY AND FREEDOM: THE DEBATE IN DOCUMENTS, VOL. I (Susan Groag Bell and Karen M. Offen eds.) (Stanford: Stanford University Press, 1983), at p. 33. (Under British common law, once wed a woman and a man merged into one creating a circumstance by which, according to Sir William Blackstone, "the very being or legal existence of the woman is suspended during marriage, or at least is incorporated and consolidated into that of the husband: under whose wing, protection, and cover, she performs everything; and is therefore called in our law-French a *feme covey*, or under the protection and influence of her husband, her baron or lord; and her condition during her marriage is called her coverture.")

96   *See* Marjorie Wall Bingham, WOMEN AND THE CONSTITUTION: STUDENT TEXTBOOK (Atlanta, Georgia: The Carter Center of Emory University, 1990), at p. 21. ("While the majority of women were probably most affected by ideas of the home being women's sphere, the minority of women reformers had a lasting effect on American history.") *See also* Ann Ferguson, BLOOD AT THE ROOT: MOTHERHOOD, SEXUALITY & MALE DOMINANCE (London, England: Pandora Press, 1989), at p. 104.

97   For further reading on this topic, *see* Sylvia A. Law, *The Founders on Families*, in THE UNITED STATES CONSTITUTION: ROOTS, RIGHTS, AND RESPONSIBILITIES (Washington: Smithsonian Institution Press (A.E. Dick Howard ed.), 1992), at pp. 213, 216–17.

98   *See* THE ADAMS PAPERS: ADAMS FAMILY CORRESPONDENCE, Vol. I, edited by L.H. Butterfield, *Abigail to John, March 31, 1776*, at 120–121. (Reprinted by permission of the publisher of THE ADAMS PAPERS: ADAMS FAMILY CORRESPONDENCE, Vol. I, edited by L.H. Butterfield, Cambridge, Massachusetts: The Belknap Press of Harvard University Press, © 1963 by the Massachusetts Historical Society.)

99   *See* Norton, *supra* note 5, at p. 58.

100   *See* Bingham, *supra* note 96, at p. 7 (citing Linda Kerber, *History Can Do It No Justice: Women and the Interpretation of the American Revolution*, in WOMEN IN THE AGE OF THE AMERICAN REVOLUTION (Ronald Hoffman and Albert, Peter J., eds.), at p. 29.)

101   *Id*.

102   *Id*.

103   *Id*. at 45.

104   *See* Norton, supra note 5, at p. 72.

105   *Id*.

106   *Id*. (citing LAWES RESOLUTIONS, 79–90, pp. 116–229; MD. ARCHS, XLI, 43; WP, IV, p. 147).

107   Others scholars write of this period that "[i]n the colonial states, where old English common law applied, the wife did eventually acquire some rights to previously owned property. In the middle of the nineteenth century, some states passed the Married Women's Property Acts. The first one was enacted in Mississippi in 1839; it allowed women to keep control of the property they brought with them to the marriage. In 1848 New York passed a Married Women's Property Act that prohibited a husband from disposing of a wife's previously owned property (Deckard 1983). Another act was passed in 1860 in New York which gave married women rights to their earnings as well (Schneir 1972). However, the old underlying assumption about the competence of women prevailed in the implementation of the law until it was officially changed in 1971 in *Reed v. Reed*, when the U.S. Supreme Court ruled that women were to be included as persons under the Constitution." *See* Winnie Hazou, THE SOCIAL AND LEGAL STATUS OF WOMEN, A GLOBAL PERSPECTIVE (New York: Praeger, 1990), at p. 57.

108   *See* Hazou, *supra* note 107, at p. 57.

109   *Id*.

110   *See* BINGHAM, *supra* note 96, at p. 4 (Chart A); Hazou, *supra* note 107, at p. 38.

111   For a contrast of how women were treated in the criminal context at a time when women had no legal civil identity, *see, e.g.,* Anne Butler, GENDERED JUSTICE IN THE AMERICAN WEST: WOMEN PRISONERS IN MEN'S PENITENTIARIES (Urbana, Illinois: University of Illinois Press, 1997).

112   *See* Zemon Davis & Ker Conway, *supra* note 1, ENDNOTES FOR INTRODUCTION, at p. 84. ("When enlightenment ideas came to America, the debate about women's rights found a new context, since the most powerful form of social hierarchy there was not gender but race. And the American Constitution, by dispensing with hereditary rank and monarchical institutions, immediately granted women a new role: teaching republican values to young Americans. The new republic opened many avenues to women: social, economic, political, educational, and religious. Evangelical Christianity made the home, not the church, the site of religious instruction.")

113   *See* Pair, *supra* note 80, at p. 28.

114   *See* Bingham, *supra* note 96, at p. 28.

115   *See, e.g.,* Barbara Allen Babcock *et al.,* SEX DISCRIMINATION AND THE LAW: HISTORY, PRACTICE, AND THEORY (Boston: Little Brown (2nd ed. 1996)), at p. 45.

116   *See also* Ferguson, *supra* note 10, ENDNOTES FOR INTRODUCTION, at p. 104.

117   404 U.S. 71 (1971). (Specifically, the Idaho statute declared that where there were equal candidates to serve as administrator of an estate, "males must be preferred to females...." After Richard Lynn Reed died, both his mother, Sally Reed, and his father, Cecil Reed, filed to serve as administrator. A probate judge held, in accordance with the statute, that Cecil Reed should serve. Sally Reed appealed. In striking down the Idaho statute, the Justices of the Supreme Court held that the Idaho statute cannot stand, because "[b]y providing dissimilar treatment for men and women who are thus similarly situated, the challenged section violates the Equal Protection Clause.") Other cases regarding gender classifications decided around that time include *Stanton v. Stanton*, 421 U.S. 7 (1975) and *Orr v. Orr*, 440 U.S. 268 (1979).

118   Five years later, in the case of *Craig v. Boren*, 429 U.S. 190 (1976), the United States Supreme Court began to apply the Equal Protection Clause analysis to gender discrimination cases.

119   60 U.S. (19 How.) 393, 404–06, 417–18, 419–20 (1857).

120   *See* Norton, *supra* note 5, at p. 103.

121   *Id.*

122   60 U.S. 393 (1856).

123   *Id.* at 450. (The "due process" clause at issue here was the Fifth Amendment Due Process Clause, which deals with federal legislation. The Fourteenth Amendment, which applies to states, had not yet been adopted. But the language of the two clauses is identical.)

124   *See* Stephen B. Presser, RECAPTURING THE CONSTITUTION (Washington, D.C.: Regnery Publishing, Inc., 1994) at p. 130.

125   *See* Wechsler, *The Court and the Constitution*, 65 COLUM. L. REV. at pp. 1001, 1008 (1965) (quoting Abraham Lincoln referring to the *Dred Scott* decision in his first inaugural address).

126   *See* Babcock, *supra* note 115, at p. 49.

127   *See* Presser, *supra* note 124, at p. 130 (citing ROBERT BORK, THE TEMPTING OF AMERICA: THE POLITICAL SEDUCTION OF THE LAW (New York: Free Press, 1990), at p. 28.)

128   See Ellen Alderman and Caroline Kennedy in THE RIGHT TO PRIVACY (New York: Alfred A. Knopf, 1995), at p. 55.

129   *See* Leslie Friedman Goldstein, THE CONSTITUTIONAL RIGHTS OF WOMEN: CASES IN LAW AND SOCIAL CHANGE (University of Wisconsin Press, 2d ed., 1988), at p. 67.

130   *See, e.g.,* Babcock *et al., supra* note 115, at p. 61.

131   *Id.* at 21. (Thus, according to the authors, "[a] wife could not enter into contracts, write wills, or sue or be sued in her own right. She could not legally manage or retain the fruits of her real property or acquire or keep personal property—these were the prerogatives of her husband. Her labor, too, belonged to her husband; his were the proceeds of any work she performed in the home, in business with him, or for others.") *See also* Law, *supra* note 97, at p. 216. ("As the American edition of *Blackstone's Commentaries* explained, when a woman married, her legal identity merged into her husband's; she was dead under civil law. She could not sue, be sued, enter into contracts, make wills, keep her own earnings, or control her own property. Her husband had the right to chastise her, restrain her freedom, and force her to engage in sexual intercourse against her will.")

132   For further discussion, *see* Bingham, *supra* note 96, at p. 53.

133   Because married women had no legal identity, they were not allowed to file suit without the permission of their husbands.

134   *See* Haselmayer, *Belle A. Mansfield*, 55 WOMEN L.J. 46 (1969).

135   The Fourteenth Amendment is a post-Civil War amendment, ratified on July 9, 1868, and intended to protect "citizens" from wrongful actions by state actors. Bradwell's lawyer argued that "...the Fourteenth Amendment opens to every citizen of the United States, male or female, black or white, married or single, the honorable professions as well as the servile employments of life; and that no citizen can be excluded from any one of them. Intelligence, integrity, and honor are the only qualifications that can be prescribed as conditions precedent to any entry upon any honorable pursuit or profitable avocation, and all the privileges and immunities which I vindicate to a colored citizen, I vindicate to our mothers, our sisters, and our daughters." BINGHAM, *supra* note 96, at p. 53 (citing Deborah L. Rhode, JUSTICE AND GENDER: SEX DISCRIMINATION AND THE LAW (Cambridge: Harvard University Press, 1989), at p. 23).

136   83 U.S. (16 Wall.) 130 (1872).

137   *Bradwell v. Illinois* was actually the first case argued under the newly enacted Fourteenth Amendment, though the Supreme Court's decision in the *Slaughter-House Cases*, 77 U.S. 273 (1873), was delivered first to the express defeat of the arguments made in *Bradwell v. Illinois*. *See* FRIEDMAN, *supra* note 129, at p. 66. (According to Friedman, Justice Miller reasoned, in writing for the Court, that the ruling in the *Slaughter-House Cases* rendered elaborate argument unnecessary in *Bradwell v. Illinois*. *See Bradwell*, 83 U.S. at 139.)

138   The Fourteenth Amendment states in pertinent part: "All persons born or naturalized in the United States, and subject to the jurisdiction thereof, are citizens of the United States and of the State wherein they reside. No State shall make or enforce any law which shall abridge the privileges or immunities of citizens of the United States; nor shall any State deprive any person of life, liberty, or property, without due process of law; nor deny to any person within its jurisdiction the equal protection of the laws."

139 There is a distinction to be noted here. The Fourteenth Amendment contains several clauses: the Due Process, the Equal Protection, and the Privileges and Immunities clauses as they apply to the state. There is no telling whether Myra Bradwell's case might have been decided differently were it brought under another of these clauses. With regard to the Privileges and Immunities Clause, Justice Miller reasoned further that "the right to control and regulate the granting of license to practice law in the courts of a State is one of those powers which are not transferred for its protection to the Federal Government, and its exercise is in no manner governed or controlled by citizenship in the United States in the party seeking such license." *Bradwell v. Illinois*, 83 U.S. (16 Wall.) at 139. If the Court were ruling on this case today, however, it is safe to assume that it would be decided differently.

140 83 U.S. (16 Wall.) 130 (1872).

141 *Slaughter-House Cases, In re*, 83 U.S. 36 (1872).

142 *See* Friedman Goldstein *supra* note 129, at p. 66.

143 Legal scholars have long noted that the Court's decision in the *Slaughter-House Cases* spelled doom to most early cases interpreting the Fourteenth Amendment's Privileges and Immunities Clause, which was so "thoroughly eviscerated" by the Court's decision in the *Slaughter-House Cases*, 77 U.S. 273 (1873), "that on only one occasion since has that clause been invoked by the Court to invalidate state legislation" (*Colgate v. Harvey* (1935), a decision that was quickly overruled in *Madden v. Kentucky* (1940)). See Saul K. Padover, (revised by Jacob W. Landynski), THE LIVING U.S. CONSTITUTION, (3d revised ed., Meridian New York 1995 (1953)), at p. 212. More recently, however, scholars have noted that the once-formidable force of the Slaughterhouse cases may have waned in the last century. See, e.g., Roger Pilon, *"Slaughter-House Cases" Undone?*, NAT'L L.J., May 31, 1999, at A22.

144 *See Bradwell*, 83 U.S. at 139.

145 For review of the various clauses of the Fourteenth Amendment, *see supra* note 139.

146 *Bradwell v. Illinois*, 83 U.S. (16 Wall.) at 139.

147 *See, e.g.*, Roger Pilon, *"Slaughter-House Cases" Undone?*, NAT'L L.J., May 31, 1999, at A22.

148 *Bradwell v. Illinois*, 83 U.S. (16 Wall.) at 140–141.

149 *Id.* (Justice Bradley added further that by social convention "a woman had no legal existence separate from her husband, who was regarded as her head and representative in the social state; and, not withstanding some recent modifications of this civil status, many of the special rules flowing from and dependent upon this cardinal principle still exist in full force in most States. One of these is, that a married woman in incapable, without her husband's consent, of making contracts which shall be binding on her or him. This very incapacity was one circumstance which the Supreme Court of Illinois deemed important in rendering a married woman incompetent fully to perform the duties and trusts that belong to the office of an attorney and consellor [*sic*].")

150 88 U.S. (21 Wall.) 162 (1874). (The Supreme Court held that even if women were "citizens" the Constitution did not guarantee women the right to vote. Therefore, if states prohibited such action, there was nothing women could do.)

151 *Id.* at 163.

152 *Id.*

153 *See* Pair, *supra* note 80, at p. 76.

154 *Id.*

155 For review of the language of the Fourteenth Amendment, *see supra* note 143.

156 88 U.S. (21 Wall.) at 170.

157 *Id.*

158 *Id.*

159 The Nineteenth Amendment was ratified on August 18, 1920. The language of that amendment expressly provides that "[t]he right of citizens of the United States to vote shall not be denied or abridged by the United States or by any State on account of sex. Congress shall have power to enforce this article by appropriate legislation." But even that was not without controversy. Some scholars argue that as the abolition movement grew, "[t]he argument for suffrage then became more expedient: white women's votes would balance those of newly enfranchised black males and immigrants. The majority that ratified the 19th Amendment in 1920 was built on these racist grounds." *See, e.g.*, Zemon Davis & Ker Conway, *supra* note 112 at p. 84.

160 *See* Bingham, *supra* note 96, at pp. 2–5.

CHAPTER TWO

Biology, Sex, and the Obligation of Motherhood

WOMEN AND THE "GIFT:"
A Life Defined by Biology

Historians taking the measure of our lives may one day conclude that the modern hymns of sexual liberation were best found on the pages of women's magazines and popular fiction. From Erica Jong's *Fear of Flying* to monthly dispatches graphic enough to make Dr. Ruth blush, the stories of the latter half of the twentieth century for women were about "great sex": who was having it, how to get it, and what to do to make it *even better*.[1]

But sex has always been a problem for women. Or perhaps more precisely, the possibility that women might have sex for reasons other than procreation has always been a problem for women. As set forth in Chapter One, women have long derived social value from their ability to bear children: heirs during the feudal period,[2] extra hands in agricultural times.[3] And, thus, sex as a necessary precursor to childbearing has always held a utilitarian place in society. But what if a woman did not intend to bear children? Could she still have sex? And was there even the question of pleasure for her?

The last four decades of the twentieth century were marked by a series of gains for women in the area of reproductive rights, and that is what people tend to remember. But this expansive period stands in stark contrast to the previous two centuries, when the efforts of women to gain rights and reforms met Biblical quotes, prosecution, and the zealous efforts of state officials to "preserve the family" by reaffirming the role women were meant to play in American society.

"Victorian women," for example, "were commonly characterized as 'angels in the house,' ethereal spirits lacking sensual and sexual needs, less lusty and 'purer' than men," gender historian Marilyn Yalom notes. "This view was furthered not only by nineteenth-century novels featuring innocent brides and virtuous wives, but also by medical treatises promoting an ideology of female sexlessness. The esteemed British doctor William Acton was convinced that 'many of the best mothers, wives, and managers of households know little of...sexual indulgence. Love of home, of children, and of domestic duties are the only passions that they feel.'"[4]

And of course, out-of-wedlock sex had no place in an ordered society. "[I]f men and women engaged in sexual activity only within marriage, and if dependents showed appropriate deference to their real and their metaphorical parents, the cornerstones of civilized society would successfully be laid," seventeenth- and eighteenth-century British and American leaders believed, Norton notes.[5]

In accordance with these notions, the social identity historically assigned to women was that of wife, subordinate, caregiver, and mother. Women were "nurturers"—*their biological function*—and caregivers—*a natural extension of that function*—mothers to their own children and the "mothers of the nation" with an obligation to serve the family of mankind.[6] Thus, an independent female sexual identity—one devoid of maternal instincts or disinclined to produce heirs—was a threat to society, as dangerous as terrorism, viral and contagious, and downright unpatriotic.

But if marriage was the "goal" of proper women,[7] it was the requirement of men of a certain class. And the best evidence of a loving marriage, seventeenth-century contemporary wisdom went, was children.[8] But "...because an unmarried man could not have legitimate children, marriage necessarily preceded the relationship between a father and his sons, which many theorists interpreted as the foundation for all political authority," historian Norton explains.[9]

And they quickly took possession.

"Men's first step to control was the establishment of patriliny," author Marilyn French argues, "which overturned the ancient tradition of naming children for the known parent, the mother. Tracing children's descent through the male line gave men an excuse to guard women's sexuality by forcing [women] into marriage and childbearing at very young ages. They killed or enslaved women for losing virginity (even if they were raped), put them in purdah, denied them rights to divorce or child custody, and killed them for abortion or extramarital sex."[10]

The parables of the Bible and literature taught that virginity was a possession to be protected by ostracism, sometimes violence, and the law. Shakespeare's Prospero curses the union of his daughter, for example, should her intended "break her virgin-knot before [a]ll sanctimonious ceremonies may [w]ith full and holy rite be minist'red."[11] But even women who were not virgins were expected to obey the rules of social decorum (*i.e.*, no sex out of wedlock) or they would pay the price. Among early American writers, Nathaniel Hawthorne offers the passion play of the condemned Hester Prynne, whose figurative branding was a disappointment to those within her community who would have preferred that a real iron be put to her flesh.[12]

Of course, there was misogyny to this pattern of community "protection," dating at least as far back as the Medieval Period when young men were "allowed the freedom of their 'youth' in the form of liaisons with girls of lower station, concubines, and prostitutes," while daughters "were carefully supervised and allowed little opportunity to lose their precious virginity before they married, usually at an early age," Yalom explains.[13]

An element of commerce was also involved. Virginity increased a young girl's chances of a good marriage. Assurance of a child's "purity" could be traded for land or dowry by the middle class. In that sense, a young girl's "maiden's head" was the commodity of empires with the power to join territories. And, although America had no royalty of its own, similar rules would make their way into the laws of this new country.

MODERN EUROPE, EARLY AMERICA:
Protecting Society—Guarding Sexuality

Like the British before them, the leaders of the young American states were concerned about out-of-wedlock sex and what it might do to society were it allowed to go unchecked. But in England, church courts overwhelmingly dealt with such matters. There were no church courts in America.[14] That left communal bodies and emerging legislatures. To magistrates and legislators in the new colonies, "marriage primarily required parental consent and a formal wedding ceremony, whether performed by a clergyman or a magistrate. To ordinary colonists, marriage…consisted of a mutual contract by the parties and the act of sexual intercourse," Norton argues.[15]

"Fornication"—defined as "sexual intercourse by any man with a single woman"[16]—was a crime in all of the American colonies. There were relatively few prosecutions in Chesapeake Bay, for example. But "fornication" was frequently the basis of prosecutions in New England. There were more than 150 prosecutions for "premarital fornication" in New England during the early decades of the seventeenth century.[17] Indeed, prosecutions for the offense were reportedly so vigorously pursued that in the northern colonies they constituted nearly half of all criminal charges filed against married couples and approximately one-fifth of all prosecutions of married women.[18] By contrast, the numbers for men were considerably smaller; a mere "5 percent of all male criminals faced such allegation," according to Norton.[19]

But predatory conduct towards maids and minor females also drew the attention of legislators, prompting passage of a Plymouth law in 1638, equating the "deflowering" of girls younger than sixteen by disingenuous, dishonest, or forcible means with stealing. Though this might simply have been considered the "freedom of youth" in Medieval Europe, this sort of "practicing" created a barrier to the "contracting of valid marriages," Plymouth lawmakers reasoned.

Few men would voluntarily agree to marry a woman who was not a virgin.[20] Rhode Island authorities passed a similar law in 1647. The Bay Colony followed a year later and New Haven joined in passing a similarly worded law in 1656.[21]

There were real consequences to sex: it wreaked havoc on "ordered societies," early lawmakers argued. And in some ways, it did. During the Victorian Age, "indiscriminate activity" brought on a near epidemic of sexually transmitted disease, some scholars note. And though men—who outnumbered women in the early United States—were often more involved, women bore the blame.[22]

The structure of the female reproductive system was (as it is now) such that a woman could be infected and continue to spread disease without knowing she had it. By contrast, symptoms of infection were often more apparent to men, who could seek treatment. Thus, the female body once again became a "contagion." And there was another problem.

Turn-of-the-twentieth-century British newspapers warned of the horrors sexually active unmarried women wrought on society. "[I]gnorance and fear of the body and sexuality affected women of all classes," writes Sheila Rowbotham, author of A Century of Women.[23] That "fear of sex as well as poverty"[24] stoked classist fires, raising the alarm of "the tragic consequences" of sex out of wedlock. Among the consequences, moralists argued, were the "suicides of pregnant servants, corpses of abandoned babies, and the 'bastardy-order courts', when desperate unmarried mothers took fathers to court."[25]

A similar problem was emerging in America, and while it may or may not have made the papers, it made it to court. In terms of numbers, between 1916 and 1925, at least 150 "bastardy" cases were heard in courts across the United States.[26] Of course, "unmarried mothers" and pregnant servants did not impregnate themselves. (This was well before the time of assisted reproduction.) Men were clearly involved somewhere along the way.

And yet, it was single, poor, immigrant, and other "statusless" women, their bellies swollen with the betrayal of secret or forced trysts, who were branded the literal bearers of ill-tidings; "mothers of the underclass."[27] In the echoes of a controversial notion that would resurface periodically throughout the twentieth century, the public debate over "race suicide" among whites and a world populated by "undesirables" got underway, scholars suggest.

"[C]lass bias and racism crept into the birth control movement when it was still in its infancy," argues Angela Davis in Racism and Reproductive Rights.[28] "More and more, it was assumed within birth control circles that poor women, black and immigrant alike, had a 'moral obligation to restrict the size of their families.' What was demanded as a 'right' for the privileged came to be interpreted as a 'duty' for the poor."

As set forth below in greater detail, this has remained a recurrent theme in the debate over birth control in America. But what would be demanded of poor immigrants and minorities or held as appropriate for "imbeciles" by the nation's highest court would be resisted with great vigor by authorities who would battle in and out of court to preserve the obligation of women regarding "children" well into the next century.

WOMEN AND THE WOMB:
The Emerging Birth Control Debate

The twentieth century dawned in America on a falling white birth rate. In 1800, an average of seven children were born to each "American-born white wife," historians report. [29] By 1900, that number had fallen to roughly half.[30] Though there may have been several factors, some historians suggest that this decline—occurring as it did among young white women—may have been due to the use of contraceptives or abstinence, though few talked openly about it.[31]

"In spite of all the rhetoric against birth control, the birthrate plummeted in the late nineteenth century in America and Western Europe (as it had in France the century before); family size was halved by the time of World War I," notes Shari Thurer in *The Myth of Motherhood*.[32]

As issues go, the "plummeting birthrate" among whites was a powder keg, sparking outcry as the "failure" of the privileged class to have children was contrasted with the "failure" of poor immigrants and minorities to control the number of children they were having. Criticism was loud and rampant. "The upper classes started the trend, and by the 1880s the swarms of ragged children produced by the poor were regarded by the bourgeoisie, so Emile Zola's novels inform us, as evidence of the lower order's ignorance and brutality," Thurer notes.[33]

But the seeds of this then-still nearly invisible movement had been planted much earlier. In the late 1700s, British political theorists began disseminating information on contraceptives as concerns of overpopulation grew among some classes.[34] Despite the separation of an ocean, by the 1820s, this information was "seeping" into the United States.

"Before the introduction of the Comstock laws, contraceptive devices were openly advertised in newspapers, tabloids, pamphlets, and health magazines," Yalom notes. "Condoms had become increasing popular since the 1830s, when vulcanized rubber (the invention of Charles Goodyear) began to replace the earlier sheepskin models."[35] Vaginal sponges also grew in popularity during the 1840s, as women traded letters and advice on contraceptives.[36] Of course, prosecutions under the Comstock Act went a long way toward chilling public discussion.

Though Margaret Sanger's is often the first name associated with the dissemination of information on contraceptives in the early United States, in fact, a woman named Sarah Grimke preceded her by several decades. In 1837, Grimke published the *Letters on the Equality of the Sexes*, a pamphlet containing advice about sex, physiology, and the prevention of pregnancy.[37]

Two years later, Charles Knowlton published *The Private Companion of Young Married People*, becoming the first physician in America to do so.[38] Near this time, Frederick Hollick, a student of Knowlton's work, "popularized" the rhythm method and douching. And by the 1850s, a variety of material was being published providing men and women with information on the prevention of pregnancy. And the advances weren't limited to paper.

"In 1846, a diaphragm-like article called *The Wife's Protector* was patented in the United States," according to Marilyn Yalom.[39] "By the 1850s dozens of patents for rubber pessaries 'inflated to hold them in place' were listed in the U.S. Patent Office records," Janet Farrell Brodie reports in *Contraception and Abortion in 19th Century America*.[40] And, although many of these early devices were often more medical than prophylactic, by 1864 advertisements had begun to appear for "an India-rubber contrivance" similar in function and concept to the diaphragms of today.[41]

"[B]y the 1860s and 1870s, a wide assortment of pessaries (vaginal rubber caps) could be purchased at two to six dollars each," says Yalom.[42] And by 1860, following publication of James Ashton's *Book of Nature*, the five most popular ways of avoiding pregnancy—"withdrawal, douching, the vaginal sponge, condoms, and the rhythm methods"—had become part of the public discussion.[43] But this early contraceptives movement in America would prove a victim of its own success. The openness and frank talk that characterized it would run afoul of the burgeoning "purity movement."

"During the second half of the nineteenth century, American and European purity activists, determined to control other people's sexuality, railed against male vice, prostitution, the spread of venereal disease, and the risks run by a chaste wife in the arms of a dissolute husband," says Yalom. "They agitated against the availability of contraception under the assumption that such devices, because of their association with prostitution, would sully the home."[44]

Anthony Comstock, a "fanatical figure," some historians suggest, was a charismatic "purist," who, along with others in the movement, "acted like medieval Christians engaged in a holy war," Yalom says.[45] It was a successful crusade. "Comstock's dogged efforts resulted in the 1873 law passed by Congress that barred use of the postal system for the distribution of any 'article or thing designed or intended for the prevention of contraception or procuring of abortion'," Yalom notes.

Comstock's zeal would also lead to his appointment as a special agent of the United States Post Office with the authority to track and destroy "illegal" mailing, *i.e.*, mail deemed to be "obscene" or in violation of the Comstock Act. Until his death in 1915, Comstock is said to have been energetic in his pursuit of offenders, among them Dr. Edward Bliss Foote, whose articles on contraceptive devices and methods were widely published.[46] Foote was indicted in January of 1876 for dissemination of contraceptive information. He was tried, found guilty, and fined $3,000. Though donations of more than $300 were made to help defray costs, Foote was reportedly more cautious after the trial.[47] That "caution" spread to others, some historians suggest.

MARGARET SANGER AND OTHER REBELS:
Women Who Would "Injure" Society

Some women are who they are in spite of their mothers. Others become who they become *because* of their mothers. In 1869, right around the time that the advertisement of contraceptives was reaching its height, a 21-year-old Catholic woman named Anne Purcell married an equally young man named Michael Higgins in New York state. Though they were available, Anne Purcell would never choose to use artificial contraceptives. Instead, for nearly two of the next three decades, she was pregnant. In 1899, Anne Purcell died of consumption, leaving eleven children behind. One of those children was a girl named Margaret.

"The memory of her mother was undoubtedly a major factor in Margaret Sanger's work to make contraceptives legal and available to married women," Yalom and others theorize.[48] "Trained as a nurse and married in 1902 at the age of twenty-three to a young architect, Sanger limited her own progeny to three children during a period of eight years. When her family moved from Hastings, New York, to the city in 1910, she took up work as a part-time nurse in the immigrant districts of New York's Lower East Side. The plight of women who, like her mother, wore themselves out with continuous childbirth awakened her social conscience."

But Sanger told part of that story in her own words, recalling her time in the tenements: "Pregnancy was a chronic condition among the women of this class,"[49] with the "remedies" offered up as preventives (and seized upon by the women) ranging from "herb teas" to "turpentine, steaming, rolling downstairs, inserting slippery elm, knitting needles, [and] shoe-hooks." These "doomed" women, as Sanger described them, did all they could to avoid pregnancy, begging druggists and Sanger for practical—as opposed to theoretical and religious—advice. When the remedies and advice failed, they resorted to more dangerous things.

"On Saturday nights I have seen groups of from fifty to one hundred with their shawls over their heads waiting outside the office for a five-dollar abortionist," Sanger recalled.

By 1911, Sanger had begun to lecture on issues of reproduction and sexuality. But it was the experience of watching a desperate young mother die from a second self-induced abortion in 1912 that made Sanger a crusader. "[O]ne stifling mid-July day in 1912, I was summoned to a Grand Street tenement," Sanger wrote. "My patient was a small, slight Russian Jewess, about twenty-eight years old, of the special cast of feature to which suffering lends a madonna-like expression.... Jake Sachs, a truck driver scarcely older than his wife, had come home to find the three children crying and her unconscious from the effects of a self-induced abortion. He had called the nearest doctor, who in turn had sent for me...."[50]

Sanger and the doctor worked frantically to save the woman and prevent infection, and within two weeks she had recovered physically, although she remained spiritually troubled. "At the end of three weeks," Sanger continued, "as I was preparing to leave the fragile patient to take up her difficult life once more, she finally voiced her fears, 'Another baby will finish me, I suppose?' 'It's too early to talk about that,' I temporized. But when the doctor came to make his last call, I drew him aside. 'Mrs. Sachs is terribly worried about having another baby.' 'She well may be,' replied the doctor, and then he stood before her and said, 'Any more such capers, young woman, and there'll be no need to send for me.' 'I know, doctor,' she replied timidly. 'But,' and she hesitated as though it took all her courage to say it, 'what can I do to prevent it?'"

"The doctor was a kindly man, and he had worked hard to save her, but such incidents had become so familiar to him that he had long since lost whatever delicacy he might once have had. He laughed good-naturedly. 'You want to have your cake and eat it too, do you? Well, it can't be done.' Then picking up his hat and bag departed he said, 'Tell Jake to sleep on the roof.'"

But Jake didn't sleep on the roof, and so the telephone rang at Sanger's house some three months later. "Jake Sachs's agitated voice begged me to come at once; his wife was sick again and from the same cause. For a wild moment I thought of sending someone else, but actually, of course, I hurried into my uniform, caught up my bag, and started out," Sanger wrote.[51]

"All the way I longed for a subway wreck, an explosion, anything to keep me from having to enter that home again. But nothing happened, even to delay me. I turned into the dingy doorway and climbed the familiar stairs once more. The children were there, young little things. Mrs. Sachs was in a coma and died within ten minutes. I folded her still hands across her breast, remembering how they had pleaded with me, begging so humbly for the knowledge which was her right. I drew a sheet over her pallid face. Jake was sobbing, running his hands through his hair and pulling at it like an insane person. Over and over again he wailed, 'My God! My God! My God!'"[52]

That year, Sanger began writing the weekly column, *What Every Girl Should Know*, for the Socialist Newspaper, *The Call*. Coining the phrase "birth control," Sanger also began publishing the newsletter, *The Woman Rebel*, which offered information on contraceptives.[53] Though Sanger was pushing her agenda on several fronts, it was an article in *The Call* on venereal disease that "brought [Sanger] into direct confrontation with her antagonist and nemesis, Anthony Comstock, who outlawed her column in 1913. From this point on, Sanger was often in conflict with the law," Yalom notes.[54] Sanger was indicted on nine counts for violating the Comstock Act.[55]

"One morning [in August of 1914] I was startled by the peremptory, imperious, and incessant ringing of my bell. When I opened the door, I was confronted by two gentlemen," Sanger wrote in her autobiography. "'Will you come in?' They followed me into my living room, scrutinized with amusement the velocipede and wagon, the woolly animals and toys stacked in the corner. One of them asked, 'Are you the editor and publisher of a magazine entitled the *Woman Rebel*?' When I confessed to it, he thrust a legal document into my hands. I tried to read it, threading my way slowly through the jungle of legal terminology. Perhaps the words became a bit blurred because of the slight trembling of my hands, but I managed to disentangle the crucial point of the message. I had been indicted—indicted on no less than nine counts—of alleged violation of the Federal Statutes [regarding the Comstock Act]. If found guilty on all, I might be liable to forty-five years in the penitentiary."[56]

Voicing objections that resonate today, Sanger's critics argued that the distribution of information and birth control devices would spark illicit sexual activity by rendering *inconsequential* an act meant by God and nature to produce children.[57] Sanger was arraigned in the United States District Court for Southern New York beside a United States Attorney who argued that distributing information on birth control was the equivalent of disseminating "...articles advocating bomb throwing and assassination."[58]

Facing the possibility of prison, Sanger fled to Montreal, where she assumed a false name and boarded a ship for Europe. During the voyage, Sanger authorized release of another pamphlet, *Family Limitations*, which also contained information on birth control. But Sanger would decide to return to the United States to stand trial. She was greeted with such overwhelming support that prosecutors dropped the charges.[59]

Some legal scholars suggest that Sanger's initial defense of birth control was "vehemently feminist."[60] And yet, the reasoning underlying her approach to contraceptives was in line with the reasoning articulated nearly fifty years later by the Justices of the United States Supreme Court in declaring "fundamental" and "private" a person's decision to use birth control.[61] Sanger and the Justices saw "women's ability to control their own reproduction as essential to their freedom and equal participation in society."[62] Indeed, Sanger wrote in her 1920 book, *Woman and the New Race*[63] that "[n]o woman can call herself free who does not own and control her own body. No woman can call herself free until she can choose consciously whether she will or will not be a mother."[64]

A half century later, the Justices of the United States Supreme Court wrote that "...[i]f the right of privacy means anything, it is the right of the *individual*, married or single, to be free from unwarranted governmental intrusion into matters so fundamentally affecting a person as the decision whether to bear or beget a child."[65] Although Sanger was vocal about the right to birth control and both she and the Justices would ultimately conclude that it was an issue of "individual freedom," a fundamental right to choose birth control would not become *substantive* until the Justices breathed life into the concept in 1965 in deciding *Griswold v. Connecticut*,[66] a contraceptives case involving a married couple, and in 1972, *Eisenstadt v. Baird*,[67] when the Court extended the same right to single persons.

And yet, for the roughly fifty years in between, Sanger and other supporters of contraceptive choice were forced to continue efforts to push the envelope on women's reproductive rights. In 1916, Sanger opened the first birth control clinic in the United States in Brownsville, Brooklyn, where pessaries were given out.[68] Lines reportedly formed in the street, snaking around the corner and catching the eye of police. Ten days after it opened, the clinic was raided. Sanger and her sister[69] were taken to jail.[70]

"When she was tried in 1917 for distributing birth control information and devices to immigrant women…thirty of her clients were subpoenaed and came to the courtroom with numerous babies in tow, presumably to indicate their need for family limitation. Found guilty and given the choice of a $5,000 fine or thirty days in prison, Sanger chose the latter," according to Yalom.[71] And though the judge would uphold Sanger's conviction on appeal in 1918, he would also declare that while contraceptives could not be used to prevent pregnancy, they could be used to prevent venereal disease.

"This interpretation would allow Sanger and other birth control advocates some leeway in the decades to come," Yalom suggests.[72] But Sanger's legacy lives on for another reason: two of her books, *Woman and the New Race* and *The Pivot of Civilization*, were extraordinarily popular in their time, selling more than half a million copies during the 1920s.[73] The message was clearly getting out as supporters grew.

"Despite ongoing opposition, the movement found many allies in unlikely places, including some of the more progressive religions," says Yalom. "In 1930, the bishops of the Anglican Church issued from London a carefully worded statement condoning the use of artificial contraception within marriage when spouses felt a moral obligation to limit parenthood. A year later, the Federal Council of the Churches of Christ in America, chaired by theologian Reinhold Niebuhr and representing some 22 million Protestants, formally endorsed birth control on medical and economic grounds."[74]

Though the Roman Catholic Church and other conservative Christian sects would continue to oppose birth control, supporters of birth control would continue to disseminate information and to oppose the Comstock Act, though in 1927, the debate would take an ironic turn in the most public of arenas: the United States Supreme Court. That year the Court delivered a decision in the now infamous case of *Buck v. Bell*.[75] At issue before the Court was a Virginia statute permitting the involuntary sterilization of "feeble-minded" people if state officials believed sterilization was in the person's "best interests."

Carrie Buck, the named plaintiff opposing the law, was an eighteen-year-old girl at the time of the case. Buck was young, fertile, white, and a citizen and, thus, Carrie Buck might have been the poster-girl for the anti-contraceptives movement were it not for the fact that Carrie Buck was reportedly "slow." As a result, she could be sterilized, according to the Justices on the United States Supreme Court, because "three generations of imbeciles is enough…." The decision was consistent with the efforts of an era to preserve the "integrity" of American society by shaping its progeny. By some estimates, more than 70,000 American citizens have undergone compulsory sterilization since the first sterilization statute was passed in 1907,[76] many under laws like the one at issue in *Buck v. Bell*.

Though *Buck v. Bell* was heard by the Court more than seventy years ago, its legacy has proved lasting. The involuntary sterilization of "feeble-minded" people has never been held unconstitutional, although the federal government has made some efforts to end the practice. In 1973, federal legislation was adopted intending to ensure that all sterilizations funded by Medicaid were "voluntary."[77] Even so, fourteen states still deem it permissible to sterilize mentally challenged citizens in a throwback to the debates of the turn-of-the-twentieth century when the "bourgeoisie" argued that "the poor" were having too many children.

Still, throughout the 1930s and 1940s, conservatives continued to oppose the broad use and availability of artificial contraceptives, even by "feeble-minded persons," though the arguments asserted often offered other concerns. It was argued during this time, for example, that taxpayer dollars should not be spent on birth control.[78] "Were I on the board of birth control, I imagine I would rather focus my mind on solving not how to eradicate poverty by birth control, but to eradicate poverty by getting rid of birth control money," Father Charles Coughlin told Congress in January of 1934, testifying against a proposed amendment to the Comstock Act that would have allowed doctors to prescribe contraceptives in some circumstances.[79]

"[T]oday, believing as a Christian, not only as a Catholic but a Presbyterian, a Baptist, a Lutheran, an Episcopalian, and all of other sects of Christianity, believing that marriage was invented by God for what purpose? For the primary purpose of procreation and educating children," Coughlin continued, "I still think there is enough intelligence in the married man and the married woman of our land to consider that matrimony is not simply a legalized bed of prostitution, and consider that matrimony means something more than every man and woman to live like two animals. Surely Christianity has taken that into consideration. They want a man and a woman to be married before there is such a thing as conception, before there is such a thing as birth; and after marriage they want a man to so love his wife that he does not make her simply his play toy. It was not done before they were married and it is not done after they are married."[80]

For two hundred years this has been the reasoning of women's lives. It has been used to limit women's choices; to foreclose options. And as some have no doubt argued, to keep women *women*. As a result, the efforts of women to "control their bodies," as Sanger argued, or to do much outside of the home, including work, because of their bodies, has been a source of political and social tension in the United States for as long as the United States has been the United States. And yet, there came a point during the 1960s and 1970s—with the nation in the midst of upheaval—when the United States Supreme Court would issue a trio of decisions so significant to the nearly hundred-year-old reproductive rights debate that they would free women from (at least some of) the burden of this history. Among the new "freedoms" granted were the right to choose birth control and abortion.

But with greater reproductive choice and the greater array of sexual freedoms this choice has created have come "unresolved problems about sexual behavior," some researchers suggest.[81] And that appears to be the epicenter of the reproductive rights debate today. Though the landmark precedents of the

1960s and '70s still stand (some of them despite continued challenge), they do so amid the swirl of new or continued arguments over whether women should really have reproductive choice. And despite the medical advances of the twenty-first century, battles continue to include religious and legislative declarations that life begins at the inexact moment of "conception." Attempts by conservative lawmakers have also been made to resurrect "chastity" by forced abstinence and bans on advice on contraceptives and abortion. These things, conservatives have argued, will help preserve an ordered society and ensure women continue to do what they are supposed to do.

ENDNOTES FOR CHAPTER TWO

1   A relative few recent examples from a few mainstream media outlets include: *An Orgasm is in Your Stars*, JANE, January/February 2001, at p. 81; Catherine Perry, *What's the Best or Worst Way a Woman Has Ever Initiated the Big Deed?*, GLAMOUR, March 2001, at p. 150; Marcelle Karp, *You'll Have Sex Like 6,000 Times in Your Life*, JANE, January/February 2001, at p. 118; Stephanie Klein, *What Are Your Sexy Dreams Telling You?*, MADEMOISELLE, March 2001, at pp. 68–70; Catherine Perry, *What Are You Secretly Wanting That She's Never Suspected*, GLAMOUR, February 2001, at p. 124; Andrea Baird, *The Shy Girl's Guide to Whoa!*, GLAMOUR, February 2001, at pp. 126–127; Leslie Yazel and Amy Spencer, *Make Your Bed & Fly in It*, GLAMOUR, February 2001, at pp. 197–199; *Dear Sex Diary (suffocating during orgasm)*, JANE, April 2001, at p. 115; Alix Strauss, *How Often Do You Have Sex?*, MARIE CLAIRE, April 2001, at p. 124. Alex Kuczynski of *The New York Times* also noted that although it may go unnoticed, many mainstream outlets also run ads for escort services and massage parlors. "The *Village Voice*," wrote Kuczynski, "publishes several pages of ads each week for escort and massage services. *The New York Observer* prints as much as two broadsheet-size pages each week." *See* Alex Kuczynski, *Racy Magazine Ads Expose Inconsistency in Publishers's Stance*, N.Y. TIMES, March 12, 2001, at p. C1.
2   *See* Otten, *supra* note 8, ENDNOTES FOR INTRODUCTION, at p. 36.
3   For discussion and review, *see* Ryan, *supra* note 9, ENDNOTES FOR INTRODUCTION, at p. 162.
4   *See* Yalom, *supra* note 18, ENDNOTES FOR CHAPTER ONE, at p. 294.
5   *See* Norton, *supra* note 2, ENDNOTES FOR INTRODUCTION, at p. 38 (citing MD. ARCHS, X, pp. 293–96).
6   *See* Murphy, *supra* note 7, ENDNOTES FOR INTRODUCTION, at pp. 15–16.
7   *See* Norton, *supra* note 5, at p. 58.
8   *Id.* at 76.
9   *Id.* at 57 (citing Keith Wrightson, ENGLISH SOCIETY 1580-1680 (London: Hutchinson, 1982), Chap. 6); Susan Dwyer Amussen, AN ORDERED SOCIETY: GENDER AND CLASS IN EARLY MODERN ENGLAND (Oxford: Basil Blackwell, 1988)).
10 *See* Marilyn French, THE WAR AGAINST WOMEN (New York: Summit Books, 1992), at p. 105. *See also* Ferguson, *supra* note 10, ENDNOTES FOR INTRODUCTION.
11 See William Shakespeare, THE TEMPEST, Act 4, Scene I, reprinted in THE ALEXANDER TEXT OF WILLIAM SHAKESPEARE: THE COMPLETE WORKS (London: Collins Clear-Type Press (first printed in 1951, reprinted in 1953, 1954, 1956, 1957, 1959, 1960, 1962, 1963, 1964 (twice), 1965, 1966, 1968, 1970, 1971)), p. 19. ("Then, as my gift, and thine own acquisition Worthily purchas'd, take my daughter. But if thou dost break her virgin-knot before All sanctimonious ceremonies may With full and holy rite be minist'red, No sweet aspersion shall the heavens let fall To make this contract grow; but barren hate, Sour-ey'd disdain, and discord, shall bestrew The union of your bed with weeds so loathly That you shall hate it both. Therefore take heed, As Hymen's lamps shall light you.")
12 In the Hawthorne classic, Hester Prynne was not physically branded, though scarring of that sort was proposed when she seemed to critics to be wearing the embroidered "A" too proudly. *See* Nathaniel Hawthorne, THE SCARLET LETTER (New York: Washington Square Press, 1994), at p. 51. ("The magistrates are God-fearing gentlemen, but merciful overmuch,—that is a truth," added a third autumnal matron. "At the very least, they should have put the brand of a hot iron on Hester Prynne's forehead. Madam Hester would have winced at that, I warrant me. But she,—the naught baggage,—little will she care what they put upon the bodice of her gown! Why, look you, she may cover it with a brooch, or such like heathenish adornment, and so walk the streets as brave as ever!")
13 *See* Yalom, *supra* note 4, at p. 49.
14 *See* Norton, *supra* note 5, at p. 66 (citing Ingram, *Church Courts*, chap. 7, on the handling of premarital fornication in English ecclesiastical courts; and the articles of P.E.H. Hair, *Bridal Pregnancy in Rural England in Earlier Centuries*, POPULATION STUDIES XX (1966), pp. 233–43, and *Bridal Pregnancy in Earlier Rural England Further Examined*, POPULATION STUDIES, XXIV (1970), pp. 59–70).

15 *Id.* at 69.

16 This was different from adultery, a more serious offense involving sex with a married woman.

17 *See* Norton, *supra* note 5, at p. 66, n. 28 (citing L& L, 23; NHCP *Recs*, II, 590; and NPCL, 43). (Norton notes further that "[c]oding identified just seven southern men and six women accused of premarital fornication;" four of the Chesapeake trials occurred at one 1639 court session in Accomack County, Virginia (AN CT. *Recs*, I, 151).)

18 *Id.* n. 34 (Norton notes that her "New England data set includes 336 married couples charged with crimes of all description, of which 45.5% (N=153) were for premarital fornication. The Bay Colony was the site of 71% (N=109) of those prosecutions. Married women were the objects of 804 New England prosecutions; of the 781 cases in which crimes are known, 163 were identified as fornication (10 married women were accused of fornication before marriage with men other than their eventual husbands.) Most such women were never charged with any other crime; the handful (13) who appeared in court on other occasions had usually committed such minor offenses as not attending church services.")

19 *Id.* at 69 n. 35.

20 *Id.* at 65.

21 *Id.* (citing NPCL, 61; RI *Col Recs*, I, 174; L&L, 37; NHCP *Recs*, II, 600).

22 *See* Tannahill, *supra* note 41, ENDNOTES FOR CHAPTER ONE, at pp. 364–65.

23 *See* Sheila Rowbotham, A CENTURY OF WOMEN: THE HISTORY OF WOMEN IN BRITAIN AND THE UNITED STATES (New York: Viking, 1997), at p. 32.

24 *See, e.g.,* Dorothy Roberts, KILLING THE BLACK BODY: RACE, REPRODUCTION, AND THE MEANING OF LIBERTY (New York: Pantheon Books, 1997), at pp. 106–108 (offering evidence of a similar modern trend).

25 *See* Rowbotham, *supra* note 23, at p. 30. (Bastardy proceedings in the United States were plentiful during the early years of the twentieth century. For example, during a nine-year period from 1916 to 1925, roughly 150 "bastardy" cases were heard across the United States.)

26 A sampling of bastardy cases for just a five year period include: *Sims v. Birden*, 73 So. 379 (Ala. 1916); *Williams v. Wilson*, 97 So. 911 (Ala. 1923); *Reichert v. Jerome H. Sheip, Inc.*, 102 So. 440 (Ala. 1924); *Harkrader v. Reed*, 5 Alaska 668 (1917); *Rowland v. Taylor*, 203 S.W. 1034 (Ark. 1918); *Boyd v. Epperson*, 232 S.W. 939 (Ark. 1921); *Ex Parte Madalina*, 164 P. 348 (Cal. 1917); *In re Baird's Estate*, 223 P. 974 (Cal. 1924); *Appeal of Eva*, 104 A. 238 (Conn. 1918); *Petition of Frisby*, 110 A. 673 (Del. Orph. 1920); *Harrison v. Odum*, 96 S.E. 1038 (Ga. 1918); *Poss v. Clark*, 123 S.E. 873 (Ga. 1924); *In re Alexander*, 27 Haw. 158 (Hawaii 1923); *People v. Baker*, 222 Ill.App. 451 (Ill. App. 1921); *Glansman v. Ledbetter*, 130 N.E. 230 (Ind. 1921); *Luce v. Tompkins*, 158 N.W. 535 (Iowa 1916); *Erickson v. Erickson's Estate*, 180 N.W. 47 (Iowa 1920); *Arndt v. Arndt*, 167 P. 1055 (Kan. 1917); *Doughty v. Engler*, 211 P. 619 (Kan. 1923); *Vanover v. Steele*, 190 S.W. 667 (Ky. 1917); *Steele v. Crawford*, 248 S.W. 197 (Ky. 1923); *Perkins v. Brownell-Drews Lumber Co.*, 84 So. 894 (La. 1920); *Minor v. Young*, 89 So. 757 (La. 1921); *Van Dickson v. Mayfield*, 104 So. 315 (La. 1925); *Stripe v. Meffert*, 229 S.W. 762 (Me. 1921); *In re Crowell's Estate*, 126 A. 178 (Me. 1924); *O'Leary v. Lawrence*, 113 A. 638 (Md. 1921); *Dilworth v. Dilworth*, 108 A. 165 (Md. 1919); *Green v. Kelley*, 118 N.E. 235 (Mass. 1918); *Taylor v. Whittier*, 138 N.E. 6 (Mass. 1922); *King v. Penisular Portland Cement Co.*, 185 N.W. 858 (Mich. 1921); *Kotzke v. Kotzke's Estate*, 171 N.W. 442 (Mich. 1919); *State v. Juvenile Court of Ramsey County*, 179 N.W. 1006 (Minn. 1920); *Geisler v. Giesler*, 200 N.W. 742 (Minn. 1924); *Welford v. Harvard*, 89 So. 812 (Miss. 1921); *Crum v. Brock*, 101 So. 704 (Miss. 1924); *Busby v. Self*, 223 S.W. 729 (Mo. 1920); *Laumeier v. Laumeier*, 229 S.W. 762 (Mo. 1925); *Craig v. Shea*, 168 N.W. 135 (Neb. 1918); *Schmidt v. State*, 194 N.W. 679 (Neb. 1923); *In re Forney's Estate*, 184 P. 678 (Nev. 1919); *In re Parrott's Estate*, 203 P. 258 (Nev. 1921); *State v. Byron*, 104 A. 401 (N.H. 1918); *Jackson v. Jackson*, 113 A. 495 (N.J.1922); *Ex Parte Wallace*, 190 P. 1020 (N.M. 1920); *Hiser v. Davis*, 194 N.Y.S. 275 (N.Y. 1922); *Stillman v. Stillman*, 196 N.Y.S. 356 (N.Y. 1925); *Croom v. Whitehead*, 93 S.E. 854 (N.C. 1917); *Thayer v. Thayer*, 127 S.E. 553 (N.C. 1925); *Eichorn v. Zedaker*, 144 N.E. 258 (Ohio 1924); *Copeland v. Copeland*, 175 P. 764 (Okla. 1918); *Page v. Roddie*, 218 P. 1092 (Okla. 1923); *Westfall v. Westfall*, 197 P. 271 (Or. 1921); *Laberee v. Laberee*, 228 P. 460 (Or. 1924); *In re Bisbing's Estate*, 74 Pa. Super. Ct. 317 (1920); *In re Russell's Estate*, 110 S.E. 791 (S.C. 1922); *Tarleton v. Thompson*, 118 S.E. 421 (S.C. 1923); *Blue v. Holman*, 245 S.W. 722 (Tex. Civ. App. 1922); *Hicks v. State*, 263 S.W. 291 (Tex. Cr. App. 1924); *Jensen v. Earley*, 228 P. 217 (Utah 1924); *Hoover v. Hoover*, 109 S.E. 424 (Va. 1921); *Vanderpool v. Ryan*, 119 S.E. 65 (Va. 1923); *Pierson v. Pierson*, 214 P. 159 (Wash. 1923); *State v. Williams*, 213 P. 921 (Wash. 1923); *In re Ecker's Estate*, 182 N.W. 977 (Wis. 1921); *Riley v. State*, 203 N.W. 767 (Wis. 1925).

27 *See* Davis, *supra* note 41, ENDNOTES FOR CHAPTER ONE, at pp. 19–20.

28 *Id.* at 20.

29 *See* Yalom, *supra* note 4, at p. 298.

30 *Id.*

31 *See* Shari Thurer, THE MYTHS OF MOTHERHOOD, at p. 217. (Excerpt reprinted by permission of Houghton Mifflin Company, © 1994 by Shari L. Thurer. All rights reserved. Thurer notes that "Jane Austen's letters…contain the advice to a friend that to avoid continual childbearing she should adopt 'the simple regimen of separate rooms.'")

32   *Id.*
33   *Id.*
34   Robert Thomas Mathus and Francis Place were among the leaders of this movement. For more reading, *see* Yalom, *supra* note 4, at p. 299.
35   *Id.* at 300.
36   *Id.* at 301. (According to Yalom, "John D'Emilio and Estelle Freedman in their book INTIMATE MATTERS include several examples of married women sharing contraceptive knowledge. In 1876, Mary Hallock Foote wrote to her friend Helene Gilder that 'a sure way of limiting one's family' was for her husband to 'go to a physician and get shields of some kind. They are to be had also at some druggists. It sounds perfectly revolting, but one must face anything rather than the inevitable result of Nature's methods.")
37   *See* Janet Farrell Brodie, CONTRACEPTION AND ABORTION IN 19TH-CENTURY AMERICA (Ithaca, New York: Cornell University Press, 1994), at p. 89.
38   *See* Yalom, *supra* note 4, at p. 299. (Yalom explains that "Knowlton recommended postcoital douching as an effective means of evacuating the sperm. Women were advised to douche right after intercourse with a pint of water mixed with one of the following substances: alum, sulphate of zinc, saleratus, vinegar, and liquid of soda. In Knowlton's opinion, these methods were sure, cheap, harmless, did not cause sterility, and did not interfere with coitus. Moreover, control was placed in the hands of the women, which was considered a good thing.")
39   *Id.* at 300.
40   *See* Brodie, *supra* note 37, at p. 218.
41   *Id.*
42   *See* Yalom, *supra* note 4, at p. 300.
43   *Id.* at 299 (citing Brodie, *supra* note 37, at p. 185).
44   *Id.*
45   *Id.* at 300.
46   Among these publications were: *Medical Common Sense; Plain Home Talk*, HOME ENCYCLOPEDIA; *Words in Pearl;* and the periodical, *Health Monthly* (1876–1883).
47   *See* Norman Hines, MEDICAL HISTORY OF CONTRACEPTION (Baltimore: The Williams Wilkins Co., 1936), at pp. 276–278.
48   *See* Yalom, *supra* note 4, at p. 305.
49   *See* Brodie, *supra* note 37, at p. 88.
50   *Id.* at 89–92.
51   *Id.*
52   *Id.*
53   *See* Brodie, *supra* note 37, at p. 89.
54   *See* Yalom, *supra* note 4, at p. 305.
55   Passed by Congress in 1873 and named after "anti-obscenity" crusader Anthony Comstock, the Comstock Act prohibited distribution of "obscene" material via United States mail. The Comstock Act did not prohibit the distribution of material regarding contraception and abortion outright. But it allowed states that had already passed anticontraception laws to foreclose the possibility of having such literature shipped into their state from elsewhere. *See* Comstock Act (17 Stat. 599 (1873)). Scholars note that "[i]t was Comstock's doing…that caused the key words 'for the prevention of conception and procuring of abortion' to be inserted into the federal legislation of 1873." *See* Brodie, *supra* note 37, at p. 263. Those "key words" would appear for the next century in most federal and state legislation outlawing abortion and the distribution of contraceptives.
56   *See* Sanger, *supra* note 11, ENDNOTES FOR INTRODUCTION, at p. 114.
57   *See* Davis, *supra* note 27, at pp. 18–19. ("It was no coincidence that women's consciousness of their reproductive rights was born within the organized movement for women's political equality. Indeed, if women remained forever burdened by incessant childbirths and frequent miscarriages, they would be unable to exercise the political rights they might win. Moreover, women's new dreams of pursuing careers and other paths of self-development outside of marriage and motherhood could be realized if they could limit and plan their pregnancies." But there was, in fact, another issue, which goes to the depiction of women as the literal bearers of the race. The rate of white births fell significantly towards the end of the 19th century as American society grew increasingly urban. Scholars note that farm life had demanded large families. In cities, however, there was no such need. The prospect of "race suicide" rang so many bells that in 1905 President Theodore Roosevelt ended a Lincoln Day speech by noting that "race purity must be maintained.")
58   Sanger described the events in SANGER: AN AUTOBIOGRAPHY, *supra* note 56, at p. 115.
59   For more reading on Margaret Sanger and the history of contraceptives in the United States, *see* Sanger, *supra note* 56. *See also* Gordon, *supra* note 41, ENDNOTES FOR CHAPTER ONE.
60   *See* Roberts, *supra* note 24, at p. 57.
61   *See Griswold v. Connecticut*, 381 U.S. 479 (1965), and *Eisenstadt v. Baird*, 405 U.S. 438 (1972).
62   *See* Roberts, *supra* note 24, at p. 57.
63   *See* Margaret Sanger, WOMAN AND THE NEW RACE (New York: Brentano's, 1920), at p. 94.
64   *Id.*

65   *Eisenstadt v. Baird*, 405 U.S. 438, 453 (1972) (holding that even unmarried people had a funda-
     mental right to birth control and that such a right was with the fundamental notions of personal
     privacy) (emphasis in the original). *See also Griswold v. Connecticut*, 381 U.S. 479 (1965) (holding
     that such rights were within the "marital" relationship).
66   In *Griswold v. Connecticut*, the Justices wrote the now famous words: "Would we allow the police to
     search the sacred precincts of marital bedrooms for telltale signs of the use of contraceptives? The
     very idea is repulsive to the notions of a privacy surrounding the marriage relationship." With those
     words, the Justices "breathed" life into the concept of "liberty" to create what would become a "fun-
     damental right" to privacy, because privacy was seen by the Justices as part of "liberty." Decisions
     of this sort, involving the "uncovering" of an implied fundamental right where one is not expressly
     enumerated, involve what is known as "substantive due process," a complex legal doctrine
     explained perhaps most concisely by Ellen Alderman and Caroline Kennedy. *See* Alderman &
     Kennedy, *supra* note 128, ENDNOTES FOR CHAPTER ONE, at p. 55. ("Constitutional protection of a
     woman's decision to end a pregnancy is based upon the Due Process Clause of the Fourteenth
     Amendment. That clause declares that no person will be denied 'life, liberty, or property, without
     due process of law.' Beginning nearly a hundred years ago, the Supreme Court interpreted 'liberty'
     as encompassing certain fundamental rights not specifically listed in the Bill of Rights. Giving sub-
     stance to the term 'liberty' in this way is known as 'substantive due process.' In this view, rights
     'deeply rooted in this nation's history and tradition' and 'implicit in the concept of ordered liberty
     such that neither liberty nor justice would exist if they were sacrificed,' are protected.")
67   405 U.S. 438 (1972).
68   *See* Brodie, *supra* note 37, at p. 218.
69   Sanger's sister's name was Ethel Byrne, who served as the clinic's nurse.
70   *People v. Sanger*, 166 N.Y.S. 1107 (1917). Byrne was also prosecuted. *See People v. Byrne*, 163 N.Y.S.
     682 (1917).
71   *See* Yalom, *supra* note 4, at pp. 305–306.
72   *Id.* at 306.
73   *Id.*
74   *Id.* at 306–307.
75   274 U.S. 200 (1927).
76   *See* HUMAN BETTERMENT ASSOCIATION OF AMERICA, SUMMARY OF UNITED STATES STERILIZATION LAWS
     (1957) (cited by James B. O'Hara and T. Howland Sanks, *Eugenic Sterilization*, 45 GEO. L. REV. 20
     n. 3 (1956)).
77   *See* U.S.C. Sec. 300 A-5.
78   The modern-day argument in the public realm has centered most often around Title X and block
     grant funding allocated for family planning. In 1995, the Republican-controlled Congress moved
     to block Title X funding for contraceptives. The measure failed outright. But in recent years con-
     servatives have turned their efforts away from funding and instead toward initiatives aimed at
     requiring parental consent for minors who want to use birth control and who would be covered by
     Title X. Title X of the Public Health Service Act, Medicaid, and two federal block grant programs
     provide federal funding for family planning services.
79   *See, e.g., Testimony of Father Charles E. Coughlin Opposing an Amendment to the Comstock Act*,
     which would allow doctors to prescribe contraceptives, before the United States Congress, on the
     Judiciary Hearing on Birth Control, 73rd Congress, 2d session, January 18-19, 1934, at pp. 126–130
     (quoted in THE ABORTION CONTROVERSY: A DOCUMENTARY HISTORY (Eva R. Rubin ed., 1994) (West-
     port, Conn.: Greenwood Press, 1994), at pp. 29–31).
80   *Id.*
81   *See* Zemon Davis & Ker Conway, *supra* note 1, ENDNOTES FOR INTRODUCTION, at p. 85.

CHAPTER THREE

Working Women and the Issue of "Protection"

WOMEN WORKING IN AMERICA:
"Frailty, thy name is woman!"[1]

Women have always worked in the United States—despite myths to the contrary—as hard as Lewis's Shoshones where home was concerned, cooking, cleaning, and stirring everything in hot pots from stew to candle wax. Indeed, as late as the 1920s in a still largely rural America, for example, "[f]arm work was still the most common form of women's labor," researchers Rosalyn Baxandall and Linda Gordon wrote in *America's Working Women*. "Farm women's unpaid labour [*sic*] was crucial on the vast plains of the Midwest, as well as the Western frontier. In the poorer farms without piped water, gas, or electricity, this meant seasonal fieldwork on top of housework."[2]

But women also worked outside of the home, where they found jobs most commonly as servants, maids, and governesses—jobs thought suitable for women who had to work. More rarely, in early America women were publishers,[3] small business owners,[4] and occasional "cowgirls,"[5] spies,[6] and "doctors."[7] As yet, where payment was concerned, women trying to make a go in the working world have always run into obstacles. This was particularly true where jobs fell outside the realm of the traditional "female" professions.

Part of the reason for this was that in the early United States, female "disabilities" and a woman's biological ability to bear a child held sway. Thus, the constraints on women's lives were painted in broad strokes. Women had an obligation to procreate. This foreclosed the right to own property in a practice of ancient reasoning that tangled marriage, household, and motherhood.[8]

Specifically, because women bore children—were, in fact, *predestined* for the *divine mission* of motherhood[9]—they should be married.

But once married, there was little left for women. Property became the asset of husbands and women were not allowed to bring suit or enter contracts without her spouse's assistance.[10] In addition, given the "innocence" of their minds and their place as the "gentler" of the two within society, the rough and tumble world of politics was deemed not to suit them.

And though women struggled alongside men to build a new land and continued to do so well into the twentieth century, the "constitutions" of women were deemed to be weaker and women, therefore, unsuited for "*many of the occupations of civil life.*"[11] As set forth in Chapter Two, that is exactly what at least one of the Justices of the United States Supreme Court concluded in *Bradwell v. Illinois*, in upholding a decision by the Supreme Court of Illinois denying a married woman a license to practice law.[12]

And yet, despite this far-reaching declaration, women did work in the United States. They took in laundry and boarders and looked after children in rural areas, where only these sorts of positions were available. In more settled areas, women worked as domestics. In addition, women occupying the lowest social rungs found jobs in agricultural sectors, and in urban areas, women found work in crowded factories and makeshift sweat shops.

"Thousands [of women] toiled in such desperate conditions for so little that many fell into prostitution," argues journalist Marci McDonald.[13]

When "social investigators tramped up tenement steps" in turn-of-the-twentieth century New York, for example, they found "Italian homeworkers finishing clothing, making artificial flowers, or cleaning ostrich plumes, Syrians doing lace work or making kimonos and Jewish women producing straw hats and women's neck wear," historian Sheila Rowbotham notes. "The latter were also to be seen selling fruit, fish, or clothing on the streets, running candy stores, groceries, butcher's shops, [and] cleaning and dyeing shops."[14]

Drawing immigrants and unskilled labor to American shores—in addition to the desire to start a new life in a new and often more prosperous nation—were turn-of-the-twentieth century advances in machinery and new methods of production. The factory model for assembly line mechanized production had begun. And women wanted part of it, taking jobs alongside new immigrants in the expanding textile and garment industries. But the hours were long, the work fraught with danger, and the wages low, forming a vicious economic circle.

"Women's dependence on men in the family was reinforced by their low rates of pay," Rowbotham writes. "It was assumed from the start of their working lives that their position as wage earners was temporary."[15]

Assumed by others, perhaps. But events of the early decades of the twentieth century suggest that women had another plan in mind. By the opening of that first year, women were pushing for improvements in working conditions. They were also testing their clout and making demands as the American labor movement got underway with a series of planned demonstrations and protests mirroring similar actions in England at about the same time.[16] By 1900, for example, female steam laundry workers in San Francisco had unionized, and over the next twelve years, they would secure important safety concessions and a 30 percent pay raise.[17]

With the burgeoning movement proving larger than their differences, women of the various classes began to join ranks nationwide, and, thus, janitors marched alongside candymakers and teachers during the 1903 Labor Day Parade in Chicago. A year later, clerks in Chicago began to organize.[18] "Less downtrodden women were mobilizing too," Rowbotham notes. "The telephone operators, from upper- and working-class, often Irish-American backgrounds, were stylishly dressed high-school graduates. [By] 1907 they were demanding an eight-hour day, two-week vacations, standardized pay scales with automatic pay increases, improvements in their shift arrangements, and clearer grievance procedures."[19]

As efforts to unionize and calls for clear-cut grievance procedures grew, an era of labor unrest and strikes got under way, with one of the defining moments for women coming on November 22, 1909, when "[a] young Jewish clothing worker, Clara Lemlich..., walked to the front of a strike meeting in New York's Cooper Union Hall called by the International Ladies' Garment Workers' Union (ILGWU) and passionately demanded a general strike," says Rowbotham.[20] Lemlich made the call in Yiddish.

Between 20,000 and 40,000 workers responded to the call, filling the streets in protest. But "[w]ithout funds and repeatedly beaten and arrested on the picket lines, the strikers called on the Women's Trade Union League for help," Rowbotham notes. That call too was answered. "When middle-class feminists and socialists joined the pickets, the strike received increasing publicity, and this intervention marked closer links between working women and the feminist movement."[21]

Although many of the strikers' demands ultimately went unanswered, historians suggest that some factory owners demonstrated a willingness to negotiate with women and the union, a significant victory. An even more significant gain, however, was that the strike "lifted the work of immigrant women out of obscurity and into public consciousness," author Elizabeth Ewen suggests.[22] The devastating fire at the Triangle Shirtwaist Company in March 1911, resulting in the deaths of 146 people—most of them women—drew even more attention. Though many of the 800 workers had reportedly complained prior to the fire of locked exits, their complaints were ignored. Those locked exits prevented many workers from fleeing during the blaze.

The tragedy sparked outrage, leading to the promulgation of early safety laws. The push toward unionization also continued with safety issues, wages, and working conditions still of primary concern. Between 1905 and 1915, an estimated 100,000 workers in the garment and textile industries were involved in some type of labor dispute. In addition, by some estimates roughly half of all women working in the garment industry between 1909 and 1919 belonged to unions.[23]

From the start of the early union movement, a "... militant spirit of the rank and file persisted in the subsequent wave of strikes in the garment industries of Rochester, Chicago, Philadelphia, and Cleveland, in which women demanded better pay and conditions and an end to the system of subcontracting work out," says Rowbotham.[24]

This was the context of the twentieth century's earliest legal challenges to restrictive or "protective" legislation and it would present an interesting dichotomy: while some union organizers and social reformers led the push for legislation that would "protect" women from long hours and abusive employment practices, others were challenging the legislation as it was applied.

WORKING WOMEN GO TO COURT:
Efforts to Overcome the Mission Divine

The labor unrest of the early twentieth century—with its gritty street protests and work-related riots—left a mark on American history, at times shaping early work-related practices; at others laying the ground work for eventual (and perhaps even inevitable) legal challenge. The events of this period had a lasting effect on the lives of women. Under pressure from women's and national advocacy groups—the National Consumers' League among them—states began passing laws specifically designed to protect women and children. Minimum standards for "ventilation, adequate washing facilities, seats, and mandatory rest periods," were among the workplace improvements put into effect during this period.[25]

But there was a double edge to this sword where women were concerned: as applied, laws of this sort sometimes became obstacles to opportunity and work. And the first decade of the twentieth century would open with a United States Supreme Court challenge to "protective legislation." In 1908, attorneys representing a group of women challenged an Oregon statute limiting work hours for female laundry employees.

Under Oregon law, women—married or single—were deemed to have equal contractual and personal rights with men.[26] But in 1903, the Oregon legislation passed a law mandating that women "shall not work more than ten hours during the twenty-four hours of any one day."[27] In September of 1905, Curt Muller, a laundry owner, was fined for "require[ing] a female, to-wit, one Mrs. E. Gotcher, to work more than ten hours in said laundry."[28] He was convicted at trial and ordered to pay $10 in penalty. The conviction was upheld on appeal by the State Court of Oregon.[29]

Though the law was clearly aimed at the conduct of employers who might overwork women, the effect of this legislation, early women's rights groups argued, was to limit the rights of women to enter freely into contracts. In 1908, attorneys representing a group of women challenged the Oregon statute, arguing that it was violative of the Oregon law creating equal contractual rights between men and women. On the federal level, the case became *Muller v. Oregon,*[30] and as the Justices of the United States Supreme Court saw it, the "single question" before them was "the constitutionality of the statute under which the defendant was convicted so far as it affects the work of a female in a laundry."[31]

But what makes *Muller v. Oregon* significant both in terms of outcome and a clear statement of the Court is that the attorneys for the female plaintiffs brought their challenge in reliance upon the United States Supreme Court's 1905 decision in *Lochner v. New York*.[32] In *Lochner*, the Justices struck down a New York law limiting the number of hours bakery employees could work per week by "breathing" life into the otherwise flat and constitutionally undefined notion of "liberty" in a practice generally referred to by scholars today as the "substantive due process approach."[33] Critics of the substantive due process approach argue that during this period the Supreme Court was peppered with "activists...hostile towards labor regulation" tending, instead, toward a "conservative economic ideology."[34]

As applied in *Lochner v. New York*, in striking down the New York law as repugnant to the "fundamental" and constitutionally protected "right of liberty" of the male bakers, whose work time would have been limited to sixty hours per week or ten hours a day were the statute upheld,[35] the Justices declared definitively that "[t]he question of whether this [New York] act is valid as a labor law, pure and simple, may be dismissed in a few words. There is no reasonable ground for interfering with the liberty of person or the right of free contract, by determining the hours of labor in the occupation of a baker. There is no contention that bakers as a class are not equal in intelligence and capacity to men in other trades or manual occupations, or that they are not able to assert their rights and care for themselves without the protecting arm of the State, interfering with their independence of judgment and or action."

It was an impressive and seemingly broad statement. And in a nation where legal precedent is revered, *Lochner v. New York* would seem to have established a new rule on work-hour limitations. "Seem," however, is the operative word. Three years after the Court's decision in *Lochner v. New York*, attorneys for the women challenged the Oregon statute. The Oregon statute was similar in form and limitation to the New York law struck down in *Lochner*. Like the New York statute, the Oregon law sought to limit the number of hours laundry employees—women—could work per day to ten. Given the similarities of the two cases, attorneys for the women in Oregon relied, in support of their challenge, on the strong language and precedent of *Lochner v. New York*.

But the Justices of the United States Supreme Court dismissed this reliance as misplaced.[36] "We held in *Lochner v. New York*," the Justices wrote, "that a law providing that no laborer shall be required or permitted to work in bakeries more than sixty hours in a week or ten hours in a day was not, as to men, a legitimate exercise of the police powers of the State, but an unreasonable, unnecessary, and arbitrary interference with the right and liberty of the individual to contract in relation to his labor, and, as such, was in conflict with, and void under, the Federal Constitution. That decision is invoked by plaintiff *in error* as decisive of the question before us. But this assumed that the difference between the sexes does not justify a different rule respecting a restriction of the hours of labor."[37]

Indeed, in light of the "difference between the sexes," it might fairly be said that the Court's decision in *Muller v. Oregon* began and ended with the first footnote.[38] It is a side note made of layer upon layer of citation to restrictive European and American labor law, culminating in the self-serving declaration of a health inspector, who argued that "[t]he reasons for the reduction of the working day to ten hours [for women was]—(a) the *physical organization of women*, (b) *her maternal functions*, (c) the rearing and education of children, (d) maintenance of the home—are all so important and so far reaching that the need for such reduction need hardly be discussed."

The Justices were apparently so convinced by these words that they would go on to declare in *Muller v. Oregon* "[t]hat a woman's physical structure and the performance of maternal functions place her at a *disadvantage* in the struggle for subsistence is obvious. This is especially true when the *burdens* of motherhood are upon her. Even when they are not, by abundant testimony of the medical fraternity continuance for a long time on her feet at work, repeating this from day to day, tends to injurious effects on the body, and as healthy mothers are essential to a vigorous offspring, *the physical well-being of woman becomes an object of public interest and care in order to preserve the strength and vigor of the race*."[39]

The United States Supreme Court's decision in *Muller v. Oregon* set the stage for a spate of rulings upholding "protective" statutes of this sort, limiting the hours women could work. The reason most frequently articulated for work-hour limitations during this period was always the same: the physical well-being of women was of public interest and concern. In 1914, for example, the Supreme Court heard the case of *Hawley v. Walker*,[40] and would eventually uphold an Ohio statute limiting the hours women could work. What makes the case noteworthy, however, is that the decision was apparently deemed to be of so little public interest that the Justices offered only an abbreviated memorandum.[41]

In 1915, the Justices returned to full-blown declaration on the nature of things, with the decision in *Miller v. Wilson*,[42] in which the Court held that "[w]omen are admittedly weaker than men in the struggle of economic competition and *may be* protected by legislative enactment against the oppressive bargaining or control of their employer, whether arising *from cupidity* or such a mistaken philanthropy as that of the hospital here, which admittedly works its undergraduate girl nurses the equivalent of twelve hours a day for six day week [*sic*] to make a better showing of the number of poor people cared for."[43] A California statute limiting work hours for women was upheld.

Later that year, the Supreme Court reaffirmed this holding in *Bosley v. McLaughlin*,[44] a case brought by Ethel Nelson, a licensed female pharmacist, who argued that the California statute limiting the number of hours she could work "interfered with [her] liberty to contract and denied to [her] the equal protection of the law contrary to the Fourteenth Amendment." In rejecting

Nelson's arguments and upholding the law instead, Justice Hughes wrote, in delivering the opinion for the Court, that "[i]n view of the nature of their work, and the extreme importance to the public that it should not be performed by those who are suffering from over-fatigue, there can be no doubt as to the legislative power reasonably to limit the hours of labor in that occupation."[45] But wouldn't concerns of "over-fatigue" apply to *all* pharmacists?

And in 1917, the United States Supreme Court heard another case from Oregon, and again upheld a ten-hour work limitation for women in *Bunting v. Oregon*[46] reaching both sexes, though some scholars argue that women were disproportionately affected. Seven years later, the Justices upheld a New York law prohibiting women from working in city restaurants between 10 p.m. and 6 a.m. in *Radice v. New York*,[47] as an appropriate measure to protect the health of women. Dozens of state courts held similarly during this period,[48] raising the question of what, if anything, *Muller v. Oregon* came to mean.

PROTECTIONIST LEGISLATION:
A Place at Work for Women and a Place for Muller in History

Though it was decided nearly a century ago, the theory of social placement underlying *Muller v. Oregon* (*i.e.*, of women as "mothers of the nation," who were, therefore, obligated to procreate) remains a central construct for conservative politicians and religious leaders opposed to birth control and abortion. And yet for some women, their efforts during the early decades of the twentieth century in pushing labor practices were about forcing "the State" to view them not just as "mothers of the nation," with limited choices as a result, but rather as wholly separate individuals with contractual rights of their own—like men.[49]

As set forth above, in permitting states to set limits on the number of hours women could work, the Justices of the United States Supreme Court conceded in *Muller v. Oregon* that "[t]he limitations which [the Oregon] statute places upon [a woman's] contractual powers, upon her right to agree with her employer as to the time she shall labor, are not imposed solely for her benefit, *but also largely for the benefit of all*. Many words cannot make this plainer. The two sexes differ in structure of body, in the functions to be performed by each, in the amount of physical strength, in the capacity for long-continued labor, particularly when done standing, the influence of vigorous health upon the future well-being of the race, the self-reliance which enables one to assert full rights, and in the capacity to maintain the struggle for subsistence. This difference justified a difference in legislation and upholds that which is designed to compensate for some of the burdens which rest upon her."[50]

In other words, because women bear children, laws intended to protect women "and their unborn children" were permissible, even where protective legislation curtailed a woman's individual "liberty" interests. Of course, there were instances where "protective" legislation helped women at the expense of others. For example, in 1912, a laundry operator named Quong Wing filed a discrimination suit, challenging a Montana statute as gender-biased because it exempted women who ran laundries from certain tax requirements.[51]

Quong Wing won the case at the trial court level. But the Supreme Court of Montana reversed. Quong Wing appealed. He got no help from the United States Supreme Court, which ruled in *Quong Wing v. Kirkendall*,[52] that if the State of Montana "deems it advisable to put a lighter burden upon women than upon men with regard to employment...the Fourteenth Amendment does not interfere by creating a fictitious equality where there is a real difference."

It was not an isolated case. In *Breedlove v. Suttles, Tax Collector*,[53] the United States Supreme Court again upheld "tax breaks" for women, reasoning that "[t]he tax being upon persons, women may be exempted on the basis of special considerations to which they are *naturally* entitled. In view of the burdens necessarily borne by them for the preservation of the race, the State reasonably may exempt them from the poll taxes." Further, because "[d]iscrimination in favor of all women" was permissible, "appellant may not complain because the tax is laid only upon some, or object to registration of women without payments of taxes for previous years," the Court held.

Decisions like those of *Quong Wing v. Kirkendall* and *Breedlove v. Suttles, Tax Collector* have long driven the debate over the "legitimate" use of "protectionist" legislation. Or, in the parlance of the current debate, "reverse discrimination."[54] And, indeed, so clearly biased were decisions of this sort, some scholars suggest, that they reveal a clear "willingness" on the part of the United States Supreme Court of the turn-of-the-twentieth century "to swallow any argument in defense of legislation providing special treatment to women."[55]

Review of case law from this period suggests that this is largely true. And yet, there were a few notable exceptions. In 1923, the United States Supreme Court heard the case of *Adkins v. Children's Hospital*,[56] which would result in a decision that seemed to do away with gender-based "protective" statutes. *Adkins v. Children's Hospital* involved a congressional statute creating a three-member board empowered to set a minimum wage for women and children in the District of Columbia.

The hospital employed many women and, thus, challenged application of the statute. The hospital was joined in the challenge by a woman who worked as a hotel elevator operator. The woman argued that setting a minimum wage would interfere with her right to contract by driving her out of a job. Her employers, she said, would not pay a "minimum wage" that was higher than the wage she was earning.[57] Supporters of the statute and the wage board argued that setting a minimum wage, especially where women were involved, was a matter of public health.[58]

Similar "public health" arguments had succeeded in the past. But in *Adkins v. Children's Hospital*, the Justices were not persuaded. Instead, the Court began its analysis of the issues by noting that "...the ancient inequity of the sexes, otherwise than physical, as suggested in the *Muller* case has continued 'with diminishing intensity.' In view of the great—not to say revolutionary—changes which have taken place since that utterance, in the contractual, political, and civil status of women, culminating in the Nineteenth Amendment, it is not unreasonable to say that these differences have now come almost, if not quite, to the vanishing point."[59]

In striking down the minimum wage statute as an arbitrary interference with the right to contract, the Supreme Court held that "while the physical differences must be recognized in appropriate cases, and legislation fixing hours or conditions of work may properly take them into account, we cannot accept the doctrine that women of mature age, *sui juris*, require or may be subjected to restrictions upon their liberty of contract which could not lawfully be imposed in the case of men under similar circumstances. To do so would be to ignore all the implications to be drawn from the present day trend of legislation, as well as that of common thought and usage, by which a woman is accorded emancipation from the old doctrine that she must be given special protection or be subjected to special restraint in her contractual and civil relationships."[60]

The Court's decision in *Adkins v. Children's Hospital* was a victory for women in that women seemed finally to be on an equal footing with men. According to the Court, women were now free to contract without "the undue interference of the state." Thus, it would also seem that women were free of the historic notion that as the weaker sex they were in need of "special protection" under the law. And yet, the realities of the world were such that although women *could* contract, when they did, they were still inevitably paid less than men, which led to attempts to set a "fair" or "living" minimum wage for women and children in the first place. But were women really finally free of the restraints of biology? The answer to that question can be found in the 1937 United States Supreme Court case of *West Coast Hotel Co. v. Parrish*.[61]

Elsie Parrish was a maid at the West Coast Hotel. After a Washington state minimum wage statute went into effect, she brought suit to recover the difference between the wages she was paid by the hotel and the amount she should have received under the minimum wage law.[62] In the decade-and-a-half since the United States Supreme Court's decision in *Adkins v. Children's Hospital*, this area of the law had begun to swirl with contradictions, a fact the United States Supreme Court noted in undertaking review of *West Coast Hotel Co. v. Parrish*, in an attempt to settle the legal issues once and for all.[63] On this point, the Court wrote:

> The history of the litigation of this question may be briefly stated. The minimum wage statute of Washington was enacted over twenty-three years ago. Prior to the decision in the instant case it had twice been held valid by the Supreme Court of the State.[64] The Washington statute is essentially the same as that enacted in Oregon in the same year.[65] The validity of the latter act was sustained by the Supreme Court of Oregon in *Steller v. O'Hara*[66] and *Simpson v. O'Hara*.[67]
>
> These cases, after reargument, were affirmed here by an equally divided court, in 1917.[68] The law of Oregon thus continued in effect. The District of Columbia Minimum Wage Law was enacted in 1918.[69] The statute was sustained by the Supreme Court of the District in the

Adkins case. Upon appeal the Court of Appeals of the District first affirmed that ruling, but on rehearing, reversed it and the case came before this Court in 1923. The judgment of the Court of Appeals holding the Act invalid was affirmed, but with Chief Justice Taft, Mr. Justice Holmes and Mr. Justice Sanford dissenting, and Mr. Justice Brandeis taking no part.

The dissenting opinions took the ground that the decision was at variance with the principles which this Court had frequently announced and applied. In 1925 and 1927, the similar minimum wage statutes of Arizona and Arkansas were held invalid upon the authority of the *Adkins* case. The Justices who had dissented in that case bowed to the ruling and Mr. Justice Brandeis dissented.[70] The question did not come before us again until the last term in the *Morehead* case,[71] as already noted. In that case, briefs supporting the New York statute were submitted by the States of Ohio, Connecticut, Illinois, Massachusetts, New Hampshire, New Jersey, and Rhode Island. Throughout this entire period the Washington statute now under consideration has been in force."[72]

After considered analysis, the Court in *West Coast Hotel Co. v. Parrish* would "dramatically revers[e] itself in upholding minimum wage legislation essentially indistinguishable from legislation struck down only the year before in *Morehead v. New York ex rel. Tipaldo,*" renowned Harvard constitutional scholar Laurence Tribe explains.[73] The Justices also held "that the case of *Adkins v. Children's Hospital,*" which the hotel relied upon, "should be, and it is, overruled."[74] It was a retreat, and women again needed protection, according to the Court.

What can be closer to the public interest than the health of women and their protection from unscrupulous and overreaching employers?" asked the Justices. "And if the protection of women is a legitimate end of the exercise of state power, how can it be said that the requirement of the payment of a minimum wage fairly fixed in order to meet the very necessities of existence is not an admissible means to that end? The legislature of the State was clearly entitled to consider the situation of women in employment, the fact that they are in the class receiving the least, that their bargaining power is relatively weak, and that they are the ready victims of those who would take advantage of their necessitous circumstances. The legislature was entitled to adopt measures to reduce the evils of the 'sweating system,' the exploiting of workers at wages so low as to be insufficient to meet the bare cost of living, thus making their very helplessness the occasion of a most injurious competition. The legislature had the right to consider that its minimum wage requirements would be an important aid in carrying out its policy of protection.[75]

After *West Coast Hotel Co. v. Parrish* "protective" legislation again became the rule. In 1941, for example, the United States Supreme Court heard the case of *United States v. Darby*.[76] Though the case was heard in 1941, the history of *United States v. Darby* began in 1938 when the Roosevelt Administration proposed legislation that would later become the federal Fair Labor Standards Act (FLSA). The Act would require employers to pay overtime and establish a national minimum wage. The catalyst for this movement was the Great Depression. According to historians, President Roosevelt is said to have believed that a national minimum wage would help struggling Americans.[77]

In upholding the Fair Labor Standards Act, the Court declared in *United States v. Darby* that "[s]ince our decision in *West Coast Hotel Co. v. Parrish*, it is no longer open to question that the fixing of a minimum wage is within the legislative power [of the government] and...the bare fact of its exercise is not a denial of due process under the Fifth more than under the Fourteenth Amendment. Nor is it any longer open to question that it is within the legislative power to fix maximum hours."

Did the Court's decision in *United States v. Darby* render the working world suddenly equal? Not quite. Though the FLSA mandated wages, women still faced discrimination in the jobs they were "allowed" to take. In Michigan for example, seven years after *United States v. Darby*, state law prohibited a woman from working as a bartender and serving liquor at night unless she was the "wife or daughter of the male owner" of a licensed liquor establishment. Again, the proffered reason for this prohibition was that women were in need of protection, especially in bars.

But would "protective" legislation of this sort be in line with the spirit of the Fair Labor Standards Act and the hopes of getting and keeping Americans employed in jobs that paid "living" wages? Or was it gender discrimination plain and simple? What would the court say?

Margaret and Valentine Goesaert were mother and daughter, who tended bar in a tavern they owned. They, along with Caroline McMahon, another tavern owner; Gertrude Nadroski, a bartender, and twenty-two other women challenged the Michigan statute prohibiting women from working in taverns at night. Though the language of the legislation was cloaked in suggestions of "public health," some legal scholars suggest that the Michigan statute was the result of an "unchivalrous desire by male bartenders" to control the tavern and liquor business.[78] The Justices of the United States had a response to suggestions of this sort as well as to the challenges of the women in *Goesaert v. Cleary Liquor Control Commission of Michigan*[79] and it was downright Shakespearian.

We are, to be sure, dealing with a historic calling," the Justices wrote. "We meet the alewife, sprightly and ribald, in Shakespeare, but centuries before she played a role in the social life of England.[80] The Fourteenth Amendment did not tear history up by the roots, and the regulation of the liquor traffic is one of the oldest and most untrammeled of legislative powers. Michigan could, beyond question, forbid all women from working behind a bar. This is so despite the vast changes in the social and legal position of women.... The Constitution does not require legislatures to reflect sociological insight, or shifting social standards, any more than it requires them to keep abreast of the latest scientific standards.

And there it was. With the twirl of its collective pen, the United States Supreme Court had turned women back into the "alewives" of old. Saucy, perhaps, given the times. But still subordinate and necessarily unable to freely choose the professions they would enter, the jobs they would take and the hours they would work. For the first half of the twentieth century, work-related discrimination of this sort was deemed permissible given the biology of a woman's body, its meaning to society, and the historic fact that the physical well-being of women—especially when they are with child—has long been "*an object of public interest.*"[81] And it was not until the late 1960s and early 1970s that laws of this kind began to change as the working world changed and a new thicket of legislation was passed, aimed specifically at discrimination based upon race, religion, and gender.

ENDNOTES FOR CHAPTER THREE

1   William Shakespeare, HAMLET, Act I, Scene 2.

2   *See* Rowbotham, *supra* note 23, ENDNOTES FOR CHAPTER TWO, at pp. 50–51 (citing AMERICA'S WORK-ING WOMEN: A DOCUMENTARY HISTORY, 1600 TO PRESENT (New York: Vintage, 1976, Rosalyn Baxandall and Linda Gordon, ed.); updated and revised by Baxandall and Gordon and published by W.W. Norton (New York, 1995), at p. 147).

3   In the late 1760s, Mary Katherine Goddard, and her mother, Sarah Updike Goddard, published almanacs, newspapers, (the *Providence Gazette* among them), and the first signed copy of the Declaration of Independence. *See* Vicki Leon, UPPITY WOMEN OF THE NEW WORLD, (Berkeley, California: Conari Press, 2001), at pp. 28–30.

4   Margaret Brent and her sister reportedly owned and operated Sisters Freehold, a livestock yard in Maryland during the 1600s. In addition, in 1647, Margaret Brent was named "executrix" of the estate of Lord Baltimore, founder of the State of Maryland. Brent was also granted power of attorney over the estate of Lord Baltimore, who was absent from the state. Leon, *supra* note 3, at pp. 22–23.

5   *See* Rowbotham, *supra* note 2, at p. 51. (According to Rowbotham, "[a]mong the stereotypical Wild West cowboys and gunfighters were a few famous cowgirls, such as Goldia Fields Malone, an early twentieth-century trick-rider, as well as a farmer.")

6   Lydia Darraugh was a spy against the British during 1777. *See* Leon, *supra* note 3, at pp. 42–43.

7   Harriot Kezia Hunt practiced as a "doctor" for several years, though she was repeatedly denied formal instruction by Harvard, whose leaders declared that "[w]e are not opposed to allowing [a] woman her rights, but do protest against her appearing in places where her presence is calculated to destroy our respect for the modesty and delicacy of her sex.") Leon, *supra* note 3, at pp. 36–37.

8   *See* Hazou, *supra* note 107, ENDNOTES FOR CHAPTER ONE, at p 57.

9   *See, e.g.,* Paula England & George Farkas, HOUSEHOLDS, EMPLOYMENT AND GENDER: A SOCIAL, ECO-NOMIC, AND DEMOGRAPHIC VIEW (New York: Aldine De Gruyter, 1986), at pp. 73–101.

10   For discussion of *feme covert, see* Bingham, *supra* note 96, ENDNOTES FOR CHAPTER ONE, at p. 21.

11   *See Bradwell v. Illinois*, 83 U.S. (16 Wall.) 130 (1872).

12   *Id.*

13   *See* Marci McDonald, *Work on Their Own,* U.S.NEWS & WORLD REPORT, February 24/March 3, 2003, at p. 60.

14   *See* Rowbotham, *supra* note 2, at pp. 51–52.

15   *Id.* at 19. (According to Rowbotham, "[a] study in Birmingham, for example, by E. Cadbury, M. Cecile Matheson and G. Shawn, '*Women's Work and Wages: A Phase of Life in an Industrial City*', found that in 1901 the average wage of young women was only 10s. a week, 4s. less than they judged was necessary to keep healthy and respectable. In the woolen manufacturing region of Colne Valley in Yorkshire, wages for young girls began at 5s. and slowly rose to £1 at (p. 22) the beginning of the First World War. Moreover, the custom of tipping the money into their mothers' aprons left the young workers with only a penny for every shilling.")

16   *Id.* at 19–25.

17   *Id.* at 50.

18   *Id.* (Rowbotham notes, however, that "fluctuation in the economy caused them to lose members three years later.")

19   *Id.*

20   *Id.* at 45.

21   *Id.*

22   *Id.* (citing Elizabeth Ewen, IMMIGRANT WOMEN IN THE LAND OF DOLLARS: LIFE AND CULTURE ON THE LOWER EAST SIDE, 1890–1925 (New York: Monthly Review Press, 1985), at p. 260).

23   *Id.* at 46.

24   *Id.*

25   *Id.* at 52.

26   *See Muller v. Oregon,* 208 U.S. 412, 418 (1908) (citing *First National Bank v. Leonard,* 36 Or. 390, 396).

27   208 U.S. at 417.

28   *Id.*

29   *See State v. Muller,* 48 Or. 252.

30   208 U.S. 412 (1908).

31   *Id.*

32   In *Lochner v. People of State of New York,* 198 U.S. 45 (1905), the Supreme Court rejected the notion that state regulations prescribing the number of hours bakery employees could work to 60 per week promoted health and well-being.

33   *Lochner* marked the start of a period in legal history called the *Lochner* era, during which Supreme Court Justices began to "give substance" to the otherwise abstract notion of "liberty." Critics of the Substantive Due Process approach argue that the Supreme Court of the time was peppered with "activists" who were "hostile towards labor regulation" and tended towards a "conservative economic ideology." The *Lochner* era came to an end with the Court's ruling in *West Coast Hotel v. Parish,* 300 U.S. 379 (1937), in which the Justices of the Supreme Court upheld minimum wage legislation in what legal historians argue was a dramatic turn away from the Substantive Due Process approach.

34   In 1949, the Supreme Court expressly rejected the "*Allgeyer-Lochner-Adair-Coppage* constitutional doctrine" with the ruling in *Lincoln Federal Labor Union v. Northwestern Iron and Metal Co.,* 335 U.S. 525, 535 (1949) and the *Lochner* doctrine lay legally dormant until the reproductive privacy cases of the 1960s.

35   *See Lochner v. New York,* 198 U.S. 45, holding that a law providing that no laborer shall be required or permitted to work in bakeries more than sixty hours in a week or ten hours in a day was not, as to men, "a legitimate exercise of the police powers of the State, but an unreasonable, unnecessary, and arbitrary interference with the right and liberty of the individual to contract in relation to his labor, and, as such, was in conflict with, and void under, the Federal Constitution."

36   Some legal scholars note that *Muller v. Oregon* marked the start of a period during which the states and courts generally sought to "protect" women as the weaker sex. Thus, the "protection" of women by state statute spelled the decline of the substantive due process approach to the analysis of governmental regulations begun in *Lochner v. New York. See, e.g.,* Friedman Goldstein, *supra* note 129, ENDNOTES FOR CHAPTER ONE, at p.19.

37   *See Muller v. Oregon,* 208 U.S. at 419.

38   The substance of that footnote is as follows:

The following legislation of the States impose restrictions in some form or another upon the hours of labor that may be required by women: Massachusetts: ch. 221, 1874 Rev. Laws 902, ch. 106, Sec. 24; Rhode Island: 1885, Acts and Resolves 1902, ch. 994, p. 73; Louisiana: Sec. 4, Act 43, p. 55, Laws of 1886, Rev. Laws 1904, ch. 139, 1887, Rev. Stat. 1903, ch. 40, Sec. 48, p. 402; New Hampshire: 1887, Laws 1907, ch. 94, p. 95; Maryland: ch. 445, 1888, Pub. Gen. Laws 1903, art. 100, Sec. 1; Virginia: p. 150, 1889–1890, Code 1904, Tit. 51A, ch. 178A, Sec. 3657b; Pennsylvania: No. 26, p. 30, 1897, Laws 1905, No. 226, p. 352; New York: Laws 1899, Sec. 1, ch. 560, p. 752, Laws 1907, ch. 507, Sec. 77, subdiv. 3, p. 1078; Nebraska: 1899, Comp. Stat, 1905, Sec. 7955, p. 1986; Washington: Stat. 1901, ch. 68, Sec. 1, p. 118: Colorado: Acts 1903, ch. 138, Sec. 3, p. 310; New Jersey: 1892, Gen. Stat. 1895, p. 2350, Secs. 66, 67; Oklahoma: 1890, Rev. Stat. 1903, ch. 25, art. 58, Sec. 729; North Dakota: 1877, Rev. Code 1905, Sec. 9440; South Dakota: 1877, Rev. Code (Penal Code, Sec. 764), p. 1185; Wisconsin: Sec. 1, ch. 83, Laws of 1867, Code 1898, Sec. 1728; South Carolina: Acts 1907, No. 233, p. 487. In foreign legislation Mr. Brandeis calls attention to these statutes: Great Britain: Factories Act of 1844, ch. 15, pp. 161,161; Factory and Workshop Act of 1901, ch. 22, pp. 60,71; and see 1 Edw. VII, ch. 22. France, 1848; Act Nov. 2, 1892, and March 30, 1900. Switzerland, Canton of Glaurus, 1848; Federal Law 1877, art. 2, Sec 1. Austria, 1855; Acts 1897, art. 96a, Secs. 1-3. Holland, 1889; art. 5, Sec. 1. Italy, June 19, 1902, art. 7. Germany, Laws 1891. Then follow extracts from over ninety reports of committees, bureaus of statistics, commissioners of hygiene, inspectors of factories, both in this country and in Europe, to the effect that long hours of labor are dangerous for women, primarily because of their special physical organizations. The matter is discussed in these reports in different aspects, but all agree as to the danger. It would of course take too much space to give these reports in detail. Following them are extracts from similar reports discussing the general benefit of short hours form an economic aspect of the question. In many of these reports individual instances are given tending to support the general conclusion. Perhaps the general scope and character of all these reports may be summed up in what an inspector for Hanover says: "The reason for the reduction of the working day to ten hours—(a) the physical organization of women, (b) her maternal functions, (c) the rearing and education of the children, (d) the maintenance of the home—are all so important and so far reaching that the need for such reduction need hardly be discussed."

39   208 U.S. at 421.

40   232 U.S. 718 (1914).

41   The complete substance of that decision is as follows:
      No. 217. ANNA HAWLEY, PLAINTIFF IN ERROR, V. JOSEPH W. WALKER, CONSTABLE, ETC. In error to the Supreme Court of the State of Ohio. Argued January 30, 1914. Decided February 24, 1914. Per Curiam. Judgment affirmed with costs upon the authority of Muller v. Oregon, 208 U.S. 412; Lindsey v. Natural Carbonic Gas Co., 220 U.S. 61, 78–79. Mr. J. M. Sheets for the plaintiff in error. Mr. Louis D. Brandeis, Mr. Timothy S. Hogan, Mr. Frank Davis, Jr., and Mr. Clarence D. Laylin for the defendant in error.

42   236 U.S. 373 (1915). The Supreme Court upheld a California statute that limited the hours that women could work.

43   Id. at 377 (emphasis added).

44   236 U.S. 385 (1915). (At issue was a California statute prohibiting the employment of women for more than eight hours a day.)

45   Id. at 392.

46   243 U.S. 426 (1917).

47   264 U.S. 292 (1924).

48   See NOTE, Constitutional Law—Regulation of Conditions of Employment of Women, 13 B.U.L. REV. at 276 (1933). For an overview, see, e.g., Commonwealth v. Hamilton Manufacturing Co., 120 Mass. 383 (1876) (upholding a ten-hour law for women employed by manufacturing companies); Commonwealth v. Beatty, 15 Pa. Super. Ct. 5 (1895) (also upholding a ten-hour Pennsylvania law); Wenham v. State, 65 Neb. 405 (1902) (upholding a statute similar in language to the Massachusetts statute); State v. Buchanan, 29 Wash. 602 (1902) (also upholding a statute similar to the Massachusetts law); Withey v. Bloom, 163 Mich. 419 (1910) (upholding a Michigan law on the authority of Muller v. Oregon); State v. Somerville, 67 Wash. 638 (1910) (upholding an eight-hour law); People v. Bowes-Allegretti Co., 244 Ill. 557 (1910) (upholding a hour limitation in what scholars see as an implied reversal of Ritchie v. Wayman); Commonwealth v. Riley, 210 Mass. 387 (1912) (Massachusetts court extended the principle to include the posting of hours and times for meals). But see, Ritchie v. People,155 Ill. 98 (1895) (striking down a law limiting the hours that a woman may work); and, People v. Williams,189 N.Y. 131 (1907) (also striking down such a law).

49   Many of the cases decided by the Supreme Court during the Lochner era struck down state legislation that tended to interfere with an individual's "liberty" interest in contracting for labor. As Muller v. Oregon suggests, however, several laws that were said to interfere with the rights of women to contract, however, were not struck down.

50   208 U.S. at 422–23. (Scholars note that the Supreme Court effectively reversed itself in Bunting v. Oregon, 243 U.S. 426 (1917), in upholding an Oregon statute that limited the workday to ten hours for employees of mills and manufacturing plants. This, scholars says, was due to the fact that "[t]he Supreme Court could not for long endure the logical tension created by their position that maximum-hours legislation as a health measure was wholly irrational for men, whereas the same legislation was entirely rational for women.") See FRIEDMAN GOLDSTEIN, supra note 36, at p. 23.

51   Quong Wing argued that the Montana statute violated the Equal Protection Clause of the Fourteenth Amendment.

52   223 U.S. 62, 64 (1912).

53   302 U.S. 277, 282 (1937).

54   For discussion of this subject, see Babcock, supra note 115, ENDNOTES FOR CHAPTER ONE, at pp. 741–776.

55   See, e.g., Friedman Goldstein, supra note 36, at p. 96.

56   261 U.S. 525 (1923).

57   Specifically, the elevator operator argued that her wages were sufficient and that she was within her rights to sell her labor for less than the minimum wage. If the minimum wage law were upheld, the hotel would be forced to let her go because it could not afford to pay her the minimum wage. See Adkins v. Children's Hospital, 261 U.S. at 542.

58   The issue before the Court was whether the statute violated the Fifth Amendment Due Process Clause. The United States Constitution contains two "due process clauses." One, that contained in the Fifth Amendment, applies to federal legislation. The other, that contained in the Fourteenth Amendment, applies to state legislation. The wording of the clauses, however, is identical.

59   Adkins v. Children's Hospital, 261 U.S. at 553.

60 *Id.*
61 300 U.S. 379 (1937).
62 The Washington state law at issue was similar in most respects to the Washington, D.C. statute challenged and upheld in *Adkins v. Children's Hospital.*
63 Among the cases heard during this period were: *Larsen v. Rice,* 100 Wash. 642; *Spokane Hotel Co. v. Younger,* 113 Wash. 359; *Steller v. O'Hara,* 69 Or. 519; *Simpson v. O'Hara,* 70 Or. 261; *Murphy v. Sardell,* 269 U.S. 530; *Donham v. West-Nelson Co.,* 273 U.S. 657.
64 *West Coast Hotel Co. v. Parrish,* 300 U.S. at 390–91 (citing *Larsen v. Rice,* 100 Wash. 642; *Spokane Hotel Co. v. Younger,* 113 Wash. 359).
65 *Id.* (citing Laws of 1913 (Oregon) ch. 62).
66 69 Or. 519.
67 70 Or. 261.
68 243 U.S. 629.
69 40 Stat. 960.
70 *West Coast Hotel Co. v. Parrish,* 300 U.S. at 390–91 (citing *Murphy v. Sardell,* 269 U.S. 530; *Donham v. West-Nelson Co.,* 273 U.S. 657).
71 *Morehead v. New York ex rel. Tipaldo,* 298 U.S. 587 (1936).
72 *West Coast Hotel Co. v. Parrish,* 300 U.S. at 390–91.
73 *See* Laurence H. Tribe, AMERICAN CONSTITUTIONAL LAW (Mineola, New York: The Foundation Press, Inc., 1988) (2d ed.), at p. 28, n. 9.
74 *West Coast Hotel Co. v. Parrish,* 300 U.S. at 400.
75 *Id.* at 398–99.
76 *United States v. Darby,* 312 U.S. 100 (1941).
77 *See* Ronnie Ratner, *The Paradox of Protection: Maximum Hours Legislation in the United States,* 119 INT'L LAB. REV. at pp. 185, 188 (1980); Elizabeth Brandeis, *Labor Legislation,* in HISTORY OF LABOR IN THE UNITED STATES, 1896–1932, (John Commons et al., eds., 1935), at pp. 339, 462.
78 *See, e.g.,* Elizabeth Ungar Natter, GOESAERT V. CLEARY: A HISTORY (May 1984, unpublished manuscript) (cited in Babcock, *supra* note 115, ENDNOTES FOR CHAPTER ONE).
79 *Goesaert v. Cleary, Liquor Control Commission of Michigan,* 355 U.S. 464 (1948).
80 To support this point, the Court cited Jusserand, ENGLISH WAYFARING LIFE IN THE MIDDLE AGES, at pp. 133–134, 136–37 (1889).
81 208 U.S. at 421.

SECTION TWO

Twentieth Century Developments

CHAPTER FOUR

The Nation Goes to War and "Rosie" is Born

"MEN'S WORK," THE GREAT DEPRESSION, AND WORLD WAR II:
Unemployment, War, and Opportunities for Women

With the folding of traditional notions of male superiority into the formative ideas of the new American state, women became second-class citizens and paid labor—in addition to many other "natural privileges"—the near-exclusive province of men. As the presumed breadwinners of families, men were granted the right, by tradition and law, to contract for the sale of their labor free from the unreasonable intrusion of the state.[1] But women were not.

Though they could trundle away in the heavy labor of farms and primitive households, getting paid for their labor so troubled the *status quo* (given the upheaval it would surely wrought on society), that public debate on the issue often turned from tense male-driven opposition to court battle as women challenged laws obstructing their right to sell their labor as freely as men did. Women also took to the streets during the first two decades of the 1900s to protest low wages and poor working conditions. But many of the gains made during this period would become a source of dispute.

By 1912, Massachusetts lawmakers had passed the first minimum-wage law in the nation. By the end of World War I, seventeen other states had followed Massachusetts's lead.[2] In addition, that same year the United States Supreme Court declared it permissible for states to exempt women from certain tax requirements, reasoning that because the working hours of women were *properly* limited, given the obligations of procreation, women were entitled to a lighter tax burden.[3]

Women in favor of these measures rejoiced. Those opposed attempted to regroup and to plan their next attack. It was an uphill battle. As set forth in greater detail in Chapter Three, statutes limiting the paid working hours for women have a long history in the United States, and though often challenged by women's groups, the nation's courts have tended overwhelmingly to let them stand.[4] Beginning in 1908 and continuing through the early 1920s, women's groups opposed to "protective" legislation challenged state laws limiting the number of hours women could work five times in the United States Supreme Court. And they lost every time.[5]

But in 1923, with the United States Supreme Court's decision in *Adkins v. Children's Hospital*,[6] the interests of these two opposing factions dovetailed. But this time, opponents of "protective legislation" won. *Adkins v. Children's Hospital* involved the creation of a board empowered to set a minimum wage for women and children in the District of Columbia. In challenging the minimum wage ordinance, the hospital was joined by a female elevator operator who argued that a minimum wage requirement would interfere with her right to contract by driving her out of a job—because the hospital would not be able to meet the mandated wage, she would be fired.[7]

In striking down the wage statute as an arbitrary interference with the right to contract, the Supreme Court held that "while the physical differences [between men and women] must be recognized in appropriate cases...we cannot accept the doctrine that women of mature age...require or may be subjected to restrictions upon their liberty of contract which could not lawfully be imposed in the case of men under similar circumstances."[8]

Thus, "...emancipation from the old doctrine that [women] must be given special protection or be subjected to special restraint in...contractual and civil relationships" was appropriate, the Court held.[9] Though the reach of the Court's decision might have seemed endless at the time, the practical effect was not immediately felt. And the intervention of history would delay further discussion of the issue with express regard to women on the federal level for the next two decades as the nation preoccupied itself first with economic collapse, then war.

In the fall of 1929, the American stock market crashed. What followed "Black Tuesday," as the day became known, was a roiling period of financial ruin when banks failed, jobs slid away, and a survival standard of living evaporated. In 1920, 50 percent of the American population was officially "poor." But during the Great Depression, that roughly ten-year period following the stock market collapse, poverty became a new animal in United States as the number of poor or newly destitute people spiked.

By 1932, more than 30,000 American businesses had failed, pushing the national unemployment rate to nearly 25 percent. The production of steel, formerly the steam of the modern industrial engine, fell to one-sixth of its capacity.[10] One in every four families was without the traditional (male) breadwinner.[11] Farmers were among the hardest hit. Also suffering, however, were single young women who had previously been able to find work, but who were among the first to be dismissed as the nation tightened its belt. In adumbrations of the kind of social devastation not seen again for five decades, "homeless young women roamed the streets, sleeping rough in railway stations or behind the heating ducts in subway bathrooms," historian Sheila Rowbotham notes.[12]

Economic despair sparked exodus among ethnic groups, at times to unanticipated locations. Some 25,000 Finnish-Americans, for example, made their way to the Soviet Union during the 1930s, according to London-based journalist and author Anne Applebaum.

"Encouraged by Soviet propaganda…Soviet recruiters traveled around Finnish-speaking communities in the United States, speaking of the wonderful living conditions and work opportunities in the USSR," Applebaum writes.[13] In response, thousands of American-born or -based Finns "flocked" to the Karelian Republic of the Soviet Union, where their native language was still spoken freely.

"These were Finnish-speaking Finns, some had immigrated to America, some had been born there, all of whom [went] to the Soviet Union during the 1930s, the years of the Great Depression in the United States," Applebaum explains. But their independent ideas would be a problem for Soviet authorities, which "[m]any loudly pointed out to anyone who would listen, then tried to return," says Applebaum, "and wound up in the Gulag in the late 1930s instead."

At home, the most desperate of Americans began to wander in the quest for phantom jobs and vanishing work. Like characters in John Steinbeck's *The Grapes of Wrath*, two million people followed Route 66, "…through Oklahoma, El Reno, and Clinton…across the Panhandle of Texas" to "Shamrock and McLean, Conway and Amarillo" into "…the New Mexican mountains to Albuquerque, where the road comes down from Santa Fe"[14] coming to rest in roadside squatter camps called "Hoovervilles" in dubious tribute to then-President Herbert Hoover.

The policies of the Hoover administration were widely blamed for the collapse of the American economy. And Hoover would lose his bid for reelection in 1932 to Franklin Roosevelt, who would preside over a nation in turmoil from 1933 to 1945. Adopting a comforting persona, President Roosevelt cuddled under a blanket during his famous "fireside" chats. But the Roosevelt Administration would prove hard-edged and calculating as the President's advisors aggressively engineered passage of an array of previously contested economic legislation. The immediate goal was to create work and a web of social programs that would prevent people from falling through the proverbial cracks.[15] Roosevelt would also establish a practice frequently relied upon by later administrations of "stacking" the courts to create "liberal" bastions supportive of his New Deal.[16]

By 1935, Congress had passed the Federal Social Security Act, creating old age, survivors', and unemployment insurance funds by permitting taxation of wages under the newly enacted Federal Insurance Contributions Act and Federal Unemployment Act.

Three years later, Frances Perkins—then Secretary of Labor under Roosevelt—oversaw promulgation of legislation later to become the Fair Labor Standards Act. Under this new law, employers would be required to pay overtime and a national minimum wage applicable to women as well as men would be set.[17] Historians suggest that Roosevelt believed a national minimal wage would help struggling Americans.[18]

That may also have been the opinion of the Justices of the United States Supreme Court. As set forth in greater detail in Chapter Three, during the first three decades of the twentieth century, the Justices repeatedly struck down minimum wage laws, holding—in all but those cases involving women—that statutes of this kind interfered with the rights (of men) to freely sell their labor. But in 1937, after years of staggering hardship, the Court would "dramatically revers[e] itself" in upholding a Washington minimum wage law in the case of *West Coast Hotel Co. v. Parrish*.[19]

Scholars looking into history note that the Court's decision in *West Coast Hotel v. Parrish* marked the return of "protective legislation" and the hazards of the sociopolitical debate surrounding it. But for those living through it, the Depression appears to have changed the language of the challenge: no longer was the issue one of protecting the contractual rights of men (or women from themselves). Rather, in the desolation of the time, the question on the mind of the nation's leaders was how best to help families. Women were struggling alongside men to put food on their tables. Minimum wage legislation was among the proposed solutions to the problem of starving Americans.

And it was challenged.

But in 1941, the United States Supreme Court upheld the Fair Labor Standards Act, expressly declaring in the case of *United States v. Darby*[20] that "[s]ince our decision in *West Coast Hotel Co. v. Parrish*, it is no longer open to question that the fixing of a minimum wage is within the legislative power [of the government] and...the bare fact of its exercise is not a denial of due process under the Fifth more than under the Fourteenth Amendment. Nor is it any longer open to question that it is within the legislative power to fix maximum hours."

That settled the issue of wage legislation from the legal perspective for a time. And as it happened, fixing the number of maximum hours a person— male or female—could work was of less concern in 1941 than getting the job done. That year, the United States entered World War II, and although the need for war goods exploded, American factories echoed with a tomb-like emptiness. It would be a boon for women and an historic turning point for American labor.

HISTORY REDRAWN AT THE ROOTS:
Women and the New American Workforce

"Newspapers…splashed everywhere: *Help Wanted, Help Wanted, Jobs, Jobs, Jobs,*" recalls Juanita Loveless, who went to work for a California oil company in 1941. "Propaganda on every radio station: 'If you're an American citizen, come to gate so-and-so….'"[21] Juanita Loveless—and millions of other American women—took the job.

Among the founding notions of the Unites States was that men, as the heads of households, took charge of most things. Men made the decisions for their families and were supposed to build lives for their wives and children. This was the role of the man.

But there was a social contract for women as well. Women—certainly married women—were supposed to maintain the home and raise the children. It was all about order.

In this way, as part of the "social contract" the lives of men and women were "rightfully" divided into those tasks belonging to men and those belonging to women. And thus, working women who were married—except in the most dire of circumstances (and sometimes not even then)—were, if not an outright threat to the social fabric, then certainly an embarrassment to their husbands and families. And during the early decades of the twentieth century, these and other traditional notions were reflected in the law.

But with the backdrop of the Great Depression, traditional roles began to break down as survival in a time of world economic crisis claimed center stage. Within four months of Roosevelt taking office, public confidence began to push stock prices up. But by midsummer, prices had again fallen by 20 percent.[22] Economic recovery would prove slow. With their men struggling to find work, women scrambled to help feed their children, often cobbling together a series of low-paying jobs—"doing homework, going out cleaning, taking in lodgers, [and] setting up bakeries, restaurants, or beauty parlors in their homes."[23]

Throughout the 1930s, "[t]he Roosevelt administration moved from the New Deal…into a popular social patriotism," according to historians.[24] Though the administration's policies were initially aimed at getting unemployed men back to work, this goal gave way to wage legislation benefiting both sexes and "make work" projects with a dual purpose: getting the unemployed back to work on national infrastructure programs; as military spending—an integral part in the Roosevelt recovery plan—rose.

"In June of 1933, following Hoover's landslide defeat by Franklin D. Roosevelt, Congress approved an administration proposal to stimulate the economy by spending $238 million in Public Works Administration funds on the construction of twenty-four warships," according to University of Wisconsin historian Stuart Brandes. "Roosevelt reasoned that 80 percent of naval spending went to labor, and he also argued that a naval buildup was necessary in the face of a growing Japanese threat."[25]

This was, in fact, more than presidential propaganda. Having served as Secretary of the Navy for eight years under Woodrow Wilson, Roosevelt was a longtime advocate of a large—or "treaty"—navy, or one as large as allowed as by treaties signed in Washington and London in 1922 and 1930.[26] Supporters with like views "believed that American defenses in the Pacific Ocean should follow a line that extended from Alaska, through Pearl Harbor in the Hawaiian Islands, to the Panama Canal," writes Brandes.[27]

Though controversial for its time, Roosevelt would realize the first step in this long-term goal soon after his election with the passage of the Vinson-Trammell Act in 1934 and the appropriation of $470 million for naval construction.[28] Despite the often vocal criticism of opponents, America had finally entered the chase: the Imperial Japanese Navy had reached 95 percent of the permissible treaty size by 1930. And Roosevelt, history would later seem to suggest, may have been ahead of the curve in terms of war preparation, though the administration would delay America's entrance into the war until well after European nations had begun to fight. And lose.

In the spring of 1933, with the seizure of power in Germany, Adolf Hitler began shaking the world. Fear of a new war gripped the continent. Only a decade-and-a-half had passed since the end of the First World War and memory of the terror it had wrought still lingered like smoke in the skies over the continent. The panicked response of European leaders led to a frenzy of military building and spending that would begin in Europe. Arms industries were nationalized in an attempt to get things moving, and despite a worldwide depression, the price of defense-related stocks soared in France. Similarly, the profits of British airplane manufacturers climbed.[29] But it would all prove too little, too late.

"[W]hen Nazi armies invaded France, French defenders were fatally impaired by underspeed planes and underweight tanks," writes Brandes.[30]

On the other side of the pond and at a distance from the fray, the Roosevelt Administration calculated the nation's response and redoubled its military efforts.

"By 1937, the emerging danger of war compelled increased attention to American defenses. In January 1938, following new Japanese attacks in China, Roosevelt asked Congress to accelerate the ship construction program by 20 percent. In October 1938, reacting to Adolf Hitler's announcement of increased spending on fortifications, the president asked Congress to appropriate an additional $300 million, to be spent mostly on aircraft. In January 1939, he raised the figure to $500 million. These increases were only the beginning, as expenditures rose massively in every year until 1945," says Brandes.[31]

If the nation were ever to enter the war—and the United States didn't until after France had been invaded and England had been bombed—the administration was determined to roll out an American war machine capable of hitting the enemy with overwhelming force in the first "shock and awe" campaign of modern wartime. But Roosevelt would face two immediate obstacles—each capable in its own right of undoing the ultimate plan. The first was coming to terms with a production instrument whose wheels moved with the swift speed of a snail.

"When World War II opened, the United States leadership was shocked to find that the American capacity to produce war matériel was woefully inadequate," Brandes notes. "In 1940, the entire stockpile of gunpowder was too small to meet the needs of a single day of battle at 1943 levels. The rate of rifle production was so slow that had it not been speeded up, it would have taken fifty years to equip the army. Conversion of existing civilian productive capacity was vital, but it would never be enough to meet the nearly insatiable needs of the armed forces."[32]

The answer was the army, which immediately began to take stock of America's holdings—civilian as well as military. Fifteen-thousand factories were surveyed for possible use and conversion to wartime assembly lines. Nearly as many civilian managers were pressed into service as "reservists" charged with the duty of overseeing these new and often hastily put-together production lines.[33] But solving the first of these two problems brought the Roosevelt administration face to face with the second major obstacle: who was going to work these lines?

Troop involvement and the huge commitment necessary for an American rescue of Europe laid assembly lines bare at a time when a semiskilled set of hands were worth their weight in gun powder. In terms of the future for women, the desperate need for labor after the United States entered the war would strike the second—and perhaps most fatal—blow to the traditional social contract: after World War II, no longer was the place of married women so clearly only within the home.

MARCHING ON TO THE FACTORY FLOOR

"As men marched off to combat, Roosevelt's dizzying defense production goals required the mass mobilization of women to shipyards and aircraft assembly lines," recounts McDonald.[34]

As set forth above, there had always been women in the United States—married or single—who pursued work. Perhaps not "careers," given the time. But jobs. Women of that ilk were quick to join the war effort, returning to work after a respectable stint at home to raise children, or shifting from other areas of the labor force into defense-related jobs. But still more hands were needed. Thus, others—women—had to be convinced that their efforts in entering or returning to the workforce would not upset the universe.

And in a fit of calculated inspiration, one of the most powerful women of the twentieth century was born. Her name was Rosie. With the charisma of a rock star and the provocative flair of a slightly more traditional—though hardly less progressive—Madonna, Rosie was heralded as a "cover girl with a difference."[35] "In a propaganda campaign orchestrated by the government, homemakers morphed overnight into lunch-bucket-toting heroines," offers McDonald. And "Rosie the Riveter became their mythic poster girl on a 1943 *Saturday Evening Post* cover by Norman Rockwell."[36]

Trim and sassy, strong but sweet, Rosie was the subject of song and the model for major motion pictures (Claudette Colbert, a welder in *Since You Went Away* (1944) is said to have been fashioned on Rosie). Giving this paper goddess depth and something to relate to was a back story as patriotic as her portrait. With a job on the "front line" pushing tin and riveting her way to the victory Americans were praying for, Rosie was the fullest woman of her time with buffed arms, defiant fingers, a working man's coveralls and a sharp-eyed Marine named Charlie for a beau, who was doing his part, keeping an eye "out for sabotage" while "[s]itting...the fuselage."[37]

With dimensions so conscious and complete in their purpose, Rosie has been the subject of copious interpretation for years. From her position against a backdrop of the American flag, there is no doubt that Rosie is a patriot. But Rowbotham also sees "a confident, broad-shouldered figure with muscular arms, eating her lunch. Rosie, the woman war worker, has her goggles on her brow, her nose in the air, a large phallic riveting tool on her lap, and a copy of Hitler's *Mein Kampf* beneath her feet."[38]

Author Melissa Dubakis notes a departure from the "manly" style of the 1930s with "touches of frivolity" in the Rosie portrait: her name is aggressively scrawled on her lunch box in an assertion of ownership (necessary in a factory) and she sports a "line of merit buttons across her breast."[39] And yet, though Rockwell is known for his realistic "snapshots" of American life, in some ways Rosie seems more like a hologram, her image shifting and sliding with the changing eye of the interpreter. To some, there is a coquettish Rosie, "pink-cheeked" and oven-fresh. Innocent, yet war-ready.

To others, Rosie's face evinces an "expression of spiritual dedication which is in contrast to her earthly, sensual being."[40] She is a woman making sacrifices, and in her sacrifice—the sacrifice of all women—Rosie is elevated to a "quasi-religious symbol," who "transcends gender."[41] Still others see a "riveting tool [lying] in her lap like the infant Michelangelo's *Pieta*," as evidence, they argue, that "Rosie's *tryst* with production could be ended with the return of normal life."[42] And there, it seems, was the rub. "The war presented women with oppor-tunities to earn higher wages and to learn new skills," Rowbotham notes. "They became welders, electricians, and shipfitters. These were the Rosies who cap-tured the popular imagination."[43]

Even so, the prospect of married women leaving their children behind to march each morning into munitions factories did not sit well with everyone. "With the country geared to war, Roosevelt sought to persuade Americans that freedom, prosperity, and security could be achieved only through sacrifice. Ostensibly this was an appeal to all American citizens. Nonetheless, despite the need for women to be mobilized in the war effort, there was the predictable ambivalence about gender roles in state policy," Rowbotham notes.[44]

Although questions of who would do "the cooking, the washing, the mend-ing, the humble homely tasks to which every woman has devoted herself" and what would "become of the manhood of America"[45] quickly bobbed to the surface of this ancient debate, the continual pressing need for labor, and the fear of an American defeat forced the agenda in systematic fashion.

Working women and women of working age previously unemployed or displaced by the depression were targeted first. And they responded. In 1932, roughly two million women were counted as unemployed,[46] and it is not clear that things got any better in absolute terms for women as the depression wore on. But between 1940 and 1944, an estimated five million women entered the American workforce.[47] As adult women moved from the day-to-day workforce to jobs in the defense industry, high school graduates became the next target group, with Rosie and her sweet mix of moxie and fresh-faced glamour serving as the government's most revered recruiter.

As her status rose, Rosie moved from the star of a successful ad campaign to "mother" of a new breed of fiery American women. "The '*We Can Do It*' poster produced by the War Production Coordinating Committee again had a woman with muscular arms clenching her fist, but this manly gesture is belied by the glamour of her makeup," Rowbotham notes. "The recruitment poster for the U.S. Crop Corps, *Call To Farms*, showed a slender, willowy young woman giving a V-sign for victory, dressed in a figure-hugging boiler suit and driving an enormous tractor."[48]

In the need of the time, everyone got involved. Disabled persons, businessmen, and high school students worked four-hour "victory shifts" alongside women in an effort to keep supplies high. Even a young Marilyn Monroe, then a parachute factory worker named Norma Jean, had her picture snapped by an enterprising army photographer determined to marry the obligation of patriotism with the commercial dictates of an eye-pleasing subject.[49]

But even with the addition of businessmen, high school students, and women, the extraordinary need for wartime labor remained unmet. And, thus, a determined effort was made to persuade the last as-yet untapped population of stay-at-home moms to take on full-time jobs.[50] Again, women responded. Although more than 60 percent of American women are believed to have stayed at home,[51] by 1944, one in every three female defense plant workers was a former full-time homemaker. In terms of actual numbers, some researchers suggest that "2,770,000 mothers of 4,460,000 children" entered the paid labor force, pushing work-related "women's" issues to the forefront.[52]

WOMEN AT WORK:
The Issue of the "Superwoman" is Born

By the mid-1940s, women had a new image. Rosie and her necessary minions had given women confidence, muscle, a patriotic soul, and a role in the working world in a time of worldwide need. With the blessing and praise of the highest American authorities, women were urged to go forth and rivet, build, and stand in the shoes of their missing men. But only figuratively.

"Women's difference was deliberately enhanced in the new definition of female identity," feminists suggest. "Translated into a male sphere of machinery and military accoutrements, glamour distinguished wartime women and the temporary sacrifice of service to country covered the underlying maternal dedication of self. Propaganda did…shift gender norms by defining female virtue through public activity. Working-class women appeared in a new visual idiom of power and skill, no longer simply the helpless victims of exploitation portrayed in the photography of the progressive era."[53]

But with working mothers leaving home, even in pursuit of such praiseworthy service, the issue of child care—often thought of as a "contemporary problem"—would become a matter of public debate as early as the 1940s. By 1944, a significant number of married women were now working outside of the home, which translated for many into an urgent need for child care. In addition to attempting to balance the needs of wartime America, women who chose to go to work were still largely responsible for the care of their children.

This usually meant that in addition to cooking, cleaning, and nursing children after a day's work in the factories, women were also charged with the responsibility of securing private child care arrangements. And though their service was to the nation, the critics were everywhere. When women missed work because they could not find baby-sitters, they faced criticism for contributing to high rates of "absenteeism" at a time when America needed every hand. At the same time, social scientists—at times spouting the language of their own agendas—warned of a post-war generation "of juvenile delinquents" and "latchkey" childhoods.

Local governments were urged to undertake efforts to help women as the debate over who should ultimately be responsible for solving the problem got underway. And although women drew support from some government officials—notably General Louis McSherry, who urged that "adequate facilities for the care of children of working mothers" be made a priority[54]—authorities of many child advocacy programs frequently argued in response that it was in the best interests of children to have their mothers home.[55]

These differences not withstanding, in 1943, federal funds were finally approved for use in establishing child care centers. But even with the addition of federal funds, the number of children served by these centers was miniscule when compared to the number of working mothers and the number of children estimated to be left at home each morning. Rowbotham suggests that only about 140,000 children across the United States were being served by child care centers during the latter years of World War II.

But even so, "[w]artime circumstances did…affect popular assumptions and indirectly contributed to new patterns of daily life," Rowbotham says.[56] "'Can women in [the] war industry be good mothers?' asked psychiatrist Dr. Leslie Hohman in 1942, and went on to advocate a 'schedule' of household tasks and shared child care between partners so that both parents could spend engaged time with their children in 'companionship.' Suddenly women's time was of social significance."[57]

There were also new opportunities and entrepreneurial hopes that pushed progress forward. Preprepared, commercially-created, and frozen food companies—once suppliers to the military—began offering their wares for sale to the public. The intention, marketers argued, was to save harried women time. Though these new efforts would pay off better later, the optimism underlying this effort bordered on the fantastic. As late as 1941, a full third of all American households still relied upon wood or coal for heat or to cook food, and many women were still fetching it from outside.[58]

And yet, there were other more positive changes as well. Prior to the swell of married women into the nation's workforce, critics voiced fears "that the war would…change women's expectations."[59] It did. With a new understanding of their worth, many women and women's advocacy clubs and groups began to feel that the time was right to renew discussion of long dormant issues of equality. Thus, the questions of "equal pay for equal work" and the passage of an Equal Rights Amendment were put back on the table. The response was mixed.

The National War Labor Board, having noted the service of women, would eventually authorize "equal pay 'for work for comparable quantity or quality on the same or similar operations.'"[60] But this did little for the state of women's pockets. Most firms decided internally whether or not they would abide by the ruling. And if so, to what degree.

In 1943, several women's advocacy groups and professional clubs also introduced a new version of the Equal Rights Amendment, thereby re-igniting the fires of the "protectionist" debate. Says Rowbotham, "[t]he old battle was resumed between those who argued that women required special protections and those…who asked, 'are women an integral part of the democratic government or are they a class apart, unfit for the rights and freedoms that apply to them?'"[61]

The "protectionist" debate would continue with some rancor through the end of the war and well into the next four decades with issues of equal rights and equal pay among the many to be faced. Of more direct interest to many women during the late 1940s, however, was where they would fit into their new world of work after the war.

WOMEN GO HOME:
Life after the Second World War

> [O]n August 6, 1945, two B-29s flew over the Japanese city of Hiroshima. One plane carried the bomb, the other, instruments to measure the destruction. Not suspecting an air raid from only two planes, the people below did not move into the bomb shelters. At 8:16 a.m. a Los Alamos-built uranium bomb nicknamed 'Little Boy' exploded 2,000 feet above the city. No one knows how many died outright in the firestorm, perhaps 70,000, with a like number left dying of injuries and severe radiation poisoning.

Seventy-five hours later, barely time for the Japanese government in Tokyo to confirm that the attack had been from a single bomb—a nuclear bomb—and to digest the fact, Nagasaki was destroyed by an even larger blast. Two days later Japan surrendered.

—Dan O'Neill, *The Firecracker Boys*[62]

With the war at an end and America victorious, the nation basked in the pride of having beaten down the dangerous forces of "world oppression." There was pride to be taken "in the production miracle" that had made so extraordinary a victory possible. And yet for many Americans there remained a "deep anxiety that the hard days of the Depression would return."[63]

Though "[p]ersons who have been severely disadvantaged in the prewar period—farmers, blacks, southerners, and unskilled white men"—made some gains during the war or as a result of the New Deal,[64] the question on the minds of many Americans—women among them—after the war was what would become of them now. The war machine that had made victory possible would still have some work, given America's commitment to help rebuild Europe. But it would certainly be on a smaller scale than the wartime effort. For servicemen returning home, there was an immediate answer.

"When the hostilities ceased, the government expressed its gratitude in a fresh version of the New Deal. Although Congress rejected Harold Ickes's idea of directly transferring government-owned tools and factories to the GIs, and John Maynard Keynes's concept of a capital levy with proceeds going to the veterans…never seriously considered, veterans of World War II received postwar compensation of great value," writes Brandes.[65]

Among the spoils were "mustering-out pay," the right to reclaim old jobs, educational opportunities, loan guarantees, civil service job preferences, unemployment compensation, and a first-come right to buy surplus governmental property. And buy they did. "By January 1947, former GIs had purchased $501 million worth of surplus property—22 percent of the total. In the first decade after the war, 7,800,000 veterans undertook educational training," Brandes asserts.[66] All of this seemed to bode well for one-half of the American population.

By contrast, women—who had also been part of the victory effort—were now the forgotten Rosies of the war, facing "rewards" far less bountiful in a nation suddenly less enamored of their wartime efforts. The first thing that happened after the close of the war was the displacement of women, who were pushed out of jobs by men returning home, either by force of legislation or force of personal preference.

"When men came marching home, most Americans assumed that women were going to return to being housewives," Rowbotham writes. "Indeed, a substantial number of people thought women with husbands who could afford to support them should not be allowed to work. Most women workers, however, said they wanted to continue in paid employment and, having experienced well-paid jobs and learned new skills, resisted going back into 'women's work' in laundries or domestic service."[67]

A survey conducted by the United States Department of Labor after World War II found that "80 percent of U.S. women wanted to keep their jobs."[68] And yet, the number of women in the workforce fell from 36 percent in 1944 to 12 percent in 1948.[69] In addition, discrimination with regard to what jobs women should be allowed to take—all but invisible during the war—began to reemerge and was again to be upheld as valid by the nation's courts. Indeed, despite their efforts during the war, it was not until the late 1960s and early 1970s that laws of this kind would begin to change with the passage of a thicket of legislation aimed at discrimination based upon race, religion, and gender.

And yet, although the law did not begin to change until the mid-1960s and early 1970s, the landscape of the debate began to change as early as the 1950s, when women simply began to defy convention, tradition, and sometimes even husbands in an attempt to begin economically independent lives. It was the start of women and careers.

"Despite the *Ozzie and Harriet* image of the decade, women were, in fact, slipping back into the job market at a brisk rate," McDonald notes.[70] Indeed, statistics show that by the 1950s, roughly one-quarter to one-third of all married women in America were working,[71] and for the next three decades, these numbers continued to rise.[72] A reported 40 percent of all employees in the United States were women at the start of the 1960s.[73] It was a sociological shift that would mean a great deal to women and to history.

ENDNOTES FOR CHAPTER FOUR

1   See *Lochner v. New York*, 198 U.S. 45 (1905).

2   See McDonald, supra note 13, ENDNOTES FOR CHAPTER THREE, at p. 60.

3   See *Quong Wing v. Kirkendall*, 223 U.S. 62 (1912). (Two and a half decades later, the Court would rule similarly in *Breedlove v. Suttles, Tax Collector*, 302 U.S. 277 (1937)).

4   See, e.g., *Commonwealth v. Hamilton Manufacturing Co.*, 120 Mass. 383 (1876) (upholding a ten-hour law for women employed by manufacturing companies); *Commonwealth v. Beatty*, 15 Pa. Super. Ct. 5 (1895) (also upholding a ten-hour Pennsylvania law); *Wenham v. State*, 65 Neb. 405 (1902) (upholding a statute similar in language to the Massachusetts statute); *State v. Buchanan*, 29 Wash. 602 (1902) (also upholding a statute similar to the Massachusetts law); *Withey v. Bloom*, 163 Mich. 419 (1910) (upholding a Michigan law on the authority of *Muller v. Oregon*); *State v. Somerville*, 67 Wash. 638 (1910) (upholding an eight-hour law); *People v. Bowes-Allegretti Co.*, 244 Ill. 557 (1910) (upholding an hour limitation in what scholars see as an implied reversal of *Ritchie v. Wayman*); *Commonwealth v. Riley*, 210 Mass. 387 (1912) (Massachusetts court extended the principle to include the posting of hours and times for meals). But see, *Ritchie v. People*, 155 Ill. 98 (1895) (striking down a law limiting the hours that a woman may work); and, *People v. Williams,*189 N.Y. 131 (1907) (also striking down such a law).

5   See *Muller v. Oregon*, 208 U.S. 412 (1908); *Hawley v. Walker*, 232 U.S. 718 (1914); *Miller v. Wilson*, 236 U.S. 373 (1915); *Bosley v. McLaughlin*, 236 U.S. 385 (1915); *Bunting v. Oregon*, 243 U.S. 426 (1917); *Radice v. New York*, 264 U.S. 292 (1924).

6   261 U.S. 525 (1923).

7   See *Adkins v. Children's Hospital*, 261 U.S. at 542.

8   *Id.* at 553.

9   *Id.*

10   See Stuart D. Brandes, WARHOGS: A HISTORY OF WAR PROFITS IN AMERICA (Lexington, Ky.: University Press of Kentucky, 1997), at p. 234.

11   See Paul Dickson and Thomas Allen, *Marching on History*, SMITHSONIAN, Feb. 2003, pp. 84–94, at p. 86.

12   See Rowbotham, *supra* note 23, ENDNOTES FOR CHAPTER TWO, at p. 209.

13 *See* Anne Applebaum, GULAG: A HISTORY (New York: Doubleday, 2003), at pp. 123–124 (citing Michael Gelb, *Karelian Fever: The Finnish Immigrant Community During Stalin's Purges*, 45 EUROPE-ASIA STUDIES (No. 6), 1993, at pp. 1091–1160). (Applebaum adds, however, that "[a]lmost immediately, [these émigrés] caused problems for the authorities. Karelia was not, it turned out, much like America. Many loudly pointed this out to anyone who would listen, then tried to return—and wound up in the Gulag in the late 1930s instead.")

14 *See* John Steinbeck, THE GRAPES OF WRATH (New York: Bantam Books, 1969) (original publication New York: Viking, 1939), at pp. 127–128.

15 One such program was the W.P.A. For a readable overview, *see* Christine Bold, THE WPA GUIDES: MAPPING AMERICA (Jackson, Miss.: University of Mississippi Press, 1999); Joannie Fischer, *Casting a Wide Net*, U.S.NEWS & WORLD REPORT, Sept. 22, 2003, at pp. 68–72.

16 For review of the issue in the modern context, *see* Deborah Sontag, *The Power of the Fourth*, N.Y. TIMES MAG., March 9, 2003, at pp. 38–77.

17 *Id.*

18 *See* Ratner, *supra* note 77, ENDNOTES FOR CHAPTER THREE, at pp. 185, 188; Brandeis, *supra* note 77, ENDNOTES FOR CHAPTER THREE, at pp. 339, 462.

19 *See* Tribe, *supra* note 73, ENDNOTES FOR CHAPTER THREE, at p. 28, n. 9.

20 *United States v. Darby*, 312 U.S. 100 (1941).

21 *See* Rowbotham, *supra* note 12, at p. 251, n. 81 (cited Juanita Loveless as quoted in Sherna Berger Gluck (ed.), ROSIE THE RIVETER REVISITED: WOMEN, THE WAR, AND SOCIAL CHANGE (Boston: Twayne Publishers, 1987), at p. 135).

22 *See* Lewis Lord, *The Great Depression Escape*, U.S.NEWS & WORLD REPORT, July 28/August 4, 2003, at p. 16.

23 *See* Rowbotham, *supra* note 12, at p. 209.

24 *Id.* at 251.

25 *See* Brandes, *supra* note 10, at p. 201.

26 *Id.* at 203. (For review, *see* Jacob Vander Meulen, THE POLITICS OF AIRCRAFT: BUILDING AN AMERICAN MILITARY INDUSTRY (Lawrence: University Press of Kansas, 1992), at p. 141; Robert Dallek, FRANKLIN D. ROOSEVELT AND FOREIGN POLICY, 1932–1945 (New York: Oxford University Press, 1979), at p. 75; Wayne S. Cole, ROOSEVELT AND THE ISOLATIONISTS, 1932–1945 (Lincoln: University of Nebraska Press, 1983), at p. 264.)

27 *Id.*

28 *Id.* at 228.

29 *Id.* at 206.

30 *Id.* at 223.

31 *Id.* at 230 (citing Cole, *supra* note 26, at pp. 265–66; Dallek, *supra* note 26, at pp. 172–73).

32 *Id.* at 259 (citing R. Elberton Smith, THE ARMY AND ECONOMIC MOBILIZATION (Wash., D.C.: U.S. Army, 1959), at pp. 437–38).

33 *Id.* at 204.

34 *See* McDonald, *supra* note 2, at p. 60.

35 *See* Rowbotham, *supra* note 12, at p. 249.

36 *See* McDonald, *supra* note 2, at p. 60.

37 *See* Rowbotham, *supra* note 12, at p. 250.

38 *Id.* at 249.

39 *Id.* (citing Melissa Dubakis, *Gendered Labor*, in GENDER AND AMERICAN HISTORY SINCE 1890 (Barbara Melosh, ed.) (London: Routledge, 1993), at p. 196).

40 *Id.*

41 *Id.*

42 *Id.* at 249–250 (citing Dubakis, *supra* note 39).

43 *Id.* at 258.

44 *Id.* at 251–252.

45 *Id.* at 254 (citing debate over the issue of the Women's Auxiliary Army Corps (WAAC) as quoted by John Costella in LOVE, SEX, AND WAR, 1939–1945 (London: Pan Books, 1986), at p. 64).

46 *Id.* at 209.

47 *Id.* at 250.

48 *Id.*

49 *See* Donald Spoto, MARILYN MONROE: THE BIOGRAPHY (London: Arrow Books, 1994), at pp. 98–100.

50 *See* Rowbotham, *supra* note 12, p. 252.

51 *Id.* at 261.

52 *Id.* at 252.

53 *Id.* at 251.

54 *Id.* (citing General Louis McSherry as quoted by Robert L. Daniel, AMERICAN WOMEN IN THE 20ᵀᴴ CENTURY: THE FESTIVAL OF LIFE (Orlando, Fl.: Harcourt Brace Jovanovich, 1987), at p. 140).

55 *Id.*

56 *Id.* at 261.

57   *Id.* (citing Dr. Leslie Hohman, as quoted in MAJOR PROBLEMS IN AMERICAN HISTORY, Vol. 77, No. 2 (Mary Beth Norton (ed.)) (Lexington, Mass.: D.C. Heath and Co., 1989), at pp. 354–355).

58   *Id.* at 262.

59   *Id.* at 254.

60   *Id.* at 253.

61   *Id.* at 254 (quoting Daniel from AMERICAN WOMEN IN THE 20ᵀᴴ CENTURY, *supra* note 54, at p. 142).

62   *See* Dan O'Neill, THE FIRECRACKER BOYS (New York: St. Martin's Griffin, 1994), at p. 13.

63   *See* Brandes, *supra* note 10, at p. 269.

64   *Id.* at 270.

65   *Id.* at 271.

66   *Id.*

67   *See* Rowbotham, *supra* note 12, at p. 268.

68   *Id.* at 250.

69   *Id.*

70   *Id.*

71   *See* England & Farkas, supra note 9, ENDNOTES FOR CHAPTER THREE, at p. 99.

72   *Id.*

73   *Id.*

CHAPTER FIVE

The Birth Control Debate Begins

AMERICA AFTER THE WAR:
Turning from Rosie to June

For three centuries, the lives of women in the new American nation were ruled by their ability to bear children. One of the areas where this was most obvious was in employment. Women were deemed the "lesser part" of husbands. Thus, jobs thought to be too difficult or too intellectually demanding for women—a category tending overwhelmingly to include the traditional white-collar professions—were historically closed to women. At times by social convention. At others, by law.

But with the start of World War II, few of the old rules seemed to apply. With men leaving for the battlefields of Europe and the world in need of hands, Rosie the Riveter was born. Made of glossy strong arms and curves apparent even under a man's coveralls, Rosie was the wartime "pin-up girl" for all time, thrilling to the men of the Roosevelt administration and a role model for millions of Americans who would follow her lead.

By 1944, five million women across the United States were working, many of them former homemakers and the mothers of small children. Though it would scarcely register for many at the time, the age of the "working mother"—defined as married women with children (as opposed to single or widowed women with children)—had begun. It would prove a revelation, though not until much later, because in 1945, World War II would end. And by 1946, men were returning in large numbers to jobs held by women during their absence.

The result was the displacement of the wartime female workforce and the start of a debate pitting "traditionalists"—scholars and academics among them—against progressive theorists, advocates for women, and sometimes "the girls" themselves. At issue was the question of whether women should be returned to their "God-given" and "proper" places in society, or *allowed* to work outside of the home, even if their husbands could afford to support the family.

Of course, open debate was on the vocal end of a *blizkrieg* of social, academic, popular, and commercial programming, all touting the virtues of domesticity and the rewards of selfless dedication in service of the family. Other less verbal forms of persuasion were put to use as well, and like the propaganda of the 1940s—though less the result of a government-orchestrated plan than a reemerging mindset—the collective goal of these efforts was to change the hearts and minds of women: the overweening message of the time being that women should be "women" again.

Happiness for the softer gender, so the urgings went, was a home on a tree-lined street in one of the planned communities of America's newborn suburbia. From behind the proverbial white picket fence, wives—and all women should again aspire to be wives—would kiss husbands good-bye each morning before packing children off to school with brown paper bags filled with lunch. And for the rest of the day, the biggest worry women were supposed to have was what to serve for dinner. Or so went the plan.

And it went.

Sewing became a "million-dollar" industry as lovingly-tiled mosaics and hand-painted murals climbed kitchen walls in a late 1940s decorating trend intended to reaffirm the hearth as "the center of women's lives," feminist author Betty Friedan notes.[1] The self-appointed "experts" of the time instructed women on how best "to catch a man and keep him; how to breast-feed children and handle their toilet training; how to cope with sibling rivalry and adolescent rebellion; how to buy a dishwasher, bake bread, cook gourmet snails, and build a swimming pool with their own hands; how to dress, look, and act more feminine and make marriage more exciting; how to keep their husbands from dying young and their sons from growing into delinquents."[2]

As if to erase all memory of Rosie's coveralls, fashion cinched in the waists of women and pushed their feet into high heels. And, thus, where the silhouette of the 1940s was boxy and unisex by necessity, the silhouette of the 1950s was made of exaggerated curves; of tiny middles and a blossom of hips gliding gracefully above blushing calves honed to pencil-point sharpness at the ends of shoes as far removed from the rounded toes of Rosie's workaday loafers as possible. Women should look like women.

It was a debate that spilled over into academia with social scientists offering dire predictions of what would become of society if "the gentler sex" continued the *mannish* pursuit of work and higher education. With the 1947 publication of *Modern Women: The Lost Sex*, for example, social critic Ferdinand Lundberg[3] sounded a nearly 500-page alarm on an age-old warning: that "...careers and higher education [would] lead to the 'masculinization of women with enormously dangerous consequences to the home, the children dependent on it, and the ability of the woman, as well as her husband, to obtain sexual gratification."[4]

In other words, if women weren't *women*; men wouldn't be *men*. Though hardly an original position and certainly not a new construct where the social order was concerned, the conclusions put forth in *Modern Women: The Lost Sex* were quickly echoed by the editors of popular women's magazines in a glossy resurrection of lain-aside traditional male-female hierarchies.

Articles—with such titles as "Femininity Begins at Home;" "Have Babies While You're Young;" and "Are You Training Your Daughter to be a Wife?"—trumpeted the "new" femininity[5] as the public image of women moved backward. By the end of 1949, according to Friedan, "only one out of three heroines in the women's magazines was a career woman—and she was shown in the act of renouncing her career and discovering that what she really wanted to be was a housewife."[6]

And after 1949, "[f]ulfillment as a woman had only one definition—the housewife-mother," Friedan writes.[7] *Voilà!* The age of the "happy housewife" began as "[t]he feminine mystique…spread through the land grafted onto old prejudices and comfortable conventions which so easily [gave] the past a stranglehold on the future."[8] At its roots was the notion that "the highest value and the only commitment for women [was] the fulfillment of their own femininity."[9]

"Under valuation of…femininity" (a force deemed so mysteriously "close to the creation and origin of life" that "man-made science" was incapable of understanding it) was among the great mistakes of Western civilization, it was argued.[10] These claims, when taken together, conspired to create a "new" image of women—that of housewife, *i.e.*, "housewife-mothers, who never had a chance to be anything else, the model for all women: it presupposes that history has reached a final and glorious end in the here and now, as far as women [were] concerned," Friedan argues.[11]

The hype seems to have worked: the number of women attending college fell from 47 percent to 35 percent between 1920 and 1958,[12] and roughly 60 percent of women attending college or universities left school, fearing that "too much education" would rule them out as potential wives.[13] The age of marriage for women also fell. By the mid-1950s, roughly fourteen million girls were engaged by the time they were seventeen.[14]

But there was a problem with the illustration of wifehood and motherhood as it was being drawn—women who were already married were having trouble living up to the myth and they were beginning to talk about it openly.

"What a circus act we perform every day of our lives," wrote Anne Morrow Lindbergh in *Gift From the Sea*,[15] a 1955 bestseller described by reviewers as a "philosophical meditation" that became a "source of inspiration for a whole generation of wives and mothers."[16]

Anne Morrow Lindbergh, the wife of the famed aviator, Charles Lindbergh, was an aviation icon in her own right. The first woman in the United States to be granted a glider pilot's license, Anne Morrow Lindbergh served as navigator and copilot during the couple's celebrated 1930 transatlantic flight. She also went on to become a critically-acclaimed poet and writer. Through it all, Anne Morrow Lindbergh was a wife and mother who began sounding off early about the difficulties of balancing work and family.

"Look at us," Morrow Lindbergh wrote of women struggling to reconcile real life with the myth of the new American housewife. "We run a tightrope daily, balancing a pile of books on the head. Baby-carriage, parasol, kitchen chair, still under control. Steady now! This is not the life of simplicity but the life of multiplicity that the wise men warn us of. It leads not to unification but to fragmentation. It does not bring grace; it destroys the soul."

But the men of Hollywood seemed to disagree, and with a new propaganda/mass marketing tool known as television, they set about to persuade. On October 4, 1957, the nation got a glimpse of the new American archetype of woman-housewife-and-mother when *Leave It To Beaver* made its network debut. In a skirt that may or may not have sported a poodle, a top made of well-tailored lines, and a face aglow in makeup, June Cleaver baked cookies in high heels, offered sensible, ladylike advice to stymied children, and smiled lovingly over dinner with Ward. She was the "perfect" *fictional* wife, mother, and woman.

And lest the fact that June was a televised fictional depiction of woman tend to suggest that her influence was limited, it should be noted that *Leave It to Beaver* hit the small screen midway through a television revolution: the number of television sets in use across America in 1946 was estimated at roughly 10,000. But by 1960—three years after the debut of *Leave It To Beaver*—the number had risen to roughly 54 million televisions in use across the United States.[17] The flutter of June's eyelashes, it seems, would shape a generation.

IMAGES OF THE NEW AMERICAN FAMILY:
Women in the Shadow of June

But it wasn't only June. There were others. For three straight years, for example—from 1957 through the 1959-60 seasons—the soft and blurry Jane Wyatt, of TV's *Father Knows Best*, took home the Emmy for outstanding performance by an actress in a weekly series[18] as historic notions of "natural" hierarchy came full circle. Despite the efforts of women during World War II and the fact that they had flooded the workforce without destabilizing American society—father still knew best.

And yet, there was another reason that "family" remained the focus of politicians and television producers during the 1940s, 1950s, and even early 1960s. Among the many hard-fought spoils of war was a decade-long surge in the birthrate of children in America. The generation of children born during this period would later become known as the "baby-boomers."

"The century-long decline in the United States's fertility was briefly and dramatically interrupted by an unexpected upsurge in fertility between 1946 and the early 1960s," note University of Texas sociologists Paula England and George Farkas.[19] "Demographers expected fertility rates to rise temporarily [as] couples who had been apart 'made up for lost time' after the war. Unexpected, however, was the continued elevation of these rates through the 1950s, much longer than can be explained by pent-up demand for children that was unmet during the war."[20]

And yet, despite the birth boom, the renewed emphasis on family, and the eternal praise of June and Jane, women were breaking with tradition. The vast majority of women who were part of the workforce during World War II wanted to remain there.[21] And though many were forced out by 1948, as men returned home to reclaim jobs,[22] during the 1950s, women quietly began slipping back into the workforce.[23] By the close of the decade, roughly one-quarter to one-third of all married women were working.[24]

But the picture was even more complex than that. Although the 1950s are often "remembered" as a moral, family-oriented time, there was a decidedly less moral side of the time. Despite the precepts, premarital and extramarital sex were a reality during the 1950s, argues researcher and author David Allyn.[25] "[I]n 1957 alone 200,000 babies were born out of wedlock in the United States," according to Allyn.[26]

Single women—many of them mothers—have always been part of the American labor force. They were joined during this period by married women, boosting the number of women overall in the workplace until, by the start of the 1960s, an estimated 40 percent of all employees in the United States were women.[27] And their numbers continued to climb. By the 1980s, the number of married women working rose to roughly fifty percent of the population,[28] and by the early 1990s, "nearly two-thirds of all married women with children were in the labor force," according to *U.S.News & World Report*.[29]

The dynamic of the American workplace was changing and it would change even further. The women's and civil rights movements of the late 1950s and early '60s would lead to sweeping changes in the law, making it easier for women to enter and remain in the workforce. In addition, although some women undoubtedly went to work to help their families financially, also thrown into the mix, some feminists say, was the growing disillusionment of women.[30]

Thus, while Anne Morrow Lindbergh's assessment of the troubled balance of the lives of working women may have served as a "source of inspiration for a...generation of wives and mothers,"[31] it was a gathering of words and ideas brought together by a former freelance writer[32] and reportedly once-battered wife[33] that gave substance into the "problem that has no name."[34]

"The problem lay buried, unspoken, for many years in the minds of American women," wrote Betty Friedan in *The Feminine Mystique*. "It was a strange stirring, a sense of dissatisfaction, a yearning that women suffered in the middle of the twentieth century in the United States. Each suburban wife struggled with it alone. As she made the beds, shopped for groceries, matched slipcover material, ate peanut butter sandwiches with her children, chauffeured Cub Scouts and Brownies, lay beside her husband at night—she was afraid to ask even of herself the silent question—'Is this all?'"[35]

The Feminine Mystique went on to become the number-one nonfiction best-selling paperback of 1964. It also seemed to give rise to the debate over whether white, heterosexual, middle-class women should embrace—or rebuff—the doctrine of woman according to June. By the mid 1960s, it was clear that many had decided to rebuff it.

In stark contrast to the family-oriented decade of the 1950s, the 1960s were punctuated by war protests, student uprisings, and civil and women's rights movements. The focus had turned from family sacrifice to individual rights, and a series of legal challenges before the United States Supreme Court involving such anti-June questions as whether a woman (and her husband) should have the right to try to prevent getting "in the family way."[36] But there was, of course, yet another image of women.

THE CHANGES OF THE 1960s:
Sex and the Modern Woman

In almost the time it took to change channels (before the advent of the remote control, of course)—everything changed for women again with the obligation of femininity—the feminine *mystique* of the 1950s—morphing seamlessly into the open sexuality of the 1960s as poodle-skirted Junes became bikini-clad Annettes, leather-encased Cat Women, and Mata Hari spy girls whose jobs seemed to necessitate thigh-grazing miniskirts.

In a quantum leap, "obligated femininity" blossomed into straight-on glamour as women—their eyes smoldering with kohl outlines, a perfect flip to their hair—strut their stuff on the job and then at home. It was the age of "powder-puff" lunches, peddle-pushers, and pajama parties. There were pillbox hats and three-quarter coats for "career girls;" short pants, shorter skirts, and bathing suits for the sporty girls. And a peek-a-boo bit of both for the truly sporty among them.

"Sex was going to leap into the open in post-World War II America no matter what, and the 1950s was the last time that show business's pop-culture factories tried to swat it down," entertainment writer Frank Rich commented recently.[37]

By the 1960s, the swatting had turned to disrobing as arms, legs, and throats went bare. The often-contrived excuse for this newfound exposure was the sudden discovery that women could be "athletic." But within reason, of course. Piled high, one on top of the other on water skis, for example. Or bounding long-legged and lean down the beach.

There was a sassy edge to this new woman. She was sexy and fun. But most of all, she was smart enough to know—whether arguing politics or trying to catch a millionaire—that she should "never, never let him forget" he's a man. This, it seems, was the ultimate aphrodisiac as sexual suggestion became the new vogue and sex an emerging pastime as the pattern of partnership and marriage began to change in America.

"Since the 1960s, the route to the altar is no longer so predictable as it used to be," the authors of *Sex in America: A Definitive Survey* suggest.[38] "In the first half of the twentieth century, almost everyone who married followed the same course: dating, love, a little sexual experimentation with one partner, sometimes including intercourse, then marriage and children. It also was a time when there was a clear and accepted double standard—men were much more likely to have had intercourse with several women before marrying than women were to have had intercourse with several men."[39]

But that changed dramatically during the 1960s when the rate of marriage fell as "pairings" increased. Between 1933 and 1942, 84.5 percent of first-time "partnerships" among men and 93.8 percent of first partnerships among those women surveyed were marriages. Between 1953 and 1962, however, those numbers fell to 46.6 percent of men and 57.3 percent of women surveyed between 1953 and 1962. And they fell even further during the nine-year period between 1963 and 1974, to 33.9 percent for men and 35.3 percent for women surveyed.[40]

Today, "[s]ome people still marry at eighteen, [while] others [marry] at thirty, leading to very different numbers of sexual partners before marriage," findings suggest.[41] And social class appears to still play a role—"less educated people marry earlier than better-educated people;" African American people "tend to marry much later than whites, and a large number of [African Americans] do not marry at all."[42]

"But a new and increasingly common pattern has emerged" as well in recent years: "affection or love and sex with a number of partners, followed by affection, love, and cohabitation. This cycles back to the sexual marketplace, if the cohabitation breaks up or leads to marriage. Pregnancy can occur at any of these points, but often occurs before either cohabitation or marriage," the study suggests.[43]

The emerging sexuality of the 1960s—especially as it is increasingly related to and/or involved women and the fear of what that might mean to society— served to reignite the longstanding public debate over birth, a woman's obligation to society, and conception, bringing with it all of the bitterness and acrimony that have long surrounded these issues, beginning with perhaps the most obvious one of them all—sexism.

"As long as one championed sexual restraint for both sexes, there was no need to fear," writes Allyn. "But as soon as one advocated sexual freedom for women as well as men, the public responded with outrage."[44]

From an historic perspective, the 1960s and the 1970s would prove an extraordinary time for women, who would learn in the span of roughly ten years that laws articulating male gender preference were illegal.[45] Women would also learn that they had some measure of control and ownership of their bodies.[46] It was a significant change for women.

And yet, in terms of the landmark United States Supreme Court decision that might fairly be said to have changed the landscape of the modern reproductive rights debate, the underlying case involved not a single woman seeking clarification of her sexual rights in light of the times. But rather two doctors who sought to answer the question of whether married adults had the right to choose—in the privacy of their own bedroom—not to have children.

UNCOVERING FUNDAMENTAL RIGHTS:
Redefining Zones of Privacy

"No woman can call herself free who does not own and control her own body. No woman can call herself free until she can choose consciously whether she will or will not be a mother."

—Margaret Sanger[47]

In November of 1961, two doctors, one of them the executive director of the Planned Parenthood League of Connecticut, were arrested for providing married couples with information on birth control devices, then a violation of Connecticut law.[48] But the doctors didn't take the charges lightly. They appealed the case all the way to the United States Supreme Court, arguing that the Connecticut statute violated the Fourteenth Amendment of the United States Constitution.

Although the question before the Court was framed as one of legality—specifically the legality of the Connecticut statute in light of the enumerated protections of the Constitution—the subtext of the debate was whether married couples had the right, in the privacy of their own bedrooms, to choose birth control to prevent pregnancy upon the advice of their doctor. And whether medical professionals had the right to offer such advice.

The issue harkened back to the arrest and conviction nearly fifty years before of Margaret Sanger and her sister, Ethel Byrnes, for disseminating information on birth control devices in violation of "anti-obscenity" laws.[49] A half-century later, the potential use of birth control remained a troubling issue in America. Rooted in the legal questions raised by the prospect of the widespread use of birth control were religious and spiritual concerns regarding the essence of *life*.

The Catholic Church, religious leaders, and lawmakers have long opposed the widespread use of birth control, and their efforts were apparent even in traditionally "liberal" states. In New York, for example, authorities continued to prosecute people for the sale of "any article for the prevention of conception" well into the 1940s.[50] Massachusetts,[51] Pennsylvania,[52] and Iowa[53] had similarly worded statutes on the books, and continued to prosecute offenders as well. There was also at least one prosecution under a federal law at about the same time.[54]

Some historians suggest that the United States Supreme Court's decision in *Skinner v. Oklahoma*[55] set the stage for the landmark reproductive rights cases in the 1960s. *Skinner v. Oklahoma* involved challenge to an Oklahoma statute permitting the forced sterilization of "habitual criminals" or persons convicted on three or more "felonies involving moral turpitude."

ISSUES IN REPRODUCTIVE PRIVACY

There are dark periods within the reproductive rights debate that often go unnoticed. Forced sterilization presents such a moment. Throughout the twentieth century, state officials across the United States repeatedly sought ways to eliminate "undesirables" from the general population. Prisons, many argued then as they argue today, offered a solution to the problem. Simply lock them away forever. A sort of "three strikes, you're out" in the reproductive arena. But wouldn't it, in fact, be far easier for everyone involved if *eventual* criminals and the rest of the "dregs" were never born? Believe it or not, that question was actually considered by the Justices of the United States Supreme Court in the 1942 case of *Skinner v. Oklahoma.*[56]

SKINNER v. OKLAHOMA vs. THE *BUCK v. BELL* STANDARD

At issue in *Skinner v. Oklahoma* was an Oklahoma statute permitting the sterilization of "habitual criminals" convicted of committing three or more "felonies involving moral turpitude." Jack Skinner was a failed chicken thief and a convicted armed robber, and in accordance with the 1935 law, the Oklahoma attorney general sought to have Skinner sterilized. But the Justices of the Supreme Court ultimately held the Oklahoma statute unconstitutional, violative of the Fourteenth Amendment's Equal Protection Clause. It is important to note, as scholars always have, that "at the time of the *Skinner v. Oklahoma* decision, the United States was engaged in a declared war against the combined forces of world fascism. The Court was not unaware of the popularity of eugenics theories among the nation's enemy."[57]

In other words, it is possible that America's involvement in World War II encouraged the Court to publicly condemn statutes providing for the sterilization of "undesirable" members of the race. It is also possible that Jack Skinner had the luck of the biological draw on his side when he went before the Court, because he was a man. Less than two decades before the Court's decision in *Skinner v. Oklahoma*, the Justices heard another case involving the issue of sterilization, and in that case, the outcome was markedly different. But that case involved a woman.

In 1927, the plight of Carrie Buck's reproductive future was at issue before the Court in the infamous case of *Buck v. Bell,*[58] with the Justices ultimately ruling that Carrie Buck, then an 18-year-old girl, could be sterilized because "three generations of imbeciles is enough...." *Buck v. Bell* involved a Virginia statute permitting the involuntary sterilization of persons thought to be "feeble-minded" if state officials believed sterilization was in the individual's "best interests." Although *Buck v. Bell* was heard by the Court more than seventy years ago, as a matter of law, several states still have statutes similar to the Virginia sterilization law upheld by the United States Supreme Court in *Buck v. Bell,* and some states still use them as the State of Virginia sought to apply the statute against Carrie Buck.

Despite the landmark precedents of *Griswold v. Connecticut, Eisenstadt v. Baird,* and even the embattled *Roe v. Wade,* the forced sterilization of "feeble minded" people has never been held unconstitutional, though the federal government made some attempt to end the practice. In 1973, the federal government adopted regulations intended to ensure that all sterilizations funded by Medicaid payments were "voluntary."[59] Cases immediately testing these regulations were *Relf v. Weinberger*[60] and *National Rights Organization v. Weinberger*.[61] Reasoning that mentally challenged persons could not give informed consent, a federal court enjoined the use of public funds for the sterilization of persons under 21 who cannot give informed consent.

But in 1977, that decision was vacated in favor of a federal standard of voluntariness. Proposed standards were initially published in the *Federal Register*, and in November 1978, a set of final regulations were enacted. But the informed consent provision remained at issue until in 1979 federal authorities adopted regulations prohibiting the use of federal funds for the sterilization of persons under 21 years of age.[62]

Federal regulations also promulgated requirements meant to ensure that individuals to be sterilized had given proper informed consent. These, however, were the efforts of federal officials. Considerably less was done on the state level, and today at least fourteen states still have statutes that authorize sterilization in certain situations,[63] which has led to some not so insignificant numbers. By some estimates, more than 70,000 American citizens have undergone compulsory sterilization procedures[64] since the first sterilization statute was passed in 1907.

THE STATE AND STERILIZATION TODAY

But what do these statutes mean today? They mean trouble for people like Sophia Truesdell. In the early 1980s, the Mecklenberg County social services department petitioned for an order to have Sophia Truesdell involuntarily sterilized. Sophia Truesdell was eighteen at the time and described in court papers as a "mentally retarded" female. The case became known as *In the Matter of Sophia Truesdell*.[65] County officials argued that sterilization would be in Sophia's best interest, because she could not care for herself while pregnant, and she would not be able to care for a child after birth. Where there is a showing of mental illness or retardation, the North Carolina statute provided that a county official could seek involuntary sterilization if the procedure was thought to be in a person's "best interest" and there was a showing that the individual to be sterilized was sexually active and likely to conceive.

But the North Carolina Appellate Court was not convinced. Noting that "...sterilization not only affects the individual's fundamental right to procreate, recognized by the United States Supreme Court in *Skinner v. Oklahoma*, it forever deprives the individual of that basic liberty,"[66] the court held that Sophia Truesdell could not be involuntarily sterilized because county officials could make no showing of sexual activity. Thus, county officials had failed to prove that the proposed "sterilization of Sophia Truesdell at this time—will further the state's interest in preventing the conception and birth of a child whose parent is unable to adequately care for it."

The North Carolina sterilization statute was eventually challenged as unconstitutional in *N.C. Association for Retarded Children v. State of N.C.*,[67] because the law authorized involuntary as well as voluntary sterilization for "mentally defective persons housed in state institutions and those who are not patients in state institutions..."[68] if sterilization was "considered in the best interest of the mental, moral, or physical improvement" of the "retarded people, or for the public good." The North Carolina court hearing the case struck the above paragraph,[69] upholding the constitutionality of the statute without it.

In reaching this conclusion, the court explained that "[w]e interpret Article 7 as narrowly drawn to express only the legitimate State interest of *preventing the birth of a defective child or the birth of a nondefective child that cannot be cared for by its parents*, and that so viewed, the State's interest rises to the dignity of a compelling one."[70] The court held similarly in *In re Sterilization of Moore.*[71]

Not surprisingly, mentally challenged persons generally faired better in federal court. In *Ruby v. Massey*,[72] for example, a federal district court in Connecticut held that the parents of three severely challenged minors could "neither veto nor give valid consent to the sterilization of their children." The case was before the court because officials at the hospital where the girls had been taken refused to perform sterilization procedures. In a twist on things, their parents brought suit. But the girls' parents could not consent to their sterilization, because "...the Constitution protects the freedom of even an immature teenager to decide for herself whether to bear or beget a child, [and] no case has considered the question of who may make the sterilization decision for the child who is mentally incapable of deciding for herself," the Connecticut court held.

The promulgation of federal regulations clearly suggests that federal officials would like to see an end to sterilization statutes. Yet many states continue to perform sterilization procedures on mentally challenged persons under the umbrella of state police powers, and only Oregon had legislation pending in 2001 that would require a court to hear testimony about a person's ability to consent to sterilization from the *person to be sterilized*.[73] Thus, if there is a general rule regarding the sterilization of mentally challenged people, it is that some states still stand by and enforce compulsory sterilization statutes, apparently ignoring the constitutional questions they tend to raise in addition to federal court rulings and federal regulations that urge the opposite.

But in light of the near religious fervor many states have demonstrated in recent years for "unborn children," the question again comes to the fore. Why sterilization? State officials have long argued that sterilization is necessary because mentally challenged persons are unable to care for children. But why not adoption? As set forth in greater detail in this chapter, as a requirement of most informed consent statutes, state-prepared materials (often including information on adoption and adoption agencies) are given to women seeking abortion. The argument often asserted to justify the dissemination of materials of this sort is that women should be told they can give their children up for adoption.

Couldn't mentally challenged women also give their babies up for adoption? Of course, they could. But historic notions of states' rights, ancient prejudices, and persistent stigmas still govern the reproductive rights debate. Thus, some state officials have clearly determined, as the battle rages over whether a woman should have a continued right to choose abortion, that the potential risk of bringing "damaged" children into the world is sufficient enough to justify foreclosing the right of some people to reproduce.

What is frightening from a legal perspective is that some judges apparently think so too. For example, in *Smith v. Superior Court,*[74] a baby died and the dead child's parents were later convicted of child abuse. At their sentencing, the judge ordered the pair to serve two and a half years in jail. But the judge then offered to reduce their sentences if they would *voluntarily* agree to sterilization at their own expense. The Smiths appealed, arguing that the judge's suggestion was unconstitutional and illegal. The Arizona Supreme Court agreed, holding that the judge had exceeded his authority in ordering sterilization as a condition of a lesser sentence.

But there were others. Until recently, the only criminal case on record authorizing sterilization without specific statutory authority was *People v. Blankenship,*[75] in which the California appellate court upheld "chemical sterilization" as a condition of probation for a defendant who had syphilis and who had pled guilty to the rape of a child. But the case was later implicitly overruled by *People v. Dominiquez.*[76] And yet, court-ordered *voluntary* sterilization would appear to be an idea whose time has yet to come and go. At least for some.

Chemical sterilization, considered a less intrusive and reversible alternative to surgical procedures, was at issue in *Gauntlett v. Kelly.*[77] Roger Gauntlett pled guilty to first degree criminal sexual conduct. After presentencing skirmishes with the judge, Gaunlett was sentenced to five years probation with three conditions. The only one of those conditions of concern to this chapter is the requirement that he submit "to castration by chemical means...." The "chemical means" was Depo-Provera. Like the Arizona judge in *Smith v. Superior Court,* the judge in *Gauntlett v. Kelly* informed Gauntlett that if he did not submit to all of the conditions, probation would be revoked and he would be sent to jail. Due to other events, Gaunlett was ultimately sentenced to jail. Thus, he never had to submit to the Depo-Provera treatment.

Though the above cases generally illustrate how the "sterilization" issue has played out for men convicted of crimes there is, however, no general rule of thumb when it comes to incarcerated women, except to say that judges across the country often deny women their right to choice under the law. Since 1966, "there have been at least 20 cases in which judges have ordered individuals to be sterilized, [to] use contraception, or not [to] become pregnant," reports the National Abortion and Reproductive Rights Action League (NARAL).[78] That count most likely includes those cases in which judges have demanded, as a condition of probation or release, that women abstain from having more children for a certain period.

But there have also been cases, according to the NARAL, in which individual judges deliberately thwarted a female detainee's efforts to have an abortion. Among those specific instances, NARAL reports, are the following.

- In 1998, in Ohio, Yuriko Kawaguchi pled guilty to forgery and was sentenced to six months in prison, though most offenders would have received probation. The apparent reason for the prison sentence was Ms. Kawaguchi's spoken desire to have an abortion. At the sentencing hearing, Judge Patricia Cleary reportedly said: "I'm saying that she is not having a second-term abortion." The judge then dismissed Ms. Kawaguchi's lawyer for questioning the sentence, leaving Ms. Kawaguchi unrepresented during sentencing and forcing her to obtain a new attorney at a crucial time in the proceedings as well as in the pregnancy. In addition, the judge: (1) refused to free Ms. Kawaguchi on bond while she appealed the prison sentence; (2) had Ms. Kawaguchi "transported to a state prison outside of the jurisdiction of state and federal courts in Cuyahoga County to thwart Ms. Kawaguchi's Writ of Habeas Corpus, which would have allowed her to obtain an abortion;" and, (3) "improperly and without authority vacated another judge's order releasing Ms. Kawaguchi to prevent Ms. Kawaguchi from obtaining an abortion." After Ms. Kawaguchi served four and one-half months, the state appellate court released her pending her appeal. She sued Judge Clearly and others for violating her constitutional rights.[79]

- In a highly publicized Florida case, a judge refused a woman's request to delay a 60-day jail sentence so that she could have an abortion, even though attorneys for both sides had agreed to a 10-day delay. Upon denying Pamela Fomey's request, County Judge Dan C. Rasmussen stated: "[Y]ou want a continuance so you can murder your baby, is that it?" In addition, the judge criticized the woman, saying, "It seems to me, Ms. Forney, this is another indication of your irresponsibility." In a jail interview following the judge's decision, Ms. Forney stated: "I thought it was my choice.... He's telling me I don't have a choice. It's not right that he can choose for me.... He could have given me two or three days.... But now I may have to have a baby because the judge doesn't believe in abortion."[80]

- In 1997, when a 33-year-old pregnant women requested that her bail be reduced so that she might be released to terminate her pregnancy, New Jersey Superior Court Judge Leonard Arnold appointed an antiabortion activist attorney to represent the fetus.[81]

- When sentencing a woman convicted of a felony, an Illinois judge cited the woman's three abortions as an aggravating factor necessitating a harsher sentence, stating "what value...does she place on human life?" An Illinois appellate justice sitting on a three-judge panel agreed, writing that the woman deserved a harsh sentence because of her abortions and noting "that the abortions were 'relevant to the defendant's moral character' in that she 'indicates a conscious disregard for human life.'" The other two justices sitting on the panel disagreed, noting that abortion is legal and that a woman should not be punished for committing a legal act.[82]

- In 2001, the Wisconsin Supreme Court upheld a lower court ruling involving a probation order that prohibited the future procreation of a 34-year-old man convicted of the failure to pay child support and owing a reported $25,000, unless or until he is able to show that he can afford to support more children.[83]

Though judges considering the conditional release of persons convicted of crimes may impose certain conditions on that release and have wide discretion, they cannot generally impose any condition. In other words, though probation is a form of conditional release, the courts recognize that a liberty interest may be implicated.[84] Thus, "[c]onstitutional due process…require[s] that a probationer accused of violating a condition of his probation receive prior notice of the charges against him and that he or she be given an opportunity to meet and refute the charges."[85]

In addition, procreation has been deemed a "liberty" issue, which raises the question of whether it is permissible for a judge to require as a condition of release that women not get pregnant. Finally, holding the choice of abortion to be an aggravating factor justifying a higher sentence would appear to be the kind of invidious conduct the Pregnancy Discrimination Act would not tolerate in the employment context. Is it reasonable, then, that women should have to tolerate it in the courts?

In 2001, a Rhode Island legislator proposed a bill that, if passed, would prohibit the state from interfering in a woman's decision to: prevent, begin, or continue a pregnancy.[86] And a Texas bill, if enacted, proposes a constitutional amendment prohibiting the state from requiring a woman to complete a pregnancy.[87] In order for bills or laws of this sort to work, however, state judges will have to comply.

OTHER SIMILAR OR RELATED REPORTED INCIDENTS

- In September 2001, the Ninth Circuit Court of Appeals ruled—in a case involving a prisoner serving life who argued that he should be allowed to ship his semen out of the prison so that his wife could be artificially inseminated—that male prisoners have a constitutionally protected right to procreation. Specifically, the court held that procreation is "not inherently inconsistent with one's status as a prisoner."[88]

- In late 2001, the Third Circuit Court of Appeals re-instated claims on the behalf of Elizabeth Arnold, who was sterilized in 1977 as a teenager after giving what some have described as "questionable consent." The consent form at the heart of the case reportedly contains Arnold's name printed in block letters. Hospital records list Arnold "mentally retarded." Prior to sterilization, there was allegedly assertions than Arnold was "promiscuous."[89]

• In 2003, flyers began appearing along telephone poles in Brooklyn offering $200 to men and women who agreed to be sterilized. The group behind the flyers—Children Requiring a Caring Kommunity (CRACK), started in California a half-decade before—purports an interest in preventing the birth of drug-addicted children and has drawn criticism almost since its inception for the active recruitment in urban areas of "drug-addicted men and women."[90]

But others argue that the upheaval of the 1960s and the general march toward greater equality by women and minorities led to fundamental changes in the law and a series of United States Supreme Court decisions in which the Justices "uncovered" *fundamental* rights for women and minorities. And this "unveiling" would profoundly alter the essence of their relationship to the state.

"Rights," researchers and authors Robert Blank and Janna C. Merrick argue, "are 'valuable commodities,' because to claim that one has a right is to demand or to insist that one's claim be recognized.... Rights are thus entitlements...to do, have, omit, or be something and to demand that others act or refrain from acting in certain ways."[91]

In other words, in a nation like the United States, where the Constitution clearly enumerates the rights of citizens, "[e]ach person [is presumed to have]...a sphere of autonomy that others cannot violate," Blank and Merrick explain.[92]

But women traditionally did not have this autonomy. Indeed, with specific regard to reproductive rights, there was very little public discussion in America prior to the mid-twentieth century of allowing women to choose <u>not</u> to have children, even though birth control and abortion have ancient histories.[93] But during the 1960s, as women went to work and filled the streets in protests and rights marches, the question of whether the state still had the right to require women to have "unwanted children"—a previously inconceivable circumstance—made its way into the foreground.

THE BIRTH CONTROL DEBATE:
Getting from B to A

> If the right of privacy means anything, it is the right of the individual, <u>married or single</u>, to be free from unwarranted governmental intrusion into matters so fundamentally affecting a person as the decision whether to bear or beget a child.
>
> —*Eisenstadt v. Baird*, 405 U.S. 438, 453 (1972).

"Sometimes the Supreme Court leads the nation" as it did in "commanding school desegregation" with the establishment-shattering decision in *Brown v. Board of Education*,[94] offers legal writer Marcia Coyle in analyzing the 2002-2003 Supreme Court term.[95]

And sometimes the Court "follows," riding the threads of an emerging national consensus, the Justices granting it relevance by agreeing to hear it and the force of precedent with their decision. Perhaps more than any other time in recent history, that is what happened—repeatedly—during the 1960s, and the result was a greater array of rights and protections for women than ever before.

The United States Supreme Court is often thought of as an aloof body: scholarly, learned, determinedly apolitical, and above the emotional fray of day-to-day disputes. Or so it has long been argued, although there have always been clear exceptions to the above assertions. But during the 1960s, the Court seemed particularly attuned to the new American accord regarding women. Women were working, earning their own money, making their way in the world, and reluctant to have to give it all up due to an "unplanned pregnancy," a phrase that had finally become part of the lexicon of the debate. Birth control was available, albeit still largely only by prescription, and women (and many men) wanted to use it.

And even the Justices of the Supreme Court seemed to be taking note of a nation in transition. As early as 1915, Margaret Sanger argued that women were not truly "free" until they were able to control their own bodies.[96] By the 1960s, many women were determined to grasp this kind of "freedom." But there was a problem: a majority of states still had laws prohibiting the dissemination of information regarding the use of birth control—even by medical profession-als—in addition to the sale of such products. It was under one such statute that the two doctors in Connecticut were arrested in November of 1961.[97] As dis-cussed earlier, however, the doctors appealed their convictions all the way to the United States Supreme Court where the Justices found the issue "ripe" for review.

In *Griswold v. Connecticut*,[98] as the case became known (the surname of one of the doctors was Griswold), the doctors argued that the Connecticut statute violated the Fourteenth Amendment of the United States Constitution, which holds that "[n]o State shall make or enforce any law which shall abridge the privileges and immunities of citizens of the United States; nor shall any State deprive any persons of life, liberty, or property, without due process of law; nor deny any person within its jurisdiction the equal protection of the laws."[99]

In terms of modern constitutional analysis, the Fourteenth Amendment—a post-Civil War amendment—has been read to include two distinct clauses that have proved extraordinarily significant in carving out the individual rights of women and minorities in the past 40 years. They are the Equal Protection Clause and the Due Process Clause.[100]

The Equal Protection Clause provides that all citizens are entitled to the "equal protection of the law." Women and minorities would use this clause alone or with federal legislation to begin successfully challenging gender and race discrimination in the late 1960s and early 1970s. The *Due Process Clause*, however, is far broader.

There are two kinds of due process: *procedural due process*, which generally involves ensuring that all of the procedural requirements of the law are met before state or federal authorities take certain actions. In other words, the Due Process Clause has been read to guarantee individuals certain procedural protections sufficient to prevent arbitrary government action.[101]

By contrast, at set forth in Chapter Three, *substantive due process* involves the "breathing" of life into the constitutionally undefined concept of "liberty."[102] As interpreted by the courts, the construct of substantive due process requires that all "legislation...be fair and reasonable in content as well as application: such may be broadly defined as the constitutional guarantee that no person shall be arbitrarily deprived of his [or her] life, liberty, or property."[103]

The constitutional guarantees of the Due Process Clause date back to the ratification of the Fourteenth Amendment in 1868. But widespread, court-ordered application of these guarantees to the rights of women is a relatively new event. It was not until the 1960s, for example, that the United States Supreme Court began to define the "liberty" interests of women as definitively as it had the interests of men as far back as 1905. And yet, the "Pandora's box" of substantive due process was as troubling a construct to conservative scholars in 1965 as it was in 1905, due in large part during the 1960s to the questions being asked.[104]

In *Griswold v. Connecticut*, for example—one of the earliest cases during the 1960s involving the reemergence of the substantive due process approach—the doctors argued that the Connecticut statute impinged upon the protections and guarantees of the Fourteenth Amendment. That may have been what they argued. But the subtext of the challenge involved in the question of whether these sorts of laws allowed the state to wander into those areas of intimate conduct that should rightfully be deemed private.

Politicians and lawmakers argued, then, as they often do now, that with regard to the use of birth control, they had a duty to protect "citizens," even those who were as-yet "unborn" as well as those who were as-yet "unconceived."[105] Religious leaders spat fire and brimstone about "sinners" having to live with the consequences of their "bad" behavior as traditionalists fretted the ruin of American society if punishment and deterrence fell away. What would keep women from having indiscriminate sex? What would become of the institution of marriage?

Proponents of birth control argued that women—not the state—should choose whether or not they would have children, grounding their arguments in historic notions of personal privacy. From feminist corners rose protests of patriarchy (restricting birth control kept women in the subordinate role of "breeder," some argued), despite the sweeping changes in the actual role of women in society. Still others grounded challenges in general assertions of equality and freedom.

And yet, as "freedom" arguments of the 1960s gained steam, debate turned inevitably to consideration of the concept of "liberty." But "liberty" has always been a fuzzy concept, one clarified with regard to men in 1905, but rarely thought of prior to the 1960s with regard to women. Thus, the question ultimately considered by the Justices of the United States Supreme Court in *Gris-*

wold v. Connecticut was whether the notion of "liberty" included privacy and the freedom to make reproductive choices and whether these choices superseded the interests of the state.

RESURRECTING SUBSTANTIVE DUE PROCESS:
The Lochner Doctrine is Reborn

In 1905, the Justices of the United States Supreme Court declared in *Lochner v. New York* that implicit within the concept of "liberty" was *the right* to contract for men. This notion of "implicit rights" would similarly be applied by the Justices sixty years later in the case of *Griswold v. Connecticut,* though the Justices would begin analysis of the issues at bar by expressly declaring that they were "declin[ing] the invitation" to let *Lochner* be their guide.

Instead, the Justices purported to find "peripheral" notions of privacy within "the First Amendment guarantees of certain freedoms."[106] The First Amendment "has a *penumbra* where privacy is protected from government intrusion," the Justices held. In addition, past precedents suggest "...specific guarantees in the Bill of Rights have *penumbras*, formed by emanations from those guaranteed that help give them life and substance," the Justices wrote.[107] And, finally, the Justices took note that the "Fourth and Fifth Amendments" also offer protections "against all governmental invasions of the sanctity of a man's home and the privacies of life."

Though the Justices reached only as far back as the Constitution in searching for the basis of "privacy," historian Mary Beth Norton suggests that "zones of privacy"—for some people—is older than the Constitution. In the Massachusetts Bay colonies, "...men, particularly those who held public office, were not required to reveal 'private crimes or offenses' that posed no danger to the province or to any individual settler," Norton explains.[108]

Still, with a gaggle of precedents and penumbras thus enumerated, the Justices held that *Griswold v. Connecticut* "concern[ed] a relationship lying within the zone of privacy created by several fundamental constitutional guarantees." And once that was settled, the Justices got right to the matter at hand in striking down the Connecticut statute.

In doing so, the Court reasoned that the law could not stand "in light of the familiar principle, so often applied by this Court, that a 'governmental purpose to control or prevent activities constitutionally subject to state regulation may not be achieved by means which sweep unnecessarily broadly and thereby invade the area of protected freedoms.'[109] Would we allow the police to search the sacred precincts of marital bedrooms for telltale signs of the use of contraceptives? The very idea is repulsive to the *notion of privacy surrounding the marriage relationship....* We deal with a right of privacy older than the Bill of Rights...."[110]

But if the "right of privacy" involved were truly older than the Bill of Rights, as the Justices suggest, why didn't the Founding Fathers address it in the Constitution?

There are two schools of thought on this question. The first is that the Founding Fathers took traditional notions of decency and privacy so much to heart that there seemed little reason to address them in writing. In other words, the notion of privacy was within those "innate feelings of right and wrong" understood to be part of the common law by the common man. The other school of thought suggests, however, that the Founding Fathers did not include explicit suggestions of privacy within the Constitution because they did not intend people to have that kind of privacy.

Nearly two centuries later, of particular concern to the Justices in *Griswold v. Connecticut,* was the possibility of a search of the "sacred precincts of the marital bedroom." But what if a couple wasn't married? Were the precincts of the bedroom in such an instance still "sacred?" Did the penumbras protect unmarried people?

Griswold v. Connecticut was the first in a line of cases to craft the boundaries of "reproductive privacy." In 1972, for example, the Justices took on the question of whether unmarried people were entitled to the same "right of privacy" in the bedroom as married couples. The case was *Eisenstadt v. Baird,*[111] and it would ultimately answer the question of what rights apply where the couple is "unsacred." And yet, again the story of the case would begin with a third party outside of the bedroom.

William Baird gave a lecture to a group of students at Boston University, "exhibiting" several "contraceptive articles" during the talk. At the end of the lecture, he was approached by a young woman whom he eventually left with a "package of Emko vaginal foam."[112] For it, William Baird was arrested and later convicted of violating a Massachusetts law similar in force to the Connecticut statute struck down by the Court in *Griswold v. Connecticut.*

William Baird, it seems, was not "an authorized distributor" of contraceptive devices. Under Massachusetts law, only "a registered physician" could administer or prescribe birth control. Baird appealed, arguing that the Massachusetts statute unfairly denied single people access to birth control. Up for grabs was the recent precedent of *Griswold v. Connecticut.*

Would the Court's 1965 decision be revealed as the mistake critics believed it to be? After all, Supreme Court precedent could not be used to establish a two-tier set of fundamental rights—one for married people and one for unmarried people. Or could it? Who did this fundamental right of privacy belong to, anyway? Women, men, families, or "others?" Those were the questions facing the Justices in *Eisenstadt v. Baird.* Again, the Court undertook tortured analysis in an effort to determine whether a "right of privacy" existed for unmarried people. Unabashed by the statement the Court was about to make, the Justices went right to it.

"It is true," they wrote in *Eisenstadt v. Baird,* "that in *Griswold* the right of privacy in question inhered in the marital relationship. Yet the marital couple is not an independent entity with a mind and heart of its own, but an association of two individuals each with a separate intellectual and emotional makeup. If the right of privacy means anything, it is the right of the *individual*, <u>married or single</u>, to be free from unwarranted governmental intrusion into matters so fundamentally affecting a person as the decision whether to bear or beget a child."[113]

Five years later, with the 1977 decision in *Carey v. Population Services Int'l*,[114] the Justices extended the "right of privacy"—which includes the right to choose birth control—to minors. Specifically, the Court held that minors could not be denied an opportunity to buy birth control because of their age.

The rebellion and upheaval of the 1960s and 1970s clearly brought sweeping change to the United States. Not all of it in the realm of reproductive rights. Civil and women's rights movements ushered in change in the workplace and a challenge to an Oregon statute articulating a preference for male executors over women led to the 1971 United States Supreme Court decision in *Reed v. Reed*,[115] which struck down gender-preference statutes as unconstitutional.[116]

And yet, for women one of the most significant, controversial, and emotional changes of all time would come about two years after its decision in *Reed v. Reed*, with the decision of the United States Supreme Court in *Roe v. Wade*, which legalized abortion.

BIRTH CONTROL AND MINORS:
Privacy vs. a Parent's Right to Know

For teenagers, condoms and other forms of contraceptives seem to be the thing to do. Statistical data suggests that contraceptives are playing an increasingly significant role in the lives of minor females by serving their intended purpose: preventing pregnancies. In 1999, the national rate of pregnancy among female teenagers between the ages of 15 and 17 fell to its lowest level in 40 years.[117] In addition, among girls between the ages of 10 and 14, the pregnancy rate declined to the lowest since 1969.[118]

But "low" is, in fact, a relative term, because the teen birthrate in the America still far exceeds that of other industrialized nations.[119] In other words, rather than reflecting rates comparable to those of Sweden, Great Britain, and France, the rate of teen pregnancy in the United States is closer to that of the Philippines, Indonesia, Thailand, and Turkey.[120] What that means in terms of actual numbers is that in 1994, for example, more than one million young women between the ages of 15 and 19 became pregnant.[121] However, by 1996, the above number had fallen to roughly 880,000.[122]

Continued decline is part of a decade-old trend. According to researchers, pregnancy rates among teenagers fell consistently in 47 states between 1985 and 1996.[123] The rate in some states, however, remains high. In 1996, California reported the highest number of adolescent pregnancies in a state-by-state comparison with roughly 126,300 instances.[124] Texas, New York, Florida, and Illinois followed with between 40,000 to 80,000 adolescent pregnancies each.[125] States posting the lowest rates of teenage pregnancy for that same period were Vermont, North Dakota, Wyoming, South Dakota, and Alaska, which reported fewer than 2,000 pregnancies among women between 15 and 19.[126]

The decline in the rate of teen pregnancy appears to be real. But sorting out the reasons for that decline opens the door to a different controversy. According to some research, "[m]ost young people begin having sex in their mid-to-late teens, about eight years before they marry; more than half of 17-year-olds have had intercourse."[127] Further, the proportion of sexually active teenagers rose from 47 percent in 1982 to 53 percent in 1988, and 58 percent of teenagers surveyed as part of a 1990 study who admitted to being sexually active also admitted to having two or more sexual partners.[128] And yet, other researchers report a decline in sexual activity among teenagers in America.

"There has definitely been a decline in sexual activity among teenagers, both boys and girls," argued Stephanie Ventura, a government researcher and author of a 1999 report on teen sexual activity.[129] Greater efforts to promote teen abstinence, including "virginity pledges,"[130] peer support groups, and "dollar-a-day" incentive programs have proven effective in some instances, recent studies suggest.[131] In addition, there is some evidence that teenage mothers who have given birth at least once are increasingly interested in preventing new pregnancies.[132]

But also in the mix is "a more consistent use of birth control, especially condoms," Ventura explains.[133] The numbers certainly seem to bear that out. Among teenagers in America, contraceptive "use at first intercourse rose from 48% to 65% during the 1980s, almost entirely because of a doubling in condom use."[134] And by 1995, "use at first intercourse reached 78%, with two-thirds of it condom use."[135] Further, roughly "one in six teenage women practicing contraception combine two methods, primarily the condom and another method."[136]

That may explain why in the dinosaur of throw-back politics, lawmakers in Mississippi proposed a bill in 2001 that would have prohibited minors under the age of 18 from obtaining condoms without a prescription.[137] It is an aggressively regressive measure. And yet, condoms are not the most widely used contraceptive among female teenagers. Roughly 44 percent of female teenagers using contraceptives rely upon the pill.[138] Condoms do follow as a close second, relied upon by roughly 38 percent of female teenagers.[139] Another 10 percent of female teenagers reportedly rely upon injectable forms of birth control. Four percent more rely upon withdrawal, and roughly three percent of female teenagers depend upon implanted contraceptives.[140]

Since 1977, minors have had the fundamental right to choose to use birth control. In *Carey v. Population Services Int'l*,[141] the Justices of the United States Supreme Court extended the "right of privacy"—which has been held to include the right to choose birth control—to minors, *i.e.,* that minors could not be denied an opportunity to buy birth control because of their age. Yet the law in this area remains far from settled, and the rights of all women—minor as well as adult—to choose anything that might prevent conception and/or pregnancy appears to be under attack on a number of fronts.

In addition to persistent legislative and court challenge, in the past two decades funding for abortion and birth control has drawn the attention of political and religious conservatives.[142] And where female minors and poor women are concerned, there is a new and fairly specific wrinkle. In 1965, federal funds were made available for family planning as part of the "war on poverty." Two years later, Title IV-A of the Social Security Act was amended to allow state welfare departments to provide information on family planning to women receiving public aid. Then, in 1970, President Nixon signed legislation creating Title X of the Public Health Service Act, the nation's only federal program dedicated to funding family planning and reproductive services.

EMERGING ISSUES TODAY:
And a Conservative Challenge

At its inception, the intent of Title X was to provide confidential family planning services to low-income adult women and minor females. In recent years, as many as 4.5 million low-income young women received care and advice at one or more of the 4,400 Title X-supported clinics across the country,[143] which may explain why the Title X program became the target of conservative lawmakers in the last half-decade. In 1995, for example, then-Representative Bob Livingston[144] proposed elimination of the Title X program and redirection of Title X funds to community block grants. The measure failed.

But in 1996, Representative Ernest Istook[145] stepped into the debate, proposing an amendment to Title X to include the requirement that Title X providers obtain written parental consent from minors at least five days in advance of dispensing services.[146] Supporters of the Istook measure argued that parents should be informed and/or involved in minors' decisions regarding contraceptives. Opponents argued that requiring clinics to inform parents of a minor's personal conduct would destroy the minor's right to "confidential" treatment.[147] In 1998, the House of Representatives passed alternative parental notification requirements by a 293–232 vote.[148] The new measure required only that providers encourage parental participation as provided by Title X. The bill failed in the Senate, however, and was never enacted.[149]

And yet, after all is said and done, Livingston and Istook may prove more pioneers than zealots, at least as far as conservatives are concerned. In 1997, the Texas legislature prohibited the use of state family planning funds for birth control and treatment for sexually transmitted disease until minors obtained written parental consent.[150] Although a Texas court invalidated the measure as violative of the state constitution and Title X, then-Governor George W. Bush vowed to appeal, and on June 7, 1999, Bush signed an amended version of the bill into law, asserting that the "law both respects families and protects life."[151]

Although public discussion of the Texas law focused largely on the requirement of parental consent to a minor's abortion, the new law is also said to "promote" sexual abstinence among teenagers. Wisconsin, Maine, and South

Carolina legislators considered similar bills in 2000.[152] The South Carolina bill prohibited the use of state funds to distribute condoms and other types of contraceptives to minors younger than sixteen whose parents had registered objections to their children receiving services of this kind with South Carolina health department officials.[153] Although the South Carolina House of Representatives passed the bill, the Senate dropped it in committee.[154]

The momentum has continued, however, with an attempt by lawmakers in at least one state to outlaw the over-the-counter sale of condoms. If the Mississippi proposal, prohibiting the purchase of condoms without a prescription, had passed, it would have been the first law of its kind in the nation.[155] Although the Mississippi bill died in committee, lawmakers in other states seemed poised in 2001 to limit a minor's access to contraceptives. South Carolina legislators were scheduled to begin considering a bill that would allow government agencies to refuse to provide contraceptives, including condoms, to minors whose parents have registered their objections to such dispersals in a state-administered database.[156]

Bills proposed by New York and Mississippi lawmakers to be considered during the same session would prohibit health care providers in school-based health clinics from dispensing contraceptives and/or from counseling on issues of contraception or abortion.[157] Maryland officials began considering a bill that would amend existing law to allow only minors over the age of fifteen to consent to receive advice or treatment about pregnancy, contraception, sterilization, and/or sexually transmitted diseases.[158] And if a handful of legislators in other states have their way, minors might never begin to ponder the use of contraceptives because they may never learn about "human sexual development" in schools. Lawmakers in Florida, Massachusetts, and Mississippi proposed bills to be considered during the 2001 session that would require written parental consent before minors in public schools could "receive instruction in human sexual development" and/or "human sexual behavior."[159] Such stilted language was clearly intended to anticipate formal as well as informal "instruction."

Of course, conservative efforts to hobble contraceptive use by minors and adult women would likely increase the use of abortion to end unwanted pregnancies. For example, according to the New York based Alan Guttmacher Institute, a not-for-profit reproductive research and analysis corporation, "[v]irtually all American women who are sexually active but wish to avoid becoming pregnant use some form of birth control, since they have concluded that contraception is the most effective way to reduce the likelihood of a crisis pregnancy and the possibility of an unwanted birth or abortion."[160]

What that means in actual numbers is that roughly 49 percent of the 6.3 million pregnancies occurring each year among American woman are unintended.[161] Roughly one-half of these pregnancies are terminated by abortion.[162] The majority of unintended pregnancies are not the result of irresponsibility. Rather, in 1995, for example, roughly 58 percent of the women having abortions were using contraceptives when they became pregnant.[163] Only 11 percent of women having abortions that year reported having never used contraceptives.[164]

Statistics of this sort establish in numbers what women have known for a long time: that the choice of abortion is often less about sexual irresponsibility than about realistic necessity. And yet, discussion of abortion as a "choice" has been the subject of a near half-century of emotional, sometimes even violent, debate. Yet the fact that absent contraceptives, pregnancy, and abortion are interrelated appear to be part of a larger reality that conservative lawmakers and the Religious Right seem aggressively intent to ignore for purposes of foreclosing reproductive choices for women.

And as equations of foreclosure go, this one is fairly simple: minor females—like their adult counterparts—cannot use contraceptives if they are not available. The difference between contraceptive use among adult women and contraceptive use among minor females is that it is easier for the state to put hurdles in the way of minor females. Adult women don't generally have to ask their parents for permission to use contraceptives.

THE ABORTION DEBATE:
"Unborn Life" vs. Women's Rights

> We again consider the right to an abortion. We understand the contro-
> versial nature of the problem. Millions of Americans believe that life
> begins at conception and consequently that an abortion is akin to caus-
> ing the death of an innocent child; they recoil at the thought of a law that
> would permit it. Other millions fear that a law that forbids abortion
> would condemn many American women to lives that lack dignity, depriv-
> ing them of equal liberty and leading those with the least resources to
> undergo illegal abortions with the attendant risks of death and suffering.
> Taking account of these virtually irreconcilable points of view, aware that
> constitutional law must govern a society whose different members sin-
> cerely hold directly opposing views, and considering the matter in light of
> the Constitution's guarantees of fundamental individual liberty, this
> Court, in the course of a generation, has determined and then redeter-
> mined that the Constitution offers basic protection to the woman's right
> to choose.[165] We shall not revisit those legal principles. Rather, we apply
> them to the circumstances of this case.
>
> —JUSTICE STEPHEN BREYER
> *Stenberg v. Carhart,* JUNE 28, 2000[166]

That was the issue in 2000. But the essential question of whether a woman *should* be allowed to choose not to have a child has been kicking around the halls of the nation's highest court since the 1960s, tangled—for all of that time—in often emotional arguments involving societal standards, political tra-ditions, personal beliefs, and religious convictions.

A year after the United States Supreme Court's decision in *Eisenstadt v. Baird,*[167] the Justices issued the mother of all reproductive choice decisions with

Roe v. Wade,[168] in which the Court invalidated a Texas abortion statute prohibiting all abortions not necessary to save the life of the mother. At the time of the Court's decision, similar laws were in force in at least forty-one other states and the District of Columbia.

For women, *Roe v. Wade* dismantled the traditional relationship between women and the state by preempting the state's ability to foreclose certain sexual and reproductive choices. For example, where the state had once ensured—via criminal statute—that pregnant women carried fetuses to term, after *Roe v. Wade* motherhood became a choice that women could make without state intrusion during the first trimester.

"We had just formed NARAL (the National Abortion and Reproductive Action League), in February 1969 at a meeting in Chicago," Lawrence Lader, then-chairman of the National Association for Repeal of Abortion Laws, recently remarked.[169] "We decided at that first meeting to concentrate on New York State as our breakthrough state. We felt that New York represented our best opportunity, and we knew that other states often looked to New York as setting an example. So we set up tables and gathered petitions in key districts in New York."[170]

"We were living in a time of enormous change," Manfred Ohrenstein, a former Democratic New York State Senator from Manhattan noted in recalling passage of the state's 1970 abortion law.[171] "There was the [Vietnam] war. There was the women's movement, which was really bringing the abortion issue to a crescendo. It was the end of the civil rights era, and we viewed this as a civil right. In '65, we had repealed the death penalty, which people thought was impossible. There was a sense that extraordinary things were possible."[172]

Although Hawaii was actually the first state to approve a broad abortion law, within its provisions was a citizenship requirement. Only legal residents of Hawaii could get abortions in Hawaii. By contrast, the New York abortion law had no such requirement, which drew women to the state in droves. Passage of the New York law snowballed into an avalanche of support for the national availability of abortion.[173] Although pro-choice advocates generally framed the abortion issue as a woman's right to control her destiny by exercising autonomy over her body,[174] in many ways this was an after-the-fact innovation. And though "nontherapeutic" abortions have often been the whipping boy of opponents, there were other reasons that women sometimes sought abortion.

ACCIDENTS, EPIDEMICS, BIRTH DEFECTS, AND CONSEQUENCES:
In Sickness and For Health—Abortion as a Solution

During the 1960s, the issue of abortion was framed as a matter of privacy, reproductive freedom, liberty, and choice by advocates of women's rights. But during the mid-1950s, the abortion debate revolved around discussions of health. In 1959, for example, in an effort to stop clandestine illegal, and often fatal, abortions,[175] the

American Law Institute tentatively endorsed measures to reform abortion laws, lowering the high hurdles a bit.[176]

Then, in 1962, in a lesser-known—though equally poignant—moment during the abortion debate, an Arizona mother of four found herself pregnant and afraid.[177] Sherri Finkbine was the host of a television show for preschoolers. She went to her obstetrician after learning that the drug Thalidomide caused serious birth defects. Although not available in the United States, the drug was sold in Europe, where her husband bought it. Finkbine had been taking Thalidomide as a tranquilizer near the time of conception.

After an examination, the fetus she was carrying was found to be deformed. Finkbine's doctor recommended abortion. But because "elective" abortions were illegal, Finkbine was instructed to write to a nearby hospital's abortion committee to request a therapeutic abortion. She did. While awaiting an answer, Finkbine attempted to warn others of the dangers of the drug by cooperating with a friend who wrote an article about Finkbine's circumstances. Though not identified by name, Finkbine's identity was uncovered after publication and she found herself at the center of a firestorm. When it was all over, the hospital had denied her request for an abortion and Finkbine was fired from her job.

As a woman of means, Finkbine flew to Sweden, where she had an abortion. As her doctor predicted, the fetus was severely deformed. Despite the criticism, Finkbine's story vaulted discussion of the "need" for abortions into the public realm.[178] And the possibility of abortion as an alternative—though not yet a constitutionally protected choice—gained further ground on the heels of a national outbreak of rubella. Before its end in 1965, the eruption would result in the births of some 15,000 children with birth defects. The march towards the forbidden practice of abortion had begun, some scholars suggest.

Prior to 1969, the annual rate of abortion across the United States was between 200,000 and 1.2 million, almost all of them illegal, many of them fatal.[179] As a point of contrast, in the decade following the Court's 1973 decision in *Roe v. Wade*, the number of *legal* abortions across the country rose to almost 1.6 million per year.[180] The decision in *Roe v. Wade* had "a dramatic impact on women's health," medical researchers suggest.[181] Although there were more abortions, women were less likely to die or suffer permanent ill health effects. Medical professionals also argued that the procedure improved with practice.

"Women who caught rubella in the early stages of pregnancy ran a 50 percent chance of delivering seriously damaged fetuses," writes Edward Lazarus, author of *Closed Chambers: The First Eyewitness Account of the Epic Struggles Inside the Supreme Court*."[182] "And, in response, many hospitals flouted state laws and performed abortions on women with the illness."[183]

It is not clear whether this was the beginning of a new consensus on abortion that may have influenced the Court's collective mind as it rewrote the rules on reproductive choices during the 1960s and '70s. What is clear is that by 1973, the Court was ready to move toward granting women the freedoms rights advocates had urged for years.

ABORTION AND ADULT WOMEN:
A History of Fragmentation

The relationship between women and the state goes back to the birth of the nation. Among the founding principles of the American State is federalism, mandating the "sharing of power between the national government and the fifty state governments."[184] Federalism has generally served the United States well. After all, who better to know the needs of a community than local representatives?

Within the realm of reproduction, however, federalism has led to "fragmentation"[185] and the decentralization of "reproductive decision making...[so that] responsibility for public health rest[ed, and still largely rests] primarily with the states, despite the increase in federal power in the area of health care since the mid-1930s."[186]

Though it may not seem so today, abortion was not always illegal in America. Rather, in the burgeoning United States many territories followed English common law, which provided that "[n]o law officer of the Crown ever brought criminal proceedings...against anyone for aborting a *willing* woman before quickening."

Long before there was a trimester framework to be adopted and then dismantled by the United States Supreme Court, there was the quickening rule. The "quickening rule" was articulated during the thirteenth century by Henry de Bracton, chancellor of Execter Cathedral, who declared that "[i]f there be anyone who strikes a pregnant woman or gives her a poison whereby he causes an abortion, if the foetus be already formed or *animated*, and especially if it be animated, he committed homicide."[187]

Thus, a "quickened" fetus was an animated fetus. During the late 1800s, following a spate of deaths from poison—misguided attempts to end unwanted pregnancies—laws based upon the "quickening" rule began to develop in the United States.[188] In 1821, for example, Connecticut became the first American territory to enact an abortion law making it a crime to attempt abortion by poison after quickening.[189] In 1827, it became a crime in Illinois to use "any noxious substance upon any pregnant woman."[190] New York, Ohio, Missouri, Arkansas, and the "territorial legislation of Iowa" followed soon after with their own laws, as did Indiana and Alabama.[191]

But at about the same time, five other states adopted more broadly worded laws, with language suggesting or specifically providing that no one could be "indicted for aborting a willing woman *before quickening*."[192] Among those five states were two that had previously passed abortion laws.[193] Eleven other states followed.[194] But two states enacted laws directly to the contrary: Pennsylvania and North Carolina.

At other times, later laws would prove as aggressive as they seemed irrational. A 1916 New York State law held, for example, that a person could be convicted of attempting abortion, even if the woman involved *was not pregnant*.[195] Oklahoma lawmakers did a little better, passing a 1919 state law declaring an essential element of the crime of abortion to be that the woman involved be pregnant.[196]

In modern times, "[t]he United States has experienced three phases of availability of legal abortion: general nonavailability, regional availability, and finally, national availability," notes medical writer Willard Cates Jr.[197] In terms of division, prior to 1970, when New York state passed an abortion law, legal abortion was generally unavailable to women except in cases of medical emergency. This period is considered the First Phase by medical historians.

"Before 1969, the best estimates of the annual range of induced abortions in the United States were between 200,000 and 1.2 million.[198] Nearly all these abortions were illegal, which caused many deaths and complications among U.S. women of reproductive age," says Cates.[199]

The period between 1970 and 1973, when legal abortion was available on a regional basis—with the overwhelming number of procedures occurring in New York and California—is known as the Second Phase.[200] The Third Phase was the period after the legalization of abortion in 1973.

It was during the first two phases that a vocal demand for legal abortion grew as cases challenging restrictive abortion laws in Texas and Georgia made their way to the United States Supreme Court. Those cases were *Roe v. Wade*,[201] which involved constitutional challenge to the Texas abortion law, and *Doe v. Bolton*,[202] which involved challenge to a Georgia abortion statute. Though often overshadowed by the more well-known *Roe v. Wade*, the Court's decision in *Doe v. Bolton* was handed down on the same day and is considered a companion case.

HOW "CHOICE" BECAME LAW:
"Jane Roe" Takes on Texas

At its simplest, history came undone with the United States Supreme Court's 1973 decision in *Roe v. Wade*. "Jane Roe" was an unskilled worker whose real name is Norma McCorvey. Although originally protected by anonymity, McCorvey would later reveal her identity in speaking out against abortion, even though she became part of history as the "named" plaintiff in this landmark case.

McCorvey was a high school dropout who got married and became pregnant while she was still a teenager. But when she sought an abortion in the State of Texas, where she was living at the time, McCorvey was advised to travel to a more liberal state. Because she could not travel, McCorvey carried the fetus to term, giving birth later to a child she would put up for adoption.[203]

The case was allowed to proceed on to the United States Supreme Court despite the birth, because midway through the pregnancy McCorvey agreed to serve as the named plaintiff in a suit challenging the Texas abortion law as unconstitutional.[204] At issue before the Court was the question of whether a Texas statute criminalizing abortion unduly interfered with "a right; said to be possessed by the pregnant woman"—implicit within the "concept of 'personal liberty' embodied in the Fourteenth Amendment's Due Process Clause; or in personal, marital, familial, and sexual privacy said to be protected by the Bill of Rights or its penumbras [of privacy]."[205]

With all eyes watching in a nation struggling with social upheaval, the Justices began analysis of the issues, noting that although the United States Constitution "does not explicitly mention any right of privacy..." decisions dating as far back as 1891 have "recognized that a right of personal privacy, or a guarantee of certain areas or zones of privacy, does exist under the Constitution."[206]

And given so considerable a body of law, the Justices would ultimately hold that "[t]his right of privacy, whether it be founded in the Fourteenth Amendment's concept of personal liberty and restrictions upon State action, as we feel it is, or as the District Court determined, in the Ninth Amendment's reservation of rights to the people, is broad enough to encompass a woman's decision whether or not to terminate her pregnancy."[207]

From this language came the modern notion of "reproductive privacy" and a shift in the landscape of women's rights. The decision legalized first-trimester elective abortion, setting forth a cleanly-divided trimester framework to be used by the courts in balancing the rights of women against the interests of states. It was an important intersection of law and medicine.

According to biographers, after the oral arguments had been made in *Roe v. Wade* and its companion case *Doe v. Bolton*, the talents of Justice Blackmun were tapped in researching and writing the decision on behalf of the majority of the Court. Prior to joining the Supreme Court, Blackmun spent several years as general counsel for the Mayo Clinic in Rochester, Minnesota.[208] And it was there—in the clinic's medical library—that Justice Blackmun returned in the summer of 1972 to work on the monumental draft that would become *Roe v. Wade*.

Prior to the Supreme Court's decision in *Roe v. Wade*, the law of the reproductive realm fell into gray areas straddling asserted state and federal interests. The end result for women was a patchwork of conflicting statutory laws that did little to protect women.[209]

OVERVIEW OF ABORTION LEGISLATION BEFORE *ROE v. WADE*

• In 1969, a Washington, D.C., statute made abortion a felony unless performed to save the life of the mother.[210]

• Under a 1970 Georgia abortion law, once there was a fetus, the decision to have an abortion was no longer purely private and/or deemed to affect only one man and one woman.[211]

• Also during 1970, permissive abortion laws, allowing therapeutic abortions were passed in Hawaii and New York.[212]

• In 1971, a federal district court in Washington, D.C., upheld a District of Columbia statute making abortion illegal unless done to preserve the life of the mother.

• That same year, an Illinois law foreclosed abortion to all but the life-threatened.[213]

• In 1972, a Connecticut district court held that a woman's right to an abortion could not be completely abridged by the state.[214] And in Kansas, a district court struck provisions of an abortion law requiring a near clipboard of certification of explanatory letters before a woman could have an abortion.[215]

• By 1973, the state of Washington and the District of Columbia had legalized elective abortion.[216]

• But at the same time, Mississippi permitted a woman an elective abortion only in a case of rape,[217] and Louisiana, New Hampshire, and Pennsylvania prohibited abortion.[218]

Thirteen states permitted abortion only to protect the mental and physical well-being of a woman. Twenty-nine others allowed abortion only to save the life of the woman,[219] and three states prohibited abortion outright.[220]

"There he examined the Constitution for precedents relevant to the crucial question of how to reconcile the woman's right to privacy with the state's interest in protecting both the women's health and the fetus' potential life," argues Willard Cates Jr. in *Justice Blackmun and Legal Abortion—A Besieged Legacy to Women's Reproductive Health.*[221]

Justice Blackmun also reportedly "sought a scientific basis" for the opinion. "Since obstetricians had, rather arbitrarily, divided the technical management of pregnancy into trimesters, he used this measure as the basis for his reasoning. The data presented to the Court in 1972 showed that within the first trimester, abortion was generally safe, certainly much safer for the woman than continuing the pregnancy to childbirth. In its *amicus curiae* brief filed in *Doe v. Bolton*, the American College of Obstetricians and Gynecologists estimated that early abortion was twenty-three times safer than carrying and delivering a child.

"Blackmun used this concept of the relative safety of first-trimester pregnancy termination compared with that of childbirth, as the foundation of *Roe v. Wade*. Because early induced abortion was so much safer than continuing the pregnancy, the Court recognized the right of the woman and her physician to make the abortion decision during the first third of gestation, independent of any statutory limitations," notes Cates.[222]

Roe v. Wade ushered in the era of national availability. In addition, legal scholars have come to view the Court's decision as the definitive moment in modern history when the fundamental rights of the women were recognized as superior to those of a developing fetus. In that sense, *Roe v. Wade* and its companion case of *Doe v. Bolton*[223] may also represent the metaphoric instant when women overcame historically assigned biological obligations of motherhood.

After *Roe v. Wade*, and throughout the 1970s, "the number of legal abortion increased to almost 1.6 million, where it remained stable until the 1990s,"[224] according to Cates. "Initially the increase in legal abortions in the 1970s was accompanied by a progressive decline in the estimated number of illegal abortions. Thus, most of the initial increase in legal abortions was primarily due to a corresponding decrease in the number of illegal abortions."[225]

By the late 1970s, the national birthrate fell from four children per woman in America to two children per woman.[226] A declining birthrate among whites has always been part of the reproductive rights debate, and it remains part of the reason that *Roe v. Wade* has been challenged almost since the day the decision was issued.[227]

Although traditionalists may have been part of these challenges, few would dispute that most—if not all—of the twenty-plus major decisions issued by the Justices of the Supreme Court in the years following *Roe v. Wade* have been driven by pro-Life, Christian, or Conservative forces and/or politicians whose goal has always been to see *Roe v. Wade* overturned.[228] The first case of significance in what would become a near annual cycle of legal challenge was *Planned Parenthood of Central Missouri v. Danforth.*[229]

CHALLENGING *ROE* (OVER AND OVER):
Attempting to Turn Back the Clock

On June 14, 1974, the General Assembly of the State of Missouri passed House Bill No. 1211, to become effective via emergency clause. The intent of the bill was to "control and regulate" the practice of abortion during all stages of pregnancy. Specific provisions of the bill included that: (1) a woman must sign an informed consent waiver before she could have an abortion; (2) a wife must obtain written consent from her husband to have an abortion; (3) an unmarried minor must obtain consent from a parent to have an abortion; (4) doctors must preserve the life of a fetus at all stages of pregnancy; and (5) the use of saline amniocentesis as part of the abortion procedure was prohibited.

Three days after its enactment, two doctors, joined by Planned Parenthood of Central Missouri, filed suit in the United States District Court for the Eastern District of Missouri, challenging the Missouri statute on nine points, including that: (1) the statute's definition of "viability" was contrary to the holding of *Roe v. Wade*; and (2) requiring written consent was invasive and spousal consent was unconstitutional.[230]

In 1976, the Supreme Court issued a decision in *Planned Parenthood of Central Missouri v. Danforth,* siding with arguments raised by the doctors in striking down four of the statute's provisions outright,[231] including the parental consent, fetal care, and saline requirements. The Justices also held that a woman need not obtain spousal consent for an abortion. In reaching this specific conclusion, the Justices held that "...we cannot hold that the State has the constitutional authority to give the spouse <u>unilaterally</u> the ability to prohibit the wife from terminating her pregnancy, when the State itself lacks that right."

But that did not mean that the state was without the ability to regulate other issues regarding abortion. The Justices held, for example, that a state could require a woman to sign a generally-worded informed consent notice,[232] even during the first trimester. "We could not say," the Justices wrote, "that a requirement imposed by the states that a prior written consent for any surgery would be unconstitutional. As a consequence, we see no constitutional defect in requiring it only for some types of surgery, as, for example, an intracardiac procedure, or where the surgical risk is elevated above a specified mortality level, or, for that matter, for abortions."

Thus, despite the precedent of *Roe v. Wade*, *Planned Parenthood of Central Missouri v. Danforth* has been held to mean that while the "right of privacy" at issue in abortion cases is an "individual right," it may still be subject to minor intrusions by the state. And, in fact, some states were just beginning their efforts to intrude. Often pushing the envelope on these "intrusions" were conservative politicians, who simply do not believe—either due to religious convictions or sexist notions of a "woman's obligation"—that women should have the right to choose. And the problem for women is that so many of them seem to hold positions of power.

The "Danforth" in *Planned Parenthood v. Danforth*, for example, was John Danforth, who, in a cycle of power politics, would later become *Senator* John Danforth, perhaps the most vocal champion of United States Supreme Court Justice Clarence Thomas during Thomas's troubled confirmation process in 1991. In another turn of that power wheel, Thomas, a staunch antiabortion opponent, would be tapped by President George W. Bush, an abortion foe, in early 2001 to swear-in controversial Attorney General appointee, John Ashcroft, after a troubled confirmation process of his own when his appointment was challenged by minority leaders, civil rights advocates, and women's rights scholars.

Clarence Thomas served under John Ashcroft in the Missouri Attorney General's Office after Danforth left. Like Danforth before him, Ashcroft sought to impose severe restrictions on abortion as Attorney General, arguing the case on behalf of the State of Missouri himself in *Planned Parenthood Assn. v. Ashcroft* in November, 1982. And yet, in addition to direct attacks on the precedent of *Roe v. Wade*, beginning in the mid 1970s, antiabortion lawmakers also began to explore new avenues of assault, among them the ability (or inability) of women to pay for abortion.

In 1976, Congress passed the "Hyde Amendment," which would take effect in 1977 and prohibit the use of public funds for abortion.[233] Several of the Supreme Court decisions issued after 1977 involve interpretation of welfare and Medicaid requirements in light of the Hyde Amendment. And with the mean-spirited force of its design, the Hyde Amendment proved a damaging weapon in the war against abortion as states drafted regulations adopting the scope of its provisions.

Indeed, as Pennsylvania officials probably knew as they drafted the regulation that would later be at issue in *Beal v. Doe*,[234] by denying women the ability to pay for abortions, the state could deny them—if not the right to choose abortion—then certainly the means to achieve it. The plaintiff in *Beal v. Doe* was a woman who was poor, but eligible for medical assistance under the federal Title XIX program.[235] But when she sought an abortion, she was denied financial assistance in accordance with a Pennsylvania regulation limiting assistance for use in only "medically necessary" abortions.

Doe filed suit in a case that would move through the appeals process and up to the United States Supreme Court, where the Justices would find that Title XIX did not expressly speak of funding for abortions. Rather, the statute spoke of furnishing medical assistance to people whose resources were insufficient and the services were necessary. "We therefore hold," six of the Court's nine Justices concluded, "that Pennsylvania's refusal to extend Medicaid coverage to nontherapeutic abortions is not inconsistent with Title XIX.... We make clear, however, that the federal statute leaves a State free to provide such coverage if it so desires." Pennsylvania did not desire to do so.

Neither did Connecticut, which would ultimately lead to the Supreme Court's decision in *Maher v. Roe*.[236] The facts of *Maher v. Roe* were essentially the same as those of *Beal v. Doe*, except that the Connecticut Welfare Department limited Medicaid benefits to first trimester abortions deemed "medically necessary." The appellees in *Maher v. Roe* were two indigent women. Under the Connecticut statute, women seeking abortions were required to make their request in writing to an accredited hospital or clinic. Once the request had been made, a doctor had to certify that the abortion was "medically necessary" before Medicaid funding could be used as payment.

In challenging the Connecticut law, Doe and Roe alleged discrimination in violation of the Equal Protection Clause, arguing that similar restrictions were not applied to other medical procedures. Although the Justices conceded that the question before the Court was "whether the Constitution requires [pursuant to Title XIX that] a participating State to pay for nontherapeutic abortions when it pays for childbirth,"[237] the majority went on to find that "[t]he Constitution imposes no obligation on the states to pay the pregnancy-related medical expenses of indigent women, or indeed to pay any of the medical expenses of indigents." In other words, "[t]his case involves no discrimination against a suspect class," six of the nine Justices concluded.

"An indigent woman desiring an abortion does not come within the limited category of disadvantaged classes so recognized by our cases," the majority wrote. "Nor does the fact that the impact of the regulation falls upon those who cannot pay lead to a different conclusion. In a sense, every denial of welfare to an indigent creates a wealth classification as compared to nonindigents who are able to pay for the desired good or services. But this Court has never held that financial need alone identifies a suspect class for purposes of equal protection analysis.[238] Accordingly, the central question in this case is whether the regulation 'impinges upon a fundamental right explicitly or implicitly protected by the Constitution.'" The Connecticut regulation did not, and the "District Court [had] misconceived the nature and scope of the fundamental right recognized in *Roe*," the Justices held.

The third and final decision in the trilogy of financial regulation cases decided on the same day in 1977 by the United States Supreme Court was *Poelker v. Doe*,[239] which involved an Equal Protection challenge asserted by "Jane Doe" on behalf of a class of women, who sought and were refused an abortion by one of the City of St. Louis's two city-owned public hospitals. Doe was poor. In accordance with a policy directive issued by the mayor, the city used public funds to finance hospital services for childbirth. But only abortions involving a "threat of grave physiological injury or death to the mother" were covered by the directive. Doe argued that the policy was unlawful and discriminatory.

To the majority's ears, Doe's challenge was familiar, and in light of the two previous decisions issued that day, the Justices apparently saw no reason for a long decision. "We agree that the constitutional question presented here is identical in principle with that presented by a State's refusal to provide Medicaid benefits for abortion while providing them for childbirth. This was the issue before us in *Maher v. Roe*. For the reasons set forth in our opinion in that case, we find no constitutional violation by the city of St. Louis in electing, as a policy choice, to provide publicly financed hospital services for childbirth without providing corresponding services for nontherapeutic abortions."[240]

Three years later, the constitutionality of "the Hyde Amendment" and its force on Title XIX of the Social Security Act, which established the Medicaid program in 1965, was at issue before the Court in *Harris v. McRae*.[241] The Hyde Amendment prohibited the use of federal Medicaid funds for abortions. Opponents of the Hyde Amendment argued that in addition to imposing undue hardship on a woman's right of choice, the measure violated the Equal Protection Clause. And that was the test before the Court in *Harris v. McRae*.

As a matter of procedure, "[o]n September 30, 1976, the day on which Congress enacted the initial version of the Hyde Amendment, these consolidated cases were filed in the District Court for the Eastern District of New York. The plaintiffs—Cora McRae, a New York Medicaid recipient then in the first trimester of a pregnancy she wished to terminate, the New York City Health and Hospitals Corp., a public benefit corporation that operates 16 hospitals, 12 of which provide abortion services, and others—sought to enjoin enforcement of the funding restriction on abortion," the Court explained in reciting the underlying facts of the case.[242]

Among the allegations were that the Hyde Amendment "violated the First, Fourth, Fifth, and Ninth Amendments of the Constitution insofar as it limited the funding of abortions to those necessary to save the life of the mother, while permitting the funding of costs associated with childbirth."[243] The United States Supreme Court was not persuaded. "Since the Congress that enacted Title XIX did not intend a participating state to assume a unilateral funding obligation for any health service in an approved Medicaid plan, it follows that Title XIX does not require a participating state to include in its plan any services for which a subsequent Congress has withheld federal funding.[244] Title XIX was designed as a cooperative program of shared financial responsibility, not as a device for the

Federal Government to compel a state to provide services that Congress itself is unwilling to fund.

"Thus, if Congress chooses to withdraw federal funding for a particular service, a state is not obligated to continue to pay for that service as a condition of continued federal financial support of other services. This is not to say that Congress may not now depart from the original design of Title XIX under which the Federal Government shares the financial responsibility for expenses incurred under an approved Medicaid plan. It is only to say that, absent an indication of contrary legislative intent by a subsequent Congress, Title XIX does not obligate a participating State to pay for those medical services for which federal reimbursement is unavailable [under the Hyde Amendment]," the Justices concluded.[245]

And because all things involving finances and abortion seemed destined by the Court to be decided in twos, the companion case to *Harris v. McRae*, decided on the same day, was *Williams v. Zbaraz*,[246] which involved suit by a doctor, a welfare rights organization and an indigent woman named "Jane Doe," all of whom filed suit to enjoin Illinois from enforcing a statute that prohibited the use of Medicaid funding for all but those abortions "necessary for the preservation of the life of the woman seeking such treatment." The statute was challenged for alleged violations of the Equal Protection Clause of the Fourteenth Amendment.

But again, the United States Supreme Court was not convinced. In upholding the statute, the Justices concluded that the funding restrictions of the Illinois statute did not violate the Equal Protection Clause. "[W]e have concluded in *McRae* that the Hyde Amendment does not violate the equal protection component of the Fifth Amendment by withholding public funding for certain medically necessary abortions, while providing funding for other medically necessary health services," the Justices wrote. "It follows, for the same reasons, that the comparable funding restrictions in the Illinois statute do not violate the Equal Protection Clause of the Fourteenth Amendment."[247]

ASSESSING THE FALLOUT AS THE CHALLENGES CONTINUE:
Roe Under Attack—Two Decades of Battle

With the apparent approval of the Court, Congress and lawmakers in several states have forged ahead on this track, drafting regulations and statutes prohibiting the use of public money for abortions. Their efforts have met success. By January 1997, thirty-four states had enacted similar bans on federal money used to pay for abortions.[248] Lawmakers in Massachusetts and New Jersey states were considering similar laws in 2001.[249]

Supporters of such restrictions argue that they are strictly economic and not meant to punish women for their "lifestyle" or reproductive choices. Others admit, however, that refusal to pay for all but medically necessary abortions was meant to serve as a deterrent, and according to some researchers, it has achieved that goal. But still others suggest, however, that it has not worked nearly as well as antiabortion opponents had hoped. The information, itself, is contradictory on this point.

"The year before the implementation of the Hyde Amendment, about 300,000 abortions in the United States were obtained by low-income women through Medicaid," Cates notes.[250] "During the following 2 years, the number of federally funded abortions averaged only 3,000 per year, or just 1% of the previous number. The amendment, therefore, effectively stopped federally funded abortions.[251] However, limiting federal funds was primarily a symbolic exercise. Even today most low-income women manage to obtain legal abortions via other funding sources. Many states continue to finance abortions using state revenues, thus blunting the amendment's impact."[252]

Blunted, perhaps. But not rendered completely without effect. According to the Centers for Disease Control in Atlanta, which tracks abortion rates on a continual basis, adult women in America have fewer abortions.[253] In 1990, the number of legal abortions performed across the United States reached an estimated 1.61 million.[254] But for every year after that, the numbers fell until by 1996, the number of legal abortions performed across the United States had plunged to an estimated 1.37 million[255] in a decade-long slide[256] that reportedly left clinics scrambling for clients.[257]

Researchers suggest that the decline "probably reflects the decreasing rate of unintended pregnancies; reduced access to abortion services; and changes in contraceptive practices, including increased use of contraception, particularly an increased use of condoms among young women."[258]

And yet, there is more to the overall picture than that.

In addition to financial efforts to foreclose the choice of abortion for women by foreclosing the ability of some to pay, there were continued efforts by the states to limit the reach of *Roe v. Wade*. For example, after *Planned Parenthood v. Danforth*, perhaps the next most significant direct challenge to *Roe v. Wade* came by way of a Pennsylvania law requiring doctors to "preserve the life of the fetus." The case was *Colautti v. Franklin*,[259] and it had a substantial legal history even before its appeal to the United States Supreme Court.

At issue in *Colautti v. Franklin* was a Pennsylvania statute requiring a near laundry list of obstacles, among them various types of consent, private payments, and that doctors performing abortion observe a prescribed standard of care should they determine "that the fetus is viable or if there is sufficient reason to believe that the fetus may be viable." That provision alone went before the Justices in what was viewed by many as a direct attack on the underpinnings of *Roe v. Wade*. The United States Supreme Court struck down the law 6–3 as unconstitutionally vague and in conflict with the definition of fetal "viability" as established in *Roe v. Wade*.

The next attack on the practice and availability of abortion came in the case of *City of Akron v. Akron Center for Reproductive Health, Inc.*[260] In February 1978, representatives of the City of Akron passed an ordinance setting forth seventeen provisions regulating how abortions were to be performed within the city limits. A lawsuit was immediately filed on behalf of doctors and abortion agencies. Nearly every provision of the ordinance was challenged. But after decisions by the lower and appellate courts, only five of the challenged provisions remained to be heard by the United States Supreme Court. The first involved the issue of whether Akron could require that all abortions in cases beyond twelve weeks take place in hospitals. The Court struck this provision down as placing "a significant obstacle in the path of women seeking an abortion."

The Court also struck down a provision requiring parental consent for minors seeking abortions. Such a requirement, the Court held, foreclosed a minor female's right to exercise the right to choose an abortion in the event of a parental veto. Also struck down was a provision regarding the disposal of fetal remains. But the Court then considered the ordinance's two "informed consent" provisions, the first of which involved the requirement that doctors counsel women to ascertain whether a woman's consent to an abortion was truly "informed." The second involved requiring a 24-hour waiting period between the signing of a consent form and the performance of an abortion.

Both provisions were struck down with the Justices concluding that the underlying aim of each was to require doctors to recite a litany on the ills of abortion. That, the Court determined, went far beyond achieving informed consent. Accordingly, the Justices ruled that by demanding that doctors recite a long and inflexible list of information, drafters of the ordinance had placed unreasonable "obstacles in the path of the doctor upon whom [the woman is] entitled to rely for advice in connection with her decision."[261] Finally, with regard to the 24-hour waiting period, the Court held that the City of Akron had "failed to demonstrate that any legitimate state interest is furthered by an arbitrary and inflexible waiting period."

The assaults continued, however, with the battles intensifying as time moved on. And much to the chagrin of women's rights advocates, the arguments got better. Indeed, although early challenges failed to overturn *Roe v. Wade*, with each decision the Court seemed to mete out a reverse recipe for success in detailing the challenged laws deficiencies and analytical failures. Thus, even in defeat, abortion opponents grew smarter about drafting laws that would survive judicial review. In addition, states and pro-life groups began to aggressively assert a "compelling" interest in potential life.

In *Planned Parenthood v. Ashcroft*,[262] for example, two doctors challenged a broadly worded Missouri statute requiring that: abortions performed after twelve weeks be done in hospitals; pathology reports be filed after every procedure; a second physician be present to attend to the fetus for abortions performed after viability; and, that minors seeking abortions obtain consent from parents or a court.

Planned Parenthood v. Ashcroft represented a second go-around in less than a decade for Missouri officials in a case proceeding all the way up to the United States Supreme Court. And although the Justices directly struck down the first requirement of the Missouri statute citing the recent decision in *City of Akron v. Akron Center for Reproductive Health, Inc.,* the Court upheld the second physician requirement, expressly acknowledging that the state has a compelling "interest in the life of a viable fetus." The Court also held that the pathology report requirement was an "insignificant" burden. And this time, given that the lawmakers had articulated an alternate procedure to acquiring consent should a parent either refuse or be unavailable, the Court upheld the requirement of parental or court consent for minors.

The next direct challenge to *Roe v. Wade* was *Thornburgh v. American College of Obstetricians and Gynecologists,*[263] and it provoked some of the strongest language of rebuke by the Justices to date. Pennsylvania lawmakers are among the leaders in the effort to overturn *Roe v. Wade,* engaging in more than a decade of state-sponsored litigation by the time *Thornburgh v. American College of Obstetricians and Gynecologists* made its way to the United States Supreme Court.

A quick glimpse of that history is as follows: shortly after the Court's decision in *Roe v. Wade,* the Pennsylvania legislature passed the Abortion Control Act of 1974, overriding a governor's veto to do so. The Act led to protracted court action at the end of which several of the Act's provisions were held unconstitutional. Even so, in 1978, the Pennsylvania legislature again tried to restrict access to abortion, this time by limiting funding. Again, the state went to court. Again, its efforts were declared unconstitutional.

In 1982, the Pennsylvania legislature enacted another version of the Pennsylvania Abortion Control Act, and six provisions of the 1982 Abortion Control Act went before the Court in *Thornburgh v. American College of Obstetricians and Gynecologists.*[264] Not a moment of the Act's previous history was lost on the Justices, who scolded, prior to undertaking formal analysis of the issues in *Thornburgh v. American College of Obstetricians and Gynecologists,* that "[t]he states are not free, under the guise of protecting maternal health or potential life, to intimidate women into continuing pregnancies."

Among the provisions before the Court under the 1982 Act was the requirement that physicians give women detailed information of the ills of abortion and the development of a fetus during all stages of pregnancy. Pennsylvania authorities argued that information of this sort fell within the "informed consent" provision. The Justices, however, were not convinced, and they struck down the provision because it advanced "no legitimate state interest." The second provision, which required physicians to file reports following abortion procedures, was also struck down. In reaching this conclusion, the Justices reasoned that "Pennsylvania's reporting requirements raise the spectre of public exposure and harassment of women who choose to exercise their personal, intensely private, right, with their physician, to end a pregnancy." Several other provisions were also struck down one by one, and in the end, the Court found the 1982 Pennsylvania statute facially invalid.

In 1989, Missouri was back again, this time with a statute drafted by lawmakers who apparently chose to ignore the language of *Roe v. Wade* altogether. In 1986, the governor of Missouri signed into law Missouri House Bill No. 1526, which consisted of twenty provisions and a preamble declaring that "the life of each human being begins at conception." House Bill No. 1526 also amended existing state law to extend to "unborn children...all rights, privileges, and immunities available to other persons, citizens, and residents" of Missouri. The Act itself demanded that physicians perform "viability" tests on fetuses suspected of being 20 weeks or older. It also prohibited the use of public employees and public facilities to perform or assist abortions not necessary to save the life of the mother. These were among the five provisions challenged before the United States Supreme Court in the case of *Webster v. Reproductive Health Services, Inc.*[265]

After torturous and sometimes circular analysis, the "viability" provision as well as the provision regarding abortion in public facilities and public employees were upheld by the Justices in a 5–4 decision. Of far greater significance, however, was that *Webster v. Reproductive Health Services, Inc.*, marked the first time less than a majority of the Supreme Court voted to uphold the central holding of *Roe v. Wade*. Further, some legal scholars argue that the Court's decision in *Webster v. Reproductive Health Services, Inc.* so confused reproductive issues that it set the stage for clarification, which the Supreme Court acknowledged it was attempting in opening its decision in *Planned Parenthood of Southeastern Pennsylvania v. Casey*.[266] In other words, Pennsylvania was back again, and the resulting decision would prove damaging to the once widely-held notion of independent reproductive rights of women.

By almost all accounts, *Planned Parenthood of Southeastern Pennsylvania v. Casey* represents an enormous setback for women. At issue before the Court in 1992 were five provisions of the latest version of the Pennsylvania Abortion Control Act.[267] All but one were ultimately upheld in a clear turning point for women. And yet, in starting their analysis, a fractured majority expressly declared that the "essential holding of *Roe v. Wade* should be retained." But further restrictions were deemed permissible. Specifically, the Court held that a 24-hour waiting period between the time a woman requests an abortion and when the procedure may be performed was not unconstitutional.[268]

Next, the Justices held that information that was truthful and not misleading could be given to women seeking abortions, even information that might tell of the ill-effects of abortion. As set forth above, the Justices had struck down similar provisions in earlier decisions. Consent requirements for minors were also upheld. What was not upheld was a provision that would have required that a married woman sign forms indicating that she had told her husband of her intent to have an abortion. In other words, a pregnant woman could not be forced to carry a fetus to term or to become a "mother" by a partner or husband.

But what made *Planned Parenthood of Southeastern Pennsylvania v. Casey* most significant was what the majority gave away. At the start of its analysis, the Justices declared that although the state's interests were not strong enough prior to viability to support a prohibition of abortion, "the state has legitimate interests *from the outset of pregnancy* in protecting the health of the woman and the life of the fetus that may become a child." This was a significant shift. As set forth above, a decade earlier an angry Supreme Court reminded Pennsylvania officials in *Thornburgh v. American College of Obstetricians and Gynecologists* that "[t]he states are not free, under the guise of protecting maternal health or potential life, to intimidate women into continuing pregnancies."

A state's legitimate interests in protecting the health "of the fetus that becomes a child" from the outset of pregnancy, however, offered the state an argument for attempting to do so, the Court held in *Planned Parenthood v. Casey*. But even more damaging to the once-strong precedent of *Roe v. Wade* was the Court's removal of the trimester system, which had long served to demarcate the legal areas of competing interests. Under the precedent of *Roe v. Wade*, a woman's right to choose abortion during the first trimester was almost absolute (*i.e.,* it took a showing of a very strong compelling interest by the state to overcome this *fundamental* right of choice). But as the pregnancy moved into the second and third trimesters, a state's interest in the viability of the fetus grew. That was the trimester framework at work.

But in *Planned Parenthood of Southeastern Pennsylvania v. Casey*, the Justices erased this framework, declaring it "too rigid." As a result, today "...states are free to enact laws to provide a reasonable framework for a woman to make a decision that has such profound and lasting meaning," the Justices wrote. "This, too, we find consistent with *Roe's* central premises, and indeed the inevitable consequence of our holding that the State has an interest in protecting the life of an unborn."[269] In the end, the Court held that any law that places an undue burden on a woman's right to obtain an abortion before viability is unconstitutional.

Viability, however, was left by the Justices to the states to define. Thus, where that line had once been drawn at 24 to 26 weeks, since the Court's decision in *Planned Parenthood v. Casey*, the line has steadily crept downward to anywhere from 12 to 20 weeks at the urging of some lawmakers.[270] And yet, sometimes not even that is enough. In a resurrection of ancient history chock-full of modern politics, at the start of 2001, one Wisconsin lawmaker proposed enacting a law that would increase penalties for intentionally destroying or consenting to the destruction of one's "unborn *quick* child."[271]

OVERVIEW OF SUPREME COURT LAW ON CONTRACEPTIVES AND ABORTION

Griswold v. Connecticut, 381 U.S. 479 (1965).

> In a series of concurring opinions ultimately leading to a vote of 7–2, the Supreme Court held that a Connecticut statute making it a crime for any person to use any drug or article to prevent conception presented an unconstitutional invasion of the privacy of married couples. [272]

Eisenstadt v. Baird, 405 U.S. 438 (1972).

> The Justices held, by a vote of 6–1, that the constitutional right of privacy extends to unmarried as well as married people. Accordingly, a Massachusetts law making it a crime to dispense any contraceptive article to an unmarried

person, except for purposes of preventing disease, was unconstitutional, the Court held.[273]

Roe v. Wade, 410 U.S. 113 (1973).

"Jane Roe" challenged a Texas abortion statute criminalizing all abortions, except those performed to save the life of the pregnant woman. By a vote of 7–2, the Court held that the right to privacy reached a woman's decision on whether to have an abortion. Though the state has a compelling interest in a viable fetus and a woman's health as a pregnancy progressed, during the first trimester, a woman's choice of whether or not to continue a pregnancy could not be unduly burdened by the state.[274]

Doe v. Bolton, 410 U.S. 179 (1973).

"Mary Doe" was a 22-year-old mother of three[275] when she became pregnant with a fourth. Doe, who was poor and had been institutionalized, challenged a Georgia statute permitting abortions only under certain proscribed circumstances, among them that the procedure be performed only in accredited hospitals and available only to state residents. Also required was that the procedure be approved by a hospital staff committee and two licensed physicians. In this companion case to Roe, the Court struck down the Georgia statute as unconstitutional by a 7–2 vote.[276]

Bigelow v. Virginia, 421 U.S. 809 (1975).

A Virginia statute declaring it a misdemeanor to encourage abortion, by sale or circulation of abortion-related material, was challenged by the editor of a weekly newspaper who published an out-of-state abortion advertisement and was charged under the statute. By a 7–2 vote, the Supreme Court struck down the statute as violative of the protections of the First Amendment.[277]

Connecticut v. Menillo, 423 U.S. 9 (1975).

Before the Court was the question of whether a Connecticut statute criminalizing the performance of an abortion by "any person" could be applied in prosecutions of nonphysicians convicted of "procuring" an abortion for another.[278] The Court held, per curiam, that "[a]s far as this Court and the Federal Constitution are concerned, Connecticut's statute remains fully effective against performance of abortions by nonphysicians."

Planned Parenthood of Central Missouri v. Danforth, 428 U.S. 52 (1976).

Doctors challenged a Missouri abortion law requiring: women to sign consent forms and obtain consent from husbands; physicians to exercise "professional care to preserve the fetus's life and health"[279]; and the consent of parents for minor females seeking abortion. The Missouri law also included a definition of "viability." By a 5–4 vote, the Court struck down the requirements of parental and spousal consent, though the "informed consent" requirement was upheld, along with several other provisions.[280]

Bellotti v. Baird (I), 428 U.S. 132 (1976).

Noting that in some instances a minor "woman" may be required to obtain parental consent to abortion, the Justices unanimously held that a district court should have passed on deciding the constitutionality of a Massachusetts statute requiring parental consent until the state court had an opportunity to interpret the statute.

Carey v. Population Services, 431 U.S. 678 (1977).

By a vote of 7–2, the United States Supreme Court held unconstitutional a New York law that made it a crime: (1) "for any person" to sell or distribute contraceptives to minors under the age of 16; (2) "for anyone other than" a licensed pharmacist to distribute contraceptives to persons 16 years or older; and, (3) "for anyone" to advertise or display contraceptives.[281]

Beal v. Doe, 432 U.S. 438 (1977).

Decided the same day as *Maher v. Roe, Beal v. Doe* involved challenge to a policy by the Pennsylvania Department of Welfare prohibiting the use of public funds for all but "medically necessary" abortions. The plaintiffs, poor women, filed suit, challenging the policy as inconsistent with Title XIX of the Social Security Act.[282] By 6–3 vote, the Court upheld the Pennsylvania regulation.[283]

Maher v. Roe, 432 U.S. 464 (1977).

The companion case to *Beal v. Doe, Maher v. Roe* involved an equal protection challenge brought by two indigent women to a Connecticut statute prohibiting the use of public Medicaid funds for all but "medically necessary" abortions during the first trimester. By a vote of 6–3, the Justices held that even though the state provides funding for childbirth, the Connecticut law was not unconstitutional or discriminatory, because indigent women desiring abortions did not fall within the "limited category of disadvantaged class" traditionally recognized by the Court in equal protection cases.[284]

Poelker v. Doe, 432 U.S. 519 (1977).

"Jane Doe" sought an abortion in one of two St. Louis city-owned hospitals. When she was refused, she became the named plaintiff in a class action lawsuit against the Mayor and City of St. Louis's Director of Health and Hospitals, alleging violations of the Equal Protection Clause. The city offered publicly financed services for childbirth, but not for abortion. The Supreme Court upheld the hospital's refusal to provide publicly funded abortions. "We agree that the constitutional question presented here is identical in principle with that presented by the state's refusal to provide Medicaid benefits for abortion while providing them for childbirth," the Court wrote.

Colautti v. Franklin, 439 U.S. 379 (1979).

At issue before the Court was a challenge to the constitutionality of Section 5(a) of the Pennsylvania Abortion Control Act.[285] The provision required doctors to determine the viability of a fetus prior to abortion, and, if viable, to exercise the same level of care in preserving the life of the fetus as doctors would in handling a "born alive" fetus. By a vote of 6–3, the Justices struck down the provision as impermissibly vague.[286]

Bellotti v. Baird (II), 443 U.S. 622 (1979).

"Mary Moe," representing a "class of unmarried minors in Massachusetts who have adequate capacity to give valid and informed consent [to abortion], and who do not wish to involve their parents," challenged a Massachusetts abortion statute.[287] By an 8–1 decision, the Justices held that given the inadequacies of the statute's judicial waiver provision, the law violated the Due Process Clause of the Fourteenth Amendment.[288]

Harris v. McRae, 448 U.S. 297 (1980).

Following passage in 1976 of the "Hyde Amendment,"[289] a class of indigent women, with Cora McRae as the named plaintiff, sued the New York City Health and Hospital Corporation.[290] "This case," the Court wrote, "presents statutory and constitutional questions concerning the public funding of abortions under Title XIX of the Social Security Act,…and recent annual Appropriations Acts containing the so-called 'Hyde Amendment.'"[291] In a 5–4 decision, the Court upheld the Hyde Amendment as constitutional.[292]

Williams v. Zbaraz, 448 U.S. 358 (1980).

Decided the same day as _Harris v. McRae_, _Williams v. Zbaraz_ involved a class action lawsuit brought on behalf of poor women, who alleged that refusal by the State of Illinois to provide Medicaid coverage for abortions, "whether or not the life of the pregnant woman is endangered" violated the Equal Protection Clause.[293] Illinois is the home state of Henry Hyde, author of the Hyde Amendment. After declaring that the lower court lacked jurisdiction to hear the claims, a 5–4 majority of the Supreme Court noted that "we…concluded in _McRae_ that the Hyde Amendment does not violate the equal protection component of the Fifth Amendment by withholding public funding for certain medically necessary abortions, while providing funding for other medically necessary health services. It follows, for the same reasons, that the comparable funding restrictions in the Illinois statute do not violate the Equal Protection Clause of the Fourteenth Amendment."[294]

H.L. v. Matheson, 450 U.S. 398 (1981).

H.L. was an unmarried 15-year-old girl who, while still living with her parents, learned that she was pregnant. She was advised to have an abortion after consulting a social worker and a doctor. But under Utah law, physicians were required to "[n]otify, if possible the parents of a dependent, unmarried minor girl prior to performing an abortion." H.L. challenged the constitutionality of the Utah statute.[295] The Supreme Court held, in a 6–3 decision, that because H.L. had neither plead nor shown that she was a "mature" or emancipated minor, she lacked standing to challenge the constitutionality of the Utah statute.[296]

City of Akron v. Akron Center for Reproductive Health, 462 U.S. 416 (1983).

Several doctors and abortion agencies challenged several provisions of the City of Akron ordinance. Among the ordinance's requirements were that: (1) all abortions after twelve weeks be performed in hospitals; (2) minors obtain parental consent for abortion; (3) attending physicians insure that "consent for an abortion be truly informed;" and (4) adult women wait 24 hours between signing a consent form and having an abortion. By a 6–3 vote, the Court invalidated provisions requiring that D&E abortions be performed only in hospitals, that doctors provide "informed consent" material declaring that an "unborn child is a human life from the moment of conception." Also invalidated were 24-hour waiting periods, the parental consent requirement where there was no waiver provision, and obligations of fetal remains disposal.[297]

Planned Parenthood Association of Kansas City v. Ashcroft, 462 U.S. 476 (1983).

Before the Court was a challenge to a broadly-worded Missouri statute similar in breadth to the Akron ordinance at issue in City of Akron v. Akron Center for Reproductive Health.[298] By a 6–3 vote, the Supreme Court struck down the Missouri provision that would have required all second-trimester abortions to take place in hospitals.[299] But the Court upheld, by a 5–4 vote, provisions requiring that: two doctors be present during later term abortions; parental consent for minors or judicial waiver; and pathology reports following abortions.

Simopoulos v. Virginia, 462 U.S. 506 (1983).

By 8–1 vote, the Justices upheld the conviction of a doctor, who performed a second-trimester abortion outside of a licensed hospital, as required by Virginia law. In comparing the Virginia regulation to the Missouri law, the Justices noted that the definition of "hospital" differed. But the goal of the two after the first trimester was the same: to preserve the health of women obtaining abortions.[300]

Thornburgh v. American College of Obstetricians and Gynecologists, 476 U.S. 747 (1986).

In a third direct challenge to Roe v. Wade, the Governor of Pennsylvania approved the Abortion Control Act of 1982,[301] and as with the two previous attempts, six provisions of the 1982 Act were challenged by plaintiffs offering forty-one affidavits to support their position.[302] By a 5–4 vote, the Justices struck down provisions: requiring doctors to give women antiabortion information, including pictures of fetuses at various stages of development; permitting disclosure of physician and patient information; and post-viability "degree of care" obligations to attend and preserve the life of the "unborn child."[303]

Webster v. Reproductive Health Services, 492 U.S. 490 (1989).

Five provisions of a Missouri abortion law were challenged. Also at issue was the language of the statute's preamble, which declared that "[t]he life of each human being begins at conception" and that "unborn children have protectable interests in life, health, and well-being."[304] Finding that the preamble was merely "precatory," and thus passing on a decision regarding its constitutionality, the Court upheld, by a 5–4 vote in a fractious decision, several of the Missouri statute's provisions.[305] Among them was the foreclosure of the use of public hospitals and facilities for abortion and requirements regarding gestational fetal age tests. For the first time since the Court's decision in _Roe v. Wade_, only four Justices voted to affirm the precedent's central holding.

Hodgson v. Minnesota, 497 U.S. 417 (1990).

Minnesota's 1981 amended Minors' Consent to Health Services Act required a minor female's physician or agent to notify the minor's parent personally or via certified mail at least 48 hours in advance of an abortion. The Act was challenged on due process and equal protection grounds by two doctors, four clinics, six pregnant minors representing a class of minors, and the mother of a pregnant minor. In a surprise given the trend, the Court held, by a 5–4 vote, that two parent notification without judicial waiver was unconstitutional. An alternate judicial bypass procedure saved the statute, however, the Court held.[306]

Ohio v. Akron Center for Reproductive Health, 497 U.S. 502 (1990).

An Ohio statute made it a crime in all but four instances for doctors to perform abortions on unmarried, unemancipated females younger than eighteen years old "unless the physician provides timely notice" to the minor's parents or to a juvenile court with the power to grant consent. The Akron Center for Reproductive Health, a doctor and "Rachael Roe," an "unmarried, unemancipated minor woman who sought an abortion" challenged the provision. In a vote of 6–3, the Justices upheld the statute.[307]

Rust v. Sullivan, 500 U.S. 173 (1991).

In 1988, the Secretary of Health and Human Services promulgated new regulations prohibiting recipients of Title X funds from engaging in counseling, referrals, and other activities advocating abortion as a method of family planning. The regulations also required recipients to maintain independence from prohibited abortion-related activities by use of separate facilities, personnel, and accounting records.[308] The regulation was challenged as facially unconstitutional by Title X grantees and doctors who supervised Title X funds. By a 5–4 decision, the Supreme Court upheld the regulations.[309] Although the prohibition was later lifted by President Clinton in 1993, it was limited in 2001 with regard to families overseas by President George W. Bush.

Planned Parenthood of Southeastern Pennsylvania v. Casey, 505 U.S. 833 (1992).

Before the Court were five provisions of the latest version of the Pennsylvania Abortion Control Act.[310] In a fragmented decision upholding several provisions of the Act, the Justices articulated the now infamous but functionally ambiguous words: "Liberty finds no refuse in a jurisprudence of doubt. Yet, 19 years after holding that the Constitution protects a woman's right to terminate her pregnancy in its early stages, *Roe v. Wade*, that definition of liberty is still questioned." The Justices then upheld a provision requiring that doctors give patients information on health risks related to abortions as well as on adoption; 24-hour waiting period; and single parent consent requirements for minors.[311]

Bray v. Alexandria Women's Health Clinic, 506 U.S. 263 (1993).

Several abortion clinics filed suit under the "Ku Klux Klan" Act,[312] seeking to enjoin Operation Rescue and other antiabortion groups and individuals from obstructing access to abortion clinics. Although the approach was clearly inventive, the Court wasn't buying. Instead, the Justices held, by a 5–4 vote, that antiabortion obstructionists were not engaged in gender-based discrimination for purposes of the statute.[313]

National Organization for Women v. Scheidler, 510 U.S. 249 (1994).

In a rare unanimous decision, the United States Supreme Court held that under the Racketeer Influenced and Corrupt Organizations Act, the National Organization for Women did not have to show an economic motive to pursue a civil suit against antiabortion activist, Joseph Scheidler, and a coalition of antiabortion groups referred to collectively as the Pro-Life Action Network.[314]

Madsen v. Women's Health Center, 512 U.S. 753 (1994).

Upholding a Florida court-ordered injunction in a 5–4 decision, the United States Supreme Court held permissible a 36-foot buffer and "quiet" zone intended to keep antiabortion protesters from obstructing clinic entrances and disturbing patients. The Court ruled with regard to a 300-foot radius zone around the clinic, however, that there did not appear to be sufficient justification in the record for it.[315]

Schenck v. Pro-Choice Network, 519 U.S. 357 (1997).

By a vote of 8–1, the Justices upheld an injunction issued by a New York court imposing a 15-foot "fixed bubble" buffer zone intended to facilitate persons and vehicles attempting to enter or leave abortion clinics in upstate New York. With regard to a "floating" buffer zone provision, however, the Justices held that it "burden[ed] more speech than necessary to serve the relevant government interests."[316]

Mazurek v. Armstrong, 520 U.S. 968 (1997).

> Without full briefing or oral arguments, the Supreme Court reversed a lower court ruling that might have advanced challenges by health care providers to a Montana statute banning licensed physician assistants from performing abortions, even under the supervision of doctors. The Court held, *per curiam*, that in applying the "undue burden" test articulated in *Planned Parenthood of Southeastern Pennsylvania v. Casey*, the physician-only requirements are not unconstitutional.

Stenberg v. Carhart, 530 U.S. 914 (2000).

> Dr. Leroy Carhart challenged a Nebraska statute criminalizing "partial-birth" abortions unless they were for the sole purpose of saving the life of the pregnant woman. By a 5–4 vote, the Court held the statute to be unconstitutionally overbroad. As such, it created an undue burden for women, whose doctors might decline to perform the procedures for fear of prosecution.[317]

Hill v. Colorado, 530 U.S. 703 (2000).

> Before the Justices was a 1993 Colorado statute making it unlawful for "any person within 100-foot of a health care facility's entrance to 'knowingly approach' within 8 feet of another person, without that person's consent, in order to pass 'a leaflet or handbill to, displa[y] a sign to, or engag[e] in oral protest, education, or counseling with [that] person..." Antiabortion "sidewalk counselors" challenged the statute as facially invalid. In upholding the statute as content neutral by a 6–3 vote, the Court reasoned that a state's interest in the safety of its citizens "may justify a special focus on unimpeded access to health care facilities and the avoidance of potential trauma to patients associated with confrontational protests."[318]

Scheidler v. National Organization for Women, Inc., 537 U.S. 393 (2003).

> The Court held that members of a "coalition" of antiabortion organizations had not committed extortion as defined by Sec. 1951(b)(2) of the Hobbs Act "because they did not 'obtain' property from the respondents as required by the Hobbs Act. We further hold that our determination with respect to extortion under the Hobbs Act renders insufficient the other bases or predicate acts of racketeering supporting the jury's conclusion that petitioners violated RICO," the Justices wrote.

ABORTION AND MINORS:
Do Young Women Have the Right to Choose?

The cases above suggest that conservative politicians and antiabortion activists have gone to great lengths to try to foreclose on a woman's right to choose abortion. It should come as no surprise, then, to learn that similar efforts have been made with regard to minor females. Except that with minor females it is easier, because the law already permits parental involvement in many cases. And, as with most things apparent in these times of change, several states are currently contemplating legislation that would allow parents even more involvement in the private decisions of their daughters.

Among teenagers in the United States, pregnancy has been on the decline for nearly a decade.[319] (*See* Chart on Pregnancy Rates for Teens, pp. 132–133.) Though some researchers suggest that the reason for this decline may be due to the increased use of contraceptives,[320] others suggest that abstinence may play a part.[321] But, as is often the case in the area of reproductive rights, the information is contradictory. Although some researchers suggest a rise in the number of teenagers abstaining from sex, others report that the proportion of sexually active teenagers rose from 47 percent in 1982 to 53 percent in 1988, and that 58 percent of the teenagers surveyed as part of a 1990 study admit to having two or more sexual partners.[322] Still other data suggest that young people in United States begin to have sex "in their mid-to-late teens, about eight years before they marry."[323]

But studies tend to tell less truth than numbers. According to current numbers, one in every four girls in the United States becomes pregnant at least once before she reaches the age of 18, researchers suggest.[324] And what that means in actual terms is that roughly one million young women between the ages of 15 and 19 became pregnant in 1990.[325] That number did decline some to roughly 905,000 in 1996.[326] And fewer pregnancies mean fewer abortions.

"Several factors may have influenced this decline in the abortion ratios among adolescents," note researchers for the Centers for Disease Control in Atlanta. "First, teenage pregnancies decreased; therefore, abortions decreased. Second, the age distribution of reproductive-age women obtaining abortions shifted from younger women to older, less fertile women. Third, access to abortion services changed, and abortion laws that affect adolescents (*e.g.*, parental consent or notification laws and mandatory waiting periods) have undergone continual change."[327]

And yet, despite a continued decline, the pregnancy rate among teenagers in America is still one of the highest among industrialized nations. In addition, despite a rise in the use of contraceptives, teenagers—like adult women—sometimes still find themselves pregnant. Nearly 80 percent of all teen pregnancies are "unplanned," according to researchers.[328] And more than half of these teenagers carry the fetuses to term. In 1996, for example, more than half—56 percent—of the 905,000 teen pregnancies cited above resulted in births.[329] Fourteen percent ended in miscarriages and 30 percent ended in abortions.

But are minors allowed to have abortions?

That was the question before the United States Supreme Court, which declared in 1976 that like adult women, minor females have a privacy right when it comes to the choice of abortion. But for minor females, it is a more narrowly defined "right" crafted out of a thinner set of "protections" that some state lawmakers are clearly intent on rendering even thinner by—of all things—asserting an interest in the minor's well-being and the parents' right to intervene.

PLANNED PARENTHOOD v. DANFORTH

Interests of this sort were asserted, for example, by State of Missouri officials in *Planned Parenthood of Central Missouri v. Danforth.*[330] Before the Court was a 1974 Missouri statute requiring that minors seeking abortions first obtain consent from parents, which state officials argued was appropriate for a number of reasons. Among them was that "the law properly may subject minors to more stringent limitations than are permissible with respect with adults...."[331] Missouri officials also argued that state law was "replete with provisions reflecting the interest of the state in assuring the welfare of minors."[332]

In further detailing the State of Missouri's proffered reasoning, the Court explained that "[c]ertain decisions are considered by the State to be outside the scope of a minor's ability to act in his [or her] own best interest or in the interest of the public, [with the Missouri officials] citing statutes proscribing the sale of firearms and deadly weapons to minors without parental consent, and other statutes relating to minors' exposure to certain types of literature, the purchase by pawnbrokers of property from minors, and the sale of cigarettes and alcoholic beverages to minors.... Thus, a state's permitting a child to obtain an abortion without the counsel of an adult 'who has responsibility or concern for the child' would constitute an irresponsible abdication of the State's duty to protect the welfare of minors.[333] Parental discretion, too, has been protected from unwarranted or unreasonable interference from the State...."[334]

But "[c]onstitutional rights do not mature and come into being magically only when one attains the state-defined age of majority," the majority of the Court held.[335] And "[m]inors, as well as adults, are protected by the Constitution and possess constitutional rights.[336] The Court indeed...long has recognized that the state has somewhat broader authority to regulate the activities of children than of adults.[337] It remains, then, to examine whether there is any significant state interest in conditioning an abortion on consent of a parent or person *in loco parentis* that is not present in the case of an adult."[338]

The matter-of-fact reasoning of the majority took into consideration—in weighing the competing interests of the state and the pregnant minor; constitutional precedent, and permissible "parental involvement"—that once a minor female becomes pregnant, in some ways she has become a "woman," required, by dint of her condition to endure the rigors of pregnancy and child birth if State officials had their way. Thus, the Justices took a closer look at the asserted intention of the statute's parental consent provision.

"One suggested interest is the safeguarding of the family unit and of parental authority," the Justices wrote. "It is difficult, however, to conclude that providing a parent with absolute power to overrule a determination, made by the physician and his minor patient, to terminate the patient's pregnancy will serve to strengthen the family unit. Neither is it likely that such veto power will enhance parental authority or control where the minor and the nonconsenting parent are so fundamentally in conflict and the very existence of the pregnancy already has fractured the family structure. Any independent interest the parent may have in the termination of the minor daughter's pregnancy is no more weighty than the right of privacy of the competent minor mature enough to have become pregnant."[339]

Thus, "the state may not impose a blanket [parental consent] provision [as included within the Missouri statute]…requiring the consent of a parent or person *in loco parentis* as a condition of abortion on an unmarried minor during the first twelve weeks of her pregnancy," the Court held. "Just as with the requirement of consent from the spouse, so here, the state does not have the constitutional authority to give a third party an absolute, and possibly arbitrary, veto over the decision of the physician and his patient to terminate the patient's pregnancy, regardless of the reason for withholding the consent."[340]

BELLOTTI v. BAIRD

Abortion foes would clearly have preferred that the Court uphold the "parental consent" provision. When it didn't, the brawl began anew. This time with an emphasis on defining the intrusions of the state that the Court would bear. In other words, what's a minor to do when parental consent cannot be achieved? She can attempt to achieve judicial consent instead,[341] which is what "Mary Moe" tried to do in *Bellotti v Baird*.[342] "Mary Moe" represented a "class of unmarried minors in Massachusetts who have adequate capacity to give valid and informed consent [to abortion], and who do not wish to involve their parents."[343]

PREGNANCY, BIRTH, AND ABORTION RATES PER 1,000 WOMEN AGED 15–19, AND ABORTION RATIO (ABORTIONS PER 100 PREGNANCIES) BY RACE, 1990–1996.

Race and Measure	1990	1991	1992	1993	1994	1995	1996
TOTALS:							
Pregnancy Rate*							
All Women 15–19	117.1	115.8	111.9	109.3	106.1	101.1	97.3
Sexually Active							
Women 15–19	224.3	222.4	215.5	211.1	205.4	196.3	189.5
Birthrate	60.4	62.1	60.7	59.6	58.9	56.8	54.4
Abortion Rate	37.6	35.5	34.3	34.3	32.2	30.0	29.2
Abortion Ratio†	40.2	37.7	36.9	36.5	35.3	34.6	34.9
WHITE							
Pregnancy Rate*	98.3	97.0	93.0	90.9	88.9	86.0	82.6
Birthrate	50.8	52.8	51.8	51.1	51.1	50.1	48.1
Abortion Rate	33.9	30.5	28.1	26.9	25.1	23.5	22.6
Abortion Ratio†	40.1	36.6	35.2	34.5	33.0	32.0	32.0
NONWHITE							
Overall							
Pregnancy Rate*	189.6	189.6	185.2	180.4	172.5	158.7	153.3
Abortion Rate	96.5	98.4	95.5	92.5	89.1	82.2	78.1
Abortion Ratio†	67.1	65.1	64.2	63.1	59.6	54.6	54.2

Race and Measure	1990	1991	1992	1993	1994	1995	1996
BLACK							
Pregnancy Rate*	224.3	223.7	218.7	212.7	202.1	184.8	178.9
Birthrate	113.1	115.5	112.4	108.6	104.5	96.1	91.4
Abortion Rate	80.5	77.5	76.2	74.9	69.7	63.2	62.9
Abortion Ratio†	41.6	40.1	40.4	40.8	40.0	39.7	40.8

*Includes estimated number of pregnancies ending in miscarriages. †Denominator excludes miscarriages. *Notes*: Data are tabulated according to the woman's age at the pregnancy outcome, and for births, according to the mother's race (not the child's). No data are presented separately for nonwhite women other than blacks because of small numbers and the heterogeneity of the group.

SOURCE: *Teenage Pregnancy: Overall Trends and State-by-State Information,*
THE ALAN GUTTMACHER INSTITUTE (April 1999).

On behalf of the class, Moe challenged a Massachusetts statute requiring the consent of both parents before an abortion can be performed on an unmarried woman under the age of 18.[344] In addressing the constitutionality of the statute, the Court explained that "...if the state decides to require a pregnant minor to obtain one or both parents' consent to an abortion, it must [also] provide an alternative procedure whereby authorization for the abortion can be obtained."[345] The Massachusetts statute provided "an alternative procedure" by which a minor could obtain an abortion by order of a superior court judge upon a showing of good cause. But the constitutional sufficiency of that procedure was at issue before the Court.

In enjoining enforcement of the statute, the United States Supreme Court explained that a decision by the Massachusetts Supreme Judicial Court's statement "reflects the general rule that a state may require a minor to wait until the age of majority before being permitted to exercise legal rights independently.[346] But we are concerned here with the exercise of a constitutional right of unique character.[347] As stated above, if the minor satisfies a court that she has attained sufficient maturity to make a fully informed decision, she then is entitled to make her abortion decision independently. We therefore agree with the District Court that [Massachusetts Statute Section 12S, the provision that detailed the judicial alternate procedure] cannot constitutionally permit judicial disregard of the abortion decision of a minor who has been determined to be mature and fully competent to assess the implications of the choice she has made."[348]

The reasons for this, the Court held, were that "[Section] 12S falls short of them in two respects. First, it permits judicial authorization for an abortion to be withheld from a minor who is found by the superior court to be mature and fully competent to make this decision independently. Second, it requires parental consultation or notification in every instance, without affording the pregnant minor an opportunity to receive an independent judicial determination that she is mature enough to consent or that an abortion would be in her best interests. Accordingly, we affirm the judgment of the District Court insofar as it invalidates this statute and enjoins its enforcement."[349] Accordingly, the provision was struck down.

H.L. v. MATHESON

The question of the "maturity" of the minor, already old enough to be pregnant—and apparently thought wise enough by antiabortion legislators to bear a child—was again before the Supreme Court in *H.L. v. Matheson*.[350] At issue was a Utah statute requiring doctors to "[n]otify, if possible," the parents or guardian of a minor upon whom an abortion is to be performed." H.L. was an unmarried 15-year-old girl still living with her parents when she discovered she was pregnant. After consulting a social worker as well as a physician, H.L. was advised that an abortion would be in her "best medical interest." But given the Utah law, the doctor refused to perform it unless she notified her parents.[351] Violation of the law was a misdemeanor punishable by up to a year's imprisonment and a $1,000 fine.

Despite the doctor's urgings, H.L. and her social worker endeavored to proceed with the abortion without notifying H.L.'s parents. While still in her first trimester, H.L. filed suit in the Third Judicial District Court, challenging the Utah statute as unconstitutional and seeking to represent a class of similarly situated unmarried "minor women who are suffering unwanted pregnancies and [who] desire to terminate the pregnancies but may not do so" given the requirements of the Utah law.[352] But in upholding the Utah statute, the United States Supreme Court distinguished parental consent laws from parental notification statutes. And because notifying a parent of a minor child's intent to have an abortion did not grant her parents a right to veto, the Court held that the Utah law did not violate the protections of the United States Constitution.

Though "...the requirement of notice to parents may inhibit some minors from seeking abortions," the Court acknowledged, that reality did not form a "valid basis to void the statute as applied to appellant and the class properly before us. The Constitution does not compel a state to fine-tune its statutes so as to encourage or facilitate abortions. To the contrary, state action 'encouraging childbirth except in the most urgent circumstances' is 'rationally related to the legitimate governmental objective of protecting potential life.'"[353]

Thus, the tide and the Court began to turn.

OHIO v. AKRON CENTER

In November of 1985, the Ohio Legislature enacted Amended Substitute House Bill 319, which amended Ohio law criminalizing the performance of abortions "on an unmarried and unemancipated woman under eighteen years of age, unless the physician provided timely notice to the minor's parent or to a court."[354] But the statute provided four exceptions. The first two of these exceptions involved parental consent.[355] The second two involved judicial bypass procedures.[356] Max Pierre Gaujean, a doctor at the Akron Center for Reproductive Health, and Rachel Roe, "an unmarried, unemancipated minor woman who sought an abortion" at the facility, both challenged the constitutionality of the Ohio law.

After the Ohio District Court permanently enjoined enforcement of the statute[357] and the Sixth Circuit Court of Appeals affirmed that decision,[358] the cases were consolidated before the United States Supreme Court as *Ohio v. Akron Center*.[359] In opening analysis of the issues before it, however, the Court explained that it had "…decided five cases addressing the constitutionality of parental notice or parental consent statutes in the abortion context.[360] We do not need to determine whether a statute that does not accord with these cases would violate the Constitution, for we conclude that H.B. 319 is consistent with them."[361]

With precedent as the starting point, the Court held that "[t]he Ohio statute…does not impose an undue, or otherwise unconstitutional, burden on a minor seeking an abortion." The Court held further that the Ohio legislature had acted in a rational manner in enacting H.B. 319. And into the picture came mention again of destiny and the obligation of "motherhood." "A free and enlightened society may decide that each of its members should attain a clearer, more tolerant understanding of the profound choices confronted by a woman who is considering whether to seek an abortion. *Her decision will embrace her own destiny and personal dignity, and the origins of the other human life that lies within the embryo,*" the Justices wrote.[362]

"The state is entitled to assume that, for most of its people, the beginnings of that understanding will be within the family, society's most intimate association," the Court held in an apparent reversal of the reasoning adopted by the Court in *Planned Parenthood of Central Missouri v. Danforth.*[363] "It is both rational and fair for the state to conclude that, in most instances, the family will strive to give a lonely or even terrified minor advice that is both compassionate and mature. The statute in issue here is a rational way to further those ends. It would deny all dignity to the family to say that the state cannot take this reasonable step in regulating its health professions to ensure that, in most cases, a young woman will receive guidance and understanding from a parent. We uphold H.B. 319 on its face, and reverse the Court of Appeals."[364]

HODGSON v. MINNESOTA

Of course, in battles there are skirmishes, and if the list of above cases represent those dogfights, then it can fairly be said that minor women won some and they lost some. In contrast to *Ohio v. Akron Center*, in *Hodgson v. Minnesota,*[365] a case decided the same year, minors won one, at least on the issue of parental consent, when the Supreme Court held unconstitutional a Minnesota statute requiring notification of both of a pregnant minor's parents. Of particular trouble to the Court was a 1981 amendment to the Minnesota Minors' Consent to Health Services Act, authorizing an "'unemancipated minor'[366] to give effective consent to an abortion by requiring that either her physician or an agent notify 'the parent' personally or by certified mail at least 48 hours before the procedure is performed."[367]

But the term "parent" was defined by the amendment as "both parents of the pregnant women if they are both living."[368] In striking down the two-parent provision, the Court held that "[n]ot only does two-parent notification fail to serve any state interest with respect to functioning families, it disserves the state interest in protecting and assisting the minor with respect to dysfunctional families." But the 48-hour waiting period between the signing of a consent and the performance of an abortion, as established by the amendment, was a different story. That requirement, the Court held was constitutional, because it "impose[d] only a minimal burden of the right of the minor to decide whether or not to terminate her pregnancy," the Court held.

A RESTRICTED RIGHT TO CHOOSE

So minors *do* have the right to choose abortion. But it is a restricted right increasingly under attack by antiabortion forces and politicians, who may or may not have a pregnant minor's best interests in mind. Thus, in accordance with Supreme Court precedent, states may require minors to seek parental consent before they have abortions, provided parental consent statutes also include alternate consent provisions, the most common of which involve judicial intervention. States may also require 24- or 48-hour waiting periods between the signing of consent forms and performance of the procedure.[369]

Abortion is clearly of interest to minors, because even minor females realize that having a child will almost certainly change their lives. Indeed, that is the reason most often given by teens for choosing to have abortions, researchers at the Alan Guttmacher Institute note.[370] And statistically speaking, it does. Although seven out of ten teenage mothers manage to finish high school, they are less likely than other girls to go to college,[371] which tends often to lead to a cycle of low-wage jobs and poverty. Or in some cases, to a repeat of the cycle of poverty. Among those teenagers who carry a fetus to term and give birth, 83 percent are more "likely to come from poor or low-income families than are teenagers who have abortions (61 percent) or teens in general."[372]

In addition, one-fourth of all teenage mothers will have a second child within two years of giving birth to the first.[373] Finally, even given the steep decline in the rate of abortion among teenagers, in 1999, teenage pregnancies accounted for 31 percent of all nonmarital births and thirteen percent of all United States births.[374] Women's rights activists and critics of "parental involvement" and consent statutes have long argued that while some state officials may actually be concerned for minors, others know that parental consent statutes will prevent some minors from having abortions.

Though empirical data on this issue is hard to come by, there have been one or two fairly sound offerings tending to lend support to these cries. Data compiled by the Mississippi Health Department and analyzed by Stanley K. Henshaw for *Family Planning Perspectives*,[375] found a 16 percent decrease in the ratio of abortions among minors during the five-month period immediately after a Mississippi parental consent law went into effect in 1993.

"During the first five months of 1993," Henshaw wrote, "the number of abortions performed in Mississippi for minors equaled 0.126 of the number obtained by older women. In July through December, after the parental consent law took effect, the ratio was 0.106, 16 percent lower than the earlier ratio of 0.126. This result supports the hypothesis that the law affected the number of minors obtaining abortions in the state."[376]

CHILD CUSTODY PROTECTION ACT:
Divide and Conquer in the Name of Family

Not too long ago, a young man in Pennsylvania got a 13-year-old girl pregnant, and a lot of people got angry. But not so much about the pregnancy. Rather, what seems to have really riled politicians is that the boy's mother took the girl out of state to have an abortion. It is this kind of "hijacking" of a minor by a "stranger" that drove Representative Ileana Ros-Lehtinen[377] to sponsor the Child Custody Protection Act (CCPA), which, Ros-Lehtinen argues would "assure that the rights of parents across the nation are not trampled by strangers, who, without the knowledge of the parents, take minor girls to obtain an abortion."[378] Of course, the woman in the case that got Ros-Lehtinen so angry wasn't really a "stranger."

First introduced in February 1998, and gaining overwhelming approval in the House of Representatives in July of that year before failing in the Senate, the Child Custody Protection Act would have made it a crime for anyone who is not a child's parent to take her out of the state for an abortion without parental consent. And, incidentally, "anyone" may mean grandparents, siblings, members of the clergy, or even medical professionals. If convicted, a person could be sentenced to up to one year in jail and a $100,000 fine.[379] At the center of this relatively recent storm in a sky that rains new controversies each week was what is always at the center of the storm—the right to choose an abortion.

With regard to minors, pro-life activists and conservative politicians have long argued that parental involvement is important because abortion is a surgical procedure. Thus, the Child Custody Protection Act was intended to curb a minor's efforts to get around notifying her parents of her pregnancy, supporters argue. And yet, that is what makes the debate over the Child Custody Protection Act as much trouble as it is worth. Although the numbers are growing, not all states require parental consent, notice, or involvement in a minor female's choice of abortion. However, because the intent of the Child Custody Protection Act is not to require consent in all states, but rather to add force to current state consent laws, the Child Custody Protection Act would affect only those young woman under 18 years of age, who live in states requiring parental consent, who don't inform their parents, or seek a court order.

In July 1998, the House of Representatives voted 276–150 in favor of the proposed Child Custody Protection Act. But on September 22, 1998, the act stalled in the United States Senate, falling short of the 60 votes needed to prevent debate.[380] The Act was reintroduced in the House of Representatives and the Senate in 1999. The states have begun to step up efforts to close their borders as well.[381] Illinois House Bill 690, proposed in February 2001, would amend the Illinois Abortion Act of 1975 to provide that minor residents of bordering states traveling to Illinois for an abortion would have to provide that they have complied with the parental consent or notice requirements of their home states.

ENDNOTES FOR CHAPTER FIVE

1   *See* Betty Friedan, THE FEMININE MYSTIQUE (New York: W.W. Norton, 1983) (20ᵗʰ Ann. Ed.) (original copyright 1963), at p. 17.

2   *Id.* at 15.

3   *See* Ferdinand Lundberg, MODERN WOMAN: THE LOST SEX (New York and London: Harper & Brothers, 1947).

4   *See* Friedan, *supra* note 1, at pp. 42–43.

5   Among these articles were: *Femininity Begins at Home; It's a Man's World Maybe; Have Babies While You're Young; How to Snare a Male; Should I Stop Work When We Marry?; Are You Training Your Daughter to be a Wife?; Do Women Have to Talk So Much?; Why GIs Prefer Those German Girls; Really a Man's World, Politics; How to Hold on to a Happy Marriage; Don't Be Afraid to Marry Young;* and, *Cooking to Me is Poetry. See* Friedan, *supra* note 1, at p. 44.

6   *Id.* at 44.

7   *Id.*

8   *Id.* at 43.

9   *Id.*

10   *Id.*

11   *Id.*

12   *Id.* at 16.

13   *Id.*

14   *Id.*

15   Anne Morrow Lindbergh, GIFT FROM THE SEA (New York: Pantheon, 1955).

16   Geoffrey C. Ward wrote the text for THE AMERICAN EXPERIENCE: LINDBERGH (Insignia Films, WETA-TV, 1990). He was quoted by Eric Pace in *Anne Morrow Lindbergh Is Dead at 94: Author Was Charles Lindbergh's Widow,* N.Y. TIMES, Feb. 8, 2001, at A26.

17   *See* Walt Mueller, UNDERSTANDING TODAY'S YOUTH CULTURE (Wheaton, Illinois: Tyndale House Publishing, Inc., 1994), at p. 125 (citing George Comstock, TELEVISION IN AMERICA (Beverly Hills: Sage, 1980), at ix).

18   *See* A&E ENTERTAINMENT ALMANAC 1998 (Boston: Information Please L.L.C., 1997 (Beth Rowan, ed.)), at pp. 530–532.

19   *See* England & Farkas, supra note 9, ENDNOTES FOR CHAPTER THREE, at p. 77.

20   *Id.*

21   *Id.*

22   *Id.*

23   *Id.*

24   *Id.*

25   *See* David Allyn, MAKE LOVE, NOT WAR, THE SEXUAL REVOLUTION: AN UNFETTERED HISTORY (New York: Routledge 2001), at pp. 15–16. (Allyn notes, for example, that "[i]n 1953, Alfred Kinsey, a zoologist turned sex researcher at Indiana University, reported in his book SEXUAL BEHAVIOR IN THE HUMAN FEMALE ("the Kinsey Report") that roughly 50 percent of the 5,940 white American women he surveyed admitted to having had sex before marriage. He also noted that approximately 25 percent admitted to having had an extramarital encounter. Since Kinsey's sample was not random, his findings cannot be treated as nationally representative, but they do suggest a discrepancy between official morality and private behavior.")

26   *Id.* at 15.

27   *See* England & Farkas, *supra* note 19, at p. 99.

28   *Id.*

29   *See* McDonald, *supra* note 13, ENDNOTES FOR CHAPTER THREE, at p. 61.

30   *Id.*

31   *See* Pace, supra note 16.

32   Friedan reportedly wrote for CHARM, PARENTS, and REDBOOK before penning THE FEMININE MYSTIQUE.

33   According to Judith Hennessee, author of BETTY FRIEDAN: HER LIFE (New York: Random House, 1999), reviewed by Daphne Merkin for *The New Yorker* magazine, (June 14, 1999), during the first of the sit-ins Friedan organized "… in 1969, in the Oak Room of the Plaza Hotel, where women were excluded from noon to three" Friedan was reluctant to appear on camera "because her bruised face had to be heavily made up before she could appear in public." Further, according to Merkin, Friedan "was what would nowadays be called a battered wife, except that she never called herself one and she gave as good as she got." *See* Daphne Merkin, *Sister Act: Did Betty Friedan Go Wrong, or Did Feminism?,* NEW YORKER, June 14, 1999, at pp. 78, 81.

34   *See* FRIEDAN, *supra* note 1, at p. 15.

35   *Id.*

36   *See, e.g., Griswold v. Connecticut,* 381 U.S. 479 (1965); *Eisenstadt v. Baird,* 405 U.S. 438 (1972).

37   *See* Frank Rich, *Pretty Boys,* N.Y. TIMES MAG., Dec. 30, 2000, at 22.

38   *See* Robert T. Michael *et al.*, SEX IN AMERICA: A DEFINITIVE SURVEY (New York: Warner Books, 1995), at p. 96.
39   *Id.*
40   *Id.*
41   *Id.*
42   *Id.*
43   *Id.*
44   *Id.*
45   *See Reed v. Reed*, 404 U.S. 71 (1971); *Craig v. Boren*, 429 U.S. 190 (1976) (holding that gender preference statutes were unconstitutional).
46   *See Roe v. Wade*, 410 U.S. 113 (1973) (holding that a woman had the fundamental right to choose abortion).
47   *See* Sanger, *supra* note 11, ENDNOTES FOR INTRODUCTION, at p. 114.
48   The two sections of the Connecticut statute challenged by *Griswold* were Section 53-32, which provided that: "Any person who uses any drug, medicinal article, or instrument for the purpose of preventing conception shall be fined not less than fifty dollars or imprisoned not less than sixty days nor more than one year or be both fined and imprisoned;" and Section 54-196, which provided that: "Any person who assists, abets, counsels, causes, hires, or commands another to commit any offense may be prosecuted and punished as if he were the principal offender."
49   163 N.Y.S. 680 (1916) and 163 N.Y.S. 682 (1917). For fuller discussion, *see* CHAPTER TWO, *The Emerging Birth Control Debate*.
50   Well into the 1940s, New York was still prosecuting people for the distribution of birth control. *See, e.g., Barretta v. Barretta*, 46 N.Y.S.2d 261 (1944).
51   Similar prosecutions continued in Massachusetts. *See Commonwealth v. Allison*, 116 N.E. 265 (Mass. 1917); *Commonwealth v. Gardner*, 15 N.E.2d 222 (Mass. 1938); *Commonwealth v. Corbett*, 29 N.E.2d 151 (Mass. 1940); *Commonwealth v. Werlinksy*, 29 N.E.2d 150 (Mass. 1940).
52   Pennsylvania was active in birth control prosecutions as well. *See Commonwealth v. Cohen*, 31 D&C 249 (Pa. O & T 1937); *Commonwealth v. Mosholder*, 46 D&C 31 (Pa. Com. Pl. 1943).
53   Iowa also prosecuted people for distributing birth control. *See State v. Chenoweth*, 284 N.W. 110 (Iowa 1939).
54   *See Davis v. U.S.*, 62 F.2d 473 (C.C.A. Ohio 1933) (At issue was the interpretation of a statute that prohibited the deposit on common carriers of "any article for preventing conception.")
55   316 U.S. 535 (1942). (At issue in *Skinner v. Oklahoma* was the constitutionality of an Oklahoma statute permitting compulsory sterilization for recidivist criminals. In striking down the statute as violative of the Equal Protection Clause, the Justices held that "[m]arriage and procreation are fundamental to the very existence and survival of the race.")
56   316 U.S. 535 (1942).
57   *See* Friedman Goldstein, *supra* note 129, ENDNOTES FOR CHAPTER ONE, at p. 305; Tribe, *supra* note 73, ENDNOTES FOR CHAPTER THREE, at pp. 1339–1340.
58   274 U.S. 200 (1927).
59   *See* 42 U.S.C. 2000a Sec 300 a–5.
60   372 F. Supp. 1196 (D.D.C. 1974), *final disposition*, 403 F. Supp. 1235 (D.D.C. 1975), *vac. as moot per curiam*, 565 F.2d 722 (D.C. Cir. 1977).
61   372 F. Supp. 1196 (D.D.C. 1974).
62   *See* 42 C.F.R. Secs. 50.203–50.205; 441.253, 441.257, 441.258 (1993); Dorothy McBride Stetson, WOMEN'S RIGHTS IN THE U.S.A.: POLICY DEBATES AND GENDER ROLES 108 (2d ed. 1997).
63   Those states are: Arkansas (Ark. Code Ann. Sec. 20-49-204); Colorado (Colo. Rev. Stat. Secs. 27-10.5-128 to -132); Connecticut (Conn. Gen. Stat. Sec. 45-78r); Delaware (Del. Code Ann. tit. 16, Sec. 5702(a); Georgia (Ga. Code Ann. Sec. 31-20-3); Idaho (Idaho Code Secs. 39-3901 to 3910); Maine (Me. Rev. Stat. Ann. tit. 34, Sec. 2474); Mississippi (Miss. Code Ann. Secs. 41-45-1 to -19); North Carolina (N.C. Gen. Stat. Secs. 35-36 to -50); New Jersey (N.J. Rev. Stat. Sec. 30:60-5); Oregon (Or. Rev. Stat. Secs. 436.010 to .150); Utah (Utah Code Ann. Secs. 64-10-1 to -13); Vermont (Vt. Stat. Ann. tit. 18, Secs. 8705 to 16); and, West Virginia (W.Va. Code Secs. 27-16-1 to -5). Some scholars argue that the actual number of states to permit compulsory sterilization is seventeen.
64   *See* HUMAN BETTERMENT ASSOCIATION OF AMERICA, *supra* note 76, ENDNOTES FOR CHAPTER TWO.
65   304 S.E.2d 793 (N.C. App. 1983).
66   *Id.*
67   420 F. Supp. 451 (1976).
68   *Id.* at 455.
69   *Id.* at 456. (The paragraph struck provided that the "next of kin or legal guardian" could also seek sterilization. In striking this paragraph, the judges reasoned that such a provision "grants to the retarded person's next of kin or legal guardian the power of a tyrant....")
70   *Buck v. Bell* was decided on similar grounds.
71   289 N.C. 95 (1976).
72   452 F. Supp. 361, 366 (1978).
73   *See* OR. HOUSE BILL 2616 (2001).

74   725 P.2d 1101, 1102 (Ariz. 1986).
75   16 Cal. App. 606 (1936).
76   *See People v. Dominiquez,* 256 Cal. App. 2d 623, 627–29 (1967).
77   658 F. Supp. 1483 (W.D. Mich. 1987), 849 F.2d 213 (6th Cir. 1988), *rehearing denied.*
78   *See* NARAL FACT SHEET: *Unjust Punishment, Forced Contraception, and Poor Treatment of Women by the Courts and Prisons* (citing Marie McCullough, *Inmate's Abortion Request Stirs Temptest: When the Prison Refused, She Turned to the Courts and Won, Amid Controversy, She Changed Her Mind,* PHILADELPHIA INQUIRER, Dec. 2, 1998, Metro Section).
79   *Id.* at 2 (citing *State v. Kawaguchi,* CR 365106C (Ct. Common Pleas Cuyahoga County transcript from Oct. 6, 1998). *Kawaguchi v. Cleary,* No. 369172 (Ct. Common Pleas Cuyahoga County complaint filed Nov. 5, 1998); Memorandum of *Amici Curiae* National Abortion and Reproductive Rights Action League and The NARAL Foundation in Support of Plaintiffs' Opposition to Certain Defendants' Motions to Dismiss (Ct. Common Pleas Cuyahoga County, Feb. 25, 1999) (No. 369172) (motion to file brief denied March 23, 1999). A court dismissed portions of Ms. Kawaguchi's complaint in March 1999. *Kawaguchi v. Cleary,* No. 369172 (Ct. Common Pleas Cuyahoga County March 26, 1999)).
80   *Id.*
81   *Id.* (citing Bev McCarron, *Pregnant Inmate is Released, Clearing Way for an Abortion,* STAR-LEDGER, Feb. 2, 1997, at p. 031).
82   *Id.* (citing *National Briefs,* ASSOCIATED PRESS, April 16, 1985; "*Woman's Sentence Voided in Death,*" CHI. TRIB., April 17, 1985, p. 3; Eric Zorn, "*Sloppiness Goes Long Way in Court,*" CHI. TRIB., June 28, 1994, at p. 1).
83   *See* Tamar Levin, *Father Owing Child Support Loses Right to Procreate,* N.Y. TIMES, July 12, 2001, at A14; Sarah Wyatt, *Court: No More Kids For Man,* CHI. SUN-TIMES, July 11, 2001, at p. 31; Vivian Berger, *Bedroom Sentence,* NAT'L L.J., Sept. 17, 2001, at A21 (citing *State v. Oakley,* 2001 WL 767556 (Wis. July 10, 2001)).
84   *See, e.g., Holton v. State of Alaska,* 602 P.2d 1228, 1238 (Alaska 1979) (holding that "[i]n order to comport with the requirements of constitutional due process, a condition of probation must be sufficiently precise and unambiguous to inform the probationer of the conduct that is essential so that he may retain his liberty").
85   *See, e.g., Burrell v. State of Alaska,* 626 P.2d 1087, 1089 (Alaska App. 1981); *State of Alaska v. Martin,* 517 P.2d 1399, 1402 (Alaska 1974). *Accord, United States v. Simmons,* 812 F.2d 561, 565 (9th Cir. 1987) ("When...the proscribed acts are not criminal, due process requires that the probationer receive actual notice. The record must be closely scrutinized to determine whether the defendant did, in fact, receive the requisite warning. Therefore, unless [the offender] received prior fair warning that his acts could lead to revocation, the district court's revocation violated due process and was an abuse of discretion.")
86   *See* R.I. HOUSE BILL 5581 (2001).
87   *See* TEX. HJR 32 (2001).
88   *See* William Glaberson, *Skepticism Follows Court Ruling In Favor of Inmate Procreation,* N.Y. TIMES, Sept. 8, 2001, at A7.
89   *See What Did She Know and When Did She Know It?,* NAT'L L.J., July 30, 2001, at B9.
90   *See* Cecilia M. Vega, *Cash-for-Sterilization Plan Starts Slowly in New York,* N.Y. TIMES, Jan. 6, 2003, at A16.
91   *See* Robert Blank and Janna C. Merrick, HUMAN REPRODUCTION, EMERGING TECHNOLOGIES, AND CONFLICTING RIGHTS, (Washington, D.C.: C.Q. Press 1995), at pp. 2–3 (citing Richard Wasserstrom, *Rights, Human Rights, and Racial Discrimination,* 61 THE JOURNAL OF PHILOSOPHY 628-641 (1964)).
92   *Id.*
93   *See* Maguire, *supra* note 42, ENDNOTES FOR CHAPTER ONE, at pp. 32–34. (Maguire notes that "...Christianity was born in a world in which contraception and abortion were both known and practiced. The Egyptians, Jews, Greeks, and Romans used a variety of contraception methods, including *coitus interruptus,* pessaries, potions, and condoms; abortion appears to have been a widespread phenomenon.")
94   347 U.S. 483 (1954).
95   *See* Marcia Coyle, *Follow The People,* NAT'L L.J., Aug. 4, 2003, at p. S1.
96   *See* Sanger, *supra* note 47, at p. 114.
97   See *supra* note 48.
98   381 U.S. 479 (1965).
99   *See* U.S. CONST. amend XIV, Sec.1.
100   There is also a "due process" clause within the Fifth Amendment, which deals with review of federal legislation. The Due Process Clause of the Fourteenth Amendment, by contrast, deals with review of state legislation.
101   Constitutional scholar Laurence Tribe defines procedural due process as "...procedural safeguards [that] have their historical origins in the notion that conditions of personal freedom can be preserved only when there is some institutional check on arbitrary government action." *See* Tribe,

supra note 73, ENDNOTES FOR CHAPTER THREE, at pp. 663–664 (citing Kadish, *Methodology and Criteria in Due Process Adjudication—A Survey and Criticism*, 66 Yale L.J., at pp. 319, 340 (1957)).

102 For a brief overview, see *supra* note 33, ENDNOTES FOR CHAPTER THREE.

103 *See* BLACK'S LAW DICTIONARY (6ᵗʰ ed.) (St Paul, Minn.: West Publishing Co., 1990), at p. 997.

104 *See* Presser, *supra* note 124, ENDNOTES FOR CHAPTER ONE, at p. 130 (citing Robert Bork, THE TEMPTING OF AMERICA: THE POLITICAL SEDUCTION OF THE LAW (New York: Free Press, 1990), at p. 28.)

105 Among the recent examples of this effort was that, in 2001, Mississippi lawmakers were considering passage of a bill that would prohibit minors under the age of 18 from obtaining condoms without a prescription. *See, e.g.*, MISSISSIPPI HOUSE BILL 153 (which would have prohibited, were it passed, a person under 18 years of age from obtaining condoms without a prescription. The bill would also have imposed a $1,000 fine on an adult who purchased condoms for a minor). The measure apparently died, however, in committee.

106 The Court cited *NAACP v. Alabama*, 357 U.S. 449, 462 (1958), to support this proposition, reasoning that "we protected the 'freedom to associate and privacy in one's associations,' noting that freedom of association was a peripheral First Amendment right." *Griswold v. Connecticut*, 381 U.S. at 483.

107 Cases cited to support the evolution of a notion of personal privacy included: *Pierce v. Society of Sisters of the Holy Names of Jesus and Mary*, 268 U.S. 510 (1925); *Meyer v. Nebraska*, 262 U.S. 390 (1923); *Martin v. Struthers*, 319 U.S. 141 (1943); *Sweezy v. New Hampshire*, 354 U.S. 234 (1957); *Barenblatt v. United States*, 360 U.S. 109 (1959); *Baggett v. Bullitt*, 377 U.S. 360 (1964); *NAACP v. Alabama*, 357 U.S. 449 (1958); *Schware v. Board of Bar Examiners*, 353 U.S. 232 (1957); *De Jonge v. Oregon*, 299 U.S. 353 (1937).

108 *See* Norton, *supra* note 2, ENDNOTES FOR INTRODUCTION, at p. 44.

109 In support of this notion, the Court cited *NAACP v. Alabama*, 357 U.S. 449 (1958).

110 381 U.S. at 483-86.

111 405 U.S. 438 (1972).

112 Great pains were taken in this case to note that "the recipient of the foam [w]as 'an unmarried adult woman.'" *Eisenstadt v. Baird*, 405 U.S. at 440, n. 1.

113 405 U.S. at 453 (*emphasis in the original*). In reaching this conclusion, the Court cited: *Stanley v. Georgia*, 394 U.S. 557 (1969); *Skinner v. Oklahoma*, 316 U.S. 535 (1942); and, *Jacobson v. Massachusetts*, 197 U.S. 11, 39 (1905).

114 431 U.S. 678 (1977).

115 404 U.S. 71 (1971). (The case involved an Idaho statute, which declared that were equal candidates to serve as administrator of an estates, "males must be preferred to females...." After a child, Richard Lynn Reed, died, both his mother, Sally Reed, and his father, Cecil Reed, filed to serve as administrator. A probate judge held, in accordance with the statute, that Cecil Reed should serve. He was a man. Sally Reed appealed. In striking down the Idaho statute, the Justices of the Supreme Court held that the Idaho statute cannot stand, because "[b]y providing dissimilar treatment for men and women who are thus similarly situated, the challenged section violates the Equal Protection Clause.") Other cases regarding gender classifications decided around that time include *Stanton v. Stanton*, 421 U.S. 7 (1975) and *Orr v. Orr*, 440 U.S. 268 (1979).

116 Five years later, in the case of *Craig v. Boren*, 429 U.S. 190 (1976), the United States Supreme Court began to apply the Equal Protection Clause analysis to gender discrimination cases.

117 *See* Marc Lacey, *Teen-Age Birth Rate in U.S. Falls Again*, N.Y. TIMES, Oct. 27, 1999, at A14; Dave McKinney, *Teen Births in Illinois Hit 40-Year Low in '99*, CHI. SUN-TIMES, Dec. 15, 2000, at p. 42.

118 *See* Lacey, *supra* note 117, at A14.

119 *Id.*

120 *See also* Susheela Singh and Jacqueline E. Darroch, *Adolescent Pregnancy and Childbearing: Levels and Trends in Developed Countries*, 32 FAMILY PLANNING PERSPECTIVES, (Jan./Feb. 2000) at pp. 14–23.

121 *See* Lee Smith, *The New Wave of Illegitimacy*, FORTUNE, April 19, 1994, at pp. 81–90.

122 *See Teenage Pregnancy: Overall Trends and State-by-State Information* (April 1999), published by the ALAN GUTTMACHER INSTITUTE, at p. 1. (According to the Alan Guttmacher Institute, roughly 62 percent of these reported pregnancies occurred in young women 18 to 19 years of age.)

123 *Id.*

124 *Id.*

125 *Id.*

126 *Id.*

127 *See, e.g.*, FACTS IN BRIEF, *Teen Sex and Pregnancy*, published by the ALAN GUTTMACHER INSTITUTE (1999), at p. 1.

128 *See* Singh & Darroch, *supra* note 120.

129 *See* Lacey, *supra* note 117, at A14.

130 *See* Diana Jean Schemo, *Virginity Pledges by Teenagers Can Be Highly Effective, Federal Study Finds*, N.Y. TIMES, January 4, 2001, at A16. (According to Schemo, "[w]hen researchers controlled for characteristics associated with delaying sexual intercourse, they found that those who had taken chastity pledges delayed sex about 18 months longer than virgins who had never taken a pledge. [¶] 'Adolescents who pledge,' wrote Peter S. Bearman of Columbia University and Hannah Bruck-

ner of Yale University, the authors of the report, 'are much less likely than adolescents who do not pledge to have intercourse. The delay effect is substantial and robust. Pledging delays intercourse for a long time. In this sense, the pledge works.' [¶] The report was, however, couched in layers of caveats. It found that virginity pledges did not hold when only one teenager took them, but required the support of like-minded classmates, within limits. Conversely, the pledges' effectiveness began to decline and teenagers stopped delaying sex when the percentage of students signing virginity pledges increased to more than 30 percent.")

131 *See, e.g.,* Stevens-Simon, C., Dolgan, J., Kelley, L., and Singer, D., *The Effect of Monetary Incentives and Peer Support Groups on Repeat Adolescent Pregnancies: A Randomized Trial of the Dollar-a-Day Program,* 277 JAMA at pp. 977–982 (March 26, 1997). (The Denver, Colorado, study involved 286 "primiparous girls younger than 18 years, whose infants were younger than 5 months." Although "...participation in interventions was generally low," according to the authors, monetary incentive programs, such as Dollar-a-Day, "were supported: 58 percent of those offered a monetary incentive participated in the support groups, compared with 9 percent of those who were not offered the incentive." By contrast, the "peer-support group" approach was roundly rejected by participants. Indeed, "the peer-support group experience failed to prevent repeat pregnancies," the author wrote. In exact numbers, "[t]he incidence of second pregnancies at 6 months (9 percent, 22/248), at 12 months (20 percent, 49/248), at 18 months (29 percent, 72/248), and at 24 months (39 percent, 97/248) following delivery did not vary significantly in relation to intervention strategy.")

132 *See, e.g.,* Stevens-Simon, C., White, M., *Adolescent Pregnancy,* 20 PEDIATR. ANN., at pp. 322–331 (1991); Stevens-Simon, C., Reichert, S., *Child Sexual Abuse and Adolescent Pregnancy,* 149 ARCH. PEDIATR. ADOLESC. MED. at pp. 23–27 (1994); Klerman, L.V., *Adolescent Pregnancy and Parenting Controversies of the Past and Lessons for the Future,* 14 J. ADOLESC. HEALTH at pp. 553–561 (1993); Stevens-Simon, C., Fullar, S.A., McArarney E.R., *Teenage Pregnancy,* 28 CLIN. PEDIATR. at pp. 282–283 (1989); Daley, J., Delbanco, T., Hartman, E., *A 17-Year-Old Mother Seeking Contraception, 1 Year Later,* 227 JAMA at p. 1976 (June 25, 1997).

133 *See* Lacey, *supra* note 117, at A14.

134 *See* FACTS IN BRIEF, *supra* note 127, at p. 1.

135 *Id.*

136 *Id.*

137 *See, e.g.,* MISS. HOUSE BILL 153 (which would have prohibited, were it passed, a person under 18 years of age from obtaining condoms without a prescription. The bill would also have imposed a $1,000 fine on an adult who purchased condoms for a minor). The measure apparently died, however, in committee.

138 *See* FACTS IN BRIEF, *supra* note 127, at p. 1.

139 *Id.*

140 *Id.*

141 431 U.S. 678 (1977).

142 In *Maher v. Roe,* 432 U.S. 464 (1977), and then *Harris v. McRae,* 448 U.S. 297 (1980), for example, the United States Supreme Court upheld state regulations denying state and federal funding for abortions and birth control in a series of calculated restrictions, some legal scholars argue, intended to foreclose the ability of at least some women—mainly the poor—to exercise the right of choice. *See, e.g.,* Catherine A. MacKinnon, *Privacy v. Equality: Beyond Roe v. Wade,* in APPLICATIONS OF FEMINIST LEGAL THEORY TO WOMEN'S LIVES, at pp. 985, 986–87 (D. Kelly Weisberg ed., 1996) ("In 1981 the Supreme Court in *Harris v. McRae* decided that this right to privacy did not mean that federal Medicaid programs had to fund medically necessary abortions. Privacy, the Court had said, was guaranteed for 'a woman's decision whether or not to terminate her pregnancy.' The Court then permitted the government to support one decision and not another: to fund continuing conceptions and not to fund discontinuing them. Asserting that decisional privacy was nevertheless constitutionally intact, the Court stated that 'although the government may not place obstacles in the path of a woman's exercise of her freedom of choice, it need not remove those not of its own creation.' It is apparently a short step from that which the government has a duty not to intervene in to that which it has no duty to intervene in.") For further reading on the subject, *see* Deborah Haas-Wilson, *Women's Reproductive Choices: The Impact of Medicaid Funding Restrictions,* 29 FAMILY PLANNING PERSPECTIVES (Sept.-Oct. 1997), at p. 228; Theodore Joyce and Robert Kaestner, *The Effect of Expansions in Medicaid Income Eligibility of Abortion,* 33 DEMOGRAPHY (May 1996), at p. 181; THE RIGHTS OF WOMEN: THE BASIC ACLU GUIDE TO WOMEN'S RIGHTS (Susan Deller Ross *et al.,* 3rd ed. 1993), at pp. 188–193.

143 *See* ISSUES IN BRIEF , *U.S. Policy Can Reduce Cost Barriers to Contraception,* (1999 Series, NO. 2), published by the ALAN GUTTMACHER INSTITUTE REPORT, at p. 3. (According to research compiled by the Alan Guttmacher Institute, "[i]n addition to financing the provision of contraceptive services, Title X funds support a wide range of reproductive health care, including pelvic and breast examinations, blood pressure checks, Pap smears, and testing and treatment for sexually transmitted diseases.")

144   At the time, Livingston was a Republican from Louisiana. He resigned on the eve of his expected elevation to Speaker of the House after confessing "numerous" adulterous affairs in the last two decades.

145   Istook is a Republican from Oklahoma.

146   A similar regulation was proposed by the Reagan Administration in 1982. That effort would also have required clinics to notify parents by registered mail that their children had visited the clinic. As a point of legal history, the regulation was finalized in 1983, despite more than 40,000 letters in protest. But judges in two federal appeals courts would eventually bar enforcement of the legislation. It was eventually withdrawn.

147   *See* ISSUES IN BRIEF, *Title X and the U.S. Family Planning Effort*, published by the ALAN GUTTMACHER INSTITUTE REPORT, at pp. 4–5. (By statute, Title X allow clients to offer clients a range of contraceptives on a confidential basis.)

148   *See* ISSUES IN BRIEF, *Minors and the Right to Consent to Health Care*, ISSUES IN BRIEF (2000 Series, NO. 2), published by the ALAN GUTTMACHER INSTITUTE, at p. 1. (The Istook Amendment was apparently never enacted by either the House or the Senate.)

149   *Id.*

150   *See Bush Signed Law Requiring Notice To Parents on Minors' Abortions*, N.Y. TIMES, June 8, 1999, at 1.

151   *Id.*

152   *See* ISSUES IN BRIEF, *supra* note 148, at p. 1.

153   *Id.*

154   *Id.*

155   *See* MISS. HOUSE BILL 153, *supra* note 137.

156   *See* S.C. HOUSE BILL 3093 (2001).

157   *See, e.g.*, N.Y. SENATE BILL 1604 (2001) and MISS. HOUSE BILL 445 (2001).

158   *See* MD. HOUSE BILL 448 (2001).

159   *See, e.g.*, FL. SENATE BILL 214 and FL. HOUSE BILL 169 (2001); MASS. SENATE BILL 324 (2001); and MISS. HOUSE BILL 445 (2001).

160   *See* ISSUES IN BRIEF, *The Role of Contraception in Reducing Abortion*, published by the ALAN GUTTMACHER INSTITUTE (1997), at p. 2.

161   *See* FACTS IN BRIEF, *Induced Abortion*, published by the ALAN GUTTMACHER INSTITUTE (2000), at p. 1.

162   *Id.*

163   *See* ISSUES IN BRIEF, *supra* note 160, at p. 2.

164   *Id.*

165   *Stenberg v. Carhart,* 120 S. Ct. 865, 870 (2000) (citing *Roe v. Wade,* 410 U.S. 113 (1973) and *Planned Parenthood of Southeastern Pa. v. Casey,* 505 U.S. 833 (1992)).

166   *Id.*

167   405 U.S. 438 (1972).

168   410 U.S. 113 (1973).

169   *See* Richard Perez-Peña, '*70 Abortion Law: New York Said Yes, Stunning the Nation*, N.Y. TIMES, April 9, 2000, at A1.

170   *Id.*

171   *Id.*

172   *Id.*

173   For a brief overview of the evolution of abortion law, *see* Willard Cates, Jr., *et al.*, TOPICS FOR OUR TIMES: *Justice Blackmun and Legal Abortion—A Besieged Legacy to Woman's Reproductive Health*, 85 AM. J. OF PUB. H'LTH at p. 1204 (Sept. 1995).

174   For reading on the construction of legal arguments before the United States Supreme Court, *see* Edward Lazarus, CLOSED CHAMBERS: THE FIRST EYEWITNESS ACCOUNT OF THE EPIC STRUGGLES INSIDE THE SUPREME COURT (New York: Times Books, 1998), at pp. 344–345.

175   *See, e.g.*, H.W. Lawson, *et al.*, *Abortion Mortality, United States, 1972 through 1987*, 171 AM. J. OBSTET. GYNECOL, at pp. 1365–1372 (1994); P.G. Stubblefield and D.A. Grimes, *Septic Abortion*, 331 N. ENGL. J. MED., at pp. 310–314; H.K. Atrash, H.W. Lawson and J.C. Smith, *Legal Abortion in the U.S.: Trends and Mortality*, (1994) 35 CONTEMP OB/GYN., at pp. 58–69 (1990).

176   *See* Lazarus, *supra* note 174, at p. 344. (According to Lazarus, "[s]pecifically, the ALI model statute permitted abortion whenever two doctors agreed that there existed a 'substantial risk' that continued pregnancy would 'gravely impair the physical or mental health of the mother,' the fetus had a 'grave physical or mental defect,' or the pregnancy resulted from rape or incest" (citing David J. Garrow, LIBERTY AND SEXUALITY: THE RIGHT TO PRIVACY AND THE MAKING OF ROE V. WADE (New York: Macmillan, 1994), at p. 272)). The above language became the foundation of modern choice law.

177   *See* Blank & Merrick, *supra* note 91, at p. 22; Lazarus, *supra* note 174, at p. 344.

178   *See, e.g.*, Barbara Hinkson Craig & David M. O'Brien, ABORTION AND AMERICAN POLITICS (Chatham, N.J.: Chatham House 1993), at p. 41.

179   *See* Cates, *supra* note 173, at p. 1204.

180   *Id.* at 1205.

181 *Id.* (Specifically the according wrote that "[d]eath from illegal and legal abortions decreased pre-
     cipitously and have remained at a low level thereafter. Morbidity trends for abortion paralleled
     mortality and morbidity have occurred primarily because legal abortion is safer than other options
     available to pregnant women: illegal abortion or carrying the pregnancy to delivery. [¶] The
     increased availability of legal abortion in the United States in the 1970s also improved both the
     safety of abortion methods and the skill of physicians performing abortion methods and the skill
     of physicians performing abortions. For example, clinicians recognized the dilation and evacuation
     could terminate pregnancies at 13 weeks' gestation or later more safely than intrauterine instilla-
     tion methods, thus, the rigid trimester-threshold concept (the basis for the decisions in *Roe v. Wade*
     and *Doe v. Bolton*) became irrelevant. Physician skill improved as well. The legalization of abortion
     allowed physicians to learn different surgical techniques and to manage the complications associ-
     ated with these techniques. Improvements in anesthesia, use of more appropriate methods of dila-
     tion, less reliance on major operations for abortion, greater willingness to reevaluate a uterus in
     cases of suspected retained tissue, and expertise in managing abortion complications—all these
     factors may have plated a role.")

182 *See* Lazarus, *supra* note 174, at p. 344.

183 *Id.*

184 *See* Blank & Merrick, *supra* note 91, at p. 22.

185 *Id.*

186 *Id.*

187 *See* H. de Bracton, *The Laws and Customs of England,* III, at pp. ii, 4, (quoted in original Latin in D.
     Davis, *The Law of Abortion and Necessity,* 2 MODERN L. REV. at pp. 126, 133 (1938) (author's trans-
     lation).

188 *See* Cyril C. Means, Jr., *The Law of New York Concerning Abortion and the Status of the Feotus,
     1664–1968: A Case of Cessation of Constitutionality,* 14 NEW YORK LAW FORUM, No. 3 (Fall 1968), at
     pp. 411, 426. Early cases include: *Rex v. Enoch,* 5 Carr. & P. 539 (1833); *Rex v. Brain,* 6 Carr. & P. 349
     (1834); *Rex v. Crutchley,* 7 Carr. & P. 814 (1836); *Rex v. Sellis,* 7 Carr. & P. 850 (1836); *Reg. v. Reeves,*
     9 Carr. & P 25 (1839); *Reg. v. Wright,* 9 Carr. & P. 754 (1841); *Reg. v. Trilloe,* Carr. & M. 650 (1842).

189 *See* Eugene Quay, *Justifiable Abortion—Medical and Legal Foundations,* 49 GEO. LJ. at pp. 395, 434,
     (Spring 1961). *See also* Conn. Stat. tit. 22, Secs. 14, 16 (1821).

190 *Id.* (citing Ill. Rev. Code Sec. 46, at 131 (1827)).

191 In 1828, New York attempted to make trying to abort a quickened fetus manslaughter (N.Y. Rev.
     Stat. pt. iv, ch. I, tit. II, Secs. 8,9, at 550; N.Y. Rev. Stat. pt. IV, ch I, tit. IV, Sec. 21 at 578 (1828–1835).
     In 1834, it became a misdemeanor in Ohio to attempt an abortion on a pregnant woman unless it
     was to save her life. (Ohio Gen. Stat. Secs. 111 (1), 112 (2), at 252 (1841). In 1835, the Missouri leg-
     islature enacted a similar statute. (Mo. Rev. Stat. art. II, Sec. 10, at 168 (1835). Arkansas declared a
     "successful attempt to destroy a quick child" manslaughter in 1838. (Ark Rev. Stat. ch. 44, div. III,
     art II, Sec. 6 (1838). The territory of Iowa adopted a preexisting statute which proposed three years
     in prison for an attempt to abort by poison. (Iowa (Terr.) Stat. 1st Legis., 1st Sess., Sec. 18, at 145
     (1838–1839). Alabama adopted what would today be considered a typical abortion statute. (Ala.
     Acts ch. 6, Sec. 2 (1840–1841). Indiana was the last of this lot, waiting until 1881 to make it a felony
     to attempt abortion on a pregnant woman. But this was a revision of a 1838 statute that made such
     an act a misdemeanor.

192 Those states were: Massachusetts, New Jersey, Iowa, Alabama, and Kentucky.

193 Iowa and Alabama were those two states.

194 Those states were: Maine, Florida, Maryland, Nebraska, Ohio, Oregon, Wisconsin, Virginia, Con-
     necticut, Michigan, Texas, and the District of Columbia. However, a person could be convicted on
     assault in procuring an unlawful abortion under Oregon law. *See, e.g., State v. Farnam,* 161 P. 417
     (Or. 1916).

195 *See, e.g., People v. Axelsen,* 119 N.E. 708 (N.Y. 1918).

196 *See Williams v. State,* 182 P. 718 (Okla. Cr. App. 1919).

197 *See* Cates, *supra* note 173, at p. 1204 (citing W. Cates Jr., *Legal Abortion: The Public Health Record,*
     215 SCIENCE at pp. 1586–1590 (1982)).

198 *Id.* (citing J.R. Abernathy, B.G. Greenberg, D.G. Horvitz, *Estimates of Induced Abortion in Urban
     North Carolina,* 7 DEMOGRAPHY at pp. 19–29 (1970)).

199 *Id.* at 1205. ("The increased availability of legal abortion in the United States in the 1970s," Cates
     notes, "also improved both the safety of abortion methods and the skill of physicians performing
     abortions. For example, clinicians recognized that dilatation and evacuation could terminate preg-
     nancies at 13 weeks' gestation or later more safely than intrauterine instillation methods, thus, the
     rigid trimester-threshold concept (the basis for the decisions in *Roe v. Wade* and *Doe v. Bolton*)
     became irrelevant. Physician skill improved as well. The legalization of abortion allowed physicians
     to learn different surgical techniques and to manage the complications associated with these tech-
     niques. Improvements in anesthesia, use of more appropriate methods of dilatation, less reliance
     on major operations for abortion, greater willingness to reevacuate a uterus in cases of suspected
     retained tissue, and expertise in managing abortion complications—all these factors played a

role.") *See also* D.A. Grimes, *et al., Midtrimester Abortion by Dilatation and Evacuation: A Safe and Practical Alternative,* 296 New Eng. Journal of Med. at pp. 1141–1145, (1977).

200 *Id.* (citing A.A. Frye, H.K. Atrash, H.W. Lawson, and T. McKay, *Induced Abortion in the* at pp. 131–136, (1994)).

201 410 U.S. 113 (1973).

202 410 U.S. 179 (1973). The Court's decision in *Doe v. Bolton* was issued the same day as was the decision in *Roe v. Wade. Doe v. Bolton* involved a similar challenge to the Georgia abortion statute, which required written certification by hospital committee of the extenuating circumstances leading to the need for an abortion. By a 7-2 vote, the Justice struck down the Georgia statute as unconstitutional. The Justices voted in the same 7-2 margin in *Roe v. Wade.*

203 The child was a boy.

204 McCorvey's attorneys were Sarah Weddington and Lynda Coffee, who were recent graduates of law school. *See* Blank & Merrick, *supra* note 91, at pp. 26–27.

205 410 U.S. at 129. (The Texas statute was similar to statutes in effect in at least forty-one states across the country at the time.)

206 110 U.S. at 152.

207 *Id.* at 153 (*emphasis added*).

208 *See* F. Helminski, *Law, Medicine, and Justice Blackmun,* 68 Mayo Clin. Proc. at pp. 698–699, (1994).

209 This is similar in form to what they appear to be on their way to becoming again today.

210 *See, e.g.,* D.C.C.E. Sec. 22-201; *U.S. v. Vutich,* 305 F. Supp. 1092, *rev'd,* 402 U.S. 62 (1971).

211 *See* Ga. Code Sec. 26-1201 *et. seq.; Doe v. Bolton,* 319 F. Supp. 1048, *jurisdiction postponed,* 402 U.S. 941, *appeal dismissed,* 402 U.S. 936, and *Unborn Child of Doe v. Doe,* 410 U.S. 179, *rehearing denied,* 410 U.S. 959. (Of course, the companion case of *Roe v. Wade,* is *Doe v. Bolton,* 410 U.S. 179 (1973), in which the Court struck down the Georgia statute.)

212 *See* Blank & Merrick, *supra* note 91, at p. 37; Cates, *supra* note 173, at p. 1204.

213 *See* S.H.A. Ill. ch. 38, Sec. 23-1(b); *Doe v. Scott,* 321 F. Supp. 1385, *vac., Hanrahan v. Doe,* 410 U.S. 950 (1973).

214 *See Abele v. Markle,* 351 F. Supp. 224 (D.C. Conn. 1972).

215 *See Poe v. Menghini,* 339 F. Supp. 986 (D.C. Kan. 1972).

216 *See* Blank & Merrick, *supra* note 91, at p. 36.

217 *Id.*

218 *Id.* (citing Hinkson Craig & O'Brien, *supra* note 178, at p. 75). *See also Topics for Our Times: Justice Blackmun and Legal Abortion—a Besieged Legacy to Women's Reproductive Health,* 85 Am. J. of Pub. H'lth. No. 9 (Sept. 1995), at p. 1204; *Blackmun Bust Plan Blocked,* Nat'l L.J., April 3, 2000, at A6.

219 *See* Blank & Merrick, *supra* note 91, at p. 36.

220 *Id.*

221 *See* Cates, *supra* note 173, at p. 1204.

222 *Id.* (citing B. Woodward and S. Armstrong, The Brethren (New York: Simon & Schuster, 1979)).

223 *See supra* note 202.

224 *See* Cates, *supra* note 173, at p. 1204 (citing S.K. Henshaw, J. Van Vort, *Abortion Services in the United States 1991–1992,* 26 Family Planning Perspectives at pp. 100–106, 112 (1994)).

225 *Id.* (Council on Scientific Affairs, American Medical Association, *Induced Termination of Pregnancy Before and After Roe v. Wade: Trends in the Mortality and Morbidity of Women,* 268 JAMA at pp. 3231–3239 (1992); C. Tietze, L Bongaarts, *The Demographic Effect of Induced Abortion,* 31 Obstet. Gynecol. Surv. at pp. 699–709 (1976)).

226 *See* Thurer, *supra* note 31, Endnotes for Chapter Two, at p. 247.

227 Among the cases heard by the Court since *Roe v. Wade* are: *Connecticut v. Menillo,* 423 U.S. 9 (1975); *Planned Parenthood v. Danforth,* 428 U.S. 52 (1976); *Belotti v. Baird,* 428 U.S. 132 (1976); *Beal v. Doe,* 432 U.S. 438 (1977); *Maher v. Roe,* 432 U.S. 464 (1977); *Poelker v. Doe,* 432 U.S. 519 (1977); *Colautti v. Franklin,* 439 U.S. 379 (1979); *Harris v. McRae,* 448 U.S. 297 (1980); *Williams v. Zbaraz,* 448 U.S. 358 (1980); *H.L. v. Matheson,* 450 U.S. 398 (1981); *City of Akron v. Akron Center for Reproductive Health, Inc.,* 462 U.S. 416 (1983); *Planned Parenthood Ass'n of Kansas City, Mo., Inc. v. Ashcroft,* 462 U.S. 476 (1983); *Simpoulous v. Virginia,* 462 U.S. 506 (1983); *Thornburgh v. American College of Obstetricians and Gynecologists,* 476 U.S. 747 (1986); *Webster v. Reproductive Health Services,* 492 U.S. 490 (1989); *Hodgson v. Minnesota,* 497 U.S. 417 (1990); *Ohio v. Akron Center for Reproductive Health,* 497 U.S. 502 (1990); *Rust v. Sullivan,* 500 U.S. 173 (1991); *Planned Parenthood v. Casey,* 505 U.S. 833 (1992).

228 *See* Friedman Goldstein, *supra* note 129, Endnotes for Chapter One, at p. 360.

229 428 U.S. 52 (1976). For an overview of the controversy in newspaper clippings, *see* Abortion: The Continuing Controversy (New York: Facts on File Publications, 1984) (Carol C. Collins, ed.).

230 All nine of those points were: (1) that the Missouri statute's definition of "viability" was contrary to the holding of *Roe v. Wade;* (2) that requiring a written consent from a woman seeking an abortion was unconstitutional; (3) that requiring written spousal consent was unconstitutional; (4) that requiring an unmarried woman of less than 18 to offer parental consent forms was unconstitutional; (5) that a provision requiring that doctors "preserve" the life of a fetus was unconstitutional; (6) and (7) that provisions requiring record-keeping were burdensome to doctors; (8) that pro-

hibiting the use of saline for later-term abortions was unreasonable; and, (9) that fetuses that survived abortion become "abandoned" wards of the state. Planned Parenthood challenged the statute on behalf of its doctors and patients.

231   Those struck down as unreasonable or unconstitutional were: (1) the prohibition of saline in later-term abortions; (2) requirements that doctors take steps to preserve the life of a fetus; and, (3) in its current form, requirements that a minor female get consent.

232   Other provisions upheld including a requirement that doctors keep records of abortions. Also upheld was the "viability" standard as set forth by the state.

233   The "Hyde Amendment" was sponsored by Henry Hyde, a Republican from Illinois.

234   432 U.S. 438 (1977).

235   Title XIX is a federal program established under the Medicaid program with the participation of the states. The goal is to provide federally funded Medicaid assistance to people in need.

236   432 U.S. 464 (1977).

237   *Id.* at 466.

238   *Id.* at 471 (citing *Dandridge v. Williams*, 397 U.S. 471 (1970)).

239   432 U.S. 519, 520 (1977).

240   *Id.* at 521.

241   448 U.S. 297 (1980).

242   *Id.* at 303.

243   *Id.* at 304.

244   *Id.* at 309 (noting that "[i]n *Preterm, Inc. v. Dukakis*, 591 F.2d 121, 132 (1st Cir. 1979), the opinion of the court by Judge Coffin noted: 'The Medicaid program is one of federal and state cooperation in funding medical assistance; a complete withdrawal of the federal prop in the system with the intent to drop the total cost of providing the service upon the states, runs directly counter to the basic structure of the program and could seriously cripple a state's attempts to provide other necessary medical services embraced by its plan," (further citation omitted)).

245   *Id.* at 310.

246   448 U.S. 358 (1980).

247   *Id.* at 369.

248   As of January 1997, states enforcing the ban on federal Medicaid funding for abortions included: Alabama, Arizona, Arkansas, Colorado, Delaware, Florida, Georgia, Indiana, Iowa, Kansas, Kentucky, Louisiana, Maine, Michigan, Mississippi, Missouri, Nebraska, Nevada, New Hampshire, New Mexico, North Carolina, North Dakota, Ohio, Oklahoma, Pennsylvania, Rhode Island, South Carolina, South Dakota, Tennessee, Texas, Utah, Virginia, Wisconsin, and Wyoming.

249   *See, e.g.*, MASS. SEN. BILL 925 and MASS. HOUSE BILL 851 (2001); N.J. SEN. BILL 845, N.J. ASS. COMM. RES. 75 and N.J. ASS. BILL 772 (2000). Rhode Island and Tennessee were considering amendments to current law. *See, e.g.*, R.I. HOUSE BILL 5305 and R.I. HOUSE BILLS 5719 and 5722 (2001); TENN. SEN. BILL 32 and TENN. HOUSE BILL 531 (2001).

250   *See* Cates, Jr., *supra* note 173, at p. 1205.

251   *Id.* (citing W. Cates, Jr., *The Hyde Amendment in Action: How Did the Restriction on Federal Funds for Abortion Affect Low-Income Women?*, 246 JAMA at p. 112 (1981).

252   *Id.* (citing K.J. Meier, D.R. McFarlane, *State Family Planning and Abortion Expenditures: Their Effect on Public Health*, 84 AM. J. OF PUB. H'LTH at pp. 1468–1472 (1994).

253   *See* Lisa M. Koonin, *et al.*, *47 Abortion Surveillance 1995*, Centers for Disease Control Surveillance Summaries, MORBIDITY AND MORTALITY WEEKLY REPORT, No. SS-2 (July 3, 1998), at pp. 31–68.

254   *See* FACTS IN BRIEF, *Induced Abortion*, *supra* note 160, at p. 1.

255   *Id.*

256   *See* Jacqueline Darroch Forrest and Susheela Singh, *The Sexual and Reproductive Behavior of American Women, 1982–1988*, FAMILY PLANNING PERSPECTIVES, Sept./Oct. 1990, at p. 206.

257   *See, e.g.*, Gina Kolata, *As Abortion Rate Decreases, Clinics Compete for Patients*, N.Y. TIMES, Dec. 30, 2000, at A1.

258   *See* Koonin, *supra* note 253.

259   439 U.S. 379 (1979).

260   462 U.S. 416 (1983).

261   In support of this decision, the Court cited *Whalen v. Roe*, 429 U.S. 589, 604 n. 33 (1977).

262   462 U.S. 476 (1983). At the time of the case, John Ashcroft, a conservative Christian, was attorney general of Missouri. In 2001, following a bitterly fought presidential campaign, Ashcroft became President-Elect George Bush's choice for Attorney General of the United States. Ashcroft lost an embarrassing race to retain his Senate seat against then-deceased Governor on Missouri, Mel Canahan, whose wife was later appointed to the Senate seat. Following the designation, Ashcroft became the subject of sometimes scathing articles and editorials. *See, e.g.*, David Sanger, *Conservative for Justice Post; Whitman Chosen to Head E.P.A.*, N.Y. TIMES, Dec. 23, 2000, at A1; Anthony Lewis, *An Unfit Nominee*, N.Y. TIMES, Dec. 30, 2000, at A31; David Johnson & Neil A. Lewis, *Religious Right Made Big Push to Put Ashcroft in Justice Dept.*, N.Y. TIMES, Jan. 7, 2001, at A1; William Safire, *Gunning for Ashcroft*, N.Y. TIMES, Jan. 8, 2001, at A21; Bob Herbert, *Far, Far From the Center*, N.Y. TIMES, Jan. 8. 2001, at A21.

263   476 U.S. 747 (1986).

264   The six provisions involved: (1) informed consent; (2) dissemination of printed material detailing the harms of abortion; (3) reporting requirements for doctors; (4) viability tests of fetuses; (5) a degree of care provision for postviability; and (6) a second physician requirement.

265   492 U.S. 490 (1989).

266   505 U.S. 833 (1992).

267   Those provisions were: (1) 24-hour waiting period; (2) consent of at least one parent where a minor was concerned; (3) the signing of a form by married women indicating that they told their husbands; (4) provisions for medical emergencies in late-term abortions; and (5) reporting requirements.

268   States across the country began requiring consent waivers following the Supreme Court's decision. Even as recently as the fall of 2000, a ballot measure was proposed that, if passed into law, would require a 24-hour waiting period before a woman could actually have the abortion.

269   505 U.S. at 873.

270   *See, e.g.,* FL. HOUSE BILL 497 (2001) (amending a vehicular homicide statute to define a "viable fetus" as a fetus after the 20th week of gestation); MISS. SEN. BILL 2215 (2001) (would permit a pregnant woman to be charged with manslaughter if death of a fetus 20 weeks or older was the result of substance abuse); MONT. HOUSE BILL 547 (2001) (would create the Fetal Protection Act, which defines an "unborn child" as a human fetus conceived and more than 12 weeks old but not yet born); N.J. SEN. BILL 1397 and NEW JERSEY ASS. BILL 2558 (2000) (prohibiting doctors from performing abortions on "unborn children" of 20 weeks or more until viability tests have been performed); R.I. HOUSE BILL 5069 (2001) (provides that assaulting a pregnant woman thereby causing a miscarriage or stillbirth is punishable by 30 years imprisonment if the fetus was 12 weeks or older).

271   *See* WIS. ASS. BILL 3 (2001).

272   Delivering the opinion for the Court was Justices Douglas. Joining in total or concurring in parts were: Chief Justice Warren and Justices Clark, Goldberg, Brennan, Harlan, and White. Dissenting were Justices Black and Stewart.

273   Joining in the decision were: Justices Brennan, Douglas, Stewart, and Marshall. Concurring were Justices White and Blackun. Dissenting was Chief Justice Burger.

274   Joining or concurring with the majority decision were: Justices Blackmun, Douglas, Brennan, Stewart, Marshall, Powell, and Chief Justice Burger. Dissenting were Justices White and Rehnquist.

275   But two of those three children were in foster care at the time of the case.

276   Not surprisingly, given that it was the companion case to *Roe v. Wade*, either joining or concurring with the majority's decision in *Doe v. Bolton* were: Justices Blackmun, Douglas, Brennan, Stewart, Marshall, Powell, and Chief Justice Burger. Dissenting were Justices White and Rehnquist.

277   Joining in or concurring with the majority decision were: Justices Blackmun, Douglas, Brennan, Stewart, Marshall, Powell, and Chief Justice Burger. Dissenting were Justices Rehnquist and White.

278   The Connecticut statute specifically provided that "[a]ny person who gives or administers to any woman, or advises or causes her to take or use anything, or uses any means, with intent to procure upon her a miscarriage or abortion, unless the same is necessary to preserve her life or that of her unborn child, shall be fined not more than one thousand dollars or imprisoned in the State Prison [for] not more than five years or both."

279   The penalty for failing to do so is a criminal charge of manslaughter and potential civil damages.

280   Joining in the majority decision were: Justices Blackmun, Brennan, Stewart, Marshall, and Powell. Dissenting in all or part were: Justices Stevens (on parental consent), White, Rehnquist, and Chief Justice Burger.

281   Joining the majority or concurring were: Justices Brennan, Stewart, Marshall, and Blackmun. Specifically concurring were: Justices White, Powell, and Stevens. Dissenting were Chief Justice Burger and Justice Rehnquist.

282   In 1965, Title XIX of the Social Security Act established the federal Medicaid program, which provides federal assistance to those states that chose to reimburse medical costs for "needy" persons. Specifically, as the Court explained in *Beal v. Doe*, Title XIX "establishes the Medicaid program under which participating states may provide federally funded medical assistance to needy persons." The statute requires participating states to provide qualified individuals with financial assistance in five general categories of medical treatment. Those five categories of "needy" persons, as outlined for purposes of the Aid to Families with Dependent Children program were: (1) inpatient hospital services; (2) outpatient hospital services; (3) other laboratory and X-ray services; (4) skilled nursing facilities services, periodic screening and diagnosis of children, and family planning services; and (5) services of physicians. (*See* 42 U.S.C. Secs. 1396(a) (13)(B) (1970 ed. Supp.V); 1396d(a)(1)-(5) (1970 ed. and Supp. V). Though "[p]articipating states are not required to extend Medicaid coverage to the 'medically' needy,...Pennsylvania has chosen to do so," the Court noted. *See Beal v. Doe*, 432 U.S. at 448. "Although Title XIX does not require states to provide funding for all medical treatment falling within the five general categories, it does require that state Medicaid plans establish 'reasonable standards...for determining...the extent of medical assistance under the plan which ... are consistent with the objectives of [Title XIX]." *Id.* at 440. Thus, the question before

the Court was whether "Title XIX of the Social Security Act, as added, 79 Stat. 343, and amended, 42 U.S.C. 1396 *et seq.* (1970 ed. and Supp. V), requires states that participate in the Medicaid Assistance (Medicaid) program to fund the cost of nontherapeutic abortions.")

283 Delivering the opinion for the Court was Justice Powell. Joining were Chief Justice Burger and Justices Stewart, White, Rehnquist, and Stevens. Dissenting were Justices Brennan, Marshall, and Blackmun.

284 Delivering the opinion for the Court was Justice Powell. Joining were Chief Justice Burger and Justices Stewart, White, Rehnquist, and Stevens. Dissenting were Justices Brennan, Marshall, and Blackmun.

285 *See* 1974 Pa. Laws, Act No. 209, Pa. Stat. tit. 35, Sec. 6605(a) (Purdon 1977).

286 Justice Blackmun delivered the opinion for the Court. Joining were Justices Brennan, Stewart, Marshall, Powell, and Stevens. Dissenting were Justices White, Rehnquist, and Chief Justice Burger.

287 The specific language of the challenged provision provided that: "[i]f the mother is less than eighteen years of age and has not married, the consent of both the mother and her parents [to an abortion to be performed on the mother] is required. If one or both of the mother's parents refuse such consent, consent may be obtained by order of a judge of the superior court for good cause shown, after such hearing as he deems necessary. Such a hearing will not require the appointment of a guardian, or any person who had assumed the care and custody of the mother is sufficient. The commissioner of public health shall prescribe a written form for such consent. Such form shall be signed by the proper person or persons and given to the physician performing the abortion who shall maintain it in his permanent files." *See Belotti v. Beard,* 443 U.S. at 626–627.

288 Delivering the decision for the Court was Justice Powell. Joining him were Justices Stewart, Rehnquist, and Chief Justice Burger. Concurring were Justices Stevens, Brennan, Marshall, and Blackmun. Dissenting was Justice White.

289 According to the Court, "[s]ince September 1976, Congress has prohibited—either by an amendment to the annual appropriations bill for the Department of Health, Education, and Welfare or by a joint resolution—the use of any federal funds to reimburse the cost of abortions under the Medicaid program except under certain specified circumstances. This funding restriction is commonly known as the 'Hyde Amendment,' after its original congressional sponsor, Representative [Henry] Hyde. The current version of the Hyde Amendment, applicable for fiscal year 1980, provides:

> [N]one of the funds provided by this joint resolution shall be used to perform abortions except where the life of the mother would be endangered if the fetus were carried to term; or except for such medical procedures necessary for the victims of rape or incest when such rape or incest has been reported promptly to a law enforcement agency or public health service."

See Harris v. McRae, 448 U.S. at 303–304 (citing Pub. L. 96-123, 109, 93 Stat. 926).

290 Cora McRae, described by the Court as "a New York Medicaid resident then in the first trimester of a pregnancy that she wished to terminate," sued along with a group of similarly situated women, the New York City Health and Hospitals Corp., "a public benefit corporation that operates sixteen hospitals, twelve of which provide abortion services. On September 30, 1976, "the day on which Congress enacted the initial version of the Hyde Amendment," a series of cases were consolidated and filed in the District Court for the Eastern District of New York. The cases alleged that the Hyde Amendment "violated the First, Fourth, Fifth, and Ninth Amendments of the Constitution insofar as it limited funding of costs associated with childbirth. Although the sole named defendant was the Secretary of Health, Education, and Welfare, the District Court permitted Senators James L. Buckley and Jesse A. Helms and Representative Henry J. Hyde to intervene as defendants." *See Harris,* 448 U.S. at 304.

291 *Id.* at 301. ("The statutory question is whether Title XIX requires a state that participates in the Medicaid program to fund the cost of medically necessary abortions for which federal reimbursement is unavailable under the Hyde Amendment. The constitutional question, which arises only if Title XIX imposes no such requirement, is whether the Hyde Amendment, by denying public funding for certain medically necessary abortions, contravenes the liberty or equal protection guarantees of the Due Process Clause of the Fifth Amendment, or either of the Religious Clauses of the First Amendment.")

292 Delivering the opinion for the Court was Justice Stewart. Joining were Chief Justice Burger and Justices White, Powell, and Rehnquist. Dissenting were Justices Brennan, Marshall, Blackmun, and Stevens.

293 *See Williams v. Zbaraz,* 448 U.S. at 362 (Specifically, the Court noted that "[t]his suit was brought as a class action under 42 U.S.C. 1983 in the District Court for the Northern District of Illinois to enjoin the enforcement of an Illinois statute that prohibits state medical assistance payments for all abortions except those 'necessary for the preservation of the life of the woman seeking such treatment.' The plaintiffs were two physicians who perform medically necessary abortions for indigent women, a welfare rights organization, and Jane Doe, an indigent pregnant woman who alleged that she desired an abortion that was medically necessary, but not necessary to save her life. The defendant was the Director of the Illinois Department of Public Aid, the agency charged with administering the state's medical assistance programs. Two other physicians intervened as defendants. [¶] The plaintiffs challenged the Illinois statute on both federal statutory and constitutional grounds.

They assert, first, that Title XIX of the Social Security Act, commonly known as the 'Medicaid' Act, 42 U.S.C. [Secs.] 1396 et seq. (1976 ed. and Supp. II), requires Illinois to provide coverage in its Medicaid plan for all medically necessary abortions, whether or not the life of the pregnant woman is endangered. Second, the plaintiffs argued that the public funding by the state of medically necessary services generally, but not of certain medically necessary abortions, violated the Equal Protection Clause of the Fourteenth Amendment.")

294 Delivering the opinion for the Court was Justice Stewart. Joining were Chief Justice Burger and Justices White, Powell, and Rehnquist. Dissenting were Justices Brennan, Marshall, Blackmun, and Stevens.

295 The statute in question was Utah Code Ann. 76-7-304 (1978), which provided in pertinent part:
> To enable the physician to exercise his best medical judgment [in considering a possible abortion], he shall:
> (1) Consider all factors relevant to the well-being of the woman upon whom the abortion is to be performed including, but not limited to,
> (a) Her physical, emotional, and psychological health and safety,
> (b) Her age, and
> (c) Her familial situation.
> (2) Notify, if possible, the parents or guardian of the woman upon whom the abortion is to be performed, if she is a minor; or the husband of the woman, if she is married.

296 Chief Justice Burger delivered the opinion for the Court. Joining were Justices Stewart, White, Powell, and Rehnquist. Concurring was Justice Powell. Dissenting were Justices Marshall, Brennan, and Blackmun.

297 Justice Powell delivered the decision for the Court. Chief Justice Burger and Justices Brennan, Marshall, Blackmun, and Stevens joined. Dissenting Justices were O'Connor, White, and Rehnquist.

298 In the Court's description, "Missouri statutes require abortions after twelve weeks of pregnancy to be performed in a hospital; require a pathology report for each abortion performed; require the presence of a second physician during abortions performed after viability; and require minors to secure parental consent or consent from the Juvenile Court for an abortion." See Planned Parenthood Association of Kansas City, Missouri, Inc., et al. v. Ashcroft, 462 U.S. 476 (1983).

299 Delivering the opinion for this issue only was Justice Powell. He was joined by Justices Brennan, Marshall, Blackmun, Stevens, and Chief Justice Burger. Dissenting on this issue were Justices O'Connor, White, and Rehnquist.

300 Justice Powell delivered the opinion for the Court. He was joined by Chief Justice Burger and Justices Brennan, Marshall, Blackmun, White, Rehnquist, and O'Connor. The lone dissenter was Justice Stevens.

301 It was a fact that even the staid Justices of the United States Supreme Court seemed to notice. "The 1982 Act was not the Commonwealth's first attempt, after this Court's 1973 decision in Roe v. Wade, 410 U.S. 113, and Doe v. Bolton, 410 U.S. 179, to impose abortion restraints," the Court wrote. "The state's first post-1973 Abortion Control Act, 1974 Pa. Laws, Act No., 209, was passed in 1974 over the Governor's veto. After extensive litigation, various provisions of the 1974 statute were ruled unconstitutional, including those relating to spousal or parental consent, to the choice of procedure for a postviability abortion, and to the proscription of abortion advertisements." Thornburgh v. American College of Obstetricians and Gynecologists, 476 U.S. at 751 (citing Planned Parenthood Assn. v. Fitzpatrick, 410 F. Supp. 554 (E.D. Pa. 1975), summarily affirmed in part sub nom; Franklin v. Fitzgerald, 428 U.S. 9011 (1976), and summarily vacated in part and remanded sub nom.; Beal v. Franklin, 428 U.S. 901 (1976), modified on remand (No. 74-2440) (E.D. Pa. 1977), aff'd sub nom.; Colautti v. Franklin, 439 U.S. 379 (1979). See also Doe v. Zimmerman, 405 F. Supp. 534 (M.D. Pa. 1975)).

302 See Thornburgh, 476 U.S. at 753.

303 Justices Blackmun, Brennan, Marshall, Powell, and Stevens joined in the Court's decision. Dissenting were Chief Justice Burger, White, Rehnquist, and O'Connor.

304 According to the Court's description of the issues before it, "[i]n June 1986, the Governor of Missouri signed into law Missouri Senate Committee Substitute for House Bill No. 1596 (herein Act of statute), which amended existing state law concerning unborn children and abortions. The Act consisted of twenty provisions, five of which are now before the Court. The first provision, or preamble, contains 'findings' by the state legislature that '[t]he life of each human being begins at conception,' and that 'unborn children have protectible interests in life, health, and well-being.' Mo. Rev. Stat. 1.205.1(1), (2) (1986). The Act further requires that all Missouri laws be interpreted to provide unborn children with the same rights enjoyed by other persons, subject to the Federal Constitution and this Court's precedents. 1.205.2. Among its other provisions, the Act requires that, prior to performing an abortion on any woman whom a physician has reason to believe is twenty or more weeks pregnant, the physician must ascertain whether the fetus is viable by performing 'such medical examinations and tests as are necessary to make a finding of the gestational age, weight, and lung maturity of the unborn child.' 188.029. The Act also prohibits the use of public employees and facilities to perform or assist abortions not necessary to save the mother's life, and it prohibits the use of public funds, employees, or facilities for the purpose of 'encouraging or

counseling' a woman to have an abortion not necessary to save her life. 188.205, 188.210, 188.215." *Webster v. Reproductive Health Services*, 492 U.S. at 500.

305   Chief Justice Rehnquist delivered the opinion for the Court with concurrences by Justices White, O'Connor, Scalia, and Kennedy. Dissenting were Justices Blackmun, Brennan, Marshall, and Stevens.

306   The five Justices concurring in the majority opinion were: Justices Stevens, Brennan, Marshall, Blackmun, and O'Connor. Dissenting were Kennedy, White, Scalia, and Chief Justice Rehnquist.

307   Justice Kennedy delivered the opinion for the Court with Chief Justice Rehnquist and Justices White, Stevens, O'Connor, and Scalia joining. Dissenting were Justices Blackmun, Brennan, and Marshall.

308   *See Rust v. Sullivan*, 500 U.S. at 173.

309   Chief Justice Rehnquist delivered the opinion for the Court. Concurring were Justices White, Kennedy, Scalia, and Souter. Dissenting were Blackmun, Marshall, O'Connor, and Stevens.

310   As the Court set forth in describing the case, "[a]t issue in these cases are five provisions of the Pennsylvania Abortion Control Act of 1982, as amended in 1988 and 1989. 18 Pa. Cons. Stat. 3203-3220 (1990)....The Act requires that a woman seeking an abortion give her informed consent prior to the abortion procedure, and specifies that she be provided with certain information at least 24 hours before the abortion is performed. For a minor to obtain an abortion, the Act requires the informed consent of one of her parents, but provides for a judicial bypass option if the minor does not wish to or cannot obtain a parent's consent. Another provision of the Act requires that, unless certain exceptions apply, a married woman seeking an abortion must sign a statement indicating that she has notified her husband of her intended abortion. The Act exempts compliance with those three requirements in the event of a 'medical emergency,' which is defined in Sec. 3203 of the Act. See 18 Pa. Cons. Stat. Secs. 3203, 3205(a), 3206(a), 3209(c). In addition to the above provisions regulating the performance of abortions, the Act imposes certain reporting requirements on facilities that provide abortion services. See Secs. 3207(b), 3214(a), 3214(f)." *See Planned Parenthood of Southeastern Pennsylvania v. Casey*, 505 U.S. at 845.

311   Dissenting were Justices Blackmun, and Stevens. Joining in the Court decision were Chief Justice Rehnquist, Justices White, Scalia, and Thomas. Writing for the Court were Justices O'Connor, Kennedy, and Souter.

312   In restating the plaintiffs' cause of action, the Court wrote: "Our precedents establish that, in order to prove a private conspiracy in violation of the first clause of 1985(3), a plaintiff must show, *inter alia*, (1) that 'some racial, or perhaps otherwise class-based, invidiously discriminatory animus [lay] behind the conspirators' action,' *Griffin v. Brenkenridge*, 403 U.S. 88, 102 (1971), and (2) that the conspiracy 'aimed at interfering with rights' that are 'protected against private, as well as official, encroachment,' *Carpenters v. Scott*, 463 U.S. 825, 833 (1983). We think neither showing has been made in the present case." *See Bray v. Alexandria Clinic*, 506 U.S. at 268.

313   Delivering the decision for the Court was Justice Scalia. Joining were Chief Justice Rehnquist and Justices White, Kennedy, and Thomas. Dissenting were Justices Souter, Stevens, Blackmun, and O'Connor.

314   Chief Justice Rehnquist delivered the decision for a unanimous Court.

315   The Court's decision was delivered by Chief Justice Rehnquist and joined by Justices Blackmun, O'Connor, Souter, and Ginsburg. Dissenters included Justices Stevens, Scalia, Kennedy, and Thomas.

316   Chief Justice Rehnquist delivered the opinion for the Court, which was unanimous in Part I with seven other Justices joining for the remaining issues. Those Justices were Stevens, O'Connor, Scalia, Kennedy, Souter, Thomas, and Ginsburg. Justice Breyer dissented in part.

317   Justice Breyer delivered the opinion for the Court. Joining in it were Justices Stevens, O'Connor, Souter, and Ginsburg. Dissenting were Chief Justice Rehnquist and Justices Scalia, Kennedy, and Thomas.

318   Delivering the decision for the Court was Justice Stevens. He was joined in the decision by Chief Justice Rehnquist and Justices O'Connor, Souter, Ginsburg, and Breyer. Dissenting were Justices Scalia, Thomas, and Kennedy.

319   *See Teenage Pregnancy, supra* note 122.

320   *See* FACTS IN BRIEF, *Contraceptive Use*, published by the ALAN GUTTMACHER INSTITUTE (1998), at p. 2. (According to the Guttmacher Institute, "[o]f the 2.7 million teenage women who use contraceptives, 44 percent—more than 1 million women—rely on the pill." [¶] More than one-third (37 percent) of teenage women using contraceptives choose condoms as their primary method. Condom use declines as women grow older and marry." In addition, "[t]he proportion of female contraceptive users relying on condoms increased between 1988 and 1995—from 15 percent to 20 percent among all women, from 20 percent to 30 percent among never-married women and from 33 percent to 37 percent among adolescents.")

321   *See, e.g.,* Tamar Levin, *Cut Down on Out-of-Wedlock Births, Win Cash*, N.Y. TIMES, Sept. 24, 2000, at 5; *Pregnancies Down Among Teens*, CHI. SUN-TIMES, July 14, 2000, at 31; *Teens Rally to Promote Abstinence*, CHI. SUN-TIMES, July 20, 2000, at 13.

322   *See* Darroch Forrest and Singh, *supra* note 256, at p. 206.

323   *See* FACTS IN BRIEF, *Teen Sex and Pregnancy*, published by the ALAN GUTTMACHER INSTITUTE (1999),
        at p. 2. Some researchers, however, put that number at roughly 880,000 in 1996. *See Teenage Preg-
        nancy, supra* note 122, at p. 1.
324   *See* Samantha Rice, *Nine Months of Secrecy*, TEEN, Dec. 1998, at p. 66.
325   *See* Atrash *et. al, supra* note 175, at pp. 58–69.
326   *See Teen Sex and Pregnancy, supra* note 323, at p. 2.
327   As of January 1997, twenty-nine states had adopted and/or were enforcing parental consent, noti-
        fication, or involvement statutes where the abortion of a minor was involved.
328   *See Teen Sex and Pregnancy, supra* note 323, at p. 2.
329   *Id.*
330   428 U.S. 52, 74–75 (1976).
331   To support this argument, attorneys for the State of Missouri cited *Prince v. Massachusetts*, 321 U.S.
        158 (1994), and *McKeiver v. Pennsylvania*, 403 U.S. 528 (1971).
332   Among those laws cited for the Court were "statutes relating to a *guardian ad litem* for a court pro-
        ceeding, to the care of delinquent and neglected children, to child labor, and to compulsory edu-
        cation," the Court noted. *Danforth*, 428 U.S. at 72.
333   *Id.* at 72–73.
334   *Id.* (the Court noted citation by the State of Missouri of *Meyer v. Nebraska*, 262 U.S. 390 (1923);
        Pierce v. Society of Sisters, 268 U.S. 510 (1925); *Wisconsin v. Yoder*, 406 U.S. 205 (1972)).
335   428 U.S. 52, 74–75 (1976).
336   *Id.* at 75 (citing *Breed v. Jones*, 421 U.S. 519 (1975); *Goss v. Lopez*, 419 U.S. 565 (1975); *Tinker v. Des
        Moines School Dist.*, 393 U.S. 503 (1969); *In re Gault*, 387 U.S. 1 (1967)).
337   *Id.* (citing *Prince v. Massachusetts*, 321 U.S. 158, 170 (1944); *Ginsberg v. New York*, 390 U.S. 629
        (1968)).
338   *Id.*
339   *Id.* at 75.
340   *Planned Parenthood v. Danforth*, 428 U.S. at 74.
341   *See Ohio v. Akron Center for Reproductive Health, Inc.*, 497 U.S. 502 (1990).
342   *Bellotti v. Baird*, 443 U.S. 622 (1979).
343   *Id.* at 627 (citing *Baird v. Bellotti*, 393 F. Supp. 847, 850 (Mass. 1975)). The procedural history of the
        case is a little complex. Originally filed in the District Court, following an appeal, the Massachu-
        setts Supreme Judicial Court should have sustained and certified several questions on the meaning
        of the statute. On remand, the District Court certified several questions to the Supreme Judicial
        Court. Among them, according to the United States Supreme Court's description was "whether the
        statute permits any minors—mature or immature—to obtain judicial consent to an abortion with-
        out any parental consultation whatsoever. The Supreme Judicial Court answered that, in general, it
        does not; that consent must be obtained for every nonemergency abortion unless no parent is
        available; and that an available parent must be given notice of any judicial proceedings brought by
        a minor to obtain consent for an abortion. Another question certified was whether, if the superior
        court finds that the minor is capable of making, and has, in fact, made and adhered to, an informed
        and reasonable decision to have an abortion, the court may refuse its consent on a finding that a
        parent's, or its own, contrary decision is a better one. The Supreme Judicial Court answered in the
        affirmative. Following the Supreme Judicial Court's judgment, the District Court again declared
        the statute unconstitutional and enjoined its enforcement." *Id.* at 622. The United States Supreme
        Court affirmed this ruling.
344   Specifically, Mass. Gen. Laws Ann., ch. 112, 12S (West Supp. 1979) provided in part: "If the mother
        is less than eighteen years of age and has not married, the consent of both the mother and her par-
        ents [to an abortion to be performed on the mother] is required. If one or both of the mother's
        parents refuse such consent, consent may be obtained by order of a judge of the superior court for
        good cause shown, after such hearing as he deems necessary. Such a hearing will not require the
        appointment of a guardian for the mother. If one of the parents has died or has deserted his or her
        family, consent by the remaining parent is sufficient. If both parents have died or have deserted
        their family, consent of the mother's guardian or other persons having duties similar to a guardian,
        or any person who had assumed the care and custody of the mother is sufficient. The commission
        of public health shall prescribe a written form for such consent. Such form shall be signed by the
        proper person or persons and given to the physician performing the abortion who shall maintain
        it in his permanent files."
345   443 U.S. at 641.
346   *Id.* at 651, n. 23. ("The nature of both the state's interest in fostering parental authority and the
        problem of determining 'maturity' makes clear why the state generally may resort to objective,
        though inevitably arbitrary, criteria such as age limits, marital status, or membership in the Armed
        Forces for lifting some or all of the legal disabilities of minority. Not only is it difficult to define, let
        alone determine, maturity, but also the fact that a minor may be very much an adult in some
        respects does not mean that his or her need and opportunity for growth under parental guidance
        and discipline have ended. As discussed in the text, however, the peculiar nature of the abortion

decision requires the opportunity for case-by-case evaluations of the maturity of pregnant minors.")

347   *Id*. (citing *Id*. at 642–643).

348   *Id*.

349   *Id*. at 652.

350   450 U.S. 398 (1981).

351   *See supra* note 295.

352   450 U.S. at 401.

353   *Id*. at 413–414 (citing *Harris v. McRae*, 448 U.S. at 325; *accord, Maher v. Roe*, 432 U.S. at 473–474).

354   *See* Ohio Rev. Code Ann. Sec. 2919.12 (1987), creating Secs. 2151.85 and 2505.073 (Supp. 1988) *See also* Sec. 2919.12(B); Sec. 2919(D) (providing that the first offense would be a misdemeanor with the subsequent offenses becoming felonies); and, Sec. 2919.12 (E)(imposing civil liabilities).

355   *See Ohio v. Akron Center*, 497 U.S. 502, 507 (1990). (As described by the Justices of the United States Supreme Court, "[t]he first and second circumstances in which a physician may perform an abortion relate to parental notice and consent. First, a physician may perform an abortion if he provides 'at least twenty-four hours actual notice, in person or by telephone,' to one of the woman's parents (or her guardian or custodian) of his intention to perform the abortion. [See Sec.] 2919.12(B)(1)(a)(i). The physician, as an alternative, may notify a minor's adult brother, sister, stepparent, or grandparent, if the minor and the other relative each file an affidavit in the juvenile court stating that the minor fears physical, sexual, or severe emotional abuse for one of her parents. [See Secs.] 2919.12(B)(1)(a)(i), 2919.12(B)(1)(b), 2919.12(B)(1)(c). If the physician cannot give the notice 'after a reasonable effort,' he may perform the abortion after 'at least forty-eight hours constructive notice,' by both ordinary and certified mail. [*See* Sec.] 2919.12(B)(2). Second, a physician may perform an abortion on the minor if one of her parents (or her guardian or custodian) has consented to the abortion in writing. [See Sec.] 2919.12(B)(1)(a)(ii).")

356   *Id*. at 508–509. (As described by the Court, "[t]he third and fourth circumstances depend on a judicial procedure that allows a minor to bypass the notice and consent provisions just described. The statute allows a physician to perform an abortion without notifying one of the minor's parents or receiving the parent's consent if a juvenile court issues an order authorizing the minor to consent, [See Sec.] 2919.12 (B)(1)(a)(iii), or if a juvenile court or court of appeals, by its inaction, provides constructive authorization for the minor to consent, [See Sec.] 2919.12(B)(1)(a)(iv). [¶] The bypass procedure requires the minor to file a complaint in the juvenile court, stating (1) that she is pregnant; (2) that she is unmarried, under 18 years of age, and unemancipated; (3) that she desires to have an abortion without notifying one of her parents; (4) that she has sufficient maturity and information to make an intelligent decision whether to have an abortion without such notice, or that one of her parents has engaged in a pattern of physical, sexual, or emotional abuse against her, or that notice is not in her best interests; and (5) that she has or has not retained an attorney. [See Sec.] 2151.85(A)(1)(5). The Ohio Supreme Court, as discussed below, has prescribed pleading forms for the minor to use. [¶] The juvenile court must hold a hearing at the earliest possible time, but not later than the fifth business day after the minor files the complaint. [See Sec.] 2151.85(B)(1). The court must render its decision immediately after the conclusion of the hearing. Failure to hold the hearing within this time results in constructive authorization for the minor to consent to the abortion. At the hearing, the court must appoint a *guardian ad litem* and an attorney to represent the minor if she has not retained her own counsel. [See Sec.] 2151.85(B)(2). The minor must prove her allegation of maturity, pattern of abuse, or best interests by clear and convincing evidence, [See Sec.] 2151.85(C), and the juvenile court must conduct the hearing to preserve the anonymity of the complainant, keeping all papers confidential. [See Sec.] 2151.85(D), (F). [¶] The minor has the right to expedited review. The statute provides that, within four days after the minor files a notice of appeal, the clerk of the juvenile court shall deliver the notice of appeal and record to the state court of appeals. [See Sec.] 2505.073(A). The clerk of the court of appeals dockets the appeal upon receipt of these items. The minor must file her brief within four days after the docketing. If she desires an oral argument, the court of appeals must hold one within five days after the docketing and must issue a decision immediately after oral argument. If she waives the right to an oral argument, the court of appeals must issue a decision within five days after the docketing. If the court of appeals does not comply with these time limits, a constructive order results, authorizing the minor to consent to the abortion.")

357   *See Akron Center for Reproductive Health v. Rosen*, 633 F. Supp. 1123 (1986).

358   *See Akron Center for Reproductive Health v. Slaby*, 854 F.2d 852 (1988); 492 U.S. 916 (1989).

359   497 U.S 502 (1990).

360   *Id*. at 510 (citing *Planned Parenthood of Central Mo. v. Danforth*, 428 U.S. 52 (1976); *Bellotti v. Baird*, 443 U.S. 622 (1979); *H.L. v. Matheson*, 450 U.S. 398 (1981); *Planned Parenthood Assn. v. Kansas City. Mo., Inc. v. Ashcroft*, 462 U.S. 476 (1983); *City of Akron v. Akron Center for Reproductive Health, Inc.*, 462 U.S. 416 (1983)).

361   *Id*.

362   *Id*. at 520.

363   428 U.S. 52, 74–75 (1976).

364   497 U.S at 520.
365   497 U.S. 417 (1990).
366   *Id.* at 424 n. 3 (The Court noted that "[a]lthough there is no statutory definition of emancipation in Minnesota, *see Streitz v. Streitz,* 363 N.W.2d 135, 137 (Minn. App. 1985), we have no reason to question the state's representation that Minn. Stat. 144.341 and 144.342 (1988) apply to the minor's decision to terminate her pregnancy....Those sections provide that a minor who is living separate and apart from her parents or who is either married or has borne a child may give effective consent to medical services without the consent of any other person.")
367   *Id.* n. 4. (The Court explains that Subdivision 2 provides:
Notwithstanding the provisions of section 13.02, subdivision 8, no abortion operation shall be performed upon an unemancipated minor...until at least 48 hours after written notice of the pending operation has been delivered in the manner specified in subdivisions 2 to 40.
(2) The notice shall be addressed to the parent at the usual place of abode of the parent and delivered personally to the parent by the physician or an agent.
(3) In lieu of the delivery required by clause (a), notice shall be made by certified mail addressed to the parent at the usual place of abode of the parent with return receipt requested and restricted delivery to the addresses, which means postal employee can only deliver the mail to the authorized addresses. Time of delivery shall be deemed to occur at 12 o'clock noon on the next day on which regular mail delivery takes place, subsequent to mailing.)
368   *Id.* at 424.
369   *See, e.g.,* HAW. SEN. BILLS 7, 47, 746, 809, and HAW. HOUSE BILLS 454 and 895 (2001); KAN. HOUSE BILL 2419 and KAN. HOUSE BILL 2517 (2001); MD. SEN. BILL 643 (2001); MASS. HOUSE BILL 848 (2001); MONT. SEN. BILL 416 and MONT. SEN. BILL 417 (2001); NEB. LEG. BILL 340 (2001); N.J. SEN. BILL 1352, N.J. SEN. COMM. RES. 86 and N.J. ASS. COMM. RES. 2 (2000); N.M. SEN. BILL 298 and N.M. HOUSE BILL 372 (2001); OK. SEN. BILL 59, OK. SEN. BILL 720, OK. SEN. BILL 740, OK. SEN. BILL 760, and OK. SEN. BILL 1032 (2001); OR. HOUSE BILL 2071 (2001); R.I. BILL 5620 (2001); VT. HOUSE BILL 218 (2001); WASH. SEN. BILL 5985 and WASH. HOUSE BILL 1928 (2001).
370   *See Teen Sex and Pregnancy, supra* note 323, at p. 2.
371   *Id.*
372   *Id.*
373   *Id.*
374   *Id.* (In addition, roughly one in every five infants born to unmarried minor females are fathered by men five or more years older than the teenage mothers.)
375   Stanley Henshaw was then deputy director of research for the ALAN GUTTMACHER INSTITUTE in New York.
376   *See* Stanley K. Henshaw, *The Impact of Requirement for Parental Consent on Minors' Abortions in Mississippi,* 27 FAMILY PLANNING PERSPECTIVES No. 3 (May/June 1995), at pp. 120–121.
377   Ros-Lehtinen is a Republican from Florida.
378   *See* Rebekah Saul, *The Child Custody Protection Act: A 'Minor' Issue at the Top Of the Antiabortion Agenda, Issues & Implications,* THE GUTTMACHER REPORT ON PUBLIC POLICY, August 1998, at p. 1.
379   The Act was reintroduced earlier this year and is currently pending.
380   *Anti-abortion Bill Stalled,* CHI. SUN-TIMES, September 23, 1998, at p. 42.
381   Former Illinois Governor George Ryan reportedly considered stoking the flames for passage of such a law, for example, in an effort to "slow the tide of underage, out-of-state girls coming [to Illinois] for abortions" in July 2000. *See, e.g.,* Dave McKinney, *Ryan Makes New Push for Abortion Consent Law,* CHI. SUN-TIMES, July 22, 2000, at 5. In May 1999, then New Jersey Governor Christine Todd Whitman endorsed a measure requiring parental notification for teenagers seeking abortions. *See* Jerry Gray, *A New Political Strategy is Energizing Opponents of Abortion,* N.Y. TIMES, May 24, 1999, at A27.

CHAPTER SIX

The 1960s and an Era of Change

WOMEN, WORK, AND THE QUESTION OF EQUALITY:
The Struggle to Find a Balance

It is true, as the Justices noted in *Goesaert v. Cleary Liquor Control Commission of Michigan*[1] that the Fourteenth Amendment does not "tear up history by the roots." Nor does it require state, local, or federal authorities to strain the law's reach in service of "political correctness," as conservatives have been wont to argue of late. But as society changes, so usually does the law. Not as quickly, perhaps, as some would like. But change it does. And American society was stretching in extraordinary ways during the 1960s.

Women continued to make their way into the American workforce, for example, until by the start of the 1960s, some 40 percent of all employees in the United States were women.[2] And yet this increase involved more, some argue, than merely an increased desire to work on the part of women.

"Women's work, long an outlet for the lower classes, suddenly became a middle-class pursuit," journalist Marci McDonald suggests,[3] which may explain why their numbers continued to grow until "nearly two-thirds of all married women with children were in the labor force" by the start of the 1990s, according to *U.S.News & World News Report*.[4]

It was also during the 1960s that long-accepted racist and discriminatory practices began to bend under the weight of a sustained Civil Rights movement that actually began to rock the nation a half-decade before, even as—or perhaps because—Ward and June were being touted as the template for American life and family. There was another side to the picture, and the world was about to get a shameful glimpse.

For most of the first half of the twentieth century, the lives of whites and "coloreds" were separate, often by law. They used separate bathrooms and drinking fountains. They walked through separate entrances and exits. Whites were allowed to sit in the front of the bus, while "coloreds" were assigned to seats in the back. They lived in separate neighborhoods and their children went to separate schools.

But that all changed in 1954, when the United States Supreme Court declared with its decision in *Brown v. Board of Education*[5] that state constitutional or statutory provisions mandating segregation in public schools on the basis of race were violative of the Equal Protection Clause of the United States Constitution. And with that, the shaking began.

With desegregation and issues of racial equality pushing the national agenda and a burgeoning Civil Rights movement gaining momentum, in a bow to public pressure, Congress passed the Civil Rights Act of 1957. It was by all accounts a pyrrhic victory and the end of a cynical political power play.

"President Eisenhower was not an enthusiastic supporter of desegregation," argues Georgetown University Professor of Law Mark Tushnet, "but his Attorney General Herbert Brownell came to believe that excluding African Americans from voting was deeply wrong and, incidentally, that the Republican Party could gain some political advantage from sponsoring legislation aimed at securing the right to vote."[6]

But there were other motives at work as well.

"In the Senate, Democratic majority leader Lyndon Johnson planned to seek the party's nomination for president in 1960 and knew he had to demonstrate that he supported civil rights," Tushnet explains further. "The interests of the administration and Johnson converged to produce the Civil Rights Act in 1957, after a protracted struggle against segregationists in the Senate."[7]

But in last minute deals, proponents of the Act "were forced to omit provisions that civil rights advocates regarded as most important, especially one that would have authorized the Justice Department to enforce all constitutional rights…," says Tushnet.[8] The result was an Act full of declarations and mandates with few real means of enforcing them, civil rights activists complained. And with such a large potential voting block at stake, their cries were heard.

In 1963, then-President John F. Kennedy proposed an updated version of the Act, in which he reintroduced many of the far-reaching provisions so determinedly stripped from the 1957 version. Following President Kennedy's assassination, President Lyndon Johnson took up the cause, famously twisting arms in a bid to ensure passage of an even stronger third version of the Act.

But segregationist and political opposition was vehement for all of the "right" and "rational" reasons. In voting against the Civil Rights Act of 1964,[9] Barry Goldwater somewhat famously declared, for example, that "[t]he problem of discrimination cannot be cured by laws alone."[10] And yet, the Civil Rights Act, which was finally signed into law by President Johnson on July 2, 1964, after one of "the longest filibusters in history," according to journalist Sara Ann Friedman,[11] is generally viewed today as "a principal cause of black progress" during the 1960s, narrowing the earnings gap specifically between "blacks and whites" until the mid-1970s.[12]

Far-reaching in scope, the Civil Rights Act of 1964 was intended to end discrimination based upon "race, color, religion, or national origin."[13] Title I of the Act, for example, removed obstructive voter registration requirements, while Title II prohibits discrimination or apartheid-like segregation in public accommodations, particularly those involved in interstate commerce.[14] Discrimination in the "equal utilization of any public facility" is prohibited by Title III.[15]

The desegregation of public schools was mandated under Title IV.[16] Title V expanded federal authority to reach financial assistance and loan programs,[17] while Title VI prohibits racial discrimination in any program receiving governmental assistance.[18] Finally, Title VII prohibits discrimination in employment, where the employer has fifteen or more workers, based upon "race, color, religion, *sex*, or national origin."[19] This language, which is broad in tone and is reflected throughout the statute, has proved an important tool in advancing the economic and social progress of minorities and women since its passage forty years ago.

MODERN EQUATIONS OF WOMEN AT WORK:
After the Civil Rights Act of 1964

Proposed at a time when southern senators like Richard Russell of Georgia were arguing vehemently that "mongrelization" would be the ruin of the American nation,[20] "Title VII...was skillfully steered to passage by a handful of determined women activists, and has since become one of the best-used pieces of legislation" in history, "accounting for thousands of lawsuits and many millions of dollars of awarded damages," argues Friedman.[21]

Especially for women. Like minorities, who faced discrimination based upon race prior to passage of the Act, working women lived with systematic discrimination based upon gender that was so widely accepted that women came to understand it as the natural course of things.

"If you were a school teacher in Texas, you could be told you had to quit if you got pregnant, or you'd be fired," attorney Sarah Weddington recently said, recalling the 1960s.[22] As a young lawyer, Weddington would argue the groundbreaking *Roe v. Wade* case before the United States Supreme Court.

But with more and more women entering the workforce, preventing and punishing discrimination became part of the national debate. Though federal law clearly defines "gender discrimination" as discrimination "because of sex" today, despite the passage of the Civil Rights Act of 1964 and Title VII, it wasn't until the early 1970s that claims of "pregnancy discrimination" began making their way into the courts.

Some of these challenges were brought under the newly-enacted Title VII. But many others were grounded in reliance upon more traditional constitutional approaches, often in the form of the due process or equal protection challenges, leaving it up to the Justices of the United States Supreme Court to bring the two together, a coupling that would matter a great deal to women.

"PREGNANCY DISCRIMINATION" AND THE CONSTITUTION:
Does the Equal Protection Clause Apply?

Prior to the 1970s, laws permitting discrimination or preference of gender were common and often upheld by the courts. But in 1971, with the Supreme Court decision in *Reed v. Reed*,[23] the Equal Protection and Due Process Clauses of the Fourteenth Amendment began to reach some of the potential women's rights groups had always hoped for. *Reed v. Reed* involved a challenge to an Idaho statute declaring that where equal candidates sought to serve as administrator of an estate, "males must be preferred to females...."

After Richard Lynn Reed died, his mother, Sally Reed, and his father, Cecil Reed, sought separately to serve as administrator of his estate. A probate judge appointed Cecil Reed, the deceased's father, citing the statute. Sally Reed appealed, arguing that the statute was discriminatory and a violation of the Equal Protection Clause.

In simplest terms, the touchstone of the Equal Protection Clause is equality under the law. But the question regarding this and other constitutional amendments has always been interpretation. And during the latter part of the last half century, constitutional law—as created by the United States Supreme Court—has begun to "reflect sociological insights" and "shifting social standards" of the time.

That appears to have been the case in *Reed v. Reed*, in which the Justices held—in striking down the Idaho statute—that "[t]he Equal Protection Clause of [the Fourteenth Amendment] does...deny the states the power to legislate that different treatment be accorded to persons placed by statute into different classes on the basis of criteria wholly unrelated to the objective of that statute."[24]

Although the ruling in *Reed v. Reed* was specific to an Idaho statute, it was part of a larger trend. With its decisions on birth control in the 1960s, the Supreme Court had resurrected the dormant "substantive due process" approach to interpreting the Constitution. With a greater set of choices and greater personal freedoms, women were more actively involved in society than ever before. Could it really be, then, that at a time when more women were working than ever before, states could still lawfully articulate preferences in gender?

Reed v. Reed seemed to settle the question: statutes articulating gender preferences were not reasonably related to the goals of the statute and were, therefore, vulnerable. And when state statutes fall, private industry and federal and state agencies tend to fall in line. After *Reed v. Reed*, states could no longer deny women jobs or equal opportunities based solely on their gender.

GEDULDIG v. AIELLO

And that is what Justices Brennan, Douglas, and Marshall held the rule of *Reed v. Reed* to mean in their 1974 dissenting opinion in *Geduldig v. Aiello,* a case involving an Equal Protection challenge to a 30-year-old California disability insurance program's exclusion from coverage of pregnancy and pregnancy-related conditions and complications.[26]

"In the past, when a legislative classification has turned on gender, the Court has justifiably applied a standard of judicial scrutiny more strict that generally accorded economic or social welfare programs," the dissenting Justices wrote in *Geduldig v. Aiello,*[27] comparing the Supreme Court decisions in *Reed v. Reed*[28] and *Frontiero v. Richardson*[29] to the Court's decisions in *Dandridge v. Williams*[30] and *Jefferson v. Hackney.*[31]

But this was the view of the dissenting Justices. The majority in *Geduldig v. Aiello* had a different idea rooted in a greater history. Five months before the decision in *Geduldig,* the Court struck down two maternity leave policies mandating the removal of pregnant teachers from the classroom when they reached a certain month whether or not they were able to continue teaching in a case called *Cleveland Board of Education v. LaFleur,*[32] holding that the policy created the irrebuttable presumption that pregnant women were not able to continue work in violation of the Due Process Clause on the United States Constitution.[33]

At the time, *Cleveland Board of Education v. LaFleur* seemed another promising victory for women as these historic amendments seemed likely, in light of recent events, to begin to reach new antidiscriminatory applications.[34] But five months later, with the ruling in *Geduldig v. Aiello,*[35] the Court would seem to dash these hopes.

Carolyn Aiello, Augustina Armendariz, Elizabeth Johnson, and Jacqueline Jaramillo were the named plaintiffs in *Geduldig v. Aiello.* Geduldig was the director of the California Department of Human Resources Development. As a case, *Geduldig v. Aiello* was significant because it would set the stage for a showdown that would pave the way for the promulgation of the Pregnancy Discrimination Act. And just what happened in *Geduldig v. Aiello* to bring all of this about? Carolyn Aiello, Augustina Armendariz, Elizabeth Johnson, and Jacqueline Jaramillo got pregnant. And when they were denied benefits, they decided to fight.

At issue before the United States Supreme Court was a California statute authorizing payment of disability benefits to "persons in private employment who are temporarily unable to work because of disability not covered by workmen's compensation."[36] The California disability program was funded entirely by employee contributions unless the employees opted out of the fund in favor of a private plan approved by the state. In exchange for contributions, an employee was "insured against the risk of disability from a substantial number of 'mental or physical illness[es] and mental or physical injur[ies].'"[37]

Aiello and the three other plaintiffs paid into the fund and would later argue that they should be eligible to collect benefits under the disability program. Each was pregnant, and although Jaramillo argued that her pregnancy was in and of itself a disability, Aiello, Armendariz, and Johnson each reportedly experienced "abnormal complications."[38] Those complications, the women argued, rendered them "disabled" within the meaning of Section 2626 of the California Unemployment Insurance Code, which provides in pertinent part:

> *"Disability" or "disabled" includes both mental or physical illness and mental physical injury. An individual shall be deemed disabled on any day in which, because of his physical or mental condition, he is unable to perform his regular or customary work. In no case shall the term "disability" or "disabled" include any injury or illness caused by or arising in connection with pregnancy up to the termination of such pregnancy and for a period of 28 days thereafter.*[39]

Because the plaintiffs sought to enjoin enforcement of the statute on the basis of discrimination, a three-judge district court was convened to hear the case.[40] By divided vote, the court held that Section 2626 violated the Equal Protection Clause of the United States Constitution.[41] But California officials appealed to the United States Supreme Court. The Court granted *certiorari*, which essentially means it agreed to review the issues in the case. And although the case was before a federal court, the Justices apparently felt compelled to consider the decision by the California Court of Appeals in *Rentzer v. Unemployment Insurance Appeals Board*[42] handed down just ten days before the three-judge panel's decision.

The claim in *Rentzer* was brought by a woman who, like Aiello, Armendariz, and Johnson, suffered "abnormal complications" to a pregnancy. Hers was an ectopic pregnancy.[43] According to the California appellate court, Section 2626 did not foreclose the dispersal of benefits where a "disability" arises from medical complications to a pregnancy.[44] The Justices of the United States Supreme Court saw it differently.

Declaring that a "limited construction" should be given to the California appellate court's decision in *Rentzer*,[45] the Justices began disposition of the issues in *Geduldig* by noting that the complaints filed on behalf of Aiello, Johnson, and Armendariz were moot, because the three women were ultimately deemed eligible for benefits (though on the grounds other than pregnancy). Thus, only Jaramillo's claim remained before the Court.

And in the Court's view of the facts, the issue regarding Jaramillo's claim was "whether the California disability insurance program invidiously discriminates against Jaramillo and others similarly situated by not paying insurance benefits for disability that accompanies normal pregnancy and childbirth."[46] But this seemed merely to have been a preliminary statement of the issue.

In restating the ultimate question, Justice Stewart concluded, in writing for the Court, that "[t]he essential issue…is whether the Equal Protection Clause requires [policies like the California code] to be sacrificed or compromised in order to finance the payment of benefits to those whose disability is attributable to normal pregnancy and delivery."[47]

In analyzing Jaramillo's claim in this light, Justice Stewart seemed almost to set the stage for what would come, declaring that "[i]t is not every disabling condition...that triggers the obligation to pay benefits under the program. As already noted, for example, any disability of less than eight days' duration is not compensable, except when the employee is hospitalized. Conversely, no benefits are payable for any single disability beyond 26 weeks. Further, a disability is not compensable if it results from the individual's court commitment as a dipsomaniac, drug addict, or sexual psychopath. Finally, Sec. 2626 of the Unemployment Insurance Code excludes from coverage certain disabilities that are attributable to pregnancy. It is this provision that is at issue in the present case."[48]

The Supreme Court held that the exclusion of normal pregnancies from coverage under the California Code did not amount to invidious discrimination in violation of the Equal Protection Clause.[49] "The classification challenged in this case relates to the asserted underinclusiveness of the set of risks that the state has selected to insure," Stewart wrote.[50]

"Although California has created a program to insure most risks of employment disability, it has not chosen to insure *all* such risks, and this decision is reflected in the level of annual contribution exacted from participating employees. This Court has held that consistently with the Equal Protection Clause, a state 'may take one step at a time, addressing itself to the phase of the problem which seems most acute to the legislative mind....The legislature may select one phase of one field and apply a remedy there, neglecting the others...'[51] Particularly with respect to social welfare programs, so long as the line drawn by the state is rationally supportable, the courts will not interpose their judgment as to the appropriate stopping point. '[T]he Equal Protection Clause does not require that a state must choose between attacking every aspect of a problem or not attacking the problem at all.'"[52]

The decision riled the dissenting Justices, who argued that "by its decision...the [majority of the] Court appears willing to abandon that higher standard of review without satisfactorily explaining what differentiates the gender-based classifications employed in this case from those found unconstitutional in *Reed* and *Frontiero*."

Then, in even harsher language, the dissenters argued that "[t]he [majority's] decision threatens to return men and women to a time when 'traditional' equal protection analysis sustained legislative classifications that treated differently members of a particular sex solely because of their sex."[53] Whether or not it really could, the rebuff was enough to spur women's groups into action.

TITLE VII OF THE CIVIL RIGHTS ACT OF 1964
And the Evolution of the Pregnancy Discrimination Act

> "There is employment discrimination whenever an employee's pregnancy
> is a motivating factor for the employer's adverse employment decision."
> —3rd Circuit Court of Appeals, *In re Carnegie Center Associates*[54]

Gender discrimination, or discrimination based upon "sex," has long been part of the American legal system. But it wasn't until the late 1960s and early 1970s, with the great influx of women into the workplace that "pregnancy discrimination" cases began making their way into the courts. With the apparent uncertainty of a constitutional challenge, women began looking for another possible tool in the war for workplace equality.

The sweeping language of Section 703(a)(2) of Title VII of the Civil Rights Act of 1964 seemed to fit the bill. Generally administered by the Equal Employment Opportunities Commission,[55] Title VII expressly prohibits discrimination "against any individual with respect to [her] compensation, terms, conditions, or privileges of employment, because of such individual's race, color, religion, sex, or national origin."[56] The statute covers most employers[57] and it establishes an administrative and procedural structure for dealing with complaints.[58]

In one of the earliest cases involving a claim brought under Title VII, the United States Supreme Court would reverse a decision by the Fifth Circuit in the 1971 case of *Phillips v. Martin Marietta Corp.*,[59] deeming it unlawful for an employer to deny a woman a job because she had small children. "Section 703(a) of the Civil Rights Act of 1964 requires that persons of like qualifications be given employment opportunities irrespective of their sex," the Justices wrote.[60]

Spurred on by victory, perhaps, women continued to challenge the *status quo* in court. In 1976, for example, the Court handed down its ruling in *General Electric Co. v Gilbert*,[61] a case involving a class action lawsuit brought on behalf of a group of female employees at the company's Salem, Virginia, plant. The women sought a judgment declaring an exclusion within the company's disability policy—similar to the provision upheld by the Court in *Geduldig v. Aiello*—discriminatory on the basis of sex and, thus, a violation of Section 703 of Title VII of the Civil Rights Act.[62]

With *Geduldig v. Aiello* as one of the Court's most recent precedents in the area many assumed the complaint in *General Electric Co. v. Gilbert* would be summarily dismissed. But some argued that there was reason to hope. After all, there was a difference between *Geduldig v. Aiello* and *General Electric Co. v. Gilbert*: The claims in *Geduldig v. Aeillo* were brought under the Equal Protection Clause of the United States Constitution while the challenges in *General Electric Co. v. Gilbert* were brought under Title VII.

The district court had held, given the provisions of Title VII, that the exclusion was discriminatory. It also held that the precedent of *Geduldig v. Aiello* did not control the reasoning because *Geduldig v. Aiello* involved the Equal Protection

Clause.[63] But the Justices of the United States Supreme Court overruled the district court, reasoning that:

> [w]hile there is no necessary inference that Congress, in choosing [the language of Section 703] intended to incorporate into Title VII the concepts of discrimination which have evolved from court decisions construing the Equal Protection Clause of the Fourteenth Amendment, the similarities between the congressional language and some of those decisions surely indicate that the latter are a useful starting point in interpreting the former.[64]
>
> Particularly in the case of defining the term 'discrimination,' which Congress has nowhere in Title VII defined, those cases afford an existing body of law analyzing and discussing that term in a legal context not wholly dissimilar to the concerns which Congress manifested in enacting Title VII. We think, therefore, that our decision in *Geduldig v. Aiello*...dealing with a strikingly similar disability plan, is quite relevant in determining whether or not the pregnancy exclusion did discriminate on the basis of sex.[65]

As a case, *General Electric Co. v. Gilbert* was "...a far cry from cases like *Reed v. Reed*[66] and *Frontiero v. Richardson*,[67] involving discrimination based upon gender as such," the majority opined. "[I]t is true that only women can become pregnant," the Justices noted. But "it does not follow that every legislative classification concerning pregnancy is a sex-based classification like those considered in *Reed*,...and *Frontiero*.... Normal pregnancy is an objectively identified physical condition with unique characteristics. Absent a showing that distinctions involving pregnancy are mere pretexts designed to effect an invidious discrimination against the members of one sex or the other, lawmakers are constitutionally free to include or exclude pregnancy from the coverage of legislation such as this on any reasonable basis, just as with respect to any physical condition."[68]

But there was no distinction of that kind under the General Electric plan, the Court concluded. Because the "package" offered by General Electric "cover[ed] exactly the same categories of risk, and is facially nondiscriminatory in the sense that '[t]here is no risk from which men are protected and women are not,'"[69] and because "...there is no risk from which women are protected and men are not," the plan was not discriminatory, the majority held. "Likewise, there is no risk from which women are protected and men are not," the majority held.

"As there is no proof that the package is in fact worth more to men than to women, it is impossible to find that any gender-based discrimination does result simply because an employer's disability-benefits plan is less than all-inclusive.[70] For all that appears, pregnancy-related disabilities constitute an additional risk, unique to women, and the failure to compensate them for this risk does not destroy the presumed parity of the benefits, accruing to men and women alike, which results from the facially even-handed inclusion of risks,"[71] the majority held.

But there were a few victories for women under Title VII as it stood in at the time.[72]

In *Nashville Gas Co. v. Satty*,[73] the Supreme Court held that an employment policy requiring pregnant employees to take a leave of absence that would then cause them to lose their seniority violated Title VII. "It is beyond dispute that petitioner's policy of depriving employees returning from pregnancy leave of their accumulated seniority acts both to deprive them 'of employment opportunities' and to 'adversely affect [their] status as an employee,'" the Court wrote.[74] But the Court upheld the company's sick-leave policy.[75]

Five months after the Court's decision in *Nashville Gas Co. v. Satty*, the Justices issued a decision in *Los Angeles Department of Water & Power v. Manhart*,[76] a case involving Title VII challenge of a practice by the Los Angeles Department of Water & Power of withdrawing larger pension contributions from the wages of women because women live longer than men, and would, therefore, perhaps collect pension payments longer.[77] In rejecting this reasoning, the Court held that "[i]t is true...the average man is taller than the average woman; [but] it is not true that the average woman driver is more accident prone than the average man.[78] Before the Civil Rights Act of 1964 was enacted, an employer could fashion his personal policies on the basis of assumptions about the difference between men and women, whether or not the assumptions were valid."[79]

But "[i]t is now well recognized that employment decisions cannot be predicated on mere 'stereotyped' impressions about the characteristics of males and females," the Court wrote.[80] "Myths and purely habitual assumptions about a woman's inability to perform certain kinds of work are no longer acceptable reasons for refusing to employ qualified individuals, or for paying them less. This case does not, however, involve a fictional difference between men and women. It involves a generalization that the parties accept as unquestionably true: women, as a class, do live longer than men."[81]

And while it was true the Los Angeles Department of Water & Power might have treated its female employees "differently from its men employees because the two classes are in fact different. It is equally true...that all individuals within the respective classes do not share the characteristic that differentiates the average class representatives."[82] Thus, the question before the Court was "whether the existence or nonexistence of 'discrimination' is to be determined by comparison of class characteristics or individual characteristics."[83]

By both, according to the Court.

"An employment practice that requires 2,000 individuals to contribute more money into a fund than 10,000 other employees simply because each of them is a woman, rather than a man, is in direct conflict with both the language and the policy of the Act. Such a practice does not pass the simple test of whether the evidence shows 'treatment of a person in a manner which but for that person's sex would be different.'[84] It constitutes discrimination and is unlawful unless exempted by the Equal Pay Act of 1963 or some other affirmative justification,"[85] the majority ruled, finding no such affirmative justification.[86]

And yet, the law in the area of "pregnancy discrimination" was far from settled. Indeed, despite the rulings of *Nashville Gas Co. v. Satty* and *Los Angeles Department of Water & Power v. Manhart*, the Supreme Court's decision in *General Electric Co. v. Gilbert* clearly represented a hurdle for women in the workplace, and women's rights advocates knew it. Within days of the decision in *General Electric Co. v. Gilbert*, a coalition of feminist, civil rights, labor, and religious organizations founded the Campaign to End Discrimination Against Pregnant Workers.[87] Their collective goal was to lobby Congress for a change in the law. In March 1977, their efforts led to the introduction of the Pregnancy Discrimination Act,[88] which, if passed, would amend Title VII to prohibit employment discrimination "because of sex." On October 31, 1978, President Jimmy Carter signed the Pregnancy Discrimination Act into law.[89]

A NEW TOOL IN THE BATTLE:
The Pregnancy Discrimination Act of 1978

Though it certainly seemed promising, as with most newly enacted laws, the meaning and scope of the Pregnancy Discrimination Act of 1978 was not immediately clear. But in an ironic twist, one of the first cases to test the new law involved a challenge brought by a man. On September 20, 1979, a male employee of the Newport News Shipbuilding & Dry Dock Company filed a complaint with the Equal Employment Opportunities Commission, alleging unlawful discrimination after his employer "refused to provide full insurance coverage of his wife's hospitalization caused by pregnancy."[90]

The EEOC would later file suit on behalf of the employee, alleging "sex discrimination" in violation of Title VII. The United Steelworkers union filed a similar complaint on behalf of several individuals.[91] The cases were consolidated on appeal and brought before the United States Supreme Court as *Newport News Shipbuilding & Dry Dock v. EEOC.*[92]

The insurance plan at issue defined specific categories of employee dependents and provided coverage for hospitalization as well as medical and surgical costs.[93] Coverage categories included an employees' "spouses, unmarried children between fourteen days and nineteen years of age, and some older dependent children."[94] Although the Pregnancy Discrimination Act took effect on October 31, 1978, it did not apply to fringe-benefit programs until April 29, 1979. Prior to that, coverage for an employees' "eligible defendants" was identical to that of employees with the singular exception of a limit on hospital coverage for pregnancy.[95]

But after April 1979, the company's medical plan offered equal hospitalization for male and female employees for medical conditions. It "differentiated," however, "between female employees and spouses of male employees in its provision of pregnancy-related benefits."[96] Thus, the question before the United State Supreme Court was whether the company's amended plan complied with the amended federal statute.[97] That brought the Court's analysis full-circle, beginning with the precedent of *General Electric Co. v. Gilbert* and ending with interpretation of the Pregnancy Discrimination Act.

"In 1978 Congress decided to overrule our decision in *General Electric Co. v. Gilbert*, by amending Title VII of the Civil Rights Act of 1964 'to prohibit sex discrimination on the basis of pregnancy,'" Justice Stevens explained in writing for the Court.[98] Prior to the 1978 amendment, Title VII did not define the term "discrimination," which led the Court to apply "an analysis derived from cases construing the Equal Protection Clause of the Fourteenth Amendment to the Constitution."[99] But "[w]hen Congress amended Title VII in 1978, it unambiguously expressed its disapproval of both the holding and the reasoning of the Court in the *Gilbert* decision. It incorporated a new subsection in the 'definitions' applicable '[f]or the purposes of this subchapter,'" Justice Stevens explained.[100]

And with this new subsection came a specific definition of discrimination "because of sex."[101] When considered in light of the newly amended definition, the "[p]etitioner's practice" was unlawful, the Court held. "Its plan provides limited pregnancy-related benefits for employees' wives, and affords more extensive coverage for employees' spouses for all other medical conditions requiring hospitalization. Thus the husbands of female employees receive a specified level of hospitalization for all conditions; the wives of male employees receive such coverage except for pregnancy-related conditions. Although *Gilbert* concluded that an otherwise inclusive plan that singled out pregnancy-related benefits for exclusion was nondiscriminatory on its face, because only women can become pregnant, Congress has unequivocally rejected that reasoning. The 1978 Act makes clear that it is discriminatory to treat pregnancy-related conditions less favorably than other medical conditions. Thus petitioner's plan unlawfully gives married male employees a benefit package for their dependents that is less inclusive than the dependency coverage provided to married female employees."[102]

CALIFORNIA FEDERAL SAVINGS AND LOAN ASSOCIATION v. GUERRA

General Electric Co. v. Gilbert was finally dead. But challenges to the Pregnancy Discrimination Act were just beginning with echoes of the old as well as the new. *California Federal Savings and Loan Association v. Guerra*,[103] for example, coupled allegations of "protectionist" legislation towards women with assertions of reverse discrimination towards men. And it all started so simply.

In 1982, after years of working at California Federal Savings & Loan Association as a receptionist, Lillian Garland became pregnant and took maternity leave.[104] But when she tried to return to work the following April, Garland was told there were no receptionist jobs or similar positions available. Garland filed a complaint with the California Department of Fair Employment and Housing, which issued an "administrative accusation" on Garland's behalf, alleging that California Federal Savings & Loan had violated Section 12945(b)(2) of the California Fair Employment and Housing Act.[105]

In response, California Federal Savings & Loan, joined by the Merchants and Manufacturers Association and the state Chamber of Commerce, sought declaratory judgment and injunctive relief in federal district court, alleging that Section 12945(b)(2) was inconsistent with, and preempted by, Title VII.[106] In granting summary judgment in favor of California Federal Savings & Loan, the district court held that "California employers who comply with state law are subject to reverse discrimination suits under Title VII brought by temporarily disabled males who do not receive the same treatment as female employees disabled by pregnancy."[107] In other words, the district court held that the California law was "preempted by Title VII" and was, therefore, "null, void, invalid, and inoperative under the Supremacy Clause of the United States Constitution."[108]

The Ninth Circuit reversed, holding that the district court's "conclusion, that section 12945(b)(2) discriminates against men on the basis of pregnancy defies common sense, misinterprets case law, and flouts Title VII and the PDA [Pregnancy Discrimination Act]."[109] California Federal Savings & Loan appealed. But this was neither a simple case, nor a simple appeal. Dozens of *amicus curiae* briefs were filed with the United States Supreme Court[110] with parties on both sides arguing for and against the law, amid assertions that the PDA was just another form of "protectionist" legislation designed to defeat women's true bid for equality.

Though discussion of "protectionist" legislation and "reverse discrimination" present the "sexier" side of the debate, on the legal side, the issue argued on appeal before the Supreme Court by California Federal Savings & Loan Association was one of preemption, and thus, the Justices began their analysis with an overview of the doctrine of preemption.

"Federal law may supersede state law in several different ways," the Court wrote.[111] "First, when acting within constitutional limits, Congress is empowered to preempt state law by so stating in express terms.[112] Second, congressional intent to preempt state law in a particular area may be inferred where the scheme of federal regulation is sufficiently comprehensive to make reasonable the inference that Congress 'left no room' for supplementary state regulation.[113] Neither of these bases for preemption exists in this case. Congress has explicitly disclaimed any intent categorically to preempt state law or to 'occupy the field' of employment discrimination law."[114]

A third alternative is present, however, "...in those areas where Congress has not completely displaced state regulation, federal law may nonetheless preempt state law to the extent it actually conflicts with federal law," the Court wrote. "Such a conflict occurs either because 'compliance with both federal and state regulations is a physical impossibility,'[115] or because the state law stands 'as an obstacle to the accomplishment and execution for the full purposes and objectives of Congress.'[116] Either way, preemption is not to be lightly presumed."[117] Thus, "[i]n determining whether a state statute is preempted by federal law and therefore invalid under the Supremacy Clause of the Constitution, our sole task is to ascertain the intent of Congress,"[118] the Justices explained.

The third circumstance of preemption was at issue in *California Federal Savings & Loan v. Guerra,* the Court ruled. In interpreting the reach of the Civil Rights Act of 1964, Justice Marshall explained that "Congress has indicated that state laws will be preempted only if they actually conflict with federal law."[119] But the Court found no conflict. "We...find it significant that Congress was aware of state laws similar to California's but apparently did not consider them inconsistent with the PDA," Justice Marshall wrote.[120] In addition, "Title VII, as amended by the PDA, and California's pregnancy disability leave statute share a common goal," the Court held.[121]

"The purpose of Title VII is 'to achieve equality of employment opportunities and remove barriers that have operated in the past to favor an identifiable group of...employees over other employees,'" Justice Marshall wrote.[122] "Rather than limiting existing Title VII principles and objectives, the PDA extends them to cover pregnancy.[123] 'The entire thrust...behind this legislation is to guarantee women the basic right to participate fully and equally in the workforce, without denying them the fundamental right to full participation in family life.'"[124]

Did that make the PDA discriminatory and, thus, unenforceable?

The Court found it was not.

"[E]ven if we agreed with petitioners' construction of the PDA, we would nonetheless reject their argument that the California statute requires employers to violate Title VII.[125] Section 12945(b)(2) does not prevent employers from complying with both the federal law (as petitioners construe it) and the state law. This is not a case where 'compliance with both federal and state regulations is a physical impossibility,'[126] or where there is an 'inevitable collision between the two schemes of regulation.'[127] Section 12945(b)(2) does not compel California employers to treat pregnant workers better than other disabled employees; it merely establishes benefits that employers must, at a minimum, provide to pregnant workers. Employers are free to give comparable benefits to other disabled employees, thereby treating 'women affected by pregnancy' no better than 'other persons not so affected but similar in their ability or inability to work.' Indeed, at oral argument, petitioners conceded that compliance with both statutes 'is theoretically possible.'"[128]

But what does the Pregnancy Discrimination Act mean to working women today? Probably not what most women think it means, despite heated suggestions of "preferential" treatment. In recent years, Title VII has been held to offer a surprisingly broad spectrum of protection. Chapter Seven offers a practical overview of the evolution of Title VII and the Pregnancy Discrimination Act— the failures as well as the victories.

RELEVANT EXCERPTS FROM
CALIFORNIA FEDERAL SAVINGS & LOAN ASSOCIATION v. GUERRA:
479 U.S. 272, 284-286 (1987)

Petitioners argue that the language of the federal statute itself unambiguously rejects California's "special treatment" approach to pregnancy discrimination, thus rendering any resort to the legislative history unnecessary. They contend that the second clause of the PDA forbids an employer to treat pregnant employees any differently than other disabled employees. Because "[t]he purpose of Congress is the ultimate touchstone" of the preemptive inquiry,[129] however, we must examine the PDA's language against the background of its legislative history and historical context. As to the language of the PDA, "[i]t is a 'familiar rule, that a thing may be within the letter of the statute and yet not within the statute, because it is not within its spirit, nor within the intention of its makers.'"[130]

It is well established that the PDA was passed in reaction to this Court's decision in *General Electric Co. v. Gilbert*.[131] "When Congress amended Title VII in 1978, it unambiguously expressed its disapproval of both the holding and reasoning of the Court in the *Gilbert* decision."[132] By adding pregnancy to the definition of sex discrimination prohibited by Title VII, the first clause of the PDA reflects Congress' disapproval of the reasoning in *Gilbert*.[133] Rather than imposing a limitation on the remedial purpose of the PDA, we believe that the second clause was intended to overrule the holding in *Gilbert* and to illustrate how discrimination against pregnancy is to be remedied.[134] Accordingly, subject to certain limitations, we agree with the Court of Appeals' conclusion that Congress intended the PDA to be "a floor beneath which pregnancy disability benefits may not drop—not a ceiling above which they may not rise."[135]

The context in which Congress considered the issue of pregnancy discrimination supports this view of the PDA. Congress had before it extensive evidence of discrimination against pregnancy, particularly in disability and health insurance programs like those challenged in *Gilbert* and *Nashville Gas Co. v. Satty*.[136] The reports, debates, and hearings make abundantly clear that Congress intended the PDA to provide relief for working women and to end discrimination against pregnant workers.[137] In contrast to the thorough account of discrimination against pregnant workers, the legislative history is devoid of any discussion of preferential treatment of pregnancy,[138] beyond acknowledgments of the existence of state statutes provides for such preferential treatment. Opposition to the PDA came from those concerned with the cost of including pregnancy in health- and disability-benefits plans and the application of the bill to abortion,[139] not from those who favored special accommodations of pregnancy.

In support of their argument that the PDA prohibits employment practices that favor pregnant women, petitioners and several *amici* cite statements in their legislative history to the effect that the PDA does not require employers to extend any benefits to pregnant women that they do not already provide to other disabled employees. For example, the House Report explained that the proposed legislation "does not require employers to treat pregnant employees in any particular manner…[140] in no way requires the institution of any new programs where none currently exist."[141] We do not interpret these references to support petitioners' construction of the statute. On the contrary, if Congress had intended to prohibit preferential treatment, it would have been the height of understatement to say only that the legislation would not require such conduct. It is hardly conceivable that Congress would have extensively discussed only its intent not to require preferential treatment if in fact it had intended to prohibit such treatment.

We also find it significant that Congress was aware of state laws similar to California's but apparently did not consider them inconsistent with the PDA. In the debates and reports on the bill, Congress repeatedly acknowledged the existence of state antidiscrimination laws that prohibit sex discrimination on the basis of pregnancy.[142] Two of the states mentioned then required employers to provide reasonable leave to pregnant workers.[143] After citing these laws, Congress failed to evince the requisite "clear and manifest purpose" to supersede them.[144] To the contrary, both the House and Senate Reports suggest that these laws would continue to have effect under the PDA.[145]

Title VII, as amended by the PDA, and California's pregnancy disability leave statute share a common goal. The purpose of Title VII is "to achieve equality of employment opportunities and remove barriers that have operated in the past to favor an identifiable group of…employees over other employees."[146] Rather than limiting existing Title VII principles and objectives, the PDA extends them to cover pregnancy.[147] As Senator Williams, a sponsor of the Act, stated: "The entire thrust…behind this legislation is to guarantee women the basic right to participate fully and equally in the workforce, without denying them the fundamental right to full participation in family life."[148]

Section 12945(b)(2) also promotes equal employment opportunity. By requiring employers to reinstate women after a reasonable pregnancy disability leave, 12945(b)(2) ensures that they will not lose their jobs on account of pregnancy disability.[149] California's approach is consistent with the dissenting opinion of Justice Brennan in *General Electric Co. v. Gilbert*, which Congress adopted in enacting the PDA. Referring to *Lau v. Nichols*,[150] a Title VI decision, Justice Brennan stated:

> [D]iscrimination is a social phenomenon encased in a social context and, therefore, unavoidably takes its meaning from the desired end products of the relevant legislative enactment, end products that may demand due consideration of the uniqueness of the 'disadvantaged' individuals. A realistic understanding of conditions found today's labor environment warrants taking pregnancy into account in fashioning disability politics.[151]

By "taking pregnancy into account," California's pregnancy disability-leave statute "allows women, as well as men, to have families without losing their jobs."[152] [¶] We emphasize the limited nature of the benefits [Section] 12945(b)(2) provides. The statute is narrowly drawn to cover only the period of actual physical disability on account of pregnancy, childbirth, or related medical conditions. Accordingly, unlike the protective labor legislation prevalent earlier this century,[153] [Section] 12945(b)(2) does not reflect archaic or stereotypical notions about pregnancy and the abilities of pregnant workers. A statute based on such stereotypical assumptions would, of course, be inconsistent with Title VII's goal of equal employment opportunities.[154]

ENDNOTES FOR CHAPTER SIX

1   *Goesaert v. Cleary, Liquor Control Commission of Michigan*, 355 U.S. 464 (1948).
2   *See* England & Farkas, *supra* note 9, ENDNOTES FOR CHAPTER THREE, at p. 99.
3   *See* McDonald, *supra* note 13, ENDNOTES FOR CHAPTER THREE, at p. 61.
4   *Id.*
5   347 U.S. 483 (1954).
6   *See* Mark Tushnet, MAKING CIVIL RIGHT LAW: THURGOOD MARSHALL AND THE SUPREME COURT, 1936–1961 (New York: Oxford University Press, 1994), at p. 307 (citing Steven Lawson, BLACK BALLOTS: VOTING RIGHTS IN THE SOUTH, 1944–1969 (NEW YORK: COLUMBIA UNIVERSITY PRESS, 1976), at pp. 146–202).
7   *Id.*
8   *Id.*
9   *See* 42 U.S.C. Sec. 2000e-17.
10   *See* Alan B. Krueger, ECONOMIC SCENE, *Equality in Hiring Remains the Key of Civil Rights Goals*, N.Y. TIMES, June 22, 2000, at C2.
11   *See* Sara Ann Friedman, WORK MATTERS (New York: Viking, 1996), at pp. 7–8.
12   *Id.*
13   *See* 42 U.S.C. Sec. 2000a *et seq.*
14   *See* 42 U.S.C. Sec. 2000a. *See also Heart of Atlanta Motel v. U.S.*, 379 U.S. 241 (1964); *Katzenbach v. McClung*, 379 U.S. 294 (1964).
15   *See* 42 U.S.C. Sec. 2000b.
16   *See* 42 U.S.C. Sec. 2000c. For reading on the topic, *see* Geoffrey R. Stone *et. al*, CONSTITUTIONAL LAW (Boston, Mass.: Little, Brown & Co., 1996), at p. 537.
17   *See* 42 U.S.C. Sec. 2000d.
18   *See* 42 U.S.C. Sec. 2000e. *See also Fullilove v. Klutznick*, 448 U.S. 448 (1980).
19   *See* 42 U.S.C. Sec. 2000e at Sec. 703(a)(1).
20   *See* Robert A. Caro, *The Compassion of Lyndon Johnson*, THE NEW YORKER, April 1, 2002, pp. 56–78, at p. 61.
21   *See* Friedman, *supra* note 11, at pp. 7–8.
22   *See* Tara McKelvey, *Your Right to Choose Is Not Guaranteed*, MARIE CLAIRE, Feb. 2003, at p. 94.
23   *Reed v. Reed*, 404 U.S. 71 (1971).
24   404 U.S. at 77.
25   *See Geduldig v. Aiello*, 417 U.S. 484 (1974).
26   *See Geduldig*, 417 U.S. at 486–87 (In the description of the Court, "[f]or almost 30 years California has administered a disability insurance system that pays benefits to persons in private employment who are temporarily unable to work because of disability not covered by workmen's compensation. The appellees brought this action to challenge the constitutionality of a provision of the California program that, in defining 'disability,' excludes from coverage certain disabilities resulting from pregnancy. Because the appellees sought to enjoin the enforcement of this state statute, a three-judge court was convened pursuant to 28 U.S.C. Secs. 2281 and 2284.")
27   *Id.*
28   404 U.S. 71 (1971).
29   411 U.S. 677 (1973).
30   397 U.S. 471 (1970).
31   406 U.S. 535 (1972).
32   414 U.S. 632 (1974).
33   414 U.S. at 644–48.
34   *See, e.g., Griggs v. Duke Power Co.*, 401 U.S. 424, 431 (1971) (holding that where a practice of excluding "Negroes" is not shown to be related to job performance, it is discriminatory); *McDonnell Douglas Corp. v. Green*, 411 U.S. 792 (1973) (articulating the burden shifting framework in the employment discrimination context).
35   *See Geduldig*, 417 U.S. at 486–87.
36   *Id.* at 486.
37   *Id.* at 489 (citing Cal. Unemp. Ins. Code Sec. 2626).
38   *Id.* (Aiello and Johnson both suffered ectopic pregnancies, while Armendariz suffered a miscarriage.)
39   *Id.*
40   These steps were taken pursuant to 28 U.S.C. Secs. 2281 and 2284.
41   *See Geduldig*, 417 U.S. at 487 (citing the underlying case at 359 F. Supp. 792).
42   32 Cal. App. 3d 604 (1973).

43   *See Rentzer v. Unemploy. Ins. Appeals Bd.*, 32 Cal. App. 3d 604 (1973).
44   *See Geduldig*, 417 U.S. at 490.
45   *Id.* at 491–92. (The Court's specific language in detailing the meaning of *Rentzer* was that "[a]lthough *Rentzer* was decided some ten days before the District Court's decision in this case, there was apparently no opportunity to call the court's attention to it. The appellant, therefore, asked the court to reconsider its decision in light of the construction that the California Court of Appeals had given to 2626 in the *Rentzer* case. By a divided vote, the court denied the motion for reconsideration. Although a more definitive ruling would surely have been preferable, we interpret the District Court's denial of the appellant's motion as a determination that its decision was not affected by the limiting construction given to 2626 in *Rentzer*.")
46   *See Geduldig*, 417 U.S. at 492.
47   *Id.*
48   *Id.* at 489.
49   *Id.* at 495.
50   *Id.*
51   *Id.* (citing *Williamson v. Lee Optical Co.*, 348 U.S. 483, 489 (1955); *Jefferson v. Hackney*, 406 U.S. 535 (1972)).
52   *Id.* (citing *Dandridge v. Williams*, 397 U.S. 471, 486–487 (1970)).
53   *Id.* at 503.
54   *See In Re Carnegie Center Associates*, 129 F.3d 290, 294 (3d Cir. 1997).
55   *See* 29 C.F.R. Sec. 1600. (In some instances, however, the United States Department of Justice has jurisdiction.)
56   *See* Title VII, Sec. 703(a)(1) as codified at 42 U.S.C. 2000e-2(a)(1).
57   Under Title VII, "[t]he term 'employer's' means a person engaged in an industry affecting commerce who has fifteen or more employees for each working day in each of twenty or more calendar weeks in the current or preceding calendar year, and any agent of such a person, but such a term does not include (1) the United States, a corporation wholly owned by the Government of the United States, an Indian tribe, or any department or agency of the District of Columbia subject by statute to procedures of the competitive service (as defined in section 2102 of Title 5), or (2) a bona fide private membership club (other than a labor organization) which is exempt from taxation under section 501(c) of Title 26, except that during the first year after March 24, 1972, persons having fewer than twenty-five employees (and their agents) shall not be considered employers." *See* 42 U.S.C.A. Sec. 2000e(b).
58   Section 703(a) of the Civil Rights Act of 1964, codified as 42 U.S.C. 2000e-2(a)(1) provides in pertinent part: "It shall be an unlawful employment practice for an employer…to fail or refuse to hire or to discharge any individual, or otherwise to discriminate against any individual with respect to his compensation, terms, conditions, or privileges of employment, because of such individual's race, color, religion, sex, or national origin."
59   400 U.S. 542, 543 (1971).
60   *Id.* (The Justices further explained that "[t]he Court of Appeals therefore erred in reading this section as permitting one hiring policy for women and another for men—each having preschool-age children. The existence of such conflicting family obligations, if demonstrably more relevant to job performance for a woman than for a man, could arguably be a basis for distinction under 703(e) of the Act. But that is a matter of evidence tending to show that the condition in question 'is a bona fide occupational qualification reasonably necessary to the normal operation of that particular business or enterprise.' The record before us, however, is not adequate for resolution of these important issues" (citing *Kennedy v. Silas Mason Co.*, 334 U.S. 249, 256-257 (1948)).)
61   429 U.S. 125 (1976).
62   *See* Title VII, Sec. 703(a)(1) as codified at 42 U.S.C. 2000e-2(a)(1).
63   *See Gilbert*, 429 U.S. at 125.
64   *Id.* at 134.
65   *Id.*
66   404 U.S. 71 (1971).
67   411 U.S. 677 (1973).
68   *See Gilbert*, 429 U.S. at 134–35 (citing *Geduldig*, 417 U.S. at 496-497, n. 20).
69   *Id.* at 138–140.
70   *Id.*
71   *Id.*
72   On these cases, often the language that was deemed to protect women that, as set for above in text, Section 703(a)(2) of Title VII, codified at 42 U.S.C. 2000e-2 (a)(2) (1970), which deemed it unlawful for an employer to "limit, segregate, or classify his employers or applicants for employment in any way which would deprive or tend to deprive any individual of employment opportunities or otherwise adversely affect his status as an employee because of such individual's…sex.…" *See, e.g., Nashville Gas Co. v. Satty*, 434 U.S.136, 141 (1977).
73   *Id.* at 142.
74   *See Nashville*, 434 U.S. at 142.

75 *Id.* at 143–144 (holding that "[r]espondent failed to prove even a discriminatory effect with respect to petitioner's sick-leave plan").

76 435 U.S. 702 (1978).

77 *Id.* at 705–706 (As the Court explained, "[b]ased on a study of mortality tables and its own experience, the Department determined that its 2,000 female employees, on the average, will live a few years longer than its 10,000 male employees. The cost of a pension for the average retired female is greater than for the average male retiree because more monthly payments must be made to the average woman. The Department therefore required female employees to make monthly contributions to the fund which were 14.84% higher than the contributions required of comparable male employees. Because employee contributions were withheld from paychecks, a female employee took home less pay than a male employee earning the same salary.")

78 *Id.* at 708 (citing *Developments in the Law, Employment Discrimination and Title VII of the Civil Rights Act of 1964*, 84 HARV. L. REV. 1109, 1174 (1971)).

79 *Id.*

80 *Id.* at n. 13. (In that footnote, the Court stated that "[i]n forbidding employers to discriminate against individuals because of their sex, Congress intended to strike at the entire spectrum of disparate treatment of men and women resulting from sex stereotypes. Section 703(a)(1) subjects to scrutiny and eliminates such irrational impediments to job opportunities and enjoyment which have plagued women in the past." *Sprogis v. United Air Lines, Inc.*, 444 F.2d 1194, 1198 (7th Cir. 1971).) *See also* EQUAL EMPLOYMENT OPPORTUNITY COMMISSION, GUIDELINES ON DISCRIMINATION BECAUSE OF SEX, 29 C.F.R. 1604.1 (a)(1)(ii); *Bowe v. Colgate-Palmolive Co.*, 416 F.2d 711 (7th Cir. 1969); *Weeks v. Southern Bell Tel. & Tel. Co.*, 408 F.2d 228 (5th Cir. 1969); *Neal v. American Airlines, Inc.*, 1 CCH Employment Practices Guide 6002 (EEOC 1968); *Colvin v. Piedmont Aviation, Inc.*, 1 CCH Employment Practices Guide 6003 (EEOC 1968); 110 CONG. REC. 2578 (remarks of Rep. Bass).

81 *Id.*

82 *Id.*

83 *Id.* at 709.

84 *Id.* at 712, n. 21 (To support this point, the Court cited *Development in the Law, supra* note 78, at p. 1170. *See also Sprogis, supra* note 80, 444 F.2d at 1205 (Stevens, J., dissenting).)

85 *Id.*

86 *Id.* at 716–717. (Specifically, in finding that the precedent of *Gilbert* did not apply, the Court explained that "[i]n this case…the Department argues that the absence of a discriminatory effect on women as a class justifies an employment practice, which, on its face, discriminated against individual employees because of their sex. But even if the Department's actuarial evidence is sufficient to prevent plaintiffs from establishing a *prima facie* case on the theory that the effect of the practice on women as a class was discriminatory, that evidence does not defeat the claim that the practice, on its face, discriminated against every individual woman employed by the Department. [¶] In essence, the Department is arguing that the *prima facie* case showing of discrimination based on evidence of different contributions for the respective sexes is rebutted by its demonstration that there is a like difference in the cost of providing benefits for the respective classes. That argument might prevail if Title VII contained a cost-justification defense comparable to the affirmative defense available in a price discrimination suit. But neither Congress nor the courts have recognized such a defense under Title VII" (further citations omitted). The Court decided similarly in *Arizona Governing Committee v. Norris*, 463 U.S. 1073, 1085 (1983) (holding, with regarding to a Arizona compensation, that "it is just as much discrimination 'because of…sex' to pay a woman lower benefits when she has made the same contributions as a man as it is to make her pay larger contributions to obtain the same benefits.")

87 For fuller discussion, *see* J. GELB & M. PALLEY, WOMEN AND PUBLIC POLICY (1982), at 159–160.

88 UNITED STATES SENATE BILL NO. 995 (1977).

89 Title VII of the Civil Rights Act of 1964 was amended in 1978 to include the Pregnancy Discrimination Act, which can be found at 42 U.S.C. Sec. 2000e[k], which holds in pertinent part that discrimination "one the basis of sex" includes, "but is not limited to: discrimination on the basis of pregnancy, childbirth, or related medical conditions; and women affected by pregnancy, childbirth, or related medical conditions, shall be treated the same for all employment-related purposes, including receipt of benefits under fringe benefit programs, as other persons not so affected but similar in their ability or inability to work…."

90 *See Newport News*, 462 U.S. 669, 674 (1983).

91 *Id.*

92 *Id.* at 674.

93 *Id.* at 672, n. 3 (The Court noted that "[o]n the first day following three months of continuous service, every active, full-time production, maintenance, technical, and clerical area bargaining unit employee becomes a plan participant.")

94 *Id.* at n. 4. ("For example," the Court wrote, "unmarried children up to age 23 who are full-time college students solely dependent on an employee and certain mentally or physically handicapped children are also covered.")

95   *Id.* at 672, no. 6 (According to the Court, the exception provided that "[f]or hospitalization caused by uncomplicated pregnancy, petitioner's plan paid 100 percent of the reasonable and customary physicians' charges for delivery and anesthesiology, and up to $500 of other hospital charges. For all other hospital confinement, the plan paid in full for a semiprivate room for up to 120 days and for surgical procedures, covered the first $750 of reasonable and customary charges for hospital services (including general nursing care, X-ray examinations, and drugs) and other necessary services during hospitalization; and paid 80 percent of the charges exceeding $750 for such services up to a maximum of 120 days.")

96   *Id.* at n. 7 ("Thus, as the Equal Employment Opportunity Commission found after its investigation," the Court noted, "'the record reveals that the present disparate impact on male employees had its genesis in the gender-based distinction accorded to female employees in the past.'")

97   *Id.* at 676.

98   *Id.* at 671–72, n. 1 (citing Pub. L. 95-555, 92 Stat. 2076 (quoting title of 1978 Act)).

99   *Id.* at 677.

100   *Id.*

101   *Id.* (The language that Justice Stevens describes as the "first clause of the Act" is as follows: "The term 'because of sex' or 'on the basis of sex' include, but are not limited to, because of or on the basis of pregnancy, childbirth, or related medical conditions." The Pregnancy Discrimination Act as codified in 42 U.S.C. Sec. 2000e[k], provides that "the term 'sex' included prohibitions on discrimination on the basis of 'pregnancy, childbirth, or related medical conditions; and women affected by pregnancy, childbirth, or related medical conditions, shall be treated the same for all employment-related purposes.'"

102   *Id.* at 684.

103   479 U.S. 272 (1987).

104   *See Guerra,* 479 U.S. at 279.

105   *Id.* at 276–279. (According to the Court, "[i]n September 1978, California amended the FEHA to proscribe certain forms of employment discrimination on the basis of pregnancy. *See* Cal. Labor Code Ann. 1420.35, 1978 Cal. Stats., ch. 1321, 1, pp. 4320–4322 (West Supp. 1979).)

106   *Id.* at 279.

107   *Id.* (citing 34 FEP Cases 562, 568 (1984)).

108   *Id.* at 280.

109   *Id.* (citing California *Federal Sav. & Loan Ass'n v. Guerra,* 758 F.2d 390, 393 (1985)).

110   *Amici Curiae* briefs filed in support of reversal included court papers filed on behalf of the United States by Solicitor General Fried, Assistant Attorney General Reynolds, Deputy Solicitor General Geller, Deputy Assistant Attorney General Carvin, Richard J. Lazarus, Brian K. Landsberg, David K. Flynn, and Mary E. Mann; and for the Equal Employment Advisory Council by Robert E. Williams, Douglas S. McDowell, and Lorence L. Kessler. Briefs of *amici curiae* urging affirmance were filed for the State of Connecticut *et al.* by Joseph I. Lieberman, Attorney General of Connecticut; Clarine Nardi Riddle, Deputy Attorney General, Brian J. Comerford, Assistant Attorney General, Philip A. Murphy, Jr., Corinne K. A. Watanabe, Attorney General of Hawaii, Michael Greely, Attorney General of Montana, and Kenneth O. Eikenberry, Attorney General of Washington; for the American Federation of Labor and Congress of Industrial Organizations by Laurence Gold and Marsha S. Berzon; for California Women Lawyers *et al.* by Cheryl Houser, Janet M. Koehn, and Lorraine L. Loder; for Equal Rights Advocates *et al.* by Judith F. Kurtz, Nancy L. Davis, and Herma Hill Kay; for Human Rights Advocates *et al.* by Richard F. Ziegler and Andrew Weissmann; for the National Conference of State Legislatures *et al.* by Benna Ruth Soloman, Todd D. Peterson, and Barbara Etkind; and for Lillian Garland by Joan M. Graff, Robert Barnes, and Patricia Shiu. Briefs of *amici curiae* were filed for the American Civil Liberties Union *et al.* by Joan E. Bertin, Isabelle Katz Pinzler, George Kannar, and Charles S. Sims; for the Chamber of Commerce of the United States by Robin S. Conrad; for the Coalition for Reproductive Equality in the Workplace *et al.* by Christine Anne Littleton and Judith Resnick; and for the National Organization for Women *et al.* by Susan Deller Ross, Sarah E. Burns, and Wendy Webster Williams.

111   *Guerra* at 282.

112   *Id.* (citing *Jones v. Rath Packing Co.,* 430 U.S. 519, 525 (1977)).

113   *Id.* (citing *Rice v. Santa Fe Elevator Co.,* 331 U.S. 218, 230 (1947)).

114   *Id.* (citing 42 U.S.C. Secs. 2000e-7 and 2000h-4).

115   *Id.* (citing *Florida Lime & Avocado Growers, Inc. v. Paul,* 373 U.S. 132, 142–43 (1963)).

116   *Id.* (citing *Hines v. Davidowitz,* 312 U.S. 52, 67 (1967); *Michigan Canners & Freezers Assn., Inc. v. Agricultural Marketing and Bargaining Bd.,* 467 U.S. 461, 478 (1984); *Fidelity Federal Savings & Loan Assn. v. De la Cuesta,* 458 U.S. 141, 156 (1982)).

117   *Id.* (citing *Maryland v. Louisiana,* 451 U.S. 725, 746 (1981)).

118   *Id.* (citing *Shaw v. Delta Air Lines, Inc.,* 463 U.S. 85, 95 (1983); *Malone v. White Motor Corp.,* 435 U.S. 497, 504 (1978)).

119   *Id.* at 281–282 (comparing Secs. 708 and 1104). (Wrote the Court, "Section 708 of Title VII provides: 'Nothing in this title shall be deemed to exempt or relieve any person from any liability, duty, penalty, or punishment provided by any present or future law of any state or political subdivision

of a state, other than any such law which purports to require or permit the doing of any act which would be an unlawful employment practice under this title'" (citing 78 Stat. 262, 42 U.S.C. 2000e-7). By contract, the Court explained, "Section 1104 of Title XI, applicable to all titles of the Civil Rights Act, establishes the following standard for preemption: 'Nothing contained in any title of this Act shall be construed as indicating an intent on the part of Congress to occupy the field in which any such title operates to the exclusion of state laws on the same subject matter, nor shall any provision of this Act be construed as invalidating any provision of state law unless such provision is inconsistent with any of the purposes of this Act, or any provision thereof'" (citing 78 Stat. 268, 42 U.S.C. 2000h-4).)

120 *Id.* at 286.

121 *Id.* at 288.

122 *Id.* (citing *Griggs v. Duke Power Co.*, 401 U.S. 424, 429–430 (1979); *Hishon v. King & Spalding*, 467 U.S. 69, 75, no. 7 (1984); *Franks v. Bowman Transportation Co.*, 424 U.S. 727, 763 (1976); *Alexander v. Gardner-Denver Co.*, 415 U.S. 36, 44 (1974); *McDonnell Douglas Corp. v. Green*, 411 U.S. 792, 800 (1973)).

123 *Id.* at 289. (The Court noted that "[p]roponents of the bill repeatedly emphasized that the Supreme Court had erroneously interpreted congressional intent and that the amending legislation was necessary to reestablish the principles of Title VII law as they have been understood prior to the *Gilbert* decision" (citing *Newport News Shipbuilding & Dry Dock v. EEOC*, 462 U.S. at 679).)

124 *Id.* (citing 123 CONG. REC. 29658 (1977)).

125 *Id.* at 290. (The Justices note that "[p]etitioners assert that even if 12945(b)(2) does not require employers to treat pregnant employees differently from other disabled employees, it permits employers to do so because it does not specifically prohibit different treatment. Of course, since the PDA does not itself prohibit different treatment, it certainly does not require the states to do so. Moreover, if we were to interpret the term 'permit' as expansively as petitioners suggest, the state would be required to incorporate every prohibition contained in Title VII into its state law, since it would otherwise be held to 'permit' any employer action it did not expressly prohibit. We conclude that 'permit' in 708 must be interpreted to preempt only other state laws that expressly sanction a practice unlawful under Title VII; the term does not preempt state laws that are silent on the practice.")

126 *Id.* at 291 (citing *Florida Lime & Avocado Growers, Inc. v. Paul*, 373 U.S. 132, 142–143 (1963)).

127 *Id.* (citing *Florida Lime & Avocado Growers*, 373 U.S. at 143).

128 *Id.* (citing Transcript of Oral Argument 6).

129 *Id.* at 284 (citing *Malone v. White Motor Corp.*, 435 U.S. 497, 504 (1978) (quoting *Retail Clerks v. Schermerhorn*, 375 U.S. 96, 103 (1963))).

130 *Id.* (citing *Steelworkers v. Weber*, 443 U.S. 193, 201 (1979) (quoting *Church of the Holy Trinity v. United States*, 143 U.S. 457, 459 (1892))).

131 *Id.* (citing *Gilbert*, 429 U.S. 125 (1976)).

132 *Id.* (citing *Newport News Shipbuilding & Dry Dock Co. v. EEOC*, 462 U.S. 669, 678 (1983)).

133 *Id.* (citing *Newport News*, 462 U.S. at 678–79)).

134 *Id.* at 285 (citing *id.*, n. 14 ("The meaning of the first clause is not limited to the specific language in the second clause, which explains the application of the general principle to women employees") (further citation omitted)).

135 *Id.* (citing 758 F.2d at 396).

136 *Id.* (citing *Satty*, 434 U.S. 136 (1977)).

137 *Id.* at 286.

138 *Id.* (In this footnote, the Court explained that "[t]he statement of Senator Brooke, quoted in the dissent, post, at 300, merely indicates the Senator's view that the PDA does not itself require special disability benefits for pregnant workers. It in no way supports the conclusion that Congress intended to prohibit the states from providing such benefits to pregnant workers" (further citation omitted).)

139 *Id.* (citing S. REP. No. 95-331, p. 9 (1977); LEG. HIST. 46 (discussing cost objections); H. R. CONF. REP. No. 95–1786, pp. 3–4 (1978); LEG. HIST. 196–197 (application of the PDA to abortion)).

140 *Id.* at 287 (citing H. R. 6075).

141 *Id.* (citing H. R. REP. No. 95-948, at p. 4 (1978); LEG. HIST. 150. *See also* S. REP. NO. 95-331, *supra* note 139, at p. 4, LEG. HIST. 41; 123 CONG. REC. 7540 (1977) (remarks of Sen. Williams); *id.*, at 10582 (remarks of Rep. Hawkins); *id.*, at 29387 (remarks of Sen. Javits); *id.*, at 29664 (remarks of Sen. Brooke)).

142 *Id.* (citing 123 CON. REC. 29387 (1977) (remarks of Sen. Javits), LEG. HIST. 67 ("[S]everal state legislatures…have chosen to address the problem by mandating certain types of benefits for pregnant employees"); S. REP. No. 95-331, *supra* note 139, at p. 3, LEG. HIST. 40; H. R. REP. NO. 95-948, *supra* note 141, at pp. 10–11, LEG. HIST. at pp. 156–157; 123 CONG. REC. 29648 (1977) (list of states that require coverage for pregnancy and pregnancy-related disabilities); *id.*, at 29662 (remarks of Sen. Williams)).

143 *Id.* (citing Conn. Gen. Stat. 31-126(g) (1977), now codified at 46a-60(a)(7)(1985); Mont. Rev. Codes 41-2602 (Smith Supp. 1977), now codified at Mont. Code Ann. 49-2-310 and 49-2-311 (1986). "The Connecticut statute provided, in relevant part: 'It shall be unfair employment prac-

tice…"(g) For an employer…(ii) to refuse to grant to [a pregnant] employee a reasonable leave of absence for disability resulting from such pregnancy…(iii) Upon signifying her intent to return, such employee shall be reinstated to her original job or to an equivalent position with equivalent pay and accumulated seniority, retirement, fringe benefits, and other service credits unless, in the case of a private employer, the employer's circumstances have so changed as to make it impossible or unreasonable to do so." Conn. Gen. Stat. 31-126(g) (1977). The Montana statute in effect in 1977 was virtually identical. Both have been recodified in current statutory compilations, but the leave and reinstatement requirements are unchanged. *See also* Mass. Gen. Laws 149: 105D (1985) (providing up to eight weeks maternity leave). The dissent suggests that the reference to the Connecticut and Montana statutes should be disregarded, because Congress did not expressly state that it understood that "these statutes required anything more than equal treatment." *Post,* at 301. However, we are not as willing as the dissent to impute ignorance to Congress. Where Congress has cited these statutes in the House and Senate Reports on the PDA, we think it is fair to assume that it was aware of their substantive provisions'").

144   *Id.* at 288 (citing *Pacific Gas & Electric Co. v. State Energy Resources Conservation and Development Comm'n,* 461 U.S. 190, 206 (1983)).

145   *Id.* (The Court noted to support this point that "[f]or example, the Senate Report states: 'Since [T]itle VII does not preempt state laws which would not require violating [T]itle VII…these states would continue to be able to enforce their state laws if the bills were enacted" (citing S. REP. NO. 95-331, *supra,* note 139, at p. 3, n. 1, LEG. HIST. 40).)

146   *Id.* (citing *Griggs v. Duke Power Co.,* 401 U.S. 424, 429–430 (1979); *Hishon v. King & Spalding,* 467 U.S. 69, 75, n. 7 (1984); *Franks v. Bowman Transportation Co.,* 424 U.S. 727, 763 (1976); *Alexander v. Gardner-Denver Co.,* 415 U.S. 36, 44 (1974); *McDonnell Douglas Corp. v. Green,* 411 U.S. 792, 800 (1973)).

147   *Id.* at 289, n. 26. (The Court noted that "[p]roponents of the bill repeatedly emphasized that the Supreme Court had erroneously interpreted congressional intent and that the amending legislation was necessary to reestablish the principles of Title VII law as they have been understood prior to the *Gilbert* decision" (citing *Newport News Shipbuilding & Dry Dock v. EEOC,* 462 U.S. at 679).)

148   *Id.* at 289 (citing 123 CONG. REC. 29658 (1977)).

149   *Id.* at n. 27. ("As authoritatively construed by respondent Commission, the provision will 'insure that women affected by pregnancy, childbirth, or related medical conditions have equal employment opportunities as persons not so affected,'" the Court explained, citing CALIFORNIA FAIR EMPLOYMENT AND HOUSING COMMISSION'S PROPOSED REGULATION.)

150   414 U.S. 563 (1974).

151   *Guerra,* 479 U.S. at 289 (citing 429 U.S. at 159).

152   *Id.* at 290.

153   *Id.* (citing B. Brown, A. Freedman, H. Katz & A. Price, WOMEN'S RIGHTS AND THE LAW (1977), at pp. 209–210). "In the constitutional context," the Court wrote, "we have invalidated on equal protection grounds statutes designed 'to exclude or "protect" members of one gender because they are presumed to suffer from an inherent handicap or to be innately inferior.'" *See, e.g., Mississippi University for Women v. Hogan,* 458 U.S. 718, 725 (1982)).

154   *Id.* (citing *Los Angeles Dept. of Water & Power v. Manhart,* 435 U.S. 702, 709 (1978); *Phillips v. Martin Marietta Corp.,* 400 U.S. 542, 545 (1971)(Marshall, J., concurring)).

CHAPTER SEVEN

The Law of Pregnancy in the Workplace

THE TOUGH TASK OF PROVING
PREGNANCY DISCRIMINATION:
Title VII and the PDA at Work

The Pregnancy Discrimination Act created a specific cause of action for claims of adverse treatment based upon pregnancy or conditions related to pregnancy. Given the language of the 1978 amendment, "pregnancy discrimination" would seem to be a category of discrimination all its own, and there have been cases decided under the Pregnancy Discrimination Act, a handful of which are presented below for illustrative purposes.

But PDA is an amendment to Title VII, which, among others things, prohibits "gender discrimination," a broad category of offenses that includes: (1) "sex discrimination" or discrimination based upon one's gender; (2) sexual harassment or claims of discrimination based upon the creation of a hostile environment or inappropriate sexual conduct; and, (3) pregnancy discrimination or discrimination based upon pregnancy or a related condition.

By current standards, "pregnancy discrimination" is an antiquated term which has been folded into that category of offenses more commonly referred to today as "gender discrimination." And yet, definitions—even those intended to offer women relief—have proved simpler to devise than to apply. Indeed, as the cases below show, this area of law is complicated, in part because managing pregnancy in the workplace is complicated. But also because the language of the PDA, though seemingly simple on its face, has proved staggeringly complicated in its application.

THE LAW IN PRACTICE:
Applying the Pregnancy Discrimination Act

As interpreted following its amendment in 1978, "Title VII was amended to pro-hibit discrimination based on pregnancy after the Supreme Court in *General Electric Co. v. Gilbert* held that pregnancy discrimination was not based on gender," the Eighth Circuit Court of Appeals wrote in *Piantanida v. Wyman Center, Inc.*[1] The Eighth Circuit held further that, as amended, Title VII sets forth:

> [t]he terms 'because of sex' or 'on the basis of sex' include, but are not limited to, because of or on the basis of pregnancy, childbirth, or related medical conditions; and women affected by pregnancy, childbirth, or related medical conditions, shall be treated the same for all employment-related purposes, including receipt of benefits under fringe benefit programs, as other persons not so affected but similar in their ability or inability to work, and nothing in section 2000e-2(h) of this title shall be interpreted to permit otherwise.[2]

Given the sweep of this language, it would be tempting to conclude that the PDA has always been read and applied so broadly. But the nation's courts have often read it more conservatively. The Seventh Circuit Court of Appeals held, in *Ilhardt v. Sara Lee Corp.*, for example, that "[t]he Pregnancy Discrimination Act amended Title VII of the Civil Rights Act to clarify that pregnancy discrimination is included in Title VII's prohibition on sex discrimination. The PDA provides that '[w]omen affected by pregnancy, childbirth, or related medical conditions shall be treated the same for all employment related purposes...as other persons not so affected but similar in their ability or inability to work.'"[3] (For further reading, *see* summary of *Ilhardt v. Sara Lee Corp.*, *infra*, pp. 179.)

In contrast, the First Circuit Court of Appeals concluded in *Smith v. F.W. Morse*, that "an employee (pregnant or not) runs a risk of suffering the ordinary slings and arrows that suffuse the workplace every day she goes to work and every day she stays away. Title VII is neither a shield against this broad spectrum of employee actions nor a statutory guaranty of full employment, come what may."[4] Echoing this language, the Third Circuit held, in *In re Carnegie Center Associates*, that the PDA "is neither a shield against discrimination, nor a sword in the hands of a pregnant employee."[5]

Three different federal appeals circuits, three different interpretations. But what protections, then, does the Pregnancy Discrimination Act provide? According to the First Circuit, "Title VII provides...that it is an unlawful employment practice for an employer to discharge an individual because of her sex. Like other Title VII plaintiffs, an employee claiming discrimination on the basis of pregnancy may proceed under either a disparate treatment or a disparate impact theory."[6]

That may sound like a simple task. But except in the most egregious cases, until recently, allegations of pregnancy or gender discrimination were very difficult to prove. In addition, despite the 1978 amendment, the analysis of allegations of purposeful discrimination in violation of Title VII is complex, full of shifting burdens, intricate and judicially devised balancing tests, court-drawn distinctions, and procedural requirements. And the analysis gets even more complicated when a woman alleges disparate treatment as Kathy Smith did in *Smith v. F.W. Morse & Co.*, Inc.

WHEN SHE IS NO LONGER NEEDED:
Smith v. F.W. Morse & Co., Inc.[7]

Despite the passage of Title VII and the Pregnancy Discrimination Act, one of the most dangerous times for a woman professionally is during maternity leave. In that sense, the 1996 case of *Smith v. F.W. Morse & Co., Inc.* helps illuminate some of the issues surrounding the "problem" of pregnancy in the workplace and the analysis used by courts to work through claims of this sort.

According to court documents, Kathy Smith had worked for Damar Plastics & Metal Fabricators, Inc. for more than ten years when the company was bought by F.W. Morse & Company.[8] Following a brief period of reorganization, Smith was interviewed, evaluated, and promoted by the new owners, who created the position of materials manager for her.

ILHARDT v. SARA LEE CORP.,
118 F.3d 1151 (7th Cir. 1997)

In June 1994, the Sara Lee Corporation began a company-wide reduction of its workforce. One of the employees "reduced" was Lora Ilhardt, an in-house attorney. Ilhardt had worked for Sara Lee since 1988, when she was hired as the first female lawyer in the Chicago office. Ilhardt was promoted several times during her tenure, noted the Seventh Circuit.[9]

After a three-month maternity leave in October 1989, Ilhardt was allowed to return to work on a three days a week schedule. In 1991, the legal department began a planned move to new offices. As she planned for maternity leave prior to having her second child, Ilhardt noticed that her name and title did not appear on a diagram of the new quarters.

Concerned, Ilhardt asked the company's general counsel about the omission. According to the court, Ilhardt was told by the general counsel "that he wanted to wait to see if she returned to work and then determine what their needs were."[10] Ilhardt then spoke to her direct supervisor, who told her "that although Sara Lee reserved its right to reevaluate its need for a full-time attorney in the future, she could return to work part-time after her maternity leave."

Reassured, Ilhardt went on maternity leave, returning to work without incident. But in the fall of 1992, rumors of a force reduction began to circulate, and the company's general counsel concluded it would be best to eliminate Ilhardt's position, because it was part-time and the full-time employees could absorb her work.[11] The general counsel testified that he informed Ilhardt of the decision. Ilhardt argued she was never told her position might be eliminated. There is no dispute the legal department later created another full-time attorney position in response to an upturn in business in Latin America. Ilhardt was offered the position and told she might be able to preserve her job if she were working full-time.

Ilhardt declined the full-time position, in part because it involved extensive travel. Ilhardt was also "contemplating another pregnancy," according to the court, although she had not informed Sara Lee officials of that fact. Then, in April of 1993, Ilhardt announced her third pregnancy, volunteering—given the impending job eliminations—to extend her maternity leave for six months in an effort to save her job and help the department's budget. But that same month, the president of Sara Lee announced a force reduction plan and began meeting with company department heads.

During these discussions, the company agreed to Ilhardt's proposal, but with two conditions: (1) that the leave would last for eight months; and (2) that after the leave ended, there was no guarantee Ilhardt would have a job. Only if the law department's budget permitted it would Ilhardt be invited to return. But Ilhardt rejected the company's offer. Company officials then informed Ilhardt that she could choose to receive a severance package either before maternity leave or after should the budget not allow her return. Then, "[t]hinking that Ilhardt would accept the company's offer of taking leave in lieu of termination, [a company official] told the rest of the law department that none of them would be affected" by the force reduction, the court held.

But at some point later, Ilhardt asked Sara Lee officials if returning full-time after maternity leave would save her job. She was told that was no longer an option. Another attorney had been hired to fill the position Ilhardt declined. In June of 1993, Ilhardt's name was placed on a list of personnel to be laid off with a note that Ilhardt was on extra "nonpaid maternity leave." But on a later list, Ilhardt was listed as "status to be determined."

In September of 1993, Ilhardt was told that her position had been eliminated, the court found. Ilhardt went on maternity leave in October, requesting a date of return in January 1994. She was told by company officials that her position had been eliminated the previous June. Ilhardt was also reminded that more than a year before, she had been told her part-time position would be eliminated were there a need to reduce staff in the legal department. At the time, Ilhardt "agreed that would be a fair decision," an official testified.[12]

Ilhardt contacted the EEOC, which issued a right-to-sue letter. Ilhardt filed suit alleging disparate treatment in violation of the Pregnancy Discrimination Act; a claim under the Family and Medical Leave Act; and a disparate impact allegation under Title VII. A district court granted summary judgment in favor of Sara Lee, ruling that Ilhardt had failed to make a *prima facie* case of discrimination. Specifically, the court concluded that Ilhardt could not show that she had been treated less favorably than nonpregnant employees. Rather, the facts seemed to suggest Ilhardt had been treated better than some nonpregnant employees.

The district court also held that Ilhardt's disparate impact claim failed because she could not prove that selecting employees for elimination based upon part-time status or that her selection as a part-time employee had a disparate impact on women. Reconsideration of these claims was at issue before the Seventh Circuit. Affirming the district court's ruling, the Seventh Circuit reviewed the lower court's analysis of the issue in light of *McDonnell Douglas* test. Because Sara Lee acknowledged that Ilhardt satisfied the first three elements of the case, only the fourth element remained in dispute (*i.e.*, Sara Lee did not dispute that: Ilhardt was "pregnant and, thus, a member of a protected class; officials knew she was pregnant; Ilhardt was performing her duties satisfactorily, but was still discharged or demoted).

These admissions left only the question of whether "[s]imilarly situated employees not in the protected class were treated more favorably" than Ilhardt. But even this singular analysis proved tricky given the facts of the case. "The difficulty here is obvious," the Seventh Circuit wrote. "[W]e must compare Ilhardt's treatment with that of a group of similarly situated nonpregnant employees to see if she was treated worse because she was pregnant, but because Ilhardt was the only part-time member of the law department, there are no other similarly situated employees with whom to compare her."

"It is also clear, however, that we cannot compare Ilhardt with the nonpregnant full-time attorneys, as she suggests, because full-time employees are simply not similarly situated to part-time employees," the court continued. "There are too many differences between them; as illustrated in Ilhardt's case, part-time employees work fewer hours and receive less pay and fewer benefits. In order for us to make the inference that Sara Lee discriminated against her because of her pregnancy, Ilhardt must show that 'she was treated less favorably than a nonpregnant employee under identical circumstances.' But because she was the only part-time attorney, she could not do this," the court ruled.[13]

Further, Ilhardt could not prove she had been treated less favorably because of her pregnancy, because she could not "contradict the fact that [her supervisor] decided to eliminate her part-time position *before* she became pregnant," the court explained. "Regardless of whether he communicated this decision to her, the fact that he made the decision six months before she announced her pregnancy necessarily means he could not have made the decision because of her pregnancy." For these reasons, Ilhardt could not establish a *prima facie* case, the court held.[14]

At about the time of the purchase, Smith told Chris Bond, the new owner of the company, that she was pregnant and would need maternity leave.[15] Though F.W. Morse had no formal maternity leave policy, Smith testified that Bond "assured her" her position would be secure even if she took time off.[16]

But two things happened while Smith was on maternity leave. First, company officials found that "the plant functioned very well" without Smith.[17] Second was that company officials "grew suspicious" that Smith did not intend to return to work after maternity leave, although Smith visited the company while on leave and told F.W. Morse officials she intended to return. There is no clear explanation for this "suspicion," though the court seems to suggest that someone at F.W. Morse may have started the rumor. According to the court:

> Smith visited the plant on May 1 and informed [Plant Supervisor Maryann] Guimond that she wished to return to work one week earlier than originally anticipated. Guimond inquired about whether Smith desired more children and Smith replied affirmatively. The following day, Guimond queried Karen Vendasi, Smith's sister and coworker, about Smith's plans to have a larger family. Vendasi relayed this conversation to Smith and told her of nascent rumors that she might not return to work. Smith contacted Guimond and demanded an explanation. Guimond denied any knowledge of the rumors, dismissed them as idle "buzznacking," and again assured Smith that her job was secure. Guimond repeated those assurances during a chance meeting on May 4.[18]

But a few days after the May 4 conversation, Guimond "concluded that the materials manager's position was superfluous."[19] On May 11, Guimond called Smith to tell her of the decision. During that conversation, according to the court, Guimond asked Smith if she wanted Guimond to tell her coworkers that Smith had decided to stay home with her baby. "Smith rejected the suggestion," the court noted. "Nevertheless, a Morse employee repeated this canard to several customers."[20] The employee was later reprimanded.[21]

Smith filed suit in a New Hampshire state court, alleging wrongful discharge based upon gender discrimination. Smith also filed state claims for intentional infliction of emotional distress and breach of contract.[22] But because the gender discrimination allegation invoked Title VII, a federal claim, attorneys for F.W. Morse removed the case to federal court.[23] Once there, a federal district court granted summary judgment in favor of the company on Smith's common law claims for wrongful discharge and emotional distress.[24]

To succeed on a Motion for Summary Judgment, the moving party (F.W. Morse) must show that there is no dispute as to the material facts underlying a claim before the court.[25] By contrast, the person hoping to stave off such a motion (Smith) must show that there are facts in dispute best resolved by a jury. In addition to granting summary judgment for F.W. Morse on Smith's wrongful discharge and emotional distress claims, the district court entered a Judgment as a Matter of Law in favor of F.W. Morse on Smith's breach of contract claim,[26] which left only the Title VII claim before the federal district court.

As set forth above, Smith alleged the elimination of her job was gender/pregnancy discrimination. But F.W. Morse argued that the company "scrapped the materials manager's position and laid off...[Smith] as part of an overall strategy intended to streamline a top-heavy managerial structure."[27] The company argued further that "even if Smith had not been on maternity leave she would have been flattened by the downsizing steamroller."[28] The district court agreed, entering judgment in favor of the company.

But on appeal before the First Circuit Court of Appeals, Smith attempted again—in the court's estimation—to assert a disparate treatment argument. "Consequently, she has the burden of proving that the defendant purposefully terminated her employment because of her pregnancy," the First Circuit court explained.[29] "In cases predating the Civil Rights Act of 1991, the framework for proving intentional discrimination varies depending on the availability of direct evidence.[30] Absent the evidentiary equivalent of a 'smoking gun,' the plaintiff must attempt to prove her case by resorting to a burden-shifting framework."[31]

That, however, is where it gets really complicated and involves discussion of a recent history, a history of women's issues tangled with the history of minorities in the United States.

THE *McDONNELL DOUGLAS* STANDARD:
Racial Discrimination Creates a Framework for Gender Discrimination Claims

Title VII reaches allegations of discrimination based upon gender. It also reaches claims of discrimination based upon race. And, thus, in continuing its analysis of the claims before it in *Smith v. F.W. Morse & Co., Inc.,* the First Circuit Court of Appeals referred back to the precedent of the United States Supreme Court decision in the 1973, case of *McDonnell Douglas Corp. v. Green.*[32]

But the plaintiff in *McDonnell Douglas Corp. v. Green* was not a woman. He was an African American man, a self-styled civil rights activist who worked at McDonnell Douglas Corporation as a mechanic and laboratory technician from 1956 until 1964. When he was laid off "in the course of general reduction," according to the company, and not rehired, Green filed a complaint with the Equal Employment Opportunities Commission, alleging violations of Section 704(a) of Title VII.[33] Green argued that the company refused to rehire him because of his race and his political outspokenness.

McDonnell Douglas Corp. v. Green involved a claim of racial discrimination. But the case has been held to establish the proper framework for analysis of most, if not all, employment discrimination claims arising under Title VII.[34] In terms of standards, according to the United States Supreme Court, "[t]he complainant in a Title VII trial must carry the initial burden under the statute of establishing a *prima facie* case of racial discrimination. This may be done by showing (i) that he belongs to a racial minority; (ii) that he applied and was qualified for a job for which the employer was seeking applicants; (iii) that, despite his qualifications, he was rejected; and (iv) that, after his rejection, the position remained open and the employer continued to seek applicants from persons of complainant's qualifications."[35]

For use in the pregnancy discrimination context, the *McDonnell Douglas* "shifting burden" test has been slightly modified to require that the plaintiff seeking to establish a *prima facie* case of discrimination must show: (1) she is a member of a protected class; (2) she satisfactorily performed the duties required by the position; (3) the employer, nonetheless, dismissed her (or took some other adverse employment action); while, (4) continuing to have her duties performed by a comparably qualified person (and/or that her position remained open and was ultimately filled by a nonpregnant employee).[36]

It is an early burden. But establishing a *prima facie* case by meeting the requirements of this four-part test does not end the court's analysis. Rather, it merely creates "a rebuttable presumption that discrimination may have sparked an adverse employment action[37] and imposes upon the employer a burden to put forward a legitimate, nondiscriminatory motive for the action," the First Circuit Court of Appeals explained in *Smith v. F.W. Morse & Co., Inc.*[38]

"If the defendant clears this modest hurdle, the presumption of discrimination vaporizes,[39] and the plaintiff (who retains the ultimate burden of persuasion on the issue of discriminatory motive throughout) must then prove that the employer's proffered justification is a pretext for discrimination," the court noted in *Smith v. F.W. Morse & Co., Inc.*[40]

In applying the burden-shifting test to Smith's claims, the First Circuit Court of Appeals held that she had failed to establish a *prima facie* case.

"There is little doubt that an employer, consistent with its business judgment, may eliminate positions during the course of a downsizing without violating Title VII, even though those positions are held by members of protected groups (pregnant women included)...[41][T]he undisputed evidence before the district court indicates that after Guimond dismissed Smith, the position that Smith had occupied—materials manager—fell into desuetude.[42] ...[T]he second round of the reorganization (which cost Smith her job) bore a striking resemblance to the first round (which gave Smith her promotion to materials manager). Given these facts, the district judge's determination that Morse eliminated the appellant's position is unimpugnable," the court ruled.[43]

SHIFTING BURDENS IN REAL LIFE:
Differing Interpretations Among the Courts

But the application of the "shifting burdens" test to "real life" facts has led to less than uniform results than might be expected, despite the seemingly formulaic nature of the test. Thus, some courts have agreed with the reasoning of the First Circuit in *Smith v. F.W. Morse & Co., Inc.,* in reviewing "pregnancy discrimination" claims while others have expressly held the opposite. A federal district court in Ohio agreed, for example, in *Soreo-Yasher v. First Office Management,*[44] with the reasoning of the First Circuit in *Smith v. F.W. Morse & Co., Inc.,* while the Second Circuit in *Quarantino v. Tiffany & Company* relied upon the opposite reasoning.

What these cases suggest is that while the law prohibits the outright firing of women due to pregnancy, some courts have held that a woman can be permanently replaced at work because she is absent from her job, even if the reason for that absence is maternity leave. Loopholes in the legislative "shield" that was supposed to be the the PDA have long formed the basis of arguments of feminists and women's rights scholars. The trouble for women, however, is that these and other "women's" issues are part of a larger societal scheme. And the reproductive choices of women, it seems, continue to be shaped by work and work-related issues.

Some research suggests, for example, that career interests and professional concerns have led a generation of American women to postpone childbearing until later in life, sometimes even beyond the point of "natural" biological possibility. Economist Sylvia Hewlett, author of *Creating a Life*, notes that among 1,000 women surveyed with incomes of $55,000 or above, "childlessness"—as Hewlett terms it—"is a huge problem. Thirty-three percent of them don't have children at age 40....They're at the end of the road, as it were. And if you look at corporate America, 42 percent of these women don't have kids."[45]

Why so much "childlessness" among women in the corporate world? As set forth in greater detail in Chapters 4–6, extraordinary amounts of social and political capital have been spent attempting to ensure that all but the most dangerous pregnancies are carried to term. And yet, at a time when more women are working than ever before and "childlessness" is growing, caselaw suggests that where working women do choose to have children, they continue to face challenges in the workplace, despite laws intended to protect them. And as often as they are subtle, perhaps even elusive, the means of harassment may be overt and mean-spirited.

QUARANTINO v. TIFFANY & CO.,
71 F.3d 58 (2nd Cir. 1995)

Mary Quarantino worked for the famed retailer Tiffany & Company for seven years, having been promoted and given favorable evaluations several times until she discovered she was pregnant in 1991.[46] In May of that year, Quarantino reported her condition to her supervisor whose "...immediate response to this news was an expletive and he avoided her throughout the following week," the Second Circuit court found.[47]

Quarantino alleged that soon after, her supervisor became "highly critical of her; continued to avoid her; 'acted' unfriendly towards her; and sent her a memo in July 1991 'accusing' her of 'consistently poor performance with regard to tardiness' and threatening 'more serious action.'" [48] In the months leading up to maternity leave, Quarantino alleged that her job title was eliminated.

Tiffany's officials said Quarantino's duties were expanded, but characterized the move as part of a "reorganization." Quarantino also alleged she was told by a supervisor "not to worry and that her [new] job in the corporate department would be waiting when she returned."[49] But that same supervisor also allegedly told Quarantino "a mother should stay home with her child, and explained how his wife had quit working and stayed home with their child."[50]

Quarantino eventually took maternity leave, communicating regularly with the company while away. But upon her return, Quarantino found that she had no job, and another woman—who was single with no children—was working in her office. Quarantino was later notified by mail that she had been discharged. According to the company, a reorganization had resulted in the termination of Quarantino and two other "managers."[51] Quarantino challenged this assertion, arguing that the other "managers" said to have lost their jobs were still with the company.

In January 1993, the EEOC issued a Notice of a Right to Sue on Quarantino's behalf. Quarantino filed suit against Tiffany and two supervisors, alleging unlawful discrimination in violation of the Pregnancy Discrimination Act and the New York State Human Rights Law.[52] In reviewing an appeal of summary judgment at the district court level, the Second Circuit noted that "[t]he language of Title VII reveals Congress' intent to assure equality of employment opportunities and to eliminate discriminatory practices on the basis of race or any other impermissible classifications."[53]

The court then looked to whether Quarantino had met the requirements of the modified *McDonnell Douglas* test,[54] finding ultimately that she had. "Employers," the Second Circuit held, "have the right to restructure jobs and job responsibilities, but they cannot use that process to implement discrimination objectives.[55] An employee may always show that her employer's decisions on restructuring—as applied to her—were made to displace her for impermissible reasons such as taking maternity leave. Whether the former position remained open or had been eliminated presented a question of fact that should have been determined by a jury, not by the trial court judge."[56] That and other disputed facts foreclosed the grant of summary judgment, the court ruled, which cleared the way for a trial before a jury.

SOREO-YASHER v. FIRST OFFICE MANAGEMENT,
926 F.Supp. 646 (N.D.Ohio 1996)

Marie Soreo-Yasher worked for nearly three years as a property manager for the company's Lakewood, Ohio, office. But in July of 1990, Yasher told her employers she was pregnant and would want to take maternity leave. First Office Management had a policy of allowing eight weeks of leave, during which time other employees would assume the absent worker's position, she was told by a company administrator.

While Yasher alleged that she was never told she could be permanently replaced if she took maternity leave, First Office Management had a written policy, providing that "[t]he company will not hold a position open for an employee nor guarantee that a position will be available when an employee returns from a leave of absence."[57] But Yasher alleged that she did not receive a copy of the policy statement until just before her maternity leave was to begin. An Ohio district court found, however, that Yasher had "signed an agreement which stated that she would accept the leave under the terms and conditions of the policies of the company."[58]

While on leave, Yasher's position was filled by a man, an alleged friend of her supervisor's. The supervisor would later assert that he filled the position because "he felt that the Lakewood property needed an onsite manager."[59] Although Yasher was aware someone was carrying out her duties during her absence, it is not clear that she understood her position had been permanently assigned to someone else.

In March of 1991, Yasher informed her supervisor that she intended to return to work. But since someone else had her job, Yasher's supervisor told her she had no position to return to. She could apply for a different position, Yasher was told. Instead, she filed suit, alleging pregnancy discrimination in violation of Title VII.

In granting summary judgment in favor of the company, the federal district court held "[that] '[i]f a company's business necessitates the adoption of particular leave policies, Title VII does not prohibit the company from applying these policies to all leaves of absence, including pregnancy leaves....'[60] 'The Pregnancy Discrimination Act requires the employer to ignore an employee's pregnancy, but...not her absence from work, unless the employer overlooks the comparable absences of nonpregnant employees.'"[61]

The court held further that "[d]ue to the nature and duties of a property manager for an apartment complex, [First Office Management] believes that it needed an onsite manager. There is no evidence in the record that Yasher was treated any differently than nonpregnant employees who were on leave for a similar period of time. There is simply no causal connection between Yasher's pregnancy and [First Office Management']s decision to replace her. Therefore, the [c]ourt finds that Yasher was not discriminated against on the basis of her pregnancy."[62]

BEYOND THE *McDONNELL DOUGLAS* TEST:
The Evidentiary Requirements

> "Absent the evidentiary equivalent of a 'smoking gun,' the plaintiff must attempt to prove her case by resorting to a burden-shifting framework."
> *Smith v. F.W. Morse & Co., Inc.*[63]

In terms of the law, the courts have generally held that a plaintiff may prevail in a gender or pregnancy discrimination claim "if she submits enough believable evidence for a jury to find that an adverse employment decision resulted because of discrimination."[64] But, as set forth above, several "burdens" must first be met (*i.e.*, the plaintiff must offer sufficient "believable evidence" to establish a *prima facie* case of pregnancy or gender discrimination). And in answering the primary question of just how much "believable evidence" is "enough" to meet the burden of establishing a *prima facie* case for "pregnancy discrimination," the courts have declared that this evidentiary burden "is not onerous."[65]

This is technical stuff. And yet, even with the bar set so low, some courts note that there are few occasions when a plaintiff can offer direct evidence sufficient—in and of itself—to establish a *prima facie* case.[66] Indeed, "[a]bsent the evidentiary equivalent of a 'smoking gun,' the plaintiff must attempt to prove her case by resort to a burden-shifting framework," the First Circuit Court of Appeals has held, for example.[67] When such an absence has been established, direct or circumstantial evidence may be offered instead by the plaintiff hoping to assert a *prima facie* discriminatory case.[68] But what is the difference?

"Direct evidence" has been defined in the most concise terms as "[e]vidence that directly proves a fact, without an inference or presumption, and which in itself, if true, conclusively establishes that fact."[69] By contrast, "circumstantial evidence" has been defined as "[t]he proof of various facts or circumstances which usually attend the main fact in dispute, and therefore tend to prove its existence, or to sustain, by their consistency, the hypothesis claimed. Or as otherwise defined, it consists in reasoning from facts which are known or proved to establish such as are conjectured to exist."[70]

And yet, there are those occasions—rare though they may be—"when a smoking gun is discernible."[71] Or would seem to be. In such cases, direct evidence of a discriminatory motive—an admission, for example, by the employer that an agent took a woman's actual or anticipated pregnancy into account in making an adverse employment decision—immediately shifts the burden of persuasion from the employee to the employer,[72] who must then prove that he or she would have made the same decision whether or not the plaintiff was pregnant.[73]

But just how "direct" does that evidence have to be in order to be considered a "smoking gun" by the courts? Would threatening to push a pregnant employee down a flight of stairs to induce a miscarriage qualify as direct evidence? Would harassing an employee with the intent of coercing her into having an abortion be considered a "smoking gun?" What about making her lift heavy crates?

BERGSTROM-EK v. BEST OIL CO.:
A Smoking Gun or a Loose Cannon?

Nicole Bergstrom-Ek began working as a sales clerk earning minimum wage in a Minnesota convenience store in October 1993. By early 1995, she was about to be promoted to assistant manager, a job she was already training for when, on January 12, 1995, she "received an excellent review for her job performance and was given a $.30 per hour raise," wrote the Eighth Circuit Court of Appeals in *Bergstrom-Ek v. Best Oil Co.*[74] The raise was supposed to take effect on January 29, 1995.

It never happened.

For the duration of Ek's employment with The Little Store, her supervisor was a woman named Lola Aune, who told Ek she "would have a good chance of becoming the manager…[of the store where she worked] because at some point

Aune would probably move to a new store...."[75] For most of her tenure, Ek "had an excellent working relationship" with Aune.[76] The two women occasionally socialized outside of work.[77] But a few days after the glowing work review, Ek learned she was pregnant, and when she told Aune, everything changed.

"During their first conversation about the pregnancy," according to the court, "Aune told Ek to get an abortion." And it didn't stop there. "Aune said Ek was 'stupid,' that the father would never 'stick around' and that Ek would end up on welfare. Aune offered to take Ek to the Twin Cities to get an abortion," even offering to pay. But "Ek refused to have an abortion. Lynette Lone, a sales clerk at West End, witnessed the negative change in Aune's behavior toward Ek after Aune learned of Ek's pregnancy. Lone heard Aune tell Ek to get an abortion on more than six different occasions."[78]

Although "Aune did not deny that she discussed the issue of abortion with Ek"...she testified "that rather than telling Ek to get an abortion, she told Ek if *she were* in Ek's situation she might have an abortion,"[79] the Eighth Circuit found. But the incidents seemed only to begin there: "On one occasion, Aune called Ek's home and talked to Ek for a long period of time trying to persuade her to get an abortion.... Once Ek refused to have an abortion, Aune said she would push Ek down a flight of stairs to cause a miscarriage, that Ek would have no way to pay for a baby, and that insurance would not cover the cost of delivering the baby because Ek was pregnant before she was promoted.... On another occasion, Aune invited her cousin to come into West End and tell Ek how much it costs for the birth of a baby."[80]

And then there were Aune's efforts at work.

"In January 1995, Aune, Ek and Curt Solomon (Aune's supervisor) met to discuss Ek's promotion to assistant manager," according to the court. "During this conversation Aune told Solomon that Ek was pregnant and that Aune told her to get an abortion. Solomon inquired whether Ek wanted to have an abortion. Ek told him 'no.' Aune was not disciplined for discussing Ek's pregnancy on work premises or for suggesting that Ek have an abortion."

Among Ek's regular duties was stocking the store's coolers, which involved lifting heavy crates of soda. According to the findings of the court, the pattern among Aune and other supervisors was to order pregnant employees to lift heavy items.[81] In Ek's case, "Aune made Ek lift such items more often than she was required to do before she became pregnant," the Eighth Circuit found.[82] Ek felt that lifting such items might be dangerous to the fetus and brought in a note from her doctor, requesting she not work in the evenings.[83] Aune responded to the note by telling Ek that if her pregnancy was going to cause any restrictions on her work, Aune would reevaluate Ek's position.[84]

That seemed to be what happened.

"In February 1995, Aune and another Little Stores manager told Ek she would not be able to move up in the company because she could not take care of a child and manage a career," the court held.[85] As a matter of law, withholding a promotion because an employee became pregnant would certainly seem to qualify as an adverse employment action. But that does not appear to have been the focus of the court. Nor was it the breaking point for Ek. That came on March 10, 1995, when Ek was ordered to stock a soda cooler by Denise Bond, another of the company's supervisors who happened to be Aune's aunt.

Ek refused the order and called Aune in an effort to settle the dispute. Aune told Ek to stock the cooler, assuring Ek that the lifting probably would not hurt the fetus, because Ek "was not that far along in her pregnancy." Ek asked to speak to another supervisor who happened to be working alongside Aune that day. When Aune refused to let her speak to the other supervisor, Ek quit. She would later file suit against The Little Stores and its parent company, Best Oil, alleging constructive discharge and discrimination on the basis of pregnancy in violation of Title VII and the Minnesota Human Rights Act.[86]

Among the questions considered by the court was whether Aune's alleged conduct reached the "smoking gun" standard.[87] To meet the "smoking gun" standard, legal scholars explain that a plaintiff must offer the most direct kind of evidence, *i.e.*, evidence that, if believed, "proves [the] existence of" discrimination based upon the fact that Ek was pregnant "without inference or presumption."

In *Bergstrom-Ek v. Best Oil Co.*, according to the Eighth Circuit's findings, Ek was slated for promotion as of January 12, 1995. But after she informed her supervisors a few days later that she was pregnant, Ek was told to have an abortion; harassed and bullied because she was pregnant; threatened with possible termination; and denied that previously promised promotion. These were the Eighth Circuit's findings, but would that same court hold these incidents to be "direct evidence" of gender discrimination?

DIRECT VS. CIRCUMSTANTIAL EVIDENCE:
Balancing the Facts in Pregnancy Discrimination Claims

If the First Circuit Court of Appeals were hearing *Bergstrom-Ek v. Best Oil Co.*, the determination of the court might have been that Ek offered evidence tending to prove the "existence of [the] fact in issue without inference or presumption."[88] It was the First Circuit Court of Appeals, after all, that expounded on the "smoking gun standard." Ek's claim was grounded in a disparate treatment theory. Given that approach, the Eighth Circuit Court of Appeals—the court actually hearing the case—explained, prior to reviewing the evidence, that "[t]o prevail on a sex discrimination claim under a disparate treatment theory, Ek must present proof of discriminatory intent," which it seems she could not do directly.[89]

Under the law, if Ek had offered direct evidence of discrimination, the burden of persuasion would have shifted to Aune and The Little Store to establish that Aune and other agents of the company would have behaved the same way and/or acted in the same manner had Ek not been pregnant.[90] But Ek could offer only "circumstantial evidence," the Eighth Circuit held.

Absent direct evidence, "Ek relied upon *circumstantial* evidence to prove discriminatory intent…" the court wrote. As a result, the court was obligated to analyze the evidence before it "under the burden-shifting test set forth in the *McDonnell Douglas Corp. v. Green* line of cases."[91] Further complicating the analysis, however, was Ek's allegation of constructive discharge, which added yet another layer of inquiry. In accordance with the *McDonnell Douglas* framework, "Ek [was] required to establish a *prima facie* case by presenting evidence demonstrating: '(1) she is a member of a protected group; (2) she was qualified for her position; and (3) she was discharged under circumstances giving rise to an inference of discrimination,'" the court explained.[92]

Ek easily established the first two requirements of the test: She was "a member of the protected class of pregnant women and The Little Stores does not dispute that Ek was qualified for her position," the Eighth Circuit found. The question should have been, then, whether Ek was discharged because she was pregnant. But Ek had not been discharged in the traditional sense. Rather, she quit, alleging "constructive discharge." State and federal law hold that "[a]n employee is constructively discharged 'when an employer deliberately renders the employee's working conditions intolerable and thus forces her to quit her job.'"[93]

For purposes of a Motion for Judgment as a Matter of Law, which was the motion before the Eighth Circuit, the standard is whether a plaintiff can offer evidence "sufficient" enough "to support a jury verdict in her favor on this element to support constructive discharge." Ek had reached this standard, the court held, noting that "Aune constantly tried to convince Ek to have an abortion even after Ek told Aune she would not have an abortion." Further, "[s]ome of these statements, and other statements regarding Ek's pregnancy, were made in front of Ek's co-employees and customers at West End. Aune required Ek to lift heavy items more often than before Aune learned of Ek's pregnancy. Aune's behavior towards Ek's changed from friendly and courteous to mean and hostile," the court held.[94]

Finally, on the issue of "intent" (*i.e.*, whether employees for The Little Store intended to discriminate against Ek), the court concluded that Ek had presented evidence that "in the absence of justifiable cause to fire an employee, The Little Stores' method of getting an undesirable employee to quit was to reduce such employee's hours. Moreover, despite [a supervisor's] knowledge of other young pregnant females who complained of Aune's discriminatory conduct, no disciplinary action was taken against Aune, except the verbal warning in connection with [another pregnant employee] not to discuss employees' pregnancies on work premises. Based upon this evidence, a reasonable jury could conclude it was reasonably foreseeable to The Little Stores that other pregnant employees would quit because of Aune's discriminatory conduct."[95]

Although the Eighth Circuit did not find the evidentiary equivalent of a "smoking gun" to exist in *Bergstrom-Ek v. Best Oil Co.*, the court's decision shows how previous knowledge of actual or potentially discriminatory conduct on the part of an employee can expose employers to liability under the Title VII. Thus, it might fairly be argued that *Bergstrom-Ek v. Best Oil Co.*, sets the bar on the "loose cannon" standard.

And yet, the larger point with regard to *Bergstrom-Ek v. Best Oil Co.* is that according to the Eighth Circuit, Ek, a convenience store clerk earning barely more than minimum wage, went to work to face threats to push her down a flight of stairs; harassment; name-calling; and disparate treatment because she was pregnant. Preventing behavior of this kind—to the extent that any law can—was clearly the intent of the Pregnancy Discrimination Act.

In that sense, the Eighth Circuit court's decision in *Bergstrom-Ek v. Best Oil Co.* may represent a triumph of the law at work. But it also illustrates the kind of treatment pregnant women still sometimes endure. The Eighth Circuit court decided the issues of the case in 1998. That's hardly ancient times, and the incidents seem to run the gamut from less egregious events to those so troubling that women are forced to quit their jobs. At other times, women are still fired outright—despite the PDA—though employers usually attempt to offer another—sometimes pretextual—reason for a pregnant worker's dismissal. After all, pregnancy discrimination is against the law.

DEFINING INTENT:
The Pretext Question

What is a pretext and why would consideration of such an issue matter to women in the workplace? In the legal context, the term "pretext" has been defined as an "[o]stensible reason or motive assigned or assumed as a color or cover for the real reason or motive [behind an act]; false appearance, pretense."[96] Questions of "pretext," (*i.e.*, whether someone has assigned or offered a false reason to cover a "real motive") are often raised in the discrimination context, in part because if employers accused of impermissible discrimination based upon race or sex could offer an alternate reason for their actions, liability might not attach.

The 1995 case of *Nilson v. Historic Inns Group Ltd.*[97] offers an example of the "pretextual" issue. From December 1, 1993, until March 1994, Stacey Nilson worked as a banquet manager for Historic Inns Group Limited. Before Nilson was hired, another woman, Joan Quimby, held the position of banquet manager, and when she was promoted, Nilson was hired to fill the vacant position. Quimby was assigned to train Nilson in the duties of the job.

But on March 17, 1994, Nilson was summoned to the office of Joseph Holzman, who was food and beverage manager for Historic Inns Group. When she arrived, Nilson found Quimby already there. In short order, "Holzman informed Nilson…it had come to his attention that Nilson had altered the time of some of her subordinates' time cards," the court found. "Although Holzman asked for an explanation from Nilson about the alterations, it appears from the record that Nilson was either unwilling or unable to offer any reasons for the alterations at that time. Holzman terminated her employment immediately."[98] The reason offered by the company was that Nilson had committed a discharge-worthy offense by altering employee time cards.

But Nilson filed suit in federal court, arguing that the "real reason" for her termination was that she was pregnant.[99] Thus, Historic Inns Group had violated Title VII, the Pregnancy Discrimination Act and the Americans with Disabilities Act in firing her, Nilson argued.[100] The latter claim was dismissed with prejudice by the court, which left only the issue of whether Nilson had offered sufficient evidence to show that there was a dispute as to the material facts of the case. After evaluating Nilson's proffered pleadings under the *McDonnell Douglas* standard, the court held that Nilson had.[101]

According to the Historic Inns Group employee manual, "falsification of time records"[102] and "[f]alsification or unauthorized altercation of any hotel records" are acts that "may be considered to be of such a serious nature that they will be grounds for immediate discharge...." Company officials argued that because Nilson had trouble keeping her unit's payroll on budget, she altered time cards "to reduce the number of hours that the employees under her supervision were paid."[103] But after evaluating Nilson's pleadings under the *McDonnell Douglas* standard, the court held that summary judgment was not appropriate.[104]

"It is undisputed that Nilson was pregnant at the time of her termination," the court held. "Moreover, her educational and employment background demonstrate her qualifications for the position,[105] and although the actual motivation behind her 90-day evaluation is in dispute, it appears to demonstrate that she was meeting or exceeding her job requirements just days before her termination."[106] In addition, "Aaron Luna (a male), who ultimately replaced Nilson as banquet manager, had been originally passed over...for that position because it was believed that he was not ready for such responsibility. In fact, the record reveals that he was not immediately chosen to succeed Nilson because doubts as to his abilities still lingered. Therefore, at first glance, it would *appear* that Nilson has established a *prima facie* case."

Among the findings leading the court to this conclusion were that although Historic Inns Group argued Nilson had been fired for altering time cards, testimony established that the practice was common among the company's employees. Quimby told the court, for example, that "there were clearly times when it was proper to make alterations to a time card. She explained, for instance, that she would have altered an employee's time card '[i]f a mistake was made on the punch, if somebody punched a card that wasn't their [*sic*] card, if they forgot to clock in or out, if they have punched in on the wrong shift,'" the court noted.

Also convincing, the court found, was the fact that "Nilson did not dispute...she altered the employee time card. She contends, however, that when her employment began in December 1993, Quimby trained her to make time card alterations in the event that an employee had not punched out when he stopped working for the day."

During her deposition, Nilson recalled an instance when Quimby instructed her on how and when to "properly" change an employee's time card. These instructions came, according to Nilson, when Quimby noticed an employee who was supposed to have left an hour earlier, punched out at the same time that the employee's commuting partner did. "[Quimby] showed me what to do if I needed to change their time cards. She said change the time and initial it," Nilson testified.[107]

"Nilson also stated that she changed the time on the time cards if her employees '[e]ither...have been there when they shouldn't be, or the time clock wasn't working, or you could not read a punch that they punched,'" according to the court. Nilson also testified that she asked why these alterations had not been brought to her attention if there was a problem. "As for her inability to articulate her reasons for the alterations when questions by Holzman at the time of her termination, Nilson maintains that she was overwhelmed,"[108] the court held. She explained, for instance, that she would have altered an employee's time card "[i]f a mistake was made on the punch, if somebody punched a card that wasn't their card, if they forgot to clock in or out, if they have punched in on the wrong shift," the court wrote.[109]

Among the facts foreclosing a grant of summary judgment, according to the court, was Quimby's admission that "she had instructed Nilson to alter a clock in or clock out time to reflect the actual number of hours worked by an employees for payroll accuracy."[110] Despite this admission, Quimby argued that she had "[n]ever...instruct[ed Nilson] to change or alter the clock in or clock out times in order to reduce the number of hours worked." The district court's decision allowed the allegations to proceed to trial before a jury.

EEOC v. CLEAR LAKE DODGE,
60 F.3d 1146 (5th Cir. 1995)

Rhonda Goerlitz was hired as a Customer Service Representative by Gulf Coast Dodge in 1990. According to the Fifth Circuit Court of Appeals, "Goerlitz was about one month into a pregnancy" on her first day of work. Though it is not clear that company officials knew of the pregnancy at the time of the hire, the Fifth Circuit found that after "about one and a half months on the job, and several weeks after she revealed her pregnancy, Goerlitz was removed from her job as a CRS and...assigned temporarily as a dispatcher to fill in for vacationing employees."[111]

Goerlitz's supervisor, Don McMillan, said that the reason for the reassignment was that Goerlitz "was 'too big' to enter vehicles properly" while showing them to customers. McMillan also allegedly told Goerlitz that when she was "no longer needed as a dispatcher, he would look into finding her a clerical position." But after a few weeks as a dispatcher, Goerlitz fell in the company's service driveway, spraining her ankle. When Goerlitz was able and attempted to return to work, she was sent home and told to contact McMillan the following week.

According to the court, "[o]n September 17, Goerlitz called McMillan to ascertain her employment status. McMillan told her he did not need anyone to work in dispatch that day. In response to Goerlitz's inquiry about her status, McMillan replied that it had not changed since their conversation in August when he transferred her.... According to McMillan, he told Goerlitz that he thought they could put together a job for her doing filing and possibly keypunch. Goerlitz asked several times during the conversation if she had been fired; McMillan answered that she had not."[112]

But according to the court, even as he continued to discuss a file clerk's job with Goerlitz, McMillan "prepared a Personal Action Report and had dated it effective September 12, 1990. On the form, the box labeled 'Termination' was checked and the following comment was written: 'unable to perform her duties properly due to pregnancy.'"[113] McMillan would later testify "that this report was not a termination notice, but merely a transfer slip indicating to the company's payroll clerk which department was responsible for the employee's pay."

In February 1992, a district court ruled that the "EEOC and Goerlitz [had] established through direct testimony and documentary evidence that Goerlitz's pregnancy was a substantial factor in Gulf Coast's decision to reassign her."[114] The district court held further that "Gulf Coast had failed to prove by a preponderance of the evidence that the decision to reassign Goerlitz and then discharge her would have been made absent her pregnancy," or that "Goerlitz's pregnancy interfered with her ability to perform either her job as [CSR] or her job in Dispatch."[115]

The Fifth Circuit later affirmed this decision, holding that Gulf Coast had transferred Goerlitz because of her pregnancy and then fired her for the same "impermissible" reason. "The evidence, for example, reveals the undisputed fact that McMillan completed and signed a Personnel Action Report regarding Goerlitz on which he checked the option labeled 'TERMINATION' and noted 'UNABLE TO PERFORM DUTIES PROPERLY DUE TO PREGNANCY.' McMillan also authorized that Goerlitz be given severance pay when he filled out the Personnel Action Report."[116] Finally, the evidence "fully supports the finding that Goerlitz was fired from her job; it adequately refutes Gulf Coast's contention that she was transferred and that she quit. In short, the evidence will support the finding that the reason for Goerlitz's termination was her pregnancy. Although other evidence may support a contrary finding, we hold that the district court committed no error in entering judgment against Gulf Coast on the Title VII case."[117]

VAZQUEZ GONZALEZ v. K-MART CORP.,
940 F.SUPP. 429 (D.PUERTO RICO 1996)

Lynette Vazquez Gonzalez was hired as a part-time employee for K-Mart in Caguas, Puerto Rico, in 1990. By 1994, she was a full-time, "above-average employee" having received several salary raises.[118] In the fall of 1994, Roberto Arana, a supervisor at a K-Mart store in El Señorial, offered Vazquez a position as jewelry manager if she would transfer.[119] Vazquez, pregnant at the time and "[t]empted by the new title and the additional money," accepted, according to the district court.[120] But almost immediately Vazquez complained to Arana. "Because she live[d] near Caguas, Vazquez had to fight traffic congestion before and after work. The additional stress of arriving to work every day in traffic was especially difficult for Vazquez because she was pregnant and frequently experienced terrible morning sickness. Moreover, her new job impeded her from arriving to her classes at a local university on time."[121]

Arana initially tried to accommodate Vazquez, allowing her to arrive at 7:00 a.m. and leave at 4:00 p.m. Still, within three days of transferring to the El Señorial store, Vazquez told Arana she wanted to transfer back to the Caguas store.[122] Arana reluctantly agreed to the transfer, although the court noted that Arana had been initially "inconsiderate" towards Vazquez.[123] Indeed, in a comment the district court deemed worth noting, the justices outlined that "Arana said...[Vazquez] was 'in trouble' and 'screwed.' Whether Arana meant that she was in trouble because she was requesting a transfer within three days of beginning a new job, or that she was in trouble because she was complaining about the difficulty of traffic, or that she was in trouble because she was pregnant is, at best, ambiguous," the court wrote.[124]

But "[w]hat is clear," the court held, "is that Arana agreed to the transfer. He asked her, however, to stay for at least one week to permit him time to find a replacement."[125] Vazquez waited the week as asked. In the interim, she contacted Gina Jimenez, a supervisor with the Caguas store. Jimenez offered Vazquez a part-time position to begin as soon as Arana could find a replacement. But when Vazquez told Arana of Jimenez's offer, he "stated that such an offer did not exist and questioned whether Jimenez could make that kind of offer."[126]

Although the court concluded that Vazquez believed "...Arana was doing everything he possibly could to keep her from leaving El Señorial," because she could offer no direct evidence to support these and other facts, the court declined to consider them.[127] Vazquez continued to report to work at the El Señorial for six more days. On October 5, 1994, she told Arana it was her final day at the El Señorial store, because she was returning to the Caguas store. "Arana, apparently disturbed by her transfer before he had an opportunity to find a replacement and hoping that she would stay at his store, threatened to fire her if she left," according to the court.[128]

The next morning, Vazquez reported to work at the Caguas store. But Jimenez was not prepared for her arrival and told Vazquez to return the following Monday. When Vazquez arrived the next Monday at the Caguas store, she was told to report to the El Señorial store. When she did, with her husband at her side, Arana approached her and "shouted 'you are fired, and that is all. And in fact, you are fired from all the stores. And I talked to all the different stores, and nobody is going to hire you,'" the court found.[129] Later that day, Arana filed a K-Mart Separation Report, noting that he had fired Vazquez for "abandoning" her job."[130] Although Vazquez was later offered a temporary night position, the offer was withdrawn after input from Arana, because "they said...they couldn't trust me anymore," Vazquez testified.

In July 1995, Vazquez filed suit against the K-Mart Corporation, alleging unlawful discrimination based upon pregnancy in violation of Title VII. She also alleged that the company violated Puerto Rico's Civil Code, which outlaws discrimination based upon sex. After an extended period of discovery, attorneys for the K-Mart Corporation moved for summary judgment. A district court would eventually review the pleadings to determine whether Vazquez established a *prima facie* case.

"Under the *McDonnell Douglas* framework, Vazquez bears the initial burden of establishing a *prima facie* case of discrimination on the basis of her pregnancy," the court wrote.[131] "The elements of the *prima facie* case are analogous to four links in a chain.[132] Should Vazquez fail to present sufficient proof of any one link, the connection between her pregnancy and her dismissal is broken, and her case must be dismissed accordingly."[133] Though it was not "immediately apparent" that Vazquez had met that burden, the court held that Vazquez "presented sufficient proof of all four links in a *prima facie* case of sex discrimination."[134]

But that was just the first hurdle, and where Vazquez stumbled in her later obligations, in the court's estimation, was in failing to refute K-Mart's proffer of a "legitimate, nondiscriminatory" reason for her dismissal, which was the second hurdle required to show discrimination. As set forth above, Arana argued that Vazquez was fired because she abandoned her job. This was a "clear and reasonably specific" reason for dismissal, the court held.[135]

To prevail on her claim, given Arana's assertions, Vazquez would have to show that "K-Mart's proffered explanation for her dismissal was a pretext invented to disguise intentional discrimination," the court set forth.[136] In other words, it was not be enough for Vazquez to "prove that K-Mart's justification is pretextual," the court held. Rather, "Vazquez must also prove that her dismissal was motivated by discrimination."[137]

This second hurdle is considerably higher than the first, and Vazquez's failure to overcome it established grounds for the ruling. "Vazquez relied on one isolated, ambiguous remark to prove that K-Mart's proffered explanation is pretextual and that her dismissal was motivated by discrimination," the district court wrote. "The First Circuit Court of Appeals, however, has held that isolated, ambiguous statements are not sufficiently probative of discriminatory animus."[138]

Further, "Vazquez's proof of discriminatory animus rests entirely upon the comment that Arana made when she informed him that she was pregnant and wished to return to the Caguas store. Although Arana agreed to permit the transfer, he stated that she was 'in trouble' and she was 'screwed.' According to Vazquez, this was Arana's only comment regarding her pregnancy. It was clearly an isolated remark,"[139] the court ruled. But it was not enough to prove she was terminated for an impermissible discriminatory reason. Accordingly, the district court granted summary judgment in K-Mart's favor, dismissing Vazquez's Title VII claim with prejudice.[140] The court then declined to exercise pendent jurisdiction over Vazquez's remaining claims under Puerto Rico's Civil Code and Constitution.[141]

"In the instant case," the court wrote, "determinations as to whether Nilson was satisfactorily performing her job, and whether her termination for altering time cards could be deemed pretextual, rely heavily on the relative credibility of Nilson and Quimby. [Thus,] [m]anifestly a grant of summary judgment would be erroneous."[142]

The district court's decision allowed the allegations to proceed to trial before a jury.

Many of these cases suggest that despite the Pregnancy Discrimination Act and the seemingly formulaic nature of the *McDonnell Douglas v. Green* test, establishing a *prima facie* case for "pregnancy" discrimination remains a formidable task,[143] one made more difficult where, as in *Vazquez Gonzalez v. K-Mart Corp.* and several of the other cases following, an employer—accused of impermissible gender or "pregnancy discrimination"—offers an alternative explanation for the allegedly wrongful conduct.

As a result, employers often assert any number of alternate explanations— from a woman's alleged failure to do her job to her alleged failure to perform satisfactorily—in defense of claims that their alleged conduct was not wrongful and discriminatory. And in many cases, the courts have found for employers. Among the alternate explanations are "bad employee" claims, which have often proved fatal to a Title VII claims. This is why discussion of the "pretext" issue remains central to the overall discussion of gender and "pregnancy discrimination."

SORTING OUT THE FACTS:
The "Bad Employee" Defense

Employment discrimination suits are "a staple of federal court as we consider hundreds of cases each year falling under its general banner," the Seventh Circuit Court of Appeals wrote in *Hunt-Golliday v. Metropolitan Water*.[144] And in most cases, courts "revisit old principles and restate and apply them to the unique facts of the case at hand. Consider, for example, the decision 24 years ago by the Supreme Court in *McDonnell Douglas Corp. v. Green*, 411 U.S. 792 (1973). In 1996, in published opinions alone, we [the Seventh Circuit] restated and applied the '*McDonnell Douglas*' methodology for resolving discrimination claims in twenty-six cases where district courts granted defense motions for summary judgment."[145]

There are ninety-one federal districts in America with federal courts in every one. In addition, there are eleven federal circuits, each of them—along with the District of Columbia—including a high federal appellate court. And among the "staples" of these courts, according to the Seventh Circuit Court of Appeals, are employment discrimination cases.

HUNT-GOLLIDAY v. METROPOLITAN WATER

Though the Seventh Circuit published 26 employment discrimination decisions in 1996, that number does not include cases resolved without published decision or by mutual settlement. It also does not include cases heard by any of the other circuits. And many of these cases involve the "pretext" versus the legitimate nondiscriminatory reason for dismissal or adverse employment action question, though the courts don't always see it that way. In the 1997 case of *Hunt-Golliday v. Metropolitan Water*,[146] for example, the Seventh Circuit held there to be no legitimate "pretext" argument, though Pasha Hunt-Golliday attempted to raise the issue. *Hunt-Golliday v. Metropolitan Water* is a legally and factually complex case.

In 1987, Golliday was a laborer with the Metropolitan Water Reclamation District of Greater Chicago. But by all accounts, she was ambitious, inquiring, the court found, "about a promotion to a higher position—'Operating Engineer I.'" By 1990, Golliday had "obtained civil service" status. But each time she asked, Golliday was told by the supervisor at the plant that she had to be certified by the National Institute of Power Engineers. Once she received this certification, the water district would write a Letter of Verification allowing her to take a citywide engineer's exam.

Golliday took classes and received certification.[147] By then she had been promoted to fireman-oiler and transferred to the Chicago plant. But as instructed, Golliday returned to her former supervisor to request a Letter of Verification. Only then did the supervisor tell her of another requirement: to get the verification letter, the City of Chicago required two years of high-pressure boiler experience. This was a problem. High-pressure boiler experience was not available to Golliday at her current plant. High-pressure boilers were only found at the Stickney plant.[148]

And yet, Golliday's former supervisor had issued verification letters for other employees without requiring high-pressure boiler experience, testimony suggested.[149] But these were "good workers in his section at the Stickney plant who had two years in the fireman-oiler position" and who had received at least a "meets standards" on evaluations, the supervisor later testified. "Because Golliday at that time did not work in his section and did not have the two years as a fireman-oiler, she did not meet" the supervisor's requirements, according to the court.[150] But when Golliday asked her new immediate supervisor for a letter, he too declined on similar grounds.[151]

Golliday continued to try to get the letter, until in January 1991, "she was told by her head supervisor…that Metro Water did not have to issue her a letter of verification and if she persisted in asking for one she would 'be given a hard time,'" the Seventh Circuit found. "Golliday persisted nonetheless."[152] She also contacted the agency's equal employment officer, "for consultation only," stating that she believed the continued refusals were gender and race related. As a point of fact, the court found that "[n]o black woman held an operating engineer position."[153]

But later events would have greater bearing on the case. In early 1991, Golliday hurt her back while at work and remained on disability leave for several months.

When she was finally certified to return to work, the agency's doctor put a fifty-pound restriction of the amount she was safely allowed to lift. Then, in February 1993, when she still had not received a Letter of Verification, Golliday filed an internal complaint with the equal employment officer. Although the officer found no evidence of discrimination, she recommended that Metro Water review the way its supervisors issued Letters of Verification.

In April 1993, Golliday filed a formal complaint with the EEOC, alleging sex and race discrimination. A month later, Golliday would be found "physically able to work without any restrictions" by a Metro Water doctor. Golliday would later argue that she was never told of the doctor's conclusions. But on May 18, during her performance evaluation, Golliday suffered a panic attack and passed out. By this time, she had been transferred back to the Stickney plant and the evaluation was being done by the supervisor who had refused her requests for a Letter of Verification.

Golliday was hospitalized for depression, "allegedly brought on by her work environment, and...placed on disability leave while receiving psychological treatment for depression and anxiety," the Seventh Circuit noted. Golliday was disabled for twenty-one weeks. But as five months neared, Golliday pleaded with her doctor to be allowed to return to work. A collective bargaining agreement provided that an employee off work for more than five months could be terminated. In anticipation of her return, Golliday was examined by a Metro Water doctor, who told her she was pregnant.

Golliday returned to work only to learn from her supervisor that her workload would double and included heavy lifting. Golliday protested the lifting given the pregnancy and the previous back injury. Golliday's supervisor reportedly asked Golliday if she was refusing to do her job. Golliday said no and went to work, where, according to the court's findings of fact, Golliday and her work partner "were forced to move some heavy tool boxes (weighing 300-400 pounds) with wheels that were defective." According to Golliday, "this heavy job re-injured her back and caused her to develop abdominal pain." Golliday "went to a hospital, where she was allegedly told she was in danger of miscarrying," the court wrote.

Golliday left early the day she complained of the re-injury to her back and called in sick the next day. As a result, she was suspended by the Metro Water District for "uncooperative behavior," and three weeks later, the agency's civil service board recommended Golliday be discharged, turning the action into a "suspension pending discharge." Also figuring into the board's decision was Golliday's alleged "history of being uncooperative with supervisors, failure to return to work as directed, making a false injury claim on October 12, and the inability to perform the essential function of her job without posing a threat to herself or others due to her mental condition."[154]

In December of 1993, Golliday filed a retaliation discrimination complaint with the EEOC. In April 1994, she received a right-to-sue letter from the agency. Golliday filed suit against the Water District. Among the claim's shortcomings, however, were that even the court seemed to have had a tough time sorting the issues out. Golliday, the court wrote, "tossed everything in the kitchen, including the sink, at her former employer.... She said the District engaged in race discrimination; gender discrimination; pregnancy discrimination and sexual harassment (two subsets of sex discrimination); discrimination due to her disabilities; and retaliation against her for exercising rights under the Americans with Disabilities Act. She also claimed that Metro Water intentionally inflicted emotional distress on her and that a conspiracy was afoot to deprive her of her rights."[155]

Given the complexity of the analysis involved, the only claim to be reviewed here is Golliday's pregnancy discrimination claim. Prior to the appeal before the Seventh Circuit, a district court ruled that Golliday had failed to establish she had been treated less favorably than other nonpregnant employees. Thus, she had failed to establish a *prima facie* case. On appeal, the Seventh Circuit held that although Golliday was able to show she was suspended the day after informing her supervisor she was pregnant, her assertion "requires a presumption or at least an inference that the two events are related."

Though "[s]uspicious timing does constitute circumstantial, or indirect, evidence to support a claim of intentional discrimination or disparate treatment," the Seventh Circuit Court of Appeals concluded that Golliday had offered "absolutely no direct evidence proving that the two events were related—that any supervisor or decision maker regarding her employment admitted she was suspended because she was pregnant." Therefore, although Golliday argued that her case had been improperly analyzed under the *McDonnell Douglas* framework by the district court, the Seventh Circuit determined the analysis had been proper.

And in accordance with the *McDonnell Douglas* standard, Golliday had failed to show that "others who were not pregnant (or incapable of becoming pregnant) were treated more favorably than her," the court explained. "Golliday presented no evidence showing, for instance, that a nonpregnant employee returning from extended leave who left her job and called in sick after one day back would not have been suspended." In other words, even though supervisors knew she was pregnant, "Golliday has shown no evidence that the person with authority...failed to treat her just like any other worker with similar work problems would have been treated," the Seventh Circuit held.

KENNEDY v. SCHOENBERG, FISHER & NEWMAN, LTD., 140 F.3d 716 (7th Cir. 1998)

After Denise Kennedy was fired by a Chicago law firm, she filed suit in the federal district court, alleging wrongful termination and discrimination in violation of the Pregnancy Discrimination Act.[156] For nearly four years, Kennedy worked as a staff attorney for the National Office Machine Dealers Association. In January 1991, she was hired away by the law firm of Schoenberg, Fisher & Newman.

But almost instantly the problems began. In July of 1991, Kennedy received a less than glowing performance evaluation,[157] following a series of mistakes allegedly made by

Kennedy in the filing of an *amicus curiae* brief that resulted in its rejection twice by the United States Supreme Court and additional costs of nearly $2,000 for the firm.[158] In August of that same year, Kennedy was reportedly asked to complete the analysis of a contract. The firm alleged that she failed to do so, costing a client "a business opportunity."

In November 1991, Kennedy told her supervisor, Robert Goldberg, that she was pregnant. Although the firm had no express policy regarding pregnancy leave, in light of Kennedy's announcement, the firm adopted a paid-leave policy. Pursuant to the policy, the firm began keeping track of Kennedy's absences to calculate how many paid sick and vacation days she would be entitled to during maternity leave, the firm would later argue. But according to the court, Kennedy did not "feel [the firm's] paid-leave policy was generous enough and would have preferred more in terms of paid leave."

In June 1992, Kennedy went on leave. And during that leave, two things happened. The first was that Kennedy told Goldberg she was interested in returning to work only part-time when her leave ended. The second was that she asked to attend the National Office Machine Dealers Association's annual convention in Las Vegas. The firm agreed to allow Kennedy to return to work part-time, despite initial objections. Kennedy was also allowed to attend the convention in Las Vegas. Following her return from the convention, Kennedy submitted an expense report which included charges that would later form the basis of a dispute between Kennedy and Goldberg.[159] Kennedy was eventually fired and she filed suit.

There are those times when the court's recitation of the facts of a case offers a road map of where it intends to go. And in this case, it is clear that Kennedy won't prevail, because as the court offered: "[i]n addition to her conflict with Goldberg, plaintiff remained unproductive after her maternity leave."[160] It should come as no surprise, then, that the court would find Kennedy's claims of discrimination and wrongful termination based upon pregnancy, without merit."[161] Specifically, Kennedy offered no "direct or circumstantial evidence" tending to show that her termination was related to her pregnancy, the court held.

In terms of what was actually alleged, Kennedy said that Goldberg's comments and conduct towards her were evidence of his intent. Among the alleged conduct was that: "(1) soon after Goldberg became aware that plaintiff was pregnant, he 'repeatedly told [Kennedy]..."if you were my wife, I would not want you working after having children," and [he] told other [law firm] employees that plaintiff "should be home with her kids now, with her child now, that she shouldn't be working;" (2) less than four weeks after plaintiff announced her pregnancy, Goldberg wrote a memorandum...criticizing [her] work performance; (3) Goldberg responded 'Yes' to plaintiff's inquiry as to whether he was building a 'case' against plaintiff; and (4) while Goldberg and plaintiff were friendly before [she] announced her pregnancy, plaintiff claims that '[s]hortly after Goldberg learned of Ms. Kennedy's pregnancy, [Goldberg] became distant, cold, and acrimonious toward [her]."[162]

A federal district court held that Kennedy's assertions as to Goldberg's alleged conduct were not enough to create a factual dispute and, thus, did not prevent a ruling of summary judgment, which the court granted in favor of the law firm. Kennedy appealed to the Seventh Circuit, which affirmed the district court's decision, holding that "[d]irect evidence of discriminatory intent in pregnancy discrimination cases generally is in the form of an admission by a superior or decision maker that the employee was suspended because of pregnancy.[163] To rise to the level of direct evidence of discrimination, this [c]ourt has stated that "isolated comments must be contemporaneous with the discharge or casually related to the discharge decision-making process."

But that did not end the analysis. The Seventh Circuit then moved to the question of whether Kennedy could establish her claims via circumstantial evidence. Three basic categories of circumstantial evidence: "(1) a mosaic of evidence which, taken together, would permit a jury to infer discriminatory intent; (2) comparative evidence showing that employees similarly situated to the plaintiff other than in the protected characteristic received systematically better treatment; and (3) pretext evidence, where the plaintiff is qualified for and fails to receive the desired treatment, and the employer's stated reason for the difference is unworthy of belief."[164]

But Kennedy fell short of the requirements of even these "lesser" categories as well, according to the court. "Although plaintiff claims...Goldberg first criticized her work after he learned she was pregnant, she was aware of the substance of his criticisms prior to that time. Plaintiff's testimony establishes that she was aware of Goldberg's dissatisfaction with her handling of the *Kodak* brief before it was filed in September 1991. In addition, plaintiff was aware of other failures regarding her...work which occurred before she announced her pregnancy," the court found.

In addition, Kennedy's assertion that she was treated differently by the firm, because only her absences were tracked also failed, the court determined, because she "was the first and only associate attorney to take a disability leave after institution of the new policy." And finally, Kennedy's assertion that Goldberg's "letter writing campaign" to shareholders following a disputed expense report was driven by discriminatory intent was less than sound, the court held.

"Goldberg was not motivated by plaintiff's pregnancy in bringing the issue of plaintiff's expense reports to the attention of the shareholders." He was concerned with incorrectly billing a client, the court held. Thus, "Goldberg's conduct provides no basis for inferring that the plaintiff was terminated due to her pregnancy."[165] Rather, the shareholders maintain that Kennedy's termination was due to the "acrimonious dispute" with Goldberg; her lack of productivity; and the slowdown in corporate work at the firm. None "of the evidence presented by plaintiff regarding Goldberg's alleged comments or conduct comprise a mosaic of circumstantial evidence linking plaintiff's termination with her pregnancy," the court wrote.

Pasha Hunt-Golliday and Denise Kennedy failed, in the eyes of the court, to offer evidence sufficient to establish a *prima facie* case for discrimination, though in Golliday's case, the facts seemed to suggest some measure of favoritism towards other employees and animus towards Golliday on the part of her supervisors. Among the shortcomings of the evidence presented, the court found, was that neither woman could offer direct evidence of discrimination. But how often is it, really, that an employer or agent says, "Yes, I fired employee X because she was pregnant?"

According to the Seventh Circuit Court of Appeals, the mere suggestion of animus was not enough to prove that Golliday's dismissal was related to the impermissible motives as opposed to legitimate reasons. Similarly, the court held in Kennedy's case that isolated comments—even those that are sexist—did not necessarily establish a *prima facie* case. In both cases, the women were successfully portrayed as surly, "uncooperative" and/or possibly dishonest employees. These cases stand in contrast to those involving dismissals of women who are performing their jobs "satisfactorily". In those cases, the general rule appears to be that unless a woman claiming discrimination can prove she was treated differently due to pregnancy or a related condition, her dismissal—though unsettling—may be deemed permissible.

MARKET FORCES AND JOB ELIMINATION:
"Layoff Litigation" and Maternity Leave

"What a difference a change in seasons makes," wrote legal editor Daryl Van Duch, commenting on the economic bubble of the late 1990s that drove impossible expansion before bursting in 2001, sparking a flood of what is known in legal circles as "layoff litigation."[166] In the fall of 2000, "many of America's employment lawyers were advising corporate clients on how to beef up their workforces quickly to handle new orders," wrote Van Duch. "But before breaking for the holidays, many of those same lawyers were suddenly fielding an uncommon number of urgent queries from general counsels asking how to downsize safely."[167]

With so many women in the American workforce, it should come as no surprise that women—like men—are at work in a world of commerce subject to the ebbs and flows of the marketplace. As a result of the rise and fall in profitability, jobs held by women are often eliminated in market downturns alongside those of men. And yet, despite "market forces" arguments, allegations of pregnancy discrimination have arisen where job eliminations seem only to reach pregnant—or formerly pregnant—women. In *Ilhardt v. Sara Lee Corp.*,[168] for example, a female attorney filed suit after her part-time position was eliminated. Although there is some suggestion that Ilhardt may have been told of the possibility that her position might be eliminated before she went on maternity leave, it was not until she was on maternity leave that she learned she would not be returning to work.

Attorneys for the Sara Lee Corporation argued that the position was eliminated as part of a company-wide reorganization intended to cut costs and reduce overhead. Ilhardt alleged in a lawsuit, however, that the company had engaged in disparate treatment in violation of the Pregnancy Discrimination Act and Title VII. A federal district court granted summary judgment in favor of Sara Lee, finding that Ilhardt had failed to establish a *prima facie* case for discrimination. Specifically, the court held that Ilhardt failed to show she had been treated less favorably than nonpregnant employees. The facts suggested, instead, that Ilhardt had been treated better than some nonpregnant employees, the court held.

In affirming the district court's ruling, the Seventh Circuit held that although it is customary to "compare Ilhardt's treatment with that of a group of similarly situated nonpregnant employees to see if she was treated worse because she was pregnant,...because Ilhardt was the only part-time member of the law department, there are no other similarly situated employees with whom to compare her."[169]

In addition, because she could not "contradict the fact that [her supervisor] decided to eliminate her part-time position before she became pregnant," the court held that Ilhardt also failed to prove she had been treated less favorably because of her pregnancy. The court held further that "[r]egardless of whether [her supervisor] communicated this decision to her, the fact that he made the decision six months before she announced her pregnancy necessarily means he could not have made the decision because of her pregnancy."[170]

For these reasons, Ilhardt could not establish a *prima facie* case, though she was formally notified that her job had been eliminated while on maternity leave. (For a more detailed reading of the facts of *Ilhardt v. Sara Lee Corp.*, *see* INSET, *supra* pp. 179–181.)

Ilhardt v. Sara Lee Corp. offers a look at how some courts handle pregnancy discrimination claims in the context of economic downturns and force reductions where a large company is involved. As a point of contrast, *In re Carnegie Center Associates*[171] represents the force reductions–market forces argument from the perspective of a smaller company. It also offers a glimpse of how another federal court of appeals addresses issues of this sort.

In April 1989, Deborah Rhett accepted a temporary job as a secretary at a real estate company. Three months later, the job became full-time and Rhett continued to work there without apparent incident until June 1990, when Rhett told her supervisors she was pregnant. Soon after this announcement, Rhett alleges that the company's controller and chief financial officer/counsel "both asked if she was going to get married."[172] Rhett also alleged that the company's controller cautioned her that "being a single parent was difficult"[173] while the chief financial officer allegedly opined that "getting married was: 'in society's eyes...the right thing to do.'"[174] Finally, before she went on maternity leave, Rhett "...claimed...[the company's controller] became irate with her" and "stated that she was on 'thin ice.'"[175]

Though Carnegie Center Associates had no formal maternity leave policy, the company's practice was to try to hold an employee's position open if they could "so that '[w]hen they wanted to come back, if they contacted us and there was something open that was suitable, we would offer it to them,'" a company representative testified.[176] Rhett informed the company that she intended to take maternity leave from December 21, 1990, until April 15, 1991. In apparent accordance with that effort, Carnegie Center Associates hired a temporary secretary to fill Rhett's position while she was on leave.[177] But company officials testified that Carnegie Center Associates was experiencing financial difficulties that worsened during Rhett's leave, and shortly before Rhett's scheduled return, several positions were eliminated, including Rhett's position and the position of her supervisor.

In November 1993, Rhett filed suit against the company in federal district court. In her complaint, Rhett alleged violations of Title VII, as well as the New Jersey Law Against Discrimination.[178] But because the company was undergoing bankruptcy reorganization, the district court proceedings were automatically stayed. Rhett filed a proof of claim with the bankruptcy court in February 1994. The case would eventually become known as *In re Carnegie Center Associates.*[179] Following a three-day bench trial, the bankruptcy court concluded that Rhett's position had been eliminated for "the legitimate nondiscriminatory reason that she was away from work, and not because of discrimination on the basis of race, gender, or pregnancy."[180] Accordingly, the court found in favor of the company.

The United States District Court for the District of New Jersey affirmed the bankruptcy court's ruling, and Rhett appealed to the Third Circuit Court of Appeals, arguing that the rationale of both the lower court decisions ignored the reality of the situation. Before the Third Circuit, Rhett argued that while it was true she had been away from work when her position was eliminated, she was away from work because she was pregnant. Thus, the Third Circuit wrote in analyzing the claim before it, that this "case largely boil[ed] down to a dispute over one issue: whether terminating an employee because she is absent on maternity leave is a violation of the PDA."[181]

"The bankruptcy and district courts found that Carnegie eliminated Rhett's position because she was not at her place of employment at this time, not because of her pregnancy. Carnegie argues, and the bankruptcy and districts found at least implicitly, that Rhett was not employed by Carnegie at the time Carnegie eliminated her position." But "Rhett asserts that she was an employee on unpaid leave at the time," the Third Circuit wrote in setting forth the competing arguments.[182] And the Third Circuit seemed, at least tentatively, to agree with Rhett.

Although the company had no formal maternity leave policy, the Third Circuit noted that it was Carnegie Center Associates' practice to "hold open" an employee's job while she was on leave, and though the company would later argue that Rhett was no longer an employee once she went on "leave," Carnegie Center Associates continued Rhett's health insurance while she was away.

"It is undisputed that Carnegie maintained Rhett's medical insurance until it eliminated her position on March 25, 1991," the court found. "Therefore, it appears that Rhett was an employee of Carnegie on an unpaid leave of absence who sought reinstatement."[183]

And yet, this determination was not definitive in the eyes of the court: "[e]ven assuming that Carnegie still employed Rhett when it abolished her position, under the *Armbruster* reduction in force framework, she is still entitled to no relief," the court held.[184]

FORCE REDUCTIONS ANALYSIS:
The Armbruster Test

What is the *Armbruster* reduction in force framework? As legal explanations go, this one is almost as simple as it sounds, at least initially. The *Armbruster* reduction in force framework is a scheme of analysis set forth in the Third Circuit Court of Appeals' decision in *Armbruster v. Unisys Corp.*,[185] a case that involved claims of discrimination arising in the context of labor force reductions. It is simplest, perhaps, to think of the *Armbruster* standard as a modification of the analysis framework articulated by the United States Supreme Court in *McDonnell Douglas Corp. v. Green.*[186]

The Third Circuit Court of Appeals further modified the *McDonnell Douglas* framework for cases in its jurisdiction involving allegations of pregnancy discrimination arising out of the circumstances of force reduction. That modification, as articulated by the Third Circuit in *Armbruster v. Unisys Corp.*, provides that in order for a plaintiff to establish a *prima facie* case for pregnancy discrimination in the forces reduction context, she must show that: "(1) she belonged to a protected class, (2) she was qualified for the position from which she was terminated, (3) she was terminated, and (4) persons outside of the protected class were retained."[187]

In applying the *Armbruster* test to the complaints made in *In re Carnegie Center Associates*, the Third Circuit held that "[t]he interpretative question and answer section accompanying [Title VII][188] specifies that an employer must hold open the job of a woman absent because of pregnancy 'on the same basis as jobs held open for employees on sick or disability leave for other reasons.'"[189] But "[o]n the other hand, the PDA does not require that employers treat pregnant employees better than other disabled employees."[190]

But considering an employee's absence in determining whether to terminate her employment while she is on maternity is discrimination *per se*, Rhett argued.[191] Although the court noted that the case was "unusual in that Carnegie terminated an employee who had performed satisfactorily solely because of an economically justified reduction in the force while she was away on maternity leave,"[192] the Third Circuit held, citing the Seventh Circuit's decision in *Troupe v. May Department Stores Co.*,[193] that consistent with the PDA, "an employer legitimately can consider an employee's absence on maternity leave in making an adverse employment decision."[194]

Even more fatal to Rhett's claim, according to the court, however, was that Rhett made no "showing that Carnegie treated her differently than it would have treated a nonpregnant employee absent on disability leave. Of course, it was difficult for her to make such a showing because Carnegie never has had an employee on disability leave for a protracted period for any reason other than pregnancy," the Third Circuit wrote.[195] But because an employer is entitled to judgment when an employee fails to show "by a preponderance of the evidence that she received disparate treatment when compared to nonpregnant employee," the Third Circuit upheld the district court's finding in favor of Carnegie Center Associates.[196]

It is a decision that would appear, rationally, to make sense. And yet, it begs the question—if a woman can be fired while on maternity leave—what protection can the Pregnancy Discrimination Act truly be said to offer? That is among the questions federal courts have attempted to answer since the PDA became law in 1978. What seems certain, from review of these and other cases, is that the task of proving "pregnancy discrimination" remains considerable, though courts have suggested that the burden of proving a *prima facie* case is not "onerous."

MODERN ISSUES IN THE WORKPLACE TODAY:
A Love-Hate Relationship with "Protective" Measures

> [I]t was fated that he should stand upon a certain square foot of floor from seven in the morning until noon, and again from half-past twelve till half-past five, making never a motion and thinking never a thought, save for the setting of lard cans. In summer the stench of the warm lard would be nauseating, and in winter the cans would all but freeze to his naked little fingers in the unheated cellar. Half the year it would be dark as night when he went in to work, and dark as night again when he came out, and so he would never know what the sun looked like on weekdays. And for this, at the end of the week, he would carry home three dollars to his family, being his pay at the rate of five cents per hour—just about his proper share of the total earnings of the million and three-quarters of children who are now engaged in earning their livings in the United States."
>
> —Upton Sinclair, *The Jungle*[197]

Women entered the twentieth century workplace alongside men, and, according to some historians, they were all "in need of protection." Journalist Marci McDonald notes, for example, that "[i]t was the maids and mill girls of the early twentieth century who provoked the first labor laws that now affect all U.S. workers, male and female alike."[198] Working conditions in early America were deplorable and as dangerous for men as they were for women. And yet, the alleged "weaknesses" of women were long used to rationalize treating women differently or denying them work altogether.

In the early 1900s, the question facing working women—if they were allowed to work outside of the home—was whether they should be allowed to keep their jobs once they reached childbearing age. As set forth above, it was a question taken on by the courts, because so frail was the constitution of women that it was deemed to be the *benefit of all*[199] if they were allowed to rest, particularly while in the state of pregnancy.

And where women failed to exercise a fitting level of deference to their biology, laws were enacted to help, limiting, for example, the number of hours women could work. Many of these laws remained in place for the better part of the century. But then came the 1970s, when things began to change and the courts began to undo gender preference laws tending to reinforce ancient and stereotypical notions of women as "the weaker sex." Often, in challenging laws of this type, the question came down to how much a woman should be permitted to lift.

In 1971, for example, the Ninth Circuit Court of Appeals held in *Rosenfeld v. Southern Pacific Co.*[200] that a California statute limiting the number of hours women could work to ten and the weight they could lift to no greater than fifty pounds was a violation of Title VII. Similar challenges were raised in *Ridlinger v. General Motors Corp,*[201] a case heard by a federal district court in Ohio, and *Weeks v. Southern Bell Telephone & Telegraph,*[202] heard by the Fifth Circuit Court of Appeals, as an often heated "protectionist" legislation-versus-equality debate raged on, creating unexpected advocates and allies.

During the bitterly argued case of *California Federal Savings and Loan Association v. Guerra,*[203] for example, feminist and liberal advocacy groups challenged the Pregnancy Discrimination Act[204] as did political conservatives, asserting the PDA was another piece of "protectionist" legislation that would serve to defeat women in their bid for true equality. In its *amicus* brief, for example, the American Civil Liberties Union argued on behalf of the bank, noting that:

> Protectionist laws reflect an ideology which values women most highly for their childbearing and nurturing roles. Such laws reinforce stereotypes about women's inclinations and abilities; they deter employers from hiring women of childbearing age or funnel them into less responsible positions; and they make women appear to be more expensive, less reliable employees.[205]

The Justices of the United States Supreme Court disagreed, holding instead that by "taking pregnancy into account," lawmakers involved in crafting both the PDA and the California statute bank officials invoked in an attempt to thwart it had intended to ensure that women as well as men could have families without losing their jobs. "Accordingly, unlike the protective labor legislation prevalent earlier in this century, [the California law] does not reflect archaic or stereotypical notions about pregnancy and the abilities of pregnant workers. A statute based on such stereotypical assumptions would, of course, be inconsistent with Title VII's goal of equal employment opportunity."

Though some scholars have criticized the Court's decision in *California Federal Savings and Loan Association v. Guerra* as out of step with the issues of the times, others suggest that the Justices were likely attempting to resolve issues raised in the lower courts while also quietly responding to the swell of the nation's citizens, namely women, who sought an end to protectionist laws of the past. "By 1973," legal scholars explain, "federal courts had invalidated the hours laws of nine jurisdictions as well as the weight limitation laws of three jurisdictions and two job prohibition laws. Fourteen states had repealed their hours laws; the attorneys generals of twenty-one jurisdictions had ruled that the laws did not apply to employers covered by Title VII; and three states had exempted employees from maximum-hours coverage if they were covered by the [Federal Labor Standards Act]."[206]

That was the 1970s. But in the decades since, there appears to be some movement on the part of women towards turning back the clock, an irony given that women's groups fought so hard to overcome the limitations of protectionist legislation. Though parity is still in the distant future, women have made tremendous strides in the professional world in the last half century. Women are police officers, firefighters, corporate executives. By 2003, six women held the lofty title of CEO for Fortune 500 companies,[207] and a full 15 percent of active military personnel in the United States were women, though women are still barred from direct ground combat.[208]

And yet, progress of this sort seemed to have resurrected the "protectionist" debate with the central question before the courts today appearing to be whether women are entitled to—or should be granted—special "accommodations" by employers while they are pregnant, if accommodations of this sort might arguably protect a developing fetus. Are such accommodations required by the PDA? A corollary to this debate is whether an employer can—or should—intervene to protect a developing fetus where the employer fears a pregnant employee's duties might cause injury.[209] But these questions are pitted against another set: might an employer's attempts at intervention be viewed as discriminatory and in violation of Title VII and the PDA?

"PREFERENCE" OR "PROTECTIONISM":
Reassigning the Pregnant Employee and the Question of Accommodation

In June 2000, a female police officer vowed to file a complaint with the Equal Employment Opportunity Commission against the tiny town of Palacios, Texas, in a case that shines a bright light on the hard choices and the blurred lines that exist between "protecting" pregnant women and developing fetuses from potential harm in the workplace and discriminating against women on the job because they are pregnant.

Media reports suggest the events underlying the dispute in the Palacios case began in April 2000, when a then 25-year-old Denise Janssen, a patrol officer with the city's eight-member police department, answered a domestic call that turned out to be a "knock-down, drag-out fight."[210] Janssen, who was pregnant at the time, told a local newspaper and Court-TV that in seeing the fight, she immediately grew fearful that she or her unborn fetus might be injured. Thus, she stayed clear of the fray, allowing her husband—who had accompanied her to the scene—and another police officer to handle the battling parties.[211]

Soon after the incident, Janssen's obstetrician wrote a letter to city officials urging that Janssen should avoid "police-related work that could result in an altercation."[212] Janssen then sought desk duty—in lieu of street patrol—for the remainder of her pregnancy.[213] But Palacios officials rejected Janssen's request, arguing that in a department so small all officers have to patrol,[214] including the department's former chief, city officials explained.[215]

"We need an officer out there on the street," City Manager Charles Winfield said in response to questions.[216] "Yes, there's a danger to her and the baby, but there's a danger to the public. For her to not be patrolling is not an option."[217]

In lieu of "light duty," Janssen was offered what other municipal employees are offered in cases of emergency or disability: a thirty-day leave without pay, plus exhaustion of unused sick or leave time the employee has accrued.[218] Though there were additional fits and starts by both sides in an effort to craft a workable solution,[219] on May 2, Janssen was sent home from work with "in effect a termination letter," media reports suggest.[220] On June 14, as Janssen's final days of leave were set to expire, she vowed to seek review by the EEOC[221] if she were terminated, which city policy allows. Palacios officials defended the city's position in the wake of a wave of publicity that accompanied the case.

"The city believes that its policies and practices are in compliance with all state and federal laws and we're confident we are not discriminating against anybody," said Palacios City Attorney Randy Strong.[222] "We are sure that our actions would be sustained if it were to get to court, but hopefully it won't get to that point."

Palacios officials appear to base their views of compliance of city policies on the fact that the police department employs only eight officers. The language of the Pregnancy Discrimination Act provides that "[t]he term 'employer' means a person engaged in an industry affecting commerce who has *fifteen or more employees* for each working day in each of twenty or more calendar weeks in the current or preceding calendar year, and any agent of such a person."[223]

The above definition would appear to foreclose the possibility of sustaining a suit brought by Janssen under Title VII and the Pregnancy Discrimination Act and many courts have held that employers with fewer than fifteen employees are exempt from the provisions of the PDA. For these reasons, although Janssen's claims drew considerable media attention, it is not clear that Janssen could maintain a cause of action for discrimination should she file a case. And yet, in 1997,

Christine Raciti-Hur filed a similar suit for similar reasons against the Livingston County Sheriff's Department of Michigan.

According to the facts as established by the court, Christine Raciti-Hur was hired by the Livingston County Sheriff's Department in 1989. At the time of her hire, the then-acting sheriff endorsed an "unwritten policy" that allowed deputies to be reassigned from regular road to "light duty" during periods of "temporary disability."[224] In accordance with this "policy," when Raciti-Hur was diagnosed with Bell's Palsy in 1992,[225] she was assigned light duty as a dispatcher, though the Sheriff's Department continued to pay her at the rate of road patrol officer. A year later, when Raciti-Hur was pregnant with her first child, she was again assigned light duty as a dispatcher and again she was paid as though she were still working as a road patrol officer.[226] Other officers were treated similarly.[227]

But in 1994, the Sheriff's Department decided to discontinue the practice of reassigning employees to light duty during periods of temporary disability.[228] Although the president of the deputies union was told of the change, employees were not notified individually. When Raciti-Hur became pregnant again in 1996, she again requested light duty. But this time, the Sheriff's Department initially declined to reassign her. Raciti-Hur admitted in her deposition that her pregnancy did not render her medically disabled. She also admitted there were no medical complications with the pregnancy. Rather, "she simply felt that it was not safe for her unborn child, her fellow officers, or for herself to be working road patrol during any time of her pregnancy."[229]

But Raciti-Hur was told that light duty was no longer an option. Instead, her choices were to stay on the road patrol; take medical leave; or, to work as a dispatcher at the dispatcher rate, which represented a $10,000 cut in pay. Raciti-Hur wrote the Undersheriff, requesting transfer to a dispatcher post, but with maintenance of her road patrol salary and benefits. Raciti-Hur knew that her rate of pay prior to maternity leave would affect her rate of pay during maternity leave.[230] The Undersheriff informed Raciti-Hur there were no openings in dispatch. He promised, however, to consider Raciti-Hur should a position open. In May 1996, Raciti-Hur was offered a dispatch position at a dispatcher's salary. Raciti-Hur tentatively agreed to the transfer, but later refused after reviewing a drafted agreement.

The agreement would have required Raciti-Hur to waive all rights to future legal claims.[231] After she refused the transfer to dispatch, Raciti-Hur was sent back to road patrol, and on June 5, Raciti-Hur informed the Undersheriff that she was taking a medical leave. On June 25, she filed a complaint with the EEOC, alleging sex discrimination, retaliation, and violations of the Equal Protection Clause of the Fourteenth Amendment of the United States Constitution. In October, the EEOC issued a right-to-sue letter. Raciti-Hur brought suit.

But in finding for the Sheriff's Department, a federal court for the Eastern District in Michigan held in *Raciti-Hur v. Homan* that while "[i]t is clear... [Raciti-Hur] would have preferred that the Defendant allow her light duty work during her pregnancy, at no loss of pay, in lieu of taking leave,…it is also clear that the Defendant had no such policy in place in 1994, nor was required to have one."[232] The court further explained: "[i]t is important to note that the inquiry in a pregnancy discrimination case is not whether the employer could have been more accommodating to its pregnant employees. Rather, all the law requires is that the employer treat its pregnant employees the same as others similar in their ability or inability to work. The [Pregnancy Discrimination Act] does not require an employer who does not provide light duty work to other temporarily disabled employees to provide it for pregnant workers."[233]

For these reasons, Christine Raciti-Hur was not entitled to reassignment to light duty under the Pregnancy Discrimination Act, the Michigan court held. The Eighth Circuit Court of Appeals concurred in *Deneen v. Northwest Airlines, Inc.*,[234] declaring it permissible, despite the Pregnancy Discrimination Act "...for an employer to discriminate on the basis of sex or pregnancy 'in those certain instances' where sex 'is a bona fide occupational qualification reasonably necessary to the normal operation of that particular business or enterprise'.... The [Pregnancy Discrimination Act] 'does not create substantial rights to preferential treatment.'"[235]

But is seeking to "protect" a developing fetus by requesting "light duty" in the later months of pregnancy really an attempt to gain preferential treatment? Or is it a prudent, common sense step that women in physical jobs must be allowed to take—or be assigned to—for the protection of *all* involved? It could be argued that it would be not only reasonable, but wise to allow a pregnant patrol officer to be reassigned to light or desk duty during the later months of a pregnancy. But this would appear to be an emerging conflict in the area of "workplace law."

And yet, where the question has arisen, the courts have generally held that while an employer may voluntarily reassign an employee upon request, the law does not require employers to do so. But what have the courts said when an employer decides to reassign an employee although she has not sought reassignment and does not want it? These were the issues before the court in *Richards v. City of Topeka*,[236] and though Michelle Richards tried to fight, asserting ultimate arguments of equality, she lost.

WHEN A FIREFIGHTER IS A WOMAN:
Richards v. City of Topeka

Michelle Richards had been a firefighter for nearly eight years when she informed her employers that she was pregnant. The department's response was to immediately reassign her to "light duties" as required by a collective bargaining agreement previously agreed upon by the City of Topeka and the firefighters' union. But Richards wanted none of it and sought to be transferred back to her regular duties of "driving a fire truck, operating water pumps, and dragging hoses to the appropriate location for use by the Fire Department."[237]

To support her request, Richards offered a medical release from her obstetrician in which the physician detailed that Richards would be able to perform regular duties until her twenty-eighth week of pregnancy. Richards was reassigned to "light duties" during her tenth week.[238] But the City of Topeka refused to return Richards to regular duties, citing the collective bargaining agreement. Richards filed suit in federal court under Title VII, the Pregnancy Discrimination Act and the Americans with Disabilities Act.

The City of Topeka offered three affirmative defense arguments in response to Richards' suit.[239] The first was that the city was obligated by the collective bargaining agreement to reassign Richards. The second was that Richards should be estopped from challenging that agreement because she helped negotiate it.[240] And the third asserted defense was that Richards' reassignment fell within the "bona fide occupational qualification" exception to Title VII and the Pregnancy Discrimination Act.[241]

In a complex case handled in two parts, a district court granted summary judgment in favor of the City of Topeka on the claim brought by Richards under the Americans with Disabilities Act. As the court noted, although Richards conceded in testimony that "her pregnancy did not impair or substantially limit a major life duty, nor did it impair her ability to work,"[242] she nonetheless sought to suggest that she was "disabled within the meaning" of the Americans with Disabilities Act.[243] On appeal, the Tenth Circuit found that Richards's "argument [was] premised on a faulty reading of the ADA and the regulations promulgated under it."[244]

But Richards's claim arising under the Pregnancy Discrimination Act was allowed to go to trial at the district court level. After a jury found in favor of the City of Topeka, Richards appealed, arguing that the district court erred in denying summary judgment in her favor. In other words, according to Richards, there never should have been a trial. But the Tenth Circuit Court of Appeals found that the district court properly "denied the motion [for summary judgment] because it found disputed factual issues in the City's assertion of two affirmative defenses; the 'bona fide occupational qualifications' (BFOQ) exception to Title VII and the PDA, and estoppel against Richards because she assisted in the union negotiations that resulted in the collective bargaining agreement the City followed in reassigning her."[245]

Estoppel is a legal construct often used to foreclose one's ability to assert certain arguments given his or her previous conduct. In this case, the City of Topeka argued that Richards should be estopped from challenging the terms of the collective bargaining agreement, because she had helped draft it. The court agreed, which left only the question of the "bona fide occupational qualifications" exception.

Section 703(a) of Title VII of the Civil Rights Act reaches claims of discrimination based upon: allegations of a failure to hire; unlawful termination; wages; and benefits and/or various other privileges of employment. But Section 703(e) holds that it is not unlawful for an employer to hire an employee on the basis of sex where sex is a "bona fide occupational qualification." What the courts have read this language to mean in a practical sense is that although the "bona fide occupational qualification exception as to sex should be interpreted narrowly,"[246] even under Title VII an employer may lawfully discriminate in accordance with Section 703(e) where it "is reasonably necessary to the normal operation of [a defendant's] particular business or enterprise."[247]

Courts also have held that the bona fide occupational qualifications exception is available as an affirmative defense to allegations of discrimination where "pregnancy actually interferes with the employee's ability to perform the job."[248] In approaching Richards's claim of discrimination in light of the City of Topeka's use of the bona fide occupational qualifications defense, the Tenth Circuit Court of Appeals ruled that "[u]nder the PDA, the City can raise a BFOQ as an affirmative defense."[249]

Richards argued that the City of Topeka should be barred from asserting the BFOQ defense because less discriminatory means were available to the city in handling pregnant firefighters. But the Tenth Circuit held that at best, "[Richards's] summary judgment motion raised a mixed question of law and fact, rather than a pure question of law. We therefore do not review Richards's appeal of the district court's denial of her motion for summary judgment."[250] Accordingly, the Tenth Circuit affirmed the district court's decision in favor of the City of Topeka.

The issues before the court in *Richards v. City of Topeka* present not only the other side of those in *Raciti-Hur v. Homan*. But they seem also to encapsulate the arguments of the "protectionist"-versus-the-equality debate that has long raged. Christine Raciti-Hur, a police officer, sought "light duty"—or "special accommodations," some might argue—during her pregnancy, because she was pregnant. By contrast, Michelle Richards, a firefighter, was reassigned to light duty upon informing her employers that she was pregnant, although she never asked for it and did not want it.

Which should be honored? Should pregnant fire fighters be automatically reassigned to light duty during pregnancy for the protection and of well being of the woman? The fetus? Society? Such was clearly the reasoning at work in *Richards v. City of Topeka*. But what, then, do we do with pregnant police officers? Of course, decisions like the Tenth Circuit's in *Richards v. City of Topeka* and requests by female police officers for light duty harken back, some argue, to a time in American history when men—often from their positions of authority as lawmakers and judges—argued that these issues would not present a problem if women were not allowed to hold certain kinds of jobs when the burdens of motherhood were upon them. But, of course, the PDA does not allow employers to apply that kind of reasoning to the lives of women anymore.

LAVALLEY v. E.B. & A.C. WHITING CO.,
692 A.2d 367 (Vt. 1997)

In 1991, Carrie Lavalley was a cutter/packer on a plastics production line at the E.B. & A.C. Whiting Company in Vermont earning $359.20 per week. As a cutter/packer, Lavalley was responsible "for cutting long bundles of plastic fibers." But in March of that year, Lavalley told her supervisors she was pregnant and unable to continue to lift large bundles. Lavalley asked to be temporarily reassigned to "lighter duty" or to have a coworker assigned to help with the heavy lifting.[251] In support of her request, Lavalley offered a note from her doctor, who explained that Lavalley could not stand for long periods or lift heavy items.[252]

The company denied Lavalley's request for light duty. Instead, pursuant to its disability policy, Lavalley was classified as an employee with a "long-term disability, non-work-related injury."[253] She was placed on disability leave with half pay. Lavalley filed suit alleging gender discrimination in violation of Vermont's Fair Employment Practices Act, which provides that "[i]t shall be an unlawful employment practice…[f]or any employer…to discriminate against any individual because of…sex…." [254] The Vermont law was patterned on Title VII of the Civil Rights Act of 1964.

Lavalley alleged specifically that E.B. & A.C. Whiting Co. had violated the Fair Employment Practices Act "[b]y placing [her] into a class of persons (those injured away from the job) [because she was pregnant] and treating her differently from others who are disabled (those injured on the job)."[255] After a lower state court found in favor of E.B. & A.C. Whiting Co., holding that "[h]ere the Plaintiff has not presented evidence proving discriminatory motive,"[256] Lavalley appealed and the case eventually made its way to the Supreme Court of Vermont.

"It is clear that Congress viewed the Pregnancy Discrimination Act as a reenactment of the proper meaning of Title VII, rather than the creation of expanded civil rights protection for pregnant workers," the Supreme Court of Vermont wrote.[257] But "[t]here was no allegation below that the employer treated nonpregnant employees with non-work-related injuries more favorably by providing them with job accommodation.[258]

"On the contrary," the court wrote, "[Lavalley] appears to have been accorded exactly the same rights as were available to all other employees, whether male or female. Nor was there any allegation that defendant departed from its policy in a discriminatory manner, or that the employer implemented the policy to intentionally discriminate against pregnant women.[259] Unlike the employment policy in [*General Electric Co. v. Gilbert*][260] and virtually all of the pregnancy discrimination cases,[261] the policy does not specifically condition any employment or benefit rule on pregnancy. Indeed, the policy is facially neutral and affects pregnant women because of their temporary disability…" the court wrote.[262]

As a point of law, the court explained that although neutral on their face, disability schemes may still be the subject of disparate impact claims.[263] And "[u]nder a disparate impact theory, [Lavalley] is relieved of the burden of having to show that the employer acted with discriminatory intent; rather, [Lavalley] need only show that the employment practice has a discriminatory impact on a protected class and is not justified by business necessity."[264] But because Lavalley failed to do so, her claim of disparate impact was "reduced to one that [suggests] defendant's policy is sex discrimination *per se* because it excludes pregnant women from doing some job that they might be capable of performing.[265] In other words, plaintiff's claim is that [Vermont's Fair Employment Practices Act] prevents an employer from making disability-related employment decisions on the basis of whether the disability is work-related. We disagree that the policy violated FEPA on its face," the court wrote.[266]

Finally, the Vermont Supreme Court held that "[p]laintiff would have been treated no differently had she suffered a nonwork disability unrelated to pregnancy. [E.B. & A.C. Whiting Co.] was not required to grant to plaintiff benefits that were otherwise not available to other employees with non-work-related disabilities.[267]...If we accept plaintiff's argument here, we are necessarily holding that the governmental foundation for the distinctions defendant's policy draws are also discriminatory. We conclude that defendant did not discriminate against plaintiff on account of sex in violation of 21 V.S.A. Sec. 495(a)(1)."[268]

RIGHTS OF PREGNANT EMPLOYEES v. DEMANDS OF THE WORKPLACE

What about a 75-pound lifting requirement? (*See Deneen v. Northwest Airlines, Inc.* and *Urbano v. Continental Airlines, Inc., infra*, pp. 218–219.) Working with chemicals? (*See Leeker v. Gill Studios, Inc.* and *Cleese v. Hewlett-Packard Co., infra*, pp. 220–221.) Caring for patients with HIV? (*See Armstrong v. Flowers Hospital, Inc., infra*, pp. 223–224.) Questions of this sort have been asked in the nation's courts in the past decade in an effort to balance the rights of pregnant employees with the demands of the workplace.[269]

One woman's caution and concern is another's "preferential treatment." It should be clear at this point that the "pregnancy discrimination" law is complex, difficult to decipher, harder to enforce, and that the decisions of courts are often contradictory in their results. Among the many reasons for this is that although legislation like the Pregnancy Discrimination Act was originally heralded as a panacea, it has proved a far less aggressive tool for women. Indeed, as several courts have noted, the law is a "shield," not a sword.

Thus, the PDA requires that a plaintiff make a *prima facie* showing of discrimination, a task the courts do not consider "onerous," but that involves satisfying the requirements of a four-part test. Despite the PDA, a woman may be dismissed or terminated while on maternity leave or because she is absent due to pregnancy. Given her pregnancy, a woman may be reassigned to "light duty" against her will where supervisors deem it "reasonably necessary to the normal operation of [a defendant's] particular business or enterprise."[270] Or, she may be denied reassignment to light duty because it may be thought to smack of preferential treatment or "reverse discrimination." These are just a few of the issues facing women in the workplace today.

DENEEN v. NORTHWEST AIRLINES, INC.,
132 F.3d 431 (8th Cir. 1998)

The question before the court was whether Northwest Airlines had discriminated against Ruth Deneen by refusing to allow her to return to work after an initial call-back, because she was pregnant and company officials suspected she was experiencing complications. As a customer service agent, Deneen's duties included handling customers at the ticket counter, securing customer baggage, and gate service.[271]

In January 1993, Deneen was laid off as part of a general reduction in force. At the time, Deneen was pregnant with a July due date. Northwest Airlines knew of Deneen's pregnancy. Still in April of that year, Deneen was offered a part-time customer service agent's position for the duration of the airline's busy season. But after Deneen accepted the position, the secretary making the call on behalf of the airline "casually asked" about Deneen's pregnancy. Despite the question, things seemed to proceed as planned. Deneen was later told, during a follow-up call, that she would be working five-hour shifts.[272]

In early June, Deneen began experiencing pregnancy-induced hypertension, and she was ordered by her doctor to spend 48 hours in bed. The airline learned indirectly of the order. Deneen's husband, who took time off to be with his wife, also worked for the airline. Soon afterwards, Deneen was told by airline officials that she would not be allowed to return to work "because of her pregnancy complication."[273] Following a heated discussion with one of her supervisors, Deneen was told she could return to work. But when she reported to her assignment she found no time card and that her name had been crossed off the schedule. She was listed as being on medical leave.

Deneen testified that during a conversation with her supervisors, she was told: "It's been brought to my attention that you are having problems with your pregnancy, and we need you to bring in a note."[274] Deneen brought a note from her doctor, detailing "that she could perform most of the job functions."[275] The only exception was lifting very heavy bags. Throughout the case, Deneen argued that she "had not previously been aware…she would have to comply with any particular lifting requirements."[276] But soon after her meeting with supervisors, Deneen was sent a letter outlining the requirements of the customer service agent job. Among them was that all customer service agents must be able to lift up to 75 pounds.[277]

Deneen protested that she had never been able to lift 75 pounds, pregnant or not, and that she could perform the other requirements of the job. Still, the next day, Deneen received a letter telling her she was not qualified to return to work due to the medical restriction of light duty. Four months later, after she had given birth, Deneen was allowed to return to work without a showing of her ability to lift 75 pounds. Deneen filed suit, alleging discrimination of the basis of pregnancy.

In response to Deneen's suit, Northwest Airlines argued that her pregnancy had nothing to do with the company's decision not to allow her back to work. Rather, it was her need for "light duty" and the fact that she admitted she could not lift bags weighing as much as 75-pound bag, which rendered her unable to meet the requirements of the job.[278] In finding in favor of Deneen, a federal district court held that Deneen "had submitted sufficient direct evidence of discrimination to justify submitting the case to the jury as a mixed-motives case."[279] A jury later found in favor of Deneen.[280] The federal Appeals Court for the Eighth Circuit later affirmed the lower court's decisions.[281]

URBANO v. CONTINENTAL AIRLINES, INC., 138 F.3d 204 (5th Cir. 1998)

For four years Mirtha Urbano worked in several capacities for Continental Airlines, including as a ticket sales agent and passenger check-in representative, which meant lifting bags. In October 1994, Urbano learned that she was pregnant, and soon after, she began suffering lower back pains and discomfort. Her doctor ordered her to refrain from lifting anything over twenty pounds for the remainder of her pregnancy.[282]

Given her doctor's orders, Urbano asked to work as a service center agent, which did not require heavy lifting. Continental Airlines denied Urbano's request pursuant to the airline's policy of allowing transitional light-duty only to employees injured on the job. Employees with nonoccupational injuries were required to bid for alternative positions. The assignment of these new positions was based upon seniority. Urbano was deemed ineligible for a light-duty position. As a result, she was forced to use sick days, ninety days of family leave, and finally, unpaid medical leave to fill out the remainder of her pregnancy.

In March 1995, Urbano filed a complaint with the Equal Employment Opportunities Commission. After receiving a right-to-sue letter, Urbano filed suit in federal court, alleging pregnancy discrimination. The Fifth Circuit held, however, that Urbano had failed to establish a *prima facie* case for disparate treatment, because "Continental treated Urbano in exactly the same manner as it would have treated any other worker who was injured off the job." The court noted specifically that "Urbano was not denied a light-duty assignment because of her pregnancy, but because her back troubles were not work related."[283]

In other words, "[w]ithout a showing that Continental adhered to the requirements of the light-duty policy only in cases involving its pregnant workers, Urbano cannot maintain that she was a victim of discrimination under the PDA," the Fifth Circuit held.[284] "In this case, Continental treated Urbano the same as it treats any other worker who suffered an injury off-duty. There is no probative evidence that Continental's distinction between occupational and off-the-job injuries was a pretext for discrimination against pregnant women or that it had a disparate treatment on them. Urbano's claim is thus not a request for relief from discrimination, but rather a demand for preferential treatment; it is a demand not satisfied by the PDA."[285]

LEEKER v. *GILL STUDIOS, INC.,*
21 F.Supp. 2d 1267 (D.Kan. 1998)

Rhonda Leeker was hired by Gill Studios in March 1996, as a printing production worker. One of her duties was to refill 814 cleaning solvent containers, a task that took twenty minutes to complete, and the job was working out well for Leeker until December 1996, when Leeker learned she was pregnant. On January 3, 1997, Leeker told a supervisor she no longer thought it was a good idea for her to continue to fill the containers, given the pregnancy. The supervisor agreed to have someone else fill the containers.

A few days later Leeker presented her supervisor with a note from her physician. The note urged that Leeker "should not be around high concentrations of chemicals until further notice from her OB doctor."[286] Not long after, Leeker missed three days of work due to first trimester bleeding. When she returned to work on January 10, she gave her supervisor a note from another physician again noting that Leeker should not be near chemicals. Leeker would later assert that she was fired following an argument during which her supervisor allegedly said "[i]f [she] would have the doctor lift [her] restrictions" she would not be made to fill the chemical containers.

In an effort to get her job back, Leeker called another supervisor to ask if the company could find something else for her to do that did not involve filling the chemical containers. A nurse from her doctor's office also called to tell the company that Leeker could do anything else at the studios as long as she "did not inhale that chemical." The nurse reportedly "begged them to give [Leeker] back her job."[287] The company refused, citing the restrictions. A week after she was "terminated," Leeker was told to come to Gill Studios to fill out a disability form.

Leeker did as she was told, and from January through July, she collected disability benefits of $122.54 per week. Leeker also continued to receive health benefits. After the birth of Leeker's child, Gill Studios wrote her a letter, asking about her return to work. Leeker did not reply to the letter. Gill Studios then called, following up that telephone conversation with a letter, dated October 16, informing Leeker that her disability leave had expired on October 13, and that she was now being terminated for failure to return to work.

Leeker filed suit, arguing that by placing her on disability leave, then terminating her employment "due to her pregnancy," Gill Studios had violated the Pregnancy Discrimination Act. Leeker argued specifically that the medical restrictions related to her pregnancy only prohibited her from filling the containers, which was not an essential part of her job. Thus, she remained a qualified employee who had been discriminated against by Gill Studios, because company supervisors refused to allow her to continue to work.[288]

A Kansas district court ruled that Leeker "presented her employer with a medical restriction, which the employer logically determined prevented her from performing her job." Leeker then "proceeded to collect disability payments and insurance benefits while working for a new employer. [But Leeker] now claims that her former employer discriminated against her when it followed her physicians' restrictions."[289] But that is not the purpose of the Pregnancy Discrimination Act, the court held. "In any event, [Leeker] has failed to meet her burden of producing evidence from which a rational trier of fact could find that Gill Studios discriminated against her because she was pregnant." Accordingly, the court sustained the studio's motion for summary judgment.

CLEESE v. HEWLETT-PACKARD CO.,
911 F.Supp. 1312 (D.Or. 1995)

Slightly more novel and considerably more successful was the pregnancy discrimination claim brought by Loretta Cleese against Hewlett-Packard Company after Cleese was terminated for an alleged "failure to be truthful with her coworkers and management" concerning medical restrictions. According to the district court of Oregon's recitation of the undisputed facts of the case, Loretta Cleese began her career with Hewlett-Packard in 1989 in San Jose, California. But in June 1992, she moved to Oregon and began working at the company's Corvallis plant.

When Cleese left the San Jose plant, the court suggests that she knew she had exhausted or nearly exhausted the "flexible time off" permitted by the company. Evaluations from the San Jose plant allegedly reflected a "low dependability" rating. When Cleese arrived at the Corvallis plant, she informed employers that she wanted to get pregnant. She was undergoing fertility treatments. But this only raised questions of her "reliability." According to the court, "Cleese left work two hours early on June 17 due to illness; missed work on June 23 for a doctor's appointment; and was ill on June 24," though there was some dispute as to whether Cleese obtained permission for the June 24 incident.[290]

In July of 1992, Cleese was warned for the first of many times in a pattern that continued for months.[291] Among the various warnings, verbal as well as written, were specific articulations that Cleese had demonstrated "unacceptable behavior in the area of dependability."[292] Troubles abounded for Cleese at the Corvallis plant. On December 2, 1992, company officials circulated the results of a health study, which found that "women who worked in semiconductor fabrication facilities (clean rooms) had an increased rate of miscarriages and took longer to conceive than women who did not work in such areas."

Glycol ethers were "the suspected cause," and although the memo noted that "the Corvallis site does not use glycol ethers in any of its manufacturing processes," women employees working in the "fab areas who are either pregnant or trying to conceive" were urged to "consult their managers to discuss any health concerns."[293] On December 14, Cleese asked to be transferred out of the "clean room" because she was trying to get pregnant. The results of the study had caused her concern.

In an effort to accommodate the request, Cleese was offered a job in the drill room. Cleese refused, because she had a previous back injury that would have made the work difficult. Cleese's supervisor was unaware of the restrictions due to the back injury. As a result, Cleese was "placed on probation on December 22, 1992, for 'integrity' and 'judgment' concerns." Once on probation, Cleese was no longer eligible for transfer to another department, and because she could not be transferred to the drill room—even after her back injury had been confirmed—Cleese remained in the clean room.

Another complicating factor was that during her tenure at the Corvallis plant, Cleese "was subjected to offensive comments by her coworker, Steven Ciarla," the court wrote. Cleese would complain to her supervisor about Ciarla's alleged sexual harassment in mid-April 1993. That same month, Cleese learned she was pregnant. Shortly thereafter, "Hewlett-Packard management received complaints from three employees that Cleese was not performing the laminating aspect of her job and claiming that she had restrictions to prevent her from working with chemicals."

Cleese denied the allegations. Still, she was placed on leave pending an investigation. Later she presented company officials with a note from her physician restricting her from working with toxins for the duration of her pregnancy. Hewlett-Packard terminated Cleese on May 15, alleging a "failure to be truthful with her coworkers and management concerning her restrictions." Cleese filed suit, claiming that Hewlett-Packard had discriminated against her by terminating her "because [the company] knew that she was planning to become pregnant and probably would become pregnant in the near future."

In determining whether Cleese could establish a *prima facie* case, the Oregon court held, with regard to the first prong of the *McDonnell Douglas* test, that "there is no reason not to extend protected class status to Cleese," because although "Cleese did not actually learn of her pregnancy until April 1993, a month before her termination, she indicated to her supervisor at the time of her hiring in June 1992 that she was planning to become pregnant."

With regard to the second prong, *i.e.*, whether Cleese had been performing her job satisfactorily, the court noted that "[b]ecause Cleese was never reprimanded for the quality of her work, she satisfies the second element of her *prima facie* case."[294] The court held further that "[t]he third element of Cleese's *prima facie* case—that she suffered an adverse employment decision—is easily met…Cleese was suspended without pay on April 30, 1993, and terminated on May 15, 1993."

That left only the fourth prong, *i.e.*, whether Cleese could show she had been treated differently than others outside her protected class. "Based on records provided by Hewlett-Packard, Cleese argues that the dependability guidelines were enforced against her, but were not enforced against other nonpregnant employees," the court explained. "In particular, she notes that 30 of the 83 employees, for whom records were provided, were absent from work more than 15 hours per month, almost twice their available" time on the floor.

Cleese was also able to offer "direct evidence that Ciarla...was treated more favorably than she," according to the court. "Although Ciarla took 88 consecutive hours of unapproved and unplanned [leave without pay] in November 1991, he was given only a written warning, the same disciplinary action Cleese received for taking one day of approved [leave without pay] and being eight minutes late for work. Cleese points to the 'Application Examples' to argue that Ciarla should have received probation instead of merely a written warning."[295] Hewlett-Packard attempted to refute Cleese's claims, noting that Ciarla had been disciplined. The court held that while it is "possible there was no differential treatment in Hewlett-Packard's discipline of Cleese and Ciarla,...[the company] has not adequately countered Cleese's allegation." Thus, for purposes of summary judgment, Cleese had established a *prima facie* case.

ARMSTRONG v. FLOWERS HOSP., INC.,
33 F.3d 1308 (11th Cir. 1994)[296]

In August 1990, Pamela Armstrong took a job as a home health care nurse with Flowers Hospital in Alabama with a caseload of about twenty-five patients. But on December 12, 1990, Armstrong was told that beginning on December 14, she would have a new patient who was HIV-positive and had been recently diagnosed with cryptococcal meningitis. Given the state of the patient's health, Armstrong was told the patient would require four hours of her time each day and she would be required to draw blood.

The addition of an HIV-positive patient reportedly caused Armstrong "considerable alarm." According to the court, Armstrong "had recently learned that she was pregnant, and her primary concern was that caring for an HIV-positive patient would put her fetus at risk."[297] Armstrong testified that "she was in her first trimester of pregnancy and believed that her fetus was more vulnerable during this period." Armstrong also believed that because she had gestational diabetes, her immune system might be less resilient.

Armstrong told a supervisor she was pregnant and voiced her objections about handling the new patient. The supervisor, Carol Wynn, informed Armstrong that she had been assigned the patient because her schedule best permitted it. Wynn also reviewed the hospital's policy on refusal to treat a patient, which was grounds for termination. Although much of the conversation between Armstrong and Wynn would later be in dispute, in the end "Armstrong understood that Wynn would consider the possibility of reassigning this patient to another nurse..." the court found.[298]

And Wynn did arrange to have another nurse see the HIV-positive patient. But the change "was made simply in anticipation of Armstrong's refusal to treat him." After the conversation with Armstrong, Wynn spoke to her supervisor, and together they concluded that they "did not understand why Armstrong would refuse to see an HIV-positive patient." At no time did Wynn or her supervisor "consider modifying the policy requiring nurses to treat all patients," the Eleventh Circuit explained.

But the issue came to a head on December 14, when Wynn confirmed that Armstrong would not treat the patient. Armstrong chose to be terminated rather than resign, and in January 1992, she filed suit against Flowers Hospital, Inc., alleging violations of Title VII and the Pregnancy Discrimination Act. Although one other nurse had refused to treat an HIV-positive patient and been terminated as a result, three other nurses, who were also pregnant at the time, treated AIDS patients, hospital officials noted.

But Armstrong alleged that the hospital's policy of requiring nurses, including those who are pregnant, to treat HIV-positive patients, had a disparate impact on pregnant women, who were essentially forced to choose between their jobs and the health of their unborn fetuses. But she could not prove it, the Eleventh Circuit held. "Armstrong has not provided evidence sufficient to establish a *prima facie* case of discrimination. It may be that an evidentiary basis for discrimination cannot be established because the policy modification Armstrong seeks is, in reality, a form of preferential treatment. We need not speculate on this matter. Armstrong's discrimination claims fail for lack of evidence."[299]

TITLE VII AND GENDER DISCRIMINATION:
Four Cases and the Making of a Turning Point

On October 11, 1991, an obscure law professor from Oklahoma testified during the Senate confirmation hearings of United States Supreme Court nominee Clarence Thomas.[300] And for it, she was demonized. But soon after, this long ignored and nearly impossible to prove offense became the issue of the decade. Suddenly, sexual harassment as a reality in women's lives was *the* topic of public discussion as complaints began to reach the previously deaf ears of politicians until the walls came tumbling down.[301]

"The Thomas-Hill hearings were followed by the Tailhook scandal, in which a group of naval aviators were charged with lewd behavior toward women at a convention," journalists Jane Mayer and Jill Abramson recall.[302] And though "the court cases bogged down in a welter of conflicting accounts, the incident claimed the navy's top officer as a political casualty. Then, shortly after the 1992 election, a group of women accused Oregon's Senator Robert Packwood of a variety of harassing incidents, some dating from the early 1970s.[303]

"President Clinton himself became a target of allegations of sexual harassment, a development that forced even liberals to wonder about the appropriateness of such charges. And the private sector was equally affected. The EEOC experienced a surge of harassment complaints after Thomas's confirmation hearings, registering a 50 percent increase (to nearly five thousand complaints) in the first six months of 1992 alone," Mayer and Abramson note further.[304]

Although the five thousand complaints are believed to have been the result of an initial spark of renewed awareness, "more than nine thousand cases of sexual harassment were brought before the EEOC in the following year, a rise of 50 percent from the year before," researchers suggest.[305] By 1995, that number had risen to 15,691.[306] But until 1998—a year when the Equal Employment Opportunity Commission reportedly handled 19,114 charges of discrimination-based retaliation—little changed with regard to the law.[307]

Then suddenly, the nation was in the middle of a resurrection—and later a recasting—of Title VII. "Gender discrimination" today encompasses several legal causes of action, including allegations that a woman was denied employment or fired because she was pregnant or "could get pregnant;" complaints of direct requests for sex in exchange for favors or to prevent adverse action—"*quid pro quo*" claims;[308] or "hostile work environment" claims.[309]

THE "GENDER REVOLUTION" AND THE 1990S:
Title VII and a Flood of Modern Cases

In 1997, *Essence* magazine reported that a national survey of large corporations conducted by the American Management Association "found that 72 percent of the responding companies had recently processed at least one sexual harassment report—a high figure when one considered that on average only about 10 percent of all incidents are reported."[310]

Yet, so "small" a relative percentage has translated in actual terms into some very large numbers with the claims in such cases running the gamut from alleged slurs or derogatory name calling; to direct requests for sex; to clear or obstructed denials of professional opportunity based upon gender. And although sexual harassment as a "social problem" has long been relegated to the back rooms of thought where unscrupulous and indecent individuals were said to live, during the 1990s, even some of the nation's most venerable institutions proved not to be immune.

In 1996, Wall Street giant Smith Barney, Inc., was sued on behalf of a nationwide class of women, who alleged dozens of counts of sexual harassment and gender discrimination.[311] Among the thousands of other sexual harassment or gender discrimination cases heard by courts during this period was the case of *Humphreys v. Medical Towers, Ltd.*,[312] involving a suit by a female former building manager who brought a "a hostile work environment" claimed against a former employer, alleging that a building engineer had called her a "bitch," a "whore," and threw a paperweight at her.[313] The employer moved for summary judgment, but the United States District Court for the Southern District of Texas held that "because there [were] outstanding issues of material fact" that the case should be heard by a jury.[314]

That same year, the Seventh Circuit Court of Appeals issued a decision in the case of *Knox v. State of Indiana*,[315] which involved a Title VII claim by a female on "the line" corrections officer, whose transfer to a new shift in October 1990 resulted in a federal lawsuit. According to the findings of the court, at some point during December 1990, Knox's supervisor, Captain Robert Stewart, "began sending [Knox] electronic mail messages asking her for sex. He often propositioned [her] using acronyms; for example, he frequently asked her whether she wanted to have a HGTWM, which was later translated as a 'horizontal good time with me.'"[316]

The captain "also repeatedly asked [Knox] out on dates, calling her on the telephone and leaving messages reminding her to check her email. Whenever [Knox] would tell Stewart that she was not interested in dating him, or in having sex with him, he would ask why not and pursue her further. On one occasion, when Knox turned him down (because she was involved with another man, who she eventually married), Stewart responded, 'Well, then, we can just maybe have sex.' After Knox again rejected him, Stewart replied that he 'definitely saw a shift change in [her] future.'"[317] Knox "was frightened," according to the court, "because she needed her job and Stewart was in a position to recommend, and perhaps effect, such a change."[318]

Things finally came to a head after Stewart called [Knox] at home to ask for a date. Knox filed a formal complaint, and about a month later, Stewart was found "guilty of engaging in sex discrimination and in conduct unbecoming staff" by the Internal Affairs Division of the Department of Corrections.[319] In the interim, Stewart had complained to friends and fellow workers about [Knox's] complaints and Stewart's friends "began to make insulting and demeaning statements about [Knox] around the institution, both to staff and in front of inmates," the court found. After complaining to corrections officials with no satisfactory response, the officer filed suit under Title VII in federal court, alleging a hostile work environment and *quid pro quo* sexual harassment.[320]

In April 1996, the United States District Court for the Eastern District of Pennsylvania issued a decision in *Ascolese v. Southeastern Pennsylvania Transportation Authority*,[321] a case involving allegations of gender discrimination and sexual harassment brought by a woman who claimed she was asked to take a pregnancy test as part of the physical exam. The test was needed, the transportation authority argued, to determine whether the woman was healthy enough for the job. The court held that although the authority may generally have a "very strong interest" in conducting fitness tests, the record of the case did not demonstrate that the transportation association had "a particularly strong interest in conducting the pregnancy test...."[322]

In *Brooks v. Fonda-Fultonville Central School District,* the United States District Court for the Northern District of New York upheld a lower court's decision, finding that the school district refused to hire Brooks as a pool cleaner, because the man who might have been her immediate supervisor told her did not want to hire a woman for that job.[324] And in *Morrison v. Carleton Woolen Mills, Inc.*,[325] a woman filed suit alleging she had suffered sex discrimination as well as sexual harassment. Among the many and various offenses alleged by the plaintiff were that her supervisor prevented her transfer to better jobs; repeatedly thwarted her efforts to move on; told her she was taking a job from a man; and gave her a piece of paper marked "Application for a Piece of Ass."[326]

From the center of the "New Economy" came the hostile work environment claim of a former female employee of Juno Online Services, who alleged that her supervisor and former boyfriend, along with other men in the company, created a hostile work environment by "discussing which female employees they wanted to have sex with and referred to others with vulgar terms such as 'slut' and 'whore.'"[327]

But the new openness that has accompanied discussion of sexual harassment appears not to have moved the nation's lower courts. In *Weller v. Citation Oil & Gas Corp.*,[328] for example, the Fifth Circuit Court of Appeals held that, based upon the evidence and facts before it, a jury could not have found that the conduct of a woman's supervisor in giving her "intense religious" literature dealing with the "Spirit of Jezebel" was outrageous or severe enough to support a Title VII complaint.[329] The following year, the United States District Court for the Northern District of New York held, in *Bush v. Raymond Corp. Inc.*,[330] that a female plaintiff had failed to establish a *prima facie* case for discrimination where she alleged that a co-worker repeatedly made suggestive comments towards her.[331]

And in May of 1997, the United States Supreme Court allowed a sexual harassment suit filed on behalf of Paula Jones against then-President Bill Clinton to go forward.[332] Prior to the Court's decision, the case had been stayed by order of an Arkansas federal judge, who held that claims against a sitting president should not be allowed to proceed until he was out of office. Jones later settled the suit after a third party agreed to pay her roughly $900,000. Even so, the decision set the stage, some argue, for an historic series of events and four decisions by the United States Supreme Court in 1998 that would change the landscape of sexual harassment law.

THE 1998 SUPREME COURT TERM:
The Law Poised for Change

Prior to 1998, modern sexual harassment and gender discrimination law was shaped largely by the decisions of the United States Supreme Court in three cases: *Meritor Savings Bank FSB v. Vinson*,[333] decided in 1986, *Harris v. Forklift Systems*,[334] decided in 1993, and *Landgraf v. U.S.I. Film Products*,[335] decided in 1994. But the newfound awareness arising out of 1991 Senate hearings and the swirl of complaints that followed ignited claims by critics that the law was inadequate in the current environment. Also troubling women's rights advocates was the lack of uniformity and the fact that different courts tended to interpret sexual harassment laws differently. There was need for clarification, critics argued.

The Justices of the United States Supreme Court agreed, and in 1998, the Court issued rulings in four sexual harassment and gender discrimination cases that would change the face of the law. Those cases were: *Faragher v. City of Boca Raton*;[336] *Burlington Industries Inc. v. Ellerth*;[337] *Oncale v. Sundowner Offshore Services Inc.*;[338] and *Gebser v. Lago Vista Independent School District*.[339] Scholars suggest that the first two decisions "revolutionized [t]he liability standard of workplace sexual harassment." The third case set the standard for same-sex sexual harassment, while the fourth addressed the question of a school district's liability when a sexual harassment claim involves an allegation brought by a student against a teacher.

FARAGHER v. CITY OF BOCA RATON

In June 1998, the Supreme Court issued its decision in *Faragher v. City of Boca Raton*. Beth Faragher worked as a part-time ocean lifeguard for the City of Boca Raton for five years, from 1985 to 1990. During that time, Faragher's supervisors were Bill Terry, David Silverman, and Robert Gordon. In June of 1990, Faragher resigned, and in 1992, Faragher filed suit against Terry, Silverman, and the City of Boca Raton "for nominal damages and other relief, alleging, among other things, that the supervisors had created a 'sexually hostile atmosphere' at work by repeatedly subjecting Faragher and other female lifeguards to 'uninvited and offensive touching,' by making lewd remarks, and by speaking of women in offensive terms."[340] This conduct "constituted discrimination in the 'terms and conditions, and privileges' of her employment in violation of Title VII…" Faragher argued.[341]

A federal district court found the City of Boca Raton liable for the conduct of Silverman and Terry. But the Eleventh Circuit, sitting *en banc,* reversed the decision, finding that Terry and Silverman's conduct was outside the scope of their employment and that constructive knowledge of their behavior could not be imputed to the City of Boca Raton. In other words, the City of Boca Raton could not have foreseen that two of its supervisors would break the law. By a vote of 7–2, the United States Supreme Court reversed, upholding the decision of the original federal district court.

In writing for the Court, Justice Souter noted that several courts have found "…that there is a sense in which a harassing supervisor is always assisted in his misconduct by the supervisory relationship."[342] In other words, "[t]he agency relationship affords contact with an employee subjected to a supervisor's sexual harassment, and the victim may well be reluctant to accept the risks of blowing the whistle on a superior. When a person with supervisory authority discriminates in the terms and conditions of subordinates' employment, his actions necessarily draw upon his superior position over the people who report to him, or those under them, whereas an employee generally cannot check a supervisor's abusive conduct the same way that she might deal with abuse from a coworker."[343]

Stating it even more clearly, Souter wrote that "[w]hen a fellow employee harasses, the victim can walk away or tell the offender where to go. [B]ut it may be difficult to offer such responses to a supervisor, whose 'power to supervise—[which may be] to hire and fire, and to set work schedules and pay rates—does not disappear…when he chooses to harass through insults and offensive gestures rather than directly with threats of firing or promises of promotion.'[344] Recognition of employer liability when discriminatory misuse of supervisory authority alters the terms and conditions of a victim's employment is underscored by the fact that the employer has a greater opportunity to guard against misconduct by supervisors than by common workers; employers have greater opportunity and incentive to screen them, train them, and monitor their performance. [¶] In sum, there are good reasons for vicarious liability for misuse of supervisory authority."[345]

BURLINGTON INDUSTRIES INC. v. ELLERTH

On June 26, 1998, the Court also issued its decision in the case of *Burlington Industries Inc. v. Ellerth*. Decided by 7–2 vote, the case is widely held to have extended the reach of sexual harassment law into previously closed realms. According to the facts of the case, from March 1993 through May 1994, Kimberly Ellerth worked as a salesperson for a division of Burlington Industries in Chicago. During that time, Ellerth alleged that she was "subjected to constant sexual harassment by her supervisor," Ted Slowik.[346]

"Against a background of repeated boorish and offensive remarks and gestures which Slowik allegedly made, Ellerth places particular emphasis on three alleged incidents where Slowik's comments could be construed as threats to deny her tangible job benefits," Justice Kennedy set forth in writing for the Court.[347] The first of these incidents occurred, according to Ellerth, during the summer of 1993, when, "while on a business trip, Slowik invited Ellerth to the hotel lounge, an invitation Ellerth felt compelled to accept because Slowik was her boss," Justice Kennedy wrote. "When Ellerth gave no encouragement to remarks Slowik made about her breasts, he told her to 'loosen up' and warned '[y]ou know, Kim, I could make your life very hard or very easy at Burlington.'"[348]

The next incident allegedly occurred in March of 1994, "when Ellerth was being considered for a promotion, [and] Slowik expressed reservations during the promotion interview because she was not 'loose enough.'"[349] This comment was allegedly followed by Slowik's reaching over and rubbing Ellerth's knee. "Ellerth did receive the promotion; but when Slowik called to announce it, he told Ellerth, 'you're gonna be out there with men who work in factories, and they certainly like women with pretty butts/legs.'"[350]

The third incident occurred, according to Ellerth, in May 1994, when "Ellerth called Slowik, asking permission to insert a customer's logo into a fabric sample. Slowik responded, 'I don't have time for you right now, Kim—unless you want to tell me what you're wearing.' Ellerth told Slowik she had to go and ended the call. A day or two later, Ellerth called Slowik to ask permission again. This time he denied her request, but added something along the lines of, 'are you wearing shorter skirts yet, Kim, because it would make your job a whole heck of a lot easier.'"

"A short time later," according to the Court, "Ellerth's immediate supervisor cautioned her about returning telephone calls to customers in a prompt fashion. In response, Ellerth quit. She faxed a letter giving reasons unrelated to the alleged sexual harassment.... About three weeks later, however, she sent a letter explaining she quit because of Slowik's behavior," Justice Kennedy wrote.[351]

In October 1994, Ellerth received a right-to-sue letter from the Equal Employment Opportunities Commission. Soon afterwards, Ellerth filed suit in

federal court, alleging sexual harassment and constructive discharge in violation of Title VII. In granting summary judgment in favor of Burlington Industries, the district court held that even though Slowik's behavior, as alleged by
Ellerth, was "severe and pervasive enough to create a hostile work environment," it was not clear that Burlington Industries either knew, or should have
known, of Slowik's behavior, given that Ellerth had not complained to the company prior to resigning.

But "[t]he Court of Appeals *en banc* reversed in a decision which produced
eight separate opinions and no consensus for a controlling rationale. The judges
were able to agree on the problem they confronted: vicarious liability, not failure to comply with a duty of care, was the essence of Ellerth's case against
Burlington on appeal. The judges seemed to agree Ellerth could recover if
Slowik's unfulfilled threats to deny her tangible job benefits were sufficient to
impose vicarious liability on Burlington.[352] With the exception of Judges Coffey
and Easterbrook, the judges also agreed Ellerth's claim could be categorized as
one of *quid pro quo* harassment, even though she had received the promotion
and had suffered no other tangible retaliation," Justice Kennedy explained.

And yet, from there a clearly fragile consensus disintegrated, prompting
Ellerth's appeal to the United States Supreme Court, which would rule—after
similarly thorough consideration of the issue of vicarious liability—that
"[a]lthough Ellerth ha[d] not alleged she suffered a tangible employment
action at the hands of Slowik, which would deprive Burlington of the availability of the affirmative defense, this is not dispositive. In light of our decision,
Burlington is still subject to vicarious liability for Slowik's activity...."[353]

Taken together, the United State Supreme Court's decisions in *Faragher v.
City of Boca Raton* and *Burlington Industries Inc. v. Ellerth* established that
employers could be held liable for acts of sexual harassment carried out by their
employees, even where the employers had no previous knowledge of the conduct. Thus, the Court seemed to be saying it was the job of employers to police
their own workforce, because liability for wrongful or discriminatory conduct
by employees could attach even where the employers had no previous or foreseeable knowledge of incidents or the alleged conduct. Further, liability could
be attached where humiliating or degrading conduct is involved, even where no
"adverse employment action" was the result.

Several months after publication of the Supreme Court's decisions in
Faragher v. City of Boca Raton and *Burlington Industries Inc. v. Ellerth*, Mitsubishi Motor Manufacturing of America announced that the company had
agreed to set aside $34 million to settle sex harassment claims made by women,
who alleged, among other things, that men on the work floor of the company's
Normal, Illinois, plant routinely groped and grabbed female employees, exposed
them to lewd photographs, and sometimes asked them to show their breasts.[354]

ONCALE v. SUNDOWNER OFFSHORE SERVICES, INC.

In 1998, the Court also issued a decision in *Oncale v. Sundowner Offshore Services,
Inc.*,[355] a case involving a claim of same-sex sexual harassment with facts so

colorful that in delivering the unanimous decision of the Court Justice Antonin Scalia would open by noting that "[t]he precise details are irrelevant to the legal point we must decide, and in the interest of both brevity and dignity, we shall describe them only generally."[356]

But even in general terms, the facts are astounding. According to the Court's recitation in October 1991, Oncale was working on an offshore oil platform in the Gulf of Mexico with John Lyons, Danny Pippen, and Brandon Johnson. The oil platform was owned by Chevron USA, and "[o]n several occasions, Oncale was forcibly subjected to sex-related, humiliating actions against him by Lyons, Pippen, and Johnson in the presence of the rest of the crew. Pippen and Lyons also physically assaulted Oncale in a sexual manner, and Lyons threatened him with rape."[357]

But when Oncale complained, nothing was done to stop the harassment. Instead, the company's Safety Compliance Clerk "told Oncale that Lyons and Pippen 'picked [on] him all of the time too,'" and called him "a name suggesting homosexuality." Oncale eventually quit, asking that his pink slip reflect that "he voluntarily left due to sexual harassment and verbal abuse." Later, during his deposition, Oncale testified that he left because he "felt that if [he] didn't leave [his] job, that [he] would be raped or forced to have sex."[358]

Oncale originally filed suit against Sundowner in the United States District Court for the Eastern District of Louisiana, alleging he had been discriminated against in employment because of his gender. But the court held, in reliance upon a Fifth Circuit Court of Appeals decision, that "Mr. Oncale, a male, has no cause of action under Title VII for harassment by male coworkers."[359] Other courts have held similarly.[360] Oncale appealed to the Fifth Circuit Court of Appeals, which would affirm the lower court's decision.[361]

The United States Supreme Court granted *certiorari*, and the Justices would ultimately rule that they saw "no justification in the statutory language or [the Court's] precedents for a categorical rule excluding same-sex harassment claims from the coverage of Title VII."[362] In other words, Oncale could proceed and Title VII was deemed not only to cover traditional categories of sexual harassment but also same-sex sexual harassment. The Court's decision in *Oncale v. Sundowner Offshore Services, Inc.* sparked the filing of dozens of same-sex harassment lawsuits.[363]

GEBSER v. LAGO VISTA INDEPENDENT SCHOOL DISTRICT

The fourth case in this extraordinary series of decisions was *Gebser v. Lago Vista Independent School District*,[364] which involved a sexual relationship between a ninth grade student and a teacher. The ninth grader never reported the "relationship," though she would later testify that she believed the teacher's "conduct was improper." Beginning in the spring of 1992 and continuing through January of 1993, the student testified there was a sexual "relationship." But in January of 1993, the pair was discovered having sex by a police officer, which apparently brought the "relationship" to an abrupt end. During the period of their involvement, the district reportedly had no official policy or grievance procedure for handling sexual harassment complaints.

The teacher was fired after being discovered with the student. The student's mother then filed suit in state court against the school district and the teacher, alleging Title IX violations. Because there was a federal question at issue, the case was removed to a federal district court, which promptly dismissed the ninth grader's claim, opining that Title IX "was enacted to counter policies of discrimination...in federally funded education programs" and "[o]nly if school administrators have some type of notice of gender discrimination and fail to respond in good faith can the discrimination be interpreted as a policy of the school district."

But because the ninth grader involved had never complained, it could not fairly be held that the school district has ratified the "policy" by inaction, the federal district court held. The United States Supreme Court agreed, holding that it would "'frustrate the purposes' of Title IX to permit a damages recovery against a school district for a teacher's sexual harassment of a student based on principles of *respondeat superior* or constructive notice, *i.e.*, without actual notice to a school district official."

Of some apparent concern for the Justices was the fact that there was no "official" procedure for reporting such incidents at the time. "Because Congress did not expressly create a private right of action under Title IX, the statutory text does not shed light on Congress's intent with respect to the scope of available remedies. Instead, 'we attempt to infer how the [1972] Congress would have addressed the issue had the...action been included as an express provision in the statute,'" the majority of the Court declared in setting forth its mission.

And how did the case come to rest?

"The number of reported cases involving sexual harassment of students in schools confirms that harassment unfortunately is an all too common aspect of the educational experience," the Justices wrote. "No one questions that a student suffers extraordinary harm when subjected to sexual harassment and abuse by a teacher, and that the teacher's conduct is reprehensible and undermines the basic purposes of the educational system. The issue in this case, however, is whether the independent misconduct of the teacher is attributable to the school district that employs him under a specific federal statute designed primarily to prevent recipients of federal financial assistance from using the funds in a discriminatory manner. Our decision does not affect any right of recovery that an individual may have against a school district as a matter of state law or against the teacher in his individual capacity under state law or under 42 U.S.C. Sec. 1983. Until Congress speaks directly on the subject, however, we will not hold a school district liable in damages under Title IX for a teacher's sexual harassment of a student absent actual notice and deliberate indifference."

NO LONGER BUSINESS AS USUAL:
Sexual Harassment Law after the 1998 Term

The 1998–1999 United States Supreme Court term changed the landscape of modern sexual harassment law, sending quakes through the professional world. Legal scholars took note. But so did companies, many of which decided to settle—rather than fight—cases of this sort. The media also took note. In May 1999, the *Wall Street Journal* wrote:

> For a female employee, what's the difference between being repeatedly groped by a low-level manager and by a top executive?
> About $100,000.
> At least, that's the difference in value of awards made in a sexual-harassment case involving drug maker Astra USA, Inc. Early last year, Astra paid nearly $10 million to settle charges by the U.S. Equal Employment Opportunity Commission that its top managers had harassed scores of female sales representatives, after allegations of wild, alcohol-laden sales meetings and employees being forced to accompany executives to nightclubs.[365]

A study conducted by Rutgers University Law School found that as many as 2 million workers in America "were affected by intentional discrimination in 1999," a third of them women or minorities.[366] And as complaints continued to rise, so apparently did settlements. But in a fashion similar to the offenses alleged, settlement awards appear to run the gamut. In the fall of 1999, the Ford Motor Company agreed to "set aside $7.5 million to compensate female employees who were subjected to groping, pornography, insults, and other indignities at two Chicago area plants."[367]

In October 2000, a Montana state senator was accused by his former chief of staff of firing her when she refused his sexual advances.[368] That same week, a federal jury in Manhattan awarded a former Bronx police officer $1.25 million, closing a case that began when the officer, a woman, filed a sexual harassment complaint against her lieutenant in 1994, only to be forced to resign in retaliation.[369]

And during a single week in December of 2000, the following three things happened: a long-time aide and former liaison to the Hispanic community publicly accused the mayor of Milwaukee of sexual harassment.[370] A Syracuse, New York, plastics manufacturer settled a gender discrimination case for a reported $782,000. The company had been accused of paying women less, failing to promote women workers, and placing men with less time on the job in better positions.[371] And Wall Street giant Morgan Stanley–Dean Witter was ordered by a federal district court to comply with subpoenas issued as part of a sex discrimination lawsuit filed on behalf of four black women.[372]

As incidents continued to mount, so, it seems, did the settlements. In March of 2000, the United States government agreed to pay $508 million to settle a gender discrimination case filed more than two decades ago on behalf of 1,100 women denied promotions and jobs at the Voice of America because of their gender. Every woman would reportedly get at least $450,000 in settlement.[373]

But by the summer of 2001, sexual harassment complaints had reportedly begun to "level off," due in large part, researchers suggested, to new proactive efforts by companies less willing, in light of changes to the law, to risk going before a jury.[374] But claims did not stop altogether. In the spring of 2001, five of MetLife's staff of 6,000 employees—25 percent of whom are reportedly women—filed suit against the company, alleging gender bias in promotions, hiring, job assignments on its nationwide sales force, and pay.[375]

Jury awards also do not appear to have declined. In the winter of 2002, a Santa Barbara jury awarded a female worker at the DAKO Corporation in California $215,000 in damages. The woman alleged she was sexually harassed by a supervisor, whom she had not been able to resist due to a personal history of childhood abuse. The woman alleged that she was fired in retaliation for complaining to the company about the supervisor.[376]

The Texas-based national Rent-A-Center reached an agreement with the EEOC in March 2002 to set aside $47 million to settle the sex harassment and discrimination claims of 5,000 women, who complained that over a three-year period, they were discriminated against as job candidates and harassed on the job.[377] In June of 2002, "[s]ixty-six women who were temporary workers at a Chicago-area car dealership…settled a sexual harassment class action with the company for $300,000."[378]

In July of that same year, the Eighth Circuit Court of Appeals upheld a jury's verdict awarding a woman $300,000 in damages on her claim of constructive discharge. While working at a company, the woman alleged that her supervisor began making advances. But when she complained to the human resources manager, nothing was done. The woman felt she had no choice but to resign. She later filed suit for sexual harassment.[379] And on August 14, 2002, the EEOC announced a $875,00 settlement in a discrimination case brought against a Camarillo, California, company on behalf of a class of eighteen female employees (current and former), who alleged that they were "subjected to serious, mostly verbal, sexual harassment and to retaliation."[380]

The rules, it seems, have changed in the sexual harassment and gender discrimination context, and thus, the American workplace appears to be changing as well.

ENDNOTES FOR CHAPTER SEVEN

1   *See Piantanida v. Wyman Center, Inc.*, 116 F.3d 340, 341 (8th Cir. 1997).
2   116 F.3d at 342 (citing 42 U.S.C. Sec. 2000e(k) (*emphasis added by court*)).
3   *See Ilhardt v. Sara Lee Corp.*, 118 F.3d 1151, 1154 (7th Cir. 1997) (citing *EEOC v. Northwestern Memorial Hospital*, 858 F. Supp. 759, 763 (N.D. Ill. 1994); 42 U.S.C. Sec. 2000e(k) (1994)).
4   *See Smith v. F.W. Morse & Co., Inc.*, 76 F.3d 413, 425 (1st Cir. 1996).
5   *See In re Carnegie Center Associates*, 129 F.3d 290, 297 (3d Cir. 1997).

6   See *Smith v. F.W. Morse & Co., Inc.*, 76 F.3d at 420–23. (Smith involved an allegation of pregnancy discrimination by a female employee whose job was eliminated while she was on maternity leave. But because the elimination was one of many and part of a company-wide cost-cutting measure, Smith failed to establish a *prima facie* case, the court held.)

7   *Id*. at 425.

8   *Id*. at 418.

9   See *Ilhardt v. Sara Lee Corp*, 118 F.3d 1151, 1153 (7th Cir. 1997).

10 *Id*.

11 *Id*.

12 *Id*. at 1154.

13 *Id*. at 1155 (citing *Hunt-Golliday v. Metropolitan Water Reclamation District of Greater Chicago*, 104 F.3d 1004, 1010 (7th Cir. 1997); *McDonnell Douglas*, 411 U.S. at 802; *Wallace v. SMC Pneumatics, Inc.*, 103 F.3d 1394, 1398 (7th Cir. 1997)).

14 *Id*. at 1156.

15 See *Smith v. F.W. Morse & Co.*, 76 F.3d 413, 419 (1st Cir. 1996).

16 *Id*. at 419.

17 *Id*.

18 *Id*. at 418.

19 *Id*. at 419.

20 *Id*.

21 *Id*. at n. 2.

22 *Id*. at 419. (The procedural history of the case was that Smith filed suit in a New Hampshire state court alleging "wrongful discharge based upon gender discrimination, intentional infliction of emotional distress, and breach of contract." But because an allegation of gender discrimination invokes Title VII, Morse had the case removed to federal court.)

23 Jurisdiction in federal court is proper where a federal question is involved. Title VII is a federal statute, self-invoking of federal question jurisdiction. See 28 U.S.C. Secs. 1331, 1343(a)(3), 1441, 1446. See also 28 U.S.C. Sec. 1367 (which confers ancillary jurisdiction in federal court of state court claims provided those claims are related to the federal claim).

24 *Id*. at 419.

25 *Id*. (citing 34 FEP Cases 562, 568 (1984)). As a general rule of law, summary judgment has been deemed proper "if the pleadings, depositions, answers to interrogatories, and admissions on file together with affidavits, if any, show that there is no genuine issue as to any material fact and the moving party is entitled to judgment as a matter of law." See *Celotex Corp. v. Catrett*, 477 U.S. 317, 322 (1986), *cert. den.*, 484 U.S. 1066 (1988); *Herman v. City of Chicago*, 870 F.2d 400, 404 (7th Cir. 1989); *Smith v. Kurtzman*, 176 Ill.App.3d 840, 846 (1st Dist. 1988); 735 ILCS 5/2-1005 (1994). "A material fact is one that matters to the result. Material facts are framed by the complaint and answer." *Carruthers v. Christopher & Co.*, 57 Ill.2d 376 (1974). And "[a]n issue of material fact is genuine if 'fair-minded' persons could draw different inferences from the fact at issue." *Torrence v. DeFrates*, 56 Ill.App.3d 118, 120 (4th Dist. 1978). "Merely alleging a factual dispute cannot defeat the summary judgment motion." *Samuels v. Wilder*, 871 F.2d 1346, 1349 (7th Cir. 1989); *Turner v. City of Chicago*, 91 Ill.App.3d 932, 937 (1st Dist. 1980). Though "[a]ll factual inferences are to be taken against the moving party and in favor of the opposing party, *Adickes v. S. H. Kress & Co.*, 398 U.S. 144, 158 (1980), only reasonable inferences, and not all conceivable inferences, will be drawn." *DeValk Lincoln Mercury, Inc. v. Ford Motor Co.*, 811 F.2d 326, 329 (7th Cir. 1987). The nonmovant may not, however, rely solely on the pleadings to rebut a motion for summary judgment. See *Doherty v. Kill*, 140 Ill.App.3d 158 (1st Dist. 1986). In other words, "summary judgment is appropriate where the evidence supporting the nonmovant 'is merely colorable or is not significantly probative.'" *Bank Leumi Le-Israel, B.M. v. Lee*, 928 F.2d 232, 237 (7th Cir. 1991) (quoting *Anderson v. Liberty Lobby, Inc.*, 477 U.S. 242, 247–48 (1986)). In other words, "[a] scintilla of evidence in support of the nonmovant's position is insufficient to successfully oppose summary judgment." *Brownell v. Figel*, 950 F.2d 1285, 1289 (7th Cir. 1991). And even the "existence of a factual dispute will not bar summary judgment unless 'the disputed fact is outcome determinative under governing law.'" *Howland v. Kilquist*, 833 F.2d 639 (7th Cir. 1987) (citation omitted). In other words, if the nonmovant does not come forward with evidence that would reasonably permit the finder of fact to find in his or her favor on a material question, then the court must enter summary judgment against him or her. See *Estate of Henderson*, 185 Ill.App.3d at 530.

26 *Id*.

27 *Id*. at 420.

28 *Id*.

29 *Id*.

30 *Id*. at 420–21 (citing *Fields v. Clark Univ.*, 966 F.2d 49, 51–52 (1st Cir. 1992), *cert. den.*, 506 U.S. 1052 (1993); *Cumpiano v. Banco Santander P.R.*, 902 F.2d 148, 153 (1st Cir. 1990)).

31 *Id*. at 421 (citing *Texas Dep't of Community Affairs v. Burdine*, 450 U.S. 248, 254–56 (1981)).

32 See *McDonnell Douglas Corp. v. Green*, 411 U.S. 792, 802 (1973).

33   Section 704(a) of the Civil Rights Act of 1964, provides in pertinent part that "[i]t shall be an unlawful employment practice for an employer to discriminate against any of his employees or applicants for employment…because he has opposed any practice made an unlawful employment practice by this subchapter." *See* 42 U.S.C. 2000e-3(a).

34   *See McDonnell Douglas Corp. v. Green*, 411 U.S. at 802. (According to the Court, "[t]he complainant in a Title VII trial must carry the initial burden under the statute of establishing a *prima facie* case of racial discrimination. This may be done by showing (i) that he belongs to a racial minority; (ii) that he applied and was qualified for a job for which the employer was seeking applicants; (iii) that, despite his qualifications, he was rejected; and (iv) that, after his rejection, the position remained open and the employer continued to seek applicants from persons of complainant's qualifications.")

35   *Id.*

36   *See Quarantino v. Tiffany's & Co.*, 71 F.3d 58, 64 (2nd Cir. 1995); *Bergstrom-Ek v. Best Oil Co.*, 153 F.3d 851, 857 (8th Cir. 1998); *Smith v. F.W. Morse & Co., Inc.*, 76 F.3d 413, 420–421 (1st Cir. 1996); *In re Carnegie Center Associates*, 129 F.3d 290, 294–295 (3rd Cir. 1997); *Vargas v. Globetrotters Engineering Corp.*, 4 F. Supp. 2d 780, 785 (N.D. Ill. 1998); *Schwartz v. Paralyzed Veterans of America*, 930 F. Supp. 3, 9 (D.D.C. 1996); *Nilson v. Historic Inns Group Ltd.*, 903 F. Supp. 905, 907 (D. Md. 1995); *Millner v. District of Columbia*, 932 F. Supp. 345, 351 (D.D.C. 1996); *Kennedy v. Schoenberg, Fisher & Newman, Ltd.*, 140 F.3d 716, 722–723 (7th Cir. 1998); *Boyd v. Harding Academy of Memphis, Inc.*, 88 F.3d 410, 413 (6th Cir. 1996); *Ilhardt v. Sara Lee Corp.*, 118 F.3d 1151, 1154–1155 (7th Cir. 1997); *LaValley v. E.B. & A.C. Whiting Co.*, 692 A.2d 367, 370-371 (Vt. 1997); *Armstrong v. Flowers Hosp., Inc.*, 33 F.3d 1308, 1314 (11th Cir. 1994); *Cleese v. Hewlett-Packard Co.*, 911 F. Supp. 1312, 1316 (D. Or. 1995); *Garcia v. Woman's Hosp. of Texas*, 143 F.3d 227, 230-231 (5th Cir. 1998); *Urbano v. Continental Airlines, Inc.*, 138 F.3d 204, 206 (5th Cir. 1998); *Ensley-Gaines v. Runyon*, 100 F.3d 1220, 1224 (6th Cir. 1996); *Byrd v. Lakeshore Hosp.*, 30 F.3d 1380, 1382 (11th Cir. 1994); *Gleason v. Mesirow Financial, Inc.*, 118 F.3d 1134, 1140-1141 (7th Cir. 1997); *EEOC v. Yenkin-Majestic Paint Corp.*, 112 F.3d 831, 834 (6th Cir. 1997); *Shafir v. Ass'n of Reform Zionists of America*, 998 F. Supp. 355, 360 (S.D.N.Y. 1998); *Vazquez Gonzalez v. K-Mart Corp.*, 940 F. Supp. 429, 434 (D. P.R. 1996).

37   *Smith v. F.W. Morse & Co. Inc.*, 76 F.3d at 421 (citing *Cumpiano v. Banco Stantander P.R.*, 902 F.2d 148, 153 (1st Cir. 1990)).

38   *Id.* (citing *Texas Dep't of Community Affairs v. Burdine*, 450 U.S. 248, 254-56 (1973); *Lipsett v. University of P.R.*, 864 F.2d at 881, 899 (1st Cir. 1988)).

39   *Id.* (citing *Mesnick v. General Elec. Co.*, 950 F.2d 816, 823 (1st Cir. 1991), *cert. den.*, 504 U.S. 985 (1992)). It should be noted that although *Mesnick* was decided under the Americans with Disabilities Act, the same burden shifting framework applies. Therefore, the precedent may be held persuasive.

40   *Id.* (citing *St. Mary's Honor Ctr. v. Hicks*, 509 U.S. 502 (1993); *Mesnick*, 950 F.2d at 823-24).

41   *Id.* at 422 (citing *LaBlanc v. Great Am. Ins. Co.*, 6 F.3d 836, 844–45 (1st Cir. 1993), *cert. den*, 114 S. Ct. 1398 (1994); *Goldman v. First Nat'l Bank*, 985 F.2d 1113, 1118–19 (1st Cir. 1993); *Montana v. First Fed. Sav. & Loan Ass'n.*, 869 F.2d 100, 105–107 (2d Cir. 1989); *Dister v. Continental Group Inc.*, 859 F.2d 1108, 1115 (2d Cir. 1988); *Pearlstein v. Staten Island Univ. Hosp.*, 886 F. Supp. 260, 268–69 (E.D.N.Y. 1995)).

42   *Id.* at 423.

43   *Id.* at 424.

44   *See Soreo-Yasher v. First Office Management*, 926 F. Supp. 646 (N.D. Ohio 1996).

45   *See* 60 MINUTES, CBS, April 7, 2002 (Leslie Stahl, interview with Hewlett), p. 3 (transcript). *See also supra* note 27, ENDNOTES FOR INTRODUCTION.

46   *Quarantino v. Tiffany & Co.*, 71 F.3d 58, 61 (2nd Cir. 1995). (The Second Circuit Court of Appeals noted, however, that during that evaluation, there was a moment of strangeness when Quarantino's supervisor told Quarantino "… he had asked her co-worker Shelley Rajman and now he was asking her, 'Are you really serious about your career, or are you just going to go home and get pregnant?'" The court noted that in response, Quarantino "chose not to confide in [her supervisor] that she was pregnant." Instead, she reportedly said, "David, I'm *very* serious about my career." But after the conversation was over, Quarantino compared notes "with Rajman—the only other married women in the department—who reported that [the supervisor] had asked her the same question." Then the two women asked another Tiffany's employee whether she had been similar questions. The employee answered, "No. Probably because I'm 40 and past my prime.")

47   *Id.* at 61.

48   *Id.*

49   *Id.*

50   *Id.*

51   *Id.*

52   The New York State Human Rights Law is codified at N.Y. Exec. Law Sec. 296(1)(a) (McKinney 1993).

53   *See Quarantino*, 71 F.3d at 63 (citing *McDonnell Douglas Corp. v. Green*, 411 U.S. 792 (1973)).

54   *See McDonnell Douglas Corp. v. Green*, 411 U.S. at 802.

55   *See Quarantino*, 71 F.3d at 65.

56   *Id.*

57   *Soreo-Yasher v. First Office Management*, 926 F. Supp. 646, 649 (N.D. Ohio 1996) (citing *Nashville Gas Commission v. Satty*, 434 U.S. 136, 143 (1977)).
58   *Id.* at 649.
59   *Id.*
60   *Id* (citing *Nashville Gas Commission v. Satty*, 434 U.S. 136, 143 (1977)).
61   *Id.* (citing *Troupe v. May Department Stores Company*, 20 F.3d 734, 738 (7th Cir. 1994)).
62   *Id.*
63   *Smith v. F.W. Morse & Co., Inc.*, 76 F.3d at 421 (citing *Texas Dep't of Community Affairs v. Burdine*, 450 U.S. 248, 254–56 (1981)).
64   *Id.*
65   *See, e.g., Quarantino v. Tiffany & Co.*, 71 F.3d 58 (2nd Cir. 1995) (citing *Texas Dept' of Community Affairs v. Burdine*, 450 U.S. 248, 253 (1981)).
66   *Smith v. F.W. Morse & Co., Inc.*, 76 F.3d at 421 (citing *Troupe v. May Dept. Stores Co.*, 20 F.3d 734, 736 (7th Cir. 1994)).
67   *Id.* (citing *Texas Dep't of Community Affairs v. Burdine*, 450 U.S. 248, 254–56 (1981)).
68   *See Troupe v. May Dept. Stores Co.*, 20 F.3d 734, 736 (7th Cir. 1994); *Tyler v. Bethlehem Steel Corp.*, 958 F.2d 1176, 1187 (2nd Cir.), *cert. den.*, 506 U.S. 825 (1992)).
69   *See* BLACK'S LAW DICTIONARY, *supra* note 103, ENDNOTES FOR CHAPTER FIVE, at p. 316.
70   *Id.* at 166.
71   *See, e.g., Smith v. F.W. Morse & Company*, 76 F.3d at 423 (citing *Fields v. Clark Univ.*, 966 F.2d 49, 52 (1st Cir. 1992), *cert. den.*, 506 U.S. 1052 (1993)).
72   *See Price Waterhouse v. Hopkins*, 490 U.S. 228, 258 (1989) (plurality op.).
73   *Id.*
74   *Bergstrom-Ek v. Best Oil Co.*, 153 F.3d 851 (8th Cir. 1998). (Given the legal posture of the case, all factual disputes were to be resolved in Ek's favor. The reason for this, the Eighth Circuit explained, was that Bergstrom-Ek appealed a final judgment entered at the district court level in favor of Best Oil Co., doing business as The Little Stores. Best Oil was granted summary judgment on several state law counts as well as a judgment as a matter of law on Bergstrom-Ek's pregnancy discrimination claim. As the Eighth Circuit explained, however, "[j]udgment as a matter of law is appropriate only where the nonmoving party has presented insufficient evidence to support a jury verdict in his or her favor, and this is judged by viewing the evidence in the light most favorable to the non-moving party and giving him or her the benefit of all reasonable inferences from the evidence, but without assessing credibility." *See Bergstrom-Ek*, 153 F.3d at 856 (citing *Harvey v. Wal-Mart Stores, Inc.*, 33 F.3d 994, 997 (8th Cir. 1994)).
75   *Bergstrom-Ek*, 153 F.3d at 854.
76   *Id.*
77   *Id.*
78   *Id.*
79   *Id. (emphasis in original).*
80   *Id.* at 855.
81   *Id.*
82   *Id.*
83   *Id.* (The court notes that "Ek did not have a doctor's order restricting her activities, but Ek believed lifting such heavy items would harm her pregnancy.")
84   *Id.*
85   *Id.*
86   *See* 42 U.S.C. Sec. 2000e *et seq.*, as amended by the Pregnancy Discrimination Act of 1978, 42 U.S.C. Sec. 2000e(k); Minn. Stat. Sec. 363.01-363.15.
87   *Bergstrom-Ek*, 153 F.3d at 855. (During pleadings, similar behavior in two other instances was alleged on Aune's part. In one case, another sales clerk was fired "two or three days after informing Aune she was pregnant." And Aune was allegedly unrelenting. According to the court, "Aune required Ranua to lift heavy items and was hostile to her after learning of Ranua's pregnancy." When she refused, Aune and her supervisor reportedly mocked Ranua. But Aune was even worst, according to the court, to a third former Little Stores employee, calling her a "bitch" and a "whore" after Aune was informed of her pregnancy. Aune again made the former employee "lift heavy items and shovel snow more often than she made [her] prior to learning [the employee] was pregnant." She also allegedly "approached the father of [the employee's] baby while he was a customer at West End and told him he was 'stupid,' he was messing up [the employee's] and his lives and asked him whether he had heard about condoms.")
88   *See* BLACK'S LAW DICTIONARY, *supra* note 69, at p. 316.
89   *Bergstrom-Ek v. Best Oil Co.*, 153 F.3d at 857.
90   *Id.* (citing *Lang v. Star Herald*, 107 F.3d 1308, 1311 (8th Cir.) *cert. den.*, 118 S. Ct. 114 (1993) (further citation omitted)).
91   *See, e.g., St. Mary's Honor Ctr. v. Hicks*, 509 U.S. 502, 506–508 (1993); *United States Postal Service Board of Governors v. Aikens*, 460 U.S. 711, 713–715 (1983); *Texas Dep't of Community Affairs v. Burdine*, 450 U.S. 248, 252–256 (1981); *McDonnell Douglas Corp. v. Green*, 411 U.S. 792, 802 (1973).

92   *See Bergstrom-Ek*, 153 F.3d at 857 (citing *Hanenburg*, 118 F.3d at 574 (further citation omitted)).

93   *Id.* at 858 (citing *West v. Marion Merrell Dow, Inc.*, 54 F.3d 493, 497 (8th Cir. 1995) (quoting *Smith v. World Ins. Co.*, 38 F.3d 1456, 1460 (8th Cir. 1995)). *See also Bersie v. Zycad Corp.*, 399 N.W.2d 141, 146 (Minn. App. 1987) (holding that "[a] constructive discharge occurs when an employee resigns in order to escape intolerable working conditions caused by illegal discrimination" (quoting *Continental Can Co., Inc. v. State*, 297 N.W.2d 241, 251 (Minn. 1980)). "The employer must have acted with the intention of forcing the employee to quit. *See Johnson v. Bunny Bread Co.*, 646 F.2d 1250, 1256 (8th Cir. 1981). "Constructive discharge plaintiffs...satisfy *Bunny Bread's* intent requirement by showing their resignation was a reasonably foreseeable consequence of their employers' discriminatory actions." *Hukkanen v. International Unions*, 3 F.3d 281, 285 (8th Cir. 1993). An objective standard is employed to determine whether an employee was constructively discharged. "A person may not be unreasonably sensitive to her working environment. A constructive discharge arises only when a reasonable person would find her working conditions intolerable." *West v. Marion Merrell Dow, Inc.*, 54 F.3d at 497 (quoting *Bunny Bread*, 646 F.2d at 1256). If an employee quits without giving her employer a reasonable chance to work out the problem, the employee is not constructively discharged. *West v. Marion Merrell Dow*, Inc., 54 F.2d at 498.

94   *Id.*

95   *Id.*

96   BLACK'S LAW DICTIONARY, *supra* note 69, at p. 823.

97   *Nilson Historic Inns Groups Ltd.*, 903 F. Supp. 905 (D. Md. 1995).

98   *Id.* at 906.

99   *Id.* at 905.

100 The Americans with Disabilities Act is codified at 42 U.S.C. Sec. 12102, *et seq.*

101 In this case, the court articulated the test to be that Nilson "must demonstrate the following: (1) That at the time in question she was indeed pregnant; (2) That she was performing her position of banquet manager satisfactorily; (3) That she was terminated from her position as banquet manager; and (4) That after her termination, the position remained open or was filled by someone of comparable qualifications who was not pregnant." *See Nilson*, 903 F. Supp. at 907.

102 *Id.* at 908.

103 *Id.*

104 *Id.*

105 *Id.* at 908, n. 2. (To support this point, the court noted that "Nilson attended Johnson and Wales University, where she received an AA degree in Food and Beverage Management and a BA degree in Hotel and Restaurant Management. Prior to her employment with Historic Inns, Nilson had worked in a number of hotels and restaurants. Her prior positions included bartender, server hostess, and assistant banquet manager. Moreover, Joan Quimby recommended that Nilson be hired. Quimby's 'overall impression of her was positive, and [she] had no reason to think [Nilson] couldn't do the job.'")

106 *Id.* at 906.

107 *Id.* at 909 (citing Nilson's deposition at p. 77).

108 *Id.*

109 *Id.*

110 *Id.*

111 *EEOC v. Clear Lake Dodge*, 60 F.3d 1146, 1149 (5th Cir. 1995).

112 *Id.*

113 *Id.*

114 *Id.* at 1150.

115 *Id.*

116 *Id.* at 1152.

117 *Id.* at 1152–53.

118 *Vazquez Gonzalez v. K-Mart Corp.*, 940 F. Supp. 429, 430 (D. P.R. 1996).

119 Though the author would normally refer to Lynette Vazquez Gonzalez in the full hyphenation of Vazquez Gonzalez, throughout the case, the court referred to her only as Vazquez. Thus, in an effort to avoid confusion, the author will also refer to her only as Vazquez.

120 *Id.* at 431.

121 *Id.*

122 *Id.* (According to pleadings filed with the court, Vazquez Gonzalez reportedly told Arana: "Look, I don't feel well and I am pregnant, and I have some symptoms. I don't feel well, and the trip is being somewhat difficult for me. I have terrible morning sickness, very terrible morning sickness." Pls. Opp'n Mot. Dkt. No. 18, Ex. 3 at 8).

123 *Id.*

124 *Id.*

125 *Id.*

126 *Id.* at 432.

127 *Id.* at n. 1. (The court detailed that "Vazquez makes no reference whatsoever in her motion to several allegations that she made in her complaint. For example, in her complaint Vazquez alleges that

Arana granted her request to leave work and visit a doctor because of her pregnancy on October 3, 1994. Pls.' Compl., Dkt. No. 1, at ¶ 12. She also alleges that the doctor warned her not to continue working under strenuous conditions which could affect her health and the well-being of her baby. *Id.* at ¶ 13. Finally, she states that she informed Arana about the doctor's report and reminded him of her desire to leave El Señorial. *Id.* at ¶ 14. Because Vazquez can not [*sic*] rely on mere allegations in her complaint without any evidentiary support, the court shall not consider these assertions when ruling upon K-Mart's motion. See *LaBlanc v. Great American Ins. Co.*, 6 F.3d 836, 841 (1st Cir. 1993), *cert. den.*, 114 S. Ct. 1398 (1994) (holding that nonmoving party may not rest on mere allegations of pleadings alone to overcome motion for summary judgment).

128 *Id.*
129 *Id.* (citing Pls. Opp'n Mot. Dkt. No. 18, Ex. 3 at 21).
130 *Id.*
131 *Id.* at 434.
132 That test as articulated by the district court as that Vazquez would have to prove she: (1) was a member of a protected classes of persons; (2) was adequately performing her job and was not dismissed because of poor job performance, (3) suffered an adverse employment action, and (4) another employee with similar qualifications continued to perform her duties. See *Vazquez*, 940 F. Supp. at 434.
133 *Id.*
134 *Id.* at 435.
135 *Id.* (That other evidence included statements from Vazquez' deposition, Arana's sworn affidavit as well as his Separation Report.)
136 *Id.*
137 *Id.* (citing *St. Mary's Honor Center v. Hicks*, 509 U.S. 502, 515–517 (1993)).
138 *Id.* (citing *Lehman v. Prudential Ins. Co. of America*, 74 F.3d 323, 329 (1st Cir. 1996)); *Phelps v. Yale Security, Inc.*, 986 F.2d 1020, 1026 (6th Cir.), *cert. den.*, 510 U.S. 861 (1993); *Shenker v. Lockheed Sanders, Inc.*, 919 F. Supp. 55, 60–61 (D. Mass. 1996); and, *Nakai v. Wickes Lumber Co.*, 906 F. Supp. 698, 705 (D. Me. 1995)). But compare *Ayala-Gerena v. Bristol Myers-Squibb Co.*, 95 F.3d 86, 96 (1st Cir. 1996)). The court noted further that "[a]s a matter of law, one isolated, ambiguous remark by itself is insufficient to support a claim of discrimination under Title VII. Consequently, the court hereby grants K-Mart's motion for summary judgment. Vazquez's Title VII claim is hereby dismissed with prejudice. Pursuant to 28 U.S.C. Sec. 1367(c) (1996) and *United Mine Workers of America v. Gibbs*, 383 U.S. 715, 725 (1966), the Court declines to exercise pendent jurisdiction over Vazquez's remaining claims under Puerto Rico's Civil Code and Constitution and are hereby dismissed without prejudice.")
139 *Id.* at 436.
140 When a claim is dismissed with prejudice, it generally means that the claim cannot be refiled.
141 The court could have exercised pendent jurisdiction over these claims pursuant to 28 U.S.C. Sec. 1367(c) (1996), and *United Mine Workers of America v. Gibbs*, 383 U.S. 715, 725 (1966). Instead, Vazquez's claims arising under Puerto Rico's Civil Code and Constitution were dismissed "without prejudice," which suggests that Vazquez could conceivably refile those claims in state court.
142 *Nilson*, 903 F. Supp. at 909.
143 See cases listed, *supra* note 36.
144 *Hunt-Golliday v. Metropolitan Water*, 104 F.3d 1004, 1006–1007 (7th Cir. 1997).
145 *Id.* (citing *Pasqua v. Metropolitan Life Ins. Co.*, 101 F.3d 514 (7th Cir. 1996); *Bultemeyer v. Fort Wayne Community Schools*, 100 F.3d 1281 (7th Cir. 1996); *Denisi v. Dominick's Finer Foods, Inc.*, 99 F.3d 860 (7th Cir. 1996); *Geier v. Medtronic, Inc.*, 99 F.3d 238 (7th Cir. 1996); *Testerman v. EDS Technical Prod. Corp.*, 98 F.3d 297 (7th Cir. 1996); *Cheek v. Peabody Coal Co.*, 97 F.3d 200 (7th Cir. 1996); *Wohl v. Spectrum Mfg., Inc.*, 94 F.3d 353 (7th Cir. 1996); *EEOC v. United Parcel Service*, 94 F.3d 314 (7th Cir. 1996); *Helland v. South Bend Community School Corp.*, 93 F.3d 327 (7th Cir. 1996); *McKenzie v. Illinois Dept. of Transp.*, 92 F.3d 473 (7th Cir. 1996); *Miranda v. Wisconsin Power & Light Co.*, 91 F.3d 1011 (7th Cir. 1996); *Johnson v. City of Fort Wayne, Ind.*, 91 F.3d 922 (7th Cir. 1996); *Ford v. Wilson*, 90 F.3d 245 (7th Cir. 1996); *Rabinovitz v. Pena*, 89 F.3d 482 (7th Cir. 1996); *Smart v. Ball State University*, 89 F.3d 437 (7th Cir. 1996); *Adler v. Glickman*, 87 F.3d 956 (7th Cir. 1996); *Vitug v. Multistate Tax Comm'n*, 88 F.3d 506 (7th Cir. 1996); *Ost v. West Suburban Travelers Limousine, Inc.*, 88 F.3d 435 (7th Cir. 1996); *Piraino v. International Orientation Resources, Inc.*, 84 F.3d 270 (7th Cir. 1996); *Mills v. First Federal Sav. & Loan Ass'n*, 83 F.3d 833 (7th Cir. 1996); *Fuka v. Thomson Consumer Electronics*, 82 F.3d 1397 (7th Cir. 1996); *Weisbrot v. Medical College of Wisconsin*, 79 F.3d 677 (7th Cir. 1996); *Bratton v. Roadway Package Sys., Inc.*, 77 F.3d 168 (7th Cir. 1996); *EEOC v. Our Lady of Resurrection Med. Center*, 77 F.3d 145 (7th Cir. 1996); *Wolf v. Buss (America) Inc.*, 77 F.3d 914 (7th Cir. 1996); *Smith v. Cook County*, 74 F.3d 829 (7th Cir. 1996). The Seventh Circuit went on to note that it had "affirmed the district courts in 21 of the 26 cases but found that the existence of disputed material facts in five cases made summary judgment inappropriate. *Bultemeyer v. Fort Wayne Community Schools*; *Wohl v. Spectrum Mfg., Inc.*; *EEOC v. United Parcel Service*; *Johnson v. City of Fort Wayne, Ind.*; *Piraino v. International Orientation Resources, Inc.*" See *Hunt-Golliday*, 104 F.3d at 1107.

146 *Id.* at 1010.
147 *Id.* at 1007.
148 *Id.*
149 *Id.*
150 *Id.* at 1008.
151 *Id.* (According to the court's description of the established facts, "Golliday next asked her immediate supervisor at Calumet, Terry Nolan, for a letter of verification. He confirmed that she needed two years of high-pressure boiler experience and so he declined to issue the letter. She made several additional requests for the letter, and in January 1991, she was told by her head supervisor, Greg Cargell, that Metro Water did not have to issue her a letter of verification and if she persisted in asking for one she would 'be given a hard time.' Golliday persisted nonetheless.")
152 *Id.*
153 *Id.*
154 *Id.* at 1009.
155 *Id.* at 1006.
156 *Kennedy v. Schoenberg, Fisher & Newman, Ltd.*, 140 F.3d 716 (7th Cir. 1998). Kennedy also filed defamation and tortious interference with the employment relationship claims.
157 *Id.* at 720. (Specifically, the court detailed that "[i]n July 1991, defendant SF&N conducted a review of plaintiff's performance which indicates that plaintiff's 'overall analytical ability and problem-solving skills,' her 'writing ability,' and her 'overall contribution to the firm's legal work' needed improvement. Defendant SF&N also voiced concern that plaintiff was not delegating enough of her [National Office Machine Dealers Association] work to other SF&N employees. An SF&N shareholder also told plaintiff that she was not performing enough non-NOMDA billable work to justify her salary. In order to help plaintiff shift 30 to 40 percent of her NOMDA work to other employees, defendant SF&N agreed to provide plaintiff with assistance from clerical personnel and/or paralegals.")
158 *Id.* (According to the Seventh Circuit's description of these events, "[i]n the beginning of July 1991, plaintiff voiced an interest in drafting an *amicus curiae* brief to be filed with the United States Supreme Court on behalf of NOMDA in a pending antitrust appeal involving the Eastman Kodak Company. [Robert] Goldberg, as General Counsel for NOMDA, was responsible for the brief and permitted plaintiff to draft it. Plaintiff had at least two months to complete the brief. In that time, Goldberg set various deadlines for plaintiff to submit drafts, which plaintiff missed. Plaintiff ultimately submitted a draft to Goldberg ten days before the brief was due, to which Goldberg responded that he would have liked more time to edit the brief and that he had inadequate time for revisions and additional research. Goldberg was dissatisfied with the final brief and expressed his disappointment to plaintiff. Additionally, plaintiff made mistakes that incurred significant added costs for defendant SF&N. Plaintiff did not have the brief typeset until two days before it was due, which resulted in additional costs for expedited printing. Plaintiff also submitted the brief to the Supreme Court with the wrong color cover, which resulted in rejection of the brief by the Supreme Court and a $1,600 cost for resubmission. The Supreme Court rejected the brief a second time because the brief was submitted again with the wrong cover. Resubmission another time cost another $260.")
159 *Id.* at 721. (According to the court, the specifics of the dispute began after Kennedy submitted her expense form. "Because plaintiff had not received prior approval for the car rental and because she had not rented the car from the company NOMDA selected, Goldberg questioned the car rental expense. In a memo to Goldberg, plaintiff responded that Goldberg did not notify her as to which rental company had been selected by NOMDA. Plaintiff then modified her expense report, deleting the car rental expense. [¶] Goldberg continued to withhold approval of the expense report, questioning plaintiff's dinner charge of $25.75 on July 17, since plaintiff attended an awards banquet that evening where dinner was served. In response to Goldberg's refusal to approve the report, plaintiff submitted an amended expense report which omitted the $25.75 charge and added two dinners of $10 each for July 15, 1992, and July 16, 1992, and a breakfast of $5.75 for July 16, 1992, resulting in a total charge of $25.75. During her deposition, plaintiff admitted that she fabricated the subsequent three meal charges which totaled $25.75 and that the original dinner charge was for a meal eaten by her parents who were at the convention to look after her baby. [¶] Goldberg informed plaintiff that he was submitting the expense report to NOMDA without his approval. In response to NOMDA accounts payable Kay Nedrud's inquiry as to why Goldberg had not approved the expense report, Goldberg sent Nedrud a letter necessary in order for the report to pass muster under NOMDA's standards. Goldberg sent copies of the letter to the executive director, personnel chairman, and accounting manager of NOMDA. None of these recipients viewed the letter as accusing plaintiff of dishonesty, lacking moral integrity, defrauding NOMDA, or padding or falsifying her expenses. [¶] Upset with Goldberg's letter, plaintiff wrote a memorandum to Goldberg, charging him with making 'false' accusations against her in the letter. In response, Goldberg wrote a memorandum addressing plaintiff's claims. Plaintiff responded with another memorandum, and then she circulated one of her memos to all SF&N partners. Goldberg in turn forwarded his most

recent memo to the same partners of SF&N. Plaintiff also discussed her conflict with Goldberg with individuals at SF&N who advised her to attempt to resolve her differences with him.")

160   *Id.*

161   According to the court, during this meeting, "Goldberg refrained from speaking substantively about plaintiff."

162   *Id.* at 723.

163   *Id.* (citing *Troupe v. May Dept. Stores Co.*, 20 F.3d 734, 736 (7th Cir. 1994)).

164   *Id.* at 725 (citing *Piraino v. International Orientation Resources, Inc.*, 84 F.3d 270, 274 (7th Cir. 1990).

165   *Id.*

166   See Darryl Van Duch, *Layoffs Can Lead to Litigation*, NAT'L L.J., Jan. 22, 2001, at B1.

167   *Id. See also* Sam Lubbell, *No Pink Slip. You're Just Dot-Gone*, N.Y. TIMES, March 18, 2001, at wk2.

168   *Ilhardt v. Sara Lee Corp*, 118 F.3d 1151 (7th Cir. 1997).

169   *Id.* at 1155 (citing *Hunt-Golliday v. Metropolitan Water Reclamation District of Greater Chicago*, 104 F.3d 1004, 1010 (7th Cir. 1997); *McDonnell Douglas*, 411 U.S. at 802; *Wallace v. SMC Pneumatics, Inc.*, 103 F.3d 1394, 1398 (7th Cir. 1997)).

170   *Id.* at 1156.

171   *In re Carnegie Center Associates*, 129 F.3d 290 (3rd Cir. 1997).

172   *Id.* at 293.

173   *Id.*

174   *Id.* (The court notes, however, that "Turndorf [the company's chief financial officer] testified that the fact that Rhett was unmarried played no role in Carnegie's later decision to abolish her position.")

175   *Id.* (Because the company was in bankruptcy proceedings at the time of Rhett's suit, the case was heard by a bankruptcy court that attributed those comments to Rhett's work. Jurisdiction of the bankruptcy court was proper under 28 U.S.C. Sec. 157(b)(2)(B), (O) and 28 U.S.C. Sec. 1334(b).)

176   *Id.* (citing Bankruptcy Court Opinion at 5-6, "discussing two employees who left on maternity leave and subsequently returned to the same or similar positions").

177   *Id.*

178   *See* N.J.S.A. Sec. 10:5-12.

179   *In re Carnegie*, 129 F.3d at 294.

180   *Id.*

181   *Id.* at 295.

182   *Id.* at 294.

183   *Id.* at 295.

184   *Id.*

185   *Armbruster v. Unisys Corp.*, 32 F.3d 768 (3rd Cir. 1994).

186   *See McDonnell Douglas Corp. v. Green*, 411 U.S. 792, 802 (1973).

187   *See Armbruster*, 32 F.3d at 777.

188   This is a legal historical fact perhaps best explained by the United States Supreme Court in *Newport News Shipbuilding & Dry Dock v. EEOC*, 462 U.S. 669, 673 n. 8 (1983), in which the Court noted that "[a]fter the passage of the Pregnancy Discrimination Act,...the Equal Employment Opportunity Commission issued 'interpretive guidelines' in the form of questions and answers." Those "[i]nterim interpretive guidelines were published for comment in the FEDERAL REGISTER on March 9, 1979. 44 FED. REG. 13278–13281. Final guidelines were published in the FEDERAL REGISTER on April 20, 1979. *Id.* at 23804–23808. The EEOC explained: 'It is the Commission's desire...that all interested parties be made aware of EEOC's view of their rights and obligations in advance of April 29, 1979, so that they may be in compliance by that state.' *Id.* at 23804. The questions and answers are reprinted as an appendix to 29 C.F.R. 1604 (1982)."

189   *In re Carnegie*, 129 F.3d at 295 (citing 29 C.F.R. Sec. 1604.10(b), which provides that "[d]isabilities caused or contributed to by pregnancy, childbirth, or related purposes, shall be treated the same as disabilities caused or contributed to by other medical conditions....Written or unwritten employment policies and practices involving matters such as the commencement and duration of leave....[and] reinstatement...shall be applied to disability due to pregnancy...on the same terms and conditions as they are applied to other disabilities").

190   *Id.* (citing *Troupe v. May Dep't Stores Co.*, 20 F.3d 734, 738 (7th Cir. 1994) (further citation omitted).

191   *Id.* at 297.

192   *Id.* at 296–297 (citing *Grier v. Medtronic, Inc.*, 99 F.3d 238, 243 (7th Cir. 1996) (holding that a fired employee was not qualified for the job because she could not meet performance quota); *Troupe*, 20 F.3d at 735 (involving pregnancy employee fired for tardiness prior to maternity leave); *Soreo-Yasher v. First Office Management*, 926 F. Supp. 646, 649 (N.D. Ohio 1996) (upholding replacement of employee while on maternity leave due to "business need"); *Morrisey v. Symbol Techs.*, 910 F. Supp. 117, 121 (E.D.N.Y. 1996) (upholding the firing of an employee whose maternity leave extended beyond the period when the company guaranteed reinstatement); *Rudolph v. Hechinger*, 884 F. Supp. 184, 186 (D. Md. 1995) (involving termination of an employee while on maternity leave for reasons unrelated to pregnancy); *Ulloa v. American Express Travel Related Servs. Co.*, 822 F. Supp. 1566, 1570–71 (S.D. Fla. 1993) (involving an employee terminated in force reduction while

on maternity leave, but after guaranteed period of reinstatement had elapsed); *Crnokrak v. Evangelical Health Sys. Corp.*, 819 F. Supp. 737, 743 (N.D. Ill. 1993) (involving demotion of an employee while on maternity leave); *Felts v. Radio Distrib. Co.*, 637 F. Supp. 229, 233 (N.D. Ind. 1985) (holding that employer's argument for termination of employee based upon alleged financial difficulties was a pretext).

193   *Troupe v. May Dep't Stores Co.*, 20 F.3d 734 (7th Cir. 1994).

194   *In re Carnegie Center Associates*, 129 F.3d at 297.

195   *Id.*

196   *Id.* (citing *Ulloa*, 822 F. Supp. at 1571).

197   Upton Sinclair, THE JUNGLE (New York: New American Library of World Literature, Inc., 1980 (original copyright 1905), at p. 76.

198   *See* McDonald, *supra* note 13, ENDNOTES FOR CHAPTER THREE, at p. 60.

199   *Muller v. Oregon*, 208 U.S. 412, 421–22 (1908).

200   *Rosenfeld v. Southern Pacific Co.*, 444 F.2d 1219 (9th Cir. 1971).

201   *Ridlinger v. General Motors Corp.*, 325 F. Supp. 1089 (S.D. Ohio 1971).

202   *Weeks v. Southern Bell Telephone and Telegraph*, 408 F.2d 228 (5th Cir. 1969).

203   *California Federal Savings and Loan v. Guerra*, 479 U.S. 272 (1987).

204   The Pregnancy Discrimination Act of 1978 was passed expressly to prevent that possibility. As codified at 42 U.S.C. Sec. 2000e(k) (1988), the Act provides that "[t]he terms 'because of sex' or 'on the basis of sex' include, but are not limited to, because of or on the basis of pregnancy, childbirth, or related medical conditions; and women affected by pregnancy, childbirth, or related medical conditions shall be treated the same for all employment-related purposes, including receipt of benefits under fringe benefit programs, as other persons not so affected but similar in their ability or inability to work, and nothing in Section 2000e-2(h) of this title shall be interpreted to permit otherwise. This subsection shall not require an employer to pay for health insurance benefits for abortion, except where the life of the mother would be endangered if the fetus were carried to term, or except where medical complications have arisen from an abortion: *Provided,* that nothing herein shall preclude an employer from providing abortion benefits or otherwise affect bargaining agreements in regard to abortion."

205   The American Civil Liberties Union's brief submitted in support of California Federal Savings and Loan Association (quoted in Friedman Goldstein, *supra* note 129, ENDNOTES FOR CHAPTER ONE, at p. 51).

206   See, *e.g.*, Babcock *et al.*, *supra* note 115, ENDNOTES FOR CHAPTER ONE, at p. 129 (citing Barbara Babcock *et. al.*, SEX DISCRIMINATION AND THE LAW: CAUSES AND REMEDIES (1975), at p. 271.)

207   *See* McDonald, *supra* note 198, at p. 60.

208   Reported on ABC WORLD NEWS TONIGHT, Feb. 28, 2003 (directions for transcript availability can be found on ABCNews.com); Jodi Wilgoren, *A New War Brings New Role for Women*, N.Y. TIMES, March 28, 2003, at B1.

209   For an overview of the issue, see Robert Blank, FETAL PROTECTION IN THE WORKPLACE: WOMEN'S RIGHTS, BUSINESS INTERESTS, AND THE UNBORN (New York: Columbia University Press, 1993).

210   See Valerie Kalfrin, *No Room for Pregnant Cop in Texas Town*, May 22, 2000, APBNEWS.COM (published by APB ONLINE, Inc.).

211   *Id.* (According to Kafrin, "…the pregnant officer's limits became clear at the end of April, when she was called to break up a domestic dispute that had degenerated into a 'knock-down, drag-out fight,' she said. [¶] Her husband was with her when the call came in and accompanied her to the scene. While David Janssen helped, and a Palacios police officer who was called for backup subdued the angry man, his wife stayed out of the way and later cited her condition as a reason she didn't enter the fray.")

212   *Id.*

213   See Valerie Kalfrin, *Fate of Pregnant Cop in Limbo*, June 9, 2000, APBNEWS.COM (published by APB ONLINE, Inc.).

214   *Id.* at 2 (citing the comments of Palacios City Administrator Charles Winfield).

215   *Id.* (quoting Palacios City Manager, Charles Winfield, who reportedly said: "Everybody has to patrol. Even our chief [who retired May 15] was a patrol officer").

216   *Id.* at 1.

217   *Id.*

218   *Id.* (The City of Palacios had a temporary disability leave policy, which doubles for its maternity leave policy, providing that "[e]mployees with illnesses arising from pregnancy, maternity, or other nonoccupational illness or injury, shall be entitled to benefits on the same basis as employee's with other illnesses. Accrued sick leave or vacation leave may be used for any such temporary disability, including maternity purposes prior to delivery and for a reasonable time following as may be determined as necessary by her doctor. An employee who has exhausted all leave may request leave of absence without pay from mayor/city council. This leave shall not exceed thirty (30) days. If the employee does not report to work at the end of thirty (30) days, his or her employment will be terminated. For maternity purposes, at least ten (10) days' [*sic*] notice of leave, which shall include a statement of the employee's intentions concerning resumption of work is required, except in emer-

gencies. A medical clearance is required for all employees desiring to return to work after leave caused by a temporary disability.")

219 Those fits and starts reportedly included discussion of whether the city council was empowered to create a "light duty" officer position. *See* Stacy Hagaman Novak, *Pregnant Officer Battling City Policy*, THE MATAGORDA ADVOCATE, May 11, 2000, at 1E.

220 *See* Kalfrin, *supra* notes 210 and 213.

221 *See Pros & Cons*, COURT-TV, June 14, 2000 (reported by Helen Luciatus) (for transcript information, see Court-TV website).

222 *See* Stacy Hagaman Novak, *City Stands Behind Policy Interpretation*, THE MATAGORDA ADVOCATE, May 18, 2000, at 1E.

223 *See* 42 U.S.C.A. Sec. 2000e(b) ("[B]ut such term does not include: (1) the United States, a corporation wholly owned by the Government of the United States, an Indian tribe, or any department or agency of the District of Columbia subject by statute to procedures of the competitive service (as defined in section 2102 of Title 5), or (2) a bona fide private membership club (other than a labor organization) which is exempt from taxation under Section 501(c) of Title 26, except that during the first year after March 24, 1972, persons having fewer than twenty-five employees (and their agents) shall not be considered employers.")

224 *See Raciti-Hur v. Homan*, 8 F. Supp. 2d 958, 959 (E.D. Mich. 1998), *aff'd*, 181 F.3d 103 (N.D. Ohio 1999).

225 *Id.* at 959. (According to the court's explanation, Bell's palsy is a "condition causing partial facial muscle paralysis.")

226 *Id.* at 960.

227 *Id.*

228 *Id.*

229 *Id.*

230 *Id.* at 961.

231 *Id.* (Specifically, "[o]n May 29, 1996, Plaintiff wrote to the Undersheriff tentatively accepting the offer presented at the May 28th meeting, and requested that it be put in writing. An agreement was subsequently drafted and a meeting was held between Plaintiff [Raciti-Hur] and Undersheriff Wright, at which the Plaintiff was presented with a written agreement for her signature. The agreement provided that: (1) Plaintiff would be assigned to dispatch at dispatch pay and benefits; (2) after her pregnancy she would be returned to her road patrol position with no loss of seniority, and (3) she would waive any legal claims arising out of her reassignment as a dispatcher.")

232 *Id.* at 963.

233 *Id.* at 963–64. (Other courts have reached similar decisions. *See, e.g., Atwood v. City of Des Moines*, 485 N.W.2d 657, 660 (Iowa 1992) (holding that a police department's change in its "light duty" policy was not discrimination on the basis of pregnancy where the new policy accorded present police officers the same rights as all other employees).)

234 *Deneen v. Northwest Airlines, Inc.*, 132 F.3d 431, 436 (8th Cir. 1998).

235 *Id.* (citing 42 U.S.C. Sec. 2000e-2(e)(1)) (citing *Lang v. Star Herald*, 107 F.3d 1308, 1312 (8th Cir. 1996), *cert. denied*, 118 S. Ct. 114 (1997)).

236 *Richards v. City of Topeka*, 173 F.3d 1247, 1250 (10th Cir. 1999).

237 *Id.* at 1250.

238 *Id.*

239 In the decision, the court counts the City of Topeka's affirmative arguments as two. The author of this book counts them as three.

240 *Id.* at 1252.

241 *Id.*

242 *Id.* at 1250.

243 As a matter of law, several courts have held that normal pregnancies that proceed without complications do not qualify as "disabilities" under the Americans with Disabilities Act at 42 U.S.C. Sec. 12102(2)(A). See, *e.g., Gabriel v. City of Chicago*, 9 F. Supp. 2d 974, 980–81 (N.D. Ill. 1998); *Gudenkauf v. Stauffer Communications, Inc.*, 922 F. Supp. 465, 473 (D. Kan. 1996); *Jessie v. Carter Health Care Ctr.*, 926 F. Supp. 613, 616 (E.D. Ky. 1996). In addition, regulations promulgated by the Equal Employment Opportunities Commission expressly hold that "conditions such as pregnancy, that are not the result of a physiological disorder are…not 'impairments.'" *See* 29 C.F.R. Sec. 1630 app. Sec. 1630.2(h).

244 See *Richards*, 173 F.3d. at 1251. (The specific language of the Court's consideration of Richards's assertions regarding a disability, the Court held that "Richards's argument is premised on a faulty reading of the ADA and the regulations promulgated under it. In order for Richards to satisfy the statutory definition of 'regarded as' having an impairment, she must prove she (1) has a physical or mental impairment that does not substantially limit major life activities but is treated by a covered entity as constituting such limitations; (2) has a physical or mental impairment that substantially limits major life activities only as a result of the attitudes of others towards such impairment; or (3) has none of the impairments defined in paragraphs (h)(1) or (2) of this section but is treated by a covered entity as having a substantially limiting impairment. 29 C.F.R. Sec. 1630.2(*l*). Richards

argues that the city illegally discriminated against her under Sec. 1630.2(*l*)(3) by treating her as having a 'substantially limiting impairment,' although her pregnancy does not constitute a physical impairment under paragraphs (h)(1) and (2). Her interpretation of Sec. 1630.2(*l*)(3) reads an exception into the ADA's definition of disability that would swallow that statute itself, enabling prospective plaintiffs to claim discrimination against disabilities that are excluded from coverage by the Act. Moreover, the EEOC's interpretive guidelines for the term 'substantial limitation in a major life activity' clearly bars appellant's argument, 'An individual satisfies the third part of the "regarded as" definition of "disability" if the employer or other covered entity erroneously believes the individual has a substantially limiting impairment that the individual actually does not have.' 29 C.F.R. Sec. 1630 app. Sec. 1630.2(*l*). Because Richards concedes her pregnancy is not a substantially limiting impairment under the ADA, her claim does not remotely fall within this definition.")

245   *Id.* at 1252.

246   For fuller explanation of the standard and how it has been interpreted, *see Phillips v. Martin Marietta Corp.*, 400 U.S. 542, 546 n. 3 (1971). (According to the Court, "[t]he [Equal Employment Opportunity] Commission's regulations provide: Sex as a bona fide occupational qualification. (a) The Commission believes that the bona fide occupational qualification exception as to sex should be interpreted narrowly. Labels—'Men's jobs' and 'Women's jobs'—tend to deny employment opportunities unnecessarily to one sex or the other. (1) The Commission will find that the following situations do not warrant the application of the bona fide occupational qualification exception: (i) The refusal to hire a woman because of her sex, based on assumptions of the comparative employment characteristics of women in general. For example, the assumption that the turnover rate among women is higher than among men. (ii) The refusal to hire an individual based on stereotyped characterizations of the sexes. Such stereotypes include, for example, that men are less capable of assembling intricate equipment; that women are less capable of aggressive salesmanship. The principle of nondiscrimination requires that individuals be considered on the basis of individual capacities and not on the basis of any characteristics generally attributed to the group. (iii) The refusal to hire an individual because of the preferences of coworkers, the employer, clients, or customers except as covered specifically in subparagraph (2) of this paragraph. (iv) The fact that the employer may have to provide separate facilities for a person of the opposite sex will not justify discrimination under the bona fide occupational qualification exception unless the expense would be clearly unreasonable. (2) Where it is necessary for the purpose of authenticity or genuineness, the Commission will consider sex to be a bona fide occupational qualification, *e.g.*, an actor or actress. (b)(1) Many states have enacted laws or promulgated administrative regulations with respect to the employment of females. Among these laws are those which prohibit or limit the employment of females, *e.g.*, the employment of females in certain occupations, in jobs requiring the lifting or carrying of weights exceeding certain prescribed limits, during certain hours of the night, or for more than a specified number of hours per day or per week. (2) The Commission believes that such state laws and regulations, although originally promulgated for the purpose of protecting females, have ceased to be relevant to our technology or to the expanding role of the female worker in our economy. The Commission has found that such laws and regulations do not take into account the capacities, preferences, and abilities of individual females and tend to discriminate rather than protect. Accordingly, the Commission has concluded that such laws and regulations conflict with Title VII of the Civil Rights Act of 1964 and will not be considered a defense to an otherwise established unlawful employment practice or as a basis for the application of the bona fide occupational qualification exception.")

247   *See* 42 U.S.C. Sec. 2000e-2(e)(1) (allowing, under Title VII, an employer to discriminate where a BFOQ "is reasonably necessary to the normal operation of [a defendant's] particular business or enterprise"); *International Union UAW v. Johnson Controls*, 499 U.S. 187 (1991) (concluding that a BFOQ defense is available under the PDA when "pregnancy actually interferes with the employee's ability to perform the job").

248   *Richards*, 173 F.3d at 1252.

249   *Id.* (citing 42 U.S.C. Sec. 2000e-2(e)(1) (allowing, under Title VII, an employer to discriminate where a BFOQ "is reasonably necessary to the normal operation of [a defendant's] particular business or enterprise"); *International Union UAW v. Johnson Controls*, 499 U.S. 187 (1991) (concluding that a BFOQ defense is available under the PDA when "pregnancy actually interferes with the employee's ability to perform the job").

250   *Id.* at n. 3. (In a footnote, the Tenth Circuit explained that "[b]ecause we base our refusal to review the district court's denial of the appellant's summary judgment motion on the disputed material facts concerning the City's BFOQ defense, we need not address the question of whether estoppel is available as a matter of law where a plaintiff may have assisted in the bargaining over a contract whose provisions the plaintiff challenges under Title VII and the PDA.")

251   *Lavalley v. E.B. & A.C. Whiting Co.*, 692 A.2d 367, 368 (Vt. 1997).

252   *Id.* at 368.

253   E.B. & A.C. Whiting Co. has a policy dividing "workers into those whose disability is work-related and qualified them for workers' compensation benefits, and those whose disability is not work-related. The former are encouraged to accept whatever accommodations are possible, and compat-

ible, with their ability to work. If alternative work is available, workers in this category are placed in it. Whatever the accommodation, including the placement in alternative work, the employees in this category receive full pay as long as they work....The second category, those with non-work-related disabilities, is further divided into two subcategories. The first subcategory is made up of minor and short-term disabilities that are handled by shift supervisors through accommodations that enable the employee to continue at full pay. The second subcategory is made up of those with long-term disabilities that render the worker unable to substantially perform his or her responsibilities. According to defendant's union contract, these employees are placed on disability leave at 50 percent of salary up to a maximum of $160 per week." *Lavalley v. E.B. & A.C. Whiting Co.,* 692 A.2d at 368.

254   *See* V.S.A. Sec. 495(a)(1).

255   *See Lavalley,* 692 A.2d at 369.

256   *Id.* at 368.

257   *Id.* at 370.

258   *Id.* (citing *Adams v. Nolan,* 962 F.2d 791, 796 (8th Cir. 1992) (finding discrimination on the basis of pregnancy where an employer accommodated the non-work related disability of an employee for one month, but failed to accommodate a pregnant employee, who sought similar accommodation)).

259   *Id.* at 371.

260   429 U.S. 125 (1976).

261   Among the cases cited by the Supreme Court of Vermont were: *Colorado Civil Rights Comm'n v. Travelers Ins. Co.,* 759 P.2d 1358, 1365 (Colo. 1988); *Massachusetts Elec. Co. v. Massachusetts Comm'n Against Discrimination,* 375 N.E.2d 1192, 1199 (1978); *Minnesota Mining & Mfg. Co. v. State,* 289 N.W.2d 396, 398–99 (Minn. 1979); *Bankers Life & Casualty Co. v. Peterson,* 866 P.2d 241, 244 (1993); *Castellano v. Linden Bd. of Educ.,* 386 A.2d 396, 402 (1978), *rev'd in part on other grounds,* 400 A.2d 1182, 1183 (1979); *Brooklyn Union Gas Co. v. New York State Human Rights Appeal Bd.,* 390 N.Y.S.2d 884, 888–89 (1976); *Anderson v. Upper Bucks County Area Vocational Technical Sch.,* 373 A.2d 126 (1977); *Frank's Shoe Store v. West Virginia Human Rights Comm'n,* 365 S.E.2d 251 (1986); *Kimberly-Clark Corp. v. Labor & Indus. Review Comm'n,* 291 N.W.2d 584, 586 (1980).

262   *See Lavllley* at 371 (citing *Adams v. Nolan,* 962 F.2d 791, 794–95 (8th Cir. 1992) (holding that an internal policy providing the "light duty" for employees, even those suffering "nonwork-related injury or illness," was not discriminatory if applied to everyone without intent to discriminate against pregnant workers); *Ulloa v. American Express Travel Related Servs. Co.,* 822 F. Supp. 1566, 1571 (S.D. Fla. 1993) (holding that there was no disparate treatment where a pregnant employee, terminated while taking a leave that was longer than twelve weeks, failed to show that she had been treated less favorably than nonpregnant women who took leave that exceeded twelve weeks); *Atwood v. City of Des Moines,* 485 N.W.2d 657, 660 (Iowa 1992) (holding that a police department's change in its light duty policy was not discrimination on the basis of pregnancy where the department's new policy accorded pregnant police officers the same rights for all employees); *Wimberly v. Labor & Indus. Relations Comm'n,* 479 U.S. 511 (1987) (holding that a state's unemployment compensation rule denying benefits for employees leaving work for nonwork-related reasons was facially neutral, and did not discriminate against pregnant employees)).

263   *Id.* (citing *Scherr v. Woodland Sch. Community Consol. Dist. No. 50,* 867 F.2d 974 (7th Cir. 1988)).

264   *Id.* at 372 (citing *EEOC v. Warshawsky & Co.,* 768 F. Supp. 647 (N.D. Ill. 1991)).

265   *Id.* at 373.

266   *Id.* (citing *Wimberly v. Labor & Indus. Relations Comm'n,* 479 U.S. 511 (1987)).

267   *Id.* (In reaching this holding, the court reasoned that "[t]he policy distinction that plaintiff challenges is fundamentally rooted in the workers' compensation laws, which provide that a worker who 'receives a personal injury by accident arising out of and in the course of his employment' is entitled to compensation as provided by law" (citing 21 V.S.A. Sec. 618)." If the worker 'is unable to perform work for which the employee has previous training or experience, the employee shall be entitled to vocational rehabilitation services, including retraining and job placement, as may be reasonably necessary to restore the employee to suitable employment.'")

268   *Id.*

269   See, *e.g., Piantanida v. Wyman Center, Inc.,* 116 F.3d 340 (8th Cir. 1997) (involving the question of whether a pregnancy discrimination claim may be based upon the allegation that an employer took unlawful action against a female employee given her status as a new mother); *Boyd v. Harding Academy of Memphis, Inc.,* 88 F.3d 410 (6th Cir. 1996) (involving a pregnancy discrimination suit against a religious institution by an unmarried woman).

270   *See supra* note 247.

271   *Deneen v. Northwest Airlines, Inc.,* 132 F.3d 431 (8th Cir. 1998).

272   *Id.* at 433. (According to the findings of the court, "[i]n January 1993, NWA laid off Mrs. Deneen as part of a reduction in force. She was pregnant at that time with an expected delivery date of July, and she had informed NWA of her pregnancy. In April, the secretary to Steve Holme, director of ground operations, offered her a temporary part-time CSA position during the busy travel months of June through September 1993. Mrs. Deneen orally accepted the position. The secretary inquired

casually about Mrs. Deneen's pregnancy. In late May, another NWA representative informed Mrs. Deneen that she would be working five-hour shifts, beginning on June 9, 1993.")

273   *Id.* (According to the court's finding of fact, "[o]n June 2, 1993, the doctor restricted Mrs. Deneen to 48 hours of bed rest and relaxation due to pregnancy-induced hypertension. Mrs. Deneen's husband, who also worked as a CSA for NWA, took some time off work to be with her. On June 8, 1993, concerned about their family finances, Mr. Deneen called Mr. Holme's office to inquire about how long a person must be 'on the clock' at work to receive earned benefits. The secretary knew of Mrs. Deneen's pregnancy, and the office apparently knew that Mr. Deneen had taken some leave to be home with his wife. The secretary referred the call to Mr. Holme, who responded that Mrs. Deneen would not be allowed to return to work, 'because of her pregnancy complication.' Mr. Deneen was surprised that anyone at NWA would even know whether or not Mrs. Deneen suffered complications. The conversation became heated, and Mr. Holme concluded by stating that Mrs. Deneen could only return to work if she produced a doctor's note verifying her fitness to work. [¶] Mrs. Deneen complied and obtained a doctor's note releasing her to work her five-hour shift with light duty. When she reported to work as scheduled on June 9, 1993, Mrs. Deneen discovered that no time card was prepared for her and her name had been crossed off the work list with a notation by Mark Horvath, the CSA manager, that she was on a medical leave of absence. Neither Mr. Holme nor Mr. Horvath had ever spoken to Mrs. Deneen about her medical condition—they were acting on an assumption that she had a pregnancy-related complication that would not allow her to perform her job functions.")

274   *Id.* at 434.

275   *Id.*

276   *Id.*

277   *Id.*

278   *Id.* at 433. (According to the court, upon reporting to work one day, "Mr. Holme and Mr. Horvath met with Mrs. Deneen after she reported to work. Mr. Holme said, 'It's been brought to my attention that you are having problems with your pregnancy, and we need you to bring in a note.' She then presented her note along with her own explanation that she could perform most of the job functions, with the exception of lifting bags. She had not previously been aware that she would have to comply with any particular lifting requirements. Mr. Horvath then presented Mrs. Deneen with a letter outlining the physical requirements of the CSA job, including the ability to lift up to 75-pound bags of luggage onto a conveyor belt. Mrs. Deneen said that she was never able to lift 75-pound bags, even when she was not pregnant, and she named many CSA duties and job functions that she could perform with her present limitation. Mr. Holme responded, 'If I let you come back now, you would just go out and take your sick leave, and that would be preventing another person from working.' He told her that she could not come back to work unless she had a doctor's note verifying that she could perform all the listed job functions. [¶] The next day, Mrs. Deneen received a letter notifying her that she was not qualified to return to work because of her medical restrictions to light duty. The letter informed her that the decision could be reviewed if her doctor certified her as fit to perform all of the physical aspects of the job.")

279   *Id.* at 434. ("The district court concluded as a matter of law that Mrs. Deneen had submitted sufficient direct evidence of discrimination to justify submitting the case to the jury as a mixed-motives case. On this basis, the jury entered a special verdict finding that NWA 'did not allow Ruth Deneen to return from layoff status on June 9, 1993, and that her pregnancy was a motivating factor' in its decision.' The jury also found that NWA would not have made the same decision had she not been pregnant.")

280   Deneen was awarded $3,500 in lost wages; $10,000 compensatory damages; and, $10,000 in punitive damages.

281   *Id.* at 438. (The Eighth Circuit expressly held that "[w]e conclude that there is sufficient evidence from which a reasonable jury could conclude that NWA intentionally discriminated against Mrs. Deneen on the basis of her pregnancy-related medical condition in an attempt to deny her earned benefits.")

282   *Urbano v. Continental Airlines, Inc.,* 138 F.3d 204 (5th Cir. 1998).

283   *Id.* at 206.

284   *Id.*

285   *Id.* at 208.

286   *Leeker v. Gill Studios, Inc.,* 21 F. Supp. 2d 1267, 1269 (D. Kan. 1998).

287   *Id.* at 1269.

288   *Id.* at 1270.

289   *Id.* at 1273.

290   *Cleese v. Hewlett-Packard Co.,* 911 F. Supp. 1312 (D. Or. 1995).

291   *Id.* at 1315. (Specifically, the court noted that "Cleese left work two hours early on June 17 due to illness; missed work on June 23 for a doctor's appointment; and was ill on June 24. It is disputed whether she obtained prior approval for taking time off on June 24. Therefore, on July 1, 1992, Cleese received a verbal warning for unacceptable attendance based on the 2-1/2 days of work she missed in June 1992. She was warned that she could be terminated if she failed to follow all depend-

ability guidelines. [¶] On October 27, 1992, Cleese received a 'Written Warning' that her 'perform-ance was unacceptable' in the areas of judgment and dependability. It mentioned that Cleese had taken off September 8 for reasons not agreed to by management, showing 'unacceptable perform-ance in the area of judgment.' It was further noted that Cleese had been late for work on October 9 and 26, demonstrating 'unacceptable behavior in the area of dependability.' Cleese was warned that in future she must be prompt for work, not take an unapproved [leave without pay], and that her 'communication to all members of the management team must be done with complete accuracy.'")

292 *Id.*

293 *Id.*

294 *Id.* at 1318.

295 *Id.* at 1319.

296 *Armstrong v. Flowers Hosp., Inc.,* 33 F.3d 1308 (11th Cir. 1994).

297 *Id.* at 1310.

298 *Id.* at 1311.

299 *Id.* at 1317.

300 *See* Jane Mayer & Jill Abramson, STRANGE JUSTICE: THE SELLING OF CLARENCE THOMAS (Boston: Houghton Mifflin Co., 1994), at p. 352.

301 See *e.g.,* Patricia Phillips & George Mair, KNOW YOUR RIGHTS: A LEGAL HANDBOOK FOR WOMEN ONLY (New York: Macmillan/Arco, 1997), at p. 27. (According to Phillips and Mair, "[t]he number of harassment charges filed with the Equal Employment Opportunity Commission...has more than doubled since 1990. Of course, that may be due in part to the fact that women are now aware of the law that provides protection from sexual harassment that gives them a reasonable remedy for job harassment. Another possibility, women are invading job areas that have traditionally been dominated by men. For example, in mining and construction there is a ratio respectively of 90 and 52 sexual harassment complaints for every 100,000 women workers as contrasted with 17 in the fields of real estate, insurance, and service industries.")

302 *See* Mayer & Abramson, *supra* note 300, at p. 352.

303 *Id.*

304 *Id.*

305 *See* Friedman Goldstein, *supra* note 205, at p. 8.

306 *See* Mair, *supra* note 301, at p. 27 (citing Ellen Neuborne, *Cover Story,* USA TODAY, May 3–5, 1996).

307 *See* Michael Higgins, *Ok, Your Move,* A.B.A. J., May 1999, at p. 26.

308 "*Quid pro quo*" harassment "occurs when an employee is forced to choose between acquiescing to sexual demands or suffering adverse employment consequences, including losing her job." See FRIEDMAN, *supra* note 205. For case law, see *e.g., Williams v. Saxbe,* 413 F. Supp. 654 (D.D.C. 1976), *rev'd on other grounds sub nom., Williams v. Bell,* 587 F.2d 1240 (D.C. Cir. 1978)).

309 Although the courts have worked hard to come up with a meaningful interpretation of the term, a simple definition is that hostile work environment harassment "occurs when workplace practices constituting unwelcome 'verbal or physical conduct of a sexual nature' has the 'purpose or effect of unreasonably interfering with an individual's work performance or creating an intimidating, hos-tile, or offensive working environment.'" *See* Scott E. Friedman, SEX LAW: A LEGAL SOURCEBOOK ON CRITICAL SEXUAL ISSUES FOR THE NONLAWYER (Jefferson, North Carolina: McFarland & Co., 1990), at p. 107 (citing 29 C.F.R. Sec. 1604.11(a)).

310 *See* Dawn M. Baskerville, *Hands Off!,* ESSENCE, May 1997, at pp. 135, 196.

311 *See Martens v. Smith Barney, Inc.,* 181 F.R.D. 243 (S.D.N.Y. 1988).

312 *See Humphreys v. Medical Towers, Ltd.,* 893 F. Supp. 672 (S.D. Tex. 1995).

313 *Id.* at 678.

314 *Id.* at 684. (This case, incidentally, involved issues of vicarious liability. For tort and sexual miscon-duct cases involving similar claims, see, *e.g., Worcester Ins. Co. v. Fells Acres Day School,* 408 Mass. 393 (1990); *Medlin v. Bass,* 327 N.C. 587 (1990); *Stephens v. A-Able Rents Co.,* 101 Ohio App. 3d 20 (1995); *Lisa N. v. Henry Mayo Newhall Memorial Hosp.,* 48 Cal. Rptr. 2d 510 (1995); *Deloney v. Board of Education,* 281 Ill.App.3d 775 (1996); *Mackey v. U.P. Enterprises,* 935 S.W.2d 446 (Texas 1996); *Doe v. Hartford Roman Catholic Diocesan Corp.,* 45 Conn. Supp. 388 (1998); *Porter v. Harsh-field,* 329 Ark. 130 (1998); *Stern v. Ritz Carleton Chicago,* 299 Ill.App.3d 374 (1998)).

315 *Knox v. State of Indiana,* 93 F.3d 1327 (7th Cir. 1996).

316 *Id.* at 1330.

317 *Id.*

318 *Id.*

319 *Id.* at 1331.

320 *Id.*

321 *Ascolese v. Southeastern Pennsylvania Transportation Authority,* 925 F. Supp. 351 (E.D. Pa. 1996).

322 *Id.* at 355.

323 *Brooks v. Fonda-Fultonwille Central School Dist.,* 938 F. Supp. 1094 (N.D.N.Y. 1996).

324 *Id.* at 1099.

325 *Morrison v. Carleton Woolen Mills, Inc.,* 108 F.3d 429 (1st Cir. 1997).

326 *Id.* at 433–434.

327   See Susan E. Reed, *New Economy, Same Harassment Problems*, N.Y. TIMES, Aug. 12, 2001, Sec. 3, at pp. 1, 11.
328   *Weller v. Citation Oil & Gas Corp.*, 84 F.3d 191 (5th Cir. 1996).
329   As the court noted "[t]o state a claim for relief under Title VII for gender discrimination based on theory of a hostile work environment, a plaintiff must prove: (1) that she belongs to a protected class, (2) that she was subject to unwelcome harassment, (3) that the harassment was based on sex, (4) that the harassment affected a term, condition, or privilege of employment, and (5) that the employer knew or should have known about the harassment and failed to take prompt remedial action." *Weller*, 84 F.3d at 194. For other 1996 decisions, see, *e.g.*, *Maher v. Associated Services for the Blind*, 929 F. Supp. 809 (E.D. Pa. 1996); *Iannone v. Frederic Harris*, 941 F. Supp. 403 (S.D.N.Y. 1996); *Fisher v. Vassar College*, 70 F.3d 1420 (2nd Cir. 1995), *reh'g den.*, 523 U.S. 1041 (March 28, 1998).
330   *Bush v. Raymond Corp. Inc.*, 954 F. Supp. 490 (N.D.N.Y. 1997).
331   Among the alleged comments made by her supervisor were: "I have to get away from you before anything happens;" "You've got a really good-looking wife (said to her husband);" "How did she look in a two-piece bathing suit?;" If I tell you what your raise is, will I get a kiss and a hug?;" "That feels great," after putting his arms around plaintiff; "God you smell great;" "Let me know if you ever decide to leave your husband;" "Don't worry, if you ever leave him you can move in with me.") *See Bush v. Raymond Corp. Inc.*, 954 F. Supp. at 492.
332   See David Savage, *The Trial Must Go On*, AM. BAR J., July 1997, at p. 18.
333   *Meritor Savings Bank FSB v. Vinson*, 477 U.S. 57 (1986). (The general facts of the case were that Michelle Vinson took a job as a bank teller in 1974, and over the course of the next four years, as she was consistently promoted, Vinson alleged she was bullied into having sex with her supervisor forty or fifty times until she took indefinite leave and was fired.)
334   *Harris v. Forklift Systems*, 510 U.S. 17 (1993). (Teresa Harris sued Forklift Systems, Inc., after her supervisor continued to make sexist or sexually suggestive remarks to her. Among them were: "You're a woman, what do you know?" and "We need a man as a rental manager." The supervisor was also alleged to ask female employees to take something out of his pocket and he was known, the plaintiff alleged, to deliberately drop things on the floor and then demand that female employees pick them up.)
335   *Landgraf v. U.S.I. Film Products*, 511 U.S. 244 (1994).
336   *Faragher v. City of Boca Raton*, 118 S. Ct. 2275 (1998).
337   *Burlington Industries Inc. v. Ellerth*, 118 S. Ct. 2257 (1998).
338   *Oncale v. Sundowner Offshore Services, Inc.*, 523 U.S. 75 (1998).
339   *Gebser v. Lago Vista Independent School District*, 118 S. Ct. 1989 (1998).
340   See *Faragher*, 118 S. Ct. at 2277.
341   *Id.*
342   *Id.* at 2290 (citing *Rodgers v. Western-Southern Life Ins. Co.*, 12 F.3d 668, 675 (7th Cir. 1993); *Taylor v. Metzger*, 152 N.J. 490, 505 (1998). *Cf. Torres*, 116 F.3d at 631. *See also White v. Monsanto Co.*, 585 So.2d 1205, 1209-1210 (La. 1991); *Contreras v. Crown Zellerbach Corp.*, 88 Wash. 2d 735, 740 (1977); *Alcorn v. Anbro Engineering, Inc.*, 2 Cal. 3d 493, 498–499, and n. 2).
343   *Id.* at 2291.
344   *Id.* (citing Susan Estrich, *Sex at Work*, 43 STAN. L. REV. 813 (1991), at p. 854.
345   *Id.*
346   See *Burlington Industries*, 118 S. Ct. at 2259.
347   *Id.* at 2262.
348   *Id.*
349   *Id.*
350   *Id.*
351   *Id.* at 2263.
352   *Id.* (citing *Jansen v. Packing Corp. of America*, 123 F.3d 490, 494 (7th Cir. 1997)).
353   *Id.* at 2271.
354   See Reed Abelson, *Can Respect be Mandated? Maybe Not Here*, N.Y. TIMES, Sept. 10, 2000, Sect. 3, at p. 1. (According to Abelson, despite the settlement, things have not changed dramatically as the plant.)
355   *Oncale v. Sundowner Offshore Services, Inc.*, 523 U.S. 75 (1998).
356   *Id.* at 77.
357   *Id.*
358   *Id.*
359   *Id.* (citing *Garcia v. Elf Atochem North America*, 28 F.3d 446, 451–452 (1994)).
360   *See, e.g.*, *Martin v. Norfolk Southern Ry. Co.*, 926 F. Supp. 1044 (N.D. Ala. 1996); *Miller v. Vesta, Inc.*, 946 F. Supp. 697 (E.D. Wis. 1996); *Peric v. Board of Trustees of the University of Illinois*, 68 EPD 44,265 (N.D. Ill. 1996); *Johnson v. Hondo, Inc.*, 940 F. Supp. 1403 (E.D. Wis. 1996); *Ton v. Information Resources, Inc.*, 1996 WL 5322 (N.D. Ill. 1996); *Rushing v. United Airlines*, 919 F. Supp. 1101 (N.D. Ill. 1996); *Kaplan v. Dacomed Corp.*, 1996 WL 89148 (N.D. Ill. 1996); *Griffith v. Keystone Steel and Wire*, 887 F. Supp. 1133 (C.D. Ill. 1995); *Boyd v. Vonnahmen*, 66 EPD 43,620 (S.D. Ill. 1995); *Blozis v. Mike Raisor Ford, Inc.*, 896 F. Supp. 805 (N.D. Ind. 1995); *Wright v. Methodist Youth Ser-*

vices, Inc., 511 F. Supp. 307 (N.D. Ill. 1981); *Barlow v. Northwestern Hospital*, 67 EPD 43,831 (N.D. Ill. 1980); *Doe by Doe v City of Belleville, Ill.*, 119 F.3d 563 (7th Cir. 1997); *Womack v. Runyon*, 147 F.3d 1298 (11th Cir. 1998). *Compare, Shermer v. Illinois Dep't of Transp.*, 937 F. Supp. 781 (C.D. Ill. 1996); *Schoiber v. Emro Marketing Co.*, 941 F. Supp. 730 (N.D. Ill. 1996); *Torres v. National Precision Blanking*, 943 F. Supp. 952 (N.D. Ill. 1996); *Vandeventer v. Wabash National Corp.*, 867 F. Supp. 790 (N.D. Ind. 1994); *Guluszek v. H.P. Smith*, 697 F. Supp. 1452 (N.D. Ill. 1988).

361 *See Oncale v. Sundowner Offshore Services, Inc.*, 88 F.3d 118 (1996).

362 *Oncale*, 523 U.S. at 79.

363 *See, e.g., Mota v. University of Texas*, No. 00-20009 (5th Cir. Aug. 9, 2001); *'Equal Op' Harassment is Legal Under Title VII*, NAT'L L.J., June 12, 2000, at B4; *Men, Increasingly, Are the Ones Claiming Sex Harassment by Men*, N.Y. TIMES, June 10, 2001, at A1; *Homosexual Liable for Harassing Heterosexual*, NAT'L L.J., March 25, 2002, at B2; Deborah L. Rhode, *Harassment is a Work Issue*, NAT'L L.J., July 12, 1999, at A19; Allen Weitzman & Justin Senior, *Same-Sex Harassment*, NAT'L L.J., July 12, 1999, at B6; Michael Tinaglia, *Same-Sex Harassment in Illinois After Oncale v. Sundowner Officer Service*, 86 ILL. BAR J. at pp. 310–329, (June 1998).

364 *Gebser v. Lago Vista Independent*, 118 S. Ct. 1989 (1998).

365 *See* Mark Maremont, *A Case Puts a Value on Touching and Fondling*, WALL ST. JOUR., May 25, 1999, at B1.

366 *See* Reed Abelson, *Study Finds Bias on the Job Is Still Common*, N.Y. TIMES, July 24, 2002, at C2.

367 *See* Gary Wisby, *Bias Costs Ford $7.5 Million*, CHI. SUN-TIMES, Sept. 8, 1999, at 3; Reed Abelson, *If Women Complain, Does Ford Listen?*, N.Y. TIMES, Jan. 28, 2001, Sect. 3, at p.1.

368 *See Senator Sued for Sex Harassment*, NAT'L L.J., Oct. 30, 2000, at A6.

369 *See Award in Harassment Case*, N.Y. TIMES, Oct. 14, 2000, at B16.

370 *See* Pam Belluck, *Aide Charges Harassment in Milwaukee*, N.Y. TIMES, Dec. 6, 2000, at A16.

371 *See* Steven Greenhouse, *Plastics Company Is to Pay $782,000 to Settle Charges of Sex Discrimination*, N.Y. TIMES, Dec. 7, 2000, at C17.

372 *See Morgan Stanley Must Comply*, NAT'L L.J., Dec. 11, 2000, at B3; Patrick McGeehan, *U.S. Sues Morgan Stanley, Charging Sex Bias in a Firing*, N.Y. TIMES, Sept. 11, 2001, at C1; Patrick McGeehan, *Wall Street Highflier to Outcast: A Woman's Story*, N.Y. TIMES, Feb. 10, 2002, Sec. 3, at 1.

373 *See* Irvin Molotsky, *Government Offers $508 Million in a Record Sex-Bias Settlement*, N.Y. TIMES, March 23, 2000, at A1; Peter Kilborn, *For Women in Bias Case, the Wounds Remain*, N.Y. TIMES, March 24, 2000, at A11.

374 *See* Jonathan D. Glater, *New Guards to Lessen Liability*, N.Y. TIMES, Aug. 8, 2001, at C1.

375 *See* Joseph B. Treaster, *Five Women Sue MetLife, Charging Bias in Promotions*, N.Y. TIMES, March 14, 2001, at C4.

376 *See Worker Wins $215,000 in Sex Harassment Suit*, NAT'L L.J., Feb. 11, 2002, at B3.

377 *See* Andrew Harris, *Sex Bias Case Settles for $47M*, NAT'L L.J., March 18, 2002, at A17.

378 *See* Gary Young, *Temps Settle Harassment Case*, NAT'L L.J., June 10, 2002, at A17.

379 *See Jaros v. Lodge Net Entertainment Corp.*, No. 01-3325 (cited in NAT'L L.J., July 22, 2002, at A19).

380 *See EEOC Settlement*, NAT'L L.J., Aug. 19, 2002, at A9 (citing *EEOC v. Technicolor Inc.*, No. CV 01-06791-GAF).

CHAPTER EIGHT

Guerrilla Tactics and Reproductive Rights Today

IN THE BEDROOM:
Issues of Sex and Privacy

On July 29, 1998, nearly thirty years after the liberating and seemingly far-reaching reproductive rights decisions of the late 1960s and early 1970s, the question of what a person may or may not do in the privacy of the home was at issue before an Alabama federal district court in a suit filed on behalf of six women. The women argued that a state ban on the purchase and sale of sexual stimulation devices unduly burdened their right to privacy,[1] an intimate, fundamental, and personal privacy clearly protected by the precedents of the '60s, they argued.

The plaintiffs opposed a 1998 amendment to the Alabama statute, making it illegal "to produce, distribute, or otherwise sell sexual devices that are marketed primarily for the stimulation of human genital organs." B.J. Bailey was among the named plaintiffs in the Alabama case. A "modern woman on a mission," according to writers, Bailey was the owner of Saucy Lady,[2] a boutique that specialized in the sale of stimulation and sex-related devices. Helping women to "overcome sexual dysfunction while improving their relationships" was the motivation behind the business, Bailey argued.

With nearly half of all American women reportedly suffering from some form of sexual dysfunction,[3] Bailey's wares would seem to fill a niche. But Alabama officials saw it differently, arguing in defense of the amendment that proscribing the sale of such devices was necessary to protect children and unwitting adults from exposure to obscene matter. Persons convicted of selling such material under the 1998 amendment faced a possible one-year jail sentence and a $10,000 fine. At the time of the suit, seven other states had statutes prohibiting the sale and promotion of such devices.[4]

Victory for Bailey and the other plaintiffs seemed swift.

On March 29, 1999, a federal judge struck down the amendment. In finding that the state's efforts bore no rational relationship to the articulated interest of protecting the public, the district court held that "[t]he right to privacy is broad enough to encompass the lawful sexual practices of adults free from the government's purview. Alabama simply has no business entering the bedrooms of its citizens and proscribing their most intimate affairs. While the challenged statute does not purport to directly regulate [these] affairs, by choking off the supply and availability of sexual aids, Alabama authorities will have largely accomplished indirectly what they could not have done directly. The Constitution forbids this type of manipulation of fundamental rights."[5]

Had it stood on appeal, the district court's ruling might have marked the articulation of a new standard of privacy where the issue involves the question of sexual pleasure and there is no direct connection to procreation or family. But opening the door to that issue had the effect of pushing the debate away from the specific challenge to "sex toys" legislation raised by the plaintiffs and toward discussion of legal precedents involving the broader issue of privacy rights where "nonprocreative" activities are in controversy (*i.e.*, same-sex sexual conduct).

In October 2000, the Eleventh Circuit Court of Appeals reversed the district court ruling in reliance upon the 1986 United States Supreme Court decision in *Bowers v. Hardwick*.[6] *Bowers v. Hardwick* involved a consensual sexual relationship between two men in the privacy of one of the men's homes. "In light of *Bowers*, there would be no violation of any fundamental constitutional right to the extent the application of Alabama's statute infringed upon the sexual activity of homosexuals," the Eleventh Circuit concluded.

Further, the Alabama amendment was "rationally related to the state's legitimate government interest in public morality," the Eleventh Circuit held. For these reasons, the district court erred in invalidating the amendment, the appeals court reasoned. Though the Eleventh Circuit would modify its decision in January 2001 to exclude all reference to homosexuality,[7] the decision—combined with events occurring at about the same time[8]—would re-ignite the debate of sexual privacy and eventually lead to reconsideration and the fall of *Bowers v. Hardwick*.[9]

Eisenstadt v. Baird,[10] *Roe v. Wade*,[11] and several of the other well-regarded precedents of 1960s and '70s are often thought—if not singularly, then certainly collectively—to establish an absolute and far-reaching fundamental right to sexual privacy. But the language of these decisions is, in fact, more closely grounded in the private choices of consenting adults involved in sexual conduct directly related to procreation and/or the private choice of whether or not to procreate. *Eisenstadt v. Baird* involved the private choice of contraception, for example, while *Roe v. Wade* addressed the question of whether the right to privacy included the choice of abortion. In both cases, the United States Supreme Court held that the fundamental right to privacy encompassed these choices.

But where the issue was one of sexual pleasure in-and-of-itself or the case involved sex acts not directly related to procreation, the nation's courts have repeatedly declined to extend the same level of protection, often noting that the United States Supreme Court similarly declined such an extension with the "controversial" decision in *Bowers v. Hardwick,* reasoning as the Supreme Court had, that because same-sex acts did not relate to procreation, marriage and child-rearing, the same rule regarding privacy did not apply. This was so even where the acts involved occur in the "privacy" of one's bedroom, a distinction Michael Hardwick learned of by litigating through it.

In August of 1982, the Atlanta police entered the apartment and then bedroom of a man identified in court documents only as "respondent Hardwick." Once there, an officer discovered Hardwick in the throes of a sex act with another man. Hardwick and his companion were arrested in an incident so invasive, according to Harvard's Laurence Tribe, that the officer "refused even to leave the room or turn his back while Hardwick and his companion dressed."[12]

Hardwick was charged with violating a Georgia statute criminalizing sodomy.[13] Although the prosecutor declined to present the case to a grand jury, Hardwick challenged the constitutionality of the statute in federal court.[14] Tribe would eventually argue the constitutional issues arising out of the challenge before the United States Supreme Court.

In framing the issue of same-sex relations as the majority perceived it, Justice White set forth—in writing for that five-justice majority[15]—that "[t]he issue presented [was] whether the Federal Constitution confers a fundamental right upon homosexuals to engage in sodomy and hence invalidate the laws of the many states that still make such conduct illegal and have done so for a very long time."[16]

The majority chose not to invalidate those laws or the Georgia statute, finding instead that "none of the rights announced in [*Pierce v. Society of Sisters*[17] and *Meyer v. Nebraska,*[18] involving decision of child rearing and education; *Prince v. Massachusetts,*[19] involving family relationships; *Skinner v. Oklahoma*[20] involving decisions of procreation; *Griswold v. Connecticut*[21] and *Eisenstadt v. Baird* involving the choice of contraception; and *Roe v. Wade* legalizing abortion] bears any resemblance to the claimed constitutional right of homosexuals to engage in acts of sodomy that is asserted in this case."[22]

This was so, according to the majority, because "[n]o connection between family, marriage, or procreation on the one hand, and homosexual activity, on the other, has been demonstrated, either by the court of appeals or by respondent."[23] The majority held further that "...any claim that these cases nevertheless stand for the proposition that any kind of private sexual conduct between consenting adults is constitutionally insulated from state proscription is unsupportable. Indeed, the Court's opinion in *Carey v. Population Services International*]*[24] twice asserted that the privacy right, which the *Griswold* line of cases found to be one of the protections provided by the Due Process Clause, did not reach so far."[25]

In a further glimpse at the majority's reasoning, Justice White explained that "[s]triving to assure itself and the public that announcing rights not readily identifiable in the Constitution's text involves much more than the imposition of the Justices' own choice of values on the states and the federal government, the Court has sought to identify the nature of the rights qualifying for heightened judicial protection. In *Palko v. Connecticut*,[26] it was said that this category includes those fundamental liberties that are 'implicit in the concept of ordered liberty,' such that 'neither liberty nor justice would exist if [they] were sacrificed.' A different description of fundamental liberties appeared in *Moore v. Cleveland*,[27] where they are characterized as those liberties that are 'deeply rooted in this nation's history and tradition.'[28]

"It is obvious to us that neither of these formulations would extend a fundamental right of homosexuals to engage in acts of consensual sodomy. Proscriptions against that conduct have ancient roots.[29] Sodomy was a criminal offense in common law and was forbidden by the laws of the original thirteen states when they ratified the Bill of Rights.[30] In 1868, when the Fourteenth Amendment was ratified, all but five of the thirty-seven states in the Union had criminal sodomy laws.[31] In fact, until 1961, all fifty states outlawed sodomy, and today, twenty-four states and the District of Columbia continue to provide criminal penalties for sodomy performed in private and between consenting adults," the majority held.[32]

REEXAMINING SEXUAL PRIVACY:
Through the Prism of Same-Sex Activity

Some scholars suggest that the Court's decision in *Bowers v. Hardwick* marked the second death of the Substantive Due Process.[33] And yet, the majority's reasoning and its grounding in morals legislation would prove less sound over time. Although twenty-four states had "sodomy laws" on the books in 1986, prosecutions were relatively rare by the mid- to late-1980s. And by the late 1990s, state laws had begun to reflect a fundamental change in attitudes towards gay and lesbian persons nationwide.

In the fall of 1998, in an almost prophetic sign of things to come, the Supreme Court of Georgia struck down the Georgia sodomy law famously at issue in *Bowers v. Hardwick*, with the justices stating that they could not "... think of any other activity that reasonable persons would rank as more private and more deserving of protection from governmental interference than consensual, private, adult sexual activity."[34]

A few weeks earlier, the legality of a Maryland sodomy law, enacted in 1916, was called into question when Maryland Circuit Court Judge Richard Rombro ruled that the statute violated the Equal Protection Clause, because it "considered sex not criminal when committed by a heterosexual couple," but a crime "when practiced by a homosexual couple."[35]

Although occurring close in time, the Georgia and Maryland decisions are on the far end of the nation's response to what writer Stacey D'Erasmo calls a "[a] gay-liberation movement that began with [the Stonewall] riot[s]" in June of 1969,[36] followed throughout the next two decades by "ferocious battles over what one may or may not do in one's bedroom, AIDS, a young man beaten and left for dead against a fence, lesbian mothers losing custody of their children, [and] the relentless policing of every gradation of sexual difference."[37]

By the start of the 1990s, gay and lesbian rights activists had redoubled their efforts in pushing an agenda of equality by embracing their "differences,"[38] talking openly about violence,[39] and by taking their claims—big and small—to court. James Dale sued the Boy Scouts of America for discrimination in 1992, for example, after the group learned that Dale was gay and moved to revoke his adult membership. Dale had been a scout as a child and sought to stay involved with the organization as an adult. But after his involvement in a gay and lesbian student organization at his college became the subject of a newspaper article, the Boy Scouts sought to kick him out.

In 1998, the New Jersey Superior Court's Appellate Division held that the Boy Scout's actions violated a state law prohibiting discrimination in public accommodations.[40] The New Jersey Supreme Court affirmed. The Boy Scouts of America appealed to the United States Supreme Court, which granted *certiorari*.[41] The United States Supreme Court would ultimately hold, however, that "[a]pplying New Jersey's public accommodations law to require the Boy Scouts to admit Dale violated the Boy Scouts's First Amendment right to expressive association."[42]

Although Dale did not win, the decision sparked widespread debate, and out of that debate sprang unexpected veins of support. Schools in Illinois reportedly considered whether an organization that openly discriminates should be allowed to use school property.[43] Methodist ministers defied church rules to officiate at the union ceremonies of same-sex couples,[44] and the debate over where and whether homosexuals "fit" seemed to begin anew.

Adding significantly to the tide of the debate was the October 1998 death of a 21-year-old freshman at the University of Wyoming named Matthew Shepard. Shepard was not the only—or even the first—gay person assaulted that year. According to FBI statistics, more than seven thousand "hate crimes" were reported in 1998,[45] which is where crimes motivated by sexual orientation are categorized. But Shepard's apparent air of innocence and the way he would be left to die—tied to a fence and bleeding—would capture the nation's attention.

"Parents throughout the country felt that Matthew could have been their son, an idea many [had] never contemplated before about a gay person," Melanie Thernstrom wrote in March 1999, in offering an overview of the Shepard case.[46] "In part, this may have been a result of the fact that while he was described as gay, the press—in unwitting collusion with homophobia—did not portray Matthew as a sexual adult. He was depicted as having parents, rather than partners—loving, affluent, married American parents. He had an allowance; he wore braces. He was a member of the U.W. Episcopal Canterbury Club."

And yet, by shining a light on Shepard's childhood, his family, and his involvement in his church, there were those who argued that "the press" finally got it right, because gay people have families, lives, and childhoods that are often quite "normal." And they often go to church. Even so, "…aside from the Pansy Craze during Prohibition, when heterosexuals flocked to drag balls and clubs, it was rare for homosexuality to be discussed in mainstream news sources before Stonewall," offer Harvard School of Business alumnae and authors, Annette Friskopp and Sharon Silverstein.[47]

In more modern times and in less tolerant states, same-sex conduct was offered as *outings* "in local newspapers after someone was arrested—for being caught in a raid in a gay bar, for public sex, or for soliciting," Friskopp and Silverstein note further.[48] It was still happening well into the 1990s. Following publication of their names by the *San Antonio Express News* in 1994, for example, one gay man was reportedly fired from the job he had held for more than thirteen years, while another hanged himself in his garage.[49]

The "sin conception of same-sex sexual activity,"[50] scholars note, has allowed discrimination, ostracism, and violence against gay and lesbian persons to flourish for almost as long as America has been a nation. The depiction of "sinner" and/or antisocial "deviant" led to the even more widespread notion that homosexuals—especially gay men—were/are promiscuous, one-dimensional (perhaps even predatory) loners with few ties to family or community. And certainly devoid of social and religious grounding. Was the law expected to protect "those kinds" of people? For a long time, it didn't, gay rights activists argue. And that again seemed to be the question among Laramie, Wyoming residents as Shepard lay dying in a nearby hospital.

Upon learning of the battering of a "gay guy" from the girlfriend of one of the men later convicted of beating Matthew Shepard into a coma, a Laramie limousine driver who reportedly knew Matthew—but didn't understand that the "gay guy" beaten and the young man he had befriended were one and the same—tried to put the girl's mind at ease, according to Thernstrom, by reminding her that "in the state of Wyoming you don't go to jail for beating on a gay guy."[51] The two men allegedly involved in the beating were charged, and in December 1998 the District Attorney announced that he would seek the death penalty.

By the mid-1990s, gay and lesbian persons had become an accepted part of American society, though some conservative politicians and religious leaders continued to condemn "their lifestyle." Gay and lesbian actors appeared regularly on prime time television shows, where their characters are integral to the plot lines of sitcoms, soap operas, and "reality shows."[52] "Ambiguous" advertising campaigns—showing "dads" sitting with a child between them—began to appear.[53] Openly gay students attended high school and college and defended their right to do so.[54] Gay "families" lived alongside straight families in the suburbs,[55] and "gay issues" had become part of the public debate.

In addition, by 1995, hundreds of companies, agencies, and municipalities had adopted specific written nondiscrimination policies expressly prohibiting discrimination based upon "sexual orientation,"[56] even though the American Civil Liberties Union still noted in 2001 that thirty-nine states did not have laws "banning private sector job discrimination based on sexual orientation."[57]

"What I think has happened is that over the last ten or so years, we have seen an unprecedented increase in the visibility and identity of gay and lesbian people as families," Paula Ettelbrick of the National Gay and Lesbian Task Force Policy Institute told *The New York Times* in 2000. "We have claimed that identity and the world has allowed us increasingly to claim that identity."[58]

This may be due in part to the fact that in the last two decades, gays and lesbians have emerged as a persuasive voting block with the "gay vote" not only one to be considered these days, but at times courted.[59] For example, although gay and lesbian voters reportedly remained wary of the Republican Party, inaugural events during President George W. Bush's first week in office in January 2001, included a first-time celebratory breakfast for the Republican Unity Coalition, a rising political group that includes several gay Republican Party members.[60]

This newfound clout, coupled with the constant threat of lawsuits, has made the extension of domestic-partner benefits an increasingly common choice of municipalities and corporations.[61] And there have been other changes as well. Same-sex adoptions—once deemed a "family-shattering," perhaps even "dangerous" proposition—have grown in public acceptance, even though some states continue to oppose them.[62] And same-sex "marriage" notices have begun to appear alongside announcements of heterosexual couples in American newspapers. Even *Brides* magazine, that mainstay of nuptial traditions, began running articles on same-sex weddings in September of 2003, as gay rights groups continued to push for the legal recognition that only the formalization of marriage can bring.[63]

THE SAME-SEX MARRIAGE CHALLENGE:
With This Ring, I Do Change the Rules

By the mid-1990s, same-sex marriage had become the next challenge for gay and lesbian persons, and although the legal questions have since been answered, the issue seems likely to remain one of debate. Adding fuel to this particularly incendiary blaze were decisions by the Supreme Court of Canada in May 1999, finding that the word "spouse" may include persons of the same sex, and the German Constitutional Court in July of 2001, rejecting efforts by authorities in Bavaria and Saxony to block legislation that would allow same-sex couples to "marry."[64] By January of 2001, church officials in Toronto were preparing to perform "the modern world's first legal gay wedding."[65] Nine months later, same-sex couples began quietly registering as "partners" in Germany as a new law formalizing their unions took effect.[66] And in 2002, lawmakers in Argentina approved a law granting legal states to same-sex couples.[67]

FIRST THERE WAS HAWAII...

Same-sex marriage is not recognized in the United States, though by the end of 1996, legal scholars were so confident that same-sex unions would soon be recognized that they began answering "conflict of law" questions that seemed likely to arise.[68] The reason for the confidence was that on December 3, 1996, a Honolulu judge struck down a portion of the Hawaii Revised Statute interpreted by the Director of the Department of Health and a lower court to prohibit same-sex marriage. According to the judge, the prohibition was tantamount to sex discrimination in violation of the Equal Protection Clause.

The decision was the culmination of a case that began on December 17, 1990, when Nina Baehr, Genora Dancel, Tammy Rodrigues, Antoinette Pregil, Pat Lagon, and Joseph Melillo applied for marriage licenses and their requests were denied. The reason for the denial in each case was that they were same-sex couples. On May 1, 1991, the couples filed suit, seeking a judgment declaring the Hawaii law discriminatory. They also sought an injunction to prevent the future application of the statute section.[69]

When their claims were dismissed, the couples appealed to the Supreme Court of Hawaii, which held that the essential issue before it was "whether the 'right to marry' protected by Article I, Section 6 of the Hawaii Constitution extends to same-sex couples."[70] According to the court, "Article I, Section 6 of the Hawaii Constitution states that '[t]he right of the people to privacy is recognized and shall not be infringed upon without the showing of a compelling state interest.'"[71] Further, the framers of the Hawaii Constitution deemed that the "'privacy concept' embodied in Article I, Section 6 is to be 'treated as a fundamental right,'" the court held.[72]

That may sound simple enough. But the proper inquiry in such a case, according to the Hawaii Supreme Court, was "whether the right involved 'is of such a character' that it cannot be denied without violating those fundamental principles of liberty and justice which lie at the base of all our civil and political institutions." In applying this standard to the case, the justices held that they did not "believe...a right to same-sex marriage is so rooted in the traditions and collective conscience of our people that failure to recognize it would violate the fundamental principles of liberty and justice that lie at the base of all our civil and political institutions." [73]

"Neither do we believe that a right to same-sex marriage is implicit in the concept of ordered liberty, such that neither liberty nor justice would exist if it were sacrificed. Accordingly, we hold that the applicant couples do not have a fundamental constitutional right to same-sex marriages arising out of the right to privacy or otherwise," the justices ruled.[74] But the couples were "free to press their equal protection claim," the court held. And "[i]f they are successful, the State of Hawaii will no longer be permitted to refuse marriage licenses to couples merely on the basis that they are of the same sex."[75]

In other words, the court found "sex" to be a "'suspect category' for purposes of equal protection analysis under Article I, Section 5 of the Hawaii Constitution and [Hawaii Revised Statute] Section 572-1."[76] As such, the denial of marriage licenses based upon "sex" was necessarily subject to the constitutional "strict scrutiny test," the court held.[77]

"It therefore follows, and we do hold that (1) HRS Section 572-1 is presumed to be unconstitutional (2) unless Lewin [the director of the Department of Health], as an agent of the State of Hawaii, can show that (a) the statute's sex-based classification is justified by compelling state interests and (b) the statute is narrowly drawn to avoid unnecessary abridgments of the applicant couples' constitutional rights," the court held. In other words, "in accordance with the 'strict scrutiny' standard, the burden will rest on Lewin to overcome the presumption that [Hawaii Revised Statute] Section 572-1 is unconstitutional by demonstrating that it furthers compelling state interests and is narrowly drawn to avoid unnecessary abridgments of constitutional rights."[78]

The decision sparked widespread anticipation that Hawaii would be the first state to legalize same-sex marriage.[79] But two things happened during 1994 that would lead to equally widespread disappointment, exposing the scorching heart of the debate: the first was that the Hawaii legislature amended state law to provide that only marriages between "a man and a woman" would be deemed valid by the state. The second was that another county was heard from.

THEN CAME ALASKA...

On August 4, 1994, two men—Jay Brause and Gene Dugan—filed an application for a marriage license with the Office of Vital Statistics in Alaska. Brause and Dugan had been together for nearly 20 years, and they met the statutory requirements for the grant of a marriage license in every way except for one: they were both men. An Alaska presiding judge had previously issued a "policy directive stating that 'a marriage license shall not be issued for the purpose of marrying two persons of the same sex' since 'marriage between two persons of the same sex is not contemplated by our statutory scheme.'"[80]

Perhaps in fear of a repeat of events in Hawaii—which were still without final resolution at the time—or out of conservative or traditional furor, in March of 1996, Bill 308 was introduced before the Senate Health, Education, and Social Services Committee of the Alaska Legislature. The bill provided that "[m]arriage is a civil contract entered into by one man and one woman.... A marriage entered into by persons of the same-sex, either under common law or under statute, that is recognized by another state or foreign jurisdiction is void in this state, and contractual rights granted by virtue of the marriage, including its termination, are unenforceable in this state.... A same-sex relationship may not be recognized by the state as being entitled to the benefits of marriage."

The Alaska Marriage Code was formally amended later that year to provide that "[a] same-sex relationship may not be recognized by the state as being entitled to the benefits of marriage." Brause and Dugan filed suit, challenging the amendment as violative of the Equal Protection Clause and of the right to privacy.[81] An attorney for Brause and Dugan argued that upholding the amendment would violate the express provision of the Alaska Constitution that prohibits gender-based discrimination. But the arguments being made in Alaska would be forced to take a back seat to events taking place in Hawaii.

On December 3, 1996, Honolulu Circuit Court Judge Kevin S. C. Chang held that "[t]he sex-based classification in HRS 572-1, on its face as applied, is unconstitutional and a violation of the Equal Protection Clause of Article I, Section 5 of the Hawaii Constitution."[82] "Defendant Lawrence H. Miike, as Director of Department of Health, State of Hawaii, and his agents, and any person in acting in concert with Defendant or claiming by or through him, is enjoined from denying an application for a marriage license solely because the applicants are of the same sex."[83]

Gay and lesbian rights activists across the country saw promise in the ruling. So did scholars, who began unfolding the possible implications in the law. New York University Law School Professor, Larry Kramer, remarked, for example, in a May 1997, article published in the *Yale Law Journal* that "[i]t finally happened. On Tuesday, December 3, 1996, a Honolulu judge struck down a Hawaiian law permitting only opposite-sex couples to marry, and Hawaii became the first state to recognize same-sex marriages. Of course, the ruling hardly came as a surprise. [84]

"The surprise had come three years earlier, when the Hawaii Supreme Court ruled in *Baehr v. Lewin* that a restriction on same-sex marriage constituted sex discrimination under the state constitution and remanded the case to give the state an opportunity to show that its law served a compelling interest. Still, the trial court's finding that it did not brings a further degree of closure to one chapter in the same-sex marriage controversy: we can confidently predict that Hawaii will recognize same-sex marriages, for while the trial court stayed its mandate pending appeal, it is very unlikely that the decision will be overturned," Kramer wrote.[85]

But that is not what happened in Hawaii. Or in Alaska. Instead of same-sex marriage becoming the law in either state, by the late-1990s, supporters of same-sex marriage were facing a backlash that had made its way to Washington. "The popular media raised questions about whether [same-sex marriage] laws were permissible or whether states would be required as a matter of full faith and credit to recognize marriages celebrated lawfully in Hawaii. So opponents of gay and lesbian marriage went to Congress," Kramer explained. "They found a receptive audience, and Congress soon enacted the ironically named 'Defense of Marriage Act' (DOMA), which permits states to refuse recognition to 'any public act, record, or judicial proceeding of any other state...respecting a relationship between persons of the same sex that is treated as a marriage under the laws of such other state.'"[86]

DOMA, which defines "marriage" as a *legal union between one man and one woman* and "spouse" as a *person of the opposite sex who is a husband or a wife*, was signed into law by President Bill Clinton and has spawned passage of a flurry of similar legislation on the part of the states. Some thirty-six states have adopted "mini-DOMA" laws since 1996,[87] many of them expressly providing that marriage must be between a man and a woman.

In February of 1998, the Alaska Senate Health, Education, and Social Services Committee introduced Resolution 42, a joint Senate resolution. The resolution sought to amend the Alaska Constitution to include Section 15, which would declare that "[e]ach marriage contract in [Alaska] may be entered into only by one man and one woman. The legislature may, by law, enact additional requirements relating to marriage." This language was scheduled for submission to Alaska voters as "Measure 2," during the then-upcoming election in November of 1998.

On February 27, 1998, just 24 days after the introduction of "Measure 2," Alaska Superior Court Judge Peter Michalski ruled in *Brause v. Office of Vital Statistics*, that "...the choice of a life partner is personal, intimate, and subject to the protection of the right to privacy. Failure of the state to provide public recognition of that private choice, whether it is the choice of a life partner of the opposite sex or of the same sex, is analogous to the unwillingness of the school in *Breese*[88] to allow the presence of a student who made a personal choice to wear long hair."[89]

"It is the duty of the court," Judge Michalski explained, "to do more than merely assume that marriage is only, and must only be, what most are familiar with. In some parts of our nation mere acceptance of the familiar would have left segregation in place. In light of Brause and Dugan's challenge to the constitutionality of the relevant statutes, this court cannot defer to the legislature or familiar notions when addressing this issue.[90]

"[G]overnment intrusion into the choice of a life partner encroaches on the intimate personal decisions of the individual," Judge Michalski wrote. "This the Constitution does not allow unless the state can show a compelling interest 'necessitating the abridgment of the...constitutionally protected right.'"[91]

But the fate of same-sex marriage in Alaska and Hawaii would prove fatally linked. In November of 1998, voters in Hawaii approved Constitutional Amendment 2, granting the legislature the power to "reserve marriage to opposite-sex couples."[92] And in Alaska, although more than 61,000 Alaskans reportedly voted against the measure, Ballot Measure 2, was "overwhelmingly approved," CNN reported.[93] The measure mandates that in order for marriage to be recognized in Alaska, it must be "between one man and one woman."[94]

On September 22, 1999, nearly a year after the Ballot Measure 2 became law in Alaska, the case of *Brause v. Bureau of Vital Statistics* was dismissed by an Alaska court as moot, though Brause and Dugan vowed to appeal. The Hawaii Supreme Court similarly dismissed the same-sex marriage challenge brought by the three couples as moot that same year, given the language of the 1998 amendment. [95]

AND FINALLY THERE WAS VERMONT...

But neither the incidents in Alaska, nor the events in Hawaii seemed to settle the issue of same-sex marriage. Rather, it was about to meet with historic success. A little over a year after the November 1998 ballot initiatives in Hawaii and Alaska, the Supreme Court of Vermont ruled that the Common Benefits Clause of that state's constitution decrees that the "plaintiffs [three same-sex couples] may not be deprived of the statutory benefits and protections afforded persons of the opposite sex who choose to marry."

"We hold," wrote Chief Justice Jeffrey Amestoy, "that the state is constitutionally required to extend to same-sex couples the common benefits and protections that flow from marriage under Vermont law. Whether this ultimately takes the form of inclusion within the marriage laws themselves or a parallel 'domestic partnership' system or some equivalent statutory alternative, rests with the Legislature. Whatever system is chosen, however, must conform with the constitutional imperative to afford all Vermonters the common benefit, protection, and security of the law."[96]

The decision grew out of a challenge brought by three couples—Ms. Puterbaugh and Ms. Farnham, Stan Baker and Peter Harrigan, and Nina Beck and Stacy Jolles—that began in 1997, with a suit brought by the couples after they were refused marriage licenses by local town clerks. After a superior court judge turned down their request, the couples appealed to the Vermont Supreme Court, which heard oral arguments in November 1998."[97]

At the time of the 1999 Vermont ruling, only California and Hawaii had statewide domestic partnership systems. But they paled in comparison to the system the Vermont Supreme Court decision was expected to put into place. And the expectation that same-sex marriage might still be an option remained on the table. Opponents of same-sex marriage in Vermont suggested that they would attempt strategies similar to those used so successfully in defeating same-sex challenges in Alaska and Hawaii.

The battle also drew outsiders, among them the infamous antiabortion activist, Randall Terry, of the militant Operation Rescue, who reportedly told the *Rutland Herald* that he "plan[ned] to stay 'for the duration' of the fight."[98] In the heyday of his exaltation, Terry, with his well-known mane of bristly hair, was the face of the antiabortion movement. He and members of Operation Rescue reportedly harassed employees at women's clinics, flashed placards of aborted fetuses, and sat for hours in blockages. But during the late 1990s, as the movement began to lose steam under the weight of civil suits and federal and state prosecutions,[99] Terry turned his tirades to the decline of morality in the United States.[100]

In February 2000, the Vermont House Judiciary Committee set to work drafting this new and inclusive law.[101] Two months later, lawmakers in Vermont approved far-reaching and historic legislation that stopped short of the formal recognition of same-sex marriages many gay rights advocates had sought. But the new law allows same-sex couples to enter into "civil unions," a designation effectively creating a parallel marriage-like structure, entitling same-sex couples to most of the same benefits that married opposite-sex couples in Vermont enjoy.[102]

Under the new law, passed by 79-to-68 vote by the Vermont House of Representatives, persons seeking to join in a civil union—like those seeking to marry—were required to register with town clerks and to have their unions performed or certified by a justice of the peace or a member of the clergy. Conversely, a couple so joined would be required, under the law, to go to family court to lawfully dissolve the union. The law does not change the "unmarried" status of same-sex couples in the eyes of the federal government, however, for purposes of immigration, Social Security, and federal income tax filing.[103] Then-Governor Howard Dean, who became presidential candidate Dean during the 2003–2004 presidential election primaries, signed the measure into law.[104]

Within a year of the civil unions law, a minor "boomlet" seemed to be underway. More than three thousand gay and lesbian persons had traveled to Vermont to be "married," according to *Time* magazine,[105] while others continued on to Canada in 2003, to be "joined in holy matrimony."[106] And yet, there has been a backlash of sorts. Lawmakers on both sides of the issue lost political ground in Vermont,[107] while Nebraska voters went to the polls in October 2000 to vote on what was then being described as "the country's most sweeping effort to bar gay unions—a proposed amendment to the [Nebraska] Constitution that not only bans gay marriages but also declared same-sex civil unions and domestic partnerships invalid."[108]

In addition, courts in other jurisdictions have rebuffed all forms of the same-sex union movement. The American Civil Liberties Union of New Jersey was reportedly preparing in September of 2000, for example, to appeal a judge's refusal to allow a lesbian to hyphenate her last name to include that of her partner, though there are normally few prohibitions on name changes. The judge refused to allow the name change, because he did not want to give the impression that the court condoned same-sex relationships.[109]

And despite the reliance of courts in Hawaii and Alaska on equal protection arguments in finding that denying same-sex couples marriage licenses was tantamount to state-sanctioned sex-discrimination, in the fall of 2000, the Seventh Circuit Court of Appeals ruled that homosexuals were not a "protected class" within the meaning of Title VII, and therefore, were not entitled to use the law to assert claims of discrimination.[110]

"There is a difference between one's sex and one's sexuality under federal law," Judge Daniel A. Manion wrote for the unanimous three-judge panel decision in *Hamner v. St. Vincent Hospital and Health Care Center, Inc.*[111] Congress, Judge Manion asserted further, intended the term "sex" to refer to a person's biological gender as opposed to one's sexual orientation.[112]

And the Vermont law itself continued to face challenges. In December of 2001, the Supreme Court of Vermont ruled against two specific claims brought by town clerks, legislators and taxpayers opposed to the civil unions law.[113] Legislators opposed to the law alleged that the final vote was invalid because several members of the state House of Representatives had allegedly bet on the outcome, while several town clerks argued that it was against their religious principles to issue licenses to "homosexuals."[114]

The answer from the Vermont Supreme Court to the allegations was to defer the legislative abuse claim to the legislature and to note that the clerks were merely being asked to perform the requirements of their jobs. If they were opposed to doing that, they might seek other employment, the justices inferred. The debate, and efforts to challenge, curtail, or scale back legislation granting rights to same-sex couples, is likely to continue, as are simple statements on both sides, some of them remarkably poignant.

"You can go on Fox television and marry someone you have never met before. And you have a marriage recognized in all fifty states," offers writer Andrew Sullivan in the documentary *A Union in Wait*,[115] detailing the efforts of two lesbians to "marry." "But people who have lived together in a committed relationship for sixty years sometimes are told that they cannot marry."[116]

MASSACHUSETTS WEIGHS IN ON THE ISSUE...

Though they may join in "civil unions," same-sex couples cannot "marry" as a matter of law, despite the decision by the Vermont Supreme Court. But this is not to say that same-sex marriage may not one day become a reality. On November 18, 2003, the Massachusetts Supreme Judicial Court held, by decision of 4 to 3, that same-sex couples were entitled—as a constitutional matter—to "marry." Then, as Vermont had, the Massachusetts court left it to the state legislature to rewrite the law in a constitutional way. The decision was a victory for the 14 partners who challenged the law. But it drew criticism from as high up as the White House.

"Marriage is a sacred institution between a man and a woman," President Bush said in a statement issued in response to the ruling. "Today's decision of the Massachusetts Supreme Judicial Court violates this important principle. I will work with Congressional leaders and others to do what is legally necessary to defend the sanctity of marriage."[117]

Conservative politicians and religious leaders may try to stem the flood in the future. But even before the Massachusetts court's decision, national debate on the issue had served to move the rights of same-sex couples forward in other significant ways. In December 2002, for example, New York Governor George Pataki signed a law extending civil rights protection to lesbians and gays living in that state.[118] In June 2002, an Ohio court declared a state law unconstitutional that made same-sex solicitations illegal.[119]

THE FALL OF *BOWERS v. HARDWICK*:
Changing Times Lead to New Laws

There is little dispute that the same-sex debate of the 1990s set the stage for one of the most significant victories for gay rights activists of the new millennium, though it would seem more like housekeeping by 2003 than a significant shift in thinking. As set forth above, the question of the 1990s with regard to same-sex couples was whether they could "marry." It would seem backwards, then—if not a bit ironic—that the question before the United States Supreme Court in 2003 was whether they could sleep together.

By the turn of the millennium, shifts in American tolerance had led to the repeal of criminal "sodomy" laws in all but four states: Texas, Oklahoma, Kansas, and Missouri. It was the Texas sodomy law that would be at issue before the Court in *Lawrence v. Texas*,[120] in a challenge brought by two men in a case that began much like *Bowers v. Hardwick*, but that would lead to the precedent being overturned.

During the 1990s, while courts in Hawaii, Alaska and Vermont were upholding the right of same-sex couples to be "joined" one way or another, Texas officials and some of its citizens were reestablishing the state as an aggressive foe of gay and lesbian rights. During this period, gay men were murdered in a series of violent attacks across the state; "outings" in local newspapers were commonplace; and state and local officials demonstrated their will to preserve laws proscribing "homosexual conduct,"[121] sometimes at the potential cost of millions of dollars in revenue.

In November of 1993, for example, commissioners in Williamson County, Texas, voted against property tax abatements for Apple Computer. The company was considering building an $80 million office complex in the county, which would obviously mean jobs and revenue for the county. But several county commissioners voted against tax breaks for the company, proposed as incentives, because it is Apple's policy to grant benefits to unmarried partners.[122]

"If I had voted yes, I would have had to walk into my church with people saying, 'There is the man who brought homosexuality to Williamson County,'" County Commissioner David S. Hays said after the vote.[123] Then-Governor Ann Richards is said to have intervened to push the project through.[124]

In addition, in a single year, Republican Party officials in Galveston passed a resolution advocating the quarantine of people who are HIV-positive, while conservative Christian members of the Plano School Board encouraged the board to stop condom-use demonstrations as part of AIDS-related sex education, and Austin residents voted to repeal insurance benefits for unmarried domestic partners.

At about the same time, participants in the student government at Austin State University moved to cancel funding for the university's gay and lesbian student organization, because, in the words of one student senator, they "didn't want to have a group on campus that might in some way champion violation of Texas law."[125]

The law gay and lesbian students might champion the violation of was, of course, the Texas "sodomy" law. Gubernatorial candidate George W. Bush vowed in January of 1994 that if elected, he would preserve laws against "homosexual conduct" by vetoing all attempts to repeal them. According to then-Candidate Bush (who would become not only the Governor of Texas, but the President of the United States in a controversial election in 2000) although the law was rarely enforced, it was worth preserving as a "symbolic gesture of traditional values."[126]

LAWRENCE v. TEXAS

That "rarely enforced" law was at issue in *Lawrence v. Texas* before the United States Supreme Court in 2003. In the fall of 1998, Houston police responded to a call that a man with a gun was "going crazy" in an apartment nearby. The claim was false and a neighbor would later be convicted of filing a false police report.[127] But at the time of the call, authorities were directed to the apartment of John Geddes Lawrence. Although the officers found no gun, Lawrence and his partner, Tyrone Garner, were arrested and convicted by a justice of the peace of engaging in "deviant sexual intercourse" in violation of Texas law.

Lawrence and Garner challenged the Texas law as a violation of the Fourteenth Amendment's Equal Protection Clause and the Texas Constitution. Although the initial challenge appears to have been brought only under the Equal Protection Clause, the Texas Court of Appeals reviewed Lawrence's claims under both the Due Process and Equal Protection clauses only to reject the allegations in light of the precedent in *Bowers v. Hardwick*. Lawrence appealed to the United States Supreme Court, which agreed to hear the case, reconsidering the holding of *Bowers v. Hardwick* in the process.

"We conclude the case should be resolved by determining whether the petitioners were free as adults to engage in the private conduct in the exercise of their liberty under the Due Process Clause of the Fourteenth Amendment to the Constitution," Justice Kennedy wrote in delivering the decision on behalf of the majority.

But the prospect that the "gay lifestyle" might be embraced as part of mainstream society was met with scathing challenge from traditionalists, conservative politicians, and lawmakers, who seemed to view it as a first step towards dismantling a "proper and moral" way of life, vowing to fight acceptance of a "pro-gay" decision regardless of the outcome of *Lawrence v. Texas*.[128] In the interim, a concerted pattern of prepared responses began to make their way into the media.

Indeed, before the decision in *Lawrence v. Texas* was issued—at a time when it might fairly be argued that the Justices were still mulling over the issues—the possibility that the Court might strike down *Bowers v. Hardwick* sparked earnest and repetitive claims that "incest" and "bestiality" would be the consequence of such a ruling. In March 2003, for example, Alabama Solicitor General Nathan Forrester warned in an interview with the *National Law Journal* that "[p]edophilia, incest, polygamy, bestiality—all will be protected...if the [C]ourt says the fundamental right of privacy protects private consensual sexuality between adults."[129]

A few weeks later in one of the most derisive moments of this media-aided debate, Pennsylvania Senator Rick Santorum told the *Associated Press* that "[i]f the Supreme Court says...you have the right to consensual sex within your home, then you have the right to bigamy, you have the right to incest, you have the right to adultery. You have the right to anything."[130]

Heightened rhetoric of this sort at a time when the nation appeared to be moving away from such presumptions may explain why Justice Kennedy and the majority seemed to feel obligated to note the context giving rise to the Court's decision in *Bowers v. Hardwick*.

"It must be acknowledged, of course, that the Court in *Bowers* was making the broader point that for centuries there have been powerful voices to condemn homosexual conduct as immoral," Justice Kennedy wrote. "The condemnation has been shaped by religious beliefs, conceptions of right and acceptable behavior, and respect for the traditional family. For many persons these are not trivial concerns but profound and deep convictions accepted as ethical and moral principles to which they aspire and which thus determine the course of their lives."

The majority, then, expressly rejected this history, with Justice Kennedy noting that "[t]hese considerations do not answer the question before us. The issue is whether the majority may use the power of the state to enforce these views on the whole society through operation of the criminal law."

In finding that the state could not do so, Justice Kennedy pointed to two cases—both decided after *Bowers v. Hardwick*—which, in the majority's estimation, cast the holding of *Bowers* in doubt. "In *Planned Parenthood of Southeastern Pennsylvania v. Casey*,[131] the Court reaffirmed the substantive force of the liberty protected by the Due Process Clause," Kennedy wrote. "The *Casey* decision again confirmed that our laws and tradition afford constitutional protection to personal decisions relating to marriage, procreation, contraception, family relationships, and child rearing and education."[132]

As the *Casey* Court saw it, "[t]hese matters, involving the most intimate and personal choices a person may make in a lifetime, choices central to personal dignity and autonomy, are central to the liberty protected by the Fourteenth Amendment. At the heart of liberty is the right to define one's own concept of existence, of meaning, of the universe, and of the mystery of human life. Beliefs about these matters could not define the attributes of personhood were they formed under compulsion of the state."[133]

Although the *Casey* decision arose in the context of the abortion debate, the majority held that "[p]ersons in a homosexual relationship may seek autonomy for these purposes, just as heterosexual persons do. The decision in *Bowers* would deny them this right."[134]

The second case tending to dismantle the reasoning of *Bowers*, according to the majority, was the 1996 decision by the Court in *Evans v. Romer*.[135] "There the Court struck down class-based legislation directed at homosexuals as a violation of the Equal Protection Clause. *Romer* invalidated an amendment to Colorado's constitution which named as a solitary class persons who were homosexuals, lesbians, or bisexuals either by 'orientation, conduct, practices, or relationships,'[136] and deprived them of protection under state antidiscrimination laws," Justice Kennedy explained.[137]

Some scholars note that Kennedy has begun to occupy a "pivotal position" on the Court.[138] As a Justice, Kennedy also wrote the majority decision in *Evans v. Romer*. But a demonstrative "judicial acknowledgment of gay rights" on Kennedy's part dates back at least to 1980, scholars note, when—as a judge on the Ninth Circuit Court of Appeals—he opined in *Beller v. Middendorf*,[139] that there was at least an academic argument to be made suggesting that "...the choice to engage in homosexual action is a personal decision entitled, at least in some instances, to recognition as a fundamental right to full protection as an aspect of the individual's right to privacy."

The language of that decision reportedly almost cost Kennedy a seat on the United States Supreme Court, although the Ninth Circuit would uphold the discharge of persons for homosexual conduct by the navy. But on the Supreme Court, Kennedy has emerged, some argue, as a moderate voice on "gay" issues. In expounding on the notion of equality for homosexual citizens in *Romer v. Evans*, Kennedy noted, in the majority's invalidation of the Colorado amendment, that the provision was "'born of animosity toward the class of persons affected' and...that it has no rational relation to a legitimate governmental purpose."[140]

By contrast, the question in *Lawrence v. Texas* was not one of animosity, but rather dignity and equal treatment for all citizens, even those involved in same-sex relationships, the majority reasoned.

"Equality of treatment and the due process right to demand respect for conduct protected by the substantive guarantee of liberty are linked in important respects, and a decision on the latter point advances both interests," Justice Kennedy wrote. "If protected conduct is made criminal and the law which does so remains unexamined for its substantive validity, its stigma might remain even if it were not enforceable as drawn for protection reasons. When homosexual conduct is made criminal by the law of the state, that declaration in and of itself is an invitation to subject homosexual persons to discrimination both in public and the private spheres."

In conclusion, Kennedy wrote that "*Bowers* was not correct when it was decided, and it is not correct today. It ought not to remain binding precedent. *Bowers v. Hardwick* should be and now is overruled."[141] And then, because the "Texas statute furthers no legitimate state interest which can justify its intrusion into the personal and private life of the individual," it, too, was struck down taking with it, by inference, the last three remaining state sodomy statutes.

And yet, as painstaking as the majority was in setting forth its reasons for striking *Bowers* down, the three dissenting justices were just as aggressive in their support of the now disfavored precedent with the most scathing dissenting opinion delivered by Justice Antonin Scalia, whose comments echoed the refrain of Forrester and Santorum.

"It seems to me," Justice Scalia wrote, "that the 'societal reliance' on the principles confirmed in *Bowers* and discarded today has been overwhelming. Countless judicial decisions and legislative enactments have relied on the ancient proposition that a governing majority's belief that certain sexual behavior is 'immoral and unacceptable' constitutes a rational basis for regulation.[142] We ourselves relied extensively on *Bowers* when we concluded, in *Barnes v. Glen Theatre, Inc.*,[143] that Indiana's public indecency statute furthered 'a substantial government interest in protecting order and morality....'[144]

"State laws against bigamy, same-sex marriage, adult incest, prostitution, masturbation, adultery, fornication, bestiality, and obscenity are likewise sustainable only in light of *Bowers's* validation of laws based on moral choices.

Every single one of these laws is called into question by today's decision: the Court makes no effort to cabin the scope of its decision to exclude them from its holding."[145]

The ultimate meaning of *Lawrence v. Texas* appears to be an open question. Gay rights advocates and liberals applauded the ruling as the clear defeat of the conservative Christian movement and "family values" platform that have dominated the national agenda for the last two decades. And some would argue that as surely as *Bowers v. Hardwick* marked the "second death" of Substantive Due Process, *Lawrence v. Texas* marked the end of a two-tier justice system that all but encouraged discrimination against homosexuals by stigmatizing them.

But that may be too optimistic. Challenges to the precedent of *Lawrence v. Texas*—probably via legislation specifically introduced with the intent of driving court contests—seem likely, given the emotion of the debate. And yet, the reach of the decision may—as Justice Scalia feared—quickly move beyond those cases involving same-sex issues. Constitutional law decisions tend to flow by analogy in the United States from one case to another. Thus, just as the challenge of women in Alabama to "sex toy" legislation moved quickly into discussion of *Bowers v. Hardwick*, the Court's decision in *Lawrence v. Texas* might be used to defeat not only legislation banning the sale of such devices and sex toys, for example, but an array of other "morality-based" legislation as well, which is clearly what conservative politicians and religious leaders feared.

In that sense, as unlikely as it may seem, *Lawrence v. Texas* may prove as significant a victory for women as for same-sex couples. And not just women involved in lesbian relationships or plaintiffs like the women involved in the Alabama case. Although the context of *Lawrence v. Texas* was same-sex sexual conduct, the fundamental question it raised involved the reach of constitutional protections where the conduct was indisputably "private," but not related to procreation or, heretofore, traditional models of family. The majority chose to grant private conduct—even where it is not related to procreation or "family"—the same protection as sexual conduct related to family and procreation.

Critics argued—both before and after the majority issued the decision—that such a ruling would open the door to "bigamy, . . .adult incest, prostitution, masturbation, adultery, fornication, bestiality," and obscenities of all kinds. But for women, the decision may further foreclose challenges to their private choices. The choice of birth control—a private decision impacting "family" and procreation—was clearly settled more than two decades ago.

The majority's decision in *Lawrence v. Texas* would appear to settle the question of private sexual choices where procreation is not related and may not be the goal. In that sense, the majority's decision may serve—at least for women—as the long-awaited third piece of the puzzle. In other words, *Lawrence v. Texas* may be one of the most significant reproductive rights decisions in recent years. But even so, the decision seems unlikely to settle the never-ending questions surrounding the choice of abortion that continue to inspire rage. Far from being settled, despite a thirty-year-old precedent that should have made choice the "law of the land," the question of a woman's right to choose remains at the center of an often violent debate that will likely continue for as long as the procedure is legal in the United States.

LIFESTYLE CHOICES vs. MEDICAL TREATMENT:
Current Issues in Reproductive Rights Law

In *Griswold v. Connecticut*, a majority of the United States Supreme Court found that decisions regarding contraceptives fell "...within the zone of privacy created by several fundamental constitutional guarantees," a "privacy older than the Bill of Rights...."[146] Though some religious and conservative leaders would have it another way, for the most part, the debate over contraceptives is settled: women have the right to them. The debate in recent years has instead involved the question of money. Lots of money.

Sixty million women of childbearing age (between the ages of 15 and 44) live in the United States. Some 42 million of them are sexually active, but do not want to become pregnant. Research suggests that "a sexually active woman between ages 20 and 45 who wants two children, will spend, on average, almost five years of her life trying to become pregnant, or being pregnant or postpartum, and more than *four times that long* trying to avoid pregnancy."[147] Roughly three-quarters of all American women of childbearing age rely upon private insurance to defray medical costs,[148] and many low-income women rely upon Title X funding.[149]

And yet, for decades most private insurers have refused to cover the cost of prescription contraceptives for women, although they have covered the cost of the male potency drug Viagra since it made its way to the market, women's groups charged. That dichotomy gave rise in the summer of 2000 to the first of what some thought would be the beginning of dozens of class-action lawsuits against insurers brought by women.[150] The story of how it all got started involves a little bit of folklore.

As the chroniclers of modern history tell it, the male, middle-aged world has been "achatter" since former presidential candidate, Bob Dole, recovering from prostate surgery, leaned over during a break in taping of *Larry King Live* and whispered that now magic word: "V-i-a-g-r-a."[151] And the controversy began. An angina drug turned male impotency miracle, Viagra rocketed the "contraceptives equality" issue to the forefront of the reproductive rights debate.

First-year sales of Viagra topped $1 billion, making Pfizer, the drug's manufacturer, the world's second-largest drug company.[152] Though Viagra sales reportedly "leveled off," in 2000 "nearly 200,000 prescriptions [were still being] filled each week. Seventeen million Americans are believed to have used the drug."[153] And most insurance companies covered the cost of Viagra without dispute, sparking anticipation in late 1999 that lawsuits would quickly follow.[154]

Those expectations proved true, but not as expected. Men—a federal judge among them—and four male employees of Oxford Health Plans[155] filed suits against insurers in 1999,[156] seeking coverage. Women's groups also filed suit, alleging that covering the cost of Viagra while refusing to cover female contraceptives was gender discrimination[157] that costs women millions of dollars a year.[158]

But insurance industry officials have defended coverage of Viagra, arguing that it is a "medical treatment" while female contraceptives are a "lifestyle choice."[159] Critics have long argued in this vein (i.e., that women wouldn't need artificial intervention if they didn't have sex for reasons other than procreation). As set forth in Chapter Two, for example, similar assertions were made before the United States Congress in 1934, during hearings on a possible amendment to the Comstock Act.[160] That amendment would have allowed doctors to prescribe contraceptives.[161] It was also argued in 1934 that "common monies" should not be used to pay for birth control.[162]

Of course, the reasoning of these "lifestyle choice" arguments cuts both ways: some critics have argued that Viagra is also a "lifestyle choice" in the guise of medical treatment, and that men who take Viagra *choose* to be sexually active against the natural—albeit failing—function of their bodies. Though some lawsuits were filed and resolved in favor of women,[163] legislative intervention would strike a blow for equality. Since 1998, twenty states have passed laws requiring insurers to cover the cost of all prescriptions, including contraceptives.[164] Congress has enacted similar legislation requiring coverage for all federal employees insured through the Federal Employees Health Benefits Program.[165]

But there are partisans in this debate. In July 2001, the Bush administration denied a proposal submitted by New York Governor George Pataki to the federal Health Care Financing Administration, seeking to use federal Medicaid funds to subsidize contraceptive services for poor women.[166] The proposed plan would not pay for abortion. What it sought, instead, was to provide medical coverage for "the working poor," i.e., men and women who made too much money to qualify for Medicaid. Included in the proposal was coverage for contraceptive devices and drugs. Nine states have made similar proposals.[167] All have been blocked.

BLOCKING CHOICE, ASSERTING "LIFE"

Like the abortion debate, battles over birth control are often grounded in two contrasting views of "life." As set forth in greater detail below, lawmakers in Connecticut and Texas proposed legislation in 2001, defining the "beginning of life" as "the moment of fertilization" as opposed to birth, and that an "unborn human organism" is alive and entitled to the rights, protections, and privileges accorded any other person in the state.[168] Though this might seem to be more of an argument for the abortion context—and it is certainly an argument used there—it has also driven challenges by pro-life groups against health care plans and coverage.

During an often-heated debate over the inclusion of coverage for contraceptives for federal employees, Republican Representative Chris Smith[169] proposed an amendment to a 1998 bill that would have allowed that coverage to 1.2 million female federal employees, excluding abortifacients. Because abortions were already excluded from coverage under the bill, questions arose as to what Smith really intended with the amendment.

According to Lisa Kaeser, of the Alan Guttmacher Institute,[170] "Smith soon made it clear that his intent was to exclude from the mandate intrauterine devices (IUDs) and [Emergency Contraceptive Pills] EPCs on the grounds that they sometimes act to prevent implantation of a fertilized egg."[171] Members of pro-life groups have long argued that once an egg and a sperm cell have met, a "baby" has been made.

And yet, the science of the thing has always been explained differently. If medical texts can be deemed informative and, thus, read on the House and Senate floors during arguments over so-called "partial-birth abortion," it seems fair to look at the medicine of life. According to medical professionals, "[t]he fertilization of human gametes initially creates one two-cell entity whose medical name changes based upon its development stage and the continued division of its cells during the gestational process. After the earliest stage of fertilization, the union of the egg and sperm is called a zygote or preembryo.[172] Shortly thereafter, the conceptus becomes an embryo.[173] Eight weeks later, it becomes a fetus[174] until birth."[175]

In challenging the basis of Smith's proposed amendment, Representative Nancy Johnson[176] began by asking a simple question: "Is there no limit to my colleague's willingness to impose his concept of when life begins on others? Conception," Johnson continued, "is a process. Fertilization of the egg is part of that process. But if that fertilized egg does not get implanted, it does not grow.... For those who do not believe that life begins upon fertilization, but believe, in fact, that that fertilized egg has to be implanted, the gentleman is imposing his judgment as to when life begins on that person and, in so doing, denying them what might be the safest means of contraception available to them."

And that, it seems, is exactly what is happening.

WHERE WOMEN FIT IN THE BIRTH CONTROL DEBATE

Almost half—49 percent—of all pregnancies in the United States are unplanned, and 31 percent of all pregnancies amongst married women are a surprise.[178] Though religious and pro-life groups would have women carry fetuses to term every time there is a pregnancy, women seem to have different ideas.

Since 1982, voluntarily sterilization has been the most common form of "birth control" for women over 34 years of age with less than a high school education, who are poor or nearly poor by federal guideline standards.[179] Sterilization is more common among African American and Hispanic women, while "the pill" is widely used by white women.[180] Fifty percent of all women between the ages of 40 and 44 have been sterilized (voluntarily); another 20 percent have a partner who has had a vasectomy.[181]

As it has among adult women, the rate of abortion among minors has fallen to its lowest rate since the procedure was legalized in 1973. Greater use of contraceptives among teenagers is among the reasons for this. The percentage of teenagers using contraceptives rose from 24 percent in 1982 to 32 percent in 1988, according to researchers.[182] Since the United States Supreme Court's decision in *Carey v. Population Services Int'l*,[183] it has generally been held that there are few permissible prohibitions on a minor's ability to buy over-the-counter contraceptives, spermicides, and condoms among them.

More than one-third of teenagers using contraceptives report the choice of condoms as their primary method of birth control. They number among the 9.8 million women total who choose "barrier" forms of birth control, such as the diaphragm or the male condom (which prevent sexually transmitted diseases) or female condom (which is used as a primary method of contraception only one percent of the time by all women). In addition to over-the-counter products, more than one million teenagers reportedly use the pill. In 1973—before the Supreme Court decision in *Carey*—the pill was the leading method of birth control amongst married couples. Today, the pill is the most widely used form of contraceptive among women in their twenties. The pill requires a prescription and, thus, has been part of the lifestyle choices versus medical treatment debate.

Also part of the debate are injectable and implantable contraceptives. According to the Alan Guttmacher Institute, "[i]n 1995, the first year national data were collected on the injectable and the implant, women younger than 24 were the age group most likely to rely on those methods. Among women aged 15–17,…15 percent were using the injectable and 4 percent were relying on the implant."[184]

Injectable contraceptives include Depo-Provera and Lunelle. Both are hormone shots taken several times a year and are said to be as effective in preventing unwanted pregnancies as the pill.[185] Implanted contraceptives include Norplant, which was at the center of a controversy in 1990, after a newspaper columnist proposed linking mandated use to welfare benefits.

THE NORPLANT CONTROVERSY: SIX EASY PIECES AND "THE EDITORIAL"

During the early 1990s, Norplant seemed the perfect contraceptive to some. In 10 minutes, six matchstick-sized tubes of synthetic hormone could be placed under the skin of a woman's arm, and for 5 years she was protected from unwanted pregnancies as the tubes release low dosages of hormones that prevented ovulation and thickened mucus at the opening of the cervix, preventing sperm cells from reaching the egg. It appeared to be a breakthrough.

But much of protocol's notoriety would arise from a controversial proposal made by then-deputy editorial page editor, Donald Kimelman, of the *Philadelphia Inquirer*, who argued in a December 12, 1990, editorial that "the main reason more black children are living in poverty is that [the] people having the most children are the ones least capable of supporting them."[186] The editorial linked poverty and single motherhood. Norplant, with a possible link to welfare benefits, was suggested as a solution to "the problem."

Kimelman's assertions were old news. Politicians throughout the twentieth century have blamed women—especially single, poor woman—for the "epidemics" of pregnancy and poverty and have warned that "they" would be the ruin of society as a result of having too many babies they could not afford.[187] But in the political context of the times, they were widely considered outrageous. According to Dorothy Roberts, author of *Killing The Black Body: Race, Reproduction, and the Meaning of Liberty*,[188] the editorial set off shock waves, with criticism rising from within the *Inquirer's* own ranks.

"The *Inquirer's* Metro Columnist, Steve Lopez, issued a stinging rebuttal the following Sunday," Roberts writes. "What we have, basically, is the *Inquirer* brain trust looking down from its ivory tower and wondering if black people should be paid to stop having so many damn kids," Lopez fumed. "By combining contraception and race, the voice of the *Inquirer* calls to mind another David, David Duke."[189]

The 1980s were punctuated by "anti-urban" politics and a blaming of many of society's problems on poor, inner-city residents. Though the paper would formally apologize in writing eleven days later, "[j]ournalists immediately came to the *Inquirer's* defense," Roberts notes, citing pieces supportive of not only Kimelman, but also of Norplant-for-benefits arguments published in *Newsweek*,[190] the *Richmond Times-Dispatch*,[191] the *New Republic*,[192] and the *Washington Post*.[193]

In 1991, Darlene Johnson became the first woman to be ordered by a judge to have Norplant implanted as a condition of release.[194] Johnson, a 27-year-old pregnant mother of four receiving welfare benefits, pled guilty to charges of child abuse. After remanding Johnson to custody because he was "concerned about drug use"— though there was no evidence of drug use, according to NARAL—a California judge ordered Johnson to begin using Norplant as a condition of release.[195] Though isolated decisions of this sort probably continue, the broad promise of Norplant as a solution to society's troubles fizzled on its own. Only four percent of women appear to choose implanted contraceptives as their primary method of birth control.

EMERGENCY CONTRACEPTIVES AND THE MORNING AFTER

On September 2, 1998, the Food and Drug Administration approved the sale of the Preven Emergency Contraceptive Kit.[196] It is one of several "morning after" remedies to be taken within 72 hours of having unprotected sex.[197] The kit contains a combination of drugs that prevent ovulation and the implantation of a fertilized egg.[198] Four to five percent of childbearing age women have used "emergency" or "post coital" contraception.[199] And advocates of the protocol argue that "emergency contraceptives" are little known.[200] In March 2002, California Governor Gray Davis ordered the state's HMOs to cover "morning-after" pills.[201] Still, "morning-after pills" drew the attention of conservatives who view postcoital contraceptives as a means of ending "life."[202]

Other post-sex products include progestin or copper intrauterine devices that can be used within five days of having unprotected sex. Progestin IUDs are similar in function to "morning after" pills. But copper IUDs release copper ions, which affect the uterine lining, making implantation of an egg impossible. This method is said to reduce the risk of pregnancy substantially. It too has been roundly criticized by pro-life groups. IUDs have declined in use generally as a primary form of contraception, from two percent in 1995 to one percent in 1998.[203]

But a huge development in this area is mifepristone. Technically known as "medical abortion," because it involves ending an established pregnancy, mifepristone, formerly RU-486, was approved in September 2000, by the FDA. It was expected to make surgical abortions less necessary during the early weeks of pregnancy. Mifepristone has been successfully used by roughly 500,000 women in Europe.[204]

In the fall of 1996, after years of positive results in Europe, the FDA sent a letter of approval for mifepristone to federal authorities, opening the door to clinical trials in the United States of the protocol. As of January 1998, 1,600 American women had used mifepristone at 12 sites across the country.[205] In an attempt to head off FDA approval, pro-life politicians swung into action. In July 1998, the House of Representatives voted 223 to 202 to amend the nation's annual spending bill to include a measure blocking the FDA from researching, testing, or approving any drug that induces abortion, including mifepristone.[206]

The amendment, sponsored by Representative Tom Coburn,[207] was defeated. After difficulties finding a company willing to make the drug, mifepristone was finally approved in September 2000. Though hundreds of thousands of women have safely used the protocol in Europe and the United States, former Wisconsin Governor, Tommy Thompson, tapped by George Bush to head the Department of Health and Human Services, expressed "safety concerns" and talked of "revisiting" the FDA's decision.[208] In March 31, 2001, federal authorities began notifying state officials that women whose abortions would not be covered by Medicaid would also be ineligible for reimbursement of federal funds for medical abortions unless the pregnancies were the result of rape or incest, or where the woman's life was in danger.[209] Between September 2000 and September 24, 2003, more than 165,000 American women had safely used mifepristone.[210]

ABORTION AND THE CHALLENGE OF THE 1990s:
Murder and Mayhem in the Name of "Life"

"Terrorism is a high-cost option, a weapon of the weak, a tool of last resort. But if your movement suddenly collapses or suffers political reversals, then many activists will be tempted to go for terrorism," University of Maryland sociologist, Christopher Hewitt, told reporter Bruce Barcott in an article on the subject published in the April 7, 2002, edition of *The New York Times Magazine*.[211]

Adding to the initial threads of this thought, Hewitt offered "[t]wo examples: many antiwar advocates believed that President Johnson's decision not to seek a second term in 1968 signaled the end of the Vietnam conflict. When his successor, Richard Nixon, expanded the war, the most radical activists gravitated to the Weather Underground, a group responsible for several high-profile bombings during the 1970s. Similarly, Ronald Reagan's 1980 election led antiabortion advocates to expect the demise of *Roe v. Wade*. But by decade's end, abortion remained legal, and the tactics of radical activists…escalated from pickets to blockades to bombings. With the election of Bill Clinton in 1992, the hopes raised by Reagan were finally crushed. That's when abortion doctors started getting assassinated."[212]

On September 30, 2000, a Roman Catholic priest drove his car through the front doors of the Abortion Access Northern Illinois Women's Center. He then jumped out of the car and began wielding an ax, stopping only when he was confronted, according to news reports, by the building's owner, who met the charge with a shotgun, firing two rounds.[213] "I thank God and my shotgun that I'm alive," Gerald W. Webster told reporters. The priest, identified by authorities as Reverend John Earl, was arrested, booked and released on bond.[214]

Despite the endurance of *Roe v. Wade* and the fact that abortion is still legal after 30 years of taxpayer-funded court challenge, during the 1990s, women— and the doctors determined to ensure that women would continue to have the choice of abortion—faced a new and dangerous challenge: violence as the spine of a campaign of terror intended to close clinics.

In terms of character, where the 1980s were about legal challenge and Supreme Court decisions that chipped away at the gains of the 1970s, the 1990s were about mayhem and murder in a "debate" where the language graduated from pleas and jeers with bloody placards and psychological warfare to emotional semantics, stalking, death threats, and bullets. Opponents, who approached the task of "ending abortion" with the zeal of crusaders, threw themselves under buses and in front of cars to prevent women from entering clinics. Their battle was undertaken in the name of God, they often argued. Many were members of church groups and the clergy.[215] One of the leaders in this fight, the National Right to Life Committee, for example, was founded in 1973, five months after the Court's decision in *Roe v. Wade* by Monsignor James McHugh acting on behalf of the National Conference of Bishops.[216]

More than 6,000 clinics faced human blockades; at least 200 clinics were targets of arson or attempted arson; and since the rise of a militant antiabortion movement in the late 1970s, more than 130 death threats were called in against clinics.[217] Among the "lesser instances" of violence also occurring during this time, clinic employers were reportedly stalked; the locks to clinic doors were sealed with Krazy Glue; antiabortion activists stormed medical offices, smashing furniture, tearing phones out of walls, and vandalizing desks and records, then locking themselves inside counseling rooms.[218]

And although incidents of this sort slowed during the late 1990s, they did not stop. Between May and July of 1998, for example, isobutyric acid attacks were reported at twenty clinics.[219] In February 1999, clinics in Indiana, Tennessee, Kansas, and Kentucky were sent letters said to contain anthrax.[220] And in July 2001, the only women's clinic in Baton Rouge, Louisiana, was destroyed by fire. Though authorities had no comment on the cause of the fire at the time, four men were convicted of firebombing that same clinic in 1987.[221] Nearly fifty percent of all abortion clinics and providers were still reporting violent incidents in the late 1990s. Among these reported incidents was murder.

THE SWORDS OF THEIR JUSTICE

Three months after the Illinois priest wielded his ax, sightings of James Kopp began to appear in the media. Kopp, "one of the most avid followers" of antiabortion activist Randall Terry, according to media reports,[222] had been previously identified by law enforcement officials as a suspect in the murder of Dr. Barnett Slepian. On October 23, 1998, Dr. Slepian was killed by a shot through the kitchen window of his Buffalo home as he stood near his wife and two sons. Dr. Slepian worked at a Buffalo-area women's clinic.

Prior to the murder, Dr. Slepian's name was posted on an Internet website called *The Nuremberg Files*. The site is where Neal Horsley admitted collecting "the names, addresses, and photos of hundreds of doctors across the country who perform abortions."[223] After the murder, Horsley reportedly tapped the "strike" key on his computer keyboard. "It drew a black line through [Dr.] Slepian's name," Daniel Voll reported in *Esquire* magazine after interviewing Horsley.[224]

James Kopp reportedly fled the country after the murder of Dr. Slepian. In December of 2000, he was believed to be in the United Kingdom.[225] Kopp was finally tracked down in France in March 2001, in an investigation that led authorities from New York to Ireland; back to Brooklyn and then to France. Kopp was aided in eluding authorities by a "loose-knit group of violent antiabortion activists," according to media reports.[226] In March of 2003, Kopp admitted killing Dr. Slepian in a New York court.[227] He was sentenced to 25 years to life in prison.[228]

But Dr. Slepian's murder was not an isolated incident. In December of 1994, John Salvi walked into two separate Massachusetts abortion clinics, where he opened fire with a gun, wounding five workers and killing two receptionists. Salvi was arrested the day after the incidents and convicted of murder. He committed suicide in prison. In addition to the murders committed by Salvi, seven doctors, nurses, and volunteer escorts have been killed in bombings and ambushes at abortion clinics across the country in the last decade with Pensacola, Florida, a hot spot during 1993 and 1994.

According to media reports, John Burt was leading a protest outside a Pensacola women's clinic in 1993, for instance, when Dr. David Gunn was shot and killed by Michael Griffin, an associate of Burt's.[229] Griffin, who reportedly volunteered at a home for troubled girls run by Burt, was convicted of the murder and is currently serving a life sentence. The following year, Dr. Bayard Britton, the doctor who replaced Dr. Gunn, was shot and killed along with a volunteer escort outside the same clinic by a 45-year-old former Presbyterian minister named Paul Hill. According to some reports, Hill stalked Dr. Britton prior to the murder.[230] And in the months following the murder of Dr. Gunn in 1993—but prior to the murder of Dr. Britton—Hill became a spokesman of sorts for violence against abortion providers, appearing on *Nightline* and *Donahue*.[231]

Although Hill would attempt at trial to argue that the murder of Dr. Britton was "justifiable homicide," it failed as an affirmative defense. Hill, who said he aimed at Dr. Britton's head because he suspected the doctor might be wearing a bulletproof vest, was convicted of killing Dr. Britton and James Barrett, a 74-year-old retired Air Force lieutenant, who volunteered to drive Dr. Britton to the clinic. Barrett's wife was also injured. In September of 2003, Hill was put to death by lethal injection in Florida, becoming the first person convicted of killing an abortion provider to be put to death in the United States.[232]

At the height of the violence, the question of whether the government had an obligation to intervene to protect citizens—even citizens who may be on their way to abortion clinics—became a topic of political and public debate. And if not the intervention of "government" via marshals, then might federal legislation be used to combat the violent tactics of protesters? The latter question became an issue before the United States Supreme Court in *Bray v. Alexandria Women's Health Clinic*,[233] a case that brought the tactics of the pro-life group Operation Rescue to the fore. Michael Bray, the author of a book that justifies the murder of doctors as a means of stopping abortion, reportedly served nearly four years in prison on charges related to arson attacks and bombing at abortion clinics.[234]

Several women's clinics sought to enjoin Operation Rescue and other abortion opponents from obstructing entrances to abortion clinics in the Washington, D.C., area. In what the United States Supreme Court described as "an expedited trial," a federal district court held that the antiabortion protesters "had violated [42 U.S.C. Section] 1985(3) (commonly known as the "Ku Klux Klan Act") by conspiring to deprive women seeking abortions of their right to interstate travel."[235] In addition to enjoining the protesters, the district court ruled in favor of the clinics' pendent state law claims of trespass and public nuisance.[236] The protesters were ordered to pay $27,687.55 in attorney's fees.[237]

The protesters appealed to the United States Supreme Court, where, in a 5 to 4 decision, the Justices held that "in order to prove a private conspiracy in violation of the first clause of 1985(3),[238] a plaintiff must show,...(1) that 'some racial, or perhaps otherwise class-based, invidiously discriminatory animus [lay] behind the conspirators' action,'[239] and (2) that the conspiracy 'aimed at interfering with rights' that are 'protected against private, as well as official, encroachment.'[240] We think neither showing has been made in the present case," the Court wrote.

"To begin with, we reject the apparent conclusion of the district court...that opposition to abortion constitutes discrimination against the 'class' of 'women seeking abortion.' Whatever may be the precise meaning of a 'class' for purposes of [*Griffin v. Breckenridge's*] speculative extension of 1985(3) beyond race,[241] the term unquestionably connotes something more than a group of individuals who share a desire to engage in conduct that the 1985(3) defendant disfavors.... As Justice Blackmun has cogently put it, the class 'cannot be defined simply as the group of victims of the tortious action.'[242] 'Women seeking abortion' is not a qualifying class," the Court held.[243]

And finally, "[w]hether one agrees or disagrees with the goal of preventing abortion, that goal in itself (apart from the use of unlawful means to achieve it, which is not relevant to our discussion of animus) does not remotely qualify for such a harsh description, and for such derogatory association with racism. To the contrary, we have said that 'a value judgment favoring childbirth over abortion' is proper and reasonable enough to be implemented by the allocation of public funds,[244] and Congress itself has, without approval, discriminated against abortion in its provisions of financial support for medical procedures.[245] This is not the stuff of which a 1985(3) 'invidiously discriminatory animus' is created," the Court concluded.[246]

But sometimes, when the Justices of the United States Supreme Court find no protectable interest, Congress responds by inventing one. One of these relatively rare instances occurred in 1994. Following the Court's decision in *Bray v. Alexandria Women's Health Clinic*, Congress passed the Freedom of Access to Clinic Entrances Act (FACE),[247] which created a framework for the prosecution of individuals carrying out the kind of violent or obstructive acts that had nearly intimidated or harassed many providers out of the business during the late-1980s and mid-90s.

Prosecutions under FACE reportedly resulted in a drop in the number of reported incidents to 20 percent of what they once were. By April 2001, twenty-seven criminal prosecutions and seventeen civil cases have been brought under FACE.[248]

NATIONAL ORGANIZATION FOR WOMEN v. SCHEIDLER

Nineteen-ninety-four was also the year of the United States Supreme Court's decision in *National Organization for Women v. Scheidler*,[249] a case that began in 1986 in a federal court in the Northern District of Illinois, when the National Organization for Women (NOW) and two health care providers sued "a coalition of antiabortion groups called the Pro-Life Action Network (PLAN)," which included Joseph Scheidler, the executive director of the Pro-Life Action League, and several unnamed individuals and antiabortion organizations.

According to an amended complaint (filed on behalf of the National Organization for Women) PLAN, Scheidler, and others were "members of a nationwide conspiracy to shut down abortion clinics through a pattern of racketeering activity including extortion in violation of the 1951 Hobbs Act."[250] Scheidler apparently gave congressional testimony admitting that the closing down of clinics performing abortions was his group's goal.[251] The Hobbs Act defined extortion as "the obtaining of property from another, without his consent, induced by wrongful use of actual or threatened force, violence, or fear, or under color of official right."[252] The National Organization for Women also asserted a claim under the federal Racketeer Influenced and Corrupt Organizations Act (RICO).

The district court dismissed the case, finding that because the activities at issue "involve[d] political opponents, not commercial competitors, and political objectives, not marketplace goals," the law, as invoked by the plaintiffs, did not apply. The district court also dismissed the RICO claims, reasoning that the "income" at issue had been derived from voluntary donations and, thus, was not the result of the "pattern of racketeering alleged in the complaint."[253]

The Seventh Circuit Court of Appeals affirmed the district court's decision.[254] To resolve a conflict among the federal circuits, the United States Supreme Court granted *certiorari*. And in a decision met with enormous enthusiasm, the Court would eventually rule that the National Organization for Women "may maintain this action if respondents conducted the enterprise through a pattern of racketeering activity. The questions of whether the respondents committed the requisite predicate acts, and whether the commission of these acts fell into a pattern, are not before us. We hold only that RICO contains no economic motive requirement."[255]

MADSEN v. WOMEN'S HEALTH CENTER

In another noteworthy 1994 case, the Court upheld the provision of an injunction issued on behalf of a Melbourne, Florida, clinic by a state court permanently enjoining antiabortion protesters from blocking or otherwise interfering "with public access to the clinic, and from physically abusing persons entering or leaving the clinic." Six months later, the clinic sought to broaden the injunction, arguing that the protesters were still impeding access to the clinic. Attorneys for the clinic also alleged that antiabortion protesters sought to discourage "potential patients from entering the clinic" and that their actions had "deleterious physical effects on others."

In addressing the center's request for a broader injunction, the Florida court found that:

> despite the initial injunction, protesters continued to impede access to the clinic by congregating on the paved portion of the street—Dixie Way—leading up to the clinic, and by marching in front of the clinic's driveways. [The first court also] found [that as] vehicles heading toward the clinic slowed to allow the protesters to move out of the way, "sidewalk counselors" would approach and attempt to give the vehicle's occupants antiabortion literature. The number of people congregating varied from a handful to 400, and the noise varied from singing and chanting to the use of loudspeakers and bullhorns.
>
> The protests...took their toll on the clinic's patients. A clinic doctor testified that, as a result of having to run such a gauntlet to enter the clinic, the patients "manifested a higher level of anxiety and hypertension causing those patients to need a higher level of sedation to undergo

the surgical procedures, thereby increasing the risk associated with such procedures. The noise produced by the protesters could be heard within the clinic, causing stress in the patients both during surgical procedures and while recuperating in the recovery rooms. And those patients who turned away because of the crowd to return on a later date, the doctor testified, increased their health risks by reason of the delay.

Doctors and clinic workers, in turn, were not immune even in their homes. [Antiabortion protesters] picketed in front of clinic employees' residences; shouted at passersby; rang doorbells of neighbors and provided literature identifying the particular clinic employee as a "baby killer." Occasionally, the protesters would confront minor children of clinic employees who were home alone.[256]

Based upon this and other testimony, the Florida court determined that the original injunction was not sufficient. Thus, it broadened the order to include two "buffer zones." The first buffer zone enjoined antiabortion protesters "[a]t all times on all days, from congregating, picketing, patrolling, demonstrating or entering that portion of public right-of-way or private property within 36 feet of the property line of the clinic...."[257]

The second buffer zone enjoined protesters "[a]t all times on all days, from approaching, congregating, picketing, patrolling, demonstrating or using bullhorns or other sound amplification equipment within 300 feet of the residence of any of the [clinic's] employees, staff, owners, or agents, or blocking or attempting to block, barricade, or in any other manner, temporarily or otherwise, obstruct the entrances, exits or driveways of the residences of any of the [clinic's] employees, staff, owners, or agents."[258]

The Florida Supreme Court upheld the constitutionality of the injunction. But shortly before the Florida Supreme Court's ruling, the United States Court of Appeals for the Eleventh Circuit had struck down a similar injunction in a separate and unrelated case involving a clash "between an actual prohibition of speech and a potential hindrance to the free exercise of abortion rights," as a violation of the First Amendment. With an eye towards resolving the difference of these decisions, the United States Supreme Court granted *certiorari*, agreeing to hear *Madsen v. Women's Health Center*.[259] Before the Court was the constitutionality of the Florida injunction's two "buffer zone" provisions.

With regard to the first buffer zone provision, the Court ruled that "[o]n balance,...the 36-foot buffer zone around the clinic entrances and driveway burdens no more speech than necessary to accomplish the governmental interest at stake."[260] In other words, although "[t]he need for a complete buffer zone near the clinic entrances and driveways may be debatable,...some deference must be given to the state court's familiarity with the facts and the background of the dispute between the parties even under our heightened review. Moreover, one of petitioners' witnesses during the evidentiary hearing before the state court conceded that the buffer zone was narrow enough to place petitioners at a distance no greater than ten to twelve feet from cars approaching and leaving the clinic. Protesters standing across the narrow street from the clinic can still be seen and heard from the clinic parking lots. We also bear in mind the fact that the state court originally issued a much narrower injunction, providing no buffer zone, and that this order did not succeed in protecting access to the clinic. The failure of the first order to accomplish its purpose may be taken into consideration in evaluating the constitutionality of the broader order."

But with regard to the second, larger buffer zone provision, the Court held that "the 300-foot zone around the residences in this case is much larger than the zone provided for" by other Supreme Court precedent, because "the 300-foot zone would ban '[g]eneral marching through residential neighborhoods, or even walking a route in front of an entire block of houses.' The record before us does not contain sufficient justification for this broad a ban on picketing; it appears that a limitation on the time, duration of picketing, and number of pickets outside a smaller zone could have accomplished the desired result."[261]

SCHENCK v. PRO-CHOICE NETWORK OF WESTERN NEW YORK

In terms of consistency, the provision of a New York court injunction creating a 15-foot "floating" buffer zone around people and vehicles seeking access to four New York medical clinics in Rochester and Buffalo was similarly struck down by the United States Supreme Court in *Schenck v. Pro-Choice Network of Western New York*.[262] The provision violated the First Amendment because it burdened "more speech than necessary to serve the relevant government interests," the Court held. A 15-foot "fixed" buffer zone reaching clinic doorways, driveways, and parking lot entrances was upheld.

Schenck v. Pro-Choice Network of Western New York involved a series of "large scale blockades" against the clinics during which "protesters would march, stand, kneel, sit, or lie in parking lot driveways and in doorways," thereby hindering the entrance of patients, doctors, nurses, and clinic employees, as well as cars attempting to enter parking lots.[263] "In addition to these large scale blockades, smaller groups of protesters consistently attempted to stop or disrupt clinic operations. Those trespassers who remained outside the clinics crowded around cars or milled around doorways and driveway entrances in an effort to block or hinder access to the clinics," the Court noted.[264]

And "[p]rotesters sometimes threw themselves on top of the hoods of cars or crowded around cars as they attempted to turn into parking lot driveways," the Justices found. "Other protesters on clinic property handed [out] literature and talked to people entering the clinics—especially those women they believed were arriving to have abortions—in an effort to persuade them that abortion was immoral. Sometimes protesters used more aggressive techniques, with varying levels of belligerence: getting very close to women entering clinics and shouting in their faces; surrounding, crowding, and yelling at women entering the clinics; or jostling, grabbing, pushing, and shoving women as they attempted to enter the clinics. Male and female clinic volunteers who attempted to escort patients past protesters into the clinics were sometimes elbowed, grabbed, or spit on. Sometimes the escorts pushed back. Some protesters remained in the doorways after the patients had entered the clinics, blocking others from entering or exiting."[265]

This is what many women faced when they tried to exercise their right to choose abortion. But when doctors became targets of violence, the Clinton administration took an aggressive stance. Following Dr. Slepian's murder, United States Attorney General Janet Reno announced the creation of a national task force to address the issue of violence against women's clinics. Reno promised to investigate "any connections that may exist between individuals engaged in criminal conduct" involving abortion clinics.[266]

The tide in the nation's courts also seemed to turn, although the victories didn't always stand. On February 2, 1999, a federal jury in Oregon ordered the creators of *The Nuremberg Files*—two organizations and twelve individuals[267]— to pay $107 million[268] in punitive damages to a group of doctors and clinics. Attorneys for the plaintiffs had brought the suit under FACE, and the Oregon jury's decision was seen by many as an extraordinary civil victory.

ANTIABORTION VIOLENCE AND THE FIRST AMENDMENT

Following the $107 million award, there was speculation that the case might be open to appeal on First Amendment grounds.[269] And on March 28, 2001, that speculation seemed borne out when a three-judge panel of the United States Court of Appeals for the Ninth Circuit held that the content of *The Nuremberg Files* was protected by the First Amendment.

"If defendants threatened to commit violent acts, by working alone or with others," there would have been a proper foundation for the verdict, Judge Alex Kozinski concluded. But where their acts "merely encouraged unrelated terrorists, then their words are protected by the First Amendment."[270]

The plaintiff sought a hearing on the issues by the full panel, and upon rehearing *en banc,* the Ninth Circuit concluded that "[u]nder our cases, a threat is 'an expression of an intention to inflict evil, injury, or damage on another.'"[271] Specifically, Judge Rymer wrote for the majority that "[a]lleged threats should be considered in light of their entire factual context, including the surrounding events and reaction of the listeners.[272] 'The fact that a threat is subtle does not make it less of a threat.'[273] A true threat, that is one 'where a reasonable person would foresee that the listener will believe he will be subjected to physical violence upon his person, is unprotected by the First Amendment."[274]

In other words, "[i]t is not necessary that the defendant intend to, or be able to carry out his threat; the only intent requirement for a true threat is that the defendant intentionally or knowingly communicate the threat," Judge Rymer explained.[275]

The "threat" in this case, the six-judge majority found, arose out of the listing of "Wanted" posters on *The Nuremberg Files* by the American Coalition of Life Activists (ACLA). Specifically, it was the pattern of postings followed by murders that resulted in the perception "by physicians, who are providers of reproductive health services, [of]…a serious threat of death or bodily harm."

"After a 'Wanted' poster on Dr. David Gunn appeared, he was shot and killed. After a 'Wanted' poster on George Patterson appeared, he was shot and killed. After a 'Wanted' poster on Dr. John Britton appeared, he was shot and killed," the majority wrote. This pattern—of postings followed by murders—was perceived by the doctors filing suit as a "a serious threat of death or bodily harm," even though "[n]one of these 'Wanted' posters contained threatening language...," the majority wrote.[276]

"The posters are a true threat because, like Ryder trucks or burning crosses, they connote something they do not literally say, yet both the actor and the recipient get the message. To the doctor who performs abortions, these posters meant 'You're wanted or you're guilty; you'll be shot or killed.' This was reinforced by the scorecard in *The Nuremberg Files*. The communication was not conditional or casual. It was specifically targeted," the majority held.[277]

"Violence is not a protected value. Nor is a *true threat* of violence *with intent to intimidate*," according to the majority.[278] [¶] "A 'threat of force' for purposes of FACE is properly defined in accordance with our longstanding test on 'true threats,' as 'whether a reasonable person would foresee that the statement would be interpreted by those to whom the maker communicates the statement as a serious expression of intent to harm or assault.' This, coupled with the statute's requirement of intent to intimidate, comports with the First Amendment."[279]

"There is substantial evidence that these posters were prepared and disseminated to intimidate physicians from providing reproductive health services. Thus, ACLA was appropriately found liable for a true threat to intimidate under FACE," the majority concluded.[280] [¶] "Holding [the coalition] accountable for this conduct does not impinge on legitimate protest or advocacy. Restraining it from continuing to threaten these physicians burdens speech no more than necessary."[281] [¶] "Therefore, we affirm the judgment in all respects but for punitive damages, as to which we remand."[282]

In June 2003, the United States Supreme Court declined to hear an appeal of the Ninth Circuit's ruling filed on behalf of the American Coalition of Life Activists in a decision applauded by health care providers for women.[283] And in an untraditional pairing, Solicitor General Ted Olson filed a nineteen-page brief on behalf of the Bush administration opposing review of the appeal by the Court.[284]

But even before the Ninth Circuit's decision in 2003, the lower courts appear to have begun applying this sort of reasoning. In August of 2001, a federal judge in Albany, New York, fined several members of a family $80,000 for leaving an unmarked paper bag in the lobby of a women's clinic (the providers thought it was a bomb); standing in front of cars trying to enter the clinic's parking lot; offering to pay for the personal information of clinic doctors; and leaving posters outside of the director's home that said she had the blood of babies on her hands.[285] The decision drew the approval of New York State Attorney General Eliot Spitzer.

"It's a complete win in the sense [that] the legal precedent we got was precisely what we wanted," Spitzer said of the ruling.[286]

RICO, BLOCKADES, AND A DECISION
SEVENTEEN YEARS IN THE MAKING

But the issue of penalties for such activity under the RICO statute remained an open question. In 2003, the case of *Scheidler v. National Organization for Women*,[287] begun seventeen years earlier, made its way back to the United States Supreme Court. In the years between the 1994 decision and the parties' reappearance in 2003, a seven-week trial had taken place, at the end of which a six-member jury found that the antiabortion protesters had violated the RICO statute.

"By answering a series of special interrogatory questions, the jury found...that petitioners' alleged 'pattern of racketeering activity' included 21 violations of the Hobbs Act;[288] 25 violations of state extortion law; 25 instances of attempting or conspiring to commit either federal or state extortion; 23 violations of the Travel Act,"[289] the Court noted in summing up the earlier proceedings of the case.[290]

The jury awarded the National Women's Health Organization of Delaware, Inc. $31,455.64 and the National Women's Health Organization of Summit, Inc. $54,471.28. Under Section 1964(c) of the RICO statute, the damages were trebled. The district court also entered a permanent and nationwide injunction "prohibiting petitioners from obstructing access to clinics, trespassing on clinic property, damaging clinic property, or using violence or threats of violence against the clinics, their employees, or their patients."[291]

The Seventh Circuit Court of Appeals affirmed, rejecting Scheidler's and the other appellants' claims that the protesters had not obtained "property" within the meaning of the Hobbs Act. The National Organization for Women argued during the trial and previous phases of the case that the rights of women to seek medical services at clinics and the rights of clinics to provide medical services and to do business was "property" for purposes of the Act. The Seventh Circuit agreed, noting that it had "repeatedly held that intangible property such as the right to conduct a business can be considered 'property' under the Hobbs Act."[292]

Also dismissed by the Seventh Circuit was Scheidler and the other appellants' assertion that the protesters had not actually "claimed" the property. Rather, they had merely forced their challengers "to part with it." The Seventh Circuit noted in response to this argument that "'as a legal matter, an extortionist can violate the Hobbs Act without either seeking or receiving money or anything else. A loss to, or interference with the rights of, the victim is all that is required.'"[293]

Scheidler and the other protesters appealed. Again, the United States Supreme Court granted *certiorari*, and upon review, reversed the Seventh Circuit's ruling. "There is no dispute in these cases that petitioners interfered with, disrupted, and in some instances completely deprived respondents of their ability to exercise their property rights. Likewise, petitioners' counsel readily acknowledged at oral argument that aspects of his clients' conduct were criminal. But even when their acts of interference and disruption achieved their ultimate goal of 'shutting down' a clinic that performed abortions, such acts did not constitute extortion because petitioners did not 'obtain' respondents property," the Justices wrote.

"Petitioners may have deprived or sought to deprive respondents of their alleged property right of exclusive control of their business assets," the majority conclude, "but they did not acquire any such property. Petitioners neither pursued nor received 'something of value from' respondents that they could exercise, transfer, or sell.[294] To conclude that such actions constituted extortion would effectively discard the statutory requirement that property must be obtained from another, replacing it instead with the notion that merely interfering with or depriving someone of property is sufficient to constitute extortion."[295]

"Because petitioners did not obtain or attempt to obtain respondents' property, both the state extortion claims and the claim of attempting or conspiring to commit state extortion were fatally flawed," the Court held. "The 23 violations of the Travel Act and the 23 acts of attempting to violate the Travel Act also fail. These acts were committed in furtherance of allegedly extortionate conduct. But we have already determined that petitioners did not commit or attempt to commit extortion.

And finally, "[b]ecause all of the predicate acts supporting the jury's finding of a RICO violation must be reversed, the judgment that petitioners violated RICO must be reversed. Without an underlying RICO violation, the injunction issued by the district court must necessarily be vacated. We therefore need not address the second question presented—whether a private plaintiff in a civil RICO action is entitled to injunctive relief under 18 U.S.C. Section 1964," the Court held.[296]

ACCEPTANCE OF VIOLENCE BEGINS TO CHANGE

Although incidents of violence against abortion clinics, doctors and providers continue to occur, the tide of the acceptance of such tactics appears to have passed and the movement—along with many of its leaders—seems to have fallen out of favor. State and local governments no longer seem as willing to tolerate violence, for example, caselaw suggests that supporters of abortion have learned, not only how to fight back, but also how to force politicians to respond. This is despite the fact that the United States Supreme Court has struck down the use of the RICO statute against violent antiabortion protesters.

Attorney General John Ashcroft, a staunch antiabortion foe, reportedly ordered United States marshals to protect Dr. George Tiller, a Kansas doctor who performs abortions, for example, after criticism from women's groups and health care providers in July of 2001. Dr. Tiller, who was shot twice in 1993, was targeted, according to media reports, as part of a commemoration of the 1991 "summer of mercy" rally in Wichita, during which nearly 3,000 protesters were arrested.[297]

But the issue of antiabortion-related violence was making nation headlines again nine months later, this time in connection with stalled bankruptcy legislation five years in the making. In addition to sweeping changes to existing law, one version of the proposed bill sought to bar abortion opponents—convicted of offenses related to violence, harassment, or intimidation towards providers and ordered to pay judgments—from using bankruptcy procedures to discharge these debts.[298]

"...[A] number of prominent abortion foes have used the bankruptcy laws for that purpose, among them Randall Terry, the founder of Operation Rescue," reporter Philip Shenon wrote in April of 2002 as the stalemate over two dueling bills—one with the provision reportedly put forth by liberal and pro-choice leaders in the Senate; one without it supported by antiabortion opponents in the House—continued. "In declaring bankruptcy in 1998, Mr. Terry said he wanted to avoid paying debts, which then totaled more than $1 millions, 'to those who would use my money to promote the killing of the unborn.'"[299]

Among the most vocal opponents to the provision was Illinois Republican Representative Henry Hyde, who reportedly called the measure "bad policy" that "single[d] out a narrow class of debtors for punishment."[300] "This is a matter of principle," Representative Hyde reportedly said. "There's no reason to have something so lopsided in this legislation."[301]

Of specific concern to Hyde was that the provision did not include an exception for "peaceful opponents of abortion" and, thus, could have a "chilling effect on expressive conduct that is protected by the First Amendment.'"[302] Hyde is the author of the Hyde Amendment,[303] which foreclosed the possibility of abortion to an entire class of poor women, critics say.

Arguing just as vehemently in response as part of an often heated debate, however, was Vermont Senator Patrick Leahy, who is said to have "...angrily reminded his colleagues that he had been designated as a target for violent attacks, even assassination, on a website [*The Nuremberg Files*] run by abortion opponents who later declared bankruptcy to avoid paying court judgments." [304]

"I don't take *The Nuremberg Files* lightly, and I don't take this issue lightly. This is not sticks-and-stones. This loophole has to be closed," Senator Leahy reportedly argued.[305] The bill including the provision ultimately failed to pass, a spokesman for Senator Leahy's office said.

AFTER THE VIOLENCE;
THE DECLINING AVAILABILITY OF ABORTION:
Where Choice Exists—The Procedure May Not

Despite the decline in violence, the hostility of the 1980s and 1990s aimed at abortion clinics and providers appears to have had the desired effect. Researchers and even some clinic operators suggest that a decline in the number of abortion providers nationwide is due, at least in part, to the harassment and violence.

There is the anecdotal evidence to support this point. Robin Rothrock has reportedly run a women's clinic in Shreveport, Louisiana, for more than two decades. And she thinks about giving it up often, because for "almost every day [that the clinic has been open] she has been practically under siege by a Christian group (run by an ex-Marine who thinks he's a prophet)," writer Robert Sullivan reports.[306]

Their numbers have plummeted. In all of Minnesota, for example, there are only four public abortion clinics. Its neighbor, Wisconsin, is doing a little better: that state has five public clinics; three of them in Milwaukee, where there used to be twelve.

In just four years—between 1996 and 2000—the number of abortion providers in the United States fell 11 percent, from 2,042 providers to 1,819, according to researchers at the Alan Guttmacher Institute.[307] The national rate of abortion for that same period fell only 5 percent[308] (decreases among the rates of individual states are harder to register, due largely to women traveling out of state to have abortions).[309] By 2000, more than 85 percent of the counties in America had no abortion provider at all though more than a third of all women of childbearing age live in these areas.[310]

Clinic consolidations, as well as increasing legal constraints and stringent new zoning, licensing, and inspection requirements have contributed to the decline in the number of providers nationwide.[311] This has led to an even greater impact perhaps than might otherwise be understood: only 7 percent of all abortions were performed in nonclinical facilities in 2000.[312] In other words, more than 90 percent of all abortions are performed in clinics, hundreds of which faced blockades or became targets of arson, bombings, and other violence during the 1990s.[313]

"Despite the reported decline in severe forms of harassment of abortion providers,[314] several high-profile incidents of violence have occurred since 1996," argue Lawrence Finer and Stanley Henshaw in *Perspectives on Sexual and Reproductive Health*.[315] "These incidents may have increased providers' fear of physical threats and, thus, contributed to the drop in the number of providers."[316]

The decline in providers was concentrated primarily among facilities "with small caseloads," with the greatest impact felt among women in rural areas and small towns, Finer and Henshaw note. By 2000, abortion providers could be found in only three percent of "nonmetropolitan" counties, most of them performing no more than 400 abortions overall.

But there was also a decline among providers in metropolitan areas. Though the Northeastern and Western parts of the United States have higher rates of abortion and greater access to providers than, for example, the Midwest and the South,[317] only 30 percent of all metropolitan counties had a "large abortion provider" in 2000.[318] And "86 of the country's 276 metropolitan areas and almost all nonmetropolitan areas had no abortion provider," according to Finer and Henshaw.[319]

But violence or the threat of violence was not the only reason for the number of abortion providers. According to the Centers for Disease Control in Atlanta, which tracks abortion rates on a continual basis, the number of legal abortions performed across the United States reached 1.61 million in 1990.[320] But for every year after that, the number fell, until in 1996, the number of legal abortions performed across the United States was an estimated 1.37 million,[321] a trend that reportedly left clinics scrambling for clients.[322]

The decline "probably reflects the decreasing rate of unintended pregnancies; reduced access to abortion services; and changes in contraceptive practices, including increased use of contraception, particularly an increased use of condoms among young women," C.D.C. researchers suggest.[323] In addition, some of the consolidations or closings were also likely due to the medical finance crisis that shuttered hospitals and outpatient clinics throughout the 1990s, a circumstance that caught even nonabortion provider facilities in the undertow.

HOSPITALS, THE CATHOLIC CHURCH, AND ABORTION POLICY

Abortion services are accessed by women of all religions. The majority of Americans—roughly 56 percent—identify themselves as Protestants, compared to 28 percent who identify themselves as Catholic, and two percent who identify themselves as Jewish.[324] These percentages are similar among women who chose to have abortions in 2000: 43 percent identified themselves as Protestant, while 27 percent identified themselves as Catholic.[325] And yet, it is the Roman Catholic Church that plays a major role in abortion policy around the world and in hospital administration in the United States.

"...[T]he Catholic Church is the only world religion with a seat in the United Nations," writes Marquette University Professor of Ethics, Daniel Maguire. "From its unduly privileged perch in the United Nations, the Vatican, along with the 'Catholic' nations—now newly allied with conservative Muslim nations—managed to block reference to contraception and family planning at the 1992 United Nations conference in Rio de Janeiro. This alliance also delayed proceedings at the 1994 United Nations conference in Cairo and impeded any reasonable discussion of abortion."[326]

During the 1990s, the Catholic Church exercised a similar will in America.[327] In a move toward diversity perhaps, or in an effort to end the practice of abortion once and for all, the Church, through various organizations, began buying up hospitals and health care systems across the United States. In terms of specific numbers, since 1990, there have been more than 120 reported mergers between Catholic and non-Catholic hospitals and health care facilities.[328]

By 2000, it was estimated that "four out of ten of the largest health-care systems in America" were controlled by the Roman Catholic Church,[329] serving an estimated 85 million patients, many of them non-Catholics, and most without any idea of the hospital-Church connection unless or until they sought a type of care that was against Church doctrine. "When a Catholic hospital merges with a non-Catholic hospital, the Catholic partner often insists that religious doctrine be one of the terms of the deal," 60 Minutes correspondent Morley Safer reported in December 2000.[330]

For female patients of childbearing age at most facilities that means no access "to family planning, [or] to contraceptives. They would not have access to condoms or to education about condoms. They would not have access to sterilization (currently the leading method of birth control for adult women who have already had all of the children they want). They would not have access to most treatments for fertility. And they would not have access to abortion, although abortion is the least of the services that we are worried about," argues Frances Kissling, president of Catholics for a Free Choice, an advocacy group that wants to keep Church doctrine out of medicine.[331]

After Elliot Hospital in Manchester, New Hampshire, merged with Catholic Medical Center, for example, the hospital's stated policy of conducting abortion where medically necessary became increasingly difficult to negotiate, according to Kathleen Hutchins, a former patient at the facility, and her doctor, Wayne Goldner.

When Hutchins was 12 weeks pregnant, her water broke. After examination by two doctors, the fetus was given a two percent chance of survival. Hutchins was advised of the possibility of infection or the need for a hysterectomy—perhaps even death if she continued the pregnancy. Hutchins decided to seek an abortion. But her doctor's initial request for permission to perform the procedure was denied by the head of his department, who reportedly told Hutchins's doctor that she did not think the church and the hospital board would approve.

It was suggested that Hutchins should go elsewhere for the procedure. But the nearest hospital was 80 miles away, and according to her doctor, Hutchins had no way to get there. It was a problem Finer and Henshaw identified in their research when they noted that "[f]or most American women, access to abortion is directly tied to where they live."[332] But denying access to these women is exactly what the church intends, argues Kissling.

"In many of the mergers, what the Catholic partner has said to the non-Catholic partner is, 'Don't worry. If the pregnancy is threatening to the life of the woman, of course we will provide the abortion.' But I know of several cases where doctors have said, 'My patient must have an abortion,' and they've said, 'no, no these women have not yet reached a life-threatening stage,'" according to Kissling.[333]

According to Father Michael Place, head of the Catholic Health Association in America, who was interviewed at the time that the story broke, the Church's position is simply that "[w]e cannot attack human life. Either life of the unborn or the life of someone at the end of life. And we honor our understanding of human sexuality."[334]

It is an inflexible definition, Hutchins's doctor, Wayne Goldner, suggests.

"When I made it clear to [Elliot Hospital officials] that I would make [Hutchins's situation] public knowledge, they called me up and said, 'Can you change the diagnosis so we can get her in under something else?' I said, 'Are you asking me to lie?' 'Well, not lie. Just change it a little bit. Say that she's infected. Does she have a fever?' I said, 'No,' 'Isn't she infected?' I said, 'No.' I said, 'She's not. I'm not going to alter the records so you can slip this around the church policy.' But that's what I was asked to do."[335]

Attorneys for the hospital defended their handling of the case, suggesting that Hutchins's doctor failed to follow hospital policy in having his diagnosis confirmed.[336] Dr. Goldner argued in response to this allegation, however, that the diagnosis had been confirmed as medically necessary by four of his partners. In the end, Dr. Goldner reportedly hired a car and driver himself to take Hutchins the 80 miles to another hospital. Still, the controversy generated so much protest that the merger was reportedly dissolved. Many other mergers have stood, however.

Stories of mergers and statistics detailing shrinking numbers fueled speculation that the number of abortion providers is likely to decline even further in the next decade. A 1997 survey of doctors who perform abortions found that more than half—57 percent—were 50 or older.[337]

And yet, there are signs of hope. Despite a decade-long campaign of violence and a sustained effort to end legal abortion, a 2000 survey conducted by the National Abortion Federation found that "from 1992 to 1998, ob-gyn residency programs reporting routine first trimester abortion training increased almost four-fold, to 46 percent from 12 percent."[338]

Roughly half of all medical residency programs in the United States offered training in the performance of abortion procedures in 2002, with schools in California, Massachusetts, Michigan, and New York adding programs in recent years and programs reportedly under development in twenty other schools.[339] This renewed interest may be the end result of enormous efforts by supporters of abortion, who have lobbied for the preservation of the protocol in teaching programs.

But even so, the greatest challenge to abortion remains. That "challenge" is a grassroots campaign that has made its way into boardrooms and state houses across the country, shaping policy and determinedly rewriting the law in an effort to go around, as often as it directly challenges, *Roe v. Wade*.

"The combined efforts of grassroots groups throughout the country have already succeeded in implementing a barrage of state restrictions," Sullivan notes. "On the East Coast, New Hampshire Right to Life persuaded state legislators to pass a parental-notification law, the first restriction on abortion in the state since the nineteenth century. In the Midwest, Minnesota Concerned Citizens for Life worked with state legislators to slip a law mandating a waiting period for abortions into a seemingly benign bill repealing a ban on circuses coming to town at the same time as the state fair. Only a few of these attempts make news, like the partial-birth abortion measure, which didn't pass but was a major contributing factor in nudging public opinion in the antiabortionists' favor. Others that have passed do not seem overtly anti-*Roe v. Wade* but in fact are—like the 2002 Born-Alive Infants Protection Act, granting federal rights to human fetuses 'born alive' at any stage of development. Pro-life groups vigorously supported the law; pro-choice groups, for the most part, just watched," Sullivan argues.[340]

THE BATTLE THAT NEVER ENDS:
Abortion and Where Women Stand

On January 22, 2003—the thirtieth anniversary of the United States Supreme Court's decision in *Roe v. Wade*—Cristina Page, a program director with the National Abortion and Reproductive Rights Action League, joined Amanda Peterman, media director for Right to Life of Michigan, in urging that the "tactics" previously used by both sides in the struggle to maintain—or overturn—*Roe* be "reexamine[d]."[341]

"The slogans are old, the battle is tired," Page and Peterman wrote, noting their births in the early 1970s. "Those older than us have said that Americans born after *Roe v. Wade* cannot truly comprehend what is at stake. Maybe that is so. But we think we have a fresh understanding of how to achieve real progress."[342]

With that in mind, Page and Peterman argued that while foes of abortion and opponents of foes accept that they may "never find a solution to the most fundamental disagreements [they] hold…[b]oth sides must unite publicly against the use of violent measures in the movement and must isolate extremists who employ them. We can no longer tolerate inflammatory terms that serve only to divide us further and create conflict."[343]

These are the best hopes of idealistic women, which may seem prophetic at this moment in time, because what many women's rights activists already know is that the violence of the mid- to late-1980s has, in fact, largely come to a close. Replacing it instead in this battle that never ends in recent years has been a campaign designed to dismantle women's rights by stealth. And though the tactics of this "kinder, gentler" movement may largely have gone unnoticed by the younger public, they are just as deliberate and inflammatory as they ever were. It is just that today, instead of bomb threats, blockades, and vandalism, the fight to shatter women's rights is more often presented in the form of bills, laws, and executive orders.

OPPOSING *ROE* BY STEALTH

Since the mid-1990s, when the tide began to turn and it seemed clear that opponents of abortion would not win an outright challenge to *Roe v. Wade* in the nation's courts, a new kind of effort to defeat the precedent has been afoot—one whose goals are just a determined; its energies just as endless. One whose strategies are quieter. But just as hostile.

Today, politicians, lawmakers and sometimes even judges opposed to the enduring precedent—which remains the prevailing law—have taken to mocking it outright in public or simply pretending that it does not exist when they rule or draft new laws. On January 5, 2001, for example, the Kentucky Senate adopted a resolution mourning the anniversary of the 1973 decision.[344] Seventeen days later, pro-choice politicians in California began circulating a bill in that state's legislature urging President Bush and the United States Congress to "take necessary action to preserve the integrity" of *Roe v. Wade*.[345]

But there is a no reason to believe that will happen. Rather, the opposite seems far more likely. White House Chief of Staff, Andrew Card, has said he does not believe President George W. Bush "feels that he'll be able to eliminate abortions," because although doing so is "a high moral priority" for the President, it does not appear to be a "high public-policy priority."[346] Even so, President Bush has made his views on the issue abundantly clear, stating publicly on a number of occasions that he believes there are "too many abortions" and filling many of the positions in his cabinet with like-minded individuals. But what does "too many abortions" mean in terms of real numbers?

That the procedure is "commonplace" is understood, though it is less widely available than it once was in the United States. In addition, "[a]bortion is taken so much for granted in America today that most women [informally] surveyed by a group of clinics in Washington State did not know that it had ever been illegal," Kate Zernike wrote in January 2003.[347] Despite the rancor that generally surrounds it, in medical terms abortion is not really an "epidemic." Nor is it used by women in America as an easy alternative to birth control, as is often alleged.

On average worldwide, there are only 35 abortions per every 1,000 women of childbearing age each year (40 percent of them illegal).[348] Spain has one of the lowest rates with 5.7 abortions per every 1,000 women between the ages of 15 and 44, while Vietnam has one of the highest, with 83.3 abortions per every 1,000 women. Romania, with 78 abortions per every 1,000 women of childbearing age, was next followed by Cuba, with 77.7 abortions per 1,000 women, and Russia, with 68.4 abortions per every 1,000 women of childbearing age.[349]

By contrast, the rate among women of childbearing age in the United States is roughly 21.3 abortions per 1,000 women, for a total of 1.31 million, down five percent from the total in 1996.[350] But these numbers—even as they fall—remain the ammunition of antiabortion opponents as often for socio-political, as for the religious, reasons. And the convictions they carry—whatever they may be—have long been used to justify everything from violence to "legislative intervention" intended to correct the travesty of Roe v. Wade.

Of course the motivations are often tangled. From a cultural as well as a religious perspective, the choice of abortion moves women away from the traditional role of caretaker, mother, and submissive partner. For centuries this has been the social ideal for women, which may explain why overcoming it, even today, appears to be a factor for some women.[351]

According to the Alan Guttmacher Institute, "[o]n average, women give at least three reasons for choosing abortion: three-fourths say that having a baby would interfere with work, school, or other responsibilities; about two-thirds say they cannot afford a child; and one-half say they do not want to be a single parent or are having problems with their husband or partner."[352]

But even in these days of heightened sexuality and elevated freedoms, there are those who would argue that women should not be allowed the make the choice of abortion. "The seed of man should not be destroyed simply because a woman wants to further her career or her education," Norma McCorvey—formerly known as "Jane Roe" of the landmark *Roe v. Wade* decision.[353] According to media reports, McCorvey had not furthered her own education at the time of the ruling. Media reports have described her as "an unskilled worker" who had previously dropped out of high school. Since 1995, after she was baptized in the swimming pool of Reverend Flip Benham, of Operation Rescue, McCorvey has been an outspoken critic of abortion.[354]

And though her presence on the "other side of the line" adds an unexpected twist to the debate, her comments are anything but unexpected. Women who choose abortion have long been demonized and accused of being "heartless," "selfish," "evil," and as "baby killers"—violent themselves. And yet, negative characterizations of this kind set fire to one of the troublesome truths of the debate: half of all women who choose abortions are mothers. It is true that 75 percent of all abortions are among women who have never been married.[355] But more than 60 percent of all abortions are among women—some of them married, some unmarried—who already have one or more children.[356]

Of course, the dynamics of the public debate are often different from the dimensions of the private battle. And though statistics are often thought of as troublesome endnotes in the arena of public relations, the demographic profile of who chooses to have abortions has long informed the strategies used by antiabortion opponents to challenge that choice. Research suggests, for example, that more than half of all women who have abortions in the United States are younger than 25. In terms of breakdown, a third of all abortions are among women between the ages of 20 and 24 years old. Nineteen percent are among teenagers.[357]

It is any wonder, then, that the efforts of antiabortion opponents in recent years have included a push for new parental consent and informed consent laws in addition to legislation making it a crime for adults to take a minor out of the state to have an abortion where the adult is not the minor's parent?

By 2003, thirty-two states had passed parental consent or notification laws for minors seeking abortion.[358] The assumption of antiabortion lawmakers in pushing these measures, of course, is that a young woman's parents may not give a minor child consent to have an abortion. But research suggests that almost half—45 percent—of minors who have abortions tell their parents, and 61 percent undergo the procedure with the knowledge and consent of at least one parent.[359] "The great majority of parents support their daughter's decision," researchers at the Alan Guttmacher Institute suggest.[360]

Of course, the "choice" of young women is not the only right assailed. In addition to efforts to obstruct the ability of minors to choose abortion, efforts were made to hobble choice by limiting the number of women who can pay. What makes this an ironic choice today is that research suggests that "[i]ncreasingly, the common denominator for women having abortions is poverty," reporter Kate Zernike wrote in commemorating the 30th anniversary of the decision.[361]

In 1977, Congress expressly prohibited the use of federal Medicaid funds for abortions with the exception of those procedures deemed medically necessary to save the life of the mother.[362] In ruling on the constitutionality of a similar provision on the state level, the United States Supreme Court held in *Beal v. Doe*,[363] "...that Pennsylvania's refusal to extend Medicaid coverage to nontherapeutic abortions is not inconsistent with Title XIX.... We make clear, however, that the federal statute leaves a State free to provide such coverage if it so desires."

Pennsylvania did not desire to do so. And although the issue was repeatedly litigated over the next two decades, by 2000, only seventeen states still used public funds to cover the costs of abortions for indigent women.[364] Only 14 percent of all abortions performed in the United States today are paid for with "public funds," provided solely by the states in nearly all instances.[365]

Requiring consent and draining the potential pool of money to pay for abortions have proved effective tools. But the most effective form of attack in recent years has involved words and the changing of "fetuses" into "unborn children." In 2001, legislators in ten states proposed the inclusion of "unborn children"—fetuses under *Roe v. Wade*—in criminal homicide, assault, and/or manslaughter statutes.[366] Many states have historically allowed third parties to be held criminally liable for harm to viable fetuses.[367] Others have acknowledged fetal rights in the domestic violence context,[368] and still others have provided that lawsuits could be maintained in some instances of fetal harm.[369] But the language of these and other statutes historically, and especially after *Roe v. Wade*, was "fetuses."

In the last decade, however, the language of these and other statutes has been changed or amended to reach "unborn children" as opposed to "fetuses" in a deliberate attempt, in some cases, to thwart *Roe*. At the start of 2001, for example, a Wisconsin lawmaker proposed a bill that would increase penalties for intentionally destroying, or consenting to the destruction of, one's "unborn *quick* child,"[370] while Montana lawmakers proposed cause of death listings on fetal death certificates.[371] At about the same time, legislators in Massachusetts were set to consider prohibiting abortions sought solely on the basis of the sex of the fetus.[372]

And when all else fails, the final line of attack appears to be to simply attempt to replow well-tilled soil as though *Roe v. Wade* and its progeny did not exist. In August of 2002, women across the United States watched astounded as a Pennsylvania judge wreaked havoc on the life of a 22-year-old woman, who was nine-weeks pregnant, sought an abortion, and had to argue about it in court—despite the precedent of *Roe v. Wade*.

Tanya Meyers reportedly dated John Stachokus for less than a year. When they broke up, Meyers was pregnant, but planned to have an abortion. But the afternoon before the morning of her appointment, Stachokus filed suit, seeking to prevent her from having the procedure. In papers filed with a Pennsylvania court, Stachokus argued that his "...pre-born child at this moment is a living being whose heart beats, who moves in Tanya's womb, who had brain activity, and fully functioned organ systems. He or she is a living human being.'"[373]

That was good enough for Judge Thomas F. Burke Jr., of the Court of Common Pleas in Wilkes-Barre. On July 29, 2002, Judge Burke entered a temporary restraining order, prohibiting Meyers from having an abortion. Two days later, another judge, Michael T. Conahan, held a hearing to reconsider the order. Judge Conahan allowed the order to stand.[374] Attorneys for Meyers tried to have the case heard by the Pennsylvania appeals court as well as the Pennsylvania Supreme Court. Their requests were declined.[375]

As a state, Pennsylvania has a long history of antiabortion activism. Four major decisions issued by the United States Supreme Court between 1977 and 1992 involved the constitutionality of abortion laws drafted by Pennsylvania lawmakers with the clear intent of—if not foreclosing the precedent of *Roe v. Wade*—then certainly of limiting it.[376] The final decision in this series of challenges was issued in 1992. *Planned Parenthood of Southeastern Pennsylvania v. Casey*, as the case was known, involved challenge to five provisions of the Pennsylvania Abortion Control Act.[377]

Coming at the end of a long line of challenges, the decision was expected by antiabortion forces to mark the end of legal abortion in the United States. Instead, a majority of the Court held that the "essential holding of *Roe v. Wade* should be retained," though further restrictions were deemed permissible.[378] The majority then upheld four of the five provisions of the Pennsylvania law, striking down only one: a proposed measure that would require married women to sign forms indicating they had told their husbands of the intent to have abortions. That is the law of the land, and it formed the basis of the challenge brought by attorneys on behalf of Meyers.

"If you don't have to notify a spouse [of the intent to have an abortion, as a matter of clearly established law], you certainly don't give a veto right to a former boyfriend,'" said Linda Rosenthal, of the Center for Reproductive Law and Policy, in commenting on the decisions by Judges Burke and Conahan.[379]

By contrast, Stachokus's attorney reportedly argued that the law was "unsettled in this area" and that he thought his client had a strong case. "What's at issue here," said John P. Williamson, Mr. Stachokus's attorney, "is a child's life. A baby doesn't realize that all these lawyers are trying to abort it.'"[380] Under *Roe*, that "baby" is a fetus.

Given the precedent of *Planned Parenthood of Southeastern Pennsylvania v. Casey*, courts in several states and jurisdictions, including Pennsylvania, have rejected similar suits and issues.[381] And eventually—after a week of delays—so did Judge Conahan, who reportedly found both Meyers and Stachokus "credible and sincere."

But as a matter of law, Meyers "has a constitutional right to have an abortion," Judge Conahan declared. "This right is not subject to being vetoed by a woman's husband or partner. Neither an ex-boyfriend nor a fetus has standing to interfere with a woman's choice to terminate her pregnancy.... The delay in her procedure has inflicted significant and extreme emotional distress on Meyers, and she faces increased medical risks due to the delay in her procedure." [382]

"I felt extremely violated," Meyers said. "I still feel violated that my life was made so public. It's just been emotional torture." [383]

On August 5, 2002, an order was issued clearing the way for Meyers to have an abortion. Judge Conahan reportedly gave no reason for the court-ordered delay. But according to Meyers, the court should never have entertained Mr. Stachokus's objection, given the precedents of *Roe v. Wade*, which established a legal right to abortion, and *Planned Parenthood of Southeastern Pennsylvania v. Casey*, which established that while other restrictions may apply, a woman does not need the permission of her husband to have an abortion.

THE LANDSCAPE OF THE NEW DEBATE:
A Conservative Agenda and an Administration Open to It

"For most of the twenty-eight [now thirty] years since the Supreme Court handed down *Roe v. Wade*, the political debate over abortion has remained, essentially, frozen in time. Science has changed, the culture has changed, public attitudes have changed, but the politics of abortion unfold like a Kabuki play, stylized and familiar . . .," reporter Robin Toner argues. [384]

"Thirty years after *Roe*, it is still unknown what the...future of abortion in this country will look like when that smoke clears," Roger Smith, of *U.S. News & World Report*, wrote in January 2003. [385]

We may not know what the future of abortion will look like in America. But as long as President George W. Bush remains in the White House, pundits and scholars say they have a few ideas on what the future of the battle to preserve the right to choose abortion may look like. And what they say is that America has seen it before.

Midway through what supporters hope will be his first term, Bush has invited public comparisons not to his father, but to Ronald Reagan. Journalist Bill Keller has argued, for example, that Reagan and Bush "...are alike in their outlooks and career paths, [386] in their agendas of tax-cutting and confrontational deployment of American power, in the ideological mix of their advisors." [387] And, indeed, Bush's list of appointments hasn't strayed far from Reagan's. [388]

Bush is—as Reagan was, political commentators say—an "unashamedly spiritual" man, whose "personal faith...goes well beyond churchgoing." [389] Like Reagan, Bush's use of the "born-again vernacular" has drawn the support of evangelical voters and the religious right. [390] "More than other presidents of recent times, [Reagan and George W. Bush] imbued their civil rhetoric with evangelical themes and suggested that America has a divine assignment...to spread what Reagan called 'the sacred fire of human liberty,'" Keller suggests. [391]

The two also embrace a similar strain of political ideology. Former aides to Reagan who organized tutorials on policy issues to help Bush prepare for appearances during the presidential campaign reportedly saw a resemblance. "On taxes, on education, it was the same. On Social Security, Bush's position was exactly what Reagan always wanted and talked about in the '70s. I just can't think of any major policy issue on which Bush was different," Martin Anderson, an advisor on domestic policy under Reagan, has said.[392]

"I think he's the most Reagan-like politician we have seen in the White House," former Reagan aide Michael Deaver suggests. "I mean, his father was supposed to be the third term of the Reagan presidency—but then he wasn't. This guy is."[393]

And then there are those who suggest that Bush may prove even more politically effective than Reagan—the man who is said to have launched a "revolution." Keller argues, for example, that "[Bush] stands a good chance of advancing a radical agenda that Reagan himself could only carry so far. Bush is not, as Reagan was, an original, but he has adapted Reagan's ideas to new times, and found some new language in which to market them."[394]

But with regard to the reproductive rights of women, this could be a sign of bad things to come. As likely as Bush may be to follow the roadmap laid out by Reagan, it is equally likely that he may decide to go beyond it. Bush has already said that he believes there are "too many abortions," a comment that his policies suggest may apply not only to the United States, but to the world. In other words, it seems likely that as Bush sees it, *all* abortions—regardless of when they occur or for what reason they are sought—simply should not happen. Thus, the question currently facing the nation and women is what the Bush administration may do to push a legal agenda further to foreclose that right. And it is this single issue, some scholars suggest, that may ultimately prove to be the difference between Reagan and the younger Bush.

Despite a public perception generally to the contrary, Reagan was not a "hardliner" when it came to the issue of abortion, Keller argues, though some women's rights advocates would almost certainly have a different perspective. In more than a thousand speeches, Reagan reportedly referred to the procedure only once, Anderson suggests,[395] and then only in justifying its use in cases of rape. As governor of California, Reagan signed "one of the most liberal state abortion laws" and "did little directly" as president to challenge "the essentially permissive" state of the law surrounding *Roe*, Keller says.[396]

One reason for this, Keller says, is that although Reagan was adored by antiabortion groups, his sympathies towards the religious right "bumped up against his hands-off view of government, and against his reading on the public mood." And thus for the most part he left things alone.[397] It is here, however, that predictions, conventional wisdom and reality seem to diverge. Keller suggests that with regard to traditional "culture war" issues—abortion, gay rights, school prayer—Bush, like Reagan, has "managed to champion both 'traditional' values and 'inclusiveness' and when the two are hard to reconcile—on gay rights, for instance—he avoids the issue."[398]

"Bush's concessions to the culture warriors may be meaningful," Keller argues, "but they will not be frontal. He can, and has, cut off aid to family-planning programs overseas. He can, and will, sign a bill outlawing the procedure critics call partial-birth abortion. And he will appoint federal judges whom the right finds congenial."[399]

That may be the prediction. But it does not appear to be the approach Bush has decided to take, though admittedly his movements on abortion appear to alternate between public displays and private concessions, which have tended to rotate these issues between the front and back pages of the nation's newspapers.

REPRODUCTION, ONE MAN'S FAITH, AND THE POLITICS OF "LIFE"

Stem-cell research was among the hot-button issues relating to abortion during the 1990s, the deep emotions swirling around it sparking passage of the Dickey-Wicker Amendment in 1996. That amendment barred the use of federal funding for research leading to the "destruction" of such cells, largely because conservative, religious, and pro-life groups view them as "life."

During the Clinton administration, government officials interpreted the language of the amendment to mean that stem-cell research could go on with federal funding as long as private monies paid for the actual destruction of the cells. With Bush's election to the presidency, religious and conservatives "pro-life" groups reportedly expected him to "appeal to the antiabortion movement by restricting new technologies," including stem-cell research.[400]

But by the time of his inauguration, the scientific debate over whether stem-cell research might lead to a potential cure for Alzheimer's, Parkinson's and other debilitating diseases was in full swing.[401] Joining scientists in support of stem-cell research were some traditionally antiabortion Republicans, family members of sufferers, and Nancy Reagan, an outspoken supporter of such research. Ronald Reagan suffers from Alzheimer's disease.[402]

But conservative leaders have long been troubled by the potential experimentation on "life" that research involving stem cells could lead to. Republican Representative Christopher Smith had reportedly said that "[w]e have to look at these cryogenic tanks as frozen orphanages rather than some kind of material that—that scientists can manipulate for whatever reason they would like to."[403]

In August 2001, in what some deemed an unexpected move, "Bush acknowledged the benefits that researchers sought, and the utilitarian calculations that would allow them to seek those benefits," reported Richard Brookhiser, an author and senior editor for the *National Review*.[404] "If frozen embryos 'are going to be destroyed anyway,' [Bush] said, 'shouldn't they be used for a greater good?'"[405]

But even in the midst of this considerable concession, Bush rejected a proposal by Dr. Bill Frist permitting the use of federal funds for research of some "newly destroyed embryos." The reason for this, Brookhiser suggests, is that "[i]n Bush's view, embryos fell within the definition of human life—a 'sacred gift from our creator.' He decided, however, that the federal government could rightly fund research on existing stem-cell lines, 'where the life-and-death decision has already been made.'"[406]

By contrast, however, Bush has adopted a less "balanced" approach with regard to the issue of abortion, where he has moved swiftly and decisively. On his third full day in office, for example, President Bush reversed the Clinton-administration policy of providing financial support to international family planning groups.[407] "[T]axpayer funds should not be used to pay for abortions or advocate or actively promote abortion either here or abroad," Bush told reporters in announcing the measure.[408]

Critics of the announcement argued that in light of such measures and the appointment of a number of vocally antiabortion politicians to cabinet positions, Bush clearly intended to use the power of the presidency "to restrict a woman's right to choose."[409]

Two months after reversing the Clinton-era policy, Bush seemed to be on the path to proving them right when he issued a second order imposing restrictions on foreign aid to clinics that offer birth control and abortion services in an effort to scuttle a bid by members of Congress to prevent reinstatement of the "Mexico City Policy," so named because the policy was originally announced by the Reagan administration at a 1984 population conference there.[410]

"The president has determined the most effective way to have his Mexico City policy carried out is through the issuance of a presidential memorandum, as opposed to rule-making at a government agency," Ari Fleischer, then-White House press secretary, told reporters.[411]

But the Bush administration's efforts to turn back the clock appear to be global. During a three-day Special Session on Children at the United Nations in May 2002, the efforts of an international panel of delegates to reach an agreement on the language of a declaration outlining global standards on issues ranging from immunization to child labor were stalled by the American contingent. The Americans sought not only to change the language of the proposal before it, but also to change the language of previous declarations to reflect the current administration's religious-based and antiabortion positions. The stall prompted journalist Somini Sengupta to quip that despite all of the issues facing the world's children—war, famine, strife, and exploitation—"[s]ex has proved the most contentious topic."[412]

"The United States delegation, upholding the White House stance against abortion, seeks to amend language arrived at in previous United Nations conferences so that it excludes abortion from the menu of reproductive health services to teenagers," Sengupta reported. "Since in some countries abortion is one of the range of basic health services while in others it is against the law, language from previous conferences contained no proscriptions against it, holding only that in countries where the service is legal, it ought to be safe."[413]

The Bush administration clearly did not intend to fund these services, even where they may be the only safe procedures available to sexually exploited or foolish teenagers. But it is this "blind-eye-in-the-face-of-a-troubling-reality" strategy in a time of HIV that as has led to further comparisons between the Bush and Reagan administrations. Critics of the policy hear echoes of the "Just Say No" chorus of the '80s, offered instead of rehabilitation as the nation tumbled head first into a crack cocaine epidemic that left families ravaged and prisons full. The Bush administration's position on sex among teenagers appears to be just as unrealistically hard-nosed.

BUSH AND THE ABSTINENCE DEBATE

As a presidential candidate, Bush pledged to spend as much on programs that teach sexual abstinence to teenagers as on medical services that include dissemination of contraceptives and information on their proper use. After his election, Bush kept that promise. In February of 2002, Bush proposed a $33 million increase in spending on this package of cherished "abstinence only" education, bringing the total spent on such programs to $135 million."[414]

"Abstinence is the surest way, and the only completely effective way, to prevent unwanted pregnancies and sexually transmitted disease," Bush said on February 26, 2002, in outlining the spending scheme. "When our children face a choice between self-restraint and self-destruction, government should not be neutral."[415]

The Bush Administration has not been neutral. The language of initial proposals appeared to suggest that abstinence and contraceptive education programs would be funded equally with medical services in a coordinated effort to preserve the health and well-being of sexually active minors while attempting—through abstinence education programs—to convince them that sex outside of marriage is not the best choice for a young person to make.

Such an approach would be in line with research on the subject, which tends to suggest that the only reliable way to reduce pregnancy and the spread of sexually transmitted diseases among teenagers is contraceptives in conjunction with abstinence education programs.[416] But in defiance of the research, the Bush administration has made it an either or proposition for clinics and other agencies: accept funding for "abstinence-only" programs and there will be no talk of contraceptives, except to discuss their drawbacks.

It is an aggressive effort on the part of administration officials with grants being given to institutions whose previous work may have focused on the reduction of AIDS via the promotion of condom use. The AIDS Resource Center of Wisconsin, for example, which promoted condom use among teens, received an "abstinence-only" grant from the Bush administration, which the agency accepted. As a result, despite the center's previous commitment to contraceptive-use education, "[t]here won't be any conversation or education about condoms," Mike Gifford, deputy executive director of the center reportedly said.[417] "Our message is going to hone in substantially on the fact that the only 100 percent pure way to protect yourself from HIV is to abstain."[418]

But the new policy has drawn criticism from Republican and Democratic representatives alike. In a letter to Bush, Republican Representative James Greenwood argued that "[t]here is no scientific evidence [suggesting] that 'abstinence only until marriage' programs work." [419] In addition to Greenwood, the letter was signed by California Democrats Lynn Woolsey and Barbara Lee.

But the teenage birthrate has declined in the last decade from 117 pregnancies per 1,000 women between the ages of 15 and 19 to 93 pregnancies,[420] prompting some to suggest that abstinence may be responsible. Analysis of the decline of teen pregnancy rates between 1988–1995, suggest, however, that while about one-fourth of the reduction could be attributed to the "delayed onset of sexual intercourse," three-fourths of the decline "was due to the increased use of highly effective and long-acting contraceptive methods among sexually experienced teenagers."[421]

But even with the numbers in apparent decline, the pregnancy rate among teenagers in the United States—at 950,000 a year—is twice as high as the rate in England, Wales, or Canada and nine times as high as the pregnancy rate among teens in the Netherlands and Japan.[422] Of course, pregnancy is by definition proof of "unprotected sex," which opens the door to the potential exposure to HIV and other sexually transmitted disease.

According to the Centers for Disease Control, sexually transmitted disease is a problem among teenagers. Of the estimated 300 million reported cases of sexually transmitted disease worldwide each year, one in every twenty cases involves an adolescent.[423] One in every four sexually active teenagers in the United States contracts a sexually transmitted disease, research suggests,[424] amounting to an annual total of roughly 4 million infections among teenagers each year.[425]

Abstinence may be the Bush ideal, but American teenagers are having sex. Two-thirds of the nation's young people are believed have had sexual intercourse by the time they graduate high school,[426] and many are doing so without protection.

"Adolescents were more likely than women aged 30 or older to attribute nonuse to ambivalence about contraception or to fear that their parents would find out they were having sex," research compiled by the Alan Guttmacher Institute shows. "Adolescents younger than 18 were the most likely to indicate that unexpected sex was a reason for nonuse, but the least likely to indicate that partner preferences were a reason. Adolescents aged 18 to 19 were more likely than women aged 30 or older to cite concerns about methods as a reason for nonuse. Women in their twenties were less likely than older women to indicate that perceived low risk was a reason for pregnancy."[427]

Still, abstinence is the Bush plan, which has raised the charge among critics that the president remains a zealot at home—toying with the lives of American teenagers—as he attempts to establish himself as a humanitarian abroad. In August 2003, Bush pledged $15 billion over the next five years as part of global campaign against AIDS.[428]

The Bush administration has also proposed promoting marriage as a solution to poverty, spending between $100 and $300 million on experimental programs, media reports suggest.[429] "If marriage is good for communities, why should government be shy about promoting and strengthening it?" Wade Horn, the Bush administration's point man for the initiative, has said.[430] The premise of the initiative is simple: married couples have higher incomes even if they are poor; and children raised by two parents are better off than children raised by one.

Depending upon how one views it, the initiative is either an extreme measure that is out of step with the modern trend of cohabitation and the birth and rearing of children outside of marriage. Or, as Bush administration officials and their supporters view it, the administration's efforts to promote marriage are in line with the greater good of putting American society back on the firm footing necessary to "right" the nation. Marriage, Bush officials argue, is the right thing for families. And there seemed, at least initially, to be something more than words behind the notion.

In 1998, some media outlets began to suggest that America was on the verge of a "marriage boom" in what appeared to be a reversal of a more than 40-year trend toward decline.[431] But these predictions proved prematurely, and over the course of the next six months a picture of the "changing American family" began to emerge. To begin with, the percentage of households made up of married couples with children in the United States fell from 45 percent in the early 1970s to 26 percent in 1998. In addition, more than 4 million unwed couples were living together, and during this same period the number of African American families headed by married couples fell.[432] In the wake of this evolving trend, antiquated laws prohibiting "cohabitation" began to fall.[433]

And by the turn of the millennium, scholars had begun to talk of a "post-marriage" society, where: marriage was no longer the dominant social institution in the United States and one-third of all children were born out of wedlock; the number of "never-marrieds" grew over the course of three decades by 50 percent; and the median age of marriage is now the "oldest in history" (25 for women and 27 for men)—all of it threatening to "unglue" the fabric of society, according to a Rutgers University study.[434]

Among Americans taking the time to tie the knot, the number of interracial marriages grew significantly.[435] There are also more "blended" families in the United States than ever before,[436] and the number of fathers serving as primary caregivers of children has risen sharply in recent years.[437] In other trends, pre- and even post-nuptial agreements have become more commonplace than ever, even for people without wealth,[438] as are engagement ring suits as hopes fizzle.[439] In addition, half of all marriages in America end in divorce.

By 2003, the shift in the American household showed no signs of slowing down. Though the number of married couples in the United States was still higher—at 55.5 million—nationwide, and there are still roughly 2.3 million marriages a year in the United States, increases in the number of unmarried couples continue and the institution of family continues to change.[440] The number of unmarried couples living together in 2003 rose to 5.5 million—nine percent of "coupled" households and five percent of all households.[441] During this same period, same-sex couples accounted for 594,000 "live-in households."[442]

But it is this "trend" toward social *chaos* that has so troubled conservatives.

"It's not a healthy thing. The commitments that go with cohabitation are not as firm or strong as marriage," Allan Carlson of the Family Research Council said in March 2003.[443]

President Bush is clearly of the same mind. The $100 million proposed for the promotion of marriage was, of course, part of a broader social agenda that conservatives and party officials expected to push through starting in January 2003, with the help of then-Senate Majority Leader Trent Lott, when the Republicans regained control of the Senate.[444] But after comments that were widely seen as supportive of racial segregation, Lott was forced to step aside and has maintained a low profile ever since. But even without the public support and political maneuverings of Lott, Bush's "pro-family" initiatives have rolled on.

During the same month that he revealed his spending plan for "abstinence-only" programs, Bush announced the allocation of $100 million for a "faith-based initiative" called the Compassion Capital Fund, and another $10 million to be spent on group homes for pregnant young women.[445] The money would be used to support "faith-based" and antiabortion programs. Though the administration appears to be moving its agenda forward, "faith-based" initiatives have not been without challenge.

In April 2001, a woman filed suit in federal court against the Kentucky Baptist Homes for Children, accusing agency officials of discrimination. Specifically, the woman alleged that she was fired after her supervisors learned she was a lesbian. At about the time that the specifics of the suit were coming to light, a proposal was pending in Congress—that was reportedly being "pushed hard" by members of the Bush administration—that would have allowed religious agencies to consider an employee's "religious practices" in hiring and work-related decisions.

Though religious institutions have traditionally been exempt from discrimination laws, the Bush administration's "faith-based" initiatives funneled federal money to religious agencies and institutions. Thus, the question expected to be asked by attorneys at the trial of the fired Kentucky Baptist Home for Children employee was whether discrimination by religious institutions, where those institutions received federal funding, is permissible.[446] The American Civil Liberties Union assisted the woman in her suit.

Meanwhile, as the debate gained steam in Congress, the proposal drew criticism from gay rights groups, who alleged that the proposal would give religious agencies *carte blanche* to discriminate against gays and lesbians. A coalition of civil rights groups sent the president a letter urging him to "oppose 'government-funded' discrimination in any form."[447] By July of 2001, the administration had begun to back away from a proposal.[448]

And in a blow to the current governmental "no abortion" policy, a federal judge in Massachusetts held in June 2002 that the Department of Defense had violated Maureen Britell's rights by denying medical coverage for the abortion of a fetus with a brain condition that would not have allowed it to survive outside of the womb. Britell was married to an Air Force National Guard captain. When she was 20 weeks pregnant, Britell was told by doctors that the fetus was missing part of its brain and would certainly die outside of the womb. When she sought an abortion, the Civilian Health and Medical Program of the Uniformed Services refused to cover the costs. Britell had the abortion, paying for it herself. In ruling against the Department of Defense, Judge Nancy Gertner, of the federal district court in Boston, ordered the agency to reimburse the couple.[449]

STALWARTS ON THE FRONT LINE—
THE BUSH ADMINISTRATION AND
THE FIGHT FOR THE COURTS

Among the other efforts to further a determinedly "conservative social agenda"—as it has been called by supporters—Bush has sought, as has every president since Franklin Roosevelt, to pack the nation's federal courts with sympathetic or like-minded judges in a move that has been lauded by antiabortion groups hoping to finally see an end to *Roe v. Wade*. Ken Connor, president of the Family Research Council, noted, for example, that he is "'cautiously optimistic'...Bush will be able to overturn *Roe v. Wade* through his appointments to the Supreme Court."[450] It is an effort started two decades ago.

As President, Ronald Reagan and later George Bush Sr., both announced intentions to overturn the precedent of *Roe v. Wade* by government initiated litigation.[451] And like Roosevelt before them, both men understood that the success of the cases the administration hoped to bring would depend upon federal courts that saw the issue as they did. It was during the Reagan-Bush Sr. terms that Justice William Rehnquist, a vocal critic of *Roe v. Wade*, was elevated to Chief Justice, and Justices Antonin Scalia and Clarence Thomas were appointed to the Court and confirmed.

Though there have been no retirements from the United State Supreme Court since he took office, "Bush has nominated two hundred federal judges [and] more than half of them have been confirmed, as will the rest," according to author and legal affairs journalist, Jeffrey Toobin.[452] Bush has said publicly that his two favorite justices are Clarence Thomas and Antonin Scalia,[453]—two of the most conservative (and in the case of Scalia, religious[454]) Justices on the Court. And they appear to be the template for his appointments. In terms of actual numbers, though there has been some noise, only a relative few of the candidates the current President Bush has proposed have been opposed vigorously enough to draw public notice.

In February 2003, Deborah Cook became the subject of scrutiny not only by the Senate, which opposed her nomination to a seat on the Sixth Circuit Court of Appeals. But also by editorial writers, at least one of whom approached discussion of her judicial resume with a mixture of fury and dismay. Adam Cohen wrote in an editorial published in *The New York Times* on February 25, 2003, for example, that "Deborah Cook, a 51-year-old, one-time corporate lawyer from Akron, Ohio, may actually be the most utterly typical of the Bush administration's judicial nominees. Which is why, based on her judicial record, we should all be very worried about the future of the federal courts."[455]

"In eight years on the Ohio Supreme Court, Justice Cook has been a steady voice against injured workers, discrimination victims, and consumers. The court's most prolific dissenter, she frequently breaks with her Republican colleagues to side with big business and insurance companies. Often she reaches for a harsh legal technicality to send a hapless victim home empty-handed," Cohen wrote.[456] "The Bush administration has a long list of Deborah Cooks—

nominees who are not stirring controversy, but who will radically reshape the federal judiciary for a generation."

Another name on that "long list" was Judge Charles Pickering Jr., nominated by Bush administration officials to fill a seat on the United States Court of Appeals for the Fifth Circuit, which sits in New Orleans. Haunting Pickering in his dealings with the Senate, according to media reports, was an incident several years before in Improve, Mississippi, involving a cross-burning and three white men—one of them "feeble-minded;" another a juvenile; and the third a man named Daniel Swan.[457]

In terms of background, Swan and the two other men reportedly got drunk one night and decided to scare a local interracial couple by burning a cross on their lawn. Swan would later call it a "joke." Though Pickering is said to have denounced the cross-burning as "a heinous and despicable act," when the case was before him, Pickering also "referred to it at times as a simply drunken and foolish prank."

But the problem for Pickering before the Senate confirmation committee was the reported suggestion that Pickering undertook "an extraordinary effort to press prosecutors to reduce the sentence of Swan" after Swan was convicted at trial.[458] But Pickering argued in his defense that he sought to reduce Swan's sentence as a matter of justice.

The other two young men involved were sentenced to a few months of home detention after pleading guilty, while Swan was facing several years. Swan was eventually sentenced to 27 months in prison. Several senators opposed Pickering's nomination, suggesting that the leniency he showed toward Swan was evidence of racial insensitivity. They continued to oppose the nomination even after Bush renominated him for the post.

Among the longer battles over a Bush nominee was the near-war over Miguel Estrada. A graduate of Columbia College and Harvard Law School, Estrada clerked for Justice Anthony Kennedy after graduation. And if he had survived the nomination process to take a seat on the District of Columbia Circuit Court, many believed he eventually would have become the first Hispanic to sit on the United States Supreme Court. Three of the current Justices—Justices Antonin Scalia, Clarence Thomas, and Ruth Bader Ginsburg—served on the District of Columbia Circuit Court prior to being appointed to the United States Supreme Court.

Although Estrada was a former federal prosecutor and a one-time assistant solicitor general, senators reviewing his record reportedly found little that was clearly his to go on. "Unlike many nominees, he has never written anything, he has never given speeches, plus he was very vague in his answers to the committee," California's Dianne Feinstein told Toobin during an interview.[459] Faced with what some termed "evasive" answers regarding his feelings about *Roe v. Wade* and unable to gain access to memorandum he created while at the solicitor general's office, a majority of the Democrats on the committee voted to block Estrada's confirmation.[460] The process stalled for months. Estrada would eventually withdraw his name from consideration.

And yet, "...despite the occasional Democratic filibuster, [Bush] appears poised to transform the federal judiciary—which includes 179 appeals judges at full strength—back into an overwhelmingly conservative bench," Deborah Sontag wrote in March 2003. "In the 12 years between them, Ronald Reagan and George H.W. Bush established a Republican majority on every appeals court. Clinton, facing stiff resistance from an opposition Senate for six of his eight years, pushed that back somewhat so that Bush inherited a Republican majority on 8 of the 13 appellate courts, with 3 more poised to swing Republican through his appointments. And those appointments, because they are for life, could reverberate for generations."[461]

Efforts to nominate conservative justices or judicial candidates sympathetic to "the conservative agenda" and opposed to abortion will remain an integral part of the long-range strategy for the Bush administration in the battle to end the practice. A more immediate challenge to be mounted, however, that might allow abortion opponents to further chip away at the beleaguered precedent of *Roe v. Wade* may be found in the resurrection of the so-called "partial-birth abortion" issue, which administration officials clearly had in their sights from the day George W. Bush took office.

In late 2002, Trent Lott "promised a vote next Congress to outlaw a procedure that critics call 'partial-birth abortion,'" wrote Jim VanderHei of the *Washington Post*.[462] As set forth earlier, Lott has all but disappeared from public view since. But the goal remains and the challenge is likely. According to VanderHei, "[t]he House can easily pass the ban on late-term abortions, and it appears that Republicans should have the 60 Senate votes they need to follow suit and send it to the president."[463]

Antiabortion activists reportedly boasted at the time that "at least 62 incoming senators will support the ban, which if enacted is destined for a Supreme Court challenge," according to VanderHei.[464] And that is how it shook out in the fall of 2003, setting the stage for the next clear challenge to the precedent of *Roe v. Wade*.

A DIRECT CHALLENGE AND FAILURE:
The Partial-Birth Abortion Debate

Leroy Carhart probably does not fit most people's image of an "abortionist." A former Air Force Lieutenant Colonel and a physician who happens to perform abortions as part of his practice, Carhart filed suit in a federal district court in 1997, challenging a Nebraska law banning so-called "partial-birth" abortions as violative of the United States Constitution.[465] Abortion supporters and women's rights activists note that "partial-birth" abortion is a political—as opposed to a medical—term intended to inflame the rhetoric of the debate.

At the time of the challenge, Carhart was also the only physician in the state to perform the procedure after 14 weeks. The law provided that "[n]o partial-birth abortion shall be performed in [Nebraska]..., unless such procedure is necessary to save the life of the mother, whose life is endangered by a physical disorder, physical injury, including a life-endangering physical condition caused by or arising from the pregnancy itself."[466]

The statute defined "partially delivers vaginally a living unborn child before killing the unborn" to mean "deliberately and intentionally delivering into the vagina a living unborn child, or a substantial portion thereof, for the purpose of performing a procedure that the person performing such procedure knows will kill the unborn child and does kill the unborn child."[467] Violation of the Nebraska law was a "Class III felony" carrying a possible prison sentence of up to 20 years, a $25,000 fine, and the automatic revocation of a doctor's medical license.[468]

At a trial on the merits, both sides offered expert testimony, which would ultimately serve to convince the district court that the Nebraska law was unconstitutional.[469] The decision was later affirmed by the Eighth Circuit Court of Appeals.[470] But the Nebraska "partial-birth" abortion law was part of a larger movement and would become part of the larger debate over abortion and reproductive freedom.

On October 8, 1997, Congress passed a bill intended to ban so-called "partial-birth abortions." Then-President Bill Clinton vetoed the measure. But that didn't stop the rising effort from gaining momentum. Nearly 90 percent of all abortions in the United States are performed during the first trimester of pregnancy.[471] And the United States Supreme Court has repeatedly held, despite repeated challenges to *Roe v. Wade*, that a woman's right to choose to have an abortion during this early period is fundamental and, therefore, cannot be easily interfered with by the state, though some minor restrictions may apply.

Only ten percent of all abortions are performed after the first trimester.[472] By contrast, the number of D&X procedures nationwide—which is the procedure "partial-birth" abortion laws advocates report to be concerned with—is tiny. In 2000, for example, the total number of D&X procedures was 2,200, one-sixth of one percent of all abortions performed that year.[473] But this exceedingly small number of procedures became the stated focus of antiabortion groups and conservative lawmakers during the late 1990s.

In 1992, the United States Supreme Court upheld the "essential holding" of *Roe v. Wade*—though with restrictions—in *Planned Parenthood of Southeastern Pennsylvania v. Casey*. At that point, *Roe v. Wade* had been the subject of court challenge for nearly two decades. The nation had lived through battles in the street and a determined minority that seemed to rule the majority. What remained in wake of this strife was a thoroughly-litigated, well-defined, and finally settled body of law with regard to the right of women to choose abortion during the first trimester.

After *Casey*, first trimester abortions were "safe." And, thus, the battle turned toward other areas of the *Roe* precedent that were less well-defined. And an obvious next line of attack involved the question of late-term abortions. As a fetus develops, moving closer to viability outside of the womb, the state's interest grows. If certain state-imposed restrictions could be imposed on women and providers during even the "sacred" first trimester, what restrictions might be deemed appropriate during other trimesters? Getting that question before the nation's courts and into the public domain was the goal of abortion opponents during the mid- to late-1990s. And, thus, the so-called issue of "partial-birth abortion" began to make headlines.

That was the first goal.

But there was a second goal, as well as one that was part of a stealth movement that continues today. It is a movement of words and ferocious descriptions intended—as surely as the placards of the 1980s—to turn the "fetuses" so clearly defined by the Court in *Roe* as "nonpersons" into "murdered babies" and brutalized "unborn children." The medical protocol of the procedure was trotted out to help make the point. In the spring of 1993, a description of the "intact dilation and extraction" (D&X)—publicly known as "partial-birth" abortion—was printed in the Congressional Record.[474]

Depending upon the way the procedure is done, the head of a fetus may be crushed to allow it to pass through the cervix. "It is this combination of coming so close to delivering a live child with the death of the fetus by reducing the size of the skull that not only distinguishes D&X from D&E (the most common form of abortion) medically but also causes the adverse public (and legislative) reaction," the Seventh Circuit Court of Appeals explained in 1999 in hearing appeals on the issues.[475]

Doctors who regularly perform abortions say the procedure is rarely performed, but is the safest protocol. The crushing of the bones is necessary, Dr. Carhart explained in *Stenberg v. Carhart*, to reduce "the dangers from sharp bone fragments passing through the cervix" or to "lessen the likelihood of uterine perforations."[476] The procedure also involves less jabbing with surgical instruments into the uterus. But there seemed to be little concern for the health of women on the part of those who oppose abortion.

Although the federal "partial-birth" abortion bill was rejected, the president's veto proved all but inconsequential. On March 12, 1998, the General Assembly of Virginia passed a law modeled on the vetoed congressional bill. On April 13, 1998, that state's governor signed the Virginia Partial-Birth Abortion Act into law. To no one's surprise, it promptly became the subject of a lawsuit. In May of 1998, several abortion care providers and two doctors filed suit in the federal district court for the Eastern District of Virginia, seeking to bar state officials from enforcing the provisions of the Act.

The doctors and abortion providers argued in *Richmond Medical Center for Women v. Gilmore*[477] that the Virginia Partial-Birth Abortion Act was "vague," and therefore, unconstitutional. They argued further that if enforced, the new law would impose a "facially unconstitutional burden on the abortion rights of the women of the Commonwealth of Virginia."[478]

The district court granted an injunction, concluding that the language of the statute was so vague as to possibly prohibit nearly every abortion. Virginia officials appealed to the United States Court of Appeals for the Fourth Circuit, a court so historically right-wing that it has been called "the shrewdest, most aggressively conservative federal appeal court in the nation."[479]

Although the case was before the Fourth Circuit, it was heard by a single judge: the Honorable J. Michael Luttig. A native of Texas, Luttig was found by the law journal, *Judicature*, during an evaluation of six possible Bush nominees to the United States Supreme Court, to be the "second least conservative of the six."[480] But that was a relative finding that tends to suggest more about other Bush nominees than about Luttig. Luttig has been described as "[d]own-to-earth and likable in private" and "intense, austere, and unsentimental" in public. He has reportedly described himself as "a legal 'nerd' [a person who] worships analytical rigor and composes a hard-boiled, sometimes mathematically logical opinion."[481]

Without knowing his personal views on abortion, the structure, calculation, and near-mathematical precision with which Luttig dispatched the issues before the court in *Richmond Medical Center for Women v. Gilmore*, while at the same time crafting a judgment so devastating in its use of "Discovery-Channel-like" imagery, seems to suggest that whatever his views on first trimester abortions, he is no supporter of second or later term abortions. And, thus, the structure of the ruling appears calculated for maximum impact.

Or, it could be, as Justice Breyer offered in the United States Supreme Court's decision in *Stenberg v. Carhart*, that where the legal questions before the Court involve consideration of medical procedures and the termination of potential life, the discussion may at times "seem clinically cold or callous to some, perhaps horrifying to others. There is no alternative way, however, to acquaint the reader with the technical distinctions among the different abortion methods and related factual matters, upon which the outcome of this case depends."[482]

To be fair, Judge Luttig may simply have taken a direct and unsentimental approach to the issues in *Richmond Medical Center for Women v. Gilmore*. Or he may have been showing his true colors. In either event, after just one paragraph reciting the procedural background of *Richmond Medical Center for Women v. Gilmore*, Judge Luttig launches into the graphic language of the Virginia Partial-birth Abortion Act in clear, logical, laudatory fashion.

"The undisputed purpose of Virginia's Partial-birth Abortion Act," he wrote in the decision's second paragraph, "is to prohibit the late-term abortion procedure in which:

> the physician pulls a lower extremity into the vagina and then uses his fingers to deliver the lower extremity and then the torso, followed by the shoulders and the upper extremities. At that point, the skull is lodged at the internal cervical os. Usually the dilation is insufficient for the skull to pass through. At that point, the surgeon slides his or her fingers along the back of the fetus; uses a pair of blunt curved scissors to rupture the base of the skull; and uses a suction catheter to evacuate the contents of the skull and then applies traction to the fetus to remove it from the patient."[483]

Under the Virginia law, a doctor could be prosecuted for performing a "partial-birth abortion" where it was not necessary to save the life of the mother, but only if the doctor knew at the time of the procedure that the mother was not in jeopardy.[484]

As Luttig would interpret it, "...to violate the statute, an abortion provider must (1) deliver an *intact fetus or a substantial portion thereof*, (2) while the fetus is *living*, (3) *into the vagina*. In addition, in provisions barely mentioned by the district court, the statute also provides two critical *mens rea*. Thus, the statute does not prohibit the mere delivery of a living fetus or substantial portion thereof into the vagina, but rather, prohibits only the *deliberate* and *intentional* delivery of such a fetus into the vagina. Indeed, even the intentional and deliberate delivery of a living fetus into the vagina does not violate the statute unless it is performed *for the specific purpose* of performing a procedure the provider knows *will kill* the fetus."[485]

Judge Luttig would offer several pages of thoughtful review of the various mistakes the district court had made in misreading and misinterpreting the statute. But in the end, a fact completely outside of this painstaking analysis, would decide the case. And thus his decision would not be based upon whether or not the Virginia Partial-Birth Abortion Act were legal. Instead, although the doctors and providers had fought for, and won, an injunction asserting potential prosecution arguments, none of the plaintiffs, "according to their own concessions and the findings of the district court, perform this procedure," Luttig noted.[486]

"[T]he plaintiffs, having failed to establish the likely applicability of Section 18.2-74.2 to the procedures they perform, and thus to establish the likelihood that they will ultimately be held to have standing to pursue their action, the stay of the district court's injunction requested by the Commonwealth of Virginia is granted," Judge Luttig held.[487]

STENBERG v. CARHART

The Eighth Circuit Court of Appeals would rule that same year in *Carhart v. Stenberg*,[488] however, that a similarly worded Nebraska "partial-birth" abortion law was unconstitutional.[489] A little over a year later, the Seventh Circuit Court of Appeals in Chicago would consolidate appeals involving challenges to "partial-birth" abortion laws in Illinois and Wisconsin in *Hope Clinic v. Ryan*. The Seventh Circuit would ultimately hold that "...both laws can be applied in a constitutional manner. Whether that will occur depends on state courts, which alone can settle questions about the construction of statutes."[490]

And yet, "[t]o ensure that physicians are not deterred from performing other medical procedures while issues went their way through state tribunals, we hold that both sets of plaintiffs [those in Illinois as well as those in Wisconsin] are entitled to injunctive relief that will limit the statutes application to the medical procedure that each state insists is its sole concern," the court directed further.[491]

It was here that the atypical "abortionist," Leroy Carhart reentered the picture and stepped into the national debate. The federal circuit courts were split on the issue of "partial-birth" abortion. Federal appeals courts in Ohio, Virginia, Nebraska, and Illinois had reached divergent views of the constitutionality and enforceability of state "partial-birth" abortion laws.[492] In the wake of the 1997 Congressional "partial-birth" abortion bill, nearly 39 states passed or begun debating passage of mini-"partial-birth" abortion laws.[493] In an attempt to settle the emerging and conflicting body of law in this area, the United States Supreme Court agreed to hear the appeal filed by Nebraska officials.

"The question before us is whether Nebraska's statute, making criminal the performance of a 'partial-birth abortion,' violates the Federal Constitution, as interpreted in *Planned Parenthood of Southeastern Pennsylvania v. Casey*, and *Roe v. Wade*," Justice Breyer wrote in delivering the June 28, 2000, decision in *Stenberg v. Carhart*[494] on behalf of the majority. "We conclude that it does for at least two independent reasons. First, the law lacks any exception 'for the preservation of the...health of the mother.'[495] Second, it 'imposes an undue burden on a woman's ability to choose a d&e abortion, thereby unduly burdening the right to choose abortion itself."

"Partial-birth" abortion marked the most significant challenge to *Roe v. Wade* since *Casey*, and *Carhart*—clearly a determined, perhaps even stubborn man— would see it through to the United States Supreme Court. In the process, he would stumble into an ancient debate over when life begins and what constitutes a "living unborn child" from a legal perspective. When *Roe v. Wade* was decided, the Court leaned heavily on a trimester system, which marked the phases of pregnancy in clear bright lines.

But the trimester system was effectively retired with the decision in *Casey*. The states should be "free to enact laws to provide a reasonable framework for a woman to make a decision that has such profound and lasting meaning," the majority reasoned in *Casey*.[496] Though the "viability" standard remains, advances in science have blurred the line in the last three decades. In 1970, for example, fewer than half of all babies weighing less than four pounds at birth survived. Today, more than 90 percent of these extreme "preemies" survive with the help of sometimes extraordinary medical intervention.[497]

Of course, what *Casey*, *Carhart*, and all of the other reproductive rights decision of modern times involve—indirectly, if not clearly stated—is religion and arguments of when "life" begins, which has reemerged in recent years as a justification for governmental intervention. As set forth earlier, God has long been part of the debate. And yet, "Christianity," according to Marquette's Maguire, "was born in a world in which contraception and abortion were both known and practiced. The Egyptians, Jews, Greeks, and Romans used a variety of contraception methods, including coitus interruptus, pessaries, potions, and condoms; abortion appears to have been a widespread phenomenon. Knowledge of all of this was available to Christians, and although church leaders tried to suppress it, they were never fully successful."[498]

"The Bible does not condemn abortion," Maguire argues further. "The closest it gets is Exodus 21:22, which speaks to accidental abortion. This imposes a financial penalty on a man who caused a woman to miscarry 'in the course of a brawl.' The issue…is the father's right to progeny; he could fine you for the misdeed, but he could not claim 'an eye for an eye' as if a person had been killed. Thus, as conservative theologian John Connery, S.J., said, 'the fetus did not have the same status as the mother in Hebrew Law.'"[499]

But during the 1930s, Pope Pius is said to have articulated what is commonly thought of today as the "Catholic position" on birth control and abortion.[500] Specifically, in "tidying up" a frayed tradition,[501] the Pope declared that the use of contraceptives was a "sin against nature." But abortion was a "sin against life."[502] Though the political hierarchy has attempted to portray "the Catholic position is an univocal, an unchanging negative wafting through twenty centuries of untroubled consensus," early Christian teachings deemed abortion permissible "unless a 'fully formed' fetus were involved," Maguire argues.[503]

This was due in part to the idea that a fetus did not have a soul until near-viability. "Borrowed from the Greeks, [the theory of ensoulment] taught that the spiritual human soul did not arrive in the fetus until as late as three months into the pregnancy," Maguire notes. "Prior to that time, the life did not have the moral status of person."[504] By the fifteenth century, Christian scholars were expounding on the notion of *crudelitas necessaria*—a necessary cruelty—or what would be called a "partial-birth abortion" today, which was deemed permissible in the later months of pregnancy.[505]

"This idea of delayed *ensoulment* survived throughout the tradition. Saint Thomas Aquinas, the most esteemed of medieval theologians, held this view. Thus the most traditional and stubbornly held position in Catholic Christianity is that early abortions are not murder," says Maguire. "Since the vast number of abortions done today in the United States, for example, are early abortions, they are not murder according to this Catholic tradition. Also, according to this Catholic tradition of delayed ensoulment, all pregnancy terminations resulting from the use of RU-486 would not qualify as the killing of a human person."[506]

Though grounded in medical theory, the underpinnings of *Roe v. Wade* involved a notion not unlike *ensoulment*. In the case of *Roe*, the conclusion of the Court was that fetuses do not become "persons" until perhaps the latter moments of viability. But more properly, until after birth. In deciding *Roe v. Wade*, for example, the Justices held that the word "person" did not have a "prenatal application." The specific language of the Court was that although:

> [t]he Constitution does not define "person" in so many words[,] Section 1 of the Fourteenth Amendment contains three references to a "person." The first, in defining "citizens," speaks of "persons **born** or naturalized in the United States." The word also appears both in the Due Process Clause and in the Equal Protection Clause. "Person" is used in other places in the Constitution: in the listing of qualifications for Representatives and Senators, Art. I, Section 2, Cl. 2, and Section 3, Cl. 3; in the Appointment Clause, Art. I, Section 2, Cl. 3; in the Migration and Importation provision, Art. I, Section 9, Cl. 1; in the Emolument Clause, Art. I, Section 9, Cl. 8; in the Electors provisions, Art. II, Section 1, Cl. 2, and the superseded Cl. 3; in the provision outlining

qualifications for the office of President; Art. II, Section 1, Cl. 5; in the Extradition provisions, Art. IV, Section Cl. 2, and the superseded Fugitive Slave Clause 3; and in the Fifth, Twelfth, and Twenty-second Amendments, as well as in Sections 2 and 3 of the Fourteenth Amendment. But in nearly all these instances, the use of the word is such that *it has application only postnatally*. None indicates, with any assurance, that it has any possible prenatal application.[507]

Fetuses are not "persons" as a matter of law under *Roe v. Wade*. And yet, most of the "partial-birth" abortion laws enacted after 1997—including the Nebraska law before the Court in *Stenberg v. Carhart*—spoke of protecting or preventing the death of "living unborn children" in a shift of language clearly intended—especially when coupled with graphic depictions of how these "children" would die—to untie one of the central holdings of *Roe*.

Although the 5-to-4 majority of *Stenberg v. Carhart* did not speak directly to the issue of "personhood," except to note that while "the Nebraska law applies both to pre- and postviability…, [t]he state's interest in regulating abortion previability is considerably weaker than postviability,"[508] what troubled the majority most was that the language of the act could be interpreted to foreclose all abortions.

"[A] state may promote but not endanger a woman's health when it regulates the methods of abortion[509]…[it] cannot subject women's health to significant risks both in that context, and also where state regulations force women to use riskier methods of abortion," the majority wrote. "Our cases have repeatedly invalidated statutes that in the process of regulating the *methods* of abortion, imposed significant health risks. They make clear that a risk to a women's [*sic*] health is the same whether it happens to arise from regulating a particular method of abortion, or from barring abortion entirely."[510]

That was the first basis for the majority's finding that the Nebraska law was unconstitutional. The second basis was that although the statute purported to reach only later-term abortions, the language, as written, imposed an "undue burden" on the woman's right to terminate her pregnancy before viability, the majority found.

"The statute forbids 'deliberately and intentionally delivering into the vagina a living unborn child, or a substantial portion thereof, for the purpose of performing a procedure that the person performing such procedure knows will kill the unborn child,' Justice Breyer set forth in writing for the majority. "We do not understand how one could distinguish, using this language, between D&E (where a foot or arm is drawn through the cervix) and D&X (where the body up to the head is drawn through the cervix). Evidence before the trial court makes clear that D&E will often involve a physician pulling a 'substantial portion' of a still-living fetus, say, an arm or leg, into the vagina prior to the death of the fetus."[511]

For the majority this was a significant constitutional hurdle. One that could not be overcome by reasoning around it or assertions from the Nebraska attorney general's office that the state did not intend to apply the statute to D&E procedures, the majority held.

"Even if the statute's basic aim is to ban D&X, its language makes clear that it also covers a much broader category of procedures," Justice Breyer wrote. "The language does not track the medical differences between D&E and D&X—though it would have been a simple matter, for example, to provide an exception for the performance of D&E and other abortion procedures.[512] Nor does the statute anywhere suggest that its application turns on whether a portion of the fetus' body is drawn into the vagina as part of a process to extract an intact fetus after collapsing the head as opposed to a process that would dismember the fetus.

"Thus, the dissenters' argument that the law was generally intended to bar D&X can be both correct and irrelevant," Justice Breyer continued. "The relevant question is not whether the legislative wanted to ban D&X; it is whether the law was intended to apply only to D&X. The plain language covers both procedures.... Justice Thomas's dissent...will make clear why we can find no difference, in terms of this statute, between the D&X procedure as described and the D&E procedure as it might be performed. Both procedures can involve the introduction of a 'substantial portion' of a still-living fetus, through the cervix, into the vagina—the very feature of an abortion that leads Justice Thomas to characterize such a procedure as involving 'partial-birth.'"[513]

For these reasons, the Nebraska law was unconstitutional, the majority held.

THE LAW AFTER *STENBERG v. CARHART:*
The Battle Moves to Washington

For many women's rights activists, the majority's decision in *Stenberg v. Carhart* was an enormous victory. But for others it represented little more than another judicial finger in the dike of the continued flood of determined antiabortion activism[514] that would flow on almost as though the Court hadn't spoken. By the spring of 2001, lawmakers in nine states were considering passage of new or amended "partial-birth" abortion laws.[515] Kansas was the only state whose lawmakers were scheduled to discuss repealing the state's "partial-birth" abortion statute at that time.[516]

With regard to Leroy Carhart, who stared down a movement; he has been paying for it ever since. In the months immediately following the decision in *Stenberg v. Carhart*, the building housing the clinic where Dr. Carhart practiced was bought by a real estate partnership that reportedly included Nebraska Senator D. Paul Hartnett. An open opponent of abortion, Harnett admitted that although he "bought the building partly because it was a good business investment," he also "wanted to oust 'the occupant.'"[517] Research suggests that efforts of this kind nationwide have led to the decline in the number of abortion providers in America.[518] And that was clearly the goal of some Nebraska officials.

"It would be one of my greatest accomplishments if he left," Bellevue Mayor Jerry Ryan reportedly said.[519] "I hope no one would give him another facility in Bellevue."[520]

Joining Ryan in the push was a local antiabortion group, which reportedly sent a letter to the mayors of thirteen nearby communities asking them not to allow Carhart to move his practice to their towns.[521] Carhart also filed suit against the University of Nebraska Medical Center's College of Medicine after he was removed from a position as an unpaid member of the faculty. Medical center officials argued publicly that Dr. Carhart was one of 200 volunteer faculty members terminated in an overall pool of 1,300 people let go. But a newspaper source identified only as "a high-ranking university official," speaking on the condition of anonymity, reportedly admitted that the outcry of abortion opponents "influenced the decision."[522] Carhart vowed to fight the dismissal,[523] and in August 2001, the university settled with Carhart, agreeing to reinstate his faculty position and to pay $65,000 in legal fees in exchange for Carhart dropping the suit.[524]

In January 2003, with Republicans poised to take control of the Senate, the debate over "partial-birth" abortion and other restrictive measures began to gain momentum with Senator Bill Frist, a medical doctor, assuming the role that Trent Lott had been expected to play. Frist is seen by many as a "strong ally" of antiabortion groups—the National Right to Life Committee among them, which has reportedly given Frist a "100 percent rating on major votes for the last six years."[525]

Antiabortion forces moved swiftly. By June of 2003, the House had voted 282 to 139 to approve legislation that would outlaw the controversial and contested D&X procedure. A similar measure was approved by the Senate earlier in the year. President Bush voiced his support for the bill and was expected to sign it once it crossed his desk.[526] Some states were quick to respond. By late June, Virginia had passed the nation's first "partial-birth infanticide" law.[527] The measure was immediately challenged, and on July 1, 2003, United States District Court Judge Richard L. Williams blocked enforcement of the law.[528]

In October 2003, "[b]y a vote of 281 to 142, the House approved final passage of a similarly worded federal measure."[529] Should the bill become law, Leroy Carhart said he is ready to go to court again.

"I would have to stop doing abortions between the fourteenth and eighteenth weeks because I'm not able to use the safest medical procedure—the D&X protocol—that we now use. We'd have to use procedures that have greater risks of infertility, infection, and bleeding, and even death, and I just don't feel that that's tolerable," Carhart said in an interview on a *National Public Radio* broadcast October 15, 2003.[530]

Although supporters of the bill argue that its reach is limited to D&X procedures, because the law is written so broadly, it could be interpreted to include D&E procedures, Carhart attorneys argue. Thus, he would have to stop performing D&E abortions in addition to D&X procedures or risk prosecution, Carhart argues. The majority reached a similar conclusion in *Stenberg v. Carhart*.

But even some supporters of the measure concede that it will likely fail, given the precedent of *Stenberg v. Carhart*, unless a Justice on the United States

Supreme Court retires and Bush is allowed to appoint a new one, which could shift the fragile balance of the Court. And yet, even in failure there will be success, they say.

According to antiabortion activist Gary Bauer, "the partial-birth abortion battle inevitably focused attention, from our standpoint, on the humanity of the unborn child. Whether it was diagrams being shown on the floor of the Senate or descriptions in news articles, more and more Americans were forced to think about the fact that at a particular point of gestation, the baby has a heartbeat and so forth. And I think that's been very damaging to the other side and very helpful to the pro-life movement."[531]

Planned Parenthood, the American Civil Liberties Union, and several other groups were poised to file suit as soon as President Bush signed the measure into law, which would keep the issue in the news, some suggest, for the next three to five years.[532] But that hardly seems likely to stop the movement. Conservative lawmakers across the country are engaged in a crusade intended simply to legislate the precedent of *Roe v. Wade* away where court challenge fails.

And the most potent weapon in this campaign has been language.

The "fetuses" of *Roe* have become the "unborn" or "preborn children" of today, *humanized*, largely during the last decade, by state and federal statutes expressly created to challenge *Roe*, albeit it in a quieter fashion. So quiet at times that their efforts have slipped by most Americans. Also all but invisible is that in addition to debating the legal rights of "as-yet-unborn-citizens," some legislators have begun the push for laws protecting "life" from the moment of "fertilization."

Lawmakers in Arkansas, Kentucky, Michigan, and Mississippi proposed amendments to current laws in 2001, for example, intended to protect "viable fetuses" and/or "unborn children" *from fertilization onward* in wrongful death actions,[533] while lawmakers in Arizona and Colorado proposed enhancing penalties for offenses committed against pregnant women.[534] And several versions of a bill were introduced before the Montana legislature in 2001, with language intended to require certified nurses to prepare fetal "death" certificates.[535]

The "essential holding" of *Roe* may have been upheld by the Supreme Court in *Planned Parenthood of Southeastern Pennsylvania v. Casey*, but it seemed to matter little to the nation's lawmakers. With this shift in language has come another dynamic that is worth nothing for women. As unborn fetuses are humanized for purposes of the political and legal debate, the women carrying them are necessarily dehumanized—literally reassigned the status of the lesser of the two in the contest of rights. Nowhere is this more apparent, incidentally, than in the context of a rain of drug and alcohol prosecutions across the United States throughout the 1990s.

On November 5, President Bush signed the Partial-Birth Abortion Ban Act of 2003 into law.[536] Judges in New York and Nebraska immediately blocked enforcement of the law.[537]

HUMANIZING FETUSES—DEHUMANIZING WOMEN:
And the Creation of "Unborn Children"

In 1998, a young and arguably foolish native Canadian woman effected a change in Canadian law. And she did it by sniffing glue. The young woman, pregnant at the time, was sentenced by a Winnipeg court to drug treatment. The case wound its way through the Canadian courts until in 1998, the High Court of Canada ruled that the lower court could not attempt to control a pregnant woman's behavior, even if her actions pose a potential threat to a developing fetus. Feminists hailed the decision as a victory for women, while religious and conservative groups argued that the law should "protect the unborn."[538]

Canada is America's closest neighbor, and a nation with a shared history. Thus, the contrast between the Canadian and the American approach to this issue is worth noting. At about the same time that the Canadian court was declaring that a woman's rights are superior to those of a fetus, South Dakota officials were attempting to fashion the first law in the United States that would require pregnant women found to be using drugs or alcohol while pregnant to undergo mandatory rehabilitation.[539] The leverage of the bill involved classifying the use of drugs and alcohol by a pregnant woman as *child abuse*. In addition to mandatory rehabilitation, the South Dakota law also permitted relatives of pregnant women to have them committed to emergency detox centers for up to two days.

In a further bit of protection, the South Dakota law also reportedly allowed judges to confine pregnant drug and alcohol users for up to nine months, the full period of gestation. The South Dakota law, which took effect on July 1, 1998, was one of several "fetal abuse" statutes considered or passed by state legislatures during the mid- to late-1990s. By 1998, for example, South Carolina and Wisconsin had passed "fetal abuse laws," while legislators in Alaska, California, Delaware, Georgia, Indiana, Maryland, Massachusetts, Minnesota, Tennessee, and Virginia were considering similar bills.[540]

With "children"—as opposed to fetuses—as the rationale, these laws shifted the balance of power in favor of the state and the language of the debate began to change. Developing fetuses so clearly defined by the Justices in *Roe v. Wade* became "unborn children" in need of the protection of the state. "Child abuse" statutes were used to bully or prosecute women in aggressive, heavy-handed campaigns undertaken—as often, no doubt, in the stated effort to "help people"—as part of a larger political effort intended to change the nation's perspective on "unborn children" by taking aim at the easiest targets: poor, downtrodden, drug- and alcohol-addicted women.

For example, Angela M. W. was pregnant. She was also a drug addict who was reported to Wisconsin authorities by her doctor. As a result, on September 5, 1995, the Waukesha County Department of Health and Human Services filed a "Motion to Take An Unborn Child Into Custody," pursuant to the Wisconsin child abuse and neglect statute.[541] But "taking the *unborn child* into custody" meant taking Angela M.W. into custody. The "unborn child"—expressly defined as a "nonperson" until birth by *Roe*—was in Angela M.W.'s womb. And, thus, taking Angela M.W. into custody—where she had not been charged with a crime—would be a violation of her Fourth and Fourteenth Amendment rights, legal experts argued.[542]

As state officials prepared to take her into custody, Angela M.W. agreed to enter an inpatient drug treatment center. The court amended the custody order to reflect Angela M.W.'s placement in an inpatient center. But the court also ordered that if Angela M.W. attempted to leave, "both she and the fetus were to be detained and transported to Waukesha Memorial Hospital."[543] In the interim, the state petitioned the juvenile court, arguing that Angela M.W.'s "viable fetus was in need of protection" because Angela M.W. had "neglect[ed], refuse[d] or [was] unable for reasons other than poverty to provide necessary care, food, clothing, medical or dental care, or shelter so as to seriously endanger the physical health of the child."

But there were problems to come, and they began when Angela M.W. didn't want to be in custody anymore. Not even "protective" custody. But Angela M.W. was still pregnant. Wisconsin officials wanted Angela M.W.'s "unborn child" to remain in custody, which meant that Angela M.W. had to remain in custody. Angela M.W. got a lawyer, and when all was said and done, a divided Court of Appeals held that the juvenile court had not exceeded its jurisdiction in reaching a fetus.[544] On appeal, the Wisconsin Supreme Court was asked to determine whether a "viable fetus" was a "child" as defined by Wisconsin abuse and neglect statute. The court held that it was not.

Such a finding may be unlikely today. Wisconsin is among the states that have passed "fetal abuse" statutes. But even before enacting such a law, Wisconsin was not alone in attempting to reach beyond the rights of a pregnant woman to protect "*unborn children.*" Between 1988 to 1992, more than 150 women were arrested and prosecuted for allegedly "abusing or neglecting" *unborn children.*[545] By 2003, that number had grown to more than 200.[546]

Many of these cases hinged upon inventive arguments grounded in "prenatal child abuse," though under *Roe* there are no "prenatal children." Other states sought to prosecute women for harms to "newborn children," though the conduct underlying these allegations was clearly prenatal. In 1989, for example, Jennifer Johnson became the first woman in the United States to be convicted of "delivering" cocaine to her unborn fetus via the umbilical cord.[547] Similar prosecutions took place in Arizona,[548] California,[549] Connecticut,[550] Florida,[551] Georgia,[552] Ohio,[553] Kentucky,[554] Michigan,[555] Nevada,[556] Pennsylvania,[557] Texas,[558] Washington,[559] Wisconsin,[560] and Washington, D.C.,[561] during the late 1980s and through the 1990s with some thirty-four states involved in prosecutions of this sort by 1995.[562]

Some argued that these cases and similar prosecutions of the time were evidence of a burgeoning "fetal rights" movement. But "[t]he term fetal rights is a distortion of the real issue and obscures what ought to be the primary concern—the health of the child when born," author Robert Blank explains. "It is not the fetus that has rights; rather it is the child once born that must be protected from avertable harm during gestation.... The unfortunate but conscious focus on fetal rights instead of the rights of the newborn intensified opposition without contributing to resolution of the problem. Although the fetus may have 'interests' to be protected that will materialize after birth, it is clear under *Roe v. Wade* that fetuses do not even have a 'right' to be born, at least throughout the first two trimesters."[563]

Thus, the "fetal rights" movement was little more than an extension of the antiabortion movement. It is a movement with teeth and prosecutors, who regularly ordered pregnant women be taken into custody to protect the "unborn children" they are carrying, even where there was little or no proof of criminal conduct and state action was grounded in little more than a hunch. In no other area of the law would prosecutors be allowed to order that a person be taken into custody for crimes that cannot be proved or that have not yet occurred. There has also been some suggestion that although women are often prosecuted, birth defects, miscarriages, and some childhood cancers can be caused by the defective sperm of men.[564]

Rebecca Corneau, for example, was a member of a religious sect that, according to the *Christian Science Monitor*, "evolved from a Bible study group, [and] rejects what it calls the 'seven systems' of mainstream society: banking, education, entertainment, government, medicine, religion, and science."[565] Religious activity is generally protected by the First Amendment. After two "children" born into the sect died—one of them Corneau's—a Massachusetts district attorney sought a court order to have an again-pregnant Corneau see a doctor.[566] By some reports the Corneau "baby" was stillborn while others suggest a failure to clear the lungs caused the death.[567] Authorities argued that the "children" might have lived had the women seen doctors.

When a pregnant Corneau refused to have a physical examination, citing her religious faith, a court declared her an "unfit mother." She was taken into custody. Although Corneau was questioned regarding the whereabouts of the missing "children," she was never charged with a crime.[568] Still, she remained in jail for three months, until she gave birth in October 2000, to a 7-pound, 15-ounce baby girl. After the birth, authorities said Corneau was free to go when she felt well enough.[569] The baby was placed in foster care. Rebecca Corneau and her husband were later granted immunity from prosecution, and David Corneau testified before a grand jury looking into the sect's activities. He also led authorities to an area in the Maine wilderness where state officials uncovered two pine coffins.[570]

STATE OF WISCONSIN v. ZIMMERMAN

By contrast, Deborah Zimmerman wasn't religious. She was an unhappy woman who drank, which led the State of Wisconsin to arrest and charge her with intentional attempted homicide in 1996, following a series of events that began about a week before her due date. While drinking in a bar, Zimmerman reportedly thought she was going into labor. She was taken to a hospital by her mother, where she was described by personnel as "uncooperative, belligerent at times, and very intoxicated." Her blood alcohol level was reportedly 0.30 percent.[571]

But the fireworks began when Zimmerman allegedly told a nurse, "if you don't keep me here, I'm just going to go home and keep drinking and drink myself to death and I'm going to kill this thing because I don't want it anyways." She also reportedly "expressed fear about the baby's race, an abusive relationship she was in, and the pain of giving birth." Clearly, Zimmerman was a troubled—as opposed to a malicious—woman. She would eventually consent to a cesarean section and gave birth to M.M.Z., a girl.

Wisconsin authorities moved at some point later to charge Zimmerman with attempted first-degree intentional homicide and first-degree reckless injury. Despite the language of *Roe*, Zimmerman was held for trial after a circuit court found probable cause to support the state's charges. Zimmerman appealed the denial of a Motion to Dismiss the charges by a lower court. Upon review, the Wisconsin Court of Appeals would hold that "an unborn child is not a 'human being' because it is not one who has been born alive as required in [the Wisconsin homicide statute], and probable cause did not exist to charge Deborah with the crimes of attempted first-degree intentional homicide and first-degree reckless injury. As a result, we reverse the circuit court's denial of the motion to dismiss the information."

Although Zimmerman prevailed, the case of *State of Wisconsin v. Zimmerman*[572] was closely watched by legal scholars for three reasons. The first reason was that it was not the first time a pregnant woman had been charged with a criminal offense for drinking while pregnant, which seemed to suggest a trend. In 1990, amid declarations that "prosecutors should not have to wait until a child is born with defects to act to protect it," a nearly five months pregnant Diane Pfannensteil was charged with felony child abuse for drinking while pregnant after hospital officials measured her blood alcohol level.[573] Pfannensteil had gone to the hospital after being beaten by her husband. The charges in that case were later dismissed.[574]

Women's rights groups suggest that this a typical fact pattern for many of these prosecutions. "Most of the women [prosecuted] are of color, poor, or both, and they often suffer a range of socioeconomic problems, such as domestic violence, sexual abuse, drug addiction, or poor health and lack of health care—problems that many experts agree call for treatment, not prison time," Cynthia L. Cooper wrote in reporting on the trend.[575]

The second reason for the widespread interest in *State of Wisconsin v. Zimmerman* involved the seriousness of the charges. Zimmerman had been charged with attempting to kill a "child." The third reason was that drinking is *legal conduct*, permissible for everyone of sufficient age. Were state officials attempting to assert that women were not entitled to engage in certain legal acts because they were pregnant? If so, wouldn't that be "pregnancy discrimination" in violation of Title VII and the Equal Protection Clause? And if the state could proscribe drinking, what else could it demand pregnant women do or not do under threat of criminal charge?

By charging women for offenses involving alcohol, state officials appeared to be setting up another potential test of women's rights, which had women's rights scholars concerned. And it is a question, incidentally, that some courts have considered. The Kentucky Supreme Court noted the following, for example, in *Commonwealth v. Kentucky*:

> [t]he mother was a drug addict. But, for that matter, she could have been a pregnant alcoholic, causing fetal alcohol syndrome; or she could have been addicted to self abuse by smoking, or by abusing prescription painkillers, or over-the-counter medicine, or for that matter she could have been addicted to downhill skiing or some other sport creating serious risk of prenatal injury, risk which the mother wantonly disregarded as a matter of self-indulgence. What if a pregnant woman drives over the speed limit, or as a matter of vanity doesn't wear the prescription lenses she knows she needs to see the dangers of the road? The defense asks where do we draw the line on self-abuse by a pregnant woman that wantonly exposes to risk her unborn baby? The Commonwealth replies that the General Assembly probably intended to draw the line at conduct that qualifies as criminal, and then leaves it to the prosecutor to decide when such conduct should be prosecuted as child abuse in addition to the crime actually committed.

WHITNER v. STATE OF SOUTH CAROLINA

The opinion of the Supreme Court of Kentucky stands in sharp contrast, however, to the Supreme Court of South Carolina's in an illustration of the fracture among the states and the courts on this issue. While the courts in dozens of cases have held that prosecutors could not turn an "unborn fetus" into a "child" with little more than a word,[576] the Supreme Court of South Carolina in *Whitner v. State of South Carolina*,[577] held just the opposite in a case involving a broadly worded children's code.[578]

On April 20, 1992, Cornelia Whitner pled guilty to criminal "child" neglect. The charges in the case stemmed from the fact that Whitner gave birth to a newborn who tested positive for cocaine metabolites in the blood.[579] The circuit court sentenced her to eight years in prison. Whitner filed an application for Post-Conviction Relief.[580] The petition was granted. The state appealed.

The issue on appeal to the South Carolina Supreme Court was whether a "viable fetus" was within the South Carolina Children's Code, which defined a "child" to be a "person under the age of eighteen."[581] As the South Carolina Supreme Court read it, the basis of Whitner's appeal was that interpreting the statute to include viable fetuses "would lead to absurd results not intended by the legislature."[582] In other words, "every action by a pregnant woman that endangers or is likely to endanger a fetus, whether otherwise legal, would constitute unlawful neglect under the statute. For example, a woman might be prosecuted under Section 20-7-50 for smoking or drinking during pregnancy."[583]

The court disagreed, noting that "...the same arguments against the statute can be made whether or not the child has been born. After the birth of a child, a parent can be prosecuted under Section 20-7-50 for an action that is likely to endanger the child without regard to whether the action is illegal in itself. For example, a parent who drinks excessively could, under certain circumstances, be guilty of child neglect or endangerment even though the underlying act—consuming alcoholic beverages—is itself legal. Obviously, the legislature did not think it 'absurd' to allow [the] prosecution of parents for such otherwise legal acts when the acts actually or potentially endanger the 'life, health or comfort' of the parents' born children. We see no reason such a result should be rendered absurd by the mere fact the child at issue is a viable fetus."[584]

Whitner appealed to the United States Supreme Court, citing "an intolerable conflict among the nation's high courts regarding the scope of federal constitutional guarantees embodied in the Fourteenth Amendment."[585] This conflict, Whitner argued, stemmed from the fact that "[t]he high courts of Kentucky and Nevada have squarely held that the due process guarantee of notice and its prohibition against vague criminal statutes preclude the use of child neglect statutes to punish women for their conduct during pregnancy."[586] In May 1998, the United States Supreme Court declined to grant *certiorari* in *Whitner v. State of South Carolina*, thereby leaving open the question of whether fetuses have become "unborn children" for the purposes of prosecution regarding otherwise legal conduct.

It was a decision that seemed to rally forces. In August 1999, Oklahoma authorities jailed Julie Stark, alleging that the fetus she was carrying was in danger, after a trailer she was in was raided by police as a methamphetamine lab. Stark tested negative for drugs. Her lawyers argued that she had simply been in the wrong place at the wrong time.[587] Prosecutors argued that "fumes" in the trailer were harmful to the fetus. After 36 days in jail, Stark was released and would eventually give birth to a healthy 8-pound, 2-ounce boy, who tested negative for drugs or toxins in his system. But at trial, Stark was convicted of depriving a "child" of a safe environment. In January 2001, the Supreme Court of Oklahoma vacated the conviction.[588]

Similar prosecutions during this time involved a New Jersey woman threatened with the loss of custody of a newborn child for taking part in a medically prescribed methadone program; a Kentucky woman charged with "child abuse" for taking the painkiller OxyContin during pregnancy,[589] and the homicide conviction, in May 2001, of a 24-year-old South Carolina woman who (authorities argue) killed the fetus she was carrying by smoking crack cocaine.[590] Medical personnel reportedly disagreed on the actual cause of the stillbirth and testified so at trial. More than 26,000 stillbirths occur in the United States each year, and the cause is unclear in many of them. But prosecuting attorneys pushed the theory of homicide because they reportedly wanted to extend the use of the charge in such cases.

"If the child had been smothered by its mother two weeks after being born, there'd be no question about prosecution," prosecutor Greg Hembree said in an interview. "The only difference here is, this was two weeks before the child would have been born. It is still part of a parent's fundamental responsibility to protect children."[591]

FERGUSON v. CITY OF CHARLESTON

Although the United States Supreme Court declined to hear an appeal in *Whitner v. State of South Carolina*, the Justices agreed to hear the case of *Ferguson v. City of Charleston*,[592] another South Carolina case of importance to women because it underscored a decade of questions regarding a hospital's right (or wrong) to perform drug tests on pregnant women, the results of which were later turned over to police where they were positive. The facts underlying *Ferguson v. City of Charleston* apparently began in the fall of 1988, when staff members at a public hospital in Charleston run by the Medical University of South Carolina (MUSC) grew "concerned about an apparent increase in the use of cocaine by patients who were receiving prenatal treatment."[593]

In what may or may not have been a true attempt at medical assistance, MUSC staff personnel began performing drug screens on the urine samples of maternity patients suspected by hospital officials of using cocaine. If the patient tested positive, she was referred by MUSC staff to county substance abuse commissioners for counseling and treatment. Despite these referrals, the problem of substance abuse by drug-addicted pregnant women continued. Enter Nurse Shirley Brown. According to the United States Supreme Court's recitation of the facts, Nurse Brown had "heard a news broadcast reporting that the police in Greenville, South Carolina, were arresting pregnant users of cocaine on the theory that such use harmed the fetus and was therefore child abuse."[594]

Nurse Brown "discussed the story with MUSC's general counsel," who got in touch with the City of Charleston's Solicitor "in order to offer MUSC's cooperation in prosecuting mothers whose children tested positive for drugs at birth," according to the Court.[595] After the meeting, the city solicitor began promulgation of a coordinated policy statement and cooperative plan to "prosecute women who tested positive for cocaine while pregnant." The policy, outlined in a 12-page document known as Policy M-7, dealt "with the...Management of Drug Abuse During Pregnancy, involving police officials; MUSC staff members; the county substance abuse commission and the department of social services."

But in the Court's view of it, the policy seemed far more criminal in nature than medical. In analyzing the document, the Court found:

> The first three pages of Policy M-7 set forth the procedure to be followed by the hospital staff to 'identify/assist pregnant patients suspected of drug abuse.' The first section, entitled the 'Identification of Drug Abusers,' provided that a patient should be tested for cocaine through a urine drug screen if she met one or more of nine criteria.[596] It also stated that a chain of custody should be followed when obtaining and testing urine samples, presumably to make sure that the results could be used in subsequent criminal proceedings. The policy also provided for education and referral to a substance abuse clinic for patients who tested positive. Most important, it added the threat of law enforcement intervention that 'provided the necessary "leverage" to make the [p]olicy effective.' That threat was, as respondents candidly

acknowledge, essential to the program's success in getting women into treatment and keeping them there.

The threat of law enforcement involvement was set forth in two protocols, the first dealing with the identification of drug use during pregnancy, and the second with identification of drug use after labor. Under the latter protocol, the police were to be notified without delay and the patient promptly arrested. Under the former, after the initial positive drug test, the police were to be notified (and the patient arrested) only if the patient tested positive for cocaine a second time or it she missed an appointment with a substance abuse counselor.[597] In 1990, however, the policy was modified at the behest of the solicitor's office to give the patient who tested positive during labor, like the patient who tested positive during a prenatal care visit, an opportunity to avoid arrest by consenting to substance abuse treatment.

The last six pages of the policy contained forms for the patients to sign, as well as procedures for the police to follow when a patient was arrested. The policy also prescribed in detail the precise offenses with which a woman could be charged, depending on the stage of her pregnancy. If the pregnancy was 27 weeks or less, the patient was to be charged with simple possession. If it was 28 weeks or more, she was to be charged with possession and distribution to a person under the age of 18—in this case, the fetus. If she delivered 'while testing positive for illegal drugs,' she was also to be charged with unlawful neglect of a child. Under the policy, the police were instructed to interrogate the arrestee in order 'to ascertain the identity of the subject who provided illegal drugs to the suspect.' Other than the provisions describing the substance abuse treatment to be offered to women who tested positive, the policy made no mention of any change in the prenatal care of such patients, nor did it prescribe any special treatment for the newborns.[598]

Ten women who tested positive and were arrested during various stages of the policy's implementation[599] challenged the constitutionality of Policy M-7. Among the challenges asserted was that the MUSC had engaged in "warrantless and nonconsensual drugs test[ing] conducted for criminal investigatory purposes." As a result, those tests were "unconstitutional searches" in violation of the Fourth Amendment of the United States Constitution.

The women sued the City of Charleston, several of the law enforcement officials charged with development and enforcement of the policy, and representatives of MUSC. The hospital defended the tests, arguing that petitioners had "consented" to them. The hospital argued further that even without consent, the tests were neither unlawful, nor unreasonable. Rather, they were justified for "special nonlaw-enforcement purposes."

But the case would have a procedural history nearly as troubling as the allegations. At the district court level, the court rejected the "consent" defense offered by MUSC and law enforcement officials, reasoning that the tests had been "searches." In other words, the tests had not been "done by the medical university for independent purposes. [Instead,] the police came in and there was an agreement reached that the positive screens would be shared with the police," the district court held.

Given this finding, the district court issued jury instructions requiring in finding "a verdict in favor of [the ten women] unless the jury found [that] consent [had been given]."[600] The jury found for MUSC and law enforcement officials. The ten women appealed to the ultraconservative Court of Appeals for the Fourth Circuit, arguing that the evidence before the district court was "insufficient to support the jury's consent finding."

The Fourth Circuit affirmed the jury verdict, holding—without reaching the issue of consent—that the "searches were reasonable as a matter of law under [its] line of cases recognizing that 'special needs' may, in certain exceptional circumstances, justify a search policy designed to serve nonlaw-enforcement ends."[601] In other words, the Fourth Circuit was convinced that MUSC "personnel conducted the urine drug screens for medical purposes wholly independent of an intent to aid law enforcement."

The women appealed again. The United States Supreme Court agreed to review the Fourth Circuit's decision, but only on the "special needs" issue. A determination on the issue of consent was remanded to the Fourth Circuit for yet another determination. But "given the posture in which the case comes to us, we must assume for purposes of our decision that the tests were performed without the informed consent of the patients," the Supreme Court noted.[602]

With regard to the "special needs" claim, the Court explained that the urine tests conducted by MUSC staff members were "indisputably searches within the meaning of the Fourth Amendment" and "[b]ecause MUSC is a state hospital, the members of its staff are government actors, subject to the strictures of the Fourth Amendment." With these facts established, the question before the Court, as the Justices saw it, was whether the tests were "reasonable" and lawful as defined by the body of law that has developed around interpretations of the Fourth Amendments protections.

One of those well-established protections is that warrantless searches must be supported by a probable cause belief by law enforcement officials or state actors that a crime has been committed and that the person to be searched has committed it. But "[n]either the District Court nor the Court of Appeals concluded that any of the nine criteria used to identify women to be searched provided either probable cause to believe that [the women] were using cocaine, or even the basis for a reasonable suspicion of such use," the majority of the United States Supreme Court wrote.

"Rather, the District Court and the Court of Appeals viewed the case as one involving MUSC's right to conduct searches without warrants or probable cause.[603] The argument of MUSC and law enforcement officials was that the drug tests were not within the purview of traditional Fourth Amendment analysis. But rather within a "closely guarded category of constitutionally permissible suspicionless searches," the majority wrote.

But there was a distinction. At issue in those cases in which "suspicionless drug tests" were upheld by the Court were screening for railway employees involved in train accidents;[604] drug tests for United States Customs officials seeking promotions to "sensitive positions;"[605] and high school students participating in interscholastic sports.[606] In each of those cases, the Court "weighed the intrusion [of the tests] on the individual's interest in privacy against the 'special needs' that supported the program," the Justices explained.

By contrast, the intrusion at issue in *Ferguson v. City of Charleston* was far more "substantial than in those cases," the Justices explained, because "the use of an adverse test result to disqualify one from eligibility for a particular benefit, such as promotion or an opportunity to participate in an extracurricular activity, involves a less serious intrusion on privacy than the unauthorized dissemination of such results to third parties."

As a general rule, patients undergoing diagnostic tests in hospitals have a far more substantial privacy interest in those test results not being shared with nonmedical personnel without their consent, the Justices concluded. As a constitutional right, that privacy interest only grows when the "special need" asserted to justify the absence of a warrant or "individualized suspicion [is] not…divorced from the state's general interest in law enforcement," the Court held.

"[T]he central and indispensable feature of [Policy M-7] from its inception was the use of law enforcement to coerce the patients into substance abuse treatment. This fact distinguishes this case from circumstances in which physicians and psychologists, in the course of ordinary medical procedures aimed at helping the patient herself, come across information that under rules of law or ethics is subject to reporting requirements, which no one has challenged here," the Justices wrote. "In this case, a review of the M-7 policy plainly reveals that the purpose actually served by the MUSC searches '[was] ultimately indistinguishable from the general interest in crime control.'"[607]

Therefore, although "the ultimate goals of the program may well have been to get the women in question into substance abuse treatment and off of drugs, the immediate objective of the searches was to generate evidence *for law enforcement purposes*[608] in order to reach that goal.[609] The threat of law enforcement may ultimately have been intended as a means to an end, but the direct and primary purpose of MUSC's policy was to ensure the use of those means. In our opinion, this distinction is critical. Because the law enforcement involvement always serves some broader social purpose or objective, under [MUSC's and law enforcement officials'] view, virtually any nonconsensual suspicionless search could be immunized under the special needs doctrine by defining the search solely in terms of its ultimate, rather than immediate, purpose.[610] Such an approach is inconsistent with the Fourth Amendment.

"Given the primary purpose of the Charleston program, which was to use the threat of arrest and prosecution in order to force women into treatment, and given the extensive involvement of law enforcement officials at every stage of the policy, this case simply does not fit within the closely guarded category of 'special needs,'"[611] the Court held. Thus, "[w]hile state hospital employees, like other citizens, may have a duty to provide the police with evidence of criminal conduct that they inadvertently acquire in the course of routine treatment, when they undertake to obtain such evidence from their patients *for the specific purpose of incriminating those patients*, they have a special obligation to make sure that the patients are fully informed about their constitutional rights, as standards of knowing waiver require."[612]

Ferguson v. City of Charleston, with a decade of arrests and litigation behind it, offers a compelling portrait of the larger debate and the efforts of state officials to protect "unborn children" in defiance of *Roe* and at the determined expense of living women.

There was, of course, a context to the drug-related cases that tended to allow the nation to look the other way on this activity. During the 1980s and early 1990s, America was lasting out the devastating effects of a cocaine and crack epidemic as hobbling to inner-city communities and populations as any war would be.

"Pregnant women [are] not immune to the allure of these substances," researcher Michelle D. Mills wrote in *Fetal Abuse Prosecutions: The Triumph of Reaction Over Reason* in 1998, in commenting on the trend of the '90s.[613] "Although studies do not agree on a figure, as many as 100,000 to 375,000 infants each year [were] born after being exposed to some type of drug in the womb.[614] This trend shows no signs of slowing down. One commentator has estimated that by the year 2000, well beyond 500,000 cocaine-exposed infants will be born each year in this country."[615]

That was an estimate. It may not, in fact, be the case. Statistics compiled by the United States Department of Justice suggest that the use of crack and cocaine by the general population has declined sharply, which suggests that the use has likely declined among pregnant women as well. If that is true, then the number of fetuses exposed to crack should decline. But that was not happening in the late 1980s in South Carolina. The response of MUSC officials was to test, threaten, and then have pregnant women arrested.[616]

And yet, as troubling as the facts of *Ferguson v. City of Charleston* may be what is far more dangerous for women and the precedent of *Roe* today is that lawmakers seem determined to legislate around it. Statutes that turned fetuses into "unborn children" for their protection were and are an example of this. And legislatures continue to enact them. As set forth earlier, in early 2001, for example, representatives in Arkansas, Kentucky, Michigan, and Mississippi proposed amendments to current law that they argue will protect "viable fetuses" and/or "unborn children" *from fertilization onward* in wrongful death actions,[617] while lawmakers in Arizona and Colorado proposed enhancing penalties for offenses committed against pregnant women.[618]

That same year, lawmakers in Mississippi considered a bill in 2001 that would allow the state to charge a women with manslaughter in the death of an "unborn child" of 20 weeks of more dies as a result of its "mother's" use or abuse of an illegal controlled substance.[619] Also, that same year, Iowa lawmakers were considering a civil commitment statute for "chronic substance abusers," a definition that includes pregnant women who "habitually lack self-control as to the use of chemical substances" and who are, therefore, likely to cause injury to themselves or the fetuses "if allowed to remain at liberty without treatment."[620]

Of course, ingesting cocaine, smoking crack, and shooting heroin are illegal activities. But where is the law with regard to legal conduct, such as drinking? Except for *State of Wisconsin v. Zimmerman*, the majority of the cases involved the use of illegal drugs by pregnant women. But crack and cocaine do not appear to represent the crisis of the future. Crack abuse was "epidemic" in the 1980s, according to the Department of Justice.[621] But as set forth above, data suggests that crack use has been on decline in most major cities since the mid-1990s.[622]

But that does not mean that prosecutions of pregnant women will slow. Drinking amongst pregnant women is on the rise, according to researchers at the Centers for Disease Control (CDC).[623] And just who is drinking may hold a few surprises. A recent CDC study of 138,496 women interviewed over a period of years found that alcohol consumption among pregnant women fell between 1988 and 1992. Between mid-1992 and 1995, however, the use of alcohol by pregnant women increased more than 60 percent.

But this class of users was not made up of the downtrodden, undereducated, or terminally impoverished. According to the CDC, the "pregnant women who were at risk for alcohol use were college educated, unmarried, employed...students, [with] annual household incomes of more than $50,000, or were smokers. Pregnant women who were at high risk for frequent alcohol use were more likely to be unmarried or smokers."[624]

Between 1995 and 1999, the overall number of pregnant women appeared to decline. But "rates of binge drinking and frequent drinking during pregnancy did not decline and remained higher than the 2010 Healthy People objectives," the CDC reports. Again, the pregnant women involved in this study were "unmarried, and older" women who tend[ed] to have higher rates of alcohol use. Women who drink alcohol are more likely than other women to be white, unmarried, younger, and working full-time outside the home."[625]

Does that mean that white, middle-class women may become the subject of prosecutions for endangering the welfare of a minor, for example, for drinking during pregnancy? In terms of cultural equations of power—which are and have always been part of the reproductive rights debate—wealthy women remain largely unaffected by a great deal of the current legislation. But if we are talking about the desire of the state to assert its perceived right to protect "unborn children," the answer to that question should be yes. And it could expand even further.

Recent studies suggest that some common hair dyes used by women during pregnancy may cause birth defects. And although smoking during pregnancy reportedly declined between 1988 and 1998, the rates still seems to range between 12 and 22 percent.[626] Women wearing three-inch stilettos walk the streets at 8 months. Do these acts pose a risk to "unborn children"? If so, do women who have their hair dyed, smoke, or wear tall shoes run the risk of prosecution for harms to their unborn "children"? Women's rights groups argued that this was the path courts were taking and it raised the specter—once again—of women as vessels with no individual rights, obligated to carry the "state's children."

But it is precisely these sorts of acts—those that would seek to elevate the status of unborn fetuses over those of living women—that *Roe v. Wade* was supposed to settle. The rights of women were supposed to be superior to those of the "fetuses." For the last three decades, however, legislators and other elected officials who don't agree with the United States Supreme Court's decision in *Roe v. Wade* had simply decided to ignore, and/or not to follow that particular law as they waste million of tax-payer dollars enacting laws that are clearly unconstitutional and tossing pregnant women in jail as they argue that the state's interest is in promoting and preserving the health of "unborn children."

THE POLITICS OF DECONSTRUCTION:
Redefining "Life" to Dismantle Roe

Though issued more than thirty years ago, the decision in *Roe v. Wade* continues to divide the nation as deeply on a symbolic level as it does in real life. Members of the Kentucky Senate[627] mourned the anniversary of that decision, for example, in January of 2001, when California lawmakers asked the President to preserve its integrity. And, thus, the debate continues.[628]

But by the start of the new millennium the battle over abortion had turned from a noisy, violent public debate into an effective campaign of stealth tactics intended ultimately to foreclose the right to abortion. And in large part, it has worked. By some accounts, more than 335 laws have been passed by the states since 1995, further restricting the practice and access to abortion. And by 2000, the simple and determined strategy of antiabortion opponents seemed to be to legislate around the plain language of *Roe* and its progeny.

In a single year—2001—for example, the following things happened: Texas legislators began debating passage of a bill whose language declared that "life" begins "at the moment of fertilization" (as opposed to birth) and that an "unborn human organism" is alive and entitled to the rights, protections, and privileges accorded any other *person* in the state.[629] Texas is the home state of *Roe v. Wade*. That same year, a Connecticut lawmaker proposed a bill declaring "that no infant member of the species *Homo sapien* who is born *at any age state of development* may be denied appropriate medical treatment;"[630] and representatives in Arizona, Colorado, Massachusetts, Iowa, and Montana considered bills requiring the issuance of "death" certificates for fetuses.[631]

In February 2002, the Idaho Senate sent competing bills to the Idaho House. The first, sponsored by Republican Senator Harold R. Bunderson, would include fetuses and even embryos in the state's manslaughter and murder laws. The second, sponsored by Bunderson's opponents, would increase the penalties for attacks against pregnant women resulting in stillbirths or miscarriages.[632]

Not all of these bills became law. But this is clearly where the law is not only going, but has gone. In that sense, it seemed that more than a few of these proposed measures will be reintroduced until they are finally defeated or they succeed. It is a strategy that has gone a long way toward changing the hearts and minds of the American public, though few—outside of women's rights scholars and activists—seemed to notice. Therefore, although abortion remains legal, geographic, political and legal accessibility has declined as "fetuses" have effectively become "unborn children."

"I've seen things go from being very open to very restrictive," Susan Hill, director of the National Women's Health Organization in North Carolina, said in an interview. "The restrictions start in Mississippi because they know they can get anything through the state legislature, and then they move to other states."[633]

It is an approach that has been remarkably effective. But in addition to this under-the-radar approach, opponents of abortion have also been careful to craft laws that appear to be not only sensible and fair, but moderate and utilitarian, as opposed to radical and clearly anti-woman.

"These laws are written by middle-class people with nice homes. The laws don't seem like an undue burden, until you have seen a woman sleeping in a car with her four children," Hill explained, remarking on an incident involving a woman who traveled to a Mississippi clinic. The woman could not afford a motel. In accordance with the state's 24-hour mandatory waiting law, however, she had to wait to have an abortion. She reportedly slept in her car in 100-degree heat, along with her four daughters.[634]

In addition to being written by middle-class Americans, these laws are supposed to appeal to middle-class Americans. For soccer moms and PTA parents. For the "middle of America" and people who have settled—usually comfortably—into child rearing and, who, therefore, cannot imagine, or don't care to consider, the harsh realities of other people's lives. It is toward these people that state officials have aimed when announcing the prosecutions of poor, urban, and (mainly minority) women for drinking or living out the tragedies of addiction while pregnant. It is for these people—middle-class parents—that graphic arguments about "partial-birth" abortion are made and for whom placards were waved.

Kate Michelman, president of the National Abortion and Reproductive Action League (recently renamed NARAL Pro-Choice America), admitted in January 2003, that the group and abortion supporters in general were facing the "most hostile atmosphere for abortion in 30 years."[635]

Indeed, efforts to end legal abortion in the United States take many forms today, from the seemingly inconsequential to the plainly significant with the shifts in reasoning at times clearly apparent. In October of 2002, the Michigan Court of Appeals held that a pregnant woman may use deadly force to defend the fetus she is carrying, even if she does not fear for her own life. Jaclyn Kurr alleged that she stabbed Antonio Pena in the chest with a kitchen knife after he punched her in the stomach. At the time, Kurr was between 16 and 17 weeks pregnant with quadruplets. Pena was reportedly her lover and biologically related to the fetuses she carried.

Kurr was sentenced to from five to twenty years in prison after a jury rejected her claims of self—or fetus—defense. It was recognized on both the trial and appellate levels that the fetuses would not have survived outside of the womb, and Kurr miscarried a few weeks after the event. Though Michigan law allows the use of deadly force to protect oneself as well as in defense of others, the self-defense argument reportedly troubled Judge Richard Lyon Lamb of the Kalamazoo County Circuit Court.

"I believe in order to be able to assert a defense of others there has to be a living human being existing independent of [the person asserting the defense]," which would constitute "the other" under the statute. "Under 22 weeks, there are no others," Judge Lamb reportedly said.[636]

In reversing the conviction and ordering a new trial, the appellate court reasoned that the concept of defending others with deadly force could and "should also extend to the protection of a fetus, viable or nonviable, from an assault against the mother."[637] Though the court noted that the defense could be used only in the context of assault, as opposed to cases involving destruction of frozen embryos, for example, the creeping nature of the ruling seemed to trouble some.

"One is left with a most peculiar legal situation. Although she may use deadly force to protect the viable or nonviable fetus, thereby ending someone's life, she also has the constitutional right to terminate the pregnancy herself without consequence," Atlanta attorney John C. Mayoue, a specialist in reproductive rights law told *The New York Times* in commenting on the Michigan appellate court's decision.[638]

In April 2003, the Missouri Supreme Court held that an unwed "father" could maintain a wrongful death action against the convenience store where his pregnant girlfriend was shot and killed during a robbery. The man brought the action alleging that the store's negligence resulted in the death of his "unborn child." A lower court initially dismissed the suit, reasoning that because the "child" died before being joined as a party to the claim, the "father" was required by the Uniform Paternity Act to show that he was, in fact, the "father." Because he had failed to do so, the suit could not be maintained, the lower court reasoned.[639]

The Missouri Supreme Court reversed, holding—despite precedents to the contrary—that the requirement of establishing paternity in wrongful death actions need not be followed in this case. The case was remanded to the lower court with the direction of the Missouri Supreme Court that in order to prevail, the perspective "father" would have to prove that he was, in fact, the "father" of the "unborn child;" that the "child" died as a result of negligence on the part of the store owner; and that he had suffered damages.[640]

Of course, litigation is a constant in the war. In recent years, for example, Alabama, Florida, Louisiana, Oklahoma, and South Carolina enacted "*Choose Life*" license plates laws to the ire of pro-choice supporters. The brainchild of a

Florida Commissioner who originally sought in 1996 to raise money for adop-
tions, the nation's first *"Choose Life"* license plate law was introduced before the
Florida legislation in 2000. It would eventually be vetoed by then-Governor
Lawton Chiles.

But the veto sparked national interest and the commissioner was reportedly
contacted by groups in 35 states, all of them interested in producing *"Choose
Life"* licenses plates of their own.[641] With the election of Jeb Bush as Florida Governor, the measure was signed into law the second time around. *"Choose Life"* is
scrawled in a childlike hand on the Florida plates, which also include cartoon
images of a girl and a boy.

But shortly after the Florida *"Choose Life"* law was enacted, it was challenged,
unsuccessfully, by the National Organization for Women.[642] Money raised from
the sale is reportedly earmarked for pregnancy centers where women are educated about adoption, but not abortion.[643] In addition to the Florida suit,
women's rights groups in other states have also sued, challenging the laws as
governmental fundraisers "for the private fight against abortion."[644] Others go
farther, suggesting that *"Choose Life"* license plates are a form of "antichoice
propaganda" spread with the assistance of the government.[645]

But these are costly, often lengthy challenges. In December 2001, for example, a case involving challenge to the Louisiana law went before the United
States Court of Appeals for the Fifth Circuit."[646] A lower court issued an injunction, blocking the production and distribution of such plates in Louisiana.
"Choose Life" appears on the Louisiana plate near the state bird, the pelican,
which happens to be carrying a "bundle of joy" in its beak as a stork might.

Supporters of the license plates argue that their sale has raised more than
$600,000 in Florida, and Louisiana Assistant Attorney General Roy Mongrue,
who argued the state's case before the appeals court, has reportedly called challenges to the law "the ultimate in subterfuge."[647]

INFORMED CONSENT AND
A NEW DEVICE IN THE PROPAGANDA WARS

In addition, "informed consent" laws have also provided opponents of abortion
another avenue of attack, women rights groups charge. Since the Court's decision
in *Planned Parenthood of Southeastern Pennsylvania v. Casey,* in which the Court
held that information on the ills and risks associated with abortion could be given
to women prior to abortion as long as it was truthful, several states have adopted
"informed consent" statutes requiring recitation or review of state-prepared material. What lawmakers in some states have sought to include in this material, however, has not always been medical information.

Alabama officials considered passage of a so-called "informed consent" law in
2001, for example, providing—as part of state-prepared "informational
materials"[648]—that women should be told "...[t]here are many public and private
agencies willing and able to help you to carry your child to term, and to assist you
and your child after your child is born, whether you choose to keep your child or
to place her or him for adoption. The State of Alabama strongly urges you to con-

tact those agencies before making a final decision about abortion. The law requires that your physician or his or her agent give you the opportunity to call agencies like these before you undergo an abortion."[649]

At about the same time, New Jersey legislators began considering an "informed consent" draft that would require women in that state to review state-prepared materials that would include: "a description of the probable anatomical and physiological characteristics of the fetus at two-week increments, including survival rates, pictures, and information about brain and heart function; information on common abortion procedures and their medical risks, including the risks of infection, hemorrhage, danger to subsequent pregnancies, breast cancer, 'possible adverse psychological effects associated with an abortion,' and the medical risks of carrying a pregnancy to term; a comprehensive, geographically indexed list of agencies and services available to assist the woman during pregnancy, upon childbirth, and while the child is dependent; a toll-free, 24-hour hotline providing this list; the support obligations of the 'father'; that it is unlawful to coerce a woman to have an abortion; and that if a minor is denied financial support by the minor's parents due to the minor's refusal to have an abortion, the minor shall be considered emancipated for the purposes of eligibility for medical assistance benefits."[650]

Authorities in Hawaii and Texas considered requiring doctors or their agents to "offer information and counseling on fetal pain prior to an abortion of a fetus" 20 weeks or older,[651] while a Mississippi bill involved the question of screening women seeking abortion for a variety of "ailments," including whether "she is a vulnerable person."[652] That particular bill happens to have died in committee. But the award for plain-speaking and honesty may go to Nebraska, where lawmakers considered deleting the requirement that "informational materials" provided prior to abortion in favor of material reflecting the "state's public policy favoring childbirth over abortion."[653] Lawmakers in Oklahoma began debating the creation of a civil cause of action that would allow women to sue doctors for "failing" to provide enough information, prior to abortion, to allow them to give informed consent.[654]

And yet, the war of information has proved larger than "informed consent" laws, though this modern controversy has often been tangled. Eleven states proposed informed consent provisions or statutes listing breast cancer as a potential risk to abortion along-side possible "hemorrhage, danger to subsequent pregnancies and infertility."[655] The Illinois Senate Committee on Rules prepared, in early 2001, to begin discussion of the resolution that would create the Abortion-Breast Cancer Task Force, which would study the supposed link between breast cancer and abortion.[656]

Critics argue, however, that science has uncovered no discernible link between abortion and breast cancer. Dr. Nancy Snyderman, physician and medical correspondent for *Good Morning America*, has been a vocal critic of the effort, calling it "bad science" that has been misused in an attempt to dictate social policy.[657] "There seem to be many causes [for breast cancer]," Snyderman said. "But when you go back and try to link it to abortion, there are huge loops, huge holes in retrospective studies like this."

The only study considered by many doctors to be scientifically sound enough to be of use on the question is a Danish study that followed 1.5 million women who had abortions between 1935 and 1978. After reviewing all of the data with an eye towards increased cancer risks, Danish scientists found "no link."[658]

Though there have always been questions of whether arresting a woman's menstrual cycle may alter estrogen levels spurring the growth of potentially cancerous cells, Snyderman notes that roughly half of all pregnant women suffer "some kind of spontaneous abortion or miscarriage," which suggests that if women who have abortions are at risk for breast cancer, so too are women who miscarry. But no link in that regard has been proved either.

But even so, media reports suggest that officials of the Bush Administration removed information stating that there is no link between abortion and breast cancer after Christopher H. Smith, a Republican from New Jersey who also serves as co-chair of the House of Representative's Pro-Life Caucus, reportedly "wrote a letter of protest to Secretary Tommy Thompson calling the research cited by the National Cancer Institute 'scientifically inaccurate and misleading to the public.'"[659]

In addition to "Choose Life" license plate laws and "informed consent" laws that tend to inform women only of adoption, opponents of abortion have also continued to build upon the gains of the past, especially where the use of tax-payers funds are involved. As set forth in greater detail in Chapter Two, as far back as 1934, Father Charles Coughlin, a Catholic priest well respected enough to be invited to testify before Congress, told lawmakers that it would be wiser for the nation to focus not on "how to eradicate poverty by birth control, but to eradicate poverty by getting rid of birth control money."[660]

Illinois Republican Henry Hyde proposed something similar with regard to abortion in the mid-1970s. It would change the course of the debate and the ability of poor women to choose abortion. In the years immediately following the Court's decision in Roe v. Wade, "the number of legal abortions increased to almost 1.6 million, where it remained stable until the [start of the]1990s,"[661] medical researcher Willard Cates Jr. wrote.[662] As the number of legal abortions increased, the number of illegal abortions fell, resulting in an improvement in the health of women having abortions, Cates suggested.[663]

But with passage of the Hyde Amendment in 1976, which prohibited the use of public taxpayer funds for all abortions except those that were "medically necessary,"[664] the choice of abortion was effectively foreclosed for thousands of poor women across the nation. And then, their numbers fell.

According to Cates, "[t]he year before the implementation of the Hyde Amendment, about 300,000 abortions in the United States were obtained by low-income women through Medicaid."[665] But in the two years following its passage, "the number of federally funded abortions averaged only 3,000 per year, or just one percent of the previous number. The amendment, therefore, effectively stopped federally funded abortions," says Cates.[666]

The Hyde Amendment was challenged repeatedly over the course of the next twenty years—on several grounds initially, including under the Equal Protection Clause, by women's rights advocates who argued that denying federal funding was tantamount to denying poor women the fundamental right to choose abortion. But the United States Supreme Court would repeatedly uphold the amendment, noting that there was no fundamental right to taxpayer-funded abortion.

While supporters of these restrictions argue that they are strictly economic and not meant to punish women for "lifestyle" or reproductive choices, others admit that the refusal to pay for all but medically-necessary abortions was intended to deter women from having an abortion. Cates argues, however, that "...limiting federal funds was primarily a symbolic exercise. Many states continue to finance abortions using state revenues, thus blunting the amendment's impact."[667]

And yet, the Hyde Amendment has been a roadmap in recent years for those state officials who do not want to pay. By January 1997, thirty-four states had quietly passed laws similarly banning the use of public funds for elective abortions.[668] By 2001, similar measures were pending before the legislatures of Massachusetts, New Jersey, Rhode Island, and Tennessee.[669]

Among the latest rulings in this area was the decision by the Supreme Court of Texas in January of 2003, holding that state restrictions on Medicaid funding for all but medically necessary abortions did not violate the Texas constitution.[670]

The unanimous decision in *Bell v. Low Income Women of Texas*,[671] reversed a lower court ruling of December 2000, in which that court held that the denial of funding to poor women who sought abortions where there was no threat of death was a violation of the Texas Equal Rights Amendment.[672]

Passed in 1967, the Texas Medicaid Assistance Program (TMAP) limits the state funding to Medicaid to subsidies offered by the federal funds, which effectively incorporates the Hyde Amendment.[673] Three clinics and three Dallas doctors filed suit in 1993, arguing that the funding restrictions of the TMAP were sex discrimination in violation of the Equal Rights Amendment and the Texas constitution. The state's Motion for Summary Judgment was granted by a court in Austin in 1997. The Third District court reversed.[674] After languishing before the Texas Supreme Court for more than a year—the court heard arguments in November 2001—the decision of the Third District Court was reversed.

"We hold that the TMAP's abortion funding restrictions do not violate the Texas Constitution's Equal Rights Amendment, Equal Protection Clause, or right to privacy," Texas Supreme Court Justice Harriet O'Neill wrote in the court's opinion.[675]

And yet, although violence, the declining availability of providers, oppressive consent laws, misinformation and restrictive funding have succeeded in staggering *Roe v. Wade*, perhaps the greatest threat to legal abortion in the United States is that the constant barrage of newly-created legislation defining fetuses as "unborn children" has begun to overwhelm once clearly-established law.

THE NEO-SEMANTICS OF THE CONTINUED DEBATE:
Turning the "Fetuses" of Roe into the
"Unborn Children" of Today

"The early strategy of the pro-life movement, as designed by the Catholic Church, was to concentrate on passage of a human life amendment," authors Robert Blank and Janna Merrick explain in *Human Reproduction, Emerging Technologies, and Conflicting Rights.*[676] "In the mid-1970s, it became apparent that this strategy would fail because there were not enough pro-life votes in Congress. Therefore, its next strategy focused on getting more pro-life legislators elected: by 1978, pro-life campaign activities were in full swing. Old-fashioned electoral strategies were combined with high-tech direct mail. Candidates—especially incumbents—who were identified as pro-choice and electorally vulnerable were targeted for defeat.

"Iowa pro-life groups produced a leaflet designed to appeal to the emotions, depicting a fetus with a caption that read, 'This little guy needs your help.'[677] Thousands of leaflets were distributed at churches in Iowa on the Sunday before election day in 1978. Pro-life groups also organized a voter identification program in order to establish a name bank of pro-life volunteers and to develop lists for mass mailings," Blank and Merrick further note. "The Iowa strategies were repeated by pro-life organizations in other states in the 1980 election. *Right to Life* organizations held electoral strategy training sessions at their national conferences and used their national newsletters to keep members informed about successful strategies."[678]

The "fortunes of the pro-life movement" would certainly change,[679] but due as much in part to large amounts of cash, as to strategies. By some accounts, antiabortion groups associated with the Christian right raise upwards of $40 million per year.[680] It is money that abortion opponents have used to lobby Congress and state lawmakers unrelentingly. And though the gains they initially made were incremental and, thus, seen by many as unrelated and insignificant, for antiabortion activists, every step was part of the plan. By the mid-1970s—within four years of the decision in *Roe*—the Hyde Amendments had made abortion less available to poor women mainly. But less available nonetheless.

By 1980, politicians—in particular presidents—sympathetic to the cause were reportedly helping the efforts of antiabortion opponents along, critics suggest, pointing specifically to the twelve-year run of Presidents Reagan and George H.W. Bush. During this time, a "Christian, family-values" agenda moved to the forefront of American policy; roughly 60 percent of the appointments to federal judgeships were made (to lifetime appointments); and, governmental challenges to abortion came about as promised. The plan was clearly taking shape and having an effect.

While supporters of the right to choose and the privacy of women engaged in a highbrow debate on the meaning of the law and the failure of lawmakers to respect and/or properly apply it, opponents of abortion commenced a guerrilla war of back door tactics determined to undermine *Roe v. Wade* by turning the fetuses of *Roe* into "unborn children" everywhere else, though the Justices clearly held in deciding *Roe* that the term "person" had no "prenatal application."[681]

It is a strategy that has proved so successful in the last two decades that the once-clear language of *Roe* has been overwhelmed by an avalanche of legislation—some successfully passed, some not—intended to protect prenatal "infants" and as-yet-"unborn children." As set forth above, for example, a Connecticut lawmaker drafted a bill requiring medical treatment for *any infant* "born at any state of development."[682] Bills in New Hampshire and Washington proposed protecting "born-alive infants,"[683] though under *Roe*, there are no *infants* until they are "born alive."

Massachusetts lawmakers introduced a bill in 2001, that would protect *the unborn* from "sex-selection-motivated" abortions,[684] and a bill introduced before the Nebraska legislature that same year proposed a change in the language of the state's abortion-related laws by replacing the term "fetus" with that of "unborn child."[685] And though the "unborn children" movement might naturally be expected to infuse the reproductive rights debate, as Claremont University Professor Jean Reith Schroedel notes in *Is the Fetus a Person?* the push towards "fetal rights" has generally expanded across policy lines.[686]

This trend suggests not only that the beleaguered holding of *Roe* has fallen out of favor among legislators, but that the sensibilities it once seemed to dictate have also gone by the wayside. For many years, for example, legislators deferred to the ultimate meaning of *Roe* in devising laws in other areas. Thus, in many states it was impossible after *Roe* to murder a developing—as opposed to a viable—fetus. But today, that appears to be no more.

In a reversal of the earlier trend, state legislators have begun drafting laws in recent years recriminalizing harm to fetuses in the womb, an initiative that nearly disappeared after the decision in *Roe v. Wade*. Bills were introduced before the legislatures of Arizona, Colorado, Rhode Island, Texas, and Virginia in 2001, increasing the sentences for offenses committed against a pregnant woman.[687] That same year, a Connecticut bill was introduced with language that would permit a charge of homicide for the *killing* of "an unborn person."[688]

A proposal before New Hampshire lawmakers suggested amending the law to include the term "fetus" within the definition of "another" for purposes of the negligent homicide statute.[689] Florida legislators considered a similar amendment to that state's vehicular homicide statute to reach viable fetuses.[690] A Mississippi bill similarly sought to amend the law to make the death of "an unborn fetus" actionable—perhaps even manslaughter—under the state's driving under the influence statute.[691]

And in February 2001, a bill that would amend current state law to include sentencing guidelines for killing or injuring an "embryo" or "fetus" went before the Michigan Senate.[692] Again, it should be noted that not all of these bills became laws. But they were clearly part of a larger movement.

"Since late 1994 pro-life groups have experienced a dramatic upsurge in their effectiveness in getting measures adopted both at the national and state levels. NARAL labeled members of the 104th and 105th Congresses as 'the most antichoice since *Roe*' on the basis of a record number of antiabortion votes," notes Schroedel. "They classified only 131 or 145 members of the House of Representatives and 33 senators as fully supportive of the pro-choice position on abortion. Of the eighty-one votes on reproductive issues since 1995, abortion rights supporters prevailed on only ten."[693]

This shift was further reflected on the state level.

"In 1997 state legislatures considered 84 percent more antiabortion measures than in the preceding year and enacted almost three times more of them. Nearly two-thirds (thirty-two) of the states passed restrictive abortion statutes in 1997, compared to only nine states in 1996. The trend is not abating. In 1998 twenty-seven states enacted a total of sixty-two laws restricting abortion."[694] Though some of the above proposed legislation no doubt included express exceptions for abortion,[695] supporters of abortion fear that those exceptions will eventually disappear," says Schroedel.

In addition to criminal amendments to protect the fetus, proposals in the civil arena have been made as well. Arkansas lawmakers considered amending the language of a state law to make the death of a viable fetus a "person" for purposes of wrongful death actions.[696] Kentucky and Mississippi lawmakers were considering similar bills.[697] And then there was the federally initiated legislation that seemed almost certain to give rise to a form of "federally initiated litigation" perhaps once contemplated—as a tool in the war—by President Ronald Reagan.

In July 2001, the Bush administration announced promulgation of a new policy under the Children's Health Insurance Program, that would allow states to define "an unborn child" as a person for purposes of eligibility for medical coverage under the program. Administration officials argued that the program would allow states to offer medical coverage to previously ineligible persons.[698]

"The purpose is simple. This will increase access to prenatal care for pregnant women, the ultimate goal being healthier babies and healthier children. It could help many pregnant women who are not eligible for Medicaid or the children's health program," Department of Health and Human Services Spokesman William Pierce said in defending the program.[699]

In February 2002, administration officials announced a "clarification" and the "broadening" of the definition of children under the Children's Health Insurance Program, including "unborn children" with coverage to begin at "conception."[700] The move was immediately denounced by women's rights groups.

"The Bush [a]dministration's proposal demonstrates its commitment to the strategy of undermining a women's right to choose by ascribing legal rights to embryos," said Kate Michelman, president of NARAL Pro-Choice America.[701]

In August 2002, with the debate over the Children's Health Insurance Program still relatively fresh, the Born-Alive Infants Protection Act was signed into law by President Bush during a heavily covered visit to Pennsylvania to see nine men rescued after being trapped in a mine.[702] The federal law amends the legal definition of "person," "human being," "child," and "individual" to include "fetuses," which it appears to assume will be "born alive." And, thus, the fetuses of *Roe v. Wade* have become the "unborn children" of today.

Then, as though it were a follow-up, the Bush administration issued the final guidelines on eligibility under the Children's Health Insurance Program in September of 2002, defining "child" as an "individual under the age of 19, including the period from conception to birth."[703]

Adding force to the arguments of antiabortion opponents, of course, is science. With medical assistance, even the nearly one-pound fetus has a chance at survival today.[704] Powerful new machinery allows the viewing of fetuses in 3-D and prebirth medical intervention has allowed physicians to repair sometimes life-threatening developmental flaws.[705] While these achievements are often remarkable, the fact that they occur has further complicated the reproductive rights debate as abortion foes cite advances of this sort to bolster their assertions regarding the "unborn." President Bush evoked science, for example, in announcing the signing of the Born-Alive Infants Protection Act into law.

"Today, through sonograms and other technology, we can see clearly that unborn children are members of the human family. They reflect our image, and they are created in God's own image," Bush told an audience that reportedly included several members of the clergy. "The Born-Alive Infants Protection Act is a step toward the day when every child is welcomed in life and protected in law. It is a step toward the day when the promises of the Declaration of Independence will apply to everyone, not just those with the voice and the power to defend their rights."[706]

Even before President Bush took up the course so publicly, attempts to spark a "fetal rights" movement has been extremely political, in large part because a "fetal rights" movement necessarily challenges the once-clearly established rights of women. Thus, the states have tended to divide with regard to the "fetal rights" issue along political lines.

"Existing fetal case and statutory laws reveal huge disparities in the rights accorded fetuses," Schroedel explains. "Case and statutory laws can be sorted into a fetal rights continuum, ranging from consistently pro-fetal states to consistently anti-fetal states. At the pro-fetal rights pole are Utah and North Dakota, which consistently accord personhood or near personhood status to the fetus in all policy domains, have legislatively declared their commitments to protect the 'unborn,' and have among the most restrictive abortion statutes in the nation.[707]

"At the opposite end of the continuum are pro-choice New Jersey and Vermont, whose courts have ruled that their constitutions more fully protect women's reproductive rights than does the federal Constitution and whose case and statutory law consistently deny legal rights to the fetus. Hawaii also is a strong pro-choice state, with case and statutory laws that consistently do not accord rights to the fetus but a constitution that does not exceed the federal Constitution in guaranteeing reproductive rights for women."[708]

But while George Washington University Professor of Law Jeffrey Rosen argues that the debate is, indeed, political, some of the shift in perspective—which would allow, for example, an ex-boyfriend to be charged with attempted murder for beating his pregnant girlfriend, while preserving the right to choose abortion—may be due to a "more nuanced vision of fetal personhood" among the American public.

"Despite the theatrics of interest groups on both sides of the abortion debate," Rosen argues, "...the public sees no contradiction in punishing fetal homicide and protecting a woman's right to choose early-term abortion. In recent surveys, more than 90 percent of Americans say they would support a federal law that increases punishment for perpetrators who harm an unborn child, while more than two-thirds oppose laws that restrict first-trimester abortions. The public's intuitions are not only reasonable. They reveal a far more nuanced vision of fetal personhood than the black-and-white vision adopted by the Supreme Court in *Roe v. Wade*. The fetal homicide statutes provide a model for a legislative solution to the abortion debate that would treat potential life differently in different contexts."[709]

The problem as women's rights activists see it, however, is that opponents of abortion seek to have "potential life" treated the *same* way in *all* contexts—and that is as an "unborn child" who has, from the moment of "conception," a right not only to medical benefits and the protections of the state, but to life. That suggestion necessarily conflicts with a woman's right to choose abortion as stated by *Roe v. Wade*.

Another problem for pro-abortion supporters is that the nation has visited the issue of the "unborn" before. In 1986, William Webster, then governor of Missouri, signed Missouri House Bill No.1526. The then-new law included some twenty provisions and a preamble declaring that "the life of each human being begins at conception." House Bill No. 1526 also sought to amend existing state law to grant "unborn children...all rights, privileges, and immunities available to other persons, citizens, and residents" of Missouri.

At the time, the Missouri was criticized by women's rights groups as a direct challenge to the meaning of *Roe v. Wade*. Though the United States Supreme Court would consider the constitutionality of other parts of Missouri House Bill 1526 at issue in *Webster v. Reproductive Health Services*, the majority would decline to reach the issue of whether asserting a protectable interest in the "life, health, and well-being" of an "unborn child" invalidated all provisions of a law in the abortion context. Instead, the majority handled the issue in the following way:

> [t]he Act's preamble...sets forth "findings" by the Missouri Legislature that "[t]he life of each human being begins at conception," and that "[u]nborn children have protectable interests in life, health, and

well-being."[710] The Act then mandates that state laws be interpreted to provide unborn children with "all the rights, privileges, and immunities available to other persons, citizens, and residents of this state," subject to the Constitution and this Court's precedents.[711] In invalidating the preamble, the [Eighth Circuit] Court of Appeals relied on this Court's dictum that "a state may not adopt one theory of when life begins to justify its regulation of abortions."[712] It rejected Missouri's claim that the preamble was "abortion-neutral," and "merely determine[d] when life begins in a nonabortion context, a traditional state prerogative."[713] The court thought that "[t]he only plausible inference" was that "the state intended its abortion regulations to be understood against the backdrop of its theory of life."[714]

The state contends that the preamble itself is precatory and imposes no substantive restrictions on abortions, and that appellees therefore do not have standing to challenge it.[715] Appellees, on the other hand, insist that the preamble is an operative part of the Act intended to guide the interpretation of other provisions of the Act.[716] They maintain, for example, that the preamble's definition of life may prevent physicians in public hospitals from dispensing certain forms of contraceptives, such as the intrauterine device.

In our view, the Court of Appeals misconceived the meaning of the Akron *dictum*, which was only that a state could not "justify" an abortion regulation otherwise invalid under *Roe v. Wade* on the ground that it embodied the state's view about when life begins. Certainly the preamble does not by its terms regulate abortion or any other aspect of appellee's medical practice. The Court has emphasized that *Roe v. Wade* "implies no limitation on the authority of a state to make a value judgment favoring childbirth over abortion."[717] The preamble can be read simply to express that sort of value judgment.

We think the extent to which the preamble's language might be used to interpret other state statutes or regulations is something that only the courts of Missouri can definitively decide. State law has offered protections to unborn children in tort and probate law,[718] and can be interpreted to do so much more than that. What we have, then, is much the same situation that the Court confronted on *Alabama State Federation of Labor v. McAdory*.[719] As in that case:

> We are thus invited to pass upon the constitutional validity of a state statute which has not yet been applied or threatened to be applied by the state courts to petitioners or others in the manner anticipated. Lacking any authoritative construction of the statute by the state courts, without which no constitutional question arises, and lacking the authority to give such a controlling construction ourselves, and with a record which

> presents no concrete set of facts to which the statute is to be applied, the case is plainly not one to be disposed of by the declaratory judgment procedure.[720]

> It will be time enough for federal courts to address the meaning of the preamble should it be applied to restrict the activities of appellees in some concrete way. Until then, this Court "is not empowered to decide...abstract propositions, or to declare, for the government of future cases, principles or rules of law which cannot affect the result as to the thing in issue in the case before it."[721] We therefore need not pass on the constitutionality of the Act's preamble.

It appears, however, that the time may have come for the United States Supreme Court to reach the question of that long-ago Act's preamble, though it has assumed a different form today. As set forth earlier, several states have sought to turn the language of the *Webster v. Reproductive Health Services*[722] preamble into free standing law. And thus, the apparent question to be considered is whether these law are constitutional in light of *Roe v. Wade.*

As the Court explained in *Webster v. Reproductive Health Services*, "[s]tate law has offered protections to unborn children in tort and probate law,[723] and can be interpreted to do so much more than that." That may, in fact, be the setup for the next constitutional challenge of *Roe*, after the latest "partial-birth abortion" case is heard, should the Court agree to hear a case that involves a federal law that is nearly identical to the Nebraska law that was struck down in 2000.

With an ever-graying Supreme Court and continued predictions of impending retirements, President Bush (should he be re-elected) and a handful of his closest legal advisors—many of them conservative Christians—may be charged, as planned, with appointing successors to the Court who may hear these cases.

A SHIFT IN PERSPECTIVE AND CHANGING LAW IN PLAY:
Where the Law Stands Today

Few decisions having to do with abortion last very long in their entirety. The once-hallowed decision of the United States Supreme Court, *City of Akron v. Akron Center for Reproductive Health, Inc.*, was no exception. In that case the majority struck down an "informed consent" provision that would have required doctors to "counsel" women seeking abortion to be sure that their decisions involved "informed consent."[724]

A decade and a half after *City of Akron v. Akron Center for Reproductive Health, Inc.*, the Justices had a change of heart, holding in *Planned Parenthood of Southeastern Pennsylvania v. Casey*, that information that was truthful and not misleading could be given to women seeking abortions, even information that might tell of the ill-effects of abortion. In other words, gone was the ban on recitation of the litany of ills.

At the start of the millennium, questions of mental coercion and the presentation of misleading information by states to women seeking abortions began to reemerge. Since the Supreme Court's decision in *Planned Parenthood of Southeastern Pennsylvania v. Casey*, several states have either adopted or proposed "informed consent" statutes that require recitation or review of state-prepared material.[725]

In 2001, legislators in Oklahoma prepared to debate the creation of a civil cause of action for women who could prove that doctors failed to provide "enough" information on the possible ills and injuries associated with the procedure prior to abortion, thereby denying then the opportunity to give proper informed consent.[726] Though it might initially seem simple and innocent enough—the product, perhaps, of zealous personal injury lawyers—the Oklahoma debate was part of a larger movement orchestrated by "pro-life organizations," according to Schroedel.

"Pro-life organizations and legislators also have mounted a campaign to expand the group of possible litigants who can file civil claims against abortion providers," Schroedel explains.[727] That was one area of attack. Another came in the guise of "informed consent" laws by states lawmakers pretending to believe that if a woman wanted to have an abortion she simply didn't know that there were other options. Hence the current movement.

Alabama and Rhode Island lawmakers considered passage of a "informed consent" statute in 2001, for example, requiring that women be told "[t]here are many public and private agencies willing and able to help you to carry your *child* to term, and to assist you and your *child* after your *child* is born, whether you choose to keep your *child* or to place her or him for adoption. The State of Alabama strongly urges you to contact those agencies before making a final decision about abortion. The law requires that your physician or his or her agent give you the opportunity to call agencies like these before you undergo an abortion."[728]

Though New Jersey has traditionally been a "pro-abortion" state, in 2000 bills began circulating on the House floor that would have permitted state-prepared materials to include: "a description of the probable anatomical and physiological characteristics of the fetus at two-week increments, including survival rates, pictures, and information about brain and heart function; information on common abortion procedures and their medical risks, including the risks of infection, hemorrhage, danger to subsequent pregnancies, breast cancer, 'possible adverse psychological effects associated with an abortion,' and the medical risks of carrying a pregnancy to term; a comprehensive, geographically indexed list of agencies and services available to assist the woman during pregnancy, upon childbirth, and while the child is dependent; a toll-free, 24-hour hotline providing this list; the support obligations of the 'father'; that it is unlawful to coerce a woman to have an abortion; and that if a minor is denied financial support by the minor's parent due to the minor's refusal to have an abortion, the minor shall be considered emancipated for the purposes of eligibility for medical assistance benefits."[729]

Bills proposed in Hawaii and Texas in 2001 would require a physician or a physician's agent to "offer information and counseling on fetal pain prior to an abortion of a fetus" 20 weeks or older.[730] A Mississippi bill would have permitted the screening of women seeking abortion for a variety of "ailments," including whether "she is a vulnerable person."[731] That bill died in committee. But if the trend continues, dozens more will be introduced this year and several may pass.

In addition to "informed consent" laws, the homicide statutes in many states have been rewritten to reach "unborn children." As of 1999, some courts appeared to be resisting the rush toward a new type of judgment. Robert Courchesne was charged in June 1999, for example, with murder and two counts of capital felony in the stabbing death[s] of a "mother" and a "daughter" in Waterbury, Connecticut. The "mother," Demetris Rodgers, died of stabs wounds allegedly inflicted by Courchesne. She was eight-and-a-half months pregnant at the time of the attack. The fetus she was carrying was delivered by emergency Cesarean section, and survived for six weeks on life support.[732]

Attorneys for Courchesne moved to dismiss the charges underlying one set of charges, arguing that the fetus—identified as Antonia Rodgers in media reports—could not have been murdered in the stabbing attack, because she was not "alive" at the time. In other words, because she hadn't been born, she did not fit the definition of "person." Within the state's murder statute, a "person" is a "human being who has been born alive." Only "persons" can be killed. But a Connecticut Superior Court judge held that there was probable cause to charge Courchesne with the murder of Antonia Rodgers.

The murder charge for Antonia Rodgers's death could stand "as long as the fetus was born alive and subsequently died of injuries inflicted *in utero*," the judge held, in distinguishing the case from another in which a Connecticut judge held that a defendant could not be charged with murdering a fetus. In that case, the fetus was stillborn.[733] The judge held that the requirement of "intent" necessary to support a murder charge could be inferred from the doctrine of transferred intent (*i.e.*, Robert Courchesne intended to murder Rodgers, who was pregnant). Therefore, he intended to murder Antonia Rodgers, the fetus she was carrying.

The attempts of Courchesne's attorneys to assert "nonperson" arguments harken back to *Roe v. Wade* and the 1970 California case of *Keeler v. Superior Court*,[734] and a judicial finding that may soon achieve urban myth status given how far removed the law is today. The facts underlying *Keeler v. Superior Court* involved a man apparently unhappy upon finding that his ex-wife was pregnant by another man. His response was to intercept her on a mountain road, report the rumors, and upon catching sight of her protruding belly, add: "You sure are. I'm going to stomp it out of you."

With that, he reportedly rammed his knee into her abdomen, fracturing the skull of the fetus, which was later stillborn. Keeler was charged with murder for the "unlawful kill[ing] [of] a human being, to wit Baby Girl Vogt, with malice aforethought." His attorneys moved to dismiss the charge, arguing that an unborn fetus was not a "human being" within the meaning of the California penal statute. State prosecutors argued, however, that given the advances of medicine, a viable fetus had an excellent chance of survival. Therefore, it should be assumed that "Baby Girl Vogt" would have become a human being but for Keeler's actions.

But the Supreme Court of California ruled that it could not "hold this petitioner to answer for murder by reason of his alleged act of killing an unborn—even though viable—fetus," because "[t]o such a charge there are two insuperable obstacles, one 'jurisdictional' and the other constitutional." In enumerating the jurisdictional obstacle, the California court explained that "[w]e recognize that the killing of an unborn but viable fetus may be deemed by some to be an offense of similar nature and gravity" but as Chief Justice [John] Marshall warned long ago[:]

> It would be dangerous, indeed, to carry the principle, that a case which is within the reason or mischief of a statute, is within its provisions, so far as to punish a crime not enumerated in the statute, because it is of equal atrocity, or of kindred character, with those which are enumerated.[735]

In other words, the courts are not entitled to rewrite, misapply, or extend the California penal code to reach a fetus for purposes of murder, the California Supreme Court held. Construction of statutory law fell strictly within the province of Legislature. Further, because the murder statute did not clearly reach fetuses, the court reasoned that there was also a due process question involved the issue of notice (*i.e.*, "fair warning of the act which is made punishable as a crime").

Because it was not clear that an unborn fetus was a "human being" for purposes of the California murder statute, the court held that "the judicial enlargement of Section 187 now urged upon us by the People would not have been foreseeable to this petitioner, and hence that its adoption at this time would deny him due process of law."

That does not appear to be the prevailing law, or the trend in the law, today. After the decision in *Roe v. Wade* was handed down, only fifteen states passed laws making it a crime to kill a fetus.[736] But by the mid-1990s, antiabortion activists had begun to consider manslaughter and homicide laws as ripe for expansion. In 1997, Ohio and Pennsylvania lawmakers made it an offense to kill "an unborn child." In 1998, legislators in Tennessee[737] and Wisconsin[738] passed a similar measure.

By January 1998, thirteen states—in addition to the original twelve—had amended the language of existing law or enacted new homicide and manslaughter statutes to reach fetuses. In 1999, Arkansas joined the count with that state's lawmakers revising murder, manslaughter and negligent homicide statutes to reach fetuses of at least 12 weeks.[739]

Among the galvanizing events during this period, by some reports, was the death of an eight-month-old fetus in a car accident. When the family of the pregnant woman learned that the driver of the other car could not be prosecuted under Pennsylvania law for the death of the fetus, they lobbied state officials to extend the state's homicide law to reach not only fetuses, but embryos as well.

According to Schroedel, "[t]he Pennsylvania Pro-Life Federation and the Catholic Family Institute worked with pro-life state legislators in developing H.B. 1299/S.B. 45, which closely resembled the [Americans United for Life] model fetal homicide statute that Ohio passed in 1996.[740] The legislation defines the killing of an 'unborn child' at any state of prenatal development as murder or manslaughter. In House debates, the primary sponsor of H.B. 1299, Dennis O'Brien (R-Philadelphia), was asked if a person who intentionally knocked over a petri dish of fertilized eggs could be charged with 'multiple homicide.' O'Brien responded, 'If you knew, and it was your intent, then yes.'[741] The bill easily passed the House and Senate with strong bipartisan majorities and was signed into law by the state's pro-life Republican governor, Tom Ridge."[742]

By 1999, the move to criminalize the "murder" or "battery" of fetuses had begun to emerge as an issue on both the state and national levels. Perhaps the clearest sign of this was the 254-to-172 vote in the House of Representatives in favor of the "Unborn Victims of Violence Act of 1999." The primary sponsor of the bill was conservative Republican Representative Lindsey Graham,[743] who was reportedly "given a 100 percent approval rating from the Christian Coalition in 1998."[744] But the bill—of which there were competing versions in the House and Senate—stalled, leaving antiabortion and Christian activists struggling to get it back on track.

KNOCKING ON THE BACK DOOR:
Connor's Law and the "Unborn Victims of Violence Act"

Her mother asked for it and that only adds to the story's compelling nature. And yet, in so many ways, it is perfect for a media blitz. An attractive young woman—the picture most often shown is a portrait of a wholesome, healthy life. She has a broad, perfect smile, delicate features and a peaches and cream complexion. She is indisputably lovely.

And since May 5, 2003, conservatives—joined by Laci Peterson's family—have endeavored to use her picture, her memory, the story of her life, and her "unborn child" to push the stalled "Unborn Victims of Violence Act," which—though supported by George Bush and passed by the House of Representatives twice—faltered after its introduction in 1999 to pass into law.

The Unborn Victims of Violence Act, which began shuffling through the Congress the first time in 1999, then again in early 2001, would make injuring or killing a fetus a separate crime if the such injury or "death" occurred during the commission of a predicate federal crime.[745] The National Right to Life

Committee "helped originate the bill in 1999, and was instrumental in winning approval of the bill in the House of Representatives in 1999 and again in 2001,"[746] when House members voted 252-172 in favor of the bill's passage.

The bill was reintroduced in May 2003,[747] by conservative Republican Senator Mike DeWine of Ohio, and though the language of both the Senate and House versions exempt abortion providers from prosecution, supporters of women's rights see the bill as yet another cynical attempt to unravel what is left of the precedent of *Roe v. Wade*. Specifically, supporters of the right to choose argue that *Roe v. Wade* once granted women a baseline level of protection, long interpreted to include the notion that a living woman's rights are paramount to those of the fetus.

The Unborn Victims of Violence Act would seem—at least arguably—to conflict with that. It also moved "the fetus" one step closer to a "living" child, which would necessarily set up a potential conflict of rights between the "mother" and the "unborn child," with the state stepping in to argue the "rights" of the "unborn child," where the "mother" may not want to do as the state says she should. That would effectively defeat the meaning of *Roe*, they argue.

THE WHITE HOUSE WEIGHS IN:
Religious Initiatives and George W. Bush

"On the anniversary of the landmark decision in *Roe v. Wade* establishing American women's right to reproductive choice, President Bush reinstated a rule denying that right to poor women outside our borders," Stanford Law Professor Deborah L. Rhode noted.[748] Though the move sparked a lawsuit by a privately funded group that works for abortion rights overseas,[749] few seemed to notice.

He has announced his support for the Unborn Victims of Violence Act and his intent to sign it, should it ever pass. His administration adopted a policy that would allow the states to extend medical coverage to "unborn children." He has made efforts to stack the federal bench with judges who oppose abortion. Many of his cabinet appointments were made in the same way, legal observers suggest.

"As in 2000, Bush would choose between the pro-choice and pro-life wings of the [Republican] Party," author Jeffrey Toobin suggests. "If the President wanted a moderate, [Colin] Powell and Tom Ridge would be obvious possibilities. But if Bush wanted an experienced, pro-life former Cabinet member—as Cheney was in 2000—Ashcroft would fit the bill. In a recent talk at the American Enterprise Institute, Karl Rove, Bush's top political adviser, said the Republicans' biggest failure in the last race was their inability to rally enough religious conservatives to the polls. 'We probably failed to marshal support of the base as well as we should have,' Rove said. 'There should have been nineteen million of them, and instead there were fifteen million.' At this point, few would rally the Republican base like John Ashcroft."[750]

Among the most controversial of Bush's cabinet appointments, Ashcroft, a former Missouri Senator,[751] is a conservative Christian and staunch antiabortion opponent, who presided over challenges to *Roe v. Wade* while he was Attorney General of Missouri.[752] Though he has vowed to uphold the nation's laws—which presumably include Supreme Court law[753]—Ashcroft's history has made him "the most polarizing figure of the Bush Cabinet," Toobin argues.[754]

That Ashcroft is socially conservative, few dispute. That he is the "most socially conservative figure to become attorney general—far more so than, say Edwin Meese III—many accept. What they find unacceptable, however, is that he may be "using his popularity from the antiterrorism campaign to push his agenda on social issues, particularly abortion and gun control," says Toobin.

"In many ways, Ashcroft has created a far more political department than any Justice Department since I've been here," Senator Leahy has reportedly said. "I think it's beneath the dignity of the Justice Department."[755]

But Ashcroft does have his supporters. Utah Senator Orrin Hatch, a conservative man himself who once sold religious songs via a television shopping club, has said that he believes "Ashcroft's people have a lot more professional approach toward the work of the Justice Department." [756] And, indeed, it should be noted that despite his personal opposition to abortion, as Attorney General Ashcroft—whom many feared would not enforce the law with regard to abortion—announced in August 2003, that the Justice Department would defend the Freedom of Access to Clinic Entrances Act from constitutional challenge in court.[757]

Also appointed to head the Department of Health and Human Services was former Wisconsin Governor Tommy Thompson, who reportedly told the Senate committee overseeing his confirmation hearings that he would "revisit" the Food and Drug Administration's approval of medical abortion pill mifepristone (formerly known as RU-486).[758] "Safety concerns are something that's in question," Thompson reportedly said.[759]

But the drug has proved safe and very effective, according to its manufacturer, which reported after the death of an 18-year-old who used the drug that between September 28, 2000—the day mifepristone was finally approved for use by the FDA—and September 24, 2003, more than 165,000 American women have safely used it.[760]

Safety may have been the stated concern. But the administration may, in fact, have simply had other ideas about allowing an "abortion pill" to gain a foothold in the United States. Mifepristone had a long journey to the market in the United States, though it has been used safely and successfully for at least a decade throughout Europe. Though the FDA originally found mifepristone "approvable" in 1996, after reviewing test results the agency delayed final formal approval until a manufacturer could be found. Fearful of a conservative Christian backlash, no major drug maker would agree to manufacture mifepristone. In 1998, a new pharmaceutical company offered to bring the drug to market.

With the widespread use of mifepristone, antiabortion would lose "...a major public relations battle because the public's image of abortions will radically change from the gruesome images conjured by partial-birth abortions to a much less troubling imagine," Schroedel noted. "As Robertson wrote, 'Preventing a fertilized egg from implanting or interrupting implantation shortly after an embryo has developed is less morally or symbolically problematic than surgically destroying a much more developed fetus."[761]

In August of 2002, a loose-knit coalition of religious and Christian groups— the American Association of Pro-Life Obstetricians and Gynecologists, Concerned Women for America, and the Christian Medical Association—sought to halt the sale of mifepristone, alleging that the FDA had violated its own rules in approving the protocol. The group reportedly cited an agency report and one death in making the claims.[762]

Four months later, in December 2002, Dr. W. David Hager was appointed to the FDA's Advisory Committee for Reproductive Health Drugs. Hager, an opponent of abortion like Thompson, has reportedly questioned the safety of mifepristone.[763]

The Bush administration has also been accused of "clouding science" by requiring that certain words that are distasteful to the "Christian" lifestyle be stricken from scientific proposals and information. Anything that doesn't comport with the religious-based message administration officials want to send has been removed from agency reports, critics charge.

In November 2002, Adam Clymer of *The New York Times* reported that "[i]nformation on condom use, the relation between abortion and breast cancer and ways to reduce sex among teenagers has been removed from government websites, prompting critics to accuse the Department of Health and Human Services of censoring medical information in order to promote a philosophy of sexual abstinence."[764]

"Over the last year, the department has quietly expunged information on how using condoms protects against AIDS, how abortion does not increase the risk of breast cancer and how to run programs proven to reduce teenage sexual activity," Clymer suggests. The posting that found no link between abortion and breast cancer was removed from the department's website last June, after Representative Christopher H. Smith, a New Jersey Republican who is co-chairman of the House Pro-Life Caucus, wrote a letter of protest to Secretary Tommy Thompson calling the research cited by the National Cancer Institute 'scientifically inaccurate and misleading to the public.'"[765]

In August of 2003, California Representative Henry Waxman presented a forty-page report to the House Committee on Government Reform, concluded that "[t]he administration's political interference with science has led to misleading statements by the president, inaccurate responses to Congress, altered websites, suppressed agency reports, erroneous international communications, and the gagging of scientists."[766]

The report also found that "federal agencies have jeopardized scientific integrity in many ways, including stacking scientific advisory committees with unqualified officials or industry representatives, blocking publication of findings that could harm corporate interests, and defending controversial decisions with misleading information."[767, 768]

Responding to the report, White House spokesman Scott McClellan argued that the Bush administration "looks at the facts, and reviews the best available science based on what's right for the American people. The only one who is playing politics about science is Congressman Waxman. His report is riddled with distortion, inaccuracies, and omissions."[769]

McClellan also accused Waxman, the ranking Democrat on the committee, of trying to score political points, noting that the California Congressman had conducted a noisy and aggressive inquiry into the tobacco industry.[770]

The Bush administration has been a controversial one so far, filled with officials determined to redefine individual "privacy" in favor of the state. Since he took office, Bush and the administration officials have fought the extension of essential privacy to gay and lesbian persons in their homes; they have opposed gay marriage, despite the administration's emphasis on "family" (homosexuals aren't the kind of "families" the Bush administration wants to include); and they have overwhelmingly taken up the cause of the religious right in attempting to turn back the clock on women's reproductive rights, with the eventual undoing of *Roe v. Wade* as the ultimate goal.

Whether the administration's apparent zeal in these and other areas reflects the attitude of the nation's Commander in Chief—a man who was "born again" after a "misguided youth" spent on things he has sought to keep private (he has been reluctant to comment on the specifics) and who is said to be grateful for God's love (he credits it with turning his life around)—is not known to those not privy to the inner workings of the White House. Although critics see parallels.

But it is equally likely, say others, that administration officials have simply endeavored to reactivate the religious glory of the past (*i.e.*, that Bush—a "Reagan imprint"—has simply surrounded himself by men (and a few women) who are ideological absolutists and who have been part of conservative administrations for decades). Donald Rumsfeld, for example, served in Congress before serving on the White House domestic policy staff under Richard Nixon. While working for Nixon, Rumsfeld hired a 28-year-old graduate student named Dick Cheney.[771]

Dick Cheney, Paul Wolfowitz, Richard Pearle, Colin Powell, and Dr. Condolezza Rice—all members of the current Bush inner circle—served under Ronald Reagan, during a time when "Christian family values" dominated American domestic policy in the form of government-made challenges to abortion and women's reproductive rights.[772]

Driven by the conviction with which he has marched American troops into conflicts in Afghanistan and Iraq, critics charge that the Bush administration has resumed the antichoice war against women. But this time, instead of straight-out battle, the arguments are cloaked, wrapped in assertions of safety and the protections needed for "unborn children." The approach is not new. But what is different this time is that the President and his conservative allies have racked up a series of victories that—although all but invisible to the general public—have begun to equal a great deal.

ENDNOTES FOR CHAPTER EIGHT

1   *See Williams v. Pryor*, (No. CV-98-01928-CV-S-NE) (filed July 29, 1998), at p. 1. See *also Williams v. Pryor*, 41 F. Supp. 2d 1257 (N.D. Ala.1999).

2   *See* Pamela Coyle, *Public Morality vs. Privacy Rights: Ruling on Sale of Sexual Devices Has Gay Activists Worried*, 30 A.B.A. J. (March 2001).

3   *See* Edward O. Laumann, Anthony Paik and Raymond C. Rosen, *Sexual Dysfunction in the United States: Prevalence and Predictors*, 281 JAMA at p. 537, (Feb. 10, 1999).

4   Those states include: Colorado (Colo. Rev. Stat. Secs. 18-7-101, 102); Georgia (Ga. Code Ann. Sec. 16-12-80); Kansas (Kan. St. Ann. Sec. 21-4301), Louisiana (La. Rev. Stat. Ann. Sec. 14:1206.1); Mississippi (Miss. Code Ann. Sec. 97-29-105); Texas (Tex. Penal Code Ann. Secs. 43.21, 43.23); and Virginia (Va. Code Ann. Sec. 18.2-373).

5   *See Williams v. Pryor*, 41 F. Supp. 2d 1257 (N.D. Ala. 1999).

6   *See Williams v. Pryor*, 229 F.3d 1331 (11th Cir. 2000); *Williams v. Pryor*, 240 F.3d 944 (11th Cir. 2001).

7   *See, e.g., Change of Appeal: 11th Circuit Deletes References to Gays in Ruling on Sexual Devices*, A.B.A. J., May 2000, at p. 28.

8   See *Dale v. Boy Scouts of America*, 308 N.J. Super. 516 (1998); *cert. granted*, 528 U.S. 1109 (2000); *Boy Scouts of America v. Dale*, 530 U.S. 640 (2000).

9   *Bowers v. Hardwick*, 478 U.S. 186 (1986).

10   *Eisenstadt v. Baird*, 405 U.S. 438 (1972).

11   *Roe v. Wade*, 410 U.S. 113 (1973).

12   *See* Tribe, *supra* note 73, ENDNOTES FOR CHAPTER THREE, at p. 1425.

13   As it stood at the time, the Georgia statute provided that: "A person commits the offense of sodomy when he performs or submits to any sexual act involving the sex organs of one person and the mouth or anus of another." Ga. Code Ann. Sec. 16-6-2 (1988).

14   *Bowers*, 478 U.S. at 188.

15   Justices White, Burger, Powell, Rehnquist, and O'Connor joined in the majority decision, though Justices Burger and Powell would file separate concurring opinions as well. Justices Stevens, Brennan, and Marshall would join in the dissent.

16   *Bowers*, 478 U.S. at 190.

17   *Pierce v. Society of Sisters*, 268 U.S. 510 (1925).

18   *Meyer v. Nebraska*, 262 U.S. 390 (1923).

19   *Prince v. Massachusetts*, 321 U.S. 158 (1944).

20   *Skinner v. Oklahoma*, 316 U.S. 535 (1942).

21   *Griswold v. Connecticut*, 381 U.S. 479 (1965).

22   *Bowers*, 478 U.S. at 190.

23   *Id.* at 191.

24   *Carey v. Population Services International*, 431 U.S. 678 (1977).

25   *Bowers*, 478 U.S. at 191.

26   *Palko v. Connecticut*, 302 U.S. 319, 325, 326 (1937).

27   *Bowers*, 478 U.S. at 192 (citing *Moore v. East Cleveland*, 431 U.S. 494, 503 (1977) (Powell, J)).

28   *Id.* (citing *Moore v. East Cleveland*, 431 U.S. at 503, (Powell, J.); *Griswold v. Connecticut*, 381 U.S. at 506).

29   *Id.* (citing *Survey on the Constitutional Right to Privacy in the Context of Homosexual Activity*, 40 U. MIAMI L. REV. 521, 535 (1986)).

30   *Id.* (Support for the assertion that "[s]odomy was a criminal offense at common law," Justice White, writing for the majority, noted that: "[c]riminal sodomy laws in effect in 1791: Connecticut: 1 Public Statute Laws of the State of Connecticut, 1808 Title LXVI, ch. 1, Sec. 2 (rev. 1672). Delaware: 1 Laws of the State of Delaware, 1797, ch. 22 Sec. 5 (passed 1719). [¶] Georgia had no criminal sodomy statute until 1816, but sodomy was a crime at common law, and the General Assembly adopted the common law of England as the law of Georgia in 1784. The First Laws of the State of Georgia, pt. 1, p. 290 (1981). [¶] Maryland had no criminal sodomy statute in 1791. Maryland's Declaration of Rights, passed in 1776, however, stated that 'the inhabitants of Maryland are entitled to the common law of England,' and sodomy was a crime at common law. 4 W. Swindler, Sources and Documents of United States Constitutions 372 (1975). [¶] Massachusetts: Acts and Laws passed by the General Court of Massachusetts, ch. 14, Act of Mar. 3, 1785. [¶] New Hampshire passed its first sodomy statute in 1718. Acts and Laws of New Hampshire 1680–1726, p. 141 (1978). [¶] Sodomy was a crime at common law in New Jersey at the time of the ratification of the Bill of Rights. [¶] The State enacted its first criminal sodomy law five years later. Acts of the Twentieth General Assembly, Mar. 18, 1796, ch. D.C., Sec. 7. New York: Laws of New York, ch. 21 (passed 1787). [¶] At the time of ratification of the Bill of Rights, North Carolina had adopted the English Statute of Henry VII outlawing sodomy. *See* Collection of the Statutes of the Parliament of England in Force in the State of North Carolina, ch. 17, p. 314 (Martin ed. 1792). [¶] Pennsylvania: Laws of the Fourteenth General Assembly of the Commonwealth of Pennsylvania, ch. CLIV, Sec. 2 (passed 1790). [¶] Rhode Island passed its first sodomy law in 1662. The Earliest Acts and Laws of the Colony of Rhode Island and Providence Plantations 1647–1719, at p. 142 (1977)). [¶] South Carolina: Public Laws of the State of South Carolina, p. 49 (1790). [¶] At the time of the ratifica-

tion of the Bill of Rights, Virginia had no specific statute outlawing sodomy, but had adopted the English common law. 9 Hening's Laws of Virginia, ch. 5, Sec. 6, p. 127 (1821) (passed 1776).

31   *Id.* at 193, n. 6 (That footnote, as the Court sets forth includes that, "[c]riminal sodomy statutes in effect in 1868: Alabama: Ala. Rev. Code Sec. 3604 (1867). Arizona (Terr.): Howell Code, ch. 10, Sec. (1865). Arkansas: Ark. Stat., ch. 51, Art. IV, Sec. 5 (1858). California: 1 Cal. Gen. Laws, ¶ 1450, Sec. 48 (1865). Colorado (Terr.): Colo. Rev. Stat., ch. 22, Sec. 45, 46 (1868). Connecticut: Conn. Gen. Stat., tit. 122, ch. 7, Sec. 124 (1868). Delaware: Del. Rev. Stat, ch. 131, Sec. 7 (1893). Florida: Fla. Rev. Stat., div. 5, Sec. 2614 (passed 1868) (1892). Georgia: Ga. Code Sec. 4286, 4287, 4290 (1867). Kingdom of Hawaii: Haw. Penal Code, ch. 13, Sec. 11 (1869). Illinois: Ill. Rev. Stat., div 5, Sec. 49, 50 (1845). Kansas (Terr.): Kan Stat., ch. 53 Sec. 7 (1855). Kentucky: 1 Ky. Rev. Stat., ch. 28, art. iv, Sec. 11 (1860). Louisiana: La. Rev. Stat., Crimes and Offenses, Sec. 5 (1856). Maine: Me. Rev. Stat., tit. XII, ch. 160, Sec. 4 (1846). Maryland: 1 Md. Code, art. 30, Sec. 201 (1860). Michigan: Mich. Rev. Stat., tit. 30, ch. 158, Sec. 16 (1846). Minnesota: Minn. Stat., ch. 96, Sec. 13 (1859). Mississippi: Miss. Rev. Code, ch. 64, Sec. LII, art. 238 (1857). Missouri: 1 Mo. Rev. Stat., ch. 50, art. viii, Sec. 7 (1856). Montana (Terr.): Mont. Acts, Resolutions, Memorials, Criminal Practice Acts, ch. IV, Sec. 44 (1856). Nebraska (Terr.): Neb. Rev. Stat., Crim. Code, ch. 4, Sec. 47 (1866). Nevada (Terr.): Nev. Comp. Laws, 1861-1900, Crimes and Punishments, Sec. 45. New Hampshire: N.H. Laws, Act. of June 19, 1812, Sec. 5 (1815). New Jersey: N.J. Rev. Stat., tit. 8, ch. 1, Sec. 9 (1847). New York: 3 N.Y. Rev. Stat., pt. 4, ch. 1, tit. 5, Sec. 20 (5th ed. 1859). North Carolina: N.C. Rev. Code, ch. 34, Sec. 6 (1855). Oregon: Laws of Ore., Crimes — Against Morality, etc., ch. 7, Sec. 655 (1874). Pennsylvania: Act of Mar. 31, 1860, Sec. 32, Pub. L. 392, in 1 Digest of Statute Law of Pa. 1700-1903, p. 1011 (Purdon 1905). Rhode Island: R.I. Gen. Stat., ch. 232, Sec. 12 (1872). South Carolina: Act of 1712, in 2 Stat. at Large of S.C. 1682-1716, p. 493 (1837). Tennessee: Tenn. Code, ch. 8, art. 1, Sec. 4843 (1858). Texas: Tex. Rev. Stat., tit. 10, ch. 5, art. 342 (1887) (passed 1860). Vermont: Acts and Laws of the State of Vt. (1779). Virginia: Va. Code, ch. 149, Sec. 12 (1868). West Virginia: W. Va. Code, ch. 149, Sec. 12 (1868). Wisconsin (Terr.): Wis. Stat. Sec. 14, p. 367 (1839).

32   *Id.* at 193–194 (citing SURVEY U. MIAMI L. REV., *supra*, at p. 524, n. 9).

33   See *e.g.*, Conkle, *The Second Death of Substantive Due Process*, 62 IND. L.J. 215, 232–235, 242 (1987).

34   *See* Kevin Sack, *Georgia's High Court Voids Sodomy Law*, N.Y. TIMES, Nov. 24, 1998, at A14; Debra Cassens, *New Court Rejects Ga. Sodomy Law*, A.B.A. J., Feb. 1999, at p. 30 (citing *Powell v. State*, No. S98A0755 (Nov. 23, 1998)).

35   *See Maryland Ditched Sodomy Law*, THE ADVOCATE, November 24, 1998, at p. 16.

36   The "Stonewall Riots" as the series of clashes became known, erupted on June 27, 1969—a Friday night—when New York City police officers raided a Greenwich Village gay bar called the Stonewall Inn. Raids of this kind were reportedly not uncommon at the time, and they often met little or no resistance. But on this night, violence and violent protests broke out and continued for several nights. *See Village Raid Stirs Melee*, N.Y. POST, June 28, 1969; *4 Policemen Hurt in 'Village Raid,'* N.Y. TIMES, June 29, 1969; *Police Again Rout 'Village' Youths*, N.Y. TIMES, June 30, 1969; *Hostile Crowd Dispersed Near Sheridan Square*, N.Y. TIMES, July 3, 1969; *Gay Power Comes to Sheridan Square*, THE VILLAGE VOICE, July 3, 1969. This was the beginning of the gay rights movement, historian suggest. *See, e.g.*, GAY FREEDOM 1970: A COMMEMORATIVE PICTORIAL ESSAY OF THE FIRST ANNIVERSARY OF THE GAY LIBERATION MOVEMENT (New York: Queen's Quarterly Publishing, Co., 1970); Donn Teal, THE GAY MILITANTS (New York: Stein & Day, 1971); Leigh W. Rutledge, THE GAY DECADES: THE PEOPLE AND EVENTS THAT SHAPED GAY LIVES (New York: Penguin Books, 1992); Martin Duberman, STONEWALL (New York: Penguin, 1993); Eric Marcus, MAKING HISTORY: THE STRUGGLE FOR GAY AND LESBIAN EQUAL RIGHTS, 1945–1990 (New York: HarperCollins, 1992).

37   *See* Stacey D'Erasmo, *Polymorphous Normal: Has Sexual Identity—Gay, Straight, or Bi—Outlived its Usefulness?*, N.Y. TIMES MAG., Oct. 14, 2001, at 104–11, at p. 106. (That young man was Matthew Shepard, a 21-year-old freshman at the University of Wyoming, whose death sparked wide-spread discussion about the issues of violence against homosexuals. See, *e.g.*, Robyn Meredith, *Illinois Mulls New Tactic Over Violence Based on Sex*, N.Y. TIMES, Feb. 9, 2000; John LeLand, *Silence Ending About Abuse in Gay Relationships*, N.Y. TIMES, Nov. 6, 2000, at A14; Melanie Thernstrom, *The Crucifixion of Matthew Shepard*, VANITY FAIR, March 1999, at pp. 209–275.

38   *See, e.g.*, Kristin Eliasberg, *Making a Case for the Right to Be Different*, N.Y. TIMES, June 16, 2001, at p. A17; Larry Kramer, *Same-Sex Marriage, Conflict of Laws, and the Unconstitutional Public Policy Exception*, 106 YALE L. J. at pp. 1965–2008 (May 1997).

39   *See, e.g.*, Craig Garrett, *Poll: Local Gays More Likely to Be Victims of Assaults*, DETROIT NEWS, March 11, 1997, at 5C; H.G. Bissinger, *The Killing Trail*, VANITY FAIR, Feb. 1995, at pp. 80–145.

40   See *Dale v. Boy Scouts of America*, 308 N.J. Super. 516 (1998).

41   528 U.S. 1109 (2000).

42   *Boy Scouts of America v. Dale*, 530 U.S. 640 (2000).

43   *See* Lucio Guerrero, *Schools May Evict Scouts*, CHIC. SUN-TIMES, Sept. 14, 2000, at p.3.

44   *See* Ernest Tucker, *84 Methodist Ministers to Conduct Same-Sex Marriage*, CHIC. SUN-TIMES, Jan. 15, 1999, at p. 24; *Seeing a Liturgical, Minister Defies a Ban on Same-Sex Unions*, N.Y. TIMES, Jan. 2, 2001, at A10.

45   *See* Barbara Dozetos, *FBI Releases Latest Statistics on Hate Crimes in the U.S.*, GAY.COM NETWORK, Feb. 13, 2001. (In point of fact, it was actually not until 2000 that the House of Representatives voted 232 to 192 to make crimes against gay and lesbian persons a federal hate crime.)

46   *See* Thernstrom, *supra* note 37, at p. 272.

47   *See* Annette Friskopp and Sharon Silverstein, STRAIGHT JOBS, GAY LIVES (New York: Scribner, 1995), at p. 38.

48   *Id.* at 39.

49   *See* Bissinger, *supra* note 39, at p. 85.

50   See SEXUAL ORIENTATION AND THE LAW (eds. Harvard Law Review), (Cambridge, Mass.: Harvard University Press, 1989), at pp. 1–44.

51   *See* Thernstrom, *supra* note 37, at p. 210.

52   *See* Vicky Hallett, *Who do You Love?*, U.S.NEWS & WORLD REPORT, July 14, 2003, at p. 38.

53   *See* William L. Hamilton, *Messages That Are Both Ambiguous and Direct*, N.Y. TIMES (July 20, 2000), at B1. ("In Mitchell Gold furniture ads running in national magazines now, two smiling young men sit on a white sofa, with a blond little girl between them on a child's chair. A) They are college friends with a sister. B) They are an attractive couple. The girl is their daughter Dorothy. And you aren't in Kansas anymore.")

54   In 2001, for example, two lesbian medical students sued Albert Einstein College of Medicine alleging discrimination in housing on the basis of sexual orientation. *See* Somini Sengupta, *New York's Top Court Hears Gay Students' Housing Suit*, N.Y. TIMES, April 25, 2001, at A18.

55   *See* Jane Gross, *Gays Thrive as Part of a Quiet New Jersey Community*, N.Y. TIMES, Dec. 4, 2000, at A.28; Erica Goode, *A Rainbow of Differences in Gays' Children*, N.Y. TIMES, July 17, 2001, at D1.

56   For a list of some of the hundreds of companies with such policies, *See* Friskopp & Silverstein, *supra* note 47, at pp. 491–508.

57   *See* American Civil Liberties Union ad, THE NEW YORKER (and other national publications), April 9, 2001, at p. 41.

58   *See* Carey Goldberg, *Gay Couples Welcoming Idea of Civil Union*, N.Y. TIMES, March 18, 2000, at A1, A10.

59   *See* Dan Gilgoff, *Gays Force the Issue*, U.S.NEWS & WORLD REPORT, Aug. 18–Aug. 25, 2003, at pp. 12–14.

60   *See* Elizabeth Becker, *Gays See Bush With Wariness and Optimism*, N.Y. TIMES, Jan. 26, 2001, at A1.

61   By 2000, for example, several major corporations—Coors, Levi Strauss, American Express, IBM and Disney among them—and nearly 60 American cities and one state have extended benefits to domestic partners. For review of the issue in terms of headlines, *See, e.g.,* Mireya Navarro, *2 Decades Later, Miami Passes Gay Rights*, N.Y. TIMES, Dec. 2, 1998, at A1; *Same-sex Partners Would Get Benefits Under Ruling*, N.Y. TIMES, Feb. 2, 2000, at p. A21; Daniel B. Kennedy, *'Til Death Do Us Part: Same-sex Survivor Seeks Assets of Partner Under Equitable Doctrine Governing Heterosexuals*, A.B.A. J., Jan. 2001, at p. 22; *Spitzer Joins ACLU in Suit*, N.Y. TIMES, Sept. 7, 2000, at A27; *Minnesota: Benefits Blocked for Gay Partners*, N.Y. TIMES, May 5, 2001, at A9; *Constructive Trust for Same-sex Couple*, NAT'L L.J., June 18, 2001, at A6; *Domestic Partners Win Benefit Battle*, NAT'L L.J., July 2, 2001, at A6; Adam Clymer, *House Approves D.C.'s Law on Rights of Domestic Partners*, N.Y. TIMES, Sept. 26, 2001, at p. A12. States and municipalities that have approved same-sex adoptions include: Alaska: Anchorage and Juneau; California: Alameda, Butte, Contra, Costa, Fresno, Los Angeles, Marin, San Diego, San Francisco, San Luis Obispo, San Mateo, Santa Clara, Santa Cruz, Sonoma; Massachusetts (whole state); Michigan: Washtenaw and other counties; Minnesota: Aitkin and Hennepin counties; New Jersey: Essex and Middlesex counties; New York: Monroe, Rochester, and Washington (same-sex adoptions have been invalidated by courts across the state and in New York City); Oregon: Multnomah and Portland; Pennsylvania: York; Texas: San Antonio and Tarrant; Vermont (whole state); Washington: King, Spokane and Thurston.

62   For a review of the evolution of the issues, *See* Nancy Polikoff, *This Child Does Have Two Mothers: Redefining Parenthood to Meet the Needs of Children in Lesbian-Mother and Other Nontraditional Families*,78 GEO. L. REV. 459-517 (1990); *Kulla v. McNulty*, 472 N.W.2d 175 (Minn. App. 1991); *McGuffin v. Overton*, 542 N.W.2d 288 (Mich. App. 1995); *N.C., Virginia Courts Split on Parenting*, THE ADVOCATE, Sept. 1, 1998, at p. 16 (noting that a Virginia court granted a "divorced lesbian and her partner custody of her 6-year-old boy and 8-year-old girl, while the North Carolina Supreme Court denied a gay father custody of his 9- and 12-year-old sons); *Judge Gives Lesbian Joint Custody of Child*, ASSOC. PRESS, Nov. 3, 1998 (reprinted on CNN.COM, Nov. 3, 1998); *Pending Texas Law Targets Gay Foster Parents, Consensual Sex Acts*, ASSOC. PRESS, Jan. 7, 1999; *Unmarried Life Partner Cannot Adopt Child*, NAT'L L.J., Feb. 15, 1999, at B25 (citing case of *In re the Adoption of Baby Z.*, No. 15868 (Conn. 1999); Andrienne Drell, *Lesbian Asks Court for Parental Rights*, CHIC. SUN-TIMES, May 11, 1999, at p. 16; Tim Novak, *Lesbian Denied Visitation to Child of Former Lover*, CHIC. SUN-TIMES, Dec. 17, 1999, at p. 18; *Lesbian Custody Ruling Stands*, NAT'L L.J., Oct. 23, 2000, at A6; Mike KcKee, *Gay Guardianship Rights Get Boost*, NAT'L L.J., Nov. 27, 2000, at A4; Robert Hanley, *Appeals Court Says Lesbian May Add Companion's Name*, N.Y. TIMES, Aug. 3, 2001; *U.S. Fund for Tower Victims Will Aid Some Gay Partners*, N.Y. TIMES, May 30, 2002, at A1; *Same-Sex Visitation*, NAT'L L.J., June 3, 2002, A6; *Michigan: Gay Adoption*, N.Y. TIMES, June 6, 2002, at A23; *Court Allows Vote on*

Barring Same-Sex Union, N.Y. TIMES, June 14, 2002, at A21; *Lesbian Can't Co-parent Her Partner's Children*, NAT'L L.J., Sept. 9, 2002, at B6; *Domestic Partner Ruling*, NAT'L L.J., Dec. 23– Dec. 30, 2002, at A6; Peter Whorisky, *A New Year's Baby with an Additional Difference: 2 Moms*, WASH. POST, Jan. 2, 2003, at A01.; Erica Goode, *Group Backs Gays Who Seek to Adopt a Partner's Child*, N.Y. TIMES, Feb. 4, 2002, at A1; Fred Bernstein, *Married or Not, It's a Full House*, N.Y. TIMES, Nov. 20, 2003, at D1.

63   See SEXUAL ORIENTATION AND THE LAW (eds. Harvard Law Review), (Cambridge, Mass.: Harvard University Press, 1989), at p. 95. ("Marriage has always been regarded as a central institution in American society. Alongside its strong symbolic meaning to the partners, marriage bestows concrete legal advantages on the couple: tax benefits, standing to recover damages for certain torts committed against spouses, rights to succession, and insurance benefits, to name a few.") See *also* NOTE, *Marital Status Classifications: Protecting Homosexual and Heterosexual Cohabitors*, 14 HASTINGS CONST. L.Q., III, pp. 115–116 (1986). For case law, See *Turner v. Safley*, 107 S. Ct. 2254, 2265 (1987).

64   See *Canada Overturns Definition of 'Spouse' as Heterosexual*, REUTERS, May 20, 1999 (reprinted in N.Y. TIMES, May 21, 1999), at A10; *Germany: Court Upholds Gay Marriage*, N.Y. TIMES, July 21, 2001, at A8.

65   See James Brookes, *Banns Being Read for Gay Weddings in Canada*, N.Y. TIMES, Dec. 28, 2000; Clifford Krauss, *Court Rules That Ontario Must Recognize Same-Sex Marriages*, N.Y. TIMES, July 14, 2002, at p. 11.

66   See *Same-Sex Partners Win Legal Status in Germany*, REUTERS, Aug, 2, 2001 (reprinted in N.Y. TIMES, Aug. 2, 2001, at A3).

67   See *Argentina: Legal Status for Homosexual Couples*, N.Y. TIMES, Dec. 14, 2002, at A6.

68   So promising that scholars began "confidently" predicting that Hawaii would recognize same-sex marriages after the state supreme court's decision in *Baehr v. Lewin*, 852 P.2d 44 (Hawaii 1993). See, *e.g.*, Larry Kramer, *Same-Sex Marriage, Conflict of Laws, and the Unconstitutional Public Policy Exception*, 106 YALE L. J. (May 1997), 1965–2008; Mark Strausser, 48 *Natural Law and Same-Sex Marriage*, DEPAUL L. REV. (Fall 1998), 51–82; Deborah M. Henson, *Will Same-Sex Marriages Be Recognized in Sister States?: Full Faith and Credit and Due Process Limitations on States' Choice of Law Regarding the Status and Incidents of Homosexual Marriages Following Hawaii's Baehr v. Lewin*, 32 U. LOUISVILLE J. FAM. L. 551, 560–76 (1993–1994); Joseph W. Hovermill, *A Conflict of Laws and Morals: The Choice of Law Implications of Hawaii's Recognition of Same-Sex Marriages*, 53 M.D. L. REV. 450, 454–66 (1994); Candice L. Sage, NOTE, *Sister-State Recognition of Valid Same-Sex Marriages; Baehr v. Lewin—How Will It Play in Peoria?*, 28 IND. L. REV. 115 (1994); Victoria Slind-Flor, *Same-Sex Case Poses Many Questions*, NAT'L L.J., Dec. 16, 1996, at A8; David Savage, *Combustible Cases: Will a Car Crash Ruling Lead to Recognition of Gay Marriages?*, A.B.A. J., March 1998, pp. 42–44.

69   See *Baehr v. Lewin*, 852 P.2d 44 (Hawaii 1993). Cases involving related challenges include: *Dean v. Dist. of Columbia*, 653 A.2d 307 (D.C. App. 1995); *Gajovski v. Gajovski*, 610 N.E.2d 431 (Ohio App. 9 Dist. 1991); *Braschi v. Stahl Associates Co.*, 543 N.E.2d 49 (N.Y. 1989); *Singer v. Hara*, 522 P.2d 1187 (Wash. App. 1974).

70   *Baehr* at 55. (As part of its analysis, the court set forth that "article I, section 6 of the Hawaii Constitution expressly states that '[t]he right of the people to privacy is recognized and shall not be infringed upon without the showing of a compelling state interest.' HAW. CONST. ART. I, Sec. 6 (1978). The framers of the Hawaii Constitution declared that the 'privacy concept' embodied in article I, section 6 is to be 'treated as a fundamental right[.]' *State v. Kam*, 69 Haw. 483, 493, 748 P.2d 372, 378 (1988) (citing Comm. WHOLE REP. NO. 15, in 1 Proceedings of the Constitutional Convention of Hawaii of 1978, at 1024 (1980).")

71   *Id.* at 57 (citing HAW. CONST. ART. I, Sec. 6 (1978)).

72   *Id.* (citing *State v. Kam*, 69 Haw. 483, 493 (1988) (citing COMM. WHOLE REP. NO. 15, in 1 Proceedings of the Constitutional Convention of Hawaii of 1978, at p. 1024 (1980))).

73   *Id.*

74   *Id.*

75   Specifically, the court held that "sex is a 'suspect category' for purposes of equal protection analysis under article I, section 5 of the Hawaii Constitution and that [Hawaii Revised Statute] Sec. 572-1 is subject to the 'strict scrutiny' test. It therefore follows, and we do hold that (1) HRS Sec. 572-1 is presumed to be unconstitutional (2) unless Lewin [the director of the Department of Health], as an agent of the State of Hawaii, can show that (a) the statute's sex based classification is justified by compelling state interests and (b) the statute is narrowly drawn to avoid unnecessary abridgments of the applicants couples' constitutional rights." *Id.* at 67. In other words, "in accordance with the 'strict scrutiny' standard, the burden will rest of Lewin to overcome the presumption that [Hawaii Revised Statute] Sec. 572-1 is unconstitutional by demonstrating that it furthers compelling state interests and is narrowly drawn to avoid unnecessary abridgments of constitutional rights." *Id.* at 69.

76   *Id.* at 67.

77   *Id.*

78   *Id.* at 69.

79   See Carey Goldberg, *Couple Who Stirred Issue of Same-Sex Marriage Still Hopeful*, N.Y. TIMES, July 28, 1996, at A12; Melissa Healy, *Senate OKs Bill Against Same-Sex Marriage*, L.A. TIMES, Sept. 11,

1996, at A1; John E. Yang, *Senate Passes Bill Against Same-Sex Marriage*, WASH. POST, Sept. 11, 1996, at A1; *Hawaii Seeks Law to Block Gay Marriage*, N.Y. TIMES, April 18, 1997, at A 15; David Coolidge, *At Last, Hawaiians Have Their Say on Gay Marriage*, WALL ST. JOUR., April 23, 1997, at A19.

80   *See Brause v. Bureau of Vital Statistics*, Case No. 3AN-96-6562 CI.

81   *See* Jim Clarke, *Alaska Men Want Court to Throw Out Same Sex Marriage Ban*, ASSOCIATED PRESS, Nov. 16, 1997.

82   *See Baehr v. Miike*, 1996 WL 694235 (Haw. Cir. Ct. Dec. 3, 1996), at * 19.

83   *Id.*

84   *See* Kramer, *supra* note 68, at p. 1965.

85   *Id.*

86   *Id.* at 1966 (citing DEFENSE OF MARRIAGE ACT, PUB. L. NO. 104-99, Sec. 2(a), 1996 USC CAN (110) 2419, 2419)); PUBLIC LAW 104-199 [H.R. 3396]; September 21, 1996.

87   Among those states are: Alaska, Arizona, Delaware, Georgia, Indiana, Illinois, Kansas, Michigan, Missouri, North Carolina, Oklahoma, Pennsylvania, South Carolina, South Dakota, Tennessee, and Utah. For fuller review, *See* Evan Wolfson, *Anti-Marriage Bills 1997—State-by-State Status Report. See also* Shannon P. Duffy, *Pushing the States on Gay Unions*, NAT'L L.J., Dec. 4, 2000, at A1.

88   *Breese v. Smith*, 501 P.2d 159 (Alaska 1972).

89   *See Brause v. Bureau of Vital Statistics*, Case No. 3AN-96-6562 CI, at * 4.

90   *Id.* at * 2.

91   *Id.* at *4 (citing *Breese v. Smith*, 501 P.2d at 170).

92   *See Hawaii Gives Legislature Power to Ban Same-Sex Marriage*, CNN.com, Nov. 3, 1998.

93   *Id.*

94   *Id.*

95   *See Baehr v. Miike* (1999).

96   *See Baker v. Vermont*, No. 98-032; Carey Goldberg, *Vermont's High Court Extends Full Rights to Same-Sex Couples*, N.Y. TIMES, Dec. 21, 1999, at A1, A23.

97   *See* Goldberg, *supra* note 95, at A23.

98   *See* Carey Goldberg, *Forced to Act on Gay Marriage, Vermont Finds Itself Deeply Split*, N.Y. TIMES, Feb. 3, 2000, at A1, A14.

99   *See* Dan Barry, *Icon for Abortion Protesters Is Looking for a Second Act*, N.Y. TIMES, July 20, 2001, A1, at A20. (According to Barry, Terry's "former pastor and colleagues say he is an unrepentant sinner who betrayed the faith by abandoning his wife, using foul language and drinking alcohol in the presence of children, and who nevertheless still seeks to raise money from those who are unaware of how far he has fallen.")

100 *Id.*

101 *See* Goldberg, *supra* note 98, at A14.

102 *See* Ross Sneyd, *Vt. House OKs Gay Unions*, CHI. SUN-TIMES, March 17, 2000, at p. 34.

103 *Id.* at p. 34. See *also* Carey Goldberg, *Vermont Gives Final Approval to Same-Sex Unions*, N.Y. TIMES, April 26, 2000, at A12.

104 *Id.*

105 *See* Tammerlin Drummond, *The Marrying Kind*, TIME, May 14, 2001, at p. 52.

106 *See* Lois Smith Brady, *For Gay Couples, New Rituals at the Altar*, N.Y. TIMES, Nov. 23, 2003, at p. 2.

107 *See Vermont Law on Gay Rights Proves a Factor in Primaries*, N.Y. TIMES, Sept. 14, 2000, at A20.

108 *See* Pam Belluck, *Nebraskans to Vote on Most Sweeping Ban on Gay Unions*, N.Y. TIMES, Oct. 21, 2000, at A7.

109 *See ACLU to Appeal Denial of Name Change to Lesbian*, N.Y. TIMES, Sept. 22, 2000, at A25.

110 *See* Darryl Van Duch, *Gays Held Unprotected by Title VII*, NAT'L L.J., Sept. 11, 2000, at B1.

111 *Hamner v. St. Vincent Hosp. and Health Care Center*, No. 99-3086 (7th Cir. Aug. 24, 2000).

112 *See* Van Duch, *supra* note 110, at B1.

113 *See* Sneyd, *supra* note 102, at p. 34.

114 *See Vermont Law on Gay Rights Proves a Factor in Primaries, supra* note 107, at A20.

115 A UNION IN WAIT (2000), airing on SUNDANCE, September 21, 2003.

116 *Id.*

117 *See* Pam Belluck, *Marriage by Gays Gains Big Victory in Massachusetts*, N.Y. TIMES, Nov. 19, 2003, A1, A19.

118 *See* Shaila K. Dewan, *New York Approves Measures Protecting Gays' Civil Rights*, N.Y. TIMES, Dec. 18, 2002, at A1.

119 *See Same-Sex Solicitations Decriminalized in Ohio*, NAT'L L.J., June 3, 2002, at B4.

120 *Lawrence v. Texas*, 123 S. Ct. 2472 (2003).

121 *See* Bissinger, *supra* note 39, at p. 87.

122 *Id.*

123 *Id.*

124 Texas officials along with individual companies have proved particularly aggressive in their efforts to block the arrival of agencies and industries that are generally disapproved of. In November 6, 2003, for example, cement companies opposed to abortion refused to deliver supplies to a con-

struction site where a women's health clinic was being built. *See* TEXAS: *Abortion Dispute*, N.Y. TIMES, Nov. 6, 2003, at A22.

125   *See* Bissinger, *supra* note 39, at p. 87.

126   *Id.*

127   *See* Linda Greenhouse, *Justices, 6-3, Legalize Gay Sexual Conduct in Sweeping Reversal of Court's '86 Ruling*, N.Y. TIMES, June 27, 2003, at A1, A17.

128   *See* Sarah Kershaw, *Adversaries on Gay Rights Vow State-By-State Fight*, N.Y. TIMES, July 6, 2003, at A8.

129   *See* Marcia Coyle, *In the Bedroom: Gay Rights Are at the Center of the Sodomy Case at the Supreme Court*, NAT'L L.J., March 24, 2003, at A1, A6.

130   *See* Sheryl Gay Stolberg, *Persistent Conflict for Gays and G.O.P.*, N.Y. TIMES, April 23, 2003, at A20 (citing *Associated Press* article of April 21, 2003).

131   *Planned Parenthood of Southeastern Pennsylvania v. Casey*, 505 U.S. 833 (1992).

132   *Lawrence v. Texas*, 123 S. Ct. at 2481 (Kennedy, J., majority).

133   *Casey*, 505 U.S. at 851.

134   *Lawrence*, 123 S. Ct. at 2481.

135   *Evans v. Romer*, 517 U.S. 620 (1996).

136   *Id.* at 624.

137   *Lawrence*, 123 S. Ct. at 2482.

138   *See* Richard Brust, *The Man in the Middle*, A.B.A. J., October 2003, pp. 24–25.

139   *Beller v. Middendorf*, 632 F.2d 788 (9th Cir. 1980).

140   *Lawrence*, 123 S. Ct. at 2482 (citing *Evans v. Romer*, 517 U.S. at 622–624).

141   *Id.* at 2484.

142   *Id.* at 2490 (Scalia, J., dissenting) (citing *Williams v. Pryor*, 240 F.3d 944, 949 (11th Cir. 2001), and noting citation to *Bowers* "in upholding Alabama's prohibition on the sale of sex toys on the grounds that '[t]he crafting and safeguarding of public morality...indisputably is a legitimate government interest under rational basis scrutiny'"); *Milner v. Apfel*, 148 F.3d 812, 814 (7th Cir. 1998) (noting citation to *Bowers* to support the proposition that "'[l]egislatures are permitted to legislate with regard to morality...rather than confined to preventing demonstrable harms'"); *Holmes v. California Army National Guard*, 124 F.3d 1126, 1136 (9th Cir. 1997) (noting the reliance "on *Bowers* in upholding the federal statute and regulations banning from military service those who engage in homosexual conduct"); *Owens and State*, 352 Md. 663, 683, 724 A.2d 43, 53 (1999) (noting a reliance on "*Bowers* in holding that 'a person has no constitutional right to engage in sexual intercourse, at least outside of marriage'"); *Sherman v. Henry*, 928 S.W.2d 464, 469–473 (Tex. 1996) (noting reliance on "*Bowers* in rejecting a claimed constitutional right to commit adultery")).

143   *Barnes v. Glen Theatre, Inc.*, 501 U.S. 560, 569 (1991).

144   *Lawrence*, 123 S. Ct. at 2490 (Scalia, J., dissenting).

145   *Id.*

146   *Griswold*, 381 U.S. at 483–86.

147   *See* Rachel Benson Gold, ISSUES & IMPLICATIONS, *The Need for and Cost of Mandating Private Insurance Coverage of Contraception*, published within THE GUTTMACHER REPORT ON PUBLIC POLICY, Aug. 1998, at pp. 1, 5.

148   *See* ISSUES IN BRIEF, *U.S. Policy Can Reduce Cost Barriers to Contraception*, 1999 SERIES (NO. 2), published by the Alan Guttmacher Institute, at p. 1.

149   *Id.* at 2. (According to the Alan Guttmacher Institute, "Title X of the Public Health Service Act, the only federal program devoted solely to the provision of family planning service. These programs have a long history of success in providing contraceptive services and reducing unintended pregnancy among low-income women, teenagers and other women in need of subsidized services; they also have made their mark by improving the health and financial well-being of women and their children. [¶] Each year, publicly funded contraceptive services help women avoid 1.3 million unintended pregnancies, which would result in 534,000 births, 632,000 abortions and 165,000 miscarriages. Services provided by clinics receiving funds under Title X are responsible for averting one million of these pregnancies.")

150   *See Viagra Spawns Birth Control Issue*, A.B.A. J., at pp. 36–37 (August 1998); Michael Grunwald, *Judge Sues to Get More Viagra*, CHI. SUN-TIMES, March 29, 1999, at p. 41 (reprinting story first published in WASH. POST) (reporting that a federal bankruptcy judge was preparing to file a class action lawsuit against the federal government, arguing that his federal health plan should cover payments for the full prescription of Viagra each month, and not just a small set number of pills); *See Sibley-Schreiber v. Oxford Health Plans*, 98 CV 3671. (The case, being heard by a federal judge in Brooklyn, was certified in September 1999, as a class after Oxford announced that the company would pay for no more than six Viagra pills per employee per month, regardless of the dosage prescribed); Bruce Balestier, *Angry Judge Clears Way for Viagra Class Action*, NAT'L L.J., Sept. 6, 1999, at A5; Tamar Lewin, *Insurance Should Cover Cost of Contraceptives, Suit Says*, N.Y. TIMES, July 20, 2000, at A16. (In July 2000, Jennifer Erickson, a 26-year-old pharmacist from Washington State, was among the named females plaintiffs who brought suit under Title VII of the Civil Rights Act of 1964, alleging that paying for the "basic health care needs of men" while refusing to pay for contraceptives for women rose to the level of gender discrimination.)

151   That version of the story was recounted by Jack Hitt in *The Search for the Female Viagra and Other Tales from the Second Sexual Revolution*, N.Y. TIMES MAG., Feb. 20, 2000, at p. 34.

152   *Id.*

153   *Id.* at 36. (Other interesting asides, according to Hitt, were that "Viagra has been embraced by the well off (4 percent of the total population of Palm Beach County has a prescription), but not only the well off. Not long ago, Wal-Mart and Kmart had a Viagra war that drove the per-pill price down from $10 to $7.80.")

154   *See Viagra Spawns Birth Control Issue*, A.B.A. J., at pp. 36–37 (August 1998).

155   *See Sibley-Schreiber, supra* note 150; *Balestier, supra* note 150.

156   *See Grunwald, supra* note 150.

157   *See Lewin, supra* note 150.

158   *See* ISSUES IN BRIEF, *U.S. Policy Can Reduce Cost Barriers to Contraception*, published by the Alan Guttmacher Institute (1999 SERIES, NO. 2), at p. 1. (According to the Alan Guttmacher Institute, though the majority of American women rely on private insurance,… "many private insurance plans provide inadequate coverage of contraceptive services and supplies. This gap increases many women's risk of experiencing an unintended pregnancy and helps explain why women of reproductive age spend 68% more on out-of-pocket health care costs than do men.")

159   That statement was attributed to Richard Coorsh, spokesman for the Health Insurance Association of America, (quoted in *Viagra Spawns Birth Control Issue, supra* note 150, at p. 36).

160   *See, e.g., Testimony of Father Charles E. Coughlin*, at pp. 126–130 (quoted in THE ABORTION CONTROVERSY: A DOCUMENTARY HISTORY, *supra* note 79, ENDNOTES FOR CHAPTER TWO, at pp. 29-31).

161   *Griswold*, 381 U.S. 479 (1965).

162   The modern day argument in the public realm has centered most often around Title X and block grant funding allocated for family planning.

163   *See, e.g.,* Tamar Lewin, *Judge Says Some Employees Must Cover Contraceptives*, N.Y. TIMES, June 13, 2001, at A18.

164   Those states are: Arizona; California; Connecticut; Delaware; Georgia; Hawaii; Iowa; Maine; Maryland; Massachusetts; Missouri; Nevada; New Hampshire; New Mexico; New York; North Carolina; Rhode Island; Texas; Vermont; Washington. (Under the Connecticut law, religious employers are not allowed to opt out of coverage and Texas will allow some companies to offer insurance without contraceptive coverage as of Jan. 1, 2004.) *See* STATE POLICIES IN BRIEF: *Insurance Coverage of Contraceptives*, published by the Alan Guttmacher Institute, Sept. 1, 2003.

165   *See* ISSUES IN BRIEF, *The Cost of Contraceptive Insurance Coverage*, published by the Alan Guttmacher Institute, April 2003.

166   *See* Raymond Hernandez, *U.S. Balks at New York Plan to Subsidize Contraceptives*, N.Y. TIMES, July 28, 2001.

167   Those states are: Colorado; Georgia; Kentucky; Mississippi; New York; North Carolina; Virginia; Washington; and, Wisconsin.

168   *See, e.g.,* CONN. HOUSE BILL 5672 (2001) and TEXAS HOUSE BILL 213 (2001).

169   Representative Chris Smith is a Republican from New Jersey.

170   The Alan Guttmacher Institute is a not-for-profit corporation for reproductive health research, policy analysis, and public education with offices in Washington, D.C. and New York.

171   *See* Lisa Kaeser, *What Methods Should Be Included in a Contraceptive Coverage Insurance Mandate?*, THE GUTTMACHER REPORT ON PUBLIC POLICY, October 1998, at p. 1.

172   *See* Gloria J. Banks, *Traditional Concepts and Nontraditional Conceptions: Social Security Survivor's Benefits for Posthumously Conceived Children*, 32 LOYOLA OF LOS ANGELES L. REV., at pp. 251, 272 (citing generally STEDMAN'S MEDICAL DICTIONARY, 876 (26th ed. 1995) at pp. 559, 638, 1976 (defining an embryo, fetus, and zygote in relation to the gestational process.))

173   *Id.* (citing STEDMAN, *supra* note 172, at p. 1976).

174   *Id.* (citing STEDMAN, *supra* note 172, at p. 638).

175   *Id.* (Banks notes that "the legal status and constitutional safeguarding of human conceptus has historically been based upon the stage of fetal development. The United States Supreme Court has, in its litany of abortion cases, conferred the greatest degree of protection upon viable fetuses. *See Planned Parenthood of Southeastern Pennsylvania v. Casey*, 505 U.S. 833 (1992). The moral dilemma in assigning rights to human conceptus has exploded with the advent of assisted reproductive techniques. The Court's reliance on viability is rather tenuous as technology threatens to expand fetal viability into the embryonic and zygote stages of human development.")

176   Johnson is also a Republican, who is from Connecticut.

177   *See* Kaeser, *supra* note 171, at p. 2.

178   *See* Katy Koontz, *22 Birth Control Blunders Even Smart Wives Make*, REDBOOK, February 1999, at p. 96.

179   *See* William Mosher, *Contraceptive Practice in the United States, 1982–1988*, FAMILY PLANNING PERSPECTIVES, Sept./Oct. 1990, at p. 198.

180   *See* FACTS IN BRIEF, *Contraceptive Use*, published by the Alan Guttmacher Institute, 1998. Programs like C.R.A.C.K (Children Requiring A Caring Kommunity) started in Orange County, California, pays crack-addicted women $200 to have their fallopian tubes tied. In July 1999, C.R.A.C.K moved

its efforts to Chicago. For background, *See* Pam Belluck, *Cash-for-Sterilization Plan Draws Addicts and Critics*, N.Y. TIMES, July 24, 1999, at A7.

181   *See* FACTS IN BRIEF, *supra* note 180.

182   *See* Mosher, *supra* note 179, at p. 199.

183   *Carey v. Population Services International*, 431 U.S. 678 (1977).

184   *See* FACTS IN BRIEF, *supra* note 180.

185   *See* Jim Ritter, *Monthly Shot Equal to Pill*, CHI. SUN-TIMES, May 19, 1999, at p. 4; *Taking Control*, MODE, October 1999, at p. 62; Mary Ann Marshall, *Morning Becomes Prophylactic*, Ms., Aug./Sept. 1999, at p. 40.

186   *See* Donald Kimelman, *Poverty and Norplant: Can Contraception Reduce the Underclass?*, PHIL. INQUIRER, Dec. 12, 1990, at A18.

187   At the turn of the century in Britain, as Sheila Rowbotham notes in *A Century of Women*, for example, similar issues sparked sensational newspaper reports that detailed "the tragic consequences: suicides of pregnant servants, corpses of abandoned babies, and the 'bastardy-order courts', when desperate unmarried mothers took fathers to court." *See* Rowbotham, *supra* note 23, ENDNOTES FOR CHAPTER TWO, at p. 30.

188   *See* Roberts, *supra* note 24, ENDNOTES FOR CHAPTER TWO, at p. 107 (noting that Lopez was referring to editorial-page editor, David Boldt, who reportedly okayed the editorial).

189   *Id.*

190   *Id.* (Roberts notes that Kimelman's proposal was praised by other NEWSWEEK writers. Jonathan Alter wrote, for example, that "[h]owever offensive the editorial, Kimelman was clearly on to something....The old answers have mostly failed. After the shouting stops, the problem will remain. It's too important to become taboo." *See* Jonathan Alter, *One Well-Read Editorial*, NEWSWEEK, Dec. 31, 1990, at pp. 85–86.)

191   The *Richmond Times-Dispatch* offered even more support, suggesting in an editorial of its own that Norplant "offers society yet another way to curb the expansion of an underclass most of whose members face futures of disorder and deprivation." *See Journalistic Thought Police*, RICHMOND TIMES-DISPATCH, Dec. 27, 1990, at A12.

192   Finally, the *New Republic's* Matthew Rees argued that Norplant may be the solution to the "current threat to children in our inner cities...." *See* Matthew Rees, *Shot in the Arm: the Use and Abuse of Norplant; Involuntary Contraception and Public Policy*, NEW REPUBLIC, Dec. 9, 1990, at A12.

193   *See* Roberts, *supra* note 188, at pp. 107–108. ("David Frankel, director of population sciences at the Rockefeller Foundation, made light of the tensions at the *Inquirer*, writing in the *Washington Post*, 'Despite the infantile reaction of some black staffers...birth control incentives would not be genocide. Such incentives would be human inducement to social responsibility,'" Roberts notes. In addition, then-mayor Marion Barry voiced support for tying Norplant to welfare benefits. "You can have as many babies as you want," Barry reportedly said. "But when you start asking the government to take care of them, the government now ought to have some control over you." *See* Sally Quinn, *Childhood's End*, WASH. POST, Nov. 27, 1994, at C1 (quoting Barry).)

194   *See* NARAL FACT SHEET: *Unjust Punishment*, *supra* note 78, ENDNOTES FOR CHAPTER FIVE, at p. 9.

195   *Id.* at 3 (citing Melissa Burke, *The Constitutionality of the Use of Norplant Contraceptive Device as a Condition of Probation*, 20 HASTINGS CONST. L. QUAR. at pp. 218–219 (Fall 1992)(quoting Reporter's Transcript [hereinafter RT] from Judgment Proceedings, at 3–4, in Clerk's Transcript [hereinafter CT] on Appeal, No. F015316, *People v. Johnson* (Super. Ct. Tulare County, Cal. No. 29390), at 41–42, and additional sources, Madeline Henley, *The Creation and Perpetuation of the Mother/Body Myth: Judicial and Legislative Enlistment of Norplant*, 41 BUFFALO L. REV. at p. 739 (Spring 1993) (further citation omitted.)))

196   Preven Emergency Contraceptive Kit is distributed by Gynetics, Inc.

197   *See* MEDICAL LETTER ON DRUGS AND THERAPEUTICS, Oct. 23, 1998, at pp. 102–103.

198   Two of the four tablets should be taken as soon as possible after unprotected sex. Studies shows that as much as 50 percent of the time women were nauseous and some were even sick enough to vomit after taking the first two pills. Women who vomit within one hour of taking the first two pills are warned to take a new dose. Twelve hours later, the second two of the original four pills must be taken.

199   *See* Jeff Stryker, *Emergency Birth Control: Access Issues*, N.Y. TIMES, March 11, 2003, at D5.

200   *See* ISSUES IN BRIEF, *Emergency Contraception: Increasing Public Awareness*, published by the ALAN GUTTMACHER INSTITUTE, Jan. 2003; Kate Zernike, *Use of Morning-After Pill Rising and It May Go Over the Counter*, N.Y. TIMES, May 19, 2003, at A1.

201   The 1998 proposed amendment by New Jersey Republican Representative Chris Smith was among these challenges. As set forth above, Smith sought to exclude from coverage contraceptives such as Preven as well as certain IUDs. The amendment was defeated 222–198.

202   *See California: 'Morning-After' Pill Coverage*, N.Y. TIMES, March 29, 2002, at A20.

203   *See* FACTS IN BRIEF, *supra* note 180.

204   *See The New Abortion*, THE VILLAGE VOICE, January 27, 1988, at 57.

205   *The Fight to Make RU 486 Available to U.S. Women: A Chronology in Brief*, MEMORANDUM, Oct. 7, 1998, THE FEMINIST MAJORITY FOUNDATION AND NEW MEDIA PUBLISHING INC.

206   *See French Trials of RU 486 Find 96 Percent Abortion Rate in Pregnancies of Less Than Seven Weeks,* FAMILY PLANNING PERSPECTIVES, May/June 1990, at p. 134.
207   Coburn is a Republican from Oklahoma.
208   *Id.* (The full context of Thompson's quote was reportedly: "I do not intend to roll back anything unless it is proven to be unsafe," Thompson reportedly told Senator Hillary Rodham Clinton in response to questions. "Safety concerns are something that's in question.")
209   *See Government Limits Abortion Pill Coverage,* N.Y. TIMES, April 1, 2001, at A19.
210   *See* Gina Kolata, *Death at 18 Spurs Debate Over a Pill for Abortion,* N.Y. TIMES, Sept. 24, 2003, at A18.
211   *See* Bruce Barcott, *From Tree-Hugger to Terrorist,* N.Y. TIMES MAG., April 7, 2002, pp. 56–81.
212   *Id.* at 59.
213   *See Abortion Clinic Damaged by Priest Wielding Ax,* N.Y. TIMES, Oct. 1, 2000, at 16. (The full content of the story is "[a] Roman Catholic priest drove a car into an abortion clinic today, then chopped at the building with an ax until the owner confronted him with a shotgun, the authorities said. The clinic was not open at the time and no one was injured. [¶] The priest, the Rev. John Earl, 32, drove through a door at the Abortion Access Northern Illinois Women's Center around 8:15 A.M. He was swinging an ax when the building's owner, Gerald W. Webster, fired a 12-gauge shotgun twice. [¶] 'I thank God and my shotgun that I'm alive,' Mr. Webster said. [¶] Father Earl was arrested and charged with burglary and felony damage to property, said Deputy Police Chief Dominic Iasparro. The priest, who was released on $10,000 bond, is the pastor at St. Patrick's Catholic Church in Rochelle, about 30 miles south of Rockford. [¶] The clinic houses the offices of Dr. Richard Ragsdale, who filed a landmark lawsuit challenging Illinois abortion restrictions.")
214   *Id.*
215   Interviews with some of these "crusaders" can be found in *Soldiers in the Army of God,* AMERICA UNDERCOVER, HBO TELEVISION (Producers, Daphne Pinkerson, Marc Levin and Daniel Voll), originally airing, April 1, 2001.
216   *See* Jean Reith Schroedel, IS THE FETUS A PERSON: A COMPARISON OF POLICIES ACROSS THE FIFTY STATES (Ithaca, New York: Cornell University Press, 2000), at p. 40 (citing Keith Cassidy, *The Right to Life Movement: Sources, Development, and Strategies* in THE POLITICS OF ABORTION AND BIRTH CONTROL IN HISTORIC PERSPECTIVE (Donald T. Critchlow ed.) (University Park, Penn.: Pennsylvania State University Press, 1996).
217   *See* Babcock, *et. al, supra* note 115, ENDNOTES FOR CHAPTER ONE, at p. 1059.
218   *See* Susan Faludi, BACKLASH: THE UNDECLARED WAR AGAINST AMERICAN WOMEN (New York: Crown Publishers, Inc. 1991), at p. 411.
219   *See* Annys Shin, *Feds Revisit Clinic Violence,* MS. April/May 1999, at p. 30.
220   *See Planned Parenthood Gets Anthrax Threat,* N.Y. TIMES, Feb. 23, 1999.
221   *See Louisiana: Fire Destroys Abortion Clinic,* N.Y. TIMES, July 17, 2001, at A13.
222   *See, e.g.,* Dan Barry, *Icon for Abortion Protesters Is Looking for a Second Act,* N.Y. TIMES, July 20, 2001, A1, at A20.
223   *See* Daniel Voll, *The Righteous Man With His Hit List Rocks on the Front Porch of His Glass House,* ESQUIRE, February 1999, at pp. 111–112.
224   *Id.*
225   As of December 2000, Kopp had not been captured. Authorities reportedly had information that Kopp may be in the United Kingdom. Reported on *Newsbreak,* COURT-TV, Dec. 15, 2000.
226   *See* David Johnston, *France Arrests Foe of Abortion in 1998 Murder,* N.Y. TIMES, March 30, 2001, at A1; Dan Barry, *Tracing Antiabortion Network to a Slaying Suspect in France,* N.Y. TIMES, March 31, 2001, at A1; James Risen, *Arrests May Reopen Question of Antiabortion Conspiracy,* N.Y. TIMES, March 31, 2001, at A13; WORLD NEWS TONIGHT, ABC TV, March 29, 2001, (Pierre Thomas reporting).
227   *See* Thomas J. Lueck, *Doctor's Killer Waives Right to Jury Trial,* N.Y. TIMES, March 12, 2003, at A23; *Potential Jurors Are Surveyed on Abortion,* N.Y. TIMES, March 4, 2003, at A25; Randal C. Archibold, *Man Denies Killing a Doctor Who Performed Abortions,* N.Y. TIMES, June 7, 2002; *Suspect Tells Newspaper He Killed Physician,* N.Y. TIMES, Nov. 21, 2002, at A31.
228   *See* David Staba, *Abortion Foe Who Killed Obstetrician Is Sentenced to 25 Years to Life,* N.Y. TIMES, May 10, 2003, at A15.
229   In June 2003, John Burt was arrested on charges of molesting a 15-year-old girl at the home he ran and where Griffin had volunteered. See *Florida: Man Charged In Molestation,* N.Y. TIMES, June 11, 2003, at A23.
230   *Id.* at A23.
231   *See* Abby Goodnough, *Florida Executes Killer of an Abortion Provider,* N.Y. TIMES, Sept. 4, 2003, at A12.
232   *Id.*
233   *Bray v. Alexandria Women's Health Clinic,* 506 U.S. 263 (1993).
234   *See, e.g., Award Overturned in Abortion Doctor 'Wanted Posters',* N.Y. TIMES, March 29, 2001, at A18.
235   *Bray,* 506 U.S. at 267.
236   As set forth above, 28 U.S.C. Sec. 1367 confer ancillary or pendent jurisdiction in federal court over state law claims as long as those claims are reasonably related to a federal claim properly brought in federal court.
237   *Id.*

238 Section 1985(3) of the Civil Rights Act states that "[i]f two or more persons...conspire or go in dis-
     guise on the highway or on the premises of another, for the purpose of depriving, either directly or
     indirectly, any person or class of persons of the equal protection of the laws, or of equal privileges
     and immunities under the laws; or for the purpose of preventing or hindering the constituted
     authorities of any State or Territory from giving or securing to all persons within such State or Ter-
     ritory the equal protection of the laws...."

239 *Bray*, 506 U.S. at 268 (citing *Griffin v. Breckenridge*, 403 U.S. 88, 102 (1971)).

240 *Id.* (citing *Carpenters v. Scott*, 463 U.S. 825, 833 (1983)).

241 It should be noted that *Griffin v. Breckenridge* involved a claim of racial discrimination.

242 *Bray*, 506 U.S. at 270–271 (citing *Carpenters, supra* note 240, at 850). (The Justices also note that if
     this were allowed,..."innumerable tort plaintiffs would be able to assert causes of action under
     1985(3) by simply defining the aggrieved class as those seeking to engage in the activity the defen-
     dant has interfered with. This definitional ploy would convert the statute into the 'general federal
     tort law' it was the very purpose of the animus requirement to avoid.")

243 *Id.*

244 *Id.* at 274 (citing *Maher v. Roe*, 432 U.S. at 474).

245 *Id.* (citing *Harris v. McRae*, 448 U.S. 325).

246 *Id.*

247 *See* 18 U.S.C. Sec. 248 (1994).

248 In April 2001, the United States Supreme Court refused, without written comment, to hear consti-
     tutional challenge to the Freedom of Access to Clinic Entrances Act.

249 *National Organization of Women v. Scheidler*, 510 U.S. 263 (1994).

250 The Hobbs Act is codified at 18 U.S.C. Sec. 1951.

251 *See NOW v. Scheidler*, 510 U.S. at 251 (citing Abortion Clinic Violence, Oversight Hearings Before
     the Subcommittee on Civil and Constitutional Rights of the House Committee on the Judiciary,
     99th Cong., 1st and 2d Sess., 55 (1987) (statement of Joseph M. Scheidler, Executive Director, Pro-
     Life Action League).

252 *See* 18 U.S.C. Sec. 1951(b)(2).

253 *NOW v. Scheidler*, 510 U.S. at 251.

254 968 F.2d 612 (7th Cir. 1992).

255 *NOW v. Scheidler*, 510 U.S. at 254.

256 *Madsen v. Women's Health Center*, 512 U.S. 753, 755 (1994).

257 *Id.* at 757.

258 *Id.*

259 *Id.* at 753.

260 *Id.* at 768.

261 *Id.* at 773.

262 *Schenck v. Pro-Choice Network of Western New York*, 117 S. Ct. 855 (1997).

263 *Id.* at 857.

264 *Id.*

265 *Id.*

266 For some background on the use of the Ku Klux Klan Act, FACE and RICO, *See* Rhonda Copelon,
     *The Applicability of Sec. 241 of the Ku Klux Klan Acts to Private Conspiracies to Obstruct or Preclude
     Access to Abortion*, 10 NAT'L BLACK L.J. 183 (1987).

267 *See, e.g., Award Overturned in Abortion Doctor 'Wanted Posters,'* N.Y. TIMES, March 29, 2001, at A18.

268 *Id.* (Some media reports put the award at $109 million.)

269 *See Antiabortionists Liable for Threats*, NAT'L L.J., February 15, 1999, at A8.

270 *See Award Overturned, supra* note 267, at A18.

271 *See Planned Parenthood v. American Coalition of Life Activists*, No. 99-35320 (D.C. No. CV-95-
     01671-REJ (District of Oregon), at 7079, 7114 (May 16, 2002) (citing *United States v. Gilbert
     (Gilbert II)*, 884 F.2d 454, 457 (9th Cir. 1989); *United States v. Orozo-Santillan*, 903 F.2d 1262, 1265
     (9th Cir. 1990)).

272 *Id.* (citing *Orozco-Santillan*, 903 F.2d at 1265; *United States v. Mitchell*, 812 F.2d 1250, 1255 (9th Cir.
     1987); *Watts v. United States*, 394 U.S. 705 (1969)).

273 *Id.* (citing *Orozco-Santillan*, 903 F.2d at 1265; *United States v.Gilbert (Gilbert II)*, 884 F.2d at 457).

274 *Id.*

275 *Id.* (upholding Sec. 871 conviction of defendant with no capacity to carry out [the] threat); *Roy v.
     United States*, 416 F.2d 874, 877 (9th Cir. 1969).

276 *Id.* at 7137–7138.

277 *Id.* at 7138.

278 *Id.* at 7139.

279 *Id.* at 7142.

280 *Id.* at 7143.

281 *Id.*

282 *Id.*

283 *See, e.g., U.S. Supreme Court Sides with Planned Parenthood Against Terrorists: Leaves Intact Court Holding That "Wanted" Posters Targeting Doctors Are Illegal Threats of Violence,* PLANNED PARENTHOOD FEDERAL OF AMERICA, INC. PRESS RELEASE, June 27, 2003.

284 *See* Charles Lane, *U.S. Opposes "Wanted" Posters in Abortion Case,* WASH. POST, at A03.

285 *See* James C. McKinley, Jr., *A Family is Fined Over Abortion Protests,* N.Y. TIMES, Aug. 28, 2001, at A15.

286 *Id.*

287 *Scheidler v. National Organization for Women,* 537 U.S. 393 (2003).

288 *See supra* note 250.

289 The Travel Act is codified at 18 U.S.C. Sec. 1952.

290 *Scheidler, supra* note 287.

291 *Id.*

292 *Id.* (citing *Scheidler v. National Organization for Women,* 267 F.3d 687, 709 (7th Cir. 2001)).

293 *Id.* (citing *United States v. Stillo,* 57 F.3d 553, 559 (7th Cir. 1995)).

294 *Id.* at 405 (citing *United States v. Nardello,* 393 U.S. 286, 290 (1969)).

295 *Id.*

296 *Id.* at 411.

297 *See* David Johnston, *Ashcroft Orders U.S. Marshals to Protect Abortion Doctor,* N.Y. TIMES, July 13, 2001, at A15.

298 *See* Philip Shenon, *Abortion Issue Holds Up Bill on Bankruptcy,* N.Y. TIMES, April 30, 2002, at A1, A20.

299 *Id.*

300 *Id.*

301 *Id.* at A20.

302 *Id.*

303 For review of the Hyde Amendment, *see supra* Chapter Five. Cases include: *Harris v. McRae,* 448 U.S. 297 (1980); *Williams v. Zbaraz,* 448 U.S. 358 (1980); *Planned Parenthood Association of Kansas City v. Ashcroft,* 462 U.S. 476 (1983); *Rust v. Sullivan,* 500 U.S. 173 (1991).

304 *See* Philip Shenon, *Abortion Debate Stalls Bankruptcy Bill,* N.Y. TIMES, May 23, 2002, at A18.

305 *Id.*

306 *See* Robert Sullivan, *Roe No More,* VOGUE, October 2003, pp. 162–168, at p. 168.

307 *See* FACTS IN BRIEF, *Induced Abortion,* published by the Alan Guttmacher Institute, Jan. 2003, at p. 1.

308 *See* Lawrence B. Finer & Stanley K. Henshaw, *Abortion Incidence and Services in the United States in 2000,* 35 PERSPECTIVES ON SEXUAL AND REPRODUCTIVE HEALTH at pp. 6–15 (Jan./Feb. 2003).

309 *Id.* at 13. (In some states, abortion decreases may be due to regulatory requirements placed on women seeking abortion. For example, in Wisconsin, the imposition of a two-day delay may have contributed to the 21% decline in the abortion rate (although women there may increasingly have gone to Illinois, particularly Chicago, to obtain abortions). In other states, rates may decline because many women travel out of state to have abortions. This may occur when the barriers to obtaining an abortion—such as gestational limited or other restrictions, or expense—are lower in neighboring states.)

310 *See* FACTS IN BRIEF, *supra* note 307.

311 *See* Finer & Henshaw, *supra* note 308, at p. 13.

312 *Id.*

313 *See* Babcock, *et al., supra* note 115, ENDNOTES FOR CHAPTER ONE, at p. 1059.

314 *See* Finer & Henshaw, *supra* note 308, at p. 14 (citing S.K. Henshaw and L.B. Finer, *The Accessibility of Abortion Services in the United States,* 2001, 35 PERSPECTIVES ON SEXUAL REPRODUCTIVE HEALTH at pp. 16–24, (2003)).

315 *Id.*

316 *Id.* (citing National Abortion Federation (NAF), Violence Statistics).

317 *Id.* (citing *Mandatory Waiting Periods for Abortion,* STATE POLICIES IN BRIEF, published by the Alan Guttmacher Institute, 2002; *State Funding of Abortion Under Medicaid,* STATE POLICIES IN BRIEF, published by the Alan Guttmacher Institute, 2002; and *Parental Involvement in Minors' Abortions,* STATE POLICIES IN BRIEF, published by the Alan Guttmacher Institute, 2002).

318 *Id.*

319 *See* Henshaw & Finer, *The Accessibility of Abortion Services, supra* note 314, at p. 16.

320 *See* Lisa M. Koonin, *et al., Abortion Surveillance 1995,* Centers for Disease Control Surveillance Summaries, MORBIDITY AND MORTALITY WEEKLY REPORT, Vol. 47, No. SS-2 (July 3, 1998), at pp. 31–68; Jacqueline Darroch Forrest and Susheela Singh, *The Sexual and Reproductive Behavior of American Women, 1982–1988,* FAMILY PLANNING PERSPECTIVES, Sept./Oct. 1990, at p. 206.

321 *Id.*

322 *See, e.g.,* Gina Kolata, *As Abortion Rate Decreases, Clinics Compete for Patients,* N.Y. TIMES, Dec. 30, 2000, at A1.

323 *See* Koonin, *supra* note 320.

324 *See* Maguire, *supra* note 42, ENDNOTES FOR CHAPTER ONE, at pp. 31–32 (referring to the work of theologian Christine Gudorf).

325 *Id.*

326   *Id.* at 31. (Maguire's exact title is Professor of Ethics within the Theology Department at Marquette University. Maguire is also the President of the Religious Consultation on Population, Reproductive Health and Ethics.)

327   *See* Robin Toner, *Testing the Church's Influence in Politics*, N.Y. TIMES, Jan. 26, 2003, Sec. 4, at p. 1.

328   *Id.* at 10.

329   *See God, Women and Medicine*, 60 MINUTES, CBS, airing December 10, 2000 (Morley Safer, reporting), at 9 (transcript) (available through Burrell's Transcripts).

330   *Id.*

331   *Id.*

332   *See* Finer & Henshaw, *supra* note 308, at p. 14.

333   *Id.*

334   *Id.* at 12.

335   *Id.* at 11.

336   *Id.*

337   *See* ISSUE UPDATE, *Abortion*, published by the Kaiser Family Foundation (Menlo Park, Ca., May 1999).

338   *See* Linda Villarosa, *Newest Skills for Future Ob-Gyns: Abortion Training*, N.Y. TIMES, June 11, 2002, at D6; Jim Ritter, *Shift in Ob-Gyn Specialty*, CHI. SUN-TIMES, Feb. 14, 2000, at p. 6; Finer & Henshaw, *supra* note 308, at pp. 6–7.

339   *Id.*

340   *See* Sullivan, *supra* note 306, at p. 166.

341   *See* Cristina Page & Amanda Peterman, *The Right To Agree*, OP-ED, N.Y. TIMES, Jan, 22, 2003, at A23.

342   *Id.*

343   *Id.*

344   *See* KEN. SEN. RES. 18 (2001) (Sponsor Roeding).

345   *See* CAL. SEN. JUD. RES. 3 (2001).

346   *See* Roger Smith, *The Argument that Never Ends*, U.S.NEWS & WORLD REPORT, Jan. 20, 2003, at p. 24.

347   *See* Kate Zernike, *30 Years After Abortion Ruling, New Trends but the Old Debate*, N.Y. TIMES, Jan. 20, 2003, at A1.

348   *See* THE WORLD IN NUMBERS: *Abortion Decision*, THE ATLANTIC MONTHLY, April 2003, 38–40, at p. 38 (citing numbers collected and compiled by the Alan Guttmacher Institute).

349   *Id.*

350   *See* Finer & Henshaw, *supra* note 308, at p. 6.

351   Some scholars argue that this was also the position of the Roman Catholic Church. *See, e.g.,* Maguire, *supra* note 324, at pp. 31–32. ("The sudden rapport between the Vatican and conservative Muslim states is interesting," writes Maguire. "For fourteen centuries, the relationship was stormy to the point of war and persecution. During that time, abortions were known to be happening, and yet this produced no ecumenical coziness. Is the issue really fetuses, or is it that these two patriarchal bastions are bonded in the face of a new threat—the emergence of free, self-determining women? Questions like these and all of the above summon us to visit Roman Catholicism first in our examination of the world religions.")

352   *See* FACTS IN BRIEF, *Induced Abortion, supra* note 307.

353   *See* Sullivan, *supra* note 306, at p. 168.

354   *Id.* at 162.

355   *Id.*

356   *See* FACTS IN BRIEF, *Induced Abortion, supra* note 307.

357   *Id.*

358   *Id.* (Those states are: Alabama, Arkansas,; Arizona, Delaware, Georgia, Iowa, Idaho, Indiana, Kansas, Kentucky, Louisiana, Massachusetts, Maryland, Michigan, Minnesota, Missouri, Mississippi, North Carolina, North Dakota, Nebraska, Ohio, Pennsylvania, Rhode Island, South Carolina, South Dakota, Tennessee, Texas, Utah, Virginia, Wisconsin, West Virginia, and Wyoming.)

359   *Id.*

360   *Id.*

361   *See* Zernike, *supra* note 347, at A1.

362   *Id.*

363   432 U.S. 438 (1977).

364   Those states are: Alaska, Arizona, California, Connecticut, Hawaii, Illinois, Massachusetts, Maryland, Minnesota, Montana, New Jersey, New Mexico, New York, Oregon, Vermont, Washington, and Wyoming.

365   *See* FACTS IN BRIEF, *Induced Abortion, supra* note 307, at p. 2.

366   *See, e.g.,* CONN. HOUSE BILL 6243 (2001) (if enacted would provide that a person may be charged with homicide or assault when the victim is an "unborn child"); FLOR. HOUSE BILL 497 (2001) (if enacted would amend vehicular homicide statute to include "viable fetus" of 20 weeks or more); KEN. HOUSE BILL 189 (2001) (if enacted would amend wrongful death statute to include "unborn child"); MICH. SENATE BILLS 70 and 71 (2001) (if enacted would amend penal code to include killing or injury of "an embryo" or fetus"); MISS. SENATE BILL 2215 and HOUSE BILL 794 (2001) (if enacted would provide that a woman could be charged with manslaughter resulting from the death of an

"unborn child" 20 or more weeks old if a controlled substance is involved, and includes death of an "unborn fetus" in DUI manslaughter statute); NEW HAMP. HOUSE BILL 319 (2001) (includes fetus as "another" for purposes of negligent homicide statute); OR. HOUSE BILL 2769 (2001) (amending current homicide and assault law to include "unborn children," with "unborn children" defined at every state of gestation beginning with fertilization); RHODE ISLAND HOUSE BILL 5069 (2001) (providing that punishment for causing a miscarriage or stillbirth via assault is punishable by up to 30 years, but if the fetus is 12-weeks or older, the punishment is life in prison); SOUTH CAROLINA SENATE BILL 312 (2001) (including "unborn child" at every state of gestation in utero from conception until live birth in the definition of other for purposes of unlawful battery statute); WIS. ASSEMBLY BILL 3 (2001) (increases penalty for intentionally destroying the life of one's "unborn quick child" or consenting to its destruction by another).

367 For an overview, *See* Renee J. Solomon, NOTE AND COMMENT, *Future Fear: Prenatal Duties Imposed by Private Parties*, 17 AM. J.L. & MED. 411, 413 & n. 6 (1991). (By 1991, eighteen states have passed feticide statutes.)

368 *Id.* at 413 (citing *e.g., Gloria C. v. William C.*, 476 N.Y.S.2d 991 (Fam. Ct. 1984)).

369 *See, e.g., Womack v. Buchhorn*, 187 N.W.2d 218 (Mich. 1971) (permitting suit against a person alleged to have negligently inflicted prenatal injuries); *Grodin v. Grodin*, 301 N.W.2d 869, 870 (Mich. Ct. App. 1980)(permitting a child to sue its mother for "negligent" ingestion of tetracycline during pregnancy).

370 *See* WIS. ASSEM. BILL 3 (2001).

371 *See, e.g.,* MON. SENATE BILL 290 (2001) (if enacted, would provide that certified advanced practice registered nurses could make medical certification of the cause of death on a fetal death certificate).

372 *See, e.g.,* MASS. HOUSE BILL 849 (2001) (if enacted, would prohibit abortion sought solely for purposes of sex selection).

373 *See* Adam Liptak, *Ex-Boyfriend Loses Bid to Halt an Abortion*, N.Y. TIMES, August 6, 2002, at A10.

374 *Id.*

375 *Id.*

376 *See Beal v. Doe*, 432 U.S. 438 (1977); *Colautti v. Franklin*, 439 U.S. 379 (1979); *Thornburgh v. American College of Obstetricians and Gynecologists*, 476 U.S. 747 (1986); *Planned Parenthood of Southeastern Pennsylvania v. Casey*, 505 U.S. 833 (1992).

377 Those provisions were: (1) 24 hour waiting period; (2) consent of at least one parent where a minor was concerned; (3) the signing of a form by married women indicating that they told their husbands; (4) provisions for medical emergencies in late term abortions; and, (5) reporting requirements.

378 States across the country began requiring consent waivers following the Supreme Court's decision. Even as recently as the fall of 2000, a ballot measure was proposed that, if passed into law, would require a 24-hour waiting period before a woman could actually have the abortion.

379 *See* Liptak, *supra* note 373, at A10.

380 *Id.*

381 *Id.*

382 *Id.*

383 *Id.*

384 *See* Robin Toner, *The Abortion Debate, Stuck in Time*, N.Y. TIMES, Jan. 21, 2001, at Section 4 at 1.

385 *See* Roger Smith, *supra* note 346, at p. 24.

386 *See* Bill Keller, *Reagan's Son*, N.Y. TIMES MAG., Jan. 26, 2003, pp. 26–63, at p. 27. (According to Keller, Reagan and Bush both defied "…the advice of the experts, they launched seemingly hopeless campaigns against popular incumbent governors and astonished their own party by winning. Each went on to win a second term by large margins. Reagan's executive experience was more meaningful. (California has a strong-governor system, while in Texas the governor defers to rambunctious, independently appointed agency heads.) Both managed to work with Democratic legislatures, which often entailed ruthlessness in California but in Texas required mainly charm.")

387 *Id.* (Keller argues that "[w]hatever you read about the president's inheritance from his father and Gerald Ford, the Reagan DNA is dominant in the staffing, training and planning of the Bush administration."); *See also* Richard Brookhiser, *The Mind of George Bush*, THE ATLANTIC MONTHLY, April 2003, at pp. 55–69.

388 Vice President Dick Cheney, Defense Secretary Donald Rumsfeld, Deputy Defense Secretary Paul Wolfowitz, National Security Adviser Condolezza Rice, Richard Pearle, and Secretary of State Colin Powell are all veterans of the Ford, Reagan or first Bush administration. *See* Brookhiser, *supra* note 387, at pp. 55–69; David Rosenbaum, *10 Years Spent Building the House Into a Home for the Reagan Revolution*, N.Y. TIMES, July 26, 2000, at A17; *Dick Cheney's Political Resume*, N.Y. TIMES, July 26, 2000, at A25.

389 Keller argues, for example, that "Bush bonded with Vladimir Putin over the Russian's story of a lost crucifix and opens cabinet meetings with prayers. Reagan would sometimes astonish visitors by talking about Armageddon in a way that did not seem to be merely allegorical."

390 *See* Keller, *supra* note 386, at p. 28. (In Bush's case, it has also drawn criticism, especially after American forces went to war with Iraq. *See, e.g.,* Kenneth T. Walsh, *Sticking to His Guns*, U.S.NEWS & WORLD REPORT, March 10, 2003, pp. 14–23.)

391 *Id.*

392 *Id.*

393 *Id.* at 27. (According to Keller, "Peggy Noonan, Reagan's gifted speechwriter and a torchbearer for his memory, has portrayed Bush in one of her books as eager to be likened to Reagan, but she insists that the two men are incomparable. Bush, she says, represents 'the triumph of the average American man.' He is, she told me, 'like a successful local businessman in the boring local business who becomes a school board president.' (She meant that it a good way.) Reagan, on the other hand, was 'hardly your basic man on the street.'")

394 *Id.*

395 *Id.* at 43.

396 *Id.*

397 *Id.*

398 *Id.* at 43–44.

399 *Id.* (According to Keller, when "[a]sked during the campaign to identify his favorite Supreme Court justices, Bush named Clarence Thomas and Antonin Scalia, exciting conservatives to the point of ecstasy.")

400 *Id.* at 44. Also for further background on the issue, *see* Blank and Merrick, *supra* note 91, ENDNOTES FOR CHAPTER FIVE, at pp. 176–198.

401 *See, e.g.,* Sheryl Gay Stolberg, *Scientists Create Scores of Embryos to Harvest Cells*, N.Y. TIMES, July 11, 2001, at A1; Kevin Sack and Gustav Niebuhr, *After Stem-Cell Rift, Groups Unite for Antiabortion Push*, N.Y. TIMES, Sept. 4, 2001, at A1; Nell Boyce, *A Law's Fetal Flaw*, U.S.NEWS & WORLD REPORT, July 21, 2003, at pp. 48–51.

402 *See* Nicholas Wade, *Pennsylvania Researchers Turn Stem Cells to Egg Cells*, N.Y. TIMES, May 2, 2003, at A29.

403 *See* WORLD NEWS TONIGHT, ABC-TV, airing July 9, 2001, (Terry Moran, reporting), at p. 3 (transcript), available through ABCNews.com; Robin Toner, *Conservatives Pressing Bush on Stem Cells*, N.Y. TIMES, July 12, 2001, at A1.

404 *See* Brookhiser, *supra* note 387, at p. 62.

405 *Id.*

406 *Id.*

407 *See* Robert Pear, *Thompson Says He Will Order a New Review of Abortion Drug*, N.Y. TIMES, Jan. 20, 2001, at A11. (During the presidential campaign, Bush reportedly remarked that he "was disappointed in the ruling [by the FDA approving the use of RU 486] because I think abortions ought to be more rare in America. And I'm worried that that pill will create more abortion, will cause more people to have abortions.")

408 *See* Frank Bruni and Marc Lacey, *Bush Acts to Deny Money Overseas Tied to Abortion*, N.Y. TIMES, Jan, 23, 2001 (citing an "executive memorandum to the Agency for International Development, which administers and monitors family planning aid to overseas groups"). Critics of the move note that a great many choices that might ordinarily be deemed unpopular may be accomplished by executive order. *See, e.g.,* David Rosenbaum, *Bush Rules! It's Good to be the President*, N.Y. TIMES, Jan. 28, 2001, at A16. (Critics of the measures vowed, however, to overturn the measure. *See, e.g.,* Robin Toner, *Critics Seek to Overturn Abortion Rule*, N.Y. TIMES, Feb. 16, 2001, at A14.)

409 *See* Toner, *supra* note 408, at A14 (quoting Kate Michelman, president of the National Abortion Rights Action League).

410 *See New Bush Tactic in Fight Over Aid and Abortions*, N.Y. TIMES, March 25, 2001, at p. 17.

411 *Id.*

412 *See* Somini Sengupta, *U.N. Forum Stalls on Sex Education and Abortion Rights*, N.Y. TIMES, May 10, 2002, at A3.

413 *Id.*

414 *See* Sheryl Gay Stolberg, *Grants Aid Abstinence-Only Initiatives*, N.Y. TIMES, Feb. 28, 2002, at A18.

415 *Id.*

416 *Id.* (According to Stolberg, "[t]he scientific literature, including a recent report by former Surgeon General David Satcher, carries quite a different message. With scant research on abstinence-only programs, studies conclude there is insufficient evidence that they delay sex. The only proven method for reducing pregnancy and sexually transmitted disease, the studies say, is to combine the abstinence message with one that teaches young people how to protect themselves against pregnancy and disease.")

417 *Id.*

418 *Id.*

419 *Id.*

420 *See* FACTS IN BRIEF, *Sexuality Education*, published by the Alan Guttmacher Institute, 2002, at p. 1.

421 *Id.*

422 *Id.*

423   *See* JUST THE FACTS, *Population*, MS., Dec. 1999-Jan. 2000, at p. 8.

424   *See* Rachel K. Jones, Jacqueline E. Darroch & Stanley Henshaw, *Contraceptive Use Among U.S. Women Having Abortions in 2000-2001*, 34 PERSPECTIVES ON SEXUAL AND REPRODUCTIVE HEALTH 294–303, at p. 297 (Nov.–Dec. 2002).

425   *See* FACTS IN BRIEF, *supra* note 420, at p. 1.

426   *See* Jones, Darroch & Henshaw, *supra* note 424, at p. 297; FACTS IN BRIEF, *supra* note 420, at p. 1.

427   *Id.*

428   *See* Lawrence K. Altman, *South Africa Says It Will Fight AIDS with a Drug Plan*, N.Y. TIMES, Aug. 9, 2003, at A1, A5.

429   *See* Katherine Boo, *The Marriage Cure*, THE NEW YORKER, Aug. 18, & 25, 2003, pp. 104–120; Robin Toner, *Welfare Chief is Promoting Marriage*, N.Y. TIMES, Feb. 19, 2002, at A1.

430   *Id.*

431   *See, e.g.,* Suzi Parker, *More Rings, Tuxes, Bells, and Brides*, THE CHRISTIAN SCIENCE MONITOR, July 20, 1998, at pp. 1, 14.

432   *See* Debra Baker, *Beyond Ozzie and Harriet*, A.B.A. J., Sept. 1998, at pp. 58–63; Susan Dodge, *Meet the New 'Family'*, CHI. SUN-TIMES, Nov. 24, 1999, at p. 4; *Poll Reveals Another Sign of Changing U.S. Family*, ASSOCIATED PRESS, Nov. 25, 1999 (reprinted in N.Y. TIMES, Nov. 26, 1999, at A22); Randolph E. Schmid, *4 Million Unwed Couples Live Together*, CHI. SUN-TIMES, July 27, 1998, at p. 18; *Black Married Couples Continue Decline*, CHI. SUN-TIMES, July 30, 1998.

433   For some background on the issue, *See, e.g., Donahue v. Fair Emp. and Housing Com'n*, 2 Cal. Rptr. 2d 32 (Cal. App. 2 Dist. 1991); *Friedman v. Friedman*, 24 Cal. Rptr. 2d 892 (Cal. App. 1 Dist. 1993); Steve France, *Not Under My Roof You Don't: Courts Split on Religious Liberty vs. Discrimination in Landlord/Tenant Dispute*, A.B.A. J., April 1999, pp. 26–28; *Cohabiting Case Dropped*, N.Y. TIMES, April 5, 2000, at A17.

434   *See* Eric Schmitt, *For First Time, Nuclear Families Drop Below 25% of Households*, N.Y. TIMES, May 15, 2001, at A1; Tamar Lewin, *Is Social Stability Subverted If You Answer 'I Don't'?*, N.Y. TIMES, Nov. 4, 2000, at A21; Ethan Watters, *In My Tribe*, N.Y. TIMES MAG., Sec. 6, Oct. 14, 2001, at p. 25; Alex Kuczynski, *Guess Who's Coming to Dinner Now?*, N.Y. TIMES, Sec. 9, Dec. 23, 2001, at p. 1.

435   *See Shacking Up*, THE ATLANTIC MONTHLY, Oct. 2003, at p. 47; Christopher Marquis, *Total of Unmarried Couples Surged in 2000 U.S. Census*, N.Y. TIMES, March 13, 2003, at A18; *Happy Families: How We're Related*, MARIE CLAIRE, Jan. 2000, pp. 52–56; Leah Ginsberg, *The Color of Love: Mixed Race Relationships*, MARIE CLAIRE, Feb. 2000, pp. 38–44.

436   *See Shacking Up, supra* note 435, at p. 47; Schmitt, *supra* note 434, at A1; *Poll Reveals Another Sign of Changing U.S. Family*, *supra* note 432, at A22; Baker, *supra* note 432, at pp. 58–63; Dodge, *supra* note 432, at p. 4; Schmid, *supra* note 432, at p. 18; *Black Married Couples*, *supra* note 432. *See also* Alex Kuczynski, *Guess Who's Coming to Dinner Now?*, N.Y. TIMES, Dec. 23, 2001, Sec. 9, at p. 1; Julie Salamon, *Staticky Reception for Nuclear Families on Prime-Time TV*, N.Y. TIMES, July 30, 2001, at B1.

437   *See* Marc Parent, *A Dad at the Final Frontier*, N.Y. TIMES, June 16, 2001, at A27.

438   *See, e.g.,* Sharon Edelson, *Protection Racket*, W, March 1999, at p. 408; David Rovella, *Pre-Nups No Longer Just for the Wealthy*, NAT'L L.J., Sept. 6, 1999, at A1; Mark Hansen, *Split-Up Insurance*, A.B.A. J., Nov. 1999, at p. 30; Abby Ellin, *Marriage Insurance for the Young*, N.Y. TIMES, June 18, 2000, at p. 15; *A Prenuptial Agreement That Ran Around*, N.Y. TIMES, June 25, 2000, at p. 14; Laura Caldwell, *Postnuptial Agreement in Illinois*, 88 ILL. BAR J., Aug, 2000, pp. 473–480; Tamar Lewin, *Among Nuptial Agreements, Post- Has Now Joined Pre-*, N.Y. TIMES, July 7, 2001, at A1.

439   *See, e.g., Rose v. Elias*, 576 N.Y.S.2d 257 (A.D. 1 Dept. 1991); *Bergen v. Wood*, 18 Cal. Rptr. 2d 75 (Cal. App. 2 Dist. 1993); *Widley v. Springs*, 840 F. Supp. 1259 (N.D. Ill. 1994); *Widley v. Springs*, 47 F.3d 1475 (7th Cir. 1995).

440   *See* Rebecca Mead, *You're Getting Married*, THE NEW YORKER, April 21 & 28, 2003, at pp. 76–91.

441   *See Shacking Up, supra* note 435.

442   *See* Marquis, *supra* note 435, at A18.

443   *Id.*

444   *See* Jim VandeHei, *GOP Looks to Move Its Social Agenda*, WASH. POST, Nov. 25, 2002, at A01.

445   *See* Matthew Benjamin, *A Bold Plan, Inked in Red*, U.S.NEWS & WORLD REPORT, Feb. 17, 2003, pp. 40–42, at pp. 40–41.

446   *Id.* at 64.

447   *See* Eyal Press, *Faith-Based Furor*, N.Y. TIMES MAG., April 1, 2001, pp. 62–65, at p. 63; Laura Meckler, *Bush Drops Regulation Backing Gay Bias*, CHI. SUN-TIMES, July 11, 2001, at p. 28.

448   *See* Meckler, *supra* note 447, at p. 28.

449   *See Massachuetts: Abortion Case Ruling*, N.Y. TIMES, June 1, 2002, at A11.

450   *See* Smith, *supra* note 346, at p. 24.

451   *See* Blank and Merrick, *supra* note 400, at p. 41.

452   *See* Jeffrey Toobin, *Advice and Dissent*, THE NEW YORKER, May 26, 2003, pp. 42–48, at p. 43.

453   *Id.* at 43. *See also* Keller, *supra* note 386.

454   Scalia has argued, for example, that he believes the United States Supreme Court has "gone overboard in keeping God out of government." *See Scalia Attacks Church-State Rulings*, N.Y. TIMES, Jan. 13, 2003, at A19.

455   *See* Adam Cohen, *Deborah Cook Is the Typical Bush Nominee—So Watch Out*, N.Y. TIMES, Feb. 25, 2003, at A28.

456   *Id.*

457   *See* Neil A. Lewis, *A Judge, A Renomination and the Cross-Burning Case That Won't End*, N.Y. TIMES, May 28, 2003, at A16.

458   *See* Toobin, *supra* note 452, at p. 43.

459   *Id.*

460   *Id.* at 46–47.

461   *See* Deborah Sontag, *The Power of the Fourth*, N.Y. TIMES MAG., March 9, 2003, pp. 38–68, at p. 40.

462   *See* VandeHei, *supra* note 444, at A01.

463   *Id.*

464   *Id.*

465   *See Carhart v. Stenberg*, 11 F. Supp. 2d 1099 (Neb. 1998) (trial court finding statute unconstitutional).

466   *See* Neb. Rev. Stat. Ann. Sec. 28-328(1) (Supp. 1999).

467   *Id.*

468   *Id.*

469   *See Carhart*, 11 F. Supp. 2d at 1099.

470   Record of affirmance can be found at 192 F.3d 1142 (8th Cir. 1999).

471   *See Centers for Disease Control and Prevention, Abortion Surveillance—United States, 1996* (July 30, 1999), at p. 41.

472   *Id.*

473   *See* Robin Toner, *Senate Revisits Ban on Abortion Procedure; Passage Expected and Bush Gives Support*, N.Y. TIMES, March 11, 2003, at A14 (quoting statistics provided by the Alan Guttmacher Institute).

474   As the Seventh Circuit noted in *Hope Clinic v. Ryan*, 195 F.3d 857, 861–62 (7th Cir. 1999), "[a] D&X is a variant of a D&E in which the fetus is removed without dismemberment. The American College of Obstetricians and Gynecologists (ACOG) defines D&X as follows: '1. deliberate dilatation of the cervix, usually over a sequence of days; 2. instrumental conversion of the fetus to a footling breech; 3. breech extraction of the body excepting the head; and 4. partial evacuation of the intracranial contents of a living fetus to effect vaginal delivery for dead but otherwise intact fetus' (citing 139 CONG. REC. E 1092 (Apr. 29, 1993)).

475   *See Hope Clinic v. Ryan*, 195 F.3d 857, 861–62 (7th Cir. 1999).

476   *See Stenberg v. Carhart*, 530 U.S. 914 (2000).

477   *Richmond Medical Center for Women v. Gilmore*, 144 F.3d 326 (4th Cir. 1998).

478   *See Richmond Medical Center for Women v. Gilmore*, 144 F.3d 326 (4th Cir. 1998).

479   *See* Sontag, *supra* note 461, at p. 40.

480   *See* Toobin, *supra* note 452, at p. 43–44.

481   *Id.*

482   *See Stenberg v. Carhart*, 530 U.S. 914 (2000).

483   *See Richmond Medical Center*, 144 F.3d at 327.

484   *Id. See* Va. Code 1950 Sec. 18.2-74.2(A) which provides as follows: "Notwithstanding the provisions of Sec. 18.2-72 and 18.2073 and 18.2-74, a physician shall not knowingly perform a partial-birth abortion that is not necessary to save the life of the mother. A violation of this section shall be punishable as a Class I misdemeanor."

485   *Richmond Medical Center*, 144 F.3d at 328 (emphasis in original).

486   *Id.* at 327.

487   *Id.* at 332.

488   *Carhart v. Stenberg*, 192 F.3d 1142 (1999).

489   *Id.*

490   See *Hope Clinic v. Ryan*, 195 F.3d 857, 861 (7th Cir. 1999).

491   *Id.*

492   *See, e.g., Women's Medical Professional Corp. v. Voinovich*, 130 F.3d 187 (6th Cir. 1997); *Richmond Medical Center for Women v. Gilmore*, 144 F.3d 326 (4th Cir. 1998); *Carhart v. Stenberg*, 192 F.3d 1142 (8th Cir. 1999); *Little Rock Family Planning Services, P.A. v. Jegley*, 192 F.3d 794 (8th Cir. 1999) (Arkansas); *Planned Parenthood of Greater Iowa, Inc. v. Miller*, 195 F.3d 386 (8th Cir. 1999) (Iowa); *Hope Clinic v. Ryan*, 195 F.3d 857 (7th Cir. 1999).

493   By November 1999, ten states had passed "partial-birth" abortion laws. Those states were: Indiana, Kansas, Mississippi, North Dakota, Oklahoma, South Carolina, South Dakota, Tennessee, Utah and Virginia. "Partial-birth" abortion laws were being enforced after the point of "viability" in Alabama and Georgia as well. Laws in sixteen others states were blocked by state and federal courts. Those states were: Alaska; Arizona, Arkansas, Florida, Idaho, Iowa, Kentucky, Louisiana, Michigan, Missouri, Montana, Nebraska, New Jersey, Ohio, Rhode Island, and West Virginia. In Sept. of 1999, "partial-birth" abortion laws were struck down in Arkansas, Iowa and Nebraska by a federal appeals court, sitting in St. Louis. But on October 26, 1999, the Seventh Circuit Court of Appeals upheld the constitutionality of "partial-birth abortion" laws in Illinois and Wisconsin. *See Hope Clinic v. Rust*, 195 F.3d 857 (7th Cir. 1999). The United States Supreme Court's decision in *Stenberg v. Carhart* in 2000, seemed to settle the issue—at least temporarily. *See* John Gibeaut, *Strategic*

Adjustments: Abortion Opponents Focusing on Protection of the 'Partially Born,' A.B.A. J., Feb. 1999, at 27; Schroedel, *supra* note 216, at pp. 170–171.

494 530 U.S. 914 (2000).

495 *Id.* (citing Casey, 505 U.S. at 879 (joint opinion of O'Connor, Kennedy, and Souter, J.J.)).

496 *Casey*, 505 U.S. at 873.

497 *See* Lise Funderburg, *Saving Jason*, LIFE, May 2000, at pp. 48–62; Jim Ritter, *Little Mia's Strong Will Helped Her Beat Odds*, CHI. SUN-TIMES, July 11, 2001, at p. 3; Dana Wechsler Linden and Mia Wechsler Doron, *Eyes of Texas Fasten on Life, Death and the Premature Infant*, N.Y. TIMES, April 30, 2002, at D5.

498 *See* Maguire, *supra* note 324, at pp. 32–33.

499 *Id.*

500 *Id.* at 34.

501 *Id.* at 34–35. (According to Maguire, "...'both contraception and abortion were generally forbidden' in previous teaching, but both were often thought to be associated with sorcery and witchcraft. In the Decretals of 1230, Pope Gregory IX treated both contraception and abortion as homicide. Some of the Christian Penitentials of the early Middle Ages prescribed seven years of fasting on bread and water for a layman who committed homicide—one year for performing an abortion, but seven years for sterilization. Sterilization was considered more serious than abortion because the issue was not framed as pro-life. Rather, the driving bias was antisexual. Traditional Christian attitudes towards sexuality were so negative that only reproduction could justify sexual activity. Abortion frustrated fertility once; sterilization could frustrate it forever and therefore was more serious. Also, since the role of the ovum was not learned until the nineteenth century, sperm were thought to be little homunculi, miniature people, and for this reason male masturbation was sometimes called homicide. Christian historical sexual ethics is clearly a bit of a hodgepodge.")

502 *Id.* at 34.

503 *Id.* at 36–37. (According to Maguire, "[w]ith a view towards the larger meaning, Augustine reportedly pondered the question of resurrection with regard to miscarried fetuses. He concluded that they would not rise as Christ had. Sperm spent in any number of ways not leading to successful fertilization also would not rise, Augustine determined. Catholic theologians and religious scholars have recently concluded, after studying the issue, that "the texts condemning abortion in the early church refer to the abortion of a fully formed fetus.' The early fetus did not have the status of person, nor would killing it fit the category of murder.")

504 *Id.* at 36. (Augustine pondered the question of resurrection with regard to miscarried fetuses, Maguire explains. He concluded that miscarried fetuses would not rise as Christ had. Sperm spent in any number of ways not leading to successful fertilization also would not rise, Augustine determined. Catholic theologians and religious scholars have recently concluded, after studying the issue, that "the texts condemning abortion in the early church refer to the abortion of a fully formed fetus." The early fetus did not have the status of person, nor would killed it fit the category of murder." Maguire notes further that "[t]hough sexist efforts were made to say the male soul arrived sooner—maybe a month and a half into the pregnancy—the rule of thumb for when a fetus reached the status of baby was three months (or even later).")

505 *Id.*

506 *Id.*

507 *See Roe v. Wade*, 410 U.S. at 157.

508 530 U.S. 914, 919 (2000).

509 *Id.* (citing *Thornburgh v. American College of Obstetricians and Gynecologists*, 476 U.S. 747, 768-769 (1986); *Colautti v. Franklin*, 439 U.S. 379, 400 (1979); *Danforth*, 428 U.S. at 76–79; *Doe v. Bolton*, 410 U.S. 179, 197 (1973)).

510 *Id.* at 920.

511 *Id.* at 922.

512 To support this point, Justice Breyer cited the Kansas Stat. Ann., Sec. 65-6721(b)(1) (Supp. 1999).

513 *Id.* at 923.

514 Indeed, *Stenberg v. Carhart* appears to be the case that actually made it to the United States Supreme Court. Others before it were denied a Writ of Certiorari. *See, e.g., Women's Medical Professional Corp. v. Vionovich*, 130 F.3d 187 (6th Cir. 1997), *cert. den.*, 118 S. Ct. 1347 (1998).

515 *See, e.g.,* HAW. HOUSE BILL 1484 (2001) (if passed would prohibit "partial-birth" abortion in language nearly identical to language and definitions prohibited by United States Supreme Court in *Stenberg v. Carhart*); IN. HOUSE BILL 1246 (2001) (would alter "partial-birth" abortion statute to prohibit "an abortion in which a living fetus is removed intact from the uterus until only the head remains in the uterus; all or part of the intracranial contents of the fetus are evacuated; the head of the fetus is compressed; and following fetal demise, the fetus is removed from the birth canal); ME. SENATE PROP. 37 (2001) (would prohibit "partial-birth" abortion as defined in terms similar to those struck down by the Court in 2000); ME. HOUSE PROP. 115 (2001) (would amend current law to provide that "partial-birth" abortions may only be performed to save the life of a pregnant woman); MASS. SENATE BILL 807 (2001) (prohibits "partial-birth" abortion in language similar to Nebraska statute since declared unconstitutional, except to save the life of the woman); MASS. HOUSE BILL 842

(2001) (would prohibit "intentionally caus[ing] the death of a living intact fetus while that living intact fetus is partially born"); MINN. HOUSE BILL 42 (2001) (would prohibit "deliberately and intentionally deliver[ing] into the vagina a living fetus, or a substantial portion thereof, for the purposes of performing a procedure the physician knows will kill the fetus, and kill[ing] the fetus"); NEW YORK SENATE BILL 2293 (2001) (would prohibit "partial-birth" abortion, with an exception to save the life of the woman); OKLAHOMA SENATE BILL 736 (2001) (would amend the prohibition on "partial-birth" abortion to add an exception for preserving a woman's health); VIR. HOUSE BILL 2125 (2001) (would amend definition of "partial-birth" abortion to prohibit the "deliberate dilation of the cervix"); and, MISS. HOUSE BILL 207 (2001) (would prohibit all second and third trimester abortions, except to preserve the life of the woman endangered by a physical disorder or illness or in the case of rape or incest).

516 *See, e.g.,* KAN. SENATE BILL 310 and HOUSE BILL 2371 (2001) (repealing the state's "partial-birth" abortion law).

517 *See* Pam Belluck, *After Abortion Victory, Doctor's Troubles Persist,* N.Y. TIMES, Nov. 7, 2000, at A18.

518 *See* Finer & Henshaw, *supra* note 308, at p. 14 (citing L. Osby, ECONOMIC FACTORS CLOSE GREENVILLE ABORTION CLINIC, July 18, 2002.

519 *See* Belluck, *supra* note 517, at p. 14.

520 *Id.* (According to Belluck, Ryan likened Dr. Carhart's practice to "a porno shop: the porno shop may be legal, but there are not too many people that want to set up next to that.")

521 *Id.*

522 *Id.* (The context of this statement is as follows: "And the University of Nebraska Medical Center's College of Medicine, to which Dr. Carhart has been supplying fetal tissue from abortions for research, removed him from his unpaid faculty position. Officially, the university said abortion has nothing to do with Dr. Carhart's removal, noting that he was one of 200 volunteer faculty members, among about 1,300, who were terminated. But a high-ranking university official who spoke on the condition of anonymity said an outcry from abortion opponents had influenced the decision.")

523 *See Abortion Provider Fights University Dismissal,* N.Y. TIMES, March 13, 2001, at A13.

524 *See Nebraska: Doctor and University Settle,* N.Y. TIMES, August 24, 2001, at A12.

525 *See* Robin Toner, *Foes of Abortion Ready Major Bills for New Congress,* N.Y. TIMES, Jan. 2, 2003, at A1.

526 *See Abortion Redux,* U.S.NEWS & WORLD REPORT, June 16, 2003, at p. 10; Robin Toner, *As Abortion Battle Escalates, Both Sides Look to the Supreme Court,* N.Y. TIMES, March 17, 2003, at A17.

527 *See* Steve Ginsberg, *Va.'s Laws on Abortion Get Tougher,* WASH. POST, July 1, 2003, at B01.

528 *See* Michael D. Shear, *Judge Blocks Va. 'Partial-birth' Abortion Ban,* WASH. POST, July 2, 2003, at B01.

529 *See* Sheryl Gay Stolberg, *Bill Banning Abortion Procedure Advances,* N.Y. TIMES, Oct. 3, 2003, at A23; *Abortion Wars,* U.S.NEWS & WORLD REPORT, Oct. 13, 2003, at p.10.

530 Interview broadcast during MORNING EDITION, October 15, 2003 (Julie Rovner reporting), at p. 17 (transcript) (available through Burrelle's transcripts).

531 *Id.*

532 *Id. See also Fetus Not Child Under Ind. Wrongful Death Law,* NAT'L L.J., March 25, 2002, at B8; *State's High Court Rejects Action for 'Wrongful Life,'* NAT'L L.J., Feb. 11, 2002, at B7; William Saletan, *What's the Value of a Fetus?,* N.Y. TIMES, Oct. 26, 2003, at wk. 11.

533 *See, e.g.,* ARK. HOUSE BILL 1132 (2001) (if enacted could include "viable fetus" in the definition of "person" for purposes of wrongful death action); KEN. SENATE BILL 157 (2001) (if enacted, would amend current wrongful death statute to include an "unborn child" from fertilization onward, without regard to age, health, or condition of dependency); KEN. HOUSE BILL 232 (2001) (same wording as Kentucky Senate Bill 157); MICH. SENATE BILL 70 (2001) (if enacted, would amend sentencing guidelines for killing or injuring "an embryo" or "fetus"); MISS. HOUSE BILL 793 (2001) (if enacted, would amend wrongful death statute to include "unborn fetus" in coverage).

534 *See, e.g.,* ARIZ. HOUSE BILL 2268 (2001) (if enacted, would provide for increasing sentence in domestic violence cases where the assault is on a pregnant woman); COLO. HOUSE BILL 1204 (2001) (if enacted, would enhance penalties for offenses committed against pregnant women).

535 *See, e.g.,* MON. SENATE BILL 290 (2001); MON. HOUSE BILL 547 (2001).

536 *See* Richard Stevenson, *Bush Signs Ban on a Procedure for Abortions,* N.Y. TIMES, Nov. 6, 2003, at A1.

537 *See* Susan Saulny, *Court Blocks New Statute That Limits Abortion,* N. Y. TIMES, Nov. 7, 2003, at A12.

538 *See Some Words on Fetal Rights,* OFF OUR BACKS, July 1998, at 10.

539 *See* Shawn Zeller, *Fetal Abuse Laws Gain Favor,* NAT'L JOURNAL, July 25, 1998, at 1798. The South Dakota law was declared in force on July 1, 1998.

540 *Id.*

541 Wis. Stat. Sec. 48.19(1)(c) (1993–94). The Wisconsin statute provided that: (1) A *child* may be taken into custody under any of the following; (c) An order of the judge if made upon a showing satisfactory to the judge that the welfare of the child demands that the child be immediately removed from his or her present custody. The order shall specify that the child be held in custody under Sec. 48.207.

542 Constitutional challenges would likely have involved the Fourth and Fourteenth Amendments.

543 *State ex rel. Angela M.W. v. Kruzicki,* 561 N.W.2d 729, 732 (Wis. 1997).

544   *Angela M.W.*, 561 N.W. at 733.

545   *See* Deller Ross, *supra* note 142, ENDNOTES FOR CHAPTER FIVE, at pp. 212–13.

546   *See* Cynthia L. Cooper, *This Woman Was Thrown in Jail for Being Pregnant*, MARIE CLAIRE, Jan. 2003, pp. 74–78, at p. 76.

547   *See State v. Johnson*, No. E89-890-CFA, slip. op. at 1 (Fla. Cir. Ct. July 13, 1989), *aff'd*, 578 So.2d 419 (Fla. App. 5 Dist. 1991). The conviction was later reversed by the Florida Supreme Court, *State v. Johnson*, 602 So.2d 1288 (Fla. 1992).

548   *See Reinesto v. Superior Court*, 894 P.2d 733, 736 (Ariz. App. Div. 1, 1995). Arizona prosecutors argued that Teresa Lopez Reinesto should be prosecuted for "knowingly caus[ing] injury to the child *in her womb* in a manner likely to cause death or serious physical injury." Reinesto was a heroin addict. It was further argued that Reinesto's conduct during pregnancy caused Baby Jane to suffer <u>after</u> her birth. The case was ultimately dismissed because "[d]ue process requires 'that criminal offenses be defined in terms sufficient to give a person of ordinary intelligence fair notice that his contemplated conduct is forbidden by the statute. The underlying principle for the requirement is that no person should be required, at the risk of his liberty, to speculate as to the meaning of a criminal statute.'"

549   *See Reyes v. Superior Court*, 75 Cal. App. 3d 214, 141 Cal. Rptr. 912 (1977). Margaret Velasquez Reyes gave birth to twins who were addicted to heroin, and she was charged with felony child endangerment in violation of California Penal Code section 273a. The California statute provided: Any person who, under circumstances or conditions likely to produce great bodily harm or death,…having the care or custody of any *child*,…willfully causes or permits such child to be placed in such situation that its person or health is endangered, is punishable by imprisonment in the county jail not exceeding a year, or in the state prison for not less than 1 year nor more than 10 years. *See also In re Stephen*, 126 Cal. App. 3d 23 (1981); and, Susan Stefan, *Whose Egg is it Anyway?, Reproductive Rights of Incarcerated, Institutionalized and Incompetent Women*, 13 NOVA L. REV. at p. 444 (Spring 1989).

550   *See In re Valerie D.*, 613 A.2d 748 (1992). A 23-year-old Connecticut woman shot cocaine into her arm just before going into labor. A little girl, Valerie D., was born with cocaine in her blood, and the State moved to terminate the mother's parental rights. The Supreme Court of Connecticut reversed, holding that the fetus was not a "child' until after it was born. Thus, the 23-year-old was not a parent. Accordingly, she could not be held accountable for "parental conduct."

551   *See State v. Gethers*, 585 So.2d 1140 (Fla. App. 4 Dist. 1991). Cassandra Gethers used cocaine while pregnant and the State of Florida attempted to prosecute her for aggravated child abuse. The charge was made under Florida Statutes Sec. 827.04 (1987) which provides: Whoever, willfully or by culpable negligence deprives a child of, or allows a child to be deprived of , necessary food, clothing, shelter, or medical treatment, or who, knowingly or by culpable negligence, permits physical or mental injury to the child, and in so doing causes great bodily harm, permanent disability, or permanent disfigurement to such child, shall be guilty of a felony of the third degree, punishable as provided by Florida Statute Sec. 775.082; Sec. 775.083, or Sec. 775.084.

552   *See State v. Luster*, 204 Ga. App. 156 (1992) Georgia officials argued that Darlene Michelle Luster "did unlawfully deliver and distribute…cocaine…to Tiffany Luster," while the unborn child was still in the womb. The appellate court held that Luster could not be charged with two counts of possessing cocaine and "unlawfully deliver[ing] it to her infant daughter while still in the womb."

553   *See State v. Gray*, 62 Ohio St. 3d 514 (1992). Ohio officials filed child endangerment charges against Tammy Gray after she gave birth to a baby girl who had cocaine in her bloodstream.

554   *See Commonwealth of Kentucky v. Welch*, 864 S.W.2d 280 (Ky. 1993). A Kentucky grand jury indicted Connie Welch for criminal abuse after her newly born infant tested positive for nicotine and caffeine. Prosecutors argued that such chemicals were the possible side-effects of other already ingested drugs. The court held that the legislature did not intend to impose criminal abuse sanctions on a pregnant woman who uses drugs.

555   *See People v. Hardy*, 188 Mich. App. 305 (1991). Kimberly Hardy was charged with delivering 50 grams of a drug mixture containing cocaine to an unborn fetus through her umbilical cord under a Michigan criminal drug statute.

556   *See Sheriff v. Encoe*, 885 P.2d 596 (Nev. 1994). Cathy Encoe was charged by Nevada with child endangerment after she gave birth to a baby who tested positive for amphetamines and methamphetamines.

557   *See Commonwealth v. Kemp*, No. 2707 C 1991, slip. op. at 12 (Ct. C.P. Westmoreland Co., Penn. Crim. Div. 1991)).

558   *See Collin v. Texas*, 890 S.W.2d 893 (Tex. App. El Paso 1994). Prosecutors in Texas argued that a woman had "committed injury to a child by introducing cocaine" into the baby's body while he was still in the womb. The court held that a woman charged with abuse of child for ingesting cocaine while pregnant did not have notice that her actions were violative of the law.

559   *See Washington v. Dunn*, 916 P.2d 952 (Wash. App. Div .3 1996). Selena Dunn gave birth to a little girl who tested positive for cocaine. Dunn was promptly charged by Washington State authorities with "recklessly creat[ing] an imminent and substantial risk of death or great bodily harm…" The child was diagnosed with fetal intrauterine growth retardation and placenta abruptio attributed to

Dunn's use of cocaine. The condition was described as "life threatening." It was later learned that the child was blind with the blindness also attributed to Dunn's cocaine use.

560 *See State of Wisconsin v. Zimmerman,* 96-CF-525 (Wis. Cir. Ct. Racine Cty. Sept. 18, 1996). Deborah Zimmerman was charged by Wisconsin authorities with intentional attempted homicide of the fetus she was carrying after a night of heavy drinking. But on May 26, 1999, the Court of Appeals for the State of Wisconsin held that Deborah Zimmerman should never have been prosecuted. Specifically, the court held that "an unborn child is not a 'human being' because it is not one who has been alive as required by Sec. 939.22(16) [of the Wisconsin statute] and probable cause did not exist to charge Deborah with the crimes of attempted first-degree intentional homicide and first-degree reckless injury. As a result, we reverse the circuit court's denial of the motion to dismiss the information."

561 *See United States v. Vaughn,* 117 Daily Wash. L. Rep. 441, 446–47 (D.C. Super. Ct. Aug. 23, 1988).

562 *See* Cooper, *supra* note 546, at p. 76. In addition to those states listed above, prosecutions of pregnant women for substance-abuse related offenses occurred in: Alabama, Alaska, Arizona, California, Connecticut, Florida, Georgia, Idaho, Illinois, Indiana, Kentucky, Maryland, Massachusetts, Michigan, Mississippi, Missouri, Nebraska, Nevada, New York, North Carolina, North Dakota, Ohio, Oklahoma, Oregon, Pennsylvania, South Carolina, South Dakota, Tennessee, Texas, Utah, Virginia, Washington, Wisconsin and Wyoming. For review of the issue, see Schroedel, *supra* note 216, at pp. 100–135.

563 *See* Robert Blank, FETAL PROTECTION IN THE WORKPLACE: WOMEN'S RIGHTS; BUSINESS INTERESTS, AND THE UNBORN (New York: Columbia University Press, 1993), at p. 10.

564 *See, e.g., Toxic Dads,* PARENTING, Oct. 1998, at pp. 94–102.

565 *See* Kris Axtman, *A Jailed Expectant Mom—and a Case of Tangled Rights,* CHRIST. SCIENCE MONITOR, Sept. 8, 2000, at 2.

566 *See Confined Sect Member Gives Birth to Baby Girl,* N.Y. TIMES, Oct. 17, 2000, at A23.

567 *See* Axtman, *supra* note 565; Pam Belluck, *State Seeks Child Parents Don't Acknowledge,* N.Y. TIMES, Feb. 3, 2002, at p. 18.

568 *See* Axtman, *supra* note 565.

569 *See Confined Sect Member, supra* note 566, at A23.

570 *See Sect Leaders Charged in Infant Son's Death,* N.Y. TIMES, Nov. 15, 2000, at A25; Belluck, *supra* note 567, at p. 18.

571 *See State of Wisconsin v. Zimmerman,* No. 96-2797-CR96-2797-CR (Ct. App. May 26, 1999). (unpublished decision).

572 *State of Wisconsin v. Zimmerman,* 96-CF-525 (Wis. Cir. Ct. Racine Cty. Sept. 18, 1996). (unpublished decision).

573 *See Pregnant Woman is Charged with Child Abuse for Drinking,* N.Y. TIMES, Jan. 22, 1990, at B8.

574 *See Case Against Pregnant Woman is Dismissed,* N.Y. TIMES, Feb. 3, 1990, at 10.

575 *See* Cooper, *supra* note 546, at p. 75.

576 *See State v. Luster,* 204 Ga. App. 156 (1992) (holding that a mother could not be charged with two counts of possessing cocaine and "unlawfully deliver[ing] it to her infant daughter while still in the womb"); *In re Valerie D.,* 223 Conn. 492 (1992) (holding that the statute permitting termination of parental rights for certain abusive conduct did not include the prenatal conduct of injecting cocaine several hours before the onset of labor); *State v. Ashley,* 701 So.2d 338 (Fla. 1997) (holding that a teenager who shot herself in the abdomen, causing the death of her unborn fetus could not be charged with manslaughter); *Commonwealth of Kentucky v. Welch,* 864 S.W.2d 280 (Ky. 1993) (holding that the legislature did not intend to impose criminal abuse sanctions on a pregnant woman who uses drugs); *State v. Gray,* 62 Ohio St. 3d 514 (1992) (holding that a woman who gave birth to a drug addicted child may not be prosecuted for child endangerment for substance abuse occurring before birth); *Collin v. Texas,* 890 S.W.2d 893 (Tex. App. El Paso 1994) (holding that a woman charged with abuse of child for ingesting cocaine while pregnant did not have notice that her actions were violative of the law); *In re J.B.C.,* No. 94194 (Okla. 2001) (holding that a fetus is not a "child" under the Oklahoma Children's Code, which permits emergency temporary custody).

577 *Whitner v. State of South Carolina,* 492 S.E.2d 777 (S.C. 1995).

578 *Whitner,* 492 S.E.2d at 779.

579 The state alleged that when Whitner used cocaine during the third trimester of her pregnancy, she violated S.C. Code Ann. Sec. 20-7-50 (1985) which provides: Any person having the legal custody of any child or helpless person, who shall, without lawful excuse, refuse or neglect to provide, as defined in Sec. 20-7-490, the proper care and attention for such child or helpless person, so that the life, health or comfort of such child or helpless person is endangered or is likely to be endangered, shall be guilty of a misdemeanor and shall be punished within the discretion of the circuit court. (Section 20-7-50 was amended in 1993 to make violation of the section a felony and to make the maximum term of imprisonment conform to the new crime classification system. *See* S.C. Code Ann. Sec. 20-7-50 (Supp. 1994).

580 She argued that the court lacked subject matter jurisdiction. Therefore, the court could not properly have accepted her guilty plea. Whitner also alleged that she had received ineffective assistance

of counsel because her attorney had failed to advise her that the statute under which she had been charged might not apply to prenatal drug use.

581   *Id.* at 780. In starting its review, the South Carolina court held that "South Carolina law has long recognized that viable fetuses are persons holding certain legal rights and privileges." The court added that "[t]he policies enunciated in the Children's Code also support our plain meaning reading of 'person.' S.C. Code Ann. Sec. 20-7-20(C) (1985), which describes South Carolina's policy concerning children.... [T]he consequences of abuse and neglect which takes place after birth often pale in comparison to those resulting from abuse suffered by the viable fetus before birth. This policy of prevention supports a reading of the word 'person' to include viable fetuses. Furthermore, the scope of the Children's Code is quite broad. It applies 'to all children who have need of services.' S.C. Code Ann. Sec. 20-7-20(b) (1985). When coupled with the comprehensive remedial purposes of the Code, this language supports the inference that the legislature intended to include viable fetuses within the scope of the Code's protection."

582   *Whitner*, 492 S.E.2d at 781.

583   *Id.*

584   *Id.* at 781–782 (emphasis added).

585   *See Whitner v. South Carolina*, 492 S.E.2d 777, *Petition for Writ of Certiorari*, at 9, *cert. den.*, 523 U.S. 1145 (1998).

586   *Id.* (citing *Sheriff v. Encoe*, 110 Nev. 1317, 1319 (1994); *Commonwealth v. Welch*, 864 S.W.2d 280, 283 (Ky. 1993)).

587   *See* Cooper, *supra* note 546, at p. 75–76.

588   *Id.* at 76–77.

589   *Id.* at 76.

590   *Id. See also* David Firestone, *Woman Is Convicted of Killing Her Fetus by Smoking Cocaine*, N.Y. TIMES, May 18, 2001, at A12.

591   *Id.* at A12.

592   *See Ferguson et al. v. City of Charleston et al.*, 532 U.S. 67 (2001).

593   *Id.*

594   *Id.* n. 2. (The Court noted that "[u]nder South Carolina law, a viable fetus has historically been regarded as a person; in 1995, the South Carolina Supreme Court held that the ingestion of cocaine during the third trimester of pregnancy constitutes criminal child neglect. *Whitner v. South Carolina*, 492 S.E.2d 777 (1995), *cert. den.*, 523 U.S. 1145 (1998).")

595   *Id.* n. 3 (To support this point, the Court noted that "[i]n his letter dated August 23, 1989, [MUSC's General Counsel, Joseph C.] Good wrote: 'Please advise us if your office is anticipating future criminal action and what if anything our Medical Center needs to do to assist you in this matter.'")

596   *Id.* n. 4. (The Court noted that "[t]hose criteria were as follows: 1. No prenatal care; 2. Late prenatal care after 24 week gestation; 3. Incomplete prenatal care; 4. Abruptio placentae; 5. Intrauterine fetal death; 6. Preterm labor 'of no obvious cause'; 7. IUGR [intrauterine growth retardation] 'of no obvious cause'; 8. Previously known drug or alcohol abuse; 9. Unexplained congenital anomalies.")

597   *Id.* n. 5. (The Court explained that "[d]espite the conditional description of the first category, when the policy was in its initial stages, a positive test was immediately reported to the police, who then promptly arrested the patient.")

598   *Id.* at 71–73.

599   Four of these women were arrested prior to the 1990 modification to the policy. The latter six after.

600   *Id.* n. 6. (The majority of the Court cited the instructions which read: "There were no search warrants issued by a magistrate or any other proper judicial officer to permit these urine screens to be taken. There not being a warrant issued, they are unreasonable and in violation of the Constitution of the United States, unless the defendants have shown by the greater weight or preponderance of the evidence that the plaintiffs consented to those searches." In the dissenting opinion, the Court noted that "[u]nder the judge's instructions, in order to find that the plaintiffs had consented to the searches, it was necessary for the jury to find that they had consented to the taking of samples, to the testing for evidence of cocaine, and to the possible disclosure of the test results to the police. Respondents have not argued, as Justice Scalia does, that it is permissible for members of the staff of a public hospital to use diagnostic tests 'deceivingly' to obtain incriminating evidence from their patients.")

601   *Id.* n. 7. (As explained by the Court, "[t]he term 'special needs' first appeared in Justice Blackmun's opinion concurring in the judgment in *New Jersey v. T.L.O.*, 469 U.S. 325, 351 (1985). In his concurrence, Justice Blackmun agreed with the Court that there are limited exceptions to the probable-cause requirement, in which reasonableness is determined by 'a careful balancing of governmental and private interests,' but concluded that such a test should only be applied 'in those exceptional circumstances in which special needs, beyond the normal need for law enforcement, make the warrant and probable-cause requirement impracticable....' *Ibid.* This Court subsequently adopted the 'special needs' terminology in *O'Connor v. Ortego*, 480 U.S. 709, 720 (1920) (plurality opinion), and *Griffin v. Wisconsin*, 483 U.S. 868, 873 (1987), concluding that, in limited circumstances, a search unsupported by either warrant or probable cause can be constitutional when 'spe-

cial needs' other than the normal need for law enforcement provide sufficient justification." *See also Vernonia School District 47J v. Acton*, 515 U.S. 646, 652–653 (1995)).

602   *Id.* n. 11. (The five Justices joined in the Court's decision noted that "[t]he dissent would have us do otherwise and resolve the issue of consent in favor of respondents. Because the Court of Appeals did not discuss this issue, we think it more prudent to allow that court to resolve the legal and factual issues in the first instance, and we express no view on the those issues." *See, e.g., Glover v. United States*, 531 U.S. 198 (2000); *National Collegiate Athletic Assn. v. Smith*, 525 U.S. 459, 470 (1999)).

603   *Id.* n. 10 (The Court explained that "[i]n a footnote to their brief, respondents do argue that the searches were not entirely suspicionless. They do not, however, point to any evidence in the record indicating that any of the nine search criteria was more apt to be caused by cocaine use than by some other factor, such as malnutrition, illness, or indigency. More significantly, their legal argument and the reasoning of the majority panel opinion rest on the premise that the policy would be valid even if the tests were conducted randomly.")

604   *See, e.g., Skinner v. Railway Labor Executives' Assn.*, 489 U.S. 602 (1989).

605   *See, e.g., Treasury Employees v. Von Raab*, 489 U.S. 656 (1989).

606   *See, e.g., Vernonia School Dist. 47J v. Acton*, 515 U.S. 646 (1995).

607   *Ferguson et al. v. City of Charleston et al.*, 532 U.S. 67 at 81 (citing *Indianapolis v. Edmond*, 531 U.S. 32 (2000) (slip op., at 15).

608   *Id.* at 82-83 (*emphasis in original*). (The Court explained that it had "italicized those words lest our reasoning be misunderstood. In none of our previous special needs cases have we upheld the collection of evidence for criminal law enforcement purposes. Our essential point is the same as Justice Kennedy's—the extensive entanglement of law enforcement cannot be justified by reference to legitimate needs.")

609   *Id.* n. 21. ("Accordingly," the Court wrote, "this case differs from *New York v. Burger*, 482 U.S. 691 (1987), in which the Court upheld a scheme in which police officers were used to carry out administrative inspections of vehicle dismantling businesses. That case involved an industry in which the expectation of privacy in commercial premises was 'particularly attenuated' given the extent to which the industry in question was closely regulated. *Id.* at 700. More important for our purposes, the Court relied on the 'plain administrative purposes' of the scheme to reject the contention that the statute was in fact 'designed to gather evidence to enable convictions under the penal laws....' *Id.* at 715. The discovery of evidence of other violations would have been merely incidental to the purposes of the administrative search. In contrast, in this case, the policy was specifically designed to gather evidence of violations of penal laws. [¶] This case also differs from the handful of seizure cases in which we have applied a balancing test to determine Fourth Amendment reasonableness. *See, e.g., Michigan Dept. of State Police v. Sitz*, 496 U.S. 444, 455 (1999); *United States v. Martinez-Fuerte*, 428 U.S. 543 (1976). First, those cases involved roadblock seizures, rather than 'the intrusive search of the body or the home.'" *See Indianapolis v. Edmond*, 531 U.S. at 32 (slip op., at 7–8) (Rehnquist, C.J., dissenting); *Martinez-Fuerte*, 428 U.S. at 561 ("[W]e deal neither with searchers nor with the sanctity of private dwellings, ordinarily afforded the most stringent Fourth Amendment protection") Second, the Court explicitly distinguished the cases dealing with checkpoints from those dealing with "special needs." *Sitz*, 496 U.S. at 450.)

610   *Id.* n. 22. ("Thus, under respondents' approach," the Court wrote, "any search to generate evidence for use by the police in enforcing general criminal laws would be justified by reference to the broad social benefits that those laws might bring about (or, put another way, the social harms that they might prevent).")

611   *Id.* n. 23. ("It is especially difficult to argue that the program here was designed simply to save lives," the Court held. "*Amici* claim a near consensus in the medical community that programs of that sort at issue, by discouraging women who use drugs from seeking prenatal care, harm, rather than advance, the cause of prenatal health (citing Brief of American Medical Association as *Amicus Curiae* 6–22; Brief for American Public Health Association *et al. as Amici Curiae* 17-21; Brief for NARAL Foundation *et al., as Amici Curiae* 18–19.)

612   *Id.*

613   *See* Michelle D. Mills, *Fetal Abuse Prosecutions: The Triumph of Reaction Over Reason*, 47 DePaul L. Rev. No.4 (Summer 1998), at p. 989 n. 3 (citing Note, Derk B.K. Van Raatle VI, *Punitive Policies: Constitutional Hazards on Non-Consensual Testing of Women for Prenatal Drug Use*, 5 Health Matrix at pp. 443–444 (1995) (in turn citing a 1990 survey of public and private hospitals conducted by the American Academy of Pediatrics finding that 11% of new mothers who used controlled substances during pregnancy)).

614   *Id.* at 989 n. 4 (citing Nancy J. Bennett, *Drug Exposed Newborns: Alternatives to Punitive Sanction of the Mother—A Coordinated Response*, 24 J. Health & Hosp. L. 182, 185 (1991)). (According to Mill, "[t]he 1989 National Drug Control Strategy estimates that there are 100,000 cocaine-exposed newborns each year, and the National Association for Perinatal Addiction Research and Education (NAPARE) claims 375,000 infants are born drug-exposed. A survey of hospital discharges performed by the National Center for Heath Statistics found that less than 14,000 drug-exposed infants are born each year. The discrepancies result from the sample used in the survey and whether the hospitals tested for multiple substances; higher numbers generally result when women and

newborns are universally tested for exposure to many different drugs. *Id.* The Center for Health Statistics survey, for example, was conducted in hospitals that did not routinely test all women and infants. *See also* Judy Howard, *Chronic Drug Users as Parents*, 43 HASTINGS L.J. at pp. 645, 647 (1992) (indicating that the 100,000 figure did not include prenatal exposure to heroin, methamphetamine, or phencyclidine (PCP); Page McGuire Linden, *Drug Addiction During Pregnancy: A Call for Increased Social Responsibility*, 4 AM. U. J. GENDER & L. at pp. 105, 107 (1995) (citing a study claiming as many as 739,000 drug-exposed infants are born each year). *But See* Dorothy E. Roberts, *Unshackling Black Motherhood*, 95 MICH. L. REV at pp. 948–49, (1997). Roberts criticized the media after an examination of articles citing the NAPARE figures revealed that most had exaggerated or misinterpreted the statistics. *Id.* The study's numbers included any amount of exposure to any drug for any length of time, but many articles extrapolated the statistics to mean that all 375,000 infants were actually harmed and/or exposed to cocaine. *Id.* In fact, the study did not indicate that all 375,000 suffered any injury and revealed that only 50,000 to 100,000 infants were specifically cocaine-exposed." *Id.*)

615   *Id.* at 990 (citing Margaret P. Spencer, *Prosecutorial Immunity: The Response to Prenatal Drug Use*, 25 CONN. L. REV. at pp. 393–394 (1994), (suggesting that the actual number of cocaine-exposed newborn babies may number between 500,000 and 4,000,000 each year)).

616   *See Ferguson*, 532 U.S. 67 n. 1. (As the Court explained, "[a]s several witnesses testified at trial, the problem of 'crack babies' was widely perceived in the late 1980's as a national epidemic, prompting considerable concern both in the medical community and among the general populace.")

617   *See, e.g.*, ARK. HOUSE BILL 1132 (2001) (if enacted could include "viable fetus" in the definition of "person" for purposes of wrongful death action); KEN. SENATE BILL 157 (2001) (if enacted, would amend current wrongful death statute to include an "unborn child" from fertilization onward, without regard to age, health, or condition of dependency); KEN. HOUSE BILL 232 (2001) (same wording as KENTUCKY SENATE BILL 157); MICH. SENATE BILL 70 (2001) (if enacted, would amend sentencing guidelines for killing or injuring "an embryo" or "fetus"); MISS. HOUSE BILL 793 (2001) (if enacted, would amend wrongful death statute to include "unborn fetus" in coverage).

618   *See, e.g.*, ARIZ. HOUSE BILL 2268 (2001) (if enacted, would provide for increasing sentence in domestic violence cases where the assault is on a pregnant woman); COLO. HOUSE BILL 1204 (2001) (if enacted, would enhance penalties for offenses committed against pregnant women).

619   *See, e.g.*, MISS. SENATE BILL 2215 (2001).

620   *See* IOWA SENATE BILL 23 (2001).

621   *See* RESEARCH IN BRIEF, *Crack's Decline: Some Surprises Across U.S. Cities*, NATIONAL INSTITUTES OF JUSTICE (July 1997).

622   *Id.* at 6–11.

623   *See* Shahul H. Ebrahim *et al.*, *Alcohol Consumption by Pregnant Women in the United States During 1988–1995*, 92 J. OBSTET. & GYNECOL., No. 2 (August 1998), at p. 187.

624   *Id.*

625   *See Alcohol Use Among Women of Childbearing Age—United States*, 1991–1999, 51 MORBIDITY AND MORTALITY WEEKLY REPORT, April 5, 2002, at pp. 273–276.

626   *See Tobacco Use and Reproductive Outcomes*, SURGEON GENERAL'S REPORT ON WOMEN AND SMOKING. *See also Smoking Behavior of Recent Mothers 18–44 Years of Age, Before and After Pregnancy: United States, 1990*, June 18, 2002.

627   *See* KEN. SEN. RES. 18 (2001) (Sponsor Roeding.)

628   *See* CALIFORNIA SEN. JUD. RES. 3 (2001).

629   *See, e.g.*, TEXAS HOUSE BILL 213 (2001) (declaring that because life begins at the moment of fertilization, an "unborn human organism" is alive and entitled to the rights, protections, and privileges accorded any other person in the state).

630   *See, e.g.*, CONN. HOUSE BILL 5672 (2001).

631   *See, e.g.*, ARIZ. HOUSE BILL 2416 (2001) (would require a birth certificate in cases of fetal death occurring after 20 weeks of gestation); COLO. HOUSE BILL 1308 (2001) (would authorize funeral parlors to treat fetal death the same as a dead body); COLO. HOUSE BILL 1325 (2001) (would require a death certificate for every stillborn death, not including induced termination of pregnancy); MASS. SEN. BILL 453 (2001) (would allow state officials to establish certificate of birth resulting in stillbirth for fetal deaths occurring for gestation period of at least 20 weeks); IOWA SEN. BILL 78 (2001) (birth certificates for fetuses 20 weeks or more); MON. SENATE BILL 290 (2001) (would permit medical personnel to certify cause of death on fetal death certificate).

632   *See Idaho: Abortion Debate*, N.Y. TIMES, Feb. 27, 2002, at A19.

633   *See* Sullivan, *supra* note 306, at p. 168.

634   Alan Fisk, *Abortion Fight Takes to the Highways*, NAT'L L.J., Dec. 24—Dec. 31, 2001, at A4; *South Carolina: Abortion Fight*, N.Y. TIMES, Sept. 6, 2001, at A20.

635   *See* Jennifer 8. Lee, *Abortion Rights Group Plans a New Focus and a New Name*, N.Y. TIMES, Jan. 5, 2003, at p. 17.

636   *See* Adam Liptak, *Ruling Opens New Arena in the Debate on Abortion*, N.Y. TIMES, Oct. 16, 2002, at A16.

637   *Id.*

638   *Id.*

639 *See Could-be Dad Can Sue Over Unborn Child's Death*, NAT'L L.J., May 5, 2003, at B4.

640 *Id.*

641 *Id.*

642 *Id.*

643 *See* Fisk, *supra* note 634, at A4; *South Carolina: Abortion Fight*, N.Y. TIMES, Sept. 6, 2001, at A20.

644 *Id.*

645 *Id.*

646 *Id.*

647 *Id.*

648 For review of recently proposed "informed consent" legislation, *See, e.g.,* ALASKA SEN. BILL 91 and HOUSE BILL (2001); ARIZ. SEN. BILL 1380 (2001); ARK. SEN. BILL 336 (2001); and GEOR. SEN. BILL 209 (2001); VIR. SENATE and HOUSE BILLS 1211and 2570 (2001).

649 *See* AL. HOUSE BILL 151 (2001); R.I. SENATE BILL 466 (2001).

650 *See* N.J. ASSEM. BILL 1892 (2000) and N. J. SEN. BILL 1176 (2000).

651 *See* HAW. HOUSE BILL 1477 (2001); TEXAS HOUSE BILL 1244 (2001).

652 *See* MISS. SEN. BILL 2383 (2001) (According to NARAL, the bill would have created the Protection from High Risk and Coercive Abortion Act and permitted "screening a woman prior to an abortion for risk factors, including gonorrhea or chlamydia infection, a family history of breast cancer, prior history of gestational trophoblastic tumor, history of caesarean section, a history of prior abortion, adolescence, feelings of being pressured to have the abortion, feelings of attachment to the unborn child, a history of psychological illness or emotional stability, lack of support from the partner or parents, strong religious convictions against abortion, a second or third trimester pregnancy, and low expectations of coping well." The bill also required a "qualified person to evaluate the woman, prior to an abortion, to determine if she is a vulnerable person, and provide counseling if she is determined to be a vulnerable person.")

653 *See* NEB. LEG. BILL 341 (2001).

654 *See* OKLA. HOUSE BILL 1331 (2001).

655 *See, e.g.,* ARK. HOUSE BILL 1074 (2001); GEOR. HOUSE BILLS 244 and 462 (2001); HAW. SEN. BILL 580 (2001); ILL. HOUSE BILL 1864 (2001); MASS. SENATE BILLS 609, 610 and 924 (2001); MINN. SEN. and HOUSE BILLS 217 and 262 (2001)(before Senate and House Committees on Health and Family Security); MISSOURI SEN. BILL 34 (2001); NEB. LEG. BILL 342 (2001); NEV. ASSEM. BILL 169 (2001); N.J. ASSEM. BILL 640 (2000); N.M. HOUSE BILL 477 (2001); R.I. SEN. BILL 200 (2001); TEXAS HOUSE BILL 17 (2001).

656 *See* ILL. SEN. RES. 8 (2001).

657 *See* Dr. Nancy Snyderman, GOOD MORNING AMERICA, March 5, 2001, at 2 (*transcript*). (Transcripts available through ABCNews.com.)

658 *Id.*

659 *See* Adam Clymer, *Critics Say Government Deleted Sexual Material From a Web Site to Push Abstinence*, N.Y. TIMES, Nov. 26, 2002, at A18.

660 *See Testimony of Father Charles E. Coughlin*, *supra* note 79, ENDNOTES FOR CHAPTER TWO, at pp. 126–130.

661 *See* NARAL: FACT SHEETS. The Department of Justice and Reproductive Freedom. See also S.K. Henshaw, J. Van Vort, *Abortion Services in the United States 1991–1992*, 26 FAMILY PLANNING PERSPECTIVES at pp. 100–106, 112 (1994).

662 *See* Willard Cates, Jr., *et al., Topics for Our Times: Justice Blackmun and Legal Abortion—A Besieged Legacy to Woman's Reproductive Health*, 85 AM. J. OF PUB. H. at p. 1205 (Sept. 1995); W. Cates, Jr., *The Hyde Amendment in Action: How Did the Restriction on Federal Funds for Abortion Affect Low-Income Women?*, 246 JAMA at pp. 1109–1112 (1981).

663 *Id.* (COUNCIL ON SCIENTIFIC AFFAIRS, AMERICAN MEDICAL ASSOCIATION, *Induced Termination of Pregnancy Before and After Roe v. Wade: Trends in the Mortality and Morbidity of Women*, 268 JAMA at 3231–3239 (1992); C. Tietze, L. Bongaarts, *The Demographic Effect of Induced Abortion*, 31 OBSTET. GYNECOL. SURV. at 699–709 (1976)).

664 The "Hyde Amendment" was sponsored by Henry Hyde, a Republican from Illinois.

665 *See* Cates Jr., *supra* note 662, at p. 1205.

666 *Id.* (citing W. Cates, Jr., *The Hyde Amendment in Action: How Did the Restriction on Federal Funds for Abortion Affect Low-Income Women?*, 246 JAMA at pp. 1109–1112 (1981)).

667 *Id.* (citing K.J. Meier, D.R. McFarlane, *State Family Planning and Abortion Expenditures: Their Effect on Public Health*, 84 AM. J. OF PUB. H'LTH at pp. 1468–1472 (1994)).

668 As of January 1997, states enforcing the ban on federal Medicaid funding for abortions included: Alabama, Arizona, Arkansas, Colorado, Delaware, Florida, Georgia, Indiana, Iowa, Kansas, Kentucky, Louisiana, Maine, Michigan, Mississippi, Missouri, Nebraska, Nevada, New Hampshire, New Mexico, North Carolina, North Dakota, Ohio, Oklahoma, Pennsylvania, Rhode Island, South Carolina, South Dakota, Tennessee, Texas, Utah, Virginia, Wisconsin, and Wyoming.

669 In 2001, similar bans were being considered in Massachusetts, New Jersey, Rhode Island and Tennessee. *See* MASS. SENATE BILL. 925 and HOUSE BILL 851 (2001); N.J. SENATE BILL 845, ASSEMBLY COMMITTEE RESOLUTION 75 and ASSEMBLY BILL 772 (2000). RHODE ISLAND and TENNESSEE were

considering amendments to current law. *See, e.g.,* R.I. HOUSE BILL 5305 and HOUSE BILL 5719 and 5722 (2001) and TENN. SENATE BILL 32 and HOUSE BILL 531 (2001).

670   *See* Mary Alice Robbins, *Abortion Restrictions Upheld,* NAT'L L.J., Jan. 13, 2003, at A7.

671   See *Bell v. Low Income Women of Texas,* 95 S.W.3d 253 (2003).

672   *See* Robbins, *supra* note 670, at A7.

673   *Id.*

674   *Id.*

675   *Id.*

676   *See* Blank and Merrick, *supra* note 400, at p. 40.

677   *Id.* (citing Majorie Randon Hershey & Darrell M. West, *Single-Issue Politics: Prolife Groups and the 1980 Senate Campaign,* IN INTEREST GROUP POLITICS (Allan J. Cigler & Burdett A. Loomis, eds.) (Washington, D.C.: CQ Press, 1983), at pp. 31–59).

678   *Id.*

679   *Id.* at 41.

680   *See* Schroedel, *supra* note 216, at p. 168.

681   *See Roe v. Wade,* 410 U.S. at 157.

682   *See* CONN. HOUSE BILL 5673 (2001).

683   *See* N.H. HOUSE BILL 390 (2001); WASH. HOUSE BILL 1929 (2001).

684   *See* MASS. HOUSE BILL 849 (2001).

685   *See, e.g.,* NEB. LEG. BILL 566 (2001) (requiring employees of public schools to use the term "unborn child" instead of "fetus" when describing all stages of human development); NEBRASKA LEGISLATIVE BILLS 567 and 753 (2001) (changes all references in state related abortion laws from "fetus" to "unborn child").

686   *See* SCHROEDEL, *supra* note 216, at p. 185.

687   *See* ARIZ. HOUSE BILL 2268 (2001); COLO. HOUSE BILL 1204 (2001); R.I. HOUSE BILL 5069 (2001); TEXAS SEN. BILL 269 (2001); VIR. HOUSE BILL 2403 (defeated as of February 2001) and VIR. HOUSE BILL 2798 (2001).

688   *See* CONN. HOUSE BILL 6243 (2001).

689   *See* N.H. HOUSE BILL 319 (2001).

690   *See* FLOR. HOUSE BILL 497 (2001) (defining "viable fetus" as a fetus 20 weeks or older).

691   *See* MISS. HOUSE BILL 794 (2001).

692   *See* MICH. SENATE BILL 70 and MICH. SENATE BILL 71 (2001).

693   *See* Schroedel, *supra* note 216, at p. 168. (Schroedel notes further that "[i]n 1996 the NRLC through its political action committee contributed more than $2 million to over one hundred pro-life congressional candidates" (citing Carol Long, *National Right to Life Committee,* NRLC 1997 Yearbook (Washington, D.C.: National Right to Life Committee)).)

694   *Id.* (citing National Abortion and Reproductive Rights League, *Who Decides? A State-by-State Review of Abortion and Reproductive Rights* (7th ed.) (Washington, D.C.: NARAL Foundation, 1998d), at v-vi; National Abortion and Reproductive Rights League, *Who Decides? A State-by-State Review of Abortion and Reproductive Rights* (8th ed.) (Washington, D.C.: NARAL Foundation, 1999), at ix).

695   *See, e.g.,* MON. HOUSE BILL 547 (2001) (which would create the Fetal Protection Act, defining an unborn child as a human fetus that is conceived and is more than 12 weeks old but who is not yet born. The bill also proposes to create criminal offenses for death or injury to an unborn child. But it provides an exemption for legal abortion); N.J. ASSEMBLY BILL 2946 (2000) (provides that the intentional killing of an "unborn child" would constitute murder with the exception of the death of a fetus as a result of a therapeutic abortion); VIR. HOUSE BILL 2403 (defeated in February 2001); OR. HOUSE BILL 2769 (2001)(would amend current law to include "unborn children" at every stage of gestation within criminal homicide and assault statutes, with exception for medical procedures).

696   *See* ARK. HOUSE BILL 1132 (2001).

697   *See* KEN. SENATE BILL 157 and KEN. HOUSE BILL 189 (2001) (would amend current wrongful death law to include an "unborn child" within the definition of "person"); MISS. HOUSE BILL 793 (2001).

698   *See* Robert Pear, *Bush Plan Allows States to Give 'Unborn Children' Medical Coverage,* N.Y. TIMES, July 6, 2001, at A1; *Bush Administration Defines Fetus as "Unborn Child,"* BUST, Spring 2002, at p. 12.

699   *Id.*

700   *See* Robin Toner, *Administration Plans Care of Fetuses in a Health Plan,* N.Y. TIMES, Feb. 1, 2002, at A18.

701   *Id.*

702   *See* Mike Allen, *President Signs Bill on Abortion Procedures,* WASH. POST, Aug. 6, 2002, at A03. See *also* Adam Clymer, *Heady Days for G.O.P. Flexing its New Muscle,* N.Y. TIMES, March 10, 2001, at A7. (Given Republican control of the House of Representatives, only 60 votes would be needed—as opposed to 67—to break a Democratic filibuster were either measure to come down to a partisan battle, according to some media reports.)

703   *See* Robert Pear, *Bush Rule Makes Fetuses Eligible for Health Benefits,* N.Y. TIMES, Sept. 28, 2002, at A12.

704   *See* Funderburg, *supra* note 497, at pp. 52–53 (recounting the story of Jason Waldmann, who was born at 1.2 pounds, kept alive at a cost of roughly $500,000. Funderburg reports that "[a]bout 450,000 babies are born prematurely in the U.S. each year, but Jason is among the 25,000 consid-

ered extremely premature—27 weeks of gestation or less. In the past 10 years, the edge of viability hasn't changed much; it's still between 23 and 24 weeks. But more of these micropreenies are surviving. "Ten or 15 years ago, these babies died," says Dr. Istvan Seri, clinical director of newborn services at Children's Hospital. "In the mid-'70s, if a 28 weaker survived, that was the standard." In 1970, only 40 percent of babies born weighing less than 3.3 pounds lived. Now it's more than 90 percent. And the success rate is likely to climb as researchers develop new treatments, more precise drug regimens and better machines to treat patients born too soon.") *See also As Premature Babies Grow, So Can Their Problems*, N.Y. TIMES, May 8, 2000, at A1.

705   *See* Blank & Merrick, *supra* note 400, at p. 156; Maggie Jones, *A Miracle, and Yet*, N.Y. TIMES MAG., July 15, 2001, at pp. 39–63.

706   *See* Allen, *supra* note 702, at A03; Clymer, *supra* note 659, at A7.

707   *See* Schroedel, *supra* note 216, at p. 184.

708   *Id.*

709   *See* Jeffrey Rosen, *A Viable Solution*, LEGAL AFFAIRS, Sept./Oct. 2003, pp. 20–22, at p. 20.

710   *See Webster*, 492 U.S. at 504 (citing Mo. Rev. Stat. 1.205.1(1), (2) (1986)).

711   *Id.* n. 4. (Section 1.205 of the Missouri Rev. Stat. provided at the time that "1. THE GENERAL ASSEMBLY OF THIS STATE FINDS THAT: (1) The life of each human being begins at conception; (2) Unborn children have protectable interests in life, health and well-being; (3) The natural parents of unborn children have protectable interests in the life, health, and well-being of their unborn child. 2. EFFECTIVE JANUARY 1, 1988, the laws of this state shall be interpreted and construed to acknowledge on behalf of the unborn child at every state of development, all the rights, privileges, and immunities available to other persons, citizens, and residents of this state, subject only to the Constitution of the United States, and decisional interpretations thereof by the United States Supreme Court and specific provisions to the contrary in the statutes and constitution of this state. 3. AS USED IN THIS SECTION, the term 'unborn children' or 'unborn child' shall include all unborn child [*sic*] or children or the offspring of human beings from the moment of conception until birth at every stage of biological development. 4. NOTHING IN THIS SECTION shall be interpreted as creating a cause of action against a woman for indirectly harming her unborn child by failing to properly care for herself or by failing to follow any particular program of prenatal care.)"

712   *Id.* at 505 (citing *Webster*, 851 F.2d at 1075–1076, quoting *Akron v. Akron Center for Reproductive Health, Inc.*, 462 U.S. 416, 444 (1983), in turn citing *Roe v. Wade*, 410 U.S. at 159–162). (The basis of the Eighth Circuit's strike of the several provisions was that they violated the United States Supreme Court's decision in *Roe v. Wade*.)

713   *Id.* (citing lower court's decision st. 851 F.2d. at 1076).

714   *Id.* (The majority notes, however, that "Judge Arnold dissented from this part of the Court of Appeals' decision, arguing that Missouri's declaration of when life begins should be upheld 'insofar as it relates to subjects other than abortion,' such as 'creating causes of action against persons other than the mother,' for wrongful death or extending the protection of the criminal law to fetuses.")

715   *Id.* (citing Brief for Appellants 21–24).

716   *Id.* (citing Brief of Appellees 19–23).

717   *Webster*, 492 U.S. at 506 (citing *Maher v. Roe*, 432 U.S. at 474).

718   *Id.* (citing *Roe v. Wade, supra*, at 161–162).

719   *Alabama State Federation of Labor v. McAdory*, 325 U.S. 450 (1945).

720   *Id.* at 460.

721   *Webster*, 492 U.S. at 507 (citing *Tyler v. Judges of Court of Registration*, 179 U.S. 405, 409 (1900); *Valley Forge Christian College v. Americans United for Separation of Church & State, Inc.*, 454 U.S. 464, 473 (1982).

722   492 U.S. 490 (1989).

723   *Id.* (citing *Roe v. Wade, supra*, at 161–162).

724   For review, *See* CHAPTER FIVE, *supra*.

725   For review of recently proposed "informed consent" legislation, *See, e.g.*, ALASKA SEN. BILL 91 and ALASKA HOUSE BILL (2001); ARIZ. SEN. BILL 1380 (2001); ARK. SEN. BILL 336 (2001); and GEOR. SEN. BILL 209 (2001); VIR. SEN. AND HOUSE BILLS 1211and 2570 (2001).

726   *See* OK. HOUSE BILL 1331 (2001).

727   *See* SCHROEDEL, *supra* note 216, at p. 169.

728   *See* ALA. HOUSE BILL 151 (2001); R.I. SENATE BILL 466 (2001).

729   *See* N.J. ASSEMBLY BILL 1892 (2000) and N.J. SENATE BILL 1176 (2000).

730   *See* HAW. HOUSE BILL 1477 (2001); TEXAS HOUSE BILL 1244 (2001).

731   *See* MISS. SEN. BILL 2383 (2001).

732   *See* Paul Frisman, *Baby was "Person,' So Killer May Die*, NAT'L L.J., June 14, 1999, at A4.

733   *Id.*

734   *Keeler v. Superior Court*, 470 P.2d 617 (Cal. 1970).

735   *Id.* at 629 (citing *United States v. Wiltberger*, 18 U.S. (5 Wheat.) 76, 96 (1820)).

736   Those states were: Arizona, Arkansas, Georgia, Illinois, Indiana, Louisiana, Minnesota, New Hampshire, New Mexico, North Dakota, Ohio, Pennsylvania, Rhode Island, South Dakota, and Utah. New

Mexico and Minnesota—two states that had 19th century feticide laws—repealed those laws shortly before *Roe*, enacting new ones in 1985 and 1986.

737   *See* Tenn. Code Ann. 39-13-214, Secs. 202, 211, 213 and 215 (across the board the language was changed to include a "viable fetus" as a "victim" under first and second degree murder and voluntary manslaughter, vehicular and reckless homicide statutes).

738   *See* Wis. Stat. Sec. 940.01 (1998) (language of first-degree intentional homicide makes a person liable for a Class A felony for causing the "death of an unborn child with intent to kill that unborn child, kill the woman who is pregnant with that unborn child or kill another"); Wis. Stat. Sec. 940.05 (1998) (permitting mitigating factors to allow for a reduced charge of second degree intentional homicide). What makes the Wisconsin laws more notable, however, is that in addition to "fetuses," "embryos" are also covered. See Wis. Stat. Secs. 940.02, 940.06, 940.08, 940.09, and 940.10).

739   *See* Ark. Code Secs. 5-1-102 [13]; 5-2-501 [1]; 5-10-101 through 5-10-105, 5-61-101; 5-61-102; 20-16-704, and 20-16-806.

740   *See Schroedel, supra* note 216, at p. 127 (citing "State Bill" 1997; interview with Pennsylvania Pro-Life Federation spokesman, November 17, 1999).

741   *Id.* (citing LANCASTER NEW ERA 1997, at A1).

742   *Id.* at 127–128.

743   Graham is a Republican representative from South Carolina.

744   *See Schroedel, supra* note 216, at p. 172, n. 18.

745   *See* Robert Pear, *Led by Republicans, House Approves Bill Giving Fetus Legal Protection*, N.Y. TIMES, Oct. 1, 1999, at A22; Adam Clymer, *Heady Days for G.O.P. Flexing its New Muscle*, N.Y. TIMES, March 10, 2001, at A7.

746   *See Senate Democrats Stall Unborn Victims Bill With Amendments on Unrelated Issues*, Aug. 5, 2003, published by National Right to Life Committee.

747   In the Senate, the bill was reintroduced on: Calendar No. 89, 108th Congress, 1st Session, S. 1019, May 7, 2003. In the House, a similar version of the bill was reintroduced as Laci and Conner's Law, 108th Congress, 1st Session, H.R. 1997, introduced May 7, 2003. (The author notes that "Connor" has been spelled as "Connor" and "Conner" at various times during the debate. Prior to passage of the law, the proposed bill was widely referred to as "Laci and Connor's Law," and that is how many media outlets continue to refer to it. Indeed, if one were to google "Connor's Law," he or she would likely find contemporary stories using the above spelling. Not until "Connor's Law" was formalized as law did it become "Conner's Law" for reasons that remain unclear. On that specific point, the author notes that since neither the author—nor any of the partisans of this debate—truly know how Laci Peterson might ultimately have decided to spell it, the "correct spelling" remains a mystery.)

748   *See* Deborah L. Rhode, *Gagging on a Bad Rule*, NAT'L L.J., Sept. 10, 2001, at A21.

749   *See* Laura Mansnerus, *Abortion Rights Group Files Suit Over Bush Family Planning Rule*, N.Y. TIMES, June 7, 2001, at A22.

750   *See* Toobin, *supra* note 452, at p. 63.

751   Ashcroft was nominated after losing his seat in the Senate to then-deceased Governor of Missouri, Mel Canahan, who wife was later appointed to the vacant Senate seat. He was confirmed by the Senate Judiciary Committee by 58 to 42 vote. As Attorney General, Ashcroft will be charged with helping President Bush shape legal policy, which will likely include effort to further restrict access to abortion, given President Bush's stated concern that "too many abortions" occur in the United States. As Attorney General, Ashcroft will also likely assist in the selection of judicial candidates. Bush may appoint two, perhaps even three, United States Supreme Court Justices during his tenure.

752   *See Planned Parenthood v. Ashcroft*, 462 U.S. 476 (1983). Three years earlier, Ashcroft filed an *amici curiae* brief in *Williams v. Zbaraz*, 448 U.S. 358 (1980). (Among Ashcroft's critics is the National Abortion Rights Action League, which stated in a fact sheet that "[t]he landmark of John Ashcroft's long public career has been his dedication to taking away women's constitutional rights. He has pressed litigation and legislation seeking to curtail women's reproductive rights. He goes beyond the antichoice beliefs of many of his antichoice peers: he opposed abortion even in cases of rape and incest. He even opposes common forms of contraception, including the birth control pill. If John Ashcroft's world view becomes embodied in law, the clock would be turned back to the days of common illegal abortion and women would be disempowered socially and legally as a result of losing control over their reproductive lives." See NARAL: FACT SHEETS. The Department of Justice and Reproductive Freedom.)

753   *See* David Johnston & Neil A. Lewis, *Ashcroft Pledges to Enforce Laws That He Opposes*, N.Y. TIMES, Jan. 17, 2001, at A1.

754   *Id.*

755   *See* Toobin, *supra* note 452, at p. 52.

756   *Id.*

757   *See* Eric Lichtblau, *Ashcroft to Defend Ban on Some Abortion Protests, Angering His Longtime Allies*, N.Y. TIMES, Aug. 30, 2003, at A10.

758   *See* Robert Pear, *Thompson Says He Will Order a New Review of Abortion Drug*, N.Y. TIMES, Jan. 20, 2001, at A11.

759 *Id.* (The full context of Thompson's quote was reportedly: "I do not intend to roll back anything unless it is proven to be unsafe," Thompson reportedly told Senator Hillary Rodham Clinton in response to questions. "Safety concerns are something that's in question.")

760 *See* Gina Kolata, *Death at 18 Spurs Debate Over a Pill for Abortion*, N.Y. TIMES, Sept. 24, 2003, at A18.

761 *See Schroedel, supra* note 216, at p. 187 (citing John A. Robertson, *Children of Choice: Freedom and the New Reproductive Technologies* (Princeton, New Jersey: Princeton University Press, 1994), at p. 64).

762 *See Challenge to Abortion Pill*, N.Y. TIMES, Aug. 22, 2002, at A18.

763 *See Antiabortion Doctor to Lead Panel*, N.Y. TIMES, Dec. 27, 2002, at A15.

764 *See* Clymer, *supra* note 659, at A18.

765 *Id.*

766 *See* Christopher Marquis, *Bush Misuses Science Data, Report Says*, N.Y. TIMES, Aug. 8, 2003, at A14.

767 *See* Clymer, *supra* note 659, at A18. (Scientists seem to agree with the report. See, *e.g.,* Erica Goode, *Certain Words Can Trip Up AIDS Grants, Scientists Say*, N.Y. TIMES, April 18, 2003, at A10.)

768 *See* Goode, *supra* note 767, at A10.

769 *Id.*

770 *Id.*

771 *See* James Mann, *Young Rumsfeld*, THE ATLANTIC MONTHLY, Nov. 2003, at pp. 90–101.

772 *See* Kenneth T. Walsh, *The Man Behind the Curtain*, U.S.NEWS & WORLD REPORT, Oct. 13, 2002, at pp. 27–31; Walsh, *supra* note 390, at pp. 15–23; Brookhiser, *supra* note 387, at pp. 55–69.

CHAPTER NINE

A Woman's Worth:
Less is Still Less

A CENTURY OF QUESTIONS:
Where Women Stand Today

As Harvard Professor Aage B. Sorensen explains:

> There are two ways in which the idea that social structure is relevant for the creation of inequality can be understood. One conception of the relevance of structure, often used in labor market research, is one where 'structural effects' reflect that people, because of their location in a social structure, change their effort and skills and thus become more or less productive. These effects might, for example, be produced by the incentive structures and training arrangements developed in internal labor markets.
>
> There is, however, another conception of how social structure creates inequality. The idea is that properties of positions in social structure are relevant for how much income and other rewards occupants of these positions obtain independently of the characteristics of these occupants. Thus the advantage or disadvantage of a location in social structure is obtained independently of how this location influences the economic productivity of an individual. These kinds of advantages and disadvantages are those that we ordinarily think about when we talk about class advantages and disadvantages.[1]

In the last two decades, the American economy has come full circle and that has had a profound effect on the lives of some women. The early 1980s were heralded by supporters as one of the high points of the "Reagan Revolution," a period when, by administration accounts, 19 million new jobs were created and "exploding technology and unprecedented prosperity…rekindled national pride."[2]

"So many Americans had been making so much money that the term 'millionaire' became meaningless," argues former Assistant Attorney General Kevin Phillips in *The Politics of Rich and Poor: Wealth and the American Electorate in the Reagan Aftermath.*[3] "[I]n Manhattan, where midtown parking could cost fifty dollars a day, 'millionaire' had come to mean only persons with yearly incomes over one million dollars (a level usually bespeaking assets in the $5 million to $10 million range). A Georgia marketing expert, Thomas J. Stanley, counted almost one hundred thousand 'decamillionaires'—people worth over $10 million.[4] Back in 1960 there hadn't been that many plain-vanilla millionaires."[5]

And yet, were he alive, Dickens might have had a version of the story too, because during that same period, although wealth grew for the "well-educated," the "well-married," and the already "well-off," the 1980s were "tough on people whose weakness was a matter of education, family status, sex, age, or race…" Phillips writes.[6] And what that meant—though nearly invisible at the time— was that "a disproportionate number of women, young people, blacks, and Hispanics" were among the "casualties" of this otherwise prosperous period.

"Even as record numbers of female corporate directors, black millionaires, and twenty-six-year-old investment bankers and rock stars were entrenching themselves in Upper America, a much larger and growing underclass of high school dropouts, unwed mothers, female heads of households, unemployable young black males, and homeless persons of all races and ages was beginning to provoke worried questions about the nation's future," Phillips notes.[7]

Those worries proved legitimate. The realignment of economic opportunity away from those in need and toward those Americans already doing well "devastated the lives of many low-income Americans by removing the jobs and circumstances needed for homes and family cohesion," Phillips argues.[8] Blue-collar workers were enormously affected as unions made repeated and sometimes sizable concessions,[9] and a sluggish economy forced cuts to even "the white collar workforce (of male managers)."[10]

In the muddled give and take of the 1980s American economy, though it is often argued that women made considerable gains in an absolute sense, in terms of practical life, those gains were often instantly consumed by day-to-day necessities. Scholars note, for example, that throughout the 1980s, women claimed an astounding number of "new jobs" created during this period, thereby "narrowing the male-female salary gap."[11] And, indeed, the median weekly income for women working full-time rose from 62.5 percent of men's salaries in 1979 to 66 percent in 1983.

And yet, "the extra costs of day care, marital stress, reduced shopping opportunity, and lost leisure" were among the "dissatisfying side-effects of these gains," researchers note.[12] In addition, "[s]ingle-parent families mostly with a female head, grew from 13 percent of the total in 1970 to 22 percent in 1980, and then to 27 percent in 1987," according to Phillips. "So while the inflation-adjusted median family income of married couples was going up by almost 9 percent from 1980 to 1986, that of female-headed families rose by only 2 percent."[13]

This suggests, of course, that women with children remained among the poorest Americans, because women who are the sole financial support for families "are more likely to be poor, than married-couple families,"[14] Single-wage, single female headed households accounted for nearly half of all poor families.[15]

"Not only is the poverty rate of families maintained by women much higher than that for other families, but also the rate for black female householders with no husband present is higher than that of their white counterparts," government reports suggest.[16] Indeed, "[s]ince the mid-1960s, even with the major changes in the economy over this period, there has been relatively little fluctuation in the poverty rates for families maintained by women."[17]

By contrast, "…women in professional jobs and upper-income circumstances were achieving striking gains," notes Phillips.[18] "Female college graduates…outpaced males of equivalent education in income gains, so that women's economic circumstances polarized even more than men's during the Reagan years." And yet, "[t]he bottom 25 to 35 percent of women (working and nonworking)…represented an important portion of the decade's major losers." As a result, "a lot more women than men voted against George [H.W.] Bush for a plausible reason: a disproportion number of females were becoming a 'have-not constituency'[19]—earning 66 percent of what men made," Phillips suggests.

THE 1990s:
A Postmodern June

By 1990, there were 127,470,455 women living in the United States, 11 million more than the decade before.[20] As a decade, the 1990s would give birth to a "postmodern June…almost as mainstream as the 1950s version," journalists Barbara Kantrowitz and Pat Wingert suggest.[21] Except with a different focus, Kantrowitz and Wingert contend. The results were apparent on the political front by 2000, when women held a record number of seats in Congress.[22]

Between 1980 and 1990, the rate of college enrollment for women aged 15 through 39 approached that of men, according to the United States Bureau of the Census.[23] In addition, the percentage of women entering fields of study traditionally dominated by men increased, rising, for example, from one percent of all the bachelor's degrees in engineering earned in 1980 going to women to 14 percent by 1990.[24] There were also gains on the graduate level.

In 1970, roughly nine percent of all business degrees went to women. By 1990, 47 percent of all business degrees went to women.[25] Similar gains were made in the area of the law. Only ten percent of the students entering law schools in 1970 were women. By 2001, 49.4 percent of the 43,518 first-year students entering law schools across the country were women,[26] though research suggests that there are still fewer opportunities for women in the law once they leave school.[27]

Medicine was changing as well. "In 1975, women made up only a quarter of all entering students," wrote Rachel Sobel, in the March 10, 2003, issue of *U.S.News & World Report*. At [University of California–San Francisco medical school] today, [women make up] 57 percent of the class; the national average is close to 50 percent. Women are also increasingly going into traditional male specialties, such as surgery."[28]

And, between 1980 and 1990, "[d]espite the fact that there has been no discernible reduction in household and family responsibilities," according to the census bureau, "women have joined the labor force in record numbers."[29] In 1990, the majority of adult women were either at work or looking for work, according to government data, with 28.7 million women reporting that they held full-time jobs.[30]

And yet, although there has been some "distribution of…women and men across occupations," statistics suggest that overall the "labor market remains sharply segregated by sex."[31] In other words, "women have made progress in entering occupations predominantly held by men in the past, especially managerial and professional specialty occupations, the majority of women are still in traditional 'female' occupations," the data suggests.[32] But at the same time, women are still "over-represented in clerical (administrative support) and service occupations and underrepresented in production, craft, repair, and labor occupations."[33]

As a result, "[t]he economic position of women is considerably lower than that of men," Census Bureau officials note. "In 1989, the median family income for families with a female householder, no husband present was $17,414, significantly less than the median family income for married-couple families ($39,584)."[34]

Between 1970 and 1990, the demography of marriage and childbirth also changed. United States Bureau of the Census statistics suggest that in the last three decades of the twentieth century, an increasing number of women chose to delay marriage and childbirth in favor of college and establishing a career, a pattern more traditionally followed by men. "In 1990, 63 percent of all women in their early twenties had not yet married, compared with only 36 percent in 1970," the Census Bureau found.

There are those who suggest, of course, that this trend is responsible, at least in part, for the billion-dollar boom in assisted reproductive technology and the rise in recent years of first births among "older" women.[35] And here the statistics are worth noting, if for no other reason than they may further illuminate the trend. In 1990, 4,158,200 babies were born in the United States. According to Census data, "[t]his number was the highest reported since 1962 (4,167,362), near the end of the Baby Boom."[36] And yet, many of these mothers were not in their twenties, as they were in the 1960s.

Indeed, according to government statistics, "[i]n 1990, the birthrate for women 30 to 34 years old was the highest it has been in the past two decades (81 per 1,000 women)," and "[d]uring the past decade, birth rates for women in this age group…increased more than any other age group."[37] But "[w]omen 35 to 39 had the next highest increase. Their birthrate was the highest it has been since 1971."[38]

Data also suggests that some women may be forgoing marriage or remarriage altogether. According to government statistics, the percentage of "never-married" women rose from 11 percent of women between 25 and 29 years old and 6 percent of women 30 to 34 in 1970 to 31 percent for women in their late twenties and 16 percent for women in their early thirties by 1990.[39] "At the same time, the proportion of married women decreased from 63 percent to 55 percent."[40]

One of the reasons for this decline was divorce, and according to Census Bureau officials, "[d]ivorce has become much more common in the past twenty years," rising from 4 percent of women and 3 percent of men in 1970, who reported "divorced" as their current marital status to 10 percent of women and 7 percent of men in 1990. Some demographers note, however, that "[b]ecause women live longer than men, it is not surprising that 12 percent of women and…3 percent of men reported their marital status as widowed."[41]

PORTRAIT OF A CHANGING WORKFORCE

— In 1952, less than 30 percent of women held jobs. Today, women make up nearly half the U.S. labor force—an estimated 41 million wage earners. More than 6.2 million women own companies, contributing nearly $2.4 trillion to the national economy.

— In 1955, only 18 percent of mothers with children under 6 worked. By 2001, that number jumped to 64 percent—with about 3 million mothers of infants less than a year old holding full-time jobs.

— By 1989, 80 percent of home buyers were two-income couples. According to the U.S. Bureau of Census, most families in the 1990s needed two incomes to "maintain the standard of living...enjoyed two decades earlier."

— Since 1995, though the number of women reaching top executive levels in Fortune 500 companies has nearly doubled in the last eight years—"swelling" to 15.7 percent from 8.7—in terms of actual numbers, women executives number only 2,140 of 13,600 executives overall.

— "In 1900, women earned 50 cents for every dollar a man made. A century later, they earn 76 cents."

— Although women are leaving "corporate America" to start their own businesses in record numbers, "[o]nly 39 percent have landed loans from commercial banks, compared to 52 percent of male business owners."

—U.S.News & World Report[42]

Another reason for the apparent decline in the rate of marriage, some suggest, is that the institution of marriage is viewed by many Americans as less relevant today than it once was. "There is a very significant increase in the number of unmarried-couple households," according to Martin O'Connell, United States Census Bureau chief of fertility and family statistics. Though married couples still make up a majority of American households—at 52 percent—statistics show a steady decline.

AT THE TURN OF THE MILLENNIUM:
Money Matters and Women

In dissecting the prosperity of the 1990s, Joseph Stiglitz, chairman of the Council of Economic Advisers during the Clinton administration, explains that "[a]fter sluggishness in the 1970s and 1980s, productivity in the United States had risen sharply, to levels that exceeded even those of the boom following World War II.... Jobs were created, technology prospered, inflation fell, poverty was reduced."[43]

By 2000, the median income of American households topped $40,000 for the first time in history.[44] "It was the fifth straight increase in median income, the first time that has happened since the Bureau started keeping track of household incomes since 1967," declared Steven Holmes in *The New York Times*.[45] At the same time, Census data showed that "the percentage of households living in poverty dropped to the lowest point in more than two decades."[46]

"In its annual reports on income and poverty, the [Census] Bureau noted that median household income rose by 2.7 percent in 1999 to $40,816, up from $39,744 the prior year. It reported that 11.8 percent of the population lived below the poverty line in 1999, down from 12.7 percent the year before. The poverty rate in 1999 was defined as a household income of $17,029 for a family of four. Over the long term, the Bureau's reports describe an economy that is merely returning the country to where it was at the beginning of the 1990s," wrote Holmes.[47]

This wave of prosperity drove a surge in spending. New and larger homes were bought, statistical data from thirteen states show. More Americans finished or went back to school, earning more college and graduate degrees than in previous years. Even the elderly were flush, gaining roughly 60 percent in income.[48]

And yet there were a few downturns in an otherwise upbeat time—downturns running along gender lines. For the second straight year in 1999, the earnings gap between men and women increased, with median incomes of full-time working women falling to $26,324 from $26,433. By contrast, median incomes for men working full-time rose to $36,376 from $36,126.[49] In addition, though it is often noted that "[m]ost women's incomes rose" during the period, while those of men "stagnated or fell,"[50] most women's incomes generally still did not exceed those of men.[51]

THE "NEW ECONOMY":
A Boom or Bust for Women?

"When Heidi G. Miller quit her job in February [2000] as the highest-ranking woman at Citigroup to join Priceline.com, the online travel agency, her move was heralded as a stunning signal that the new economy was eclipsing the old one," wrote journalist Patrick McGeehan.[52] But "[n]ow that Ms. Miller has abruptly resigned from Priceline and is looking for work, her brief adventure in cyberspace is being cited as confirmation that the dot-coms are dead."[53]

The "New Economy"—the heralded shift from an "economy based on the production of physical goods to an economy based on the production and application of knowledge"[54]—was supposed to remake America. And for the latter half of the 1990s, the mere anticipation of this shift drove an economic revival. But by the start of 2001, the question of whether the "New Economy" was dead was already being asked.[55]

"In the traditional economy new technologies and products start out expensive and rare, and only gradually become cheap and common; think of refrigeration, the automobile, the long-distance call," Jonathan Rauch explained in the *Atlantic Monthly*. "In the New Economy additional capacity seems to become available so quickly and inexpensively (think of the microchip) that traditional supply constraints are almost trivial. 'In such a world,' former Treasury Secretary Lawrence H. Summers has been quoted as saying, 'the avalanche, rather than the thermostat, becomes the more attractive metaphor for economic policy.'"[56]

With the computer revolution, everything changed.

"In the three decades since 1970 the power of microprocessors increased by a factor of 7,000," writes Rauch. "Computing chores that took a week in the early 1970s now take a minute. According to the Federal Reserve Bank of Dallas, the cost of storing one megabit of information, or enough for a 320-page book, fell from more than $5,000 in 1975 to seventeen cents in 1999."[57]

Technology breathed new life into a staggering economy, opening markets and rendering efficient processes that previously were not.[58] By "the second half of the 1990s the aggregate effect on productivity became large enough to register in the national accounts...," according to Rauch.[59] The "New Economy" spurred growth; creating an "entrepreneurial revolution" as skilled workers left corporate jobs in favor of electronic start-ups. Though it was called the "new" economy, Wall Street insiders argue that the "New Economy" was actually the "third or fourth new economy since the 19th century—each one offering a similar promise—and yet none could stop a persistent downturn."[60]

During the 1990s, markets expanded with the promise of the cyber frontier. Speculation of the promise drove investment, which, in turn, drove speculation on Wall Street. Capital spending surged in 1995 as computers, software, semiconductors, telephone and telecommunications equipment was bought.[61] By 2000, capital spending had risen from 31 percent in 1995 to 40 percent in 2000, before the boom began to slow.[62]

And where were women in the New Economy?

Highly-educated women made strides in corporate America. By January 2000, *Working Women* magazine was celebrating the elections of twenty-five female chief or controlling officers of Fortune 500 companies.[63] The American Association of University Women notes, however, that these strides were still small by comparison. "Only 10 percent of the officers and only 2.4 percent of those at the pinnacle of power in Fortune 500 companies are women," the Association reported in 2000.[64]

But in terms of entrepreneurial efforts, *U.S.News & World Report*'s McDonald notes that "...women have decamped from corporations in record numbers to start their own businesses over the past decade."[65] The *Christian Science Monitor* reported in 1998 that "[t]he past decade has seen an explosion in female-owned companies, with their numbers almost doubling and their sales and employment tripling. Women now own 8 million firms—more than a third of all U.S. businesses. They employ 18.5 million people—one in five U.S. workers—and produce $2.3 trillion in annual revenues."[66]

Even so, in 1999, "[a]t a time when women are starting two-thirds of the nation's new businesses, why do so few of them tap into the record $12 billion pool of venture capital? *The Wall Street Journal* reports that a scant 2% of venture capital, the key to fast growth for most small companies, goes to women-owned firms, according to the Small Business Administration estimates."[67]

By December 2000, the New Economy had begun to retract.[68] By winter 2000, the national unemployment rate reached four percent, a tenth of a percentage point above its lowest level in three decades. By 2001, forecasters were admitting that the economy—new and old—was in a recession.[69] Women lost their jobs alongside men. But what makes that fact doubly worth noting is another statistic. According to Kantrowitz and Wingert, as the New Economy boomed, the number of families headed by single mothers was also growing, increasing "25 percent since 1990, to more than 7.5 million households" by the end of the decade.

Women tend overwhelmingly to be the custodial parents of children. Women also tend to earn less than men. As a result, women and households headed by women are likely to be among the hardest hit by the decline of the "New Economy," just as women were among the hardest hit by the decline in the economy of the 1980s.

THIS WOMAN'S WORK:
Seventy-Something Cents on the Dollar

"Women who work full-time, regardless of age, race, or educational attainment, earn less, on average, than men," according to a May 1999 Bureau of Labor Statistics Summary.[70] "Overall, in 1998, median weekly earnings of female full-time wage and salary workers were $456 compared to $598 for men."[71] In other words, by 1998, women were earning somewhere around 76 cents for every dollar earned by a man.[72]

Inequities in earnings has long been deemed a "feminist" issue. But the United States Department of Labor offers annual, quarterly, and sometimes even monthly "snapshots" of the issue as do journalists, politicians, and scholars. And what all of those "pictures" show is inequity across the board. At a time, for example, when women's tennis is among the biggest draws on the professional sports circuit (far more popular than men's tennis), the top-ranked women's champions were still slated in 2002 to receive smaller prize packages than men's champions.[73] The disparity is symptomatic.

According to Labor Department officials, the "gap between men's and women's earnings" is as historic as the gap between male and female employment opportunities. Historians agree. In the noted study of young women entering the labor force in the 1970s, researcher Clifford Adelman found that women experienced more unemployment than men; were often channeled toward and worked (as a result) in lower-paying and often traditionally "female" jobs; and generally had lower incomes.[74]

For example, in 1979, "women who were full-time wage and salary workers had earnings that were only about three-fifths those of men," Labor statistics show.[75] Though the next two decades would bring "progress," there was no equality. By 1995, despite higher levels of education, women still earned only "two-thirds of men's earnings," according to Labor Department statistics.[76] "Further, a woman with a bachelor's degree could expect to make $327 more annually than a male who achieved an associate degree ($39,271 compared to $38,944, respectively), but $21,737 less than a man with a bachelor's in 1995 ($39,271 compared to $61,000, respectively)," Labor data show.[77]

Labor officials note that there was similar progress among racial groups. Gains were even larger for minority women when compared to men of certain minority groups. "Black and Hispanic women, for example, had earnings that were around 85 percent of those of their male counterparts; among whites, the ratio was about 76 percent," the data suggest.[78] This has more to do with the fact that black and Hispanic men tend to earn less than white men,[79] as opposed to black and Hispanic women having made significant "real" gains in the labor market. In other words, the earnings gap may be smaller than that of white women and white men. But that does not mean that black and Hispanic women are not still making less overall and/or that they may not still be poor. (*See* Table 2, *infra*, at p. 390.)

TABLE 1: AVERAGE EARNINGS OF YEAR-ROUND, FULL-TIME WORKERS AGE 25 AND OLDER ACCORDING TO GENDER, AND FEMALE TO MALE EARNINGS RATIO, BY LEVEL OF EDUCATION 1995

	Males	Females	Percentages of Female Earnings as compared with Male Earnings
Totals	$41,118	$27,162	66.1
LEVELS OF EDUCATION			
Less than 9th Grade	$20,461	$13,349	65.2
9th to 12th Grade (No Diploma)	$24,377	$16,188	66.4
High School Graduates or Equivalency	$31,081	$21,383	68.8
Some College, But No Degree	$35,639	$24,787	70.0
Associate's Degree	$38,944	$26,903	69.1
Bachelor's Degree or Higher	$61,008	$39,271	64.4

U.S. DEPARTMENT OF COMMERCE. STATISTICAL ABSTRACT OF THE UNITED STATES: 1996 (WASHINGTON, D.C.: BUREAU OF THE CENSUS, 1996), AT 471.[80]

Age also appears to make a difference. According to 1998 Labor Department summaries, "[y]oung women and men (those under age 25) had fairly similar earnings (young women's earnings were about 91 percent those of men's). By contrast, women's earnings were much lower than men's in older age groups."[81] (*See* Table 1, *supra*.) But young people tend to be low or minimum wage earners.

Table 2: Median usual weekly earnings[1] of full-time[2] wage and salary workers,[3] by sex, race, and Hispanic origin, annual averages, 1990–2000

Characteristic	Year										
	1990	1991	1992	1993	1994	1995	1996	1997	1998	1999	2000
Black											
Both sexes	$329	$348	$357	$369	$371	$383	$387	$400	$426	$445	$468
Men	361	375	380	392	400	411	412	432	468	488	503
Women	308	323	335	348	346	355	362	375	400	409	429
Hispanic origin											
Both sexes	304	312	322	331	324	329	339	351	370	385	396
Men	318	323	339	346	343	350	356	371	390	406	414
Women	278	292	302	313	305	305	316	318	337	348	364
White											
Both sexes	424	442	458	475	484	494	506	519	545	573	591
Men	494	506	514	524	547	566	580	595	615	638	669
Women	353	373	387	401	408	415	428	444	468	483	500
EARNINGS RATIOS											
Black to white	77.6	78.7	77.9	77.7	76.7	77.5	76.5	77.1	78.2	77.7	79.2
Black men to white men	73.1	74.1	73.9	74.8	73.1	72.6	71.0	72.6	76.1	76.5	75.2
Black women to white women	87.3	86.6	86.6	86.8	84.8	85.5	84.6	84.5	85.5	84.7	85.8
Hispanic to white	71.7	70.6	70.3	69.7	66.9	66.6	67.0	67.6	67.9	67.2	67.0
Hispanic men to white men	64.4	63.8	66.0	66.0	62.7	61.8	61.4	62.4	63.4	63.6	61.9
Hispanic women to white women	78.8	78.3	78.0	78.1	74.8	73.5	73.8	71.6	72.0	72.0	72.8

[1] Earnings are expressed in nominal dollars.
[2] Full-time workers include persons who usually work 35 hours or more a week on their sole, or principal, job.
[3] Wage and salary workers exclude self-employed persons whether or not their businesses are incorporated.

SOURCE: Bureau of Labor Statistics, Current Population Survey.

While full-time, white, salaried men earned roughly $669 per week in 2000, according to Department of Labor statistics, white women working full-time earned weekly salaries of only $500.[82] During that same period, full-time salaried African American men earned $503, while African American women earned $429. Full-time salaried Hispanic women similarly took home less, earning $364 to the $414 of Hispanic men.[83]

Although the median weekly earnings of the nation's 100.2 million full-time working women was up 4.2 percent in the second quarter of July 2000, "[a]mong men, the $787 median weekly earnings level of 45- to 54-year olds was highest of any group."[84] By contrast, among women, although "earnings also were highest for those 45 to 54 years old," women earned only $557.[85] And "[a]mong the major occupation groups, persons employed full time in managerial and professional specialty occupations had the highest median weekly earnings—$999 for men and $697 for women."[86]

Though this might appear to be evidence of institutional bias to some, Department of Labor officials suggest that several factors have traditionally been responsible for the earnings gap. "First, although more women have achieved higher levels of education, they have been more likely than men to enter fields of study and occupations traditionally dominated by females.[87] These pay less than those traditionally held by males."[88]

In addition, "married women and women with children may have been more likely than men to take time off from a career for family. Women who leave the labor market for family reasons often return to wages lower than those of women who did not leave. Further, women who leave the labor market lose seniority and are less likely to receive on-the-job training, their job skills may depreciate, and their employers may believe they will take another leave."[89]

Thus, it is not clear that gender bias or discrimination alone are responsible for the lower wages women earn. While this may be true generally, bias is often most clearly apparent when women move into "traditionally male occupations," researchers suggests. Even in those cases, for example, where the educational level attained by women is equal to that of men and women have "invaded" fields of occupation not "traditionally dominated by females," women are still paid less.

In 2001, a survey conducted by the American Association for the Advancement of Sciences found that although the median salaries of all "life scientists"—researchers in the fields of biology, medicine, and related disciplines—rose by roughly seven percent between May 2000 and May 2001, "women employed full-time as life scientists earn some $72,000 a year, 23 percent less than the $94,000 their male counterparts make."[90]

And though the not-for-profit sector is often thought to be "kinder and gentler," a 2001 study by GuideStar found that women "lagged" behind in promotions to top positions and in pay in this arena as well. Where male CEOs made roughly $264,602, female chief executives made only $170,180. But it wasn't only in the top positions. Rather, across the board—in all areas of not-for-profits—women were paid less, according to the study.[91]

In addition to earning less, a 1999 study by the Lucile Parkard Foundation found that attitudes in the workplace towards women, particularly working mothers, have changed little, with many Americans still saying it is best for women to stay home with their children.[92] And there is a growing trend among women who—driven by dissatisfaction or quality of life issues—simply "opt out" of the corporate world after having children.[93] And then there are the extraordinary instances when women are penalized for keeping pace with men.[94]

But there is one industry where women rule, writer Susan Faludi argues. "Porn—at least porn produced for a heterosexual audience—is one of the few contemporary occupations where the pay gap operates in women's favor; the average actress makes fifty to a hundred percent more money than her male counterpart. But then she is the object of desire; he is her mere appendage, the object of the object," Faludi wrote in *The Money Shot*.[95]

Or would doing porn be an example of building "social position" as Sorensen suggests?[96] In terms of economics, these women are sometimes among the highest paid entertainers in the world. And that wealth may help them "earn" rewards and benefits. But would becoming a scientist after years of study and sacrifice be more in line with Sorensen's theory of social structure, even though research suggests that women are still paid less than their male counterparts and are, therefore, less able to partake of the advantages inherent in wealth?

Though gender discrimination law underwent a dramatic change in 1998, despite three decades of discussion on equal pay legislation and the continued promise of elected officials to ensure that women "earn equal pay for equal work," at the start of the millennium, women were still earning less. This has proved true even where women had obtained the same educational level and/or have managed to make their way into jobs traditionally occupied by men, which raises an enduring question: Will women ever obtain the same social status as men?

ENDNOTES FOR CHAPTER NINE

1   *See* Aage B. Sorensen, *The Structural Basis of Social Inequality*, 101 AM. J. SOC., No. 5 pp. 1333–1365, at p. 1334 (March 1996).

2   *See* Kevin Phillips, POLITICS OF RICH AND POOR: WEALTH AND THE AMERICAN ELECTORATE IN THE REAGAN AFTERMATH (New York: HarperPerrennial, 1989), at p. 4.

3   *Id.* (Biographic material for Kevin Phillips lists that in addition to serving as chief political analyst for the 1968 Republican presidential campaign and later served as assistant to the attorney general," Phillips also served as "editor-publisher of *The American Political Report*." In addition, Phillips has "also edited and published the *Business and Public Affairs Fortnightly*" and was, at the time of publication, "a contributing columnist to the *Los Angeles Times*, a member of the political strategists' panel of *The Wall Street Journal*, and a regular commentator for National Public Radio and CBS Radio Network," in addition to many other accomplishments. *Id.* at p. 263.)

4   *Id.* (citing Thomas J. Stanley, MARKETING TO THE AFFLUENT (Homewood, Ill.: Dow Jones-Irwin, 1988).

5   *Id.*

6   *Id.* at 202.

7   *Id.*

8   *Id.*

9   *Id.* (citing *Women Outpacing Men in Employment Gains*, CHI. TRIB., Dec. 9, 1988).

10   *Id.*

11   *Id.*

12   *Id.* at 202–203 (citing *People Patterns*, WALL ST. JOUR., Sept. 7, 1988).
13   *Id.*
14   *See We the Americans: Women,* U.S. DEP'T OF COMMERCE, ECONOMICS, AND STATISTICS ADMINISTRA-TION, BUREAU OF THE CENSUS, Sept. 1993, at p. 9.
15   *Id.*
16   *Id.*
17   *Id.* (Some of this is due to the failure of fathers to pay child support. For an overview of the issue, *See* Lydia Scoon-Rogers and Gordon Lester, *Child Support for Custodial Mothers and Fathers: 1991,* CURRENT POPULATION REPORTS, U.S. DEP'T. OF COMMERCE, August 1995.)
18   *See* PHILLIPS, *supra* note 2, at p. 203. (According to Phillip, "[w]hile males with a high school educa-tion or less lost ground in the 1980s, the only females working full-time to lose constant-dollar earn-ing power from 1980 to 1986 were high-school dropouts, many of whom became single mothers.")
19   *Id.*
20   See *We the Americans: supra* note 14, at p. 2. (Government projections suggest further that by 2050, of the 383 million people expected to live in the United States, 195 million of them will be women and girls.)
21   *See* Barbara Kantrowitz & Pat Wingert, *Unmarried With Children,* NEWSWEEK, May 28, 2001, at pp. 46, 48.
22   In September of 2001, as noted by writer Margaret Talbot, "there are thirteen women in the U.S. Senate now, more than ever before, and only one of them got there through the once-traditional route of widowhood." *See* Margaret Talbot, *In the Balance: Women and Power in 2001,* N.Y. TIMES MAG., Sept. 9, 2001, at p. 92.
23   *See* Leonhardt, *supra* note 17, ENDNOTES FOR INTRODUCTION, at A15.
24   *Id.*
25   *See* Flaherty, *supra* note 19, ENDNOTES FOR INTRODUCTION, at C1.
26   *See* Glater, *supra* note 20, ENDNOTES FOR INTRODUCTION, at A1.
27   *See* Viner Samborn, *supra* note 22, ENDNOTES FOR INTRODUCTION, at pp. 30–42; Choo, *supra* note 22, ENDNOTES FOR INTRODUCTION, at pp. 84–85.
28   *See* Sobel, *supra* note 18, ENDNOTES FOR INTRODUCTION, at p. 59.
29   *We the Americans: Women, supra* note 20, at p. 5.
30   *Id.* at 7.
31   *Id.* at 8.
32   *Id.* See *also* Deborah L. Rhode, *Job Bias Persists,* NAT'L L.J., March 4, 2002, at A21.
33   *We the Americans: Women, supra* note 20, at p. 8.
34   *Id.*
35   For an overview of the debate, *see* note 27, ENDNOTES FOR INTRODUCTION. See *also Other Issues in Reproductive Law, infra* CHAPTER TEN.
36   *We the Americans: Women, supra* note 20, at p. 6.
37   *Id.* at 5.
38   *Id.*
39   *Id.* (In terms of proportions, "women who had never married also increased between 1970 and 1990, from 21 percent to 23 percent," according to the Census Bureau.)
40   *Id.*
41   *Id.*
42   *See* McDonald, *supra* note 13, ENDNOTES FOR CHAPTER THREE, at pp. 59–62.
43   *See* Joseph Stiglitz, *The Roaring Nineties,* THE ATLANTIC MONTHLY, October 2002, at pp. 76–89.
44   *See* Steven Holmes, *Incomes Up and Poverty is Down, Data Show,* N.Y. TIMES, Sept. 27, 2000, at A12 (citing United States Census Bureau statistics).
45   *Id.*
46   *Id.*
47   *Id.*
48   *See* Peter Kilborn, *Census Shows Bigger House and Incomes, But Not for All,* N.Y. TIMES, May 15, 2002, at A14.
49   *See* Holmes, *supra* note 44, at A1. (Holmes notes that the "[m]edian household income is the level at which half of the 120 million households in the country bring in more money and half bring in less." Measuring the "median household" income in considered a more accurate measure of house-hold income by researchers than the "average household income," which can be skewed by super-wealthy families who number few, but whose earnings can have a big impact.)
50   *Id.* (Census figures for thirteen states released in 2000 showed that in the last decade women's incomes rose while middle-class men's incomes stagnated. High-paying industrial jobs like logging and mining jobs were lost during the 1990s to men, causing unemployment among men to spike in some communities. But during this same period, women made education gains, graduating in greater numbers from colleges and universities, making them eligible for white-collar jobs. The effect of these gains was to narrow the wage gap between men and women in some states. With more women in the workforce, median household incomes rose roughly 10 percent in most states.)
51   *See* Kilborn, *supra* note 48, at A14.

52   *See* Patrick McGeehan, *Executive Assesses Her Adventure at a Dot-Com*, N.Y. TIMES, Nov. 9, 2000, at C1. (Miller would later resign, prompting many to speculate that dot-coms were dead.)

53   *Id.*

54   *See* Jonathan Rauch, *The New Old Economy: Oil, Computers, and the Reinvention of the Earth*, ATLANTIC MONTHLY, Jan. 2001, at pp. 35–39.

55   *Id.* (As Rauch defines it, what was being called the "New Economy" of the 1990s was "an economy based on the production and application of knowledge" as opposed to a more traditional "economy based on the production of physical goods." In other words, "the New Old Economy" was "an economy in which technological advances have 'an aggregate effect on productivity.'")

56   *Id.*

57   *Id.*

58   *Id.* (As Rauch explains it, during the 1980s, "Old Economy businesses" tended to waste the resources put into computers by simply "drop[ping] a PC on every desk and declar[ing] themselves computerized." Once companies began to use and to understand the power of these instruments, however, American business began to change, as "each innovation enabled other innovations, none of them revolutionary but all of them combining in an accelerating cascade.")

59   *Id.*

60   *See* Louis Uchitelle, *Can the New Economy Navigate Rougher Waters?*, N.Y. TIMES, Dec. 18, 2000, at C1, C4.

61   *Id.* at C4.

62   *Id.*

63   *See* Joanne Cleaver, *Top 25 COs for Executive Women*, WORKING WOMAN, Jan. 2000, at 49–56.

64   *See* AMERICAN ASSOCIATION OF UNIVERSITY WOMEN *Dear Friend Letter*.

65   *See* McDonald, *supra* note 42, at p. 62.

66   *See Out From Under the "Glass Ceiling,"* CHRISTIAN SCIENCE MONITOR, July 17, 1998, p. 10.

67   *See* Paulette Thomas, *When Venus Seeks Funding from Mars*, WALL ST. JOUR., Feb. 24, 1999, at B1. (In the interest of fairness, it is worth noting that according to Thomas, "[w]omen's enterprises tend to be smaller and thus less interesting to high-flying venture capitalists. Also, until recently, relatively few women were launching businesses in the high-tech fields that are most intriguing to venture capitalists. But on a more basic level, it seems, the lopsided funding statistics represent yet another Mars-and-Venus standoff between two genders and two different views of relationships.")

68   *See* Uchitelle, *supra* note 60, at C1. (According to Uchitelle, "[t]hat American enterprise has been changed by asset of new technologies is beyond doubt. Ever-faster computers connected through high-speed networks or embedded in almost everything people use are putting their imprint on the nation, just as railroads once did, or the electric motor and the gasoline engine, or Eisenhower's interstate highways. Each enriched America, but could not arrest the endless cycles of a market system. And now the latest new economy—not just the dazzling dot-coms but the whole economy now that nearly every company is interlaced with computers—is caught in a slowdown.")

69   *Id.* at C1.

70   *See Issues in Labor Statistics*, U.S. DEP'T OF LABOR, BUREAU OF LABOR STATISTICS SUMMARY 99-5, May 1999, at 1.

71   *Id.*

72   That according to Elizabeth Dole, who reportedly made the comments during a speech before the Public Policy Days, an event sponsored by the Nationally Accepted Certification for Women in Business (NAWBO). *See* WORKING WOMAN, Feb. 1999.

73   *See Men Will Still Earn More at Wimbledon*, N.Y. TIMES, April 24, 2002, at C18. (At Wimbledon, for example, the women's champion was slated in 2002, to receive $700,000 in prize money while the men's champion was to be awarded $756,000. The previous year the women's champion was awarded $666,000 to the men's award of $720,000.)

74   *See Gender Differences in Earnings Among Young Adults Entering the Labor Market*, STATISTICAL ANALYSIS REPORT, NAT'L CENTER FOR EDUCATION STATISTICS, U.S. DEP'T OF EDUCATION, March 1988, at 4 (citing Clifford Adelman, LESSONS OF A GENERATION: EDUCATION AND WORK IN THE LIVES OF THE HIGH SCHOOL CLASS OF 1972 (San Francisco: Jossey-Bass, 1994), at 57).

75   *See Issues in Labor Statistics, supra* note 70, at p. 1.

76   *See Gender Differences in Earnings Among Young Adults Entering the Labor Market, supra* note 74, at p. 4.

77   *Id.*

78   *Id.*

79   *See Usual Weekly Earnings of Wage and Salary Workers: Second Quarter 2000*, UNITED STATES DEP'T OF LABOR, BUREAU OF LABOR STATISTICS, July 20, 2000. (According to Labor Department data, the "[m]edian earnings for black men working full-time jobs were $514 per week, 77.9 percent of the median for white men ($660). The difference was much less among women, as black women's median earnings ($416) were 84.2 percent of those for their white counterparts ($494). Overall, median earnings for Hispanics who worked full-time ($388) were lower than those of blacks ($467) and white ($584).")

80   *See Gender Differences in Earnings Among Young Adults Entering the Labor Market, supra* note 74, at p. 4.

81   *See Issues in Labor Statistics, supra* note 70, at p. 1.

82   *See Counting Minorities: A Brief History and a Look at the Future,* U.S. DEPT' OF LABOR REPORTS, available online, downloaded Feb. 16, 2004, at p. 36.

83   *Id.*

84   *See Usual Weekly Earnings of Wage and Salary Workers: Second Quarter 2000, supra* note 79, at p. 1.

85   *Id.*

86   *Id.*

87   *See Gender Differences in Earnings Among Young Adults Entering the Labor Market, supra* note 74, at p. 5 (citing Jerry Jacobs, *Long Term Trends in Occupational Segregation by Sex,* 95 AM. J. OF SOC. at pp. 160–173 (1989)).

88   *Id.* (citing Donald J. Treiman & Heidi I. Hartmann, WOMEN, WORK AND WAGES (Washington, D.C.: National Academy Press, 1981)).

89   *Id.* at 5 (citing Joyce P. Jacobson & Laurence Levin, *Effects of Intermittent Labor Force Attachment on Women's Earnings,* 118 MONTHLY LABOR REVIEW at 4–19 (Sept. 1995)).

90   *See* Natalie Angier, *Pay Gap Remains for Women in Life Sciences,* N.Y. TIMES, Oct. 16, 2001, at D3 (citing the American Association for the Advancement of Sciences 2001 Survey); Karen Arenson, *Uneven Progress for Women on Princeton Science Faculty,* N.Y. TIMES, Sept. 30, 2003.

91   *See* Tamar Lewin, *Women Profit Less Than Men in the Nonprofit World, Too,* N.Y. TIMES, June 8, 2001, at p. 23.

92   *See* Tamar Lewin, *Study Says Little Has Changed In Views on Working Mothers,* N.Y. TIMES, Sept. 10, 2001, at 20.

93   *See* Lisa Belkin, *The Opt-Out Revolution,* N.Y. TIMES MAG., Oct. 26, 2003, pp. 42–85.

94   *See* Susan Douglas, *So Who Gets the Kids?,* MS. June/July 1999, at pp. 48–58 (detailing, among others, the case of Alice Hector, whose children were taken away from her by a three-member panel (all men) who found that because she worked long hours at a prominent Florida law firm her husband was better suited to raise the children).

95   *See* Susan Faludi, *The Money Shot,* THE NEW YORKER, Oct. 30, 1995, at pp. 63–87, 65–66.

96   *See* Sorensen, *supra* note 1, at pp. 1333–1334.

CHAPTER TEN

The Reproductive Rights of "New Medicine"

OTHER ISSUES IN REPRODUCTIVE LAW:
When Does the State's "Concern" Go too Far?

Women have a right to reproductive privacy. That has been established. What is constantly being redebated is how far the state may lawfully go into this sacred realm before an individual's rights have been violated. It is a debate that goes on every day. For example, after 12-year-old Parker Jensen was diagnosed with an aggressive form of cancer known as Ewing's sarcoma and a tumor was removed from his mouth, doctors recommended chemotherapy. But when Parker's parents learned that chemotherapy drugs could cause blindness, sterility, and even death, his parents refused to consent to the treatment. Utah authorities moved to take Parker into custody, arguing that his parents were putting his health at risk.

"With chemo, the survival rate is approximately 70 percent," Carol Sisco, a spokesperson for the Utah Division of Child and Family Services, told reporters.[1]

The Jensens fled, taking Parker to Idaho. Utah authorities charged them with kidnapping. The Jensens eventually returned and were allowed by a Utah court to keep Parker provided they agreed to allow Parker to be examined by an oncologist and to follow the doctor's recommendations.[2] Did Utah authorities go too far? Or were their actions proper in attempting to protect a child?

"American society has traditionally shown a preference for minimal state intervention in child rearing decisions," Robert Blank and Janna Merrick argue in *Human Reproduction, Emerging Technologies, and Conflicting Rights.* "It is based on the assumption that parents are able to determine and will pursue the course of action that is in their child's best interest."[3]

It would be tempting to assume that the state makes the *same* assumption with regard to women when they are carrying fetuses. But as the cases of the last thirty years have shown, officials of some states have asserted the "state's interest into this private sphere, at times genuinely seeking to intervene on behalf of the child; at others, as part of an ideological campaign determined to redefine the relationship between women, privacy, and the state. Some women's rights groups argue that these attempts have led to the abuse of *living* women in the name of protecting unborn fetuses. Whether or not one agrees, what is clear after all is said and done in many of these cases is that the women involved appear to have little or no recourse.

For instance, at age 13, Angela C. seemed to have fought and won a battle against cancer. But at 24, Angela C.'s cancer reemerged, and five days after her twenty-fifth birthday, Angela C.'s left leg, pelvis, and hip were amputated. Still, Angela C. was determined to have "a life," and two years after the amputation she got married and she got pregnant. But not long after that, Angela C. began experiencing shortness of breath and back pain. An x-ray revealed a tumor the size of a football in her right lung, that, although large, was inoperable, leaving doctors to hope for "a healthy but motherless child." With that in mind, doctors sought to extend Angela C.'s life long enough to give the fetus a chance to grow. Angela C. was carrying a 25-week-old fetus the day she was admitted to the hospital.[4] Four days later, as Angela C. lay struggling to breathe in an intensive care unit, the fetus reached the twenty-six weeks mark, the traditional threshold of "viability," which opened the door among hospital officials to discussion of a cesarean section.

Doctors anticipated performing a postmortem cesarean section on Angela C. But when doctors discussed this possibility with Angela C.'s family, family members asked that the doctors let Angela C. die in peace without further suffering. In other words, family members were in favor of allowing Angela C. and the fetus to die. Hospital administrators discussed the case with doctors, who explained that the fetus would probably not survive given Angela C.'s "compromised" condition. Angela C.'s family was then informed that Angela C. would die "intact," given their wishes.

But at some point later, a hospital administrator called the hospital's lawyer. Counsel for the hospital feared that the institution would find itself in the middle of a firestorm, which is, in fact, what happened.[5] The hospital attorney called a superior court judge to request a hearing. The judge rushed to the hospital with a police escort and several volunteer attorneys, among them lawyers appointed to represent Angela C., the family, the fetus, the state, and the hospital. After hearing from all of the attorneys, several doctors, and the family, the judge declared that "...the court is of the view that the fetus should be given an opportunity to live."

Moments later, however, Angela C. was awake. She was then questioned by two doctors. One doctor reported that Angela C. agreed to have a cesarean section, while the second doctor reported she had not. The attorney appointed to represent Angela C. sought a stay and contacted three judges on the District of

Columbia's Court of Appeals at 6:15 p.m. But at 6:30 p.m., the sitting judge told the attorney the stay had been denied. A cesarean section was then performed on Angela C. A baby girl was delivered. Two hours later, the baby died. The following day, Angela C. died.

Although Angela C. died in June 1987, the case continued to move through the courts until on November 10, 1987, the appellate court reviewed the case, reversing the judge's original order requiring Angela C. to undergo a cesarean section as *erroneous*. "Instead of balancing [the "rights" of the fetus against the rights of the mother], the lower court should have ascertained the woman's wishes by means of the doctrine of substituted judgment. The woman's decision, *not the fetus's interest*, is the only dispositive factor. If the woman is competent and makes an informed decision, that decision will control in virtually all cases," the appellate court ruled.[6]

That would appear to be the analysis that should be applied in light of *Roe v. Wade*. But that doesn't always happen. Instead, the last two decades have been peppered by the attempts of state actors, determined to test the law by overriding the decisions of competent women who fail to give the answers they want to hear. A young woman in Illinois identified only as "Doe" in court documents, for example, was expecting her first child. On November 24, 1993, Doe had a prenatal exam. After the exam, the doctor suggested that sufficient oxygen was not moving through the placenta to the fetus. The doctor recommended an immediate cesarean section or induced labor. Doe declined, citing religious beliefs. On December 8, 1993, the hospital contacted the Office of the Cook County State's Attorney, which filed a petition for adjudication of wardship of the fetus,[7] and a swirl of legal maneuvering began.[8]

An emergency hearing was held on December 9, during which a state's attorney asked for a court order forcing Doe to undergo an immediate cesarean section. The appellate panel ruled that the court lacked jurisdiction to hear the case because no order had been entered by the circuit court. The panel noted further that jurisdiction in a circuit court was not proper, because the state brought the motion under the Juvenile Court Act, and that an order compelling a pregnant woman to submit to an invasive procedure would violate her constitutional rights.

Undaunted, state's attorneys went to a juvenile court, which later that same day ruled that the Juvenile Court Act did not apply to fetuses (it only applied to living children). The state then moved to file an amended petition. The court granted leave to file an amended petition. On December 11, 1993, the court denied the state's petition. Several notices of appeal were filed. In the midst of the fighting, Doe quietly gave birth to a healthy baby boy. Though the birth resolved the urgent controversy over whether the child was being deprived of oxygen, lawyers sought a written decision in an attempt to clarify the issue of whether a competent woman has the right to refuse a cesarean section, even if state officials believe a cesarean is in the best interests of the fetus she is carrying.

In determining that the right of privacy precludes state officials from forcing a woman to undergo invasive procedures solely for the benefit of an unborn fetus, the Illinois appellate court noted that "[c]ourts in Illinois and elsewhere have consistently refused to force one person to undergo medical procedures for the purpose of benefiting another person—even where the two persons share a blood relationship, and even where the risk to the first person is perceived to be minimal and the benefit to the second person may be great.

"The Illinois Supreme Court addressed this issue in *Curran v. Bosze*,[9] where it refused to compel twin minors to donate bone marrow to a half-sibling, despite the fact that the procedures involved would pose little risk to the twins, and the sibling's life depended on the transplant," the appellate court noted further. "Nor would the court compel the minors to undergo even a blood test for the purpose of determining whether they would be compatible donors. If a sibling cannot be forced to donate bone marrow to save a sibling's life, if an incompetent brother cannot be forced to donate a kidney to save the life of his dying sister,[10] then surely a mother cannot be forced to undergo a cesarean section to benefit her viable fetus."

Other Illinois courts have applied similar reasoning. *In re Brown*[11] began in June 1996, after Darlene Brown had surgery. Brown, a Jehovah's Witness, was 34 weeks pregnant. During surgery, Brown lost more blood than expected and her doctor ordered a transfusion. Brown refused to consent to the transfusion, citing her religion, which opposes the introduction of blood products from outside of one's body.

And Brown continued to refuse the transfusion even as doctors began suggesting that her condition was "life-threatening" to Brown and to the fetus she was carrying. Doctors attempted alternative medical procedures compatible with Brown's religious beliefs to raise her hemoglobin level. But the level continued to fall. Finally, on June 28, 1996, Illinois officials filed a petition for adjudication of wardship. They sought temporary custody of "Baby Doe," the fetus Brown was carrying.[12]

The state's petition was granted after a hearing before a court. A hospital administrator was then appointed "temporary custodian of Fetus Brown, with the right to consent to one or more blood transfusions for Darlene Brown, when advised of such necessity by any attending physician." With the consent of the custodian for the transfusion, Darlene Brown was given six units of packed red blood cells.

On July 8, 1996, the court held a status hearing on the petition and found that Brown had delivered a healthy baby a week earlier. The court vacated the temporary custody order and closed the case. But the office of the Cook County Public Guardian appealed. Darlene Brown also filed an appeal, challenging the court order appointing a temporary custodian with the ability to consent to a blood transfusion in the interest of the fetus. At issue before the court in Brown's appeal was whether "a competent pregnant woman's right to refuse medical treatment, which in this case involve[d] religiously offensive blood transfusions, may be overridden by the state's substantial interest in the welfare of the viable fetus."

The court ruled in favor of Darlene Brown, holding that in "balancing the mother's right to refuse medical treatment against the state's substantial interest in the viable fetus, we hold that the state may not override a pregnant woman's competent treatment decision, including refusal of recommended invasive medical procedures, to potentially save the life of the viable fetus. We disagree with the Baby Boy Doe court's suggestion that a blood transfusion constitutes a 'relatively noninvasive and risk-free procedure,'[13] ...We thus determine that the circuit court erred in ordering Brown to undergo a transfusion on behalf of the viable fetus."

There is a contrast, incidentally, to the Illinois court's ultimate position in *In re Brown.* The Supreme Court of New Jersey held in *Raleigh Fitkin-Paul Morgan Memorial Hospital v. Anderson,*[14] for example, that the *rights* of a woman's "unborn child" were entitled to the protection and intervention of the state. Like Darlene Brown, the woman had refused a blood transfusion. She too was a Jehovah's Witness. Still, the New Jersey court ordered that the physician in charge could—under the court's ruling—order transfusions where necessary to save the woman's life or the life of the fetus. In reaching this decision, the New Jersey court reasoned that a blood transfusion was a relatively noninvasive and risk-free procedure.

The contrast between *In re Brown* and *Raleigh Fitkin-Paul Morgan Memorial Hospital v. Anderson* illuminates the inconsistency and the troublesome trend in the law with some states simply deciding to ignore that well-established body of law that holds the rights of living women to be above those of unborn fetuses. Indeed, where review of United States Supreme Court precedent and caselaw clearly establish that a state cannot interfere with a competent woman's lawful choices during pregnancy, the apparent trend among some state officials is to do whatever is necessary to protect unborn fetuses, leaving the courts to determine whether state officials violated the once well-settled right of privacy of the women involved in the process. As set forth in the cases above, the courts have often found that state actors violated the privacy rights of women.

Women's rights groups have challenged such measures, arguing that they are part of the larger efforts of religious leaders and conservative politicians who seek to turn back the clock by elevating—in pre-*Roe* fashion—the "rights" of the unborn fetus over those of living women. Others argue that although the "fetus rights debate" has long been grounded in traditional Christian notions of when "life" begins—as opposed to the legal definition—the efforts of state officials have often demonstrated considerable intolerance for those who don't share their religious views. In overriding the wishes of Jehovah's Witnesses, for example, state officials frequently elevate traditional Christian notions over the religious tenets embraced by others who don't share their views and who also don't have the political clout of conservative Christians, critics argue.

And yet, the legal questions arising out of those circumstances where pregnant women are clearly not competent to make decisions regarding their health or the health of the fetuses they carry are often more complex and tend to go beyond mere political or religious ideologies, though these views are often injected into the debate as well. In the summer of 1999, Tammi Martin lay in a coma as her family tried to decide whether to withdraw life-sustaining support. Martin fell into a coma after being hit on the head. She was reportedly a drug and alcohol user,[15] habits state officials used throughout the late 1980s and early 1990s to justify aggressive action.[16]

As Martin's family began considering tests to determine her exact status (*i.e.*, whether she was brain dead), Martin's boyfriend of ten months moved to block examinations. He also resisted the efforts of her family to remove her from life support. The basis of the challenge was that Martin was carrying a 17-week-old fetus her boyfriend wanted to save. Despite the wishes of Martin's family, Martin's boyfriend had the law on his side. The Texas Natural Death Act forbids the removal of life support from a pregnant woman.[17] Texas has traditionally asserted an aggressive interest in "protecting life." Women's groups have long opposed the possibility of keeping a woman "alive" via life support for the sole purpose of incubating a fetus.

In May of 2003, the issue of "incubation" reemerged—this time before a national audience—when Florida Governor Jeb Bush waded into the debate, asking a judge to appoint a guardian for the fetus of a developmentally challenged 22-year-old woman, impregnated as a result of a rape. The woman, who reportedly has no family, has lived in state-run facilities for the last 18 years.[18] It was while at an Orlando group home that she is believed to have been raped.

Identified only as J.D.S., the woman has the developmental age of a preschooler. After the pregnancy was discovered, a Florida judge appointed a guardian for the woman, because she clearly could not make decisions regarding her health for herself or for the fetus. But Governor Bush sought to have a guardian appointed to protect the "rights" of the fetus. "Given the facts of this case, it is entirely appropriate that an advocate be appointed to represent the unborn child's best interests in all decisions," Governor Bush said, in defending the appointment request.[19]

His efforts drew criticism from women's groups and the ACLU. "The governor's personal agenda and political aspirations are getting in the way of providing for this woman's health and well-being," Howard Simon, executive director of the ACLU of Florida, argued.[20]

"Our take on this," said Bebe Anderson of the Center for Reproductive Rights, "is that this woman's needs, her desires, and her interests need to take precedence. If she is incompetent, someone else should represent her and her interests alone and make that decision for her." That is generally what the law is supposed to provide. Though no one sought an abortion in the case, and, indeed, it is not even clear that abortion was ever mentioned directly as an issue, efforts to appoint a guardian for the fetus drew protests from opponents of this sort of intervention for precisely the reason that religious groups applauded the governor's efforts.

"If a guardian is appointed, there would be a clear recognition that there is a human being occupying that womb," said Brian Fahling, an attorney with the

American Family Association's Center for Law and Policy.[21] "The governor has the constitutional duty to uphold the right to life."

Despite the considerable clout the governor's involvement brought to bear, on May 14, 2003, Judge Lawrence Robert Kirkwork, of the Circuit Court in Orlando, ruled that J.D.S. should remain in the protective care of the state. But he declined to consider the issue of guardianship for the fetus, noting that the issue had not been introduced prior to the status hearing scheduled. In addition, in 1989, the Florida Supreme Court reportedly declared that appointing a guardian for a fetus was "clearly improper."[22]

In August 2003, J.D.S. gave birth (via cesarean section) to Baby Girl S. But the issue of whether a guardian may be appointed for a fetus in Florida remains an issue of debate in Florida with state officials continuing to defend the governor's actions.[23]

Intervention by state officials—and even private citizens on occasion—is grounded in arguments of an "unborn child's" rights. These are arguments that open an emotional vein, tending to bleed heartfelt convictions over nothing less than the meaning of God. Thus, in recent years pregnant women seeking to exercise *their right* to make decisions regarding their health and the health of the fetus they are carrying has been challenged by zealous prosecutors, conservative politicians, and even strangers who appear to believe that their interest in protecting "unborn life" supersedes that of the women involved.

Although the courts in several states have repeatedly held that the choices of pregnant women should stand, officials in some states have made a concerted effort to effect a change in the law on the point. Thus, they continually assert the "rights" of "unborn children" as the basis for medical and legal actions against women who make choices that authorities don't agree with.

THIRD PARTY INTERVENTION OR STRANGER INTERFERENCE?

Not only the state has sought to intervene on behalf of "unborn children." On occasion, third parties—strangers—have sought to intervene. In December 1988, for example, Nancy Klein was in a car accident that left her brain-damaged and in a coma. Nancy Klein was pregnant. But the pregnancy, according to doctors, increased the strain on her already fragile system. If an abortion was performed, there was hope that Nancy Klein would make a full recovery.

In February 1989, Martin Klein, Nancy's husband, sought to have an abortion performed on his comatose wife in the hopes of saving her life. But two men—members of a pro-life action group who were strangers to the Klein family—petitioned a court in an effort to be appointed guardians in the case: one for the comatose Nancy Klein, the other for the unborn fetus. The men opposed the abortion sought by Martin Klein and his wife's family.

A flurry of legal wrangling followed. A court ultimately denied the motion of the two strangers, holding that a nonviable fetus was not a "person" for whom a guardian can be appointed. The court held further that Martin Klein's interests were not so adverse to those of his wife's as to preclude his appointment as guardian for his comatose wife.

"Ultimately, the record confirms that these absolute strangers to the family, whatever their motivation, have no place in the midst of this family tragedy," the court held.[24]

REPRODUCTIVE RIGHTS AND NEW MEDICINE:
Creating a New Universe of Choice

For three decades, opponents of abortion have fought to end the right of women to choose to have the procedure, arguing that fetuses have "rights" and that partial-birth abortions—like all abortions—are heinous, horrible procedures. More implicitly, they seem to argue that the women who choose to have these procedures are callous, mean-spirited women who don't care about "children."

And yet, it is almost as though the zeal of their mission has blinded critics to the current trend, which is that babies are back with a vengeance. Indeed, by the start of the new millennium, having children was again a "lifestyle choice," one increasingly being made by so progressive (and wealthy) a lot that even upscale stores began to make the effort to cash in on an emerging maturity market for older, more financially stable, but newly pregnant women.

Fred Segal, Liz Lange, Saks Fifth Avenue, and Barneys' New York with its new *Procreation* line, were among the high-end retailers launching maternity lines near the start of the millennium.[25] Motherhood and babies were back, though not in the fashion perhaps of the 1900s, when there were few reproductive choices.[26] Or even in the fashion of the 1950s, which was just before the social and cultural revolution that came with "the pill." It is true that fewer children have been born in recent years than in past decades.[27] But the national rates of abortion for adult women and minor females fell throughout the 1990s to the lowest levels since legalization.[28]

At the same time, single women joined married couples spending millions of dollars trying to increase the size of their families by assisted or "artificial" means where nature had apparently failed.[29] What was clearly understood by the late 1990s was that science and medicine have the potential to change every aspect of human reproduction. Pioneering procedures have allowed older or infertile women, for example, to bear children; comatose women to carry fetuses to term; widows to bear the children of their dead spouses; and women with potentially life-threatening health illnesses—HIV among them—to consider pregnancy and to carry fetuses safely to term.[30]

"We are in the midst of a revolution in biomedical technology, especially where that technology affects human genetics and reproduction," author Robert Blank argues.[31]

But the hard numbers may tell that story more clearly. According to the Centers for Disease Control, the number of Assisted Reproductive Technology (ART) procedures conducted in 1998 was 81,899, resulting in 28,873 live births, which was up from 64,724 in 1996.[32] Though once the obscure work of doctors, these procedures are very much a part of everyday life for millions of people in the United States today.

Assisted reproduction helped singer Celine Dion have the baby she longed for.[33] And if you believe what you read, then Dr. Christo Zouves gets the kind of email that would have made Aldous Huxley green with envy. Among the calls for assistance made to Dr. Zouves was: a 59-year-old woman who wanted to have a child via the fertilization of a donor egg by her husband's sperm implanted in her womb; lesbian partners who wanted to become mothers; and two gay men who wanted to have a child.[34]

"Under the microscopes, their long tails furiously lashing, spermatozoa were burrowing head-first into eggs; and, fertilized, the eggs were expanding, dividing, or if bokanovskified, budding and breaking up into whole populations of separate embryos. From the Social Predestined Room the escalators went rumbling down into the basement, and there, in the crimson darkness, stewingly warm on their cushion of peritoneum and gorged with blood-surrogate and hormones, the fetuses grew and grew or, poisoned, languished into a stunted Epsilonhood. With a faint hum and rattle the moving racks crawled imperceptibly through the weeks and the recapitulated aoens to where, in the Decanting Room, the newly-bottled babes uttered their first yell of horror and amazement," Huxley wrote in *Brave New World*,[35] considered dark satire and wildly science-fictional when it was published in 1932.[36]

The impossibility of these images has come closer. In the last three decades, the dreams of science fiction have merged with the gains of medicine in previously unimaginable ways. In November of 1999, for example, an Ohio woman gave birth to a baby boy five months after his extremely premature twin died during an early birth. After 152 days of "arrested development" achieved "by drug therapy, surgical intervention, and treatment protocols," Debbie Feitl gave birth to a baby, Jared.[37]

In October 2000, Dr. Kutluk Oktay reported at a medical conference in San Diego that a piece of a 35-year-old unnamed woman's ovaries had been successfully planted into her forearm where it began to produce eggs and female hormones.[38] The woman, a cancer survivor made infertile by treatment, hoped that eggs produced as a result of the implantation could be used in an *in vitro* fertilization procedure. Though doctors were able to retrieve mature eggs from the woman's arm, they were unable to achieve pregnancy, Dr. Oktay reported.

That appears, however, to be among the few clear failures. By contrast, the gains have been plentiful. In July 2001, for example, a healthy 7-pound, 6-ounce baby was born to a woman who had been in a coma for eight months. Chastity Cooper was in an automobile accident on November 25, 2001, resulting in severe head trauma. After two weeks in the hospital, doctors realized she was pregnant. Although comatose women had carried fetuses before, rarely had it been to term, medical experts note.[39] A healthy full-term baby was taken home by the woman's husband to join her other siblings.

Technology has changed the nature of reproduction. In the process, it has changed the dimensions of human reproduction. In 1971, there were 1,034 "higher-order multiple" births.[40] But by 1995, that number jumped to 4,973—as the use of fertility drugs increased, so did multiple births.[41] Among the most sensational "higher-order multiples" was the delivery of septuplets by Bobbi McCaughey in 1997, and the delivery of octuplets in 1998 by Nkem Chukwu, though one of the Chukwu infants died soon after birth.[42]

Assisted reproduction has changed the vocabulary of reproduction, adding phrases like "noncoital procreation," "traditional surrogacy," "heterologous artificial insemination," "human concepti," and "posthumously conceived children." It has also changed the science of mating: where life once began only in the uterus, it can be created today in the petri dish or the test tube, which has made the *right* to "procreate" artificially a cause of action worth fighting for in recent years.

One out of every six to eight marriages is infertile, researchers suggest.[43] As a result, an estimated 2.3 million couples seek help for infertility each year in the United States,[44] making it a billion dollar a year industry.[45] *In vitro* fertilization is among the most popular techniques rising steadily in numbers of procedures each year from 3,921 in 1985 to 31,900 in 1993.[46] By 1999, more than 40,000 couples were believed to have used *in vitro* fertilization.[47] Between 1995 and 1998, that number rose "from about 59,000 to about 81,000, and the number of clinics [offering the procedure] rose by 28 percent, from 281 to 360," according to Gina Kolata.[48]

But *in vitro* is just one of a half-dozen heavily relied upon assisted reproductive techniques. Some estimates also suggest that as of 1995, more than 500,000 children in the United States were conceived via artificial insemination, most with sperm from donors.[49] In a single year (1986–1987) "[a]pproximately 172,000 women underwent artificial insemination," according to Blank and Merrick.[50] The result was a reported 75,000 births.[51]

And yet, until recently, infertility treatments—which are costly procedures—were not covered by many insurance companies.[52] In the late 1990s, a handful of plaintiffs across the country decided to do something about it. They filed claims with the EEOC, arguing that denial of coverage for infertility treatments was tantamount to discrimination. More specifically, they argued that the inability to "naturally" reproduce falls within the protected categories of the Americans with Disabilities Act.[53]

As unorthodox as that argument may sound, those arguing in support of coverage found persuasive support in the language of the United States Supreme Court's decision in *Bragdon v. Abbott*,[54] in which the Justices held that a person's "ability to reproduce and to bear children constitute a 'major life activity'" within the definition of the Americans with Disabilities Act.[55] On April 28, 1999, the EEOC added its voice to the debate, finding that the refusal of the Franklin Covey company to pay for infertility treatments for an employee violated the ADA.[56]

In December 1998, the employee, Rochelle Saks, was facing her final infertility treatment if the company did not offer further coverage.[57] As a manager of a bookstore, Saks and her husband could not afford to pay for additional infertility treatments. A similar complaint brought by a Chicago police officer was decided in favor of the officer. Others complaints have been similarly settled.[58]

The new technology of conception has also changed the law. By 2000, several states have moved to amend laws, appropriate funds, or otherwise require coverage for infertility.[59] And yet, given the quantum leaps assisted reproduction techniques have made, it is inevitable perhaps that these procedures have created questions that the nation's courts have struggled to resolve, among them: who "owns" fertilized eggs? Who has a right to frozen sperm? Who are the parents of children born as a result of *in vitro* fertilization? Who is the "mom" when a surrogacy agreement comes into dispute? And whether there is—or should be—a cause of action for the "fraudulent" use of semen?[60]

MOTHERHOOD AND MODERN MEDICINE:
Oh What a Tangled Web We Weave,
When First We Practice to ~~Deceive~~ Conceive[61]

In the P.D. Eastman classic book *Are You My Mother?* a baby bird is hatched from an egg, and when he can't find his mother, he goes in search of her.

"Are you my mother?" he asks a cat.

"Are you my mother?" he asks a hen.

"Are you my mother?" he asks a dog.

"Are you my mother?" he asks a cow.

He calls to a boat. He calls to a plane. The baby bird even attempts discussion with a metal crane. But when he is unable to find her, the baby bird begins to wonder whether he has a mother.[62] Given the current state of technology, Eastman would appear to be a visionary. Intimate knowledge of the double helix—the roadmap of life as DNA is sometimes called—is only fifty years old.[63] And assisted reproduction in humans, less than thirty. And yet, no less than a dozen variations on that question are being asked every day in courtrooms across the nation.

In the summer of 1978, Louise Brown was born in England.[64] Brown was the first child conceived via *in vitro* fertilization.[65] At the time, the procedure was roundly criticized as unethical and the child studied for "defects" by international scholars. But Brown grew up to be a normal, healthy adult in a very big "family." Some 30,000 children have been born across the United Kingdom via *in vitro* fertilization since 1978,[66] "created" in more than 70 licensed clinics.

In the United States, it was not until January 1980 that a Virginia hospital obtained permission to begin *in vitro* procedures. In 1981, Elizabeth Carr became the first American child conceived *in vitro*.[67] But with science speeding assisted reproduction along, Brown and Carr would collectively come to represent a new generation of Eve: as *in vitro* protocol swept into the nation's hospitals and clinics, the number of children born via the procedure grew each year.

More than 70,000 assisted reproductive procedures were performed across the United States between 1985 and 1990, resulting in 8,200 births and 10,600 children.[68] And although a single Virginia hospital may have started the assisted reproductive technology ball rolling, by the mid-1990s, more than 200 clinics in America were offering *in vitro* fertilization as a reproductive option.[69] That number has increased each year and is likely to increase even further as insurance coverage for the diagnosis and treatment of infertility increases.[70] But *in vitro* was clearly just the beginning.

Women today may choose whether they want to have a boy or a girl.[71] But this is among the simplest of possibilities. In recent years, an explosion of technology has pushed the envelope of "choice" into once-impossible realms, rendering nearly commonplace procedures as precise as the injection of a single previously selected male sperm cell into a woman's egg in a micromanipulation technique known as *Intracytoplasmic Sperm Injection* (ICSI). The first child "conceived" in this manner was born in Singapore in 1989, according to doctors.[72] But the procedure has been criticized in recent years as a potential cause of genetic defects.[73]

Researchers in Spain, France, and Italy have reported some progress in recent years in the use of the new technique known as "egg-gluing," a protocol that may one day allow a child born of a donated egg to reflect the genetic composition as his or her "biological" parents.[74] The specifics of this delicate effort involve fusing the cytoplasm of a donor egg with the nucleus of an egg taken from the biological mother.[75] The procedure was initially developed to help women whose eggs contained defective cytoplasm, a condition that dramatically reduces the potential of developing a viable fetus.

In December 2000, doctors in Asia announced that they had outdone previous efforts with the birth of the world's first set of twins conceived of frozen eggs *and* frozen sperm.[76] Though more than thirty births using either frozen sperm *or* frozen eggs have been reported worldwide, Singapore doctors say the twins were the first born of both.[77] Because the father's semen contained no sperm, doctors extracted sperm from his testes, which was then frozen. After initial attempts to fertilize the mother's eggs were unsuccessful, doctors also froze the woman's eggs, and a second attempt at implantation led to the twins' birth.[78]

Advances made public during the first seven months of 2001 went even further. In February 2001, researchers in England announced they had successfully thawed frozen human ovarian tissue, reviving it for implantation into mice in an effort to determine whether the protocol might be used to grow human ovarian tissue.[79] If successful, the tissue might be used to help women conceive if they are infertile due to chemotherapy or age. According to the formal announcement by the researchers, some initial success was reported: immature follicles within the tissue grew in a manner similar to normally grown ovarian tissue.[80] Previous attempts by doctors to revive frozen ovarian tissue by implantation into an American woman were unsuccessful.[81]

In March 2001, the first child conceived of an egg donated by one woman, then frozen, thawed, and implanted into the womb of another woman was born.[82] But by May of that same year, scientists at the Institute for Reproductive Medicine and Science of St. Barnabas in New Jersey, had taken this advance one step further, announcing the births of as many as thirty "genetically altered" children. The children were the beneficiaries of *ooplasmic transfer*, a procedure that involves injecting genetic material from a donor egg into the egg cells of women with fertility problems. Early tests suggest that the children do not suffer infertility conditions similar to those of their mothers.[83] In that same month, advances in the MicroSorting technique, which allowed parents to select the gender of their children nine out of ten times, were also announced.[84]

THE NEW GENESIS: ASSISTING ADAM AND EVE

Fertility experts often playfully refer to themselves as "plumbers." But all jokes aside, getting women pregnant the new-fashioned way is technical stuff. And there are so many new choices after boy meets girl. For example, once a woman's egg and a man's sperm have been combined, a couple faces a near "wine list" of implantation choices, including, Gamete Intrafallopian Transfer;[85] Zygote Intrafallopian Transfer;[86] or Surrogate Embryo Transplantation.[87] If a couple wants to increase their luck even more, they might try ovum aspiration, a process often used to retrieve multiple eggs from the ovaries by using a hollow needle guided by an ultrasound image."[88]

Though science has helped doctors do miracles, this new world is not without wrinkles. Complications to the human assisted reproductive process have begun to emerge from— of all places—the freezer. This is due generally to the pragmatics of the process. Eggs and sperm are not easily retracted, and they are not items to be left lying around on counters. Thus, after coupling egg and sperm and entering the initial stages of development, fertility doctors use the icy process of "cryopreservation" to freeze unused embryos for future use. The frozen embryos are then used in embryo transfer and *in vitro* fertilizations.[89] But the process of freezing and thawing may leave embryos in a fragile state.

But advances in the realm of assisted reproduction has also raised the specter of legal challenges to child support where "noncoital procreation" or "posthumous" conception was involved in addition to other troubling issues. In other words, there are those cases today when it is *actually* true that the guy "wasn't even there," which has created a need for laws governing the use of "assisted reproductive technology" and the harms it sometimes inadvertently creates.

"The modern reality of a traditional American family structure today does not depend solely upon one's biological affiliation with those within the familial association," law professor Gloria Banks says.[90] "Of most importance is the creation of voluntary familial associations by parents who intensively accept the attending rights, responsibilities, and benefits of raising children. After all, what is the familial tie that really binds—blood or commitment?"

By July 2001, researchers at Cornell University were announcing a break-through that may one day allow infertile women with no useable eggs to become mothers. The protocol of this advance involves injecting material from any cell of the woman's body into eggs offered by a donor. Electric currents or chemicals are then used to spark the cell's natural splitting processes. Once the nucleus has been halved, it is further pared. Genetic material from the would-be father's sperm is then inserted.[91] According to Cornell researchers, the procedure could be used by women who have already experienced menopause.

And it gets even more impossible.

In a bit of feminist science fiction, attempts were made during the early 1980s to do away with the need for the traditional method of male-female cou-pling. According to Blank and Merrick, "[t]he fusion of the nuclei of two eggs could eliminate the need for the male contribution to procreation; two women could each contribute an egg, thus producing a daughter with two mothers and no father."[92] The procedure was attempted in dairy cows in the Denver area in the early 1980s.[93] But by 1995, it was still a theory.

What a difference six years make. During a July 2001, meeting of the Euro-pean Society for Human Reproduction in Lausanne, Switzerland, Dr. Orly Lacham-Kaplan, of Monash University in Melbourne, Australia, announced the kind of breakthrough that—if viable—could start an entirely new revolution. According to Lacham-Kaplan, a team of researchers at Monash had devised a technique that would permit the fertilization of eggs using genetic material from other cells in the body, *without* a single drop of sperm.[94]

At the time of the announcement, the success of the Monash team's work was limited to mice eggs. But scientists suggest that women and lesbian couples may one day be able to fertilize eggs and "conceive" girl children without any sperm.[95] The procedure would only produce female fetuses: women do not carry the genetic material necessary to produce male children without sperm. Other advances announced during 2002 and 2003 included reports by doctors both in Saudi Arabia and Sweden that they had successfully carried out uterus transplants.[96] But a uterus transplant will not be necessary if Kentucky fertility specialist Panos Zavos does what he predicts he and his colleagues will do: Zavos repeatedly said publicly that by 2003, he and colleagues would "clone a human for therapeutic purposes."[97] As of the first four months of 2004, there had been no announcement from Dr. Zavos's group.

Though the reproductive rights debate has long been dominated by the question of whether a woman should be allowed to end a pregnancy, medicinal science has offered women an ever-expanding list of ways to "conceive" a child. It is a list that includes: *in vitro* fertilization, egg selection, sperm washing, egg gluing or blending, the posthumous harvest of semen, intracytoplasmic sperm injection, MicroSorting, freezing, thawing, nucleus fusion, and one day perhaps even spermless fertilization.

But the use of these techniques has redefined social—as well as reproductive—roles, untying traditional kinship structures, leaving the courts and lawmakers to rebind them with a new set of court-imposed relations between "parents" and "children." There may be parents and children, however, who are not biologically related to each other, even though a "mother" may have carried the "child." In addition, though the paternity of fathers has long been a legal issue, science appears to be on its way to granting women a new kind of equality, one that would allow them to achieve a "family" without men. And while science has not yet done away with the need for the womb,[98] the possibility that doctors can replace one seems to have become a new reality as well.

ASSISTED REPRODUCTION:
And the Kinship of Modern Time

Advances in assisted reproductive technology and the evolution of once-controversial—but now increasingly common—techniques have given rise to the kind of "relations" that might once have formed the punchline for hillbilly jokes. Today a woman can be "mom" in the traditional sense. But advances in reproductive technology had also made it possible for "mom" to be "grandmom," "auntie," or "sister."

It sounds like a tabloid story. But on October 1, 1987, for example, a grandmother in South Africa gave birth to her own grandchildren.[99] According to news reports, Pat Anthony bore triplets for her daughter, Karen, who donated eggs for the procedure.

The sperm used to fertilize the eggs came from Karen's husband. The result is that South African laws, that might in another time have clearly marked mother and father, have turned into their own double helix.

Although she had no direct biological connection to the triplets, under South African law Pat Anthony is their legal mother. But all parties agreed that Karen would adopt the children. In formally adopting the children, Karen—the triplets' biological mother—became their adoptive mother, rather than their sister. Karen's husband—their biological father—became their adoptive father rather than a sperm donor. And once the adoption proceedings were final, Pat Anthony—the gestational surrogate—became the triplets' grandmother, rather than their mother.[100]

The social grid of most societies is organized along kinship lines. These are genealogical constructs, based in "blood" historically used to "order" society via the enforcement of social taboos. Native American communities have always had strict incest taboos, for example, traveling along clan lines that rule out potential lovers on maternal as well as paternal sides of a complex ancestral chart intended to ensure that the children are born "well." American law has similar prohibitions, which have generally taken the form of incest laws.

"[T]here are all those genealogical diagrams, those triangles and circles and lines anthropologists have been drawing for decades. Kinship in tribal societies is obviously those vertical lines between parents and children, those braces connecting siblings. But things are not that simple," says Roger M. Keesing in *Kin Groups and Social Structure.*[101]

They certainly are not today.

Once upon a time, a single straight line marked a mother's connection to her child. And there was no way to "make" a child without a father, though he later might be "absent" for a child's entire life. Only the "worst kind of woman" did not know who the father of her child was, and there was no branch on the family tree for sperm donor. Back then, one line connected a man to his father and to his grandfather before him with no sideways lines, except to reflect an uncle. Back then, it was a straight hop from mom to pop. But assisted reproduction—for all of its positive attributes—has reordered society.

Today, it is not uncommon for the triangles and circles of those geometric diagrams to overlap in the creation of parental and societal disorder that lawyers and judges struggle daily to straighten out, generally when one of these "new families" comes into being; needs a legal declaration of just who is who; or dissolves, because it is not only in South Africa that grandmothers give birth to their "grandchildren" today. In 1998, a 52-year-old Texas woman gave birth to her daughter's twins. Like the South African case, the Texas woman's daughter supplied the eggs and her daughter's husband supplied the sperm.[102] After the birth, such a family—perhaps the modern family for today—could easily be realigned in more traditional terms via the formal relinquishment of rights and an adoption.

"We're being forced to rethink the whole concept of motherhood," George Annas, chairman of the Department of Health Law at the Boston University School of Public Health said in commenting on the current state of reproductive technology.[103] "I never thought that would happen in my lifetime.[104] Once a little couplet said it all: mother's baby, father's maybe. Now DNA tests can pretty well settle the question of biological paternity, while the issue of biological maternity has been sufficiently muddied to demand the regular intercession of judges."

"Postmenopausal women have gestated their daughters' eggs and given birth to their own grandchildren," offers Pulitzer Prize winning science writer Natalie Angier.[105] "Congenitally infertile men can have their dysfunctional sperm mechanically rammed into the body of an egg, and thus sire sons who inherit the once uninheritable: the fathers' sterility. An older woman's fading egg, and the chromosomes it enfolds, can be rejuvenated through the addition of the rich, viscous cytoplasm from a younger woman's egg. If that chimeric gamete is then fertilized and transferred into the womb of a third woman for gestation, the resulting child can claim three biological mothers: chromosomal mom, cytoplasmic mom, and gestational mom."[106]

But how would the case of the Texas grandmother be decided in terms of the law? That depends on where such a case takes place. The law regarding assisted reproductive techniques or arising out of medical advances has yet to develop consistency. But some general rules have emerged. In some states, the Texas grandmother would be deemed the "mother" of the twins because she gave birth to them, though this is an older rule that appears to be declining in authority. Some states have, however, held fast to this rule in the surrogacy context, perhaps in an attempt to discourage the practice. In other states, the Texas grandmother would be considered a gestational surrogate, given that she has no *direct* biological connection to the children (*i.e.,* that the eggs were her daughter's).

For example, if the Texas grandmother's case were analyzed under California law, the legal kinship equation for the grandmother, her daughter, and her daughter's husband would likely be that the grandmother had served as a gestational surrogate and is, therefore, entitled to no parental rights, because she had no biological connection to the children.[107] Her daughter—whose eggs were fertilized—would be considered the legal mother, and the daughter's husband—whose sperm was used to fertilize the eggs—would be the legal father. This analysis would be in line with the findings of a California court in 1993 case of *Johnson v. Calvert*.[108] This case is widely viewed as having set the modern standard for gestational surrogates.[109]

As a point of explanation, surrogacy generally involves an "agreement in which a woman carries a child to term intending at the initiation of the pregnancy for another woman to raise the child as the social mother."[110] Though such agreements may be legally troublesome, surrogacy may be the only way "for a woman without a uterus to be the genetic mother of a child (through embryo transfer, for example), or to be the mother of a child whose genetic father is her husband (through artificial insemination of the surrogate with the husband's sperm)," bioethicists note.[111]

In other words, surrogacy is a form of medical intervention intended to help couples unable to conceive "naturally." But surrogacy has created social and legal complications.[112] It is possible today for a child's "birth parents" to have no biological connection to that child. It is possible for children to have what at a different time would clearly have been "two mothers." And it is possible today for a child to be born with no "legal" parents—in the traditional sense—unless or until a court declares someone to be the child's parents, all of which has led to the reinvention of "motherhood."

GETTING THE BALL ROLLING:
In the Matter of Baby M and Other Issues of Surrogacy

The term "surrogate mother" became part of the American lexicon in 1988, with the infamous case of *In the Matter of Baby M,*[113] which some suggested offered the best evidence of why surrogacy—despite its potential—was a bad idea. And yet, by the time of the *Baby M* case, the practice of surrogacy had been around for nearly a decade. Among the early participants was Denise Thane, who agreed in 1980, to bear a child for a New York couple. In accordance with an agreement reached by the parties, one of Thane's eggs would be fertilized by the husband's sperm. Though medical expenses would be paid by the couple, there would be no fee. But during pregnancy, Thane decided she would not surrender the child. Trial was threatened. In the end, however, the couple agreed to settle the matter out of court to avoid publicity.[114]

Another early case widely reported in the media involved a woman identified as Elizabeth Kane (not her real name). Kane, a 37-year-old Illinois housewife, appeared on the *Phil Donahue Show*. She also gave an interview to *People* magazine. In both instances, Kane discussed her role as a surrogate for an infertile couple. Although she admitted collecting a $10,000 fee for carrying the fetus, Kane argued that she "thought of it as a pure gift of love, no strings attached."[115] By contrast, there were clearly strings attached in the *Baby M* case.

Made for TV even before it was made into a TV movie, the *Baby M* case, as it came to be known, was a Dickensonian tale for modern times. William and Elizabeth Stern were white-collar professionals with a reported annual income of more than $90,000 per year. By contrast, Mary Beth Whitehead, the mother of two children, was married to a sanitation worker. Whitehead herself was a homemaker who had dropped out of high school.[116] The Whiteheads' annual income was $28,000.

William Stern and the Whiteheads signed a surrogacy contract on February 6, 1985. For $10,000, Mary Beth Whitehead would be artificially inseminated with William Stern's sperm. But the egg to be fertilized would be her own. That fact would prove significant. *In re Baby M* involved what is generally known today as a traditional surrogate arrangement. Elizabeth Stern reportedly had multiple sclerosis, which she believed would be exacerbated by the stress of pregnancy.

Mary Beth Whitehead carried the fetus to term with relations between the two families remaining generally cordial until just before the child's birth. After the child's birth, Mary Beth Whitehead was supposed to surrender custody and terminate her parental rights so that Elizabeth Stern could adopt the child. On March 27, 1986, Baby M was born. William Stern named the child Melissa. Mary Beth Whitehead called her Sara. Although apparently distraught, on March 30, 1986, Mary Beth Whitehead turned the child over to the Sterns. But she asked to have the child back for a week to help ease the difficulty of the departure. The Sterns obliged.

It would take four months to recover Baby M, as William Stern sought to enforce the surrogacy agreement. Mary Beth Whitehead and her husband fled to Florida with the child. But after three months on the run, authorities caught up with them and the baby was returned to New Jersey. The Sterns sought custody of the child. Mary Beth Whitehead did the same. The couples went to trial. On March 31, 1987—thirty-two days after it began—the trial court upheld the contract and ordered termination of Mary Beth Whitehead's parental rights. In reaching this decision, the court reasoned that because Whitehead had other children, she was in the best position to understand attachment issues. The court also concluded that distancing the child from Whitehead's apparent "instability" was in the child's best interests. Whitehead appealed.

In February of 1988, the Supreme Court of New Jersey unanimously ruled that the surrogacy contract was unenforceable because it was in conflict with existing state statutes prohibiting the sale or exchange of a child for money. The court also found that the surrogacy contract ran contrary to public policy. With regard to the constitutional arguments raised on both sides, the court held that the essential question was one of reproductive privacy. In restoring Whitehead's parental rights, the court held that "[t]he right to procreate very simply is the right to have natural children, whether through sexual intercourse or artificial insemination.

"It is no more than that," the court held. "Mr. Stern has not been deprived of that right. Through the artificial insemination of Mrs. Whitehead, Baby M is his child. The custody, care, companionship, and nurturing that follow birth are not parts of the right of procreation. To assert that Mr. Stern's right of procreation gives him the right to the custody of Baby M would be to assert that Mrs. Whitehead's right of procreation does not give her the right to the custody of Baby M; it would be to assert that the constitutional right of procreation includes within it a constitutionally protected contractual right to destroy someone else's right of procreation."

In addition, because there was "simply no basis, either in the statute or in the peculiar facts…to warrant termination of Mrs. Whitehead's parental rights," the New Jersey Supreme Court held "that the natural mother is entitled to retain her rights as a mother.[117] We have decided that both the statutes and public policy of this state require that the termination be voided and that her parental rights be restored."[118]

Mary Beth Whitehead was awarded visitation rights. She was divorced soon after the final decision. She later remarried and reportedly continues to have visitation rights with Melissa.[119] And in a lesser footnote to the case, in 1987, Whitehead would join Elizabeth Kane on Capitol Hill to ask Congress to make surrogacy a federal offense.[120]

But where *In the Matter of Baby M* established that a "surrogate" mother could, in some circumstances, be deemed a child's biological mother, the California case of *Johnson v. Calvert* established the reasons for denying such an extension. *Johnson v. Calvert* was not the first surrogacy case to reach the California appellate court. That case involved a woman named Nancy B. who gave birth to a little boy named Matthew. Two years earlier, Nancy B. had read an article in a newspaper, which told the story of Timothy and Charlotte M. and their inability to have children. Nancy B. got in touch with the couple and was artificially inseminated with Timothy M.'s sperm in accordance with a surrogacy agreement. Matthew was the result.

After Matthew's birth, Nancy B. was supposed to assign Timothy and Charlotte M. custody and formally consent to the child's adoption by Charlotte M. Once that had been done, Charlotte M. was supposed to file a petition for custody, which would begin adoption proceedings. Nancy B. was living with the family at the time. She reportedly gave the signed petition of consent to Charlotte M. as a 44th birthday present.

But three months later, Nancy B. began appearing on television shows and in the newspaper, declaring that she intended to seek custody of Matthew. Timothy and Charlotte M. grew concerned and decided that Matthew should have no further contact with Nancy B. In July of 1987, Nancy B. filed a petition to withdraw her consent to custody. The trial court denied Nancy B.'s petition. She appealed. The case became known as *In re Adoption of Matthew B.-M.*[121]

In her appeal, Nancy B. raised several arguments. But because the case came to the court after most of the requirements of the surrogacy agreement had been met, the California appellate court determined that the essential issue before the court was Nancy B.'s withdrawal of consent. Thus, the case fell into the realm of contract—rather than constitutional or surrogacy—law, the court concluded.

"Contract law has long played a role in the ordering of familial relationships, including the rights of child custody and visitation," the court wrote. "By using these well-settled principles to resolve the dispute in this case, we do not mean to suggest that children are commodities. The child's best interests remain the most important consideration....[¶] Nor by this opinion do we determine the validity of surrogate contracts. Surrogacy raises many constitutional, public policy, and human questions that we do not discuss in this opinion. It is, of course, for the Legislature to consider these important questions and provide answers through legislative action.[122]

"However, because the parties in this case fully performed their surrogate agreement, different public policy questions are raised. Here, Nancy's release of Matthew to the M.'s for parenting, her stipulation to Timothy's paternity, and her execution of the consent to Charlotte's adoption of Matthew moot the debate about the desirability of surrogate contracts. Rather, the best interests of Matthew must now be our paramount concern. The trial court properly recognized this fact in refusing to decide whether the surrogate contract was illegal and in denying Nancy's petition as not in Matthew's best interests. The trial court did not err,"[123] the California appellate court ruled.

In accordance with this ruling, Charlotte M. was free to become Matthew's adoptive mother, even though Nancy B. was his biological mother.[124] Though surrogacy was central to the issues in the case, the ultimate application of contract law by the court in *In re Adoption of Matthew B.-M.*[125] is the reason that the case is of little note in the surrogacy context. *Johnson v. Calvert* was, and is, of far greater note in the surrogate context because it established a standard for gestational surrogates. The case also caused a sensation in the media because it stirred the pot of social and racial taboos. [Mark Calvert is Caucasian; his wife is Filipino, and Anna Johnson is African American.]

Mark and Crispina Calvert were a married couple. Crispina could not carry children after an hysterectomy. But she could still produce eggs. Anna Johnson was a colleague of Crispina's, who offered to carry a child for the couple. Mark and Crispina Calvert signed a surrogacy contract with Anna Johnson. The agreement provided that Crispina's egg would be fertilized by Mark's sperm and then implanted into Anna's uterus. Anna Johnson would have no direct biological connection to the baby. In accordance with the contract, Anna agreed to relinquish "all parental rights" to the child. In return, Mark and Crispina agreed to pay Anna Johnson $10,000 in installments and to secure a $200,000 life insurance policy.

In February 1990, it was learned that Anna Johnson was pregnant. But good news in surrogacy cases is often conditional. It wasn't long before the parties began to fight. Mark Calvert grew concerned after he learned that Anna Johnson had suffered several stillbirths. Anna Johnson reportedly grew frustrated by the couple's slow movement in obtaining the life insurance policy. Johnson also argued later that the couple had "abandoned" her during premature labor in June. And, then, things apparently got medieval.

In July 1990, Anna Johnson sent the Calverts a letter demanding the $10,000 payment in full or she would not give up the child. The Calverts responded with a lawsuit in which they sought declaratory judgment by the court that they were the legal parents of the child in Anna Johnson's womb. Anna Johnson filed a countersuit, seeking to be declared the child's mother. The cases were consolidated, and once the child was born, blood tests were performed. The tests established that Anna Johnson was not the biological mother of the child. The child was placed in the temporary custody of the Calverts. Anna Johnson was given visitation rights.

The case presented a direct challenge to the California law of the time, which presumed that women who gave birth to children were their mothers. In finding that the common law presumption of maternity did not apply in this case and that its reading of the Uniform Parenting Act of 1975, would not permit Johnson to be declared the child's "mother," the California Supreme Court held that "...with the undisputed evidence [it is clear] that Anna, not Crispina, gave birth to the child [but] that Crispina, not Anna, is genetically related to him. Both women thus have adduced evidence of a mother and child relationship as contemplated by the [Uniform Parentage Act].

"Yet for any child California law recognizes only one natural mother, despite advances in reproductive technology rendering a different outcome [than] biologically possible. [¶] We decline to accept the contention…that we should find the child has two mothers…. The Calverts are the genetic and intended parents of their son and have provided him, by all accounts, with a stable, intact, and nurturing home. To recognize parental rights in a third party with whom the Calvert family has had little contact since shortly after the child's birth would diminish Crispina's role as mother," the court wrote.[126]

Though *Johnson v. Calvert* is not a United States Supreme Court case, it is generally considered solid and persuasive authority in the area of gestational surrogacy.

TRADITIONAL v. GESTATIONAL SURROGACY

There are two kinds of surrogacy agreements. The first is what is known as the "traditional surrogacy" agreement, which means that a woman is impregnated with the sperm of a man with the prior—often written—understanding that the resulting child will be the legal child of the married man and his wife. But the egg usually belongs to the surrogate. In a traditional surrogacy arrangement, conception is "accomplished with a needleless syringe or similar device" resulting in a child who is "genetically related to the 'intended' father and the '*un*intended mother.'"[127]

The second kind of surrogacy is called "gestational surrogacy," which involves the coupling of a man's sperm with the egg of his wife or an egg donor. The embryo is then implanted into another woman's womb. In gestational surrogacy cases, the woman who carries the fetus to term is generally not held to be the legal mother of the child, because there is generally no biological connection. As ways to conceive continue to change, however, so do the rules.

Between 1979 and January of 1993, an estimated 5,500 babies were born as a result of surrogacy agreements.[128] In the aftermath of the *Baby M* case, lawmakers in three states drafted bills declaring surrogacy contracts void and unenforceable.[129] Another "seventy-two bills pertaining to surrogacy were introduced in twenty-six legislatures and the District of Columbia," Blank and Merrick explain. "Bills were also introduced in 1988 and 1989. The arena of conflict regarding commercial surrogacy has included both the courts and state legislatures. The provisions of state statutes vary widely and have created a confusing patchwork of public policy."[130]

But drafting and adopting laws prohibiting "commercial surrogacy," as it is sometimes called, proved less urgent over time than it seemed in the wake of the emotion swirling around the *Baby M* case. Fewer than half of the states had drafted or enacted statutes outlining the state's position on surrogacy contracts by 1993. In addition, many of those same states had no guidance in the form of court decisions.[131] "Commercial surrogacy" contracts were held unenforceable by law only in thirteen states.[132]

Surrogate mothers were deemed the legal mothers and their husbands the fathers of children born as a result of surrogate contracts in Arizona, North Dakota, and Utah, while surrogacy "without compensation" was permissible in Florida, New Hampshire, and Virginia.[133] The Virginia law allows women to change their mind regarding surrender up to 180 days after the date of the last assisted reproductive procedure. As *Johnson v. Calvert* establishes, surrogacy contracts are enforceable in California, but not in New Jersey, the state of the *Baby M* case. Arkansas permits surrogacy contracts, as does Nevada, though there has been some concern that Nevada's prohibition against "baby selling" might ultimately render the surrogacy statute unenforceable if challenged.

By 2000, several states still had not adopted specific surrogacy statutes.[134] But this may be due, argues Harvard Law Professor Martha Fields, to an "excess of available law, which includes contract law, baby-selling law, adoption law, laws governing the rights of biological fathers not married to the biological mothers of their children, and laws concerning the rights and obligations of sperm donors."[135] Several states chose, for example, to cover surrogacy agreements within their versions of the Uniform Parentage Act.[136]

SURROGACY AND ARTIFICIAL INSEMINATION:
The Side-Effects of Assistance

"...[N]o matter how divergent their views, nearly all of the commentators on the relationship between law and science have fundamentally different methods of seeking the truth," argue David T. Case and Jeffrey B. Ritter in commenting on the current rift between science and the law.[137]

Except perhaps with regard to assisted reproduction.

Assisted reproductive techniques have proved enormously helpful to people who might otherwise not be able to have children. But these procedures are not without controversy. "[B]y creating new categories of mother and father [these techniques] have produced the likelihood of conflict among such categories. At least five parents are now possible," note Blank and Merrick, in *Human Repro-duction, Emerging Technology, and Conflicting Rights*. "The most significant and novel distinction is that between the genetic mother, who contributes the ova, and the gestational or biological mother, who carries the child to term."[138]

Visions of Eastman's baby bird making his way toward a cat may be dancing in your head. Defining "mom" may be that baffling these days in an area where the courts are just making do. In *Stanley v. Illinois*,[139] the United States Supreme Court held that the term "[p]arents means the father and mother of a legitimate child, or the survivor of them, or the natural mother of an illegitimate child, and includes any adoptive parent."[140]

But the Court's decision in *Stanley v. Illinois* was issued nearly three decades ago. Since then, a great deal has changed. In an effort to keep pace with these evolving issues, new parentage laws have been codified and passed by many states. Yet cases and the claims regarding the underlying relationship of one person to another continue to be decided on a case-by-case basis in large part because "mother"—and many of the other familiar relationships—are open to interpretation today.

Determining who was the legal mother of twins, for example, was the question before a New York court in *Arredondo v. Nodelman*.[141] In 1991, Luz Arredondo had several eggs removed from her ovaries to be fertilized by her husband's—Andres Arredondo's—sperm. The fertilized ova were then implanted into the womb of Judith Nodelman, who had entered into what appears to have been a gestational surrogacy agreement. The agreement included affidavits signed by Judith Nodelman and her husband. The Nodel-mans declared in those affidavits that the Arredondos were "the biological par-ents of the fertilized eggs."[142]

Things apparently went along swimmingly until Judith Nodelman gave birth in May 1992. On the birth certificate, Andres Arredondo was listed as the children's father. But Judith Nodelman was listed as the twins' mother. Andres Arredondo sought declaratory judgment from a court that he was the legal father of the children. Also sought was a declaration that Luz Arredondo was the twins' "mother." To support the petition, the Arredondos offered genetic tests performed on Judith Nodelman. The tests excluded her as the biological mother of the twins.

Of course, this case would hardly be worth discussing if there weren't a twist, and the twist in this instance made history. The purpose of the Arredondos' petition was to have the court direct the City of New York to amend the children's birth certificates to reflect that Luz Arredondo was the legal mother of the twins. What apparently stumped city officials was the fact that Judith Nodelman had given birth to the twins.

In deciding the case, the court ruled that "[f]rom the affidavits, there is no dispute that the children born by respondent Nodelman resulted from the eggs of Luz Arredondo which were fertilized by the sperm of her husband Andres Arredondo, and not from the eggs of Nodelman or the sperm of her husband. Indeed, the results of the genetic testing reveal that Nodelman could not be the mother of the children, and that it is highly probable that the Arredondos are the genetic parents of the children."[143] Accordingly, the birth certificates could be amended to reflect the proper parentage of the twins.

The facts were slightly different in the case of *McDonald v. McDonald*,[144] though the essential question remained the same. Robert McDonald and Olga Benitez were married on July 9, 1988. But because Olga Benitez—known as Olga McDonald while married—could not conceive naturally, the couple opted for *in vitro* fertilization using donor eggs and Robert McDonald's sperm. The fertilized eggs were then implanted into Olga McDonald's womb, and on February 3, 1991, Olga McDonald gave birth to twin girls. And they all lived happily ever after until Robert McDonald filed for divorce.

In his petition, Robert McDonald sought to have the twins declared "illegitimate...or, in the alternative," if the children were found to be "genetically and legally" his, Robert McDonald sought sole custody.[145] The basis for this claim was that Olga McDonald had no biological connection to the twins, because the eggs used had come from a donor. On this basis, Robert McDonald argued that he should be granted "immediate and sole custody of the infant[s]" because he was the "only genetic and natural parent available" to the twins. In other words, Olga McDonald had served as a gestational surrogate, Robert McDonald argued.

But the New York court granted temporary custody to Olga McDonald, reasoning that Olga McDonald "has been the custodial parent of the twin infants conceived during the parties' marriage since their birth on February 3, 1991, and is indisputably their birth mother."[146]

The Supreme Court of Queens County would later take up the issue. Olga McDonald was not the biological mother of the twins in the strictest sense, the court found. She was closer, in fact, to a gestational surrogate. Thus, for guidance on the issue, the Queens court looked to *Johnson v. Calvert*.[147] Like Olga McDonald, the surrogate in *Johnson v. Calvert* had no biological connection to the child, a fact that had proved determinative for the California court.

But the Queens court held that because they had a "true 'egg donation' situation" on their hands—as opposed to a situation where the women asserting her rights as "mother" had provided the egg—the reasoning of *Johnson v. Calvert* did not control. In a true egg donor case, "the wife, who is the gestational mother, is the natural mother of the children, and is, under the circumstances, entitled to temporary custody of the children with visitation to the husband,"[148] the Queens court held.

By contrast, *In re Marriage of Moschetta*,[149] involved what the California Court of Appeals called the question of enforceability where a "traditional" surrogacy contract was involved. Robert and Cynthia Moschetta wanted children. But Cynthia was sterile. So, the Moschettas did what more than a few red-blooded Americans do these days. They called a surrogacy broker, who introduced them to Elvira Jordan.

The Moschettas and Elvira Jordan entered into an agreement by which Elvira Jordan would be artificially inseminated with Robert Moschetta's sperm. The idea was that she would bear Robert Moschetta's "biological offspring." Elvira Jordan also agreed that once the child was born, Robert Moschetta would obtain sole custody. The child would then be adopted by Cynthia Moschetta, making Cynthia Moschetta the child's legal mother.

In November 1989, Elvira Jordan found herself pregnant. But by January 1990, the Moschettas' marriage was dissolving. In April, Robert Moschetta told Cynthia Moschetta he wanted a divorce. On May 27, 1990, Elvira Jordan went into labor. Only then did she learn of the Moschettas' marital difficulties. The next day, Elvira Jordan gave birth to a girl named Marissa. But when the Moschettas came to take Marissa home, Elvira Jordan refused for two days to release her, relenting only when the Moschettas promised to stay together. It didn't last. Seven months later, Robert Moschetta left the family home, taking Marissa with him. A month later, Cynthia Moschetta filed a petition for legal separation. She also filed a petition seeking to establish a parental relationship with the child, arguing that she was the child's *de facto* mother.

The case would eventually go to trial with none of the parties asking the court to enforce the surrogacy agreement. The trial court held that the legal parents of the child were Robert Moschetta, who contributed the sperm, and Elvira Jordan, whose egg was fertilized. Cynthia Moschetta could not be the child's mother, the court held, because the child "has no biological, natural or genetic connection with Cynthia [Moschetta]."[150]

Robert Moschetta and Elvira Jordan were granted joint custody. Robert Moschetta appealed, arguing that Elvira Jordan should not have been declared Marissa's mother. Instead of Elvira Jordan, his estranged wife should have been declared Marissa's legal mother under the Uniform Parentage Act, Robert Moschetta argued.[151] In support of this argument, Robert Moschetta argued that under the Uniform Parentage Act, his estranged wife—as the intended mother—was as much Marissa's mother as was Elvira Jordan.[152]

Robert Moschetta argued further that such situations must be resolved in favor of the party who "was originally intended to be the mother."[153] The problem for the court, however, was that Cynthia Moschetta had not initiated adoption proceedings. She also had not filed a motion in support of Robert

Moschetta's petition. For these reasons, the California appellate court held that "[t]he flaw in [Robert Moschetta's] argument is that Cynthia is not 'equally' the mother of Marissa. In fact, she is not Marissa's mother at all. There is no 'tie' to break."[154] Genetics tests established definitively that Elvira Jordan was Marissa's biological mother.

In challenging this ruling as well, Robert Moschetta argued that because he and Cynthia had taken Marissa home and because Cynthia had held the child out as her own, Cynthia Moschetta should be legally declared Marissa's mother. But again the court was not persuaded, holding instead that "[o]n the simplest level, [this] argument is unpersuasive because Cynthia never held Marissa out as her 'natural' child. There never was any doubt that Marissa has no biological, natural, or genetic connection with Cynthia."[155] Because "birth parents" were required to offer specific consent to an adoption in the presence of a social worker under the California Family Code, and Elvira Jordan had withdrawn her consent, the court held that "[t]here was no such consent." Thus, Elvira Jordan was Marissa's mother, the court held.

The Arizona case of *Soos v. Superior Court County of Maricopa*[156] involved a nearly identical set of facts and a nearly identical set of claims, though the larger context involved a challenge to the constitutionality of the Arizona surrogacy statute. Ronald Soos and his wife Pamela wanted a child. But they couldn't conceive naturally, because Pamela Soos had had a partial hysterectomy. Eventually, the couple got in touch with a surrogate named Debra Ballas. As agreed, eggs were removed from Pamela Soos's ovaries and fertilized with Ronald Soos's sperm. After implantation, doctors found that Debra Ballas was pregnant with triplets.

During Ballas's pregnancy, Pamela Soos filed for dissolution of the marriage. But she sought custody of the fetuses. In response to his estranged wife's petition, Ronald Soos filed a petition of his own, arguing that he should be granted custody because he was the biological father of the unborn triplets and because under the Arizona surrogacy statute,[157] Debra Ballas was the legal mother of the child. In other words, as a matter of law, his estranged wife had no standing to seek custody, Ronald Soos argued. After the children were born, a court named Ronald Soos their legal father and he was granted custody. Pamela Soos filed a motion, seeking custody of the triplets. She also challenged the constitutionally of the Arizona statute.

In declaring that "there is not a compelling state interest that justifies terminating the substantive due process rights of the genetic mother in such a summary fashion," the Arizona court held that "[t]he current law could leave a child without any mother, as a gestational mother may have no desire to do more than she was hired to do, which is to carry and give birth to the child. The current law...ignores the important role that generations of genetics may play in the determination of who a child is and becomes. The current law does not consider what is in the best interest of each individual child. The court finds ARS Section 25-218(B) to be unconstitutional."[158]

In affirming the lower court's decision, the Arizona appellate court ruled that "the surrogate statute effects a fundamental liberty interest" (*i.e.*, the *fundamental* right of procreation). But as written, the statute "violates the equal protection guarantees of the United States and Arizona Constitutions."[159] Accordingly, the statute was struck down. Ronald Soos could not defeat his wife's status as biological mother to the child.

The question of whether a child can legally have two moms was at issue in *Alison D. v. Virginia M.*[160] The context in this case was a long-term lesbian relationship. In 1977, Alison D. and Virginia M. began a relationship and by March of 1978, they were living together. Two years later, the couple decided they wanted a child and, thus, the two women planned the child's conception and agreed to share joint custody and joint responsibilities in child rearing. Virginia M. was artificially inseminated and in July 1981, she gave birth to a little boy identified only as A.D.M. The women shared the birth expenses, and as A.D.M. grew, he came to call both women "mommy."

But when he was two years old, Alison D. and Virginia M. ended their relationship. Alison D. moved out of the couple's jointly purchased home. They reached an agreement regarding visitation and Alison D. agreed to continue to pay one-half of the mortgage and other household expenses. Eventually, Virginia M. bought out Alison D.'s interest in the house. In 1987, Alison D. moved to Ireland to pursue career opportunities. But she continued to try to communicate with A.D.M. There came a point, however, when Virginia M. terminated all contact, returning Alison D.'s gifts and letters. Alison D. filed a petition for visitation rights under New York Domestic Relations Law. When the Supreme Court dismissed the proceeding, Alison D. appealed.

In restating the facts before it, the New York Court of Appeals explained that Alison D. "concedes...she is not the child's 'parent'; she is not the biological mother of the child, nor is she a legal parent by virtue of an adoption. Rather she claims to have acted as a '*de facto*' parent or that she should be viewed as a parent 'by estoppel.' Therefore, she claims she has standing to seek visitation rights. These claims, however, are insufficient under Section 70," the court held. "Traditionally, in this state it is the child's mother and father, who, assuming fitness, have the right to the care and custody of their child, even in situations where the nonparent has exercised some control over the child with the parents' consent."[161]

Because Alison D. concedes Virginia M. "is a fit parent," she "has no right to petition the court to displace the choice made by this fit parent in deciding what is in the child's best interest." Further, "[w]hile one may dispute in an individual case whether it would be beneficial to a child to have continued contact with a nonparent, the Legislature did not in Section 70 give such nonparent the opportunity to compel a fit parent to allow them to do so," the court ruled. Thus, Alison D. was not the little boy's mother or even a parent under New York law. Therefore, although she had been part of the child's early life and planned for his conception, Alison D. was not entitled to visitation unless Virginia M. chose to allow her visitation.[162]

This is increasingly becoming a minority view in many states. Courts across the country increasingly hold that gay and lesbian parents have many of the same rights as heterosexual couples with regard to child rearing, which makes *Alison D. v. Virginia M.* a bit of a relic. This seems particularly true in light of the United States Supreme Court's 2003 decision in *Lawrence v. Texas.* In addition, with the invasion of assisted reproductive technology, children being born with "two mothers" has nearly become the "norm."[163] And, thus, although the question of "Who is mom?" continues to make its way into the nation's courts, it appears to have gotten easier to answer.

By contrast, a more complicated scenario—the kind that tends to get ethicists talking—unfolded in *Seymour v. Stotski,*[164] a case pitting a nonbiological father against the intended adoptive mother. In 1982, Richard Reams and his wife, Beverly Seymour, wanted a child. In an effort to become parents, Richard Reams and Beverly Seymour orally agreed that Norma Stotski would serve as a surrogate.

After repeated attempts at conception with Richard Reams' semen failed, Norma Stotski became pregnant with a child later named Tessa Annaleah Reams. But neither Richard Reams nor Beverly Seymour had a biological connection to the child. Tessa Annaleah Reams was the biological child of Norma Stotski and Leslie Minor, the man whose sperm was ultimately used to fertilize Norma Stotski's egg.[165]

In March of 1985, Norma Stotski filed a paternity suit against Richard Reams because she believed it was a necessary first step in formal adoption proceedings.[166] Though he was not the biological father, Richard Reams acknowledged the paternity of Tessa Annaleah Reams.[167] He was granted custody of the child. But not long after that, he and Beverly Seymour began to have marital problems. The couple eventually separated and divorced. And Beverly Seymour apparently carried Tessa Annaleah off with her other cherished possessions when she moved out of the couple's home, which brought about an appearance in court.

Beverly Seymour was required under a Parentage and Custody Order to return the child to Richard Reams. Instead, Beverly Seymour filed a motion to vacate the paternity order, arguing that Richard Reams was not Tessa's biological father. The court vacated the order and all of the men—Joseph Stotski, Leslie Minor, and Richard Reams—were joined in an action to determine who was the biological father of Tessa Annaleah. Blood tests revealed that Leslie Minor was the child's biological father. Still, Richard Reams filed a petition to adopt Tessa Annaleah. Beverly Seymour also filed a petition for adoption.

Then, in September 1990, Richard Reams died, leading the Ohio court to dismiss first the custody case, then Beverly Seymour's parentage action as moot. Beverly Seymour appealed. In answering her appeal, the Ohio appellate court held that "[i]t was not because the parentage action was 'moot' that the trial court was obliged to dismiss appellant's complaint; rather, it was because [Beverly Seymour] lacked standing to prosecute her claim."

"She was without standing because she is admittedly not the biological mother of Tessa, nor was she ever determined to be Tessa's legal mother by means of the so-called 'surrogate agreement,' when considering Ohio's adoption laws, is unsettled and open to considerable scrutiny as far as enforceability. Additionally, it has been previously determined that appellant had no legal relationship to the child. In Ohio, one cannot claim the status of an adoptive parent merely through an oral agreement. Thus, appellate was in no position to bring a parentage action or claim motherhood of Tessa," the Ohio court held.[168]

An even more complicated scenario emerges in *Jaycee B. v. Superior Court (John B.)*,[169] and it presents one of the most unsettling assisted reproduction cases ever recorded. In May of 1989, a couple—John and Luanne—were married. In 1994, John filed a petition for separation, asserting that no minor children were the result on the marriage. The following year, John filed a petition for a dissolution of marriage. Luanne responded to John's petition, arguing that the parties were "expecting a child by way of surrogate contract." Luanne attached a copy of the surrogate contract to her petition. The surrogate contract was signed by John, Luanne, a woman named Pamela, who would act as the surrogate, and Pamela's husband, Randy.

The contract specified that Pamela would carry to term an implanted embryo "created with donated genetic material, unrelated to any of the parties."[170] (A woman named Erin Davidson would later tell the television news magazine *48 Hours* that she had provided the eggs and was, therefore, "the biological mother" of the child.)[171] The facts before the court at the time, however, were that John and Luanne had no biological connection to the child. But John and Luanne had "contracted" for the child while still married.

As the various petitions made their way through the courts, Luanne sought monetary support. She also sought sole custody of the child, born in April of 1995. She named the child Jaycee. In response to Luanne's petition, John argued that although he had entered into the surrogacy contract, it was not legally binding on the issue of fatherhood because paternity could not be established. He also argued that the trial court had no jurisdiction over the matter.

The case eventually made its way to the appellate court, which concluded, despite the uniqueness of the facts before it, that "[t]he present case is the functional equivalent of a paternity action, where a mother who is the caretaker of a child seeks court-ordered support from a man but for whose actions the child would never have come into existence. As a classic paternity action, this case involves the conundrum of a court's authority to order a man to pay child support before it is authoritatively adjudicated that he is the child's father.[172]

"The remarkable thing about this case is that, unless a court is to hold that the surrogate Pamela is the natural mother of the child, Jaycee has no legal parents at all," the California court noted further. "Her genetic parents are anonymous and will probably not be held to be her natural parents.[173] And Pamela, the so-called surrogate mother who could establish parenthood under the Uniform Parentage Act, never contemplated keeping the child. [¶] Holding that Pamela, the birth mother, is the natural mother (and thereby, by extension, holding that

John cannot be the father) is unlikely to comport with the ultimate result in this case. As our Supreme Court pointed out in *Johnson [v. Calvert]*, the rule that the birth mother in a gestational surrogacy arrangement is the natural mother is to burden her with 'responsibilities' she never contemplated and is directly 'contrary to her expectations.'"[174]

A clearly tentative court admitted that "[t]he unique (a word which, given the facts before us, seems rather understated) facts of the present case present us with a dilemma. The facts and the law are almost, but not quite, 'entirely clear.' This is, after all, a case of first impression coming to us at the very inception of the litigation."[175]

Jaycee B. v. Superior Court (John B.) was amongst the first cases to establish what would have been impossible in another time: that a child could be born with "no legal parents." But since *Jaycee B. v. Superior Court (John B.)*, neither time nor science has stood still since. Thus, while *Jaycee B. v. Superior Court (John B.)* may have been extraordinary in its time—way back in 1996—it may not stand alone.

And yet, there were several footnotes to *Jaycee B. v. Superior Court (John B.)*, among them the allegation that Jaycee may have been conceived of sperm stolen at the University of California–Irvine fertility clinic where egg and sperm were put together.[176] Those allegations later proved false.[177] In response to the lower court's ruling regarding her nonlegal status as Jaycee's mother and John's obligation to pay child support, however, Luanne appealed. And after two more years of battle, she won, with the California appeals court declaring succinctly that the "portion of the [superior court's] judgment which declares that Luanne Buzzanca is not the lawful mother of Jaycee is reversed. The matter is remanded with directions to enter a new judgment declaring her the lawful mother [of Jaycee]."[178]

Legal scholars declared the decision a landmark, though in the evolving area of assisted reproductive law, similar "landmarks" appear to be founded every day. Finally, though he would continue to hold that he was not the "father" of Jaycee and, thus, should not be obligated to pay child support, a California court would ultimately declare that because John had "caused" Jaycee to be brought into the world, he was her legal father, and, therefore, must pay child support.

THE WIDOWS AND SPERM:[179]
Posthumous Conception and Other Defining Issues

In late March 1999, the story of a California woman's grisly reproductive choice began sweeping the country. Her name was Gaby Vernoff and she had given birth to a baby after sperm retrieved from her husband was later used to impregnate her.[180] What made the story sensational was that Vernoff's husband, Bruce, had been dead for nearly thirty hours when retrieval took place.[181]

Gaby Vernoff was not the first to use the procedure and she probably won't be the last woman to put her dead husband's sperm to work.[182] A 1997 survey conducted by the University of Pennsylvania Center for Bioethics found that fourteen clinics in eleven states had retrieved sperm from dead loved ones, usually within 24 hours of the male's death.[183] Indeed, "retrieving sperm from the dead is now so common that the American Society of Reproductive Medicine has developed a protocol, 'Posthumous Reproduction,' for dealing with it," law professor and reproductive rights scholar Lori Andrews explains.[184] There is even a name for this "new kind of father": Sperminator.

Though the method used to retrieve the sperm in Vernoff's case was newly heralded, as set forth earlier, there have been other dead dads. On June 4, 1991, a baby girl named Judith Christine Hart was born to Nancy Young Hart and the late Edward W. Hart Jr. Judith Hart was conceived by Gamete Intrafallopian Transfer three months after her "father's" death.[185] The difference between the Vernoff and the Hart cases was that Edward Hart Jr.'s sperm was taken while he was still alive.

What makes the *Hart* case important is that a year later, Nancy Hart applied for social security survivor's benefits for her daughter based upon the earnings of her deceased husband. The Social Security Administration denied her claim in an opinion letter dated November 17, 1993.[186] Though denial of death benefits for no other reason than the timing of one's birth might seem constitutionally impermissible, survivor's insurance under the Social Security and Workers' Compensation Acts was meant to replace "lost" income that the child would have received but for the death of the wage earner.[187]

After three years of appeals, the Social Security Commission announced on March 11, 1996, that survivor's benefits would be paid to Judith Hart. In doing so, the commissioner concluded that it was good public policy in light of the "[r]ecent advances in modern medical practice, particularly in the field of reproductive medicine...."[188]

As Judith Hart and Gaby Vernoff illustrate, advancements in medical technology have made tremendous inroads in assisted reproduction in the last ten years. Yet, those "inroads have plagued the legal community with a myriad of novel issues and controversies that, before this time, could never have been contemplated by lawmaking bodies," notes Law Professor Gloria Banks.[189] "The combination of the long existing process of artificial insemination with recently developed reproductive techniques has all but made noncoital human reproduction an everyday occurrence. Unfortunately, as seen in *Hart*, the rapid growth of this technology has continued to outpace the regulatory response to government."[190]

Who, for example, does the law say must support "posthumously conceived children?" A father would normally be required to support a child. But who takes on the task if there is no father? In an effort to answer these and other questions, a nationwide campaign got underway in the late 1990s intended to drive passage of the Uniform Rights of Posthumous Conceived Children Act. Another possible approach would be to amend state paternity and inheritance laws across the country to include "posthumously conceived children,"[191] Banks notes.

Why such enormous measures?

"[P]osthumously conceived children are a newly created class of nonmarital children whose rights, entitlements, and status remains unsettled," writes Banks. "As tradition would have it, these children are conceived by nonconventional reproductive techniques and practices which have no history in the archives of normative familial or procreative infrastructures. Assuring the equal protection of laws for such after-conceived children may therefore necessitate progressive judicial activism premised on moral and ethical principles of fair treatment."[192]

Although posthumous conception is an area of that law that most state legislatures have yet to address, there has been some effort. The Uniform Status of Children of Assisted Conception Act has been described by scholars as the "most relevant legislative initiative thus far determining the relational status of posthumously conceived children."[193] Section 4(b) of the USCAC provides that "[a]n individual who dies before implantation of an embryo, or before a child is conceived other than through sexual intercourse, using the individual's egg or sperm, is not a parent of the resulting child."[194]

Three states have taken varying stances, however, in addressing the legal status of posthumously conceived children. Those states are: Virginia, North Dakota, and Florida. Virginia's version of the USCAC, which is called the Status of Children of Assisted Conception, Section 20-158(b), provides that:

> [a]ny child resulting from the insemination of a wife's ovum using her husband's sperm, with his consent, is the child of the husband and wife notwithstanding that, during the ten-month period immediately preceding the birth, either party died. However, any person who dies before *in utero* implantation of an embryo resulting from the union of his sperm or her ovum with another gamete, whether or not the other gamete is that of the person's spouse, is not the parent of any resulting child, unless (i) implantation occurs before notice of the death can reasonably be communicated to the physician performing the procedure or (ii) the person consents to be a parent in writing executed before the implantation.[195]

Florida's version provides that "[a] child conceived from the eggs or sperm of a person or persons who died before the transfer of their eggs, sperm, or preembryos to a woman's body shall not be eligible for a claim against the decedent's estate unless the child has been provided for by the decedent's will."[196] The North Dakota version of the USCAC provides that "[a] person who dies before a conception using that person's sperm or egg is not a parent of any resulting child born of the conception."[197]

Critics of "posthumous conception" argue that this form of assisted reproduction "promote[s] a society of the living dead by diminishing the structure of the traditional American family." Banks argues, however, that "[s]ociety should not punish posthumously conceived children because their parents elected to procreate by assisted reproduction."[198]

Legislation pending in at least five states would provide that a deceased husband or former spouse will not be the "parent" of the resulting child unless the spouse or deceased partner expressly consented to "parenthood" prior to death or dissolution of marriage.[199]

The courts in other states have been forced to resolve some of the issues arising out of posthumous conception. The Massachusetts Supreme Judicial Court ruled in January 2002 that the twin daughters of a man who died two years before their birth may have a right to inherit if they can show: (1) that they are biologically related to the deceased parent; (2) that the deceased person had consented prior to death to the conception; and that, (3) the deceased consented prior to death to supporting the child or children who may be born as a result of the posthumous conception.[200] This seems to be the general direction that the law is heading.

THE SPERM AND THE EGG:
Money and the Legal Issues

A great many things have changed in the wake of modern technology. Parents may no longer be "parents" in the traditional sense and children may be born well after their *mothers* and *fathers* are dead. But one thing remains: the egg still comes first, which may help explain why, in the spring of 1999, a small but enticing advertisement began to appear in the newspapers of some of the nation's most prestigious universities and colleges.

In large letters the ad read, "Egg Donor Needed," then, in smaller letters below, "Large Financial Incentive. Intelligent, Athletic Egg Donor Needed For Loving Family. You Must be at least 5 feet, 10 inches. Have a 1400+ SAT score. Possess no major family medical issues. $50,000. Free Medical Screening. All Expenses Paid."[201] More than 200 women responded.[202] The ad was placed by a well-to-do couple, described by their lawyer as "highly educated," who are tall and who want any child they might have to be smart and tall too. "We have heard that only one percent of the college population is over 5 feet, 10 inches with an over-1400 SAT score," Darlene Pinkerton, the couple's attorney, said.[203]

And so the couple did the American thing: they went shopping. Though the ad sparked debate, for infertile couples it makes perfect sense. "For a woman who is trying to get pregnant and has no viable eggs of her own, donor eggs are a last resort," writer Rebecca Mead argued in *Eggs for Sale*.[204]

Eggs are big business, and not just because a brilliant 5 foot, 10 inch wunderkind could hit the $50,000 lottery. In addition to the money being offered by wealthy couples to bright, good-looking students,[205] there is money to be made by private agencies and clinics able to boast egg donor programs with immediate availability of a carefully screened supply. And there are millions to be made in storage fees as women attempt to overcome the tick of their biological clock.

A woman's eggs are healthiest before she is thirty-five, and the possibility of being able to store healthy eggs for use later has been touted as the biggest potential equalizer ever known to women—a way to turn back the hands of the biological clock.[206]

"Young women could bank their eggs and get on with their lives," Christo Zouves said.[207] "Then when they're ready to have children, they could call up those eggs, their genetic package, and have a child."[208]

Of course, the second part of the "baby recipe" is a man's sperm. And there is plenty of money to be made there too. The Repository for Germinal Choice is a Southern California sperm bank where women can select a vial of hope from a donor field that reportedly includes "Nobel Prize winners and Olympic athletes."[209] The bank was started two decades ago by physicist Robert Graham, who "believed that America's future depended on improving the breed." There are about one hundred sperm banks across the country, including Cryobank, the nation's largest, which sent some 2,500 vials of sperm a month to clients in 2000.[210]

The commerce of coupling egg and sperm has created a thriving market.[211] But it is the combination of what these couplings have created that has led to litigation. In early 2001, a woman identified as J.B. asked the New Jersey Supreme Court to affirm a decision by the appellate court. The appellate court had previously issued a decision allowing a fertility clinic to destroy seven "pre-embryos" that remained in storage as a result of fertility attempts by the woman and her ex-husband. The ex-husband, identified in court papers as M.B., asked to receive the "embryos" so that they might be implanted in a future spouse.[212]

The New Jersey case was not the first of its kind. Rather, where the issue was once so new that it baffled courts, "custody" battles over frozen embryo are commonplace today. In April 2000, for example, the Massachusetts Supreme Judicial Court ruled that it "would not enforce an agreement that would compel one donor to become a parent against his or her will."[213] The Massachusetts case involved a 44-year-old woman, identified only as B.Z., who sought use of frozen embryos to become pregnant. The embryos were the product of a marriage between B.Z. and A.Z., the woman's ex-husband who opposed their use, though he had signed several consent forms.[214]

And in August of 1997, a Cook County, Illinois, judge issued a preliminary injunction to prevent the implantation of two frozen embryos into a woman's womb. The embryos were the remainder of fertility treatments undertaken during the six-year marriage. The court issued the injunction because the couple was in the midst of a divorce. The woman's estranged husband challenged the implantation, arguing that he had the right not to become a father against his will.[215] The reasoning of the above cases is grounded in the rationale used by the Supreme Court of Tennessee in deciding the case of *Davis v. Davis*,[216] set forth below, which is widely considered the persuasive, if not controlling, precedent in this emerging area of the law.

DAVIS v. DAVIS:
Frozen Embryos and the Coupling Problem

Mary Sue Easterly and Junior Davis were married in 1980, and for nine years they tried to have a baby. During one of their many *in vitro* attempts, several eggs were taken from Mary Sue's ovaries to be fertilized in a petri dish with Junior's sperm. Then they were frozen for possible use by the couple in the future. But the strain of the procedures, when added to the couple's other problems, led to the end of the marriage. After the couple filed for divorce, the frozen preembryo became the subject of years of litigation.

Both Mary Sue and Junior sought "custody" of the embryos in *Davis v. Davis*,[217] as the case was known, with both Mary Sue and Junior asserting that the embryos were "part of me." Mary Sue argued further that she would like to have children without Junior and that he had effectively consented to fatherhood when he agreed to allow his sperm to fertilize the eggs. But Junior Davis argued that the embryos should be destroyed because he did not want his children to be raised in a broken home. After Mary Sue remarried, she again sought "custody" of the embryos, this time so that she might donate them to an infertile couple, she argued. Junior Davis again opposed, contending that he should not be forced to become a father against his will to children he did not know.

The trial judge awarded the embryos to Mary Sue, arguing that they were not frozen fertilized eggs, but rather "children *in vitro*." Thus, it was in the "best interests of the children *in vitro*" to have a chance at life, the judge reasoned. Junior Davis appealed, and one year later an intermediate court awarded joint custody to Mary Sue and Junior Davis. Mary Sue appealed to the Tennessee Supreme Court, arguing that she would donate the embryo to a childless couple.

Junior Davis reiterated that he should not be made to be a father against his will in a reversal of the arguments used in *Roe v. Wade*. Junior Davis asked for custody of the embryos to destroy them. In the end, the Tennessee Supreme Court held that "[t]he right of procreation is a vital part of the individual's right to privacy." Therefore, Junior Davis's interest in not becoming a parent outweighed Mary Sue's interest in gaining possession of the eggs to donate to another couple.

As stated earlier, though it is not a United States Supreme Court case, *Davis v. Davis* has generally become the standard for reviewing the rights of individuals "not to become" parents against their will.

In addition to custody suits over frozen embryos, an emerging issue in the law involves the posthumous gift of sperm to a loved one and all of the wreckage this simple act of giving may cause. William Kane was a Yale-educated lawyer. In 1991, he froze fifteen vials of sperm, leaving them to his girlfriend, Deborah Hecht. Then he went to Las Vegas and committed suicide.

Kane's apparent intent was that Hecht would use the sperm to become pregnant, further evidenced by the fact that he left a letter for his "potential unborn child."[218] He also left a will, a specimen storage agreement, and a letter directing that the sperm should be given to Hecht upon his death. But the vials were initially deemed "property" and, therefore, part of Kane's estate. Deborah Hecht challenged the designation. In attempting to decipher the issues before it, a California court would wade in a quagmire of the reproductive rights debate that would eventually require answering the question of how to dispose of "human concepti" under California probate law.

But the case proved more complicated than that. After the court reasoned that Kane's sperm was "potential life," rather than property, and deserving of special status, Deborah Hecht brought suit, alleging that the court's failure to release the vials to her as directed by Kane's bequest was an infringement of *her* right to privacy and procreation—a right protected by the federal and California constitutions.[219] Legal scholars note that *Hecht v. Superior Court*[220] opened the door to a new frontier of reproductive issues.[221] But appeals in the case dragged on for years as Kane's living children joined, challenging the bequest as against public policy. The children also argued that additional heirs would take from their deceased father's estate.

The court found little merit in these arguments.[222] Deborah Hecht prevailed in her claims.[223] The vials were awarded to her. But she was never able to become pregnant, despite repeated medically aided attempts. The *Hecht* decision is generally understood to mean that "only the procreational rights of the living party to whom the deceased had determined, prior to death, would be entitled to use the frozen sperm...," according to scholars.[224]

SPERM DONORS AND DADS:
An Evolving Standard

"Sperm donors" as a class have been in the news a great deal of late, in large part because their status appears to be in flux. Once cloaked in a heavy shroud of "confidentiality," that veil has been pierced by order of the court in recent years, or for voluntary reasons by the parties involved as the first generation of children come of age.

In *Johnson v. Superior Court*, for example, the Supreme Court of California upheld a decision by the appellate court allowing the revelation of the identity of a donor at the center of a negligence, fraud, and breach of contract case brought against the facility by a young girl suffering from liver disease.[225]

But the voluntary relinquishment of privacy among men who give to these banks is becoming more commonplace as well, with some men even becoming involved with their "children."[226] There are also those instances when men who thought they could act strictly as sperm donors have changed their minds. In *Jhordan C. v. Mary K.,*[227] for example, the California Court of Appeals was essentially asked to answer a philosophical question: What is it exactly that makes a man a sperm donor—as opposed to a suitor?

The facts of *Jhordan C. v. Mary K.* were as follows: A woman and her female lover wanted to have a child. To help them out, a male doctor "privately provided" the women with the semen necessary to have a child. But instead of ending things, this altruistic act proved to be the beginning. After the child was born, the women went to court to prevent the doctor from claiming paternity. The women also sought to have their relationship as "mother" and other *de facto* parent to the child legally acknowledged.[228]

Before the court, the women argued that the parties had agreed—prior to the child's conception—that the doctor would have no parental rights to, or obligations for, the child. In other words, the doctor was a sperm donor. As a result, he was entitled to no relationship to the child. The doctor argued, however, that everyone's postagreement conduct served to nullify and/or waive any and all agreements.

The doctor pointed specifically to the fact that he had been allowed to take part in various stages of the pregnancy. He also had been allowed early visits with the child.[229] For guidance in deciding the case, the court considered the Uniform Parentage Act, of which several states have adopted a version.[230] Under California's version of the Act:

> (A) A husband of any woman who conceives a child from donated sperm, from a man not her husband through artificial insemination, is the father of that child if he consented to the process;
>
> (B) A sperm donor is not the father of a child born through assisted reproduction from any woman who is not his wife.[231]

The court held that a literal interpretation of the Uniform Parentage Act did not fit in the case. Under the California version of the act, in order for the doctor to be declared a "sperm donor," the sample would have had to have been delivered to a licensed physician for use under clinical conditions. That was not done in this case. Instead, the doctor admitted he had provided the sperm *directly to the woman*, who later carried the child.[232] That singular, but clearly significant difference led the appellate court to affirm the lower court's determination that the doctor was the legal father of the child. He was awarded visitation rights.

In the early to mid-1990s, courts in Colorado, Ohio, New York, and Oregon considered similar cases.[233] Thus, the emerging rule seems to be that a "sperm donor" is a sperm donor when he acts like a sperm donor. But he may be declared the "father" of the child when paternity is established and the "coupling" takes place in the usual and customary way. A potential hiccup with regard to the sperm donor question arises, however—as it does in other areas—when assisted reproductive techniques enter the picture.

For example, what happens when a husband and wife harvest eggs and sperm that are then coupled in a petri dish and frozen, but the couple gets a divorce? Is the former husband the "father" if the implantation of the embryos takes place after the divorce? Or is he a sperm donor? The Supreme Court of Tennessee's decision in *Davis v. Davis* would appear to govern this question: Men cannot be made to be "fathers" against their will. But what if his ex-wife clearly intends at the time of the *in vitro* procedure that her ex-husband will have nothing to do with the child? That was the set of issues facing a Texas court in *In the Interest of Olivia Grace McGill.*[234]

Don McGill and Mildred Schmit spent 20 years in a "rough marriage." But during one of several reconciliations, Don McGill agreed to have another child with Mildred Schmit because, according to court papers, he knew of his ex-wife's "strong desire to have more children." To achieve this goal, the couple began *in vitro* fertilization procedures at a clinic. At some point, however, the clinic staff was informed that in the event of a divorce, the embryos should be destroyed. In 1996, the pair divorced. But several months later, Mildred Schmit had several frozen embryos implanted into her womb, and in 1997, she gave birth to a little girl she named Olivia.

Don McGill sued for custody, and in 1998, a Texas court found Don McGill to be Olivia's biological father. He was then awarded visitation rights. Mildred Schmit was appointed Olivia's managing conservator. On appeal, Mildred Schmit argued that Don McGill may have begun the *in vitro* process as a "consenting husband." But as time wore on, he agreed to implantation procedures only if he would have "no parental or financial responsibilities for any resulting child."[235] That promise rendered Don McGill a "sperm donor," Schmit argues. Under the Texas Family Code, sperm donors have no parental rights.[236] Several states have passed similar statutes in attempts to create a workable framework for new reproductive issues.[237]

But the Texas statute may not apply, according to judges hearing the case. After all, *In the Interest of Olivia Grace McGill* is different from a typical sperm donor case. Absent a statute governing the case, what should be done? An attorney for Mildred Schmit argued that the case should be remanded to allow a jury to hear and decide the terms of Don McGill and Mildred Schmit's oral agreement. Schmit's lawyer argued further that public policy dictates Mildred Schmit be given sole custody to protect mothers in assisted reproductive cases from interference from sperm donors. Attorneys for Don McGill argued, however, that Don McGill was not a stranger or an uninvolved sperm donor. Rather, "[i]t is uncontested that he is the biological father."[238]

Hecht v. Superior Court, Jhordan C. v. Mary K, and *In the Interest of Olivia Grace McGill* raise new and difficult legal questions, critics note. Each represents a move away from the traditional definition of family. While many states still decide paternity and parental obligations in traditional biological terms, advances in "assisted reproductions" have changed the basic equation often requiring as much review of the law as consideration of common sense. For example, although sperm donors do not have parental rights, biological fathers do.

Thus, where men have acted more like husbands and boyfriends than "typical sperm donors," courts have generally held those men to be "fathers" in the traditional sense. And in accordance with their determination as "fathers," the courts have frequently ordered these men to pay child support, even where the men and women involved attempted to—or actually reached—agreements stating that the child's mother will not seek support from the "father" in the future.

In February 2002, a Florida appellate court held, for example, that a Broward County doctor—who signed an eight-page "preconception agreement" stating that he was a "sperm donor" before impregnating his girlfriend the old-fashioned way—was the child's father for purposes of support. Though Florida law provides that a sperm donor must relinquish all rights to the child born of assisted reproductive techniques, in this case the court held that the doctor was the father because he had gotten the woman pregnant in the "usual and customary" way.[239] In addition, the court held that the child's parents could not sign away the child's rights to support.

Traditional reproduction has always had its quirks and the kind of odd stories that make Shakespearian tales seem plausible after all. For example, after months of having people she didn't know wave at her and smile, Tamara Rabi, a student at Hofstra University in New York, learned an extraordinary truth in March 2003: although she was born in Mexico and adopted as a baby and raised on Manhattan's Upper West Side as an only child, she was a twin. Her identical sister, a girl named Adriana—also raised as an only child—was a student at Adelphi, not far away.[240]

The articulated fear of ethicists and critics of assisted reproduction and the "blind" use of sperm donors is that the practice may lead to generations of long-lost relations whose faces do not tell the story of their shared lineage as immediately as Tamarra Rabi's did. And, thus, biological brothers may begin to relate to biological sisters in ways that current law does not allow. And yet, of more immediate concern in this area in recent years have been the mistakes. Doctors can do miracles today, and assisted reproduction—the potential as well as the reality—has remade the genealogical landscape. But with bigger possibilities have come devastating mistakes and phenomenal accidents that few involved seem to be prepared for.

ASSISTED REPRODUCTIVE TECHNOLOGIES:
Bigger Possibilities—More Devastating Mistakes

In March 1999, an average woman from Staten Island, New York, found herself at the center of a tabloid world. Eleven months earlier, Donna Fasano had gone to a Manhattan fertility clinic, and after several procedures and a stunning mistake, Fasano left carrying an embryo created from her husband's sperm and her egg and several fertilized embryos created from the sperm and egg of an African American couple she had never met. Nine months later, Donna Fasano gave birth to "twins:" one white, as the Fasanos are; the other African American.[241]

On March 12, 1999, Deborah Perry and Richard Rodgers, an African American couple who was undergoing procedures at the clinic at the time, sued the fertility clinic and several doctors for medical malpractice and breach of contract. The Rodgers also sued the Fasanos, seeking a declaratory judgment regarding their status with regard to the African American child Fasano gave birth to.[242] Prior to the birth of the two boys, the couples were notified by the clinic of the mistake.

A state inquiry found that an embryologist made a mistake during Fasano's final *in vitro* procedure, handing the doctor a batch of embryos belonging to the Rodgers. The embryologist initially kept quiet about the mistake, because he viewed the wrongly implanted embryos as "lower grade in quality," which suggested that they probably wouldn't "take." But when Fasano became pregnant, the embryologist confessed the error to the doctor, who immediately informed the couples.[243]

DNA tests were conducted to determine the relationship to the children. On April 13, 1999, DNA tested established that the African American child was the Rodgers's child. With lawyers in the middle, the couples initially agreed that the Fasanos would relinquish custody of the child they had called Joseph. That agreement fell apart, however, when the Fasanos sought future visitations. Eventually the Fasanos would seek to vacate the agreement. They would also seek a visitation order, which would be granted on January 14, 2000. The Rodgers challenged that order.[244]

In June 2000, the New York Supreme Court, Appellate Division, reversed the Fasanos' visitation order, holding that while the court recognized that "in these rather unique circumstances, where the Rodgers's embryo was implanted in Donna Fasano by mistake, and where the Fasanos knew of the error not long after it occurred, the happenstance of the Fasanos' nominal parenthood over Akeil (the name the Rodgerses gave the child) should have been treated as a mistake to be corrected at [sic] soon as possible, *before the development of a parental relationship*. It bears more similarity to a mix-up at the time of a hospital's discharge of two newborn infants, which should simply be corrected at once, than to one where a gestational mother [is involved]. Under such circumstances, the Fasanos will not be [held] to claim the stature of parents, entitled to seek an award of visitation."[245]

As impossible as it might seem, in the assisted reproductive realm, lightning of this sort sometimes does strike twice. Or even three times. The Fasano-Rodgers debacle was the second highly publicized incident of its kind. A similar mix-up occurred at a Florida clinic in 1994. Michael and Betty Higgins underwent infertility treatments at Memorial Hospital in Jacksonville, Florida, and almost as soon as the couple's children were born, it was clear there had been a mistake. Michael Higgins is African American, while Betty is white. When the couple's twins were born, it was apparent that Betty was the biological mother. But Michael was not the biological father. The wrong sperm had been used during the procedure. The couple sued the hospital, and later they divorced.[246]

A lawsuit was the result of wrongfully implanted embryos in California after Susan B. went to a Santa Clara clinic, where she was supposed to receive "genetic material" from two strangers, which would be fertilized and then implanted in her womb.[247] Robert and Denise B., a married couple, went to the same clinic, where they were supposed to receive embryos, created from donated ovum and

Robert B.'s sperm. These embryos were supposed to go only to Robert and Denise B.

Somehow three of the thirteen embryos meant for Robert and Denise B. were implanted into Susan B.'s womb and she became pregnant. Denise B. also became pregnant as a result of implantation, and ten days apart both women gave birth to children; Daniel for Susan B. and Madeline for Robert and Denise B. Daniel and Madeline were genetic siblings. After clinic officials disclosed the error to the parties, Robert B. filed a paternity action to determine whether he was the biological father of Susan B.'s son. The test showed that Robert B. was the biological father of Susan B.'s son.

Susan B. challenged Robert B.'s paternity petition and the legal designation of Robert B. as Daniel's father, arguing that even if Robert B. were technically the child's biological father, his function in the transaction had been that of a sperm donor. Denise B. also filed suit, alleging that Susan B. had "colluded" with clinic officials to obtain the embryos. Denise B. sought to have herself declared Daniel's legal mother. The court found no evidence of collusion on Susan B.'s part. The court also held, in accordance with the development of the law in this area, that Denise B. was not Daniel's legal mother.

If it can be said that a general rule has emerged with regard to these extraordinary cases, it is that when women are mistakenly implanted with the wrong embryos, the courts have tended to conclude that their position is equivalent to that of a gestational surrogate. As a result, women mistakenly implanted are generally not granted visitation rights, because they are often not held to be the "mothers" of the children they carried and gave birth to. Though harsh, that appears to be where the law is headed. Such a ruling does not, of course, preclude a woman from filing suit against doctors and hospitals where such an incident has occurred.

EMBRYO FRAUD:
Errors, Destruction, and Deliberate Deception

In addition to mistakenly implanted embryos, the already-crowded dockets of the nation's courts have been peppered in recent years with cases of the alleged destruction or misuse of "human concepti." More than 100,000 clinics handle the storage and maintenance of frozen embryos,[248] and occasionally disputes regarding that handling have led to property—as opposed to "custody"—claims for the loss of embryos or other genetic matter.

At issue in *York v. Jones*,[249] for example, was the question of ownership of frozen prezygotes. According to the facts of the case, a young couple went to a Virginia clinic for fertility treatments. But before the procedures were complete, the couple moved to California. When they sought to have the prezygotes transferred to a California facility, the Virginia clinic refused, arguing that the clinic owned the prezygotes. The couple filed suit. In considering the claims, the court ruled that the ultimate issue involved a contract dispute because the original agreement between the couple and the Virginia clinic referred to the frozen matter as "property."[250] Accordingly, the couple had a claim against the Virginia clinic. But for the recovery of property.

By contrast, in an attempt to avoid suits of this sort, an Arizona fertility clinic began running ads in the *Arizona Republic* newspaper in June 1999, in an effort to inform former and current clients that the clinic's owner was preparing to retire and close the clinic. The ad read:

> If you feel you have embryos or sperms stored with Arizona Institute of Reproductive Medicine, please contact us immediately.[251]

The ad further informed readers that all unclaimed material still at the clinic on July 15, 1999, would be destroyed. Clients were given a choice. They could have their stored material transferred to another clinic or they could permit the clinic to destroy it.[252] Destroying "genetic matter" is controversial, in large part because religious leaders and pro-life groups view this material as "life" and have, thus, publicly criticized the destruction. John Grabowski, a theologian at Catholic University, has argued, for example, that thawing and discarding embryos "as if they were nothing more than excess lab material is morally troubling."[253]

Given the passion of the abortion debate, it should come as no surprise, then, that religious leaders and conservative politicians have made efforts in recent years to change the law in this area too. In February 2001, Maryland, New York, and New Jersey officials considered bills requiring fertility clinics and health care facilities that provide *in vitro* and assisted reproduction services to provide written notification of the policies regarding the disposal of all leftover material.[254]

But sometimes it is less about "left over" matter, than deliberately discarded matter. The deliberate destruction of a couple's genetic material led to a lawsuit in *Del Zio v. Presbyterian Medical Center.*[255] According to the facts set forth by the court, after a couple's sperm and egg were mixed as part of an experimental procedure, a doctor—who was "morally opposed" to the procedure—deliberately destroyed the material. The couple sued the medical center, and a jury awarded them damages for emotional distress.

But if the deliberate destruction of human concepti is a harm worthy of damages, would artificially inseminating unsuspecting women with one's own sperm be another? That is what Virginia doctor Cecil Jacobson did to an estimated 120 women, all the while suggesting that either their husbands or anonymous sperm donors had been of use.[256] By some counts, Jacobson may have fathered seventy children.[257] A federal grand jury would indict Jacobson on fifty-three counts of violating federal law, including mail, wire, and travel fraud, as well as perjury.[258] And in February 1992, Jacobson was convicted on all counts.[259] He was sentenced to sixty months in prison.[260]

But Jacobson's behavior pales in comparison to cases arising out of the Center for Reproductive Health, a fertility clinic run in association with the University of California at Irvine by three doctors: Dr. Ricardo Asch, Dr. Jose Balmaceda, and Dr. Sergio Stone. Of the three, Dr. Asch was the most well-known as the inventor of the fertilization process known as GIFT—Gamete Intra Fallopian-tube Transfer. But in 1994, University officials began receiving complaints accusing doctors at the center of a number of things, including: prescribing unapproved drugs to patients;[261] implanting eggs without the consent of donors; and stealing "eggs from women undergoing fertility treatments" during the late 1980s and early 1990s.[262]

The University appointed a panel to investigate the allegations. The news was not good. The panel reportedly found "plausible evidence" that the doctors implanted human eggs without donor consent, as well as evidence of some of the other alleged violations."[263] At least fifteen births were thought to have been the result of unlawful egg transfers, write Judith Fischer, professor of law at Chapman University School of Law.[264] The University filed suit against the clinic, alleging that the Center for Reproductive Health had "transplanted patients' eggs into other patients without obtaining their donors' consent."[265]

A legal landslide began.

Roughly 105 civil lawsuits were filed against the fertility clinic by former patients.[266] Seventy-five of them were settled at a cost of $15 million to the University.[267] Among the twenty cases that remained unsettled as of January 1999 were two involving claims that Cornell University may have been the recipient of some of the missing material.[268] The scandal prompted the California legislature to enact a statute criminalizing the misappropriation of eggs or embryo.[269]

In 1995, Drs. Asch and Balmaceda fled the United States.[270] Dr. Asch is said to be running a fertility clinic in his native country of Argentina and teaching at a university in Mexico City. Dr. Balmaceda is reportedly running a similar facility in his home country of Chile.[271] Dr. Stone, who remained in the United States, was convicted of nine counts of mail fraud and sentenced to one year of home detention.[272] In the wake of the scandal, several states moved to pass bills allowing the states to regulate facilities and persons offering assisted reproduction care.[273]

BABY STRAIN OR ESCAPE HATCH:
Assisted Reproduction from the Male Perspective

As set forth earlier, assisted reproductive techniques have changed the landscape of the American family. And yet, the procedures involved have raised legal questions not always limited to defining "mom." Rather, an emerging challenge involves the effort of men—husbands—to have themselves declared not to be "fathers," because their children were conceived via assisted reproduction.

In *Levin v. Levin*,[274] for example, Donald and Barbara Levin chose artificial insemination in an attempt to have a baby because Donald Levin was sterile. Barbara Levin underwent the procedure with Donald Levin's full support. And in September 1977, Barbara Levin gave birth to a son. Donald and Barbara Levin were listed as parents on the child's birth certificate. From 1977 to 1987,

Donald Levin supported the child and held him out as his son. But in 1987, the couple divorced. Barbara Levin sought child support.

Soon after, Donald Levin terminated his personal relationship with the child and requested that the court vacate all orders of child support. The basis of Donald Levin's motion? That the child was not his biological son. On a petition brought by Barbara Levin, the trial court granted a request for an increase in child support. Donald Levin appealed, asking the court to answer the following questions: (1) whether the "father" of a nonbiological child conceived via artificial insemination is obligated to pay child support; and (2) whether a child conceived via artificial insemination is a "child of the marriage" as defined by the Dissolution of Marriage Act.[275]

The Supreme Court of Indiana held that Donald Levin was responsible for child support and that the child was a "child of the marriage." Specifically, the court found that "Donald [had] induced Barbara to go forward with the artificial insemination," and he consented to it both orally and in writing. That consent was Donald Levin's promise to become the father of the resulting child and to assume his support," the court reasoned. In addition, Donald Levin held the child out as his own for fifteen years. "He made no objection to declaring the child a child of the marriage in the dissolution decree in 1987. For her part, Barbara had relied in good faith upon Donald's actions and consequently bore a child for which she believed both she and Donald would be responsible, the court determined. For these reasons, Donald is estopped from denying his obligations towards this child. To hold otherwise would be unjust."[276]

An interesting contrast to the case of *Levin v. Levin* is the Illinois case of *In re Marriage of Witbeck-Wildhagen*.[277] Eric Wildhagen asked an Illinois court to answer the same questions Donald Levin had asked of the Indiana court. But again there was one factually significant twist. Eric Wildhagen didn't want a baby, and he made that clear every chance he got. The record before the court was that Marcia Witbeck married Eric Wildhagen in 1990. The record suggests that Marcia Witbeck wanted to have a baby. But Eric Wildhagen was so disinterested that he used a condom whenever he and Marcia had sex. In addition, when Eric Wildhagen and Marcia Witbeck-Wildhagen visited a fertility clinic to learn about artificial insemination, Eric Wildhagen made clear to Marcia Witbeck-Wildhagen and the attending nurse that he did not want to participate. He also made clear that he did not consent to his wife's attempts to become pregnant.

Despite the clear and unequivocal nonconsent of her husband, Marcia Witbeck-Wildhagen remarked that she would "be all right" if she pursued the pregnancy alone. And after the initial consultation, Marcia Witbeck-Wildhagen did just that, undergoing seven artificial insemination procedures, according to court records. Eric Wildhagen was not told of these procedures by either the clinic or his wife. By October of 1993, Marcia Witbeck-Wildhagen was pregnant. By January of the following year, she was filing for a dissolution of marriage. But in her petition, Marcia Witbeck-Wildhagen argued that she did not have sufficient property or income to provide for her needs and/or those of her unborn child. Marcia Witbeck-Wildhagen sought custody of the child. She also asked the court to require Eric Wildhagen to pay maintenance, child support, and prenatal and delivery expenses.

The Illinois appellate court denied the request for support, finding that under Illinois law "a husband's written consent" is a prerequisite to "the establishment of a legal father-child relationship and the imposition of a support obligation" in artificial insemination cases.[278] But in this case, "[t]here is no evidence of consent by [Eric Wildhagen] to the artificial insemination procedure, written or otherwise," the court noted. Rather, Marcia Witbeck-Wildhagen "filed for a dissolution of marriage within two or three months of becoming pregnant. She was impregnated by the sperm of a man other than [Eric Wildhagen], without [Eric Wildhagen's] knowledge or consent, and apparently without any intention of raising the child with [him]."[279]

In her petition for support, Marcia Witbeck-Wildhagen had also argued that denying child support would be contrary to public policy. Accordingly, the court addressed two issues of public policy: M.W.'s right to support; and, Eric Wildhagen's right to choose not to be a parent.

"Just as a woman has a constitutionally protected right not to bear a child,[280] a man has a right not to be deemed the parent of a child that he played *no* part in conceiving," the court wrote. And in this case, Eric Wildhagen had made a choice not to parent a child, the court ruled. "That choice was evidenced by not giving his consent to petitioner or any support to her choice to undergo artificial insemination. But Marcia Witbeck-Wildhagen underwent the procedure unbeknownst to Eric Wildhagen, who learned from his attorney after M.W. was born of the manner of the child's conception," the court explained.

"This is not a case," the court held, "where respondent...changed his mind or is attempting to evade responsibility for his own actions in helping to conceive or encouraging the conception of a child. The facts of this case illustrate, and the trial court correctly determined, it would be inconsistent with public policy to force upon [Eric Wildhagen] parental obligations which he declined to undertake." Therefore, although there was a general public policy that recognized a child's right to support, that obligation "cannot be met by requiring a nonparent to fulfill the obligation of a parent,"[281] the court held. Accordingly, Eric Wildhagen had no financial obligation for M.W., the Illinois appellate court held.

Although the rule was ultimately inapplicable in *In re Marriage of Witbeck-Wildhagen*, the requirement of written consent to artificial insemination has been a hotly disputed issue. Several courts have imposed child support requirements in artificial insemination cases where there was no statutory requirement of written consent.[282] Given recent complications in the issues of birth, however, many states have begun to adopt statutes that require evidence of an express writing to demonstrate consent to artificial insemination before an obligation of child support will attach.

In the Illinois case of *In re Marriage of Adams*,[283] for example, the Illinois appellate court was called upon to interpret Section 3 of the Illinois Parentage Act.[284] To be deemed the "natural father" of a child conceived by artificial insemination, the Illinois statute requires consent of both a husband and a wife under the supervision of a licensed physician. Although the husband had not authored an expressed written consent in *In the Marriage of Adams*, the Illinois appellate court held that because it had been previously determined by the trial court that there was sufficient evidence of consent to his wife's insemination before, during, and after the pregnancy, the husband could be obligated to pay support.[285]

Although the court in *In re Marriage of Adams*, held that where a husband gives sufficient oral consent, he may be estopped from arguing that his consent must be in writing as required by the statute, eight years later in *In re Marriage of Witbeck-Wildhagen*, the Illinois appellate court held that the "legislature intended a husband's written consent to be a prerequisite to the establishment of the legal father-child relationship and the imposition of a support obligation."[286] Thus, the rule—at least in Illinois—appears generally to be that a husband must give written consent to artificial insemination if he is to be obligated to pay child support, though where there is sufficient evidence of other kinds of consent, the obligation may attach as well.

Oral versus written consent was at issue in *K.B. v. N.B.*,[287] a case involving an ex-husband's assertion that because he had not met the written requirement of the Texas artificial insemination statute, he could not be deemed the father of a son born of that process. Nor could he be obligated to pay child support. The husband had undergone a vasectomy that proved irreversible. The Texas appellate court held that where there is clearly ratification by a husband of a wife's efforts to become pregnant via artificial insemination, a husband may be held to be the legal father of the child and obligated to support his child.

"Here the husband knew about the artificial insemination process and participated in it willingly from the beginning," the Texas appellate court wrote. "He acknowledged the child and publicly held him out as his son for several years.... Under the unique facts of the case, he has ratified the parent-child relationship. We hold that the finding of ratification supports the court's ruling that the parent-child relationship existed. In view of this conclusion, we also hold that the court properly ordered child support, which the husband has attacked only on the ground that he is not the child's father."[288]

But the Texas court noted that its "ratification holding" in *K.B. v. N.B.*, was "narrow," and limited to "the unique facts" of this case. "Artificial insemination is not an ordinary transaction between two persons. It brings new life into being. Unlike more common contractual arrangements, this transaction could not be rescinded, and nothing like restitution is possible," the Texas court held.[289] Thus, if there is a rule to emerge from these cases, it would appear to be that a husband may be a "father," required to pay child support for a child born of artificial insemination, provided there is sufficient evidence of consent, written or oral.

PREVENTION FOILED—THE STORK HAS ARRIVED:
Fraudulent Birth and the Misuse of Sperm

It is widely understood today that motherhood—whether naturally or "artificially" achieved—can occur outside of bonds of marriage. Assisted reproductive techniques have tangled the traditional equation, forcing the courts to define once-clearly established relationships. It is the birth of a child or children in those cases that sets the wheels of litigation into motion. But what if a person—usually a man—never intended to become a parent?

Allegations of sexual trickery and/or fraud have been made in the context of pregnancy and pregnancy litigation in recent years, with the claims sometimes grounded in assisted reproductive technologies misused; at other times challenging conception that occurred the old-fashioned way. In the 1998 case of *Hong Soo Shin v. Oyoung Kong*,[290] for example, an ex-husband sued his wife's doctor for intentional infliction of emotional distress; negligent infliction of emotional distress; professional malpractice; general negligence; violation of the California Family Code; fraud and misrepresentation; invasion of privacy; and false light privacy after he learned that his wife had been artificially inseminated without the husband's knowledge, allegedly with the doctor's own sperm.[291]

The suit was eventually dismissed.[292] But this is an indication of the kind of claims that have begun in the last decade to make their way into court. Indeed, although "sexual fraud" cases are becoming increasingly more commonplace and more complicated, they weren't always. In the early days—as far back at the 1980s—suits of this sort were rarely successful and the courts tended to dismiss them as untenable. An early example of such a case, for example, is *Stephen K. v. Roni L.*[293]

Roni L. and Stephen K. were lovers, and a child was born of their coupling. But at some point things went bad. The couple parted and Roni L. brought a paternity suit to formally establish Stephen K. as the child's father. Stephen K. filed a cross-complaint, alleging that Roni L. had wrongfully induced him into having intercourse with her by falsely represented to him that she was taking birth control pills. The result of this "misrepresentation," Stephen K. argued, was the child. In other words, Stephen K. argued that he had never intended to be a father and he would not have been but for Roni L.'s alleged trickery and misrepresentation.

"Birth control fraud" has rarely proved a viable defense once a child is born, though plaintiffs in several highly-publicized cases in recent years have begun to question the practice of requiring men to continue to pay child support for children that genetic testing has revealed not to be theirs. And it didn't prove successful for Stephen K.

In dismissing Stephen K.'s cross-complaint, the California court held that "[t]he claim...is phrased in the language of the tort of misrepresentation. Despite its legalism, it is nothing more than asking the court to supervise the promises made between two consenting adults as to the circumstances of their private sexual conduct. To do so would encourage unwarranted governmental intrusion into matters affecting the individual's right to privacy.... [¶] We reject Stephen's contention that tortious liability should be imposed against Roni, and conclude that as a matter of public policy, the practice of birth control, if any, engaged in by two partners in a consensual sexual relationship is best left to the individuals involved, free from any governmental interference."[294]

But, in fact, the nation's courts are often asked to "interfere" in the relationships of (former) partners. At issue in L. Pamela P. v. Frank S.,[295] for example, was the assertion that a woman's "intentional misrepresentation that she was practicing birth control" had deprived a man of his "constitutional right to decide whether to father a child." L. Pamela P. and Frank S. met and the relationship progressed to the point of a child. After a court found by clear and convincing evidence—the standard in paternity suits—that Frank S. was the child's father, the court ordered Frank S. to pay child support. Frank S. appealed, alleging that L. Pamela P. had had the child "regardless of his wishes" and that she had "misrepresented to him that she was using contraception."[296]

This is, of course, the constitutional argument used so successfully by Junior Davis in Davis v. Davis—stood on its head. As set forth above, the Supreme Court of Tennessee held in Davis v. Davis that "[t]he right of procreation is a vital part of the individual's right to privacy." And in that case, Junior Davis's interests in *not* becoming a parent—even to unknown and as yet "unborn children"—outweighed Mary Sue's interest in gaining possession of the eggs to donate to another couple.[297]

With the decision in Davis v. Davis, the Supreme Court of Tennessee put a father's choice of whether or not to become a father on a fundamental par with that of a woman's. Courts in Illinois and Massachusetts held similarly in frozen embryo cases in 1999.[298] But the New York court hearing L. Pamela P. v. Frank S. in 1983, held that a violation of one's constitutionally protected rights is generally not enforceable against private citizens. Rather, the United States Constitution was drafted to protect citizens from wrongful state or federal action.

According to the court, in recognizing that L. Pamela P. "engaged in no state action, [Frank S.] urges that imposition of a support obligation upon him under these circumstances constitutes state involvement sufficient to give vitality to his constitutional claims."[299] Even though the lower court found that L. Pamela P. had "purposefully deceived" Frank S. with regard to her use of contraception,[300] the New York Court of Appeals held that even "[a]ssuming without deciding, that sufficient state action is present in this case, we conclude that Frank S.'s contentions fall short of stating any recognized aspect of the constitutional right of privacy," the court wrote.[301]

In other words, although Frank S. had a constitutionally protected right to decide whether to become a father, "the interest protected has always been stated in terms of governmental restrictions on the individual's access to contraceptive devices. It involves the freedom to decide for oneself, *without unreasonable governmental interference*, whether to avoid procreation through the use of contraception. This aspect of the right of privacy has never been extended so far as to regulate the conduct of private actors as between themselves," the appellate court explained.[302]

The court held further that "constitutional entitlements to avoid procreation do not encompass a right to avoid a child support obligation simply because another private person had not fully respected his desires in this regard. However unfairly Frank S. may have been treated by L. Pamela P.'s failure to allow him an equal voice in the decision to conceive a child, such a wrong does not rise to the level of constitutional violation," the court concluded.

But Frank S. was a bit of a pioneer. It is not uncommon today for "fathers" charged in paternity suits to frame their objections as constitutional challenges in an effort to defeat the requirement of child support. In the vast majority of these cases, however, courts have ordered fathers to pay. But the case of *Linda D. v. Fritz C.*[303] involved a novel approach to the challenge as well as a novel proposed solution in a case that might either have involved a misrepresentation or a miscommunication. Both seem possible.

The facts of *Linda D. v. Fritz C.*[304] are straightforward and simple. In response to a paternity suit, Fritz C. alleged that Linda D. "represented to him throughout their relationship she was using a birth control device." But Linda D. testified via affidavit that she had endometriosis, a condition that, as described by the court, "...renders women infertile."[305] Because she understood that Fritz C. was "uneasy," she "also used a contraceptive device,"[306] according to the court. Even so, in March 1981, Linda D. became pregnant. When she informed Fritz C., he asked her to have an abortion. She refused. Several months later, a baby boy was born.

Fritz C. and his mother visited Linda D. in the hospital, and Fritz C. reportedly volunteered to pay $200 a month for child-care costs, according to court documents. At some later point, Linda D. asked Fritz C. to acknowledge paternity. He refused, and soon after negotiations broke down and court proceedings began. In his pleadings, Fritz C. alleged "...damage claims against [Linda D.] by way of a set-off against the amount of child support for which he may be liable...."[307] To offset the harm resulting from Linda D.'s "misrepresentation," Fritz C. argued that his "damages" should be subtracted from the child support award. In addition, as others had done, Fritz C. attempted to assert a "right of procreation" argument.

The court was not persuaded.

"The father's right to make an individual decision regarding procreation is not restricted by refusing to allow him to assert in this action that he now had the right to avoid his child support obligations if the mother did not successfully use contraceptive measures," the Washington Appellate Court wrote in deciding *Linda D. v. Fritz C.* "The father argues that the mother's negligent use, or her misrepresentation of use, of contraceptive measures deprived him of his fundamental constitutional right to decide whether to father a child."

Again, the court noted that the most significant part of this constitutional equation is the freedom from "unwarranted governmental intrusions into matters so fundamentally affecting a person as the decision whether to bear or beget a child. No such right, however, encompasses the right of one parent to avoid a child support obligation where the other parent's choice regarding procreation is not fully respected."[308] In other words, Fritz C.—along with many of the men who have similarly attempted "birth control fraud" arguments across the country—have generally been held to be out of luck once the child was born because the child's right of support attaches.

By contrast, where there is a pregnancy but no child, the courts have tended to treat the issue differently, usually letting the damages alleged dictate. In *Barbara A. v. John G.*,[309] for example, Barbara A. filed suit against John G., a former lover, alleging that he had told her he was sterile. He apparently was not.

According to the published facts of the case, Barbara A. not only became pregnant as a result of her relationship with John G. She suffered an ectopic pregnancy, which led first to complications and later to life-saving surgery. In the end, Barbara A. was left sterile. Barbara A. sued, arguing that she consented to sex with John G. in reliance upon his knowingly false representation that he was sterile. In other words, Barbara A. asserted that she had relied upon John G.'s misrepresentation, and as a result, she had suffered permanent harm.

The trial court entered judgment in Barbara A.'s favor. But a California appellate court reversed, reasoning that Barbara A.'s complaint asserted claims for battery and deceit. In doing so, the court distinguished the case at bar from *Stephen K. v. Roni L.* "In essence," the appellate court wrote," Stephen [in *Stephen K. v. Roni L.*] was seeking damages for the 'wrongful birth' of his child resulting in support obligations and alleged damages for mental suffering. Here, no child is involved; appellant is seeking damages for severe injury to her own body."[310]

Misrepresentation and "birth control fraud" claims have become increasingly popular in recent years, due in part to burgeoning men's and fathers' rights movements. But it is also apparently due to the fact that nearly every time such an argument has been asserted, it has received national attention from the media. "Sued for Getting Pregnant" was the title of a segment on the once-trendy *Leeza Show*. The segment involved an appearance and interview with a Tennessee man who brought suit against a former lover after she became pregnant.[311] The suit was eventually dismissed. But the arguments raised by this and other cases have continued to evolve.

"Birth control fraud" was one of three defenses offered, for example, by an ex-husband in *Erwin L.D. v. Myla Jean L.*[312] And what a tangled web it was. Myla Jean L. and Erwin L.D. had a short-lived marriage, but a long and intimate relationship. Although the pair divorced after less than a year of marriage, they remained lovers, and eventually Myla Jean L. became pregnant, had a child, and sought child support. In attempting to refute paternity, Erwin L.D. argued that: (1) he might not be the father of the child; (2) Myla Jean L. told him he would not have to support a child; and (3) Myla Jean L. had committed "birth control fraud," lulling him into sexual encounters by telling him that she was using birth control, when she clearly was not.

A trial court awarded Myla Jean L. child support. The Court of Appeals for the State of Arkansas would uphold that decision, noting that the court could not "…endorse appellant's proposition that birth control fraud can act as a bar to a claim of paternity. Courts that have confronted the issue have refused to recognize misrepresentations regarding the use of contraceptives as a defense.[313] In *Paul M. v. Teresa M.*,[314] we observed that the purpose of our filiations laws was to provide a process whereby the putative father can be identified so that he may assume his equitable share of the responsibility to his child. To permit this defense, as one that assigns fault for conception, would result in the denial of support to innocent children whom the law was designed to protect."[315]

Of course, assigning fault for conception is precisely the point of many of these suits. But not all such claims directly assert allegations of "fraud." Some invoke more subtle language in the hopes, perhaps, of getting around precedent. At other times, the language is edgy, because the claim is meant to be edgy. Peter Wallis made headlines in November 1998, for example, when he brought suit against a former live-in girlfriend.

In the suit, Wallis alleged that his ex-girlfriend "intentionally acquir[ed] and [then] misus[ed]" his semen during intercourse.[316] The allegations underlying Wallis's claim are similar in essence to those of *Stephen K. v. Roni L.* Peter Wallis lived with Kellie Smith. But either before, or as a result of, Kellie Smith's becoming pregnant, the couple fell apart. Kellie Smith later gave birth to a baby girl. Not long after that Wallis brought suit, alleging that Kellie Smith made him a father against his will by promising to take birth control pills, but failing to do so.

In arguing that Kellie Smith had "misused his semen," Wallis appears to have been asserting a constitutional argument (*i.e.*, that Kellie Smith had violated *his* fundamental right to choose whether or not to become a father by "fraudulently" inducing him into sexual intercourse, then "misusing" his sperm). Although a media-savvy approach, as the cases above establish, this does not appear to be a unique approach. Nor does it appear to have been a particularly successful approach. Rather, as set forth above, courts have held that once a child is born, the father is responsible for support regardless of the circumstances of conception.

In response to Wallis's allegations, Kellie Smith argued two things the courts seemed to take silent note of. First, Smith argued that the pregnancy was accidental. Secondly, Smith alleged that she "could not have stolen Wallis's sperm because [Wallis] 'surrendered any right of possession to his semen when he transferred it…during voluntary sexual intercourse.'"[317]

It is the "voluntary" nature of a consensual sexual encounter, incidentally, that has tended generally to defeat claims of "birth control fraud" or "misuse of sperm" claims, even in those instances where participation in sexual conduct by a man—or even a boy—results in a child. This has held true even where the boy involved might arguably have been the victim of a crime.

Colleen H. was a sixteen-year-old baby-sitter hired to care for twelve-year-old Shane S.[318] At some point, Colleen H. and Shane S. began a sexual relationship, and biology took over. When Colleen H. was seventeen and Shane S. was thirteen, they became parents. Criminal charges were filed against Colleen H. She would ultimately be adjudicated as a juvenile offender for "engaging in the act of sexual intercourse with a child under the age of sixteen" in *State ex rel. Hermesmann v. Seyer.*[319] Colleen H. would later stipulate to the lesser offense of contributing to a child's misconduct, which is not a sexual offense *per se.*

But to support the child she now had to take care of, Colleen H. applied for and received benefits through the Aid to Families with Dependent Children Program. On March 8, 1991, the Kansas Department of Social and Rehabilitation Services filed a petition in the name of Colleen H., alleging that Shane S. was the father of Colleen H.'s baby daughter. As part of its petition, the agency asked the court to determine the paternity of the child and to order Shane S. to reimburse the state for the child's support, should he be declared the father. On December 17, 1991, an administrative hearing officer found that Shane S. was the baby's biological father. Shane S. was ordered to reimburse the state for the child's support up to the date of the hearing and beyond. Shane S., still a teenager at the time, appealed.

On appeal, Shane S. argued three things: (1) as a minor, he could not consent to sexual intercourse; (2) because he was unable to consent, he could not be held responsible for the birth of the child; and (3) because he could not be held responsible for the birth of the child, he could not be required to pay child support. A reasonable argument? To many it would seem so. But in taking apart the carefully crafted appeal, the Supreme Court of Kansas held that the substance of Shane S.'s first challenge was that Colleen H. "sexually assaulted him, that he was the victim of the crime of statutory rape, and that the criminal statute of indecent liberties with a child should be applied to hold him incapable of consenting to the act."[320]

The Kansas court would concede that "all of the admitted facts established, without a doubt, all of the elements necessary to prove a crime" under the state's statutory rape law. Further, the court would acknowledge the "fact that Colleen [H.] was able to plea bargain for a lesser offense did not preclude Shane S. from alleging...he was a victim of statutory rape." Still, the court would conclude that Shane S. had given consent to the sexual acts that led to the birth of his daughter.

"Although the question of whether the intercourse with Colleen [H.] was 'voluntary,' as the term is usually understood, is not specifically before us," the court wrote, "it was brought out in oral argument before this court that the sexual relationship between Shane S. and his babysitter...started when he was only twelve years old and lasted over a period of several months. At no time did Shane register any complaint to his parents about the sexual liaison with Colleen [H.]."

But could a thirteen-year-old be ordered to pay child support?

The State Parentage Act[321] "specifically contemplates minors as fathers and makes no exception for minor parents regarding their duty to support and educate their child," the Kansas court held.[322] And "[i]f the legislature had wanted to exclude minor parents from responsibility for support, it could easily have been done." The court held further that "[a]s previously stated, Shane [S.] does not contest that he is the biological father of the child. As a father, he has a common-law duty, as well as a statutory duty, to support his minor child." Finally, a criminal allegation involving sexual misconduct "does not apply to a civil proceeding and cannot serve to relieve Shane [S.] of his legal responsibilities towards his child,"[323] the court held.

There was one final argument, however, that Shane S. attempted to make: that requiring him to pay child support would violate public policy. He was, after all, a minor. And as it turned out, this argument was troublesome, given that it raised a possible conflict between two competing issues of public policy: the state's interest in protecting juveniles and the state's interests in requiring parental support of children. But which was more compelling in the case of a minor father?

According to the Supreme Court of Kansas, the state's "…interest in requiring minor parents to support their children overrides the state's competing interest in protecting juveniles from improvident acts, even when such acts may include criminal activity on the part of the other parent. Considering the three persons directly involved, Shane [S.], Colleen [H.], and Melanie [the baby], the interests of [the child] are superior, as a matter of public policy, to those of either or both her parents. This minor child, the only truly innocent party, is entitled to support from both her parents regardless of their ages."[324]

Thus, the rule appears to be that when the support of a minor child—"an innocent party"—is at issue, the requirement of child support will attach. "Criminal" conduct is not a bar to that requirement, and in many states—as it was not in Kansas—youth is not a defense. In this regard, *State ex rel. Hermesmann v. Seyer* is not an anomaly. Courts in other jurisdictions have decided similar cases similarly.

The Wisconsin case of *In re Paternity of J.L.H.*,[325] for example, dealt with the issue of child support in a case involving a 15-year-old father. In upholding the award of child support, the Wisconsin court reasoned that issues of statutory rape and a lack of consent pertains "to the guilt of a criminal defendant, not the civil rights or duties of the victim. Paternity actions are civil proceedings." The Wisconsin court held further that "[i]f voluntary intercourse results in parenthood, then for purposes of child support, the parenthood was voluntary. This is true even if a fifteen-year-old boy's parenthood resulted from a sexual assault upon him within the meaning of the criminal law."[326]

That reasoning appears to be well-founded in the law.

As far back as 1961, a Colorado court held that a sixteen-year-old father could be required to pay support for a child born of a twenty-year-old woman. The case was called *Schierenbeck v. Minor*,[327] and despite the father's age, the

Colorado court held that even though "[S.'s] assent to the illicit act does not exclude commission of the statutory crime…it has nothing to do with assent as relating to progeny. His youth is basic to the crime; it is not a factor in the question of whether he is the father of [the child].… The putative father may be liable in bastardy proceedings for the support and maintenance of his child, even though he is a minor.…"[328] If S. is adjudged to be the father of [the child] after a proper hearing and upon sufficient evidence, he should support [the child] under this fundamental doctrine."[329]

The Illinois Appellate decided similarly in *In re Parentage of J.S.*,[330] holding that "Illinois public policy has never offered blanket protection to reckless minors. At the same time, Illinois public policy has recognized the blanket right of every child to the physical, mental, emotional, and monetary support of his or her parents. The public has an interest in protecting children from becoming wards of the state. [¶] In the instant case, we find that the public policy mandating parental support of children overrides any policy of protecting minors from improvident acts," the Illinois court held.[331]

And in upholding an order requiring a sixteen-year-old father to pay eight dollars a week in child support for a child born out of wedlock, the Massachusetts court held in *Commonwealth v. A. Juvenile*,[332] that the "defendant's claim rests on an assertion that a support order is inconsistent with the statutory purpose of treating a juvenile defendant as a child 'in need of aid, encouragement, and guidance.' Although we acknowledge that purpose, we see no basis, and certainly no statutory basis, for concluding that a juvenile should be free from any duty to support his or her illegitimate child. The illegitimate child had interests, as does the Commonwealth."[333]

As a general rule, the above cases establish that the requirement of child support will attach, even if the conditions of conception were not ideal and/or may even have been "criminal." The reason for this is that courts across the country have generally held that it is within society's interests to protect children. Thus, the courts have frequently struck down arguments in which men assert that they have been "tricked," "beguiled," or even "assaulted" into fatherhood.

ENDNOTES FOR CHAPTER TEN

1   See *A Dangerous Parent Trap*, U.S.NEWS & WORLD REPORT, Oct. 13, 2003, at p. 12.
2   *Id.*
3   See Robert Blank and Janna Merrick, HUMAN REPRODUCTION, EMERGING TECHNOLOGIES, AND CONFLICTING RIGHTS (Washington, D.C.: CQ Press, 1995), at p. 12.
4   *In re A.C.*, 573 A.2d 1235 (D.C. App. 1990).
5   During the year prior to Angela C's case, a Muslim woman arrived at the hospital's door. She was carrying a full-term fetus. The woman's water broke, but the woman remained only partially dilated for two days. As the risk of infection to the child grew, the hospital recommended a cesarean section. The woman refused due to religious convictions. A hearing was eventually held. A judge ordered the hospital to deliver the baby by cesarean.
6   *In re A.C.*, 573 A.2d at 1237, 1249 (1990) (*emphasis added*).
7   Jurisdiction was based upon the Juvenile Court Act (705 ILCS 405/1-1 *et seq.* (West 1992)).
8   *In re Baby Boy Doe*, 260 Ill.App.3d 392 (1994).
9   141 Ill.2d 473 (1990).
10   See e.g., *In re Pescinski*, 67 Wis.2d 4 (1975).
11   *In re Brown*, 294 Ill.App.3d 159 (1997).

12   Both were filed pursuant to the Illinois Juvenile Court Act of 1987. 705 ILCS 405/1-1 *et seq.* (West 1996).
13   *See Baby Boy Doe*, 260 Ill.App.3d at 402.
14   41 N.J. 421 (1964), *cert. denied*, 377 U.S. 985 (1964).
15   *See* Mark Ballard, *Can the Common-law Hubby Bar Plug Pulling?*, NAT'L L.J., Aug. 23, 1999, at A4 (involving *Common Law Marriage and the 17-week-old Fetus*).
16   *See* Chapter Eight, *supra*.
17   *Id*. (In the fall of 1999, authorities were still trying to decide what to do.)
18   *See* Dana Canedy, *Gov. Jeb Bush to Seek Guardian for Fetus of Rape Victim*, N.Y. TIMES, May 15, 2003, at A25.
19   *Id*.
20   *Id*.
21   *Id*.
22   *See also Woman at Center of Fight on Fetal Rights Gives Birth*, ASSOCIATED PRESS, August 31, 2003 (reprinted in N.Y. TIMES, Sept. 1, 2003, at A8).
23   *Id*.
24   For reading regarding *In re Klein*, *see* Alderman & Kennedy, *supra* note 128, ENDNOTES FOR CHAPTER ONE at p. 121.
25   *See, e.g.*, Laura M. Holson, *Dressing for 2, Buying for 1*, N.Y. TIMES, Aug. 3, 2001, at C1.
26   According to author and population and environmental researcher, Bill McKibben, "[i]n the empty, agricultural United States of the nineteenth century, 'the more kids the better.' And in the first part of the twentieth century, as efficiency experts like the father in *CHEAPER BY THE DOZEN* came to the fore, 'mass production really permeated the American culture.'" *See* Bill McKibben, MAYBE ONE (London: Anchor, 1999), at p. 38.
27   *Id*. at 12. (According to McKibben, "Americans currently bear children at a rate of just under two per woman.")
28   For detailed discussion of the falling rate of abortion, *see supra* Chapter 5.
29   For discussion of the trend as well as the numbers, *see* Rick Weiss, *Babies in Limbo: Laws Outpaced by Fertility Advances*, WASH. POST, Feb. 8, 1998, at A1; Lisa Bennett, *High-Tech Pregnancies*, ADVOCATE, Dec. 22, 1998, pp. 47–50.
30   *See e.g.*, Linda Villarosa, *Women Now Look Beyond HIV to Children and Grandchildren*, N.Y. TIMES, Aug. 7, 2001, at D7; Gina Kolata, *Parenthood Help for Men with HIV*, April 30, 2002, N.Y. TIMES, at D1; *AIDS Drugs During Pregnancy Don't Harm Fetus, Study Shows*, N.Y. TIMES, June 13, 2002, at A27.
31   *See* Robert Blank, FETAL PROTECTION IN THE WORKPLACE: WOMEN'S RIGHTS, BUSINESS INTERESTS, AND THE UNBORN (New York: Columbia University Press, 1993), at p. 1.
32   *See Use of Assisted Reproductive Technology—United States 1996 and 1998*, Centers for Disease Control, MORBIDITY AND MORTALITY WEEKLY REPORT, Feb. 8, 2002.
33   *See Boy, Oh Boy!*, PEOPLE, Feb. 12, 2001, at pp. 92–98.
34   *See* Cynthia Gorney, *The Egg Man*, BAZAAR, Dec. 1998, at p. 264.
35   *See* Aldous Huxley, BRAVE NEW WORLD (New York: Harper & Row, 1932), at p. 98. Science appears to finally be approaching the "Huxley standard." *See e.g.*, *Promise of Production-Line Embryos*, BBC NEWS ONLINE, Aug. 16, 2000.
36   *See* Clive James, *Out of Sight: The Curious Career of Aldous Huxley*, THE NEW YORKER, March 17, 2003, pp. 143–148.
37   *See Boy Is Born 5 Months After His Twin Died*, N.Y. TIMES, Nov. 12, 1999, at A16.
38   *See Ovary Transplanted Into Arm Makes Eggs*, CHI. SUN-TIMES, Oct. 25, 2000, at 56.
39   *See Special Delivery*, ABC NEWS.COM, July 26, 2001.
40   *See* Claudia Kalb, *The Octuplet Question*, NEWSWEEK, Jan. 11, 1999, at p. 33.
41   *See also* Anne Adams Lang, *Doctors Are Second-Guessing the 'Miracle' of Multiple Births*, N.Y. TIMES, June 13, 1999, at wk. 4; Tamar Lewin, *Report Links Fertility Aids to Small Size in Newborns*, N.Y. TIMES, July 15, 2000, at A6; *Gang of Four*, PEOPLE, July 23, 2001, pp. 116–118; *Third Set of Septuplets in the World Are Born*, N.Y. Times, July 14, 2001, at A8; *Assisted Reproductive Technology Reports*, CENTERS FOR DISEASE CONTROL, REPRODUCTIVE HEALTH INFORMATION SOURCE.
42   See Kalb, *supra* note 40, at p. 33; *Gang of Four*, PEOPLE, July 23, 2001, pp. 116–118.
43   *See* Arthur C. Guyton, M.D., TEXTBOOK OF MEDICAL PHYSIOLOGY (8th ed. 1991), at p. 913; Blank & Merrick, *supra* note 3, at p. 85.
44   *See* Sharon Begley, *The Baby Myth*, NEWSWEEK, Sept. 4, 1995, at pp. 38, 41.
45   *See* Rick Weiss, *Babies in Limbo: Laws Outpaced by Fertility Advances*, WASH. POST, Feb. 8, 1998, at A1.
46   *See* Gloria J. Banks, *Traditional Concepts and Nontraditional Conceptions: Social Security Survivor's Benefits for Posthumously Conceived Children*, 32 LOY. L.A. L. REV. 251–379, at p. 268 (Jan. 1999).
47   *Id*.
48   *See* Gina Kolata, *Fertility Inc.: Clinics Race to Lure Clients*, N.Y. TIMES, Jan. 1, 2002, at D1, D7.
49   *See* Blank & Merrick, *supra* note 3, at p. 86.

50   *Id.*

51   *Id.*

52   *See* Weiss, *supra* note 45, at A1.

53   *See* Jane Gross, *Fight for Infertility Coverage: Couple's Suit Says Refusal to Pay is a Form of Bias,* N.Y. TIMES, Dec. 7, 1998, at A1.

54   Citation Number 97-156 (June 25, 1998).

55   The Americans with Disabilities Act has been read by some to offer protection to persons who suffer disabilities that impair a "major life activity."

56   In *Bragdon v. Abbott,* 97-156 (June 5, 1998), the Justices noted that "[t]he life activity upon which respondent relies, her ability to reproduce and to bear children, constitutes a 'major life activity' under the [Americans with Disabilities Act]. The plain meaning of the word 'major' denotes comparative importance and suggests that the touchstone is an activity's significance. Reproduction and the sexual dynamics surrounding it are central to the life process itself. Petitioner's claim that Congress intended the ADA only to cover those aspects of a person's life that have a public, economic, or daily character founders on the statutory language. Nothing in the definition suggests that activities without such a dimension may somehow be regarded as so unimportant or insignificant as not to be 'major.' This interpretation is confirmed by the Rehabilitation Act regulations, which provide an illustrative, nonexhaustive list of major life activities. Inclusion on that list of activities such as caring for one's self, performing manual tasks, working, and learning belies the suggestion that a task must have a public or economic character. On the contrary, the regulations support the inclusion of reproduction, which could not be regarded as any less important than working and learning."

57   *See* Gross, *supra* note 53, at A1.

58   *Id.*

59   *See, e.g.,* ARIZONA SENATE BILL 1390 (2001) (appropriating funds for infertility treatments as well as contraceptives); CONN. HOUSE BILL 5622 (2001); FLA. SENATE BILLS 142 and 464 (2001); IND. HOUSE BILL 1182 (2001); KAN. HOUSE BILL 2491 (2001) (providing for insurance coverage for artificial insemination and assisted reproduction); MASS. SENATE BILL 599 (2001) (establishing a Health Care Trust to provide publicly funded health care services, among them fertility treatments); MINN. SENATE BILL 401 (2001); MISS.HOUSE BILL 373 (2001); N.J. ASSEMBLY BILLS 1862, 2003, and 2954 (2000); N.J. SENATE BILL 1076 (2000) (requiring insurers providing benefits to groups of 50 people or more to cover diagnosis and treatment of infertility); N.Y. SENATE BILLS 739, 936, 1265, and 1411 (2001); PA. SENATE BILLS 417 and 432 (2001); R.I. HOUSE BILL 5489 (2001); VA. HOUSE BILL 1151 (2000) (amending insurance coverage requirements for state employees to include coverage for infertility treatments); NEB. LEGISLATIVE BILL 319 (2001) (requiring insurance coverage for infertility diagnosis and treatment as well as contraceptive coverage); NEB. LEGISLATIVE BILL 825 (2001) (prohibiting, as discriminatory, insurance contracts with the state from refusing to cover "reproductive health care," including diagnosis and/or treatment of infertility). See also *Insurer Law for Fertility Treatment,* N.Y. TIMES, Sept. 1, 2001, at A10.

60   *See* Barbara Vobejda, *Man's Suit Claims Fraud in Pregnancy,* CHI. SUN-TIMES, Nov. 23, 1998, at 22.

61   Sir Walter Scott, quoted in JOHN BARTLETT'S FAMILIAR QUOTATIONS (16th ed.) (Boston: Little, Brown & Co., 1992), at p. 378 (altered by the author).

62   P.D. Eastman, ARE YOU MY MOTHER? (New York: Beginner Books/ Random House, 1960) at pp. 22, 25, 29, 33.

63   For background on the discovery and the science of DNA, *see e.g.,* Nell Boyce, *Triumph of the Helix,* U.S.NEWS & WORLD REPORT, March 3, 2003, pp. 38–46; *A Conversation with James D. Watson,* SCIENTIFIC AMERICAN, April 2003, pp. 67–70; Nicholas Wade, *Double Helix Leaps From Lab Into Real Life,* N.Y. TIMES, Feb. 25, 2003, at D1.

64   *See* Blank & Merrick, *supra* note 3, at p. 89.

65   *Id.*

66   *See IVF,* BBC NEWS ONLINE, March 31, 1999, at 1.

67   *See* Blank & Merrick, *supra* note 3, at p. 89.

68   *Id.*

69   *Id.*

70   *See* Mary Duenwald, *After 25 Years, New Ideas in the Prenatal Test Tube,* N.Y. TIMES, July 15, 2003, at D5; James Trefil, *Brave New World,* SMITHSONIAN, (Dec. 2001), pp. 39–45.

71   *See, e.g.,* Lisa Belkin, *Getting the Girl,* N.Y. TIMES MAG., July 25, 1999, at 26; *Choosing Baby Sex Made Easier,* BBC NEWS, July 5, 2001 (reporting on the international fertility conference then in progress); *Concern Over Baby Sex "Guarantee,"* BBC NEWS, July 5, 2001; *The PGD Baby Battle,* BBC NEWS, July 5, 2001; Susan Sachs, *Indians Abroad Get Pitch on Gender Choice,* N.Y. TIMES, Aug. 15, 2001, at A1; Gina Kolata, *Fertility Society Opposes Choosing Embryos Just for Sex Selection,* N.Y. TIMES, Feb. 16, 2002, at A13; Gina Kolata, *Fertility Ethics Authority Approves Sex Selection,* N.Y. TIMES, Sept. 28, 2001, at A14.

72   *See* Blank & Merrick, *supra* note 3, at p. 92.

73   *See e.g., IVF Advances on the Way,* BBC NEWS ONLINE, Feb. 17, 1999; *Fertility Technique "May Cause Genetic Defects,"* BBC NEWS ONLINE, March 30, 1999; Gina Kolata, *Treatments for Fertility Are Studied for Problems,* N.Y. TIMES, March 7, 2002, at A16.

74   *See e.g., Egg Breakthrough Hailed By Scientists,* BBC NEWS ONLINE, April 26, 2001; *See Eggs "Created" for Older Women,* BBC NEWS, July 2, 2001; *Egg Breakthrough Hailed by Scientists,* BBC NEWS, July 2, 2001.

75   *See also* Denise Grady, *Pregnancy Created Using Egg Nucleus of Infertile Woman,* N.Y. TIMES, Oct. 14, 2003, at A1.

76   *See First "Frozen" Twins Born,* BBC NEWS ONLINE, December 29, 2000.

77   *Id.* (According to the BBC Online, the first child conceived of a frozen egg was born in Australia in 1986.)

78   *Id.* (Some scientists note, however, that the findings of a 2001 study suggest that sperm extracted from the testes may result in fetal "abnormalities." *See, e.g., Genetic Fears Over Sperm Retrieval,* BBC NEWS ONLINE, July 3, 2001.

79   *See Human Ovaries "Grown in Mice,"* BBC NEWS, July 10, 2001.

80   *Id.*

81   *Id.* at 2.

82   *See First "Frozen Egg IVF Baby" Born in UK,* BBC NEWS, March 12, 2001.

83   *See Genetically Altered Babies Born,* BBC NEWS ONLINE, May 4, 2001, at 1; Denise Grady, *Baby Spared Mother's Fate by Genetic Tests as Embryo,* N.Y. TIMES, Feb. 27, 2002, at A16; Bruce Howell & Amy Bryant, *Cases Require Informed Consent in Genetic Studies,* NAT'L L.J., June 3, 2002, at C6.

84   *See e.g., Choosing Baby Sex Made Easier,* BBC NEWS ONLINE, July 5, 2001, at p. 1.

85   "Gamete Intrafallopian Transfer involves the use of a laparoscope to insert eggs and sperm directly into a woman's fallopian tube. Any resulting embryo floats into the uterus." *See* Banks, *supra* note 46, at p. 271 (citing Begley, *supra* note 44, at pp. 38, 41).

86   "In a two step procedure, eggs are fertilized in the laboratory (IVF) and any resulting zygotes (fertilized eggs) are transferred to a fallopian tube. Approximately 1,500 of these procedures are performed each year, with a 24 percent success rate, at a cost of $8,000 to $10,000 per attempt." *Id.* (citing *id.*)

87   "Surrogate Embryo Transplantation involves '[t]he removal by uterine lavage of the fertilized egg a few days after artificial insemination of a surrogate mother, and its transfer to the uterus of the 'wish mother.'" *Id.* at 271–72 (citing Eugene B. Brody, *Biomedical Technology and Human Rights* (1993), p. 63–96).

88   *See* Monica Shah, COMMENT, *Modern Reproductive Technologies: Legal Issues Concerning Cryopreservation and Posthumous Conception,* 17 J. LEGAL MED. 547, 549–50 (1996) (cited in Banks, *supra* note 46, at p. 271).

89   *See* Brody, *supra* note 46, at p. 92.

90   *Id.*

91   *See Eggs "Created" for Older Women,* BBC NEWS ONLINE, July 2, 2001.

92   *See* Blank & Merrick, *supra* note 3, pp. 92–93.

93   The author of this book contacted Robert Blank in 1999 to ask him about the procedure.

94   *See Eggs Fertilised [sic] Without Sperm,* BBC NEWS ONLINE, July 10, 2001.

95   *Id. See also Have Fertility Techniques Gone Too Far?,* BBC NEWS ONLINE, July 13, 2001.

96   *See* Eliza McCarthy, *Womb with a View,* ELLE, Oct. 2003, at p. 244; Denise Grady, *Saudi Surgeons Perform First Uterus Transplant,* N.Y. TIMES, March 7, 2002, at A1.

97   *See The Clone Age,* A.B.A. J., July 1997, pp. 68–73; Cynthia Gorney, *The Egg Man,* BAZAAR, Dec. 1998 263, at 264; *Experts Support Human Cloning,* BBC NEWS ONLINE, Aug. 16, 2000; *Cloned Human Planned 'By 2003,'* BBC NEWS ONLINE, Jan. 30, 2001; ABC WORLD NEWS TONIGHT, Feb. 13, 2001 (Barry Serafin reporting), transcript at 7; *Doctors Defiant on Cloning,* BBC NEWS ONLINE, March 9, 2001; *Cloning Humans: Can It Really Be Done?,* BBC NEWS ONLINE, March 9, 2001; Sheryl Gay Stolberg, *Despite Warnings 3 Vow To Go Ahead on Human Cloning,* N.Y. TIMES, Aug. 8, 2001, at A1; Gina Kolata, *24 Cow Clones, All Normal, Are Reported by Scientists,* N.Y. TIMES, Nov. 23, 2001, at A17; Sheryl Gay Stolberg, *Cloning Executive Presses Senate,* N.Y. TIMES, Dec. 5, 2001, at A22; Sheryl Gay Stolberg, *States Pursue Cloning Laws as Congress Debates,* N.Y. TIMES, May 26, 2002, at A1; Kyla Dunn, *Cloning Trevor,* ATLANTIC MONTHLY, June 2002, pp. 31–52; *Of Clones and Clowns,* ATLANTIC MONTHLY, June 2002, pp. 54–59; Nell Boyce, *A Clone at Last?,* U.S.NEWS & WORLD REPORT, April 21, 2003, p. 52; *Pandora's Baby,* SCIENTIFIC AMERICAN, June 2003, at pp. 63–67.

98   There has been some discussion in scientific circles of the possibility of an artificial womb. *See* Natalie Angier, *Baby in a Box,* N.Y. TIMES MAG., May 16, 1999, Section 6, at pp. 87–88. (According to Angier, "in the laboratory of Yosinori Kuwabara and his colleagues at Juntendou University in Tokyo, a fetal goat floats in a clear acrylic tank the size of a large toaster oven, bathed in eight quarts of artificial amniotic fluid kept at body temperature. Its umbilical cord is threaded to two machines that jointly perform the nuts and bolts of a placenta, pumping in blood oxygen and nutrients and cleaning out waste. The fetus is almost 20 weeks old, weighs about six pounds and has been living in its eerie fishbowl of a universe since it was removed from its mother by cesarean section several days earlier. The creature behaves like any other prenatal goat, blinking its soft black eyes and kicking

its slender white limbs. Should it survive for two more weeks, to the full 21-week goat term, it will be 'born': lifted out of the tank and its umbilicus cut.")

99 See Martha A. Field, *Surrogate Motherhood: The Legal and Human Issues* (Cambridge, Mass: Harvard University Press, 1988) at p. 36.

100 *Id.*

101 Roger M. Keesing, *Kin Groups and Social Structure* (New York: Holt, Rinehart and Winston, 1975) at p. 11.

102 See Sherry Amatenstein, *My Mother Gave Birth to My Babies*, MARIE CLAIRE (March 2000), at pp. 151–152.

103 Annas was quoted in Angier, *supra* note 98, at p. 88.

104 *Id.* at 88.

105 *Id.*

106 *Id.*

107 As the triplets' grandmother, she would be entitled to visit provided Karen permitted it.

108 *Johnson v. Calvert*, 5 Cal.4th 84 (1993).

109 See Banks, *supra* note 46 (citing Helene S. Shapo, *Matters of Life and Death: Inheritance Consequences of Reproductive Technologies*, 25 HOFSTRA L. REV. 1091, 1194–1208 (1997)). *See also* Michael H., 491 U.S. at 123–30.

110 See Barry R. Furrow et al., *Bioethics: Health Care Law and Ethics* (St. Paul, Minn.: West Publishing Co., 1997 (3rd ed.)) at p. 115.

111 *Id.*

112 *Id.*

113 *In the Matter of Baby M.*, 537 A.2d 1227 (N.J. 1988).

114 For fuller review of the surrogacy issue, *see* Field, *supra* note 99, at p. 1.

115 See Blank & Merrick, *supra* note 3, at p. 119.

116 *Id.* at p. 122.

117 *In the Matter of Baby M.*, 537 A.2d at 1253.

118 *Id.* at 1255.

119 In another recent surrogacy case in New Jersey, Elvira Jordan was awarded joint custody of a child she carried and gave birth to for a couple who divorced while she was pregnant. *See In re Moschetta*, No. D324349 (Orange Co. Super. Ct. Sept. 26, 1991).

120 See Blank & Merrick, *supra* note 3, at p. 71.

121 284 Cal. Rptr. 18 (1991).

122 284 Cal. Rptr. at 37.

123 *Id.*

124 The surrogacy contract "designated Timothy as the 'Natural Father' and Charlotte as the 'Adoptive Mother.' In it, Nancy agreed to be artificially inseminated with Timothy's sperm 'so that [Nancy] may bear a Child biologically related to [Timothy], to be…subsequently adopted by [Charlotte] as her child.'"

125 284 Cal. Rptr. 18 (1991).

126 The California court found the intent of the parties particularly persuasive, holding that "[t]he parties' aim was to bring Mark's [*sic*] and Crispina's child into the world, not for Mark and Crispina to donate a zygote to Anna. Crispina from the outset intended to be the child's mother. Although the gestative function Anna performed was necessary to bring about the child's birth, it is safe to say that Anna would not have been given the opportunity to gestate or deliver the child had she, prior to implantation of the zygote, manifested her own intent to be the child's mother. No reason appears why Anna's later change of heart should vitiate the determination that Crispina is the child's natural mother."

127 *In re Marriage of Moschetta*, 30 Cal. Rprt. 2d 893, 894 (1994).

128 See e.g., Daniel Rosman, *Surrogacy: An Illinois Policy Conceived*, 31 LOY. U. CHI. L.J. at 227 n. 3, (Winter 2000) (citing Steve Johnson & V. Dion Hayes, *Surrogacy Debated, But Still the Answer for Some*, CHI. TRIB. Jan. 17, 1993, (Northwest) at 1).

129 These early states were Louisiana, which introduced the bill in July 1987; Nebraska, whose lawmakers introduced a similar bill in February 1988; and, Michigan, which introduced its own bill on June 1988. *See* Field, *supra* note 99, at p. 155.

130 See Blank & Merrick, *supra* note 3, at p. 123.

131 *Id.*

132 Those states were: Arizona; Florida; Indiana; Kentucky; Louisiana; Michigan; Nebraska; New Hampshire; New York; North Dakota; Utah; Virginia; and Washington.

133 See Blank & Merrick, *supra* note 3, at p. 125.

134 States without surrogacy statutes include: Alaska; Arizona; California; Colorado; Connecticut; Delaware; Georgia; Hawaii; Idaho; Illinois; Iowa; Kansas; Maine; Maryland; Massachusetts; Minnesota; Mississippi; Missouri; Montana; New Jersey; New Mexico; North Carolina; Ohio; Oklahoma; Pennsylvania; Rhode Island; South Carolina; South Dakota; Texas; Vermont; Wisconsin; and Wyoming.

135 See Blank & Merrick, *supra* note 3, at p. 124 (citing Field, *supra* note 99, at pp. 7–8).

136 Applicable "parentage acts" include: Ala. Code Sec. 26-17-2 (1997); Ariz. Rev. Stat. Ann. Sec. 25-501 (1997); Cal. Civ. Code Sec. 7005 (West 1983) (repealed 1994) (current version at Cal. Fam. Code Sec. 7613 (West 1994)); Colo. Rev. Stat. Ann. Sec. 19-4-106 (West 1997); Fla. Stat. Sec. 742.11 (West 1997) (except in a case of gestational surrogacy); Ill. Comp. Stat. 40/2 (West 1993); Ind. Code. Ann. Sec. 39-5405 (1997); Kan. Stat. Ann. Secs. 23-128, 23-129, 38-111(4)(f) (1997); La. Civ. Code Ann. art. 188 (West 1997); Md. Code Ann., Est. & Trusts Sec. 1-206(b)(1991); Mass. Gen. Laws. Ann. ch. 46 Sec. 4B (West 1997); Mich. Comp. Laws Ann. Sec. 700.111(2) (West 1997); Minn. Stat. Ann. Sec. 257.56 (West 1998); Mo. Ann. Stat. Sec. 210.824 (West 1996 & Supp. 1998); Mont. Code Ann. Sec. 40-6-106 (1997); Nev. Rev. Stat. Ann. Sec. 126.061 (Michie 1997); N.J. Stat. Ann. Sec. 9;17-44 (West 1997); N.M. Stat. Ann. Sec. 40-11-6 (Michie 1994); N.C. Gen. Stat. Sec. 49A-1 (1997); N.D. Cent. Code Sec. 14-18-03 (1997) (to dispute paternity, the husband must deny parentage within two years of discovering the child's birth and he must prove he did not consent to the insemination); New York Domestic Relations Law Sec. 122; Ohio Rev. Code Ann. Sec. 3111.37 (West 1996); Okla. Stat. Ann. tit. 10, Secs. 554, 555 (West 1997); Or. Rev. Stat. Secs. 109.243, 109.239 (1997); Tenn. Code Ann. Sec. 68-3-306 (1996); Tex. Fam. Code Ann. Sec. 151.101 (West 1996); Wash. Rev. Code Ann. Sec. 26.26.050 (West 1997); Wis. Stat. Ann. Sec. 891.40 (West 1997). On the federal front, *see* the Uniform Status of Children of Assisted Conception Act (U.S.C.A. Act) Sec. 4(b), 9B, U.L.A. 186 (Supp. 1996).

137 *See* David T. Case & Jeffrey B. Ritter, *Disconnects Between Science and the Law*, CHEM. & ENG. NEWS, Feb. 14, 2000, at p. 49.

138 *See* Blank & Merrick, *supra* note 3, at p. 99.

139 405 U.S. 645 (1972).

140 405 U.S. at 650.

141 163 Misc. 2d 757 (Nov. 16, 1994).

142 *Id.* at 758.

143 *Id.* at 758–59.

144 196 A.D.2d 7 (2nd Div. 1994).

145 *Id.* at 9.

146 *Id.*

147 851 P.2d 776 (Cal. 1993), *cert. den.*, 114 S. Ct. 206.

148 195 A.D.2d at 12.

149 30 Cal. Rptr. 2d 893 (1994).

150 30 Cal. Rptr. 2d at 897.

151 *See* California Family Code, Sec. 7600, *et seq.*

152 The California appellate court noted in *In re Marriage of Moschetta*, in *Johnson v. Calvert*, the California court held that a surrogacy contract "is a proper basis on which to ascertain the intent of the parties because it does not offend public policy 'on its face.'" 30 Cal. Rptr. 2d at 900.

153 30 Cal. Rptr. at 896.

154 *Id.*

155 *Id.* at 897.

156 897 P.2d 1356 (Ariz. App. Div. 1 1994).

157 At the time, the statute was A.R.S. Sec. 25-218 (1991).

158 897 P.2d at 1358.

159 897 P.2d at 1361.

160 572 N.E.2d 27 (N.Y. 1991).

161 572 N.E.2d at 29.

162 For review of discussion of the issue of lesbian motherhood and the law, *see* Nancy Polikoff, *This Child Does Have Two Mothers: Redefining Parenthood to Meet the Needs of Children in Lesbian-Mother and Other Nontraditional Families*, 78 GEO. L.J. 459 (1990).

163 *See e.g.,* Roger Highfield, *First Babies Born with Dad and Two Moms*, CHI. SUN-TIMES, May 6, 2001, at 40A; See, PRIVACY, Chapter Eight.

164 611 N.E.2d 454 (Ohio App. 10 Dist. 1992).

165 Norma Stotski released the baby into the care of the Reams in exchange for $10,000 as per the oral agreement.

166 But it seems that Norma Stotski was a little confused. Under the Uniform Adoption Act (1994) Sec. 1-102, the proper procedure was a custody petition. Section 1-102 of the Act provides that "…[a] specific individual will not be entitled to adopt a minor unless the individual is favorably evaluated as suitable to adopt, obtains custody of a minor from a person authorized to place the minor for adoption, and is permitted to adopt by a court upon a finding that the adoption is in the minor's best interests. Marital status, like other general characteristics such as race, ethnicity, religion, or age, does not preclude an individual from adopting, but, if the prospective adoptive parent is married, his or her spouse has to join the petition."

167 Neither Leslie Minor, the biological father of the child, nor Joseph Stotski, Norma Stotski's husband, were part of this action.

168 611 N.E.2d at 458.

169   49 Cal. Rptr. 2d 694 (Cal. App. 4 Dist. 1996). For a popular accounting of the story, *see Who's My Mommy?*, 48 HOURS, airing on CBS on April 17, 2001 (Bill Lagattuta reporting).

170   49 Cal. Rptr. 2d at 697.

171   *See Who's My Mommy?*, 48 HOURS, *supra* note 169, at 1.

172   49 Cal. Rptr. 2d at 698.

173   The California court noted California Fam. Code, Sec. 7613, subd. (b).

174   49 Cal. Rptr.2d at 701 (citing *Johnson v. Calvert*, 5 Cal.4th 84).

175   *Id.* at 702.

176   The couple made the allegations publicly during an interview with the news magazine show 48 HOURS. *See Who's My Mommy, supra* note 171, at p. 23.

177   The couple originally making the allegations of their embryos being stolen later discovered a consent form they had signed, indicating a willingness to donate the embryos at the clinic's discretion. *Id.* at 16–17.

178   *Id.* at p. 23.

179   *See* Banks, *supra* note 46, at p. 285 (citing E. Donald Shapiro & Benedene Sonnenblick, *The Widow and the Sperm: The Law of Post-Mortem Insemination*, 1 J.L. & HEALTH 229, 276-77 (1986–87). This article discusses the 1984 French case *Paipalaix v. CECOS*, which was credited with starting much of the early debate on the efficacy of postmortem conception. (In *Paipalaix v. CECOS*, Corinne Paipalaix, a twenty-two-year-old secretary from Marseilles, France, asked that a sperm bank return sperm deposited by her husband before his death from cancer in 1983. A French court authorized the release.) *Paiapalaix* differed from *Hecht* in that the widow's deceased husband failed to leave any written acknowledgment of his desire to have his sperm used by his wife after his death.

180   *See e.g., A Birth Spurs Debate on Using Sperm After Death*, N.Y. TIMES, March 27, 1999, at A11; *Woman Impregnated After Mate Died Gives Birth*, CHI. SUN-TIMES, March 27, 1999, at 16.

181   *See* Lori B. Andrews, *The Sperminator*, N.Y. TIMES MAG., March 28, 1999, at 62.

182   Vernoff later told her story to *Marie Claire* magazine. *See* Jennifer Rosen, *My Miracle Baby*, MARIE CLAIRE, Dec. 1999, at pp. 109–110.

183   *See* Andrews, *supra* note 181, at p. 62.

184   *Id.* at 62–64. (Sperm can be collected manually, surgically, or by drug-induced convulsions. Where these methods fail or seem undesirable, there is also the electroejaculation method, which involves inserting an instrument that looks like a cattle prod into a man's rectum. Once in place, an electric shock, designed to cause involuntary ejaculation, will be administered.)

185   *See* Banks, *supra* note 46, at p. 251. *See also* Andrews, *supra* note 181, at p. 62. (Using an in vitro procedure known as GIFT—Gamete Intrafallopian Transfer—which involves the use of a laparoscope to insert frozen sperm and eggs into a woman's fallopian tubes to then be transferred by nature to the uterus, where the embryo is implanted, Judith Hart was impregnated with the sperm of her dead husband.)

186   The administration ruled that under federal and Louisiana law, Judith was not Edward's legal child. Among the reasons was that: (1) Judith did not qualify as her father's heir for intestacy purposes under Louisiana law, therefore, she could not meet the requirements of the Social Security Act, because she had not been born within thirteen months after her biological father's death; (2) Judith had been born more than 300 days after the dissolution of her parents' marriage at her father's death; and, (3) Judith was only ten days old at the time the statute of limitations expired in her case, therefore no birth certificate was available. Finally, Judith was unable to prove paternity by showing that her father acknowledged her, prior to his death, as his biological daughter either under the laws of Louisiana, or under other relevant provisions of the Act. *See* Banks, *supra* note 46, at pp. 252–253.

187   *Id.* at 261.

188   *Id.* at 256.

189   *Id.* at 256–57.

190   *Id.*

191   *Id.* at 259.

192   *Id.* at 264.

193   *Id.* at 290.

194   *Id.* (Banks notes that "[t]he comments accompanying this section indicate that its purpose is to: provide finality for the determination of parenthood of those whose genetic material is utilized in the procreation process after their death. [Section 4(b)] deal[s] with the procreation by those who are married to each other. It is designed primarily to avoid the problems of intestate succession which could arise if the posthumous use of a person's genetic material could lead to the deceased being termed a parent. Of course, those who want to explicitly provide for such children in their wills may do so."

195   Va. Code Ann. Sec. 20-158.

196   Fla. Stat. Ann. Sec. 742.17.

197   N.D. Cent. Code Sec. 14-18-04.

198   *Skinner v. Oklahoma*, 316 U.S. 535, 541 (1942).

199 *See, e.g.,* MD. HOUSE BILL 915 (2001); MINN. HOUSE BILL 631 and SENATE BILL 617 (2001); N.Y. SEN-ATE BILL 669 (2001); TEXAS HOUSE BILL 920 (2001).

200 *See* Elizabeth Amon, *Kids of Long-Dead Dad Are Ruled His Heirs,* NAT'L L.J., Jan. 14, 2002, at A4 (citing *Woodward v. Commissioner of Social Security,* No. SJC-08490); Nell Bernstein, *The Incredible Choice I Made,* MARIE CLAIRE, Sept. 2002, pp. 170–176.

201 *See* Gina Kolata, *$50,000 Offered to Tall, Smart Egg Donor,* N.Y. TIMES, March 3, 1999, at A10.

202 *Id.*

203 *Id.*

204 *See* Rebecca Mead, ANNALS OF REPRODUCTION, *Eggs for Sale,* THE NEW YORKER, August 9, 1999, at pp. 56–65.

205 *Id.*

206 *See When Will You Be Able to Freeze Your Eggs?* MARIE CLAIRE, May 1999, at 84; *I've Frozen My Eggs Until I Meet Mr. Right,* MARIE CLAIRE, May 1999, at pp. 83, 85.

207 *See* Gorney, *supra* note 97, at p. 268.

208 *Id.*

209 *See* 60 MINUTES, October 22, 2000 (reporter, Morley Safer) (transcript at 1).

210 *Id.*

211 Indeed, according to Associate Professor of Law, Judith D. Fischer, "[i]n vitro fertilization (IVF) allows couples who have been unable to achieve coital pregnancy the opportunity to experience parenting of their own biological children. It is an expensive, arduous, and risky business. A single IVF costs approximately $7,500;" with "[t]he average cost for a successful delivery ranges from $114,286 to $800,000, depending on individual complications." *See* Fischer, *Misappropriation of Human Eggs and Embryos and the Tort of Conversion: A Relational View,* 32 LOY. L.A. L. REV. 381–431, at p. 387, (Jan. 1999) (citing Jean Voutsinas, *In Vitro Fertilization,* 12 PROB. L.J. 47, 49 (1994); Keith Alan Byers, *Infertility and In Vitro Fertilization,* 18 J. LEGAL MED. 265, 285 (1997)).

212 *See* Iver Peterson, *Fate of 7 Human Embryo Argued at High Court in Trenton,* N.Y. TIMES, Feb. 27, 2001, at A22. *See also J.B. v. M.B.,* 331 N.J. Super. 223 (2000); *Ex-Wife Wins End to Frozen Embryo,* NAT'L L.J., June 19, 2000, at A6; *People Or Property?,* CBS NEWS, Aug. 14, 2001; *Court Upholds Right to Bar Embryo Use,* N.Y. TIMES, Aug. 15, 2001, at A21.

213 *See* Carey Goldberg, *Court Says a Partner Can Veto an Embryo Implantation,* N.Y. TIMES, April 4, 2000, at A14; *See also Woman Denied Custody of 4 Frozen Embryo,* N.Y. TIMES, Feb. 11, 2000, at A20.

214 *Id.*

215 *See* Jane Peres, *Couple's Divorce Entangles Frozen Embryo,* CHI. TRIB., Aug. 7, 1999, at Front Page.

216 842 S.W.2d 588 (Tenn. 1992).

217 *Id.*

218 The content of that letter was:
I address this to my child, because although I have only two, Everett and Katy, it may be that Deborah will decide—as I hope she will—to have a child by me after my death. I've been assiduously generating frozen sperm samples for that eventuality. If she does, then this letter is for my post-humous offspring, as well, with the thought that I have loved you in my dreams, even though I never got to see you born. If you are receiving this letter, it means that I am dead—whether by my own hand or that of another makes very little difference.
The full text of the letter was quoted in Banks, supra note 46, at pp. 287–288.

219 *See Hecht v. Superior Court,* 16 Cal. App. 4th 836 (1993).

220 *Id.*

221 *See* Banks, *supra* note 46, at p. 287.

222 In reliance upon previous precedent, the court found the children's public policy argument to be without merit. And in reliance upon the Uniform Status of Children of Assisted Conception Act (U.S.C.A.C. Act) Sec. 4(b), 9B, U.L.A. 186 (Supp. 1996), and the California Probate Code, the court concluded that "it [was] unlikely that the estate would be subject to claims with respect to any such children." *See* Banks, *supra* note 46, at p. 290.

223 In a recent interview, Deborah Hecht revealed that although she tried for several years to become pregnant after the release of William Kane's sperm, the procedure ultimately failed.

224 *See* Banks, *supra* note 46, at p. 298.

225 *See* Ellen Waldman, *Fatherhood Revealed,* NAT'L L.J., Nov. 20, 2000, at A12; *Sperm Donor Must Testify,* NAT'L L.J., Sept. 4, 2000, at A5.

226 *See* Linda Villarosa, *Once-Invisible Sperm Donors Get to Meet the Family,* N.Y. TIMES, May 21, 2002, at D5.

227 179 Cal. App. 3d 386 (1986).

228 *See Jhordan C.,* 179 Cal. App. 3d at 389.

229 *Id.*

230 *See* Cal. Civ. Code Sec. 7005 (West 1983) (repealed 1994) (current version at Cal. Fam. Code Sec. 7613 (West 1994)). Applicable statutes from other states include the following: Ala. Code Sec. 26-17-2 (1997); Ariz. Rev. Stat. Ann. Sec. 25-501 (1997); Colo. Rev. Stat. Ann. Sec. 19-4-106 (West 1997); Fla. Stat. Sec. 742.11 (West 1997) (except in a case of gestational surrogacy); Ill. Comp. Stat. 40/2 (West 1993); Ind. Code. Ann. Sec. 39-5405 (1997); Kan. Stat. Ann. Secs. 23-128, 23-129, 38-

111(4)(f) (1997); La. Civ. Code Ann. art. 188 (West 1997); Md. Code Ann., Est. & Trusts Sec.1-206(b)(1991); Mass. Gen. Laws. Ann. ch. 46 Sec.4B (West 1997); Mich. Comp. Laws Ann. Sec. 700.111(2) (West 1997); Minn. Stat. Ann. Sec. 257.56 (West 1998); Mo. Ann. Stat. Sec. 210.824 (West 1996 & Supp. 1998); Mont. Code Ann. Sec. 40-6-106 (1997); Nev. Rev. Stat. Ann. Sec.126.061 (Michie 1997); N.J. Stat. Ann. Sec. 9;17-44 (West 1997); N.M. Stat. Ann. Sec.40-11-6 (Michie 1994); N.C. Gen. Stat. Sec.49 A-1 (1997); N.D. Cent. Code Sec. 14-18-03 (1997) (to dispute paternity, the husband must deny parentage within two years of discovering the child's birth and he must prove he did not consent to the insemination); Ohio Rev. Code Ann. Sec. 3111.37 (West 1996); Okla. Stat. Ann. tit. 10, Secs. 554, 555 (West 1997); Or. Rev. Stat. Secs. 109.243, 109.239 (1997); Tenn. Code Ann. Sec. 68-3-306 (1996); Tex. Fam. Code Ann. Sec.151.101 (West 1996); Wash. Rev. Code Ann. Sec. 26.26.050 (West 1997); Wis. Stat. Ann. Sec. 891.40 (West 1997).

231 See California Civil Code Sec. 7005.

232 179 Cal. App. 3d at 390.

233 For review of other cases in this area, see e.g., C.O. v. W.S., 639 N.E.2d 523 (Ohio Common Pleas); In re R.C., 775 P.2d 27 (Colo. 1989); McIntyre v. Crouch, 780 P.2d 239 (Or. App. 1989); and, In the Matter of Thomas S. and Robin Y., 618 N.Y.S.2d 356 (A.D. 1994)).

234 988 S.W.2d 473 (Tex. App. 1999).

235 See Nathan Koppel, A Tangled Web We Weave When In Vitro We Conceive, NAT'L L.J., March 15, 1999, at A9.

236 Tex. Fam. Code Ann. Sec. 151.101 (West 1996).

237 See e.g., Cal. Civ. Code Sec. 7005 (West 1983) (repealed 1994) (current version at Cal. Fam. Code Sec. 7613 (West 1994)). For applicable statutes from other states, see supra note 230.

238 See Koppel, supra note 235.

239 See He's No "Sperm Donor," He's a Father, NAT'L L.J. Feb. 18, 2002, at A4.

240 See Elissa Gootman, Separated at Birth in Mexico, United at Campuses on Long Island, N.Y. TIMES, March 3, 2003, at A25.

241 See Jim Yardley, After Embryo Mix-Up, Couple Say They Will Give Up One Baby, N.Y. TIMES, March 30, 1999, at A23.

242 See Perry-Rodgers v. Fasano, 276 A.D.2d 67 (2000).

243 See Jim Yardley, Investigators Say Embryologist Knew He Erred in Egg Mix Up, N.Y. TIMES, April 17, 1999, at A13.

244 See Perry-Rodger, supra note 242.

245 Id. at 249.

246 See Judith Fischer, Misappropriation of Human Eggs and Embryos and the Tort of Conversion: A Relational View, 32 LOY. L.A. L. REV. 381 at 395 (1999).

247 See Mike McKee, Fertile Law From Fertility Clinic Error, NAT'L L.J., June 23–June 30, 2003, at p. 4 (citing Robert B. v. Susan B., 109 Cal. App. 4th 1109 (2003).

248 Id. See also Gina Kolata, When a Cell Does an Embryo's Work, a Debate is Born, N.Y. TIMES, Feb. 9, 1999; Gina Kolata, Researchers Say Embryos in Labs Aren't Available, N.Y. TIMES, Aug. 26, 2001, at A1.

249 See York v. Jones, 717 F. Supp. 421 (E.D. Va. 1989).

250 Specifically, the agreement provided that in the event that the couple got a divorce, ownership of the pre-zygotes would be determined by a property settlement. See 717 F. Supp. at 426.

251 See Clinic Plans to Destroy Unclaimed Embryos, N.Y. TIMES, July 13, 1999, at D10.

252 Id.

253 Id.

254 See MARYLAND HOUSE BILL 723 (2001); NEW YORK SENATE BILL 671 (2001); NEW JERSEY ASSEMBLY BILLS 1116 and 2151 (2000).

255 1978 U.S. Dist. LEXIS 14450 (S.D.N.Y. Nov. 14, 1978), reprinted in Michael H. Shapiro & Roy G. Spece Jr., CASES, MATERIALS, AND PROBLEMS ON BIOETHICS AND LAW, 522, 523 (1981).

256 See Teri Sforza, Who Rules How Babies are Made?, ORANGE COUNTY REG., May 28, 1995, at A1; see also Diane M. Gianelli, Fraud Scandal Closes California Fertility Clinic, AM. MED. NEWS, June 19, 1995, at 1.

257 See Sforza, supra note 256, at A1.

258 See St. Paul Fire and Marine Ins. Co. v. Jacobson, 826 F. Supp. 155, 158 (E.D. Va. 1993).

259 Id.

260 Id.

261 The unapproved drug was HMG Massone, a fertility drug produced in Argentina, but not approved for use in the United States. Dr. Asch apparently admitted to dispensing HMG Massone to two patients, but the panel found evidence that he had given the drug to at least nine patients. See Fischer, supra note 246, at p. 398, n. 132.

262 Id. at 398.

263 See Nick Anderson & Esther Schrader, 50 Couples to get $10 Million to End UCI Fertility Clinic Suits, L.A. TIMES, July 19, 1997, at A1. See also Davan Maharaj, Fertility Doctor Charged in Egg Theft, L.A. TIMES, July 19, 1997, at A3.

264   *See* Fischer, *supra* note 246, at 398, n. 138. *See also* Lawrence Eisenberg, *What's at Stake in the Trial of Dr. Stone*, ORANGE COUNTY REG., Oct. 5, 1997, at G1.

265   *Id.* at 399 n. 141 (citing First Am. Compl. at 2, *Regents of the Univ. of Cal. v. Asch*, No. 747155 (Orange County Super. Ct., filed May 25, 1995)).

266   *See* Kim Christensen, *21 Additional Settlements in UCI Egg Cases*, ORANGE COUNTY REG., Sept. 27, 1887, at B4 available in 1997 WL 7445643 (cited in Fischer, *supra* note 246, at 399).

267   *See* Fischer, *supra* note 246, at 399 (*See* Marcida Dodson, *Fertility Patient OKs $460,000 UCI Settlement*, L.A. TIMES, Feb. 20, 1998, at B4).

268   *Id.* at 399 (citing First Am. Compl. at 74, *Dubont v. Regents of the Univ. of Cal.*, No. 755021 (Orange County Super. Ct., filed Nov. 9, 1995); *Beasley v. Regents of the Univ. of Cal.*, No. 755023 (Orange County Super. Ct., filed Oct. 31, 1995). *See also* Jack McCarthy, *Grieving over Lost Embryos*, PRESS-ENTERPRISE (Riverside, Cal.) Aug. 25, 1997 at A1 (recounting alleged shipment of three of plaintiff Kimberley Dubont's embryos to Cornell)).

269   *See* Cal. Penal Code Sec. 367(g) (West Supp. 1998).

270   Both men were indicted on federal charges of mail fraud and income tax evasion. *See Orange Country Perspective: UCI Scandal's Bottom Line*, L.A. TIMES, March 31, 1998, at B8. *See also* Anderson & Schrader, *supra* note 263, at A1.

271   *See* Fischer, *supra* note 246, at p. 401.

272   *See* John McDonald & Kim Christensen, *No Jail: Fertility Doctor Gets Home Detention, Fine*, ORANGE COUNTY REG., May 12, 1998, at B2. *See also* Michelle Nicolosi, *Indictment: Asch, Others Hid Incomes*, ORANGE COUNTY REG., June 21, 1997, at 2.

273   *See A New 'To-Do' List for Fertility Clinics*, N.Y. TIMES, July 27, 1999, at D8.

274   645 N.E.2d 601 (Ind. 1994).

275   *Id.* at 603.

276   *Id.* at 604–605.

277   667 N.E.2d 122 (Ill. App. 4 Dist. 1996).

278   *Id.* at 125.

279   *Id.* (Also persuasive to the court was that Marcia Witbeck-Wildhagen "admits she underwent the procedure relying on her doctor's written assurance [that Eric Wildhagen] would be legally responsible for her child, even though it was not his wish she have a child." There is no evidence in the record of any contact or interaction between [Eric Wildhagen] and M.W. (the baby), and [Marcia Witbeck-Wildhagen] had M.W.'s last name legally changed to her maiden name. Under the facts of this case, there is no statutory or equitable basis for concluding a father-child relationship exists between [Eric Wildhagen] and M.W.," the court held.)

280   The Illinois court cited *Roe v. Wade*, 410 U.S. 113 (1973), to support this assertion.

281   667 N.E.2d at 126.

282   *See e.g., People v. Sorensen*, 68 Cal.2d 280 (1968); *Gursky v. Gursky*, 242 N.Y.S.2d 406 (Sup. Ct. 1963); *In re Baby Doe*, 291 S.C. 389 (1987). *See also* ANNOTATION, *Legal Consequences of Human Artificial Insemination*, 25 A.L.R.3d 1103 (1969).

283   174 Ill.App.3d 595 (1988), *rev'd on other grounds*, 133 Ill.2d 437 (1990).

284   *See* 750 ILCS 40/3 (West 1994). SECTION THREE provides: "(a) If, under the supervision of a licensed physician *and with the consent of her husband*, a wife is inseminated artificially with semen donated by a man not her husband, *the husband shall be treated in law as if he were the natural father* of a child thereby conceived. *The husband's consent must be in writing executed and acknowledged by both the husband and wife. The physician who is to perform the technique shall certify their signatures and the date of the inseminations, and file the husband's consent in the medical record where it shall be kept confidential and held by the patient's physician*. However, the physician's failure to do so shall not affect the legal relationship between father and child. All papers and records pertaining to the insemination, whether part of the permanent medical record held by the physician or not, are subject to inspection only upon an order of the court for good cause shown." (*Emphasis added*.) 750 ILCS 40/3(a) (West 1994).

285   174 Ill.App.3d at 615.

286   667 N.E.2d at 125.

287   811 S.W.2d 634 (Tex. App. San Antonio 1991).

288   *Id.*

289   *Id.* at 639.

290   *See Hong Soo Shin v. Oyoung Kong*, 80 Cal. App. 4th 498 (2000).

291   *Id.*

292   *Id.*

293   105 Cal. App. 3d 640 (1980).

294   *Id.* at 644–45.

295   449 N.E.2d 713 (N.Y. 1983).

296   *Id.* at 714.

297   (For fuller discussion of *Davis v. Davis*, *see* FROZEN EMBRYOS AND THE COUPLING PROBLEM, at pp. 431–432.)

298 *See* Carey Goldberg, *Massachusetts Case Is Latest to Ask Court to Decide Fate of Frozen Embryos*, N.Y. TIMES (Nov. 5, 1999), at A19; Tim Novak, *Judge Keeps Embryos from Wife*, CHI. SUN-TIMES (Sept. 30, 1999), at Front Page.

299 449 N.E.2d at 715.

300 *Id.* at 714.

301 *Id.* at 715.

302 *Id.* at 716 (*emphasis added*).

303 687 P.2d 223 (Wash. App. 1984).

304 *Id.*

305 *Id.* at 225.

306 *Id.*

307 *Id.* at 225–26.

308 *Id.* at 228.

309 145 Cal. App. 3d 369 (1983) (*rehearing denied* Sept. 29, 1983).

310 *Id.* at 378–379.

311 "*Sued for Getting Pregnant*," LEEZA Show, March 9, 1999.

312 847 S.W.2d 45 (Ark. App. 1993).

313 In support of this note, the court cited *Faske v. Bonnano*, 137 Mich. App. 202 (1984); *Hughes v. Hutt*, 500 Pa. 209 (1983); and *Pamela P. v. Frank S.*, 59 N.Y.2d 1 (1983).

314 36 Ark. App. 116 (1991).

315 847 S.W.2d at 47–48. (This reasoning was upheld by a Pennsylvania Superior Court in *Kost v. Kost*, No. 00-1573 (2000).)

316 *See* Barbara Vobejda, *Man's Suit Claims Fraud in Pregnancy*, WASH. POST (reprinted in the CHI. SUN-TIMES, Nov. 23, 1998, at 22).

317 *Id.*

318 Although the case names the two individuals in this case fully, the editors of this book have chosen to protect what little privacy these two people—both juveniles at the time of this case—may have left by offering only their first names.

319 *State ex rel. Hermesmann v. Seyer*, 847 P.2d 1273 (Kan. 1993).

320 *Id.* at 1276.

321 *See* Kansas Statutes Ann. Sec. 38-1110 *et seq.*

322 847 P.2d at 1277.

323 *Id.* at 1278.

324 *Id.* at 1279.

325 149 Wis.2d 349 (1989).

326 *Id.* at 360.

327 148 Colo. 582 (1961).

328 To support this position, the Colorado court cited the statute section on BASTARDS, 10 C.J.S. 152 Sec. 53.

329 148 Colo. at 586.

330 193 Ill.App.3d 563 (1990).

331 *Id.* at 565.

332 387 Mass. 678 (1982).

333 *Id.* at 680.

CHAPTER ELEVEN

Sex and "Seduction" in the Time of AIDS

DATING GAMES AND STDs:
White Lies as a Cause of Action

"At lovers' perjuries they say Jove laughs," quips the heroine of Shakespeare's *Romeo and Juliet*.[1] Humor is often found in the bedroom. And yet, the "real life" search for Romeo and romance is often fraught with mistakes, dangers, disasters, and sexually transmitted diseases. According to the Centers for Disease Control, the national rates of gonorrhea, syphilis and HPV—the virus responsible for several infections, including genital warts and cervical cancer—rose in 1999, after a long period of decline.

It was an increase that spread across inner cities and the nation's "heartland."[2] Indianapolis, a city of roughly 778,000,[3] for example, had the highest rate of syphilis of any American city in 1999, a rate that was increased between 1998 and 2000 by roughly 475 percent.[4] And though the rate of syphilis infection fell during 2000, due in large part to a national prevention campaign,[5] many of the behaviors thought responsible for the rise in sexually transmitted diseases persist.

On the fringes, the sex-for-drug trade was reportedly thriving in 2000, pushing rates of infection up among heterosexual women, particularly in the American South. In addition, the reemergence of high-risk sex practices has contributed as well. Though women in the mainstream generally live safer lives than most call girls or women on the stroll, many—especially young and college-aged women—remain at risk, due in large part to the sexual choices they appear to be making.

Marriage and procreation are not necessarily part of the social equation that involves "making love" or having sex today, a fact well known and apparently well understood by women on many of the nation's college campuses, according to the authors of *Hooking Up, Hanging Out, and Hoping for Mr. Right—College Women on Dating and Mating Today*, a 74-page survey and report published by the Independent Women's Forum in 2001.[6] The trend has all but done away with the whole nine yards of past love affairs while at the same time opening the door to racy sexual practices and litigation.[7]

"In the past, social processes that guided young people toward marriage had a name: courtship," the survey's authors note. "Yet, just as the term courtship itself has faded away and has come to seem old-fashioned, the complex social networks that the term described appear also to have faded away, leaving scholars to wonder whether any comparable institutions have risen to replace them."[8]

This may represent the latest extension of the sexual revolution. Throughout the 1950s, the average age of marriage dropped steadily for women until it reached seventeen.[9] But by the mid-1960s, this downward slide had turned upward, moving the median age of first marriage back to about 20 for women by 1970.[10] By 2000, the age had risen to 25.[11] In terms of trends, women who marry later tend not to meet their husbands in college, as they did in the 1950s. They also tend to be more financially independent, more career-oriented and less inclined overall to give up work completely to stay at home.

Separations and divorces among their parents,[12] along with other social changes have made "…college women…less willing to rely on marriage for economic security," survey authors note. And that has "affected their attitudes about marriage and relationships in other ways."[13] For example, though Americans still apparently flirt, mingle, and date, women on college campuses today report that "dating in the traditional sense is rare on their campuses."[14]

"Hook ups" and one-night stands are part of the evening curriculum today, and although private conversations may include discussions of the flavor and color choices of condoms, it is what is often not said that has invited lawyers and sometimes the state back into the sacred precinct of the bedroom. Deliberate misrepresentation, deceit and even negligence have formed the basis of suits involving the actual or alleged exposure or contraction of sexually transmitted diseases. This is an evolving area of the law with cases ranging from the bizarre—a suit was filed in 2000 against the American Red Cross by a woman who claimed she contracted herpes from a CPR mannequin[15]—to the tragic as states have begun to reenter this intimate fray with the passage of new laws criminalizing this conduct.

LOVER'S PERJURIES:
Intimate Contagions and Their Force in the Law

All is fair in love and war.
—FRANCIS EDWARD SMEDLEY.[16]

In 1984, a California appellate court issued a decision in *Kathleen K. v. Robert B.*[17] According to the court, Robert B. represented that he was disease-free, although he allegedly knew he had herpes. Kathleen K. brought suit after she contracted genital herpes from Robert B. In papers filed in support of her claim, Kathleen K. alleged that Robert B: (1) acted negligently in failing to exercise a proper standard of care during intercourse given that he knew he was a carrier; (2) committed battery; (3) committed intentional infliction of emotional distress; and, (4) engaged in a fraud by misrepresentation arising out of his assurances to Kathleen K. that he was disease-free.

Through his attorneys, Robert B. sought to have the suit dismissed for "failure to state a legally recognized claim."[18] What that means in laymen's terms is that Robert B. argued that despite Kathleen K.'s alleged harms, she could not assert a cause of action under then-existing law. Robert B. also argued that it was not the business of the court to "supervise the promises made between two consenting adults as to the circumstances of their private sexual conduct." The trial court agreed.

But the California appellate court did not, holding instead that Kathleen K. had a legally cognizable cause of action, because her claims were not based upon Robert B.'s express promise that he was disease-free. Rather, Kathleen K.'s claim was grounded in a theory of tortuous harm made more grave by the fact that she had contracted a "serious and (thus far) incurable" disease. This distinction removed Kathleen K.'s claim from that class of antiquated claims more commonly known as "seduction actions," the court held. Seduction actions have generally fallen out of favor with the courts. North Carolina is one of the few states that still enforces "seduction" and heartbalm judgments.

"This is an action for damages based upon severe injury to appellant's body, which allegedly occurred because of respondent's misrepresentation that he was disease-free,"[19] the California appellate court explained in reversing the trial court's decision. Analysis of these sorts of cases appears to be fact-based, though some general rules have emerged, among them that where there is real harm, the courts may find in favor of the plaintiff. But where, by contrast, there is only a fear of harm, the courts have been less inclined to find damages.

In the 1993, Idaho case of *Neal v. Neal,*[20] for example, a soon-to-be ex-wife filed a counterclaim to her husband's petition for divorce, seeking damages for "adultery, extreme cruelty, and willful desertion." In reviewing a lower court's decision, the Idaho Court of Appeals initially held that Mary Neal's claim essentially involved a claim of tortious interference with the marital relationship, which was the legal equivalent of the abolished claim of criminal conversation.

But the Idaho appellate court also held that there could be an action for emotional injuries arising out of an extramarital affair—and the corresponding fear of sexually transmitted disease—if it could be shown there was a genuine potential of harm. Courts in other states have adopted a similar standard. The Illinois Supreme Court held in the 1998 case of *Majca v. Beekil*, for example, that a tort cause of action may exist for fear of exposure to HIV or AIDS provided the fear was based upon actually being exposed to the virus or disease.[21]

Because Mary Neal could not make a similar showing of a well-grounded fear of actual exposure to sexually transmitted disease, her claim could not be sustained. Thus, Mary Neal was not entitled to damages, the Idaho court held. And yet, with the decision in *Neal v. Neal*, the Idaho court joined others in keeping the door open to the possibility of liability arising out of deliberate misrepresentations or omissions regarding sexually transmitted diseases where those misrepresentations or omissions involved actual exposure to contagious, incurable diseases.[22] And that appears to be where the law stands today, though it continues to evolve.

In the 1994, case of *Meany v. Meany*,[23] for example, the Supreme Court of Louisiana held that an ex-wife could recover damages from an ex-husband, who gave her genital herpes. According to the court's recitation of the facts, the woman's husband contracted herpes during extramarital encounters. In another case, *Loverridge v. Chartier*,[24] the Supreme Court of Wisconsin held that a claim could exist for the negligent transmission of a sexually transmitted disease. The court also held that an insurance company could be required to pay damages resultant from that transmission. But this appears to be among the newer developments, one that insurance companies have often contested.

What exactly is a man expected to know after a visit to his doctor? That was the question before the court in *Milbank Ins. Co. v. B.L.G.*[25] According to the facts set forth in the court's decision, B.L.G. went to the doctor. During that visit, the doctor reportedly noted on B.L.G.'s chart that he had "genital sores." A few months later, B.L.G. met M.M.D., and they began a sexual relationship, according to court records. At issue before the Minnesota Appellate Court was whether B.L.G. knew he had herpes and failed to tell M.M.D. of the condition. M.M.D. sought $38,000 in damages, the costs of medical treatment.

B.L.G. filed a claim for coverage of M.M.D.'s damage claim with the Milbank Insurance Company. In response to the suit, attorneys for the insurance company sought a declaratory judgment effectively asking the court to determine whether the company was obligated to pay damages arising out of M.M.D.'s suit. In challenging coverage, attorneys for Milbank argued that because the record suggested B.L.G. probably knew he was infected, it could be argued that B.L.G. intended to infect M.M.D. Thus, B.L.G.'s actions were willful. B.L.G.'s policy with Milbank covered only accidental harms.

The issue was murky enough that it would lead the Minnesota appellate court to conclude that further finding of facts was necessary in an effort to "determine the extent and certainty of B.L.G.'s knowledge and whether he expected that he would infect M.M.D. with herpes through sexual contact." The case was then set for trial to resolve the issues. Of course, herpes and other sexually transmitted diseases, even where incurable, represent one kind of threat. HIV or AIDS represents another, because in addition to being incurable, it is always fatal. Thus, where the knowing transmission of "lesser" sexually transmitted diseases has traditionally been handled in the civil context, nearly thirty states have enacted statutes criminalizing the knowing transmission of HIV or AIDS.[26]

THE AIDS ISSUE:
An Offense of a Different Color

From the pictures he seems to be tall, and that makes sense. He is handsome and looks strong. As the center of the Si Tanka Huron University basketball team, he seemed destined to be popular on a campus of fewer than 500. He was also HIV-positive. Nikko Briteramos was an 18-year-old freshman at the tiny South Dakota college when he was arrested on April 23, 2002. Briteramos was reportedly informed by the American Red Cross in March 2002, that he was HIV-positive after he attempted to donate blood.

Briteramos was the first person in South Dakota ever charged with knowingly exposing a woman to the AIDS virus.[27] He was charged with five felony counts. But about a week after his arrest, two other men were arrested and charged with similar violations of the law.[28] The men faced up to fifteen years in prison if convicted. Briteramos reportedly faced 75 years on all of the charges. He was sentenced to four months in August of 2002.[29]

Thirteen months later, Ronald Gene Hill, a former health commissioner, was arrested and charged on September 25, 2003, with the knowing exposure or transmission of HIV to a former lover in the first such prosecution in California.[30] Hill, who was appointed to the position (reportedly reserved for a person with HIV) by Mayor Willie Brown in 1997, was held on $100,000 bail.

Twenty-four states have passed laws imposing criminal penalties for the knowing transmission and exposure of HIV and AIDS.[31] Legal research suggests that while more than 800,000 people in the United States are believed to have AIDS, only 300 prosecutions for the knowing exposure of the disease have occurred across the country.[32] Hill's former lover, Thomas Lister, reportedly began dating Hill in March 2000. Lister contended in a civil suit that he and Hill discussed AIDS and HIV and that Hill represented that he was free of the disease.

The two men reportedly had tests, but Lister says he did not see Hill's results until after he fell ill while on a cruise to Alaska in July of 2000 with flu-like symptoms. It was the onset of the disease. Lister sued Hill in court and won a default judgment of $5 million. Hill never answered the suit and reportedly could not be found at the time of the ruling.[33] Though prosecutors said in April of 2002 that they did not know whether they intended to prosecute Hill, by September 2003, they had apparently changed their minds. He asserted his innocence.

AIDS—Acquired Immunodeficiency Syndrome—was first identified as a unique medical condition in June of 1981, with little more than a blurb about five suspect cases of *pneumocystis carinii* pneumonia among gay men in Los Angeles in the Centers for Disease Control's *Morbidity and Mortality Weekly Report.*[34] But within six months, "several articles followed in which physicians from Los Angeles and New York City described a series of young, gay men who were dying from 'opportunistic' infections or malignancy and in whom laboratory studies revealed a profound suppression of the immune system that was both unexpected and unexplained," noted Drs. Helena Brett-Smith and Gerald H. Friedland.[35]

Though the likelihood that a sexually transmitted infection was responsible for this initial class of victims—given an emerging pattern of the disease's occurrence among gay men involved with multiple sexual partners apparent from early epidemiological studies—the variety of illnesses suffered were so divergent that researchers began to entertain other explanations, including theories based upon perceptions of behavioral practices.[36] But all of that changed when the number of AIDS cases began to double every six months. Soon after, several other "risk" groups were identified.

"[I]n the United States and Western Europe, these included intravenous drug users and hemophiliacs, both suggesting a blood-borne route of transmission.[37] Simultaneously, numerous cases of a virtually identical disease were noted among Haitians, and soon thereafter among central Africans, where no obvious risk behavior emerged except nonmonogamous heterosexuality," Brett-Smith and Friedland write.[38]

By 1983, researchers had given a name to the virus then known to cause AIDS. Its proper reference is Human Immunodeficiency Virus (HIV).[39] Though enormous strides were made in unwinding the mystery of how the virus eludes and attacks the body's natural defenses,[40] by 1993, AIDS had evolved into a worldwide epidemic. According to estimates published by the World Health Organization for 1993, on a global level between 8 and 10 million adults and 1 million children were believed to be infected, with those numbers expected to quadruple by 2000, health authorities predicted.[41]

And those predictions were borne out. By 2001, an estimated 40 million people worldwide were believed to be infected with the AIDS virus.[42] Another 21.8 million have died of the disease, 3 million in 2000 alone,[43] and an estimated 5.5 million people were believed to be newly infected in 2001, at a rate of 15,000 a day.[44] That total was up from the 5.3 million newly infected in 2000, according to the World Health Organization.[45]

And where the spread of the virus was once thought to be limited to the gay community and the anti-social fringes, HIV is more mainstream than ever today, with its victims getting younger. Among those infected with the virus during 2000, for example, were an estimated 600,000 children under the age of 15.[46] AIDS is the fourth largest killer worldwide. And since 1999, the virus has been the number one killer worldwide of all infectious diseases, overtaking tuberculosis, diarrheal ailments, and pulmonary illnesses.[47] The virus has continued to spread as foreseen by health experts nearly a decade before.

AMERICAN WOMEN AND HIV:
Facing the Epidemic—Changing the Law

The biggest common denominator among HIV and AIDS cases worldwide, according to experts, is poverty. According to Brett-Smith and Friedland, "[a]s AIDS has become endemic in pockets of urban poverty, this inequality has come increasingly to mirror the larger socioeconomic inequalities in America."[48] Although the initial group of victims in the United States were predominantly gay men contracting the virus via homosexual contact, as far back as 1993, people of color were disproportionately represented. The reasons for this is simple: poor people more often lead high-risk, less stable, more urgent lives. Lives that may involve trading sex for food or drugs or that may not include medical coverage or a permanent address. In this regard, though the degrees may be different, impoverished Americans infected with HIV or AIDS may not be any better off than those infected in Second and Third World countries.

"For us, it's not about patents and pharmaceutical giants and money," journalist Michael Specter was told by an Indian researcher while in that nation to work on a piece about the spread of AIDS.[49] "It's about our poverty, which is profound. If I were offered drugs or food, I would take the food, because I know it will give my patients a better quality of life. I would do that even if the drugs cost nothing. You have to distribute drugs, and they need to be used by the right date. You have to take eight glasses of water with some of them. You have to store some of them in a refrigerator. Nobody has a refrigerator here. On top of all this, there will be resistance developing to the drugs. People will take them as long as they can afford them, then they will stop."

In the United States, drugs are generally available, as are the refrigerators to keep them in. And yet, the social hurdles of the less industrialized nations appear to be a factor in the lives of poor Americans infected with HIV or suffering from AIDS as well.

AIDS is the "most serious communicable disease epidemic in contemporary times," offers medical scholar Lawrence O. Gostin.[50] It is also "uniquely problematic," because the "infection cannot currently be prevented or cured; the virus changes easily; making the future development of vaccines difficult; there is no finite incubation period, so carriers of the virus are chronically infectious; and many of those at greatest risk are vulnerable to social prejudice and private discrimination because of their race, class, or sexual orientation, posing special problems for public health officials seeking to identify people carrying the virus and capable of transmitting it."[51]

Between 650,000 and 900,000 people in the United States were believed to be infected with the HIV virus in 2000, according to the Centers for Disease Control and Prevention.[52] A third of these people do not know they are infected,

CDC officials note. Roughly 400,000 Americans are believed to be newly infected each year,[53] and since its discovery two decades ago, AIDS has killed more than 438,000 people in America,[54] many of them heterosexual,[55] with some areas harder hit than others. New York, for example, is believed to have lost 75,000 people to the disease.[56]

And though researchers reported in 2000 that young gay black men in Baltimore, Dallas, Los Angeles, Miami, New York, and Seattle were being infected at a rate of nearly 15 percent a year,[57] AIDS in America is no longer a disease of gay men, prostitutes, and intravenous drug users. Rather, it is "increasingly an epidemic of the poor, which means it is increasingly an epidemic of minorities," according to health experts. African Americans now account for more than half of all new reported HIV infections, though they make up just 13 percent of the overall population.[58]

"[O]f the second 100,000 cases reported to the [CDC during the late 1980s and early 1990s], 31 percent were among African Americans and 17 percent were among Hispanics, figures representing, respectively, two and one-half and two times the expected proportions based on the population distribution of these groups in the United States," Brett-Smith and Friedland explain.[59] "Further, death rates per 100,000 population are far higher for African Americans and Hispanics (29 and 22, respectively) than for non-Hispanic whites (9)."[60]

For these reasons, "[i]t is impossible to talk about AIDS in the United States as a single epidemic," argues Dr. Helene D. Gayle, director of several AIDS programs at the Centers for Disease Control, quoted in an article on the 20th anniversary of the first reported cases.[61] "It is multiple epidemics. There is the inner-city epidemic, the rural epidemic, the epidemic among women, among intravenous drug users, among gay men, among blacks, among non-Hispanic whites, and among Hispanics."[62]

These multiple epidemics have increasingly made AIDS a heterosexual woman's disease, though many women who contract the disease may never have engaged in any of the traditionally "high-risk" behaviors believed to attribute to the spread of AIDS. CDC researchers note that the number of HIV infections among heterosexual women has risen in recent years. The most noticeable rise was among women in the rural South where the sex-for-drugs trade was thriving. But there was also a rise in the rate among heterosexual women who were not directly involved in the sex-for-drug trade and had never used intravenous drugs.

In terms of the global perspective, there are at least 16,000 new infections a day worldwide.[63] Many of these new infections occur among heterosexual women, because in some countries, AIDS is a "heterosexual disease." The initial spread of HIV in Thailand, for example, was almost exclusively heterosexual, according to researchers. South Africa showed a similar pattern. And yet, the clearest picture of what lay beneath the emerging heterosexual "woman's AIDS epidemic" can perhaps be found in India, where "[n]ew brides are usually illiterate and are exposed to AIDS by the most highly valued factor in Indian culture: monogamous marriage," Specter notes.[64]

AIDS AND HIV AROUND THE WORLD

In 1993, researchers predicted that "the developing countries of Africa, the Caribbean, Latin America, and Southeast Asia," would bear "the greatest burden of this disease."[65] Their predictions were prophetic. Africa—the continent believed by many researchers to hold clues to the origins of the virus[66]—has been hardest hit by the disease. Sixteen African nations have AIDS rates exceeding 10 percent; 119 others currently have rates of one percent or less. Six thousand Africans die of AIDS or AIDS-related illnesses every day in a epidemic so fierce that by the end of 2000, 10.4 million African children had lost one or both parents to the disease.[67]

Statistics compiled by the World Health Organization suggest that the virus has overwhelmed the continent. In 2001, Algeria showed an infection rate of one percent of the nation's population, while Libya reportedly witnessed an outbreak of the disease among drug users. Djibouti and the Sudan were also facing growing epidemics. Infection rates in Nigeria, Burkina Faso, Cameroon, Ivory Coast, and Togo have reached 5 percent, though they were previously much lower, researchers report.[68]

By 2000, Botswana was believed to have the highest rate of infection in the world, with 35.8 percent of the adult population said to be afflicted.[69] But South Africa has also been made hollow by the disease, with an estimated 4.7 of the country's 44 million people—1 in 9— believed to be infected.[70] Ignorance, poverty, misogynist traditions, fatalism, liberal ideas about sex, a lack of drugs to fight the disease, and a staggering rate of rape—among the highest in the world—have contributed to the spread HIV across South Africa.

AIDS researchers estimate that in Hlabisa, a community of about 250,000 in the hills of KwaZulu-Natal Province, South Africa, there is a 40 percent chance of contracting the HIV virus during rape with little or no possibility of receiving the preventive medicines given in Europe and the United States immediately following a rape.[71] Ten percent of Hlabisa's adults are believed to be infected with HIV.[72]

"...[S]tudies have shown that once the rate of infection among women who are tested in birth clinics rises above one percent, it becomes nearly impossible to keep an epidemic like HIV from seeping into the rest of the population," some researchers note.[73] HIV has moved into the general population of Africa with the percentages of many of the nations already at or above the one percent mark. And yet, AIDS is not just an "African disease." According to United Nations researchers, the rate of HIV infection is rising faster in Eastern Europe and Central Asia than anywhere in world.

In 2001, more than 250,000 Eastern Europeans and Central Asians—almost a third of them in Russia—were infected.[74] By contrast, the number of new HIV infections fell in Africa to 3.4 million in 2001, down from 3.8 million in 2000. By the close of 2001, the Ukraine had the highest prevalence of the disease in the region with a measure of one percent of the population. It was the first time that any European nation had reached this level, according to researchers. The Central Asian republics of Kazakhstan, Kyrgyzstan, Tajikistan, and Uzbekistan also saw rises in the level of infections.

More than 4 million people in Asia were believed to be infected with the HIV virus by 1997.[75] By 2001, 7.1 million were believed to be infected with several countries— Cambodia, Myanmar and Thailand—reporting rates exceeding one percent. These are countries with renowned sex trades. But initial infections can come in a number of ways: via transfusion; shared needles; a non-sterile medical environment[76]—to then be spread through sexual contact.

And that is part of the reason that by 2000, China—a nation not known for its sex trade, though it has one—was also suffering the ravages of AIDS. An estimated one million people are believed to be infected in China, according to the United Nations. Nine provinces in the nation were said to be on the brink of "epidemic" status, among them one province reporting a rise in the percentage of infections among sex workers that soared from zero two years ago to 10 percent in 2000.[77] Some Chinese officials have continued, however, to refute these numbers. At least in terms of their public statements.

In November 2001, Chinese Health Minister Zhang Wenkang reported that only 600,000 Chinese citizens were infected with the HIV virus. Wenkang added, however, that Chinese authorities hope to limit the number of infections to 1.5 million by 2010.[78] But that may be more than impossible. According to an internal United Nations report summarized in *The New York Times*, "China is on the verge of a[n AIDS] catastrophe that could result in unimaginable human suffering, economic loss and social devastation."[79] China's poor response is believed to be a major obstacle to slowing the spread of the disease.

And yet, the story of AIDS in China may be worse than even United Nations' researchers can gauge, given the information before them today, because there is, in fact, a new variable at issue in China. In addition to the rise of AIDS infections among sex workers, their clients, and drug abusers, China has seen a rise in the number of cases among the general population due in part to the widespread practice of blood selling, an activity that reportedly takes place in rural communities as well as in some of China's most reputable hospitals.[80]

In rural hospitals, transfusions have been used to treat anemia. In Western nations, iron supplements are used for this purpose. Among China's poor, transfusions have also been seen traditionally as a status symbol, a gift given to the wife by her husband during or after birth. What has made this gift deadly for hundreds of Chinese families, however, according to media reports, is that the blood used was at times "collected outside official channels and in violation of basic medical practice."[81] In one reported case, a pregnant woman was given four transfusions during pregnancy "all [of them] unscreened for infectious diseases and each purchased off the street from someone paid to donate."[82] The woman later died of AIDS. The daughter and husband were also infected.

The next potential explosion—one that some professionals fear may not only rival the African tragedy, but exceed it—is expected to be in India. Second in total reported cases only to South Africa, by 2001, 3.86 million people were believed to be infected with HIV in India.[83] That number already represents slightly less than one percent of the nation's population. But surveys conducted in recent years found a 2 percent rate among pregnant women in some Indian states and a 10 percent rate among patients seeking treatment for other sexually transmitted diseases.

These and other equally troubling facts have led World Health officials to predict that "[w]ith nearly one billion people, India will have more infected people than any single country, currently estimated to be 2.5 million to 3.5 million" in the near future.[84] "Even the most conservative government estimates predict that in seven years there will be at least 10 million people infected with HIV here," Subhash Hira, professor or infectious disease and the director of the AIDS unit at Sir J.J. Hospital in Bombay (Mumbai), India, said in a December 2001 article.[85] "This is a heterosexual epidemic with the potential to destroy this society and decimate our economy. And nobody seems to be terribly concerned."

More than half of the intravenous drug users in Katmandu, the capitol of the tiny Himalayan nation of Nepal, are believed to be infected with the HIV virus.[86] Nepal and Vietnam have experienced sharp rises in the number of infections in the last three years. Eighteen percent of women working in massage parlors in Jakarta, Indonesia, and 40 percent of intravenous drug users currently being treated in clinics in that country have HIV or AIDS.[87] And 63 percent of inmates imprisoned in Iran are infected with HIV.[88]

Little information has been published on the number of HIV or AIDS cases in Japan. But the Japanese government has reportedly maintained a center in Hawaii where Japanese citizens can go to be tested for HIV,[89] some 4,000 miles from the Japanese mainland. Japanese officials have long denied that AIDS is, or should be, of concern in Japan. In 1993, during the same year that Brett-Smith and Friedland were predicting the staggering spread of HIV that we know today to be the reality, Keigo Ouchi, Japan's Health Minister, announced in a speech that the "Asian nations...surround[ing] Japan are all AIDS countries."[90] The implication was clearly that Japan was not an "AIDS country." But with a growing gay scene and the continued popularity of Thailand sex tours, AIDS researchers cautioned throughout the 1990s that Japanese officials would do well to take note.

Though AIDS is often thought to spread erratically, according to Brett-Smith and Friedland, the reality of the disease is that "[c]ommunities at increased risk are defined not just by a single, clearly identifiable risk behavior—for example, men having sex with men or intravenous drug users sharing needles—but by much broader social and economic structures within which these behaviors occur, such as geography, race, social institutions (such as prostitution), and economic class."[91]

"[T]he dispersion of HIV in Africa has been traced along trucking routes; among inner-city communities of the Northeastern United States, prevalence spreads outward from New York City along highway and railroad routes and diminishes in direct proportion to distance from New York," write Brett-Smith and Friedland.[92] There are similar findings in India. "[O]ne study of seven hundred Tamil truck drivers showed that the percentage of those infected with HIV rose from 1.5 percent in 1995 to more than 6 percent just two years later," journalist Michael Specter reported for *The New Yorker.*[93] "But last year, more than 20 percent of the drivers were infected—a figure with ominous echoes of the early epidemic in Africa, where AIDS made the inevitable leap from groups like truck drivers and prostitutes into the wider population. Many experts find it hard to believe that India can avoid a similar fate."

These are scary facts, and though it would be tempting to dismiss the "rantings" of a journalist, a 1997 article in the *Journal of the American Medical Association* tells the same story. Personal accounts are also worth noting. According to a clinic director in Madras, 95 percent of the women she sees, who are HIV-positive "have a single partner, and that is their husband."[95]

American woman have more education than women in India generally, and in many cases, a greater number of sex partners. And it is this latter fact that has alarmed researchers fearing the spread to the heterosexual community since HIV first appeared in the United States. "Although HIV has always been evenly distributed between the sexes in areas of heterosexual spread such as Haiti and Africa, its rising impact on women in the United States—and its close link, for women, with heterosexual sex—warrants attention," Brett-Smith and Friedland wrote in 1993.[96]

Men in the United States have traditionally comprised the majority of people living with HIV, and that remains true today. But the rate of infection among women and children has been on the rise for a long time, reaching epidemic proportions among some populations during the 1990s. And many of these incidents—certainly on the part of adult women—are a direct result of unprotected sex. Though women accounted for just 12 percent of the second 100,000 AIDS cases reported to health authorities during the 1980s and early 1990s, 61 percent of all AIDS cases were attributed to heterosexual contact, AIDS experts note.[97]

In addition, "[a]s early as 1988, in certain geographic areas of the United States (for example, New York and New Jersey), AIDS had become the leading cause of death for African American women between the ages of 15 and 44," Brett-Smith and Friedland wrote as far back as 1993.[98] As previously noted, the years between 15 and 44 are commonly known as "the childbearing" years for women. Statistics of this sort led some researchers to predict that AIDS would eventually supplant cancer as the leading cause of death for all women in this age group.[99] Still other studies suggest that "in some areas of the Northeast the figure [for the rate of infection among women] [was] closer to 25 percent and growing."[100]

Though these are American numbers and the focus of this book is primarily American, it is worth noting that on a global level, women appear to be on the brink of an AIDS tragedy. Though women in America may have some idea about the cause and spread of HIV, thousands of women in other countries do not, even as they contract and spread the disease. Thus, the rate of incidences and morbidity statistics are as staggering—if not more so—for women around the world as they are for women in the United States; though as a wealthy nation, the opposite would likely seem to be true.

For example, with meaningful efforts at prevention stymied by poverty, politics, antiquated and misogynist cultural practices,[101] and staggering rates of illiteracy in many countries—including most of "black" Africa—women and girls are the overwhelming new victims of AIDS today, with the disease having been spread to them by husbands, boyfriends, clients, or during rapes.[102] By 2000, women accounted for 55 percent of all HIV infections in Africa, according to the World Health Organization.[103] In addition, teenage girls across the continent were suffering the infection at five times the rate of boys, an unfortunate circumstance that led some African leaders to publicly blame women for the spread of the disease.[104] In September 2001, for example, the king of the tiny AIDS-ravaged nation of Swaziland ordered women not to have sex out of wedlock for the next five years.[105] Included in this pronouncement was the mandate that young unmarried women resume the ancient practice of wearing *umcwashos*, clusters of blue and gold or black and red wool tassels meant to signal that a woman or young girl is practicing celibacy.[106] Roughly 25 percent of Swaziland's adult population—about 900,000 people—were believed to be infected with the HIV virus, according to a United Nations' report.[107] By comparison, that is about equal to the total projected number of people estimated to be infected in the United States.

Although statistics would appear to tell one story—a story relied upon by male politicians looking for a way to avoid the reality of male participation—experts note that the current explosion in the rate of infection among heterosexual women has less to do with female promiscuity than politicians assert[108] and more to do with physiology. Scientists have long argued that the vagina is more susceptible to HIV than the penis, because the lining of the vagina is susceptible to tearing.

Tears, even those occurring on the microscopic level, may open the body to infection. The trickiness of HIV, however, is that the virus eludes the body's natural defenses. Thus, the risk of contracting HIV is higher for women generally, even for those women who engage only in "straight," heterosexual, monogamous sex with their husbands. That risk is multiplied, of course, by high-risk behavior (*i.e.*, anal sex, oral sex, unprotected sex, sex with an intravenous drug user, or sex with an intravenous drug user's partners).

But the burgeoning spread of HIV in the heterosexual community is not all about the female body. Rather, it is often about the male body, male desires, and male sexual patterns. Promiscuity among men; misogynist standards that encourage multiple sex partners and the taking of multiple wives are among the other factors contributing to the spread of HIV to women in Africa and around the world.

For example, a reliable network of roadways and the sexual activity of male truck drivers has been linked to the spread of HIV in Botswana, the African nation with one of the highest rates of infection in the world.[109] Cultural factors have also played a part. In the remote villages of Tanzania, for instance, the ancient practice of polygamy, which allows husbands to have up to ten wives, in addition to numerous lovers, coupled with the scarring ritual of female circumcision (often carried out in less than sterile circumstances) have been linked to the spread of the virus among women.[110]

Fables, self-serving superstitions, and old wives' tales also play a role in many impoverished, semiliterate nations. Among the recent fictions being reported by Western magazines, for example, is the belief—said to be prevalent among some African men—that having sex with a virgin will cure AIDS. Though baseless and absurd, this confused notion has led to an increase in the number of children infected with HIV, health experts report.[111] Indeed, though it is not clear that all of these acts were attempts to "cure" AIDS, the rape of young girls in South Africa has led to an epidemic in its own right in recent years.[112]

Seventy percent of the female tuberculosis patients at Hlabisa Hospital in South Africa in 2001 were infected with HIV.[113] Hlabisa has one of the highest rates of infection in Africa.[114] But what has stunned some researchers is that similar or higher numbers have been posted in other clinics. In the impoverished black township of Khayelitsha, just outside Cape Town, 98 percent of the pregnant women arriving at public health clinics during the 1990s tested positive for HIV, according to the medical journal *Lancet*.[115]

When there is pregnancy, by definition there has been unprotected sex. And unprotected sex assists in the transmission of HIV, which compromises the immune system, opening the body to any number of opportunistic infections. Thus, pregnancy can sometimes be a significant barometer for the infection. Researchers in the United States saw a similar rise in infections among heterosexual women in America, often for similar reasons.

American women are among the most liberated and legally and politically powerful in the world. And yet, health officials report that the cascading effect of intravenous drug use coupled with unhealthy sexual practices have led to a spike in the rate of AIDS and HIV infection among heterosexual women.

"Injection drug use is the second most frequently reported risk for AIDS, accounting for 184,359 cases through December 1995," explained researcher Lawrence Gostin and colleagues in a 1997 article published in the *Journal of the American Medical Association*.[116] "In 1995, 36 percent of all AIDS cases occurred among [intravenous drug users], their heterosexual sex partners, and children whose mothers were [intravenous drug users] or sex partners of [intravenous drug users]."[117]

By contrast, only 12 percent of all reported AIDS cases were associated with intravenous drug use in 1981.[118] In recent years, however, the spread of the virus has been acute among women and their children. "Of the 71,818 AIDS cases among women reported through December 1995, nearly 65 percent were [intravenous drug users] or were sexual partners of an [intravenous drug users]," writes Gostin.[119] "Further, of the 6,256 perinatally acquired AIDS cases reported through December 1995, 60 percent had mothers who were [intravenous drug users] or had sex with an [intravenous drug user]."[120]

That may explain why researchers predict that AIDS may become the leading cause of death for African American women between the ages of 15 and 44 in the United States.[121] And yet, as set forth above, class and economic means remain the strongest determinants of how well a person who is HIV-positive will fare. People who—by virtue of their income, education, or social status— are able to lead stable lives despite HIV and AIDS generally live longer and fare better than those who cannot. Thus, most—if not all—of the various HIV epidemics cited above may arguably stem from some form of social and cultural fracture.

Though economic inequalities have always been part of the American fabric, lawmakers in several states appeared in 2001 to have come to terms with what HIV and AIDS could mean if left unchecked. In an effort to combat this threat, legislation was introduced in several states either amending existing statutes or introducing or creating new laws mandating funding, coverage, and the distribution of HIV and AIDS drugs to those without means.[122] Other states have moved to introduce or amend previously existing laws to require testing of pregnant women and newborns.[123] HIV and AIDS education and prevention was also covered by some of these new laws.[124]

By virtue of their social position, women—along with African Americans and Hispanics as demographic populations—remain poorer and less politically and socially powerful around the world. This still holds true in America, where women continue to earn roughly two-thirds of what men earn and where the lion's share of the medical research has long been—and remains—largely focused on men.

"Despite its increasing impact on women...most of the medical and social research on HIV disease in Western societies has been based on overwhelmingly male study populations," Brett-Smith and Friedland wrote.[125] Thus, "[o]ne of the most important tasks facing current HIV programs, but those providing care and those generating research information, is to reach out to women," argued Brett-Smith and Friedland.[126]

If Brett-Smith and Friedland were writing today, they would probably amend the above statements to include children. As with all others, the "women's HIV epidemic" spills over, as it has always spilled over into other realms. Most women with HIV are—and always have been—of childbearing age. Thus, as their numbers have increased, so has the number of AIDS cases among children.

By the early 1990s, when the disease was reaching peak death rate levels in the United States "HIV infection [was] among the ten leading causes of death for children between one and four years of age," explains law professor and AIDS researcher Taunya Lovell Banks in *Reproduction and Parenting*.[127] The overwhelming majority of these cases were the result of transmissions from mother to child,[128] a circumstance that still afflicts many children in poor countries around the world. But by the late 1990s, the protocol in wealthier nations—the United States among them—was to administer neviraprane or a similar drug to HIV-positive women to prevent the virus from being passed to children during the birthing process.

Other medical and pharmaceutical protocols have helped thousands of children born HIV-positive to survive into their teens. An estimated 2,400 had reached adolescence by 2000.[129] According to the Centers for Disease Control, improved antiretroviral medicines have raised the average age of survival for children born with HIV from 9 prior to 1996, first to 13 and now to about 15.[130] And there are others who have survived even longer. Some even marking the two-decades anniversary of the disease's appearance in 1981, with personal birthdays. Among the most famous of these children is Hydeia Broadbent, a noted AIDS activist with a foundation in her name, who turned seventeen in 2001.

And yet, even advances as significantly promising as these are still darkened by the grim truth of the disease: despite 15 to 19 medications proven periodically effective when combined in what medical reports have called a "cocktail," there is no cure for AIDS, and the virus has shown a tremendous ability to wait out the effectiveness of each new cocktail, exploding with the production of new mutating poisonous cells the moment a pharmaceutical-aided battle is lost, current research suggests.[131]

THE LIMITATIONS OF HAART:
Resentment and a Backlash

By 1999, researchers in the United States were again facing an AIDS epidemic as Highly Active Anti-Retroviral Therapy (HAART) drugs began to fail and the rate of death began to creep up. Adding to this fact was a protocol that is reportedly extraordinarily difficult to follow[132] and a painful series of side effects.[133] The promise of HAART was apparently over. The infection had won, and not just by defeating the efforts of the world's best scientists. Also by spreading itself farther and wider than ever before.

"New HIV infections have continued to mount," wrote medical writer Laurie Garrett in 1999. "[B]ut often in different social groups than before. While new infection rates appear to have declined among gay white men in North America, for example, they have risen steadily elsewhere. A striking illustration of the change can be seen in the Bay Area, where until the early 1990s, by far the majority of all new HIV infections occurred among gay white men living in four key neighborhoods of San Francisco. By last year, the new-infections rate among that group, and in the city overall, had fallen."[134]

Though the protocol was expected to get easier with the development of a one-a-day pill approach for some patients, poverty, ignorance, and unhealthy sexual practices continue to change the trajectory of the disease. In the fall of 2001, for example, San Francisco officials began noticing what *The New York Times* described as "an alarming increase in syphilis among gay men, citing an almost tenfold rise in the number of cases from 1998 to this year."[135]

It was an increase that reportedly led some San Francisco officials to conclude "…that gay men were more readily engaging in risky behavior than in earlier years, confident that advances in medications would ultimately protect them," the *Times* reported.[136] That charge, coupled with an unfortunately placed statement in response to a theoretical question regarding quarantine, would lead to criminal charges of stalking and harassment filed against two AIDS activists.

According to reporter Greg Winter, "[w]hile some used the statistics to preach safe sex, [the two activists accused and], other Act Up members took the figures to task, saying they had been concocted to keep federal money flowing into the city. [¶] The acrimony intensified when an interview with Dr. [Jeffrey] Klausner [of the city's Department of Public Health published] in the *Washington Monthly* discussed coercive means of preventing HIV, including quarantining infected men who repeatedly have unprotected sex, without mentioning that neither he nor the San Francisco health department advocated those methods."[137]

The article's author, Andrew Web, would later clarify the omission.[138] But with an issue so historically emotional, the comments created a new rift. Still, researchers persisted, attempting to explain there has long been a correlation between the spread of HIV and the spread of other sexually transmitted diseases. It is a connection that takes into account the kind of behavior that can lead to the infection and spread of syphilis, gonorrhea and other sexually transmitted disease.[139]

As set forth above, gay activists also objected to what they saw as "coercive" means of preventing the spread of HIV and AIDS. But as the reproductive rights debate for women shows, "coercive" means have long been the tools of politicians and lawmakers intent on curbing certain sexual practices. But the spread of HIV and AIDS does arguably involve health issues. And in an attempt to prevent the knowing spread of HIV, two dozen states have adopted laws criminalizing the knowing exposure and/or transmission of HIV and AIDS, and state prosecutors have begun in recent years to take these kinds of cases to court.

THE SPREAD OF HIV:
And the New Law

In November 2000, a Tennessee appeals court upheld a twenty-six year sentence handed down by a circuit court judge against an HIV-positive woman convicted of having unprotected sex with perhaps as many as 50 men, because she reportedly wanted to "get even" with the ex-boyfriend who infected her.[140] All of the men were his apparent surrogate.

ATTEMPTS AT A CURE AND THE HAART PROTOCOL

AIDS has ushered in an extraordinary age of scientific research, an era that has resulted in a total of roughly 30 experimental HIV vaccines since 1987.[141] But in the early 1990s, there was little reason for hope, and HIV was a death sentence after an almost certain period of prolonged misery. But in 1996, the surprising results of an experimental combination of three or more Highly Active Anti-Retroviral Therapy (or HAART) drugs caused even the most jaded researchers to begin muttering about "eradication." Indeed, so stunning were the results of these new HAART cocktails—made up of as many as 250 possible combinations—that even the announcement of these findings has become the stuff of legend.

On January 29, 1996, Emilio Emini, of Merck Research Laboratories, reported the findings of experiments on a small number of HIV patients taking then unlicensed protease-inhibitor cocktails to scientists, medical researchers, and physicians at the annual Conference on Retroviruses and Opportunistic Infections in Washington. Then, as scientific writer Laurie Garrett reports it, "[a]s Emini's slides, depicting plummeting HIV levels in the blood of patients taking the novel cocktails, flashed before the gathering, the excitement [in this hall of thousands] was unmistakable. And the audience went electric when Emini described one of [University of Alabama researcher] Michael Saag's patients who, after taking the Merck protease inhibitor *indinavir* in combination with older drugs AZT and DDI, had no detectable HIV in his blood for nearly two years."[142]

According to Garrett, these were the cocktails drunk around the world in a grand toast to what many believed might be the end of HIV and AIDS as a murderous epidemic. "In San Francisco and New York, where large numbers of doctors handle HIV patients exclusively, the medical community eagerly prescribed the new cocktails," Garrett wrote. "By the summer of 1996, word of miraculous deathbed recoveries had spread worldwide, and at the International Conference on AIDS, convened in Vancouver that August, mountains of evidence supported Emini's battle cry."[143]

With the help of HAART cocktails, AIDS was expected to become a disease of the past. The latest medical fright rendered obsolete by medical science. A marring remembrance akin to smallpox or polio. And in the protocol's heyday, HAART cocktails seemed nearly able to achieve all of that. But more than anything, HAART seemed to hold the promise of one day allowing former AIDS and HIV sufferers to live not only disease-free, but staggeringly medication-free. In other words, there was a time when researchers believed that medicine, when taken in the right combination and in the right unforgiving order, could force the virus into a near-dormant state permanently.

"Word from Vancouver was simple and upbeat," Garrett writes.[144] "New tests allowed physicians to measure, with exquisite specificity, how many HIVs were in a droplet of an individual's blood. The number of viruses, or the viral load, correlated well with the patient's prognosis; high viral loads—more than ten thousand HIVs per milliliter of blood—spelled very bad news. But numerous studies showed that the new HAART cocktails enabled the body to slaughter HIVs by the billions, bringing viral loads down to below the limits of technological detection, which at the time was about five hundred HIVs per milliliter.

"Using even more sophisticated technology, clinical researchers such as New York's Dr. David Ho, Alabama's Dr. [Michael] Saag, and Emini showed that 'zero detectable' HIVs in blood actually equaled no viruses in the bloodstream. And on the eve of the Vancouver meeting, a small group of top HIV researchers from all over the world gathered to cautiously discuss one word: *eradication*. They dared not say 'cure'—that word was far too emotionally charged. But the group thought that powerful HAART cocktails might actually eradicate all vestiges of HIV from an individual's body."

This hope—and the discussion that lay under it—was premature.

The first person ever to take a HAART cocktail—the drug indinavir coupled with older anti-AIDS drugs—was from Alabama and is said to have experienced a "miraculous recovery."[145] That was in 1993. What scientists and researchers understand today, however, given trial and error and the crushing truth that comes with failure, is that in many patients HAART cocktails deliver only a few years of "miraculous recoveries." The Alabama patient who reportedly started the whole ball rolling, for example, died in April 1998, right around the time the truth about HIV and the HAART cocktails was becoming apparent.

It is true that with the help of the HAART bullet, the rate of death among infected people began to fall. For example, according to Garrett, "in 1996, the number of people in New York City who died of AIDS fell to 5,000, down from a 1994 total of nearly 7,000. And rough data for 1998 shows about 3,500 deaths recorded. Similar trends have been seen in most major U.S. cities. And nationally, AIDS death rates between 1996 and 1997 fell a breathtaking 47 percent."[146]

Other countries were swift to adapt the HAART protocol given the clear rate of success in America. Most notably among them was Brazil, an impoverished nation with a staggering rate of infection, which, by 1997, had pledged and begun the arduous process of providing AIDS drugs to anyone who needed it, thereby providing a laudable example of how a poor nation could afford to treat HIV and AIDS; an example to India and Africa. Except that it, too, was apparently premature.[147]

For those who know the history of the emergence of HIV in America, the woman's conduct harkens back to the 1980s urban-myth of Gaetan Dugas, the Canadian flight attendant identified by the Centers for Disease Control and Prevention as part of its efforts to track the appearance of what was initially believed to be a new cancer as a primary or secondary sex partner of 40 of the first 248 people diagnosed with HIV-related AIDS in the United States.[148] According to some reports, Dugas is said to have declared in the face of challenge that it was his "right" to do what he wanted with his body. "…I've got it

[AIDS]. They can get it too."[149] Dugas is also reported to have explained that he felt his sex partners had a "duty to protect themselves."[150]

If "they"—and society—did not know what was going on in the late 1980s, as it might be argued, Americans certainly had enough information by the late 1990s to understand the dangers of HIV, which made the story of what happened in a small town in upstate New York in 1997, all the more tragic. That is when a man identified in the media as Nushawn J. Williams went to Jamestown and cut a sexual swath through the community reminiscent of Dugas'. Except that Nushawn Williams's partners were not world-weary adult males, capable of sizing up the situation and accessing the possible risk. Many of Williams's conquests were reportedly young girls "who were unhappy with their lives and curious about his urban roots."[151]

Williams apparently had several aliases,[152] among them "Face Williams" and "Face Johnson," because he was handsome. And it was a face that Williams put to good use "in neighborhood parks in both urban and rural communities, establish[ing] relationships with young women," according to Chautauqua County health officials.[153] So many relationships with so many young women, it became apparent later, that a sense of alarm would prompt health department officials to warn—in a controversial, though widely distributed *Health Alert flier* posted in December 1997—that "[a]nyone who has had unprotected sex with a man who matches this description is at risk for HIV infection" above Williams's name and picture.[154]

Dubbed a "modern-day HIV-positive Lothario" by one media outlet,[155] authorities believed that Williams may have had unprotected sex with as many as 300 unsuspecting women.[156] "Transient" by the time of his arrest in 1997, Williams was raised by a grandmother in the Crown Heights section of Brooklyn, where he reportedly ran with a gang and sold drugs. It was the sale of drugs and the desire not to be a burden to his family that led him to Jamestown in 1997, Williams told reporters in 1999.[157]

Once there, Williams reportedly "found himself unusually successful with girls."[158] Law enforcement officials suggest that Williams had sex with at least 47 young women, one who was just 13 years old, a fact that would lead to a statutory rape charge following Williams's arrest on drug charges in September 1997. In addition, Williams is believed to have had "contact" with 20 others in New York City, Rochester, and in a series of small towns in western New York, Virginia, and North Carolina. Another 50 to 75 women were believed to have been potential victims, law enforcement officials suggest.[159] But there may have been hundreds of others—if what Nushawn Williams told reporters is true.[160]

Health officials reportedly told Williams that he was HIV-positive in 1996, prior to his arrival in Jamestown.[161] By mid-1998, between thirteen and sixteen of the young women Williams had sex with were confirmed to be HIV-positive by health officials.[162] In February 1999, Williams pled guilty to reckless endangerment for having unprotected sex with a Bronx high school student,[163] a charge separate from those involving the young women in Jamestown. Williams was later sentenced to from 4 to 12 years in prison following guilty pleas to two counts of reckless endangerment involving the knowing infection of two girls with the HIV virus and the statutory rape charge.[164]

Williams's February 1999 plea, reportedly marked the first criminal conviction related to the exposure and transmission of HIV in New York City.[165] But there have been other similar prosecutions in other states. In 1991, for example, a California man was charged with assault after having unprotected sex with a woman who later gave birth to a child born HIV-positive.[166] Similar charges were filed in an Oregon case that same year.[167] And yet, since the virus's appearance and the days of Gaetan Dugas, legislators have grappled for ways to balance sexual freedom and a diversity of desires while discouraging sexually irresponsible behavior.

Given the seriousness of the problem, it is worth noting again that AIDS is the "most serious communicable disease epidemic in contemporary times," according to medical professionals. As set forth earlier, between 650,000 to 900,000 people in the United States are believed to be infected with the HIV virus, according to the CDC. But nine out of ten of these people are believed not to know they are infected. Thus, some of them will undoubtedly spread the disease to unsuspecting or unprotected partners.

Of course, the "unknowing" spread of AIDS is different from the knowing spread of AIDS. It is this latter category of individuals that has led some lawmakers to push for the adoption of criminal statutes. In the last decade, several states have enacted laws making it a felony for a person to knowingly spread the virus that causes AIDS.[168] But there have been relatively few prosecutions. In addition, these are generally new measures, sparked in large part by the fright and outrage of the alleged escapades of people like Dugas, Williams, and the women in Tennessee. Frustrating law enforcement and government officials across the United States, however, was that many states—New York among them—did not have laws expressing criminalizing the knowing transmission of HIV and AIDS.

Given that the United States Constitution does not allow a person to be convicted of an offense that does not exist at the time of the alleged incident or harm, Williams and others could not be convicted for knowingly transmitting HIV at the time of their cases. As a matter of law, there was no such offense in most states. Instead, in these early cases involving transmission by sexual means, defendants were often charged with assault,[169] battery, or in the case of Williams, reckless endangerment and statutory rape.[170] In other cases, defendants were charged with aggravated assault or even attempted murder.[171]

But after the Jamestown story broke, there was a flurry of activity on the part of lawmakers with new laws falling largely into three main categories: (1) those creating or enhancing criminal penalties for the knowing exposure of persons to the virus; (2) statutes regarding the notification of partners and "contacts;" and, (3) HIV reporting requirements. Nearly thirty states have enacted criminal penalties for the knowing exposure to HIV or AIDS,[172] and twenty-eight have reportedly adopted tracking statutes. But only a handful of states—Arkansas,

North Carolina, Oregon, and South Carolina among them—have enacted partner notification statutes.

AIDS TRANSMISSION WITHOUT SEXUAL ACTIVITY

Though the lion's share of most recent legislative attempts to curb the willful or knowing transmission of HIV and AIDS was drafted in response to a series of well-publicized and frightening events involving sexual conduct, there were earlier "AIDS transmission" cases that made their way into the public consciousness by way of a criminal procedure that did not involve sexual activity. Generally, these cases are part of a forgotten moment of emotion in American history when little was known about HIV and everything was feared. By 1991, 300 people had been charged under a variety of criminal statutes for allegedly attempting to transmit AIDS to another by scratching, spitting, or biting.[173]

Among the most serious of the charges in these cases was an allegation of attempted murder brought against an inmate in *Texas v. Weeks*,[174] for spitting at a corrections officer. The inmate, who was HIV-positive, was sentenced to 99 years in prison. The following year, an inmate in New Jersey was similarly charged with attempted murder and assault after he allegedly bit a corrections officer and shouted "now die." The inmate was sentenced to twenty years on the attempted murder charge, plus five years for aggravated assault.[175]

In *Scroggins v. State*, a charge of "assault with intent to kill" was upheld by a Georgia appellate court in a case involving the alleged biting of a police officer.[176] Similarly, in *United States v. Moore*, the Eighth Circuit Court of Appeals upheld a charge of aggravated assault, reasoning that the defendant's teeth were a deadly weapon.[177] Though 300 cases were brought in this vein—many of them in the military context—only about fifty were ultimately upheld. Of course, critics of such aggressive tactics have long argued that many of these prosecutions failed because, despite the general hysteria surrounding HIV and AIDS, clear evidence of the defendant's intent in many of these cases to do serious harm was very thin.[178] Yet many critics acknowledge that there is a difference between spitting and "sex" prosecutions and that HIV and AIDS in the sexual context is worthy of public and legal attention.

"The 'sex without notice' cases differ from the biting and spitting ones in several important aspects," argues Yale School of Law Professor Harlon Dalton.[179] "First, HIV transmission is a real possibility in the sex cases, at least to the extent that safer sex precautions are not taken. In contrast, when biting and spitting constitutes the relevant behavior, the likelihood of transmission approaches zero. However, in the sex cases the defendants rarely can be said to have acted out of malice. Their failure to inform their sexual partners of their HIV status is, in most cases, attributable to the pursuit of pleasure or, at worst, profit. Notwithstanding the awkwardness with which we as a nation approach the subject, consensual sex can be a socially, as well as personally, rewarding activity. In contrast, there is little to be said for spitting at or maliciously biting one another."

And yet, at the same time, "...there is a different 'impulse to criminalize' at work in the two sets of cases. The sex cases tap into an incredibly deep and murky reservoir of worry, fear, excitement, and dread. Quite apart from AIDS, sex (especially, but not exclusively, casual sex) embodies, for many of us, an unsettling mix of reward and risk, pleasure and danger.[180] The thought that, unbeknownst to us, a lover might be infected with HIV serves to remind us of how vulnerable we truly are, emotionally as well as physically, when it comes to sex.... Given our unease surrounding sex, together with its near universality as a human pastime (or at least aspiration), it is not surprising that we would look for ways to *compel* others to behave responsibly. We want to feel safe, to be made safe, to be protected from bad choices, to avoid having to fully reckon with the risks of carnal knowledge."[181]

It is easy to philosophize about the ultimate meaning of HIV and AIDS to American society when the issues are remote, and because AIDS was initially thought to be a "gay" disease, they were. Thus, for a decade after the first cases began to appear in 1981, HIV and AIDS generally remained "somebody else's" disease and, therefore, "somebody else's" problem. But when AIDS and HIV began to spread to the larger suburban heterosexual community, the disease became anyone's crisis and society's problem. Thus, by the late 1990s, concerns about AIDS—while they might also have involved that "murky reservoir of worry, fear, excitement, and dread"—appear to have been grounded in a genuine health crisis.

In addition, while there may still be a great deal of cultural "unease surrounding sex," the overwhelming thrust of these statutes seems to be knowledge, as opposed to sex. In other words, the language and enforcement of many of these new laws seems to involve the knowledge of the person exposing or transmitting the disease to someone who does not know of the infection. Specifically, many of these laws presume that if a person knows he or she is infected with HIV or AIDS and does not inform the partner prior to unprotected sex, the intent was to infect that person. That may seem "coercive" or invasive to some, and it is an issue that will likely remain emotional. But this appears to be where the law in that area is headed.

In January 1998, for example, an Orange County, Florida, judge ordered a 20-year-old man (convicted after admitting he had infected a 16-year-old girl with HIV) to obtain signed consent from all future sex partners on a document witnessed by a third party, then shown to the man's probation officer. The signed consent order was a condition of the man's sentence, which included two years probation plus counseling. The man's lawyer is said to have devised the document to protect his client from future partners who might consent to sex knowing he is HIV-positive only to later claim otherwise.[182]

Given the rising rate of infection in the heterosexual community and estimates of the number of people in America who may be infected with the virus but not know it, what we know today is that unprotected sex is not only foolish, it can be deadly for women. And not just casual, unprotected sex. Or "gay" sex. But also the kind of semiconscious, alcohol-or drug-induced encounters that are part of "hooking up." In addition, prolonged incubation periods of the virus and the fact that until the onset of the disease, a person may look and feel fine have made even unprotected sex within the context of a committed monogamous relationship a risk.

FRAUD OF THE SEXUAL VARIETY:
A New Tool in an Old War
or the Battle of the Sexes Comes Full Circle

"Five Scams Men Use to Get You in the Sack" was the title of a 1999 *Jane* magazine article.[183] And true to form, the article offers a glimpse of what women face when they "date" today. Among the deceptions admitted to by the men interviewed for the article was a claim of having cancer by one of the men, molding himself into "one of those unfortunate victims she's trying so hard to comfort."[184]

Another of the men boasted spending "endless amounts of time kissing" a woman's lips, neck, and shoulders to convince her that he is "romantic" and sensitive.[185] A third asks women a set of questions in an attempt to discern whether she might be interested in a threesome,[186] while a fourth presented a checklist of ways to manipulate a woman into ending a relationship when his courage fails. But it is the second to last story, offered by Mark, 29, from Atlanta, that is perhaps the most illustrative of the litigation-ready exercise that dating and modern "love" have become.

According to Mark, should a girlfriend become pregnant and he is unable to persuade her to have an abortion, he simply "become[s] her worst nightmare," (*i.e.*, Mark will: (1) tell the woman he did "massive amounts of drugs" near the time of conception to suggest an "unhealthy baby—two arms growing out of its head"; (2) threaten never to see the woman again; (3) threaten to seek sole custody of the child; (4) suggest that during visitations he and his friends "will consume loads of drugs in front of the kid;" and (5) drive "home the fact that even pedophile fathers get visits").[187]

Would it be an understatement to say that relationships have gotten complicated in the new millennium?

And yet, there have been times when attempts by young women to socialize, mingle, perhaps even flirt a little have ended worse than that. In March 2000, three men—all still in their teens—were convicted on involuntary manslaughter in the GHB-related death of a fifteen-year-old girl.[188] According to media reports, Samantha Reid was a high school freshman from suburban Detroit, who told her mother she was going to the movies. Instead, Reid went to a small party with two female friends.[189] A few hours later, Reid was dead after having been served a drink laced with *gamma hydroxybutyrate*, or GHB.[190]

There have always been urban myths about men slipping "mickeys" into women's drinks so they might have their "way." But rarely did cases of this sort make their way to court.[191] In another time, incidents of this kind were considered private, just as relationship disasters were considered "dirty laundry," never to be discussed in polite company. But during the last twenty years, Americans have begun not only to talk about dating disasters, dating deceptions, and date rape, but also to bring civil suits for alleged injuries and harms.

Adding to their efforts have been law enforcement officials who have begun to impose criminal penalties for acts that might previously have been written off as without a supporting legal cause of action. And that has made slipping women a "mickey"—or GHB—a criminal act in most states. Authorities have finally come to realize the danger involved, and there is plenty. In the last decade, the Drug Enforcement Agency reported 65 deaths attributed to GHB. More than 5,700 cases of recreational GHB-abuse were documented, among them the death of a suburban Chicago woman shown to have ingested "a GHB-type substance."[192]

And yet, the GHB craze was not all about teen experimentation. Throughout the 1990s, GHB also proved itself to be among the most popular of "date rape drugs."[193] So much so that its increasing use led one Republican lawmaker to note publicly that the drug has been "used to facilitate sexual assaults."[194] At least fifteen incidents of GHB-related sexual assault—involving 30 victims—were reported to authorities during the 1990s.[195] These assaults—and the uproar they caused—sparked passage of the Controlled Substances Act in 2000, which toughens federal penalties for possession and use of the so-called "date rape" drug.[196]

And though the GHB-related offense in the Reid case resulted in charges of manslaughter given Reid's death, in less deadly incidents, courts have begun to analyze the use of drugs and alcohol—and anything else that tends to under-mine a woman's ability to give clear and conscious consent to sexual acts—in the criminal, sexual assault, or rape contexts.[197] That is the significance of this section, which we begin with talk of contempt.

As the *Jane* stories suggest, there are some men who prove the warnings of every woman's grandmother right: they have so much contempt for women that they value women for only "one thing," and they are not above lying, cheating, or "stealing," according to some feminist scholars, to get it.

The "one thing," of course, is "the one thing." And unlike the last century, this time around we are not talking about "making babies," though "it" arguably may entail a "reproductive" act. And that is what has brought the law back into our bedrooms, where it should be, argues University of Wisconsin Law Professor Jane E. Larson in *"Women Understand So Little, They Call My Good Nature 'Deceit': A Feminist Rethinking of Seduction."*[198]

Subterfuge, deliberate misrepresentation, and "fraudulent" conduct on the part of men leads to nonconsensual sexual encounters on the part of women, a disturbing reality that has given rise to the need for a new actionable category of harms, Larson argues.[199] And it is here, incidentally, that one *Jane's* Tarzan—or Mark, from Atlanta—becomes another Jane's Neanderthal, intent on "defrauding" women of their virtue. It is time for a change, Larson argued in the 1993 law review article. A change founded in the resurrection of ancient "seduction" actions. "In the great novels of seduction," explains Larson, the fate of the ill-treated girl "(like Donna Elvira's [in the opera Don Giovanni]) is miserable and pitiable.[200] The seduced woman murders her lover and is executed.[201] She kills her baby and is exiled to a penal colony.[202] Her baby dies and she becomes a drunken and impoverished prostitute.[203] She is imprisoned as a sexual criminal.[204] She is forced to marry a much older man whom she does not love in order to hide her pregnancy.[205] She kills herself."[206]

In other words, the picture—literary or real—is almost never pretty for the ill-treated woman. "The grim destiny of seduced women in the novels is to suffer social disgrace and isolation," writes Larson further. "This, we are told, is a woman's sexual fate.[207] Equally inevitable is that the men suffer few sexual consequences. The seducer remains welcome in respectable society, his reputation and prospects intact. Sex neither determines a man's fate, nor burdens his future. At most, the woman's seducer feels regret or guilt when he learns of the misery to which his brief, thoughtless, sexual passion has brought her."[208]

And yet, to hear Larson tell it, the Sisters of Yore have nothing on the women of today, who continue to face emotional subterfuge, sexual misrepresentation, and "fraudulent" conduct diabolical enough to serve as the plot for any of the great and tragic operas. In addition, women still face stigmas, double-standards, and the brand of sexist labels. Thus, whether one calls it dating, socializing, flirting, mingling, courting, wooing, "hooking up," or any of a dozen other modern names, women attempting to do any of these things are in need of protection, Larson says. The kind of innovative protection grounded in arguments of "sexual fraud." And just what is "sexual fraud?" According to Larson, sexual fraud is "…an act of intentional, harmful misrepresentation made for the purpose of gaining another's consent to sexual relations."

According to Larson, allowing women to sue and collect damages for "sexual misrepresentations" would serve as a tremendous equalizer for women, one "address[ing] the physical and emotional injuries caused by deceptive inducement into sex."[209] But what would dating be without "deceptive inducement into sex?" Isn't deception part of the game? In many ways, that question has long been part of the problem, feminist scholars suggest. Larson's theory appears, arguably, to have been adopted by some as part of the solution.

Though once limited to a largely academic debate, civil lawsuits and criminal liability founded in complaints of "sexual fraud" have emerged as the tort for the new century. But with a twist that even Larson might not have anticipated: in recent years, women have also been hit with suits from men for alleged abortion and birth control fraud. In addition, as set forth in greater detail below, women-against-women "seduction" and "enticement" suits have spiked in the last decade, though these causes of action have been abolished in several states.

SEDUCTION AND OTHER ENTICEMENTS

When contemporary issues of seduction and "sexual fraud" are discussed, there is often a commingling and then a confusion of terms, as though separate and distinct categories of harm were one and the same. Though they share the same root, they are not the same, having evolved along different legal lines to address different harms. One category—tort actions intended to redress "interference with the continuance of the relation [of marriage], unimpaired"[210]—appears to be dying after having been abolished in all but a mere handful of states, while the other—"sexual fraud"—seems to be coming of age.

According to *Funk & Wagnalls Standard Dictionary of the English Language*, this troublesome, often emotional word has been defined to mean: To "lead astray; *entice* into wrong, disloyalty, etc.; [to] tempt."[211] A second meaning is to "induce, as a woman, to surrender chastity; debauch."[212] *Black's Law Dictionary* defines *seduction* as "the act of seducing, *i.e.,* [inducing one "to surrender chastity. To lead away or astray]. Act of man *enticing* woman to have unlawful intercourse with him by means of persuasion, solicitation, promises, bribes, or other means without employment of force."[213]

And that is why so many nineteenth century novels and so many of the great operas are filled with stories of seduction. Seduction is a plot device—or even a "character"—in these dramas. Thus, tales of seduction serve as parables of good vs. evil where virtue is pitted against temptation, before a backdrop of chastity battling sin, lust tempting divinity, and passion challenging stoicism. All of it inevitably leads to deception, betrayal, and a fall from grace so devastating that it pushes women off bridges and in front of trains.

Of course, the tragedy was meant as a lesson, a harbinger of things to come for women who trod the forbidden path. Yet, despite the warnings—historic and otherwise—"real life" has always been filled with seduction, enticement, betrayal, and falls from grace, though women seem generally less inclined today to throw themselves off bridges and in front of trains. It is perhaps because it does occur in "real life" that cases involving issues of "seduction" have always proved so desperately compelling.

Case in point: the nineteenth century "seduction scandal" involving Theodore Tilton and Henry Ward Beecher. It was a Victorian case with tabloid flare sufficient enough to match the feeding frenzies of today for fairly obvious reasons: the parties were attractive, rich, well-known, and self-righteous. Henry Ward Beecher was the son of renowned Calvinist Lyman Beecher and the brother of Harriet Beecher Stowe. Henry Ward Beecher and his accuser, Theodore Tilton, were both authors,[214] though Beecher was the more famous and richer of the two. In addition, according to magazine articles of the time, Henry Ward Beecher was the highest paid clergyman in the United States by 1874, the year he became embroiled in the "Beecher-Tilton Scandal," as the accusation and subsequent trial came to be known.[215]

Though less renowned and less wealthy, Theodore Tilton was a devotee and former friend of Beecher's, who helped edit the religious periodical, *The Independent.*[216] But in 1874, Tilton sued Beecher for "criminal conversation" and "alienation of the affections" of his wife, Elizabeth Tilton. The specifics of this allegation, according to Richard Wightman Fox, author of *Trials of Intimacy: Love and Loss in the Beecher-Tilton Scandal,* were that "Theodore Tilton said his wife Elizabeth…confessed to adultery with his former intimate friend and mentor, the Reverend Henry Ward Beecher, but both Beecher and Mrs. Tilton denied it."[217]

It is often argued that trials are supposed to clarify the facts underlying a lawsuit. But confusion over whether Henry Ward Beecher and Elizabeth Tilton really had an adulterous affair continued to mount during the six-month trial that followed,[218] writes Fox. Salting this stew of uncertainty was none other than Elizabeth Tilton, who confessed to an "adulterous" affair with Beecher only to recant before confessing again.[219] It was a strategy that could not have worked out better if Elizabeth Tilton had planned it. Thus, the question of whether an "adulterous" affair between Elizabeth Tilton and Beecher ever really took place remained unanswered, says Fox, a fact that continues to bedevil historians today.

"What became frustratingly clear during a full year of frenzied investigation and insinuation was that in the real-life drama, no one would ever find out what had really happened," Fox explains. "No one would ever know if Beecher had engaged in 'criminal conversation' with Mrs. Tilton, thereby, as Mr. Tilton charged in Brooklyn civil court, 'alienating her affections' from him."[220]

What seems well-established, by contrast, is that there was a "special attachment" between Beecher and Elizabeth Tilton,[221] an attachment that Fox describes as "passionate,"[222] involving a welcomed exchange of gifts, books, and—according to Tilton's allegations—far too many flowers for there to be anything other than a love affair.[223]

Though an ancient incident, the "Beecher-Tilton Scandal" opens the door to discussion of what "seduction," "alienation of affections," "enticement," and "criminal conversation" means from a legal perspective. The foundations of the law of modern "seduction" can be traced as far back as "the Roman law notion that some individuals may hold property interests in the bodies and sexuality of others," Larson explains.[224] Thus, actions based upon claims of seduction "exemplified the proprietary character of master-servant law, which allowed a master to sue someone who injured his servant (defined to include his child) for loss of service," says Larson.[225]

"By the mid-seventeenth century in Britain, a father's common-law right to sue his daughter's seducer—typically, when a pregnancy had resulted—was established under this 'loss of services' framework."[226] But time marches on, and by dint of evolution, seduction and similar "enticement"-related[227] claims were soon grounded in a "common-law tort actionable by a parent against an individual for violating his daughter's virginity," an historic development still noted by some courts, among them a New Jersey Superior Court in the 1999 case of *C.M. v. J.M.*[228] The civil action of seduction "…was intended to recompense an aggrieved parent for the 'consequent degradation, mortification, and wounded feelings visited upon [the daughter] as well as upon her parents stemming from the child's 'loss of chastity,'" the New Jersey Court wrote.[229]

That remains part of the law today. Seduction suits may still be brought on behalf of children.[230] But in the last two centuries, "seduction" and other "enticement"-like claims have moved beyond this once-limited application where adults are involved. Broad interpretations, an improper intermingling of terms, and a collective history steeped in moral principles may explain why "heartbalm" claims for "seduction," "enticement," and "alienation of affections," among others, have frequently been "lumped together for identical treatment" in the media as well as the courts. But the legal differences between these close, but separate and distinct causes of action are important, because the type of claim asserted and the language used may determine whether an action can be sustained in most states today.

Though often collectively labeled "seduction" actions, the civil wrongs of "alienation of affections," "breach of promise to marry," "criminal conversation," "enticement," and adult "seduction" claims[231] were covered by a web of "heartbalm" statutes that once criss-crossed the country. As an historic point of fact, New York became the first state in 1866 to recognize the tort of "alienation of affections."[232] The New York courts also defined "seduction" to involve the "allurement, enticement, or persuasion to overcome unwill-ingness or resistance."[233]

Between 1866 and the 1930s, when states began to recognize claims of this kind, every state except Louisiana adopted similar statutes.[234] The goal of these statutes, according to proponents, was to protect marriage and the family; to deter socially "undesirable" behavior; and to compensate plaintiffs for losses.[235] And though the term "breach of promise to marry" is self-explanatory, discerning practical meanings for these intimate harms is more complicated than it may initially seem, given the inclusion of words like "seduction" and "enticement" in several legal definitions. The reason for this, of course, is that "enticement," like "seduction" can be its own offense.

The legal definition of "enticement" is "[t]o wrongfully solicit, persuade, procure, allure, attract, draw by blandishment, coax, or *seduce*. To lure, induce, tempt, incite, or persuade a person to do a thing. Enticement of a child is inviting, persuading, or attempting to persuade a child to enter any vehicle, building, room, or secluded place with intent to commit an unlawful sexual act upon or with the person of said child."[236]

Though this definition may seem simple enough to define a cause of action—one gen-erally abandoned or held to be unenforceable in most jurisdictions[237] today—confusion sometimes enters the picture when the more complex and widely used terms of "alien-ation of affections," "criminal conversation," and "seduction" are introduced. Though legally individual, these terms have long been lumped together or mistakenly used inter-changeably, a fact painstakingly acknowledged, for example, by the Utah Court of Appeals in *Hodges v. Howell*.

Courts in Utah, one of the few states to still permit alienation of affections claims, define seduction as "'the offense of inducing a woman to consent to unlawful sexual inter-course, by enticements which overcome her scruples,' and as an act involving 'some undue influence, artifice, deceit, fraud, or…some promise to induce the plaintiff to sur-render her chastity and virtue."[238] The Utah Court of Appeals noted, however, in *Hodges v. Howell*, that "it is by no means certain that…alienation of affections [and] seduction [can]…be lumped together for identical treatment."[239]

At other times, these legal terms have been read morally in the public context, and that has caused confusion. For example, the Tilton-Beecher case has long been referred to as a scandal involving "seduction," perhaps because from a moral perspective the case involved discussion of whether an alleged "seducer" had wrongfully *induced* a woman to surrender her chastity. But what was truly at issue before the court were allegations of criminal conversation and alienation of affections. And not seduction in the legal sense at all.

By the 1950s, most common-law "heartbalm" claims were expressed in two causes of actions in the United States: alienation of affections and criminal conversation. These claims were traditionally filed together because the alleged activity underlying the claim was often seen as leading from one harm to the other. But as a matter of law, there are differences between "alienation of affections," "criminal conversation," and "seduction."

Though it is known as "*criminal* conversation," there is nothing "criminal" about the civil tort of criminal conversation, a fact noted by some of the nation's courts. "...[T]he name may seem misleading today," wrote the Court of Appeals of Maryland in the 1998 case of *Jane Doe v. John Doe,*[240] "[t]hough it was logical at the time of its inception. It was '[c]riminal' because it was an ecclesiastical crime; [and] 'conversation' in the sense of intercourse."

Like the civil action of seduction, there are common-law foundations to the torts of criminal conversation and alienation of affections. "Criminal conversation and alienation of affection, [like]...the tort of seduction arose in property law," Larson explains. "[I]t evolved in the nineteenth and twentieth centuries into a hybrid of family and tort law."[241] The Maryland Court of Appeals offered a simpler explanation for the claim's evolution in its March 7, 2000, decision in *Doe v. Doe.*[242] "The common-law tort of criminal conversation was the civil tort remedy available to a husband when his wife committed adultery," the court wrote.[243]

Yet, that may be where the mistaken association with issues of "criminality" enter the picture: adultery is a criminal offense often enumerated by statute and prosecuted by the state[244] whereas civil claims are generally brought by individuals. Legal and court-made definitions for "criminal conversation" vary from state to state. But "criminal conversation" has generally been defined as "a common-law reference to adultery, which was [once] seen as 'criminal conversation with a man's wife.'"[245]

By contrast, the gist of a cause of action for alienation of affections "is the protection of the love, society, companionship, and comfort that form the foundation of a marriage and give rise to the unique bonding that occurs in a successful marriage," wrote the Utah Court of Appeals in *Howell v. Hodges.*[246] "[T]o pursue a successful action for alienation of affections, the plaintiff must prove: '(a) [t]he fact of marriage, (b) that the defendant willfully and intentionally, (c) alienated the wife's affections, (d) resulting in the loss of comfort, society, and consortium of the wife, and (e) (to justify punitive damages) a charge of malice,'" the court explained.[247]

Thus, the distinction between these claims is that the courts have generally held that "[s]exual relations with the spouse is not a necessary element of the tort" of alienation of affections.[248] But sexual relations are a necessary element of a claim for "criminal conversation." Sexual relations are also imperative to a claim of seduction.[249] The reason distinctions of this sort matter is that they matter to the law as much today as they mattered in earlier times. During the Tilton-Beecher trial, for example, the inability to definitively answer the question of whether Henry Ward Beecher ever actually had an adulterous affair with Elizabeth Tilton proved the undoing of the case.

Though Henry Ward Beecher repeatedly denied a sexual relationship, Elizabeth Tilton repeatedly confessed, then recanted, an affair. To date, historians continue to disagree on this point, which may explain why the jury hearing the case never reached an unanimous verdict. In the end, three members thought Beecher had committed the acts alleged. But nine others concluded he had not. Fox's work is just one of several written about the case.[250] Given the continued interest in a 100-year-old case, it should come as no surprise that "seduction" claims and the scandals they spawn remain the fodder for gossip columnists, and even a senatorial committee or two considering impeachment. "Heart Balm" claims[251] have become a disfavored area of the law in the last three decades, though claims are reportedly on the rise in the handful of jurisdictions that still allow them.

In 1874, eight years after the enactment of the first law in the United States recognizing "alienation of affections" and the year of the Tilton-Beecher trial, "seduction" and "enticement"-type claims were plentiful and commonplace.[252] And they remained popular well into the twentieth century.

Among the reasons to use a class of laws that included "seduction" was that working-class families could face "serious financial hardship when an unmarried daughter earning wages outside the home became pregnant and lost her income," writes Larson.[253] And there were future prospects to be considered as well. "[B]ecause access to the marriage market was economically crucial for women, the daughter's loss of opportunity to marry was still of greater consequence.[254] As a result, working-class and poor families brought forth the lion's share of seduction actions.[255] Nineteenth-century seduction plaintiffs thus sought both a remedy for economic loss and a recompense for injured social status," Larson explains.[256]

Persons historically asserting claims for seduction, alienation of affections, and criminal conversation claims were husbands and fathers. The reason for this, of course, was that wives and daughters "belonged" to husbands and fathers.[257] Though repugnant and illegal now, there was a time when misogynist notions of this sort were thought to serve society by protecting women. And that is precisely why Larson believes the cause of action for seduction should be resurrected and made applicable to adults today.[258] But unlike the claims of the previous centuries, which were generally brought by men given their protectible interest in a wife or daughter's body, women should be able to use a modern adult "seduction" tort to seek redress for economic loss, loss of social status, or perhaps in response to being seduced by deception (*i.e.,* to assert the protectible interests women hold in their bodies).

Larson's is a provocative theory, one that would allow the subject in need of redress to file suit on her (or his, to avoid gender discrimination) own behalf. There is, however, a major hurdle to the broad resurrection of "seduction" torts generally, and it is this: in the last three decades, the nation's courts have moved away from the notion of spouse or relative as sexually protectible property interest, a trend that manifests itself perhaps more clearly in the systematic, state-by-state elimination of almost all "Heart Balm" torts.

But there is a new legal trend in the arena of seduction torts. It is called fraud: "love fraud," "sexual fraud," "birth control fraud," and "child support fraud" are among the various kinds of "frauds" allegedly arising out of modern relationships. Though they have long been pled separately, some might argue that "heartbalm" claims have long been the foundation of these kinds of "fraud" claims. Below is an overview of how "fraud" has become part of modern romance.

FRAUDULENT COUPLINGS:
A New Cause of Action Gaining Ground

In 1977, a man and a woman got married. In 1991, the couple began divorce proceedings. Or more precisely, the wife began divorce proceedings. The husband filed court papers alleging fraud (*i.e.,* that his wife "defrauded" him by marrying him many years ago and taking vows promising to love him, even though she did not love him and never had). The thrust of the husband's complaint was that prior to the marriage, his wife told her husband that she "loved, desired, and cared for him."[259] In reliance upon these representations, the couple was married.

Once married, the husband began signing properties over to his new wife, five properties in all, although they were originally his property and separate from the marital property, the husband would argue in his complaint. Divorce proceedings were initiated, the husband said, after his wife told him she had never loved him. That admission, the husband argued, led to his claim of fraud.

The case was immediately dismissed by the court. Or was it? Though the wife filed for divorce, a final disposition of the couple's property was stayed pending a civil trial on the issue of fraud. In the end, a jury would award the husband $242,000 in damages arising out of the wife's misrepresentations. The wife was also ordered to convey her interest in the properties back to her husband. The deed was then reformed to list the properties as solely those of the husband.

But that was on the trial court level. The California Court of Appeals reversed the trial jury's judgment, holding that although the ex-husband's complaint had been styled as "an action for fraud," it was nothing more than a claim for "breach of promise to marry."[260] As such, it was an abolished "heartbalm" tort. The court held further that breach of promise/fraud suits are "fundamentally incompatible" with California's "no fault" divorce statutes.[261]

The promulgation of no-fault divorce statutes have been viewed by some courts to foreclose "fraud" suits. But that is not to say that sexual/emotional/relationship "fraud" is not actionable. Rather, the reality appears to be quite the opposite. Courts in several jurisdictions have allowed cases involving allegations of "sexual" or "marital" fraud to go to verdict. And, indeed, throughout the last decade, plaintiffs—often women, but sometimes men—have filed "fraud" claims that have included an ever-expanding lists of "offenses," harms, and new twists.

For example, one of the most prominent—and political—cases of "marital fraud" filed in recent years was the 1999, case of Ana Margarita Martinez. It was a case of the fairy tale turned political spy-thriller. Martinez, a woman of Cuban-American heritage and a staunch anti-Communist, met Juan Pablo Roque in Bible class in 1992,[262] and he must have seemed like more than a bit of Prince Charming.

A former Cuban Air Force officer, Roque presented himself as a defector to the people he met in Miami, a man disheartened by the current crumble of Cuba. And even today, with the benefit of hindsight, it seems unlikely that he could have played the part any truer. Embraced and applauded by anti-Castro Cubans for courage and heroism, Roque wrote a book in 1995 about the reasons for his defection. Then, in 1996, he married Martinez and commenced living the life of a Cuban-American refugee and anti-Castro, pro-democracy supporter.

Except that Juan Pablo Roque had a secret.

For the nearly four years he lived in the United States as an anti-Castro activist and Martinez's husband, Roque was really a Cuban spy, sent to Miami—under cover of defection—to "infiltrate the South Florida Cuban exile community, in particular to infiltrate and discredit Brothers to the Rescue," argued Scott W. Leeds, an attorney for Martinez in March 2001.[263] Brothers to the Rescue is an affiliation of pilots who comb the waterways between Cuban and Miami in search of Cuban refugees and rafters in distress.

As thus, as George Villiers would say, "Aye, now the plot thickens upon us."[264]

Or, for her.

On February 23, 1996, Roque told Martinez he was going on a business trip.[265] The following day, two Brothers to the Rescue planes were shot down, resulting in the deaths of four people. Two days later, Roque was "seen on CNN coming off a plane in Cuba," Leeds alleged.[266] Again, Roque was hailed a hero and lauded for his bravery. This time in Cuba, and during additional television interviews, Roque denounced Brothers to the Rescue as a "terrorist organization." He also told reporters what he missed most about Miami was his Jeep Cherokee.

And what about his marriage to Ana Margarita Martinez?

It seemed all but forgotten, save an apology Martinez reportedly received a year later from Roque. And that might have been the end of it. Except that

Roque left Martinez with debts he had amassed, Martinez alleged. In addition, she found herself a pariah, regularly "ostracized by the Cuban exile community after it was revealed that she had been married to a spy for Cuba," according to statements made by Martinez's lawyers.[267] After all, how could a wife not have known?

Given these and other damages, Martinez sued the Cuban government in August 1999, under a provision of the Foreign Sovereign Immunity Act, which allows Americans to sue foreign nations for injuries foreign state actors cause on American soil.[268] Though used in just a few albeit high profile cases since its enactment, the little-known law may have gained a new measure of importance after September 11, 2001. It was under this 1996 law that the first suit of the World Trade Center terrorist tragedy was filed.[269]

The basis of Martinez's claim under the Foreign Sovereign Immunity Act, by contrast, was sexual battery.[270] Roque's lies and "fraudulent" misrepresentations foreclosed the possibility of knowing consent to the intimate acts of marriage, Martinez alleged. Martinez argued further that her marriage to Roque "was based on a lie"[271] and that she would never have "consent[ed] to…sex with the man over the 11 months of her marriage" had she known he was a Cuban spy.[272]

What all of that means, in other words, is this: Martinez argued that because there can be no consent to sex where the initial connection is born of "fraud and concealment," Roque committed sexual battery against her by taking her to bed.[273] Given this "battery," Martinez reasoned that because her husband was in the employ of the Cuban government at the time of their marriage—and deceiving her in the course of that employment—the Cuban government was liable.

It was a provocative idea. And if there is truly a cause of action to be asserted for sexual fraud by women, as Larson argues, the Martinez case probably represents its finest moment. In March 2001, a Florida Circuit Court Judge awarded Martinez $7.1 million in compensatory damages and $20 million in punitive damages, a verdict so large that it was widely reported and celebrated in the media.[274] The reality, however, is that it may have been a victory in name only. Legal experts appear to agree that Martinez may have a nearly impossible time collecting the award, though satisfaction of the claim is meant to come from Cuban assets frozen by American authorities.

Though others have made previous claims for these assets, few have been able to collect. But among the few to have been paid were relatives of the Brothers to the Rescue pilots shot down in 1996. Some political pundits suggest the Clinton administration was reluctant to release these funds to satisfy lawsuits while others suggest that the Bush administration will take a different tact.[275] For these reasons, it remains an open question as to whether Martinez will ever see a penny. But in January 2003, Ana Margarita celebrated a victory of a sort after her lawyer filed attachment papers for a plane owned by the Cuban government. The plan was to sell the plane at auction.[276]

In the framework of Larson's "sexual fraud" approach, words form the basis of their claims. But words, like the bases of DNA, are the building blocks of conversations. It is in these conversations, according to Larson, that "fraudulent" misrepresentations, false promises, and misleading enticements are made. But from a cultural perspective, it might fairly be argued that statements later alleged to be "fraudulent" or "deliberate misrepresentations" may simply have been the result of mis- or cross-cultural communication or the troubled hazards of male-female conversation. That is what linguist Dr. Deborah Tannen suggests.[277] "Boys and girls grow up in different worlds, even if they grow up in the same house," Tannen contends. "And as adults they travel in different worlds, reinforcing patterns established in childhood. These cultural differences include differing expectations about the role of talk in relationships and how it fulfills that role."[278]

Cultural differences. Differing expectations, and almost certainly divergent ideas about the "role of talk" in relationships. Is it any wonder, then, that when "boys" and "girls" talk there are misunderstandings and miscommunications as early or promising talk falls on ears tuned to the frequency of previous experience and expectation? And, indeed, this may be where the once solid ground of dialogue is spun into the quicksand of Venus-vs.-Mars communications. In other words, innocent misunderstandings clearly account for some of the dating and relationship "confusions" that have begun to reform themselves as civil—and even criminal—claims.[279]

Innocent miscommunications are different, however, from determined lies and/or deliberately deceptive acts. When "boy-girl" talk turns to lies and deliberate misrepresentations, purposely introduced with the intent of "defrauding" a "girl" of her virtue, the "boy" has entered the realm of legally actionable "sexual fraud," argues Larson.

Though some courts have been reluctant to embrace sexual-fraud based claims, others appear to have begun to take a closer look at the "knowing" or "deliberate" nature of a respondent's actions with regard to whether it might equal fraud, even fraud of the sexual variety, and whether such a claim can stand outside of the traditional "Heart Balm" context. In addition, claims of this sort have begun to appear in the arena of criminal law.

For example, true story: on March 28, 1993, a sleeping woman is awakened by a knock at the door, and she opens it, she later testifies, expecting her boyfriend, Lenny. But after turning on the lights, she realizes that the man who has entered the apartment is her boyfriend's twin brother, Lamont. After a brief conversation, the woman tells Lamont to lock the door on his way out. She then goes back to sleep.[280]

Ninety minutes later, there was another knock at the door. Again the woman thinks it must finally be her boyfriend. Again she opens the door and falls back into bed in a fog.[281] Once her boyfriend comes to bed, the woman asks why he didn't use his key. The boyfriend answers that he has either lost—or left—it at his father's house. The woman then has sex with her boyfriend only to realize— with the utterance of two mean-spirited sentences—that he is not her boyfriend. So, what was it that the stranger says? "Was that the best sex you ever had?" and, "What are you going to tell Lenny?"[282]

Unbeknownst to the woman, she had had sex with Lamont, her boyfriend's twin brother.[283] The woman, who would very soon become the plaintiff in a criminal case, immediately turned on the lights. Only then did she realize that the man in bed was Lamont. And according to court testimony, the woman threw the man's clothes out of the door and called the police.[284] Lamont Hough was later charged with sexual misconduct. He pled not guilty, however, and moved to dismiss the charges, arguing that the woman had consented to sex.[285] And it is here that discussion of the "sexual fraud" framework comes into play: though the charge against Hough was criminal in nature, the court would analyze the case via a framework of fraud.

"Assuming arguendo that the complainant's version of the facts is correct," the court wrote, "the issue presented before this Court is whether a female actually consents to sexual intercourse with a man who procures the female's consent by impersonating the female's boyfriend." [286]

"Though New York law provides that a 'lack of consent, may result from forcible compulsion or incapacity to consent,'"[287] the court noted, "…[w]here the offense charged is sexual abuse…any circumstances in addition to forcible compulsion or incapacity to consent in which the victim does not expressly or impliedly acquiesce in the actor's conduct may be considered as lack of consent."

Of course, in the case at bar, "[t]he lack of consent which forms the basis of the charge against the defendant is not claimed to have been by forcible compulsion or the complainant's incapacity to consent," the court explained. "Rather, the lack of consent results from the complainant's mistaken belief resulting from defendant's alleged fraud that the body she made love with was that of her boyfriend."[288]

But did that meet the legal definition of sexual misconduct?

Though the court seemed genuinely sympathetic to the woman's plight, it nonetheless held that given the constitutional requirements of due process[289] and the rules of statutory construction, the court could not hold Lamont Hough criminally liable for sexual misconduct unless or until the legislature changes the law to expressly include "fraud" as an element of that crime. "In general, in the absence of a statute, where a woman is capable of consenting and does consent to sexual intercourse, a man is not guilty of rape even though he obtained the consent through fraud or surprise," the court wrote.[290]

Though other courts have held similarly in recent years, it has hardly slowed the tide of "sexual fraud," intimacy-fraud-related suits, and other suits that tend towards the previously unimaginable. A decade ago, for example, even the most creative attorney would have been hard-pressed to assert a "sexual fraud," misuse of sperm, or birth control fraud claim with a straight face. But these and similar or related claims are increasingly common today, and they appear to be a part of a creative civil wave of the future, though they may not necessarily succeed in court.

ENDNOTES FOR CHAPTER ELEVEN

1   William Shakespeare, ROMEO AND JULIET, Act II, Scene II. (Historians note that the original phrase is *perjuria ridet amantum Jupiter*—"Jupiter laughs at the perjuries of lovers.")

2   *See* Lawrence K. Altman, *Rates of Gonorrhea Rise After a Long Decline*, N.Y. TIMES, Dec. 6, 2000, at A28. (According to Altman, "[a]fter falling steadily for more than 20 years, the rate of gonorrhea increased 9 percent from 1997 to 1999, officials at the [Centers for Disease Control and Prevention in Atlanta] said. The rate peaked at 467.7 cases per 100,000 people in 1975, then fell steadily in all regions by 72 percent until stabilizing at rates of 123.2 in 1996 and 122.0 in 1997. The rate is now 133.2, with a total of 360,078 cases." In addition, the CDC "also released findings from the first national survey on human papilloma virus, or HPV It is believed to be the most common sexually transmitted infection among young, sexually active people, but the agency did not specify the age range. The 30 types of the virus have been linked to several diseases like genital warts and cancer of the cervix, penis, and anus. Papilloma virus accounts for 93 percent of cervical cancer, and one type, HPV-16, accounts for half of all such cases.")

3   The United States Census Bureau estimated in 2000 that the population of Indianapolis was roughly 778,712. *See* www.census.gov for more precise numbers.

4   *See* Altman, *supra* note 2, at A28. (According to Altman, the CDC also noted that although there were no new cases of syphilis reported, it remains "a significant health threat in specific areas." Small outbreaks were reported, for example, among gay men in Los Angeles and Seattle, according to THE NEW YORK TIMES. In addition, "[h]alf the reported cases of syphilis were from 25 counties mainly in the South. In 1999, Indianapolis had the highest syphilis rate of any American city. In the last two years, the city's rate increased by nearly 475 percent, to 50 per 100,000 people in 1997.")

5   *See Drop in Syphilis Infection Rate Raises Hopes of Elimination*, N.Y. TIMES, Nov. 29, at A18 (quoting information compiled by researchers at the Centers for Disease Control). (Specifically, the article reports that, according to CDC numbers, "5,979 cases of primary and secondary syphilis, or 2.2 cases for every 100,000 people, were reported in 2000. That was a 9.6 percent drop from the previous year, when 6,650 cases of primary and secondary syphilis were reported.")

6   See *Hooking Up, Hanging Out, and Hoping for Mr. Right: College Women on Mating and Dating Today*, commissioned by the Independent Women's Forum, at p. 4. (The report is described by its authors as an 18-month study of "attitudes and values of today's college women regarding sexuality, dating, courtship, and marriage—involving in-depth interviews with a diverse group of 62 college women on 11 campuses, supplemented by 20-minute telephone interviews with a nationally representative sample of 1,000 college women.")

7   *See, e.g.*, Lynn Darling, *Sweet Chastity*, BAZAAR, August 1999, pp. 168–170; Phoebe Hoban, *Single Girls: Sex But Still No Respect*, N.Y. TIMES, Oct. 12, 2002, at A19.

8   *See Hooking Up*, *supra* note 6, at p. 4.

9   *See* Friedan, *supra* note 1, ENDNOTES FOR CHAPTER FIVE, at p.16.

10   *See Hooking Up*, *supra* note 6, at p. 7.

11   *Id.*

12   *Id.* at 6. ("Familiarity with marital breakups has also increased among relatives, friends, neighbors, and acquaintances of families that experienced divorce," explain researchers for the Independent Women's Forum. During the 1930s, for example, "[t]he proportion of college-educated women...whose parents had divorced or separated by the time the women were age 16 was only seven percent, according to the 1972–1996 General Social Surveys." By contrast, in 2000, "...25 percent of the college women responding to the national survey underlying the Independent Women's Forum's report 'parents who had divorced or separated, though that percentage was somewhat lower when they were age 16.'")

13   *Id.*

14   *Id.* at 18.

15   *See This Suit Blows*, NAT'L L.J., Dec. 18, 2000, at A6. (Though there are few specifics, according to the *National Law Journal*, "[a] woman who claimed she caught herpes from locking lips with a mannequin at CPR classes has dropped a federal lawsuit against the American Red Cross. Jerry Jarrett, an attorney representing Brenda Nelson, said his client withdrew her complaint upon consulting another doctor. 'Basically, she came to me and told me a second opinion that said she did not have herpes.' Ms. Nelson had noticed a tingling sensation in her mouth shortly after taking the CPR class.")

16   Francis Edward Smedley, a quote from FRANK FAIRLEIGH (1850), Chapter 50.

17   *Kathleen K. v. Robert B.*, 150 Cal. App. 3d 992 (1984).

18   In the realm of the law, a formal Motion to Dismiss seeks to have a claim dismissed because it "fails to state a legally cognizable claim upon which damages can be granted."

19   *Kathleen K.*, 150 Cal. App. 3d at 997.

20   *Neal v. Neal*, 873 P.2d 881 (Idaho App. 1993).

21   *See Majca v. Beekil*, 183 Ill.2d 407 (1998) (involving a claim of being exposed to HIV).

22   *See, e.g., State v. Lankford*, 29 Del. 594 (1917); *De Vall v. Strunk*, 96 S.W.2d 245 (Tex. Civ. App. 1936); *Barbara A. v. John G.*, 145 Cal. App. 3d 369 (1984).

23   *Meany v. Meany,* 639 So.2d 229 (La. 1994).

24   *Loverridge v. Chartier,* 468 N.W.2d 146 (Wis. 1991).

25   *Milbank Ins. Co. v. B.L.G.,* 484 N.W.2d 52 (Minn. App. 1992).

26   Among the states making the knowing spread of HIV a felony in the last decade are: Arkansas, California, Florida, Georgia, Idaho, Illinois, Michigan, Missouri, Nevada, New Jersey, North Dakota, Oklahoma, South Carolina, Tennessee, Texas, and Washington. In addition, states making it a felony for HIV-positive persons to engage in acts of prostitution are: Colorado, Florida, Kentucky, Oklahoma, Pennsylvania, South Carolina, and Utah. *See also* Cal. Penal Code Sec. 647f (West Supp. 1990); Ga. Code Ann. Sec. 16-5-60(c) (Harrison Supp. 1989); Nev. Rev. Stat. Ann. Sec. 201.358 (Michie Supp. 1989). *But compare* Fla. Stat. Ann. Sec. 796.08(5) (West Supp. 1990).

27   *See* John W. Fountain, *After Arrest, Campus Queues for HIV Tests,* N.Y. TIMES, May 1, 2002, at A14.

28   *See South Dakota: More Arrests for HIV Exposure,* N.Y. TIMES, May 3, 2002, at A14.

29   *See South Dakota: Jail Term for HIV Exposure,* N.Y. TIMES, Aug. 30, 2002, at A12.

30   *See* Dee McAfree, *The Debate Over HIV Exposure Laws,* NAT'L L.J., Sept. 29, 2003, at p.4.

31   *Id. See also* Lynda Richardson, *Wave of Laws Aimed at People with HIV,* N.Y. TIMES, Sept. 25, 1998, at A1. (Florida, Illinois, and New Jersey are among the states that have enacted HIV and AIDS specific laws, while New York and Texas have not.)

32   *Id.*

33   *See* Peter Page, *AIDS-Infected Man Wins $5M From Former Lover,* NAT'L L.J., April 8, 2002, at A6.

34   *See* Helena Brett-Smith M.D. & Gerald H. Friedland, *Transmission and Treatment, AIDS Law Today: A New Guide for the Public* (New Haven, Conn.: Yale University Press, 1993), at p. 18 (citing Gottlieb *et al., Pneumocystis Pneumonia—Los Angeles,* 30 MORBIDITY AND MORTALITY WEEKLY REPORT at p. 250 (1981)). Helena Brett-Smith holds a BA from Yale and an MD from Stanford. Brett-Smith completed her residency and infectious disease training at Yale–New Haven Hospital. Since 1989 and at the time of the above article she was the director of AIDS Services at the Hospital of St. Raphael in New Haven in addition to being a member of the Yale–New Haven AIDS Care Program. Gerald Friedland was a professor of medicine, epidemiology, and public health at the Yale University School of Medicine and director of the Yale AIDS Program when the above article was published.

35   *Id.* (citing *e.g., Kaposi's Sarcoma and Pneumocystis Pneumonia Among Homosexual Men—New York City and California,* 30 MORBIDITY AND MORTALITY WEEKLY REPORT at p. 305 (1981); *Follow-up on Kaposi's Sarcoma and Pneumocystis Pneumonia,* 30 MORBIDITY AND MORTALITY WEEKLY REPORT at pp. 409–10 (1981); Siegal, *et al., Severe Acquired Immunodeficiency in Male Homosexuals, Manifested by Chronic Perianal Ulcerative Herpes Simplex Lesions,* 305 NEW ENG. J. MED. at p. 1439 (1981)).

36   *Id.* (Brett-Smith and Friedland note that "[f]or a full history of the early debates about etiology, including theories about cytomegalovirus, exposure to amyl nitrate, and cumulative damage from multiple infections, *see* R. Shilts, AND THE BAND PLAYED ON (1987), at pp. 80–92; Centers for Disease Control, *Task Force on Kaposi's Sarcoma and Opportunistic Infections, Epidemiologic Aspects of the Current Outbreak of Kaposi's Sarcoma and Opportunistic Infection,* 306 NEW ENG. J. MED. at p. 248 (1982).)

37   *Id.* (citing *Update on Kaposi's Sarcoma and Opportunistic Infections in Previously Healthy Persons—United States,* 31 MORBIDITY AND MORTALITY WEEKLY REPORT at pp. 300–301 (1982); Ehrenkranz *et al., Pneumocystis Carinii Pneumonia Among Persons with Hemophilia A,* 31 MORBIDITY AND MORTALITY WEEKLY REPORT at p. 365 (1982)).

38   *Id.* (citing Hensley *et al., Opportunistic Infections and Kaposi's Sarcoma among Haitians in the United States,* 31 MORBIDITY AND MORTALITY WEEKLY REPORT at p. 353 (1982); *Clumeck et al., Acquired Immune Deficiency Syndrome in Black Africans,* 1 LANCET at p. 642 (1983)).

39   *Id.* at 21. (In light of the tremendous amount of research that went into this discovery, Brett-Smith and Friedland note that "[p]reviously used acronyms" for HIV "are HTLV-III, or human T cell leukemia virus, type 3, and LAV, or lymphodenopathy associated virus." Brett-Smith and Friedland notes further that "[t]here is also a related but distinct virus, HIV-2, that has been identified as the cause for a significant proportion of A.I.D.S cases in West Africa.")

40   As Brett-Smith and Friedland explain it, "HIV belongs to a particular family of viruses (the retroviruses) whose members share a specific mechanism of reproduction and are characterized by two distinctive features. First, the genetic information for the virus is stored in molecules or building blocks of RNA, rather than in the usual DNA of human genes. Second, the virus possesses a unique enzyme or protein not otherwise present in human cells, called 'reverse transcriptase,' that enables it to translate its RNA into an equivalent DNA sequence. These features are basic to the reproductive strength of the virus and its capacity to survive in human cells. They also represent the Achilles' heel toward which we direct our pharmacologic attack, discussed later in this chapter. [¶] The life cycle of the virus can be summarized briefly. Each viral particle is composed of the viral genome (RNA) protected by a coating of structural proteins. These proteins enable the virus to attach to a specific receptor protein (referred to as 'CD_4') on the outside of certain human cells that are crucial to the normal functioning of the human immune system. Once attached, the virus enters these cells and activates its own reverse transcriptase to copy viral RNA into its analogous DNA

sequence. The resulting fragment of DNA then inserts itself into the DNA strands of the host cell's genes, ensuring lifelong infection of that cell and its descendants. At this point, the virus may either turn off and become latent or remain active. In the first case the infected cell continues to function normally but carries the more-or-less quiescent virus. In the second, the viral genes remain turned on, taking over the normal machinery of the cell and forcing it to produce huge numbers of new viral particles. These new viruses move on to infect other tissue, and eventually the host cell dies. In certain types of body tissue, direct cell-to-cell transfer of the virus may also occur, usually resulting in larger conglomerates of infected cells." *Id.* at 21 (noting that "[f]or an excellent but medically sophisticated summary of the basic mechanisms by which HIV causes disease, *see* Fauci, *et al., Immunopathogenic Mechanisms in Human Immunodeficiency Virus (HIV) Infection,* 114 ANNALS INTERNAL MED. at p. 678 (1991)").

41   See Brett-Smith & Friedland, *supra* note 34, at p. 19.
42   *See* Denise Grady, *Scientists Shifting Strategies In Quest for an AIDS Vaccine,* N.Y. TIMES, June 5, 2001, at D1.
43   *Id.*
44   *Id.*
45   *See* Elizabeth Olson, *AIDS Infections Rise Globally, But Sub-Saharan Cases Stabilize,* N.Y TIMES, Nov. 25, 2000, at A5 (citing statistics published by the World Health Organization).
46   *Id.*
47   *See* Robin McKie, *AIDS Becomes World's Leading Infectious Killer,* LONDON OBSERVER (reprinted in CHI. SUN-TIMES), May 24, 1999, at p. 46.
48   *See* Brett-Smith & Friedland, *supra* note 34, at p. 20.
49   *See* Michael Specter, ANNALS OF MEDICINE, *India's Plague,* THE NEW YORKER, Dec. 17, 2001, at pp. 74–78.
50   *See* Lawrence O. Gostin *et al., Prevention of HIV/AIDS and Other Blood-Borne Diseases Among Injection Drug Users,* 277 JAMA at p. 59 (Jan. 1997). (According to his bio, Gostin was, at the time of this publication, the executive director of the American Society of Law and Medicine; adjunct professor of health law, Harvard School of Public Health; and lecturer on law, Harvard Law School. Mr. Gostin also sits on policy steering committees for the World Health Organization (WHO), the Council for International Organizations of Medical Sciences (CIOMS), and the U.S. Centers for Disease Control (CDC). He was consulting legislative counsel for the U.S. Senate Labor and Human Relations Committee and conducted a bi-partisan briefing of U.S. senators in the Senate. Mr. Gostin is director of the AIDS Litigation Project, supported by the National AIDS Program Office, Department of Health and Human Services. He was also co-chair for the law and policy track of the Eighth International Conference on AIDS, sponsored by Harvard University and held in the Netherlands, July 1992. Mr. Gostin is editor of *AIDS in the Health Care System.*
51   *Id.*
52   *See* Sheryl Gay Stolberg, *In AIDS War, New Weapons and New Victims,* N.Y. TIMES, June 3, 2001, at A20 (citing CDC statistics and 2000 reports).
53   *Id.*
54   *See* Jennifer Steinhauer, *A New York Vastly Altered by AIDS,* N.Y. TIMES, June 4, 2001, at A1.
55   *Id.*
56   *Id.*
57   *See* Lawrence K. Altman, *Swift Rise Seen in HIV Cases for Gay Blacks,* N.Y. TIMES, June 1, 2001, at A1.
58   *See* Stolberg, *supra* note 52, at A20.
59   *Id.* at 20 (citing *The Second 100,000 Cases of Acquired Immunodeficiency Syndrome—United States, June 1981–December 1991,* 41 MORBIDITY AND MORTALITY WEEKLY REPORT at p. 28 (1992)).
60   *Id.* (citing *Mortality Attributable to HIV Infection/AIDS—United States, 1981–1990,* 40 MORBIDITY AND MORTALITY WEEKLY REPORT 41 (1991)).
61   *Id.*
62   For discussion of the "rural epidemic in Alabama," *See* Jacob Levenson, *Showdown in Choctaw County,* UTNE READER, May–June 2002, pp. 72–80.
63   *See* Specter, *supra* note 49, at p. 77.
64   *Id.*
65   *See* Brett-Smith and Friedland, *supra* note 34, at p. 19 (citing *The Second 100,000 Cases of Acquired Immunodeficiency Syndrome—United States, June 1981–December 1991,* 41 MORBIDITY AND MORTALITY WEEKLY REPORT 28 (1992)).
66   *See* Lawrence K. Altman, *Researchers Trace AIDS Virus to a Subspecies of Chimpanzee,* N.Y. TIMES, Feb. 1, 1999, at A1. (According to Altman, researchers reported during a meeting in Chicago in February 1999, that they had traced the roots of a virus related to a subspecies of chimpanzees in Africa.)
67   *See* Marina Cantacuzino, *The World's Worst Crisis,* MARIE CLAIRE, Nov. 2000, at p. 128.
68   *See* Lawrence K. Altman, *HIV "Explosion" Seen in East Europe and Central Asia,* N.Y. TIMES, Nov. 29, 2001, at A16 (citing United Nations statistics).
69   *See* C. Claire Ray, *AIDS in Africa,* N.Y. TIMES, June 5, 2001, at D2.

70 See Rachel L. Swarns, *South Africa's AIDS Vortex Engulfs a Rural Community*, N.Y. TIMES, Nov. 25, 2001, at A1.
71 See Donald G. McNeil, *South African Victims Face Rapists and HIV*, N.Y. TIMES, Nov. 30, 2001, at A1.
72 See Swarns, *supra* note 70, at A1.
73 See Specter, *supra* note 49, at pp. 74, 78.
74 Roughly 75,000 of the newly infected were in Russia. *See* Altman, *supra* note 68, at A1.
75 See Raman R. Gangakhedkar *et al.*, *Spread of HIV Infection in Married Monogamous Women in India*, 278 JAMA at p. 2090 (Dec. 17, 1997).
76 In describing visits to hospitals in India, for example, Specter writes that "[a]t several facilities that I visited, needles are routinely bleached and used more than once, medical instruments are sterilized in giant soup pots, and patients had better hope that a family member or friend will bring them food if they want to eat." *See* Specter, *supra* note 49, at p. 80.
77 See Elisabeth Rosenthal, *Poorly Prepared Asian Countries Warned of AIDS Epidemic*, N.Y. TIMES, Oct. 5, 2001, at A10.
78 See Elisabeth Rosenthal, *China Seems Uncertain About Dealing Openly with AIDS*, N.Y. TIMES, Nov. 14, 2001, at A3.
79 See Elisabeth Rosenthal, *With Ignorance as the Fuel, AIDS Speeds Across China*, N.Y. TIMES, Dec. 30, 2001, A1, A8. (Rosenthal does not say how the report was acquired, though she notes that it was not publicly released. But its findings appear to jive with a great deal of other published research.)
80 See Elisabeth Rosenthal, *Blood and Tears: A Chinese Family's Ordeal in a Nation in Denial of AIDS*, N.Y. TIMES, Sept. 16, 2001, at A25.
81 *Id.*
82 *Id.*
83 See Specter, *supra* note 49, at p. 74.
84 See Gangakhedkar *et al.*, *supra* note 75, at p. 2090.
85 See Specter, *supra* note 49, at p. 80.
86 See Rosenthal, *supra* note 77, at A10.
87 *Id.*
88 *Id.*
89 See Stan Sesser, *Hidden Death*, THE NEW YORKER, Nov. 14, 1994, at p. 62.
90 *Id.* at 63.
91 See Brett-Smith and Friedland, *supra* note 34, at p. 19.
92 *Id.* at 19–20 (citing D-Aquila, *et al.*, *The Association of Race/Ethnicity and HIV Infection Among Connecticut Drug Users*, 2 J. AIDS at p. 503 (1989)).
93 See Specter, *supra* note 49, at pp. 79–80.
94 See R. Raman *et al.*, *Spread of HIV Infection in Married Monogamous Women in India*, 278 JAMA at pp. 2090–2092 (December 17, 1997).
95 See Specter, *supra* note 49, at p. 80.
96 See Brett-Smith and Friedland, *supra* note 34, at 20.
97 *Id.* (citing *The Second 100,000 Cases*, *supra* note 65; *Mortality Attributable to HIV Infections/AIDS*, *supra* note 60). *See also* Chu *et al.*, *Impact of the Human Immunodeficiency Virus Epidemic on Mortality in Women of Reproductive Age, United States*, 264 JAMA at p. 225 (1990)).
98 *Id.*
99 *Id.*
100 See Taunya Lovell Banks, *Reproduction and Parenting*, AIDS LAW TODAY: A NEW GUIDE FOR THE PUBLIC (New Haven, Conn.: Yale University Press, 1993), at p. 216.
101 See STATE OF THE WORLD'S MOTHERS 2000, report by Save the Children, May 2000, at p. 9. According to Save the Children, "…Latin America has the highest female literacy rate among developing regions studied, while Africa has the lowest, at 45 percent. Within Africa, South Africa, Zimbabwe, and Mauritius have literacy rates that are close to 80 percent. But in Burkina Faso and Niger, fewer than 19 percent of women can read and write. [¶] Comparisons between sub-Saharan Africa and the industrialized world are even starker. On average, only half of all females in sub-Saharan Africa receive primary education at the appropriate age, compared with 97 percent in industrialized countries." And, incidentally, education does matter, according to Save the Children. *See Id.* at 16. ("Education provides a woman the opportunity to develop life skills that are critical to her own well-being. Literacy has a major influence on her access to information, on her self-esteem, on her capacity to identify and seize opportunities to improve her life and the lives of her children. All of these behaviors, in turn, help to break the cycle of poverty for mothers and children. [¶] Female education also directly affects a woman's economic and health status. Studies that examined the impact of primary education on women's wages found that income rose by 10 to 20 percent for each additional year of schooling. Educated women also are more likely to postpone marriage and childbirth. In Togo, for example, one in six girls who has not been to school gives birth each year, while only one in 100 with some secondary education does so. How a child grows and develops depends substantially on a mother's education. An educated mother is likely to provide her children with nutritious foods, to improve sanitary conditions in her home, and to seek appropriate health care for herself and for her children. [¶] An educated mother is much more likely to send

all her children to school, including her daughters. And when a girl attends school, she not only increases her economic opportunities, but she is much more likely to postpone marriage and childbearing, increasing the likelihood that her children will be born when she is ready and able to support and care for them.")

102 *Id.*

103 *See* Cantacuzino, *supra* note 67, at p. 130 (quoting the United Nations statistics).

104 *See* STATE OF THE WORLD'S MOTHERS 2000, *supra* note 101, at p. 9.

105 *See* Henri E. Cauvin, *To Fight AIDS, Swaziland's King Orders Girls to Avoid Sex for 5 Years*, N.Y. TIMES, Sept. 29, 2001, at A5.

106 *Id.* (Young girls and adolescents must wear blue and gold tassels, while young women are required to wear red and black tassels.)

107 *Id.*

108 *See* STATE OF THE WORLD'S MOTHERS 2000, *supra* note 101, at p. 9.

109 *See* Ray, *supra* note 69, at D2.

110 *Id.*

111 *Id.*

112 *See* McNeil, *supra* note 71, at A1.

113 *See* Rachel L. Swarns, *A South African Hospital Fights AIDS and Despair*, N.Y. TIMES, November 26, 2001, at A10.

114 *See* Swarns, *supra* note 70, at A1.

115 *See Huge Percentage of Women Volunteer for Zidovudine Project*, LANCET, Jan. 16, 1999, at 219. Researchers in India reported a similar trend, finding that 3.9 million cases of HIV infection, 3 percent of these cases were among pregnant women. *See* Stolberg, *supra* note 52, at A20.

116 *See* Gostin, *supra* note 50, at p. 53.

117 *Id.* (citing *Centers for Disease Control and Prevention, HIV/AIDS Surveillance Report, 1995* (Atlanta, Ga.: U.S. Dept. of Health and Human Services, Public Health Service, 1996).

118 *Id.* (citing Normand, J., Vlahov D., Moses, LE., eds., *Preventing HIV Transmission: The Role of Sterile Needles and Bleach* (Washington, D.C.: National Academy Press, (1995))).

119 *Id.* (*HIV/AIDS Surveillance Report, 1995, supra* note 117).

120 *Id.*

121 *See* Brett-Smith and Friedland, *supra* note 34, at p. 20.

122 *See, e.g.,* ARK. HOUSE BILL 1789 (introduced Feb. 15, 2001, and appropriating funds for HIV and AIDS medication for pregnant women living with the disease and for their "unborn children"); ARK. SENATE BILL 34 (enacted Jan. 17, 2001, with the Governor's signature, and requiring state to promulgate legislation and regulations regarding the distribution of HIV and AIDS medication to indigent state citizens); MASS. SEN. BILL 534 (filed on Senate docket Jan. 3, 2001, and requiring health care officials to provide treatment for; information to; and the option of HIV testing for women within four weeks of giving birth); N.J. ASSEM. BILL 808 (carried over from Jan. 11, 2000, and requiring HIV testing for pregnant women).

123 *See, e.g.,* ALA. HOUSE BILL 60 (prefiled Jan. 4, 2001, and amending existing law to require syphilis and HIV testing for pregnant women and newborns where law already permits testing for other sexually transmitted diseases).

124 *See, e.g.,* IN. HOUSE BILL 1177 (introduced Jan. 9, 2001, and amending existing law to require that information and instruction on HIV and sexually transmitted diseases be medically accurate); MD. HOUSE BILL 644 (introduced Feb. 7, 2001, and establishing the HIV and AIDS Media Campaign for Teenagers and Young Adults within the state's Department of Health and Mental Hygiene); MASS. SEN. BILL 239 (introduced Jan. 3, 2001, and amending existing law to include HIV and AIDS prevention in public school curriculum); MASS. SENATE BILL 534 (filed on Senate docket Jan. 3, 2001, and requiring health care officials to provide treatment for; information to; and the option of HIV testing for women within four weeks of giving birth); MASS. HOUSE BILL 2301 (introduced Jan. 3, 2001, and moving to include HIV and AIDS prevention education in public school curriculum); NEW JERSEY SENATE BILL 868 (carried over from Feb. 2, 2000, and requiring public school instruction on human sexuality to include information on prevention of HIV); N.J. ASSEM. BILL 792 (carried over from Jan. 11, 2000, and requiring public school instruction on human sexuality to include information on abstinence as well as failure rates of contraceptives and HIV); N.J. ASSEM. BILL 801 (carried over from Jan. 11, 2000, and requiring written permission from parents before children can receive instruction on human sexuality and HIV); N.J. ASSEM. BILL 808 (carried over from Jan. 11, 2000, and requiring health care providers to inform pregnant women on the importance of HIV treatment during and after pregnancy); N.J. ASSEM. BILL 1764 (carried over from Jan. 11, 2000, and requiring public schools to provide "age-appropriate" education on the prevention of HIV and AIDS); OK. HOUSE BILL 1386 (prefiled Jan. 12, 2001, and requiring HIV and AIDS prevention to be taught within the framework of the state's existing abstinence-focused curriculum).

125 *See* Brett-Smith and Friedland, *supra* note 34, at pp. 20–21.

126 *Id.*

127 *See* Lovell Banks, *supra* note 100, at p. 216 (citing UPDATE: *Acquired Immunodeficieny Syndrome— United States, 1918–1990*, 265 JAMA at p. 3226 (1991) (noting that "[i]n 1981 women made up

only 3 percent of the total cases reported to the CDC) (citing Wiessman, *Working with Pregnant Women at High Risk for HIV Infection: Outreach and Intervention,* 67 BULL. N.Y. ACED. MED. at pp. 291, 292 (1991). *See also* Gayle, Selik & Chu, *Surveillance for AIDS & HIV Infection among Black & Hispanic Women of Childbearing Age, 1981–1989,* 39 MORBIDITY AND MORTALITY WEEKLY REPORT at pp. 23–24 (1990). At the time of publication of the above article, Banks was professor of law at the University of Maryland School of Law. She has written extensively on HIV- and AIDS-related issues.

128   *Id.* (citing Zylke, *Another Consequence of Uncontrolled Spread of HIV Among Adults: Vertical Transmission,* 265 JAMA at p. 1798 (1991).

129   *See* Linda Villarosa, *A New Generation: Teenagers Living with HIV,* N.Y. TIMES, Nov. 20, 2001, at D7.

130   *Id.* (Villarosa notes that "[a]ccording to data from the Centers for Disease Control and Prevention, before the mid-1990's children with HIV lived to an average age of 9. But thanks to breakthroughs in antiretroviral medication, since 1996 the average age has risen to 13 to 15 and is going up. There are now 2,400 adolescents who were born with HIV infection, and thousands more who will turn 13 over the next five years.") *See also* Linda Villarosa, *Rescued HIV Babies Face New Problems as Teenagers,* N.Y. TIMES, March 5, 2002, at D6.

131   Researchers announced that in May 2003, attempts to create a vaccination had failed. *See* Carol Ezzell, *The Race Card,* SCIENTIFIC AMERICAN, May 2003, at p. 23. There is, however, a "morning-after" cocktail that seems to have proved somewhat successful. *See* Jim Ritter, *After-Sex Remedy for HIV Studied,* CHI. SUN-TIMES, Aug. 27, 1998, at p. 14.

132   And, indeed, according to researchers, many patients find the protocol very hard to follow. *See Maintenance Antiretroviral Treatment in HIV Infection,* 281 JAMA at pp. 497–498 (reprinting article previously published in LANCET).

133   Among the reported side effects is the redistribution of body fat (lipodystrophy), which can cause a general thickening of the trunk, a lump of fat to grow on the back of the neck (called the buffalo hump by sufferers), the development of a round belly (called the protease paunch), and the hollowing out of cheeks above skeletal limbs.

134   *See* Laurie Garrett, *The Virus at the End of the World,* ESQUIRE, March 1999, at pp. 102, 104–5.

135   *See* Greg Winter, *San Francisco AIDS Debate Leads to Criminal Charges,* N.Y. TIMES, Dec. 24, 2001, at A10.

136   *Id. See also* Erica Goode, *With Fears Fading, More Gays Spurn Old Preventive Message,* N.Y. TIMES, August 19, 2001, at A1.

137   *Id.*

138   *Id.*

139   Researchers began to note what many deemed a dangerous trend, for example, among gay men in recent years: High-risk sexual behavior, the use of drugs and Viagra. *See* David Tuller, *Experts Fear a Risky Recipe: Viagra, Drugs and HIV,* N.Y. TIMES, Oct. 16, 2001, at D5.

140   *See State v. Wiser,* 2000 Tenn. Crim. App. LEXIS 852.

141   *See* Denise Grady, *Scientists Shifting Strategies In Quest for an AIDS Vaccine,* N.Y. TIMES, June 5, 2001, at D1; Sheryl Gay Stolberg, *In AIDS War, New Weapons and New Victims,* N.Y. TIMES, June 3, 2001, at A20.

142   *See* Garrett, *supra* note 134, at pp. 102, 104–5.

143   *Id.* at 105.

144   *Id.*

145   *Id.* at 104.

146   *Id.* at 105.

147   *See* Tina Rosenberg, *How to Solve the World's AIDS Crisis,* N.Y. TIMES MAG. Jan. 28, 2001, Sect. 6, at 26.

148   *See* Randy Shilts, AND THE BAND PLAYED ON: POLITICS, PEOPLE, AND THE AIDS EPIDEMIC (New York: Penguin, 1988), at pp. 147– 200.

149   *See, e.g.,* Harlon L. Dalton, *Criminal Law,* AIDS LAW TODAY: A NEW GUIDE FOR THE PUBLIC (New Haven, Conn.: Yale University Press, 1993), at pp. 242, 261, n. 30 (citing Shilts, *supra* note 148, at p. 200 (though Dalton refers to the author as R. Schiltz)).

150   *Id.*

151   *Id.*

152   According to the name's listing on a HEALTH ALERT flier posted and widely distributed by the Chautauqua County Department of Health, "Nu Shawn Williams" was also known as: Face Williams, "E," Shyleek Johnson, Jo Jo Williams, Lashawn Fields, Headteck Williams, Shoe Williams, and Face Johnson.

153   *Id.* (reprinted in the A.B.A. J., May 1998, at p. 26). (The flier was controversial because as a matter of public policy, medical conditions have long been held confidential.)

154   *See* Chautauqua County HEALTH ALERT flier, *supra* note 152.

155   *See* Mark Hansen, *Can the Law Stop AIDS?,* A.B.A. J. May 1998, at p. 26.

156   *Id.*

157   *See* Michael Cooper, *Man Guilty of Spreading AIDS Virus Says He Had Hundreds of Sex Partners,* N.Y. TIMES, July 29, 1999, at A19.

158   *Id.*

159 *Id.*

160 *Id.*

161 *Id.*

162 *See Man with HIV is Guilty in Unprotected-Sex Case*, N.Y. TIMES, Feb. 19, 1999; Hansen, *supra* note 155, at p. 26.

163 *Id.*

164 *See* Cooper, *supra* note 157, at A19.

165 *Man With HIV Is Guilty In Unprotected-Sex Case*, *supra* note 162, at A19.

166 *See California v. Crother*, 232 Cal. App. 3d 629 (1991); *Man Sentenced to Abstinence for Knowingly Infecting Girlfriend*, 7 AIDS LIT. REP. at p. 198 (Andrews) (Nov. 22, 1991).

167 *See Oregon v. Gonzales*, No. C91-0733392 (Or. Cir. Ct. Oct. 28, 1991).

168 For a review of these state laws *see supra* note 26.

169 *See, e.g., California v. Crother*, 232 Cal. App. 3d 629 (1991).

170 *See* Cooper, *supra* note 157, at A19.

171 *See, e.g., United States v. Johnson*, 30 M.J. 53 (C.M.A. 1990); *Mississippi v. McIntyre*, No. E-367(B) (Miss. Cir. Ct. April 13, 1989).

172 *See* Hansen, *supra* note 155, at p. 26.

173 *See* Dalton, *supra* note 149, at p. 242 (citing Walt, *AIDS Exposure Laws Debated*, N.Y. NEWSDAY, Sept. 23, 1991, at p. 27).

174 58 U.S.L.W. 2343 (Tex. Dist. Ct. Nov. 4, 1989).

175 *See Inmate with AIDS Guilty of Trying to Kill by Biting*, N.Y. TIMES, April 12, 1990, at B4.

176 *See Scroggins v. State*, 401 S.E.2d 13 (Ga. 1991).

177 *United States v. Moore*, 846 F.2d 1163 (8th Cir. 1988). *But see, Brock v. State*, 555 So.2d 285 (Ala. Ct. App. 1989), *aff'd*, 580 So.2d 1390 (Ala. 1991).

178 *See, e.g.,* Dalton, *supra* note 149, at p. 242. (According to Dalton, "[m]ost of the civilian cases involve courtroom, jailhouse, or arrest-scene skirmishes in which a prisoner or detainee allegedly spit at or bit a law enforcement officer. More often than not, the detainee punctuated the hostilities by announcing that he or she was infected with HIV. In some cases, the detainee reportedly expressed the desire to transmit the virus to the officer. Not surprisingly, the officers in these cases reacted with alarm, anger, and fear, especially if they were poorly informed about the ways in which HIV is and is not transmitted. Seeking retribution, they turned to the criminal justice system that, at least at the margin, could be expected to respond sympathetically to those who serve it day in and day out.")

179 *Id.* at 244–45. "By contrast, the biting and spitting cases do not tap into anything so elemental or widespread, apart from our generalized, culturally reinforced fear of disease and death. Indeed, our impulse to criminalize seems to raise not so much from an engaged sense of vulnerability as from a kind of institutional sympathy for those who are the usual targets of spittle. Then, too, there is a more troublesome explanation for the prominence of these cases for the draconian punishments imposed in the most well-publicized ones. These cases represent a new phase is an ongoing struggle for control and respect between keepers of the peace and those who are kept. In a sense, HIV represents a new weapon possessed by HIV-positive detainees (at least to the extent that law enforcement personnel fear transmission via saliva), and major prosecutions for minor assaults represent a new weapon in the arsenal of the men and women in blue.")

180 *Id.* n. 11 (Dalton notes that he "borrow[s] this later opposition from Carol Vance, who employed it as the conceptual umbrella for an extraordinary collection of essays, PLEASURE AND DANGERS: EXPLORING FEMALE SEXUALITY, (C. Vance, ed. 1984)").

181 *Id.*

182 *See* Hansen, *supra* note 155, at p. 28.

183 *See* JANE (June/July 1999), at p. 144.

184 *Id.*

185 *Id.*

186 Among the questions was whether the woman likes dates like "salt and vinegar potato chips," because he "has heard" that an affirmative answer is an indication of bi-sexuality, and his Christmas wish would involve two women. JANE, *supra* note 183, at p. 145.

187 *Id.*

188 According to media reports, the young men: Joshua Cole, Daniel Brayman, and Nicholas Holtschlag were 18 or above at the time of their convictions. *See, e.g.,* Keith Bradsher, *3 Guilty of Manslaughter in Slipping Drug to Girl*, N.Y. TIMES, March 15, 2000, at A14.

189 *Id.*

190 A friend of Reid's, who was also served a tainted drink, fell into a coma for twelve hours, but later recovered. A third girl did not touch the drink she was served. She suffered no injuries.

191 At least one formula for "Mickey Finns" was cholylhydrate.

192 *See Drug Suspects Held*, CHI. SUN-TIMES, Sept. 14, 2000, at p. 18.

193 In addition to GHB, which is also known as Liquid Extasy and Grievous Bodily Harm, there are other common "date rape" drugs, among them: (1) Ketamine also known as Special K, Ketalar, Ketaject, and Super-K; (2) Rohypnol, which is also offered under the generic name of Fluni-

trazepam and the street names Rophies, Ruffies, Roofies, La Rocha, Roofenal, Roche, R2, Mexican Valium, Rib, and Rope.

194   See Bill Passed to Toughen Law on "Date Rape" Drug, N.Y. TIMES, Feb. 2, 2000, at A20 (quoting Republican Congressman Fred Upton of Michigan).

195   See Bradsher, supra note 188, at A14.

196   See Bill Passed to Toughen Law on "Date Rape" Drug, supra note 194, at A20.

197   See, e.g., Desnick v. American Broadcasting Companies, Inc., 44 F.3d 1345, 1352 (7th Cir. 1995) ("The law's willingness to give effect to consent procured by fraud is not limited to the tort of trespass. The RESTATEMENT gives the example of a man who obtains consent to sexual intercourse by promising a woman $100, yet (unbeknownst to her, of course) he pays her with a counterfeit bill and intended to do so from the start. The man is not guilty of battery, even though unconsented-to sexual intercourse is a battery. RESTATEMENT (SECOND) OF TORTS Sec. 892B, illustration 9, pp. 373–74 (1979). Yet we know that to conceal the fact that one has a venereal disease transforms 'consensual' intercourse into battery. Crowell v. Crowell, 180 N.C. 516 (1920). Seduction, standardly effected by false promises of love, is not rape, Pletnikoff v. State, 719 P.2d 1039, 1043 (Alaska App. 1986); intercourse under the pretense of rendering medical or psychiatric treatment is, at least in most states. Compare State v. Tizard, 1994 WL 630498, 8-10 (Tenn. Crim. App. Nov. 10, 1994); with Boro v. Superior Court, 163 Cal. App. 3d 1224 (1985). It is certainly battery. Bowman v. Home Life Ins. Co., 243 F.2d 331 (3d Cir. 1957); Commonwealth v. Gregory, 132 Pa. Super. 507 (1930)).

198   See Jane E. Larson, "Women Understand So Little, They Call My Good Nature 'Deceit'": A Feminist Rethinking of Seduction, 93 COL. L. REV. at pp. 374, 380 (1993). At the time of this article, Larson was an assistant professor of law at Northwestern University.

199   Id.

200   Id. at 377.

201   Id. n. 7 (citing Tess in Thomas Hardy's TESS OF THE D'URBERVILLES (Bantam Books 1984) (1891), at pp. 377, 390).

202   Id. n. 8 (citing Hetty Sorel in George Eliot's ADAM BEDE (John Paterson ed., Houghton Mifflin Co. 1968) (1859), at pp. 379–380).

203   Id. n. 9 (citing Maslova in Leo Tolstoy's RESURRECTION (Rosemary Edmonds trans., Penguin Books 1985) (1899), at pp. 25, 27).

204   Id. n. 10 (citing Hester Prynne in Nathaniel Hawthorne's, THE SCARLET LETTER (Harcourt Brace Jovanovich 1984) (1850), at p. 38).

205   Id. n. 11 (citing Charity Royall in Edith Wharton's, SUMMER (Harper & Row 1979) (1918), at pp. 260–278).

206   Id. n. 12 (citing Anna Karenina in Leo Tolstoy's ANNA KARENINA (George Gibian ed., Louis Maude & Aylmer Maude trans., W.W. Norton & Co. 1970) (1878), at p. 695).

207   Id. n. 13. (Larson argues in this note that "[t]his harsh message was even more bluntly conveyed in nineteenth-century literature of less lasting artistic merit. Barbara Welter documents the morality that prevailed in the highly popular magazine short stories and romance novels of the era, in which social humiliation, depravity, illness, madness, spiritual decline, and even death awaited the young woman who indulged in sex before marriage. See Barbara Welter, THE CULT OF TRUE WOMANHOOD, 1820–1860, 18 AM. Q. at pp. 151, 154–59, (1966).)

208   Larson, supra note 198, at p. 378 (citing e.g., Prince Nekhlyudov in Tolstoy, supra note 206, pp. at 95–96; Alexander D'Urberville in Hardy, supra note 201, at pp. 301–02).

209   See Hardy, supra note 201, at p. 380.

210   See PROSSER AND KEETON ON THE LAW OF TORTS, Sec. 124 (5th ed. 1984), at p. 915.

211   See FUNK & WAGNALL'S STANDARD DICTIONARY OF THE ENGLISH LANGUAGE, INTERNATIONAL EDITION (New York: Funk & Wagnalls (Albert H. Marckwardt et. al (eds., 1970)), at p. 1138.

212   Id.

213   See, e.g., BLACK'S LAW DICTIONARY, supra note 103, ENDNOTE FOR CHAPTER FIVE, at p. 945.

214   Among the published works of Henry Ward Beecher are: MAN AND HIS INSTITUTIONS (New York: Calkins & Stiles, 1856); PLYMOUTH COLLECTION OF HYMNS AND TUNES (New York: A.S. Barnes & Co., 1856); LIFE THOUGHTS (Boston: Phillips, Sampson & Co., 1858); Woman's Duty to Vote (Speech delivered at the Eleventh National Woman's Rights Convention on May 10, 1866) (New York: Office of "The Revolution," 1868); THE LIFE OF JESUS CHRIST (New York: J.B. Ford & Co., 1871); YALE LECTURES ON PREACHING (New York: J.B. Ford & Co., 1873); STAR PAPERS (New York: J.B. Ford & Co., 1873); NORWOOD: VILLAGE LIFE IN NEW ENGLAND (New York: J.B. Ford & Co., 1874); THE SUMMER PARISH: SABBATH (New York: J.B. Ford & Co., 1875); PAST PERILS AND THE PERILS OF TO-DAY (New York: The Christian Union Print, 1877); A STRING OF PEARLS (Ovington, 1888); LECTURES TO YOUNG MEN, ON VARIOUS IMPORTANT SUBJECTS (Philadelphia: H. Altemus, 1895); and, OLD CHRISTMAS CHIMES: THE OVERTURE OF ANGELS (Lancaster: J.P. McCaskey, 1913). Among the published works of Theodore Tilton are: GOLDEN-HAIRED GERTRUDE: A Story for Children (New York: Tibbals & Whiting, 1865); THE KING'S RING (New York: Hurd & Houghton, 1867); THE CONSTITUTION, A TITLE-DEED TO WOMAN'S FRANCHISE (New York: Office of the Golden Age, 1871); THE PHILADELPHIA FAILURE: A REVIEW OF GRANT'S RENOMINATION (New York: The Golden Age, 1872); THOU AND I: A LYRIC OF HUMAN LIFE (New York: R. Worthington, 1880); TEMPEST-TOSSED; A ROMANCE (New York:

J.W. Lovell Co., 1883); HEART'S EASE (London: T.F. Unwin, 1894); THE CHAMELEON'S DISH (London: T.F. Unwin, 1894); COMPLETE POETICAL WORKS (Oxford: Clarendon Press, 1897); THE FIRST DON QUIXOTE (Paris: Brentano, 1899); and, THE FADING OF THE MAYFLOWER (Chicago: A N. Marquis & Co., 1906).

215 *See* Richard Wightman Fox, TRIALS OF INTIMACY: LOVE AND LOSS IN THE BEECHER-TILTON SCANDAL (Chicago: University of Chicago Press, 1999), at p. 20 (citing Frank Leslie, *Henry Ward Beecher, The Great Pastor's End*, ILLUSTRATED WEEKLY, March 19, 1887, at p. 75). ("Frank Leslie's story took an equal interest in one other subject"—his network. It estimated his wealth at between $100,000 and $200,000. His total career income might have come to a million dollars, Leslie's [sic] added, but the events of the 1870s had cost him dearly. He had been forced to mortgage his residence at 124 Columbia Heights, and his astronomical salary, raised by the Plymouth Church board to $100,000 in 1875, was eaten up by legal bills.")

216 According to Fox, Tilton had once served as "understudy" for Beecher, "the paper's leading writer, and ultimately replaced Beecher as editor (a position Tilton held from 1863–1870)." *See* Fox, *supra* note 129, at 13.

217 *See* Fox, *supra* note 215, at pp. 15–16. Fox also writes that "[i]n the late 1860s, Elizabeth Tilton and Henry Ward Beecher became intimate friends, and the Tiltons wrote each other hundreds of letters trying to make sense of their lives, their marriage, and their friendship with their pastor. Henry and Elizabeth were spiritual soulmates [sic] who experienced some kind of passionate bond with each other. In 1870 Mrs. Tilton told her husband that she had gone too far in her knowing and loving of Beecher. After a harrowing series of encounters among the three of them in December, Beecher and the Tiltons agreed to try to keep stories about their private relations from reaching the public. [¶] In 1872, radical reformer Victoria Woodhull issued a public statement accusing Beecher of adultery with Mrs. Tilton. Her charge was assembled from conversations she had had with Theodore [Tilton] and other friends in the women's suffrage movement." *See also* Fox, *supra* note 215, at pp. 7–8.

218 According to Fox, "[i]n the fall of 1874 Tilton sued Beecher for 'criminal conversation' (adultery) and 'alienation of [his wife's] affections.' The suit was civil, not criminal; Beecher was never in any danger of imprisonment, only of suffering a damaged reputation. The trial began in January 1875 and was concluded in July 1875, when the jury announced it could not reach a decision. The only person imprisoned in connection with the Beecher-Tilton Scandal was Victoria Woodhull, who spent time in the Ludlow Street Jail in Manhattan after Anthony Comstock had her arrested for publishing the adultery charges (she was finally acquitted on a technicality)." *See* Fox, *supra* note 215, at p. 12.

219 It should be noted that in 1878, Elizabeth Tilton is said to have confessed to having committed adultery with Beecher. But Fox explains that "[o]ne of the best-known 'facts' about [Elizabeth Tilton] from 1874 on was that she was always liable to change her mind on the adultery charge, and even to endorse documents that contradicted others she had already signed." *See* Fox, *supra* note 215, at pp. 15–16.

220 *See* Fox, *supra* note 215, at I.

221 *Id.* at 20 (citing Leslie, *supra* note 215, at p. 75) ("In earlier years [Beecher] had spent money with relish, not only on his own travel, engravings, paintings, and gems, but on gifts for his friends. He and the Tiltons exchanged presents all the time in the 1850s and 1860s. During the period of their three-way friendship, Theodore copied Henry's lavish spending habits. He put down $500 on a portrait of Beecher (it required thirty hours of sitting on Beecher's part, a generous outlay for a man of his responsibilities), which he hung in his home at 174 Livingston Street, a mile from Beecher's house. When Elizabeth and Henry developed their special attachment in the late 1860s, he gave her many gifts (books especially) which Theodore claimed during the trial to have discovered, to his dismay, in a closet. Tilton's lawyers elicited the information that Mrs. Tilton had kept multiple pictures of Beecher in the mass-produced pictures of many other male public figures, also in multiple copies. She had collected them.")

222 *Id.* at 7 ("Henry and Elizabeth were spiritual soulmates, who experienced some kind of passionate bond with each other," writes Fox.)

223 According to Fox, Theodore Tilton's allegations were based in part on the fact that Henry Ward Beecher "had given Mrs. Tilton too many flowers." Henry Ward Beecher's lawyers countered this argument, however, "by admitting that Beecher had showered her with flowers, but pointed out that he had given everyone else mountains of flowers too." And then, "[u]nder re-cross-examination Tilton conceded that his house was always aglow in botanical arrangements and that Beecher's 'occasional' floral gifts had not been concealed from him." *See* Fox, *supra* note 215, at p. 20.

224 *See* Larson, *supra* note 198, at p. 382 no. 27 (citing Roscoe Pound, *Individual Interests in the Domestic Relations*, 14 MICH. L. REV. at pp. 177, 179–81 (1916)). *See also Guy v. Livesey*, 1619, Cro.Jac. 501, 79 Eng. Rep. 428; *Hyde v. Scyssor*, 1620, Cro.Jac. 538, 79 Eng.Rep. 462; *Galizard v. Rigault*, 1702, 2 Salk. 552, 91 Eng.Rep. 467, 8 HOLDSWORTH, HISTORY OF ENGLISH LAW (2d ed. 1937), at pp. 427–430; 1 STREET, FOUNDATIONS OF LEGAL LIABILITY (1906), at pp. 262–267; Wigmore, *Interference with Social Relations*, 21 AM. L. REV. at p. 764 (1887); Holbrook, *The Change in the Meaning of Consortium*, 22 MICH. L. REV. at p. 1 (1923); Lippman, *The Breakdown of Consortium*, 30 COL. L. REV. at p. 651

(1930); *Duffies v. Duffies*, 45 N.W. 522 (1890); *Doe v. Roe*, 20 A. 83 (1890); *Hodge v. Wetzler*, 55 A. 49 (1903); *Emerson v. Fleming*, 193 S.E.2d 249 (1972); *Wilson v. Hilske*, 321 A.2d 13 (1974); and, *Kline v. Ansell*, 287 Md. 585, 414 A.2d 929 (1980).

225   *Id.* n. 28 noting that '[s]eduction originates in the common law action to recover loss of services (action *'per quod servitium amisit'*) for the master's loss when another person enticed away or beat his servant. *See* 3 William Blackstone, COMMENTARIES ON THE LAWS OF ENGLAND (U. CHI. PRESS 1979) (1768), at pp. 139–142. As master of the family, the father had a legal right to claim the household labor of his children. Thus a father could sue his daughter's lover for having deprived him of her services, in the same sense as with any of his other servants. *See* W.S. Holdsworth, A HISTORY OF ENGLISH LAW (1926), at p. 428. If the father was dead or absent, other persons acting in a parental capacity could bring the seduction action, including female persons such as a widowed mother. *See* M.B.W. Sinclair, SEDUCTION AND THE MYTH OF THE IDEAL WOMAN, 5 LAW & INEQ. J. at pp. 33, 36–37, 41–45 (1978)).

226   *Id.* at 382.

227   At the risk of adding further confusion, for purposes of expedience, the author has chosen to use the phrase "other forms of enticement" to include: alienation of affections, enticement proper, and criminal conversation. The actual legal definition for "enticement," however, is "[t]o wrongfully solicit, persuade, procure, allure, attract, draw by blandishment, coax or seduce. To lure, induce, tempt, incite, or persuade a person to do a thing. Enticement of a child is inviting, persuading or attempting to persuade a child to enter any vehicle, building, room or secluded place with intent to commit an unlawful sexual act upon or with the person of said child." BLACK'S LAW DICTIONARY, (6th ed. 1991) (St. Paul: West Publishing), at p. 367.

228   *C.M. v. J.M.*, 726 A.2d 998, 1001 (N.J. Super. Ch. 1999).

229   *Id.* at 1001.

230   *Id.* (citing *Magierowski v. Buckley*, 39 N.J. Super. 534, 555 (1956)). *See also, Taylor v. Thunder*, 13 P.3d 43, 44 (Nev. 2000) (permitting a criminal, statutorily created charge of "sexual seduction" under Nevada law); *Brayman v. Deloach*, 439 S.E.2d 709, 711 (Ga. App. 1993) (holding that under Georgia statutory law "[t]he seduction of a daughter, unmarried and living with her parent, whether followed by pregnancy or not, *shall give a right of action to the father or to the mother* if the father is dead, or absent permanently, or refuses to bring an action") (emphasis supplied by court); *Franklin v. Hill*, 417 S.E.2d 721, 723 (Ga. App. 1992) (explaining that "[t]he elements of the tort of seduction contained in [the Georgia code] do not include a requirement that the seduced female be 'virtuous.' A cause of action under that section requires only that the seduced daughter be unmarried and living with her parent"); *White v. Rhodes*, 607 N.E.2d 75, 77 (Ohio App. 1992) (holding that "if a jury were to find that a tortuous seduction occurred, the [parents of a minor female allegedly seduced by an employee of the Board of Education] would at least be entitled to nominal damages and, therefore, the recovery of their costs").

231   This is as opposed to seduction actions for minors, which are still a cause of action in many states, sometimes statutorily created and in the historic context was criminal in nature. For cases, *see, e.g., Franklin v. Hill*, 417 S.E.2d 721 (1992); *White v. Rhodes*, 607 N.E.2d 75 (Ohio App. 1992); *Taylor v. Thunder*, 13 P.3d 43 (Nev. 2000); *Brayman v. Deloach*, 439 S.E.2d 709 (Ga. App. 1993); *C.M. v. J.M.*, 726 A.2d 998, 1001 (N.J. Super. Ch. 1999) (holding that "'[s]eduction' is a common law tort actionable by a parent against an individual for violating their daughter's virginity. It was intended to recompense an aggrieved parent for the 'consequent degradation, mortification, and wounded feelings visited upon [the daughter] as well as upon her parents' stemming from the child's 'loss of chastity'" (citing *Magierowski v. Buckley*, 39 N.J. Super. 534, 555 (App. Div. 1956)). For older cases, *see, e.g., Kennedy v. Shea*, 110 Mass. 147 (1872); *Lavery v. Crooke*, 9 N.W. 599 (1881); *Lawrence v. Spence*, 2 N.E. 145 (1885); *Simpson v. Grayson*, 16 S.W. 4 (1891); *Reutkemeier v. Nolte*, 161 N.W. 290 (1971); *Silva v. Mills*, 131 A. 695 (1926); *Schurk v. Christensen*, 497 P.2d 937 (1972).

232   *See* COMMENT, Jennifer E. McDougal, *Legislating Morality: The Actions for Alienation of Affections and Criminal Conversation in North Carolina*, 33 WAKE FOREST LAW REVIEW pp. 163–188, at p. 171 (March 1998) (citing James Leonard, *Cannon v. Miller: The Brief Death of Alienation of Affections and Criminal Conversation in North Carolina*, 63 N.C. L. REV. at pp. 1317, 1319 (1985). *See also Heermance v. James*, 47 Barb. 120 (N.Y. App. Div. 1866).

233   *See, e.g., People v. Hough*, 607 N.Y.S.2d 884, 885 (Dist. Ct. 1994).

234   The State of Louisiana appears never to have adopted a cause of action for either "alienation of affections" and/or "criminal conversation" because Louisiana law does not allow punitive damages in civil cases. *See, e.g., Moulin v. Monteleone*, 115 So. 447 (La. 1927).

235   *See* McDougal, *supra* note 232, at pp. 170–172.

236   *See* BLACK'S LAW DICTIONARY, *supra* note 213, at p. 367.

237   *See, e.g.,* Suzanne Reynolds, NORTH CAROLINA FAMILY LAW, Sec. 5.44 (5th ed. 1993), at p. 385. (According to Reynolds, actions for "enticement" are generally "no longer recognized in probably any jurisdiction.")

238   *See, e.g., Hodges v. Howell*, 4 P.3d 803, 805 (Utah App. 2000) (citing *Bowers v. Carter*, 59 Utah 249, 252 (1921)).

239   *See Hodges*, 4 P.3d at 805 (citing *Norton v. MacFarlane*, 818 P.2d 8, 13 n. 9 (Utah 1991)).

240 No. 99, September Term, 1998 (Md. Ct. App.), at 8, n. 2 (citing PROSSER, *supra* note 210, at p. 875 n. 75; Lippman, *The Breakdown of Consortium*, 30 COL. L. REV. 651 at pp. 654–660 (1930)).

241 *See* Larson, *supra* note 198, at p. 383.

242 *See Doe v. Doe*, 358 Md. 113 (2000).

243 *Id.* at 121 (citing *Kline v. Ansell*, 287 Md. 585 (1980); *Kohlhoss v. Mobley*, 102 Md. 199 (1905)).

244 In most states, prosecutions for adultery are no longer brought.

245 *C.M. v. J.M.*, 726 A.2d at 1001.

246 *Hodges*, 4 P.3d at 805 (citing *Norton v. MacFarlane*, 818 P.2d 8, 12 (Utah 1991)).

247 *Id.* (citing *Wilson v. Oldroyd*, 1 Utah 2d 362, 367 (Utah 1954)).

248 *Id.*

249 *See Hodges*, 4 P.2d at 805.

250 *See, e.g.*, Fox, *supra* note 215; Laura Hanft Korobkin, CRIMINAL CONVERSATIONS: SENTIMENTALITY AND NINETEENTH-CENTURY LEGAL STORIES OF ADULTERY (New York: Columbia University Press, 1998); Ann Douglas, THE FEMINIZATION OF AMERICAN CULTURE (New York: Noonday Press, 1998); Robert Shaplen, FREE LOVE AND HEAVENLY SINNERS: THE STORY OF THE GREAT HENRY WARD BEECHER SCANDAL (New York: Knopf, 1954); Paxton Hibben, HENRY WARD BEECHER: AN AMERICAN PORTRAIT (New York: G.H. Doran, 1927).

251 The phrase "heartbalm claims" generally refers to a category of alleged "love interference" actions that includes: alienation of affections, breach of promise to marry, criminal conversation, and seduction of persons over legal age of consent. *See* BLACK'S LAW DICTIONARY, *supra* note 213, at p. 498.

252 As set forth above, in 1866, New York became the first state to recognize the tort of alienation of affections, and every state—except Louisiana—adopted similar laws between 1866 and the 1930s. As these laws evolved so did the caselaw surrounding them. *See* McDougal, *supra* note 232, at p. 171 (citing Leonard, *supra* note 232, at p. 1319*). See also Heermance v. James*, 47 Barb. 120 (N.Y. App. Div. 1866). The State of Louisiana appears never to have adopted a cause of action for either "alienation of affections" and/or "criminal conversation." *See, e.g., Moulin v. Monteleone*, 115 So. 447 (La. 1927). *See, e.g., Brown v. Brown*, 121 N.C. 44 (1897); *Seiber v. Pettitt*, 49 A. 763 (Pa. 1901); *Cottle v. Johnson*, 179 N.C. 426 (1920); *Townsend v. Holderby*, 197 N.C. 550 (1929).

253 *See* Larson, *supra* note 198, at p. 383, n. 30 ("Working women rarely earned a living wage in the eighteenth and nineteenth centuries. *See* Barbara M. Werthheimer, WE WERE THERE: THE STORY OF WORKING WOMEN IN AMERICA (1977), at pp. 102–103. An unmarried mother without assistance from her birth family (or from charity) could not support herself at respectable work. Unmarried mothers often were forced into prostitution or to have abortions, *see* John D'Emilio & Estelle B. Freedman, INTIMATE MATTERS: A HISTORY OF SEXUALITY IN AMERICA (1988), at p. 64; or to commit infanticide, *see* Constance B. Backhouse, DESPERATE WOMEN AND COMPASSIONATE COURTS; INFANTICIDE IN NINETEENTH CENTURY CANADA, 34 U. TORONTO L.J. at pp. 447–448 (1984). *See* generally John R. Gillis, SERVANTS, SEXUAL RELATIONS AND THE RISK OF ILLEGITIMACY IN LONDON, 1801–1900, in SEX AND CLASS IN WOMEN'S HISTORY (J. Newton et al. eds. 1983), at p. 114 (discussing economic hardship of single mothers in Victorian Britain); Rachel G. Fuchs, POOR AND PREGNANT IN PARIS; STRATEGIES FOR SURVIVAL IN THE NINETEENTH CENTURY (1992) (same for France)).

254 *Id.*

255 *Id.* n. 31 (*See* Constance Backhouse, PETTICOATS AND PREJUDICE: WOMEN AND LAW IN NINETEENTH-CENTURY CANADA (1991), at pp. 61–62).

256 *Id.*

257 For explanation *see Moulin v. Monteleone*, 165 La. 169 (1927).

258 *C.M. v. J.M.*, 726 A.2d at 1001 (citing *Magierowski v. Buckley*, 39 N.J. Super. 534, 555 (App. Div. 1956)). *See also, Taylor v. Thunder*, 13 P.3d 43, 44 (Nev. 2000) (permitting a criminal, statutorily created charge of "sexual seduction" under Nevada law); *Brayman v. Deloach*, 439 S.E.2d 709, 711 (Ga. App. 1993) (holding that under Georgia statutory law "'[t]he seduction of a daughter, unmarried and living with her parents, whether followed by pregnancy or not, *shall give a right of action to the father or to the mother* if the father is dead, or absent permanently, or refuses to bring an action'") (emphasis supplied by court); *Franklin v. Hill*, 417 S.E.2d 721, 723 (Ga. App. 1992) (explaining that "[t]he elements of the tort of seduction contained in [the Georgia code] do not include a requirement that the seduced female be 'virtuous.' A cause of action under that section requires only that the seduced daughter be unmarried and living with her parent"); *White v. Rhodes*, 607 N.E.2d 75, 77 (Ohio App. 2 Dist. 1992) (holding that "if a jury were to find that a tortuous seduction occurred, the [parents of a minor female allegedly seduced by an employee of the Board of Education] would at least be entitled to nominal damages and, therefore, the recovery of their costs").

259 *See Askew v. Askew*, 28 Cal. Rptr. 2d 284, 294 (Cal. App. 1994).

260 The Minneapolis Court of Appeals held similarly in *M.N. v. D.S.*, 616 N.W.2d 284 (2000).

261 *See Askew v. Askew*, 28 Cal. Rptr. 2d at 294.

262 *See* Margaret Cronin Fisk, *The Spy Who Came in From the Marriage*, NAT'L L.J., March 26, 2001, at A13.

263 *Id.*

264 From *The Rehearsal*, Act III, Scene II (1663), by George Villiers, Duke of Buckingham.

265 *See* Fisk, *supra* note 262, at A13.

266 *Id.*

267 *Id.*
268 *See* Rick Bragg, *Ex-Wife Is Suing Cuba Over a Spy's Deception*, N.Y. TIMES, August 15, 1999, at A12.
269 *See* William Glaberson, *Widow of Terrorist Victim Sues bin Laden and Taliban*, N.Y. TIMES, Oct. 15, 2001, at B11. (The basis of the World Trade Center suit against Osama bin Laden and the Afghani Taliban government, filed by a woman identified only as "Jane Doe" and a widow of one of the victims, against the "intentional and willful mass murder of thousands of innocent men, women, and children.") *See also* Mark Hamblett, *Bin Laden Named in Suit*, NAT'L L.J., Oct. 22, 2001, at A4.
270 *See Martinez v. Republic of Cuba*, No. 99-18208 Div. 20 (Fla. Cir. Ct. Miami-Dade Co.).
271 *Id.*
272 *Id.*
273 *Id.*
274 *See, e.g.,* Fisk, *supra* note 262, at A13; NAT'S L.J., April 9, 2001, at A4; *Ex-Wife of Cuban Spy Is Awarded $20 Million*, N.Y. TIMES, March 24, 2001, at A28.
275 *See* Fisk, *supra* note 262. (Grain shipments from American suppliers in December 2001, to make up for Cuban crops destroyed by Hurricane Michelle suggest, however, that Cuban-American relations might have reached a turning point.)
276 *See* Peter Page, *Cuban Plane Sale a Symbolic Victory*, NAT'L L.J., Jan. 20, 2003, at A4.
277 *See* Deborah Tannen, Ph.D., THAT'S NOT WHAT I MEANT!: HOW CONVERSATIONAL STYLE MAKES OR BREAKS RELATIONSHIPS (New York: Ballantine Books, 1986 (reprinted 1992)), at p. 133.
278 *Id.*
279 *See, e.g., State v. Moorman*, 358 S.E.2d 502 (N.C. 1987) (involving a claim by a sleeping woman of rape. By contrast, the defendant argued that he had sex with the plaintiff in her dorm room, because he mistook her for her roommate, with whom he had a relationship).
280 *See People v. Hough*, 607 N.Y.S.2d 884, 885 (Dist. Ct. 1994).
281 *Id.*
282 *Id.*
283 *Id.*
284 *Id.* (The court's specific findings on this point are that: "[t]he male began to touch the complainant's breasts and complainant responded 'Oh boy, your [*sic*] drunk and horney [*sic*].' He then asked her to have sex with him and she told him to make it quick because she had to work in the morning. Complainant removed her clothing and was calling him Lenny. The male then took off his clothing and got on top of the complainant and inserted his penis into her vagina. They had intercourse for several minutes during which time complainant wasn't looking for the male's face. When the act was over, the male said, 'Was that the best sex you ever had?' and 'What are you going to tell Lenny?' Complainant got out of bed, turned the light on and saw that it was Lamont and not Lenny that she had sexual intercourse with. Complainant threw the defendant's clothes out of the door and defendant left. Shortly thereafter, complainant contacted the police.")
285 *Id.* at 885.
286 *Id.*
287 *Id.* (citing Penal Law Section 130.20, which the court held "must be read in conjunction with Sec. 130.05 which provides the definition of lack of consent. Under the statute, lack of consent results from forcible compulsion or incapacity to consent. A person is incapable of consent when he or she is less than 17 years old or mentally defective or mentally incapacitated or physically helpless.")
288 *Id.*
289 The Due Process Clause of the United States constitution requires that persons accused of crimes have fair notice that they have committed a crime, *i.e.*, that the language of the statute clearly includes the offense as actionable.
290 *Id.* at 886 (*emphasis added*).

SECTION THREE

The Politics of Female Adolescence

CHAPTER TWELVE

Pop Life and the
Legal Confusion of Girls

THE WORLD OF PRE-WOMEN:
Confounding Realities in a Quasi-Adult Universe

There is "no clear ideal biography for the female life course," researcher Gail Landman wrote in a 1995 article published in *American Anthropologist*.[1] The contradictory demands of contemporary life can be paralyzing for women struggling to define themselves amid cultural and gender roles that continue to oppose each other; social pressures that continue to take a toll and scientific marvels that can change everything in a blink.

But if it is difficult for women to hold on to themselves in the swirl of modern challenge, what must it be like for adolescent girls? Can you say: *bewilderment, confusion, emotional turmoil?*[2] Adolescent girls are lost. Drowning. Utterly and absolutely overwhelmed, argues psychologist Mary Pipher in the wildly successful *Reviving Ophelia: Saving the Selves of Adolescent Girls*.

"Most preadolescent girls are marvelous company because they are interested in everything—sports, nature, music, and books," Pipher notes. "Almost all the heroines of girls' literature come from this age group—*Anne of Green Gables, Heidi, Pippi Longstocking*, and *Caddie Woodlawn*. Girls this age bake pies, solve mysteries, and are not yet burdened with caring for others. They have a brief respite from the female role and can be tomboys, a word that conveys courage, competency, and irreverence."[3]

Then it all changes.

"Something dramatic happens to girls in early adolescence," says Pipher. "Just as planes and ships disappear mysteriously into the Bermuda Triangle, so do the selves of girls go down in droves. They crash and burn in a social and developmental Bermuda Triangle.[4] In early adolescence, studies show that girls' IQ scores drop and their math and science scores plummet. They lose their resiliency and optimism and become less curious and inclined to take risks. They lose their assertive, energetic, and 'tomboyish' personalities and become more deferential, self-critical, and depressed. They report great unhappiness with their own bodies," Pipher explains.[5]

Adolescence is a time of confounding realities, when girls are told who they are and what they ought to be by their peers, the media, popular culture, music videos, and even their own body. It is a time when a "girl" is neither full adult, nor absolute child. She is not old enough—as a matter of law—to engage in most of the sins and vices that the law outlines, though there may be few physical hurdles in her way. But what, then, is the biography of the adolescent girl?

Very simply, it is the contradiction they feel. The adolescent lives of girls are a Caliban stew of conflicting laws, twisted social policy, and bent cultural interpretations that can wreak havoc on their developing psyches. It is a schizophrenic time made that much more inconsistent by traditional expectations, power politics, and a public persona threatening to undo it all.

For example, most of society views and treats adolescent females as though they were *women*, equal to adults in all ways, with all of the rights, privileges, and choices therein. And in many ways, it may seem to be true. Given the fashion of our times, she may, in fact, "look" like a woman and there is little really stopping her from having sex. She may have a baby at any time after puberty, provided her body can manage it. And young women are increasingly being tried as adults in the criminal context alongside young men.

And yet, by most other measures and under the law of most states, adolescent and teenage girls are *pre-women*—the legal appendages of parents (or of the state where there are no parents)—until they reach majority, which is generally defined as the point at which the state says the child is an adult. In most states, that is 18 at the latest. And, thus, regardless of how she dresses or how others respond to her changing body, and regardless of how "the girl" may attempt to present herself, by most legal definitions, adolescent girls remain "minor children," legally incapable, prior to a certain age, of consenting to the very acts thought to make a girl a woman.[6]

So what is the "girl" today? Is she the "woman" at 12 that the media, popular culture, and society seem to suggest? Or is she the "child," the law, most parents, and politicians would prefer? She is both, which begins the troubling conflict between what is false and what remains true. An adolescent girl may be deemed "old enough," for example, to consent to sex between the ages of 12 and 18,[7] depending upon the state in which she lives, and she is considered "adult enough" to choose to marry by the time she is 18 in most states.[8]

She has a legal right to choose to use contraceptives and even to have an abortion, though there are constraints. And yet, on her wedding night, should she choose to marry at the relatively mature age of 18 (because some states allow marriage at younger ages), she will not be legally adult enough to have a glass of champagne without breaking the law. She will not be adult enough to order a drink in a bar or to buy a pack of cigarettes for three more years, though she may have three children in the years between the time she marries and the time she turns 21.[9]

Inconsistencies of this sort may seem like little more than minor inconveniences to some. But the confusion created by so contradictory a set of laws—and the uncertain status they create for girls coming of age—raises profound questions for society; chief among them whether it is reasonable that decisions regarding sex, marriage, and parenthood should be deemed less significant than whether an 18-year-old mother can have a drink. It is a confused dichotomy giving rise to a body of social constructs that tend to sever the lives of girls into clashing parts.[10]

One reason for such inconsistency is that lawmakers—many of them parents—write laws that parents would write. Protective, paternalistic laws that reinforce traditional notions of adolescents. Under these laws, teenage girls are "children" to be treated as such,[11] though five minutes spent channel surfing, or a quick glance through popular teen magazines offers evidence to the contrary in page after page of fashion or cosmetic spreads that routinely recast the bodies of adolescent girls as nubile, sex-ready adults. At other times, the promulgation of such increasingly conservative bills are offered up by politicians in an effort to mollify family-value lobbyists[12] and the religious right.

In terms of the law, issues of adulthood and majority are part of the States versus Parents' Rights debate, a legal space where there has always been tension, because although parents are charged with the obligation of raising children,[13] the state's relationship to the minor child has historically been paramount.[14] It is the state, after all, that decides whether minors are being properly cared for by parents. And it is the state—not an adolescent girl's parents—that decides whether "the minor female" is legally able to consent to certain acts. Finally, it is the state that decides when a minor female becomes an adult and a woman,[15] which are not necessarily the same under the law.

And the state doesn't always stop there, because it doesn't have to. Though a child may be "liberated" as a matter of law from parents at majority, for instance, the state has traditionally remained involved in the lives of young women, given its "protective" role and their apparent need for protection, raising the specter of yet another conflict on issues of sex and reproduction among "minors." For example, the law has traditionally held that when a female child is married,[16] she becomes an individual, complete and separate from her parents.[17] In other words, marriage has historically been deemed an act that emancipates or "frees" the child from her parents. Thus, marriage arguably turned child into adult.[18]

In accordance with this reading of the law, a married female would appear to be adult enough to make private and personal choices in all aspects of her life. As an adult, it would seem that she would also be free of the intrusion of the state into private areas. And yet, the state has chosen at times to remain involved in the lives of young women even after marriage. Although it is rare and may have fallen out of favor today, there is some caselaw to suggest that despite the traditional expectation of emancipation that comes with marriage, a female minor may be neither *free,* nor *adult* enough in the eyes of the state to engage in certain private acts even after marriage.[19]

As recently as the late 1960s, a married minor female in the United States could not consent to sexual activity outside of marriage in some states. When she attempted to do so, the underage female's contingent status as adult was revoked and her legal identity reverted back to that of a "minor" in need of the state's protection. In the 1967, California case of *People v. Caldwell,*[20] for example, a married-but-separated 15-year-old began dating outside her marriage. Though the proper showing of state disapproval for this kind of conduct might have been a charge of adultery filed against the "woman," who was, after all, married, it was her lover who was charged—with statutory rape.

Though she was "old enough" to be married, under California law, the "girl" had not yet reached the legal age of numeric majority, a fact apparently known to her lover. To prove that the girl's lover had knowledge of her age, the young woman's mother testified somewhat colorfully during trial that she had warned the defendant her daughter was "San Quentin quail."[21] In response to the charges, attorneys for the young woman's lover argued that statutory rape laws were never intended to protect *married* minors. Was this the proper moral standard for the state to observe?

Perhaps. But what it suggests is that as a matter of law, a married—though "underage" female—may *only* be an "adult" as long as she remains under the protection of a husband. Further, it suggests that she may consent to sex only if it occurs *during* marriage. But this was 1967. Thus, it would seem that at that time in history, California granted minor females the conditional status of adult as long as she engaged in acts that the state approved of, especially with regard to sex and matters of the family. In ruling, the California court held that "the Legislature…deemed married minors as immature for certain purposes."[22] Sex outside of marriage was one of those purposes. Accordingly, state officials were entitled to intervene for the young woman's protection.

But could *People v. Caldwell* happen today? The case was decided prior to the landmark decisions of the 1970s, and the law regarding reproductive choice for minors has moved forward since 1967. In 1976, for example, the United States Supreme Court ruled in *Planned Parenthood of Central Missouri v. Danforth,*[23] that minor females were entitled to substantially the same fundamental rights regarding procreation as were adult women.

One of those "rights" was the right of choice regarding procreation (*i.e.,* the right to decide—free from unreasonable governmental intrusion—whether or not to have a child). In reaching the decision in *Planned Parenthood of Central Missouri v. Danforth,* the Justices held that "[c]onstitutional rights do not mature and come into being magically only when one attains the state-defined age of majority. Minors, as well as adults, are protected by the Constitution and possess constitutional rights…."

A year later, in *Carey v. Population Services Int'l*,[24] the Justices ruled that minor females were also entitled to the fundamental choice of birth control. Taken together, the Court's decisions in *Parenthood of Central Missouri v. Danforth* and *Carey v. Population Services Int'l.* clearly altered a traditional landscape for young women with regard to issues of sexual choice. And yet, most states still have—and many still vigorously enforce—statutory rape laws, traditionally viewed as "benevolent intrusions"[25] by state officials and historically "…heralded by women and reformers as a way of protecting innocent young girls from the vice of adult men."[26]

But critics of statutory rape laws argue that although their stated intent is to protect minors, in fact, such laws "unduly" interfere with a young woman's choice of a mate.[27] In addition, because minor females cannot legally consent to sex until the state permits it, their fundamental choices regarding procreation and motherhood are impacted, opponents argue. Finally, critics suggest that statutory rape laws do girls a disservice by stigmatizing them. "By classifying the underage female partner to consensual sexual intercourse as a 'victim' and the male partner as a criminal, statutory rape laws perpetuate stereotypical images of female passivity and male aggression," some argue.[28]

But there are critics of the alleged failure to enforce statutory rape laws as well. Author R. Barri Flowers argues in *The Victimization and Exploitation of Women and Children*, for example, that given the "consensual nature" of intercourse (even intercourse that may later be declared a crime), "little attention or seriousness to statutory rape is applied by the public, media, or law enforcement. Indeed, the occurrence of consensual sexual relations involving children is so widespread today, it has made statutory rape laws virtually unenforceable."[29]

The sexual lives of women have always been of considerable political and legal interest. The sexual lives of girls are no different. Rather, in some ways the sexual lives of girls are of greater interest, because the actions of girls are more easily regulated. And, thus, issues of adolescent and teen sexuality remain on the front of the political burner today. Indeed, the epicenter of the current political/legal debate over the sexual lives of "girls" involves one of the pet themes of the Bush administration. Abstinence, administration officials argue, will curtail incidents of statutory rape, underage pregnancy, sexually transmitted disease, abortion, and the use of contraceptives.[30] Girls and boys are apparently supposed to "just say no" to sex.

Abstinence may be a core of the Bush administration's plan for teens. But critics suggest that limiting or foreclosing the availability of contraceptives and birth control information to minors puts the lives of minors at risk because—in addition to the hormonal flux, the war of body image, and the roller coaster of self-esteem—adolescent girls are exploring their sexuality in the face of the spread of HIV, AIDS, and Hepatitis C, an infection far more widespread and contagious than HIV and yet hardly ever spoken of, though it can cause liver failure.[31]

Of course, some of it may not be their fault. Or their choice, because regardless of how she dresses or what she says or does, adolescent girls remain a temptation.

A confection. The best part of a "woman" to some. They are young. Perky. Sexy. And thus, they are the prey of the predatory. Indeed, in addition to the traditional growing pains of youth as one's body moves into a new space, adolescent girls face the potential today of Internet predators,[32] adult stalkers, dating violence, gangs, gunfire in the schoolyard, peer sexual harassment, sexual assault, rape, and the adult media construct of the sexual teen as sexual woman. Although they are still just girls.

But even that assertion gives rise to a bit of controversy. Emerging research suggests that secondary sex characteristics associated with puberty have begun to appear in girls of elementary school age.[33] In other words, the body—indeed, the very biology of the girl—may be moving toward the realm of woman sooner. And that fact, more than any other, tends to undo Pipher's view of the world of the preadolescent girl. What, after all, might the growth of breasts at the age of nine have done to the intrepid Anne of Green Gables? The stoic Heidi? The fearless Pippi Longstocking?

Indeed, it might be argued that when faced with so defining a change, even the adventurous Alice might have taken to her bed—unsure of how to proceed—instead of taking the wondrous tumble down the rabbit hole. Further, given the state of the girl today, were Lewis Carroll writing *Alice's Adventures in Wonderland* for the new century, the notoriously playful author might well have suggested that when Alice gazes through the looking glass, she might well have found an older woman looking back at her.[34]

America is conflicted about how it is to view and treat adolescent girls. For some purposes—usually legal—adolescent girls are children. For others—those that tend to give pleasure or make money—girls are women. And that is the problem: the politics of female adolescence are astoundingly complicated. Thus, in attempting to detail the modern world of today's pre-woman, there are at least three "girls" to be spoken of: (1) Biology's Girl, the female child moving through the biological change of *becoming* a woman; (2) Society's Girl, the young person urged by the pressures of modern culture to live in the guise of a woman; and, (3) the Law's Girl, the minor who remains legally incapable of engaging in adult, "womanly," behavior unless the state has consented.

BIOLOGY'S GIRL:
Becoming a Woman and the Hormone Parade

To Shakespeare, *woman* was a Divine offspring, "[a] child of our grandmother Eve."[35] To Johann Wolfgang von Goethe, she was a "silver dish into which we put golden apples."[36] An ornament, argued Edward Young, "…made to give our eyes delight."[37] "For the comfort of men," asserted James Howell.[38] But to the oft-quoted Oliver Wendell Holmes, a woman was confusion: "Nature is in earnest when she makes a woman," Holmes argued.[39] By contrast, it may have been Victor J.E. Jouy who best captured the essence of woman as mother and partner when he wrote that "[w]ithout women, the beginning of our life would be deprived of assistance, the middle portion of pleasure, and the end of consolation."[40]

And yet, before there can be women to lend "assistance," give "pleasure," or offer "consolation," there are girls who bake mud pies and solve mysteries. Then comes the monster of puberty, characterized generally by the appearance of breasts, the growth of pubic hair, and the softening of the hard, childish line into curves. But these external changes are driven by an inner rain of chemicals. For purposes of drama, popular writers often suggest that the transition from girl to woman is instant: "Kaboom!" they say, as though puberty were an isolated and sudden event.[41] But Pulitzer prize winning writer Natalie Angier writes in *Woman: An Intimate Geography* that girls are always part physically reproductive woman.[42]

And, thus, the story of puberty appears to begin where labor ends. At birth, the healthy baby girl holds all the reproductive eggs she will ever carry.[43] Although she is not conscious of it, and could not speak of it if she were, a normal infant female child's ovaries contain—even at so early a moment—1,000,000 follicles. Follicles are "balls of cells with an immature egg in the center."[44] But inner slumber embraces the child, maintaining, not maturing, these follicles until puberty begins.

During puberty hormones spark the eggs and follicles to life, and the biological march toward womanhood begins. But puberty is a complex business, marked by ebbs and flows, fits and starts. Among the early ebbs, for example, is the decline in bone growth. Then comes the flood of hormones, leading to an increase in the mass of breast tissue. Hair begins to grow under her arms and in the pubic area.[45] As the follicles of a girl's womb mature, they secrete a consommé of sex hormones, among them estrogen and progesterone, and that is when things really go gangbusters.

In this soup, surrounded by nurturing follicles, a singular egg—after so long in "storage"—begins to age. Eventually that egg will bubble to the surface of the ovary where the follicle will open, allowing the ovum to float away.[46] The free egg moves through the funnel-shaped end of one of the fallopian tubes, where wavelike contractions motion the egg towards the uterus. The release of a mature egg, known as ovulation, is one of two interrelated processes that begin as puberty draws to a close.[47]

Thus goes the story of how a girl becomes a woman on a biological level.[48] And it would be hard enough for a 12- or 14-year-old girl.[49] But how would the onset of puberty change the life of an 8- or a 9-year-old? Researchers in the United States and Europe suggest that the growth of breast tissue and pubic hair—physiological markers for the onset of puberty—have begun to appear amongst girls of Western nations at an earlier age, a circumstance that appears to have pulled elementary-aged school girls into the mix. It is a phenomenon known in scientific circles as "precocious puberty."

PRECOCIOUS PUBERTY:
The Physical Perspective and the Problems It May Cause

"Precocious sexuality" has always been a problem in American society, legal scholars argue, Senator Hillary Rodham Clinton among them. "The so-called status offenses, incorrigibility, truancy, running away, sexual precociousness, represent a confused mixture of social control and preventive care that has resulted in the confinement of thousands of children for the crime of having trouble growing up," Rodham Clinton wrote in a 1973 article, "Children Under the Law," published in the *Harvard Education Review*.[50]

Adolescence has not gotten any easier in the last three decades. In addition to "precocious sexuality" and the other great hazards of growing up, "precocious puberty," has become a part of the public debate in the last five years. Prior to 1997, most people had never heard the term "precocious puberty." But for more than seventy years, the study of "precocious" sexual development among preadolescent girls has been a scientific discipline all its own. As far back as 1929, researchers following the development of 252 girls in California found an "onset of breast budding [among some of the girls] of 10.6 years."[51] Roughly twenty years later, a 1948 study published by researchers at the Fels Institute in Ohio found a "mean onset of breast budding at 10.8 years"[52] in some girls.

In 1969, a third team of researchers detailed the findings of a study involving 192 British girls between the ages of 8 and 18.[53] The British study, commonly referred to in scientific circles as the Marshall-Tanner study, is well-respected for its methodology,[54] and according to the finding, the mean age for breast development among the girls was about 11 years old; while the mean age for the appearance of pubic hair was about 11-and-a-half.[55] Although Marshall-Tanner researchers noted that "the girls in their study were 'not representative of the British population,'…because they researched menarche at a mean age of 13.47 years…4 months later than the population in London…;"[56] the authors note that findings tending to show that "the first sign of puberty appeared between the ages of 8.5 years and 13 years in 95 percent of girls…to have been widely accepted as a standard for the normal onset of puberty in girls."

So which is true? Has the mean age of puberty fallen? Or has it remained about the same over the course of a century? In an attempt to answer that question, scientists in North Carolina's Research Triangle undertook "a large cross-sectional study involving 17,000 girls between 3 and 12 years of age…seen in 65 different, primarily suburban practices around the United States…."[57] The findings of the 1997 study shows "that puberty is occurring significantly earlier than in the past," suggests Dr. Marcia Herman-Giddens, the study's chief author.[58] The North Carolina team also found that "the prevalence of one or more secondary sexual characteristics in girls younger than 8 years of age…is substantially higher than the commonly used figure of 1 percent [as detailed in previous studies]."[59]

In more specific terms, "on average, African American girls begin puberty between 8 and 9 years of age and white girls by 10 years age,"[60] according to the

North Carolina team. But in a bit of controversy, the 1997 study itself sparked debate over the possible need for the revision of the medical definition of "precocious puberty."[61] The outcome of that debate was a 1999 "critical examination of the new [1997] study, and a review of data concerning the benefits of treatment with gonadotropin-releasing hormone (GnRH) analogs in girls with precocious puberty."[62] The treatment had been debated as a possible medical solution that could retard precocious development in girls.

In response to proposed medical intervention, reevaluators involved in the 1999 study argued that "the onset of breast development between 7 and 8 years of age in white girls and between 6 and 8 years in African American girls may be part of the normal broad variation in the timing of puberty."[63] With regard to the onset of menses, they argued that the age of menarche[64] appears to have remained relatively consistent at about 12 years of age, though researchers note that number too has fallen from roughly 16 at the turn of the century.[65]

In 2001, the Endocrine Society and the Lawson-Wilkins Pediatric Endocrine Society challenged the 1997 study, arguing that "it is not yet established that girls typically enter puberty earlier today."[66] Though experts disagree, the lion's share of research seems to suggest that the appearance of secondary sex characteristics appears to be occurring earlier today in some girls. Though it is impossible to offer a definitive answer to the question of whether puberty is "precocious" today where scientists continue to debate, what makes this work worth noting at all is what a near-century of continual study tells us: that the sexual development of girls is as emotional and divisive an issue as the sex lives of girls.

Of course, if there is no precocious puberty, there can be no side effects. But some experts suggest that in addition to the early onset of secondary sex characteristics, "precocious puberty" changes the lives of girls in other ways.[67] "Behavior problems have been noted in girls with precocious puberty, although there are few well-designed studies on this issue," the authors of 1999 study contend.[68] "As a group, these girls appeared to be more depressed, socially withdrawn, aggressive, and moody than those in the control group."[69]

And yet, the "behavior problems" of adolescent girls are rarely among the highest of the hurdles they seem to face today. On May 24, 1999, the United States Supreme Court handed down the decision in *Davis, as next friend of LaShonda D. v. Monroe County Board of Education et al.*,[70] a case involving the question of whether sexual harassment between classmates can occur in an elementary school setting. According to the Court, school districts could be held liable for failing to halt continuous unwanted sexual advances made against a female elementary school student by a male classmate.

The decision has been criticized by some practitioners as "bad law."[71] But many feminists embraced the decision for other reasons: the suit began with a fifth grader named LaShonda, who alleged[72] that the "deliberate indifference" of school officials to a classmate's "persistent sexual advances" created "an intimidating, hostile, offensive, and abusive school environment that violated Title IX of the Education Amendments of 1972."[73]

A mistake? An overly sensitive child? Feminist hysteria?

Sexual aggression by young men in high school has long been tolerated and traditionally attributed to hormones or the fact that "boys will be boys," some women's rights scholars argue. But would a fifth grader know how to make "persistent sexual advances"? The Justices of the United States Supreme Court seemed to think so, noting, in support of the decision, that:

> According to petitioner's complaint, the harassment began in December 1992, when the classmate, G.F., attempted to touch LaShonda's breasts and genital area and made vulgar statements such as 'I want to go to bed with you' and 'I want to feel your boobs.' G.F.'s conduct allegedly continued for many months.... In early February, G.F. purportedly placed a doorstop in his pants and proceeded to act in a sexually suggestive manner toward LaShonda during physical education class.[74] G.F. allegedly rubbed his body against LaShonda in the school hallway in what LaShonda considered a sexually suggestive manner."[75]

Though LaShonda reported the incidents to school officials,[76] the assaults did not end until the following spring "when G.F. was charged with, and plead guilty to, sexual battery for his misconduct,"[77] the Justices noted.[78] The fact that school officials were aware of LaShonda's complaints and apparently did little to prevent repeated incidents opened the door to legal liability. But perhaps more troubling than the fact that a school district can be found liable for sexual harassment in a case involving elementary school children, is that *Davis v. Monroe County Board of Education* suggests the onset of the reach of the law into the lives of America's children may also be as "precocious" today as their sexuality and possible development.[79]

Manhattan psychologist Dr. Marsha Levy-Warren said in an interview in 2000, that she "is seeing more and more preteenagers who are going on junior versions of dates in fifth grade, at 10 or 11 years old. By seventh grade, they have graduated to sex."[80]

Dr. Robert W. Blum, a physician and director of pediatrics and adolescent health at the University of Minnesota, reported that "[b]esides intercourse, [adolescents] are engaging in oral sex, mutual masturbation, nudity, and exposure as precursors to intercourse."[81] Roughly seventeen percent of seventh and eighth graders surveyed as part of a study admit to having had sexual intercourse, according to Blum. The findings of the study were published in the *Journal of the American Medical Association.*[82]

Other studies suggest that one in every five teenagers may have had sex before reaching the age of 15.[83] But like the issue of precocious puberty, what may really be happening among adolescents and teenagers remains the stuff of debate. Reports in the popular media suggest that teen—and even preteen—sex practices run the gamut from oral sex to intercourse,[84] though a declining teen-pregnancy rate suggests that if teens are having more sex, they are also making greater use of condoms and other contraceptives.

Researchers and some medical professionals argue that the participation of young people in noncoital sexual activities is higher today than in the past. But others challenge these are other assertions, suggesting that "noncoital practices"—oral sex among them—may simply be talked about by young people more often than in previous years.[85] What no one seems to dispute is that "...[k]ids are overwhelmed with sexual messages, and we're seeing a younger and younger display of not only precocious sexual behavior but also aggressive sexual molestation, like holding down a student and forcibly pulling down his or her pants," says Dr. Frederick Kaeser, director of health services for District 2 of the New York Public School System.[86]

The student was not held down in *Davis v. Monroe County Board of Education*. But she was pursued for months by a sexually aggressive child. And though social scientists may debate the issue, incidents of this sort suggest that the early involvement of children in sexual or sex-related conduct is a real phenomenon that has become part of the public consciousness to be dealt with under the law. *Davis* is clearly the most significant case of sexual harassment involving an elementary school student. But it was not the first case involving a suit filed against a school district for allegedly failing to prevent repeated sexually aggressive acts made toward girls by male classmates.

Several years before the Court's decision in *Davis v. Monroe County Board of Education*, a California school district was sued on behalf of an elementary school girl who was repeatedly "taunted by her male classmates." Among the reported playground taunts: "I hear you have a hot dog in your pants."[87] While in English class, another boy allegedly asked the girl in front of the class: "Did you have sex with a hot dog?"[88] After two years of complaints to school officials, a lawsuit was filed on behalf of the girl. After the case was dismissed, the girl went to private school.[89]

And sexually aggressive behavior among school children is not all that rare. In June 2000, a 14-year-old Brooklyn student was reportedly "sexually abused by three classmates" while on a class trip to a park.[90] In that case, the "three classmates—boys 12 to 14 years old—pushed the girl into a sprinkler and groped her through her clothing," according to police.[91]

G.F.'s conduct in *Davis v. Monroe County Board of Education* clearly went beyond that, according to the findings of the Justices of the United States Supreme Court. But unlike the boys involved in the California and Brooklyn incidents, G.F. was not 12 or 14 or even in junior high school yet. At the time of the events underlying the federal lawsuit, LaShonda D. and G.F. were 10 and 11 years old[92] and G.F. would eventually plead guilty to sexual battery.[93]

"Problems at the elementary level are illustrated by the story of a 6-year-old girl who came home with a profane vocabulary as a result of the sexual taunts she was subjected to while riding to school on the bus," writes Stephanie Easland in *Attacking the "Boys Will Be Boys" Attitude: School Liability Under Section 1983 for Peer Sexual Harassment*.[94] "These comments were made to her by boys in the fourth grade."[95] But fourth grade may not even be the beginning of it. Similar behavior "has been observed even on the kindergarten level where on 'flip-up

Friday[s],' kindergarten girls at one school are afraid to wear skirts and dresses due to boys flipping up their skirts during recess," Easland says.[96]

Suggestive comments, sexual taunts on the school bus, and a fifth grader pleading guilty to sexual battery after months of aggressive, sexually suggestive behavior appear to be part of the texture of preadolescence today. But why is it that elementary school boys seem to think girls are there for the taking? Are American boys acting as they think they should act? These questions have yet to be definitively answered by researchers. But one thing is for certain: as difficult as it may be to look in the face, the notion of the "wanton" 12-year-old is part of American culture today. Adolescent girls, it seems, have an image problem.

C CUPS AND PRECOCIOUS SEXUAL CONTACT:
Because Boys Will Be Boys

> My breasts started to grow in the fifth grade, and by the time I was in the
> seventh grade, I was wearing a 'C' cup. That's when I became known in
> my suburban New York private school for something other than my ster-
> ling report cards. Before, I had been someone who kids turned to for help
> when they were stumped with vocabulary homework. Now I was the
> number-one target for bra-snapping.
>
> Leora Tanenbaum, from
> *Slut! Growing Up Female With a Bad Reputation*[97]

The budding bodies of girls provoke response. Thus, the greatest difficulty facing adolescent and teen girls today may be what grown men and their peers attempt to make of them. Rarely is it as simple these days as "bra-snapping." During the summers of 1994 and 1995, police in New York City began answering calls arising out of a new swimming pool "game" called whirlpooling. The "game" involved a group of teenage boys, who would surround a lone girl in the pool and "try to remove her bathing suit in order to 'grope' her or have sex," Cornell University Professor Joan Jacobs Brumberg explains in *The Body Project: The Intimate History of American Girls*.[98]

"...[A]dolescent girls are subject to more sexual pressure than ever before; they are more likely to become sexually active before they are 16; and all of this activity makes them more vulnerable to multiple medical risks..." says Brumberg.[99] They also appear to be vulnerable to becoming victims. "...National data reveal that 14 and 15 are two of the peak ages for becoming a victim of sexual assault; approximately 50 percent of rape victims are between 10 and 19, and half of this group is under 16," notes Brumberg.[100]

In addition to the possibility of sexual assault, a 1995 nationwide study by the Alan Guttmacher Institute found that "heightened adult male interest in the bodies of young girls is not a figment of the feminist imagination," says Brumberg.[101] "In fact, a startling number of teenage girls are having sex with adult men, instead of with boys their own age. In California, among teenage mothers

11 to 15, only 9 percent of the partners were junior high school boys; 40 percent were in high school, and 51 percent were adults."[102]

It is a national phenomenon confronted every day by social workers and child protective authorities. Crystal Taylor was a 14-year-old New Yorker, for example, when authorities entered her life. The daughter of a drug addict, Taylor was living with her boyfriend and his mother when she gave birth to a baby boy. But the birth led to a fight with social services agencies, because in the state's view—even though Crystal was now a mother—there were two minors in need of the care and protection of the state: the newborn child (Daquan) and the teenage mother.[103]

Crystal, the state argued, was at risk and could no longer live with the child's grandmother, because the child's father (Crystal's boyfriend) was a 23-year-old male. Though Crystal told authorities she consented to sex with the child's father and wanted to remain in the household, authorities noted that under state law her age rendered her incapable of granting consent to sexual intercourse. Crystal and her child were taken into protective custody while New York authorities considered whether to prosecute the baby's father.

In 1994, underage girls were among the 11.5 million teenagers having sexual relations: 6.5 million of them male, 5 million of them female.[104] In 1996, roughly 200,000 babies were born in the United States to girls between the ages of 10 and 17.[105] But others put this number much higher, suggesting that perhaps as many as "one million American girls become pregnant each year," with fully half of these pregnancies resulting in children born out of wedlock.[106]

One of the truths facing young girls is that there are adult men who think nothing of age. And there are some who will pursue girls because they are underage. Breasts, curves, and maybe even a little bit of curiosity are assumed often to be the measure of a woman, even if she is still a "child"[107] That may explain, at least in part, why some number of underage "women" bear the children of adult males each year.

But girls also appear to be having sex with boys their age, an experience that can be wonderfully intimate and magical. Or, like most other things during the teen years, humiliating and fraught with the echoes of ancient stereotypes of young women, a fact noted by Joan Didion in a 1993 article on California's notorious Spur Posse.

> "He cornered me and he tried to kiss me, then he started taking off my pants," the sweet-faced seventeen-year-old told us, first on *20/20* and then on *Montel Williams*. "He did his business and stood up, began to walk away. And I sat there crying, scrounging for my pants, and he says, 'Don't say you didn't want to,' and he walked away."
>
> "They were downright crude," a girl in a wig and dark glasses told us on *Donahue*. "They did not want to date me. They did not want to get to know me…. They went out of their way to touch me. They went out of their way to bump me…. Physically run into me. Grab me."

"It's always, you know, we're the sluts, but they're the big studs," a sixteen-year-old reported on *20/20*. "I felt used...I don't have any respect for myself. I have no self-esteem left in me at all."[108]

In March of 1993, several members of the Spur Posse were arrested on charges ranging from rape by intimidation to unlawful sexual intercourse to lewd conduct.[109] But several weeks later, the Office of the District Attorney released a statement, explaining that "[a]fter completing an extensive investigation and analysis of the evidence, our conclusion is that there is no credible evidence of forcible rape involving any of these boys.... Although there is evidence of unlawful sexual intercourse, it is the policy of this office not to file criminal charges where there is consensual sex between teenagers.... The arrogance and contempt for young women which has been displayed, while appalling, cannot form the basis for criminal charges."[110]

Though not the basis for criminal charges, the "points system" employed by Spur Posse members suggests that for some, sex has become "an essentially commercial transaction, the transfer of a commodity with depreciable value," Didion argues.[111] A simple bit of addition and subtraction, mostly for the self-esteem of the young women involved.

"Why would a girl sleep with a guy on the first date," a Spur Posse member asked somewhat rhetorically on *Maury Povich*. And in due time, he provided the answer: "They're whores." Another said that "[i]f a girl sleeps with a guy on the first night, that's not somebody that you can respect." Still a third suggested, in answering questions about how he would like his sister to be treated, that his sister was "probably one of the only virgins left in the whole city," and "she'll stay that way."[112]

It is ironic perhaps that the echoes of so ancient an equation would cross the lips of men so young. But not surprising. It is an old story in a history of double standards. But the Spur Posse incident occurred ten years ago. Conventional wisdom would suggest that great strides have not been made by girls in this particular realm. But what is the story on girls today?

THE TERRAIN OF MODERN GIRLHOOD:
From Adolescent Girl to Woman-of-the-World in a Blink

More than ever before, adolescent girls are coming of age in a world electric with sexuality. With the penetration of the sun, sexy *girls* are everywhere, their heavily made-up but-clearly-adolescent faces fronting magazines, their lips and hips pulsing in the blue spaces of a youth-oriented universe where they come alive on magazine covers; in shamelessly provocative ads; on movie screens; and on prime time television shows heavy on "adult themes."

It is in this world that the goal of girls is not only to exude sex. But to sell it. Thus, the message seen and heard by teenagers today is that they are supposed to be "sexy" and they are supposed to have sex the way the teenagers and adolescents on television do. Anywhere. Anyplace. Anytime. Sometimes for "love." Sometimes for sport. Sometimes as part of a sexual "transaction" increasingly understood as part of the cultural "norm." Of course, television has had a hand in getting these kinds of ideas across.

"A girl student is shown getting up from her knees after administering oral sex to a boy," TV critic Julie Salamon writes outlining the events of the Fox show *Boston Public*.[113] Though "[a]dminister may seem like the wrong verb, a bit formal," Salamon notes, "...as it turns out, this [was] a business arrangement. These classmates were running against one another in a school election, and she was simply campaigning for his vote."

With an average of 3.4 television sets in households where adolescents live,[114] convincing young people that they should follow the lead of their contemporaries on the screen seems to be an easy sell. From the celebration of aggressively promiscuous characters on popular shows and music videos that ride the thighs of thong-clad young women[115] to the suggestion of teenage sex as something to do to fill in the blanks, sex is so much a part of the public equation today that most Americans no longer even notice.

In addition to TV, an electronic universe of computers, cellular phones, and wireless connections offer teenagers the prospect of an "online" life. And though the Internet may be a tremendous source of entertainment and educational information,[116] its many and varied websites offer a smorgasbord of half- or fully undressed women, pornography, personal webcams, and sexually explicit documents, posted sometimes even on government websites.[117] There are also chatrooms that can open a virtual back door for adult opportunists looking for a way into teenagers' lives.[118]

All this, of course, is part of the paradox. If you believe what you see and hear, adolescent girls are supposed to have sex. On television or on the Internet, teenagers are witty and confident. Smart enough to carry condoms; wise enough to *prefer* "safe sex." But in "real life," young people—even those who admit to researchers and reporters that they engage in certain sex acts—are often far less educated and far less prepared for sex than their television counterparts.

In July 1999, the *Washington Post* reported that suburban Virginia junior high students were engaging in oral sex rather than going "all the way," because they did not view oral sex as "sex." The story caused a sensation.[119] But *Post* editors defended it as a public service, noting that sexually transmitted diseases, including HIV, can be transmitted during oral sex.[120]

Of course, TV sex only has deadly consequences if HIV is the subject of the made-for-TV movie it is in. But in real life, the nation's teenagers learned—following a series of events in the small upstate New York community of Jamestown in 1997—that in the real world, the virus that causes AIDS can be passed on by people who look healthy, who are charming, and who may even seem to care. The person at the center of that particular storm was a man identified by law enforcement officials and the media as Nu Shawn Williams, described in media reports as a "small-time drug dealer who had come to upstate Chautauqua County from Brooklyn in 1995."[121]

By the time he left town, fourteen women and girls ranging in age from 14 to 24 who had unprotected sex with Williams tested positive for the HIV virus.[122] Williams eventually pled guilty to reckless endangerment for having unprotected sex with a Bronx high school student.[123]

Law enforcement officials suggest that one of the reasons Williams was so "successful" with the young women of Jamestown is that he was charming, otherworldly, and nice to look at. And that, of course, is part of the equation.

Adolescent girls are coming of age in a world where beautiful men clad only in their underwear grace the sky-high billboards in New York's Times Square. It is in this world where perfection and youth are persuasion and where the *perfect* bodies—traditionally of America's girls, but increasingly of America's boys as well—are offered up to the ubiquitous gods of sales in an economic exchange that has *made* girls women at younger and younger ages with the suggestion of sex worn more often than clothes.

A recent ad featuring a former child-star actress, for example, has her smiling toward the camera as she caresses the head and neck of a male admirer standing behind her. The male admirer is pulling down the front of her T-shirt as he sprays her cleavage with perfume.[124] The pitch is for perfume. But is that all? In another ad, a tall blonde woman-child leans over the engine of an expensive car as though she might fix it (and she may). Behind her a burly leather-clad man stares at her rear end and thinks *only*—in a comic word bubble—"Nice Jeans."[125] And just what is the best way to sell a watch? A picture of the watch up close to show detail and workmanship? A wristwatch campaign during the late 1990s called "Skin" featured a picture of the watch alongside the youthfully thin, nude female silhouette in pigtails. The ad included one sentence: *As Light As a Shadow.*

Of course, nudity and the whiff of sexual suggestion are not limited to sales campaigns for underwear, jeans, watches, and perfumes. Sex sells TV shows and all of the commercials that run in between. "Most of the shows create fantasies or other excuses to ogle cleavage or navels—most brilliantly in *Roswell*,[126] in which the lead, Shiri Appleby, has been healed of a gunshot wound to the abdomen by a Martian teen, so she keeps having to lift her shirt to examine the iridescent handprint it left behind," critics of the 1999 fall television season note.[127]

A belly flash and an alien handprint as a pretext to offer skin may explain why the show didn't last. But prurient dashes of this kind remain the staple of the competition to draw viewers.

Since its appearance more than a decade ago, for example, *NYPD Blue* has titillated with the "southern exposures" of chiseled physiques and male backsides. And yet, what was daring then is child's play now. Of course, prime-time shows "have to compete with CNN and other reality-based entertainment," television critics note.[128] The suggestion of sex made ever more racy is often calculated to give shows an edge.[129] At other times, writers and producers suggest that the presentation of teenage sex simply reflects the real-life issues faced by teenagers today. And it sounds convincing as long as real life doesn't invade the pretense too much.

Actress Meredith Moore talked openly during an interview, for example, about the "positive approach" to teen sexuality she felt writers had taken on the then-enormously popular show *Dawson's Creek*.[130] The show undertook a gay story line and wrote in an on-screen kiss at the close of the 2000 season. Television can be a comfortable and provocative space, where artistic ideas and the best hopes for society may be freely offered up. And so on TV, when teenagers "come out," they usually do so to loving parents and supportive friends. But in the real world, when Adam Colton, a 17-year-old California high school student, announced that he was gay, and had formed the Gay-Straight Alliance at his school in September 1998, he was beaten black and blue.[131] Attacks of this kind are not uncommon, some scholars suggest, regardless of what is on TV.

"Cultural homophobia affects all adolescents," argues Elvia Arriola, assistant professor of law at the University of Texas at Austin.[132] "Harassment on campuses is not only directed at gay students; often the heterosexual children of gays and lesbians are harassed at school.[133] The wide reach of homophobia is evident in its ability to turn one set of students into victims and another set into violent perpetrators."[134]

In addition, though there is rarely a hint of it on television, in real-life law enforcement officials may still intrude upon a teenager's sex life. Legislation is often drafted and enacted for the express purpose of discouraging adolescents from moving into the erotic World of Wonders so frequently urged on MTV. Criminal penalties founded in definitions of "majority" outline the boundaries of these intrusions.[135] And these penalties tend to fall harder on gay people, including young gay people.

In June of 2003, civil libertarians and gay rights activists rallied around the cause of an 18-year-old Kansas man sentenced to seventeen years in prison following a conviction for "sodomy." The "sodomy" in this case involved consensual oral sex between the 18-year-old and a 14-year-old at a home for developmentally challenged youths where both of the young men lived. In challenging the sentence, lawyers argued that the United States Supreme Court's recently issued decision striking down sodomy laws applied. Attorneys also noted that had the young child been a girl, the maximum sentence possible would have been 15 months. On June 27, 2003, the decision was deemed vacated in light of *Lawrence v. Texas*.[136]

There is "indecent" sex with boys, it seems, that could get a person seventeen years, and "indecent" sex with girls, which could get a person fifteen months. Such are the inequities of a system that has come to "devalue" girls. And yet, the stigma of disgrace remains. Though the law may fail to adequately punish men who have sex with underage girls, as some critics argue, girls continue to face the sharp teeth of social machinery that still labels young women "whores" when they "put out." Indeed, as incongruous as it may seem in these days of aggressive sexuality, calling a girl a "slut" still packs a powerful punch, which is why it still happens. According to Tanenbaum, "[t]wo out of five girls nation-wide—42 percent—have had sexual rumors spread about them, according to a 1993 poll conducted for the American Association of University Women on sexual harassment in schools,"[137] a fact that suggests that sex is still a boy's game, and the girl is a "whore" when she gives in.

Of course, public service announcements and abstinence-only education programs tell young women that they ought to abstain from sex, because "[a]bstinence is the surest way, and the only completely effective way, to prevent unwanted pregnancies and sexually transmitted disease," according to President Bush.[138] And though teen pregnancy rates fell in 1998 and 1999,[139] the efforts of these apparently stoic youths were not helped by a gaggle of teen-idol actresses and singers making public—and, indeed, almost chic—pregnancies met by media praise, whether or not the young women were married.[140]

But, in the "real world" praise for the pregnant teen is less rare than litigation. Two female students in Covington, Kentucky,[141] and another in Xenia, Ohio,[142] were forced to file suit, for example, against school districts, alleging that they were denied memberships in local chapters of the National Honor Society because each of the young women had a child out of wedlock.[143] In commenting on the case to the media, an attorney for one of the young women described the district's action as the branding of female teenagers with "a scarlet P."[144]

A third school district was sued after the *Oakland Tribune* published a photograph of two pregnant girls with their shirts cinched up to show their swollen bellies. The picture caused an unexpected stir, even though it accompanied a story on teen motherhood. And though the teenagers were clearly participants in the photo, they later filed suit alleging—among other things—that the picture had been taken without parental consent.[145] Other legal issues raised by the case revolved around the question of whether the newspaper had a right to photograph minors on public school property.

And yet, at about the same time that the suits in Kentucky, Ohio, and California were making news, officials in a fourth school district had apparently so resigned themselves to the inevitably of pregnancy among its students that it began teaching something that most people might think went out with the hoop skirts of the 1950s: "marriage skills" classes.[146]

Of course, adolescent girls seem to understand the contradictions they are living through. "Adolescence is not what I thought it would be," offers Sara Shandler, editor of the 1999 *Ophelia Speaks: Adolescent Girls Write About their Search for Self.*[147] "Happy endings aren't inserted conveniently before the last commercial break. The peer pressure isn't unrelenting, the wild parties aren't dangerously tempting, the first loves aren't thrillingly perfect."[148]

Deborah Tolman writes in *The Dilemmas of Desire: Teenage Girls Talk About Sexuality*, "[f]or Emily, her own desire has led both to humiliating and scary encounters she regrets and to powerful experiences of connection with someone she loves. It has led to exciting, unexpected moments tinged with taboo and to frustrating, disappointing interactions that leave her confused. Emily is not sure if or how she can rely on her desire, or when it is and is not safe to do so. Yet these contradictory experiences of desire are not compartmentalized; each hangs over the other, casting shadows and shining light on the possibilities for danger and glints of pleasure."[149]

The literature of young people also reflects some of the danger young women feel. In the teen-novel *The Facts Speak for Themselves*, for example, author Brock Cole tells the story of Linda, a 13-year-old girl, whose adult lover is shot in front of her on a parking ramp by her mother's boyfriend, who then kills himself.[150] In *Speak*, Laurie Halse Anderson tells the story of a ninth grade girl who becomes a social outcast after she breaks up a summer party by calling the police. In response to the shunning, the girl stops speaking in an attempt to forget the reason she called the police in the first place: she was raped while in a drunken stupor during the party.[151]

And yet, it may be the mothers of real-life girls who tell stories of perhaps the greatest danger facing adolescent girls today: "I'm late, just a little late," Catherine Hellman recounts in *Ophelia's Mom: Women Speak Out About Loving and Letting Go of Their Adolescent Daughters*. "[My daughter] hops in the car and tells me this story: 'Mom, a man drove up to me and tried to get me to go in his car.' Emily, my 13-year-old child, is standing in the rain, this guy pulls up, rolls down his window, gives her a nod, and issues this invitation: 'Hop in. I'll give you a ride.' We're talking in front of a high school. Right in front of a high school."[152]

SOCIETY'S GIRL:
The Lolita Effect and Adoration of the 12-year-old

So when was it exactly that the female child turned from innocent playmate to compelling sexual object? In terms of world facts, children—the overwhelming majority of them girls—are a thing of value in the world sex trade. "Each year, millions of children—boys as well as girls—are bought and sold like fresh produce, commodities in a global sex industry steeped in greed and unspeakable cruelty," according to UNICEF executive director Carol Bellamy.[153]

As a "social problem" the world sex trade has been talked about in the abstract for years. But it wasn't until a 16-year-old runaway from Vermont was found dead in a New York City brothel that "the problem" acquired urgency and became a talking point of public discussion in the United States.[154] By August 2003, Congress had approved $4 million in funding to combat the sexual exploitation of children and President Bush began including it as the subject of comment in speeches. Still, there were distinctions.

Though it may not be so in the eyes of the law in some states, many people would argue that a 16-year-old is not a child. And, therefore, while child sexual exploitation may be a real issue, consensual sex with a 16-year-old—as opposed to forced prostitution—is not the kind of social problem in need of a solution. But what about an 11-year-old? In the spring of 2001, a 28-year-old Indiana principal absconded with an 11-year-old girl he claimed to be in love with. A cross-country chase ensued with the pair eventually being tracked to Las Vegas where the principal was arrested. The young girl was returned to her family.

It is hard to say and, indeed, harder to know what turns the desires of grown men toward children. Thus, it is perhaps simplest to say that some men—and it is overwhelmingly men—are attracted to children. These are people who have always been part of American society, though they often were only counted publicly in the context of criminal statistics. And yet, the apparent "dark pleasure" of underaged sex has been part of the public discourse—on an intellectual level, at least—since the word *Lolita* was uttered.[155]

Lolita, that classic read by thousands each year for pleasure or at the demand of teachers and professors, tells the story of a 12-year-old girl who is spirited away by her molester who believes he is in love with her. The molester is her stepfather, who marries the child's mother only to be close to the girl. When the child's mother realizes this, she runs in front of a car in her distraction and is killed, leaving "Lolita" to be raised by the man who wants her most.

It is not exactly the stuff of after school specials. But *Lolita* is considered serious "literature" by some scholars. Yet from the perspective of women, Vladimir Nabovok's *Lolita* offers a shattering example of the politics of female adolescence: the sexuality of girls is the trade of commerce, even when offered in the high-minded guise of literature. Some scholars argue that *Lolita* is about an aesthetic, an intellectual idea. That may be true. But it is also true that few authors survive the indulgence of writing books they do not intend to sell. And in *Lolita,* Nabokov found the kind of commercial success most writers only dream of.

It is the girl and the virgin territory her "provocative" nature (real or imagined) represents that titillates. It is the idea that the girl, even at 12, may choose the time and place for her deflowering. But most of all, *Lolita* offers the possibility that a 12-year-old girl would seduce a hapless, middle-aged man. That, more than anything else, is what has turned the pages and sold the book for decades. Critics of this assertion will likely argue that it is nothing more than feminist polemics. And that may be. But if *Lolita* were the story of an older woman's obsession with a twelve-year-old boy, would the 1955 book be *a classic*?[156]

Would the art of a close reading be encouraged by professors and scholars? In fact, America has long held such a tryst to be repugnant, especially if it results in a sexually transmitted disease. "The debased woman, who lures to her vile embrace an innocent boy and infects him with a loathsome disease, is equally liable to this action, in an injury to his master's right to service follow from her crime," a New York court wrote in the 1856 decision in *White v. Nellis.*[157] But is it any less repugnant when it results in the spread of disease or the pregnancy of an underaged girl?

Indeed, when the equation involves an adult woman and boy, even where no "loathsome" disease is involved, it is almost as though there were. Case in point: the tabloid story turned tragic opera of Mary Kay Latourneau, whose obsession with a sixth grade boy parallels Humbert's mania for "Lolita" with similarly sad results. Latourneau was a well-respected teacher and a mother who fell in love with a boy.[158] And she would be sent to prison for it, though the boy would publicly declare his love for Latourneau as well and stated intentions once upon a time to marry Latourneau when she is released from prison. The couple's second child was born to Latourneau while in prison. In an ironic twist, however, in April 2000, Latourneau's young man filed suit against the school district, alleging that officials had failed to protect him from his teacher's sexual advances.[159]

And what if Lolita had been Lolito? Would there be the same soft spot of understanding for Humbert, if the *boy* were 12 and as apparently willing? We know the answer is no, because as set forth above, when an 18-year-old man in Kansas had oral sex with a 14-year-old boy, he was convicted of "sodomy" and originally sentenced to seventeen years in prison.[160] But why, then, have scholars so readily embraced the predatory sexual conduct apparent in *Lolita*? Because it is "natural" for a man to sleep with a woman, even if that "woman" is a child. And that is the strength of *Lolita*. The connection between the two main characters is "natural" but forbidden—as opposed to what would clearly have been seen as "unnatural" if Humbert had cast his eyes so lovingly on a boy.

Even in Nabokov's time, sex with a girl-child was illegal and it is illegal in the book. But few remember the illegality of Humbert's conduct, because Nabokov does alchemy, bending adult desire for a child into mainstream passion. Indeed, the suggestion that a child could be sexually treacherous proved so lucrative a device in *Lolita* that in 1999, nearly five decades after its original publication, a French publisher released the controversial *Lo's Diary*, a page-burner brazenly marketed as a retelling of the Nabokov story "in the words of the nymphet herself."[161]

Lo's Diary was an international bestseller due in part, no doubt, to a "new and improved" Dolores, recast in this reinvention as an aggressive and insatiable "nymphet" whose desires are all woman and no child.[162] Of course, Nabokov was not the first author to explore a middle-aged man's sexual obsession with an almost teenaged girl. Nor was he the only modern author to garner commercial success for doing so. Following in Nabokov's footsteps and benefiting by comparison was Marguerite Duras, author of *The Lover*, which told the story of a poor French girl in a sometimes violent relationship with a cruel but wealthy Asian merchant.[163]

But in addition to spawning a library list of copycats, *Lolita* gave rise to a catalog of references tending to diminish girls. For example, when a young girl is thought to be sexually precocious, she is dubbed a "Lolita," even though she may have victimized.[164] Amy Fisher was dubbed a "Long Island Lolita" almost immediately by the media, for example, because as a teenager she became involved with an older married man. Or, more precisely, a married man got involved with a teenager, because that is how the law sees it. Still, Amy Fisher became "Lolita," a *nymphet* with the power to seduce a grown man.[165]

Is it any real surprise, then, that boys may be grappling with the trickle-down effect?

"America is a pluralistic culture with contradictory sexual paradigms," wrote Pipher in *Reviving Ophelia*.[166] "We hear diverse messages from our families, our churches, our schools, and the media, and each of us must integrate these messages and arrive at some value system that makes sense to us."[167]

Among these paradigms is the notion that a girl is a "girl" until she is deemed, has proven herself to be, or is imagined to be something else.[168] But what makes so simple a statement confusing is that the "proof" needed to make it so can come in any form. If an adolescent girl develops early, for example, she may become a "woman" in the eyes of male peers and older men. If her curves are too big or her breasts too full, she may be labeled a tramp and "bumped" or "run into" as a cover for groping.[169] She may become a target of harassment just because she is pretty.[170] Or worse. According to research, one in every six rape victims in the United States is under 12[171]—the age of Nabokov's "Lolita."

And the courts—where justice is supposed to prevail—are not always better. In June 2000, a South Carolina judge reportedly reduced the time served for a convicted sex offender, because the 14-year-old girl involved was "large," which the judge reasoned made her look older.[172] "The major factor in my decision (to reduce [Kevin] Tucker's sentence) was that (the girl's size) had not been brought to my attention during the original plea hearing in April," Circuit Judge Wyatt Saunders Jr., reasoned. "(Tucker) had said [the girl] appeared to be a good deal older (than 14), but there was no further explanation of why."

Tucker, a youth minister and the 14-year-old's former Sunday school teacher, was sentenced to seventeen years in prison after pleading guilty in April 2000 to second-degree criminal sexual conduct with a minor. But the judge suspended the sentence to twelve years, further reducing the sentence in June to ten years, suspending it to six years, because the 14-year-old was more than six feet tall and weighed more than 200 pounds. "In this case, (the girl's size) is in an unusual stage of maturity," Judge Saunders reportedly said.[173] "That weighed heavily in my considerations."

The judge reasoned further that the church the minor attended where Tucker taught does not keep records of its students' ages. Prosecutors objected to the sentence reduction, noting that regardless of size or appearance, "children under 16 may not legally consent to sex."[174]

The visually mature girl is now a woman. Or at least "woman" enough to provoke a man.

Of course, the "image problem" of girls does not rest entirely with literature and Nabokov. A great deal of it has to do with history and the fact that the law has always made concessions for the "needs" of men.[175] As set forth in Chapter One, a web of patriarchies dominated the lives of women throughout the nineteenth and twentieth centuries.[176] In that milieu, adolescent girls were chattel,[177] created by a divine hand to serve men as daughters and later as wives obligated to serve husbands and children.[178]

Laws enacted in the past century have helped free women from historic patriarchies. And yet, in many ways American girls are trapped in a social, legal, and literary history heavy with traditional portrayals of girls as the minor "property" of men, obligated to serve men. For all of its "provocative originality," *Lolita* falls within this traditional space.[179] Though the story is fictional, what has become "real" in recent years are the R-rated depictions of seductress children and a trend toward shameless male obsession with barely adolescent girls.

For example, Duras's *The Lover* made it into movie theaters in 1992. Nabokov's *Lolita* was made into a movie for the second time in 1997, and rushed into theaters to beat the deadline for Oscar consideration.[180] In 1998, there was *Hurlyburly*, a blur of a film featuring a heavily made-up but still clearly adolescent Anna Paquin as a homeless child "given" to a pair of Hollywood hangers-on to "practice [with] until they find a woman."[181] That appears to be exactly what is happening to adolescent and teen girls today.

THE CLOTHES THAT MAKE THE GIRL "A WOMAN":
From Simone de Beauvoir to the Commercial World

Everyone, it seems, has a Darwinian explanation for why human beings do the things they do. For example, author Wendy Steiner argues in *Venus in Exile* that "…female beauty is a competitive packaging that increases a woman's chances of perpetuating her genes; for the beauty industry, this packaging perpetuates multinational profits. One way or the other, female freedom and self-realization would seem to require resistance to such an aesthetic. But eschewing beauty comes at a high price if it forecloses passion and procreation and self-understanding."[182]

And as a result, most women do not eschew beauty. Neither do girls, perhaps because the two are one under the glare of the bright lights. The multibillion dollar cosmetics industry is carried on the faces and bodies of teenage girls, because adolescence and the teen years is the time, after all, when a "woman's" skin is freshest and the most taut. When her eyes are the brightest and the area around them as-yet still unlined. It is a time when a girl's hair is the shiniest and when her body is at its thinnest. In short, girls make a pretty picture in the push for sales to women. American women, having survived adolescence themselves, generally understand and roll with the pretense. What appears to have changed in recent years, however, is how effective the rock-n-roll, hip-hop, and rap sales pitch of our times seems to be: and young girls are not only to be lapping it up. They are eager to participate.

The story traditionally told by the marketplace is one of men exploiting the sexuality of women and girls for commercial gain. But the story being told today is that young women are increasingly doing it themselves in an approach to image management and "packaging" generally attributed to the self-promotion and overtly sexual style of Madonna, but may actually have started years earlier with Mae West, who scandalized the early twentieth century with her frank approach to sex, and Marilyn Monroe, who thrived after posing nude for a calendar.

But Mae West and Marilyn Monroe were women, whose audiences were women. Madonna, by contrast, is a sexually provocative adult who throughout the 1980s sang "bubble gum" music that struck a chord with young girls.

And yet, some argue that Madonna aside, the plight of today's adolescent girls may be due in part to one of the sisters of modern feminism, Simone de Beauvoir. During the 1950s, the French scholar and philosopher caused a minor scandal with the publication of *The Second Sex*, in which she undertook frank discussion of the female body.[183] Among the controversial revelations made was that "[t]he growth of the little girl is similar to that of the boy; at the same age she is sometimes even taller and heavier than he is. But at puberty the species reasserts its claim."[184]

This is trivial stuff today. But at the time, de Beauvoir's "reassertion"—as she called the physical changes of puberty[185]—was brazen talk.[186] Even more audacious, according to historian Sheila Rowbotham, was the suggestion that "[o]ne is not born, but rather *becomes*, a woman."[187] In Europe in the 1950s, the time of de Beauvoir's writing, her "...emphasis upon the process of 'becoming' [a woman] challenged the view that a 'changeless essence' of femininity determined women's destiny." Her "phrases resonated with a new generation ready to accept that one's womanhood was of one's own making."[188]

The genie was out of the bottle, and it would change the lives of European as well as American women and girls. With the benefit of hindsight, it is understood today that a sexual revolution was in the making, though sweeping change was by no means instant. Instead, for a time it was argued that sex "should not be made the 'be all and end all of life,' and [it] was definitely not something that people went on about in public," Rowbotham argues.[189]

"Sexuality" thus held at bay, "dwelt in half-submerged ribaldry, tantalizing allure, and a transcendent romanticism, with a nasty side of hypocrisy and prurience...,"[190] Rowbathom notes.[191] But eventually women—and a great many men—began to shun the "hypocrisy," and by the start of the 1960s a very public change was underway. Bras were burned. A second Equal Rights Amendment was proposed,[192] and a new openness undid the previously reserved universe.

In terms of commerce, female authors were suddenly able to move books through the publishing chain, even books based upon previously "taboo" subjects such as female sexuality and the plight of women in the modern world. The variety was staggering. There was Friedan's *The Feminine Mystique,* which offered a sobering snapshot of the downside of the suburban American dream.[193] There was Doris Lessing and the notorious *Golden Notebook,*[194] and Helen Gurley Brown's *Sex and the Single Girl,* made a bestseller, some argue, "not because it told you how to get married but because it told you how to have a good time with men."[195] There was even Naomi Mitchison, who, historians note, "broke into the male preserve of science fiction with *Memoirs of a Spacewoman,* a novel about sex and communication with alien life forms."[196]

By the 1960s, women—their bodies and the sex it seemed so instantly to suggest—were no longer to be hidden. With the advent and legal sale of contraceptives and birth control devices, America was riding the first "safe sex" wave. The commercial media was quick to pick up on the new identity of women. Provocative—as opposed to merely *alluring*—women appeared in television commercials, magazine ads, and movies, wedded to the suggestion that there was something to buy and they had something to sell. And sell they did to a newly and thoroughly receptive audience: teens.

For example, it could be a headline today: *Teens Grow as Top Target for Many Products.* But it is a headline from 1963,[197] a time when the very definition of *woman* was up for grabs. Indeed, if there is a genesis to the modern notion of girl-as-woman it may well have started here, with hair, makeup, and the recasting of what it meant—and took—to be a woman. It is an undertow adolescent girls have been caught in ever since.

"Teenagers uncertain of who they were anxiously did the quizzes in *Seventeen, Glamor* [*sic*], *Teen,* or *Mademoiselle* to discover their fragrance type and resolve their identity problem,"[198] writes Rowbotham. And "[t]here were all kinds of ways 'to be' on offer. Among these 'selves' were the young vulgarians, with heavy black eyeliner and back-brushed hair or beehives piled up on the top of their heads. There were blonde beach-girl beauties in scanty bikinis who dated [the] beach-boy surfers…featured in Gloria Steinem's *The Beach Book* in 1963."[199]

In the years since beehives were chic, the way "to be" a woman has morphed into the way "to be sexy," which has become synonymous in turn with less clothing and more sex. And with the female body as the workhorse of the modern advertising industry,[200] near nudity is its most common currency. In addition, advertisers, product placement agencies, and entertainment industry officials began in earnest in the last two decades to redouble their efforts to court an increasingly lucrative "teen market."

Once the most influential segment of the American population, "Baby Boomers" have begun to move into retirement, "aging out" of certain markets as they move towards fixed incomes. This has made way for successors. Kids and young adults with disposable income represent an increasingly powerful sector of the American population today.[201] With the force they once used to hook "baby boomers," corporations push everything from prison-style jumpsuits[202] and hip-hop "street cred" gear toward the fingers of adolescent boys.

"Marketers hold that adolescent boys, with their swiftly changing appetites and their enormous buying power, are the most difficult and most critical consumers to reach," journalist Rebecca Mead reported for *The New Yorker.*[203]

Toward girls, they push sexiness, sex appeal, and pieces of cloth that come closer each year to the emperor's new clothes than active wear. "Beginning with 1980 television advertising conceived by Richard Avedon and [Designer Calvin] Klein using [teenage] model Brooke Shields, Klein has steadily set and stretched the parameters of American acceptance of overt sensuality in promotion of fashion and in public display ranging from national television campaigns to Times Square (New York) billboards to print media," argues Richard Martin in *The St. James Fashion Encyclopedia: A Survey of Style From 1945 to the Present.*[204]

This is one of the ways in which adult ideals of beauty have trickled down to young girls. And in recent years, that trickle has turned into a flood as the social contract once written for women has increasingly come to rely upon the bodies of teenage—or even adolescent—girls.[205] While cereal companies may look for the "Wheaties factor," advertisers, video producers, and motion picture makers look for "sex appeal" and the kind of sexual suggestion that will translate into cash. The "commodification of the body," as Steiner calls it,[206] is meant to sell whatever *it* is supposed to sell. "Bedroom" eyes, bared backs, alluring shoulders, and bare bellies hawk everything today from beer to CDs. It should come as no surprise that with the shrinkage of clothes has necessarily come a shrinkage in years.

As a designer, Klein was among those trailblazers who helped to transport "fashion sensibility to clothing classifications prodigiously latent with sexuality such as jeans and underwear," says Martin. But Klein's work was not without controversy, often because the models used in ads looked more like children than adults, a fact that in 1995 led to the withdrawal of several ads amid criticism that Klein had gone too far.[207] But Klein was never alone in offering the mainstream a suggestion of the "forbidden fruit."

By the late-1990s, "Streetwise [record] labels were micromarketing to teens like never before, from grassroots Web campaigns to tour sponsorships with designers like Tommy Hilfiger and Abercrombie & Fitch," Sia Michel wrote in the Fall 2000 issue of *Teen Vogue*.[208] "A small army of stylists and consultants discusses every image change, like helping [Britney] Spears shed her sassy-schoolgirl look for a sleek, cyberdiva feel in the '*Oops,...[I Did It Again]*' video."[209]

Of course, these "armies" rarely extol the virtues of Mrs. Robinson, because "beauty," according to entertainment executives and advertisers, isn't timeless or ageless. It is young, hot and half-dressed. "Goldie Hawn said that in Hollywood, there are three ages of woman: babe, district attorney, and *Driving Miss Daisy*," wrote Natalie Angier, in her article *In the Movies, Women Age Faster*.[210]

Where girls are concerned, the needle appears to be stuck on "babe." In the same issue of *Teen Vogue* that Sia Michel spells out the thinking of music executives, appears an eight-page photo spread titled *Model Lives*. It is a glossy confection featuring a 15-year-old and a 17-year-old sporting backpacks and plaid and jean skirts in varying lengths. Their faces are made up and in almost every frame, both girls are wearing three-inch heels,[211] because 15-year-olds and 17-year-olds always wear three-inch-high, fire-engine-red pumps.

Though swapping girl for woman is often thought of as a new trend, Betty Friedan suggests that treating girls as sexual entities began in the late 1950s, as "...American girls began getting married in high school."[212] This occurred because "[g]irls started going steady at 12 and 13, in junior high," says Friedan. And in response to this emerging trend, "[m]anufacturers put out brassieres with false bosoms of foam rubber for little girls of 10. And an advertisement for a child's dress, sizes 3-6x, in *[T]he New York Times* in the fall of 1960, said: 'She Too Can Join the Man-Trap Set.'"[213]

In the more than four decades since, this trend has become a fixture. Nine-year-olds are still—or again—reported to be going steady[214] and advertisers continue to offer up girls as "man-traps." The female body remains the workhorse of modern commerce.[215] And by the late 1990s, the benefits of coupling woman and girl were so well established that it shocked few when Britney

Spears, an apple-cheeked former Mickey Mouse Club member and the "heir-apparent" to the legacy of Madonna,[216] played up the theme of the "Catholic schoolgirl gone bad" in her first music video.

The effect of this avalanche of sexuality and the double standard it creates can be overwhelming. Adult women—having survived adolescence and made peace with the possibility of not being cool—are often able to put the urgings of advertisements and promoters into perspective. But younger women, especially those still trying to define themselves, are more susceptible to the dictates of the market and the slickness of the "packaging." By adolescence, girls have begun to understand that "beauty" is a competitive endeavor.[217] And what that has meant in recent years is less fabric and more skin for every occasion.

"Blame HBO's *Sex and the City* or blame the decline of the ozone layer, but skin is in," wrote Jenny Lyn Bader in *All That's Bare is Fit to Wear, So Why the Stares?*[218] "American women are showing more of it than ever before. [¶] Summer itself is hotter. And over the last decade, the proliferation of the Wonderbra coincided with global warming so that just as cleavages became more pronounced, shorts became shorter." And "[w]ith the triumph of minimalism, the handkerchief has returned, not as a decoration in a man's pocket but as an entire piece of women's clothing, featured in handkerchief tops and hanky hemlines.

"…American woman are showing more of it than ever," Bader suggests, noting that in addition to the handkerchiefs as halter tops trend, low-cut, slinky, tight-fitting, and sexy are not just okay. They are all the rage, especially for girls in high school.

"Fashion is so central to our culture that we must consider it [as a cultural construct]," argues Martin.[219] "Fashion is always hard to grasp. It is a visual art of immense creativity, challenged to accommodate art to the human body. It is a pragmatic business of addressing and dressing consumers in clothing that flatters and pleases and sells.[220] It is a complex system, involving advertising—including the most controversial advertising of our time—and commerce. It is a social system in which wearers and designers are not merely expressing themselves but using apparel to negotiate daily contacts with one another and with the larger social contract."[221]

And the new "fashion" is barely there.

"I wanted a dress that was sexy, but not completely trashy, and this is it," 17-year-old Jamie Ocasio said in May of 2001, while searching for a prom dress.[222] She eventually had a designer friend create a dress described as "'very Jennifer Lopez'—a languorous confection and, like its inspiration, shamelessly provocative."[223]

Department store buyers and manufacturers report that prom dresses are now the stuff of videos—tight, sexy, bare-backed, slit, and usually very short.[224] The line between adult and female child fashion has clearly blurred in the last decade. And while this may not be a problem for a 17-year-old heading to the prom, it has proved a problem for 13- or 12-year-olds left to deal with the backlash as they try to live their day-to-day lives.

But that, too, is an equation fraught with problems of its own.

"Female exposure has been attacked by the puritanical and the macho alike," Bader notes.[225] "At the George Washington Middle School in Alexandria, Virginia, 12-year-old girls wearing shorts of the lengths recommended by *Seventeen* magazine were accused of violating the school dress code, lined up, and subjected to humiliating inspections.... And [¶] [o]n the day of the recent Puerto Rican Day parade in New York City's Central Park, women wearing the latest fashions were mauled by young men less interested in the pages of *Vogue* than in the violent imagery of traditional skin magazine."

These are among the reverberations.

SPORTS, SEX, "PACKAGING," AND FEMALE EMPOWERMENT

In the cultural divide that is adolescence, the categories used to be hard and fast. There were "good girls" and "bad girls;" party girls and punks. Rockers, rappers, and athletes. There were girls who idolized pop stars, asserting budding personalities and pushing the envelope of expression, imitating the hair, makeup and half-clothing of their idols. There were girls who hung out and girls who studied. And there were girls who worshiped athletes, a force in every school and a choice made easier in the three decades since the passage of Title IX. That 1972 law mandated equal spending on male and female sports teams.

Part of the confusion for young women today, however, is that the categories have begun to slide. Professional female athletes, the idols of young girls, have begun to take their cue from rock stars: less—as in clothing—it seems, is now more.[226] And, thus, issues of sex—though perhaps not intended have begun to invade that once sacred realm of athletics.

"Packaging" has always been part of American culture, especially when it comes to women. In the commercial context, the allure of the "package" can make or break the deal. In the months leading up to the Olympics in Salt Lake City in 2002, carefully crafted profiles of the American women expected to compete began appearing in magazines and newspapers worldwide. The stories unwound the commercial and professional prospects of those competitors who might win and who had the "good looks" to carry the momentum of their athletic prowess to market.[227]

"...[Sarah] Schleper, 23, was last year's United States slalom champion. ...[Jean] Racine, 23, is the world's number one female bobsled driver. A top candidate for Olympic medals, she possesses what marketers call the Wheaties factor: a magnetic blend of sex appeal, salty wit, wholesomeness, and spunk," journalist Ruth La Ferla explained. "Those virtues commend an athlete to advertisers, who last fall began splashing the faces and toned physiques of Olympic hopefuls on products like Corn Flakes and candy, and who plan to crank up their efforts during and after the Games."

"Claire was blonde and petite with sensuous lips and cat eyes. She was around 19 or 20, so naturally I watched her every move. When she lit up a cigarette, I immediately followed suit. Nobody reacted," model Christy Turlington said in explaining how she became a chain smoker.[228] "I remember feeling slightly less awkward from that moment on. Ever since then, whenever I found myself waiting around, I'd simply light up a cigarette, flip through a magazine, and feel a little more at ease."

The adolescent years are bumpy. "Faced with the awkwardness of puberty—and often a mouth full of braces—junior high school students have it tough," suggests Susan Dodge in *Cliques are the Rule in Middle School*.[229] "They struggle to fit in and make friends, at the same time, they are becoming more self-conscious about their looks and personality."

Like Turlington, young girls are often looking for something to put them at ease. Something that makes them feel a little more comfortable in their skin. Thus, they look to "Claire," or older, more knowledgeable friends, to peers or even professional athletes as role models, which may explain why in 2000, a topless, but hand-covered photo of Olympic swimmer Jenny Thompson published in *Sports Illustrated* caused a stir. Thompson, the most highly decorated American swimmer ever, was applauded by fellow athletes, but criticized in the media and by women's groups.

One reason for the criticism is that sports have traditionally been a "safe harbor" for girls. A sort of nonsexual alternative to the sexualized lives of girls. Studies suggest that girls who are involved in sports are more likely to have a greater sense of self and higher self-esteem than girls who are not. And they are less likely to drop out of school or to get pregnant while still in school. Thus, "sexualized" athletes—those who openly flaunted their sexuality—were not only taboo. It was the worst kind of betrayal, some argue. And that is, in fact, what they argued with regard to Thompson.

"It's incongruent to take that body you've worked so hard for and use it for sex," Donna Lopiano, executive director of the Women's Sports Foundation, told *Sports Illustrated for Women* in an article published after the publication and fallout of the "Thompson picture."[230]

But Thompson argued that the photo was about empowerment, not sex. "My stance in the picture was one of strength and power and girls rule," Thompson argued.[231] "It's nothing sexual. I wasn't pouting or giving a sexual look. It was like, here I am. I'm strong. The body is supposed to be celebrated, and Olympians have amazing bodies. So I think it's a work of art."

Thompson refused to apologize for the photo, further riling critics. Given the trend in modern athletics, however, it is not clear that she should. Though a "topless" photo of Thompson drew fire, she is one of dozens of world-class athletes who have posed semi- or fully nude in recent years.[232] Thompson's teammate Dara Torres, also an Olympic swimmer, appeared in a see-through shirt wearing what sports journalist Kelli Anderson described as a "come-hither look" on the cover of the men's magazine, *Maxim*.[233] And yet, compared to other world-class female athletes, Torres was wearing plenty.[234]

The entire 1999 Australian women's soccer team and Canadian water polo player Waneek Horn-Miller posed completely nude. The "Matildas," as the Aussie footballers are known, took off their clothes for a calendar; Horn-Miller for the Canadian edition of *Time*.[235] United States gold medal-winning soccer player, Brandi Chastain, whose professional profile went through the roof when she pulled her shirt off after scoring the winning goal in a World Cup game, volunteered even more skin for a Nike ad.[236] And the long-legged high jumper and part-time model, Amy Acuff, an athlete known to push the limits of athletic fashion even when clothed—appearing at the Millrose Games in 2002, in a sequined halter top and hot pants,[237]—posed for a calendar wearing thigh-high stockings and an American flag painted across her chest.[238]

In addition to making an "empowering" statement, some women athletes defend nude or seminude photos as simply pragmatism.[239] "It had nothing to do with women taking off their clothes for attention," Australian beach volleyball player and gold medallist Kerrie Pottharst offered in response to questions about posing nude for *Black + White* magazine. "In this country [Australia], women's sports tend to get relegated to page 28. Everyone is looking for an angle to raise their profile. Posing nude is just another angle. If you do it to raise your profile, and in turn increase your sponsorship so you can remain an athlete, why not?"[240]

Whether it is "right" for female athletes to pose nude is not really the issue. What is of interest is the contradiction these individuals or increasingly collective expressions of beauty and personal self-esteem creates for young girls. Simply put, nudity—whether done as a form of self-expression or to raise one's profile—is no longer where it is "supposed" to be. Or, perhaps more precisely, where it traditionally has been kept, which is out of the once safe realm of sports for little girls. In *Playboy*, for example, instead of *Sports Illustrated*, some would argue.

School districts up and down the East Coast have attempted to address the problem of shrinking fashion versus "provocative exposure" with the imposition dress codes enforced by hall monitors.[241] Under these codes, spaghetti straps, fishnet stockings, shorts reaching above mid-thigh, shirts that don't cover the stomach, and even Saran Wrap are forbidden. In an incident in an upstate New York School District, two girls reportedly showed up "...on Halloween dressed in Saran Wrap" with only one of them appearing "to be wearing underwear."[242]

"While dress codes of the past...revolved around matters of taste (long hair) and safety (hats or bandannas in gang colors), the latest ones try to rein in what schools see as rampant sexualization of teenagers," reported Kate Zernike in September 2001. "The way schools and psychologists see it, the continuum begins with skimpy clothes, moves into 'freak dancing' in which students grind their pelvises together in simulated sex, and ultimately, incidents like the one in Chappaqua [New York] in which parents went along as high school football players hired a stripper for a party to inaugurate the season."[243]

AND NOW THE REAL STORY:
Ophelia in Snapshots

> "I want to know how to live in an adult world, yet still be a child."
> — 13-year-old (Mississippi).[244]

So who is the adolescent girl today? Is she made in the image of the media? Is she a vamp, wild and experimental? Is she the stuff of literature—the original Ophelia—troubled, love-sick, a child who drowns herself because a confused mind offers her no alternative? Is the Ophelia of today a treacherous seducer—a *Lolita*—bending the minds of adult men like a sorcerer?

If we follow the lead of the magazines, Ophelia is a near-naked girl-woman trying to sell perfume, lipstick, jeans, and anything else that might seem to fit. But more often in the "real life" of the school yard, Ophelia is the elementary school girl being chased by classmates. Ophelia is likely to face discrimination and sexual harassment in the workplace in one form or another, according to the EEOC.[245]

An adolescent girl may have many identities, and not all of them "good." Not all of them "proper." There are the obvious ones. The majority of today's adolescent girls will probably make their way through elementary and junior high school without a major incident, such as rape or sexual assault. And "Ophelia" may shine in high school, having regained some of her footing as many girls do. But she may also find thinness in the joy of tobacco, despite years of warning.[246] In the last decade, the number of teenagers younger than 18 who began smoking, increased by roughly 73 percent.[247]

In addition, she may use drugs. Overall, "Ophelia" has begun to catch up with her male counterparts with regard to the use of alcohol, tobacco, and drugs in general, research shows.[248] Ophelia may find an identity in "designer drugs,"[249] though she is generally less interested in crack cocaine today than she once was.[250] And yet, she is more interested in marijuana,[251] powder cocaine, and other drugs than she once was.[252] Heroin use is reportedly on the rise among young people.[253]

But even more dangerous than drugs, the Ophelia of today may be a part-time hooker, straddling the worlds of home, school, and the "streets," while maintaining an otherwise "normal" life. When she was just 15, for example, Shauna Stavos[254] would leave school a few days a week and head toward "a notoriously dangerous strip in San Francisco's Mission District, where she [would make] as much as $600 in a few hours, working as a prostitute."[255] It is an atypical story from an atypical existence. It hardly makes sense, after all, that a rational teenager would choose to "work the streets," even if she could make $600 in a few hours. Or that she would be able to otherwise maintain a "normal" life. But statistics suggest that thousands of teenage girls nationwide are involved in the same kind of high-risk behavior that Shauna Stavos seems to take in stride.

Authorities in Atlanta report as many as 200 cases per year involving teen prostitutes. Of course, that number includes only those underage prostitutes who have been caught or are somehow otherwise involved in the judicial sys-tem.[256] Still, if Shauna Stavos suggests a sex-trade anomaly, here is another: not only minority or urban youths with hard luck stories are getting involved. According to *Newsweek* reporter Suzanne Smalley, suburban white girls in the heartland have taken up an "exciting" new vocation. And not by need. But, rather, by choice.

"Like many teenage girls in Minneapolis, 17-year-old Stacey liked to hang out after school at the Mall of America.... Cute, blond, and chatty, she flirted with boys and tried on the latest Gap fashions. One day last summer, Stacy[257]...says she was approached by a man who told her how pretty she was, and asked if he could buy her some clothes. 'He was an older guy, dressed really well,' she recalls. 'He said he just wanted to see me in the clothes.' Stacy agreed, and went home that night with a $250 outfit," Smalley reported.[258]

But Stacey appears to have learned a disturbing lesson that day: that her body was a money maker. Though she lives in a neighborhood that Smalley described as "upscale" and is a "good student," engaged enough in school to be interested in trying out for the tennis team, Stacey began taking secret trips to hotel rooms where she would strip for money. The money was used to buy clothes. Eventually, she moved into "more intimate activities." She even placed personal ads on telephone services, all the while continuing to make it home before her midnight curfew until the night she was detained by police and her mother had to be called.

"Over the last year, local and federal law-enforcement officials say they have noted a marked increase in teen prostitution in cities across the country," Smalley suggests. "Solid numbers are difficult to come by—a government-sponsored study puts the figure in the hundreds of thousands—[according to] law-enforcement agencies and advocacy groups that work with teen prostitutes say they are increasingly alarmed by the trend lines: kids are getting younger; according to the FBI, the average age of a new recruit is 13; some are as young as 9. The girls—many fewer are boys, most experts believe—are subjected to more violence from pimps. And while the vast majority of teen prostitutes today are runaways, illegal immigrants, and children of poor urban areas, experts say a growing number now come from middle-class homes."[259]

It should be noted that Smalley's assertions have been challenged. Jack Shafer of the online magazine *Slate* suggested, for example, that the *Newsweek* article was an exercise in "bogus trendspotting."[260] Shafer took specific aim at what he sees as "soft" or "absent" numbers in the Smalley piece. But there do appear to be numbers. According to the nonprofit group, SAGE—Standing Against Global Exploitation—which attempts to get prostitutes off the streets, an estimated 100,000 to 300,000 underage prostitutes go to work in the United States every day.[261] There is no reason to assume that all of these young people come from the inner city.

Ophelia is also more violent than she once was. Overall, teenage girls—like their male counterparts—are more violent than they used to be.[262] "It has long been known that crime rates typically peak in the late teen years, and age-specific patterns for such crimes as robbery and burglary have not changed significantly in the past 20 years," Justice Department officials note.[263] What has changed is the pattern of homicides among the young.

"From 1970 to 1985, individuals aged 18 to 24 were the most likely of any group to commit murder, and the murder rate among this group was relatively steady," Justice Department researchers note.[264] In 1985, for example, "murder by people under 24 began to increase: for those 18 and younger, the homicide rate more than doubled between 1985 and 1992." By contrast, "[d]uring that same period, the rate among those 24 to 30 remained steady, and the rate declined for those over 30."[265]

What these numbers suggest is that the rise in the nation's homicide rate during the late 1980s was due in part to a surge in killings by young people.[266] And, incidentally, not only poor, urban teenagers were committing murder. There were multiple-injury shootings in rural and remote communities across the country: Moses Lake, Washington; Bethel, Alaska; Pearl, Mississippi; West Paducah, Kentucky; Jonesboro, Arkansas; Springfield, Oregon; Littleton, Colorado; and, Conyers, Georgia, among the most noted.[267]

And Justice Department officials cautioned during the mid-1990s that there may be more to come. "Children who are now younger (about ages 5 to 15) represent the future problem, because they are larger [in number] than the current 18-year-old group. Even if current rates do not continue to rise, violent crime is likely to increase because there will be more 18-year-olds to commit violence at a higher rate."[268]

Breaking rank with tradition and a stereotype that made them "everything nice," adolescent and teenage girls were increasingly counted in projections of criminal activity, because adolescent and teenage girls have become more involved in crime in a trend that has been gaining steam for two decades. From 1981 to 1997, "violent crime by girls increased 107 percent, compared to a 27 percent for boys," Justice Department statistics suggest.[269]

More specific findings include that between 1985 and 1994, "Violent Crime Index arrest rates for juvenile females increased 125 percent, while the male rate increased 67 percent."[270] The Violent Crime Index includes statistics on four offenses—murder/nonnegligent manslaughter, forcible rape, robbery, and aggravated assault.[271] In 1985 "approximately 9,000 Violent Crime Index arrests involved a female below age 18," according to Justice Department.[272] By 1994, that "number had increased to more than 21,000."[273]

Though the number of delinquency cases—as offenses involving juveniles that remain in juvenile courts are called—still overwhelmingly involve adolescent males, girls are gaining in numbers,[274] with the turn toward violence and antisocial behavior among girls made for many of the same reasons as young men. In September 1999, the Chicago Crime Commission found that girls—some as young as 8 years old—were increasingly becoming involved in gangs and gang-related activity,[275] a trend now common in many American cities, though hidden in the so-called heartland.

"We've got kids here in Bismarck, real North Dakota kids, taking on inner-city gang identities," Bismarck Police detective Lloyd Halverson told a reporter in detailing the version of the phenomenon he sees most.[276] "It's kind of weird. You've got kids calling themselves Black Gangster Disciplines—and these are white kids."[277]

According to the experts who track them, in middle America and on the windswept plains where there is little else to do, restless teenagers in search of an identity have increasingly chosen the visible cloak of known gangs—renowned for their violence—though they have little or no real firsthand experience with them, while "real gang members" in the inner cites and urban areas tend to go "underground."

"Bloods and Crips are widely associated with red and blue, but to avoid the police, both groups now play down their colors (except at ceremonial events like funerals) and opt instead for Tommy Hilfiger and Fubu," Brian Palmer reported in *The New York Times*.[278] "Latin Kings in the East used to wear beads in the gang's color scheme; lately they've started hiding them in a pocket."[279]

And where are teenage and adolescent girls in this picture? According to Gina Sikes, author of the acclaimed, *8 Ball Chicks: A Year in the Violent World of Girl Gangs*, they are in the mix, especially in urban cities like Los Angeles. "Some 1,200 gangs roam the four thousand square miles of urban sprawl that make up Los Angeles; of the 150,000 members listed in police files, roughly 12,000 are females."[280]

Though a relatively small number when compared to the number of male gang members, girls appear not only to be gaining in numbers. They also appear to be gaining in terms of the violent lifestyle. Sikes tells stories of razor fights,[281] muggings,[282] and revenge killings[283] carried out by girls, and if their lives are half as harrowing as these stories, society may have an impossible task in reclaiming them.

Of course, it could be argued that gang members are not typical of the teen and adolescent experience today. But violence is, even in traditionally "safe" suburban communities. In 1995, for example, a beautiful, long-haired blonde girl named Crystal Shelby was attacked by three female classmates who allegedly slammed her head-first into a wall and then beat her in the head with a padlock. The assault left Shelby with permanent brain injuries requiring multiple surgeries.[284] And though it might sound like common fare for an urban high school, the incident took place in a suburban high school outside of Rochester, New York.

Much has been made in recent years of the "aggression" of middle-class girls,[285] perhaps because the middle-class girls—the products of "good homes" and "good schools"—are "supposed" to behave better than "troubled" inner city students. And yet, Justice Department statistics suggest that young women, overall, are generally more violent. Female arrests have increased, for example, "more than male rates in the high-volume violent crimes of robbery (110 percent versus 51 percent) and aggravated assault (134 percent versus 88 percent).

This same pattern is also evident in simple assault arrests (141 percent versus 102 percent)," according to Justice Department statistics.[286]

In addition, between 1978–1989, the "[a]dmission of females to juvenile facilities increased by 18 percent overall; however, female admissions to private facilities rose much faster, increasing 96 percent, compared with a 2-percent decline in admissions to public facilities," government statistics show.[287] And "[f]emales accounted for 6 percent of all known juvenile homicide offenders in 1995,"[288] according to Justice Department statistics. Girls clearly had made strides in this area.

And yet, it remains true that far more often than girls are villains, they are victims. Incidents of battery by adult men and boys against adolescent girls, for example, are widespread and sometimes deadly. Barrie Levy, editor of *Dating Violence: Young Women in Danger*, detailed how her 15-year-old daughter was stabbed to death by her boyfriend when she attempted to break up with him.[289] Gretchen Wright was 16 when she was killed by her 17-year-old boyfriend with a shot at point-blank range.[290] When Rosie Vargas was 14 and pregnant, she was killed by her 16-year-old boyfriend, who later shot himself.[291]

According to researchers, "[t]een dating violence mirrors adult domestic violence in that it exists on a continuum ranging from emotional and verbal abuse to rape and murder. The end of the abusive relationship is the most dangerous time for the victim. Perpetrators often threaten suicide and homicide. If they have access to weapons, they may present a lethal threat."[292]

Indeed, if the 1990s can be given a fitting name in this area, it might well be "the decade of the teen restraining order." More than 57 percent of all restraining orders issued by the State of Massachusetts against teenagers involved teenagers in relationships, according to a survey published by the Massachusetts Department of Probation in April 1994.[293] And yet, the law does not always protect and assist adolescents. Instead, legal issues regarding teenagers and young people has long been marked by political whims, religious and conservative schemes, and the stubborn hopes of parents determined not to let their "babies grow up too fast."

THE LAW'S GIRL:
Adolescent Women Under the Law

Scholars often argue that the law is intended to further the goals of a democratic society by creating a community of equals. The operative word in that sentence when it comes to discussion of the rights of young people, of course, is "equals." Under the law, "adolescents," "children," "minors," "teenagers," and "juveniles"—all terms used to refer to persons who have not reached majority—may be equal among themselves. But they are not equal to "adults" until the law declares them to be adults.

But that, it seems, is where the confusion comes in, because a "child" can reach majority at different times for different things. As set forth above, for example, though a young woman has the right to choose to use contraceptives and to have an abortion (with some constraints) and though she may marry at 18—the latest in most states—she cannot legally drink "hard liquor" until she is 21, a fact that tends to suggest that in the eyes of many lawmakers, young women remain "children" incapable of making decisions about their general health.

Thus, it seems incongruous that a young woman would be allowed—and, indeed, considered "adult enough"—to make choices and decisions regarding having children alone (or with the intervention of the court where parents oppose her)—when she is not allowed or considered adult enough as a matter of law to decide whether on not she wants to smoke. This, incidentally, is exactly the argument of conservatives and the religious right, who argue that "girls" are too young to make such life-altering decisions on their own.

Throughout the 1980s and 1990s, with "family values" arguments imprinting the national agenda, lawmakers seemed to find persuasion in arguments of this kind, passing parental consent and notification laws that required minor females to seek parental or judicial consent and/or to notify parents of their intent to have the procedure prior to an abortion; eliminating sex education classes from public school curricula; and obstructing the ability of poor youths to gain access to free contraceptives. In short, the push was on to turn back the clock on the reproductive rights of girls. With parents and grandparents joining the call of conservatives, this too appeared to be an easy sell.

But there were three problems. The first for conservatives and "family value" lawmakers is the problem they have faced for three decades: *Roe v. Wade*. As set forth above, *Roe v. Wade* grew out of a movement to free women from the paternalistic obligation to carry mankind's children. The decision, coupled with others regarding birth control and the right to choose contraceptives, gave women a measure of control over their bodies previously unknown in America. But, of course, if women could have control of their bodies, what about "almost-women?"

That was among the questions considered by the United States Supreme Court considered in *Parenthood of Central Missouri v. Danforth*.[294] In the end, a majority of the Justices would declare that "[c]onstitutional rights do not mature and come into being magically only when one attains the state-defined age of majority. Minors, as well as adults, are protected by the Constitution and possess constitutional rights...."

A year later, the Justices expressly ruled in *Carey v. Population Services Int'l*,[295] that minor females were entitled to the fundamental choice of birth control, a choice that could not be unduly burdened by the state. Taken together, *Danforth* and *Carey* have generally been read by the nation's courts to mean that minors are entitled to substantially the same fundamental rights regarding procreation as adult women, with some exceptions.

Thus, in the last two decades, twenty-five states and the District of Columbia have passed laws or adopted policies expressly granting minors the authority to consent to contraceptive services. In addition, twenty-seven states and the

District of Columbia have enacted laws and/or policies allowing pregnant minors to consent to, and/or to obtain prenatal care and delivery services, without parental consent or notification. All fifty states and the District of Columbia allow minors to consent to testing and treatment for sexually transmitted diseases, including HIV, with only Iowa requiring parental notification if a minor tests positive for HIV.[296] And she may *always* have a baby.

Of course, the most contentious of these "health care" issues is abortion.

And it has been the most restrained. Two states—Connecticut and Maine—as well as the District of Columbia have passed laws or adopted policies allowing minors to obtain an abortion on their own. But on the other side, thirty-one states have passed laws requiring the involvement or consent of at least one parent in their daughter's decision to have an abortion. But there is a split. In sixteen of the thirty-one states, a minor needs the consent of one or both parents, while the other fifteen states require only that a minor notify her parents prior to the abortion.[297]

Only one state—Utah—does not provide a statutory alternative to parental consent in the form of either a confidential judicial bypass procedure, by which a minor female can obtain a court's consent to an abortion without informing her parents or where parents refuse to give consent, or a "physician's bypass," as provided, for example, by Maryland law.[298] It should be noted that where a minor has married (with or without parental consent as required); has attained a certain age (usually 16); or has had a child, some states have granted an expanded array of choices. Thus, some "minors" in some states may have abortions, seek medical treatment, or request contraceptive services without requirement of parental notification or judicial consent. (For a review of these laws, *see The Contradictory State of the Law for America's "Girls,"* at pp. 561–570.)

It is worth noting that "[e]fforts to enact new parental involvement laws in the context of abortion have slowed in recent years," according to the Alan Guttmacher Institute. "Between 1991 and 1997, the number of states with laws in effect mandating parental consent or notification rose from eighteen to thirty, but between 1997 and 2000, that number increased by only one. In large part, this drop-off reflects the fact that ten other states have enacted laws that are currently blocked by courts from going into effect, leaving only seven states that have no parental involvement required on the books."[299]

Of course, it is the "exceptions," especially with regard to reproductive rights law, that tend to make the rule.

Danforth and *Carey* are relatively new decisions and as "court-made" law have been repeatedly challenged, in large part because in reaching these decisions the Court stepped squarely into a purview that has long been seen as the sole domain of the state, to be regulated and controlled in the manner in which state officials saw fit. Thus, for most of the last two centuries, state officials told women and girls who they would marry (not interracially in many states until after 1967); when they could marry (between 12 and 18 generally, though parental consent may be needed in some cases); that they had an obligation—

enforced by law—to carry fetuses to term; and who they could legally have sex with (women with men until recently and preferably of the same race).

Though most of the vestiges of the past have fallen, many states continue—through the enactment and enforcement of statutory rape laws—to tell minor girls who they can have sex with. Thus, teenage girls remain the captives of the state, feminists and critics of statutory rape laws argue. State officials defend the enforcement of statutory rape laws, even in this day and age, as necessary to protect vulnerable young women from predatory older men.

GIRLS AND SEX:
Statutory Rape Laws and a History of Protecting Virtue

"All societies seek to control and direct sexual energy in order to maintain their group structure and function," argued the editors of the *Yale Law Journal* in 1952.[300] "Unchanneled, the sex drive threatens to disrupt patterns of social and family organization.[301] Properly controlled, on the other hand, sexual energy moves people into relationships and activities which sustain the group. The channeling of sexuality into marriage is crucial to all societies and espoused as a desirable goal by virtually all component subgroups.[302] In our society, sexual taboos, often enacted into law, buttress a system of monogamy based upon the 'free bargaining' of the potential spouses."

Though it may echo the well-placed rejoinders of conservative politicians trying to make their point today, this was the thinking of lawmakers in originally enacting statutory rape laws. Sexual energy had to be directed to the "proper" channels. Nothing less than the order of society was at stake. Among the sexual taboos passed into law were restrictions on the sexuality of minors, originally enacted to protect young people from sexual exploitation.[303]

"The sheltering of females from sexual experience has been a prominent feature of our male-dominated culture, in which women were once considered the exclusive private property of the men to whom they were married (and before marriage the property of their fathers, acting in trust for the future husbands)," argue Albert D. Klassen, Colin J. Williams, and Eugene E. Levitt in *Sex and Morality in the U.S.* "Many of our sexual norms are rooted in such beliefs. Rape, for example, was until recently seen in terms of one man violating the property rights of another. Prohibitions of premarital sex and emphasis on virginity likewise can be seen as efforts to preserve the market value of females."[304]

"[B]eginning in the 1880s, the massive Women's Christian Temperance Union took an activist, reform position on the issue of protecting adolescent girls, launching a nationwide effort to raise the age of consent for sexual relations (which was as low as 10 in some states)," says Cornell's Brumberg. "The statutory rape laws that emerged from this campaign were heralded by women and reformers as a way of protecting innocent young girls from the vices of adult men."[305]

Thus, "[s]tatutory rape laws...make it a crime to engage in consensual sexual intercourse with young women below a particular age, 12 at common law and now typically higher," legal scholars note.[306]

What troubles critics of statutory rape laws, however, is not only that the reach of such laws may foreclose an emerging young woman's "choice" of a mate. But also that these laws generally tend to lack distinctions between "peer statutory rape"—which they argue should not be a crime, because both parties are of equal bargaining position—and "predatory statutory rape," which is what the law originally sought to conquer and should contemplate today now that society has advanced beyond a time when virginity is traded for a commodity.

"By criminalizing all intercourse with minors, statutory rape laws literally outlaw girls' expression of their own sexuality," Deborah Tolman and Tracy Higgins argue in *How Being a Good Girl Can Be Bad for Girls*.[307]

"The crime of statutory rape has traditionally been understood as consensual intercourse with a female under a particular age," argues Rita Eidson in *The Constitutionality of Rape Laws*.[308] "There are only two elements in the offense of statutory rape; the age of the female and the act of sexual intercourse.[309] Since the male's age is not an element of the crime, traditional statutory rape laws have failed to distinguish the consensual acts of peers from the sexual exploitation of adolescent females by older men.[310] Consent of the underage female is not a defense to statutory rape; apparently she is conclusively presumed to be incapable of understanding the nature and consequences of sexual intercourse."

Though this may have been true once, it is rarely true today that the underage female is "incapable of understanding the nature of sexual intercourse" and information on the consequences of sexual intercourse is readily available on the Internet, even if schools no longer offer a full spectrum of information. Should "girls" be allowed to choose their mates, as some critics argue? Or, does the state always have a "compelling interest" in protecting underage girls? Consider the case of Adela Cantana and Pedro Sotelo.

For ten days in 1996, the City of Houston crackled with the story of a 10-year-old rape victim, reportedly pregnant and about to give birth, and said to be on the run from authorities because she did not want to be separated from the fetus she was carrying. The young woman's name was Cindy Garcia. Or so the public was initially told. It was a sensational story that spiraled into a sensational debate centered around the question of whether adult males involved with teenage girls are always predators, as state laws seem to presume.

UNIDENTIFIED REPORTER #1 ("News 2 Houston Nightbeat"): *Now, breaking news. A race against the clock to find this 10-year-old girl.*

MS. JUDY HAY (Child Protection, Harris County): *I don't think anybody in Houston was talking about anything else.*

REPORTER #1 ("News 2 Houston Nightbeat"): *The desperate search escalates.*

MS. HAY: *You heard it everywhere.*

UNIDENTIFIED REPORTER #2 ("News 2 Houston Nightbeat"): *The pregnant 10-year-old could give birth at any time.*

> —"A Second Look—Age of Consent"
> *Dateline NBC*, February 2, 1996.[311]

In the end, the truth was more tragic and far different than most would have imagined. In the end, Cindy Garcia was not 10-year-old Cindy Garcia. She was a 14-year-old young girl/woman named Adela Cantana, whose parents had illegally purchased immigration papers with the name Cindy Garcia appearing on them because they wanted to bring their daughter from the family's poor rural village in Mexico to the United States. And there had been no rape. Or, perhaps more precisely, there had been no forcible rape. But there was sex between Cantana and her 22-year-old lover, Pedro Sotelo, about which everyone intimately concerned apparently thought it was fine because the couple intended to be married. The sex was "consensual" and Cantana's parents permitted it. Adela Cantana and Pedro Sotelo shared a bedroom in the Cantana family home and Adela Cantana's father told the media that Pedro Sotelo "took care of his daughter."[312]

By all accounts, Adela Cantana and Pedro Sotelo were in love and planning the birth of their first child. They had bought a crib for the baby, which stood in the corner of their bedroom. Though illegal in many American states, marriages between young girls and older men are reportedly common in the tiny village of Mexico where the couple was from. No one—not even Texas authorities—disputed that the two loved each other or that they had been living together "as man and wife," which, for Texas authorities, was precisely the problem. Under Texas law, Adela Cantana could not legally consent to sex for three more years.[313]

Pedro Sotelo told *Dateline NBC* he did not know that engaging in sexual intercourse with a "minor" was illegal. But it did not matter to authorities that Pedro Sotelo did not know the law in the United States. It also did not matter that he believed he had Adela Cantana and her father's consent to the relationship or that he intended to marry Adela Cantana. It also did not matter to authorities that Adela Cantana had chosen Pedro Sotelo as a lover and to be the father of her child.

VICTORIA CORDERI: (Voiceover) *Houston police investigating the case have confirmed the birth certificate is fraudulent, apparently to cover up a case of illegal immigration.*

MR. MICHAEL BAGENT (Houston Police): *The mom finally confessed that they faked this birth certificate. She is really 14, and her name really is Adela Cantana.*

CORDERI: (Voiceover) *But that was just the beginning. Littia Romero says the girl told her she wasn't a rape victim, that she and [Pedro] Sotelo had been living together with her parents' blessing.... She said that her parents approved of their situation. They had spent a year and a half together. Police have confirmed that, too.*

— "A Second Look—Age of Consent"
Dateline NBC, February 2, 1996.[314]

Legal scholars and law enforcement officials note that the United States has long prohibited the taking of "child brides."[315] And Texas authorities argued in the Sotelo case that most states prohibit treating minor "girls" as "brides" prior to marriage, especially when the person doing the "treating" is an adult male. But on the other side, critics argue that the legal system has historically punished adolescents for "sexual precociousness."[316]

CORDERI: (Voiceover) *Pedro Sotelo now sits in jail, unable to make his $200,000 bail and unable to make sense of what's happened to him.*

([Question to] Sotelo): *You had no idea that it was illegal to have sex with a minor?*

MR. SOTELO: (Through translator) *No, I had no idea. We lived a happy life with her father, and she was happy with me.*

CORDERI: (Voiceover) *Sotelo says he and Adela Garcia [sic] were from the same village in rural Mexico, where it is acceptable for a man in his 20s to date a 13-year-old.*

(Corderi interviewing Sotelo)

MR. SOTELO: (Through translator) *In my country, that's the way it is. It's sad that for love, it can be possible that I'm in jail. Is it is crime?*

CORDERI: *The law here says to love is a crime when the girl is a child.*

MR. SOTELO: (Through translator) *I understand. Now that I'm in jail, I understand.*

— "A Second Look—Age of Consent"
Dateline NBC, February 2, 1996.[317]

And while these positions may be black and white for the adults on both sides, confusing the issue for young people is the notion of love. As a society, America has always been in love with the idea of love, at the very least as a promotional device. In addition, as a nation grounded in democratic notions of free choice, it should come as no surprise that young people have bought into the promos and believe that their choices with regard to love should at least be taken into consideration.[318]

Following a whirlwind of media-driven fury, Adela Cantana was found by authorities, who promptly removed her from the custody of her parents. Pedro Sotelo was soon after arrested and charged with a first-degree felony reportedly carrying a possible 99-year sentence.[319] Texas authorities argued in defending the state's decision to so vigorously prosecute Pedro Sotelo that the "abuse" may have begun even before Adela Cantana was 14. But what does the Cantana/Sotelo case mean today—in the time of Britney Spears?

Was the public prosecution of Pedro Sotelo simply the political fallout of an exceptional case spun out of control after days of emotional media coverage? Was it racism, as some have suggested?[320] Or was his arrest and subsequent imprisonment proper intervention by state authorities obligated to protect a minor from abuse by an adult where she is clearly unable—in the state's interpretation—to properly judge the situation? As much as it provokes questions nearly impossible to answer, the Adela Cantana case offers evidence of the contradictions facing adolescent girls today.

But lawmakers defend these contradictions, and their position may perhaps best be exemplified by the story of Latif Al-Hussaini. A 34-year-old man who fled Iraq after the Gulf War, Latif Al-Hussaini made his way to the United States in 1996 to begin a new life in Nebraska. Al-Hussaini spoke "virtually no English," according to the court. But he managed to get married in an Islamic ceremony on November 9, 1996. The bride had been given away by her father[321] in a service followed by a party.

And following the ceremony, Latif Al-Hussaini and his wife consummated the marriage, which led eventually to the filing of criminal charges. The bride was 13.[322] A little over a week after the wedding, Latif Al-Hussaini's new bride did not return home from school. She had gone to authorities. Latif Al-Hussaini was arrested and later convicted of first degree assault of a child in violation of Nebraska Revised Statutes Section 28-319. Like Pedro Sotelo, who argued that his conduct was widely accepted in his culture, Latif Al-Hussaini argued that his "actions [were] legal and proper under Islamic law and [that] he had no idea...his actions violated the law in this country."[323]

Unlike Pedro Sotelo, Latif Al-Hussaini had actually "married" the girl—or, at least, attempted to—with the girl's father giving her away at the wedding. That would appear to be parental consent. Whether or not it was, however, was of no consequence to Nebraska authorities, according to the court. Latif Al-Hussaini was charged with first-degree assault on a child and sexual penetration of a female less than 16 years of age. In accordance with a plea agreement, Latif Al-Hussaini was sentenced to an indeterminate sentence of 4 to 6 years.[324]

"We recognize that this is an unusual situation," the Nebraska appellate court wrote in upholding the conviction. "To some degree, [Latif] Al-Hussaini is a victim of laws with which he has little, if any, familiarity and which are, according to him, vastly different from the customs and laws of his naive country. But as the district court observed when it imposed sentence, there is really only one victim of this crime, and that is the 13-year-old child with whom [Latif] Al-Hussaini had sexual intercourse without her consent."[325]

Is there a difference between the case of Cantana-Sotelo and *State v. Al-Hussaini*? Does it make a difference that Cantana and Sotelo loved each other and Al-Hussaini and his "bride" did not? Should it? After all, young people fall in love.[326] During the 1970s, along with others being revised at the time, the statutory rape laws of many states were rewritten. But as Eidson notes, few made the meaningful distinction between "predatory" sexual conduct by older boys and men and peer sexual relations.[327] Minors below a certain age simply cannot consent to sex in most states as a matter of law. Though prosecutions are rare when the parties are of the same age,[328] states continue to focus energy on cases involving underage women and adult males, though not as much attention as they should, some critics argue.

GIRLS AND SCHOOLS:
Issues in Equality and Discrimination

In addition to the politics of reproduction and the politics of crime, the politics of female adolescence include the politics of education. Minors in America—boys as well as girls—must attend school for a certain number of years.[329] This is a legal requirement fueled perhaps by romantic notions of education as the great equalizer. But even the once venerable institution of school is not what it used to be, and the changes make a difference in the lives of America's children.

For one thing, the nation's children are attending classes that are increasingly diverse, increasingly multicultural, increasingly underfunded, and increasingly overcrowded. "While the problems of illegal immigration to the United States have generated headlines, it is the steady increase of both legal and illegal immigrants that has transformed many communities and their schools from St. Paul to Chicago and from Detroit's suburbs to Wausau, Wisconsin," argues education researcher James G. Ward.[330]

Many of these recent immigrants, who come primarily from Asia and Latin America, "tend to be younger than the population at large and have younger children and larger families," says Ward. And "[a]s the proportion of the population that is Hispanic and Asian grows, public schools are enrolling more students who have limited English proficiency and are often poor."[331]

In addition to the influx of younger, poorer immigrants in need of services, many cities and states face a potential growing crisis as the Baby Boomer generation begins to age out of the system. "Since 1900, the number of elderly persons has doubled every thirty years in the United States," Ward suggests.[332] The steady increase in the elderly population "will raise public demands for health care and recreation, while possibly decreasing direct demand for public school services. By 2020, all of the states in the north central region except Illinois will have at least 28 elderly [people] for every 100 working-age adults. Illinois will have between 22 and 25 elderly for every 100 working-age adults," Ward predicts.[333]

And what these trends mean for adolescents is less money. An older population aging out of the workforce and the tax market coupled with a new wave of younger, poorer children could strain local budgets. "All public services will be competing against each other for the same funds," Ward points out.[334] "An increasing proportion of older Americans will mean greater voter interest in public funding for functions such as health care, recreational facilities, and police protection—functions older individuals tend to use more than public educational services."[335]

The interplay between redirected government funding, failing local school financing, and power politics has undermined public education, critics say.[336] In offering the example of funding spent at an Illinois school, for example, author Jonathan Kozol offers in *Savage Inequalities: Children in America's Schools,* that the "[t]otal yearly spending—local funds combined with state assistance and the small amount that comes from Washington—ranges today in Illinois from $2,100 on a child in the poorest districts to above $10,000 in the richest."[337]

The numbers Kozol quotes may be slightly higher today.[338] But disparities continue in large measure because "affluent voters are reluctant to raise their own taxes to pay for public services—including education—that primarily benefit families in other communities," critics argue.[339] Thus, the system continues to bear "the appearance of calculated unfairness."[340] Or, as Ward argues in more direct terms, such reluctance "raises very real equity questions about the future distribution of educational resources and access to technology, and makes the job of equalizing school financing a very difficult one."[341]

Chicago schools have historically been among those cash-starved entities that have struggled not only to find funding, but to raise national test scores amid the crumbling walls and shortages of supplies. In 1996, school officials—desperate for a solution to their image problem—announced a policy banning "social promotions" for students who were failing during the regular school year. School board officials opted for the alternative of year-round schooling intended to bring faltering students up to par.[342] But at about the time that Chicago school officials were debating the "social promotions" problem, elite magazines began running articles on a well-spun and well-connected tutoring program called IvyWise, created for students who "fall behind," but whose parents can afford to spend up to a rumored $1,000-an-hour to be personally tutored in the best ways to convince Ivy League admission officials that William Jr. or Tiffany deserves a chance to wear the crimson.[343]

Poverty is "growing, particularly among children, and public school students are becoming poorer as a result," school experts note.[344] In addition, as funding remains low and libraries and classrooms remain in disarray, children across the nation continue to fail at everything from standardized tests to sex education as lawmakers continue to vote each year to cut school funding.[345] By contrast, funding for prisons has soared throughout the last decade.

"The idea that school, by itself, cannot cure poverty is hardly astonishing, but it is amazing how much of our political discourse is implicitly predicated on the notion that it can," writes James Traub in *Schools Are Not the Answer.*[346] But failure of this romantic myth, then, may be intolerable for some. Sociologist James Coleman shook the political community when he concluded following a commissioned study during the Civil Rights Era that "the inequalities imposed on children by their home, neighborhood, and peer environment are carried along to become the inequalities with which they confront adult life at the end of school."[347]…This was, if true, astonishing and deeply unsettling news. Nobody believes in school the way Americans do, and no one is more tantalized by its transformative powers. School is central to the American myth of self-transcendence…" Traub contends.[348] But the nation's public schools appear to be failing America's children, and certainly its girls.

THE NEW ABCs OF EDUCATION:
Sexual Assault in the Classroom

In addition to funding shortfalls and overcrowding, sexual harassment and sexual assault are realities today in the nation's schools.[349] Christine Franklin was a Georgia high school student, for example, when a coach began making suggestive comments that would eventually escalate into first forced kissing, and then forced sexual intercourse, according to the complaint filed originally with a Georgia district court.

In seeking damages from the school district, Franklin would also allege that although school officials were aware of the problem, they took no action. School officials even discouraged Franklin from filing a complaint against the teacher, she alleged. Franklin sought damages under Title IX of the 1972 Education Amendments,[350] which prohibits sexual discrimination by institutions that receive federal funding for educational programs.

After dismissals by the lower courts, which reasoned generally that victims of intentional gender discrimination were entitled to injunctive relief, but not monetary damages, the case would make its way to the United States Supreme Court as *Franklin v. Gwinnett County Public Schools,*[351] where it became what some scholars consider a necessary precursor to the Court's later decision in *Davis v. Monroe County Board of Education.*[352] In finding for Franklin, the United States Supreme Court held that victims of intentional sexual harassment were entitled to the full array of damages, including monetary damages.

Monetary damages were at issue in *Davis v. Monroe County Board of Education,* in which, as set forth above, the Justices of the United States Supreme Court held that a school district could be sued where district officials were aware of peer sexual harassment, but failed to take actions to prevent further incidents. Though still evolving, the law in this area varies widely, and it is part of a very political debate made that much more complex with respect to adolescent girls by rulings like *Franklin v. Gwinnett County Public Schools*[353] and *Davis v. Monroe County Board of Education.*[354]

Below is a brief overview of the legal relationship between school and minors, with a particular emphasis on adolescent girls.

As the United States Supreme Court explained in *Vernonia School District 47J v. Wayne Acton, et. ux,*[355] "[t]raditionally at common law, and still today, unemancipated minors lack some of the most fundamental rights of self-determination, including even the right of liberty in its narrow sense (*i.e.*, the right to come and go at will). They are subject, even as to their physical freedom, to the control of their parents or guardians. When parents place minor children in private schools for their education, the teachers and administrators of those schools stand in *loco parentis* over the children entrusted to them. In fact, the tutor or schoolmaster is the very prototype of that status. As Blackstone described it, a parent 'may…delegate part of his parental authority during his life to the tutor or schoolmaster of his child; who is then in *loco parentis*, and has as such a portion of the power of the parent committed to his charge…—that of restraint and correction, as may be necessary to answer the purposes for which he is employed.'"[356]

This historic standard has been articulated repeatedly by the Court. In *Tinker v. Des Moines Independent Community School District,*[357] for example, the United States Supreme Court detailed the significance of the "comprehensive authority" school officials hold, an authority that is "consistent with fundamental constitutional safeguards, to prescribe and control conduct in schools."[358] It is not, however, an unfettered, unlimited control. Yet, balancing the authority of school officials with the expanding rights of minors has become difficult in recent years. Issues of discipline, for instance, have long been part of the emotional debate over whether school officials standing in *loco parentis* over the children are entitled to rigorously discipline children "in the same way that parents might."

The emotional answer to that question, at least on a social level, appears to be a resounding no. The legal answer, however, appears to be yes and no. And it all comes down to degrees. Corporal punishment, as the process of disciplining students in public schools is commonly referred to under the law, has been banned in recent years in twenty-seven states across the country.[359] But it remains legal in twenty-three other states, mostly southern,[360] as long as it is "reasonable" and not excessive. The "reasonable, but not excessive" standard was set forth in the 1977 United States Supreme Court case of *Ingraham v. Wright,*[361] an apparent low point in American teacher-student relations. Two junior high school boys were involved in the incidents underlying the case of *Ingraham v. Wright*. They were James Ingraham and Roosevelt Andrews. One was an eighth grader. The other was in the ninth grade. But what precisely happened to James Ingraham and Roosevelt Andrews that sent their case all the way to the United States Supreme Court?

"The evidence," the Justices wrote, "consisting mainly of the testimony of sixteen students, suggests that the regime at Drew [Junior High School] was exceptionally harsh. The testimony of Ingraham and Andrews, in support of their individual claims for damages, is illustrative. Because he was slow to respond to his teacher's instructions, Ingraham was subjected to more than twenty licks with a paddle while being held over a table in the principal's office."[362] But "[t]he paddling was so severe that [Ingraham] suffered a hematoma,[363] requiring medical attention and keeping him out of school for several days," the Court noted. With regard to Andrews, the Justices noted that "Andrews was paddled several times for minor infractions. On two occasions he was struck on his arms, once depriving him of the full use of his arm for a week."[364] Parents for the two boys argued that paddling as vicious as this violated the Eighth Amendment's prohibition against "cruel and unusual" punishment.[365]

There is just one problem. The Eighth Amendment provides that "[e]xcessive bail shall not be required, nor excessive fines imposed, nor cruel and unusual punishments inflicted,"[366] which is probably why the Justices held in *Ingraham v. Wright* that "...when public school teachers or administrators impose disciplinary corporal punishment, the Eighth Amendment is inapplicable."[367] With regard to issues of due process under the Fourteenth Amendment, however, the Court held that "[b]ecause it is rooted in history, the child's liberty interest in avoiding corporal punishment while in the care of public school authorities is subject to historical limitations. Under the common law, an invasion of personal security gave rise to a right to recover damages in a subsequent judicial proceeding.[368] But the right of recovery was qualified by the concept of justification. Thus, there could be no recovery against a teacher who gave only 'moderate correction' to a child. To the extent that force used was reasonable in light of its purpose, it was not wrongful, but rather 'justifiable or lawful.'"[369]

Courts within states that still allow corporal punishment continue to adhere today to the "reasonableness" standard for corporal punishment as a valid measure of control. In addition, as schools have grown more dangerous, courts have continued to advance the notion of the need for even greater authority on the part of school officials who hope to keep order. Reaffirming the need for school authority in the 1985 case of *New Jersey v. T.L.O.*,[370] for example, the United States Supreme Court held that "maintaining security and order in schools requires a certain degree of flexibility in school disciplinary procedures, and we have respected the value of preserving the informality of the student-teacher relationship."[371]

In the name of security, safety, and flexibility, school officials have been allowed to search the backpacks, lockers, and sometimes even the persons of school children.[372] School officials were also allowed in one instance to search a minor suspected of "crotching" drugs.[373] In another school, a student's backpack was searched after a school official heard a "thud."[374] The search of a fanny-pack by officials of a school in Oregon was deemed reasonable, given that it was based upon two "reliable" students in addition to the fact that the minor involved had once brought a gun to school before.[375] And in *New Jersey v. T.L.O.*,[376] the Court held it to be reasonable for officials to search a student's purse after the student denied she had been smoking.[377] School authorities have long been allowed to search lockers.[378] Pat-down searches for weapons that yield smaller, softer items such as marijuana may also be reasonable.[379] And the search of a student's car may not be absolutely off limits.[380]

What all of that means, of course, is that school officials have a great deal of flexibility in their dealings with students. And yet, arguments regarding safety and the need for discipline do not always justify everything.[381] For example, the nude strip-search of a 13-year-old girl suspected by school officials of possessing drugs was held to have been well out of constitutional bounds by federal court officials, who deemed the search "a humiliation."[382] And in *People v. Dilworth*,[383] an Illinois student successfully appealed a conviction based upon the unlawful possession of a controlled substance found in a flashlight on school property. On appeal, the student argued that his Fourth and Fourteenth Amendment rights had been violated by the police officer assigned to the school, who admitted deciding to search the student because he had been with another student who had previously been searched for drugs. School officials argued that because the arrest took place on school grounds, the student was entitled to less protection than the average citizen. The Illinois Appellate Court disagreed, holding that search had not been properly supported by probable cause.

What the above cases establish, of course, is that with so much authority and control comes responsibility. Or at least it should, argue critics of the current school system. "Millions of parents send their children to school each day without thinking of the possible consequences of their actions," argues James M. Kemp in *DeShaney and its Progeny—The Failure to Mandate that Public School Officials Protect Our Tender Youth*.[384] "Most know where their children are going and generally what time they will return home. Unfortunately, a majority of parents have no idea what occurs within many of the school systems throughout this country. Arguably, the level of danger facing our 'tender youth' has risen as society has become more violent. There are a tremendous number of elements which inflict disastrous harm on our children. Teachers try to prevent the possession of weapons and drugs, gang membership and activities, sexual promiscuity, harassment, assault, and other behaviors and their consequences."[385]

Although Kemp notes the "[e]fforts by some schools to install video devices, metal detectors, and security personnel are commendable," at the same time, there are schools that lack the funding to pay for such devices. What, then, is the "proper level of supervision under federal law," Kemp asks, before attempting an answer of his own. "To resolve this issue, one much first address a question which is the subject of considerable debate among judges, scholars, and parents: who is responsible for ensuring the safety of children within the school setting?"[386]

That was precisely the question in *Manchu v. Field Museum of Natural History*,[387] a case that began innocently enough—with a trip by school children to the Field Museum in Chicago. According to court documents, two teachers took a class of fifty junior high school students to the Field Museum. But one of the children, a 12-year-old boy, wandered away and was beaten up by students from another school. The student's parents sued the teachers and the museum. The Illinois court held that neither the teachers, nor the museum, was liable because neither could foresee that danger of this kind would come to the child. Were the teachers really to blame?

In another case, a California student was shot by gang members while standing in front of the school building after the school day had ended. There was a suit, which ended with the court finding that there was little school officials could have done to prevent the shooting.[388] But in another nearly identical case, a school district could be held liable where district officials directed a fifth-grader to wait outside the school building at 6:15 A.M. for a bus to take her to a gifted class. While she was waiting one morning, the girl was snatched off the street and sexually assaulted. Although a lower court found that the school was not liable, the Florida Appellate Court held that because the district directed the child to stand outside of the school, the district was obligated to provide adequate security. Because the district had failed to do so, it had breached a duty to the girl. Accordingly, liability attached.[389]

Traditionally, however, state officials as well as their entities were held immune from liability for personal injury torts if the officials were acting in the course of their employment. But that fact has prompted critics to argue that the *DeShaney* standard should apply to school officials. The *DeShaney* standard was derived from the case of *DeShaney v. Winnebago County Department of Social Services*,[390] which raised the issue of whether states have a constitutional duty to protect students from "known abuse." *DeShaney* involved the sad story of a little boy being abused by his father, a fact state officials received reports of. Despite the reports, however, the boy was never removed from the home, and eventually the child's father beat him to death.

The *DeShaney* case led to outrage and arguments that the Due Process Clause of the United States Constitution required states to protect the "life, liberty, or property of its citizens" against harm once it becomes aware of that harm, even if it should come from private citizens. But the United States Supreme Court held that the Due Process Clause granted only so much protection against the harms of private actors. Rather, "[i]t is the state's affirmative act...through incarceration, institutionalization, or other similar restraint of personal liberty...triggering the protections of the Due Process Clause."[391] In other words, because the little boy was not in the custody of the state, the protections of the Due Process Clause were not triggered. But the standard of care of one "in custody" of the state remains as a benchmark.

For example, in likening attendance and the physical situation of school to "incarceration, institutionalization, or other similar restraint of personal liberty," critics, such as Kemp, argue that the *DeShaney* standard reasonably applies to schools. What that would mean in a practical sense is that school districts would be required to exercise the highest standard of diligence to protect students from harm as opposed to the merely foreseeable standard. An impossible standard? It might have seemed so once. But not today. Although not expressly invoked, the United States Supreme Court's 1999 decision in *Davis v. Monroe*

County Board of Education,[392] appears to rely on the above logic where harms or misconduct take place on school grounds.

"Where, as here," the Justices wrote in *Davis v. Monroe County Board of Education,* "the misconduct occurs during school hours and on school grounds— the bulk of G.F.'s misconduct, in fact, took place in the classroom—the misconduct is taking place 'under' an 'operation' of the funding recipient."[393] And, indeed, the issue of funding was significant in *Davis v. Monroe County Board of Education* because the plaintiff alleged violations under Title IX. "In these circumstances, the recipient retains substantial control over the context in which the harassment occurs. More importantly, however, in this setting the Board exercises significant control over the harasser."[394]

And control over the harasser is the key to unlocking liability under Title IX.

"We have observed, for example," the Justices wrote in *Davis v. Monroe County Board of Education,* "that the nature of [the state's] power [over public school children] is custodial and tutelary, permitting a degree of supervision and control that could not be exercised over free adults.[395] On more than one occasion, this Court has recognized the importance of school officials' 'comprehensive authority'...consistent with fundamental constitutional safeguards, to prescribe and control conduct in the schools.[396] The common law, too, recognizes the school's disciplinary authority.[397] We thus conclude that recipients of federal funding may be liable for 'subject[ing]' their students to discrimination where the recipient is deliberately indifferent to known acts of student-on-student sexual harassment and the harasser is under the school's disciplinary authority."[398]

In this sense, the world has changed for adolescent girls. Although *Davis v. Monroe County Board of Education* is sometimes thought to have changed the school world for adolescent girls in the blink of an eye, in fact, the case and subsequent Supreme Court decision was the long-fought result of a ground swell of lobbying and scholarly articles.[399] Though some would clearly disagree,[400] others suggest that there was a need. A 1993 survey conducted by the American Association of University Women "found that four out of five public school students from eighth to eleventh grade reported experiencing sexual harassment, defined as 'unwanted and unwelcome sexual behavior that interferes with your life.'"[401]

Although *Davis v. Monroe County Board of Education* may eventually do a great deal to makes school hallways less hostile for adolescent girls in America's schools, the decision is not a panacea. Though it is often disputed, classrooms remain places of hidden hazard, which are at times particular to adolescent girls. For example, in addition to groping, sexual harassment, teacher come-ons, and declining self-esteem, adolescent girls also stumble in school. For instance, although boys repeat grades and drop out of school at a higher rate than girls, "the link between grade repetition and dropping out is stronger for girls than boys," say researchers.[402]

In other words, girls held back a grade are more likely to drop out at some point in their academic careers than those who are not held back. Not only does that appear to be something particularly detrimental to girls about being held back; there is something more detrimental to girls about dropping out: they are less likely than their male counterparts to return and complete school.[403] Indeed, current research shows that in 1995, "females comprised 45 percent of 15- to 24-year-olds who dropped out [of school] that year; they made up 50 percent of 16- to 24-year-olds who stayed out."[404]

As they enter adolescence, girls also tend to become more hesitant to speak in class, an event that is more than mere "stylistic difference," researchers argue. "[S]peaking out in class—and being acknowledged for it—is a constant reinforcement of a student's right to be heard, to take academic risks," writes Peggy Orenstein in *Schoolgirls: Young Women, Self-esteem, and the Confidence Gap.*[405] "Students who talk in class have more opportunity to enhance self-esteem through exposure to praise; they have the luxury of learning from mistakes and they develop the perspective to see failure as an educational tool."[406]

The adolescent girl may also walk away from science or refuse to push herself in math class because she feels that it is not what is expected of her, turning instead to the "coolness" of sex, crime, or beauty in an effort to find her worth, which leaves only the question: is there anything to be done to settle adolescent girls today? Until the adolescent girl is granted one, singular, consistent legal and social identity, the answer is probably not.

THE CONTRADICTORY STATE OF THE LAW FOR AMERICA'S "GIRLS"

Alabama:

As of 2000, minor females needed the consent of parents to be married. But they could consent to prenatal care and drug and alcohol abuse treatment. They could also drop out of high school at the age of 16. A minor female must prove that she is a high school graduate, married, pregnant, the parent of a child, or at least 14 before her consent to general medical services becomes valid. Minors older than 12 can also consent to treatment for sexually transmitted diseases, including HIV. But under state law, doctors can notify a minor's parents. A minor female needs the consent of a parent before she can have an abortion. By contrast, she may make the decision regarding adoption herself. The age of majority is 19 in Alabama.

Alaska:

Minor females need the consent of parents to be married. But they can make the choice to drop out of school after their 16th birthday. Minors may choose to use contraceptives. They also can consent to general medical services. Alaska had no express law or policy regarding the consent of parents for abortions. Attempts at consent and abortion restrictions where not in line with United States Supreme Court precedent have been blocked by the courts. The age of majority is 18.

Arizona:

Minors can drop out of high school at 16 if they choose to. They may use contraceptives without parental consent. Minors may consent to treatment for sexually transmitted diseases and alcohol and drug treatment provided the minor is older than 12. But a minor female still needs the express consent of her parents before she can marry. Arizona has no express law or policy regarding the consent of minors to abortions. Attempts at consent and abortion restrictions not in line with United States Supreme Court precedent have been blocked by the courts. The age of majority generally is 18.

Arkansas:

Parental consent is needed for the marriage of a minor. But under Arkansas law, parental consent is not necessary for the minor seeking treatment for sexually transmitted diseases, excluding surgery, but doctors may notify parents. Parental notification involving both parents of a minor is necessary prior to an abortion. The age of majority is 18.

California:

Parental consent is not necessary for minors seeking to use contraceptives, seeking prenatal care or testing, or treatment for HIV. Minors can consent on their own to treatment for alcohol and drug abuse treatment. California had no express law or policy regarding the consent of minors to abortions. Attempts at consent and abortion restrictions not in line with United States Supreme Court precedent have been blocked by the courts. The age of majority is 18.

Colorado:

Minors may choose birth control without the consent of parents and they can seek treatment for sexually transmitted diseases, including HIV, without the consent of parents, as long as the minor is 16 or older. Minors can drop out of high school after the age of 16. Colorado has no express law or policy regarding the consent of parents to abortions. Restrictions on abortion that fall outside of United States Supreme Court precedent have been blocked by the courts. The age of majority is 18.

Delaware:

While parental consent is not necessary for contraceptive use, provided the minor is at least 12 years old, authorities in Delaware may inform parents of the use. Minors may drop out of school after 16 years of age; they may seek treatment for sexually transmitted diseases. A minor may be married without parental consent if she is pregnant or already has a child. But parents may be notified. Delaware requires parental notice for abortion for minors under the age of 16, but there is a judicial bypass provision. The age of majority is 18.

District of Columbia:

Minors in the District of Columbia may choose to use contraceptives, seek treatment for sexually transmitted diseases or for alcohol and drug abuse; and agree to an abortion. But they need the consent of their parents to marry. The age of majority is 18.

Florida:

Minors may seek treatment for sexually transmitted diseases, HIV, and alcohol and drug abuse without the consent of parents. And minors who are pregnant or married do not need parental consent to use contraceptives. In addition, a pregnant minor may get married without the consent of parents. Florida was at the epicenter of the antiabortion movement during the 1990s. Restrictive parental consent proposals were part of this effort. In July 2003, the state's most recent version of the Parental Notice of Abortion Act was declared unconstitutional by a Florida court.[407] The age of majority is 18.

Georgia:

Minors in Georgia may drop out of school without parental consent at age 16; and they may choose to use birth control. They may seek treatment for sexually transmitted diseases, including HIV, without the consent of parents, except with regard to surgery. But physicians may notify parents. Pregnant minors may marry without the consent of parents. Parental notification for abortion is explicitly required for abortion. The age of majority is 18.

Hawaii:

Minors of at least 14 may use contraceptives, but their parents may be notified by doctors. The same is true with regard to treatment for sexually transmitted diseases and treatment for alcohol and drug abuse. Minors 15 or older may seek judicial approval to marry in lieu of parental consent. According to the Alan Guttmacher Institute, Hawaii has no express law or policy outlining a minor's right to consent to abortion services. The age of majority is 18.

Idaho:

Minors may drop out of school at 16. They may seek testing and treatment for sexually transmitted diseases and alcohol and drug abuse without parental consent. They also may choose to use contraceptives. But parental notification is required for minors seeking an abortion. In addition, parental consent is required for marriage. The age of majority is 18.

Illinois:

Minors in Illinois may consent to the use of contraceptives if they are married, parents themselves, or pregnant. Minors 12 or older may seek testing or treatment for sexually transmitted diseases, but doctors may notify parents. If they are employed, minors 16 years and older may drop out of high school. Minors need parental consent to marry. Illinois has no express law or policy outlining a minor's right to consent to abortion services, according to the Alan Guttmacher Institute. The age of majority is 18.

Indiana:

Indiana has no clearly stated policy on whether a minor may consent to the use of contraceptives. Minors in Indiana may consent to testing and treatment of sexually transmitted diseases and the treatment of alcohol and drug abuse. Minors who are pregnant may be married with the consent of the court, provided they are at least 15 years old. But parental consent is required for minors who want to drop out of high school and who want to have abortions. The age of majority is 18.

Iowa:

Iowa has no clearly stated policy on whether a minor may consent to the use of contraceptives. Iowa law does provide, however, that a minor may consent to testing and treatment for HIV. The parents of a minor can be notified if a minor has tested positive, according to the law. A minor may drop out of school if a court allows her to do so. Parental consent is required for marriage and parental notification is expressly necessary for a minor seeking an abortion. The age of majority is 18.

Kansas:

Kansas has no clearly stated policy on whether a minor may consent to the use of contraceptives. The general standard for evaluating whether a minor may use contraceptive appears to be, however, if a minor is "mature enough" to understand the "nature and consequences" involved with using the products. Minors in Kansas may consent to testing and treatment for HIV, but doctors may notify parents. A minor can consent to drug and alcohol treatment. Parental consent is needed for marriage. A minor may drop out of high school with the court's permission, and parental notification is required prior to abortion. The age of majority is 18.

Kentucky:

A minor may use contraceptives and request treatment for sexually transmitted diseases, as well as treatment for alcohol and drug abuse. The law provides, however, that doctors may notify the minor's parents. Minors who are pregnant may marry without parental consent. But parental notification is required for a minor who intends to drop out of high school. Only minors who are 16 or older may leave school, even with parental consent. Parental consent is required for minors seeking abortions. The age of majority is 18.

Louisiana:

Minors may consent to treatment for alcohol and drug abuse as well as for testing and treatment for sexually transmitted diseases. They may also consent to general medical treatment, but not surgery. A minor in Louisiana may drop out of high school at 17. But parental consent is needed for marriage, as well as for abortion. The age of majority is 18.

Maine:

Married minors may use contraceptives. They may also consent to testing and treatment for sexually transmitted diseases and alcohol and drug abuse. Minors may consent to abortion. Minors 17 or older may drop out of high school. But parental consent is needed for marriage. The age of majority is 18.

Maryland:

Minors may choose to use contraceptives; and to be tested and treated for sexually transmitted diseases and drug and alcohol abuse. But doctors may notify their parents. Minors may drop out of school at 16. And minors who are pregnant and at least 15 may marry without parental consent. Maryland provides a physician's bypass allowing minors who cannot obtain parental consent to still obtain an abortion. The age of majority is 18.

Massachusetts:

Massachusetts has no clearly stated policy on whether a minor may consent to the use of contraceptives. But state funds are used to support a statewide program providing confidential services to minors. Minors may consent to testing and treatment for sexually transmitted diseases as well as for treatment of drug and alcohol abuse provided the minor is at least 12 years old. A minor cannot consent, however, to methadone maintenance therapy. Minors who have jobs, are least 14 years old, and have completed the sixth grade may drop out of high school. But parental consent is required for abortion and marriage. The age of majority is 21 in Massachusetts, except where consent to health care is involved. The age of majority for heath care purposes is 18.

Michigan:

Researchers suggest that Michigan has no clearly stated policy on whether a minor may consent to the use of contraceptives. But the minor may consent to testing and treatment of sexually transmitted diseases, as well as treatment for alcohol and drug abuse, though doctors are permitted to inform parents. A minor may drop out of school. But parental consent is necessary if a minor wants to get married or have an abortion. The age of majority is 18.

Minnesota:

Minors may consent to contraceptive use; testing and treatment of sexually transmitted diseases; and treatment for drug and alcohol abuse. But minors need parental consent if they want to get married or drop out of high school. And parental notification of both parents is required before a minor female can have an abortion. The age of majority is 18.

Mississippi:

Minors who are married may consent to the use of contraceptives; testing and treatment for sexually transmitted diseases; and treatment for alcohol and drug abuse, provided the minor is at least 15 years old. Female minors who are older than 15 and male minors who are older than 17 may marry without parental consent, although the law requires parental notification for all minors under the age of 21. Minors who are 17 and older may drop out of high school. Parental consent and the "involvement" of both parents is required for minors seeking abortions. The age of majority is 18.

Missouri:

Minors may consent to treatment for sexually transmitted diseases, as well as to treatment of alcohol and drug abuse. Minors in Missouri may drop out of high school if they are employed and at least 14. Parental consent is required, however, for marriage and abortion. The age of majority is 18.

Montana:
Minors may consent to the use of contraceptives, testing and treatment for sexually transmitted diseases, and treatment for alcohol and drug abuse. Minors who are at least 16 years of age may drop out of high school, provided they have completed the eighth grade. Parental consent is required for minors seeking to marry. Attempts at consent and abortion restrictions not in line with United States Supreme Court precedent have been blocked by the courts. The age of majority is 18.

Nebraska:
Minors may consent to testing and treatment for sexually transmitted diseases and treatment for alcohol and drug abuse. Minors who are at least 17 years of age may drop out of high school. Minors who are at least 17 may marry without parental consent. Parental notification is required, however, for abortion. As of 2000, Nebraska had no clear policy or law regarding the consent of parents to use contraceptives. The age of majority is 18.

Nevada:
Minors may consent to testing and treatment for sexually transmitted diseases and treatment for alcohol and drug abuse. Minors who have graduated from the eighth grade may drop out of school without parental consent if a court determines that the minor is able to make such a potentially life-altering decision. Parental consent is required for marriage. As of 2000, Nevada had no clear policy or law regarding the consent of minors to abortion. Attempts to enact consent and abortion restrictions not in line with United States Supreme Court precedent have been blocked by the courts. The age of majority is 18.

New Hampshire:
In New Hampshire, minors who are at least 14 years old may consent to testing and treatment for sexually transmitted diseases. Minors who are 12 and older may consent to treatment for alcohol and drug abuse. But parental consent is needed for minors who want to drop out of school. Parental consent is also required for marriage. As of 2000, New Hampshire had no clear policy or law regarding the consent of minors to abortion. Attempts at consent and abortion restrictions not in line with United States Supreme Court precedent have been blocked by the courts. The age of majority is 18.

New Jersey:
Minors may consent to testing and treatment for sexually transmitted diseases and treatment for alcohol and drug abuse. Minors who are at least 16 years old may drop out of school. Parental consent is required for marriage. As of 2000, New Jersey had no clear policy or law regarding the consent of parents to abortion. Attempts at consent and abortion restrictions not in line with United States Supreme Court precedent have been blocked by the courts. The age of majority is 18.

New Mexico:

Minors can consent to the use of contraceptives in New Mexico. They may also consent to testing for sexually transmitted diseases and for treatment generally. Treatment for HIV is not covered by the law. Parental consent is required for marriage and where a minor wants to drop out of school. New Mexico did not have an express policy or law regarding a minor's consent to alcohol and drug abuse treatment in 2000. The state also had no clear policy or law regarding the consent of minors to abortion. Attempts at consent and abortion restrictions not in line with United States Supreme Court precedent have been blocked by the courts. The age of majority is 18.

New York:

Minors in New York can consent to testing for sexually transmitted diseases as well as treatment for HIV expressly included. Minors may also consent to alcohol and drug abuse treatment. Minors above the age of 16 may drop out of school. Parental consent is required for marriage where minors are concerned. New York did not have an express policy or law regarding a minor's consent to the use of contraceptives, though state funds are used to offer confidential contraceptive care to minors. The state also had no clear policy or law regarding the consent of minors to abortion. The age of majority is 18.

North Carolina:

In North Carolina, minors may consent to the use of contraceptives. They may also consent to testing and treatment for sexually transmitted disease, including HIV and treatment for alcohol and drug abuse. Minors who are above the age of 16 may decide whether or not they want to remain in school. Parental consent is required for minors who want to marry. Parental consent is also required for minors seeking abortion. But the state law expressly provides for judicial bypass. The age of majority is 18.

North Dakota:

Minors who are at least 14 may consent to testing and treatment for sexually transmitted disease. The law requires, however, that at least one parent be shown the informed consent form for HIV tests before the minor signs it. Minors who are above the age of 16 may decide whether or not they want to remain in school. Parental consent is required for minors who want to marry. Parental consent is also required for minors seeking abortion. The "involvement" of both parents is required. The age of majority is 18.

Ohio:

Although minors may consent to testing and treatment for sexually transmitted diseases, the law requires express consent to HIV testing. Treatment for HIV is not included in the law. A minor may consent to treatment for alcohol and drug abuse. Ohio does not allow minors to decide whether or not they will drop out of high school. The state did not have an express policy or law regarding a minor's consent to the use of contraceptives in 2000. Parental consent is required for minors who want to marry. Parental notification is required of minors who want to have abortion. The age of majority is 18.

Oklahoma:

If a minor has ever been pregnant, she may consent to the use of contraceptives in Oklahoma. Minors may also consent to testing and treatment for sexually transmitted diseases as well as treatment for alcohol and drug abuse. But parental consent is required for minors who want to drop out of school. A minor who is pregnant or has a child may get married with the approval of the court. The state did not have an express policy or law regarding a minor's consent to an abortion in 2000. The age of majority is 18.

Oregon:

Minors may consent to the use of contraceptives, though the law allows doctors to notify parents. Minors may also consent to testing and treatment for sexually transmitted diseases and to treatment for alcohol and drug abuse as long as the minor is at least 14. Minors may drop out of school, provided they are at least 16, have a job, and can demonstrate sufficiently before the school board that they have gained knowledge "equivalent" to course work. Parental consent is required for minors who want to marry. In 2000, the state did not have an express policy or law regarding parental consent to abortion. The age of majority is 18.

Pennsylvania:

Minors in Pennsylvania may consent to the testing and treatment for sexually transmitted disease, including HIV. They may also consent to treatment for alcohol and drug abuse. Minors who are above the age of 17 may decide whether or not they want to remain in school. Parental consent is required for minors who want to marry. Parental consent is also required for minors seeking abortion. The age of majority is 21.

Rhode Island:

Minors living in Rhode Island can consent to testing for sexually transmitted diseases with treatment for HIV expressly included. Minors may also consent to alcohol and drug abuse treatment. Minors above the age of 16 may drop out of school. Parental consent is required for minors who want to marry. It is also required for minors seeking abortions. Rhode Island had no express policy or law regarding a minor's consent to contraceptives in 2000. The age of majority is 18.

South Carolina:

Minors who are older than 16 may consent to general medical treatment, including contraceptives. They may also consent to testing and treatment for sexually transmitted diseases. In addition, minors who have completed the eighth grade may also seek the approval of a court to leave school for work. Parental consent is required for marriage and for minors seeking to have abortions. The age of majority is 18.

South Dakota:

South Dakota had no express policy or law regarding a minor's consent to contraceptives in 2000. But state law provided that minors could consent to the testing and treatment for sexually transmitted diseases, as well as to treatment for drug and alcohol abuse. Minors 16 or older are allowed to decide whether or not they will stay in school.

But they need parental consent to marry, and parental notification is required for minors seeking to have abortions. The age of majority is 18.

Tennessee:
Minors in Tennessee may consent to the use of contraceptives, as well to the testing and treatment for sexually transmitted diseases and alcohol and drug abuse. In addition, minors who are above the age of 17 may decide whether or not they want to remain in school. But parental consent is required for minors who want to marry. Parental consent is also required for minors seeking abortion. The age of majority is 18.

Texas:
Texas had no stated law or policy regarding the consent of minors for the use of contraceptives in 2000. Texas law did expressly provide, however, that state funds may not be used to provide confidential contraceptives and related services to minors. Minors may consent to testing and treatment for sexually transmitted diseases, including HIV, but the law provides that doctors are allowed to inform parents. The same was true with regard to treatment for alcohol and drug abuse. Minors are not allowed to drop out of school in Texas. Minors between the ages of 14 and 18 who want to be married may petition the court for permission. Parental notification of abortion is required prior to the procedure. The age of majority is 18.

Utah:
Like Texas, Utah had no stated law or policy regarding the consent of minors for the use of contraceptives in 2000. But Utah also does not allow state funds to be used to provide confidential contraceptives and related services to minors. Minors could consent to testing and treatment for sexually transmitted diseases. There was no law regarding their consent to treatment for drug and alcohol abuse in 2000. Minors required parental consent for marriage. Minors are not allowed to drop out of school in Utah. And parental notification is required for abortion. The Utah law regarding notification and consent does not include a provision for a judicial bypass. The age of majority is 18.

Vermont:
Vermont had no law or policy on the consent of minors to use contraceptives in 2000. But minors who have reached at least the age of 12 were allowed to consent to tests and treatment for sexually transmitted diseases. They were also allowed to agree to treatment for alcohol and drug abuse. Minors 16 years old who have completed the tenth grade are allowed to decide whether they want to leave school. But they need parental consent for marriage. Vermont had no express policy or law regarding a minor's consent to abortion in 2000. The age of majority in Vermont is 18.

Virginia:
Minors can consent to the use of contraceptives, testing and treatment for sexually transmitted diseases; and treatment for alcohol and drug abuse in Virginia. But parental consent is required for minors who want to marry, and parental notification is required

by law before a minor can have an abortion. Minors are not allowed to drop out of school, and the age of majority in Virginia is 18.

Washington:

At 16, minors in Washington can decide whether or not they will stay in school. In that state, minors 14 and above can consent to testing and treatment for sexually transmitted diseases, while minors 13 and older can consent to treatment for alcohol and drug abuse. But parental consent was required for minors who wanted to marry. Washington had no law or policy on the consent of minors to abortion in 2000. The state also had no law or policy on the consent of minors to use contraceptives. The age of majority in Washington is 18.

West Virginia:

In West Virginia, minors may consent to testing and treatment for sexually transmitted diseases as well as to treatment for alcohol and drug abuse. Minors who are 16 and employed may drop out of school. Parental consent is required for minors who wanted to marry, and parental notification is required by West Virginia law, though the statute includes a judicial bypass provision. The age of majority in West Virginia is 18.

Wisconsin:

Minors in Wisconsin may consent to testing and treatment for sexually transmitted diseases, as well as for treatment for drug and alcohol abuse. Minors cannot drop out of school. Parental consent is required for marriage, and parental notification is required for minors seeking abortions. But the law has a judicial bypass provision. The age of majority is 18.

Wyoming:

Minors in Wyoming may consent to the use of contraceptives and testing and treatment for sexually transmitted diseases, including HIV. Minors who have reached the age of 16 and have completed the tenth grade may drop out of school if they want. But they cannot get married or have an abortion without parental consent. The age of majority in Wyoming is 18.

• • • • •

If there is anything to be understood from this section it is that the world of adolescent girls is not what it used to be. Medical professionals suggest that girls are "becoming" women earlier than ever before, at a time when peers and older men appear to see—or at least to trade upon—the notion of girl as sex kitten. Sexual harassment has found its way into school hallways at a time when violence, drug use, and internal strife seem to be constant companions. In short: the world of the adolescent girl is spinning. Thus, if it is possible to ease the crisis that is adolescent "girlhood" today, it may well begin with "attacking [the] destructive stereotyping" that sometimes begins as early as birth, according to Judy Mann, author of *The Difference: Growing Up Female in America*.[408]

In today's society, girls are objectified and sexualized at an earlier age each year. It is an objectification that may spark improper assumptions on the part of peers and adult men, and even worse behavior in places once thought to be safe, such as schools. And as if that were not enough, today's adolescent girls are bombarded outside of school with sexual images of the illusive girl-women of about their age. Thus, to keep pace and the peace, adolescent girls have had to learn to live with bra-snapping, bullying, "whirlpooling" and the bumps, pinches, and gropes of peers. In addition, from the time they are little, adolescent girls are told they are not as smart as men and not as good as boys. What may be surprising to some, however, is that adolescent girls appear to buy into it, growing hesitant to speak in class as they reach puberty and even more reluctant to return to school should they drop out. For these reasons, it is not hyperbole to say that wading through the politics of female adolescence can be more than a little treacherous to today's adolescent girls.

ENDNOTES FOR CHAPTER TWELVE

1   See Gail Landman, *Negotiating Work and Womanhood*, 97 AM. ANTHROPOLOGIST 33 (March 1995), at p. 13 (citing Faye Ginsburg, CONTESTED LIVES: THE ABORTION DEBATE IN AN AMERICAN COMMUNITY (Berkeley: University of California Press, 1989)).

2   See, e.g., Amira Proweller, CONSTRUCTING FEMALE IDENTITIES: MEANING MAKING IN AN UPPER MIDDLE CLASS YOUTH CULTURE (New York: State University of New York Press, 1998); Mary Pipher, REVIVING OPHELIA: SAVING THE SELVES OF ADOLESCENT GIRLS (New York: Ballantine Books, 1994); and Naomi Wolf, PROMISCUITIES: THE SECRET STRUGGLE FOR WOMANHOOD (New York: Fawcett Columbine, 1997). See also Leora Tanenbaum, SLUT! GROWING UP FEMALE WITH A BAD REPUTATION (New York: Seven Stories Press, 1999); Judy Mann, THE DIFFERENCE: GROWING UP FEMALE IN AMERICA (New York: Time Warner, 1994).

3   See Pipher, *supra* note 2, at p. 18.

4   *Id.*; Wolf, *supra* note 2; Tanenbaum, *supra* note 2; Mann, *supra* note 2.

5   See, e.g., Pipher, *supra* note 2, at p. 18.

6   See Hillary Rodham, *Children Under the Law*, 43 HARV. ED. REV. at pp. 487–488 (Nov. 1973). ("'Children' is something a term of legal classification, but it is more common to find the categories of 'infancy' or 'minority' describing people under twenty-one, or under eighteen for some purposes. The status of infancy, or minority, largely determines the rights and duties of a child before the law regardless of his or her actual age or particular circumstances. Justification for such a broad, chronologically determined classification rely on the physical and intellectual differences between adults and children.")

7   The age of sexual consent for "minors" varies widely. See, e.g., Alaska Stat. Sec. 11.41.41(a)(3), (a)(4) (1978) (ages 13 and 18 respectively); Ariz. Rev. Stat. Ann. Sec. 13-1405 (1978) (age 18); Ark. Stat. Ann. Sec. 41-1803(1)(c) (1977) (age 11); Colo. Rev. Stat. Sec. 18-3-403(1)(e) (1978) (age 15); Conn. Gen. Stat. Ann. Sec. 53a-71(a)(1) (West Supp. 1980) (age 15); Fla. Stat. Ann. Sec. 794.05 (West 1976) (age 18); Hawaii Rev. Stat. Secs. 707-730(1)(b), -731(b) (Supp. 1976) (age 14); Ill. Ann. Stat. ch. 38, Sec. 11-4(a)(1), -5(a)(1) (Smith Hurd 1979) (age 16 and 18 respectively); Ind. Code Ann. Secs. 609.3, -4 (West 1979) (ages 12 and 14, respectively); Kan. Stat. Ann. Sec. 21-3503 (Supp. 1979) (age 16); Ky. Rev. Stat. Secs. 510.040(1)(b)(2), .050, .060(1)(b) (1975)(ages 12, 14, and 16 respectively); La. Rev. Stat. Ann. Sec. 14:42(3) (West Supp. 1980) (age 12); Me. Rev. Stat. Ann. tit. 17A Sec. 252(1)(A), 254 (1979) (age 14 and 16, respectively); Md. Ann. Code art. 27 Secs. 463(a)(3), 464C(a)(3) (Supp. 1979) (ages 14 and 16, respectively, and providing that the perpetrator must be at least four years older than the minor); Mass. Ann. Laws Ch. 265, Sec. 23 (Michie/Law. Co-op Supp. 1980) (age 16); Mich. Comp. Laws Secs. 750.520b(1)(a), .520d(1)(a) (Mich. Stat. Ann. Sec. 28.788(2)(1)(a), .788(4)(1)(a) (Callahan Supp. 1979) (ages 13 and 16 respectively); Minn. Stat. Ann. Sec. 609.342(a), .344(a) (West Supp. 1980) (age 13); Mo. Ann. Stat. Secs. 566.030(1)(2), .050 (Vernon 1979) (ages 14 and 16 respectively); Mont. Rev. Codes Ann. Sec. 94-5-503(3) (1977) (age 16); Neb. Rev. Stat. 28-319(1)(c) (defining "sexual assault in the first degree" when the actor is nineteen years of age or older and the victim is less than sixteen years of age.) Neb. Rev. Stat. 28-320(1)(c) (holding that a person commits "sexual assault of a child if he or she subjects another person fourteen years of age or younger to sexual contact and the actor is at least nineteen years of age or older." For purposes of this section, however, "the phrase 'fourteen years of age or younger' designates persons whose age is less than or under fourteen, and also designates persons who have

reached and passed their fourteenth birthday but have not reached their fifteenth birthday." *See State v. Carlson*, 223 Neb. 874 (1986)); N.H. Rev. Stat. Ann. Sec. 632-A:2 (Supp. 1979) (age 13); N.J. Stat. Ann. Sec. 2C:14-2(a) (West 1979) (age 13); N.M. Stat. Ann. Sec. 30-9-11(A)(1) (1978) (age 13); N.C. Gen. Stat. Sec. 14-27.2(a)(2) (Supp. 1979) (age 12); N.D. Cent. Code Secs. 12.1-20-30(1)(d), 2(a), -05(1),–07(1)(f) (Supp. 1979) (age 15); Ohio Rev. Code Ann. Secs. 2907.02(A)(3), -04(A) (Baldwin 1979) (ages 13, between 12 and 15 respectively); Or. Rev. Stat. Sec. 163.435 (1977) (age 18); Pa. Cons. Stat. Ann. Sec. 3122 (Purdon Supp. 1979) (age 14); R.I. Gen. Laws Sec. 11-37-2(A) (Supp. 1979) (age 13); S.C. Code Sec. 16-3-655 (Supp. 1979) (ages 11,14, and 16, respectively); S.C. Codified Laws Ann. Sec. 22-22-1(4) (1979) (age 15); Tenn. Code Ann. Secs. 39-3703(3), -3705(4) (Supp. 1979) (ages 13 and 16 respectively); Utah Code Ann. Secs. 76-5-401, -402(2) (Supp. 1979) (ages 16 and 14, respectively); Vt. Stat. Ann. tit. 13, Sec. 3252(3) (Supp. 1979) (age 16); Wash. Rev. Code Sec. 9A.44.070, .080, .090 (1979) (ages 11, 14, and 16, respectively); W. Va. Code Secs. 61-8B-3(3). -5(a)(2) (1977) (ages 11 and 16, respectively); Wis. Stat. Ann. Sec. 940.225(1)(d), (2)(e) (West Supp. 1979) (ages 12 and 18 respectively); Wyo. Stat. Secs. 6-4-303(a)(v), (c), -305 (1977) (ages 12 and 16, respectively).

8   For example, under Alabama law, the age of marriage is 18 (*see* Ala. Code Sec. 30-1-4 (1996)). Under Texas law, the age of marriage is also 18. (*See* Tex. Fam. Code Ann. Sec. 1.51 (West 1996)). Under Virginia law, the age of marriage is 18. (*See* Va. Code Ann. Sec. 20-45.1 (Michie 1996)). Under Washington State law, the age of marriage is 17. (*See* Wash. Rev. Code Ann. Sec. 26.040.010 (West 1996)). But under Maine law, the age of marriage is 14. (*See* Me. Rev. Stat. tit. 17A Secs. 252(1)(A), 254 (1979)).

9   During the Reagan administration, the legal drinking age was raised to 21.

10   Adolescent boys are confronted by many of the same issues today, but this is a book on women's rights. Thus, male issues will only be discussed as they relate to the primary women's issues.

11   *See* Rodham, *supra* note 6, at p. 491.

12   A recent example of such efforts include moves by politicians to tie Title X funding for birth control to parental consent. *See supra* Chapter Five, at 104–106, for fuller discussion. *See also* Sheryl Gay Stolberg, *Grants Aid Abstinence-Only Initiative*, N.Y. Times, Feb. 28, 2002, at A18; Facts in Brief, *Sexuality Education*, published by the Alan Guttmacher Institute, August 2002; Issues in Brief, *Teen Pregnancy: Trends and Lessons Learned*, published by the Alan Guttmacher Institute, April 2002; Issues in Brief, *Sex Education: Politicians, Parents, Teachers and Teens*, published by the Alan Guttmacher Institute, March 2001; Facts in Brief, *Teenagers' Sexual and Reproductive Health*, published by the Alan Guttmacher Institute, Jan. 2001.

13   As noted in Chapter Five, *supra*, at pp. 90–97, however, there have been efforts by the courts to prevent individuals from having children where there was a suspicion that the parents would not properly care for them. These efforts have largely been deemed unconstitutional.

14   *See* Rodham, *supra* note 6, at p. 490.

15   *Id.* at 489–90. Perhaps the clearest example of this can be found in sexual consent laws. For an historic overview of this issue, *see e.g.*, Mary E. Odem, Delinquent Daughter: Protecting and Policing Adolescent Female Sexuality in the United States, 1855–1920 (Chapel Hill: The University of North Carolina Press, 1995); Rita Eidson, *The Constitutionality of Statutory Rape Laws*, 27 UCLA L. Rev. 757 (1980). American case law on the issue dates back to the 1800s with the cases of *Holton v. State*, 28 Fla. 303. (1891); *Murphy v. State*, 120 Ind. 115 (1889). For other early demonstrative cases, *see also Altman v. Eckermann*, 132 S.W. 523 (Tex. Civ. App. 1910); *People v. Marks*, 146 A.D. 11, 12 (1911); *Watson v. Taylor*, 35 Okla. 768, 774 (1913); *State v. Adkins*, 106 W.Va. 658, 663 (1929); *Parsons v. Parker*, 160 Va. 810, 813–14 (1933); *State v. Huntsman*, 115 Utah 283 (1949).

16   Traditionally, the law has held that when a female child is married, she becomes an "adult" complete and separate from her parents. *See e.g., Kamper v. Waldon*, 17 Cal.2d 718 (1941). But she may not be a woman under the law. A relatively recent example of this reality can be found in the 1967 case of *People v. Caldwell*, 255 Cal. App. 2d 229 (1967); *People v. Courtney*, 180 Cal. App. 2d 61 (1960).

17   *See Kamper,* 17 Cal.2d 718 (holding that once a child is married, parents no longer have a legal obligation of support). (As stated in Chapter One, women and girls were thought to become part of their husband upon marriage. This legal phenomenon, known by the historic term of *feme covert*, may also explain a girl-child's emancipation upon marriage.)

18   *See* Rodham, *supra* note 6, at p. 489.

19   The theory behind this traditional rule was that sexual activity was permissible by a minor within a marriage. But that was contingent. If a minor attempted to move beyond the "safe" boundaries of marriage, her status as minor was restored and the man or men involved could be prosecuted. The rationale behind a married minor's ability to consent to sex involves the dual notions of procreation and marital consent, which also traditionally formed the basis of a woman's inability—until recently—to prove spousal rape.

20   255 Cal. App. 2d 229 (1967).

21   255 Cal. App. 2d at 229.

22   255 Cal. App. 2d at 230. The right to consent to sex was apparently one of those instances when minors remains too immature, even if the minor had consented to sex previously. *See also People v. Courtney*, 180 Cal. App. 2d 61 (1960) (holding that although a female under 18 can consent to a

second marriage without parental consent, that does not mean that she is able to consent to illicit sexual intercourse. Accordingly, she may be reached by penal law regarding statutory rape.

23   428 U.S. 52 (1976).

24   431 U.S. 678 (1977). The case involved the question of whether minor females had a fundamental right to choose birth control. In 1977, the Justices of the United States Supreme Court extended the "right of privacy," which included the right to choose birth control, to minors holding that minors could not be denied the opportunity to purchase birth control because of their age.

25   *See* Rodham, *supra* note 6, at p. 490.

26   *See* Joan Jacobs Brumberg, THE BODY PROJECT: AN INTIMATE HISTORY OF AMERICAN GIRLS (New York: Random House, 1997), at pp. 17–18. Brumberg notes further that "[a]ll of this concern—on the local and state levels—about preserving the sexual innocence of younger women resulted in a great deal of community supervision of the physical development of girls. Some of it was undoubtedly repressive and unkind; some of it was not. Most of all, this 'protective umbrella' meant that girls had many projects—other than their own bodies—to keep them busy and engaged" (citing David J. Pivar, PURITY CRUSADE, SEXUAL MORALITY, AND SOCIAL CONTROL (Westport, Conn., 1973); Ruth Bordin, WOMAN AND TEMPERANCE—THE QUEST FOR POWER AND LIBERTY, 1873–1900 (Philadelphia, 1981); and, Odem, *supra* note 15).

27   *See e.g.*, Eidson, *supra* note 15, at p. 757. (Eidson notes that "[c]ommentators have severely criticized this aspect of statutory rape laws: '[T]he law's refusal to heed the full consent of young girls, because of an inflexible test of capacity to understand, seems unjustified. Protection of the "pure and naive" should be achieved without punishing many blameless men'" (citing COMMENT, *Forcible and Statutory Rape: An Exploration of the Operation and Objectives of the Consent Standard*, 62 YALE L.J. 55, 56 (1952). *See also* COMMENT, *The Resistance Standard in Rape Legislation*, 18 STANFORD L. REV. 680 (1966).

28   *Id.* (citing Burnstein, Jr. & James, *Prostitution in Seattle*, WASH. ST. B. NEWS, Aug.–Sept. 1971, at pp. 5, 29) (in reliance upon Rosenbleet & Pariente, *The Prostitution of Criminal Law*, 11 AM. CRIM. L. REV. 373, 397 (1973), at p. 387, n. 84). ("Society considers the sex experience of a man as attributes if not milestones in his general development. Similar experiences in the life of a woman represent loss of virtue and degradation"); L. Kanowitz & A. Price, WOMEN'S RIGHTS AND THE LAW 5 (1969), at p. 23; *Forcible and Statutory Rape, supra* note 27; COMMENT, *Rape and Rape Laws: Sexism in Society and Law*, 61 CALIF. L. REV. 919, at p. 925 (1973); Karst, *Foreword: Equal Citizenship Under the Fourteenth Amendment*, 91 HARV. L. REV. (1977)). *See also* A. Flexner, PROSTITUTION IN EUROPE (1914), at p. 108.

29   *See* R. Barri Flowers, THE VICTIMIZATION AND EXPLOITATION OF WOMEN AND CHILDREN (Jefferson, N.C., McFarland & Co., Inc., 1994), at pp. 71–72.

30   *See* Stolberg, *supra* note 12, at A18.

31   *See* CENTER FOR DISEASE CONTROL AND PREVENTION VIRAL HEPATITIS C—FACT SHEET *See also*, Denise Grady, *Hepatitis C: How Widespread a Threat?*, N.Y. TIMES (Dec. 15, 1998), at D1.

32   *See, e.g.*, John Schwartz, *Internet Leash Can Monitor Sex Offenders*, N.Y. TIMES, Dec. 31, 2001, at C1; Bruce Lambert, *Man Guilty in Sex Torture of Teenager*, N.Y. TIMES, Dec. 7, 2002, at A18; Elissa Gootman, *On Stand, Girl Recalls Week of Capivity, Assault and Rape*, N.Y. TIMES, Nov. 26, 2002, at A24; Bruce Lambert, *150 Years in Sex Abuse of Teenager*, N.Y. TIMES, Feb. 12, 2003, at A33.

33   *See e.g.*, Paul B. Kaplowitz *et al.*, *Reexamination of the Age Limit for Defining When Puberty Is Precocious in Girls in the United States: Implications for Evaluation and Treatment*, Special Article, PEDIATRICS 1999; 104: 936–941; M.E. Herman-Giddens, E.J. Slora, R.C. Wasserman, et al., *Secondary Sexual Characteristics and Menses in Young Girls Seen in Office Practice: A Study from the Pediatrics Research Office in Office Settings Network*, PEDIATRICS, 1997; 99: 505–512; A.B. Nicholson and C. Hanley, *Indices of Physiological Maturity: Derivation and Interrelationships*, CHILD DEV. 1953; 24:3-38; E.L. Reynolds, J.V. Wine, *Individual Difference in Physical Changes Associated with Adolescence in Girls*, AM. J. DIS. CHILD. 1948; 75: 329-350; W.A. Marshall, J.M. Tanner, *Variations in the Pattern of Pubertal Changes in Girls*, ARCH. DIS. CHILD, 1969; 44:291-303.

34   *See* Lewis Carroll, ALICE'S ADVENTURES IN WONDERLAND and THROUGH THE LOOKING GLASS (New York: Penguin Putnam, Inc. 1998).

35   William Shakespeare, LOVE'S LABOUR'S LOST, Act I, Scene 1, Line 266.

36   *See* Johann Wolfgang von Goethe, CONVERSATIONS OF GOETHE WITH JOHANN PETER ECKERMANN (New York: Da Capo Press, 1998) (translated by John Oxenford) (J.K. Moorhead, ed.).

37   *See* Edward Young, LOVE OF FAME, THE UNIVERSAL PASSION (London: J. Robert, 1725, first printing) (reprinted with the addition of the Seventh Satire (Louisville: Lost Cause Press, 1968), at Satire VI, line 224).

38   *See* James Howell, THE FAMILIAR LETTERS OF JAMES HOWELL: TO SARGEANT D. (London: D. Nutt 1892, first print). (When the author uses the word "agreed," it is philosophical.)

39   *See* Oliver Wendell Holmes, THE AUTOCRAT OF THE BREAKFAST TABLE (Chicago: W.B. Conkey Co., 1990), at Chapter 12.

40   *See* Victor J.E. Jouy, *Maximes*. (The phrase in its original French is: *Sans les femmes le commencement de notre vie seroit privé de secours, le milieu de plaisirs, et le fin de consolation.*)

41   *See* Walt Mueller, UNDERSTANDING TODAY'S YOUTH CULTURE (Wheaton, Illinois: Tyndale House Publishing, Inc., Illinois, 1994), at p. 17.

42   *See* Natalie Angier, WOMAN: AN INTIMATE GEOGRAPHY (Boston: Houghton Mifflin, 1999), at p. 2.

43   *Id.*

44   *See* THE NEW OUR BODIES, OURSELVES (New York: Touchstone, 1992 (updated edition)), at p. 247.

45   As scientists explain, the development of breast tissue and the growth of pubic hair are driven by different hormonal events. For further explanation, *see et al., supra* note 33. ("It is generally accepted that the appearance of breast tissue is the most reliable physical sign of the activation of the pituitary-gonadal axis (gonadarche) in girls. Appearance of pubic hair, although usually occurring at approximately the same time, is attributable to a distinct hormone process, the onset of androgen secretion by the adrenal glands (adrenarche), and is not a marker for gonadarche.")

46   *See* OUR BODIES, OURSELVES, *supra note* 44, at p. 247.

47   *See* Christiane Northrup, M.D., WOMEN'S BODIES, WOMEN'S WISDOM: CREATING PHYSICAL AND EMOTIONAL HEALTH AND HEALING (New York: Bantam Books, 1994), at p. 106. (In simplest terms, the way it all works is that as ovulation gets underway, an influx of estrogen causes the uterine lining to thicken as glands that increase the blood supply to the uterus form. It is through the fallopian tube and into the uterus that the mature egg moves in a natural offering of reproduction. If there is no male sperm cell to couple with the mature egg, the uterine lining is shed, except for the bottom third, which remains full of follicles to produce estrogen and to start the process over again every month for several decades.)

48   For a fuller and more fun review, *see* Angier, *supra* note 42, at pp.164–65. (A taste of Angier's vibrant descriptions of puberty includes: "The adrenals mature at around ten years of age, and that is when a child may start fantasizing about sex and forming obsessive crushes on classmates or pop stars or teachers. The body of a ten-year-old girl may be prepubescent, but her brain is recharged, erotic again....After the adrenals have spoken, there is no turning back, and the pace and the hunger and the noise will only increase. The body will follow the lead of the mind, and it will become sexualized. [¶] At the age of twelve or so, the pulse generator in the hypothalamus is resuscitated, disinhibited. It begins squeezing out packets of hormones again. Just as we don't know what shut it off before kindergarten, we don't know why it starts ticking again. Perhaps cues from the adrenal gland have stimulated us. Or fat may be the culprit. Fat cells release a signaling molecule called leptin, and some experiments have suggested that leptin is the switch that reactivates the brain clock. It is possible that the brain judges reproductive readiness by a girl's fat content, and that a girl must attain a certain level of fatness, a certain heft, before she is capable of ovulating. One rule of thumb has long had it that when a girl reaches approximately one hundred pounds, she pubesces, regardless of her height or even her age. Fat girls menstruate earlier than thin girls or athletic girls. If a quarter of those hundred pounds are fat, then we're looking at twenty-five pounds of fat, which represents an energy reserve of 87,000 calories. The demands of pregnancy are about 80,000 calories. In theory, then, the brain may assess the leptin levels leaking forth from a growing girl's adipose tissue and start its metronome beating again at the hundred-pound mark. [¶] Whatever the trigger, the revived hypothalamus is stronger now by far than it was in its nursery days. And stronger still are the ovaries, the gray sacks of heirloom pearls. They are ready to roll. The adrenals can go only so far. The ovaries know no bounds. They are the primary source of sex hormones that sexualize the body. Before the ovaries are able to serve up a viable egg, they are quite adept at dishing out the sex hormones. The sex hormones cause pubic hair to grow, fat to gather on the breasts and hips, the pelvis to widen, and eventually menstrual blood to flow.")

49   The average onset of menstruation is twelve. Researchers note, however, that anytime between nine and eighteen is still normal. *See* OUR BODIES, OURSELVES, *supra* note 44, at p. 247.

50   *See* Rodham, *supra* note 6, at p. 491; Odem, *supra* note 15; Tanenbaum, *supra* note 2.

51   *See* Kaplowitz, *supra* note 33, at p. 937 (citing Nicholson A.B., Hanley C., *Indices of Physiological Maturity: Derivation and Interrelationships,* 24 CHILD DEV. at pp. 3–38, (1953)).

52   *Id.* at pp. 936–37 (citing Reynolds E.L., Wine J.V., *Individual Difference in Physical Changes Associated with Adolescence in Girls,* 75 AM. J. DIS. CHILD. at pp. 329–350 (1948)).

53   *Id.* at 937 (citing Marshall, W.A., Tanner, J.M., *Variations in the Pattern of Pubertal Changes in Girls,* 44 ARCH. DIS. CHILD, at pp. 291–303 (1969)).

54   *Id.* (As part of that study, each of its 192 subjects "was photographed nude at each visit, and staging of breast development and pubic hair was done by examination of the photographs (not the patient) using the rating system devised by Tanner," wrote Dr. Paul B. Kaplowitz, a pediatric endocrinologist affiliated with the Virginia Commonwealth University's Medical College in a 1999 paper published in the journal PEDIATRICS.)

55   *Id.* at 936–937. *See supra* note 33.

56   *Id.* at p. 937 (citing Marshall and Tanner, *supra* note 53).

57   *See* Kaplowitz, *supra* note 33, at p. 937 (citing Herman-Giddens M.E., Slora E.J., Wasserman R.C., et al., *Secondary Sexual Characteristics and Menses in Young Girls Seen in Office Practice: A Study from the Pediatrics Research Office in Office Settings Network,* 99 PEDIATRICS at pp. 505–512 (1997)). (Participants in this study were part of the American Academy of Pediatrics' Research in Office Settings (PROS) network.)

58 *Id.*

59 *See* Herman-Giddens, *supra* note 57, at p. 511.

60 *Id.* at 509 (citing G. Bacon, Spencer M., Hopwood, N. et al., *A Practical Approach to Pediatric Endocrinology*, Chicago, Ill.: YEAR BOOK OF MEDICAL PUBLISHERS; 1982, at p. 189). (Dr. Herman-Giddens notes that "[c]linicians completed data collection sheets on 18,549 girls. For 9.76 (5.3%), the race, ethnicity, birth dates, or all pubertal values were missing from the form, or the girls were out of the age range of the study. These girls were deleted from the study. Because races other than African American or white constituted only 2.8% of the study population, these cases were deleted from further analysis as well. The 17,077 remaining girls, of whom 90.4% were white and 9.6% were African American, comprised the study sample.") *Id.* at 507.

61 *See* Kaplowitz, *supra* note 33, at p. 936 (The authors of the 1999 study note that "[s]ince the publication of [the Herman-Giddens' study], a letter appeared in the journal *Lancet* (from a single group of pediatric endocrinologists) proposing revised guidelines for the ages at which precocious puberty should be investigated.") For review of that letter, *see* M.J. Elders, C.R. Scott, J.P. Frindik, S.F. Kemp, *Clinical Work-Up for Precocious Puberty*, 350 LANCET, at pp. 457–458, (1997).

62 *Id.* (The authors of the 1999 review note that "[t]he 4th edition of Wilkins's textbook THE DIAGNOSIS AND TREATMENT OF ENDOCRINE DISORDERS IN CHILDHOOD AND ADOLESCENCE states: 'By definition isosexual precocity is development of secondary sexual characteristics along female lines in girls who are less than 8 years of age and along male lines in boys who are less than 9 years of age.'")

63 *Id.* at 938.

64 Menarche means the commencement of menstruation.

65 *See, e.g.,* Basil A. Stoll, *Western Diet, Early Puberty, and Breast Cancer Risk*, 49 BREAST CANCER RESEARCH AND TREATMENT at pp. 187–188, (1998). *See also* Brumberg, *supra* note 26, at pp. 3–4.

66 *See* Gina Kolata, *Doubters Fault Theory Finding Earlier Puberty*, N.Y. TIMES, February 20, 2001, at A1; Gina Kolata, *2 Endocrinology Groups Raise Doubt on Earlier Onset of Girls' Puberty*, N.Y. TIMES, March 3, 2001, at A9; Michael D. Lemonick, *Teens Before Their Time*, TIME, Oct. 30, 2000, at p. 66.

67 *See* Michael D. Lemonick, *Teens Before Their Time*, TIME, Oct. 30, 2000, at pp. 66–68.

68 *See* Stoll, *supra* note 65, at p. 188. (The authors note that "Sonis *et al.* administered the Child Behavior Checklist to 33 early-maturing girls 6 to 11 years of age and an age-matched control group; 27% of the patients scored > 2 standard deviations (SD) above the means on the Total Behavior Problem scale." *See* Sonis W.A., Comite F., Blue J., *et al.*, *Behavior Problems and Social Competence in Girls with True Precocious Puberty*, 106 J. PEDIATRICS at pp. 156–160 (1985).

69 Kaplowitz, *supra* note 33, at p. 938. (On this point, Kaplowitz notes, however, that no attempt was made to relate these problems to the age of the children at diagnosis or at the time of testing, and it is not clear which, if any, of these behavior problems would have responded to hormonal therapy.)

70 *See Davis v. Monroe County Board of Education et al.,* 119 S. Ct. 1661 (1999).

71 *See e.g., Judge Blasts School Harassment Case*, NAT'L L.J., May 1, 2000, at A9. (In May 2000, New York District Court Judge Colleen McMahon "lamented the flood of litigation triggered by the U.S. Supreme Court's 1999 decision in *Davis v. Monroe County Board of Education*," 119 S. Ct. 1661. [¶] "*Davis* is classic example of the old law school maxim that 'bad facts make bad law,'" Judge McMahon said. "What happened to the plaintiff in *Davis* was horrible—indeed, she was the victim of a crime. However, despite the best efforts of the Supreme Court to restrict its reach, *Davis* will inevitably be applied to justify lawsuits over far less heinous behavior—like this one." Judge McMahon then granted summary judgment to school officials in *Manfredi v. Mount Vernon Board of Education*, No. 97 Civ. 7103, a case brought against a New York school district on behalf of a 7-year-old girl, who alleged that she was repeatedly knocked down, "tormented and teased" in the schoolyard by a male student.)

72 The allegation was made through a third person. Minors, like women before them, cannot generally bring lawsuits on their own.

73 *See Davis v. Monroe County Board of Education*, 119 S. Ct. 1661.

74 *Id.* at 1665.

75 *Id.*

76 *Id.*

77 *Id.* at 1666. (The Justices also noted that "[n]or was LaShonda G.F.'s only victim; it is alleged that other girls in the class fell prey to G.F.'s conduct. At one point, in fact, a group composed of LaShonda and other female students tried to speak to Principal Querry about G.F.'s behavior. According to the complaint, however, a teacher denied the students' request with the statement, 'If [Querry] wants you, he'll call you.'")

78 For further discussion of *Davis v. Monroe County Board of Education, see* David D. Savage, *Look the Other Way and Pay*, A.B.A. J., July 1999, at 34; Annys Shin, *Testing Title IX*, Ms. April/May 1999, at 32; Cynthia Gorney, *Teaching Johnny the Appropriate Way to Flirt*, N.Y. TIMES Mag., June 13, 1999, at 43; Susan Fineran & Larry Bennett, *Teenage Peer Sexual Harassment: Implications for Social Works Practice in Education*, 43 SOCIAL WORK 55 (Jan. 1998); COMMENT, Stephanie Easland, *Attacking the "Boys Will Be Boys" Attitude: School Liability Under Section 1983 for Peer Sexual Harassment*, 15 J.

JUV. LAW at p. 119 (1994). For discussion of a school district's liability when a school employee sexually harassed students, see *Gebser et al. v. Lago Vista Independent School Dist.*, 524 U.S. 274 (1998).

79 Media reports suggest that following the *Davis* decision, schools have begun teach sexual harassment classes. *See e.g.,* A CLOSER LOOK, *Teaching Sexual Harassment in School*, ABC WORLD NEWS TONIGHT, aired January 10, 2000, 5:30 p.m. (reporter Bob Woodruff) (transcript available through ABCNews.com).

80 *See* Anne Jarrell, *The Face of Teenage Sex Grows Younger*, N.Y. TIMES, April 3, 2000, at B1.

81 *Id.*

82 *See* Robert W. Blum, JAMA (1997).

83 *See* Tamar Lewin, *1 in 5 Teenagers Has Sex Before 15, Study Finds*, N.Y. TIMES, May 20, 2003, at A18.

84 *See* Lisa Remez, SPECIAL REPORT: *Oral Sex Among Adolescents: Is it Sex or Is it Abstinence?*, 32 FAMILY PLANNING PERSPECTIVES at 298–299 (Nov.–Dec. 2000); Tamar Lewin, *Teenagers Alter Sexual Practices, Thinking Risks Will be Avoided*, N.Y. TIMES, April 5, 1997 (suggesting that high school students—even those had had some AIDS-related education—considered oral sex a less dangerous alternative to vaginal intercourse); citing L.S. Stepp, *Parents are Alarmed by an Unsettling New Fad in Middle Schools: Oral Sex*, WASH. POST, July 8, 1999, at A1; L.S. Stepp, *Talking to Kids about Sexual Limits*, WASH. POST, July 8, 1999, at C4 (reporting on an "unsettling new fad" among suburban middle-school students, who reportedly engaged on a regular basis in oral sex in parks, on school grounds and one another's homes); L. Franks, *The Sex Lives of Your Children*, TALK, February 2000, at pp. 102–107, 157 (reporting the findings of interviews with twelve 16-year-olds, who said, among other things, that seventh grade was the "starting point" for oral sex and that by tenth grade, "well over half of their classmates were involved"; A. Jarrell, *The Face of Teenage Sex Grows Younger*, N.Y. TIMES, April 2, 2000 (quoting a Manhattan psychologist who reportedly suggested that oral sex was "like a good-night kiss to them" in detailing the sex habits of seventh- and eighth-grade virgins who were saving themselves for marriage were having oral sex in the meantime because they perceived it to be safe and risk-free); L. Mundy, *Young Teens and Sex: Sex & Sensibility*, WASH. POST MAG., July 16, 2000, at pp. 16–21, 29–34 (reporting that eighth graders described being regularly propositioned for oral sex in school); K. Toomey, Division of Public Health, Georgia Department of Human Resources, Atlanta, Ga., personal communication [by Remez], Aug. 23, 2000 (Toomey argues, for example, that "anecdotal evidence and some recent data suggest that teenagers are engaging in oral sex to a greater degree than we had previously thought, but whether this represents a true increase is difficult to say, since we have no baseline data for comparison"); S. Edwards and C. Carne, *Oral Sex and the Transmission of Viral STIs*, 74 SEXUALLY TRANSMITTED INFECTIONS at 6–10, (1998)); L. Dominquez, Planned Parenthood of New Mexico, Albuqurque, N.M., personal communication [with Remez], Sept. 7, 2000.

85 *See* Remez, *supra* note 84 (citing K. Toomey, Division of Public Health, Georgia Department of Human Resources, Atlanta, Georgia, personal communication [by Remez], Aug. 23, 2000; S. Rosenthal, Children's Hospital Medical Center, Cincinnati, Ohio, personal communication [with Remez], Sept. 5, 2000; D. Haffner, personal communication [with Remez], Oct. 4, 2000 (Haffner, a sexuality educator and former president of the Sexuality Information and Education Council of the United States, reportedly dismissed the press reports of oral sex among middle-school-aged adolescents as largely media hype, saying that only a very small number of young people are probably involved).

86 *See* Jarrell, *supra* note 80, at B8.

87 *See* Easland, *supra* note 77 (citing *Jane Doe v. Petaluma City Sch. Dist.*, 830 F. Supp. 1560, 1564 (N.D. Cal. 1993).

88 *Id.* (citing *Doe v. Petaluma*, 830 F. Supp. at 1565).

89 *Id.* (Regarding *Doe v. Petaluma*, Easland explains that "[i]n this case, the United State District Court for the Northern District of California held that student-to-student sexual harassment is actionable under Title IX of the Education Amendments of 1972." *Id.* at 1575. However, the court further held that the victim must prove intentional discrimination on the part of a school employee in order to recover. By doing this, the court rejected the Title VII employer liability standard of "knew or should have known" about the harassment. *Doe*, 830 F. Supp. at 1576.")

90 *See Girl is Groped on Class Trip*, N.Y. TIMES, June 25, 2000, at 21.

91 *Id.*

92 *See* Gorney, *supra* note 77, at 44.

93 As stated above, G.F. was a fifth grader. But, in fact, there is research to suggest that boys even older than G.F. don't grasp that sexual violence against women and girls is not appropriate. *See, e.g.,* PIPHER, *supra* note 2, at p. 206. ("A recent study of teenagers in Rhode Island documents the confusion [teens appear to suffer regarding sexual issues]. Teens were asked to respond to questions about circumstances under which a man 'has a right to have sexual intercourse with a woman without her consent.' Eighty percent said the man had the right to use force if the couple was married, and 70 percent if the couple planned to marry. Sixty-one percent said that force was justified if the couple had had prior sexual relations. More than half felt that force was justified if the woman had led the man on. Thirty percent said it was justified if he knew that she had had sex with other men, or if he was so sexually stimulated he couldn't control himself, or if the woman was drunk. More

than half the students thought that 'if a woman dressed seductively and walks alone at night, she is asking to be raped.' Clearly at least 80 percent of these teenagers didn't know that a man never has a right to force sex.")

94 *See* Easland, *supra* note 77, at p. 120 (citing Margaret Lilliard, *Sexual Harassment Spreads to First Grade*, L.A. TIMES (Oct. 3, 1993), at p. 4).

95 *Id.*

96 *Id.* (citing John M. Leighty, *When Teasing Goes Over the Line*, SAN FRANCISCO CHRONICLE (Nov. 8, 1992), at p. 12/Z1.

97 *See* Tanenbaum, *supra note 2*, at p. 29.

98 *See* Brumberg, *supra* note 26, at pp. 185–186 (citing Chuck Sudetic, *Seven Are Arrested in Groping of Girl in Pool*, N.Y. TIMES, July 24, 1995). *See also* Ellen Goodman, *Adult Men Must Not Be Left Out of the Teenage Pregnancy Question*, ITHACA JOURNAL, February 9, 1996; GOING ALL THE WAY: TEENAGE GIRLS' TALES OF SEX, ROMANCE AND PREGNANCY (New York, 1995); and, *Putting a Big Thing in a Little Hole: Teenage Girls' Accounts of Sexual Initiation*, JOURNAL OF SEX RESEARCH 27 (August 1990). *See also* Mann, *supra* note 2, at p. 257.

99 *Id.*

100 *Id.* at 186 (citing Donald E. Greydanus and Robert B. Shearin, ADOLESCENT SEXUALITY AND GYNE-COLOGY (Philadelphia, 1990), at p. 245).

101 *Id.* (citing Jennifer Steinhauer, *Study Cites Adult Males for Most Teenage Births*, N.Y. TIMES, August 2, 1995, at A10).

102 *Id.*

103 *See* Susan Sheehan, *A Lost Childhood*, THE NEW YORKER, January 11, 1993, at pp. 54–85.

104 *See* Flowers, *supra* note 29, at p. 72.

105 *See* Howard N. Snyder, JUVENILE OFFENDERS AND VICTIMS: 1999 NATIONAL REPORT, OFFICE OF JUVENILE JUSTICE AND DELINQUENCY PREVENTION (Sept. 1999), at p. 9.

106 *See* Mann, *supra* note 2, at p. 14.

107 See Brumberg, *supra* note 26, at p. 186.

108 *See* Joan Didion, *Trouble in Lakewood, Letter from California,* THE NEW YORKER (July 26, 1993), at pp. 46–50, at p. 48; Mann, *supra* note 2, at pp. 246–247.

109 *Id.* at 50.

110 *Id.* at 54.

111 *Id.* at 50.

112 *Id.* at 49–50.

113 *See* Julie Salamon, *Sex at 8: The Patridges Don't Live Here Anymore*, N.Y. TIMES, Dec. 10, 2000, at 6 wk. The 2000 season of the hit television teen show Dawson's Creek, for example, boasted "the first kiss" between two males characters.

114 *See* Walt Mueller, UNDERSTANDING TODAY'S YOUTH CULTURE (Wheaton, Illinois: Tyndale House Publishing, Inc., 1994), at p. 125 (citing George Comstock, TELEVISION IN AMERICA (Beverly Hills: Sage, 1980), at ix) (citing Jane Delano Brown *et. al., The Influence of New Media and Family Structure on Young Adolescents' Television and Radio Use*, 17 COMMUNICATION RESEARCH (February 1990), at 72)). *See also* George Comstock, TELEVISION IN AMERICA (Beverly Hills: Sage, 1980), at p. ix (citing Nancy Ten Kate, *TV Dynasty*, AMERICAN DEMOGRAPHICS, January 1991, at 16); (citing Jane Delano Brown *et al., The Influence of New Media and Family Structure on Young Adolescents' Television and Radio Use*, 17 COMMUNICATION RESEARCH at p. 72 (February 1990)).

115 On June 29, 2000, VH1 host, Rebecca Rankin, detailed the use of sex in music videos during the show *Rankin File*. See RANKIN FILE, VH1, airing June 29, 2000, at 6:30 p.m.

116 *See Why Your Kids Know More About the Future Than You Do*, NEW YORK MAG., May 17, 1999, at pp. 30–31; *See 200,000 Hooked on Sex on Internet, Study Finds*, N.Y. TIMES, March 1, 2000, at A21.) The proliferation of sexually explicit imagery on the Internet has created complex legal problems as well. *See, e.g., Image in Everything: Court Slams Child Porn Law as Covering Digital Works and Art, Too*, A.B.A. JOURNAL, May 2000, at pp. 20–21; *Journalist Loses Appeal of Pornography Verdict*, N.Y. TIMES, April 16, 2000, at p. 21.

117 The Starr Report was released online, for example. *See* John M. Broder & Don Van Natta, Jr., *Starr Finds A Case for Impeachment in Perjury, Obstruction, Tampering*, N.Y. TIMES, at A1.

118 *See, e.g.,* Tim Novak, *Sex Case MD Out on Bail*, CHI. SUN-TIMES, June 19, 1999, at p. 3 (The article describes how an Oak Park, Illinois, gynecologist was arrested after allegedly attempting to engage in a sexual relationship with a 13-year-old girl he met on the Internet); *See* Debra Baker,*When Cyber Stalkers Walk*, A.B.A. J., December 1999, at p. 50. *See also, Wisconsin Man Charged in Internet Sting*, CHI. SUN-TIMES, April 28, 2000, at 18; *'Shell-shocked,' But free*, EDITOR & PUBLISHER, July 10, 1999, at p. 8; *Stranger Danger Online*, THE OPRAH WINFREY SHOW, aired October 1, 1999, (transcripts available through Burrelle's Transcripts).

119 *See, e.g., Post Article Meant As a Wake-up Call for Parents*, EDITOR & PUBLISHER, July 24, 1999, at pp. 9–10.

120 An April 2000, *The New York Times* story seemed to find similar attitudes and conduct amongst young people. *See* Jarrell, *supra* note 80, at B8.

121 *See* JoAnn Wypijewski, *The Secret Sharer: Sex, Race, and Denial in an American Small Town*, HARPER'S, July 1998, at 35.

122 *Id.*

123 *Man With HIV Is Guilty In Unprotected-Sex Case*, N.Y. TIMES, Feb. 19, 1999, at A19. *See also supra* Chapter Eleven.

124 *See* Candies fragrance ad, © 1999, Candies, Inc.

125 *See* Gasoline wear ad, © 1999, Gasoline CD: Nakash.

126 *Roswell* was broadcast on the W.B. Network.

127 *See* Handelman, *supra* note 47, at p. 336.

128 *Id.*

129 *See* Jarrell, *supra* note 80.

130 *See Meredith Rocks the Creek*, YM, June 1999, at pp. 84–88; *Outings on the Creek*, THE ADVOCATE, March 16, 1999, at pp. 46–49.

131 *See* Evelyn Nieves, *Attacks on a Gay Teenager Prompt Outrage and Soul-Searching*, N.Y. TIMES, Feb. 19, 1999, at A.12.

132 *See, e.g.,* Elvia Arriola, *The Penalties of Puppy Love: Institutionalized Violence Against Lesbian, Gay, Bisexual, and Transgendered Youth*, 1 JOURNAL OF GENDER, RACE & JUSTICE 429, 451 (1998).

133 *Id.* (citing Diane Raymond, *"In the Best Interests of the Child": Thoughts on Homophobia and Parenting*, in HOMOPHOBIA: HOW WE ALL PAY THE PRICE (Warren J. Blumenfeld ed., 1992), at 114).

134 *Id.* at 430. (Arriola argues that "lesbian, gay, bisexual and transgender (LGBT) youth do not 'jump into existence' at the legal age of adulthood and consent. Rather, they exist at all ages of the stage in life known as 'adolescence,' and that their abandonment by social, moral, political, legal, and medical authorities makes them one of America's invisible minorities.")

135 *See* Rodham, *supra* note 6, at p. 490 (November 1973) ("...[T]he law's concern with children has been confined to those occasions when the state may limit parental control in the interest of necessary protections or justifiable punishment of the child, or in the name of some overriding state interest. The theory of benevolent intrusion into families by the state seems to embody a contradiction. On the one hand, it operates within the context of a powerful social consensus that the proper relationship between parents and the state in their joint exercise of control over a child's life favors parental dominance. On the other hand, the doctrine of *parens patriae* has long justified state interference with parental prerogatives and event termination of all parental rights. ¶ The social consensus that forms the first half of this apparent contradiction includes the following assumptions: a) America is a familial, child-centered society in which parents are responsible for their own children and have primary control over them; b) the community of adults, usually represented by the state, will not assume responsibility for the child unless the parents are unable to do so or will not do so, or until the child breaks a law; c) because ours is a child-loving society, nonparents and other adults representing the state want to and will do what is in the child's 'best interests'; and d) children need not or should not be participant with the family and the state in making decisions which affect their lives. The tenets of this consensus, legitimized in the rules of laws governing children's affairs, have represented outer limits beyond which child-oriented reforms cannot be effected. The other half of the apparent contradiction, however, involves regular challenges to family authority by state representatives. Certain social norms are enforced at the expense of family privacy, in the name of a child's best interests.").

136 *See* Linda Greenhouse, *Justices Extend Decision on Gay Rights and Equality*, N.Y. TIMES, June 28, 2003, at A10.

137 *See* Tanenbaum, *supra* note 2, at 10 (citing Felicity Barringer, *School Hallways as Gauntlets of Sexual Taunts*, N.Y. TIMES, June 2, 1993, at B7). (Tanenbaum notes that "[t]he poll, conducted by Louis Harris & Associates for the American Association of University Women Educational Foundation, surveyed 1,632 students in grades eight through eleven in seventy-nine schools across the country.")

138 *See* Stolberg, *supra* note 414, ENDNOTES FOR CHAPTER EIGHT, at A18.

139 *See* Susan Dodge, *Teen Birth Rate Decline Linked to Contraception*, CHI. SUN-TIMES, Nov. 8, 1999, at 19.

140 *See, e.g.,* Cynthia Kling, *Younger Mothers Verses Older Mothers*, BAZAAR, Sept. 1999, at p. 511. (The article offers that 20-something teen actress Reese Witherspoon, musician Bjork, model Kirsten Owen, British singer Melanie Blatt, Jade Jagger, and Spice Girl Victoria Adams all very publicly had children in their late teens or very early twenties.)

141 *See* Ethan Bronner, *Lawsuit on Sex Bias by 2 Mothers*, 17, N.Y. TIMES, August 6, 1998, at A12.

142 *See A Question of Honor*, PEOPLE, June 15, 1998, at p. 149.

143 *See* Bronner, *supra* note 141.

144 *Id.*

145 *See Trib Suit Pregnant with Possibilities*, EDITOR & PUBLISHER, July 3, 1999, at p. 12–13.

146 *See* Tamar Lewin, *High Schools Tackle Marriage Skills*, N.Y. TIMES, October 14, 1998, at A22. (Incidentally, there appears also to have been a reemergence of newly published books on the subject. *See, e.g.,* Esther Drill, Heather McDonald and Rebecca Odes, DEAL WITH IT! A WHOLE NEW APPROACH TO YOUR BODY, BRAIN AND LIFE AS A GURL (New York: Pocket Books, 1999); Evelyn Lerman, TEEN MOMS: THE PAIN AND THE PROMISE (California: Morning Glory Press, 1997).)

147 See Sara Shandler, OPHELIA SPEAKS: ADOLESCENT GIRLS WRITE ABOUT THEIR SEARCH FOR SELF (New York: HarperPerennial, 1999), at p. 3.

148 *Id.*

149 Deborah Tolman, DILEMMAS OF DESIRE: TEENAGE GIRLS TALK ABOUT SEXUALITY (Cambridge, Mass.: Harvard University Press, 2002), at p. 107.

150 *See* Brock Cole, THE FACTS SPEAK FOR THEMSELVES (New York: Puffin Books, 1997).

151 *See* Laurie Halse Anderson, SPEAK (New York, Farrar Straus Giroux, 1999).

152 *See* Nina Shandler, OPHELIA'S MOM: WOMEN SPEAK OUT ABOUT LOVING AND LETTING GO OF THEIR ADOLESCENT DAUGHTERS (New York: Crown Publishers, 2001), at p. 124.

153 *See* James Brooke, *Sex Web Worldwide Traps Children*, N.Y. TIMES, Dec. 23, 2001, at A8; Jan Goodwin, *War In Hell on Women & Children*, MARIE CLAIRE, Nov. 2002, pp. 96–108, at p. 98. (Goodwin notes that "[w]omen and children account for 28 million of the world's 35 million refugees; during wars and for years after, they are left defenseless against hunger, disease, military servitude, and sexual exploitation.")

154 *See* Dean Schabner, *Fatal Attraction: 16-year-old Vermont Girl Lured to Prostitution, Death in NYC*, ABCNEWS.COM, Feb. 6, 2000.

155 Vladimir Nabokov, LOLITA (New York: G.P. Putnam's Son, 1955).

156 Although there have been literary stories and movies made about an older woman's sexual obsession with a younger man, in America these are usually tragic tales, and the older woman is either to be pitied, psychologically examined, or laughed at in her at-first titillating, but later clearly pathetic quest for a younger lover. In other words, though these stories have the power to stir—at least initially—in the end, they are either not perverse enough, or so perverse that they make people uncomfortable. Feminist hogwash? Consider Anne Bancroft as the stunning, middle-aged bombshell Mrs. Robinson, in the 1967 hit, THE GRADUATE. Mrs. Robinson was a woman so good at adult mind games—always a concern when there is an age difference—that she had the head of Dustin Hoffman's poor little college boy spinning. Nearly from start to finish, he was never quite sure whether Mrs. Robinson was "trying to seduce him." Yet, in the end—after so much love and good humor—the young man runs away with her daughter, leaving the older woman to reflect on her folly and moviegoers to think that all is right with the world again. The message: older women belong with men their age. Granted, there are rare recent exceptions. There was Terry McMillan's 1996 novel, HOW STELLA GOT HER GROOVE BACK, which is the story of a 40+ woman who goes to Jamaica and begins a relationship with a man half her age only to spend the rest of the book and the movie fending off insults and wondering whether she should have her head examined. Was Stella the voice of societal disapproval? Eventually, the young man and the older woman get together to perhaps live happily ever after, which does happen sometimes (and it apparently did for the author), though perhaps not as often as older men coveting and claiming much younger brides.

157 *See White v. Nellis*, 31 N.Y. 405 (1856).

158 The minor involved in the Latourneau case has publicly stated that he never felt "raped" or abused. But under the law, the adult—and not the child—is to be held responsible. That is the essence of most statutory rape laws. Although high profile—given the spectacle of a mother who would risk and lose everything for an obsession with a sixth grader—in reality, the Latourneau case involved a relatively rare prosecution of a woman charged with the equivalent of statutory rape of a male child. Statistically, however, adolescent and minor girls are far more often the victims of statutory rape. (*See e.g.,* Brumberg, *supra* note 26, at p. 186.) And according to media reports, one in every six rape victims in the United States is under twelve—the age of Nabokov's notorious little girl. (*See A Second Look, infra* note 171, at p. 1.)

159 *See Teenager Seeks Damages In Teacher Sex Case*, N.Y. TIMES, April 16, 2000, at 21.

160 *See* Linda Greenhouse, *Justices Extend Decision on Gay Rights and Equality*, N.Y. TIMES, June 28, 2003, at A10.

161 Ads in well-respected print magazines such as *The New Yorker* include the description that the author, "Pia Pera shows us the world through Lo's eyes, exploring the themes of seducer and seduced, sexuality and obsession, truth and perception."

162 Indeed, far from being a victim in *Lo's Diary*, Pia Pera creates a "Lolita" who seeks a sexual predator herself. Writes Pera at the start of Chapter Fourteen, for example: "That's that. Hummie's definitely a bore in bed. He doesn't know anything interesting. In spite of his vast 'experience' he's way below Roger. He lies there like a straw man. A real sexual parasite. Aside from stammering some French poetry, he brings nothing of himself. And that's only quotations anyway. Nevertheless, a truly historic night: Miss Dolores Maze possessed Monsieur Humbert Guibert...."

163 Unlike "Lolita," the child in THE LOVER is meant to be young but on the verge of contained despair and she appears to give herself to the older man out of passivity and boredom.

164 In fact, the term "Lolita" has become a common reference for underaged girls involved with adult men. For example, Amy Fisher was portrayed in the media as "the Long Island Lolita," a reference to a young girl supposedly wily enough—on a sexual level—to seduce a grown man into forgetting himself. Under this supposed spell, her lover was apparently able to forget all, including that he had a wife.

165 In the much acclaimed 1999 film AMERICAN BEAUTY, for example, the underlying premise of the film is that the main character, played by actor Kevin Spacey, is having a midlife crisis, which manifests itself in a number of ways, including his clear lust for a high school student who is the friend of his daughter. The girl apparently lies about her sexual prowess throughout the movie until near the end when Spacey's character finally manages to get her alone on a couch. In the height of the moment, she admits that she is a virgin.

166 See Pipher, *supra* note 2, at p. 206. See also Landman, *supra* note 1, at pp. 33–39.

167 *Id.* at 205.

168 There are, incidentally, times when the imagined failings of adolescent girls have been bizarre. See, e.g., Girls Ordered to Prove Gender Lose, ASSOCIATED PRESS, June 19, 2000. (The story details a discrimination suit brought by a basketball team of Oglala Sioux girls, who were required to prove— by taking off their clothes—that they were girls after they won a basketball game, and the opposing side suggested the 10 to 12 year old girls were not, in fact, girls. The suit was dismissed in June.)

169 See Didion, *supra* note 108, at pp. 46, 50.

170 See Tanenbaum, *supra* note 2, at pp. 29–31.

171 See A Second Look—Age of Consent, DATELINE NBC, February 2, 1996 (reporter Victoria Corderi), at 1.

172 See, Tom Langhorne, HERALD JOURNAL on the Internet.

173 *Id.*

174 *Id.*

175 As radically feminist as this may sound, some male authors acknowledge as much. See, e.g., Paul Kivel, BOYS WILL BE MEN: RAISING OUR SONS FOR COURAGE, CARING, AND COMMUNITY (Gabriola Island, British Columbia: New Society Publishers, 1999).

176 See Ann Ferguson, BLOOD AT THE ROOT: MOTHERHOOD, SEXUALITY & MALE DOMINANCE (London: Pandora Press, 1989), at pp. 102–106.

177 See Rodham, *supra* note 6, at p. 489. ("In eighteenth century English common law, the term children's rights would have been a *non sequitur*. Children were regarded as chattels of the family and wards of the state, with no recognized political character or power and few legal rights. Blackstone wrote little about children's rights, instead stressing the duties owed by 'prized possessions' to their fathers. Early American courts accepted this view. In this country children have long had certain rights resulting from their attainment of some other legal status, such as parties injured by tortfeasors, legatees under wills, or intestate successors. Even these rights, however, can be exercised only vicariously through adult representatives. Older children have a few additional legal rights, granted by statutes which reflect some legal recognition of their increased competence. Examples include the right to drive a motor vehicle, the right to drop out of school, the right to vote, the right to work, and the right to marry (although before a certain age marriage can be voided in the absence of parental consent).")

178 For discussion of this destiny, *see supra* Chapter One.

179 Once Dolores's mother is killed in a freak accident upon learning of Humbert Humbert's true desires, the child he called "Lolita" is literally deemed to "belong" to him.

180 "Lolita" in the 1997 version was a very aggressive child—one who repeatedly touches Humbert in suggestive ways, and who—twenty minutes into the film—runs upstairs to jump onto his torso, long legs wrapped around his waist before planning what is clearly intended to be a sexual kiss on his mouth.

181 About twelve minutes after the title for HURLYBURLY is shown, a heavily made-up Anna Paquin appears on screen, sitting in a chair in the home of Sean Penn, a first-thing-in-the-morning-cocaine-snorting neurotic Hollywood type. Penn shares the house with Kevin Spacey, a married-but-separated man, who lecherously leers at Paquin. Into the room walks Garry Shandling, who promptly offers to "give" Anna Paquin to Penn and Spacey. "You want her?" Shandling asks, explaining that Paquin was a homeless girl living in an elevator, that he found her, and now he was "giving" her to Penn and Spacey to keep them "in practice" until they "find a woman." An exchange between the three men ensues during which Paquin is referred to alternately as "a little care package," "like a pet," "a perfectly viable piece of ass," and someone they can "keep" and "fuck" if they want to. Within three minutes of this discussion, Penn, Spacey, and Paquin are on a love seat with Spacey caressing Paquin's knee. Penn's arm is around Paquin. Within two minutes of that scene, Paquin is stripping Penn as Chaz Palminteri watches. One minute later, Penn and Paquin are in bed, laughing. In another scene, less than ten minutes later, Palminteri walks into the Penn/Spacey house, where Paquin is sitting. He proceeds to call Paquin "a ditz," "a bitch," "a stupid bitch," and "an invasion of tits and ass." Then he head butts her in the face. Paquin cries and when Penn does nothing to avenge her, she leaves, hitchhiking away. Although HURLYBURLY was probably intended as a commentary on male debauchery and the sadness it supposedly covers, most of the film is more positive than negative in its portrayal of a group of men who—in addition to conscienceless couplings with homeless Paquin before she is headbutted in the face—routinely and hatefully refer to women as "whores," "bitches," "ditzes," "that little bubble brain," and "stupid bitches." Indeed, perhaps the only positive thing either Spacey, Shandling, Palminteri, or Penn ever offer about a woman is Spacey's description of Meg Ryan's character Bonnie as "artistic" in her abilities regarding oral sex. One of the men even refers to a tiny baby girl in a blanket as a "broad of the future."

Near the end of the film, Sean Penn finally articulates the phrase intended to sum up all things: "They (women) are fucking ghouls. They eat our hearts," he declares.

182   *See* Wendy Steiner, VENUS IN EXILE: THE REJECTION OF BEAUTY IN 20TH-CENTURY ART (New York: The Free Press, 2001), at xviii.

183   *See* Simone de Beauvoir, THE SECOND SEX (New York: Vintage Books Edition, 1974 (first ed. Knopf, 1953)), at p. 29.

184   *Id.*

185   *Id.* ("Under the influence of the ovarian secretions the number of developing follicles increases, the ovary receives more blood and grows larger, one of the follicles matures, ovulation occurs, and the menstrual cycle is initiated; the genital system assumes its definitive size and form, the body takes on feminine contours, and the endocrine balance is established," de Beauvoir wrote.)

186   *See* Rowbotham, *supra* note 186, at p. 391.

187   *Id.*

188   *Id.* (quoting de Beauvoir, *supra* note 185).

189   *Id.* at 303 (quoting Jeffrey Weeks, SEX, POLITICS, AND SOCIETY: THE REGULATION OF SEXUALITY SINCE 1800 (Longman: London, 1980), at p. 238).

190   *Id.* at 303–304 (citing Barbara Schreier, MYSTIQUE AND IDENTITY: WOMEN'S FASHIONS OF THE 1960S (New York: Chrysler Museum, 1984), at p. 13).

191   *Id.*

192   The first Equal Rights Amendment for women was introduced in Congress in 1924. In 1946, the Senate undertook the first floor vote on the ERA, which passed by a simple majority, but not the two-thirds vote necessary to succeed. Between 1967–68, more than 140 ERA bills were submitted to Congress. But Congress took no action. In 1972, Congress passed the ERA, then sending it to the states for ratification. But in 1982, the ERA failed, falling short by three states of the number needed for ratification. (For further discussion of the ERA, *see* Debra Baker, *The Equal Rights Amendment Died in 1982, But Supporters Are Trying to Breathe New Life Into the Cause in Congress and State Legislatures*, 85 A.B.A. J. (August 1999), at p. 53.

193   *See* Friedan, *supra* note 1, ENDNOTES FOR CHAPTER FIVE.

194   *See* Doris Lessing, THE GOLDEN NOTEBOOK (Harmondsworth: Penguin Books, 1964).

195   *See* Rowbotham, *supra* note 86, at p. 391.

196   *Id.* at 338.

197   *See* Susan J. Douglas, WHERE THE GIRLS ARE: GROWING UP FEMALE IN THE MASS MEDIA (Harmondsworth: Penguin Books, 1995), at p. 102.

198   *See* Rowbotham, *supra* note 186, at p. 391.

199   *Id.*

200   For a look at how the nubile young body is used, *see* Sarajane Hoare, *Beauty Has Gone Global and It's About Time*, HARPERS BAZAAR (October 1999) at pp. 229–235.

201   *See, e.g.,* Shanda Deziel, *How Teens Got the Power*, MACLEAN'S, March 22, 1999, at p. 42.

202   In the summer of 2000, "incarceration chic"—orange jumpsuits and prison blues, some of them even made in prison—reportedly took urban America by storm. *See, e.g.,* Guy Trebay, *In Jailhouse Chic, an Anti-Style Turns Into a Style Itself*, N.Y. TIMES, June 13, 2000, at A23; Tracie Rozhon, *The Race to Think Like a Teenager*, N. Y. TIMES, Feb. 9, 2003, Section 3, at p. 1; Ruth La Ferla, *More and More, the Prom Dress Covers Less and Less*, N.Y. TIMES, May 29, 2001, at A14.

203   *See* Rebecca Mead, *A Man-Child in Lotusland*, THE NEW YORKER, May 20, 2001, pp. 48–67, at p. 51. See *also* Rebecca Mead, *Shopping Rebellion*, THE NEW YORKER, March 18, 2002, pp. 104–111; Ruth La Ferla, *Boys to Men: Fashion Pack Turns Younger*, N.Y. TIMES, July 14, 2002, Section 9, at p.1.

204   *See* Richard Martin, THE ST. JAMES FASHION ENCYCLOPEDIA: A SURVEY OF STYLE FROM 1945 TO THE PRESENT (Detroit: Visible Ink Press, 1997), at p. 225.

205   *See* Guy Trebay, *Beauty is as Beauty Seller*, N.Y. TIMES, March 3, 2002, at Section 9, p. 1; Cathy Horyn, *In Milan, Sex Is Subject to Interpretation*, N.Y. TIMES, March 4, 2002, at A22; Tracie Rozhon, *The Race to Think Like a Teenager*, N.Y. TIMES, Feb. 9, 2003, Section 3, at p. 1; Jenny Lyn Bader, *All That's Bare is Fit to Wear, So Why the Stares?*, N.Y. TIMES, July 2, 2000, at wk 4; Ruth La Ferla, *More and More, the Prom Dress Covers Less and Less*, N.Y. TIMES, May 29, 2001, at A14; e.g., *Diva Undone: "Diva" Means "Goddess"—But When Did Goddesses Start to Look so Cheap?*, W, June 2000, at 128.

206   See Steiner, *supra* note 186, at xvii.

207   *Id.* at x. *See also* Lisa Wolff, VIOLENCE AGAINST WOMEN (San Diego, Ca.: Lucent Books, Inc., 1999), pp. 55–57.

208   *See* Sia Michel, *Musical Chairs*, TEEN VOGUE, Fall 2000, 160, at 162.

209   *Id.*

210   *See* Natalie Angier, *In the Movies, Women Age Faster*, N.Y. TIMES, Dec. 9, 2001, at wk 3.

211   *See* *Model Lives*, TEEN VOGUE, Fall 2000, at pp. 168–175 (photos by Arthur Elgort).

212   *See* Betty Friedan, THE FEMININE MYSTIQUE (New York: W.W. Norton, 1983) (20th Ann. Ed.) (original copyright 1963), at p. 16.

213   *Id.*

214 For an overview of this trend, *see, e.g.,* Deirdre Dolan, *Love in the Time of Coloring,* N.Y. TIMES MAG., Section 6, Oct. 14, 2001, at p. 76. (The story details "serious" relationships between 9- through 12-year-olds.)

215 For a look at how the bodies of young women are used today, *see, e.g.,* Sarajane Hoare, *Beauty Has Gone Global and It's About Time,* HARPERS BAZAAR (October 1999) at pp. 229–235.

216 See *Britney Spears: Madonna's Heir Apparent,* VOGUE, November 2001.

217 *See* Steiner, *supra* note 186, at xviii.

218 *See* Jenny Lyn Bader, *All That's Bare is Fit to Wear, So Why the Stares?,* N.Y. TIMES, July 2, 2000, at wk 4.

219 *See* Martin, *supra* note 204, at viii.

220 *Id.* at vii. (As the work horse of the fashion, cosmetics, and pharmaceutical industries, the female body—in parts or as a whole—is employed routinely to sell everything from the easily conceivable, such as clothing, makeup, and fragrances, as well as to less obvious products, including computers, prescription items and alcohol. *See, e.g.,* VOGUE (August 2000), featuring 105 full or double-page ads comprised around or reliant upon the female body, some of featuring merely parts, 16 of theses ads featuring cleavage and/or partial or total nudity (or the suggestion thereof); ELLE (August 2000), featuring 95 ads, 11 of them featuring cleavage and/or partial or total nudity; HARPER'S BAZAAR (September 2000), featuring 250 ads reliant upon or comprised around the female body, 22 of those ads featuring cleavage and/or partial or total nudity; W (September 2000), featuring 198 ads comprised around or reliant upon women's faces, bodies or body parts, 15 of those ads featuring cleavage, see-through clothing and/or partial or total nudity. By contrast, *see* TOWN & COUNTRY (August 2000), featuring 14 full or double-page ads comprised around or reliant upon the female body or "body parts," only one of theses ads featuring cleavage; TOWN & COUNTRY (September 2000), featuring 88 full or double-page ads comprised around or reliant upon the female body or "body parts," 4 of theses ads featuring cleavage and/or partial or total nudity; and TOWN & COUNTRY (Oct. 2000), 45 full or double-page ads comprised around or reliant upon the female body, some of featuring merely parts, 2 of theses ads featuring cleavage. (Though women's magazines are generally wedded to women's fashions, which may by necessity require devotion to the female form. There are some designers, however, who advertise only the product. *See, e.g.,* Ralph Lauren ad for alligator purse (a picture of only the purse), HARPER'S BAZAAR (Sept. 2000), at 39; Kate Spade handbag ad (an assortment of handbags hanging on a tree), HARPER'S BAZAAR, *supra,* at 109; OPI Nail Lacquer ad (a picture of bottles of nail polish), HARPER'S BAZAAR, *supra,* at 118; Gucci jewelry ad (a picture of a golden y-necklace), HARPER'S BAZAAR, *supra,* at 124; Mauboussin watches ad (just a picture of the watch), HARPER'S BAZAAR, *supra,* at 145; Prana Gioia ad (a picture of just the jewelry), HARPER'S BAZAAR, *supra,* at 179; Faconnable Diamond Chronograph ad (just the watch), HARPER'S BAZAAR, *supra,* at 183; Coach eyewear ad (just a picture of the eye glasses), HARPER'S BAZAAR, *supra,* at 195; Tagheuer ad (watch picture), HARPER'S BAZAAR, *supra,* at 203; TechnoMarine Professional Diving Watches ad (picture of watches), HARPER'S BAZAAR, *supra,* at 211; Raymond Weil jewelry ad (just the jewelry); HARPER'S BAZAAR, *supra,* at 239–240; Andre Assous Collection ad (picture of a tote bag with matching shoe), HARPER'S BAZAAR, *supra,* at 241; Locman watches (just the watch), HARPER'S BAZAAR, *supra,* at 311; Vidal Sassoon hair products, HARPER'S BAZAAR, *supra,* at 315-317; Dooney & Bourke (picture of just the backpack), ELLE, *supra,* at 16; Clinique Turnaround Cream (a picture of the jar of the cream), ELLE, *supra,* at 29; Neutrogena Pore Refinined Mattifier (a photo of the jar), ELLE, *supra,* at 49; Bebe footwear ad (showing only the shoes), VOGUE (August 2000), at 155). By contrast, some advertisers rely upon female nudity as the foundation of an ad. *See, e.g.,* Lancome Aroma Calm Body Treatment Fragrance ad, HARPER'S BAZAAR, *supra,* at 16–17 (showing a seemingly nude woman); Calvin Klein, Truth ad, HARPER'S BAZAAR, Sept. 2000, at 67–68; Clarins Renew-Plus Body Serum (a photo of apparently nude woman), HARPER'S BAZAAR, *supra,* at 97; Tanqueray ad (the face of a hip young woman next to a bottle), ELLE, *supra,* at 37; Gucci ad (photo featuring a woman appearing to be wrapped in a fur coat and little else), VOGUE, *supra,* at 108–109.)

221 *Id.* at viii.

222 *See* Ruth La Ferla, *More and More, the Prom Dress Covers Less and Less,* N.Y. TIMES, May 29, 2001, at A14.

223 *Id.*

224 *Id.*

225 *See* Bader, *supra* note 218, at wk 4.

226 *See* Leslie Kaufman & Cathy Horyn, *More of Less: Scantier Clothing Catches On,* N.Y. TIMES, June 27, 2000, at A29.

227 *See* Ruth La Ferla, *Bringing Home Lots More Gold,* N.Y. TIMES, Jan. 27, 2002, at BW St. 7.

228 *See* Christy Turlington, *Up in Smoke,* TEEN VOGUE, Fall 2000, 152–155, at 154.

229 *See* Susan Dodge, *Cliques are the Rule in Middle School,* CHI. SUN-TIMES, Aug. 21, 2000, at pp. 6–7.

230 *See* Kelli Anderson, *The Other Side of Jenny,* SPORTS ILLUSTRATED FOR WOMEN, (November/December 2000), at 118–121.

231 *Id.* at 120.

232 Male athletes have posed nude as well, among them decathlete Dan O'Brien. But this is a women's rights book. Thus, we are concerned with the women who pose nude.

233 *Id.* at 121.
234 *Id.*
235 *Id.*
236 The ad offered a side view of Chastain in soccer shoes, holding a ball.
237 Millrose Games round-up, broadcast Feb. 3, 2002, at 3:30 p.m. (Central-time) by ESPN, Channel 29. Though considered a standout in the field, Acuff was edged out in the competition by Tisha Waller, who won with a jump of 6 feet, 4.5 inches. Acuff finished second.
238 *See* Anderson, *supra* note 230, at p. 121.
239 *See* Joan Wallach Scott, GENDER AND THE POLITICS OF HISTORY (New York: Columbia University Press, 1988), at p. 34 (citing Catherine McKinnon, *Feminism, Marxism, Method, and the State: An Agenda for Theory,* 7 SIGNS 515 (1982), at p. 541.)
240 *See* Anderson, *supra* note 230, at p. 121.
241 *See* Kate Zernike, *School Dress Codes vs. Sea of Bare Flesh,* N.Y. TIMES, Sept. 11, 2001, at A1.
242 *Id.*
243 *Id.* at A21.
244 *See* Pamela Haag, *Voices of a Generation: Teenage Girls on Sex, School and Self,* AMERICAN ASSOCIA-TION OF UNIVERSITY WOMEN (July 1999, released to the public September 15, 1999), at p. 3.
245 *See* Alexei Oreskovic, *Teenagers Are Frequent Targets,* NAT'L L.J., July 21, 2003, at A5.
246 *See Teen Smoking Is On the Rise,* NATION'S HEALTH, Nov. 1998, at pp. 9, 31; *Teen Smoking: The Longest Drag,* HEALTH, July 1999, at p. 18; *New Laws Fit for Teens,* CHI. SUN-TIMES, June 28, 1999, at p. 28.
247 *Id.*
248 *See Teen Detox?* HOSPITALS & HEALTH NETWORKS, 1999, at pp. 78–80. (This is an unfortunate occur-rence for women, because lung cancer strikes more women than men. *See Lung Cancer Strikes More Women,* CHI. SUN-TIMES, Nov. 19, 1998, at pp. 1–2.
249 *See* Linda Marsa, *Teens and Party Drugs: The Dangerous Search for a Good Time,* FAMILY CIRCLE, June 1, 1999, at pp. 90–94.
250 *See* Andrew Lang Golub and Bruce D. Johnson, CRACK'S DECLINE: SOME SURPRISES ACROSS U.S. CITIES, NATIONAL INSTITUTE OF JUSTICE RESEARCH BRIEF (July 1997).
251 *See* Lee Bowman, *Teen Marijuana Use Rises,* SCRIPPS HOWARD NEWS SERVICE (reprinted in CHI. SUN-TIMES, August 22, 1998) at p. 12.
252 *See, e.g.,* Fox Butterfield, *Teenage Drug Use is Dropping, a Study Finds,* N.Y. TIMES, Dec. 17, 2002, at A23; *Drug Use by Teenagers Increasing, Survey Finds,* N.Y. TIMES, June 9, 2000), at A26; Ernest Drucker, *Drug Prohibition and Public Health,* 114 PUBLIC HEALTH REPORTS pp. 13–29 (Jan–Feb. 1999), at p. 16; *Teen Drug Abuse: Bringing the Message Home,* SATURDAY EVENING POST, May 1998, at p. 16.
253 *See* Christopher S. Wren, *Face of Heroin: It's Younger and Suburban,* N.Y. TIMES, April 25, 2000, at A22.
254 That is not her real name.
255 *See* Ashley Craddock, *Rescuing Child Prostitutes in America,* MARIE CLAIRE (June 1999), at p. 62.
256 See Marilyn Milloy, *Girls Interrupted,* ESSENCE, Sept. 2002, pp. 160–165.
257 Smalley notes that this is not her real name.
258 *See* Suzanne Smalley, *This Could be Your Kid,* NEWSWEEK, Aug. 11, 2003.
259 *Id.* Smalley's account has been challenged by some, however. *See, e.g.,* Jack Shafer, *Newseek's Bogus Trendspotting,* SLATE, posted Aug. 12, 2003.
260 *See,* Jack Shafer, *Newseek's Bogus Trendspotting,* SLATE, posted Aug. 12, 2003.
261 *See* Craddock, *supra* note 255, at 64.
262 According to FBI statistics, during the late 1980s and early 1990s—the height of the crack era—there was a substantial relationship between drug involvement, drug sales, gang involvement, and violent crime, with studies showing "that gang membership and involvement in drug sales appear to be highly associated with gun ownership among arrestees." *See* Howard N. Snyder *et al.* JUVENILE OFFENDERS AND VICTIMS: 1996 UPDATE AND VIOLENCE, STATISTICS SUMMARY, OFFICE OF JUVENILE JUS-TICE AND DELINQUENCY PREVENTION, February 1996, at p. 21. Weapons possession charges, however, may not be readily apparent in current statistics on crime, because under FBI protocol, arrests are classified by the most serious charge involved. *Id.* (The authors of the study note, however, that "[t]he juvenile arrest rate for weapons possession is at an historic high. A weapons law violation was the most serious charge for 63,400 juvenile arrests in 1994. However, many more arrests undoubtedly involved a weapons law violation. FBI coding procedures require an arrest to be clas-sified by the most serious charge involved. Consequently, none of the arrests of juveniles for killing someone with a handgun, aggravated forcible rape, armed robbery, or aggravated assault with a firearm would be included in the arrest count for weapons law violations.") Justice Department officials note, that as found in the 1996 report, "[y]oung juveniles (under age 15) were more involved in arrests for arson, vandalism, runaway, larceny-theft, simple assault, and burglary, and less involved in arrests for drug abuse violations, murder, prostitution, and liquor law violations." *See* Snyder at p. 12.
263 *See* Alfred Blumstein, *Youth Violence, Guns, and Illicit Drug Markets,* NATIONAL INSTITUTE OF JUSTICE RESEARCH PREVIEW (June 1996), at 1.
264 *Id.*

265 *Id.*

266 *Id.*

267 *See* Susan C. Vaughan, *What Makes Children Kill*, BAZAAR, September 1998, at p. 546.

268 *See Youth Violence, Guns, and Illicit Drug Markets, supra* note 263, at p. 2.

269 *See* Terry Carter, *'Equality with a Vengeance': Violent Crimes and Gang Activity by Girls Skyrocket*, A.B.A. J. (Nov. 1999), at pp. 22–24.

270 *Id.*

271 *See* Snyder, *supra* note 262, at p. 17.

272 *Id.* at 11.

273 *Id.*

274 *See Juvenile Offenders and Victims: 1996 Update on Violence*, STATISTICS SUMMARY, OFFICE OF JUVE-NILE JUSTICE AND DELINQUENCY PREVENTION (Feb. 1996), at p. 23. (In 1993, for example, 1.2 million delinquency cases were disposed by the juvenile courts involving male adolescents. By comparison, only 297,400 similar dispositions involving adolescent females were handled by courts.) *See also Juvenile Justice Bulletin*, U.S. DEPARTMENT OF JUSTICE (July 1996), at p. 3.

275 *See* Curtis Lawrence, *Girls Increase Roles in Gangs*, CHI. SUN-TIMES (Sept. 17, 1999), at 18.

276 *See* Brian Palmer, *True Colors*, N.Y. TIMES MAGAZINE, August 15, 1999, at p. 24. The full title and subscript introduction is: *True Colors: While Politicians Debate 'Gang-Related Clothing,' the Gangs Themselves are Going Incognito.*

277 *Id.* (Palmer notes further that "[n]ot only do these kids deliberately wear far more of a gang colors than most members comfortably would, they also sometimes get tattoos for which they aren't eligible—like one that indicates a member has officially been 'jumped in' to a gang.: 'The younger kids, half of them don't even know what this stuff means,' says Donna DeCasare, a photographer who has documented two Los Angeles gangs. 'It becomes real when they find themselves in jail.' There, when someone is spotted with a tattoo that he hasn't earned the right to wear, prison gangs often give him a choice; cut it off, burn it off or let us get rid of it.")

278 *Id.*

279 *Id.* (The author writes further that "[f]or obvious reasons, though, tattoos—like three dots, which symbolize la vida loca—never completely go out of style, though, for one simple reason: 'That's all they can afford,' says Detective V.R. Bond of the Harris County, Tex., Sheriff's Department. 'If the gang has some form of finances, the identifiers are going to be a little more sophisticated.' In search of the old L.A. cholo style khakis, white undershirts, Pendelton shirt—some even turn to the Salvation Army.")

280 *See* Gina Sikes, 8 BALL CHICKS: A YEAR IN THE VIOLENT WORLD OF GIRL GANGS (New York: Anchor Books, 1997), at pp. 3–4.

281 *Id.* at xvii. (Sikes writes: At sixteen, Tiny was sweet-faced with baby-fat cheeks, pouty lips, and smooth olive skin, except for the angry purple crescent on her right cheek. Another scar sliced her laugh line. She turned to reveal yet another that snaked below her ear. "They say they'll go away in about a year," she said, but this seemed unlikely. During a fight she was winning, her opponent surprised Tiny by flicking a concealed razor blade from her mouth. Her face burning, Tiny at first thought the girl had slapped her, only harder than she'd ever been struck before. She didn't realize she'd been cut from the side of her nose to just below her right eye until the girl jabbed at her again. This time Tiny knew. She frantically felt for the wound, blood seeping between her fingers. Suddenly, in self-preservation, she grabbed the girl's neck and, blinded by her own blood, began smashing her rival's head into the concrete until Isabel, hearing a siren, dragged her away. The girl had slashed Tiny's face eleven times.)

282 *Id.* at xvii-xviii. ("One time the guys we were chillin' with tried to catch a herb." A "herb" means a victim, slang from an old Burger King commercial featuring a frail milquetoast character named Herb, who become a symbol for an easy white mark. "And Isabel was looking for a herbette, but couldn't find nobody. So when her boyfriend and all his homeboys jump this herb, she's trying to jump him, too. She goes up with a forty-ounce bottle and smashes him on the head. It goes *bad-ing!* [¶] "I guess I didn't hit him hard enough"—Isabel leaped in—"because it didn't break. He started screaming and then…he started blowing a *whistle!*" Isabel cracked up at the ridiculousness of this attempt to get help, her eyes welling with tears. "I was like, 'Man, make him eat it. Make him eat that whistle.'"…[¶] Though minutes earlier the girls insisted they formed NFL only to protect themselves, they now gave in to adolescent swaggering, seeing themselves as urban bandits. [¶] "If I see you coming down the street and I think you have money, I'll rob you," Tiny told me in lurching rapid-fire speech. "Out here we only go for Chinese or white people. They got money. I won't rob her"—she pointed to an elderly woman outside—"because she's old." The others nodded, silently agreeing with this moral code. "But I'll rob her"—Tiny poked Happy—"as fast as I'll rob you. It don't matter. We do it for fun. Sometimes to get high or to buy something to drink. If we go out dancing, we catch a herb first. We can have money in our pockets and we'll still do it.")

283 *Id.* at xi. ("TJ kept moving, fixed on the screen door. What if I trip? These stupid shoes are too big, TJ thought. What if the girls fucked up—what if he isn't here? But there he was, slouched in an overstuffed chair just inside the door, rolling a joint. The enemy didn't even glance up until TJ was inside the living room, willing the gun upward. [¶] In the moment before it went off, TJ sensed the

boy's panic. A familiar expression of dread and expectation crossed his face, a face so much like TJ's that each of them could have been staring into a mirror. The kid jerked himself up from the chair, spilling the bag of weed onto the carpet. TJ heard his sharp intake of breath. [¶] *Here's the payback for Lennox!* [¶] TJ wanted to say the words out loud but was scared they would crumble and everything would fall apart. In the end the gun spoke for itself. It sounded like someone slammed two pots together; the ringing made the room bizarrely quiet. TJ watched a pantomime of people gaping in shock at the figure writhing on the floor. Ears still ringing, TJ turned away and in a moment was back in the car.")

284 See Peter Page, *Beating May Cost School District $11.4 Million*, NAT'L L.J., July 22, 2002, at A4.

285 *See, e.g.*, Margaret Talbot, *Girls Just Want to Be Mean*, N.Y. TIMES MAG., Feb. 24, 2002, pp. 23–65; Sharon Lamb, THE SECRET LIVES OF GIRLS (New York: The Free Press, 2001), pp. 141–147.

286 Sikes, *supra* note 280 at p. 11.

287 *See* NATIONAL JUVENILE CUSTODY TRENDS 1978–1989, REPORT FROM THE OFFICE OF JUVENILE & DELINQUENCY PREVENTION (March 1992), at p. 2. (The numbers, according to the Department of Justice were: In 1979, there were 29,256 female juveniles in private facilities and 115,460 in public facilities; in 1983, there were 34,367 female juveniles in private facilities and 106,356 in public facilities; in 1985, there were 41,079 juvenile females in private facilities and 104,624 in public facilities; in 1987, there were 51,212 juvenile females in private facilities and 117,761 in public facilities; and in 1989, there were 57,212 juvenile females in private facilities and 112,872 in public facilities.) *Id.* at 7.

288 *See* Snyder, *supra* note 262, at p. 1.

289 For over all reading on the issue, *see e.g.*, DATING VIOLENCE: YOUNG WOMEN IN DANGER (Barrie Levy, ed., 1991) (Seattle, Washington: The Seal Press, 1991), at pp. 21–27.

290 *See* Ruben Castaneda, *In a Split Second, A Bright Future Is Threatened*, WASH. POST (January 5, 1994), at B1.

291 *See* BUFFALO NEWS, July 12, 1994, at LIFESTYLES 1.

292 *See Teen Dating Violence: The Hidden Epidemic*, 37 FAMILY & CONCILIATION COURTS REVIEW at p. 356 (1999).

293 *Id.* at 357.

294 428 U.S. 52 (1976).

295 431 U.S. 678 (1977). The case involved the question of whether minor females had a fundamental right to choose birth control. In 1977, the Justices of the United States Supreme Court extended the "right of privacy," which included the right to choose birth control, to minors holding that minors could not be denied the opportunity to purchase birth control because of their age. As set forth in Chapter One, however, legislative attacks against that decision appear to be under way. For discussion, *see* Chapter One, *supra*, at pp. 33–34.

296 *See* ISSUES IN BRIEF, *Minors and the Right to Consent to Health Care*, published by the Alan Guttmacher Institute (2000), at p. 4.

297 *Id. See also* Julie Flaherty, *Girls Link Their Use of Family Planning Clinics to Keeping Parents in the Dark*, N.Y. TIMES, Aug. 14, 2002, at A12.

298 *See* ISSUES IN BRIEF, *Minors and the Right to Consent to Health Care*, published by the Alan Guttmacher Institute (2000), at p. 4.

299 *Id.*

300 *See* COMMENT, *Forcible and Statutory Rape: An Exploration of the Operation and Objectives of the Consent Standard*, 62 YALE L. J. 53, 55 (Dec. 1952).

301 *Id.* (The authors note that "[t]he imperious drive of sex is capable of impelling individuals, reckless of consequences while under its spell, toward behavior which may imperial or disrupt the cooperative relationships upon which social life depends. The countless interpersonal bonds out of which human association is forged, complex and often delicately balanced, can ill suffer the strain of the frustrations and aggressions inevitably generated by indiscriminate competition over sexual favors" (citing Murdock, SOCIAL STRUCTURE (1949), at p. 260).

302 *Id.* (citing Wilson & Kolb, SOCIOLOGICAL ANALYSIS (1949), at p. 588).

303 *See* Robert Mnookin and D. Kelly Weisberg, CHILD, FAMILY, AND STATE (Boston, Mass.: Little, Brown & Co. (Second Printing)), at p. 175

304 *See* Albert D. Klassen, Colin J. Williams, and Eugene E. Levitt, SEX AND MORALITY IN THE U.S. (Middleton, Conn.: Wesleyan University Press, 1989), at p. 272.

305 *See* Brumberg, supra note 26, at pp. 17–18.

306 *See* Robert Mnookin and D. Kelly Weisberg, CHILD, FAMILY, AND STATE (Boston, Mass.: Little, Brown & Co. (Second Printing)), at p. 175.

307 *See* Deborah L. Tolman and Tracey E. Higgins, *How Being a Good Girl Can Be Bad for Girls*, published in WOMEN, SEX & POWER IN THE NINETIES (New Brunswick, N.J.: Rutgers University Press, 1996) (Nan Bauer Magli & Donna Perry, ed.), at p. 210.

308 *See* COMMENT, *The Constitutionality of Statutory Rape Laws*, 27 UCLA L. REV. (1980), pp. 757–815, at p. 757 (citing, *e.g.*, 64 AM. JUR. 2d *Rape* Sec. 15 (1972); R. Perkins, CRIMINAL LAW (2d ed.1969), at pp. 152–171.) Eidson notes further that "[i]n this COMMENT, the term 'statutory rape' will refer

only to gender-based definitions of the crime unless otherwise specified. The issues involved in protecting young persons from homosexual advances are beyond the scope of this Comment."

309 *Id.* (citing *Murphy v. State*, 120 Ind. 115 (1889) (where female was under the age of consent, it did not need to be alleged or proved that the intercourse was had forcibly or against her will). *Accord, see, e.g., People v. Marks*, 146 A.D. 11, 12 (1911); *State v. Huntsman*, 115 Utah 283 (1949)).

310 *Id.* (citing *e.g., People v. Atchinson*, 22 Cal.3d 181 (1978), in which the California Supreme Court noted that "both the state's statutory rape law protecting all females under 18. Cal. Penal. Code Sec. 261.5 (West Supp. 1980), and the statute protecting males and females under 14 from the lewd and lascivious conduct of any person, Cal. Penal Code Sec. 288 (West Supp. 1980), are directed toward protecting the young from sexual exploitation. Unlike revised sex offense statutes recently enacted in many states, neither California statute requires an age differential between the perpetrator and the victim of sexual exploitation. Yet, it has been found that persons who are convicted of non-forcible sexual relations with youngsters between the ages of 12 and 15 may be classified as other 'subculture offenders' or 'near-peer' offenders. Subculture offenders are adults who belong to a portion of society which regards anyone past puberty as a suitable sexual partner. Near-peer offenders are so close in age to their 'victims' that a sexual relationship is likely to be mutual rather than exploitative"). *See also* P. Gebhard, J. Gagnon, W. Pomeroy, and C. Christensen, SEX OFFENDERS (1965), at pp. 102–103; Slovenko, STATUTORY RAPE, MEDICAL ASPECTS OF HUMAN SEXUALITY (March 1971), at p. 155: "The 'victim' in statutory rape cases is often willing, if not seductive, while the male may be equally young and ignorant of the law.")

311 *See A Second Look—Age of Consent, supra* note 171, at 2.

312 *Id.*

313 *See Tex. Penal Code Ann.* Sec. 21.11 (West 1996) (which provides that the age of consent to sexual activity is 17).

314 *Id.* at 4.

315 Lawrence Wright notes, for example, that in 1857, "the Utah Territory" and the United States nearly went to war over the practice of multiple bride-taking (polygamy) by Brigham Young, the "area's defiant and dictatorial governor" whose legendary practice of collecting "more than thirty wives, and perhaps twice that many, with whom he 'sealed' himself in secret ceremonies," some as "young as fourteen," was among those things that irked federal officials. *See* Lawrence Wright, *Lives of the Saints*, NEW YORKER MAG., Jan. 21, 2002, 40–57, at 46. Though polygamy has been outlawed in every state, by the federal government and by the Mormon church, some women's and girls' rights advocates argue that the practice of taking minor and multiple child brides continues. *See, e.g.,* Helen Thorpe, *Rescuing America's Child Brides*, MARIE CLAIRE, March 2002, at pp. 149–154.

316 *See Rodham, supra* note 6, at p. 491.

317 *See A Second Look—Age of Consent, supra* note 171, at p. 4.

318 *See Rodham, supra* note 6, at p. 489. ("Older children have a few additional legal rights, granted by statutes which reflect some legal recognition of their increased competence. Examples include the right to drive a motor vehicle, the right to drop out of school, the right to vote, the right to work, and the right to marry (although before a certain age marriage can be voided in the absence of parental consent.")

319 *See A Second Look—Age of Consent, supra* note 171, at p. 6.

320 *Id.* at 4.

321 *See State v. Al-Hussaini*, 579 N.W.2d 561, 562 (Neb. App. 1998).

322 Her fourteen-year-old sister was also given away in marriage by their father that day.

323 579 N.W.2d at 562.

324 *Id.*

325 *Id.* at 563.

326 *See, e.g.,* Deirdre Dolan, *Love in the Time of Coloring*, N.Y. TIMES MAG., Oct. 14, 2001, Section 6, at 76. (Dolan reports on the growing trend of children as young as 8 and 9 formally committing themselves to each other.)

327 *See Eidson, supra* note 15, at p. 766, n. 51. (Eidson notes that "[f]or example, in Alabama a male 16 years of age or older who engages in sexual intercourse with a female who is less than 12 years old is guilty of 'Rape in the first degree,' a Class A felony. Ala. Code Sec.13-A-6-1 (1978). If the same male engaged in sexual intercourse with a female more than 12 but less than 16 years of age, he would be guilty of 'Rape in the second degree,' a Class C felony, provided that he was at least two years older than the female. Ala. Code Sec. 13A-6-62. Other statutes that vary the severity of the punishment with the relative ages of the participants include: Alaska Stat. Secs. 11.41.410(a)(3), 440(a)(1) (1978); Ariz. Rev. Stat. Ann. Sec. 13-1405 (1978); Ark. Stat. Ann. Secs. 41-1804 to -1810 (1977); Fla. Stat. Ann. Sec. 794.011(2)-(4) (West 1976); Ill. Ann. Stat. ch. 38, Secs. 11-4, 11-5 (Smith-Hurd 1979); Ind. Code Ann. Sec. 35-42-4-3 (Burns 1979); Iowa Code Ann. Secs. 709.3, 709.4 (West 1979); Ky. Rev. Stat. Secs. 510.040(1)(b)(2), 510.050, 510.060(1)(b) (1975); Me. Rev. Stat. Ann. tit. 17A, Secs. 252, 254 (1979); Md. Ann. Code art. 27, Secs. 463(a)(3), 464C(3) (Supp. 1979); Mich. Comp. Laws Secs. 750.520b(1)(a), 750.20d(1)(a) (Mich. Stat. Ann. Secs. 28.788(2)(1)(a), 28.788(4)(1)(a) (Callahan Supp. 1979)); Minn. Stat. Ann. Secs. 609.342(a), 609.344(a) (West Supp. 1980); Mo. Ann. Stat. Secs. 566.030, 566.050 (Vernon 1979); N.J. Stat. Ann.

Secs. 2C: 14-2, 14-3 (West 1979); N.M. Stat. Ann. Sec. 30-9-11 (1978); N.Y. Penal Law Secs. 130.25(2), 130.30, 130.35 (McKinney 1975); N.D. Cent. Code Secs. 12.1-20-03, 12.1-20-05, 12.1-20-07 (Supp. 1979); Ohio Rev. Code Ann. Secs. 2907.02(A)(3), 2907.04(a) (Baldwin 1979); Okla. Stat. tit. 21 Sec. 1114 (1958); Or. Rev. Stat. Secs. 163.355, 163.365, 163.375 (1977); S.C. Code Sec. 16-3-655 (Supp. 1979); Tenn. Code Ann. Secs. 39-3703(3), 39-3705(4) (Supp. 1979); Utah Code Ann. Secs. 76-5-401, 76-5-402(2) (1977); Va. Code Secs. 18.2-61, 18.2-63 (Supp. 1979); Wash. Rev. Code Secs. 9A.44.070, 9A.44.080, 9A.44.090 (1979); W. Va. Code Secs. 61-8B 3(3), 61-8B 5(2) (Supp. 1979); Wis. Stat. Ann. Sec. 940.225 (West Supp. 1979); Wyo. Stat. Secs. 6-4-303(a)(v), (c), 6-4-305 (1977).

328 *See* Didion, *supra* note 108, at pp. 46, 50.

329 For review of the law regarding mandatory education, *see, e.g.,* Ala. Code Sec. 16-28-3 (1975 & Supp. 1993); Alaska Stat. Sec. 14.30.010 (1993); Ariz. Rev. Stat. Ann. Sec. 15-802 (1989 & Supp. 1993); Ark. Code Ann. Sec. 6-18-201 (Michie 1993); Cal. Educ. Code Sec. 48200 (West 1992 & Supp. 1993); Colo. Rev. Stat. Ann. Sec. 22-33-104 (West 1990 & Supp. 1994); Conn. Gen. Stat. Ann. Sec. 10-184 (West 1992 & Supp. 1994); Del. Code Ann. tit. 14, Sec. 2702 (1983 & Supp. 1992); D.C. Code Ann. Sec. 31-402 (1988 & Supp. 1993); Fla. Stat. Ann. Sec. 232.01 (West 1993 & Supp. 1994); Ga. Code Ann. Sec. 20-2-690.1 (1991 & Supp. 1993); Haw. Rev. Stat. Sec. 298-9 (1985); Idaho Const. art. 9, Sec. 9; Ill. Ann. Stat. ch. 105, para. 5, Sec. 26-1 (Smith-Hurd 1989 & Supp. 1992); Ind. Code Ann. Sec. 20-8.1-3-17(b) (Burns 1987); Iowa Code Ann. Sec. 299.1(A) (West 1985 & Supp. 1994); Kan. Stat. Ann. Sec. 72-1111 (1993); Ky. Rev. Stat. Ann. Sec. 159.010 (Michie/Bobbs-Merrill 1990 & Supp 1992); La. Rev. Stat. Ann. Sec. 17:221 (West 1986 & Supp. 1994): Me. Rev. Stat. Ann. tit. 20-A, Sec. 5001-A (West 1992 & Supp. 1993); Md. Educ. Code Ann. Sec. 7-301 (1991 & Supp. 1993); Mass. Gen. Laws Ann. ch. 72, Sec. 2 (West 1993); Mich. Comp. Laws Ann. Sec. 380.1561 (West 1993 & Supp. 1994); Minn. Stat. Ann. Sec. 120.101 (West 1983 & Supp. 1994); Miss. Code Ann. Sec. 31-13-91 (1993); Mo. Ann. Stat. Sec. 167.031 (Vernon 1983 & Supp. 1993); Mont. Code Ann. Sec. 20-5-103 (1993); Neb. Rev. Stat. Sec. 79-201 (1989 & Supp 1993); Nev. Rev. Stat. Ann. Sec. 392.040 (Michie 1991); N.H. Rev. Stat. Ann. Sec. 193-1 (1993); N.J. Stat. Ann. Sec. 18A-38-25 (West 1993); N.M. Stat. Ann. Sec. 22-12 (Michie 1993); N.Y. Educ. Law Sec. 3205 (McKinney 1992 & Supp. 1994); N.C. Gen. Stat. Sec. 155C-378 (1993); N.D. Cent. Code Sec. 15-34.1-01 (1989 & Supp. 1993); Ohio Rev. Code Ann. Sec. 3321.01 (Anderson 1990); Okla. Const. art. 13, Sec. 4; Or. Rev. Stat. Sec. 339.010 (1993); Pa. Stat. Ann. tit. 24, Sec. 13-1326 (1993); R.I. Gen. Laws Sec. 16-19-1 (1990 & Supp. 1993); S.C. Code Ann. Sec. 59-65-10 (Law. Co-op. 1985 & Supp. 1993); S.D. Codified Laws Ann. Sec. 13-27-1 (1992 & Supp. 1993); Tenn. Code Ann. Sec. 49-6-3005 (1991 & Supp. 1993); Tex. Educ. Code Ann. Sec. 21-032 (West 1986 & Supp. 1994); Utah Code Ann. Sec. 53A-11-101 (1989 & Supp. 1993); Vt. Stat. Ann. tit 16, Sec. 1121 (1991 & Sup. 1993); Va. Code Ann. Sec. 22.1-254 (Michie 1991 & Supp. 1993); Wash. Rev. Code Ann. Sec. 28A-255.010 (West 1986 & Supp. 1994); W.Va. Code Sec. 18-8-1 (1993); Wis. Stat. Ann. Sec.118.15 (West 1987 & Supp. 1993); Wyo. Stat. Sec. 21-4-102 (1986 & Supp. 1993).

330 *See* James G. Ward, *Demographics and Economic Changes Facing Schools in the North Central Region,* POLICY BRIEFS, RURAL AND URBAN SCHOOL FINANCE: DISTRICTS AND EXPERTS SPEAK OUT Report 1 (1995), at 5. (At the time of this writing, James G. Ward was a professor of Educational Administration and the Associate Dean for Academic Affairs at the College of Education, University of Illinois at Urbana-Champaign, Illinois. Ward was considered an expert in the area of school finance.)

331 *Id.* at p. 2.

332 *Id.*

333 *Id.*

334 *Id.*

335 *Id.*

336 *See* Jonathan Kozol, SAVAGE INEQUALITIES: CHILDREN IN AMERICA'S SCHOOLS (New York: Crown Publishers, Inc. 1991), at pp. 56–57.

337 *Id.*

338 Sources suggest that the amount spent per child in Illinois may have risen in recent years to nearly $6,000. *See* Lynn J. Stinnette, *Hard Times Getting Harder in Urban School Districts,* POLICY BRIEFS, *supra* note 463, at 9. (At the time of this publication, Stinnette was the director of Urban Education for the North Central Regional Education Laboratory, the publisher of POLICY BRIEFS.) Stinnette's sources include statistics compiled by the *Chicago Tribune.*

339 *See* Ward, *supra* note 332, at 3.

340 *See* Kozol, *supra* note 336, at 57 (quoting John Coons, professor of law at Berkley University).

341 *See* Ward, *supra* note 332, at 3.

342 *See* Lynette Holloway, *Chicago Provides Model In Summer School's Use,* N.Y. TIMES, August 18, 1999, at A20.

343 *See Tutor Style,* W (October 1999), at 108.

344 *See e.g.,* Ward, *supra* note 336, at 3; Todd Rosenkranz, *supra* note 463, at 19 (contained within URBAN PROFILES, edited by Nancy Fulford).

345 *See* Kozol, *supra* note 336, at 54.

346 *See, e.g.,* James Traub, *Schools Are Not the Answer,* N.Y. TIMES MAG., Jan. 19, 2000, at 52.

347   *Id.* at 55.
348   *Id.*
349   *See Shante D. v. City of New York,* 638 N.E.2d 962 (N.Y. 1994); *State v. Michael,* 642 A.2d 1372 (N.J. 1994); *Davis v. Monroe County Board of Education, supra* note 70.
350   *See* 20 U.S.C. Sec. 1681 *et seq.*
351   503 U.S. 60 (1992).
352   *See supra* note 349.
353   503 U.S. 60 (1992).
354   *See Davis v. Monroe County Board of Education, supra* note 70.
355   515 U.S. 646 (1995).
356   *Id.* at 652–653.
357   393 U.S. 503 (1969).
358   *Id.* at 507.
359   States outlawing corporal punishment include: Alaska, California, Connecticut, Hawaii, Illinois, Iowa, Maine, Massachusetts, Michigan, Minnesota, Montana, Nebraska, Nevada, New Hampshire, New Jersey, New York, North Dakota, New Jersey, Oregon, Rhode Island, South Dakota, Utah, Vermont, Virginia, Washington, West Virginia, and Wisconsin.
360   States that have not prohibited corporal punishment include: Alabama, Arkansas, Arizona, Colorado, Delaware, Florida, Georgia, Idaho, Indiana, Kansas, Kentucky, Louisiana, Maryland, Mississippi, Missouri, New Mexico, North Carolina, Ohio, Oklahoma, Pennsylvania, South Carolina, Tennessee, and Texas.
361   430 U.S. 651 (1977).
362   *Id.* at 657.
363   The following note appears as a footnote in the Court's decision: "STEDMAN'S MEDICAL DICTIONARY (23d ed. 1976) defines 'hematoma' as '[a] localized mass of extravasated blood that is relatively or completely confined within an organ or tissue...; the blood is usually clotted (or partly clotted), and, depending on how long it has been there, may manifest various degrees of organization and decolorization.'"
364   430 U.S. at 657.
365   *Id.* at 659.
366   U.S. CONST., amend. VIII.
367   430 U.S. at 671.
368   To support this point, the Justices cited 3 W. BLACKSTONE, COMMENTARIES * 120–121.
369   430 U.S. at 675–676.
370   469 U.S. 325 (1985).
371   *Id.* at 340.
372   *See, e.g., Cornfield by Lewis v. Consolidated High School District No. 230* (Ca. III), No. 92-1863 April 23, 1993; *Matter of Gregory M.,* 585 N.Y.S.2d 193 (1992); *State ex. rel. Juvenile Department of Washington County v. DuBois,* 821 P.2d 1124 (1991); *New Jersey v. T.L.O.,* 83 L. Ed. 2d 720 (1985); *Com. v. Snyder,* 597 N.E.2d 1363 (1992).
373   *See Cornfield by Lewis v. Consolidated High School District No. 230,* No. 92-1863 (Ca. III), April 23, 1993).
374   *See Matter of Greogry M.,* 585 N.Y.S.2d 193 (1992).
375   *See State ex. rel. Juvenile Department of Washington County v. DuBois,* 821 P.2d 1124 (1991).
376   469 U.S. 325 (1985).
377   Drugs and drug paraphernalia were found in the car.
378   *See e.g., Com. v. Snyder,* 597 N.E.2d 1363 (1992).
379   *See e.g., Wilcher v. States,* 876 S.W.2d 466 (Tex. Ct. App. 1994).
380   *See e.g., Moore v. Florence School Dist.,* 444 S.E.2d 498 (S.C. 1990).
381   *See Mueller, supra* note 52, at 268 (citing *We're Number One!,* YOUTHWORKER UPDATE (January 1988), at 4). *See also* Lloyd D. Johnston, Patrick M. O'Malley, and Jerald G. Bachman, *Drug Use Among American High School Seniors, College Students, and Young Adults, 1975–1900,* Vol. I (Rockville, Maryland: National Institute on Drug Abuse, 1991), at 5).
382   *See Doe v. Renfrow,* 475 F. Supp. 1012 (N.D. Ind. 1979), 635 F.2d 582 (7th Cir. 1980).
383   640 N.E.2d 1009 (Ill. App. Ct. 1994).
384   *See* James M. Kemp, *Deshaney and Its Progeny—The Failure to Mandate that Public School Officials Protect Our Tender Youth,* 24 J. OF LAW & EDUCATION 679 (1995).
385   *Id.*
386   *Id.*
387   283 N.E.2d 956 (1972).
388   *See Brownell v. Los Angeles United School Dist.,* 5 Cal. Rptr. 756 (1992).
389   *See O'Campo v. School Board of Dade County,* 589 So. 2d 383 (Fla. App. 3 Dist. 1991).
390   489 U.S. 189 (1989).
391   *Id.* at 200.
392   *See Davis v. Monroe County Board of Education, supra* note 70.

393 *Id.* at 10 (citing *Doe v. University of Illinois*, 138 F.3d 653, 668 (7th Cir. 1998) (holding that private damages could be had under Title IX where fund recipient responded inadequately to complaints of student-on-student harassment)).

394 *Id.*

395 *Id.* (citing *Vernonia School District 47J v. Acton*, 515 U.S. 646, 655 (1995)).

396 *Id.* (citing *Tinker v. Des Moines Independent Community School Dist.*, 393 U.S. 503, 507 (1969); *see also New Jersey v. T.L.O.*, 469 U.S. 325, 342, n. 9 (1985)).

397 *Id.* (citing RESTATEMENT (SECOND) OF TORTS Sec. 152 (1965)).

398 *Id.*

399 *See, e.g.,* James S. Wrona, *Eradicating Sex Discrimination in Education, Extending Disparate-Impact Analysis to Title IX Litigation*, 21 PEPP. L. REV. 1 (1993); Karen Mellencamp Davis, *Reading, Writing, and Sexual Harassment: Finding a Constitutional Remedy When Schools Fail to Address Peer Abuse*, 69 IND. L.J. 1123 (1994); Stacey R. Rinestine, *Terrorism on the Playground: What Can Be Done?*, 32 DUQ. L. REV. 799 (1994); Helen K. Doloan, NOTE, *The Fourth R—Respect: Combatting Peer Sexual Harassment in the Public Schools*, 63 FORDHAM L. REV. 215 (1994).

400 *See, e.g.,* Christina Hoff Sommers, *The War Against Boys*, THE ATLANTIC MONTHLY, May 2000, at p. 59.

401 *See* GENDER GAPS: WHERE SCHOOLS STILL FAIL OUR CHILDREN, American Association of University Women (New York: Marlowe & Co., 1999), at p. 85.

402 *Id.* at 80.

403 *Id.*

404 *Id.* at 83.

405 *See* Peggy Orenstein, SCHOOLGIRLS: YOUNG WOMEN, SELF-ESTEEM, AND THE CONFIDENCE GAP (New York: Anchor Books, 1994), at 12.

406 *Id.*

407 *See Florida Abortion Act Violates Minor's Right to Privacy*, NAT'L L.J., July 21, 2003, at p. 14.

408 *See* Mann, *supra* note 2, at p. 55.

SECTION FOUR

Violence and Women

CHAPTER THIRTEEN

A Woman's Place is in the Hospital

THE STORY OF VIOLENCE:
A Toll Counted Daily

When it comes to talk of women and violence, there are some things best said without preamble; among them that within most societies, there are some people who use violence as a means of communication. At times because it is the most powerful thing one can "say." At others as a means to an end or simply out of habit.

There is a well-documented history to violence, retold each day in police reports, government documents, news stories, and trial transcripts. It is a collage of mayhem that can turn in a blink from the random to the specific, with women often in the mix. "From an historic perspective, the issue of violence has long been significant to women because within most societies, there have long been laws, religious decrees, or atavistic cultural practices outlining—in direct language or by metaphor—acts of violence (rightfully) *visited upon* women deemed to have committed unvirtuous infractions."

In more modern times, theories have abounded to *explain* male aggression, but less frequently offering ways to stem it. And, thus, violence against women remains the practice of many men. According to statistics compiled by the United States Department of Justice, women are frequently the victims of violence at the hands of strangers. But more often, they endure rough treatment at the hands of "loved ones" in incidents that range from intimidation, stalking, assault, rape or sexual battery, or the knowing transmission of HIV, to partner abuse and domestic violence.

"Violence" runs the gamut from the clearly urgent—bumps, bruises, and fractures—to the less immediate, though in many ways just as controlling.

Political parity, for example, continues to elude the "weaker sex."[1] Though women represent more than half of the population in the United States and are a strong voting bloc,[2] they hold just 12 percent of all legislative seats and less than a third of all administrative posts.[3] And yet, when women run for political office, they still may face the kind of mean-spirited misogyny specifically reserved for women.

In 2000, when former First Lady Hillary Rodham Clinton made a bid for a Senate seat (the first First Lady in history ever to do so[4]), she was hounded by reporters and attacked by conservatives with questions about her *husband's* adulterous affair,[5] the clear or implied assertion being that she had "failed" as a wife. Labeled a perjurer—though she was thoroughly investigated and never indicted—and called dishonest—though the Arkansas Bar Association never contemplated her disbarment—Hillary Rodham Clinton was chided for refusing to discuss her private life with the public media.[6]

There are those, of course, who would argue that "the Clintons" deserved everything they got. And yet, the barrage Hillary Clinton weathered on her way to becoming the junior senator from New York[7] remains illustrative of the kind of verbal violence women often still endure when they run for political office in par-for-the-course campaign measures that slip quickly from gentile political spin to bare-knuckle—specifically suggestive—name-calling, a fact noted by some political reporters.

"Usually, female candidates have to prove they're tough enough," wrote Maureen Dowd in a September 2000 editorial for *The New York Times*.[8] "Hillary Clinton is in the odd position of having to prove she's tender enough. [¶] In case anyone failed to get the Medusa message, the New York GOP chairman, William Powers, has sent out a new fundraising letter that reads, 'I have high hopes that you'll help us…stop this ambitious, ruthless, scheming, calculating, manipulating woman from fooling voters.' He ends: 'Hillary Clinton is an angry woman.'"[9]

Even after the turn of the millennium, accusing a woman of being "angry," "vengeful," "scorned," or "ambitious" still packs a good punch. And, indeed, Powers's comments appear to reflect that deep well of ancient anger long directed toward "mean-spirited" ambition, claims of preferential treatment, or "reverse discrimination." Critics of such claims insist, of course, that such arguments serve only to further gender discrimination.

"Economic violence," a phrase popularized by Jesse Jackson, has also played a role in the lives of women and continues to do so today, largely because women tend to be poorer than men. And that may make them vulnerable. In the spring of 1999, government investigators began ordering hospital officials in the Los Angeles area to stop demanding cash payments for pain medication from pregnant women, sometimes, according to media reports, as the women lay writhing in pain or in the throes of labor.[10]

Frustrated by the low rate of state and federal reimbursement, doctors and officials in some hospitals began demanding cash payments for pain medications in advance of supply, some newspaper accounts suggest.[11] Where women failed to pay in full, some say they got no relief, the reporters suggest.

"I'm not a wimp when it comes to pain," Ozzie Chavez said in an interview after one of the reported incidents. "But it was a very painful delivery. The anesthesiologist wouldn't even come into the room until she got her money. I offered her a credit card and a check, but she wouldn't accept it. I was lying there having contractions, and they wouldn't give me an epidural. I felt like an animal. It was degrading."[12]

The hospital is said to have apologized. Chavez filed suit. And although the incident may be isolated, that it could happen in one of the most advanced nations in the world suggests what many feminists and social scientists have long argued: that American society continues to embrace economic inequities and a class and race structure that favors men. Thus, financial inequities remain a part of women's lives. This is especially true where women fall within a minority group.[13]

In most societies, one's status—traditionally derived from social position, economic worth, and/or by race and gender, according to some scholars—has a perceived value, for which a person is rewarded.[14] Whether formally set forth or by default, American society mirrors this trend, and among these rewards in the United States traditionally has been preferential treatment and entree into echelons that might otherwise be closed but for one's position, wealth, race, or gender. By contrast, there is another side of the coin: when people are thought to be of "diminished" status, lesser social position or little or no wealth, they are deemed to have less value, and therefore, receive fewer rewards. And it is this part of the equation that matters to women, who still occupy a lesser social position than men with poor women at the bottom.

The majority of American women working full-time earned "only 76 cents for every dollar a man earn[ed]" in 1999.[15] Those numbers saw little substantive change during the techno-bubble of the late 1990s. Therefore, although America was experiencing the most sustained period of prosperity since the 1960s, women still earned a fourth less than men, according to the Bureau of Labor Statistics. This fact tends to suggest that the "traditional wage formula" may be unbreakable even in the wealthiest of times.[16]

As yet, economic inequities are among the lesser immediate forms of violence facing women today. Indeed, a snapshot of the problem grows darker as the context shifts towards the physical. Though the United States is often lauded for its protection of individual rights and freedoms, it is praise made by comparison. It is true that when weighed against what is deemed permissible against citizens in other countries, American laws offer more protection to individuals—and even those who are not citizens—against unlawful incidents that occur on American soil or in American waters.[17] As a result, non-American citizens have increasingly begun to use the American court system to bring suits against foreign governments in alien tort actions.[18]

In addition, given American constitutional law, women in the United States fare better than women in many other countries. Women in the United States are allowed to walk down the street unaccompanied, for example; to earn a license to drive;[19] to vote; to work; to run for political office; and to move about uncovered.[20] In addition, statutory and constitutional laws have proved to be powerful tools in moving women towards equity.[21] And yet, despite a thicket of federal and state laws, women are victims of violence all over the world—including in the United States—in numbers and in acts at times as incongruous as they are inexplicable, which makes the commonalties and comparisons between the United States and other countries worth noting.

In 1992, an 18-year-old Italian woman alleged that she was taken to a remote location outside a small town near Naples and raped by a 45-year-old instructor during a driving lesson.[22] In 1999, she became a symbol of a male-dominated legal system run amok as critics and women's rights advocates set the Italian sky on fire.[23] The reason for the uproar? The woman had been wearing jeans at the time of the alleged attack. But jeans, the third division of the Italian Supreme Court in Rome held in the winter of 1998, "cannot be easily removed and certainly it is impossible to pull them off if the victim is fighting against her attacker with all of her force." In other words, the "sex" may have been consensual, as the instructor argued, the Italian court reasoned.

"It should be noted that it is instinctive, especially for a young woman, to oppose with all her strength the person who wants to rape her," the Italian court wrote. "And it is illogical to say that a young woman would passively submit to rape, which is a grave violence, for fear of undergoing other hypothetical and no more serious offenses to her physical safety."

The language of the Italian court's decision suggests that the court deemed it less "instinctive" for an older woman to oppose rape, which raises further questions of a sexist predisposition on the part of court officials (*i.e.*, that because older women have had sex, they would not "oppose" it out of youthful fear or the preservation of virtue). But this was a rape case. Legal scholars and feminists around the world generally agree that rape is different from sex. And yet, in the Italian court's eyes, a failure of determined virtue was clearly the young woman's undoing. In other words, the girl had not fought hard enough. Thus, the instructor should be granted a new trial, the court held.[24]

But that is Italy. That could never happen in the United States.

In Gosarigaon, Bangladesh, village elders sat down one steamy afternoon in the summer of 2000, in an attempt to negotiate away the scarred, but once stunning, face of a married woman.[25] The woman's previously beautiful face had been ruined, according to news reports, by a spurned admirer who had taken his revenge in a splash of sulfuric acid, leaving a crater where one of Peyara Begum's eyes used to be and scar tissue in place of a cheekbone.[26] According to official tallies, the attack on Begum was one of 174 acid assaults in Bangladesh in 1999, most of them the work of dejected suitors obligated by traditional notions of superiority to seek revenge.[27] Though of little apparent concern at the time, acid-scarring incidents quickly grew into an international shame, prompting then Prime Minister Khaleda Zia in February 2002, to propose stiffer penalties for those convicted of such attacks.[28]

Similar attacks have been reported in Cambodia.[29] And in a related trend, a spate of permanently disfiguring attacks in Australia in the summer of 2001—overwhelmingly on poor Aboriginal women—involved blinding. According to the *Australia Herald Sun*, "[d]ozens of Aboriginal women [were] being blinded and disfigured in horrifying cases of family violence."[30] But spurned suitors don't ruin the faces of lovers in America? Do they?

In the winter of 1999, authorities in Paris sentenced an African woman to eight years in prison for the genital mutilation of 48 girls, ranging in age from one month to 10 years. The woman, along with 27 parents, were convicted of genital cuttings—an ethnic ritual said to be long practiced in Africa—and reportedly intended to control women and girls "by reducing or preventing...[their] sexual pleasure."[31] But genital mutilation is not an American issue. Is it?

And since 1993, in and around Cuidad Juárez, Mexico, a city of 2 million just across the Rio Grande from El Paso, Texas, nearly 200 women have been raped, murdered, and mutilated in a crime spree of ghastly acts.[32] In addition to rape, some of the victims had their breasts cut off. In other cases, the victims were shot, had objects forced inside them, and had their bodies stuffed into ovens to rot.[33] Though theories abound as to who may be responsible—ranging from a pack of serial killers to teenage gang members—most of the murders remain unsolved and few arrests have been made.[34]

But women are not murdered in such vast numbers in the United States each year, are they? In fact, they are in far greater numbers across the United States than many outraged Mexicans would imagine. The faces of women are also deliberately scarred in the United States and a unique form of genital mutilation is underway in America. Indeed, in one form or another, all of the incidents detailed earlier, can *and have* happened to women in the United States. For example, the question of consensual sex versus an allegation of rape has been at issue before the American courts, sometimes famously so.

On March 6, 1983, for example, a 21-year-old Massachusetts woman walked two blocks from her apartment to a New Bedford tavern. She wanted a pack of cigarettes.[35] But once there, she had a few drinks and began talking to the waitress. She stayed a little longer, talking a little more until "she was pushed to the floor by several men, her jeans forcibly pulled off, and she was carried, struggling, crying and shouting for help, to the pool table at the back of the small bar" where she was raped by six men in a notorious incident that later became known as "Big Dan's pool table rape," according to Columbia University journalism professor Helen Benedict.[36]

Sympathy for the victim was swift and far-reaching. But later, once the men involved began giving interviews in the media—the woman was vilified, portrayed by members of a close-knit community as someone who could not be trusted because she allegedly was "a prostitute." In fact, she was not a prostitute.[37] The woman was also alleged to be "indecent" because she had left her children in bed unattended while she "went out to the bar." In fact, the woman's boyfriend was at home with the children, journalist Leona Tanenbaum notes.[38] But these allegations, along with others, were printed by newspapers.

And yet the woman's most serious failing, according to self-appointed analysts, was that she "did not appear to be resisting" the removal of her jeans by men in the bar, supposed witnesses said.[39] Benedict argues, however, that the woman ran from the bar "[w]earing only a sock and a jacket,"[40] suggesting that all of her clothes had been torn off. These were not insignificant discrepancies. As the Italian court's decision indicates, from a legal perspective, the suggestion that the woman had not fought the removal of her jeans can raise the issue of consent.

In the Massachusetts case, the question was apparently whether the woman had decided to have very public consensual sex in a bar with multiple partners, only to cry rape later. Though a jury would ultimately decide the woman had been raped, prior to the trial reporters for several media agencies seemed to think otherwise. And thus, they decided that the woman deserved none of the traditional protections accorded rape victims, including anonymity.[41] Accordingly, they published her name.[42]

But that was 1983. Ancient history by all accounts, and no longer reflective of society or American law, critics would almost certainly argue.[43] And, indeed, there appeared to be change afoot. And yet, during the now infamous 1991 rape trial of William Kennedy Smith, mainstream media outlets trounced on the woman who had accused the Kennedy relation, dissecting her lifestyle, criticizing her clothing, and questioning her motives. There was public speculation that the woman was a "gold digger."[44] And during the trial, legal analysts poured over discussion of the woman's allegedly misplaced underwear, the whereabouts of which they said went to her credibility.[45]

"[I]t has been my experience," said one female television commentator, "that women usually know where they take off their underwear. And when they don't, they usually have a credibility problem."[46]

Women are living in a time when Victoria's Secret hosts "fashion" shows in prime-time and actresses expose the upper strap, singing the praise of the thong.[47] And yet, in the court of public opinion there are still "good girls" and "bad girls" and sometimes a woman's designation as a member of one class or another has to due with her underwear. Monica Lewinsky (along with a certain former president) was credited by editorial writers with ushering the word "thong" into the "political lexicon."[48] But, of course, we know that she was "a very bad girl." In the rape context, similar designations have always applied and they continue to apply today.

For example, a woman reported to police that she had been raped while at a university party. At trial, she was asked if she were wearing a bra at the time of the attack. She was also asked to describe the shorts and tank top she wore.[49] In another case, another alleged rape victim watched as a defense attorney "paraded [her] thong...in front of the jury, asking if she 'regularly wore this type of silky underwear,'"[50] though the woman reported that the attack occurred as she was closing the video store where she worked. The man charged in that incident was later identified by authorities as a "serial rapist," according to reports,[51] and despite the waving of the thong, he was later convicted.[52]

But in a Massachusetts case, a woman raped by a man and then held hostage for fourteen hours was reportedly forced to watch at trial as the alleged attacker took the stand to accuse her of supporting the "murdering [of] babies." The woman had once attended a pro-choice rally, according to writer Melba Newsome.[53]

Though not all defense attorneys use tactics of this sort, these incidents illustrate how easily the legal construct of "credibility" can be turned against women who "cry rape." It is a construct colored by societal expectations, religious and/or moral convictions, cultural assumptions, and personal bias. "Good girls," after all, don't wear thongs unless they want, or are expecting sex, the conventional wisdom goes, though lingerie companies peddle their wares in prime time.

"Good girls" also apparently don't have unprotected sex or abortions, which is why there is often such an effort to get facts of this kind before a jury. For example, the fact that a woman had an abortion four years earlier and reportedly contemplated another in a pregnancy that later ended in a stillbirth was deemed relevant in a malpractice suit against a doctor and hospital. A Philadelphia Superior Court panel reasoned that "...[i]f [the plaintiff] placed so little value on the fetus, then her level of emotional distress would not be the same as that of a woman who valued the fetus all through the pregnancy and never contemplated an abortion at any stage."[54]

The first trial on the woman's malpractice claim ended in a hung jury. A second jury ruled in favor of the doctor and hospital. But a Pennsylvania Appellate Court ruled in the late spring of 2002, that the superior court had erred in admitting this information. In remanding the case for a new trial, the appellate court noted that the trial court had "based its relevancy conclusion on the mere speculation that a prior abortion would affect the suffering felt after the loss of an entirely separate pregnancy. We discern no correlation between an abortion four years prior and the degree of emotional distress parents would feel upon hearing that their full-term baby had died *in utero* after subsequent delivery."[55]

In January 2002, the Georgia Court of Appeals decided a similar issue, this time involving attempts to introduce the medical and sexual history of a deceased women before ruling that "[e]vidence of a dead woman's abortions, adoptions, and unprotected sex may not be used to determine the value of her life in a wrongful-death case."[56] The ruling stemmed from the 1994 death of a 23-year-old woman, who lost her life after a car driven by her boyfriend, Edward Smith, collided head-on with a car driven by Dana Wedincamp. The woman, Laura Johnson Flores, left behind a then three-year-old son. After a *guardian ad litem* sued both drivers on behalf of the boy, Laura Johnson Flores's sex life became fair game.[57]

Although both Smith and Wedincamp were sued, only Wedincamp's attorneys sought inclusion of Flores's sexual history. And at a 1999 pretrial hearing, Judge Amanda F. Williams of Glynn Superior Court reportedly ruled that if the *guardian ad litem* acting on behalf of Flores's son tried to prove that Flores was a "good mother and a good person" who "liked to work with children," then evidence of her abortions and adoptions would be permitted.[58] The judge apparently reasoned that a jury could find that a "good unmarried mother" with a son of three, would not become pregnant again after his birth.

Further, a jury could conclude that "promiscuous" people have higher mortality rates than people who are in a monogamous relationship or who have protected sex.[59]

In rejecting this reasoning, Judge Anne E. Barnes held, in writing for the three-judge appellate panel, that "[t]he defendant wants to unfairly devalue the descendant's life to the jury by focusing on her sex life and sex partners, evidence that is irrelevant to the value of her life to herself. This course of action cannot be condoned."[60]

And yet, American courts have a long history of doing just that. Like their English counterparts before them, American judges and juries have long been suspect of women and "their credibility" in the rape context, argues former Harvard law professor, Susan Estrich.[61]

"Juries have never been alone in refusing to blame the man who commits a 'simple' rape. Three centuries ago the English Lord Chief Justice Matthew Hale warned that rape is a charge 'easily to be made and hard to be proved, and harder to be defended by the party accused, tho' never so innocent.'[62] [But if] it is difficult for the man to establish his innocence, far better to demand that a woman victim prove hers; under Hale's approach, the one who so 'easily' charges rape must first prove her own lack of guilt. That has been the approach of the law,'" writes Estrich.[63]

This history, coupled with persistent fears that "vindictive women" may falsely accuse men of rape, tend to dictate what is an "acceptable" question or defense in rape cases.[64] "There is a bias against women in the court," former United States Justice Department official Bonnie Campbell said in an interview in 2001. "Most of the players in the courtroom are men, and one of their greatest fears is that they will be falsely accused of rape. The question 'Is she telling the truth?' inserts itself into every case."[65]

Thus, suggestions of "consent" and/or the failure to resist are par for the course in rape cases.[66] So are acquittals where women fail to prove themselves credible enough victims. Indeed, as Campbell's comments suggest, American juries are made of human beings, who bring human emotions and prejudices with them when they hear cases; prejudices and social standards that work against women where it can be argued that they have violated societal norms.

As a result, a woman may be deemed "a bad victim" if she wears a thong, though they are apparently the stuff of dreams. She may be a "bad victim" if her skirt is "too short," though clothes have gotten smaller, shorter, and more provocative in the past decade.[67] Prior to September 11th, for example, the suggestion of violence was among the strongest elements of women's fashion.[68] Clothing was sharp, dark and offered with the suggestion, it not the feel, of Victorian bondage, fashion critics noted.

In addition, anger and attitude were prevailing themes as the leather-to-vanishing-cloth ratio moved even business attire into the realm of the dominatrix. And yet, wherever possible, the suggestion of heat and a satisfied breathlessness was at play. This, advertisers and designers offered, was the new woman in all of her four-inch-high-heeled glory. And it seems to have worked.

"For many, dressing sexily is as much about power and entitlement as about attracting mates," fashion writers Leslie Kaufman and Cathy Horyn note. "Younger women are moving the unapologetically sexy look into even the most button-down corporate suits. Mati Bonetti, 27, recently left a marketing job at the tobacco giant Phillip Morris, where she felt totally at home wearing capri pants, sheer skirts, and mules. Asked what she would say to a supervisor who questioned her attire, Ms. Bonetti, who is about to start a job at MTV, replied, 'I'd say, well, I don't think I am insulting you.'"[69]

There are those who argue that the current "lack of modesty" is responsible for everything from eating disorders[70] and female self-consciousness[71] to adultery.[72] And while an internal "women's" debate may rage over whether modesty serves women best, one thing is clear today: although "sexiness" has made its way from the catwalk to the asphalt, many judges and juries have yet to progress thus far. In December of 2000, for example, a man in Massachusetts was acquitted of an alleged GHB-assisted rape following a trial that again involved the display of a thong. But there was also testimony that the alleged victim had been drinking—which is probably how she ingested the GHB—and statements suggesting she had flirted with a friend of the man later charged with raping her.[73]

In another case, a 41-year-old Missouri woman was allegedly attacked and raped in her own home after her wine was spiked in a bar. GHB was again believed to be the drug used. The defendant, who had driven her home, was charged and convicted of rape, sodomy, and sexual assault. But a Franklin County Circuit Judge chose to disregard the jury's recommendation of a 10- to 27-year sentence, ordering instead that the man serve 120 days in jail and 5 years probation.[74] The judge apparently found the woman's actions in going to a bar unacceptable. "If anyone is listening, this is why you don't go to bars," the judge reportedly said during sentencing.[75]

Has there ever been a judge anywhere in America to say such a thing to a man?

Women have long been accused of "asking for it" if they go to bars and/or of "provoking" men to rape if, at the time of an attack, they were wearing short skirts or a thong, though that particular piece of clothing is nearly invisible when women are fully dressed.[76] In addition, judges and juries have historically concluded that in some cases the woman who was alleged raped really wanted to have "sex" with the man she had accused—even if she did not know him—because she did not fight "hard enough" to hold on to her virtue.

An old-fashioned story? Feminist rantings? Maybe. But maybe not.

"Even though the first detective to see her after her reported rape observed that [the victim] was 'hysterical,' 'bruised,' and 'roughed up,' the fact that she had accepted [William Kennedy] Smith's offer to walk along the beach on his family's estate was widely regarded as evidence that she had consented to have sex with him," author Leora Tanenbaum wrote in reviewing the treatment of the alleged victim in the Smith case.[77] "NBC News and *The New York Times* revealed her name despite their usual policy of not naming the complainant in rape cases. NBC featured a picture of [the victim]."[78]

By *evolution*, for "honor," revenge, or because men have "been taught" to believe they have the right to take what they want, violence against women is part of American society and a part of the American legal system. And so are attempted defenses that often degrade women. For example, it may be thought that the "jeans defense" would never be attempted in an American court. But it was attempted in the New Bedford case.[79]

And though several of the men charged in the "Big Dan's pool table rape" were convicted,[80] that hardly ended the woman's ordeal. Following the verdict, members of the community threatened to bomb her house.[81] The woman fled Massachusetts, and in a tragic footnote to the story nearly two years after the trial, she died in a high-speed automobile accident in Florida, an act Tanenbaum suggests may have been suicide.[82] Benedict suggests that the accident was the result of recklessness and despair.[83]

In contrast to the men in the New Bedford case, Kennedy Smith was acquitted, and in the years since the trial has reportedly completed medical school and become a conscientious citizen of the world, who has worked against the proliferation of land mines.[84] And yet, the "trauma" appears to have been a learning experience. After the trial, Florida lawmakers began debating making it a crime to publish a sexual assault victim's name.[85, 86]

Scarring of a different kind is at work when there is talk of a retaliatory acid attack. As previously set forth, women in Bangladesh survived 174 acid attacks in the spring of 2000. Reports of acid attacks are not common in the United States. But scarring women achieved through a variety of other means is. Since 1981, when a dejected suitor slashed the face of an aspiring model, effectively ending her burgeoning career,[87] it has been understood on a public level that slashing a woman's face is a particularly effective form of violence. And though they are not as sensational as they once were, slashings still occur, usually to the same effect.

On a desolate New Jersey road in November 1997, a young man held the arms and legs of a former girlfriend while a current girlfriend slashed the woman's face, legs, and scalp so deeply that at times the skull was pierced.[88] Though it does not appear that the Justice Department keeps specific numbers on slashing attacks, the agency does track of the annual number of aggravated assaults involving weapons, which would presumably include razor attacks and slashings.[89] Nearly one million aggravated assaults were carried out against women in 1994,[90] in addition to roughly 1,128,100 other "victimizations" against women involving weapons.[91]

Of course, it is pubic slashing that is at issue where there is talk of genital mutilation. But genital mutilation is not an American issue. Or is it? More than 100 million African women have been forced to undergo genital cutting, according to media reports.[92] While there is no evidence that forced genital mutilation is practiced in the United States, debate of the issue reached American shores in 1997, when Adelaide Abankwah sought political asylum in New York.

Upon arrival at New York's John F. Kennedy Airport, Abankwah told immigration officials that she feared death or the violence of the ancient practice of genital mutilation in her native country of Ghana. A member of a small tribe, Abankwah reportedly had been sexually active outside of marriage, a taboo in her culture.[93] As punishment, Abankwah was told that she would·be mutilated.[94] Or so went the story she offered.[95]

At the airport, Abankwah was taken into custody[96] and held in federal prison while American authorities debated her plight. Though the first immigration judge hearing Abankwah's case believed her fear was genuine, in order to qualify for political asylum Abankwah was required to prove that the Ghanaian government would not protect her, the judge ruled. The problem for Abankwah was that genital mutilation was officially outlawed by the Ghanaian government in 1994. But Abankwah told immigration officials that elders in the village she was from were still cutting women and young girls in 1997.

After more than two years of detention, Abankwah was granted asylum. It was later alleged, however, that the Adelaide Abankwah written about and publicly supported by Gloria Steinem and Hillary Rodham-Clinton, among others, was actually a woman named Regina Norman Danson.[97] It was further alleged that she had entered the country on documents stolen from the real Adelaide Abankwah.[98] But "Abankwah's" supporters remained loyal, her defenders staunch.[99]

Whatever the truth, what makes the "Abankwah" story relevant to the issue of women and violence in the United States is an irony: while "Abankwah" was being held in prison for refusing to submit to genital mutilation, sensational reports began to surface that women in America had begun the trend of slipping quietly into the offices of plastic surgeons in the hopes that a few intimately-placed stitches might ensure they "bled on [their] wedding night[s]."[100]

More than 7 million Americans have plastic surgery each year, according to the American Society of Plastic Surgeons,[101] with the emergence of the somewhat delicately called "hymen reconstruction," a new entry on a growing list of augmentations. Hymen reconstruction reportedly involves the sewing closed of the vagina to create the illusion of chastity, thereby arguably allowing a woman to become a virgin *again*.[102] Though hymen reconstruction is clearly the choice of women—as opposed to forced mutilation—feminists argue that the voluntary mutilation of one's genitalia to meet the misogynist expectations of men offers evidence of another kind of oppression.

And though the murders in Cuidad Juarez caused a stir in Mexico, women in America are murdered in far higher numbers each year. And unlike the killings in Mexico, which are believed to have been carried out by strangers, women in the United States are often killed by people——men——they know. On a hot summer's day in Chicago, a cab driver had an enraged argument with his wife, which led the cab driver to douse his wife with gasoline and set her on fire, according to witnesses.[103] She died soon after the charred taxi was towed away. In New York in April 1999, a husband sneaked into his wife's bedroom. But not for romance. Once inside, the man allegedly attempted to bludgeon his wife to death with a barbell. When he thought the task was complete, he exited the room, and upon running into his daughter in the hallway, announced, "I've killed Mom."[104]

In 1998, roughly 1,830 people across the United States were murdered by intimate partners; 1,320 of them women. That total represented an eight percent increase over the number of women murdered by intimate partners the year before. Though the number of violent crimes in general has fallen in recent years,[105] women continue to be murdered, mugged, assaulted, battered, and raped in the United States. And it is not always clear that laws, law enforcement officials, or the legal system deter, prevent, or have the will to prosecute the men—the partners—carrying out the crimes.

But there are not just the partner crimes. Women are also attacked by strangers. On a summer's day in New York, a 25-year-old woman walked down the street after a morning of church. In a blink, she was on the ground, suffering lacerations, broken teeth, and a fractured skull in what is commonly referred to by law enforcement officials as an act of "random violence." According to witnesses, the woman was attacked from behind by a man, who bashed her in the head with a 3- to 5-pound piece of concrete.[106] The assailant was not immediately caught.[107] But the incident bore a close resemblance to the assault of another woman in November 1999. In that incident, the victim was smashed in the head by a man wielding a six-and-a-half-pound paving stone.[108]

In August 2000, a divided New York appeals court held (in reversing a previous order of a summary judgment[109]) that a jury should decide whether a rape victim's alleged failure to look through the peephole in her apartment door before opening it relieved her landlord of liability in a claim involving negligent security.[110] Though a small case, the decision could mean a great deal to women. Had the order of summary judgment been allowed to stand, the suggestion arising out of the case might have been that the victim was responsible for her rape, though her alleged attacker, "known as a troublemaker," may have been admitted to the premises by the building's security guard.[111] The appellate court's decision will allow a jury to decide whether the building's owners met their duty regarding security.

Thousands of women are attacked and/or assaulted across America each year.[112] Data compiled by the United States Department of Justice suggest that members of "the weaker sex" remain inviting targets of crime on the streets, in their cars, on the job, and in their homes. In 1994, women survived[113] 5 million violent victimizations, according to Justice Department research.[114] And what, precisely, does "5 million victimizations" mean in real numbers to real women?

"[W]omen age 12 or older" survived more than "432,000 rapes and sexual assaults, 472,000 robberies, over 940,000 aggravated assaults, and over 3 million simple assaults," according to Justice Department research. And though the incidents of violent crime have generally fallen across the country, the numbers are still high for women. In 1999, for example, 3 of every 1,000 women across the country were raped or sexually assaulted,[115] and 4,489 females age 12 or older were victims of homicide.[116] And just where in America was the most dangerous place for a woman in 1994? The same place it was in 1995, 1996, 1997, and 1998, 1999, 2000, etc.

"Females were more likely to be victimized at a private home (their own or that of a neighbor, friend, or relative) than in any other place," Justice Department researcher note.[117] Forty-nine percent of all nonfatal assaults in 1998 were carried out against women by people unknown to them. In terms of actual numbers, roughly "six out of ten robberies were committed by strangers compared to one out of four of all rapes/sexual assaults," according to Justice Department figures.[118] But still violence against women remains "primarily partner violence," according to the Justice Department.[119] In other words, women in America are more likely to be victimized by friends, family members, or intimate partners than by strangers.[120] By contrast, men are more likely to be victimized by strangers.[121]

In addition, though women as a gender "experienced intimate partner violence at a lower rate in 1998 than in 1993,"[122] women as individuals were the "victims of intimate partner violence at a rate of about five times that of males."[123] In other words, women may come home after running the gauntlet of potential harms in the outside world[124] to find that their partners also have violent hands. And there were other clear patterns as well.

Among these trends is that violence generally occurs at a higher rate in urban areas.[125] In addition, approximately one million women are stalked each year,[126] and roughly, 1.5 million women are physically assaulted[127] and/or raped,[128] some of them multiple times,[129] events that another class of researchers suggest may have lasting psychological effects, among them Post-Traumatic Stress Disorder.[130] Finally, women are "more likely than [men][131] to sustain an injury,"[132] during assaults, and nearly one-fourth of the time, weapons are used against women during assaults.[133]

And yet, assaults and physical attacks are only part of the violence women face.

Though women have greater protections today, they have long been the victims of prejudice and bias at the hands of law enforcement officials, some scholars argue.[134] This may be particularly true where a woman is deemed "obstructive," though the real target may be the man who was her lover, some journalists suggest.[135] And yet, as "just plain victims," women sometimes hardly fare better.

Indeed, as often as there are crimes against women, there are attempted defenses, some tending to do violence with the words used. For example, almost as often as there are charges of rape, there are assertions of "consensual" sex,[136] even where the facts clearly make that impossible. In other instances, where there are charges of "date rape,"[137] there are claims of "obsessed" women crying wolf or falsely accusing men for revenge.[138] Newer to the mix are "date rape drugs,"[139] the administering of which may be "forgiven" if it happens in a bar. And these, of course, are just the things that happen in the courts.

There are also the scholars. And at the start of the millennium, the promise of enlightenment seemed to take a back seat to more primitive notions of rape and sexual violence as evolutionary "adaptations." In two books that were new and "provocative" at the time, academicians argued that rape and jealous battery may stem, not from bad behavior and/or poor impulse control on the part of men, but rather from a male biological imperative founded in the reproductive equivalent of a "survival of the fittest theory." In other words, sometimes when a man rapes a woman, he may do so for no other reason than he is unable to attract her, but still needs to place his seed, the authors argue. TRANSLATION: Men are born to breed, and they will breed, even if they have to rape to do it.[140] Of course, arguments—academic or otherwise—based upon the needs of men explain, at least in part, why violence against women remains an integral part of American society.

THE SEEDS OF VIOLENCE:
On History Repeating Itself and Then Some

> "A vital part of understanding a social problem, and a precursor to preventing it, is an understanding of what causes it."
> *Understanding Violence Against Women*[141]

In literature, brutality against women is often explained as the passion of a superior mind spun out of alignment. When the mercurial prince of Denmark assailed his beloved Ophelia as a "breeder of sin,"[142] for example, he was likely mad as a hatter, argues Robert Youngman in *The Madness of Prince Hamlet and Other Extraordinary States of Mind*.[143] Too bad for the fragile Ophelia. After so harsh an attack, she drowns herself.[144]

Dostoyevsky also hints at madness in *Crime and Punishment*,[145] though his "hero" dreams of murder prior to the act and carts a hatchet across town to achieve it.[146] Walter Morel, the besotted father of D.H. Lawrence's *Son and Lovers*, is mad with drink when he throws a drawer across the room, striking his wife in the face;[147] and the rugged Petruchio is irrational with pride when he endeavors to starve the *shrewish* Kate until she be "tamed."[148] (There are those who argue, however, that the good Kate was as mad as her dear Petruchio.[149]) And then there is Othello, a lover so possessed by jealous madness[150] that he murders the tragic Desdemona.[151]

But literature is not science. And though these stories may be classic and compelling, neither Shakespeare nor Dostoyevsky offer statistical data in support of their stories. And yet, the fables literature has to offer remain worth considering because life often does imitate art. In the "true story" of women and violence, men abuse women in ways that many Americans can only wish was the stuff of fiction.

In *Without Conscience: The Disturbing World of the Psychopaths Among Us*, for example, psychologist Dr. Robert Hare profiles a patient as dark as any rogue Shakespeare could create. Except that "Earl" is real. According to Hare, "Earl" was a prisoner and recidivist who proudly admitted engaging in personal conspiracies aimed at the women in his life.

"The most salient thing about Earl," Hare wrote, "is his obsession with absolute power.... He values people only insofar as they bend to his will or can be coerced or manipulated into doing what he wants.... His relations with women are as shallow and as predatory as the rest of his behavior. He attests to having had several hundred live-in relationships, ranging from days to weeks, and an inestimable number of sexual contacts over the years. When asked how many children he has, Earl replied, 'I don't really know. A few, I guess. I've been accused of being the father, but I'd say, "Fuck you! How do I know it's mine?"' He routinely terrorized and assaulted the women in his life, sexually abused his daughter, and raped her girlfriend. His propensities for sadistic sexual behavior carry over into prison, where he is well known for his 'aggressive homosexuality.'"[152]

Violence in the name of power, conquest, dominance, and submission are the cornerstones of ancient history. A world history made of threats, intimidation, bribery, war, and predatory relationships. Violence is part of the animal kingdom and of the kingdom of mankind. Thus, murder and other forms of violence have long been deemed the fastest way to get from A to B. More expedient than diplomacy. More compelling than words. Or in the days before the development of language, the only way to communicate. And so, Caveman A hit Caveman B on the head and dragged away his woman.

In that sense, "Earl" may simply have been born in the wrong time. In less "civilized" times, "Earl" might have been a knight. A mercenary. A feared and revered lord. Maybe even a pope.[153] Religious and political ascensions haven't always been as bloodless and "democratic" as they are today. Rather, they were historically achieved through violent means.

Conquest, expansion, religious annexation, imperialism, trade, and money have all served, at different times, as motivations in a grand history of war, violence, and civilization. In 400 B.C., for example, marauding Gauls sacked the armored guardsmen of the Roman army.[154] But it appears to have been a learning experience. In 200 B.C., the rebounding Romans waged war with Macedonia and claimed Greece. Europe, Egypt, and most of Asia followed[155] with a far-reaching Roman occupation that continued through 58 B.C., when Caesar avenged his long-fallen countrymen by routing the rugged Gauls.[156] But even the mighty tumble: by the fifth century B.C., the once puissant Roman empire had fallen to the "barbarians."[157]

And that was before "God" entered the picture.

With "God"—clothed in the vestments of a succession of not-always-so-holy popes—in the mix, ten centuries of warfare got underway.[158] Unlike the United States of modern day, there was no separation of church and state in medieval Europe.[159] Rather, religious leaders made every effort to shape state and national politics. Historians note, for example, that Gregory the Great is said to have engaged in "judicious" use of the papacy during the fifth century.[160] At other times, popes sought the help from leaders with the command of armies or money to hire mercenaries.[161] By the seventh century, this connection seemed cemented.

The defeat of the "Arian Visigoths in Aquitaine and the *heathen* Alemanni war bands of the middle Rhine," by the Christian convert Clovis established the empire of Charles Martel, historians note. And Martel's son, Pepin, would agree in 754 A.D. to fight annexation of Rome by the Lombards in exchange for papal approval of assault on the Merovingian throne.[162] Pope Stephen is said to have made the perilous journey across the Alps himself to personally plead for Pepin's help. His approval for the counterassault was freely granted, say historians.

It was Pepin's son Charlemagne, a man described by scholars as an "inexhaustible and immensely shrewd war leader," who spent his "long reign trying to impose his authority over half the peoples of northern Europe."[163] In addition to being a "shrewd war leader," Charlemagne saw himself "...as the supreme ruler of Latin Christendom, just as he believed the Byzantine emperor governed eastern Christendom." Thus, in addition to fighting the Saracens and Bavarians, Charlemagne "took a keen interest in the internal administration of his dominions," [164] working "with Church leaders, and encourag[ing] the foundation of monastic institutions and cathedral schools," historians note.

But in the scant civilization of the medieval world, few things remained consistent for long. After Charlemagne's death, medieval Europe exploded in conflict. "The Danes ravaged England, Norse raiders harried the Scottish coast and islands, and established a kingdom of their own in Ireland," historians note. Battle followed battle until "[f]inally, a wave of even more savage invaders, the Hungarians, surged in from the eastern frontiers of the old empire. Excellent horsemen, they raided Saxony, Thuringia, Bavaria, and Carinthia, and continued to be a serious menace to the Christian West until Otto I annihilated them at Lechfield in 955."

From this caldron of fire rose the nascent nations that would become Europe. And though modern civilization was in the making, the violence remained. These were the nations teeming with leaders ambitious and savage enough to inspire Shakespeare. As the battles for world dominance continued, the Normans conquered a divided England. The French conquered a stumbling Normandy. Turkish warriors crushed the Byzantine army on its way to occupy Jerusalem. And nearly three centuries of Crusades got underway.[165]

Further along in this chronicle of upheaval, conflict raged from 1568 to 1609 in the Netherlands.[166] Germany endured the Thirty Years' War[167] as military and religious mercenaries, merchants, and traders traveled land and sea in search of new trade routes and new and richer territories.[168] As commerce and conquest coupled, port cities in Italy and France rose, sparking exploration anew.

"In the modern era there emerged the old imperialism of the seventeenth and eighteenth centuries, which arose concomitantly with the Commercial Revolution and with the discovery of the New World," wrote Louis Snyder in *The Making of Modern Man: From the Renaissance to the Present.*[169] "Motivating influences were the three Gs—Gold, Glory, and God. Spain, Holland, Portugal, France, and England founded colonial empires and Europeanized the Americas. During this wave of imperialism the interests of the colonies were regarded as subservient to those of the mother country—an accurate reflection of the mercantilism of the day."[170]

Mercantilism ushered in the Industrial Revolution, which "pushed country after country into the machine age of the late nineteenth century," argues Snyder.[171] "Growing industrialization called for the discovery of new markets, new sources of materials to feed insatiable machines, more food to satisfy the hunger of increased populations, and new fields for investing excess capital. European life required many products which only tropical regions could supply."[172]

Evidence of these "European requirements" can still to be found on historic maps of the time.[173] During this period of exploration, parts of Africa were known as: the Grain (Pepper) Coast, the Ivory Coast, the Gold Coast, and the Slave Coast.[174] "Imperialists used a variety of methods and pretexts" to gain footholds in the new territories, says Snyder.[175] "In most cases they did not seek outright annexation of colonies, but preferred the more subtle process of peaceful penetration."[176]

Except when the exploitation of natives and transplants was necessary, which, of course, it was in the Americas. In 1521, the Spanish conquered the Aztecs in Mexico,[177] and by 1535, the Incas had also been subdued in Peru.[178] The expansion of the Spanish moved northward. Spain was the first to establish a permanent base in North America in 1565,[179] and although the Spanish initially wrote treaties with Native Americans,[180] the defeat of the Armada in 1588 put an abrupt end to the practice.[181] Swiftly thereafter and in the name of British,[182] French,[183] Dutch,[184] Swedish,[185] and later American expansion, war and murder became the rule in handling the "Native American problem."[186]

Though the members of some Native American tribes could be subdued and enslaved, others proved to be exceptional enemies and swift escapees. Add to this the already troubling calculation that Native Americans often knew the terrain better than pioneers, and it becomes clear that taking hostile Native Americans as part of a planned workforce generally proved to be an exceedingly bad idea. The kind of idea that could provoke a massacre. Conquering forces and early pioneers came to the same or similar conclusions. But with expansion into the New World and the riches to be gained, something had to be done.

In 1607, England began settling colonies on the Atlantic seaboard.[187] And for the next two centuries, the British and new American colonists alternately presided over a captive population of unpaid workers known as slaves. According to demographers and historians, by 1700, "indentured servants and slaves composed one-third of Virginia's population of sixty thousand."[188] But indentured servants were soon phased out in the emerging American states. And "[a]fter 1700 the labor was increasingly that of Negro slaves from Africa," historians note. And "by 1776 Negroes in America numbered a third of a million."

Of course, oppression is not difficult when one believes those being oppressed are inferior, and that was what England and many of the early American colonists believed. But not even a captive population of oppressed labor could prevent the outbreak of war when so much is at stake. Tensions between the fledgling colonies and the motherland began to mount, reaching high notes with an infamous "tea party" on a December night in 1773,[189] followed by a Revolutionary War[190] and the signing of the Declaration of Independence.[191]

But upon gaining freedom, conflicts continued to threaten the embryonic states as they set out to establish themselves by undoing an earlier civilization. During the next century, the barely United States survived the War of 1812, a war with Mexico, a Civil War, and the Spanish-American War. Elsewhere in the world, violence also reigned: England and France fought the France and Indian War; the Napoleonic Wars raged; and the First Burmese War got underway.

There was also the First Afghan War; the Opium Wars of China; the First of the Maori wars in New Zealand; and the British War with the Sikhs. Then came the Second of the Burmese Wars; the Crimean War; the Second Maori War; the Second Afghan War; the British occupation of Egypt; the Japanese defeat of China; Italy's battle with Ethiopia; and the Boer War in South Africa.

And the twentieth century was hardly better. At the start of the modern era of armed conflict, there was the Russo-Japanese War; the First and Second Balkan Wars; World War I; the Spanish Civil War; and the Holocaust and battles of World War II. There was oppression on a smaller scale as well. Among them dark political imprisonments in the former Soviet Union; racist lynchings in the American South; a cultural revolution in China. "Ethnic cleansing" in Eastern Europe. Volatile skirmishes across the Middle East. And a series of extraordinarily bloody massacres in Rwanda beginning in the summer of 1994, resulting in "nearly three times the rate of Jewish dead during the Holocaust" in what some researchers suggest was the "most efficient mass killing since the atomic bombing of Hiroshima and Nagasaki," "...all of which tends to suggest that 'ending' violence may be far harder than politicians, diplomats, and scholars suggest, even where the violence at issue falls within that smaller cultural subset of incidents generally characterized as "violence against women."[192]

THE MODERN TREND OF MAN:
Violence and Mankind; Violence and Womankind

People kill each other. People maim each other. It has always been mankind's habit to do so, especially when there was something to be gained. From an historic perspective, the seeds of violence—those same seeds that may be responsible for male violence against women—are likely ancient and as well founded in some societies as language. Is it any wonder, then, that violence has also long been an integral part of the lives of many women?

"Legal wife-beating did not disappear with the Middle Ages," Stanford's Yalom offers. Rather, "[i]t hung on in many places into the nineteenth century; and even after it was no longer legal, battering has continued to maim countless wives from every ethnic and social sector. Our recent efforts to provide shelters for battered wives and to stamp out this now-criminal offense run counter to centuries of practice."[193]

This is because wife battering was "an accepted practice, sanctioned by law and custom, that allowed husbands to enforce authority over their wives," says Yalom.[194] So accepted, in fact, that "[e]ven when concerned family members and neighbors intervened and brought the matter to the attention of the courts, the husband usually got off with only a fine or a pledge to 'receive his wife in his house and treat her agreeably.'"[195]

Feminist scholars have long noted a connection between the struggle for women's rights in early America and the abolition of slavery. The reason for this has to do with the recognition of a simple reality: state-sanctioned violence against women—(much like state-sanctioned violence against slaves and Native Americans)—was permissible, because women, like slaves and Native Americans, were, if not "uncivilized," then at least "irrational" in the fashion of a child. Thus, women, like others, were in need of discipline; discipline that could be freely offered in back-of-the-hand lessons. At other times, women were battered because—like slaves and Native Americans—they had no significant value. They were chattel, servants, and child-bearers.

Though more privileged generally than slaves in most cases, the plight of women—even white women—in America was in many ways similar to those of slaves under the law.[196] The American colonies were originally "founded for England's profit, not her glory."[197] Thus, the leaders of many of the fledgling colonies-*cum*-states borrowed heavily from the foundations of European law in constructing a governmental and legal system, one tending to foreclose a woman's "[i]ndivisibility of sovereignty."[198]

With few clearly defined rights, limited protections, and a legal civil identity that dissolved upon marriage, women in early America could be treated as men wanted to treat them.[199] One of those ways, according to history professor Anne Butler, was with a heavy hand. At the start of the nineteenth century, "...the divorce rate soared" in the rugged West "beyond other national regions, with women commonly charging verbal and physical abuse in their petitions," says Butler.[200]

And yet, self-defense (or defense of a woman by a woman) was rarely held to be legally valid defense or a legally defensible position by courts. In April 1910, a woman named Jessie Carmon shot a man, who later died.[201] For it, Jessie Carmon was sentenced to from four to fourteen years in prison[202] even though the man Jessie Carmon killed was married to a woman Carmon employed as a domestic in a boarding house Carmon managed.[203] The man's name was James McCoy, and, as described by Butler, McCoy was "an unemployed miner known for his vicious wife-beating."[204]

In the pattern of modern wife-beaters, James McCoy was violating a court order to keep away from his wife, Rose, and Jessie Carmon, on the night he skulked into the boarding house.[205] Jessie Carmon shot him as he crept up the stairs. And Jessie Carmon went to jail. But not all of her troubles were "man-made." Rose McCoy, the abused wife and a domestic servant in Carmon's boarding house, exhibited symptoms typical of "battered wife's syndrome" long before the affliction had a name. She frequently complained of her husband's brutality, filing, then withdrawing, battery complaints.

But after Jessie Carmon shot James McCoy in Rose McCoy's defense, Rose McCoy "shifted from the persecuted wife to the aggrieved widow," according to Butler.[206] And what followed then is what often follows similar events today. Jessie Carmon was shredded in the newspapers. According to Butler, her life was dissected, her divorce mischaracterized, and she was declared a sexual deviant, though no one offered any proof. "Although circumstances around the shooting made it unclear whether Jessie Carmon and Jesse Newton [the businessman who had hired Jessie Carmon to manage the house] shared a common bedroom as well as a common first name, the terms 'alleged paramour,' 'alleged affinities,' and 'free love' peppered the newspaper reports," Butler wrote.[207]

Perhaps the greatest damage to Jessie Carmon, however—at least from a woman's perspective—may have been done by her lawyer, who argued that Carmon was "'insane' at the time of the shooting, because the incident...occurred on the first day of a very difficult menses."[208] It was a strategy that nearly succeeded, Butler suggests. "The jury, after being deadlocked eleven to one in favor of acquittal, eventually convicted Jessie Berry Carmon of 'manslaughter by reason of accidental shooting,'" writes Butler.[209]

"Perhaps more forcefully than any other institution, the legal system, in concert with the press, defined the legitimacy of an individual," Butler wrote. "Legal structures, although only one of the forces at play, marked with insiders and outsiders of society with razorlike clarity. Once a woman entered its maze of constraints, the legal institution helped society rearrange the contours of her persona, transforming her from a 'respectable female' into a 'social deviant.'"[210]

Carmon served her time in the Colorado State Penitentiary, a men's prison in a little-known trend common in the American West. Though never a "sizable portion of the prisoner population, women passed in an increasingly regular parade through the penitentiary gates," according to Butler.[211] Jessie Carmon was but one of them.

The "disobedience" of women for their "sins" has also long been deemed punishable under natural law and sometimes under statutory law or simply by practice. Especially if that punishment will restore a father's or a family's honor. Women in Jordan grew furious in early 2002, for example, after a father, who had killed his daughter with a cleaver because she had premarital sex, was sentenced to six months in jail.[212] So-called "honor killings" were legal in Jordan until recently.[213]

But "honor killings" remain legal in parts of Bangladesh, Turkey, and Pakistan,[214] where a nearly parallel case was playing out in May of 2002, following the reported conviction of a 26-year-old Pakistani woman, based upon similar evidence—a baby girl—and of a nearly identical offense under strict Islamic *hudood* law.[215] She was sentenced to death by stoning.[216]

But it is not only "primitive cultures" and "primitive people" lost in "ancient times" who perceive women as the couriers of sin. There is evil in the world, and it apparently continues to hold women in its grips even in America in the twentieth century. In 1997, for example, a Glendale, California, deacon pled guilty to involuntary manslaughter after he and two other men tried to stomp the demons out of a woman in two multiple-hour sessions that left the woman with "blunt-force injuries that included sixteen broken ribs, shredded and bruised muscles, and crushed internal organs."[217] She died as a result of the injuries.[218]

Kyung Chung and her husband of more than two decades, Jae Whoa Chung, were missionaries living in Bangladesh.[219] The couple was reportedly passing through the Los Angeles area on a visit to church sponsors before heading to a religious meeting in Chicago in the summer of 1996. Their visit coincided with that of another missionary, identified in news reports as Sung Soo Choi, who had recently arrived from China, also to visit sponsors.

According to the *Los Angeles Times*, Choi "had never met the Chungs before, when, during a July 3 prayer session at a private home, he determined that a demon dwelled within [Mrs.] Chung. A healer herself, she had last undergone a demon-cleansing ritual three years earlier in Korea."[220] But "[a]fter three years, the demons were back. Once again, dark spirits were making the missionary's wife arrogant, disobedient to her husband, and constantly interfering with his work at their seminary in Bangladesh."[221]

Choi, who "had roused evil spirits from believers" five times before, reportedly "volunteered as the healer."[222] Thus, Chung's husband "shouted the name of Jesus," while Choi "prayed, sermonized, sang hymns, and laid on hands, commanding the demons to leave with all the fervor he could marshal."[223] Eventually, they "took turns pushing against [Kyung Chung's] thighs, abdomen, and chest—using their hands, a spoon, and their feet in an attempt to squeeze out the devils." Their attempts ended with Choi reportedly standing on Chung's chest in an attempt to "force the devil up through her mouth."[224] A third man, a deacon at the Glendale church, summoned authorities.[225]

Similar events were reported in Oakland two years earlier, ending in guilty pleas in 1996,[226] and in France in 1994, involving a Muslim cleric, whose attempts to drive the demons out of another woman's body included beating her with bamboo, dunking her underwater, and forcing her to drink salt water. That woman also died, and in June 1997, the cleric was sentenced to four years in jail.[227] But the demons apparently continued to invade. In March of 2002, a jury awarded a 17-year-old girl $300,000 after she was allegedly assaulted, battered, and falsely imprisoned during an attempted exorcism by a Texas reverend and several members of his church.[228]

Do exorcisms happen to men? Probably. It seems rare, however, that men are deemed to be possessed of, or by, demons. And even when they are, the dynamic is completely different. For one thing, the exorcism would involve men beating men. And never women beating the devil out of men. In addition, a cry of possession would never be based upon a husband's arrogance towards his wife, because as the pious know, women are supposed to be as obedient to husbands as they are to God.

Where they were not obedient or did not otherwise perform as they should, women might be ruled "possessed" by demons by male-dominated religious establishments. Thus, they were battered as part of an exorcism, or otherwise, until their God-ordained obedience returned. Are exorcisms few and far between? Probably, though it may also be that the practice tends only to come to the attention of the public and authorities when there is a death or when someone alerts law enforcement officials. But even if that is true, the inclination toward a belief in the sin of women or that women fall more easily under the sway of demons (and then lead others astray) is fairly well-established.

Without reason or the natural guidance of God, women would wallow in sin, it was reasoned. And not only that. *Sinful* women would then lead others—men—toward evil, injuring society. And men would not be able to do a thing about it. Instead, they would be as weak as Adam. Thus began the eternal quest for women *without sin*. A quest continually stoked by the Catholic Church and one that has led to cultural, religious, and political obsessions with the state of a woman's hymen. It is an obsession that has been used throughout the centuries to justify various forms of violence—from child rape to murder—against women.

MAIDENHOOD AND MAIDENHEADS:
Hymen Envy and a Universe Desirous of Virgins

> *Then, as my gift, and thine own acquisition,*
> *Worthily purchas'd, take my daughter. But*
> *If thou dost break her virgin-knot before*
> *All sanctimonious ceremonies may*
> *With full and holy rite be minist'red,*
> *No sweet aspersion shall the heavens let fall*
> *To make this contract grow; but barren ate,*
> *Sour-ey'd disdain, and discord, shall bestrew*
> *The union of your bed with weeds so loathly*
> *That you shall hate it both. Therefore take heed,*
> *As Hymen's lamps shall light you.*[229]
>
> PROSPERO TO FERDINAND
> *The Tempest* Act 4, Scene I.[230]

So what is it that gives women value?

Traditionally, it has been their "purity," and, thus, a young girl's virginity was a valuable commodity to be dealt away in political or financial schemes. A father's asset or the property of kingdoms with the power to join empires. Thus, while royal sons in Medieval Europe were "allowed the freedom of 'youth' in the form of liaisons with girls of lower station, concubines, and prostitutes," daughters "were carefully supervised and allowed little opportunity to lose their precious virginity before they married, usually at an early age," writes Yalom.[231]

And, indeed, if one believes that Shakespeare reflects history, more than one kingdom was made on such a thing. Thus, parents of the Middle Ages did well to lock their daughters away.

There were basic dowries to be had in more modern times. A field. A plow. A mule. One less mouth to feed. Or a better life for the girl or the person selling her worth. And this, incidentally, was not always the simple transaction of starving fathers ridding themselves of a financial drain. Rather, it was often a very sophisticated and competitive endeavor. Arthur Golden recounts, for example, the calculated machinations involved in the sale of a young girls *mizuage*—virginity—to a much older doctor, who would also become her permanent patron during pre-World War II Japan in *Memoirs of a Geisha*:

> In the end, Dr. Crab agreed to pay ¥ 11,500 for my *mizuage*. Up to that time, this was the highest ever paid for a *mizuage* in Gion, and possibly in any of the geisha districts in Japan. Keep in mind that in those days, one hour of a geisha's time cost about ¥ 4, and an extravagant kimono might have sold for ¥ 1500. So it may not sound like a lot, but it's much more than, say, a laborer might have earned in a year.[232]

"Of all the important moments in the life of a geisha, *mizuage* certainly ranks as high as any," Golden's geisha remarks,[233] and that would certainly seem true when the outcome of this transaction can change a life. But what does a fictional account of the sale of a young girl's virginity before World War II have to do with women and violence today? Although it may be the stuff of faraway lives, this is not also the stuff of fiction.

More than a few adult men have been arrested in the United States in recent months for allegedly trying to negotiate sexual encounters with minors via the Internet, law enforcement and media reports suggest.[234] And the Federal Bureau of Investigation reportedly calls the "sexual exploitation of children one of the most significant crime problems they and we have as a nation."[235] Around the world, the sexual exploitation of children still includes the purchase of a young girl, often largely because their virginity has a commercial value all its own. Writer Jan Goodwin reported on the spirited auction surrounding the sale of the virginity of a 13-year-old Afghan girl named Nadia, for example, in the April 2002, edition of *Marie Claire* magazine.[236]

"I've had offers of 20,000 rupees ($325) for her first night," Ameet, a man identified by Goodwin as a "prostitute's agent" reportedly boasted. "But I know I can get 30,000 ($485)."[237]

And yet, after the first night and the high price it may command, Nadia's price will fall precipitously and immediately to roughly $64 a night or $16 per sexual encounter "until Nadia is either too sick to work or forced to turn tricks for a rupee or two at the local bus station—literally the end of the line," Goodwin writes.[238]

VIRGINS AND VICTIMS
IN THE COMMERCIAL SEX TRADE

There are academics who will take exception, of course, at the suggestion of a worldwide problem based upon the stories told in a woman's magazine. But Goodwin's account joins thousands of others told by academics, researchers, international aid groups, and child advocates. A controversial study, published by the University of Pennsylvania School of Social Work, for example, estimated that one in every 220 children in America—roughly 325,000 in total—is a "victim of prostitution, pornography, and other forms of commercial sex."[239]

Within that number were 122,000 runaways, forced into pornography or prostitution to survive; 52,000 "throwaways;" and 73,000 children who remain at home where they are "sexually exploited by family and friends," the authors of the study found.[240] But the University of Pennsylvania study was not without its critics, among them the University of New Hampshire's Crimes Against Children Research Center, which assisted the authors by supplying data,[241] challenged the study's reported findings. And yet, even if we concede that the University of Pennsylvania authors got it wrong in terms of specific numbers, what remains clear is that a great many children around the world are being sexually exploited and otherwise abused.

The international agency UNICEF estimated in 2002, for example, that more than 300,000 children were "serving in government or rebel forces in over thirty armed conflicts in the world—as soldiers, runners, guards, sex slaves, cooks, and spies. These children are frequently abducted from their homes, schools, or refugee camps and forced into combat. They are beaten or killed if they attempt to escape. Girls are especially vulnerable—because they are often sexually exploited and forced to be 'wives.'"[242]

Another 200,000 were believed to be the victims of trafficking "every year in West and Central Africa," according to UNICEF.[243] But the really big numbers are reserved for the commercial realm and overwhelmingly for girls. "Millions of children throughout the world are being bought and sold like chattel and used as sex slaves," UNICEF Executive Director Carol Bellamy reported in December 2001.[244]

Specifically, UNICEF estimates that "…one million children, mainly girls, are forced into the multibillion dollar commercial sex trade every year. These children are often lured with promises of an education or a 'good' job. Girls appear to be forced into the sex industry at increasingly younger ages partly as a result of the mistaken belief that younger girls are unlikely to be infected with HIV/AIDS virus."[245]

Of course, a child's age may ultimately matter less than the period of time she has been involved in prostitution. In August 2002, the United States Customs Service reported arrests in connection with an international child pornography ring involving children in America and abroad ranging in age from 2 to 14.[246]

What at least some of these numbers suggest is that the international market for virgins is alive, well, and moving ever younger, because as theories apparently go in this and other realms, the younger the child, the cleaner the child. In addition, virgins are often specifically requested, because sleeping with one is thought by some men—apparently hundreds of thousands of men—to be a "very special thing." And, indeed, according to UNICEF's analysis of exploitation trends, "[r]ecent research evidence suggests that the age of the children involved [in child prostitution] is decreasing and the sexual exploitation of children as young as six is increasingly becoming pervasive."[247]

In the 1990s, international relief agencies found Southeast Asia to be among the world leaders in child prostitution. But in the last decade, Africa, Latin America, and parts of Eastern Europe have emerged as plentiful "providers."[248] For example, according to UNICEF, child prostitution is "an emerging phenomenon" in Kenya,[249] with brothels now apparent in residential areas of Mombasa, Malindi, and Nairobi.[250] In South Africa, girls as young as 8 years old have been found working in commercial sex clubs in Cape Town, Johannesburg, Pretoria, and Durban,[251] while 10-year-olds have been reported in establishments in Zambia.[252]

And though it is often thought that brothels are part of the landscape in "other countries," they also thrive in the United States, a quietly held fact that came to startling light in early 2000, for example, when a 16-year-old runaway from Vermont was found dead in a New York City brothel.[253] Even more disturbing than the existence of brothels in American cities, however, may be that the child and young adult population there may not be made only of American "country girls" drawn to the bright lights of the big city.

According to UNICEF, "[i]t is thought that Zambian girls are trafficked to third countries such as USA, Israel, and Russia via South Africa."[254] Indeed, although child trafficking is "predominantly an in-country phenomenon," UNICEF notes in analyzing international data, that "[g]irl children are the primary targets, although boy children have also been identified as victims." These are girls, UNICEF notes, who "range in age from 4 to 17 years."[255]

Though researchers and academics argue that the actual number of child abductions by strangers is relatively small in the United States—roughly 115 per year—a spate of highly publicized abductions, sexual assaults, and murders of preteen and teenage girls throughout the spring and summer of 2002 has shed some light on the desire for young girls in the United States as well. Polly Klaas, Danielle van Dam, Elizabeth Smart, and Samantha Runnion were among the young girls abducted in highly publicized incidents.[256]

Yet the problem of disappearing and abused children may not be as limited or simple as some suggest. Garnering far less attention than these high-profile incidents, yet staggering by comparison, are more than 35,000 persons under the age of 18 who disappeared within the first three weeks following the abduction of Elizabeth Smart under what authorities describe as "suspicious circumstances." In addition, according to the Polly Klaas Foundation (founded by the abducted and murdered child's father), "2,100 times a day parents and caregivers call law enforcement to report a missing child."[257]

And who is responsible for the vast majority of child abductions and disappearances?

"After studying hundreds of cases, scientists can provide at least a partial answer. The broad population of child molesters, most of whom do not abduct their victims, is too diverse to fit a single psychological profile, but the far smaller group of those who abduct and keep children for sexual abuse share common traits," health writer Mary Duenwald reports.[258]

Among the common denominators is that child abductors generally have very little contact with children in their daily lives and overwhelmingly—95 percent of the time—they are men. "In general, as everyone suspects, these people are losers," retired FBI agent and consultant for the National Center for Missing and Exploited Children, Kenneth Lanning told *The New York Times* in August 2002, as panic continued to swirl in the wake of the summer's abductions.[259] "Why do these particular child molesters abduct? Because they lack the interpersonal skills to attract, befriend, and seduce their victims."[260]

Some child abductors harbor sexual fantasies involving children and may thus be drawn to child pornography. "What motivates these people are their thoughts, their fantasies," Dr. Ann Burgess, a professor of psychiatric nursing at Boston College, told Duenwald. "They have it in their heads that they want to have sexual contact with children, and they look for the opportunity to get that. What we aren't so clear on is where do these fantasies come from? And now you have to look at the individual person."[261]

Others believe that some child abductors gravitate towards children because, although they would prefer to engage an adult woman, poor social skills keep them from doing so or because restraining an adult woman is harder than restraining a child "...they progress younger until they're finally able to find someone small enough to bring into their vehicle," Duenwald writes.[262] Five-year-old Samantha Runnion was grabbed while playing near her home by a man who threw her into his car.

But child abduction and rape, forced labor and sexual slavery are global matters as well, perhaps even more grave than in the United States, because in some countries—those where these abuses go unchecked—the marketing of young girls slides easily from "personal use" into commerce. Thus, although there may always have been a demand for child sex partners, in some countries governments do little or nothing to prevent the supply.

As a result, a global market of children—overwhelmingly young girls—has emerged as have perverse male rites of passage and social boasts. For example, although notions of the "virgin brides" have long held a place in religious tradition, the notion of the "virgin whore," *i.e.,* the young child who will soon be "turned out" into a life of prostitution, holds a coveted place of value in the global market place today.

UNICEF estimates the following numbers for victims of commercial sexual exploitation: 35,000 women and children in West Africa; 100,000 women and children each in Brazil, the Philippines, and Taiwan; 175,000 women and children in Eastern and Central Europe; 200,000 women and children in Thailand; between 244,000-325,000 women and children in the United States; and

400,000 women and children in India.[263] And what gives this otherwise isolated exploitation its international or global flare is "sex tourism."

"In the Eastern and Southern African Region, the number of tourists from western countries has increased dramatically," UNICEF research suggests. "While most of these travelers may not deliberately be seeking sex when they travel, the number of those who make use of commercial sex is considerable." Among the reasons for this, UNICEF notes, is that "[w]hen tourists come to the region there is anonymity, which releases them from the usual restraints which determine sexual behavior in their home countries."[264]

Thus, men "who would never visit brothels in their home countries end up doing so especially in the most famous tourist destination in the region," according to UNICEF. In addition, tourists often "may not understand the cultural values of the host communities. This leads them to make assumptions which are untrue, but which allow them [to] rationalize their sexual exploits. For example, it is common for western tourists exploiting children sexually to rationalize that this is a way of helping poor children and their families get some money. They see it as a way of reducing poverty."[265]

There are other factors as well, UNICEF suggests. Among them that tourism often "reinforce[s] prejudice," *i.e.,* that visitors to some African countries "hold strong ethnocentric views, whether explicit or obscure, about the inferiority of others. These attitudes," UNICEF concludes, "may lead them into exploiting children whom they consider to be inferior."[266]

In addition, the availability of and desire for children, western wealth, and the fact that "tourists are often willing to pay large sums of money for sexual services from children" has made the trade in children "lucrative to criminals" and thus commonplace in some areas." In other words, "[t]he ease with which tourists in some areas can obtain children as sexual partners is, in itself, a powerful incentive for some to try the novelty of child sexual partners," UNICEF found.[267]

But there are also endemic practices, particular to cultural—often misogynist—beliefs that may also involve sex with children, overwhelmingly girl children and virgins if they can get them.

"[E]ven if my wife was the most beautiful woman in the world, men are like this," Goodwin quotes a Peshawar pimp named Raja. "It's not only the sex we enjoy. Getting a virgin is noble and precious, like opening a hotel. There's a sense of achievement. Men can boast about it."[268]

That, of course, is part of the paradoxical story of women: men worship virginity, often with something like religious zeal. And yet, the ultimate goal of this "worship" is to destroy—or perhaps more precisely, conquer and claim—this thing that they love, at times seeking public notice of this fact. For example, within some Islamic cultures, the traditional practice was that the bride was deflowered in a private room following the wedding ceremony after which the groom was supposed to present the bloody sheet.[269]

It is a male rite of passage that many men seem to still care about, whether or not they intend to raise the sheet. A reported seventy-eight percent of men in the Philippines—a country that has long had a thriving sex trade—say marrying a virgin is important to them. It is important elsewhere in the world as well. And to help this nearly universal quest along, social structures have sprung up. Zulu girls in South Africa, for example, may be given a certificate to show they are virgins after an exam if question marks have been drawn on their thighs.[270]

And yet, it is the desire to experience this apparently enchanted "rite" outside of wedlock that has proved so problematic for women and girls on a global level. Though "getting a virgin" may be among the most cherished of the darker desires (for men), this passion is the reason that hundreds of thousands of girl children are targeted, kidnapped and sold into sexual slavery every year. It is also the reason that religious leaders world-wide continue to expound on the positives of "virtue" and the reason that slandering a woman by sexual reference still goes a long way toward trashing her social credibility, even in America today.

THE OPPOSITE OF MARY AND WORKING SHAME:
Sin and Slander by Sexual Reference

There has always been a certain authority that comes with name calling, especially where the act involves a woman and the name she was being called was the "right" one. Remember Carol Brady? The curvaceous, reservedly sexy mother of six played by Florence Henderson on the popular 1970s television show *The Brady Bunch*. The ultimate in bombshell moms with an hour-glass figure poured into polyester belly-bottoms and a matching double-knit blouse. Is it any wonder that half the nation was in love with her?

Now think "porn queen."

Does the label fit?

Florence Henderson didn't think so. And so, in March of 2000, Henderson filed suit against Serial Killer, Inc., seeking to enjoin the El Segundo, California, company from selling T-shirts bearing her likeness as Carol Brady above the words "porn queen."[271] Asserting claims for emotional distress and invasion of privacy,[272] Henderson argued that the publication and sale of the T-shirts would expose her to "contempt and ridicule." To many—feminists certainly—that would seem to have been the point, though the T-shirt makers would almost certainly argue otherwise. And yet it was a label Henderson would have to share that year.

In October 2000, a California teacher sued the school district where she worked after students portrayed her as a "porn queen" in a student newspaper.[273] The teacher, arguing that she had been forced to leave her job as a result of the label, alleged that district officials did little to prevent students from circulating the underground newspaper and that complaining to the district "...was an exercise in futility."[274] Though the teacher sought expulsion, the district reportedly chose to suspend eleven students and transferred several others. In

March 2002, the school district was found liable and the teacher, Janis Adams, was awarded $4.35 million.[275]

The verdict suggests, of course, that a change may be afoot. And yet, the practice remains, because there has always been a certain level of power in calling a woman names that suggest she lacks virtue. It was the reported practice of Puritans to mark women in scarlet.[276] And at the turn of the century, more than one marriage was ruined by a woman's alleged lack of virtue. In the time of James Dean, it was a cruel "joke" to pen the name or telephone number of a women on the wall of a men's washroom: "For a good time, call...." A joke, of course, for the men involved. Quite another for the women involved.

Women have been called names throughout the ages for many reasons and in many ways, including: religiously, emotionally (within the context of the male right of outrage towards sin and moral turpitude), as an act of revenge, or simply because it has long been understood that calling a woman those kinds of names tends to reinforce male power. Because women were (and are) supposed to be ashamed of certain acts and attitudes. And where they are not, men have always done their best to make women ashamed. Or, in the alterative, to bring shame upon them.

At the end of the now infamous four-year divorce of the Duchess of Argyll, for example, the presiding white-wigged judge reportedly frothed swirls of moral condemnation at the Duchess, given what he had heard. Margaret Whigham, her given name, was sued for divorce after her husband found a series of "compromising" Polaroids of her engaged in a sex act with a person dubbed famously as "the headless man." (The man's head and face did not appear in the frame of the picture.)

Though these racy events took place in the 1960s, they are hardly the most notorious incidents involving the British royals in this or any other century. And yet, during the proceedings, the judge was apparently so disturbed by what he heard about Whigham's behavior that he felt compelled to note in a 50,000-word decision that the Duchess was "a highly sexed woman who ha[d] ceased to be satisfied with normal sexual activities and has started to indulge in disgusting sexual activities to gratify a debased sexual appetite that can only be satisfied by a number of men. Her attitude to the sanctity of marriage was what moderns call 'enlightened,' but which in plain language was wholly immoral."[277]

Sordid, tawdry, titillating, and laden with the kind of information most people hope to keep private, the judge's tome took three hours to read aloud. And though the clear intent of the judge was to disgrace the Duchess, despite those 50,000 words, the name of the man the Duchess was clearly involved with remained one of the British Isles' greatest mysteries for nearly three decades. So great that in 2000, the Argyll divorce became the subject of a documentary shown on British television.[278]

Though speculation reportedly swirled at the time with some concluding that American actor Douglas Fairbanks, Jr. was the mystery man, Whigham is said to have told a friend that "the only Polaroid camera in the country at the time had been lent to the Ministry of Defense," a comment some writers suggest pointed directly at Duncan Sandys, then Defense Secretary and son-in-law of Winston Churchill.[279] Though Whigham was the daughter of a millionaire who was once proclaimed debutante of the year, after the divorce she was drummed out of "polite society" and reportedly died penniless in a nursing home in 1990. But is there a more befitting end for such an "immoral" woman?

In 1976, economist Glenn Loury, formerly of Harvard and the John F. Kennedy School of Government, now an economist at Boston University, pioneered the notion of "social capital" in his doctoral dissertation. "Social capital" is a theory of social placement grounded in the premise that "informal relationships and connections"—as often as money or brains—"pave the way for success in the labor market."[280] Though the context with regard to the application of social capital theories for women would historically tend to reach more "societal preferences," social positioning as a cultural construct appears to have been well understood by the Founding Fathers and by most Americans ever since.

"For women as well as men [in early America],...maintaining their 'credit' was key," argues Norton. "[J]ust as the insults that led men to file defamation suits clustered around the terms 'rogue' and 'knave,' and around accusations of theft and lying, the slanders that most bothered women alluded to sexual behavior. Since three-fourths of those insults came from women of the same rank, for women, as for men, defamation suits primarily offered a weapon against a vilifier of the same status. The most common single epithet, accounting for more than half of the lawsuits brought by female targets against women who applied such terms to them, was 'whore' or a synonym like 'jade.'"[281]

Though half of the complaints regarding insults lodged during the 1600s in New England involved allegations of sexual misconduct brought by women against other women, according to Norton,[282] it is clear that men have also long understood the power of sexual suggestion, which explains why so many men continue to try to draw on that power today. For example, during the confirmation hearings for Supreme Court Justice Clarence Thomas, several men were allowed to testify publicly about Anita Hill's alleged sexual perversions, leading conservative writer David Brock to famously proclaim that Hill was "a little bit nutty and a little bit slutty."[283]

Of course, Brock's comments did not go unnoticed or uncommented upon by female journalists, two of whom set out to set the record straight themselves.[284] Or by Hill, who addressed his attacks in her 1997 book, *Speaking Truth to Power* first via historic footnote, then directly:

> In 1925, in her prize-winning essay *On Being Young—a Woman—and Colored*, Marita O. Bonner asked, 'Why do they see a colored woman as a gross collection of desires, all uncontrolled reaching for their Apollos and Quasimodos with avid indiscrimination?' But for the timing, Miss Bonner might well have asked the question about the Senate Judiciary Committee members and Senator Danforth who sought to portray me as an erotomaniac. She could well have been referring to David Brock, whose fraudulent portrayal of me, presumptuously

entitled *The Real Anita Hill,* hinged on sexual mythology about black women and society's willingness to believe it. Because Brock supported his case with fabricated and misquoted sources, I was at first amazed that the press gave him such broad license to define me. (He admits to never having talked to anyone who was at any time close to me. On the other hand, the information which he reports on Clarence Thomas comes from many of Thomas's political allies—in some cases the same people who provided information critical of me.)[285]

Though Brock has since recanted the assassination of Hill's character, his *mea culpa* will almost certainly be forgotten long before the suggestion that Hill was "a little bit nutty and a little bit slutty" ever dies. As Hill notes, society seemed to have a willingness to believe it. And apparently to embrace Brock, who—with the publication of a new book—appears to be "...turning expiation for these and other past sins into a second career that has played out like a striptease over the past few years," suggests *New York Times* cultural writer Frank Rich.[286]

Society has always had very little use for the "sinful" or "slutty" woman, except, of course, as negative examples. Hence, the power of such allegations. Would it really have mattered to the underpinnings of Hill's allegations, after all, were it true that she were "a little bit slutty"? Absolutely not. But it sure goes a long way toward destroying a woman's reputation and, thus, anything she has to say. Which may often be the point. Though ancient—indeed, perhaps even biblical—in its foundations, staining a women by sexual reference has always had a place in American society.

And though the methods have changed in recent years given advances of technology, male attempts to shame women remain so strong and regular a practice that cases involving allegations of this sort have begun to make regular appearances in court, even at times when the stated intention is something else. Provisions of the Florida Adoption Act were challenged in the summer of 2002, for example, because the act reportedly required women seeking to put their children up for adoption through a private—as opposed to a state—procedure, who were unsure of the child's paternity or the father's whereabouts to "run a newspaper ad revealing her name, age, height, hair and eye color, race, and weight, as well as the child's name and the date and place of birth."[287]

The law also required the woman to list the name—or presumed names—of the possible fathers and to place the notice or notices in the newspapers of all cities where the father may be. The law was challenged on behalf of five women as an invasion of privacy in a story that made national headlines and quickly became the subject of editorials. Though the State of Florida did not intervene to defend the law—only private adoptions are subject to the requirement—the stated intent of the law was to give absent fathers notice of the possible impending adoption.[288]

SEXUAL REFERENCE AND LIBEL:
The Current and Historic Practice

In the spring of 2000, a Utah high-school student took part in what he considered a prank. In the process he set an avalanche of legal claims and counterclaims into motion. The 17-year-old reportedly began disseminating email messages, many of them containing offensive sexual references to female classmates. In one of the messages, for example, he allegedly referred to a female student as "a prostitute in training."[289] The reason for his actions? The student explained in an appearance on Court-TV that he wanted to avenge himself and his friends similarly insulted in email postings. On December 6, 2000, a Utah judge ruled the teenager would stand trial for criminal libel.[290]

According to the United States Census Bureau, 39 million American workers have access to email at work. But that number does not include those Americans who have access to email or the Internet via private servers or school connections. And all of those connections have given rise to an evolving area of "electronic law" encompassing cases ranging from: "email revenge," viewed by some either as defamation[292] or threat;[293] to electronic conduct, at times allegedly leading to sexual assault[294] or within the employment context;[295] to sexual harassment or discrimination claims arising out of cyber communications.[296]

And yet, given the speed with which the runaway technology of this field moves, email issues have left legislators scrambling to either amend existing—or draft new—laws to expressly prohibit harassing, obscene, or offensive electronic communications.[297] But even as new legislation was moving through some state houses, authorities were forced to operate under traditional approaches to prosecution in "cyber conduct" cases. In June 2001, for example, two Westchester County, New York, high school students were charged with harassment for allegedly posting the names and phone numbers of dozens of female classmates along with their alleged sexual exploits on a website.[298] Both men were 18.

Though teenagers may simply be the next generation to engage in the age-old practice of dirty tricks, in many ways electronic communications and the Internet raise the stakes on information—false or true—flung far and wide, rendering assertions that in another time might have been remained bathroom rumor or the gossip of a single community instantly accessible. For three days in December of 2000, for example, British and American media outlets were riveted, and Internet lines around the world crackled with the unfortunately true cautionary tale of a young woman, a public relations employee, who, after an apparently passionate date with a fresh-faced, freshly minted male lawyer, decided to send him an appreciation email.

And that might have been the beginning of a very sweet story told to grand-children were it not for what happened next: the fresh-faced, freshly minted lawyer decided to email his addition along with the original electronic note to a few friends, who emailed a few friends. Who emailed it to a few friends. Who emailed it to a few more friends until the story of the email and the once-so-promising, and clearly titillating relationship that lay beneath made its way first into British, then American newspapers.

Soon, the public relations employee, then all of 26, was said to be in hiding, and the fresh-faced, freshly minted lawyer was under investigation at the law firm where he worked for alleged email abuses. Editorials were written condemning the young man. And because the world seemed to know their private story, strangers began voting as part of an Internet poll on whether the lawyer should be retained by the law firm, though most of the people voting probably had never met or even heard of the lawyer prior to the story.[299]

AN OVERVIEW OF ELECTRONIC LIBEL

In *Strauss v. Microsoft Corp.*, 814 F.Supp. 1186, 1189 (S.D.N.Y. 1993), the United States District Court for the Southern District of New York held that when viewed in the light of other "offensive" behavior, sexually suggestive emails could be considered by the jury hearing a gender discrimination case. In answer to a Motion for Summary Judgment filed by lawyers for Microsoft, attorneys for a woman argued that "she ha[d] established a *prima facie* case for discrimination and that there [were] genuine issues of material fact as to whether Microsoft's stated reasons for not promoting her [were] pretextual."

The court agreed, noting that in support of her case: (1) Strauss had alleged that male employees engaged in inappropriate behavior in the office, namely, making comments and sending email messages that were offensive to women; (2) Strauss has adequately demonstrated an ability to perform the technical editor job; (3) Strauss has shown via comparison of her qualifications with those of male employees that she had been the recipient of; (4) differential treatment. This, in the eyes of the court, was sufficient evidence for a reasonable jury to conclude that Microsoft's failure to promote Strauss to technical editor was based on gender.

According to the court, in addition to offensive emails, Strauss alleged that her male supervisor declared himself the "president of the amateur gynecology club." *See Strauss,* 814 F. Supp. at 1889, no. 3. (The text of that footnote in its entirety is: "For example, Strauss alleges that Lazarus told her that he was 'president of the amateur gynecology club' and that he 'referr[ed] to a woman employee as the "Spandex queen."' *Id.* (citing deposition of Karen Strauss, taken 2/4/92, at 13-15). Strauss also testified during her deposition that Lazarus had referred to a black woman as 'Sweet Georgia Brown' and offered to pay her 500 dollars to allow him to continue to call her by that name. *Id.* (citing Strauss Dep., at 24-25). Additionally, Lazarus sent one email message to the entire *Journal* staff which contained sexual innuendo referring to male genitalia. [The supervisor] also sent an email message directly to Strauss entitled 'Alice in UNIX Land.' Finally, Lazarus sent two other sexually explicit e-mail messages to one *Journal* employee who subsequently sent the material to the rest of the *Journal* staff. *Id.* (citing Strauss Dep., 26-37." *Id.,* at 1888-1889, n.3 (S.D.N.Y. 1993).

Repeated electronic "invitations" sent by a male supervisor to a female subordinate employee—including suggestions that the female employee would have a "horizontal good time" if she went on a date with him—could form the basis of a formal complaint, the Federal Appeals Court for the Seventh Circuit held in the 1996 case of *Knox v. State of Indiana*, 93 F.3d 1327, 1330 (7th Cir. 1996). According to the findings of the court, the male supervisor sent sexual emails and then email messages reminding the female employee to check her email. The persistent emails were followed by threats of a shift change and later, after the filing of a complaint, by threats and insults by the supervisor's colleagues. The female employee was eventually awarded $40,000 in a split decision. (The court's exact words in detailing the facts of the case were that "[s]tarting in December 1991, [Captain Robert] Stewart began sending [Kristi] Knox electronic messages asking her for sex. He often propositioned Knox using acronyms; for example, he frequently asked her whether she wanted to have a HGTWM, which was later translated as a 'horizontal good time with me.' Stewart also repeatedly asked Knox out on dates, calling her on the telephone and leaving messages reminding her to check her email.")

A supervisor's interest in pornography viewed via Internet at work was part of a sexual harassment claim in *Scott v. Plaques Unlimited, Inc.*, 46 F.Supp.2d 1287, 1289 (M.D.Fla. 1999). According to the court, "[i]n October 1997, Plaintiff asserts she was subjected to unwelcome sexual conduct and other harassment and abuse in the workplace, including but not limited to, the following abuses: (a) [a supervisor] began making person comments about how attractive Plaintiff looked or how her legs looked. [The supervisor] commented on Plaintiff's clothes, weight, and hair. He told Plaintiff she was 'so thin' and that she had 'gorgeous hair.' On one occasion, [the supervisor] inappropriately rubbed Plaintiff's shoulders; (b) on another occasion, Plaintiff found [the supervisor] and a customer looking at pornography on the Internet. Another time, Plaintiff found a Playboy magazine in [the supervisor's] office; (c) [the supervisor] once told Plaintiff that other women who had Plaintiff's position before her had performed sexual favors for the owner,...and that [the owner] had even paid for a former secretary's breast implants; (d) [the supervisor] inquired into the type of relationship that existed between Plaintiff and [a fellow employee]; (e) that the [supervisor] frequently attempted to drive Plaintiff and [the fellow employee] apart by inciting arguments between them; and, (f) that [the supervisor] criticized how [the fellow employee] treated Plaintiff, assuring her that he would treat her much better, including sexually."

And in *Blakely v. Continental Airlines, Inc.*, 992 F.Supp. 731, 733 (D.N.J. 1998), a New Jersey court was asked to decide whether derogatory statements made by male pilots in an Internet chat room could form the basis of a gender discrimination claim brought by female pilots. Because the airline had no direct control over the chat room, the New Jersey court held that liability of the part of the airline could not attach. But liability could attach on the basis of other claims. According to the court recitation of the facts of the underlying case, "[a]fter a five-week trial, the jury found Defendant Continental Airlines, Inc. liable for sexual harassment and awarded Plaintiff Tammy S. Blakey a total of $875,000. Defendant now moves for a new trial on damages, or alternatively, a remittitur of the jury award in favor of Plaintiff. [¶] Plaintiff Tammy S. Blakey ('Blakey') has been employed as a pilot with Defendant Continental Airlines, Inc. ('Continental') since 1984. She was Continental's first female captain on the A300 Airbus aircraft. In 1993,

Blakey filed suit alleging: 1) hostile work environment sexual harassment in violation of Title VII of the Civil Rights Act of 1964, 42 U.S.C. Sec. 2000e *et. seq.*, and the New Jersey Law Against Discrimination ('LAD'), N.J.S.A. 10:5-1 *et seq.*; 2) disparate treatment sex discrimination in violation of Title VII and LAD; 3) retaliation in violation of Title VII, LAD, and the New Jersey Conscientious Employee Protection Act, N.J.S.A. 34:19-1 *et seq.* ('CEPA'); and 4) defamation. She testified that pornographic pictures were placed in the cockpits of aircraft and that obscene and harassing comments were directed toward her.

"Evidence at trial supported her claim that she informed Continental managers of these problems, but that no effective action was taken to eliminate the pornography or the comments. [¶] Blakey also alleged that she was punished for leaving early when on 'reserve position' at Newark, while male pilots on reserve were allowed to leave early with no adverse consequences. Blakey also alleged that after she complained about the unfair treatment and the sexual harassment, Continental retaliated against her by, among other things, denying her a leave of absence and requiring her to undergo a psychiatric examination and a flight simulation test before allowing her to fly. Blakey's defamation claims were based on allegedly offensive statements made about her by other pilots on a Continental pilots' computer forum. [¶] The Court granted summary judgment for Continental on Blakey's defamation claim on March 9, 1997. The remaining claims were tried for five weeks in September and October 1997. At the close of her case, Blakey voluntarily dismissed her CEPA claim. On October 16, 1997, the jury returned a verdict in favor of Blakey on her sexual harassment claim, but rejected her claims of disparate treatment sex discrimination and retaliation. The jury awarded Blakey $480,000 in back pay, $15,000 in front pay, and $500,000 for emotional distress, and pain and suffering, but did not award any punitive damages. The jury also found that Blakey had failed to mitigate damages, and subtracted $120,000 from her back-pay award of $480,000. The Court entered judgment on the jury's verdict on November 5, 1997." In the case before the court in this instance, Continental moved for a new trial on damages.

The electronic age is about more than scribbling phone numbers on obscure bathroom walls. And in this realm, the publication of not only a woman's name and phone number, but also her address is a particular favorite for adults as well as teenagers. In February 2002, *The New York Times* reported the conviction on Al Goldstein, a man it described as "the pornographer accused of harassing a former employee over her decision to resign."[300] Goldstein, the publisher of *Screw* magazine, reportedly swore at the former employee because he had to wait at an airport for a rental car. In response, the woman quit, and later she refused his efforts to lure her back to work.

In the face of this rejection, Goldstein allegedly "vowed to make her life 'a living hell,' accusing her of embezzling funds and [promising] to 'take her down,' which prosecutors said he attempted by flashing her home address and telephone number [on screen] during his weekly cable television show."[301] Goldstein was found guilty by a jury of several counts of harassment and aggravated harassment.[302] He was sentenced to sixty days in jail following the convictions. That Goldstein was sentenced to jail time at all, however, and that cases of this kind are making their way into the criminal realm more often than before is worth noting.

In the past, sexual slur or harassment-related claims were filed less often by the government than by private citizens, asserting civil—as opposed to criminal—claims. But with the passage of antistalking laws following the murder of actress Rebecca Schaeffer by an obsessed fan in 1989,[303] intimidation,[304] harassment,[305] and stalking claims—many of them based on harassment theories—have begun to make their way to the courts with greater frequency.[306]

Of course, in either the civil or criminal context, the strategy of humiliation is often the same, feminists and critics note. And the issues span more than merely the electronic. In that sense, Internet slurs and electronic harassment appear to be just the latest in a high-stakes game of reputation and ruin that has long been the end result of "name-calling" where women are concerned.

In 1993, when "New Mexico reporter Tamar Steiber filed a sex discrimination lawsuit against the newspaper where she worked because she was earning substantially less than men in similar positions, defense attorneys deposed her former lover to ask him how often they'd had sex," writes author Leona Tanenbaum.[307] Why would the number of times a woman had sex with a former lover be relevant to a discrimination lawsuit? Is she frigid? Or deviant? Either might be sufficient to cost her credibility and sympathy in the eyes of a jury.

This strategy has hardly been isolated.

"In the 1997 sexual harassment lawsuits against Mitsubishi Motor Manufacturing, a company lawyer asked for the gynecological records of twenty-nine employees charging harassment, and wanted the right to distribute them to company executives," Tanenbaum writes.[308]

Would defense attorneys ever ask for the medical records of male employees so that they might distribute them to supervisors and executives in similar circumstances? At the risk of sounding like a "ranting feminist" (though it may, in fact, be true), the answer is probably not, because no one cares about a man's prostate problems or whether he suffers chronic constipation, other than that it offers an opportunity to giggle. Further, in general the American public is more sympathetic than contemptuous of the man who suffers impotence.

Indeed, even if one assumes that a man's "personal" problems might be somehow relevant to a discrimination suit, such "revelations" are generally of little consequence for men, because there is no social stigma associated with a man who has a lot of sex or who cannot have a lot of sex due to impotency. Not even if a man's promiscuity results in a sexually transmitted disease, with the possible exception of AIDS.

It would be not only heavy-handed, but also boring this far into this book to waste acreage rattling off disseminations about institutional misogyny and a social and legal system that still believes men are supposed to "sow their oats." Thus, offering evidence in court that a man has had a lot of girlfriends and, as a result, has had a lot of sex or a series of sex-related problems has always been of limited use to attorneys hoping to blacken the character of a man, unless, for example, the case has to do with a series of Don Juan frauds. It is the converse of this, of course, that generally makes the gynecological records of female employees of interest to attorneys.

But Dorothy, we are not in Kansas anymore. Internet porn has proven about the safest way to make a profit in that medium thus far and a cottage industry of homespun videos has begun to bloom in suburbs across the country;[309] the stigma of the sexually active woman as "sinful," "dirty" and, therefore, lacking in moral rectitude, social worth, and legal credibility remains a religious, moral, social, and legal watershed, which explains why some lawyers play a zero-sum game. And why there is so much talk about underwear and subpoenas for gynecological records.

No one cares if a woman has bunions or capped teeth. That she may have had a nose job or liposuction may be fodder for gossip. But augmentation of the breasts—those organs of nutrition turned sexual asset—*may* be reason to question a woman's character. During the 2001, murder trial of Carolina Panthers's Rae Carruth, for example, one avenue of attack on an ex-girlfriend who would offer extremely damaging testimony against Carruth was that she had allegedly used student loan money to pay for breast augmentation surgery.[310]

There are those among us who would argue that everything a person does says something about him or her. Thus, everything a person does offers evidence of his or her character, and therefore may be offered—particularly in court cases—as evidence of his or her character and credibility, whether or not those acts are directly related to the events at hand. Of course, such an approach ignores life's accidents, the whims of human emotion, and the foolishness of youth. Or that an attractive, but young, girl might give in to—at times grotesque—commercial notions of beauty by seeking augmentation so that she can compete.

As a matter of law, there are evidentiary hurdles to be cleared before "evidence" of this sort may be introduced specifically. But in truth, information of this sort often makes it way into court in the guise of credibility evidence. And there it remains in wordless suggestion, provoking the question over and over in one's mind: Is this the kind of person you would believe? Of course, that matters to women, because there are still people who care about whether a woman has had an abortion or "reproductive problems" allegedly brought on by sexually transmitted disease, whether the woman is a victim or a witness. And some of those people sit on juries.

That is the reality of the American court system. Thus, in seeking the gynecological records of female plaintiffs in a sexual harassment case, it might fairly be argued that there is an implied threat: sue our client and we will do our best to call you a "whore" in public.[311] And once a woman has been branded with the scarlet *w*—whether or not it is true—there are still some people who will care less about her and whether or not she has been victimized.[312] And there are still some people who will argue—depending upon what she was doing at the time—that the woman brought whatever she got upon herself.

This is not, of course, a new phenomenon. Rather, it is a trump card with historic pedigree laid out at times to ground arguments about "safety;"[313] at others, for revenge; or—even in this relatively modern age—in frothing tones of moral condemnation. Indeed, defaming[314] a woman by sexual reference was once so well-oiled a practice that in 1891, lawmakers in England enacted the Slander of Women Act[315] in an attempt to stem the wrongful ruin of reputations. The purpose of the Slander of Women Act, according to legal scholars, was to offer women wrongfully accused of "unchastity or adultery" a legal remedy.[316]

Prior to its passage, allegations of unchaste behavior were deemed "purely spiritual matters," *i.e.*, sins against God rather than society, scholars suggest.[317] As a result, such assertions were deemed unactionable unless proof of "temporal" damages could be offered. This meant at the time showing that an "advantageous" marriage or match has been undone by false sex-related assertions.[318] "Virtue," as stated earlier, has always had commercial value.[319]

Soon after the passage of the Slander of Women Act in England, some American colony-states took notice and, throughout the nineteenth and twentieth centuries, began adopting and applying variations of the Act.[320] But with a twist. Some courts held that although the *spirit* of the Slander of Women Act did not apply, what lay beneath the suggestion that an unmarried woman had engaged in extramarital sexual intercourse was, in fact, a criminal charge of either adultery or fornication.[321] And a woman wronged in such a way might have a cause of action for defamation, given that it had been alleged that she engaged in criminal behavior.[322]

Today, the rule is generally that a false allegation of "unchastity" is actionable whether or not it suggests a crime.[323] One notable exception to that rule, however, are statements made in court or in the course of litigation.[324] It should come as no surprise, then, that a great many things—some of them not true—are said and alleged about women in court with the protection of immunity, including that women are "sluts" or "slutty." That they have sexual histories. Or that "sex" was consensual where it clearly was not.[325]

Even in these times of modern excess, when split leather and black lace thongs have become fashionable must haves and when breast augmentations are among the most common of all plastic surgery procedures in the United States, a woman's "credibility" remains tied to the historic expectations of her gender. Therefore, though she may only be taking part in the latest fashion trend when she dons a mini-skirt or wears a thong, it may still come back to haunt her in court. Even today.

ENDNOTES FOR CHAPTER THIRTEEN

1   In 2000, "the number of women in the House increased by 3, to 61 (including 2 nonvoting members), and when a too-close-to-call contest in Florida's 22nd Congressional District is finally decided, that figure could increase to 62. Similarly, in the Senate, the number of women increased by 3, to 12, and when a too-close-to-call contest in Washington State is decided, that figure could grow to 13." *See* B. Drummond Ayres Jr., POLITICAL BRIEFING, *Incremental Progress for Women in Politics*, N.Y. TIMES, Nov. 12, 2000, at A22.

2   *See, e.g.,* Mark Skertic and Art Golab, *Campaigns Target Women*, CHI. SUN-TIMES, October 23, 2000, at p. 7; Katharine Q. Seelye, *Marital Status is Shaping Women's Leanings, Surveys Find*, N.Y. TIMES, Sept. 20, 2000, at A19.

3   According to the New York-based Women's Environment and Development Organization, although women make up "more than 50 percent of the global population," they hold "only 14 percent of the seats in national legislatures, and a mere 9 out of 190 nations have a woman head of state." *See* Nurith Aizenman, *Where Do Women Have Power? Not in the U.S.*, MARIE CLAIRE, Sept. 2000, at p. 199. *See also* WOMEN AND GOVERNMENT: NEW WAYS TO POLITICAL POWER: A COMPARATIVE STUDY OF WOMEN IN GOVERNMENTS AND POLICY MAKING (1994). (By way of comparison, in Sweden, for example, women hold 42.7 percent of all legislative seats and 55 percent of all ministerial posts. In South Africa, a nation often presumed racially and politically elitist, women hold 29.8 percent of all legislative seats and 38.1 percent of all ministerial posts. But in the United States, women hold only 12 percent of all legislative seats and only 31.8 percent of all ministerial posts. In France, 9.1 percent of all legislative seats and 37.9 percent of all ministerial posts are held by women. Roughly 10 percent of all legislative seats and 14.3 percent of all ministerial posts are held by women in Barbados. Although Sri Lanka currently has a female prime minister, only 4.9 percent of all legislative seats and 10 percent of all ministerial posts are held by women. In Kuwait, women hold no seats in either the legislature or administration. In fact, it is illegal for women to run for office and to vote, according to WEDO. And in Japan, one of the world's foremost industrialized nations, only 5 percent of all legislative seats and 5.7 percent of all ministerial seats are held by women.)

4   The fact that she was the first First Lady ever to run for Senate rendered Hillary Clinton's campaign historic regardless of personal or political bent.

5   *See, e.g.,* Elizabeth Bumiller, *For Mrs. Clinton, One Topic on Voters' Minds Remains Taboo,* N.Y. TIMES, October 10, 2000, at A27.

6   *Id.*

7   *See* Adam Nagourney, *First Lady Ends 16-Month Run with Victory,* N.Y. TIMES, Nov. 8, 2000, at A1.

8   *See* Maureen Dowd, *A Man and a Woman,* N.Y. TIMES, Sept. 20, 2000, at A31.

9   *Id.*

10   *See* Robert Pear, *Mothers on Medicaid Overcharged for Pain Relief,* N.Y. TIMES, March 8, 1999, at A1.

11   *Id.*

12   *Id.* at A12. (Though Chavez's sister called a relative in England, who wired the money, by the time it arrived, Chavez had had the baby.)

13   The Institute of Medicine reported in March 2002, for example, that members of minority groups—even those with insurance—continue to face discrimination and bias within the medical community. *See* UNEQUAL TREATMENT: CONFRONTING RACIAL AND ETHNIC DISPARITIES IN HEALTH CARE (Washington, D.C., National Academy Press, 2002). The Institute of Medicine is an independent advisory panel of experts whose findings may be reported to Congress.

14   *See* Aage B. Sørensen, *The Structural Basis of Social Inequality,* 101 AM. J. SOC. 1333, 1334 (March 1996).

15   That according to Elizabeth Dole during a speech at Public Policy Days, an event sponsored by the Nationally Accepted Certification for Women Business (NAWBO), cited in WORKING WOMAN, Feb. 1999. (The exact text of that citation was: "Elizabeth Dole underscored the issue of unequal treatment during this year's Public Policy Days. 'Women who work full-time still earn only 76 cents for every dollar a man earns,' she said, and 'in Fortune 100 industries and Fortune 500 companies, 97 percent of senior managers are still white men.'") *See* Lori Leibovich, *Reversal of Fortune,* BAZAAR, August 2000, at p. 190 (citing statistics compiled by the United States Bureau of Labor Statistics). ("[A]lmost one one-third of the married women in the U.S. out-earned their husbands in 1998.")

16   According to United States Department of Labor, Bureau of Labor Statistics report released July 20, 2000, women still make considerably less than men. For example, "[a]mong the major occupational groups, persons employed full time in managerial and professional specialty occupations had the highest median weekly earnings—$999 for men and $697 for women." *See* USUAL WEEKLY EARNINGS OF WAGE AND SALARY WORKERS: SECOND QUARTER 2000, at 1; ISSUES IN LABOR STATISTICS: *What Women Earned in 1998,* U.S. DEP'T OF LABOR, BUREAU OF LABOR STATISTICS, SUMMARY 99-5 (May 1999); George F. Will, *Lies, Damned Lies, and...,* NEWSWEEK, March 29, 1999, at p. 84.

17   The Due Process Clause of the United States Constitution has long been held to protect "citizens" within America's borders. "Citizens" have been defined as corporations and aliens as well as American citizens. For reading, *see, e.g., Sinking Fund Cases,* 99 U.S. 700, 719 (1879); *Wong Wing v. United States,* 163 U.S. 228, 238 (1896); *United States v. Ju Toy,* 198 U.S. 253, 263 (1905); *Kwong Hai Chew v. Colding,* 344 U.S. 590 (1953).

18   *See* Elizabeth Amon, *Coming to America: Alien Tort Claims Act Provides a Legal Forum for the World,* NAT'L L.J., October 23, 2000, at A1; *7 Families Sue bin Laden and Others for Billions,* N.Y. TIMES, Feb. 20, 2002, at A 11.

19   Women in many Middle Eastern countries are still fighting for the right to drive.

20   *See* Christine Toomey, *Iran,* MARIE CLAIRE, July 2001, at pp. 38, 40. (According to Toomey, after Ayatollah Khomeini came to power in 1979, conservative Islamic religious law began to demand that "... every girl over the age of 9 [is] expected to observe *hejab.* This is the Islamic dress code, which consists of a *chador,* a head-to-toe black veil worn over a *roopoosh,* a shapeless, calf-length coat. They were forbidden to sing or play music. Their right to mix with members of the opposite sex was severely restricted: For example, married couples faced arrest for holding hands in public, and

women were forced to sit at the back of public buses, while men sat at the front. Women could also be stopped on the street by vice patrols and arrested, fined, or flogged for showing a wisp of hair or wearing makeup." In addition, under the laws, women "could work alongside men, but could not socialize with anyone to whom they were not related. They could serve in Parliament, but could not leave the country or go out after dark without a man's permission. Girls could be married off by their families at age 9, but could not vote until they turned 15. [¶] These codes remain in place. But over the past four years, since the reformist president Mohammed Khatami was voted into office, things have been slowly changing. Women are being given more legal rights, as well as liberty to play sports, perform music, and sing if only in the company of other women. Vice patrols are becoming less vigilant. Instead of the *chador*, many women now wear head scarves in addition to covering their bodies, often in bright colors. Some even wear lipstick or mascara, although this is still punishable by a fine of up to $25—half the average weekly wage—for each makeup worn.") By contrast, though they were still required to be covered, women in Bahrain were allowed, in 2002, to vote for the first time ever. *See* Neil MacFarquhar, *In Bahrain, Women Run, Women Vote, Women Lose*, N.Y. TIMES, May 22, 2002, at A3.

21 The Fourteenth Amendment, one of the post-Civil War amendments, includes the Equal Protection and Due Process Clauses, which have been used to create a framework for discrimination claims.

22 *See* Alessandra Stanley, *Ruling on Tight Jeans and Rape Sets Off Anger in Italy*, N.Y. TIMES, Feb. 16, 1999, at A6.

23 *Id.* (The court's decision sparked protest by women and female lawmakers, who wore jeans as a symbol of defiance.)

24 The procedural history of the case was more complicated. The instructor was initially convicted of the lesser charge of indecent exposure in a public place. The victim appealed. The instructor was then convicted on all charges. But with the Third Division of the Supreme Court of Appeals in Rome's decision, the instructor will get a new trial. *See* Stanley, *supra* note 22, at A6.

25 *See* Barry Bearak, *Women Are Defaced by Acid and Begali Society is Torn*, N.Y. TIMES, June 24, 2000, at A1.

26 *Id.*

27 *Id.*

28 *See Bangladesh: Proposal on Acid Attacks*, N.Y. TIMES, Feb. 6, 2000, at A6.

29 *See* WORLD NEWS TONIGHT, airing August 28, 2001, ABC-TELEVISION, at p. 6 (transcript), available through ABCNEWS.COM; Seth Mydans, *Vengeance Destroys Faces, and Souls, in Cambodia*, N.Y. TIMES, July 22, 2001, at p. 3.

30 *See* Tony Koch, SPECIAL REPORT, *Shameful: Women Blinded and Disfigured as Violence Grips a Community*, HERALD SUN (AUSTRALIA), June 29, 2001, at Front Page.

31 *See* Marlise Simons, *8-Year Sentence in France for Genital Cutting*, N.Y. TIMES, Feb. 18, 1999, at A3.

32 For background on these events, *see, e.g.*, Nancy San Martin, *Death in the Desert*, LATINA, Feb. 2000, at pp. 96–103; Charles Bowden & Julian Cardona, *I Wanna Dance with the Strawberry Girl*, TALK, Sept. 1999, at pp. 113–114.

33 *Id.*

34 As of August 2000, few arrests have been made. *See* Bowden and Cardona, *supra* note 32, at pp. 113–114; San Martin, *supra* note 32, at pp. 96–103. According to reports, throughout the 1990s, a variety of men were arrested and charged in connection with some of the crimes, the most recent of these arrests coming in November 2001, when two city bus drivers were charged in connection with the deaths of eight women. But there are some in Mexico who believe they may not be responsible for the crimes, and that the police may simply be responding to pressure to "solve" as many of the murders as possible. *See Bus Drivers Suspected in Slayings in Industrial Area*, ASSOCIATED PRESS, Nov. 13, 2001 (reprinted on DALLASNEWS.COM, Nov. 16, 2001).

35 *See* Benedict, *supra* note 44, ENDNOTES FOR INTRODUCTION, at p. 91.

36 *Id.* at 89. (The woman was also "forced into oral sex, hit, held down, and molested by at least four men while others watched and perhaps cheered. No one tried to stop the assault and no one called the police." *Id.* at 91.)

37 *Id.* at 106–107.

38 *See* Tanenbaum, *supra* note 2, ENDNOTES FOR CHAPTER TWELVE, at p. 152. ("Her boyfriend, in reality, was at home with [the children] (a fact mentioned only in one story in one paper)," writes Tanenbaum, noting further that "[t]he jury ultimately believed the victim, but the community did not. After guilty verdicts were decided, community members told reporters (who quoted them without providing any context) that 'If she had been home with her children, this would not have happened' (*Providence Journal*); and 'I'm also a woman, but you don't see me getting raped' (*Standard-Times*). They held street demonstrations and threatened to bomb the victim's house.")

39 *See* Benedict, *supra* note 35, at p. 102 (citing reports in the *Boston Herald*: The eyewitnesses said they saw the woman with one of the defendants at another end of the bar, hugging and kissing. [¶] The defendant suddenly grabbed the woman and pushed her to the floor, removing her pants and unbuckling his own. She did not appear to be resisting, the witnesses said, as the suspect got on top of her. [¶] The defendant was too intoxicated to have intercourse, they said, but picked up the woman and carried her to a green felt pool table at the back of Big Dan's. [¶] Two other men, who

THE BOUNDARIES OF HER BODY 633

have also been arrested, went over to the pool table and forced themselves on the woman. One of them made her perform oral sex. [¶] A fourth man has been charged in the incident, but the two witnesses said he was involved. [¶] When the other two men became involved, the woman began to cry and scream, the witnesses said. [¶] She kept saying, 'What did I do to you guys? What did I do to you guys?'" said Virgilio Medeiros.)

40   *Id* at 89.

41   The author uses the phrase "traditional protections" because such protections are really a matter of kindness and social habit. In 1975, the United States Supreme Court held in *Cox Broadcasting Corp. v. Cohn*, 420 U.S. 469 (1975), that state law could not create civil remedies for invasion of privacy where the complaint alleges that a news agency had reported the name of a rape victim obtained from court records or during proceedings in open court. At issue before the Court was a Georgia statute prohibiting publication by the media of a rape victim's name and a television station that wanted to do so. *See also Florida Star v. B.J.F.*, 491 U.S. 524 (1989).

42   *See* Benedict, *supra* note 35, at p. 114. ("Once cable television declared it would use her name, news editors struggled over whether to follow suit. Most chose not to: The *[Boston] Globe*, the *Standard-Times*, the big out-of-town papers, television channels 10 and 12, and the *Associated Press* never used her name. *United Press International* took a middle ground and passed her name along to its clients but left it to them to make the decision and did not put it in its own stories. Three of the main newspapers and one of the television stations covering the case, however, did decide to use her name: the local *Fall River Herald News*, the *Portuguese Times*, the *Providence Journal* itself, and the local television channel 6, which also unsuccessfully challenged the judge's ban on photographs of the victim.")

43   For review of rape laws and cases involving the issue of "resistance" and the conduct of the victim, *see* Chapter Fourteen, *infra*.

44   *See* Tanenbaum, *supra* note 38, at p. 153 (citing Peggy Reeves Sanday, A WOMAN SCORNED: ACQUAINTANCE RAPE ON TRIAL (Berkeley: University of California Press, 1997), at pp. 212–215).

45   *Id*.

46   *See Star Jones*, LIFETIME INTIMATE PORTRAIT, LIFETIME TELEVISION, aired July 25, 2000, at 7:00 p.m., Eastern Standard Time. (Jones, a Brooklyn prosecutor, was beginning a stint as an unpaid part-time legal consultant for COURT-TV. The text of Jones's comments on the issue of the alleged victim's credibility were as follows: "…[T]hey are talking to me about [the alleged victim], the accuser in this case against William Kennedy Smith. One of the things that the [Smith's] defense hammered her on was why she couldn't remember where she took off her panty hose. Did she take them off in the car? Outside the car? In the front seat? In the back seat? Did he take them off? Did she take them off? Were they off on the beach? All of this about panty hose. And I remember the anchor asking me why is it so relevant. And I said, 'Well it had to do with credibility.'" Jones's comments are interrupted at this point for the comments of a friend, Vanessa Bell Calloway, who remarked: "The quality that Star has is that she is able to break it down in lay people's terms." Jones appears again on scene, continuing, "I said it has been my experience that women usually know where they take off their underwear. And when they don't, they usually have a credibility problem. And that's basically what the problem [in the case] was."

47   In the June 24, 2002, issue of US WEEKLY, models, singers, and actresses Pamela Anderson, Jordan, Britney Spears, Gillian Anderson, Trina McGee-Davis, Molly Sims, Kate Moss, and Sadie Frost were all photographed either intentionally or unknowingly flashing their thong underwear. *See, e.g.,* Michael Callahan, *Sandra Bullock Plays Survivor*, MARIE CLAIRE, May 2002, at pp. 80–82.

48   *See, e.g.*, Jill Abramson, *The Legal, Political and Personal Legacies of Whitewater*, N.Y. TIMES, March 24, 2002, WEEK IN REVIEW, SECT. 4, at p. 4. (In offering an overview of the Clinton-Lewinsky scandal, Abramson writes that in addition to some serious questions, "… there were also absurd aspects to Whitewater. There were 15-minutes-of-fame walk-ons for obscure government officials, like Carolyn Huber, a Clinton aide who had the ill fortune to find Mrs. Clinton's law firm billings, and Linda Tripp, a Pentagon employee, who became an enduring symbol of the double crossing friend. The word 'thong' entered the political lexicon.")

49   *See* Melba Newsome, *Asking For It*, MARIE CLAIRE, August 2001, at pp. 80–81.

50   *Id*. at 82.

51   *Id*.

52   *Id*.

53   *Id*. at pp. 83–84.

54   *See* Lori Litchman, NAT'L L.J., June 17, 2002, at A4. (The above quote actually involves a working backwards of the issues. Specifically, according to Litchman, "[t]he superior court panel [that made the ruling] consisted of judges Stephen A. McEwen, Justin M. Johnson and Michael T. Joyce. McEwen concurred in the result only, and Joyce filed a separate concurring and dissenting opinion. Although it was unsigned, Johnson therefore wrote the majority decision. [¶] Joyce disagreed with the majority's reasoning on the admission of abortion evidence, writing, 'If [the plaintiff] placed so little value on the fetus, then her level of emotional distress would not be the same as that of a woman who valued the fetus all through the pregnancy and never contemplated an abortion at any stage.'")

55 *Id.* (citing *Bynum v. Thomas Jefferson University*).

56 *See* Jonathan Ringel, *Court Lets Dead Woman's Past Stay Buried*, AMERICAN LAWYER MEDIA SERVICE, (reprinted in NAT'L L.J., January 28, 2002, at A6). (Flores' sex life reportedly included "…abortions before and after the boy's birth, plus two adoptions after the boy was born, and missed work due to pregnancy," Ringel wrote, reportedly citing information contained in the appellate decision.)

57 *Id.* (According to Georgia attorney, Robert P. Killian, who reported prepared and argued the appeal before a three-judge panel, "… in preparing for last year's oral argument, he could not find another case in the country that dealt directly with admissibility of sexual history evidence for a wrongful death trial," Ringel reported.)

58 To be fair, Williams seemed cognizant of the importance and social implications of the decision, according to Ringel, "My Lord, can you imagine? Every wrongful death case now, we're going to go into the sexual activity of every person who's in here. There ain't no way this court's going to open that one up," Williams is reported as having said. *See* Ringel, *supra* note 56, at A6.

59 *Id.*

60 *Id.*

61 As a nation whose traditions were build on a foundation of British common law, American courts have long suspected rape victims of false claims, Estrich explains. *See* Susan Estrich, REAL RAPE: HOW THE LEGAL SYSTEM VICTIMIZES WOMEN WHO SAY NO (Cambridge, Mass.: Harvard University Press, 1987), at p. 5. ("Juries have never been alone in refusing to blame the man who commits a 'simple rape.' Three centuries ago the English Lord Chief Justice Matthew Hale warned that rape is a charge 'easily to be made and hard to be proved, and harder to be defended by the party accused, tho' never so innocent" (*id.* citing Sir Matthew Hale, THE HISTORY OF THE PLEAS OF THE CROWN, I (London: Professional Books, 1971), LVIII: * 635). "If it is difficult for the man to establish his innocence, far better to demand that a woman victim prove hers; under Hale's approach, the one who so 'easily' charges rape must first prove her own lack of guilt. That has been the approach of the law. The usual procedure guarantees and the constitutional mandate that the government prove the man's guilt beyond a reasonable doubt have not been considered enough to protect the man accused of rape. The crime has been defined so as to require proof of actual physical resistance by the victim, as well as substantial force by the man. Evidentiary rules have been defined to require corroboration of the victim's account, to penalize women who do not complain promptly, and to ensure the relevance of a woman's prior history of unchastity.")

62 *Id.*

63 *Id.* (Estrich goes on to argue that "[t]he usual procedure guarantees and the constitutional mandate that the government prove the man's guilt beyond a reasonable doubt have not been considered enough to protect the man accused of rape. The crime has been defined so as to require proof of actual physical resistance by the victim, as well as substantial force by the man. Evidentiary rules have been defined to require corroboration of the victim's account, to penalize women who do not complain promptly, and to ensure the relevance of a woman's prior history of unchastity.")

64 The victim's character is often at issue in cases involving allegation or charges of sexual assault or rape. *See, e.g., U.S. v. Powers*, 59 F.3d 1460 (4th Cir. 1995), *cert. den.*, 516 U.S. 1077; *Stephens v. Miller*, 13 F.3d 998 (7th Cir. 1994), *cert. den.*, 513 U.S. 808; *Sandoval v. Acevedo*, 996 F.2d 145 (7th Cir. 1993), *cert. den.*, 510 U.S. 916; *Wood v. State of Alaska*, 957 F.2d 1544 (9th Cir. 1992), *U.S. v. Torres*, 937 F.2d 1469 (9th Cir. 1991), *cert. den.*, 502 U.S. 1037; *Carrigan v. Arvonio*, 871 F. Supp. 222 (N.J. Dist. 1994); *Shaw v. U.S.*, 812 F. Supp. 154 (S.D. Dist. 1993), *vac. [on remand]*, 24 F.3d 1040; 892 F. Supp. 1265, *aff'd*, 92 F.3d 1189; *U.S. v. Stamper*, 766 F. Supp. 1396 (N.C. W. Dist. 1991), *aff'd*, *In re One Female Juvenile Victim*, 959 F.2d 231; *Kelly v. State*, 602 So.2d 473 (Ala. Crim. App. 1992); *Mitchell v. State*, 593 So.2d 176 (Ala. Crim. App. 1991); *Harris v. State*, 907 S.W.2d 729 (Ark. 1995); *Cupples v. State*, 883 S.W.2d 458 (Ark. 1994); *Evans v. State*, 878 S.W.2d 750 (Ark. 1994); *Drymon v. State*, 875 S.W.2d 73 (Ark. 1994), *aff'd*, 938 S.W.2d 625; *Slater v. State*, 832 S.W.2d 846 (Ark. 1992); *Samples v. State*, 902 S.W.2d 257 (Ark. App. 1995); *People v. Franklin*, 30 Cal. Rptr. 2d 376 (Cal. App. 6th Dist. 1994); *People v. Murphy*, 919 P.2d 191 (Colo. 1996); *People v. Murphy*, 899 P.2d 294 (Colo. App. 1994); *cert. granted, aff'd in part, rev'd in part*, 919 P.2d 191 (Colo. App. 1994); *People v. Braley*, 879 P.2d 410 (Colo. App. 1993); *State v. Kulmac*, 644 A.2d 887 (Conn. 1994), *aff'd*, 707 A.2d 1290; *State v. Rinaldi*, 599 A.2d 1 (Conn. 1991); *State v. Manini*, 659 A.2d 196 (Conn. App. 1995), *cert. denied*, 661 A.2d 99; *Castro v. State*, 591 So.2d 1076 (Fla. App. 3rd Dist. 1991); *Martin v. State*, 464 S.E.2d 872 (Ga. App. 1995); *Bates v. State*, 454 S.E.2d 811 (Ga. App. 1995); *Logan v. State*, 442 S.E.2d 883 (Ga. App. 1994); *Postell v. State*, 407 S.E.2d 412 (Ga. App. 1991), *cert. granted*, 412 S.E.2d 831, *rev'd on remand*, 417 S.E.2d 222, *vac.*, 417 S.E.2d 222; *In Interest of Doe*, 918 P.2d 254 (Hawaii App. 1996); *People v. Mason*, 578 N.E.2d 1351 (Ill. App. 4 Dist. 1991); *Caley v. State*, 650 N.E.2d 51 (Ind. App. 5 Dist. 1995); *Stewart v. State*, 636 N.E.2d 143 (Ind. App. 1 Dist. 1994), *aff'd*, 652 N.E.2d 490; *Tyson v. State*, 619 N.E.2d 276 (Ind. App. 2 Dist. 1993), *transferred den.*, *[denial of post conviction relief]*, *aff'd in part, rev'd in part*, 626 N.E.2d 482, *cert. den.*, 510 U.S. 1176, *hab. den.*, 883 F. Supp. 1213, *den. aff'd*, 50 F.3d 436, *cert. on reh'g den.*, 516 U.S. 1041; *Kelly v. State*, 586 N.E.2d 927 (Ind. App. 5 Dist. 1992); *Thompson v. State*, 492 N.W.2d 410 (Iowa 1992); *State v. Lewis*, 847 P.2d 690 (Kan. 1993); *State v. Arrington*, 840 P.2d 477 (Kan. 1992); *State v. Lewis*, 877 P.2d 443 (Kan. App. 1993); *Billings v. Com.*, 843 S.W.2d 890 (Ky. 1992); *Gilbert v. Com.*, 838 S.W.2d 376

(Ky. 1991); *State v. Trosclair*, 584 So.2d 270 (La. App. 1st Cir. 1991); *State v. Billings*, 640 So.2d 500 (La. App. 3 Cir. 1994), *writ den.*, 644 So.2d 631; *State v. Sargeant*, 656 A.2d 1196 (Me. 1995); *State v. Hoffstadt*, 652 A.2d 93 (Me. 1995); *Shand v. State*, 672 A.2d 630 (Md. 1996); *White v. State*, 598 A.2d 187 (Md. 1991); *Shand v. State*, 653 A.2d 1000 (Md. App. 1995), *cert. granted, Allen v. State, cert. granted*, 661 A.2d 733, *cert. granted, Bailey v. State*, 661 A.2d 733, *aff'd*, 672 A.2d 630; *Miles v. State*, 594 A.2d 634 (Md. App. 1991), *cert. den.*, 599 A.2d 477, *cert. den.*, 599 A.2d 447; *Commonwealth v. Hynes*, 664 N.E.2d 864 (Mass. App. Ct. 1996); *Commonwealth v. McGregor*, 655 N.E.2d 1278 (Mass. App. Ct. 1995); *Commonwealth v. Herrick*, 655 N.E.2d 637 (Mass. App. Ct. 1995); *Commonwealth v. Syrafos*, 646 N.E.2d 429 (Mass. App. Ct. 1995), *rev. den.*, 648 N.E.2d 1285; *Commonwealth v. Thevenin*, 603 N.E.2d 222 (Mass. App. Ct. 1992); *Commonwealth v. Fionda*, 599 N.E.2d 635 (Mass. App. Ct. 1992); *Commonwealth v. Gauthier*, 586 N.E.2d 34 (Mass. App. Ct. 1992), *rev. den.*, 597 N.E.2d 1371; *People v. Mooney*, 549 N.W.2d 65 (Mich. App. 1996); *People v. Powell*, 506 N.W.2d 894 (Mich. App. 1993); *People v. Lucas*, 484 N.W.2d 685 (Mich. App. 1992), *app. after rem.*, 507 N.W.2d 685, *app. den.*, 521 N.W.2d 606, *cert. den.*, *Lucas v. Michigan*, 513 U.S. 1023; *People v. Wilhelm*, 476 N.W.2d 753 (Mich. App. 1991); *State v. Enger*, 539 N.W.2d 259 (Minn. App. 1995); *Amacker v. State*, 676 So.2d 909 (Miss. 1996); *State v. Sloan*, 912 S.W.2d 592 (Mo. App. 1995); *State v. Danback*, 886 S.W.2d 204 (Mo. App. E.D. 1994); *State v. Weeks*, 891 P.2d 477 (Mont. 1995); *State v. Steffes*, 887 P.2d 1196 (Mont. 1994); *State v. Stuit*, 885 P.2d 1290 (Mont.1994); *State v. Ramos*, 858 P.2d 94 (N.M. App. 1993); *People v. Becraft*, N.Y.S.2d 437 (A.D. 4 Dept. 1993); *State v. Boggs*, 588 N.E.2d 813 (Ohio 1992); *State v. Jones*, 615 N.E.2d 713 (Ohio App. 2 Dist. 1992), *dis., jur. mot. over'd*, 613 N.E.2d 645; *Commonwealth v. Spiewak*, 617 A.2d 696 (Pa. 1992); *Commonwealth v. Widmer*, 667 A.2d 215 (Pa. Super. 1995), *rearg. den.*, *app. granted*, 680 A.2d 1161; *Commonwealth v. Berkowitz*, 609 A.2d 1338 (Pa. Super. 1992), *app. granted*, 613 A.2d 556, *aff'd in part, vac. in part*, 641 A.2d 1161; *Commonwealth v. Smith*, 599 A.2d 1340 (Pa. Super. 1991), *app. after rem.*, *Smith v. Penn. Bd. of Probation & Parole*, 636 A.2d 291; *Commonwealth v. Boyles*, 595 A.2d 1180 (Pa. Super. 1991), *app. dism'd*, 613 A.2d 556 (1992); *State v. DeNoyer*, 541 N.W.2d 725 (S.D. 1995); *Wofford v. State*, 903 S.W.2d 796 (Tex. App. Dallas 1995); *Neeley v. Commonwealth*, 437 S.E.2d 721 (Va. App. 1993); *Evans v. Commonwealth*, 415 S.E.2d 851 (Va. App. 1992).

65 *See* Newsome, *supra* note 49, at p. 82.
66 *See supra* note 64.
67 *See* Leslie Kaufman & Cathy Horyn, *More of Less: Scantier Clothing Catches On*, N.Y. TIMES, June 27, 2000, at A29. ("There has been a decided shift to a sexy, glamorous, almost trashy interpretation of fashion," Connie Marsh, a design manager for Sears, Roebuck & Co., told fashion writers Leslie Kaufman and Cathy Horyn in the summer of 2000. Indeed, according to Kaufman & Horyn, "[t]he appetite for styles that hug the figure or reveal much of it is causing a shift in the retail world. American Eagle Outfitters and Abercrombie & Fitch, whose baggy silhouettes made them the cool shops for teenagers of the mid-1990s, have suffered a slowdown. But comebacks are being reported at Guess, which grew to prominence in the 1980s showcasing the curvaceous bodies of Anna Nicole Smith and Claudia Schiffer in revealing tops and skintight jeans, and at the Limited, with its streetwise style.")
68 *See, e.g.* Ginia Bellafante, *Sell That Dress: Back to Basics in Spring Advertising*, N.Y. TIMES, Feb. 5, 2002, at A24. ("Last fall, the advertising campaign [American designer] Tom Ford created for Gucci revolved around a blond[e] model who seemed to need an anger-management seminar," noted fashion writer Ginia Bellafante. "In one image she was seated on wall-to-wall carpeting in an unfurnished room, her hand aggressively on her jutting hip. She wore nothing that had not begun its life in a cow pen: black leather boots, a black leather miniskirt, a black leather blazer buttoned just at the rib cage to reveal a chest no one would mistake for Sophia Loren's.")
69 *See* Kaufman & Horyn, *supra* note 67, at A29.
70 *See, e.g.*, Wendy Shalit, A RETURN TO MODESTY (New York: The Free Press, 1999), at p. 60. (According to Shalit, "[w]hen modesty was given a sanction, woman not only had the right to say no to a man's advances, but her good opinion of him was revered. Today, on the other hand, when our popular culture tells us that women should lust equally to men and feel comfortable about putting their bodies on display in coed bathrooms, on coed beaches—coed everything—women seem to be reporting that they feel only more at the mercy of male desire. The anorexic disfigures her body to become unwomanly because if she no longer has the right to say 'no,' at least she has the body language at her disposal. [¶] So natural modesty has a way of reasserting itself, even in desperate and neurotic fashion.")
71 *Id.* at 72.
72 *Id.* at 73–74. (In discussing a 1988 study on adultery by Dr. Annette Lawson and the seemingly cavalier attitude of Helen Gurley Brown's infamous suggestion that women keep "a married man or two" *as pets*, Shalit cautions that "[i]f women want men to stop behaving badly, to be faithful and devoted to us, we are going to have to leave off *How to Seduce a Married Man*. When men are unfaithful, they are unfaithful, usually, with other women. That is why, as Laura Gowing points out, women were responsible for maintaining some degree of opprobrium against adultery: they did so not because they were evil or deluded or wanted to oppress other women, but simply to preserve the sanctity of their own marriages.")

73　*See* Newsome, *supra* note 49, at p. 82.

74　*Id.* at 84.

75　*Id.*

76　For further tongue-in-cheek discussion of this issue, *see* Jenny Lyn Bader, *The Miniskirt as a National Security Threat,* N.Y. TIMES, Sept. 10, 2000, at wk 3.

77　*See* Tanenbaum, *supra* note 38, at p. 153. (citing Reeves, *supra* note 44, at pp. 212–215.)

78　*Id.*

79　*See* Benedict, *supra* note 39, at p. 102 (citing reports in the BOSTON HERALD: "The eyewitnesses said they saw the woman with one of the defendants at another end of the bar, hugging and kissing. [¶] The defendant suddenly grabbed the woman and pushed her to the floor, removing her pants and unbuckling his own. She did not appear to be resisting, the witnesses said, as the suspect got on top of her. [¶] The defendant was too intoxicated to have intercourse, they said, but picked up the woman and carried her to a green felt pool table at the back of Big Dan's. [¶] Two other men, who have also been arrested, went over to the pool table and forced themselves on the woman. One of them made her perform oral sex. [¶] A fourth man has been charged in the incident, but the two witnesses said he was involved. [¶] When the other two men became involved, the woman began to cry and scream, the witnesses said. [¶] She kept saying, 'What did I do to you guys? What did I do to you guys?'" said Virgilio Medeiros.)

80　*Id.* at 130–140.

81　*Id.* ("Carol Agus of *Newsday* did one of the best stories on [the victim's] life and death," writes Benedict. "She went to the trailer park where [the victim] had moved, deep in the Florida countryside, interviewed her friends and neighbors, and talked to a Californian librarian, Bernadine Abbot, who had bought rights to [the victim's] story. Agus's biography revealed how terrible the persecution of [the victim] had been—the story that the press had missed so glaringly." During the case no reporter mentioned [the victim's] son or that she'd had to leave him behind; another tragic consequence of her persecution. She had left him, Agus discovered, because she did not want to take him out of school. He lived with his grandparents.)

82　*See* Tanenbaum, *supra* note 38, at p. 152.

83　*See* Benedict, *supra* note 39, at pp. 130–140.

84　*See* Michael Sneed, *Doc Talk.,* CHI. SUN-TIMES, July 14, 2002, at p. 4.

85　*See, e.g., State v. Globe Communications Corp.,* 622 So.2d 1066 (Fla. App. 4 Dist. 1993) (holding that the state was overly broad and, thus, in violation of the First Amendment of the United States Constitution), *aff'd,* 648 So.2d 110 (Fla. App. 1993).

86　*See, e.g.,* Tanenbaum, *supra* note 38.

87　Aspiring model Marla Hanson's face was slashed in 1986 in a case that shook the nation. Hanson never regained her professional footing as a model.

88　*See Slashing Victim Testifies Against Murder Suspect,* N.Y. TIMES, June 30, 2000, at A23. The testimony emerged during the trial of a man alleged to have murdered another former girlfriend. The former girl, who was found in her Columbia University apartment, had her throat slashed. On July 27, 2000, the defendant was convicted. *See Ex-Boyfriend Guilty in Killing,* N.Y. TIMES, July 28, 2000, at A21.

89　Though often statutorily defined, the courts appear to have taken a broad view of what may classify as a weapon. In *Johnson v. U.S.,* 613 A.2d 888 (D.C. 1992), for example, the court determined that a hot iron could classify as a weapon.

90　*See* Craven, *supra* note 34, ENDNOTES FOR INTRODUCTION, at p. 2.

91　*Id.* at p. 1.

92　*See* Eve Ensler, *Women Fighting Against Genital Mutilation,* MARIE CLAIRE, Oct. 2000, at p. 61. For further background on the issue, see also *A Statement on Genital Mutilation,* by the Association of African Women for Research and Development, in Miranda Davies, ed., THIRD WORLD, SECOND SEX (London: Zed Books Ltd., 1983), at pp. 217–218.

93　*See* Sheryl McCarthy, *No Activism, No Asylum,* Ms., October/November 1999, at p. 21.

94　The process of female genital mutilation generally involves the slicing away of all or part of the clitoris and/or labia. By some reports, this is done with anything from unsterilized tools, kitchen knives, or even broken glass. In some cases, there is also the stitching up of the mutilated skin or the labia to prevent intercourse.

95　Abankwah's story was told in several places initially. *See, e.g.,* ALL THINGS CONSIDERED, National Public Radio, August 19, 1999 (Margot Adler reporting), at pp. 7–9 (transcript), (available through Burrelle's); McCarthy, *supra* note 93, at pp. 21–22.

96　Entering the country "illegally" is a criminal offense. While authorities heard Abankwah's case for political asylum, the young Ghana citizen sat in jail.

97　*See* ALL THINGS CONSIDERED, *supra* note 95, at pp. 4–6 (transcript) (reporting in part on an investigation by the WASH. POST).

98　*Id.* at 5.

99　*Id.* at 5–6. (In September 2002, Danson was arrested for allegedly lying under oath. *See* William Glaberson, *Woman Who Sought U.S. Asylum is Arrested,* N.Y. TIMES, Sept. 10, 2002.)

100　*See* Silvana Paternostro, *Please Make Me a Virgin Again,* MARIE CLAIRE, August 2000, at pp. 102–104.

101   See Elizabeth Hoyt, *Addicted to Plastic Surgery*, HARPER'S BAZAAR, Feb. 2002, at p. 76.

102   See Paternostro, *supra* note 100, at pp. 102–104.

103   See *Husband Charged with Woman's Burning Death*, CHI. SUN-TIMES, August 28, 2000, at p. 10.

104   See *Woman Beaten by Husband Accuses Court of Leniency*, N.Y. TIMES, August 26, 2000, at A11.

105   A possible exception to this trend began to appear, however, in late 2001 and early 2002, when the number of gang-related deaths, which had fallen in recent years in response to gang-negotiated truces and treaties, began to spike. The reasons for this, according to media reports, was a possible breakdown in these agreements. *See, e.g.,* Greg Winter, *Los Angeles Street Wars Grow Deadlier*, N.Y. TIMES, April 11, 2002, at A18.

106   See C. J. Chivers, *Woman is Attacked on Street by Man with Piece of Concrete*, N.Y. TIMES, July 10, 2000, at A21; *Wrong Man was Arrested in Attack, Prosecutors Say*, N.Y. TIMES, July 27, 2000, at A21.)

107   See C.J. Chivers & John W. Fountain, *Hunt Pressed for Attacker as Victim Leaves Hospital*, N.Y. TIMES, July 11, 2000, at A25.

108   An assailant in the November 16, 1999, assault was eventually arrested and tried. *See* Katherine E. Finkelstein, *As Trial Opens, Victim of a Brick Attack Tells of Her Ordeal*, N.Y. TIMES, November 14, 2000; Katherine Finkelstein, *Man Gets 25-Year Prison Sentence in Manhattan Brick Attack*, N.Y. TIMES, Dec. 14, 2000, at C17.

109   Though most lawyers know what an order for "summary judgment" means, this book is intended to non-lawyers as well as practitioners. Thus, BLACK'S LAW DICTIONARY defines "summary judgment" as a "[p]rocedural device available for prompt and expeditious disposition of controversy without trial when there is no dispute as to either material fact or inferences to be drawn from undisputed facts, or if only [a] question of law is involved. Federal Rule of Civil Procedure 56 permits ant party to a civil action to move for a summary judgment on a claim, counterclaim, or cross-claim when he (or she) believes that there is no genuine issue of material fact and that he is entitled to prevail as a matter of law. The motion may be directed toward all or part of a claim or defense and it may be made on the basis of the pleadings or other portions of the record in the case or it may be supported by affidavits and a variety of outside material." *See* BLACK'S LAW DICTIONARY, *supra* note 102, ENDNOTES FOR CHAPTER FIVE, at p. 1001.

110   See *Mason v. U.E.S.S. Leasing Corp.*, N.Y. Court of Appeals, October 25, 2000, No. 619. (According to the facts set forth in the case, "[s]hortly after seven o'clock in the morning of July 11, 1992, plaintiff was awakened by a phone call from her live-in boyfriend, who was in a store across the street and wanted to know if she needed anything from the store. According to plaintiff, he told her he would be upstairs in five minutes. Plaintiff then lay down again to wait for her boyfriend. Shortly thereafter, the doorbell to the apartment rang and, thinking it was her boyfriend, she opened the door without looking through the peephole in the door or asking who it was. At the door was the six foot four inch, 260 pound third-party defendant Lawrence Toole, who appeared to be 'on something' and who grabbed plaintiff by the neck, dragged her into the bedroom and raped and sodomized her." *Mason*, at p. 2. Attorneys for the management company that owned the building argue that its client had taken sufficient basic security precautions and that the intervening criminal act of a third party was so unforeseeable as to have severed any reasonable link between the duty of the building's owners and the plaintiff's injury. Based upon that argument, a lower court granted summary judgment in favor of the building's owners. In reversing that decision, however, and allowing the matter to proceed to trial, the New York Appellate Court held that "[g]iven the circumstances of this case, it cannot be said, as a matter of law, that plaintiff's opening of her apartment door, without looking through the peephole or inquiring who was at the door, was an independent intervening act which did not flow from defendants' alleged negligence in permitting a known troublemaker to enter the premises and gain access to plaintiff's apartment, thus relieving defendants of any liability." *Mason*, at 4.) For further reading on the case, *see* Cerisse Anderson, *Opened Door Raised Triable Issue of Fact*, N.Y. L.J., Oct. 25, 2000.

111   Indeed, in reversing the lower court, the New York Court of Appeals reasoned that "[d]espite the fact that the landlord had a security guard stationed in the common lobby and that the buildings of the Lefrak City complex had a working intercom system and locked inner and outer doors, a question of fact is presented as to whether or not defendants negligently permitted plaintiff's attacked into her building, 97-30-57th Avenue, where, according to plaintiff, the attacker, a non-resident who had grown up in Lefrak City, was widely known as a troublemaker to both security personnel and the complex's residents, including plaintiff. It is of no moment to the attacker's status as an intruder that his mother may have lived in a related but separate and distinct building, 97-22-57th Avenue. Furthermore, according to defendant security service, his photograph was also contained in its 'photo book & quot.,' containing pictures of persons arrested in the premises [single quotation remark in original]." *Mason*, at p. 3.

112   In 1994, for example, women survived 941,100 reported aggravated assaults and 3,176,900 simple assaults. *See* Craven, *supra* note 90, at p. 2. (Generally, Justice Department researchers define "simple assault" as an attack "without a weapon, resulting either in no injury, minor injury (for example, bruises, black eyes, cuts, scratches or swelling) or in undetermined injury requiring less than 2 days hospitalization. Also includes attempted assault without a weapon.") *See, e.g.,* Patsy Klaus and Cathy Maston, *Criminal Victimization in the United States, 1995*, U.S. DEP'T OF JUSTICE, OFFICE OF

JUSTICE PROGRAMS, BUREAU OF JUSTICE STATISTICS, at p. 41. A definition for "aggravated assault" is not expressly included. However, it seems fair to assume, given the definition for "simple assault above" that "aggravated assault" would be an attack involving a weapon, resulting in serious injury.

113   "Experienced" is the word used by Justice Department officials in their report. It is not the choice of the author. The author notes that the Department of Justice defines "women" as females as young as 12.

114   See Craven, supra note 90, at pp. 1–2. (By comparison, men experienced "almost 6.6 million violent victimizations," Craven writes. But women were more likely in 1994—and are more likely today—to be victimized by men they knew, or know, than strangers. Writes Craven, "for every 5 violent victimizations of a female by an intimate, there was 1 of a male." Men, by contrast, are more often victimized by strangers, according to Justice Department research. "Victimizations" as a category include murders, rapes, sexual assaults, robberies, aggravated assaults, and simple assaults. According to Craven, "[w]omen age 12 or older experienced 5 million violent victimizations: about 432,000 rapes and sexual assaults, 472,000 robberies, over 940,000 aggravated assaults, and over 3 million simple assaults. In addition, 4,489 females age 12 or older were victims of homicide." Id. at 3.)

115   See Warren E. Leary, Violent Crime Continues to Decline, Survey Finds, N.Y. TIMES, Aug. 28, 2000, at A10.

116   See Craven, supra note 90, at p. 3.

117   Id at 2. (By contrast, "[m]ales were most likely to be victimized in public places such as businesses, parking lots, and open areas," Craven writes.)

118   See Summary Findings, VIOLENT CRIME CHARACTERISTICS, U.S. DEP'T OF JUSTICE, BUREAU OF JUSTICE STATISTICS, Last Revised June 23, 2000, at p. 1. (Specifically, "[a]bout six out of ten robberies were committed by strangers compared to one out of four of all rapes/sexual assaults.")

119   See Tjaden & Thoennes, supra note 37, ENDNOTES FOR INTRODUCTION, at p. 3. (According to the Tjaden/Thoennes's study of 16,000 participants (8,000 women and men each), an estimated 76 percent "of women who were raped and/or physically assaulted since age 18 were assaulted by a current or former husband, cohabitating partner, or date, compared to 18 percent of men." Id. at 2.)

120   Id.

121   Id.

122   See Callie Marie Rennison & Sarah Welchans, Intimate Partner Violence, U.S. DEP'T OF JUSTICE, BUREAU OF JUSTICE STATISTICS, May 2000, at p. 2.

123   Id. at 3. (Authors of the study note that women suffered intimate partner violence 767 times versus 146 times per every 100,000 people for men in the year of the survey.)

124   Indeed, there was a literal gauntlet to be run by women in New York City's Central Park during the annual Puerto Rican Day Parade in June 2000. See, e.g., David Barstow and C.J. Chivers, Elements of Trouble Gelled in Rampage in Central Park, N.Y. TIMES, June 17, 2000, at A1 (detailing a slew of assaults upon women during the 2000 National Puerto Rican Day Parade in New York's Central Park.)

125   See Craven, supra note 90, at p. 5. (According to Craven, "[t]he patterns of victimization associated with where the victim lived ran from the highest risk in urban areas to the lowest risk in rural areas (Location is where the victim lived, not where he or she sustained the violence. Previous research has indicated that most victimizations occur in the vicinity of the victim's residence. See Crime Victimization in City, Suburban, and Rural Areas, BJS, NCJ-135943, June 1992.) Taking the victim's sex into account does not change this pattern.")

126   See Tjaden and Thoennes, supra note 119, at p. 4. (By contrast, an estimated "371,000 men are stalked annually in the United States.")

127   For purposes of the above report, "physical assault" was defined as "a range of behaviors, from slapping and hitting to using a gun." See Id.

128   For purposes of the above report, "rape" was defined as "forced vaginal, oral, or anal intercourse." See Id. at 2. See Tjaden and Thoennes, supra note 119, at p. 3. (By contrast, an estimated 834,700 men are raped and/or physically assaulted by an intimate partner each year in the United States. See Id.)

129   Id. at 6. ("Specifically, women who were raped in the previous 12 months averaged 2.9 rapes, while men averaged 1.2 rapes. According to surveys estimates, approximately 876,100 rapes were perpetrated against women and approximately 111,300 rapes were perpetrated against men in the United States during the 12 months preceding the survey.")

130   See. e.g., Kilpatrick & Saunders, supra note 32, ENDNOTES FOR INTRODUCTION, at pp. 479–489; H. Resnick, D. Kilpatrick et al., Prevalence of Civilian Trauma and Post-traumatic Stress Syndrome in a Representative National Sample of Women, 61 J. CON. & CLIN. PSYCHOL. 984 (1993). (The authors of the above articles suggest that women who suffer rape often suffer symptoms of post-traumatic stress syndrome.) Similar findings were also reported among prostitutes, reportedly due to the "exposure to physical danger." See Abigail Zuger, Many Prostitutes Suffer Combat Disorder, Study Finds, N.Y. TIMES, Aug. 18, 1998 ("The world's oldest profession may also be among its most traumatizing. A new study has found that a serious psychiatric illness resulting from exposure to physical danger is more common among prostitutes than among troops who have weathered combat duty.")

131   The word used by the authors but substituted by the author of this book was "males."

132   *See* Craven, *supra* note 90, at p. 1.

133   *Id.* (According to Craven, "[o]ffenders were armed in 34 percent of victimizations of males (2,047,502) and in 24 percent of victimizations of females (1,128,100)." But "[m]ost violent victimizations did not involved the use of weapons," Craven explains.)

134   *See, e.g.,* Vivian Berger, *Battered Women Hit Twice,* NAT'L L.J., Sept. 4, 2000, at A17. (Berger, a professor of law at Columbia University, argues in discussing the case of Kathy Chapman Clark, a Georgia woman who admitted to killing her abusive husband, that "[t]he view that women who strike back at their tormentors 'get away with murder' is a common misconception. In fact, the legal system bears down harshly on these defendants—often perpetuating their oppression." The man's son apparently felt that Clark had gotten away with murder. In fact, according to Berger, "[m]en constitute a much greater danger to their intimate partners than do women. More than half of female homicides were committed by husbands or boyfriends, according to a 1991 study, while a mere 14 percent of male homicides occurred at the hands of wives or girlfriends. Although most battered women who kill plead self-defense (and a few, insanity), an outright acquittal like Ms. Clark's is rare. Convicted of either murder or manslaughter, these women receive average sentences of 15–20 years. [¶] Such results reflect a tendency to blame the defendant on the basis of myth or misinformation.")

135   *See, e.g.,* Jane Mayer, *The Lover in Jail: In Texas, The Independent Counsel Got the Girl,* THE NEW YORKER, November 30, 1998; Helen Thorpe, *Home Leave: Questions for Henry Cisneros,* N.Y. TIMES MAG., August 27, 2000, at p. 21.

136   Judges and juries across the country continue to grapple with what the requirement of a clear lack of consent means. *See, e.g., U.S. v. Norrquay,* 987 F.2d 475 (8th Cir. 1993), *app. after rem.; U.S. v. Schoenborn,* 19 F.3d 1438, *cert. den.,* 115 S. Ct. 284 (holding that a defendant's need to employ force generally will indicate a lack of consent); *State v. Jackson,* 620 A.2d 168 (Conn. 1993) (holding that the victim of a potential rape need not resist to the point of physical injury in order to establish that she did not consent to the acts); *State v. Mezriouri,* 602 A.2d 29 (Conn. App. 1992) (holding that a woman need not say no or physically resist); *State v. Sedia,* 614 So.2d 533 (Fla. App. 4th Dist. 1993) (holding that a where a physical therapy patient had no opportunity to communicate her unwillingness to have sex, she was "physically helpless to resist" the encounter within the meaning of Florida sexual abuse law); *State v. Simmons,* 621 So.2d 1135 (La. App. 4th Cir. 1993), *amended on reh'ring* (holding that as defined by law, the act of forcible rape occurs upon a victim without consent; upon a victim who was prevented from resisting by force or threat of physical violence; and who reasonably believed that resistance would not prevent rape); *State v. Gallen,* 613 So.2d 1145 (La. App. 5th Cir. 1993) (defining that the difference between aggravated and forcible rape is the degree of force used by the defendant and the amount of resistance attempted by the victim); *Commonwealth v. Price,* 616 A.2d 681 (Pa. Super. 1992) (clarifying that the subsection of the Pennsylvania criminal statutes proscribing intercourse with "unconscious" people was intended to protect persons not able to give or refuse consent to intercourse due to their unconscious state); *Commonwealth v. Berkowitz,* 641 A.2d 1161 (Pa. 1994) (holding that where there is a lack of consent, but no showing of either a threat or physical force, "forcible compulsion" requirement of the rape statute was not met); *State v. Jackson,* 679 A.2d 572 (N.H. 1996) (holding that "consent" issue involves objective manifestation of unwillingness). *See also Portuondo v. Agard,* 529 U.S. 61 (2000), *reversing and remanding* 117 F.3d 696 (1998) (involving a defendant's claim of consensual sex where he was charged with "19 sodomy and assault counts and 3 weapons counts" and where two victims testified that they were "physically assaulted, raped, and orally and anally sodomized" at gun point.)

137   *See, e.g., State v. Thompson,* 861 P.2d 492 (Wash. App. Div. 2 1993); *Commonwealth v. Odell,* 607 N.E.2d 423 (Mass. App. Ct. 1993), *rev. den.,* 617 N.E.2d 639.

138   For beginning overview of the issue, *see, e.g.,* Benedict, *supra* note 39, at pp. 13–24. (In the introduction to this chapter, Benedict notes that "[i]n spite of the attempts by feminists and psychologists to explain away rape myths over the last two decades, studies have found that those myths are still alive and well. In his 1982 book, MEN ON RAPE, Timothy Beneke interviewed a large sample of men and found that many not only blamed female victims for having been raped, but admitted to being tempted to commit rape themselves. Other studies conducted in 1987 found that victims are still widely blamed for inviting rape, while perpetrators are seen as lustful men driven beyond endurance. In 1991, *New York Times* featured an article about rape victims who blame themselves. A telephone survey of 500 American adults taken for *Time* magazine in May 1991, found that 53 percent of adults age fifty and 31 percent of adults between thirty-five and forty believe that a woman is to be blamed for her rape if she dressed provocatively. And at the end of 1991, *Newsweek* pointed out that the public's disinclination to believe either Anita Hill during the Justice Clarence Thomas hearings on sexual harassment or [the woman], who said she was raped by William Kennedy Smith, 'show the lengths skeptics will go to deny the possibility of sexual offense.' Because rape myths continue to hold such sway, and because they lie at the root of my discussion in this book, they must be explained again.")

139   *See, e.g.,* Cam Simpson, *Man Pleads Guilty in "Date-Rape Drug" Case,* CHI. SUN-TIMES, July 14, 2000, at p. 21. *See also People v. Mack,* 15 Cal. Rptr. 2d 193 (Cal. App. 3 Dist. 1992) (holding that

where resistance is thwarted by administration of "intoxicating or anesthetic substance" by the accused via force or trick, rape conviction may still occur); *People v. Cortez*, 35 Cal. Rptr. 2d 500 (Cal. App. 5 Dist. 1994); *Stadler v. State*, 919 P.2d 439 (Okla. Crim. App. 1996), *cert. den.*, 117 S. Ct. 369.

140   *See* Randy Thornhill & Craig T. Palmer, A NATURAL HISTORY OF RAPE: BIOLOGICAL BASES OF SEXUAL COERCION (Boston: M.I.T. Press, 2000), at p. 55; R.D. Alexander, DARWINISM AND HUMAN AFFAIRS (Seattle: University of Washington, 1979); R.D. Alexander, THE BIOLOGY OF MORAL SYSTEMS (Hawthorne, N.Y.: Aldine de Gruyter, 1987); J.M. Bailey, S. Gaulin, Y. Agyei & B.A. Gladue, *Effects of Gender and Sexual Orientation on Evolutionary Relevant Aspects of Human Mating*, 66 J. PERS. SOC. PSYCHOL. at pp. 1081–1093 (1994); R.G. Bringle, *Sexual Jealousy in the Relationships of Homosexual and Heterosexual Men: 1980 and 1992*, 2 PERS. RELATIONSHIPS at pp. 313–325 (1995); H. Claypool & V. Sheets, *Jealousy: Adaptive or Destructive?* (paper presented at the annual meeting of the Human Behavior and Evolutionary Society, Evanston, Ill., June 1996) (cited in David M. Buss, THE DANGEROUS PASSION: WHAT JEALOUSY IS AS NECESSARY AS LOVE AND SEX (New York: The Free Press, 2000), at p. 241.)

141   *See* UNDERSTANDING VIOLENCE AGAINST WOMEN (Washington, D.C.: National Academy Press, 1996) (Nancy A. Crowell & Ann W. Burgess, eds.), at p. 49.

142   *See* William Shakespeare, HAMLET, Act III, Scene 1, line 103–140.

143   *See, e.g.,* Robert M. Youngson, THE MADNESS OF PRINCE HAMLET AND OTHER EXTRAORDINARY MINDS (New York: Carroll & Graf Publishers, Inc., 1999), at p. 1.

144   *See* Shakespeare, *supra* note 142, at Act IV, Scene 5.

145   *See* Fyodor Dostoyevsky, CRIME AND PUNISHMENT (Penguin Books (first published, 1951) reprinted 1982), at p. 291. ("'The old hag is all rubbish!' [Raskolnikov] thought heatedly and impetuously. 'The old woman is most probably a mistake. She doesn't matter! The old woman was only an illness—I was in a great hurry to step over—I didn't kill a human being—I killed a principle! Yes, I killed a principle all right, but I did not stop over—I remained on this side. All I could do was to kill! And it seems I couldn't even do that! A principle? Why was that innocent fool Razumikhin abusing the socialists? They're an industrious people—practical men, engaged in the business of bringing about 'the happiness of all'. No, I live only once, and I shan't ever live again: I don't want to wait for 'the happiness of all'. I want to live, or else I might as well be dead. Well? After all, I merely did not want to pass by my starving mother, holding on to my ruble in my pocket in expectation of 'happiness for all'. 'Carrying a little brick for the happiness of all mankind, and that's why my heart's at peace!' Ha, ha! Why have you overlooked me? I only live once; I, too, want—Oh, I'm an aesthetic louse and nothing more!' he added suddenly, laughing like a madman....")

146   *Id.* at 96.

147   *See* D.H. Lawrence, SONS AND LOVERS (New York: Penguin Book, 1978 (first printing Great Britain: Duckworth & Sons, 1913)), at p. 39. ("He was trying to fit in the drawer. At her last speech he turned round. His face was crimson, his eyes bloodshot. He stared at her one silent second of a threat. [¶] 'P-h!' she went quickly, in contempt. [¶] He jerked at the drawer in his excitement. It fell, cut sharply on his shin, and on the reflex he flung it at her. [¶] One of the corners caught her brow as the shallow drawer crashed into the fireplace. She swayed, almost fell stunned from the chair. To her very soul she was sick; she clasped the child tightly to her bosom. A few moments elapsed; then, with an effort, she brought herself to. The baby was crying plaintively. Her left brow was bleeding rather profusely. As she glanced down at the child, her brain reeling, some drops of blood soaked into its white shawl; but the baby was at least not hurt. She balanced her head to keep equilibrium, so that the blood ran into her eyes.")

148   *See* William Shakespeare, THE TAMING OF THE SHREW, Act IV, Scene 2, lines 172–194.

149   *Id.* at Act 3, Scene 3. (Lucentio asks Kate's sister, Bianca, what she thinks of her sister's marriage:
Lucentio:Mistress, what's your opinion of your sister?
Bianca:That, being mad herself, she's madly matched.

150   *See* William Shakespeare, OTHELLO, Act V, Scene 2, line 64–88.

151   In killing his wife, Othello proved worthy of having a syndrome named after his character, argues University of Texas Professor of Psychology David Buss. *See, e.g.,* DAVID M. BUSS, THE DANGEROUS PASSION: WHY JEALOUSY IS AS NECESSARY AS LOVE AND SEX (New York: The Free Press, 2000), at p. 6.

152   *See* Dr. Robert D. Hare, WITHOUT CONSCIENCE: THE DISTURBING WORLD OF THE PSYCHOPATH AMONG US (New York: Pocket Books, 1993), at p. 100.

153   *See* E.R. Chamberlin, THE BAD POPES (New York: Dorset Press, 1969), at p. 71; Wills, *supra* note 46, ENDNOTES FOR CHAPTER ONE.

154   *See* Niels M. Saxtorph, WARRIORS AND WEAPONS OF EARLY TIMES (New York: Macmillan Co., 1972), at p. 175. (According to Saxtorph, "[i]n the centuries before the Birth of Christ there existed a mysterious people, the Gauls, whom we come across on their migrations in many different places. They may have been the descendants of the Scythians at any rate, many details in their metalworks suggest this. About 400 B.C. we find them in Italy, where the Romans fought many battles with them— they attacked and plundered Rome in 387 B.C., for example. Some 100 years later they are in Greece and soon after that in Asia Minor. They are described as very brave warriors and are depicted as tall, handsome men.")

155   *Id.* at 164.

156 *Id.* at 175.
157 *See* THE ILLUSTRATED WORLD HISTORY (New York: McGraw-Hill Book Co., 1964, Esmond Wright & Kenneth M. Stampp, eds.), at p. 84.
158 Scholars have long reported the antics of the men serving as Pontiff throughout history. *See* Chamberlin, *supra* note 153; Wills, *supra* note 153, at p. 155.
159 For further reading, *see, e.g.,* Chamberlin, *supra* note 153; Wills, *supra* note 153.
160 *See* WORLD HISTORY, *supra* note 157, at p. 87. ("During the late sixth and seventh centuries, when the Lombardic invasions were at their most destructive, the papacy began to assume the moral and political leadership of the West, and in this the role of Gregory the Great (r. 590–604) was decisive. By building up Church lands and by the judicious use of the papal patrimony, he was able to organize poor relief and other charitable works on a large scale and with considerable success. Beyond all this was his constant care for the Church. He communicated frequently with his bishops all over Christendom, he reformed sees, established liturgical and canonical practices, and left numerous writings full of practical wisdom. His missionary activity was no less sustained and far-reaching. It was Gregory who in 597 sent the hesitant Augustine to Christianize the pagan English, while at the same time he labored to convert the Arian Visigoths of Spain and even the Lombards who were then pillaging Rome itself.")
161 For reading, *see* Chamberlin, *supra* note 153; Wills, *supra* note 153.
162 *See* WORLD HISTORY, *supra* note 157, at pp. 87–93.
163 *Id.*
164 *Id.*
165 *Id.* at 93. (According to historians, the First Crusade, lasting from 1069–1099, established the Latin Kingdom of Jerusalem. The Second Crusade, lasting from 1147–1149, was an abject failure. The Third Crusade, lasting from 1189–1192, was a large-scale endeavor led by Frederick Barbarossa. The Fourth Crusade, lasting from 1202–1204, led to the sacking of Constantinople. The Fifth Crusade, lasting from 1218–1221, culminated in an unsuccessful invasion of Egypt. The Sixth Crusade, lasting from 1228–1229, led to treaties between Frederick II and the Arab states. The Seventh Crusade, lasting from 1248–1251, led to Louis IX's failed invasion of Egypt. The Eighth Crusade, occurring in 1270, led to Louis IX's expedition to Tunis.)
166 *Id.* at 180.
167 *Id.*
168 *Id* at 166.
169 *See* Louis Snyder, THE MAKING OF MODERN MAN: FROM THE RENAISSANCE TO THE PRESENT (New York: D. Van Nostrand Co., 1967), at p. 541.
170 *Id.*
171 *Id.* at 542.
172 *Id.*
173 *See* WORLD HISTORY, *supra* note 157, at p. 219.
174 *Id.* (Of course,.slaves in America did not fare well. The debate over how severely they may have suffered, however, continues. *See, e.g.,* Annie Sweeney, *Records Detail Hardships of Former Slaves*, CHI. SUN-TIMES, Oct. 19, 2000.)
175 *See* Snyder, *supra* note 169, at p. 543.
176 *Id.*
177 *See* WORLD HISTORY, *supra* note 157, at p. 171.
178 *Id.*
179 *Id.* at 202.
180 For discussion of treaty-making between Native Americans and Spanish officials, *see, e.g.,* Debran Rowland, *Sovereignty in Indian Country: The Myth and the Reality*, 1 LOY. U. SCH. L. PUB. INT. L. REP. pp. 17–32(Fall 1996); Gloria Jahoda, THE TRAIL OF TEARS, (New York: Wings Books, 1975) (originally published New York: Holt, Rinehart and Winston, 1975).
181 *See* WORLD HISTORY, *supra* note 157, at p. 203.
182 *Id.*
183 *Id.* at 202.
184 *Id.* at 203.
185 *Id.*
186 *See* Jahoda, *supra* note 180, at p. 204.
187 *See* WORLD HISTORY, *supra* note 157, at p. 203.
188 *Id.* at 204–205.
189 *Id.* at 211.
190 The Revolutionary War lasted from 1775 to 1783, and included historically significant battles at Lexington, Concord, Bunker Hill, Saratoga, and Yorktown.
191 Adopted on June 7, 1776, by the Continental Congress, the Declaration of Independence declared that the American colonies "...are, and of right ought to be, free and independent states."
192 For overview, *see* WORLD HISTORY, *supra* note 157.
193 *See* Yalom, *supra* note 18, ENDNOTES FOR CHAPTER ONE, at p. 47.
194 *Id.*

195   *Id.* (citing Barbara A. Hanawalt, THE TIES THAT BOUND: PEASANT FAMILIES IN MEDIEVAL ENGLAND (New York and Oxford: Oxford University Press, 1986), at p. 208).

196   *See* Anne M. Butler, GENDERED JUSTICE IN THE AMERICAN WEST: WOMEN PRISONERS IN MEN'S PENITENTIARIES (Urbana, Illinois: University of Illinois Press, 1997), at pp. 21–27.

197   *See* WORLD HISTORY, *supra* note 157, at pp. 206–207.

198   *See* Bird, *supra* note 80, ENDNOTES FOR CHAPTER ONE, at p. 67 (citing Beverly Beeton, *Amending the Constitution to Include Women's Rights,* (originally printed in Beverly Beeton, WOMEN VOTE IN THE WEST: THE WOMAN SUFFRAGE MOVEMENT, 1869–1896 (New York: Garland Publishing, 1986)).

199   *Id.* at 76.

200   *See* Butler, *supra* note 196, at p. 3 (citing Glenda Riley, DIVORCE: AN AMERICAN TRADITION (New York: Oxford University Press, 1991)). Butler is a professor of history at Utah State University and an editor of the *Western Historical Quarterly.* In addition, Butler is the author of GENDERED JUSTICE IN THE AMERICAN WEST and DAUGHTERS OF JOY, SISTERS OF MISERY: PROSTITUTES IN THE AMERICAN WEST, 1865–90 (Urbana, Illinois: University of Illinois Press, 1985) and UNITED STATES SENATE ELECTION, EXPULSION, AND CENSURE CASES, 1793–1900 (Washington, D.C.: G.P.O., 1995). Butler is also a co-author along with Ona Siporin of UNCOMMON COMMON WOMEN: ORDINARY LIVES OF THE WEST (Logan, Utah: Utah State University Press, 1996).

201   *Id.* at 22.

202   *Id.* at 26.

203   *Id.*

204   *Id.*

205   *Id.*

206   *Id.* at 23.

207   *Id.*

208   *Id.* at 26. ("The jury, deadlocked for a time at eleven to one for acquittal, settled for a compromise verdict. It convicted Jessie Carmon, whose lawyer argued she was 'insane' because the murder occurred on the first day of a very difficult menses, of manslaughter by reason of accidental shooting. Judge Parmelee sentenced her to serve from four to fourteen years. Jessie Carmon became a woman prisoner in the state penitentiary system," Butler wrote.)

209   *Id.*

210   *See* Butler, *supra* note 196, at p. 26.

211   *Id.* at xiii. (Specifically, Butler explains that "[a]t some [male] institutions, women inmates trickled in sporadically, while in others the female populations rose as a constant over fifty years. While never a sizable portion of the prisoner population, women passed in an increasingly regular parade through the penitentiary gates. To limit the penal agencies considered, I centered my research on state penitentiaries built for and managed by men. Even after eliminating federal prisons, county jails, women's reformatories, industrial farms, and houses of correction, I found my numbers of women inmates climbing.")

212   *See Jordanian Man Gets Only Six Months for "Honor Killing,"* BUST, Spring 2002, at p. 12.

213   Indeed, Jordan has made considerable strides in this area. In May 2002, a Jordanian court granted a woman a divorce. In receiving the decree, the woman became the first woman in the country's history to be granted a court-ordered divorce. *See Jordan: A Milestone for Women,* N.Y. TIMES, May 15, 2002, at A6.

214   *Id.*

215   *See* Seth Mydans, *In Pakistan, Rape Victims are the "Criminals,"* N.Y. TIMES, May 17, 2002, at A3.

216   *Id.*

217   *See Korean Missionaries' Murder Case Pits Religion, Culture, and Law,* L.A. TIMES, April 6, 1997, at B1. (According to the article, "[s]ixteen of the victim's ribs were fractured. Her heart was crushed against her backbone and one of the major blood vessels was torn. The muscles of her abdominal wall were deeply bruised, as was her pancreas. Sections of her intestinal tract had shut down and showed early signs of gangrene. The muscles of her left thigh were so shredded and swollen, releasing enzymes sure to cause kidney failure. The leg injury appeared to be older than the other injuries. [¶] On her abdomen, stretching from hip to hip, were a series of odd, crescent-shaped abrasions. Their source: a large spoon the exorcist used to press on the victim after his own hand began hurting, so vigorous was his poking and prodding. The victim's left side was purple from knee to hip.")

218   For accounts of the case, *see 3 Plead Not Guilty in Deadly Exorcism Ritual,* L.A. TIMES, July 10, 1996, at B4; *Praying for Guidance,* L.A. TIMES, July 15, 1996, at B1; *Men to be Tried in Exorcism Death,* L.A. TIMES, Aug. 8, 1996, at B3; *Deacon Pleads Guilty in Exorcism; Agrees to Testify in Woman's Death,* L.A. TIMES, Feb. 22, 1997, at B1; *Deacon Testifies on Exorcism that Ended in Death,* L.A. TIMES, April 2, 1997, at B1; *Korean Missionaries' Murder Case, supra* note 219, at B1; *Man Testifies on Desire to Rid Wife of Demons,* L.A. TIMES, April 10, 1997, at B1; *Verdict in Exorcism Death Expected Today,* L.A. TIMES, April 16, 1997, at B1; *Judge Rules Exorcism Death Manslaughter,* L.A. TIMES, April 17, 1997, at A1; *2 Missionaries Guilty in Fatal Exorcism Case,* L.A. TIMES, April 17, 1997, at B3; *2 Found Guilty of Manslaughter in Exorcism,* L.A. TIMES, April 17, 1997, at B4; *2 Men Get Prison Time in Exorcism Death,* L.A. TIMES, April 25, 1997, at B3; *2 Missionaries Get Prison in Exorcism Case,* L.A. TIMES,

April 25, 1997; *Deacon Gets 3 Years' Probation in Fatal Exorcism*, L.A. TIMES, May 1, 1997, at B6; *Church Deacon Gets Probation for Role in Deadly Exorcism*, L.A. TIMES, May 1, 1997, at B4.

219　*See Korean Missionaries' Murder, supra* note 218, at B1.

220　*Id.*

221　*Id.*

222　*Id.*

223　*Id.*

224　*Id.*

225　*See Church Deacon Gets Probation for Role in Deadly Exorcism, supra* note 219, at B4. (The deacon, identified as Jin Hyun Choi, reportedly "summoned rescue workers and attempted to revive the woman when her breathing grew labored, Deputy Dist. Atty. Hank Goldberg said. He had been less involved in the rite than the other two men, prosecutors added.")

226　*See Korean Missionaries' Murder, supra* note 218, at B1.

227　The cleric involved was identified in media reports as Mohamed Kerazi. He was sentenced to four years in prison.

228　*See Teenager Gets $300,000 in Church Exorcism Case*, NAT'L L.J., April 15, 2002, at B2.

229　As explained by Peter Alexander, author and former Professor Emeritus of English Language and Literature at the University of Glasgow, the presence of Hymen "was invoked at Greek marriages, so regarded as god of marriages; the torch was one of his symbols." *See* GLOSSARY, in THE ALEXANDER TEXT OF WILLIAM SHAKESPEARE: THE COMPLETE WORKS (London: Collins Clear-Type Press) (first printed in 1951, reprinted in 1953, 1954, 1956, 1957, 1959, 1960, 1962, 1963, 1964 (twice), 1965, 1966, 1968, 1970, 1971), at p. 1360.

230　*See* William Shakespeare, THE TEMPEST, Act 4, Scene I, reprinted in THE ALEXANDER TEXT OF WILLIAM SHAKESPEARE, *supra* note 229, at p. 19.

231　*See* Yalom, *supra* note 193, at p. 49.

232　*See* Arthur Golden, MEMOIRS OF A GEISHA (New York: Alfred A. Knopf, 1997), at pp. 278–279.

233　*Id.* at 283.

234　*See, e.g.*, Steve Warmbir, *Swedish Exec. Sentenced Here in Cybersex Sting*, CHI. SUN-TIMES, July 11, 2001, at p. 20; *Virtual Playground*, 48 HOURS, CBS-TV, airing June 7, 2001 (Peter Van Sant, reporting), at p. 2–14 (transcript); John Schwartz, *Internet Leash Can Monitor Sex Offenders*, N.Y. TIMES, Dec. 31, 2001, at C1; James Brooke, *Sex Web Worldwide Traps Children*, N.Y. TIMES, Dec. 23, 2001, at A8; Tim Novak, *Sex Case MD Out on Bail*, CHI. SUN-TIMES, June 19, 1999, at p. 3, (the article describes how an Oak Park, Illinois, gynecologist was arrested after allegedly attempting to engage in a sexual relationship with a 13-year-old girl he met on the Internet.); *Wisconsin Man Charged in Internet Sting*, CHI. SUN-TIMES, April 28, 2000, at p. 18; *'Shell-shocked,' But free*, EDITOR & PUBLISHER, July 10, 1999, at p. 8; *Stranger Danger On-Line*, OPRAH WINFREY SHOW, ABC-TV, airing October 1, 1999; Debra Baker, *When Cyber Stalkers Walk*, A.B.A. J., December 1999, at p. 50.

235　*See Virtual Playground*, supra note 234 at p. 2.

236　*See* Jan Goodwin, *Afghan Girls Forced to Sell Sex—or Starve*, MARIE CLAIRE, April 2002, at pp. 82–88.

237　*Id.* at 84.

238　*Id.*

239　*See* ABC WORLD NEWS TONIGHT, airing on Sept. 10, 2001, at pp. 5–6 (transcript), available through ABCNews.com; Raymond Hernandez, *Children's Sexual Exploitation Underestimated, Study Finds*, N.Y. TIMES, Sept. 10, 2001, at A18.

240　*Id.*

241　Researchers at the Crimes Against Children Research Center reportedly criticized the study for "misrepresent[ing]" the center's data. Further, according to ABC NEWS, "[t]hey accuse the University of Pennsylvania authors of generating estimates by 'making assumptions that are very speculative, in some cases mistaken and not well supported by national research.'" Center officials suggest further that the study's authors may have counted many of the children several times. David Finkelhor, a professor at the Crimes Against Children Research Center, argued that the authors mistakes were so serious "…that if [the authors] had presented this article to be published in an ordinary scientific journal, which they did not,…it would have been rejected.") *See* WORLD NEWS TONIGHT, *supra* note 239, at p. 6.

242　*See* Bellamy and Otunnu, *Hail Entry into Force of Optional Protocol on Child Soldiers*, at p. 1.

243　*See* NEWS NOTE: *Background on Child Trafficking*, at p. 1.

244　Bellamy's remarks were made during press conferences in Geneva and New York calling for a global end to the "commercial sexual exploitation of children" in conjunction with the release of a UNICEF report on the sexual exploitation of children for commercial gain. *See UNICEF Calls for Eradication of Commercial Sexual Exploitation of Children*, December 12, 2001 at p. 1.

245　*See UNICEF Hails Entry Into Force of Optional Protocol on the Sale of Children, Child Prostitution and Child Pornography*, October 22, 2001, at p. 1. *See also* Graça Machel, *The Impact of Armed Conflict on Children: A Critical Review of Progress Made and Obstacles Encountered in Increasing Protection for War-Affected Children*, UNICEF REPORT, September 2000, (released in Winnipeg, Canada), at p. 11. (According to Machel, "[n]early all girls abducted into armed groups are forced into sexual slavery, subjected to physical and emotional violence, and forced to provide other personal services. The majority become infected with sexually transmitted diseases (STDs) and, increasingly, HIV/AIDS. Describing this experience as a 'forced' marriage is a complete misrepresentation and distortion of a child's experience. In addition, these young people are exposed relentlessly to extreme violence and suffering and become increasingly desensitized to the horror around them. In a number of cases, young people have been deliberately exposed to horrific scenes to harden them or to sever their links with their communities.")

246 See Web Child Porn Ring Broken, available online at CNN.COM, August 9, 2002.

247 See Analysis of the Situation of Sexual Exploitation of Children in the Eastern and Southern Africa Region, REPORT TO THE 2ND WORLD CONGRESS AGAINST COMMERCIAL SEXUAL EXPLOITATION OF CHILDREN, at p. 11. (UNICEF authors note in their analysis that "[t]he commercial sex services sector includes pornography, prostitution and trafficking in children for sexual purposes and for profit. Child exploiters are known to deliberately seek occupations that put them in frequent contact with children and these perpetrators of child exploitation include some of highly esteemed members of society. The child victims of commercial sexual exploitation worldwide are both boys and girls, although the vast majority are girls aged between 10 and 18 years. Recent research evidence suggests that the age of the children involved is decreasing and the sexual exploitation of children as young as six is increasingly becoming pervasive.")

248 Id. at 12.

249 Id. at 17.

250 Id.

251 Id. at 18.

252 Id.

253 See Dean Schabner, Fatal Attraction: 16-year-old Vermont Girl Lured to Prostitution, Death in NYC, ABCNEWS.COM, Feb. 6, 2000. See also 8 Accused of Smuggling Asians to Work in Brothels, N.Y. TIMES, Sept. 19, 2002, at A12.

254 See Analysis of the Situation of Sexual Exploitation of Children in the Eastern and Southern Africa Region, supra note 247, at p. 21.

255 Id.

256 See Jeffrey Toobin, The Man Who Kept Going Free, THE NEW YORKER, March 7, 1994, at p. 38 (detailing the journey of career criminal, Richard Allen Davis, from small-time break-in man to reportedly unrepentant sociopath); Kristen Green, Experts: DNA Evidence Links Defendant, Victim, SAN DIEGO UNION-TRIBUNE, June 21, 2002, at p. 1 (detailing DNA connections made between blood allegedly found on a jacket belonging to David Westerfield matching the DNA of kidnapped and later murdered Danielle van Dam); Kidnapped, PEOPLE, June 24, 2002, at p. 50; Man Sought in Utah Case Turns Up in West Virginia Hospital, N.Y. TIMES, June 22, 2002, at A8 (detailing the investigation into the kidnapping of Elizabeth Smart).

257 See One of Thousands We've Adopted Elizabeth as Our Own, But She is Not Alone, [WICHITA FALLS, TEXAS] TIMES RECORD NEWS, June 21, 2002, at p. 1. Following the abduction and murder of his daughter, Marc Klaas reportedly quit his job to work full-time for the Polly Klaas Foundation, established initially to help coordinate the search for his daughter, later the foundation's efforts turned towards preventing violence against children. According to statistics provided by the National Center for Missing and Exploited Children, however, the number of unsolved "nonfamily abductions" is reportedly relatively small—totaling 103 since 1990, including the abduction of Elizabeth Smart. See Michael Janofsky, Family Rebuilds Life Around Missing Daughter, N.Y. TIMES, July 28, 2002, at A12.

258 See Mary Duenwald, Who Would Abduct a Child? Previous Cases Offer Clues, N.Y. TIMES, Aug. 27, 2002, at D1.

259 Id.

260 Id.

261 Id. at D6.

262 Id. at D1.

263 See UNICEF Calls for Eradication of Commercial Sexual Exploitation of Children, supra note 244, at pp. 3–4.

264 See Analysis of the Situation of Sexual Exploitation of Children in the Eastern and Southern Africa Region, supra note 247, at p. 15.

265 Id.

266 Id.

267 Id. at 15–16.

268 See Goodwin, supra note 236, at p. 86.

269 See Virginity Around the World, MARIE CLAIRE (April 2000), at p. 108.

270 Id.

271 See A Very Brady Lawsuit, NAT'L L.J., March 8, 2000, at A24.

272 In her suit, Henderson asserted claims for emotional distress and invasion of privacy, arguing that the publication and sale of the t-shirts would expose her to "contempt and ridicule." As a point of explanation, the tort of "intentional infliction of emotional distress" generally involves the intentional infliction of mental suffering upon a person by acts that either cause physical symptoms of

the distress or that "exceed the limits of social tolerance." The tort of "invasion of privacy" includes the "appropriation, for the defendant's benefit or advantages, of the plaintiff's name or likeness without permission or consent." For further reading on the issue, *see* W. Page Keeton, *supra* note 210, ENDNOTES FOR CHAPTER ELEVEN, Chapter 20, Sec. 117, at pp. 851–854; Peter B. Kutner & Osborne M. Reynolds, Jr., ADVANCED TORTS: CASES AND MATERIALS (Durham: Carolina Academic Press, 1989), at pp. 385–418; Gordon, *Right of Property in Name, Likeness, Personality and History*, 55 Nw. U. L. REV. at p. 553 (1961).

273 *See Teacher Harassed by Students?*, PROS & CONS, COURT-TV, airing October 13, 2000. (The segment featured discussion with the teacher, Janis Adams, and her attorney, Gloria Allred.)

274 *Id.*

275 *See Traumatized Teacher Gets $4.3M from District*, NAT'L L.J., May 20–27, 2002, at B3 (citing *Adams v. Los Angeles Unified School Dist.*, No. BC 235 667 (Los Angeles Co., Calif., Super. Ct.)).

276 *See* Hawthorne, *supra* note 12, ENDNOTES FOR CHAPTER TWO, at pp. 52–53. (As Hawthorne describes in THE SCARLET LETTER, "[w]hen the young woman—the mother of this child—stood fully revealed before the crowd, it seemed to be her first impulse to clasp the infant closely to her bosom; not so much by an impulse of motherly affection, as that she might thereby conceal a certain token, which was wrought or fastened into her dress. In a moment, however, wisely judging that one token of her shame would but poorly serve to hide another, she took the baby on her arm, and, with a burning blush, and yet a haughty smile, and a glance that would not be abashed, looked around at her townspeople and neighbors. On the breast of her gown, in fine red cloth, surrounded with an elaborate embroidery and fantastic flourishes of gold-thread, appeared the letter A. It was so artistically done, and with so much fertility and gorgeous luxuriance of fancy, that it had all the effect of a last and fitting decoration to the apparel which she wore; and which was of a splendor in accordance with the taste of the age, but greatly beyond what was allowed by the sumptuary regulations of the colony.")

277 *See* Warren Hoge, *A Sex Scandal of the 60s Doubly Scandalous Now*, N.Y. TIMES, August 16, 2000, at A4.

278 *Id.* (Indeed, the case was thought to be so spectacular even decades after it was lived that in August 2000, it became the subject of a documentary shown on British television.)

279 *Id.*

280 *See* Adam Shatz, *About Face*, N.Y. TIMES MAG., Jan. 20, 2002, at pp. 18, 19.

281 *See* NORTON, *supra* note 2, ENDNOTES FOR INTRODUCTION, at p. 232.

282 *Id.* (citing *e.g.,* MD. ARCHS, X, 473, 477–78; SOFFOLKS CT. RECS, II, 688; EC CT. RECS, VII, 257–58; NH CT. RECS, XL, 448).

283 Formerly of the *American Spectator*, David Brock cruelly—and politically, he would later note—gave birth to this now infamous accusation.

284 For example, renowned journalists Jane Mayer and Jill Abramson note Brock's handiwork in reviewing Hill's silence and corresponding mistrust of the media following her testimony on October 11, 1991. According to Mayer and Abramson, since those nation-shaking events, Hill "had given several speeches, a few for lucrative fees, and had even sat for photo sessions and media interviews on rare occasions. But while she had occasionally commented on what she saw as the ramifications of her testimony, she had deflected all further inquiry into the details of her charges. Her silence was particularly conspicuous in light of revisionist interpretations of her behavior, such as the best-selling book that appeared in the spring of 1993 entitled THE REAL ANITA HILL. The book's author, David Brock, provided a wealth of what he presented as evidence that Hill was chronically unbalanced, sexually aberrant, and both personally and politically motivated to lie about how Clarence Thomas had treated her." It was Brock's assault, however, that "in large part" would lead Hill to eventually comment on the case. *See* Jane Mayer & Jill Abramson, STRANGE JUSTICE: THE SELLING OF CLARENCE THOMAS (Boston: Houghton Mifflin Co., 1994), at p. 2.

285 *See* Anita Hill, SPEAKING TRUTH TO POWER (New York: Doubleday, 1997), at pp. 281–282. (Among Hill's other poignant comments on the subject came after she was hired by NBC NEWS to address issues of a Supreme Court decision only to then be asked on air what she thought of David Brock's attacks. On this point, Hill wrote: "I agreed to comment on the case on the CBS MORNING NEWS and NBC'S TODAY SHOW. The night before the interview, I spent hours pouring over the briefs filed in the suit and the cases cited in Justice O'Connor's opinion. It was a labor of love. To me the Harris suit represented affirmation, a victory for working women. The interview with Harry Smith of CBS went smoothly. The case is a landmark case on a prominent problem affecting working women in this country. It did not represent a panacea for all the ills of sexual harassment but it was a start. It was all the more significant because it represented only the second time that the High Court had addressed sexual harassment in the workplace since the concept was introduced to the courts in the 1970s. [¶] I was angry and disappointed when Katie Couric of NBC asked me to address David Brock's allegations about me. The question had nothing to do with the *Harris* case and had not been raised by the show's producers as one of the subjects they were interested in hearing about. Yet the question was revealing especially in the context of the discussion of major legal decision. Ms. Couric's question reminded me that no matter what the legal breakthrough in law and in our understanding of the problem of sexual harassment, there will always be those who want to reduce us to talking about the salacious and the sordid.") *Id.* at 299–300.

286   *See, e.g.,* Frank Rich, *Ding, Dong, the Cultural Witch Hunt is Dead,* N.Y. TIMES MAG., Feb. 24, 2002, at p. 36. (As Rich explains, "David Brock, you may recall, was the bullying reporter of the late, not-so-great *American Spectator* who labeled Anita Hill 'a little bit nutty and a little bit slutty' and later broke Troopergate, the pioneering exposé (much of it culled from clandestinely paid 'sources') into Bill Clinton's Arkansas Kama Sutra. In his latest incarnation, Brock is turning expiation for these and other past sins into a second career that has played out like a striptease over the past few years. He set out on this path in 1997 by writing an article for ESQUIRE, '*Confessions of a Right Wing Hit Man,*' in which he started to recant THE REAL ANITA HILL, his bestselling and often fictionalized hatchet job that duped many reviewers (including one at *The New York Times*) with its lavishly foot-noted gossip, half-truths and slander. Next up is a new book, a memoir title BLINDED BY THE RIGHT: THE CONSCIENCE OF AN EX-CONSERVATIVE, that goes further still by serving as a *mea culpa* for an entire era, not just himself. In it, he not only takes back the falsifications in his reportage on Hill, Clarence Thomas and the Clintons (among others) but even offers an apologia for the over-the-top excesses of his *Esquire* apologia, which was accompanied by a photo of Brock in full martyr monty, lashed to a tree, his chest bared, eager to be burned at a stake.") In a contrasting professional rehabilitation piece titled *House of Lies,* written by Jane Ammeson and presented cosmetically as a book review and interview with the author, but published under the tiny marker of SPECIAL ADVERTISING SUPPLEMENT TO THE NEW YORK TIMES IN CHICAGO LIFE magazine (Summer 2002), at pp. 48–49, Brock is described by Ammeson as "vulnerable, sweet and wistful." And Brock, himself, is then quoted as having said he "…spent all those years doing a lot of things [including writing and making a great deal of money off THE REAL ANITA HILL] that I regret. When I was writing this book [BLINDED BY THE RIGHT: THE CONSCIENCE OF AN EX-CONSERVATIVE], I went back and re-read the Anita Hill book and it seemed like it was written by a different person. I was trying to put myself back into that thought and all the anger that was in that writing and it was just hard to try to imagine that it all came out of my mind and my keyboard." Could this really be remorse? That is apparently what readers are supposed to ask. Then, Brock—or Ammeson on behalf of Brock—begin to count through explanations—different from the motivation of money, of course—in an effort to elucidate Brock's political/emotional whimsy: among them that Brock's mother was allegedly pre-occupied throughout his childhood with outward appearances and critically unable to make even simple decisions; that as a young man he was like most, contrary; and, that he was and is gay but had to live a "double life" within a conservative Republican establishment that kept secret adulteries while preaching family values. It was in this environment—one where there was apparently plenty of money floating around and into Brock's hands for "exposing" it—in which the Clintons were to be "gotten." "Canny lawyers, the Clintons played things too close to the line, and gave their critics too much ammunition, but they were not murderous thugs or felons or even ethical or moral abominations, and no one in [now Solicitor General, then reported AMERICAN SPECTATOR legal adviser [Ted] Olson's set of canny conservative lawyers really thought they were," Ammeson quotes Brock as having written. "The problem for the Clintons was that they were successful—and far from perfect—*Democrats.* The Republican insiders, exaggerating every real law and exploiting every cockamamie angle they could find, were after one thing only: power for themselves and for the right-wing social and economic interests they represented." At the time Brock was more than eager to help them get it. And to be paid for it, as he apparently also has been for his current book.

287   *See* Elizabeth Amon, *Forced Publicity,* NAT'L L.J., Aug. 26, 2002, at A1, A6.

288   *Id.* at A6. *See also* Nicholas D. Kristof, *Shaming Young Mothers,* N.Y. TIMES, Aug. 23, 2002, at A17.

289   *See Online Hostility,* PROS AND CONS, COURT-TV, aired July 5, 2000. (The segment featured the story of a Utah student facing legal trouble after he sent out email messages to other students, whom he felt had insulted his friends or himself.)

290   *See* COURT-TV NEWSBREAK, airing December 6, 2000, (reporter Beth Karas), noting that a judge determined there was sufficient evidence to permit Ian Lake to be taken to trial.

291   *See* Dan Chapman, *Eyes Are Watching: Online Revolution Stirring New Boss-Worker Friction,* THE PALM BEACH POST, Sept. 3, 2000, at 4F.

292   For a legal overview of "defamation," *see infra* note 314.

293   Jilted real or potential lovers, for example, appear to have found a new outlet for their feelings. When a Manhattan music teacher was stood up for a date in the summer of 2000, for example, he decided to send the offender a virtual voodoo doll via the Internet venture PINSTRUCK.COM. And apparently, he was not alone. According to THE NEW YORK TIMES, PINSTRUCK.COM "sends 2,000 to 3,000 curses" a day. *See* Joyce Cohen, *Revenge Among the Nerds,* N.Y. TIMES, August 24, 2000, at D1. The nineteen available "curses" vary in form from "Look what you have become" to "You know you like it," and "I love you" to "It's not over yet." Though popular, the site hit a snag recently, deleting one of the most popular curses, "This is the end of you." According to Tyson Liotta, one of the designers of the site, "[p]eople interpreted it as a death threat." *Id.*

294   New York authorities began discussing a possible plea bargain in November 2000, for instance, in the case of a Columbia University graduate student who allegedly kidnapped and sexually assaulted a women he met via the Internet. *See Internet Sex-Assault Case May End with Plea Bargain,* N.Y. TIMES, Nov. 22, 2000, at A26. In December of the previous year, a New York appellate court ordered a new trial after ruling that the trial judge erred in refusing to permit the jury to see four emails

allegedly sent by the victim to her alleged attacker. In the emails, the woman alleged expressed "an interest in sadomasochism." *See* David Rohde, *Order for New Sex-Abuse Trial is Called Threat to Women's Rights*, N.Y. TIMES, Dec. 23, 1999, at A 26; Jane Fritsch with Katherine Finkelstein, *All Charges Dismissed by Judge in Columbia Sex Torture Case*, N.Y. TIMES, Nov. 2, 2001, at A17.

295   For example, the alleged downloading of pornographic photos was at issue in *U.S. v. Simons*, 29 F. Supp. 2d 324 (E.D. Va. 1998). The federal agent involved was later indicted for allegedly receiving material considered to be child pornography. He challenged the indictment, arguing that his employer improperly seized the material leading to that indictment. The court upheld the seizure as proper and allowed the indictment to stand. In other employment related incidents, in 1999, Xerox Corporation reportedly fired 40 employees for alleged "inappropriate use of the Internet." *See* Allison Michael & Scott Lidman, *Monitoring of Employees Still Growing*, NAT'L L.J., Jan. 19, 2001, at B9. In 2000, THE NEW YORK TIMES company also reportedly fired 20 employees for allegedly sharing emails containing "offensive material." That same year, Dow Chemical Company also terminated 40 employees for the alleged improper use of the company's email systems. *Id.* at B15.

296   For recent cases on the issue, see, e.g., *Batzel v. Smith*, 351 F.3d 904 (9th Cir. 2003); *Urofsky v. Gilmore*, 216 F.3d 401 (4th Cir. 2000); *Breeding v. Arthur J. Gallagher and Co.*, 164 F.3d 1151, 1158 (8th Cir. 1999); *Wallin v. Minnesota Dept. of Corrections*, 153 F.3d 681, 687 (8th Cir. 1998); *Vega-Rodriquez v. Puerto Rico Tel. Co.*, 110 F.3d 174 (1st Cir. 1997); *Mitan v. Davis*, 243 F. Supp. 2d 719 (W.D. Ky. 2003); *Cuccoili v. Jekyll & Hyde*, 150 F. Supp. 2d 646 (S.D.N.Y. 2001); *Bailey v. Turbine Design, Inc.*, 85 F. Supp. 2d 790 (W.D. Tenn. 2000); *Coniglio v. City of Berwyn*, No. 99-4475, 1999 WL 1212190 (N.D. Ill. Dec. 16, 1999); *Scott v. Plagues Unlimited, Inc.*, 46 F. Supp.2d 1287 (M.D. Fla. 1999); *Spencer v. Comm. Edison Co.*, No. 97-7718, 1999 WL 144486 (N.D. Ill. Jan. 6, 1999); *Blakey v. Continental Airlines, Inc.*, 2 F. Supp. 2d 598 (D.N.J. 1998); *Blakey v. Continental Airlines, Inc.*, 992 F.Supp. 731 (D.N.J. 1998); *Schwenn v. Anheuser-Busch, Inc.*, 1998 U.S. Dist. Lexus 5027 (N.D.N.Y. April 7, 1998); *Daniels v. Worldcom Corp.*, No. A.3:97-CV-0721-P, 1998 WL 91261 (N.D. Texas Feb. 23, 1998); *Curtis v. Citibank*, No. 97-1065, 1998 WL 3354 (S.D.N.Y. Jan. 5, 1998); *Martens v. Smith Barney, Inc.*, 181 F.R.D. 243 (S.D.N.Y. 1998); *Rudas v. Nationwide Mut. Ins. Co.*, No. 96-5987, 1997 WL 634501 (E.D. Pa. Sept. 26, 1997); *Miller v. Woodharbor Molding and Millworks Inc.*, 80 F. Supp. 2d 1026 (N.D. Iowa 2000); *Newsome v. Adm. Office of the Courts of the State of N.J.*, 103 F. Supp. 2d 1354 (S.D.Fla. 1999); *Smyth v. Pillsbury*, 914 F. Supp. 97 (E.D. Pa. 1996); *Knox v. State of Indiana*, 93 F. 3d 1327 (7th Cir. 1996); *Strauss v. Microsoft Corp.*, 814 F. Supp. 1186 (S.D.N.Y. 1993); *McLaren v. Microsoft Corp.*, 1999 Tex. App. Lexis 4103 (Texas Ct. App. May 1999). For articles, *see* generally, Jeremy Malcolm, *A New Australian Damages Benchmark in Internet Defamation;* Allison Michael & Scott Lidman, *Monitoring of Employees Still Growing*, NAT'L L.J., Jan. 19, 2001, at B9; Ellen McLaughlin & Carol Merchasin, TRAINING BECOMES IMPORTANT STEP TO AVOID LIABILITY, NAT'L L.J., Jan. 29, 2001, at B10; Michael Starr & Jordon Lippner, *Monitoring Employee E-mail*, NAT'L L.J., June 11, 2001, at B8; Charlotte Faltermayer, *Cyberveillance*, TIME, Aug. 14, 2000, at B22; *When E-Mail is Ooops-Mail*, NEWSWEEK, Oct. 16, 1995, at 82.S; Greg Miller, *Working: Fear of Abuse Leads Some Employers to Deny, Monitor Internet Access*, THE NEWS TRIB., Aug. 4, 1996; Cheryl Currid, *Be Careful What You and Your Users Say and Do on the Net—It Could Come Back to You*, WINDOWS MAG., Sept. 1, 1996; and, Christine A. Amalfe and Kerrie R. Heslin, Courts Start to Rule on On-Line Harassment, NAT'L L.J., Jan. 24, 2000, at C1.

297   Among the states to have enacted legislation making harassment via computer a crime at the time of this writing were California and Connecticut. *See, e.g.,* Calif. Penal Stat. Sec. 646.9 (g) (West 1998) and Conn. Gen. Stat. Ann. Sec. 53a-182b and 53a0183 (West 1995). Illinois law makers announced on September 1, 2000, that PUBLIC ACT 91-878, titled HARASSING AND OBSCENE COMMUNICATIONS ACT, would be amended effective Jan. 1, 2001, codified at 720 ILCS 135/1-1 *et seq.* For analysis, *see Illinois Law Update*, 88 ILL. BAR J. 626 (Nov. 2000) ("First-time offenders that place harassing telephone calls are normally guilty of a Class B misdemeanor, and repeat offenders face a minimum of 14 days in jail or 240 hours of public service work. Currently, only persons having three or more violations in the past year, those on probation, those convicted of a forcible felony in the last 10 years, or those who threaten to kill the victim in the course of the offense, are punishable as Class 4 felons. [¶] However, under a new Illinois law, some first-time offenders will soon face stricter penalties as well. Public Act 91-878 amends the Harassing and Obscene Communications Act to provide an additional category of harassment. Under the new law, persons at least 16 years old that make or knowingly induce another person to make a harassing phone call or other electronic communication (such as communication over the Internet) to a person under 13 years old are guilty of a Class 4 felony. The law previously made no distinctions based upon the age of either the caller or the recipient.")

298   *See Web Site Harassment Charge*, N.Y. TIMES, June 5, 2001, at A22.

299   *See* T.R. Reid, *Kiss and Email*, WASH. POST (reprinted in CHI. SUN-TIMES, December 2000), at 4. (At one point, the voting was reportedly 2 to 1 for the firm not to retain the lawyer.)

300   *See* Nichole M. Christian, *Pornographer Found Guilty of Harassing an Ex-Employee*, N.Y. TIMES, Feb. 28, 2002, at A22.

301   *Id.*

302 *Id.* (There seems to be some confusion on the actual number of convictions. In this article, the reporter suggested Goldstein was convicted on six counts. But in a subsequent article, the Times reported that Goldstein had been "on five misdemeanor harassment charges." *See* Andy Newman, *Pornographer Says Six Days in Jail Broke Him*, N.Y. TIMES, May 18, 2002, at A12.

303 In 1989, Robert Bardo, a man described in news reports as schizophrenic, reportedly became obsessed with actress Rebecca Schaeffer. And after making "countless phone calls" and sending "dozens of letters to the actress," he went to see her and when, according to Bardo, she "just looked—she just—she just looked down and looked at" him, he shot her. *See* 48 HOURS, Jan 31, 1999 (Harold Dow reporting), at pp. 4–5 (transcript) (available through Burrelle's).

304 For cases involving claims of intimidation, *see, e.g., State v. Meyers,* 643 So.2d 1275 (5th Cir. 1994) (holding that state must show specific intent to prove public intimidation charge); *U.S. v. Hayward,* 6 F.3d 1241 (7th Cir. 1993); *cert. den.,* 114 S. Ct. 1369, *reh'ring den.,* 114 S. Ct. 1872; *People v. Maldonado,* 187 Ill.Dec. 28 (Ill. App. 1 Dist. 1993) (clarifying that intimidation statute is intended to foreclose making of threats intended to compel person to act against his or her will), *app. den.,* 190 Ill.Dec. 902; *People v. Verkruysse,* 203 Ill.Dec. 322 (Ill. App. 3 Dist. 1994) (clarifying purpose of intimidation statute), *app. den.,* 205 Ill.Dec. 182; *People v. Libbra,* 205 Ill.Dec. 554 (Ill. App. 5 Dist. 1994) (holding that the gravaman of intimidation is threat of force), *app. den.,* 208 Ill.Dec. 365; *People v. Bergin,* 169 Ill.Dec. 20 (Ill. App. 2 Dist. 1992) (holding that alleged statement by defendant of "Don't talk or we'll kill the kids" was not sufficient to sustain conviction for intimidation); *Owens v. State,* 659 N.E.2d 466 (Ind. 1995) (holding that an objective standard is used to determine whether a communication is a "threat" for purposes of intimidation statute); *Hendrix v. State,* 615 N.E.2d 483 (Ind. App. 1 Dist. 1993) (communication of a threat is necessary to prove offense of intimidation); *Lyles v. State,* 576 N.E.2d 1344 (threat necessary to sustain intimidation charge); *State v. Ross,* 269 Mont. 347 (Mont. 1995) (holding that Montana intimidation statute not unconstitutionally overbroad on its face); *State v. Hansen,* 67 Wash. App. 511 (Div. 1 1992) (holding that the word "directs" as used in intimidation statute means communication made is such a way that the individual it is intended to reach understands it). Cases on ethnic intimidation include: *People v. Richards,* 509 N.W.2d 528 (Mich. App. 1993) (holding that statute prohibiting ethnic intimidation did not violate the First Amendment); *Stegmaier v. State,* 863 S.W.2d 924 (Mo. App. W.D. 1993) (conviction of ethnic intimidation in first degree based upon "race-related" damage to individual's car did not violate First Amendment); *State ex rel. Heck v. Kessler,* 72 Ohio St. 3d 98 (1994) (declaring state's ethnic intimidation statute constitutional); *State v. Wyant,* 64 Ohio St. 3d 566 (1992) (declaring that portion of ethnic intimidation statute deemed a "thought crime" to be unconstitutional), *cert. granted, vacated* 113 S. Ct. 2954, *on remand,* 68 Ohio St. 3d 162; *State v. Troutman,* 71 Ohio App. 3d 755 (9 Dist. 1991) (holding that pushing, forcing, threatening a person and calling him a "peeping Tom" was sufficient to sustain a conviction of intimidation); *Commonwealth v. Ferino,* 433 Pa. Super. 306 (1994) (holding that defendant did not commit ethnic intimidation when she allegedly said, "I'm going to kill you, you f—-king nigger," and reportedly fired a gun towards African American as well as Caucasian persons), *app. granted,* 539 Pa. 664, *aff'd,* 540 Pa. 51.

305 For cases generally filed by state officials throughout the 1990s, *see, e.g., Mozzochi v. Borden,* 959 F.2d 1174 (2nd Cir. 1992) (holding that newspaper article depicting slaying of several public officials, including mayor and city council members disseminated by disgruntled townspeople was sufficient to sustain charge of criminal harassment); *People v. Smith,* 862 P.2d 939 (Colo. 1993) (involving question of whether harassment statute providing that repeated use of offensive, coarse or lewd language in communications may be actionable was constitutionally overbroad); *People By and Through City of Longmont v. Gomez,* 843 P.2d 1321 (Colo. 1993) (involving question of whether city ordinance making it an offense to harass, threaten or abuse another person was unconstitutionally vague); *State v. Snyder,* 40 Conn. App. 544 (1996) (holding that direct communication between alleged harasser and accuser is not necessary to sustain a charge of second degree harassment; rather, communication may be made through a third party); *In Interest of Doe,* 869 P.2d 1304 (Hawaii 1994) (holding that harassment is a form of disorderly conduct directed at a single person as opposed to the public); *State v. Taliferro,* 881 P.2d 1264 (Hawaii App. 1994) (holding that to prove harassment by insults, taunts or challenges, state must show that: (1) defendant insulted, taunted or challenged another; (2) defendant did so in a manner likely to provoke violent response; and, (3) defendant did so with intent to harass, annoy, or alarm the individual); *State v. Orsello,* 529 N.W.2d 481(Minn. App. 1995) (holding that harassing conduct leading another to feel oppressed need only be proved by show of general intent); *rev. granted, rev'd,* 554 N.W.2d 70; *Alexander v. State,* S.W.2d 354 (Mo. App. W.D. 1993) (holding that civil pleading threatening violence may form basis of a harassment charge); *State v. Hoffman,* 290 N.J. Super. 588 (1996) (holding that intent to harass must be coupled with performance of proscribed acts to sustain a complaint), *aff'd in part, rev'd in part,* 149 N.J. 564; *State v. Long,* 266 N.J. Super. 716 (1993) (holding that conviction for harassment must be based upon proof of purposeful conduct by defendant, intended to harass or alarm); *People v. Foy,* 155 Misc.2d 81 (1992) (holding that aggravated harassment is a crime), *appeal granted,* 87 N.Y.S.2d 901, *aff'd,* 88 N.Y.S.2d 742; *People v. McDermott,* 160 Misc.2d 769 (1994) (holding that a defendant does not have to initiate a "harassing" phone call to be convicted

of aggravated harassment); *Commonwealth v. Zullinger*, 450 Pa. Super. 533 (1996) (holding that a criminal conviction of harassment must be reversed due to fatal variance between summary harassment statute and the criminal standard of proof); *Commonwealth v. Burlingame*, 448 Pa. Super. 594 (1996) (holding that "harassing" conduct in the course of a labor dispute was shielded from prosecution); *Commonwealth v. Schierscher*, 447 Pa. Super. 61 (1995) (holding that Pennsylvania harassment statute was not unconstitutionally vague); *Long v. State*, 903 S.W.2d 52 (Tex. App. Austin 1995) (holding that although the Texas statute did not define "harass," "annoy," "alarm," "torment," and "embarrass," statute was not unconstitutionally vague); *Seattle v. Allen*, 80 Wash. App. 824 (1996) (holding that threat of immediate harm may be assault, but threat to cause future harm may be harassment in accordance with city ordinance); *State v. Pollard*, 80 Wash. App. 60 (1995) (holding that conviction on charge of malicious harassment does not require a preplanned encounter between alleged defendant and victim), *rev. den.*, 129 Wash. App. 1011; *State v. Alvarez*, 74 Wash. App. 250 (1994) (holding that a showing of repeated invasions of one's privacy or a pattern of harassment is not necessary to sustain a conviction under state harassment statute), *rev. granted*, 125 Wash.2d 1001.

306 The National Institute of Justice summarizes the current state of "stalking law," concluding that "[t]hough most states define stalking as the willful, malicious, and repeated following and harassing of another person, some states include in their definition such activities as lying-in-wait, surveillance, nonconsensual communication, telephone harassment, and vandalism. While most states require that the alleged stalker engage in a course of conduct showing that the crime was not an isolated event, most states specify how many acts (usually two or more) must occur before the conduct can be considered stalking. State stalking laws also vary in their threat and fear requirements. Most stalking laws require that the perpetrator, to qualify as a stalker, make a credible threat of violence against the victim; others include in their requirements threats against the victim's immediate family; and still others require only that the alleged stalker's course of conduct constitute an implied threat." *See* Patricia Tjaden & Nancy Thoennes, *Stalking in America: Findings From the National Violence Against Women Survey*, NATIONAL INSTITUTE OF JUSTICE, CENTERS FOR DISEASE CONTROL AND PREVENTION, April 1998, at pp. 1–2. *See also* Donna Hunzeker, *Stalking Laws, State Legislative Report*, DENVER, COLORADO: NATIONAL CONFERENCE OF STATE LEGISLATURES (OCT. 1992), at pp. 1–6; NATIONAL INSTITUTE OF JUSTICE, DOMESTIC VIOLENCE, *Stalking, and Antistalking Legislation: An Annual Report to Congress Under the Violence Against Women Act* (Washington, D.C.: U.S. Department of Justice, National Institutes of Justice), April 1996. For recent cases, *see, e.g., State v. Randall*, 669 So.2d 223 (Ala. App. 1995); *Culbreath v. State*, 667 So.2d 156 (Ala. App. 1995); *Morton v. State*, 651 So.2d 42 (Ala. App. 1994); *People v. McClelland*, 49 Cal. Rptr. 2d 587 (Cal. App. 2 Dist. 1996); *People v. Tran*, 54 Cal. Rptr. 2d 650 (Cal. App. 6 Dist. 1996); *People v. Carron*, 44 Cal. Rptr. 2d 328 (Cal. App. 2 Dist. 1995); *People v. Heilman*, 30 Cal. Rptr. 2d 422 (Cal. App. 4 Dist. 1994); *State v. Culmo*, 642 A.2d 90 (Conn. Super. 1993); *Snowden v. State*, 677 A.2d 33 (Del. Super. 1996); *Bouters v. State*, 659 So.2d 235 (Fla. 1995); *Gilbert v. State*, 659 So.2d 233 (Fla. 1995); *State v. Glover*, 634 So.2d 247 (Fla. App. 5 Dist. 1994); *Pallas v. State*, 636 So.2d 1358 (Fla. App. 3 Dist. 1994); *Rooks v. State*, 474 S.E.2d 769 (Ga. App. 1996); *State v. Rooks*, 468 S.E.2d 354 (Ga. 1996); *Adkins v. State*, 471 S.E.2d 896 (Ga. App. 1996); *Johnson v. State*, 449 S.E.2d 94 (Ga. 1994); *Rooks v. State*, 458 S.E.2d 667 (Ga. App. 1995); *Robinson v. State*, 456 S.E.2d 68 (Ga. App. 1995); *People v. Soto*, 660 N.E.2d 990 (Ill. App. 1 Dist. 1995); *People v. Sowewimo*, 657 N.E.2d 1047 (Ill. App. 1 Dist. 1995); *People v. Bailey*, 657 N.E.2d 953 (Ill. 1995); *People v. Holt*, 649 N.E.2d 571 (Ill. App. 3 Dist. 1995); *People v. Krawiec*, 634 N.E.2d 1173 (Ill. App. 2 Dist. 1994); *Commonwealth v. Matsos*, 657 N.E.2d 467 (Mass. 1995); *Commonwealth v. Kwiatkowski*, 637 N.E.2d 854 (Mass. 1994); *People v. White*, 536 N.W.2d 876 (Mich. App. 1995); *State v. Cooney*, 894 P.2d 303 (Mont. 1995); *State v. Martel*, 902 P.2d 14 (Mont. 1995); *State v. Benner*, 644 N.E.2d 1130 (Ohio App. 1 Dist. 1994); *State v. Dario*, 665 N.E.2d 759 (Ohio App. 1 Dist. 1995); *Dayton v. Smith*, 646 N.E.2d 917 (Ohio. Mun. 1994); *State v. Saunders*, 886 P.2d 496 (Okla. 1994); *State v. Norris-Romine*, 894 P.2d 1221 (Or. App. 1995), *review granted*, 900 P.2d 509; *Commonwealth v. Urrutia*, 653 A.2d 706 (Pa. Super. 1995); *State v. McGill*, 536 N.W.2d 89 (S.D. 1995); *Woolfolk v. Commonwealth*, 447 S.E.2d 530 (Va. App. 1994); *State v. Lee*, 917 P.2d 159 (Wash. App. Div. 1 1996); *Garton v. State*, 910 P.2d 1348 (Wyo. 1996); *Luplow v. State*, 897 P.2d 463 (Wyo. 1995). *See also Stalking Law Withstands Constitutional Scrutiny*, NAT'L L.J., Feb. 19, 2001, at A14 (reporting on Sixth Circuit decision in *Metropolitan Opera Association Inc. v. Local 100, Hotel Employees and Restaurant Employees International Union*, 239 F.3d 172 (2001)).

307 *See* Tanenbaum, *supra* note 38, at p. 17 (citing Tamar Stieber, *Viewpoint*, GLAMOUR, August 1996, at p. 138).

308 *Id.* (citing Stieber, *supra* note 307, at p. 138). (Tanenbaum argues that "[i]t's amazing but true: Even today a common way to damage a woman's credibility is to call her a slut. Look at former CIA station-chief Janine Brookner, who was falsely accused of being a drunken 'slut' after she reprimanded several corrupt colleagues in the early 1990s." *Id.* (citing Tim Weiber, *C.I.A. To Pay $410,000 to Spy Who Says She Was Smeared*, N.Y. TIMES, Dec. 8, 1999, at A1). "Consider Anita Hill, whose accusation that Clarence Thomas sexually harassed her was dismissed by the Senate, because, in the mem-

orable words of journalist David Brock, she was 'a bit nutty and a bit slutty.'" *Id.* (citing David Brock, *The Real Anita Hill*, THE AMERICAN SPECTATOR, March 1992, at p. 27).)

309   Media reports suggest that in 1998, Internet millionaires were popping up left and right, made wealthy by a stream of electronic commerce that included the posting of sex videos created in the homes and bedrooms of suburban couples. *See, e.g., Dirty Money?,* 48 HOURS, CBS-TV, airing on April 1, 1999 (Erin Moriarty, reporting), at pp. 17–23 (transcript) (available through Burrelle's). At other times, the money has reportedly been made without the permission of the people involved. *See, e.g., Tough Cookie,* DATELINE, NBC-TV, airing June 30, 1998 (Josh Mankiewicz, reporting), at pp. 2–7 (transcript).

310   In a case crowded with ex-girlfriends and lost friends, contradictory contradictions, retractions, false statements, and ever-swirling theories, Turner, who reportedly met and began dating Carruth when she was in high school and he was a senior at the University of Colorado, was originally listed as a witness for Carruth. But for reasons COURT-TV described as "unclear," Turner reportedly called the victim's father, who eventually got her in touch with the prosecutor's office. And Turner became a witness for the state, testifying that Carruth once "threatened to kill her if she refused to abort his baby." *See Former Girlfriend: Carruth Threatened to Kill Me Over Pregnancy,* COURT-TV transcript. Carruth was charged with "masterminding the murder of Cherica Adams, a 24-year-old woman pregnant with his child." During cross-examination by Carruth's attorney, David Rudolf, the exchange quickly grew hot with sarcasm and barely disguised allegations. Rudolf challenged Turner's defection by recounting that she had once called his office to ask whether she should return a Charlotte investigator's calls. Later, according to COURT-TV, "Rudolf sought to undermine [Turner's] powerful testimony by getting her to admit that she used student loan money for breast implants. [¶] 'What does that have to do with anything?' [Turner] asked. [¶] 'It's called fraud,' Rudolf shot back." *Id.,* at pp. 3–4. But was Turner's alleged breast implant fraud enough to make Carruth hate her? Was it enough to discredit her testimony? Other more legitimate legal attempts to discredit Turner's testimony included having Turner admit that she had watched parts of the trial on television, though she was a potential witness in the case, and demonstrating that Turner had painted an entirely different picture of Carruth for *People* magazine.

311   The term *quid pro quo* literally means "[w]hat for what; something for something." *See* BLACK'S LAW DICTIONARY, *supra* note 109, at p. 867. In the sexual harassment context—cases involving claims grounded in gender discrimination or unwelcomed sexual coercion or contact—*quid pro quo* was often taken to mean a demand, request or suggestion of sex in exchange for something in the professional context. Or, as author Lynne Eisaguirre explains, "[o]ne type of sexual harassment occurs when submission to sexual requests serves as a basis for employment or educational decisions, such as employee selection, grades, graduation, performance appraisal, merit increases, promotions, or tenure." *See* Lynne Eisaguirre, SEXUAL HARASSMENT (Santa Barbara, California, ABC-CLIO, Inc., 1993), at p. 8. Though this type of harassment occurs less often today than it once did given profile of the issues following the Anita Hill–Clarence Thomas debate, one recent example of *quid pro quo* sexual harassment involved an Illinois car dealership some of whose managers reportedly "demanded sexual favors or dances in exchange for job security and pay raises." *See Car Dealer in Settlement,* N.Y. TIMES, May 25, 2002, at A12; Gary Young, *Temps Settle Harassment Case,* NAT'L L.J., June 10, 2002, at A17.

312   Within the confines of a courtroom, most things said are held immune from later civil charges of defamation under the theory that if someone under oath tells a lie, he or she can be criminals prosecuted for perjury.

313   As set forth in Chapter One, single women were traditionally viewed as "viral," the literal *bearers* of ill-tidings.

314   As a point of law, "[d]efamation is made up of the twin torts of libel and slander the one being, in general, written while the other in general is oral, with somewhat different rules applicable to each. In either form, defamation is an invasion of the interest in reputation and good name…. Consequently defamation requires that something be communicated to a third person that may affect that opinion." *See* PROSSER AND KEETON ON TORTS, *supra* note 210, ENDNOTES FOR CHAPTER ELEVEN, Chapter 19, Sec. 111, at p. 771.

315   *See* THE SLANDER OF WOMEN ACT, 54 & 55 VICT. CH. 51 (1891) (reprinted in Peter F. Carter-Ruck and Richard Walker, CARTER-RUCK ON LIBEL AND SLANDER (London: Butterworths (3rd ed., 1985)), at p. 378, Appendix I. (The Slander of Women Act of 1891 provided:
An Act to amend the Law relating to the Slander of Women
Be it Enacted etc. as follows:
    1. Amendment of law Words spoken and published after the passing of this Act which impute unchastity or adultery to any women or girl shall not require special damage to render them actionable. [¶] Provided always, that in any action for words spoken and made actionable by this Act, a plaintiff shall not recover more costs than damages, unless the judge shall certify that there was reasonable ground for bringing the action.)

316   *See* Carter-Ruck and Walker, *supra* note 316. (Prior to passage of the SLANDER OF WOMEN ACT, women were required to prove special damages. It was problematic judged interested in fairness. "Even the judges holding the highest judicial stations in that country have felt constrained to

decide, that to say of a married female that she was a liar, an infamous wretch, and that she had been all but seduced by a notorious libertine, was not actionable without averring and proving special damages," wrote Justice Clifford in *Pollard v. Lyons*, 91 U.S. 225, 235 (1875) (citing *Lynch v. Knight*, 9 H. of L. Cas. 594)).

317 *Id.* at 793 n. 98 and 794 n. 19.

318 *See, e.g., Davies v. Gardiner*, 79 Eng. Rep. 1155 (1593) (holding that a charge on incontinence made against an unmarried woman resulting in the loss of her marriage - was actionable). *See also Oxford v. Cross*, 76 Eng.Rep.902 (1599); *Matthew v. Crass*, 1614, Cro.Jac. 323, 79 Eng.Rep. 276 (1614); *Moody v. Baker*, 5 Cow. 351 (1826). *See also* PROSSER AND KEETON ON TORTS, *supra* note 314, at p. 793, n. 98 and p. 794, n. 19. *Reitan v. Goebel*, 33 Minn. 151 (1885) also involved an allegation of incontinence. By that time, however, the law seems to have progressed. "And in no other case," the court wrote, "can it be more fairly presumed that the scandal, if believed, will produce injury, than where an unmarried female is charged with incontinence."

319 For general discussion of this issue, *see e.g.,* Ferguson, *supra* note 96, ENDNOTES FOR CHAPTER ONE, at pp. 102–106.

320 *See, e.g., Smith v. Gaffard*, 31 Ala. 45 (1857); *Pink v. Catanich*, 51 Cal. 420 (1876); *Richter v. Stolze*, 158 Mich. 594 (Mich. 1909); *Vanloon v. Vanloon*, 159 Mo. App. 255 (1911). (In all of the above cases, the assertions at issue involved suggestions of a lack of chastity. What they were, however, is not always clear. In *Richter v. Stolze*, 158 Mich. at 13, for example, the court would note only that "[t]he words charged and proved to have been spoken by defendant are unprintable and imputed to plaintiff a want of chastity." Though the court details the allegedly troublesome words in *Vanloon v. Vanloon*, 159 Mo. App. at 632, they aren't illuminating. The words at issue were, "[y]ou run her, you know you did while she worked for your hotel.")

321 *See, e.g., Pollard v. Lyon*, 91 U.S. at 226 (involving the allegation that "I saw [plaintiff] in bed with Captain Denty." According to the Court, "[c]ertain words, all admit, are in themselves actionable, because the natural consequence of what they impute to the party is damage, as if they import a charge that the party has been guilty of a criminal offence [sic] involving moral turpitude, or that the party is infected with a contagious distemper, or if they are prejudicial in a pecuniary sense to a person in office or to a person engaged as a livelihood in a profession or trade; but in all other cases the party who brings an action for words must show the damage he or she has suffered by the false speaking of the other party"); *Kelly v. Flaherty*, 16 R.I. 234 (1888) (involving the assertion, made directly towards plaintiff, that "[y]ou are a bitch and a whore; you visit the Halfway House, and got your dress there"); *Miller v. Parish*, 8 Pick. 384 (with the court noting that "[i]n Massachusetts, the rule was laid down more broadly, namely: 'When an offense is charged which, if proved, may subject the party to a punishment not ignominious, but which brings disgrace upon the party falsely accused, such an accusation is actionable;' and in that case it was held to be actionable *per se* to charge an unmarried woman with fornication"). And, in fact, the rule set forth in *Miller v. Parish* became the rule in several states. *See, e.g., Patterson v. Wilkinson*, 55 Me. 42; *Woodbury v. Thompson*, 3 N.H. 194; *Symonds v. Carter*, 32 N.H. 458; *Vanderlip v. Roe*, 23 Pa. St. 82; *Ranger v. Goodrich*, 17 Wis. 80; *Mayer v. Schleichter*, 29 Wis. 646; *Hoag v. Hatch*, 23 Conn. 585, 590; *Zeliff v. Jennings*, 61 Tex. 458 (declaring that "[w]e think it the better rule; for it seems to us that the defamatory effect of the words charging a disgraceful offense is substantially the same, whatever the form of criminal procedure under which the offense may be punished. In Iowa and Ohio words charging an unmarried woman with fornication are held to be actionable *per se*, 'on the broad and plain ground that it would immediately and necessarily tend to hinder her advancement:' the presumption of damage being allowed to supply the place of actual proof."); *Cleveland v. Detweiler*, 18 Iowa, 299; *Barnett v. Ward*, 36 Ohio St. 107; 38 Amer. Rep. 561, *exceptions overruled; Davis v. Sladden*, 17 Or. 259 (Or. 1889) (involving the statement that "Fenton sent those two prostitutes to talk with my wife; meaning this plaintiff and her mother," and, according to the court, "[a]s a married woman, the plaintiff could not be a prostitute without having committed repeated adulteries. Such are the direct and legal consequences of the illicit acts which make up the character of a prostitute when the woman is married. To say of a married woman that she is a 'prostitute' is necessary to impute to her the guilt of adultery, and, as under our law adultery is indictable and punishable, such as words charge a crime, and are actionable *per se*. Such has been the holding in the several states which have statutes making adultery a punishable offense, and the decisions have gone on the ground that such charge, if true, rendered her liable to punishment under such statutes."); *Klewin v. Bauman*, 53 Wis. 244 (holding that words accusing a married woman of being a prostitute are actionable *per se*); *Ranger v. Goodrich*, 17 Wis. 82, (holding that words accusing a married woman of being a whore were actionable *per se*). *See, also, Sheehey v. Cokley*, 43 Iowa 185; *Pledger v. Hathcock*, 1 Ga. 551. In states where adultery or fornication are indictable by statute, words imputing that a person has been guilty of such either offense were *per se* actionable. *See, e.g., Stieber v. Wensel*, 19 Mo. 513; *Miller v. Parish*, 8 Pick. 385; *Truman v. Taylor*, 4 Iowa 425; *Vanderlip v. Roe*, 23 Pa. St. 82; *Burford v. Wible*, 32 Pa. St. 95; *Spencer v. McMasters*, 16 Ill. 405; *Moberly v. Preston*, 8 Mo. 462; *Wilson v. Barnett*, 45 Ind. 163; *Symond v. Carter*, 32 N.H. 458; *Stroebel v. Whitney*, 31 Minn. 384; *Klewin v. Bauman*, 53 Wis. 244; *Odgers*, SLAND. & LIB. 84, and note ("It is no longer the rule that the words alleged to be slanderous are to be construed in *mittiori sensu*, but they are to be

taken in their ordinary sense, as they would naturally be understood by those to whom they were addressed. If the words fairly import the charge of a crime, and would be so understood by mankind, the injury is inflicted on the character of the plaintiff as completely and fully as if the crime had been imputed.") *See Woolnorth v. Meadows*, 5 East 463; *Walton v. Singleton*, 7 Serg. & R. 450; *Damarest v. Haring*, 6 Cow. 76; *Duncan v. Brown*, 15 B. Mon. 186; *Dixon v. Stewart*, 33 Iowa 125; *Butterfield v. Buffum*, 9 N.H. 156; *Hancock v. Stephens*, 11 Humph. 507; *Brown v. Nickerson*, 5 Gray 1.

322   In addition to the cases cited above, see also, *Ledlie v. Wallen*, 17 Mont. 150 (1895), involving the assertion that the plaintiff was a "damned dirty whore"; *Douglas v. Douglas*, 4 Idaho 293 (1895), involving the allegation of "[t]hat woman (meaning the plaintiff) is a woman of shady character. Mrs. Douglas is a public prostitute." Many of these cases remain on the law books today, though the antiquated rule is generally no longer applied.

323   *See, e.g., Cooper v. Seaverns*, 81 Kan. 267 (1909) (involving assertions that the plaintiff was a "dirty slut"); *Barnett v. Phelps*, 97 Or. 242 (1920) (involving the allegation that the plaintiff was "a whore"); *Biggerstaff v. Zimmerman*, 114 P.2d 1098 (Colo. 1941) (involving "imputations of unchastity...so vulgarly expressed that, in the interest of decency, we [the court] refrain from quoting the language"); *Crellin v. Thomas*, 247 P.2d 264 (Utah 1952) (involving an assertion that "Mrs. Crellin was a whore"); *Hollman v. Brady*, 233 F.2d 877 (9th Cir. 1956) (Alaska law) (involving assertions that a man's wife was "an ex-whore from Butte, Montana"); *Gnapinsky v. Goldyn*, 128 A.2d 697 (N.J. 1957). Recent cases include: *Sauerhoff v. Hearst Corp.*, 388 F. Supp. 117 (D. Md. 1974); *Neiman-Marcus v. Lait*, 13 F.R.D. 311 (S.D.N.Y. 1952) (involving assertions impliedly made in the book U.S.A. CONFIDENTIAL that some models in the company's Dallas store were "call girls" and "most of the [male] staff are fairies." Legal scholars note that the above rule of law has never been applied to men, though in theory and under constitutional law, it should. As stated above, however, the law has never been applied that way because the social value of men has never been tied to their "virtue.")

324   Judges, for example, have absolute immunity against lawsuits based in defamation as long as their acts are arguably "judicial." *See, e.g., Pierson v. Ray*, 386 U.S. 547 (1967); *Holland v. Lutz*, 194 Kan. 712 (1965); *Stump v. Sparkman*, 435 U.S. 349 (1978), *reh'g den.*, 436 U.S. 951; *Rankin v. Howard*, 633 F.2d 844 (9th Cir. 1980), *cert. den.*, 451 U.S. 939; *Harris v. Harvey*, 605 F.2d 330 (7th Cir. 1979), *cert. den.*, 445 U.S. 938; *Zarcone v. Perry*, 572 F.2d 52 (2d Cir. 1978). This is so even if the judge knows that what he is saying is false and his motivations are not good. *See, e.g., Scott v. Stansfield*, L.R. 3 Ex. 220 (1868); *Irwin v. Ashurst*, 158 Or. 61 (1938); *Ginger v. Bowles*, 369 Mich. 680 (1962), *cert. den.*, 375 U.S. 856, *reh'g den.*, 375 U.S. 982; *Mundy v. McDonald*, 216 Mich. 444 (1921); *Karelas v. Baldwin*, 237 A.D. 265 (1932). A judge's opinions are covered by immunity. *See, e.g., Hanft v. Heller*, 64 Misc.2d 947 (N.Y. Sup. 1970). Judicial immunity falls from absolute to qualified when a judge handles an administrative function, such as discharging an employee. *See, e.g., Lynch v. Johnson*, 420 F.2d 818 (6th Cir. 1970). Grand juries are covered by absolute immunity. *See, e.g., Hayslip v. Wellford*, 195 Tenn. 621 (1953), *cert. den.*, 346 U.S. 911; *Ryon v. Shaw*, 77 F.2d 455 (Fla. 1955); *O'Regan v. Schermerhorn*, 25 N.J.Misc. 1 (1946); *Engelke v. Chouteau*, 98 Mo. 629 (1889). *See also*, NOTE, 31 MINN. L. REV. 500 (1937); NOTE, 8 U. FLA. L. REV. 342 (1955). Petit juries are as well. *See, e.g., Dunham v. Powers*, 42 Vt. 1 (1868); *Irwin v. Murphy*, 129 Cal. App. 713 (1933). Witnesses are also covered. *See, e.g., Seaman v. Netherclift*, 46 L.J.C.P. (1876); *Massey v. Jones*, 182 Va. 200 (1944); *Veazey v. Blair*, 86 Ga. App. 721 (1952); *Johnson v. Dover*, 201 Ark. 175 (1952); *Taplin-Rice-Clerkin Co. v. Hower*, 124 Ohio St. 123 (1931). This is true even if the testimony offered is perjured and/or malicious. *See, e.g., Felts v. Paradise*, 178 Tenn. 421 (1942); *Kinter v. Kinter*, 84 Ohio App. 399 (1949); *Buchanan v. Miami Herald Publishing Co.*, 206 So.2d 465 (Fla. App. 1968). (Witnesses who commit perjury may, however, be held criminally responsible.) The immunity is for civil liability. Testimony offered under subpoena or voluntarily is equally immune. *See, e.g., Beggs v. McCrea*, 70 N.Y.S. 864 (1901); *Buschbaum v. Heriot*, 5 Ga. App. 521 (1909); *Ginsburg v. Halpern*, 383 Pa. 178 (1955); *Weil v. Lynds*, 105 Kan. 440 (1919). Testimony offered via deposition and/or affidavit is also immune. *See, e.g., Dunbar v. Greenlaw*, 128 A.2d 218 (1956); *Dyer v. Dyer*, 156 S.W.2d 445 (1941); *Mezullo v. Maletz*, 331 Mass. 233 (1954); *Jarman v. Offutt*, 239 N.C. 468 (1954). A person who improperly undertakes or has created an affidavit is not immune. *See, e.g., Baily v. McGill*, 247 N.C. 286 (1957). Pleadings are covered by the privilege as are affidavits and what is said in open court. *See, e.g., Di Blasio v. Kolodner*, 233 Md. 512 (1964); *Taliaferro v. Sims*, 187 F.2d 6 (5th Cir. 1951); *Fletcher v. Maupin*, 138 F.2d 742 (4th Cir. 1943), *cert. den.*, 322 U.S. 750; *McClure v. Stretch*, 20 Wn.2d 460 (1944); *Greenberg v. Aetna Ins. Co.*, 427 Pa. 511 (1967), *cert. den.*, 392 U.S. 907; *Sacks v. Stecker*, 60 F.2d 73 (2d Cir. 1932); *Hager v. Major*, 353 Mo. 1166 (1945); *Stone v. Hutchison Daily News*, 125 Kan. 715 (1928); *Keeley v. Great N. Ry. Co.*, 156 Wis. 181 (1914); *Tonkonogy v. Jaffin*, 41 Misc.2d 155 (1963), *app. dism'd*, 21 A.D.2d 264; *Wells v. Carter*, 164 Tenn. 400 (1932); *Nissen v. Cramer*, 104 N.C. 574 (1889); *Clemmons v. Danforth*, 67 Vt. 617 (1895); *McDavitt v. Boyer*, 169 Ill. 475 (1897). Among the more recent cases, *see, e.g., In re IBP Confidential Bus. Documents Litig., Bagley v. Iowa Beef Processors, Inc.*, 755 F.2d 1300 (8th Cir. 1985); *Beeves v. Am.Broadcasting Companies, Inc. v. O. Giaimo*, 719 F.2d 602 (2nd Cir. 1983); *Wyatt v. Kaplan*, 712 F.2d 1002 (5th Cir. 1983); *Lepucki v. Van Wormer*, 587 F. Supp. 1390 (D.C. Cir. 1984); *Morinville v. Old Colony Cooperative Bank*, 579 F. Supp.

1498 (R.I. Dist. 1984); *Wickstrom v. Ebert*, 585 F. Supp. 924 (Wis. Dist. 1984); *Smith v. McDonald*, 562 F. Supp. 829 (N.C. Dist. 1983); *Hester v. Barnett*, 723 S.W.2d 544 (Mo. App. W.D. 1987); *McClatchy Newspapers, Inc. v. Superior Court of Fresno County*, 234 Cal. Rptr. 702 (Cal. App. 5 Dist. 1987); *Cutter v. Brownbridge*, 228 Cal. Rptr. 545 (Cal. App. 1 Div. 1986); *Defend v. Lascelles*, 500 N.E.2d 712 (Ill. App. 4 Dist. 1986); *Petyan v. Ellis*, 510 A.2d 1337 (Conn. 1986); *Rouch v. Enquirer & News of Battle Creek*, 398 N.W.2d 245 (Mich. 1986); *Surace v. Wuliger*, 495 N.E.2d 939 (Ohio 1986); *Bell v. Gellert*, 469 So.2d 141 (Fla. App. 3 Dist. 1985); *Ernst v. Ind. Bell Tel. Co.*, 475 N.E.2d 351 (Ind. App. 1985); *Fulghum v. United Parcel Serv., Inc.*, 424 Mich. 89 (1985); *Miner v. Novotny*, 498 A.2d 269 (Md. App. 1985); *Ribas v. Clark*, 696 P.2d 637 (1985); *Stilsing Elec., Inc. v. Joyce*, 495 N.Y.S.2d 999 (N.Y. 1985); *Barchers v. MoPac. RR Co.*, 669 S.W.2d 235 (Mo. App. E.D. 1984); *Erickson v. Aetna Life & Casualty Co.*, 469 N.E.2d 679 (Ill. App. 2 Dist. 1984); *Green Acres Trust v. London*, 688 P.2d 617 (Ariz. 1984); *Paros v. Hoemako Hosp.*, 681 P.2d 918 (Ariz. App. 1984); *Thomas v. Petrulis*, 465 N.E.2d 1059 (Ill. App. 2 Dist. 1984); *Wright v. Yurko*, 446 So.2d 1162 (Fla. App. 5 Dist. 1984); *Adamson v. Bonesteele*, 671 P.2d 693 (Or. 1983); *Andrews v. Steinberg*, 471 N.Y.S.2d 764 (N.Y. 1983); *Nix v. Sawyer*, 466 A.2d 407 (Sup. Ct. Del. 1983); *Park Knoll Assocs. v. Schmidt*, 464 N.Y.S.2d 424 (N.Y. App. 1983); *Perl v. Omin Int'l of Miami, Ltd.*, 439 So.2d 316 (Fla. App. D.C. 1983); *Village of Oakwood v. Makar*, 463 N.E.2d 61 (Ohio App. 1983); *Weissman v. Hassett*, 47 B.R. 462 (N.Y. Dist. 1985).

325   *See supra* note 64.

CHAPTER FOURTEEN

Current Issues in Rape and Sexual Assault Law

RAPE AND SEXUAL ASSAULT:
The Cultural Debate—The Legal Issues

"The conduct that one might think of as 'rape' ranges from the armed stranger who breaks into a woman's home to the date she invited in who takes silence for assent," argues former Harvard law professor, Susan Estrich.[1] "In between are literally hundreds of variations: the man may be a stranger, but he may not be armed; he may be armed, but he may not be a stranger; he may be an almost, rather than a perfect, stranger—a man who gave her a ride or introduced himself through a ruse; she may say yes, but only because he threatens to expose her to the police or the welfare authorities; she may say no, but he may ignore her words."[2]

It has been hotly debated, and, thus, written into law in some states,[3] that rape is not a crime "about sex," but is rather a crime of violence:[4] a deliberate, conscious, at times calculated, and always necessarily determined act on the part of the men who choose to engage in such conduct. Feminist scholar Kathleen Barry argues, for example, that "[i]n committing a crime against women, sexual satisfaction, usually in the form of orgasm, is one of the intended outcomes of sexual violence for the aggressor who united sex and violence to subdue, humiliate, degrade, and terrorize his female victim."[5]

Other feminists scholars offer a more forceful definition. "Forcible rape is the direct use of superior power to bypass consent and gain sexual access," argue Linda R. Hirshman and Jane E. Larson, in *Hard Bargains: The Politics of Sex*.[6] "When men and women come together to negotiate the exchange of sexual access, the law against rape is a key determinant of the initial distribution of their sexual bargaining power."

And yet, what if rape wasn't about any of that? What if rape were, instead, about Darwinism? What if it could be said, for example, that while rape may be a crime of violence or sex, or both, the impulse behind the act may stem not from sexual desire or the need to dominate, but rather from an evolutionary impulse?

In the spring of 2000, Randy Thornhill and Craig T. Palmer argued in *A Natural History of Rape: Biological Bases of Sexual Coercion*[7] that "[e]volutionary theory applies to rape, as it does to other areas of human affairs, on both logical and evidentiary grounds."[8] Indeed, in a nearly 200-page exploration of the issue Thornhill and Palmer lean heavily on the premise that "nothing in biology makes sense except in light of evolution."[9]

At the heart of their argument is the notion that "[t]he males of most species—including humans—are usually more eager to mate than the females, and this enables females to choose among males who are competing with one another for access to them. But getting chosen is not the only way to gain sexual access to females. In rape, the male circumvents the female's choice."[10]

Thornhill and Palmer concede that there are other ways to increase one's access to women.[11] But this concession appears to be little more than rhetorical filler. What Thornhill and Palmer clearly want to get to is the reason for the book, *i.e.,* discussion of whether human rape is an evolutionary adaptation—a bodily trait that is a product of direct selection for the adaptation's function (including psychological traits)—or a by-product of other psychological adaptations, "especially those that function to produce the sexual desires of males for multiple partners without commitment."[12]

It is a provocative theory, one that raises more questions than it can answer when applied to rape in modern society or recent events. Was Darwinian adaptation responsible, for example, for the 35-minute rampage during New York City's Puerto Rican Day Parade in June 2000, and the series of sexually charged incidents that followed? Fifty-nine women, many of whom were doused with water and beer, were grabbed, groped, and sometimes robbed. Shirts, shorts, and underwear were torn off, leaving women barely clad[13] and in one case, completely nude.[14] Even middle-aged, "properly dressed" women—clearly beyond the age of reproduction—were not safe.[15] Nearly forty men were arrested following the incidents.[16]

Was it adaptation that led law enforcement officials in two jurisdictions to demand sexual favors from women in exchange for dismissal of minor or falsely-brought charges in a series of incidents drawing public attention in 2001?[17] Or that led a married man—a father of three—to rape two little girls, ages 9 and 11, below the normal age of human reproduction?[18] Does the Darwinian *need* to procreate force a man to slip GHB into the cocktail of an unsuspecting woman?

Though the rape-as-adaptation theory Thornhill and Palmer offer is grounded in the dark science of Darwinian suggestion, the modern face of rape is very different from that of the scorpion fly, which Thornhill and Palmer use to bolster their argument. Putting scientific arguments to the contrary to the side for a moment, the fact that rape does involve "circumventing" a woman's choice is precisely the reason that rape is against the law. Somewhere in time, legislators came to terms with the fact that women—even those women who are "choosy" or who may be less "eager" than men—should not be forced to "mate."

And there is another hitch in the Thornhill/Palmer theory. The Department of Justice reported in 1994, that roughly 28 percent of the women raped were the victims of husbands or boyfriends and 35 percent of women were the victims of acquaintances.[19] But 55 percent of those women who reported rapes were the victims of relatives other than husbands.[20] There is some overlap between the latter two categories, because some relatives were so distant as to be listed in the "acquaintance." And yet, the question this particular fact poses remains: Was it the intent of these relatives to procreate as well?

In reviewing *A Natural History of Rape* for *Nature*, University of Chicago evolutionist Jerry Coyne and Harvard University Zoologist Andrew Berry conclude that although Thornhill and Palmer "argue that rape is an adaptation...[t]heir analysis...forms the basis of a protracted sales pitch for evolutionary psychology, the latest incarnation of sociology: not only do the authors believe that this should be the explanatory model of choice in the human behavioral sciences, but they also want to see its insights incorporated into social policy. Thus, in a single volume, Thornhill and Palmer give us both an inflammatory analysis of a sensitive topic, and a manifesto outlining evolutionary biology's future conquest of the social sciences."[21]

It is perhaps ironic, then, that it is the science of *A Natural History of Rape* that falls short, according to Coyle and Berry. "In their media appearances, Thornhill and Palmer cloak themselves in the authority of science, implying that the controversy over their ideas is purely political, and that the underlying biology is unimpeachable. This is a serious misrepresentation."[22]

Instead of sound science, *A Natural History of Rape* is based on an "ingenious rhetorical trick," Coyne and Berry argue.[23] A trick that includes proposing two evolutionary hypotheses in the alternative. The first of these notions is that rape is an adaptation of natural selection; the second is that if it is not an adaptation, it is an accidental by-product of natural selection. It is a device that sets up a false default conclusion: if it is not one, it must be the other, Coyne and Berry suggest.[24]

Still, the real premise is that rape is an adaptation, a contention Thornhill and Palmer attempt to support by citing "sociological studies, female rape victims of reproductive age are more traumatized by the experience than are women either too old or too young to reproduce."[25] In addition, Thornhill and Palmer appear to argue that because young women of reproductive age are conscious of the fact that pregnancy may be the result of rape, they fight harder than older women and little girls. And this, Thornhill and Palmer suggest, accounts for the fact that women in this age group tend to experience more violence during attacks.

But Coyne and Berry counter that "[w]hile is it true that women of reproductive age who resist rape may be partly motivated by the fear of unwanted conception, it is also true that such women, [are] at the peak of their bodily strength.... [c]hildren cannot fight off a full-grown man, and older women may also find resistance beyond them."[26]

Young women may also "fight harder" today—if they, in fact, do—because they don't want to die of AIDS, a virus that was around in 2000, when *A Natural History of Rape* was published. In that sense, the fact that women of reproductive age may fight harder may be a specific adaptation of women to the adaptation of men. Feminists and women's rights group argue, of course, that Thornhill and Palmer's theory is simply another attempt to let men who rape off the hook; this time by leaning on science.

Regardless of the politics one brings to the debate, Thornhill and Palmer's adaptation theory raises one other question that simply cannot be answered by rape adaptation theories based upon procreative urges: If rape is really an adaptation with the ultimate goal of procreation, why, then, do men rape other men? There is, after all, no rational procreative urge involved in such an incident. And yet, male rape is a reality. According to the United States Department of Justice, there were 32,900 rapes and sexual assaults reported against men in 1994.[27]

THE LESS CEREBRAL MEASURES OF RAPE AND SEXUAL ASSAULT: *The Statistical Dimensions*

Rapes and sexual assaults—whether Darwinian adaptation or psychological by-product—happens quite often to women in the United States. Every two minutes a woman is raped somewhere in America.[28] Across the country, more than 700 women are raped every Friday night and in August of 1992, 168 women were raped in the city of Los Angeles alone.[29] But these, some would argue, are the soft numbers: those that appear or are often quoted in women's magazines, thereby reenforcing the notion that rape is a "women's"—as opposed to a criminal—issue.

The hard numbers—those gathered and analyzed by the United States Department of Justice, Bureau of Statistics—suggest that rape is not only a national issue, but it is also a social problem that routinely reaches girls who are barely of reproductive age. "[W]omen 12 and older" experienced an estimated 5 million "victimizations" in 1994, 432,000 of them were rapes or sexual assaults.[30] In 1995, Department of Justice statistics suggested that "persons age 12 or older reported experiencing an estimated 260,300 attempted or completed rapes and nearly 95,000 threatened or completed sexual assaults other than rape."[31]

Justice Department statistics suggest that in recent years the rate of rape—along with those of most other violent crimes—has fallen, though in the case of rape only slightly.[32] Specifically, Justice Department statistics suggest that "[t]he highest rate of forcible rape recorded by law enforcement agencies since 1976 was in 1992—84 per 100,000 women, or about one forcible rape for every 1,200 women."[33] By 1995, however, the statistical incidents of forcible rape had declined by 14 percent. But that was forcible rape. There are other numbers and descriptions that further illuminate the picture of rape as a criminal phenomenon.

In the early morning hours of August 26, 1992, a California woman awoke to find her hands tied behind her back.[34] What the woman would later recall of the earlier part of the day was that she had "worked on a graphic-design project in [her] home office, had lunch with [her] boyfriend, and devoted the rest of the day to errands and chores," before falling asleep, still dressed and with the television on, at about 10 P.M.[35]

Roughly four hours later, the woman awoke to find "a stranger…on top of [her]."[36] The man had cut through the screen on her back door, made his way inside her home and tied her hands behind her back while she slept. He then cut off the woman's clothes and raped her. "One minute, he acted as if we were lovers, kissing me and asking if I liked it," the woman said later in going public with her story. "The next, he threatened my life. I didn't struggle or scream. I simply prayed for it to be over," the woman recalled.[37]

As stated earlier, some argue that rape is a crime of violence. Others contend that rape is a "crime of sex." New York sex crimes prosecutor Linda Fairstein says that rape is a crime of violence in which sex is the weapon.[38] And yet, by any name, reference or definition, rape often happens just as it happened in the case of the California woman.

Though most people imagine that the majority of rapes occur in dark alleys or lonely parking lots, in reality most women are raped in their own homes or in the home of a family member or friend; their attacker is someone they know. Six out of every ten rapes and/or sexual assaults reported took place in the victim's home or at the home of a friend, relative, or neighbor.[39]

For purposes of the National Crime Victimization Survey, one of two statistical series[40] maintained and analyzed by the Department of Justice, rape is defined as "forced sexual intercourse where the victim may be either male or female and the offender may be of the same sex or a different sex from the victim."[41] By contrast, the term sexual assault includes "a wide range of victimizations involving attacks in which unwanted sexual contact occurs between the victim and the offender," Justice Department officials explain. And "[t]hreats and attempts to commit such offenses are included in the counts."[42]

An estimated two-thirds of all rapes and/or sexual assaults take place between 6 P.M. and 6 A.M.,[43] and more than half of all rapes and/or sexual assaults reported by victims "occurred within one mile of their home or at their homes."[44] Only one in every sixteen victims reported the offender using a firearm during the attack.[45] Instead, most—84 percent—of all rape and sexual assault victims involved in the study reported that "no weapon was used by the offender."[46]

Further, the wishful thinking of pornographers not withstanding, rape and/or sexual assault remains overwhelmingly a solitary event: 9 out of 10 rape or sexual assault "victimizations involved a single offender," according to Justice Department statistics.[47] An estimated three of four rape or sexual assault victims are attacked or abused by a person or persons "with whom the victim [has] had a prior relationship" such as "a family member, intimate, or acquaintance."[48]

Though overall statistics vary slightly from year-to-year, the Justice Department estimates that 91 percent of all rape and sexual assault victims were female,[49] and nearly "99 percent of the offenders they described in single-victim incidents were male,"[50] 73.5 percent of whom were "nonstrangers" to the victim.[51] Unless the world spins off its axis and/or a new kind of adaptation takes place, that ratio is not likely to change significantly where women are concerned. But just who commits rape?

THE STATISTICAL DIMENSIONS OF RAPISTS:
Who's Playing at "Survival of the Fittest?"

Four out of every 10 rapists and/or sex offenders are 30 years or older.[52] But in about a quarter of all incidents, the offenders are under 21 years of age, and in a relatively small number of instances—10.9 percent of single offenders incidents; 4.4 percent in multiple offender incidents—minors younger than 18 are involved.[53] Though the incidents involving minor men are relatively rare, they appear plentiful, due in large part to media coverage. In other words, it becomes sensational when it happens, by dint of media coverage, which in turn makes people think that it happens more often than it really does. In October of 2000, for instance, the rape of a "40-year-old woman" by 13-year-old twins made *The New York Times*,[54] though in all likelihood, there were dozens of other rapes that day. But rape and sexual assault are not widely thought of as violent enough in most jurisdictions to require that judges deny bond.

Law enforcement agencies across the country reported that roughly half of all forcible rapes reported were cleared by an arrest in 1995. In other words, 34,650 arrests were made that year for forcible rape.[55] And yet, prior to trial, roughly half of all rape defendants charged are released.[56] People accused of most "violent crimes" are often denied bail, given the severity of the charges pending against them, statistics suggest. But rape and sexual assault are not widely thought of as violent enough in some jurisdictions to require that judges consider denying bond.

Most men convicted of rape plead guilty. In 1992, for example, 8 out of every 10 of the 21,655 felony defendants charged with rape were convicted as a result of a plea, the Justice Department reports. Though the incidents of rape may have declined, this trend has generally held. In addition, according to the Department of Justice, more than two-thirds of those convicted of rape were sentenced to prison in 1992, for an average term of 14 years. Only roughly two percent received life sentences.

What this means in terms of actual numbers is that "[o]n a given day about 234,000 offenders convicted of rape or sexual assault are under the care, custody, or control of corrections agencies," according to the Justice Department.

In addition, "[a]bout 60 percent of these sex offenders are under conditional supervision in the community."[57]

But there is a cautionary note to be struck. The most violent crimes in America are carried out by a relatively small number of offenders. With regard to rapists, two 3-year Bureau of Justice follow-up studies found that of "felons placed on probation" and "felons released from prison," rapists had "a lower rate of re-arrest for a new violent felony than most other categories of offenders convicted of violence. But rapists were more likely than others to be rearrested for a new rape."[58]

RAPE: "A CRIME OF VIOLENCE IN WHICH SEX IS THE WEAPON":
The Content and Context of "Rape Law" Today

"The woman raped at gunpoint by the intruding stranger should find most of the legal obstacles to her complaint removed," wrote well-known women's rights scholar and activist Susan Estrich in "Rape," an essay on the subject published originally in the *Yale Journal of Law*.[59] But "[t]hat was not always so...she might well have faced a corroboration requirement, a cautionary instruction [given to the jury]. A fresh complaint rule,[60] and a searing cross-examination about her sexual past to determine whether she had nonetheless consented to sex. In practice, she may still encounter some of these obstacles; but to the extent that the law communicates any clear message, it is likely to be that she was raped."

And yet, the reality is that women may still encounter more obstacles than they expect when they seek the help of law enforcement in making the initial complaint. In this sense, Justice Department statistics and history bear out what feminist and women's rights scholars—Estrich among them—have argued for years: that "...most rapes do not purely fit the traditional model [of an unknown intruder in the night]." As a result, these rape victims may not "fare as well" as the woman "fortunate enough" to have been attacked by an unknown intruder stalking her at night and wielding a gun or a knife.[61]

As set forth earlier, three out of four rapes or incidents of sexual abuse are committed against women and girls by people they in some way "know." The rapist may be a family member, an intimate, or an acquaintance.[62] And yet, where "prior relationships" exist between a victim who charges rape and the defendant who is accused of it, judges, juries, legislatures, and attorneys have long proved more skeptical of the women charging rape than of the men accused. This is true even where the "relationship" between the victim and her attacker is not "intimate" (*i.e.,* master and servant or employer and employee).

Institutional skepticism of this sort is grounded in the historic assumption that if a woman knew her attacker prior to an assault, there is reason to believe that *her* motives in bringing forth a rape or sexual assault allegation may not be pure. Another longstanding assumption in this regard is that the "intercourse" between the victim and the attacker may, in fact, have been consensual. It is this kind of reasoning, feminist and legal scholars argue, that has led even "...some appellate courts to enforce the most traditional views of women in the context of the less traditional rape."[63]

From an historic perspective, laws against rape were originally enacted to "protect rights of the male as possessor of the female body, and not the right of the female over her own body...," Susan Griffin wrote in an often-cited *Ramparts* magazine article.[64] In that same vein, Kate Millet argued that rape was viewed traditionally "'as an offense one male commits against another—a matter of abusing his woman.' In raping another man's woman, a man may aggrandize his own manhood and concurrently reduce that of another man. Thus, a man's honor is not subject directly to rape, but only indirectly, through *his* woman."

But during the late Middle Ages, "European law reconceived rape as a protection of female bodily integrity, placing the right to invoke the law in the hands of the victim," Hirshman and Larson note. And yet, "[p]erhaps because this law redistributed power from men to women (instead of from man to man, as the ancient law did), the law was weakly enforced." In other words, "[w]ith women given some power to act in their own sexual interests, the fear arose that victims would manipulate this power by lying to protect reputation, wreak revenge, or blackmail innocent men. Nowhere other than in the law of rape is the redistributive agenda of strengthening the weaker player in male-female sex more visible."[65]

The heightened political struggles of the nineteenth and twentieth centuries in the push and pull of strengthening and weakening rape laws tend to track the national trend in gender politics, reaching perhaps the highest point of sustained progress during the 1960s.[66] Still, despite the flux and great change of this period, "the standard for proof of rape remained higher in most jurisdictions than for most other crimes," argues University of Utah Professor of Law Leslie Francis in *Date Rape: Feminism, Philosophy, and the Law.*[67]

For example, in order to prove rape women frequently had to offer proof of "resistance, or corroboration beyond the victim's own testimony," Francis contends. "Proof of robbery, by contrast, required no such additional testimony; it was simply left up to the trier of fact to weigh the credibility of the victim's testimony against other evidence in the case. These requirements reflected the problematic judgment that the complainant's credibility in rape cases was inherently more suspect than credibility in other cases."[68]

The "fresh complaint" rule was the standard governing rape complaints in most jurisdictions until the mid-1970s. It was a rule generally requiring that all reports of alleged rapes be filed immediately, with women thought to lose credibility with each day they waited. The reasoning underlying the rule, of course, was that women "so violated" would be eager to come forward in the hopes of helping authorities catch her attacker. "[L]iars would be more likely to make up their stories at a distance," Francis explains.[69]

Women's rights groups and supporters of rape victim argued, however, that the "fresh complaint" rule did not take into consideration the overwhelming sense of shame or fear a victim might feel, even long after an attack. A rape or sexual assault victim's sexual history was also considered relevant in most jurisdictions, because it was thought to be a measure of her credibility. But during the 1960s, the women's rights movement ushered in a series of reforms intended to protect rape victims. For example, so-called "rape shield" laws, precluding introduction of a rape victim's sexual history, were enacted in several states during this time. The intent of these laws was to foreclose the possibility of unfair prejudice against a victim who might otherwise be forced to detail her sexual history in open court. Rape shield laws "shield" a victim's past sexual history. But they remain a source of controversy and efforts to get around them are endless, say some scholars.[70]

"One of the hot issues in evidence law today," argues University of California, Berkeley School of Law Professor Angela Harris in *A Dialogue on Evidence*, "has to do not with consent as a defense but with the defendant's argument that even though she didn't actually consent, he thought that she did. This is the 'reasonable mistake' rule. Under the rape shield statutes, the question is whether the defendant is still free to introduce evidence of the complainant's past sexual history, not to prove actual consent but to prove his own mental state as to consent. There is one federal case (*Doe v. United States*, 666 F.2d 43 (4th Cir. 1981)) that says he can. This punches a hole in the rape shield laws, for the ulterior motive of introducing evidence of the complainant's past sexual life is to trade on deeply rooted beliefs that loose women ask for it or can't be raped, and even if the jury is told to use the evidence to decide not actual consent but mistake about consent, this evidence will probably have the desired effect."[71]

As set forth in greater detail below, in 1991, the Fourth Circuit Court of Appeals seemed ready, at least initially in *United States v. Saunders*,[72] to extend that ruling much to the frustration of women's rights advocates. "In *Doe*," the *Saunders* court wrote, "when confronted with the question of whether 'evidence of the defendant's "state of mind as a result of what he knew of [the victim's] reputation"' was admissible under Fed.R.Evid. 412(a), "the [*Doe*] court concluded, 'There is no indication...that this evidence was intended to be excluded when offered solely to show the accused's state of mind."[73]

Hence, the current preoccupation with the thong.

DEFINING RAPE:
Obvious Devastations; Abstruse Standards

The United States Department of Justice studies it. The FBI keeps statistical records of its occurrence. Women—and, to a far lesser extent, men—report it. And for the last half-century, rape and the reformation of rape laws have been a source of public and political debate with lawmakers acknowledging that rape—as a criminal and social phenomenon—no longer falls squarely on the shoulders of "bad girls" or unfortunate child servants.[74] And yet, articulating what it means to be raped; who has been—or can be—raped; and what is required to prove that a rape or a sexual assault has occurred remain points of conflict on the map of a troubled debate.

"Rape is criminal. Rape is gendered. Rape is sexual," says Francis.[75]

"Rape is an act of aggression in which the victim is denied her self-determination. It is an act of violence which, if not actually followed by beatings or murder, nevertheless always carries with it the threat of death. And finally, rape is a form of mass terrorism, for the victims of rape are chosen indiscriminately, but the propagandists for male supremacy broadcast that it is women who cause rape by being unchaste or in the wrong place at the wrong time—in essence, by behaving as though they were free," feminist scholar Susan Griffin suggests.[76]

Rape is controversial given all that it involves and because it straddles both the criminal and the social realms. "Two decades ago, Susan Brownmiller's *Against Our Will: Men, Women, and Rape*, brought feminist attention to the history, sociology, and criminal law of rape. Brownmiller argued that rape is a crime of violence, not of passion. In sweeping and powerful descriptions of rape in war, in pogroms, and in slavery, Brownmiller argues that rape is 'nothing more or less than a conscious process of intimidation by which *all men keep all women* in a state of fear,'" argues Francis.[77]

Others cite the social and political costs of rape for women. Griffin argued in her time, for example, that "…the existence of rape in any form is beneficial to the ruling class of white males. For rape is a kind of terrorism which severely limits the freedom of women and makes women dependent on men. Moreover, in the act of rape, the rage that one man may harbor toward another higher in the male hierarchy can be deflected toward a female scapegoat. For every man there is always someone lower on the social scale on whom he can take out his aggressions. And that is any woman alive…."[78]

African American feminist writer Angela Davis argues in *Women, Culture & Politics*, that "[r]ape bears a direct relationship to all of the existing power structures in a given society. The relationship is not a simply mechanical one, but rather involves complex structures reflecting the interconnectedness of the race, gender, and class oppression that characterize the society."[79] Hirshman and Larson argue, as others have, that "[f]orcible rape is the direct use of superior power to bypass consent and gain sexual access."[80]

Even men seem to understand this. Eldridge Cleaver wrote in the critically acclaimed, *Soul on Ice*, for example, that "[r]ape is an insurrectionary act. It delighted me that I was defying and trampling upon the white man's law, upon his system of values, and that I was defiling his women—and this point, I believe, was the most satisfying to me because I was very resentful over the historical fact of how the white man had used the black woman."[81]

It was this pattern of ethnic revenge, incidentally, that drew the attention of Human Rights commissioners at the start of the millennium. In February 2001, the war tribunal at the Hague formally recognized "sexual enslavement" as a crime against humanity in convicting three Bosnian Serbs of rape. The men reportedly "took part in nightly gang rapes and torture of Muslim women and girls at so-called 'rape camps'" during the Bosnian War.[82] International investigators also reportedly found evidence of "...massacres, widespread destruction...mass deportations" and "rape and sexual slavery on a wide and possibly systematic scale" in East Timor, an island nation occupied by Indonesia until 1999.[83]

Widespread systematic rape hasn't been a problem in the United States for more than one hundred years,[84] except perhaps in prison, where it overwhelmingly involves men. But it may still be a form of conquest.[85] Some scholars attribute systematic rape in wartime to a "military culture" that encourages dominant behavior.[86] Sexual enslavement and the systematic rape in Bosnia may arguably fall into this category, while the more than 400,000 individual acts of rape or sexual assault that occur annually across the United States may be part of a more general and popular "rape culture."

Rape culture theories are based upon that "complex of beliefs that encourages male sexual aggression and supports violence against women," because sexual violence is—well—sexy to some. "In a rape culture, women perceive a continuum of threatened violence that ranges from sexual remarks to sexual touching to rape itself. A rape culture condones physical and emotional terrorism against women *as the norm*," feminist scholars argue.[87]

But this, of course, is part of the problem.

Rape, Francis explains, "...is viewed more ambiguously than many other offenses."[88] One reason for this is that "[a]s a social issue, rape reflects deep divisions in our attitudes about sexuality and gender. Sexual violence, inflicted by shadowy strangers leaping out from the dark, is a serious criminal offense—although not judged sufficiently serious to warrant the death penalty.[89] Yet even victims of these 'real rapes'[90] may be vilified, more subtly but no less powerfully than the rape victims of the past who were spurned by their husbands."[91]

Feminists have long argued that from an historical perspective, women have always been the "true" suspects in cases of rape.[92] After all, a "vindictive" woman could ruin the life of the man with her "false allegations." Or so the logic went. But also traditionally stirred into this hypercharged legal and political mix was the fact that until relatively recently, women were not involved in the writing of laws. Thus, men wrote rape laws that protected men and the property of men.

In addition, there were some women in America who simply could not be raped: the rape of African and African American slaves, for example, was generally not recognized, and later, depending upon the state and the person being accused, African American women often saw their complaints dismissed or struck down by judges, juries and law enforcement officials. And then there were wives. It was not until the 1970s that legislatures began to allow that a husband could "rape" his wife.

The reasoning underlying this legal tradition was founded, of course, in the vestiges of the United States' short-lived imperialist past: under British common law, a man's wife was his property. Thus, a husband could do whatever he wanted with his wife, short of killing her. After all, "property" does not have rights. Interestingly, it was not until March of 1991, feminist writers suggest, that the British Court of Appeals invalidated the "marital rape exception."[93]

By contrast, the upstart colonies of the United States were a bit more progressive. In 1977, Oregon became the first state to do away with the marital exemption to rape.[94] A handful of states followed gingerly.[95] A year later, Oregon authorities prepared to demonstrate the state's newfound resolve by bringing a man named John Rideout to trial for the alleged rape of his estranged—*or beloved*—wife, depending upon whose version of events one believes. The *Rideout* case, Helen Benedict suggests, offered the "…first national look at the law that astonished much of the public by its very existence: a law upholding the notion that a woman is the property of her husband."[96]

That does not appear, however, to be precisely true. Though the *Rideout* case was probably among the most sensational trials and cases of its time—involving the kind of media circus that is routine today with television crews from Britain and Germany, thereby offering an international audience a look at the law, as Benedict suggests—other writers suggest that a Missouri man named James Edward Drope was actually convicted of involvement in the "gang rape" of his wife in 1974.[97] Still, it was the story of John and Greta Rideout that made international headlines. What was it all about?

By most published accounts, John and Greta Rideout had a turbulent marriage. Media accounts at the time suggest that Greta was nineteen and John Rideout eighteen when they met and later began living together.[98] John was said to have been reared in a "poor, fatherless family" in Silverton, Oregon, while Greta, the daughter of a secretary and a draughtsman from Phoenix, was a high school dropout who earned an equivalency diploma before moving to Oregon to live with her sister.[99]

After they began living together, John reportedly found work as a cook and Greta became a waitress. And the pair reportedly lived this way until Greta became pregnant and John proposed. Greta declined to marry him, though she would carry and give birth to the couple's child, a daughter. A dejected John joined the army, leaving Greta and the child behind. Greta then reportedly went on welfare, but she still struggled. That was the setting for John Rideout's second proposal. Desperate, lonely, and poor, this time Greta accepted, and she reportedly flew off to Georgia for the ceremony.[100]

But the marriage was far from harmonious. There were reportedly fights over money, fights over responsibilities, and fights over sex, and Greta repeatedly left. But John Rideout would follow her and over and over he "won her back" allegedly with promises of better treatment and better behavior. Eventually, the Rideouts moved to Salem, where Greta left him twice and twice returned. Then, on October 10, 1978, the couple had "their biggest fight," one allegedly involving John hitting Greta in the face, "almost breaking her jaw;" choking Greta; and dragging her home and forcing her to have sex in front of their daughter.[101]

But this, of course, is where the stories diverge.

John Rideout reportedly admitted fighting with Greta and slapping her. But according to John, Greta "kneed him in the groin" during the fight. Later "they made up and made love," John said.[102] Greta's version of events was different.

According to Greta, she had run to a neighbor's house during the fight, where she hid under the table.[103] Later, she called a crisis hotline, and two days after that, she filed charges of rape against her husband. In other words, in her mind, they had not made love.

The complaint set flame to an emerging powder keg. As it often happens when a seemingly singular event appears to spark momentous change, Greta Rideout's charge of rape arrived not just after the recent repeal of the nation's first marital exemption law, but on the heels of an activist period for feminists, women's rights advocates, and reformers, who managed a series of changes in the law during the 1960s and 1970s.

"Prompted by shocking examples [of injustice arising out of the physical violence requirement of the rape statutes of the time], antirape activists pressed for extensive change in statutes and standards of judicial interpretation," explains University of Chicago Professor of Law Stephen J. Schulhofer, in *Unwanted Sex: The Culture of Intimidation and the Failure of Law.*[104] "[I]n Michigan a grassroots women's network grew into an intensive lobbying effort that culminated in the 1975 enactment of the first important feminist reform statute.[105] The National Organization for Women formed a National Task Force on Rape that coordinated efforts for legislative reform nationwide."[106]

Minnesota State University Professor of Women's Studies Maria Bevacqua describes the times in more detail in *Rape on the Public Agenda.* According to Bevacqua, "[i]n a number of cities, antirape campaigners of various stripes joined forces to engage in public events and actions to call attention to sexual assault as an issue and to pressure policy makers to respond to the needs of victims and anti-rape workers. To raise rape consciousness among varied feminist groups, antirape projects often used their public education talents to address women's organizations...."[107] Many of these events were covered by the media.[108]

At the same time, "[i]n other areas, various women's groups formed coalitions around the issue to increase their numbers, call greater public attention to rape, and lobby for an institution response to the problem," writes Bevacqua.[109] For example, "in New York members of the Women's Anti-Rape Group (WARG), precursor of the New York Women Against Rape (NYWAR) crisis collective, attended a gathering of New York NOW to discuss a variety of anti-rape strategies in 1973."[110] Similar efforts took place in Washington, D.C.,[111] and in Chicago, where "such diverse groups as the League of Black Women, Chicago NOW, Chicago Legal Action for Women, the Women's Rights Committee of the ACLU, and Rape Crisis, Inc., joined to form the Chicago Coalition Against Rape," Bevacqua reports.[112]

The "antirape" movement continued to "mature" throughout the 1970s, with progress soon becoming apparent. By 1974, Michigan had revised the state's rape statute, writing what Bevacqua calls "a dream law for reformers in other states."[113] Lawmakers in California, Connecticut, Florida, Indiana, Iowa, Ohio, New York, and Texas were soon also making efforts to revise the laws of their states.[114] By 1980, all of the states and the District of Columbia had either revised, or were considering revisions to, the rape statutes in their states,[115] and more than 400 rape crisis centers had been established. Even so, there are some scholars who say that the reforms of the 1970s did not go far enough, in large part because there was so much history to overcome.

HISTORY AND THE "UTMOST" RESISTANCE:
The Need to Push the Law Forward

Among the catalysts sparking "outrage" and reform were decisions like the 1972 reversal of a rape conviction by an Illinois appellate court in *People v. Bain*,[116] a case that began hopefully enough with a blind date arranged between Bain and a woman by one of the woman's friends. After picking her up at her home, Bain drove the woman to the friend's home, where they spent some time talking, listening to the radio, and drinking beer. At some point later in the evening, Bain was asked to drive a younger boy home. The woman decided to join Bain and the boy for the ride.

But on the way back to the friend's home, the woman testified that Bain "took a back way and finally stopped the car on a lonely country road" where, according to the woman, Bain told her "[y]ou will either have sex with me or you are going to eat me."[117] When the woman refused, she testified that she and Bain "argued back and forth until finally he pushed her down on the seat," hit her "in the mouth with his fist," removed "her slacks and underpants and had intercourse with her."[118]

But the appellate court found it troubling that during cross-examination the woman "admitted that after they had taken the boy home [but before the attack] she had continued to sit close to defendant with her arm around him while he drove." Further, the woman "admitted that she had kissed [Bain] twice" at her friend's house. But again, this was prior to the attack. Another "bad fact" in the appellate court's estimation was that "[w]hen asked if defendant removed her clothing she replied, 'I don't know, sometimes it is just blurred in my mind—whether he removed them or I did.'"[119] But the most fatal admission from the court's perspective was that the woman "admitted that she did not kick, scream, hit, or scratch."

The benefit of the doubt—despite the conviction by a jury that had heard all of the evidence—went to Bain with the appellate court declaring: "[i]t has often been stated that reviewing courts are especially charged with the duty of carefully examining the evidence in rape cases and that it is the further duty of the reviewing court not only to consider the evidence carefully but to reverse the judgment if the evidence is not sufficient to remove all reasonable doubt of the defendant's guilt and to create an abiding conviction that he is guilty of the crime charged."[120]

The court held further that "[i]n the case before us it is readily apparent that the girl made no serious physical effort to resist." In addition, although the woman's bruised face and cut mouth were corroborated by other evidence, this corroboration was weakened[121] by the woman's "failure to make a timely complaint" (*i.e.*, to complain at the "first or second opportunity" to do so, as opposed to waiting a few hours until she was in the comfort of family members).[122] Given these "facts," the appellate court held that it could not "say that the state's evidence creates a clear and abiding conviction of defendant's guilt, and we conclude that a reasonable doubt of guilt exists which will not permit the judgment to stand. Accordingly, the judgment of Circuit Court of Madison County is reversed, and the defendant is ordered discharged."[123]

The reversal outraged women's rights groups for several reasons. Among them, Schulhofer notes, was the apparent perception on the part of the court that the alleged victim "was the one in control," and, thus, "the one to be held accountable."

"She had encouraged the encounter by kissing Bain and by offering only perfunctory resistance instead of a 'serious physical effort.' Bain's direct use of force was not decisive because physical aggressiveness was considered a perfectly normal part of the male role in sexual interactions," Schulhofer notes.[124]

The clear message of the court was that "good girls" don't: "lead men on" by kissing them; get into their cars; or snuggle up with a man they don't want to have sex with. They DO resist with all their might should there be a *misunderstanding* and they report the incident immediately. Literature has long suggested that women are "conflicted" about sex, and, thus, *feelings* of "conflict" over sex were ascribed to women (usually by men) in the rape context.

A Note published in the *Stanford Law Review* in 1966, read, for example, that "[a]lthough a woman may desire sexual intercourse, it is customary for her to say 'no, no, no' (although meaning 'yes, yes, yes') and to expect the male to be the aggressor.... It is always difficult in rape cases to determine whether the female really meant 'no'...." Further, "[t]he problem of determining what the female 'really meant' is compounded when, in fact, the female has no clearly determined attitude—that is, her attitude was one of ambivalence. [Ralph] Slovenko explains that often a woman faces a 'trilemma'; she is faced with a choice among being a prude, a tease, or an 'easy lay.' Furthermore a woman may note a man's brutal nature and be attracted to him rather than repulsed."[125]

In other words, rape was a problem for women—but one that was made by women (*i.e.*, if women would just figure out what they really want—"sex or no sex"—there would not be a problem). Complicating the issue, however, was that "[t]he worst failures of rape law were hidden from public view," says Schulhofer.[126] "Police skepticism and insensitivity discouraged many victims from filing complaints. And when victims did complain, police and prosecutors often dismissed their complaints without pressing charges. If a woman had worn a short skirt or tight sweater, had been drinking, had gone voluntarily to a man's apartment, or had accepted a ride in his car, police usually assumed that she had really consented or had only got what she deserved."[127]

For women, *People v. Bain* represented the collision of rape myths, passé social policy, and the resurrection of Victorian virtue amid a landscape in the agonizing throes of change. By the late 1960s, "more than 90 percent of middle-class men and half of middle-class women had had sex before marriage, and even adultery was not uncommon," write Hirshman and Larson.[128] At the same time, there was an expansion of rights and a moving away from traditional notions of women as property and/or as less than equal citizens, though there was still clearly work to be done.

This "transition from a Victorian notion of female passionlessness to the ideology of female sexual capacity gave women a bargaining chip by raising the value of mutual and consensual sex," Hirshman and Larson argue.[129] And yet, the casting off of Victorian virtue and the perception of greater sexual bargaining power may, in fact, have contributed to the fiction of "consent" so often found by judges and juries.

Well into the later half of the twentieth century, courts routinely held that, given the fickle nature of women, the only way to tell that a woman really did not want to have sex with a man she later accuses of rape was to chart the level of resistance she offered to that alleged rape. If, for example, the resistance a woman offered reached the level of a "serious physical effort" or could be said to have been to the "utmost of her physical ability," and yet still an act of forced intercourse was completed, the woman had probably been raped. If not, courts often arrived at decisions much like the Illinois court's in *People v. Bain.*

But why resistance as a measure for rape?

Where there is talk is of rape in the legal context, there has also always been talk of sex—as in "consensual sex." The fact that a woman may have consented to sex (only to later change her mind) can be a defense to a charge of rape. Thus, the creation of outlandish suppositions like the "the jeans defense" or the "fight till near death" resistance requirement became the standard of the law.[130] It was, of course, a male standard.

REFORM GAINS A FOOTHOLD:
The Slow Steps to Change

The "utmost resistance" requirement had a long history in America even before it had a name. And in accordance with so rigid a standard, even "[a] simple rape might still be reversed, because the victim did not adequately resist," Estrich and other women's rights scholars argue. Or, "it could as easily be reversed on the grounds that her testimony was not corroborated. In many jurisdictions corroboration was technically required in all rape cases. But as with resistance, the absence of corroborating evidence was most critical where the case turned on questions of attitude (that is, the meaning of 'no') or where the woman's story was considered incredible or inculpatory."[131]

But in the 1950s, a scholarly, intellectual effort would spark the march toward reform. It was then that the "American Law Institute, a prestigious body of judges, lawyers, and legal scholars, began an ambitious project to examine the whole of American criminal law," Schulhofer explains. "The institute's goal was to draft a proposal for replacing the disorganized and archaic statutes of the time with a coherent, modern code. When they turned their attention to rape, the reformers were alarmed by the low rate of conviction in clear cases of serious abuse. The reformers—all of them men[132]—attributed this problem to three defects in the law: the resistance requirement, the undue preoccupation with victim consent, and the inclusion of too many diverse kinds of misbehavior within a single felony that carried extremely severe punishments."[133]

WHEN SHE CRIES RAPE
SUSPICION SETS A HIGH BAR

For the first half of the twentieth century, women in the United States were expected, if not to give their lives, then certainly to resist the will of a man as hard as they could and for as long as they could, because virtuous women will fight with every fiber of their being to avoid, if not the physical violations, then certainly the social shame of rape. Thus, emerged the theory—one that would become part of the law—that "true" rape victims resisted to the "utmost." Others—those who did not "resist" or failed to fight sufficiently in the eyes of the court—were often held to have been, in effect, *participants who had consented*, many courts concluded.

"In the eighteenth century, Blackstone defined rape as 'carnal knowledge of a woman forcibly and against her will,'"[134] writes the University of Chicago's Schulhofer. "Until the 1950s, American statutes almost uniformly preserved Blackstone's definition, with verbal differences. Rape included only a few instances of intercourse that weren't compelled by force, notably consensual intercourse with a minor and intercourse with a woman who was unconscious or asleep."[135]

Thus, the idea that a woman might have "given" herself to a man has long been a preoccupation of the courts, with virtue—or resistance as its physical manifestation—traditionally a close requirement. A woman's "virtue," after all, was supposed to be as important to her as it was (and apparently still is) to the men of the world. It should come as no surprise, then, that American courts have traditionally been "disinclined to reward" a woman for a lack of modesty and virtue. Caselaw from the late nineteenth—and through the first half of the twentieth—century offers evidence of this point.

- In 1838, for example, a New York court hearing *People v. Abbott*,[136] held, in considering the clothing worn by the woman at the time of the attack at issue, "Will you not more readily infer assent in the practical Messalina, in loose attire, than in the reserved and virtuous Lucretia?" The very same Lucretia who, legend has it, plunged a dagger into her flesh after she was raped.
- In 1847, the Georgia court hearing *State v. Camp*,[137] a case involving an allegation of rape brought by a prostitute, held that "[i]t would be absurd, and shock our sense of truth, for any man to affirm that there was not a much greater probability in favor of the proposition that a common prostitute had yielded her assent to sexual intercourse than in the case of the virgin of uncontaminated purity."[138]
- A court in Tennessee ruled similarly twenty-seven years later in *Titus v. State.*[139]

- And the New York court in the 1857 case of *People v. Jackson*,[140] allowed witnesses to testify as to the alleged "bad reputation" of a rape victim. Florida courts allowed similar testimony.[141]

Not surprisingly, in those early times, "virtue" was tangled with racism and the lesser status of women in general, but African American women specifically.

- In *Christian v. Commonwealth*,[142] a 1873 Virginia case, for example, the court considered the rape allegations of an African American woman brought against an African American man. But the woman had attended a concert with the man she later accused *and* she had two children out of wedlock. Could a woman like that be raped? The court held that "[i]t by no means appears, from the facts certified, that it was an attempt to ravish her against her will, or that it was not only an attempt to work upon her passions and overcome her virtue, which had yielded to others before—how often it does not appear...."[143]
- There is an interesting contrast to be found, however, in the 1880 Wisconsin case of *Whittaker v. State*,[144] involving an allegation of rape brought by a white woman against an African American man. According to the woman, Whittaker had grabbed her and held "[her] hands tight and [her] feet tight, and [she] couldn't move from [her] place even." The woman screamed for help. In response, the man brandished a gun and threatened to use it. Still, the woman screamed again.[145] On the subject of resistance, the woman testified that "I couldn't do any more, I got so tired out. I tried to save me so much as I could, but I couldn't save myself. And he held me, and...I couldn't help myself any more...I worked so much as I could, and I gave up."

That appears, however, to have been just the problem for the Wisconsin court. Whittaker was initially convicted of rape. But the Supreme Court of Wisconsin reversed the conviction, finding first that "[t]his is not a case where the prosecutrix was overcome by threats of personal violence." The court found further that "[t]he testimony does not show that the threat of personal violence overpowered her will, or...that she was incapable of voluntary action." In other words, "submission...no matter how reluctantly yielded, removes from the act an essential element of the crime of rape," the court ruled.[146]

It is worth noting that this was a white woman, who (at least in the court's eyes) had apparently allowed herself to be raped by an African American man. Did she deserve any other decision from the court after admitting that she had "given up"? For most of the nineteenth century, the Wisconsin court was within the majority of courts requiring a showing of the "utmost resistance" on the part of a woman alleging rape. And where there was less than the "utmost resistance," courts reasoned that whatever had happened between the parties involved, it was not rape.

- Three years after the Wisconsin court's decision in *Whittaker v. State*, the Missouri Supreme Court held, in *State v. Burgdorf*,[147] that passive resistance or "a mere halfway case" was not enough to sustain a change of rape.
- A year later, in *People v. Dohring*,[148] a New York court asked, in reversing the conviction of a man charged with raping a 14-year-old servant in his home[149]: "Can

the mind conceive of a woman, in the possession of her faculties and powers, revolting unwillingly that this deed should be done upon her, who would not resist so hard and so long as she was able? And where there was less than the "utmost resistance," courts reasoned that whatever happened between the parties, it was not rape."[150]

- Finally, in 1889, the Supreme Court of Nebraska reversed a conviction of rape in *Reynolds v. State*,[151] because the members of the jury "were not expressly told that if the carnal knowledge [of a woman] was with the consent of the woman, *no matter how tardily given*, or how much force had theretofore been employed, it is not rape."[152]

Reasoning of this sort dominated the law well into the twentieth century.

- A Texas criminal appellate court held in 1906 in *State v. Perez*,[153] for example, that "although some force be used," if a woman "does not put forth all the power of resistance which she was capable of exerting under the circumstances, it will not be rape."

- The Wisconsin Supreme Court went even further in reversing a conviction of rape in *Brown v. State*,[154] holding that a woman—in this case a 16-year-old girl—must make "the most vehement exercise of every physical means or faculty within [her] power," because "[a] woman is equipped to interpose most effective obstacles by means of hands and limbs and pelvic muscles. Indeed, medical writers insist that these obstacles are practically insuperable in the absence of more than the usual relative disproportion of age and strength between man and woman."[155]

- In 1938, the Wisconsin Supreme Court held, in *State v. Hoffman*,[156] that a woman's "failure" to resist could lead to the reversal of a conviction of rape.

- In 1948, a Nebraska court held, in *State v. Prokop*,[157] that "[w]hile the degree of resistance required is...relative, depending upon the particular circumstances, the general rule is that a mentally competent woman must in good faith resist to the utmost with the most vehement exercise of every physical means or faculty naturally within her power to prevent carnal knowledge, and she must persist in such resistance as long as she has the power to do so until the offense is consummated."[158]

- And in 1950, a Texas criminal court of appeals held, in *State v. Killingworth*,[159] in reversing a conviction of rape that "feigned and passive resistance" on the part of the victim was not enough to sustain the charge.

There were early cases, of course, that "excused" women of the resistance requirement.

- In 1877, for example, a Connecticut court "forgave" a woman assaulted by three men and later found semiconscious in *State v. Shields*.[160]

- In *Bailey v. Commonwealth*,[161] a Virginia court held, in affirming the rape conviction of a stepfather though there was no evidence of resistance on the stepdaughter's part other then that she had "forbade" her stepfather to enter her bed, that the stepfather should not be allowed to "shelter himself behind the circumstance" that the girl had not resisted where he was a figure of authority to the child and where he had sent the girl's mother and sister to a party so that he could be alone with the victim.[162] A Texas court decided similarly nearly seventy years later.[163]

- In addition, as early as 1892, a Missouri court held, in *State v. Dusenberry*,[164] that the "utmost resistance" was not required where a defendant shows a victim a knife and gun. In such a case, the 16-year-old victim had clearly "submitted" to the assault out of fear, the Missouri court reasoned.

- In the 1921 case of *Commonwealth v. Hart*,[165] a Virginia court reached a similar conclusion, holding the death penalty appropriate in a case where an African American man attempted to rape a white woman—a "simple, good, unsophisticated country girl"—though there was no showing of resistance.

- And in perhaps one of the oddest exceptions to the resistance rule, a Missouri court held in *State v. Catron*[166] that a showing of the "utmost resistance" was not required where the victim was larger than the defendant.[167]

- A decade later, in *State v. Esposito*,[168] a Connecticut court that was clearly ahead of its time in 1937, ruled that a drunk or semiconscious woman was not required to resist rape to the "utmost." In doing so, the court set forth language that other courts in other states would not use for decades; the court noting, for example, that there were "essential elements" involved in proving a claim of rape that "…the jury must be fully satisfied of. The court wrote further that "[t]he importance of resistance is simply to show two elements of the crime—carnal knowledge by force by one of the parties and nonconsent thereto by the other.… So far, resistance by the complainant is important and necessary; but to make the crime hinge on the utmost exertion the woman was physically capable of making, would be a reproach to the law as well as to common sense."[169]

- A California appellate court—demonstrating what some critics may suggest was the kind of "activism" California courts are infamous for—affirmed the conviction of a rapist, a stranger to the victim, in *People v. Kinne*[170] in 1938, though there had been no showing of resistance.

- And in 1944, California jurists held in *People v. Flores*,[171] that "[a] threat may be expressed by acts and conduct as well as by words."[172]

But these cases clearly represent the exception. The nation's courts continued overwhelmingly to require a showing of resistance on the part of women alleging rape or attempted rape. And yet, by the mid-twentieth century, a subtle turn of sorts began with courts in some states—California among them—began to view rape allegations and appeals more from the perspective of what the defendant had done, rather than from the perspective of what the victim had failed to do.

- In *People v. Cassandras*,[173] for example, a California appellate court held in 1948, in affirming a conviction for rape, that "where [a] defendant used an elaborate ploy to lure the complainant into a hotel and then threatened to have the hotel clerk report her to the police as a prostitute and to have her children taken away," such threats, in addition to "sufficient evidence of threats of physical harm…implied that mental coercion might be enough to overcome her will."

- A year later, a California court held, in *People v. Tollack*,[174] that a woman was not required to resist "to the utmost" of her abilities if she believes it will be useless.
- That same year, the California appellate went even farther in *People v. Blankenship*,[175] upholding the conviction of a rapist on four counts despite an absence of resistance.
- In *People v. Harris*,[176] sadly the California court fell headlong into that well of racism so clearly acceptable for the time, forgoing and forgiving the "resistance requirement" where the female victim was white and the male perpetrator African American. After some fairly colorful language in detailing the "acts" involved,[177] the court concluded that:

  [w]hen a young, white woman returning home from her work meets a strange, male person of the Negro race in the dead of night in a quiet vicinity and he exhibits a knife as he demands that she submit to carnal intercourse with him and pulls her into an automobile, lays her body upon the seat, proceeds to remove her clothing, compels her to perform the nameless act to stimulate his own amorous impulses, *it would border upon the stupid* to find that she freely acquiesced to his acts as he ravished her body. While she made some resistance, it may be safely presumed that she would have rebelled with a vengeance but for her fear of bodily harm.[178]

Other states held similarly.

- In 1960, a Virginia court held, in *Satterwhite v. Commonwealth*,[179] that a woman is not required to resist rape "to the utmost" of her abilities if she believes that it would be useless.[180]
- In *State v. Hazel*,[181] a Maryland court held that the threat of violence may be enough to overcome a woman's tendency towards resistance.
- The Supreme Court of Hawaii upheld a conviction of rape, despite no showing of resistance in *State v. Dizon*[182] in 1964.
- In *State v. Hunt*,[183] a Nebraska court held a year later that a showing of resistance was not necessary where the victim was attacked by three men. But again, these decisions were among the exceptions. Many other courts continued to hold the "utmost resistance" requirement to be the floor of a victim's permissible conduct.[184]

In addition, there were judges and jurists who—like their predecessors—simply did not believe the woman before them; they allowed juries to be told that its members should not believe the woman either.

- In *Commonwealth v. Childs*,[185] for example, a Pennsylvania jury was given an instruction in that 1863 case that its members *should be* suspicious of a woman accusing a man of rape.
- In *Bedgood v. State*,[186] an 1888 Indiana court held, in a case involving allegations by three men, that "…it was improbable that [one of the men who had once allegedly been 'intimate' with the women] would have resorted to violence." The court held further that "it is also improbable that he was one of several who did, and, if he was not, then the occurrence did not take place as [the victim] describes it."

- And in 1921, in expounding on the caution necessary to view allegations of rape, even in the case of a 15-year-old girl, the Nebraska Supreme Court acknowledged, in *Roberts v. State*,[187] that "[p]ublic sentiment seems preinclined to believe a man guilty of any illicit sexual offense he may be charged with, and it seems to matter little what his previous reputation has been. This natural tendency may be due to the fact that a woman is charging odium upon herself as well as charging him with a felony. Be this as it may, where statutory rape is charged, the law requires that the testimony of the complaining witness must be corroborated by facts and circumstances established by other competent evidence in order to sustain a conviction."[188]
- As a state, Minnesota proved an enormously skeptical place, with its highest court reversing the conviction of a priest charged with raping and impregnating a 17-year-old girl in 1894, in *State v. Connelly*,[189] reasoning that "where the charge [of rape] is true, there will almost always be some corroborating evidence, such as injury to the person or clothing of the prosecutrix or the fact that she made a complaint as soon as practicable...yet even young girls, like older females, sometimes concoct an untruthful story to conceal a lapse from virtue."
- And in *State v. Anderson*,[190] decided 71 years later, the court noted that corroboration in rape cases is required because "sexual cases are particularly subject to the danger of deliberately false charges, resulting from sexual neurosis, phantasy [*sic*], jealousy, spite, or simply a girl's refusal to admit that she consented to an act of which she is now ashamed."

In addition to failures of resistance, as stated earlier, friendships, previous relationships, and even short-lived acquaintances have long raised suspicions, and, thus, have allowed courts to overcome otherwise objective evidence and undo convictions, based upon the "doubt" these "friendships" seemed to create.

- In *Territory v. Nishi*,[191] for example, a Hawaiian court held that because the alleged victim of a rape and the defendant she accused were "friends and companions" and because she had accompanied him to a park, the question had been raised as to whether the woman had consented to sex.
- And an Alabama appellate court held similarly in *State v. Pitts*[192] in 1923.
- In 1941, the Alabama Supreme Court reversed the rape conviction of a defendant in *State v. Mosley*[193] due to a prior relationship.
- In *State v. Lewis*,[194] a 1953 Mississippi case, the court reversed a conviction of rape because the defendant, a field hand, had not been allowed to offer testimony of an alleged prior relationship with the victim, "regardless of how false the testimony may have been."

Naiveté, a trusting nature, or just plain stupid gullibility were never the concerns of the court where it ended in rape. Instead, courts often saw consent.

- In 1956, for example, the Supreme Court of Virginia held in *Commonwealth v. Barker*,[195] that "[i]t would be contrary to human experience and inherently incredible" to believe a woman who reports that after meeting two men in a bus terminal, she accepts a ride from them only to be beaten, raped, and then made to pay for the gas to get to her original destination. In the eyes of the court, because the woman had been foolish enough to get into a car with men she did not know, she must have wanted to have consensual sex with them.

And like "virtue," its lesser sister chastity was never far from view, though there were early instances when some seemed to waive even that long-held requirement.

- In *Shay v. State*,[196] a 1956 Mississippi case, the court held that a rape victim's alleged "want of chastity" was "immaterial and inadmissible" to a charge of rape.
- And in *People v. Walker*,[197] a California appellate court held, prior to the widespread passage of "rape shield laws," in affirming the conviction of a "stranger-rapist," that the victim's sexual past would not be admitted.[198]

But overwhelmingly, early decisions were slanted toward male defendants.

- For example, as far back as 1889, a Nebraska court considered the evidentiary question of the whether the prior rapes of a defendant were admissible in *State v. Reynolds*.[199]
- In *People v. Travis*,[200] a 1920 Michigan case, the court held that evidence of a defendant's romantic past was inadmissible, lest his virtue be used against him.
- More than three decades later, a federal court would rule in *Packineau v. United States*,[201] that although testimony of a rape victim's alleged prior "lack of chastity" should have been admitted at trial so that a jury might be able to evaluate her credibility,[202] testimony regarding the criminal histories of the men charged had been properly excluded.

By contrast, decisions have historically been biased against women.

- In keeping with the times, for example, and in an indication of things to come, a Texas court held in the 1926 case of *Stafford v. State*,[203] that a woman's sexual history may be important enough to merit reversal where excluded.
- And in an extension of this reasoning, the Kentucky Supreme Court ruled in the 1945 case of *Commonwealth v. Grigsby*,[204] that a rape victim's former lover could testify for the defendant at trial.
- The Nebraska Supreme court held similarly in 1949 in *State v. Frank*.[205] Two years later, but in that same vein, a Georgia court held in *Teague v. State*[206] that testimony of a rape victim's "reputation of an alleged lack of chastity" could be admitted.
- In 1962, the Illinois court held in *People v. Collins*[207] that similar testimony was admissible.

Courts have long been "obsessed with the idea that a woman might fabricate an accusation of rape, either because she feared the stigma of having consented to intercourse or because she was pregnant and needed an acceptable explanation for her condition," writes Schulhofer. Judges, the majority of them men, also have traditionally "worried that a woman might falsely accuse a man for reasons of revenge or blackmail" with "Lord Hail setting the tone" and courts "repeatedly cit[ing] his pronouncement, in 1680, that rape 'is an accusation easily made and hard to prove, and harder to be defended by the party accused, tho' never so innocent."[208]

Thus, the bar was set high for rape and remains so "…[T]o guard against false accusations, courts imposed strict rules of proof that were unique to rape cases."[209] For most of the twentieth century, among the hurdles a woman accusing rape had to clear in many states was showing that the victim had offered the "utmost resistance." A woman might also be required to show that the allegation was made promptly or as immediately as possible after the incident.[210] Further, corroboration by presentation of physical evidence or witness testimony was required in most states until at least the mid-twentieth century.[211]

As a point of historical accuracy, though the debate over reformation of rape law may have begun in earnest during the 1950s, the American Law Institute's overall efforts actually got underway some thirty years earlier, according to Linda Hirshman and Jane Larson, when institute officials began discussing "foundational questions about the nature of law, disputes that mirrored earlier controversies in the political world dating back to [Charles] Darwin's *Origin of the Species*."

Eventually, the drafters turned their attentions to nonconsensual sexual incidents, defined broadly as "sex that violates independent background norms of self ownership."[212] The goals of the American Law Institute appear, however, never to have been in line with those of feminists and women's rights activists, who viewed fundamental reformation of traditional rape laws among their primary aims, because as they stood, "[t]he rules all too often resulted in the victim's being violated a second time—by the criminal justice system," notes Estrich.[213]

ENORMOUS PROMISE—A MORE LIMITED REALITY:
A Model Penal Code and the Reformation of Rape Laws

Forced sex was serious. That much the drafters of the Model Penal Code acknowledged. They also took note of "the unjust law enforcement concerning black-on-white rape, particularly in the South," Hirshman and Larson explain.[214] The next step for the commission was to divide sexual incidents into categories in accordance with their perceived "seriousness." But these were the perceptions of men. Thus, the end result would fail women miserably, feminist scholars suggest."[215]

Though the drafters would define first and second degree felony rape as "sexual intercourse against the will of the victim by means of force, kidnapping, or threat of death, serious injury, or extreme pain,"[216] the commission would hold that there could be no spousal rape. And rape or sexual assault by a "social companion or a previous sexual partner" was deemed no greater than a second degree felony, regardless of the particular circumstances of a case. Finally, sex "procured by 'any threat that would prevent resistance by a woman of ordinary resolution'" was deemed by the drafters to be a "gross sexual imposition," but not rape.[217]

But this did not go far enough for many women. And, indeed, as Schulhofer notes, the drafters' recommendations "made no break with traditional assumptions." Instead, the Model Penal Code of 1962, "preserved the rules requiring a prompt complaint, corroboration of the victim's testimony, and special cautionary instructions to the jury."[218] In addition, "[t]he reformers not only preserved the 'marital exemption' but extended it: the code barred prosecution in cases of compelled intercourse when the assailant and victim were 'living together as man and wife,' regardless of whether the couple was formally married."[219] These efforts drew criticism.

"From even a short distance of history, the Model Penal Code's treatment of nonconsensual sex sounds sexist, heartless, and strangely naïve," suggest Hirshman and Larson. "This inability to engage with rape in a fair and fruitful way was an early sign of the failings of the libertine paradigm. Over time, arguments for withdrawing government from the sexual realm as unnecessary or ineffective would prove more persuasive than any effort to guarantee that the model of free exchange was truly free."[220]

But the 1960s were a decade of political upheaval and social change, a time of mass protest, sit-ins, and armed violence, which led to sweeping changes in the law. And in the midst of this swirl of activity, two waves of feminist reform swept the nation. Among other things, the first wave took aim at the evidentiary legal hurdles involved in proving the crime of rape "rather than at the crime itself," argues Francis, while "[t]he second wave...moved beyond issues of proof, to questioning the very understanding of rape itself."[221]

And that would have been where the persuasive influence of a "fairly" drawn Model Penal Code might have been felt. Persuasive as opposed to definitive, because American criminal law is statutory (i.e., drafted by lawmakers). Thus, the Model Penal Code had no "inherently legitimate law to restate," argue scholars.[222] Still, the effort would prove enormously influential, because the 1960s, legislatures across the country were revising their criminal statutes in accordance with new federal mandates and the significant change of the time. With regard to these efforts, the Model Penal Code was seen as a jumping-off point.

Except where the law regarding rape was involved.

Proposals of the revised Model Penal Code "had hardly surfaced in the public debate, when the second wave of feminism swept into the United States, taking rape law as one of its first targets of reform," write Hirshman and Larson.[223] "As a result of controversy created by feminist critics, almost no state adopted the Model Penal Code's rape provisions."[224]

In the wake of this controversy, "[m]any items on the feminist 'wish list' were quickly enacted into law," says Schulhofer.[225] Changes were made to the rules of evidence with the intent of limiting what could be held admissible in court. "Rape shield" laws were drafted, limiting the introduction of a victim's sexual history.[226] And gender-neutral language was adopted. And yet, two problems remained, according to Schulhofer: "the resistance requirement and the marital exemption."[227]

That was the context of the *Rideout* accusation and trial. Prior to *Rideout*, the general rule seemed to be the rule of *R. v. Miller*,[228] in which the court dismissed a rape indictment, finding it unreasonable "to say that the wife's implied consent to marital intercourse [had] been revoked by an act of the parties or by an act of the courts." That Rideout was brought to trial for the alleged rape of his wife was seen by many as a harbinger of things to come. It was.

John Rideout was acquitted, a fact that some argue brought the political and legal debate full circle, with critics citing the acquittal as evidence of the need for even greater change.[229] Indeed, despite a series of initial reforms that seemed to move the law forward in leaps and bounds, the momentum driving change soon ebbed, making it a reality still as late as 1991, that the legislatures in only nineteen states had passed laws making it illegal for a man to rape his wife.[230]

It was not until 1986, for example, that Virginia lawmakers enacted Va. Code Sec. 18.2-61(B), 18.2-67,2:1 (1986), a statute effectively overruling the Virginia Supreme Court's decision in *Kizer v. Commonwealth*.[231] In *Kizer*, the court set aside the conviction of a husband who broke in the door of his estranged wife's apartment and later raped her. Under the 1986 Virginia law, a man could not be prosecuted for raping his wife whether or not they were living together.[232]

And as late as 1991, marital exemption laws were still leading to trials. South Carolina was the venue for the trial of *State v. Crawford*, in which a husband was accused of dragging his wife by the throat into a bedroom where he allegedly tied her hands and legs with a belt and some rope, and duct-taped the woman's eyes and mouth shut before dressing her in a garter belt and stockings. The husband then had sexual intercourse with his bound and gagged wife, molested her with objects, and ran a knife across her breast and stomach, all the while making a video of the incident, which was later shown to a jury.[233]

The woman testified during the two-day trial that her cries—although muffled by the tape—were cries of pain; that she had not consented to any of the acts visited upon her by her husband; and that the couple had planned to separate the night of the alleged rape. But her husband testified that the noises his wife had made were clearly related to pleasure. The husband testified that he and his wife had played similar "games" in the past, which he had also videotaped. Thus, the husband said that he thought when she said "no" on this night, that she really meant yes (*i.e.*, that she wanted to engage in rough sex). And so he'd obliged.

Under South Carolina's marital exemption law, a woman's past sexual history may be admitted under certain circumstances, and in this case, the judge allowed the testimony of the woman's former husband, who also testified that she had allowed him to tie her up on several occasions and that she enjoyed violence and/or being treated abusively. By contrast, the judge held inadmissible the testimony of the husband's former wife, who alleged that he had raped her during their marriage as well.

The jury of eight women and four men took less than a hour to find the husband not guilty. In responding to the verdict, the wife echoed the sentiment underlying efforts to abolish the marital exemption: "If it had been a stranger doing that to me," said the woman, "the whole community would have been in an uproar, a lynching party. But because it was my husband, it was okay."[234]

In the last two decades, some courts have ruled the marital exemption to be unconstitutional as well as woefully out-of-step with the times.[235] In addition, research compiled by the National Clearinghouse on Marital and Date Rape suggests that every state has abolished the once absolute marital exemption.[236] Only seventeen states have abolished it outright, while several others have settled for modifications.[237] Still, by 1998, every state had moved to reform marital rape law. But this, like many of the areas of "rape law," remains a work in progress.[238] It was not until 1996, for example, that the Georgia legislature decided to do away with the "spousal exemption" to rape.[239] In addition, although the Virginia legislation allows spouses to be prosecuted for rape whether or not a couple is living together at the time of the attack, "…many other states bar prosecution for rape when spouses are living together, no matter how severe the injuries inflicted, and in some of these states, prosecution continues to be barred even for spouses living apart, until one of them obtains a formal decree of legal separation," Schulhofer notes.[240]

RAPE AND IMPLICIT VIOLENCE:
Pride Makes Resistance "Instinctive"

During the 1970s, most states began to abandon the "utmost resistance" requirement in favor of a "reasonable resistance" requirement, the measure of which appears in recent years to have softened even further in many jurisdictions. But the current trend may actually have been at the closing end of a pattern of leniency started two decades earlier with—of all things—a discriminatory inclination toward "forgiving" the resistance requirement when white women "failed" to resist the "lewd and lascivious" advances or attacks of African American men.[241] During this time, several states—Michigan, Ohio, Pennsylvania and New Jersey—repealed their states' resistance requirements.[242]

Still, the vast majority of states retained some form of the resistance requirement with the shift moving generally from one requiring a showing of the "utmost resistance" on the part of a victim of rape to one of "reasonable resistance."[243] And that is generally where the law remains today.[244] Thus, the essence of more recent debates involving the "resistance" requirement is how much resistance in necessary when the coercion is implicit, as opposed to explicit? In other words, when a man uses "mere" threats of violence, must a woman resist?

For many, the intricacies of this debate came to light in 1981 with *State v. Rusk*,[245] a case Estrich describes as one of the "most vigorously debated rape cases in recent volumes of the case reporters." Though a "classic example of simple rape," *State v. Rusk* would eventually be heard by a special panel of "all the appellate judges sitting together," *i.e.,* the Maryland Court of Special Appeals, the Court of Appeals, as well as justices from Maryland's highest court.[246]

"All told, twenty-one judges, including the trial judge, reviewed the sufficiency of the evidence. Ten concluded that Rusk was a rapist; eleven that he was not," wrote Estrich in remarking on the case.[247]

The events that would later give rise to the case of *State v. Rusk* began with a meeting between a woman and Eddie Rusk in a bar, where the two talked for a while. When the woman rose to leave, Rusk asked her to give him a ride home. The woman initially declined, but eventually she agreed. Upon arriving at Rusk's home, he asked her to come inside. The woman said no. Rusk asked again. The woman said no again. And so Rusk reached over and took the car keys, according to testimony.

When he wouldn't give them back, and because she was unfamiliar with the neighborhood, the woman followed Rusk into his apartment. Once inside, the woman begged Rusk to let her leave. He refused. Rusk then pulled the woman onto the bed and began removing her blouse. Rusk then asked the woman to remove her pants, as well as to undress him. The woman did. But when they were both undressed, the woman began trying to persuade Rusk not to force her to have intercourse.

"You can get a lot of other girls...for what you want," the woman testified she told Rusk. But Rusk just kept saying "no," the woman reported. "[T]hen I was really scared, because I can't describe, you know, what was said. It was more the look in his eyes; and I said, at that point—I didn't know what to say; and I said, 'If I do what you want, will you let me go without killing me?' Because I didn't know at that point what he was going to do; and I started to cry; and when I did, he put his hands on my throat, and started lightly to choke me; and I said, 'If I do what you want, will you let me go?' And he said 'yes,' and at that time, I proceeded to do what he wanted me to do."[248]

When it was over, Rusk reportedly walked the woman to her car and asked if he could see her again. By a 4-to-3 vote, the Maryland Court of Appeals affirmed the conviction of rape rendered by the lower court. Sparking the ire of women's groups and raising the profile of the case, however, were the comments of the three dissenting justices, who argued that:

> [w]hile courts no longer require a female to resist to the utmost or to resist where resistance would be foolhardy, they do require her acquiescence in the act of intercourse to stem from fear generated by something of substance. She may not simply say, 'I was really scared,' and thereby transform consent or mere unwillingness into submission by force. These words do not transform a seducer into a rapist. She must follow the natural instinct of every proud female to resist, by more than mere words, the violation of her person by a stranger or an unwelcomed friend. She must make it plain that she regards such sexual acts as abhorrent and repugnant to her natural sense of pride. She must resist unless the defendant has objectively manifested his intent to use physical force to accomplish his purpose.[249]

Here it was again, a giant step backwards for women, as the victim in this case suffered the criticisms of judges who'd decided that she had failed not only as a "proud female" but also as a victim of rape. "Proud females" resist rape. "Not-so-proud females," would "submit." But it was/is a proud woman's "natural instinct" to resist, just as it is, apparently, the natural instinct of the proud man to take a woman's keys, refuse to let her leave, insist she have sexual intercourse with him, choke her (or strongly caress her) if she cries, and never to tell her that he does not plan to kill her.

"In the dissenters' view, [the woman] was not a 'reasonable' victim, or even a victim at all," argues Estrich. "Rather than fight, she cried. Rather than protect her 'virtue,' she acquiesced. Far from having any claim that her bodily integrity had been violated, she was adjudged complicit in the intercourse of which she complained. As one judge put it, the approach of those who would reverse Rusk's conviction amounted to nothing less than a declaration that [the woman] was, 'in effect, an adulteress.'"[250]

Still, as set forth above, the Maryland Court of Appeals would affirm Rusk's conviction, holding that in "considering all of the evidence in the case, with particular focus upon the actual force applied by Rusk to [the woman's] neck, we conclude that the jury could rationally find that the essential elements of second-degree rape had been established."[251] Two years earlier, the Maryland Court of Special Appeals held the opposite in *Goldberg v. Maryland*.[252]

Two years after the Maryland court's decision in *State v. Rusk*, an Illinois court found the "record...devoid of any attendant-circumstances which suggest that [the] complainant was forced to submit" to rape in *People v. Warren*,[253] though testimony before the court established that the victim, a woman who had stopped along a bike path to rest, was lifted off her bike and carried into the woods by a 6-foot, 2-inch, 185-pound man. The woman, who admitted talking with the man prior to the alleged attack, testified that when she rose to leave, he put his hand on her shoulder and said, "This will only take a minute. My girlfriend doesn't meet my needs," and "I don't want to hurt you."

Apparently taking this as a threat, the woman—who stood at 5-feet, 2-inches and weighed 100 pounds—did not scream or fight, because she feared he might beat or choke her. But even if she had, it is not clear that it would have mattered. According to testimony, the bike path was isolated and there was no one in sight at the time of the incident. Still, because the man had made no explicit threats of violence, the conviction was set aside. Only explicit violence—or the threat thereof—would have excused the woman's failure to resist, the Illinois court held.

In this same vein, the Supreme Court of North Carolina reversed the rape conviction of the victim's former boyfriend in 1984 in *State v. Alston*,[254] a case that, like that of Greta and John Rideout, was tumultuous. Testimony offered at trial in *State v. Alston* suggested that the defendant was physically violent toward the victim, *i.e.*, that he would sometimes hit the victim when she refused to give him money or to otherwise do what he wanted her to do. And, according to the court, the victim "...often had sex with the defendant just to accommodate him."

"On those occasions," the court noted, "[the victim] would stand still and remain entirely passive while the defendant undressed her and had intercourse with her."[255]

Eventually, the victim had had enough, and, after the defendant struck her, she moved into her mother's home. But a month later, the defendant appeared at the victim's school, where he blocked her path and demanded her new address, grabbing her arm and telling her she was coming with him when she refused to tell him. The victim promised to walk with the defendant if he let go of her arm. The pair walked around the back of the school to "talk" about their relationship. But during this discussion, the defendant reportedly told the victim he was going to "fix" her face so that she would know that he "was not playing."

When the victim told the defendant that they were through, the defendant reportedly told the victim that he had a "right" to have sex with her again. The defendant then took the victim to the home of a friend, where he asked if she were "ready." The victim responded that she did not want to have sex with him. But the defendant had a "right." And so, according to testimony, the defendant pulled the victim up from the chair where she was sitting, undressed her, pushed her legs apart and had sex with her. The victim cried.[256]

The defendant was convicted of rape, and a court of appeals affirmed. But the North Carolina Supreme Court reversed the ruling, reasoning that the victim had not resisted the rape in any physical way. Further, in its estimation, although the threats and violence employed by the defendant outside the school "…may have induced fear" for the victim, it was "unrelated to the act of sexual intercourse," the court ruled.[257] Thus, there was no force at the time of the rape, the court held. This "lack of force" coupled with the victim's failure of resistance equaled consent for the court.

Rulings based upon this sort of reasoning continue to appear today in a sporadic bit of inconsistency that has always characterized rape law, though it appears today that many courts have begun to accept that a woman may be compelled into nonconsensual sex by fear. But still there are occasions when this area of the law feels like the mixed bag that sometimes it is. In 1990, for example, an appellate court in New York reversed the rape conviction of a father, finding that "there was no proof that the difference in size between the defendant and his daughter created an implied threat of force."[258]

Though the court seemed not to consider it, the implicit threat of retaliatory abuse in the guise of discipline or homelessness (the victim testified that her father had threatened to kick her out of the family home the day after the incident), might have been deemed by other courts, sufficiently "violent" enough to compel a young girl to give into her father's requests. Courts in Pennsylvania and Ohio have held similarly.[259]

But a year before the decision by the New York appellate court cited above, the appellate court also held, in a case involving a 9-year-old sexually abused by her father, that the man's superior size, age, and authority were sufficient enough to meet the standard of force or coercion.[260] Trial courts in Alabama, Arkansas, and Pennsylvania and appellate courts in California and New York have held similarly as has the Supreme Court of Ohio.[261] By contrast, where an adult man who is not a child's father, but who schemes and tricks the child into a situation where he can then take advantage of her, some courts have held that "subtle and psychological" force of this sort is not sufficient.[262]

That decision, Schulhofer notes, "stays remarkably close to the traditional doctrines of forty years earlier. Criminal law safeguards remain limited almost exclusively to protecting women from force, and 'force' still means direct physical violence, something more the 'ordinary' physical aggressiveness that is considered a normal aspect of the male sex role."[263] And how is a man supposed to know that a woman really means "no" when she says "no" if she doesn't resist? Or even if she does? These appear to be questions that continue to haunt the courts.

SHIELDING SEXUAL HISTORY:
Or Creating Doubt by Turning Victim into Vamp

In contrast to the protracted efforts involved in overcoming antiquated resistance requirements, "rape shield" laws were passed in relative earnest beginning with the reformation of the rules of evidence. By 1980, almost every state had enacted some form of "rape shield" law.[264]

Michigan was again at the forefront of this revolution.[265] And yet, 'rape shield" laws are not absolute. Most include exceptions. Under the Federal Rules of Evidence, for example, a victim's past sexual history may be admissible where a defendant argues that he is not responsible for DNA matter or the injury to the victim; where it is "constitutionally required;"[266] or where the defendant alleges that the woman consented. And perhaps not surprisingly, defendants and defense attorneys have tried mightily to put these exceptions to their full use.

As noted above, however, one of the hot-button issues with regard to rape today is the "mistaken consent" defense, which some legal scholars argue could be used to poke holes in rape shield laws by suggesting that evidence of a complainant's past sexual history goes to the defendant's state of mind.[267] The Fourth Circuit Court of Appeals ruled on this issue in *Doe v. United States*,[268] holding that where the issue was the defendant's state of mind, the victim's sexual history could be introduced to determine whether the defendant had mistakenly believed she had consented.[269]

Doe v. United States was decided in 1981. A decade later, the defendant in *United States v. Saunders*[270] argued before that same court that he should be allowed to do the same thing. Henry Saunders was convicted of aggravated sexual assault by a jury and sentenced to 360 months in prison following a showing by the government that he was a "career offender." Henry Saunders appealed to the Fourth Circuit, arguing that the district court had erred in excluding testimony permissible under Federal Rule of Evidence 412.

The "evidence" Saunders sought to have admitted was that the woman he had allegedly raped was, in his words, a "skeezer (a prostitute who trades sex for drugs)." Saunders argued further that the woman had falsely accused him of rape because he threw the crack she had been smoking out of the window of the car he was driving. That made her angry enough to falsely accuse him.

Of course, the victim offered a different story. And what the Fourth Circuit found to be true was that while driving a friend's car on the night of February 8, 1990, Saunders came across a friend, identified in court documents as Jackie "Tonka" Harris. With Harris was a woman, an acquaintance of Saunders. Saunders agreed to give them a ride home. But first Saunders stopped near a school so that Harris could sell some crack cocaine.

After dropping Harris off at his home, his business apparently concluded for the night, Saunders took the woman to his home, where, according to the court, they sampled some of Harris's wares. Saunders had agreed that afterwards, he would take the woman to a friend's home and then finally to her own home. But on the way, according to testimony offered at the trial, "Saunders drove [the] car off into a wooded area...where he threatened to 'bang [her] up' if she did not have sex with him."[271]

When the woman screamed in protest, "Saunders choked her, threatened to kill her, and pulled down her pants, forcing her to have sexual intercourse. After an intermission, he forced her to have sexual intercourse a second time," the court found. "Saunders then drove back on to the highway. When he stopped at a traffic signal, [the woman] jumped out of the car, ran across the street to a gas station where she told an employee she had just been raped, and asked that he call the police. After police arrived and questioned her, she was able to describe the location of the rape with specificity and to take the police to the location in the woods, where tire impressions matched those of Saunders's car."[272]

That would appear to corroborate the woman's allegations. But again, Saunders had a different story. Saunders denied having sexual intercourse of any kind—forced or consensual—with the woman in the woods. Indeed, Saunders denied even driving to the wooded area. He claims instead that earlier, during the visit to the school yard where Harris exited the car temporarily to sell crack, the woman had willingly performed oral sex because he promised he "could get her something."

After he had gotten the "something" (*i.e.*, drugs), he and the woman went to his house where they smoked crack and had consensual sex, Saunders testified. Later, when they were in the car again, Saunders testified that they began to argue because the woman was smoking and specifically "continued to smoke crack in the car." Saunders said he did not want the woman to smoke crack in the car and that he thought she was already too high. So, he grabbed the crack from her and threw it out of the window.

But the woman did not believe he had done it, Saunders testified. So, she got out of the car at a traffic light to look under the seat for the missing crack, Saunders said, and when he told her to get back in the car, she refused. So he did the gentlemanly thing of throwing her purse out of the car at her before driving off. The location? Near a gas station,[273] to which the Fourth Circuit wrote: "Apparently not crediting Saunders's version of the incidents that evening, which were totally inconsistent with [the woman's], the jury convicted Saunders of the rape of [the victim], as charged."[274]

Thus, the appeal.

In deciphering the issues before the court, the Fourth Circuit noted that prior to trial, during the phase when pretrial motions are submitted by counsel for both sides, Saunders sought to offer evidence of the woman's past sexual conduct. Specifically, Saunders sought to offer the testimony of a friend, a man identified as Kenneth Smith, who Saunders argued would testify that the woman Saunders had been accused of raping had had sex with Smith in exchange for drugs. The purpose of this offer, Saunders and his attorneys argued, was to establish Saunders's state of mind, *i.e.*, that he believed he and the woman were engaged in a "transaction," not a rape.

The trial court held an in-camera hearing on the issue, during which Saunders was allowed to testify to his own alleged prior sexual encounters with the woman, as well as to the alleged conversation he had with Smith a week before the incident. During that conversation, Smith allegedly told Saunders the woman was "skeezer" and that he [Smith] had had sex with her in exchange for drugs. But the federal rules of evidence don't allow everything said by witnesses to come into evidence unless it is testified to in some way.

Though Kenneth Smith was called a witness and would restate that he had sex with the woman, when the mention of drugs came up Smith invoked his Fifth Amendment rights against self-incrimination. Thus, the only testimony before the court was that Smith had sex with the woman a week prior to the incident. Given this turn of events, the district court held that Saunders could testify about his own prior sexual encounters with the woman. But Smith could not.

On appeal, Saunders argued that this had been a mistake on the district court's part. And citing *Doe v. United States*, Saunders argued that Smith's testimony had been relevant to the woman's reputation and, therefore, to his [Saunders's] state of mind. But the Fourth Circuit did not think so, opening its analysis of Sanders's challenge by stating, "[n]otwithstanding a question of whether the decision in *Doe*, regarding reputation evidence under 412(a), is correct, we find that the district court's ruling in this case was proper."[275]

"*Doe v. United States*," the Fourth Circuit offers in a footnote, "has been criticized for reading an exception into the flat prohibition of Fed.R.Evid. 412(a), when relevant to the defendant's state of mind."[276] But even so, Section 412(a), which applies to "reputation and opinion testimony of past sexual behavior, *prohibits* the evidence in every rape trial" under federal law,[277] "regardless of the circumstances under which it is offered."[278]

In contrast, Section (b) of 412 "…applies to other evidence of past sexual behavior, also prohibits the evidence except in three limited circumstances: (1) when the evidence is constitutionally required to be admitted…; (2) when the defendant claims that he was not the source of the semen or injury…; and, (3) when the defendant claims that the victim consented, in which case he may testify only to his prior relations with the victim.…"

The court then appears to take great pains to clarify its interpretation of the rule, noting, that "…the scheme of Rule 412 is that reputation and opinion evidence about a victim's past sexual behavior are never admissible, and evidence of specific prior acts is limited (to the extent constitutionally permitted) to directly probative evidence."[279] And then, as if for emphasis, the court adds that "[r]ule 412 is an express limitation on the general rules of admissibility of evidence about the prior conduct of witnesses otherwise applicable."[280]

Although the district court permitted Saunders to testify as to his own past sexual relations with the victim under an exception, the Fourth Circuit found no discernible constitutional basis for allowing Smith to testify as to his alleged past sexual relations with the victim, specifically that he allegedly spent three days in his home with the victim at some point prior to the rape.

Next, "Saunders contends…his knowledge that [the woman] was a 'skeezer' or prostitute corroborated his belief that she consented," the court wrote. "A defendant's reasonable, albeit mistaken, belief that the victim consented may constitute a defense to rape. When consent is the issue, however, [Rule 412] permits only evidence of the defendant's past experience with the victim."

The reason for this, the court explained, is that "[t]he rule manifests the policy that it is unreasonable for a defendant to base his belief of consent on the victim's past sexual experiences with third persons, since it is intolerable to suggest that because the victim is a prostitute, she automatically is assumed to have consented with anyone at any time."[281]

Though that, in fact, has long been the cultural assumption, there was a twist of sorts in this case in that attorneys for Saunders argued that Saunders believed the woman had consented to sexual intercourse with him, not because he knew she was a prostitute. But rather, he assumed that the woman had consented because he knew that she traded sex for drugs and he had given her drugs.[282]

Despite these assertions, the court ruled that "were [it] to require admission of Smith's testimony about his affair with [the victim], we would eviscerate the clear intent of the rule to protect victims of rape from being exposed at trial to harassing or irrelevant inquiry into their past sexual behavior, an inquiry that, prior to adoption of the rule, had the tendency to shield defendants from their illegal conduct by discouraging victims from testifying."[283]

Finally, the court noted that although the district court permitted Saunders to testify about his previous relations with the victim, in fact, that testimony was of "marginal relevance" because "consent was not the basis of Saunders's defense." Henry Saunders was charged with raping the victim in a car in the woods. But Saunders never argued that the victim consented to that encounter. Rather, he said it never happened and Saunders's "state of mind that [the victim] was a 'skeezer' is hardly relevant to that defense," the Fourth Circuit ruled. Further, the court noted, "Saunders did…provide an explanation for the presence of semen based on a consensual affair. He contended that he and [the victim] had consensual sexual intercourse earlier in the evening at Saunders's house."[284]

Because most rapes don't fit the traditional model, "rape shield" laws have hardly proved the brick wall women had hoped. As set forth above, most rapes are not carried out by strangers toting weapons or threatening life and limb. They are committed by friends, former lovers, ex-husbands or boyfriends, acquaintances and relatives. But prior relationships have traditionally blurred the lines for courts.[285] This legal "confusion" only gets worse where "rape shield" laws are involved, because "consent" has long seemed more plausible to judges and juries than rape. Thus, defendants have often argued it, whether or not the evidence shows that consent might actually have existed.[286] Thus, gray areas have made their way into the law.

THE RAPE SHIELD:
And Other Exemptions at Work in the Courts

As set forth above, there are three exceptions to Federal Rule of Evidence 412, that evidence of a rape victim's past sexual history and behavior may be admissible where: (1) the evidence is constitutionally required to be admitted; (2) the defendant claims that he was not the source of the semen or injury; and (3) the defendant claims that the victim consented, in which case he may testify only to his prior relations with the victim. In *Unites States v. Saunders*, the third exemption was at issue.

Other contemporary examples of these or similarly crafted state law exceptions at work include, for example, that during the highly publicized "Central Park jogger" case, though several of the teenage defendants reportedly gave "voluntary" video-taped confessions, the question of whether someone else might have been responsible for the semen found in the woman's badly battered body haunted the case from day one. Prosecutors argued that the woman, an avid jogger, was attacked by several youths moving through the park on a violent spree. During the attack, the woman was beaten unconscious with a lead pipe and rock until one of her eye sockets was smashed. She was left for dead in an icy puddle.[287]

Throughout the case, discussions—public and private—abounded as to whether the woman had sex with her boyfriend prior to the attack. That, it was argued, might explain the otherwise unidentified DNA matter. Though these arguments apparently failed to raise enough doubt to spark further investigation at the time, women's groups opposed what some saw as an attempt to put the victim on trial by piercing state "rape shield" laws. And yet, the case raises two significant ironies.

The first of these ironies is that the introduction of such evidence might be admissible under the second exception of Federal Rule of Evidence 412 if the state rule is similar. Several courts have held that this exception could be applied if done so, strictly.[288] The second is that in September 2002, media reports began to surface that another man—someone never suspected and, therefore, never questioned, but an established serial rapist and convicted murderer—had found religion in prison and, thus, confessed to attacking the "Central Park jogger" alone.[289] His DNA reportedly matched "mystery" samples found at the crime scene and on the victim's clothing.

This confession clearly establishes the basis for the federal rule that there are reasons to pierce rape shield laws, though in the "Central Park jogger case" it is not clear that doing so would have freed the young men wrongfully accused or have led to the real rapist, given that he had no prior relationship with jogger. In 2004, this exception was at the center of a heated debate in the Kobe Bryant case, as defense attorneys attempted to use a similar exception in the Colorado law. The basis of their arguments was that the injuries allegedly caused by Bryant during the alleged attack might have been caused by someone else.

Though the second and third exceptions to Federal Rule of Evidence 412 are fairly self-explanatory and more so in light of the above examples, exception number one, which may allow evidence of a rape victim's past sexual history and behavior to be admitted if the defendant can show that the "evidence is constitutionally required to be admitted…" is more nebulous. There is, how-ever, caselaw regarding the exception that may—or may not—offer guidance.

In 1988, the Supreme Court of New Hampshire issued a decision in the case of *New Hampshire v. Colbath*.[290] The facts of the case suggest that on June 28, 1985, Richard Colbath went to a tavern with some friends. While at the tavern, Colbath met the woman who would later become the complainant in the case. Colbath would testify that while in the bar, the woman allowed him to feel her breasts and behind. Colbath also testified that the woman rubbed his crotch while in the tavern. According to the court, there was also some evidence that the woman had directed provocative attentions toward other men in the bar as well.

Colbath and the woman eventually made their way to Colbath's trailer, where, according to the New Hampshire Supreme Court, "sexual intercourse followed; forcible according to the complainant, consensual according to the defendant." And what happened after that may be seen as unfortunate, if one believes the "sexual intercourse" was consensual; fortunate, if, one believes the complainant had just been raped, because, though not in the most pleasant of ways, it got her out of the trailer.

Colbath, it seems, had a suspicious girlfriend, who decided to return home at an odd hour, because she thought she would catch Colbath in a tryst with another woman. When she discovered Colbath with the woman who would later become the complainant inside the trailer, Colbath's companion "became enraged, kicked the trailer door open, and went for the complainant, whom she assaulted violently and dragged outside by the hair," according to the court. "It took the intervention of the defendant and a third woman to bring the melee to an end."

Upon returning to town, the complainant accused Colbath of rape. Colbath was arrested, and at trial his attorney was allowed during cross-examination to question the woman as to whether, on the afternoon of the incident while in the tavern, she sat on the lap of one of Colbath's friends. The woman said she had.

But soon after this testimony, the prosecutor made a Motion *in Limine* to fore-close any further testimony about the woman's conduct with other men that afternoon. The substance of this motion was that the woman's "conduct with others [was] not material on the issue of whether or not she consented to have sexual intercourse with" Colbath, the prosecutor argued.

The court granted the motion, holding that testimony of this kind was inad-missible as character evidence and prohibited by the state's rape shield law, which barred evidence of "[p]rior consensual sexual activity between the victim and any person other than" a defendant when offered to prove the offense of rape. But even so, the state's next witness, a woman named Candice Lepene, testified during direct examination that the complainant "left the tavern in the company of various men several times during the afternoon." The court also admitted into evidence a copy of the statement Lepene made to police, in which she told authorities she had seen a woman resembling the complainant "hanging all over everyone and making out with Richard Colbath and a few others." During cross-examination, Lepene further amplified these statements.

But at the close of the trial, as the judge issued instructions to the jury, they reflected the court's ruling regarding the Motion *in Limine*. The judge appar-ently did this by first reminding the jury of both the complainant and Lepene's testimony regarding the woman's conduct with men other than Colbath on the afternoon of the incident, only to then instruct the jury that he had allowed the testimony as background. Therefore, it was not "relevant on the issue of whether on not [the complainant] gave consent to sexual intercourse."

Colbath was convicted. He appealed, arguing that the jury should have been allowed to consider the complainant's public behavior with other men prior to the incident later leading to the accusation of rape as it related to the issue of consent. But what about the rape shield law? According to the New Hampshire Supreme Court, because "[t]hat part of the charge was tantamount to an instruction that the jury could not consider the evidence in question as bearing on guilty or innocence," it would treat it as "equivalent to an order striking the testimony about the complainant's openly observed behavior with other men during the course of the afternoon."

But was this simply the Supreme Court of New Hampshire's attempt to "right" a perceived wrong" (*i.e.*, a "trashy" woman goes to a man's home, has sex but later cries rape after the man's girlfriend beats her up)? Was Lord Hale rear-ing his head once again? Or was there a basis in the law?

As though anticipating the need to answer these questions, the court noted that "[d]espite the absolute terms of the [rape] shield law's prohibitions, our cases have consistently reflected the common recognition that such a statute's reach has to be limited by a defendant's state and national constitutional rights to confront the witnesses against him and to present his own exculpatory evi-dence. Thus, this court has held that a rape defendant must be given an oppor-tunity to demonstrate that the 'probative value [of the otherwise inadmissible evidence] in the context of that particular case outweighs its prejudicial effect on the prosecutrix."

That was the standard for evidence "constitutionally required to be admitted" as articulated by the New Hampshire Supreme Court. But how would the rule be applied?

The court answered this question by noting the "public character of the complainant's behavior," which it deemed "significant." "On the one hand," the court opined, "describing a complainant's open, sexually suggestive conduct in the presence of patrons of a public bar obviously has far less potential for damaging the sensibilities than revealing what the same person may have done in the company of another behind a closed door. On the other hand, evidence of public displays of general interest in sexual activity can be taken to indicate a contemporaneous receptiveness to sexual advances that cannot be inferred from evidence of private behavior with chosen sex partners."

These alternatives could be interpreted as "the same hand" (*i.e.*, the complainant was sexually suggestive in a public place, therefore, she would likely consent to sex in a private place; and, because the woman seemed generally interested in sex in the tavern, she would probably consent to sex in Colbath's trailer). Either way, it seems clear where the New Hampshire court wanted to go, and the justices made the trip: The jury could have found the evidence regarding the complainant's "openly sexually provocative behavior toward a group of men" indicative of her "probable attitude toward an individual within the group," the court concluded. In other words, because the woman might have wanted to have sex with any one of the men, she probably agreed to have sex with Colbath.

"Evidence that the publicly inviting acts occurred closely in time to the alleged sexual assault by one such man could have been viewed as indicating the complainant's likely attitude at the time of the sexual activity in question," the court wrote. "It would, in fact, understate the importance of such evidence in this case to speak of it merely as relevant. We should recall...the fact of intercourse was not denied, and that the evidence of assault was subject to the explanation that the defendant's jealous living companion had inflicted the visible injuries."

The court noted further that the "companion's furious behavior had a further bearing on the case as well, for the jury could have regarded her attack as a reason for the complainant to regret a voluntary liaison with the defendant, and as a reason for the complainant to allege rape as a way to explain her injuries and excuse her undignified predicament." Or the defendant might have alleged consent to explain his "undignified predicament" as a detainee.

But the court was winding up for the finale.

"Because little significance can be assigned here either to the privacy interest or to the fear of misleading the jury, the trial court was bound to recognize the defendant's interest in presenting probably crucial evidence of the complainant's behavior closely preceding the alleged rape. Thus the facts of this case well illustrate the court's previous observations that the sexual activities of a complainant immediately prior to an alleged rape may well be subject to a defendant's constitutional right to present evidence. The demand of the Constitution is all the clearer when those activities were carried on in a public setting. Because the jury instruction effectively excluded the evidence in question, the conviction must be reversed and the case remanded for a new trial," the court held.

These are examples of how the exceptions to Federal Rule of Evidence 412 and its state counterparts have been applied. A fascinating, but thankfully unanswered question, to be considered with regard to the application of the exceptions is how the Supreme Court of New Hampshire might have answered the questions raised in *United States v. Saunders*. Would the Supreme Court of New Hampshire have found Saunders's assertions that the complainant in that case was a "skeezer" indicative of her "probable attitude" toward "sex" with Saunders?

In an interesting aside to the case of *New Hampshire v. Colbath*, writing the decision for the court was New Hampshire Justice Souter, who was later appointed to the United States Supreme Court and has proved to be an extraordinary believer in precedent.

INVENTING CONSENT:
Where There is None

As set forth above, *United States v. Saunders* was a Fourth Circuit case. Though the defendant was not allowed to introduce the evidence, that hardly means that attempts to get around federal or state rules prohibiting the introduction of a victim's prior sexual history and/or that the introduction of thinly veiled arguments regarding a woman's alleged consent have slowed, even where consent seems far from a reality.

In *Portuondo v. Agard*,[291] for example, a 1998 New York case heard by the United States Supreme Court in March 2000, a defendant went on trial for "nineteen sodomy and assault counts and three weapons counts." According to one of the two victims involved, the defendant threatened one woman with a handgun. Additional testimony was also offered, suggesting the defendant had "physically assaulted, raped, and orally and anally sodomized" the woman.

In response to this testimony, the defendant argued that he and the woman he was accused of raping and sodomizing "had engaged in consensual vaginal intercourse." Specifically, according to Justice Scalia, who wrote the decision on behalf of the Supreme Court, the defendant "...testified that during an argument he had with [one of the victims], he struck her in the face. [But he] denied raping her or threatening either woman with a handgun."[292]

According to the United States Supreme Court, the defendant "was convicted of one count of anal sodomy and two counts of third-degree possession of a weapon." But "[o]n direct appeal, the New York Supreme Court reversed one of the convictions for possession of a weapon but affirmed the remaining convictions.[293] The defendant sought to appeal the other convictions, arguing that comments made by the prosecutor during summation violated his constitutional rights.[294] When he was denied leave by the New York Court of Appeals,[295] the defendant sought *habeas* relief in federal court, alleging that a prosecutor's comments regarding his credibility violated his Fifth, Sixth, and Fourteenth Amendment rights. A divided Second Circuit court found for the defendant. The United States Supreme Court reversed, upholding the convictions.

Though the ultimate issues of *Portuondo v. Agard* did not directly relate to the defendant's assertions of alleged consent—at gunpoint—what the trend towards "consent" suggests, if it is allowed to continue even where there is no evidence to support it, it may, as Harris suggests, punch holes in the nation's rape shield laws. Further, although the goal of the defendant in *Portuondo v. Agard* may simply have been to defeat the complaint of rape itself, as set forth above in other cases, the goal in introducing evidence of the complainant's past sexual life may be to trade on deeply rooted beliefs that loose women ask for it or can't be raped.

Thus, even if the jury is instructed to consider evidence of this sort to decide not actual consent, but rather mistaken consent, the testimony may still have the desired effect."[296]

RAPE AND SEXUAL ASSAULT:
And the Violence Against Women Act

In 1994, President Bill Clinton signed the Violent Crime Control Act into law.[297] Part of this omnibus crime bill was the Violence Against Women Act (VAWA), the language of which set forth that "all persons within the United States shall have the right to be free from crimes of violence motivated by gender."[298] Among the articulated purposes of the Violence Against Women Act was protecting "...the civil rights of victims of gender-motivated violence"[299] and promoting the "public safety, health, and activities affecting interstate commerce by establishing a federal civil rights cause of action for victims of crimes of violence motivated by genders."[300]

The Violence Against Women Act included several provisions, among them a criminal section permitting federal prosecution of interstate crimes of sex-motivated violence. In 1999, the United States Supreme Court declined to consider a constitutional challenge to the criminal provision of the Act.[301] The Act also established a federal civil remedy for victims of "gender-motivated" crimes,[302] an enactment that proved a source of controversy even before the Violence Against Women Act was signed into law.

"In the years leading up to its final passage, the Violence Against Women Act was a frequent target of criticism from federal judges, including Chief Justice Rehnquist, who singled it out in a 1998 speech as one of 'the more notable examples' of laws that unduly expanded the jurisdiction of the federal courts," veteran reporter Linda Greenhouse wrote in May 2000. "'Our system will look more and more like the French government, where even the most minor details are ordained by the national government in Paris,' the Chief Justice warned in a speech to the American Law Institute."[303]

The civil provision of the Violence Against Women Act provided that "[a] person (including a person who acts under color of any stature, ordinance, regulation, custom, or usage of any state) who commits a crime of violence motivated by gender and thus deprives another of the right declared in subsection (b) of this section shall be liable to the party injured, in an action for the recovery of compensatory and punitive damages, injunctive and declaratory relief, and such other relief as a court may deem appropriate."[304]

The Act defined a crime "motivated by gender" as "a crime of violence committed because of gender or on the basis of gender, and due, at least in part, to an animus based on the victim's gender.[305] In addition, a "crime of violence" was defined as:

> (A) an "…act or series of acts that would constitute a felony against the person or that would constitute a felony against property if the conduct presents a serious risk of physical injury to another, and that would come within the meaning of state or federal offenses described in Section 16 of Title 18, whether or not those acts have actually resulted in criminal charges, prosecution, or conviction and whether or not those acts were committed in the special maritime, territorial, or prison jurisdiction of the United States; and
>
> (B) an "…act or series of acts that would constitute a felony described in subparagraph (A) but for the relationship between the person who takes such action and the individual against whom such action is taken.[306]

The Act further provided, however, that "[n]othing in this section requires a prior criminal complaint, prosecution, or conviction to establish the elements of a cause of action under subsection (c) of this section."[307] In accordance with the Violence Against Women Act, litigants were granted a choice of forums: federal and state courts "shall have concurrent jurisdiction" over complaints brought this section."[308] It seems clear, however, that Congress intended the federal courts to be the primary forum.[309]

Passage of the Violence Against Women Act was the end result of four years of intensive hearings, data analysis, and public debate, following decades of feminist efforts to create a federal remedy for victims of rape and other gender-motivated crimes. Such a remedy was needed, feminists, women's rights groups, and later Congress argued, because state agencies often systematically failed to "vigorously" pursue cases involving violence against women.

Though jurisdiction—and/or the authority to bring a person to court—has historically been reserved for the state in which a crime occurs, Congress claimed "affirmative" authority for the concurrent federal and state jurisdiction of the Violence Against Women Act "…under Section 5 of the Fourteenth Amendment to the Constitution, as well as under Section 8 of Article I of the Constitution."[310]

That authority was challenged, however, by two members of the Virginia Polytechnic Institute varsity football team, attorneys for whom argued that the civil damages provision exceeded congressional authority.[311] That challenge led to a congressional–Supreme Court showdown, culminating with the Court's decision in 2000 in *United States v. Morrison*, striking down the civil provision of the Violence Against Women Act. The events leading up to that decision, however, actually began six years earlier.

BRZONKALA v. VIRGINIA POLYTECHNIC AND STATE UNIVERSITY[312]: United States v. Morrison[313]

In the fall of 1994, a young woman named Christy Brzonkala enrolled at the Virginia Polytechnic Institute. Because Christy Brzonkala courageously agreed to allow her name to be disclosed publicly, it will be used here, although throughout this book the names of other victims of sexual assaults have not been used.[314]

Sometime during her first month at school, Brzonkala met two men, Antonio Morrison and James Crawford, who were also students at the school as well as members of the varsity football team. Within thirty minutes of the meeting, Brzonkala alleged that she was assaulted and repeatedly raped in a university dorm by Morrison and Crawford. When it was over, Morrison allegedly told her, "[y]ou better not have any…diseases," Brzonkala alleged.

In the months following the alleged attack, Morrison "allegedly announced in the dormitory's dining room that he 'like[d] to get girls drunk and….'" And as though refusing to finish the description for reasons of decorum, the United States Supreme Court notes instead in its decision that "[t]he omitted portions, quoted verbatim in the briefs on file with this Court, consist of boasting, debased remarks about what Morrison would do to women, vulgar remarks that cannot fail to shock and offend."[315]

After the incident, the complaint alleged that Brzonkala stopped going to class, and because she was suffering "severe emotional disturbance," she sought help from the university psychiatrist, who prescribed antidepressants. In early 1995, Brzonkala filed a complaint against Morrison and Crawford with school officials under the university's sexual assault policy. At a university hearing on the complaint, the school's Judicial Committee found the evidence insufficient to sustain punishment for Crawford.

By contrast, Morrison admitted engaging in "sexual contact" with Brzonkala though she had twice told him "no." Morrison maintained, however, that the "sex" was consensual. Despite his protestations, a university's Judicial Committee found Morrison "guilty" of sexual assault. In accordance with that finding, Morrison was "sentenced" to a two-semester suspension. The school's dean of students later upheld the sentence. But in July 1995, officials notified Brzonkala that Morrison intended to challenge the "conviction" under the school's Sexual

Assault Policy and that a second hearing would be needed to remedy errors made during the first hearing, Brzonkala was also told.

Following that second hearing Morrison was again found "guilty" and again sentenced to a two-semester suspension. But this time, Morrison's offense was described as "sexual assault" during which he used "abusive language." Morrison appealed under the university's administrative system, and on August 21, 1995, the school's senior vice president and provost set Morrison's punishment aside, ruling it "excessive when compared with other cases where there has been a finding of violation of the Abusive Conduct Policy."[316] Brzonkala, who was never informed of this decision by the university, learned of the decision and that Morrison would be returning to the university in the fall of 1995 from the newspaper. She withdrew from the university.

In December of 1995, Brzonkala brought suit against Morrison, Crawford, and the Virginia Polytechnic Institute in the United States District Court for the Western District of Virginia, asserting claims against Morrison and Crawford under the Violence Against Women Act. Brzonkala's complaint also alleged that Virginia Polytechnic Institute's handling of her internal complaint violated Title IX of the Education Amendment of 1972.[317] It was widely reported to have been the first suit brought under the law's civil damages provision.[318]

Morrison and Crawford were represented by Michael E. Rosman, general counsel for the Center for Individual Rights, an association that has been publicly described as "a conservative public interest law firm."[319] Rosman challenged Brzonkala's complaint on two grounds. The first was that it should be dismissed for failure to state a claim upon which relief could be granted. The second basis was that the civil provision of the Violence Against Women Act was unconstitutional.

The district court agreed, dismissing Brzonkala's claims against Virginia Polytechnic Institute brought under Title IX for failure to state a claim.[320] The district court also held that Brzonkala's complaint may have stated a claim against Morrison and Crawford under the Violence Against Women Act. But because Congress lacked authority to create a civil remedy under either the Commerce Clause or Section 5 of the Fourteenth Amendment, those claims also had to be dismissed.[321] Brzonkala appealed to the Fourth Circuit Court of Appeals.

A divided panel of the Fourth Circuit Court of Appeals reversed the district court's ruling, reinstating Brzonkala's claims under the Violence Against Women Act and Title IX.[322] But the full Court of Appeals vacated the panel's opinion before rehearing the case *en banc*. An *en banc* Fourth Circuit then held that Brzonkala's complaint stated a claim under the Violence Against Women Act, because the alleged crime involved violence as well as "crude and derogatory statements regarding his treatment of women," which, taken together, "sufficiently indicated that [Morrison's] crime was motivated by gender animus."[323]

But a divided Fourth Circuit also voted to affirm the district court's conclusion that Congress lacked the constitutional authority to enact the civil provisions of the Violence Against Women Act.[324] In a 168-page opinion, written by

Judge J. Michael Luttig on behalf of the 7-to-4 majority, the court held that the Violence Against Women Act "simply cannot be reconciled with the principles of limited federal government upon which this nation is founded."[325]

Though Congress based its claim of authority for the civil provision of the Violence Against Women Act on findings tending to show that victims of gender-based crimes, or those fearful of being the victims of such crimes, declined to travel, lost job opportunities and spent more on health care,[326] the majority of the Fourth Circuit held that because violence against women had only "an attenuated and indirect relationship with interstate commerce," Congress had exceeded its authority.[327]

Prior to the Fourth Circuit Court of Appeals' decision, the journey of Brzonkala's complaint had been watched closely and was the frequent subject of commentary and scholarship. But after the Fourth Circuit's ruling, the politics of the debate were soon as bare as the law. Officials of the Clinton administration intervened, for example, to appeal the Fourth Circuit Court of Appeals decision, as did the NOW Legal Defense and Education Fund on behalf of Brzonkala.[328] And the United States Supreme Court, which had previously scheduled "three other federalism cases in its new term," granted *certiorari* in 1999.[329] The two appeals—*United States v. Morrison* and *Brzonkala v. Morrison*—were then combined.[330]

Critics of the current Court's "activist" approach to civil rights have noted that the fact the Court would agree to hear the first appeal in a case involving the Violence Against Women Act—an act publicly criticized by the Chief Justice prior to its passage—was clearly more about forwarding a "conservative federalist agenda" than concerns over a congressional overextension of its authority. In the end, women's rights gave way to state's rights and the Court effectively— and perhaps determinedly—undermined the very purpose of the law (*i.e.*, to grant women a remedy in cases of rape and sexual assault because states have often failed to pursue cases of this sort).

A CIVIL RAPE REMEDY NOT ALLOWED:
An "Activist" Court and a Federalist Agenda

"At first glance, the Violence Against Women Act appeared an unlikely battleground for the Supreme Court's continuing federalism wars," argued Greenhouse in *The New York Times*.[331] "This 1994 federal law neither told the states to do anything nor prohibited them from taking any action. By permitting private damage suits by victims of 'gender-motivated violence' against their attackers, the law did not expose the states, themselves, to any new liability."

In addition, there was "…no titanic struggle among co-equal sovereigns." Rather, the contrary was true. The Violence Against Women Act enjoyed widespread nonpartisan support. Indeed, while it was pending by Congress, "the attorneys general from 38 states urged its passage, and 36 states joined a brief supporting the law before the Supreme Court. Only one, Alabama, filed a brief asking the justices to strike the law down," says Greenhouse.[332]

In addition, although the United States Supreme Court "ordinarily waits to review a case until a disagreement has developed among the federal appeals courts," the Supreme Court agreed—enthusiastically, some critics say—to hear appeals in *United States v. Morrison* and *Brzonkala v. Morrison*.[333] Far from there being a conflict among the circuits, fourteen federal district courts had upheld the Violence Against Women Act[334] and the lower courts had reportedly applied the law some fifty times prior to the Court's intervention.[335]

The Violence Against Women Act was passed "just before the Supreme Court set itself on its current course of subjecting to searching scrutiny any Congressional action that could conceivably impinge on state sovereignty or traditional prerogatives," notes Greenhouse.[336] And in that sense, the Violence Against Women Act and the Court's expanding list of federalism concerns appear to have been on "an inevitable collision course" that ended on May 15, 2000, with the majority striking down the civil remedies provision.[337]

"Federalism concerns underlie the majority's activism in federal *habeas corpus* as much as it does its work in the commerce clause, Section 5 of the Fourteenth Amendment, and the Eleventh and Tenth Amendments," wrote the *National Law Journal's* Marcia Coyle. "Calling for finality in death penalty appeals and greater deference to state-court judgments, the majority in the past two decades has imposed major procedural hurdles to federal court review of state convictions and sentences in the absence of congressional action."[338]

In the context of this history, the majority's decision in *United States v. Morrison* represents a "key piece of the Rehnquist Court's federalism jurisprudence, itself one of two likely legacies of this conservative bench," Coyle suggests. "As with federal habeas corpus, the second legacy, the prevailing 5-to-4 majority has used its view of the constitutional framework of government to disperse power, most recently to the detriment of Congress and the federal courts."[339]

The Court's decision in *United States v. Morrison* was issued in May 2000. During the 1999-2000 term,[340] the Supreme Court decided 73 cases, a smaller number than any time since the early 1950s.[341] By contrast, the Court issued decisions in 79 cases during the 2000-2001 term.[342] Despite the relatively small number of cases heard, the docket ran the constitutional gamut from First Amendment issues, to religion, to the right to broadcast sexually explicit material on cable television, to state elections.[343]

During the 1999–2000 term, the Court also ruled that the Food and Drug Administration could not regulate the use of tobacco,[344] a decision whose echoes are widely thought to have foreclosed jurisdiction in the federal courts of health maintenance organizations accused of medical malpractice. And though that decision was unanimous, Greenhouse notes (as others have) that in fact, the Court "was more sharply divided than usual, with the middle ground often seeming to disappear.[345]

Twenty of the seventy-three cases decided during the 1999–2000 term were decided by 5-to-4 majority, compared to twenty-six of the seventy-nine cases decided by that same margin during the 2000–2001 term.[346] Generally, the conservative majority—*i.e.,* Chief Justice William H. Rehnquist and Justices Sandra Day O'Connor, Antonin Scalia, Anthony M. Kennedy, and Clarence Thomas—dominated these decisions, prevailing in 13 of the 20 cases decided by 5-to-4 majority during the 1999–2000 term and 14 of the 26 similarly decided cases during the 2000–2001 term.[347]

Justices John Paul Stevens, David H. Souter, Ruth Bader Ginsburg, and Stephen G. Breyer—or "the four liberal justices" as they have come to be known—voted as a group in the winning majority of only one of the 5-to-4 cases decided during the 1999–2000 term: *Stenberg v. Carhart,*[348] in which the Court held a Nebraska abortion law unconstitutional. In that case, Justices Stevens, Souter, Ginsburg, and Breyer were joined by Justice Sandra Day O'Connor.[349]

Court watchers suggest that where the case before the Court involved "straightforward" questions of the supremacy of federal law—as opposed to questions of whether federal law may "intrude" into areas where state law traditionally governed—the Justices were often unanimous in upholding the federal law.[350] And yet, federalism was clearly part of the majority's agenda. And though the majority's "activism on federalism" may have seemed "dramatic," it is not unheard of, Coyle notes.

"The vision of state and national boundaries of power now unfolding in recent decisions was clearly drawn by Chief Justice William H. Rehnquist years ago in his own dissenting opinions and other writings. He now enjoys the five votes necessary to implement that vision," argues Coyle.[351]

"...In a series of decisions over the last four years, culminating in June [2000] with three handed down on the final day of the Court's term, the Court invoked principles of federalism and sovereign immunity to circumscribe the power of Congress to identify problems in need of uniform national solutions," comments Greenhouse.[352]

"On the commerce clause side of the majority's work, *Morrison* ends any doubts that [*United States v.*] *Lopez*—which, for the first time in sixty years, struck down a federal law on Commerce-Clause grounds—was an aberration or a limited ruling," Coyle explained.[353]

Until then, Professor Thomas O. Sargentich, co-director of the Law and Government Program at American University College of Law told the *National Law Journal* that many people viewed the Court's decision in *United States v. Lopez* as "a shot across the bow of Congress," with the Court "trying to get Congress to do a better job, to be more attentive to what the Commerce Clause demands. But it wasn't really a grab for power by the court."[354]

In other words, "[b]efore *Morrison,* there was a belief that with careful congressional findings about the interstate nature or effect of the activity being regulated, Congress could go forward," Sargentich said.[355] After *Morrison,* what Congress may be allowed to do in the eyes of the Court is far less clear, scholars note.

"By the 5-to-4 vote that has become a familiar form of the court's increasingly bitter debate over the proper allocation of federal and state authority," writes Greenhouse, the United States Supreme Court "struck down a central provision of one federal law, the Violence Against Women Act, and invalidated the application of the federal age discrimination law to the states,"[356] Greenhouse wrote.

BRZONKALA v. VIRGINIA POLYTECHNIC:
United States v. Morrison is Decided

As set forth above, Christy Brzonkala appealed the decision by the Fourth Circuit. Attorneys for the federal government also appealed in defense of the Violence Against Women Act. The two appeals—*Brzonkala v. Morrison* and *United States v. Morrison*—were combined before the United States Supreme Court, and that is the manner in which the case came from the Court.

It has often been said that the reader can tell where the Court—any court—intends to go by the way it opens its decision. In writing on behalf of the majority in *United States v. Morrison*, Chief Justice William Rehnquist opens by noting that "[e]very law enacted by Congress must be based on one or more of its powers enumerated in the Constitution." Or, "[t]he powers of the legislature are defined and limited; and...those limits may not be mistaken or forgotten.'" Rehnquist cited the longstanding precedent of *Marbury v. Madison*.[357]

The decision then seems almost formulaic with the majority laying out the argument it would refute: "Congress explicitly identified the sources of federal authority on which it relied in enacting Section 13981 [of the Violence Against Women Act]," wrote Rehnquist. "It said that a 'federal civil rights cause of action' is established '[p]ursuant to the affirmative power of Congress...under Section 5 of the Fourteenth Amendment to the Constitution, as well as under Section 8 of Article I of the Constitution.'"[358]

Then, articulating the legal standard to be applied and setting forth the question the majority would answer: "Due respect for the decisions of the coordinate branch of government demands that we invalidate a congressional enactment only upon a plain showing that Congress has exceeded its constitutional bounds," Rehnquist wrote.[359] "[W]ith this presumption of constitutionality in mind, we turn to the question [of] whether Section 13981 falls within Congress's power under Article I, Section 8 of the Constitution. *Brzonkala* and the *United States* rely upon the third clause of the Article, which gives Congress power '[t]o regulate commerce with foreign nations, and among the several states, and with the Indian tribes.'"

The majority would conclude that it was not relying upon the 1995 precedent of *United States v. Lopez*,[360] in which the same 5-to-4 majority struck down the Gun-Free School Zones Act on similar grounds.[361] "As we discussed at length in *Lopez*," Rehnquist wrote, "our interpretation of the Commerce Clause has changed as our nation has developed. We need not repeat that detailed review of the Commerce Clause's history here; it suffices to say that, in the years since *NLRB v. Jones & Laughlin Steel Corp.*,[362] Congress has had considerably greater latitude in regulating conduct and transactions under the Commerce Clause than our previous case law permitted."

But as the majority's decision in *Lopez* made clear, "even under our modern, expansive interpretation of the Commerce Clause, Congress's regulatory authority is not without effective bounds," Rehnquist noted.[363] As the majority opined in *Lopez*, and then again saw it in *Morrison*, the Commerce Clause grants three legitimate categories of activity over which Congress may exercise authority.[364]

Congress has the authority to regulate the use of channels of interstate commerce.[365] Congress is also "empowered to regulate and protect the instrumentalities of interstate commerce, or persons or things in interstate commerce, even though the threat may come only from intrastate activities," Rehnquist noted on behalf of the majority.[366] "Finally, Congress's commerce authority includes power to regulate those activities having substantial relation to interstate commerce,...*i.e.,* those activities that substantially affect interstate commerce," according to the majority opinion.[367]

There might, arguably, have been room for interpretation of Section 13981 of the Violence Against Women Act under the grant of Congressional authority of the second category of activities—*i.e.,* the authority to protect the instrumentalities of interstate commerce, *or persons or things in interstate commerce, even though the threat may come only from intrastate activities*—given Congressional findings that "widespread violence against women, and fear of violence, had a negative effect on the nation's economy, measured in the billions of dollars a year, by impairing the productivity and...mobility of female employees and students."[368] But the majority dismissed this possibility, noting instead that "[p]etitioners do not contend that these cases fall within either of the first two of these categories of Commerce Clause regulation."[369]

Further, because Section 13981 of the Violence Against Women Act focuses "on gender-motivated violence wherever it occurs (rather than violence directed at instrumentalities of interstate commerce, interstate markets, or things or persons in interstate commerce, we agree that this is the proper inquiry," the majority concluded, before turning for precedent to their decision in *United States v. Lopez.*[370]

Then, invoking the precedent and language of the road map on the issue, Justice Rehnquist noted that "...a fair reading of *Lopez* shows that the noneconomic, criminal nature of the conduct at issue was central to our decision in that case."[371] In addition, the Gun-Free School Zones Act of 1990 had "no express jurisdictional element which might limit its reach to a discrete set of firearm possessions" that were also explicitly connected to and/or affecting interstate commerce.[372] It was significant to the majority in *Lopez* that "neither Section 922(q) 'nor its legislative history contain[ed] express congressional findings regarding the effects upon interstate commerce of gun possession in a school zone.'"[373]

Though "'Congress normally is not required to make formal findings as to the substantial burdens that an activity has on interstate commerce,'" the majority noted in *Lopez*,[374] that "the existence of such findings may 'enable us to evaluate the legislative judgment that the activity in question substantially affect[s] interstate commerce, even though no such substantial effect [is] visible to the naked eye.'"[375] But in *Lopez*, the majority held that the "link between gun possession and a substantial effect on interstate commerce was attenuated."[376]

In contrast to Lopez, the majority noted in *Morrison* that "Section 13981 [of the Violence Against Women Act] is supported by numerous findings regarding the serious impact that gender-motivated violence has on victims and their families."[377] Among those findings were that: "[t]hree out of four American women will be victims of violent crimes sometime during their life;[378] [v]iolence is the leading cause of injuries to women ages 15 to 44;[379] '[p]artial estimates show that violent crime against women costs this country at least 3 billion—not million, but billion—dollars a year;'[380] '[a]ccording to one study, close to half a million girls now in high school will be raped before they graduate;'[381] and '[125,000] college women can expect to be raped during this—or any—year.'"[382]

"But the existence of congressional findings is not sufficient, by itself, to sustain the constitutionality of Commerce Clause legislation," the majority wrote.[383] And with that, the majority rejected "…the argument that Congress may regulate noneconomic, violent criminal conduct based solely on that conduct's aggregate effect on interstate commerce.[384]

"The Constitution," the majority held, "requires a distinction between what is truly national and what is truly local.[385] In recognizing this fact we preserve one of the few principles that has been consistent since the Clause was adopted. The regulation and punishment of intrastate violence that is not directed at instrumentalities, channels, or goods involved in interstate commerce has always been the province of the states.[386] Indeed, we can think of no better example of the police power, which the Founders denied the National Government and reposed in the states, than the suppression of violent crime and vindication of its victims."[387]

The majority also struck down Brzonkala's Fourteenth Amendment claim, because, in the majority's analysis, Section 13981 was not "aimed at proscribing discrimination by officials which the Fourteenth Amendment might not itself proscribe; it is directed not at any state or state actor, but at individuals who have committed criminal acts motivated by gender bias."[388]

"In the present cases, for example, Section 13981 visits no consequence whatever on any Virginia public official involved in investigating or prosecuting Brzonkala's assault. The section is, therefore, unlike any of the Section 5 remedies that we have previously upheld," the majority wrote.[389] Review of past caselaw in this area led the majority ultimately to conclude that "Congress's power under Section 5 does not extend to the enactment of Section 13981."[390]

The majority's decision in *United States v. Lopez*, which clearly set the stage for the same majority's decision in *United States v. Morrison*, marked the first time since the New Deal that a majority of the United States Supreme Court found Congress to have exceeded its Commerce Clause authority.[391] Critics of the majority's decision in *United States v. Morrison* note that although states' rights appear clearly to have been on the minds of the majority, states' rights were never directly at issue in either *United States v. Lopez* or *United States v. Morrison*.[392]

And yet, the Court's decision represents "a convergence between the [C]ourt's focus on a Congress of limited powers and its newly found solicitude for state sovereignty, the focus of other recent federalism decisions that have carved out new immunities for the states from federal court lawsuits or federal policy 'commandeering,'" Greenhouse contends.[393] The profound "convergence" lay not perhaps "so much in anything" the majority opinion said explicitly, "but in the background music of a decision that rejected a large volume of evidence that the law's sponsors had compiled to show why a national approach to violence against women was needed."[394]

United States v. Morrison represented the "intersection of the New Deal and civil rights, coming together in a case concerning women," said Professor Judith Resnik of Yale Law School in an interview following the Court's decision. The majority's rejection of findings and arguments on violence against women as an appropriate subject for national legislation harkens back to "earlier eras, when the Supreme Court viewed labor-management issues and, even earlier, slavery, as a matter of interpersonal relations, not properly subject to federal intervention," Resnick added.[395]

Constitutional scholar and Harvard Law Professor Laurence Tribe remarked that "[t]he [C]ourt applied its own 'metatest' to the legislative record." In other words, the majority essentially concluded: "'We don't care what the findings are, if accepting them endangers our vision of state sovereignty, our view of the architecture of our system.'"[396]

Justice Souter, joined by Justices Stevens, Ginsburg, and Breyer, said essentially the same thing, though slightly more elegantly. "The business of the courts is to review the congressional assessment, not for soundness but simply for the rationality of concluding that a jurisdictional basis exists in fact."[397] Justice Souter noted further that "any explicit findings that Congress chooses to make, though not dispositive of the question of rationality, may advance judicial review by identifying factual authority on which Congress relied."[398]

Then, citing three full pages of supporting documentation offered by Congress,[399] and noting that the legislative record offered in *United States v. Morrison* was "far more voluminous than the record compiled by Congress and found sufficient in two prior cases upholding Title II of the Civil Rights Act of 1964 against Commerce Clause challenges,"[400] the four justices concluded that "[v]iolence against women may be found to affect interstate commerce and affect it substantially."[401]

As set forth earlier, however, the majority ruled otherwise, prompting critics to suggest that the "federalism counterrevolution" may have inched closer to those "core issues of civil rights for which the court for so long had given Congress wide scope."[402] By ruling that the civil provision of Violence Against Women Act was not an appropriate exercise of Congressional authority, "the

[C]ourt emphasized that in the area of civil rights, no less than interstate commerce, Congressional assertions of power [are] now to be scrutinized under a judicial microscope," wrote Greenhouse.[403]

This matters to the future of women's issues, of course, because "women's issues" are often civil rights issues. But on that front, the "gulf" between "the majority" of Justices Rehnquist, O'Connor, Scalia, Kennedy, and Thomas and "the minority" of Justices Souter, joined by Justices Stevens, Ginsburg, and Breyer is said to be "wide and growing."[404] The "gulf" in reasoning between the majority and minority opinions in *United States v. Morrison*, would certainly appear to suggest that this is true.

In writing for the minority, Justice Souter concluded that "...today's ebb of the commerce power rests on error, and at the same time leads me to doubt that the majority's view will prove to be enduring law. There is yet one more reason for doubt. Although we sense the presence of *[Carter v.] Carter Coal Co.*,[405] *Schechter [Poultry Corp. v. United States]*[406] and *[National League of Cities v.] Usery*,[407] once again, the majority embraces them only at arm's length. Where such decisions once stood as rules, today's opinion points to consideration by which substantial effects are discounted. Cases standing for the sufficiency of substance are not overruled; cases overruled since 1937 are not quite revived.

"The Court's thinking betokens less clearly a return to the conceptual straitjackets of *Schechter* and *Carter Coal* and *Usery* than to something like the unsteady state of obscenity law between *Redrup v. New York*,[408] and *Miller v. California*,[409] a period in which the failure to provide a workable definition left this Court to review each case *ad hoc*," Justice Souter continued.[410] "As our predecessors learned then, the practice of such *ad hoc* review cannot preserve the distinction between the judicial and the legislative, and this Court, in any event, lacks the institutional capacity to maintain such a regime for very long. This one will end when the majority realizes that the conception of the commerce power for which it entertains hopes would inevitably fail the test expressed in Justice Holmes's statement that "[t]he first call of a theory of law is that it should fit the facts."[411]

"The facts that cannot be ignored today are the facts of integrated national commerce and a political relationship between states and nation much affected by their respective treasuries and constitutional modifications adopted by the people. The federalism of some earlier time is no more adequate to account for those facts today than the theory of *laissez-faire* was able to govern the national economy seventy years ago," Justice Souter concluded.[412]

Others outside of the Court appear to agree that the majority's decision in *Morrison* may have created a "jurisprudence of doubt." "A law professor poses this hypothetical: on a visit to Earth, a lawyer from Mars discovers that the U.S. Supreme Court is reviewing the constitutionality of two federal laws. One bars states from selling personal data on drivers' licenses; the other has created a federal cause of action for victims of gender-based violence," wrote Coyle.[413]

"The Martian is told that the court will invalidate only one law as an intrusion on state sovereignty and asked which one.[414] 'I would argue every competent lawyer from Mars would guess wrong,'" says the hypothetical poser, separation-of-powers scholar Peter Shane, of the University of Pittsburgh School of Law, according to Coyle. "'He explains that the first law—the Driver's Privacy Protection Act—really is a limitation on the states, but it was upheld 9 to 0 by the court this term in *Reno v. Condon*.[415] The second, a provision of the Violence Against Women Act (VAWA) that was endorsed as necessary by a majority of the states, was struck down 5 to 4.... If lawyers from outer space might be confused by the Rehnquist Court's ongoing efforts to enforce constitutional boundaries between national and state sovereigns, is an earthbound Congress likely to do any better?'"[416]

Senator Joseph R. Biden Jr., the Delaware democrat who sponsored the Violence Against Women Act, had other words for the majority. According to Biden, the majority's decision would ultimately have "a lot less impact on violence against women than on the future role of the United States Congress."[417] The Court's decision, Biden said, was "really all about power: who has the power, the Court or Congress?"[418] Thus, "[t]he damage done to the Act is not as bad as the damage done to American jurisprudence," Biden said.[419]

Senator Charles Schumer, a democrat from New York who was the chief sponsor of the Violence Against Women Act as a representative from Brooklyn in the House of Representatives, commented that "[j]ust at a time when the economic and social conditions of the world demand that we be treated as one country and not as fifty states, the Supreme Court seems poised to undo decades and decades of a consensus that the federal government has an active role to play."[420]

ADDITIONAL FOOTNOTES TO
UNITED STATES v. MORRISON

Though the decision of the majority striking down the civil provision will likely be debated for years to come, there are a few final footnotes to the case of *United States v. Morrison*. Among them is that Christy Brzonkala's lawyer, Eileen Wagner, a sole practitioner from Richmond, has reported that Brzonkala and Virginia Polytechnic Institute settled the Title IX claim for $75,000 in March 2000.[421]

And, although citing no legal authority, the *National Law Journal* reported in August 2001 that an Ohio judge ordered a convicted rapist to pay a woman he stalked and then raped $7,651 in compensatory damages and medical expenses and $3 million in punitive damages. An attorney for the woman said there is no real expectation that the defendant will ever pay a single penny, he is serving a 30-year sentence.[422]

To many, the civil provision of the Violence Against Women Act was supposed to be what the future held. It was supposed to do for women what the Civil Rights Act of 1964 did for minorities. Though the Court struck down the civil provision, there have been some gains—scientific as well as legal—for women. In February of 2000, for example, the House of Representatives proposed tougher federal laws and stiffer prison sentences for the possession of the "date rape" drug gamma hydroxybutyrate.[423] On the scientific front, in July 2002, a company began advertising the sale of "Drink Safe" test strips and coasters, which are supposed to change color when a drink is contaminated with gamma hydroxybutyrate or Rohypnol. The strips reportedly fit into a purse and can be taken to a bar.[424]

Perhaps one of the most significant actions in the last decade in terms of rape prosecutions involves the filing of "John Doe" complaints based only upon a DNA profile against unknown alleged rapists. In 1999, in what was then seen as "an unusual legal strategy," a Wisconsin prosecutor filed rape and kidnapping charged against a still-unnamed assailant with the offenses based solely on his DNA profile.[425] The purpose of this act was reportedly to file charges within the state's six-year statute of limitations period.

Rape victims, among them the California woman who awoke to find "a stranger...on top of [her]" after he cut through the screen on her back door[426] have pushed for longer statutes of limitations and fought to bring the law in "line with current technology."[427] In 2001, California Assemblyman Lou Correa, was reportedly drafting a bill that, if passed, would extend the statute of limitations on rape to ten years in that state.[428] Given the newfound reliance on DNA profiles in rape cases where an assailant cannot be immediately identified, other states seem likely to consider similar action.

And in August 2002, it was widely reported that Representative Carolyn Maloney introduced The Debbie Smith Act, named for a victim of rape, which would provide grants to states for the training of law enforcement, medical personnel, and technicians in the proper handling and preservation of DNA evidence to be used later in rape prosecutions.[429] In the spring of 2002, Senator Hillary Rodham Clinton introduced a bill that would provide $200 million over the next two years to help law enforcement agencies analyze and store DNA evidence then reportedly backlogged, but unprocessed.[430] The purpose of both bills is to further the collection and creation of a DNA database that might be used to track down some of the "John Does" whose DNA profiles form the basis of rape or sexual assault complaints.

ENDNOTES FOR CHAPTER FOURTEEN

1   *See* Susan Estrich, *Rape*, included in SEX, VIOLENCE, WORK, AND REPRODUCTION (Philadelphia: Tempe University Press) (D. Kelly Weisberg, ed., 1996) (reprinted by permission of the YALE LAW JOURNAL and Fred B. Rothman & Co. from THE YALE LAW JOURNAL, Vol. 95, pp. 1087–1184), at p. 449.

2   For an overview of rape and sexual assault related issues arising out of cases in the last two decades, see e.g., *U.S. v. Reyes Castro*, 13 F.3d 377 (10th Cir. 1993); *Gov't of Virgin Island v. Pinney*, 967 F.2d 912 (3rd Cir. 1992); *Hatter v. Warden, Iowa Men's Reformatory*, 734 F. Supp. 1505 (N.D. Iowa 1990); *Edwards v. Butler*, 882 F.2d 160 (5th Cir. 1989); *Beam v. Feltz*, 832 F.2d 1401 (6th Cir. 1987); *Lee v. State*, 586 So.2d 264 (Ala. Crim. App. 1991); *Hutchins v. State*, 568 So.2d 395 (Ala. Cr. App. 1990); *Smith v. State*, 545 So.2d 198 (Ala. Cr. App. 1989); *Lockett v. State*, 518 SO.2d 877 (Ala. Cr. App. 1987); *Dillon v. State*, 844 S.W.2d 944 311 (Ark. 1993); *Wofford v. State*, 867 S.W.2d 181 (Ark. App. 1993); *People v. Hillard*, 260 Cal. Rptr. 625 (Ca. App. 2 Dist. 1989); *People v. Bell*, 248 Cal. Rptr. 57 (Cal. App. 2 Dist. 1988); *People v. Rodriquez*, 914 P.2d 230 (Colo. 1996); *People v. Shields*, 822 P.2d 15 (Colo. 1991); *People v. Shields*, 805 P.2d 1140 (Colo. App. 1990), *cert. granted, rev'd in part*, 822 P.2d 15; *State v. Osborn*, 676 A.2d 399 (Conn. 1996); *Johnson v. U.S.*, 613 A.2d 888 (D.C. 1992); *Greene v. U.S.*, 571 A.2d 218 (D.C. App. 1990); *Burlington v. State*, 616 So.2d 1036 (Fla. App. 3 Dist. 1993); *State v. Sedia*, 614 So.2d 533 (Fla. App. 4 Dist. 1993); *Taylor v. State*, 619 So.2d 1017 (Fla. App. 5 Dist. 1993); *Johnson v. State*, 430 S.E.2d 821 (Ga. App. 1993); *Shelton v. State*, 395 S.E.2d 618 (Ga. App. 1990); *Richie v. State*, 358 S.E.2d 648 (Ga. App. 1987); *In Interest of Doe*, 918 P.2d 254 (Hawaii App. 1996); *State v. Adams*, 880 P.2d 226 (Hawaii App. 1994); *State v. Gossett*, 808 P.2d 1326 (Idaho

App. 1991); *State v. Banks*, 740 P.2d 1039 (Idaho App. 1987); *People v. Jones*, 210 Ill.Dec. 92 (Ill. App. 1 Dist. 1995), *app. den.*, 214 Ill.Dec. 326; *People v. Robinson*, 205 Ill.Dec. 200 (Ill. App. 1 Dist. 1994); *People v. Ramey*, 179 Ill.Dec. 207, *app. den.*, 180 Ill.Dec. 156; *People v. Lauderdale*, 170 Ill.Dec. 868 (Ill. App. 1 Dist. 1992); *People v. Thomas*, 159 Ill.Dec. 368 (Ill. App. 1 Dist. 1991), *app. den.*, 164 Ill.Dec. 926; *People v. Fisher*, 217 Ill.Dec. 349 (Ill. App. 2 Dist. 1996); *People v. Kaminski*, 186 Ill.Dec. 4 615 (Ill. App. 2 Dist. 1996), *app. den.*, 190 Ill.Dec. 901; *People v. Singleton*, 160 Ill.Dec. 513 (Ill. App. 5 Dist. 1991); *People v. Bolton*, 152 Ill.Dec. 661 (Ill. App. 1 Dist. 1990); *People v. Geneva*, 143 Ill.Dec. 621 (Ill. App. 1 Dist. 1990); *People v. Robinson*, 145 Ill.Dec. 302 (Ill. App. 1 Dist. 1989); *People v. Rodarte*, 138 Ill.Dec. 635 (Ill. App. 1 Dist. 1989); *People v. Nelson*, 102 Ill.Dec. 275 (Ill. App. 2 Dist. 1986); *People v. White*, 142 Ill.Dec. 60 (Ill. App. 3 Dist. 1990); *People v. Douglas*, 131 Ill.Dec. 779 (Ill. App. 4 Dist. 1989); *Webster v. State*, 628 N.E.2d 1212 (Ind. 1994); *Wesby v. State*, 550 N.E.2d 321 (Ind. 1990); *Gonzales v. State*, 532 N.E.2d 1167 (Ind. 1989); *Pennington v. State*, 523 N.E.2d 414 (Ind. 1988); *Smith v. State*, 500 N.E.2d 190 (Ind. 1986); *Moore v. State*, 551 N.E.2d 459 (Ind. App. 3 Dist. 1990); *State v. Taylor*, 538 N.W.2d 314 (Iowa App. 1995); *State v. Shelly*, 635 So.2d 725 (La. App. 1 Cir. 1994); *State v. Cleveland*, 630 So.2d 1365 (La. App. 2 Cir. 1994); *State v. Harris*, 627 So.2d 788 (La. App. 2 Cir. 1993), *writ den.*, 634 So.2d 851; *State v. Thibodeaux*, 647 So.2d 525 (La.App. 3 Cir. 1994); *State v. Dixon*, 628 So.2d 1295 (La. App. 3 Cir. 1993); *State v. Johnson*, 652 So.2d (La. App. 4 Cir. 1995), *writ den.*, 688 So.2d 524; *State v. Fontana*, 624 So.2d 916 (La. App. 4 Cir. 1993); *State v. Simmons*, 621 So.2d 1135 (La. App. 4 Cir. 1993); *State v. Wright*, 598 So.2d 561 (La. App. 4 Cir. 1992), *writ. den.*, 669 So.2d 1227; *State v. Galliem*, 613 So.2d 1145 (La. App. 5 Cir. 1993); *State v. Montana*, 533 So.2d 983 (La. App. 1 Cir. 1988), *writ den.*, 541 So.2d 852; *State v. Henderson*, 566 So.2d 1098 (La. App. 2 Cir. 1990); *State v. Davis*, 550 So.2d 774 (La. App. 2 Cir. 1989); *State v. Poydras*, 514 So. 2d 516 (La. App. 3 Cir. 1987); *State v. Rosa*, 575 A.2d 727 (Me. 1990); *Rhodes v. State*, 539 A.2d 1160 (Md. App. 1988); *Commonwealth v. Waters*, 649 N.E.2d 724 (Mass. 1995); *Commonwealth v. Knap*, 592 N.E.2d 747 (Mass. 1992); *Commonwealth v. Caracciola*, 569 N.E.2d 774 (Mass. 1991); *Commonwealth v. Troy*, 540 N.E.2d 162 (Mass. 1989); *Commonwealth v. Henry*, 640 N.E.2d 503 (Mass. App. Ct. 1994); *Commonwealth v. Kickery*, 583 N.E.2d 869 (Mass. App. Ct. 1991); *People v. Brown*, 495 N.W.2d 812 (Mich. App. 1992); *People v. Russell*, 451 N.W.2d 625 (Mich. App. 1990); *People v. Proveaux*, 403 N.W.2d 135 (Mich. App. 1987); *State v. Sollman*, 402 N.W.2d 634 (Minn. App. 1987); *Hailey v. State*, 537 So.2d 411 (Miss. 1988); *State v. Storey*, 901 S.W.2d 886 (Mo. 1995); *State v. Gray*, 895 S.W.2d 241 (Mo. App. S.D. 1995); *State v. Mills*, 872 S.W.2d 875 (Mo. App S.D. 1994); *State v. Nelson*, 818 S.W.2d 285 (Mo. App. E.D. 1991); *State v. Jones*, 809 S.W.2d 37 (Mo. App. 1991); *State v. Koonce*, 731 S.W.2d 431 (Mo. App. 1987); *State v. Badakhsan*, 721 S.W.2d 18 (Mo. App. 1986); *State v. Hannett*, 713 S.W.2d 267 (Mo. App. 1986); *State v. Willis*, 394 N.W.2d (Neb. 1986); *State v. Moeller*, 510 N.W.2d 500 (Neb. App. 1993); *State v. Giles*, 672 A.2d 1128 (N.H. 1996); *State v. Williams*, 629 A.2d 83 (N.H. 1993); *State v. Lemieux*, 615 A.2d 635 (N.H. 1992); *State v. Johnson*, 547 A.2d 213 (N.H. 1988); *State in Interest of M.T.S.*, 609 A.2d 1266 (N.J. 1992); *State v. Interest of M.T.S.*, 588 A.2d 1282 (N.J. Super. A.D. 1991), *cert. granted*, 598 A.2d 897, *rev'd*, 609 A.2d 1266; *State v. Day*, 522 A.2d 1019 (N.J. Super. A.D. 1987), *cert. den.*, 527 A.2d 462; *State v. Pislo*, 889 P.2d 860 (N.M. App. 1994), *cert. den.*, 888 P.2d 466; *People v. Edkin*, 621 N.Y.S.2d 395 (A.D. 3 Dept. 1994), *habeas corpus., dism'd by Edkin v. Travis*, 969 F. Supp. 139; *People v. Cook*, 588 N.Y.S.2d 919 (A.D. 3 Dept. 1992), *leave to app. den.*, 594 N.Y.S.2d 723; *People v. Hough*, 607 N.Y.S.2d 884 (N.Y. Dist. Ct. 1994); *People v. Morales*, 528 N.Y.S.2d 286 (N.Y. Sup. 1988); *State v. Worsley*, 443 S.E.2d 68 (N.C. 1994); *State v. Green*, 443 S.E.2d 14 (N.C. 1994), *cert. den.*, 115 S. Ct. 642, *habeas corpus dism'd by Green v. French*, 978 F. Supp. 242; *State v. Baker*, 441 S.E.2d 551 (N.C. 1994); *State v. Thomas*, 423 S.E.2d 75 (N.C. 1992); *State v. Easterling*, 457 S.E.2d 913 (N.C. App. 1995), *rev. den.*, 461 S.E.2d 762; *State v. Herring*, 370 S.E.2d 363 (N.C. 1988); *State v. Rhodes*, 361 S.E.2d 578 (N.C. 1987); *State v. Langford*, 354 S.E.2d 523 (N.C. 1987); *State v. Hill*, 449 S.E.2d 573 (N.C. App. 1994), *rev. den.*, 453 S.E.2d 183; *State v. McClain*, 435 S.E.2d 371 (N.C. App. 1993); *State v. Black*, 432 S.E.2d 710 (N.C. App. 1993); *State v. Johnson*, 413 S.E.2d 562 (N.C. App. 1992), *rev. den.*, 421 S.E.2d 158; *State v. Mundy*, 650 N.E.2d 502 (Ohio App. 2 Dist. 1994); *Stadler v. State*, 919 P.2d 439 (Okla. Crim. App. 1996), *cert. den.*, 117 S. Ct 369; *Gilmore v. State*, 855 P.2d 143 (Okla. Crim. App. 1993); *Commonwealth v. Karkaria*, 625 A.2d 1167 (Pa. 1993); *Commonwealth v. Price*, 616 A.2d 681 (Pa. Super. 1992); *Commonwealth v. Ruppert*, 579 A.2d 966 (Pa. Super. 1990); *State v. Floody*, 481 N.W.2d 242 (S.D. 1992); *State v. Brobeck*, 751 S.W.2d 828 (Tenn. 1988); *State v. Tutton*, 875 S.W.2d 295 (Tenn. Crim. App. 1993); *State v. Locke*, 771 S.W.2d 132 (Tenn. Cr. App. 1988); *State v. Gann*, 733 S.W.2d 113 (Tenn.Crim.App.1987); *Dalton v. State*, 898 S.W.2d 424 (Tex. App. Fort Worth 1995); *Everage v. State*, 848 S.W.2d 357 (Tex. App. Austin 1993); *Selvog v. State*, 895 S.W.2d 879 (Tex. App Texarkana 1995); *Sanders v. State*, 834 S.W.2d 447 (Tex. App. Corpus Christi 1992); *Douglas v. State*, 740 S.W.2d 890 (Tex. App El Paso, 1987); *Alvarez v. State*, 767 S.W.2d 253 (Tex. App. Corpus Christi, 1989); *Chavez v. State*, 721 S.W.2d 508 (Tex. App. Houston, 14 Dist. 1986); *State v. Infante*, 596 A.2d 1289 (Vt. 1991); *Wilson v. Commonwealth*, 452 S.E.2d 669 (Va. 1995); *State v. Bright*, 916 P.2d 922 (Wash. 1996); *State v. Hayes*, 914 P.2d 788 (Wash. App. 1996); *State v. Thomson*, 861 P.2d 492 (Wash. App. Div. 2 1993); *State v. Aumick*, 869 P.2d 421 (Wash. App. Div. 3 1994); *State v. Gurrola*, 848 P.2d 199 (Wash. App. Div. 3 1993); *State v. Tultasi*, 729 P.2d 75 (Wash. App. 1986); *State v. George W.H.*, 439 S.E.2d 423 (W.Va. 1993); *State v. Allman*, 352 S.E.2d 103 (W.Va. 1986); *State v. Neumann*, 508

N.W.2d 54 (Wis. App. 1993); *State v. Schambow*, 500 N.W.2d 362 (Wis. App. 1993), *rev. den.*, 505 N.W.2d 139; *State v. Hubanks*, 496 N.W.2d 96 (Wis. App. 1992), *cert. den.*, 114 S. Ct. 99; *State v. Sinks*, 483 N.W.2d 286 (Wis. App. 1992); *Driskill v. State*, 761 P.2d 980 (Wyo. 1988); *Scadden v. State*, 732 P.2d 1036 (Wyo. 1987).

3   *See, e.g., State v. Willis*, 394 N.W.2d 648 (Neb. 1986) (clarifying that Nebraska's first-degree sexual assault statute delineates a crime of "violence," not of "sex"); *State v. Day*, 522 A.2d 1019 (N.J. Super. A.D. 1987) (holding that raping a victim with a coat hanger and club, dropping hot nails on her body, attempting to burn parts of her genitalia, and beating her so severely that her tongue was nearly torn from her mouth was sufficient to establish requirement of "serious bodily injury" within the New Jersey first-degree sexual assault statute); *State v. Williams*, 730 P.2d 1196 (N.M. App. 1986) (holding that the intent of the legislature in enacting criminal sexual assault statute was to protect bodily integrity and personal safety).

4   Feminist perspectives vary. Williams College Philosophy Professor Rosemarie Tong explains, for example, in WOMEN, SEX AND THE LAW (New Jersey: Rowman & Allenheld, 1984), at pp. 117–118 that: "[f]eminists who favor the rape-as-sexual-assault approach wish to stress rape's violent character without denying its sexual overtones or undercurrents. Like many psychiatrists, these feminists are convinced that the aggression of so-called anger rapists and power rapists (clinical categories into which most, though not all, rapists fit) is directed against female sexuality. That is, the anger rapist is not simply a man who, hating people in general, lashes out at a vulnerable and easily accessible subset of people, namely, women. Rather he is also a man who at some unconscious or conscious level hates women in particular. For him, the act of rape is an attempt to make up for what he perceives as the many hurtful acts that women in his life have committed against him, and so he seeks to hurt those parts of woman's body that distinguish her as a woman. Similarly, the power rapist is not simply a man who, desiring to control human beings in general, chooses to dominate a vulnerable and easily accessible subset of human beings, namely women. Rather he is also a man who at some unconscious or conscious level has a need to control women in particular. For him, the act of rape is an opportunity to assert his domination over all the women who have ever dominated him—such as his mother, wife, aunts, teachers, girlfriends" (citing Nicholas A. Groth & Ann Wolbert Burgess, *Rape, A Sexual Deviation*, 47 AM. J. ORTHOPSYCHIATRY at p. 400 (July 1970)). But there are also "[f]eminists who favor the rape-as-assault approach insist that rape is an assault like any other assault. According to this second group, the rapist's choice of the vagina or anus as the target of his aggression is no more significant than the barroom brawler's choice of a man's arm or leg as the target of his aggression. Therefore, there is no logical reason to have a separate category for assaults on the vagina or anus than there is to have a separate category for assaults on the arm or leg. Significantly, feminists who favor the rape-as-assault approach have pragmatic as well as logical reasons for their position. As they see it, special sexual-assault laws would reinforce the 'special' (unequal and lesser) status of women and their sexuality" (citing Schwartz and Clear, *Rape Law Reform and Women's Equality*, USA TODAY, November 1979, at p. 37). But author and former Harvard law professor Susan Estrich takes a different stance, arguing that "...to relabel rape 'criminal sexual conduct' is, if only accidentally, to assume a position in a debate of some vigor as to whether rape should be considered sex or violence. The 'rape as sex' position has been articulated, albeit to different ends, by individuals ranging from feminist theoreticians who argue for a more expansive understanding of coerced sex to the prosecutor in a 1983 Michigan case who claimed that the defendant's marital problems were relevant to show motive since he 'may not have had his "normal" male sexual desires satisfied prior to the assaults' on two thirteen-year-old girls." *See also* Estrich, *supra* note 61, ENDNOTES FOR CHAPTER THIRTEEN, at p. 82 (citing Catherine MacKinnon, *Feminism, Marxism, Method, and the State*, SIGNS: 8 J. WOMEN IN CUL. & SOC'Y at p. 646 (1983); Diana Russell, THE POLITICS OF RAPE: THE VICTIM'S PERSPECTIVE (New York: Stein & Day, 1975); Andrea Medea & Kathleen Thompson, AGAINST RAPE (New York: Farrar, Straus & Giroux, 1974); Lorenne Clark and Debra Lewis, RAPE: THE PRICE OF COERCIVE SEXUALITY (Toronto: Women's Press, 1977); *People v. Flanagan*, 342 N.W.2d 609, 612 (Mich. App. 1983); *People v. Travis*, 246 Mich. 516 (1920)). Estrich argues further that such a view "... encompasses as well the judge in a well-publicized South Carolina case who thought that convicted rapists should have a choice between castration and imprisonment, a choice which makes sense only if their crime (in that case, a rape by two men who also burned cigarettes on the victim's body) is understood as a problem solely of excessive, abnormal, sexual desire. The 'rape as violence' position, said to be the response of 'liberal' (as opposed to radical) feminists, has always seemed to me the better approach theoretically and strategically. Focusing on the violent aspects of rape makes clear that you are not trying to prohibit all sex and that violent men (such as rapists in that South Carolina case) must be incapacitated as dangerous criminals, not treated as only sexually aberrant. Moreover, to see rape as violence is to recognize sex should be inconsistent with violence, a message which is needed precisely because violence in sex has been accepted by so many as normal, and even justified, because of its supposed desirability to women." *See* Estrich, *supra*, at *id*. (In support of these statements, Estrich cites: Carol Goldfarb, *Practice of Using Castration in Sentence Being Questioned*, 15 CRIM. JUST. NEWSL. at p. 15 (Feb. 15, 1984) (noting that "[t]he castration option in the South Carolina case was ultimately reversed on appeal); *State v. Brown*, 326 S.E.2d 410 (S.C. 1985); *People v. Gaunlett*,

352 N.W.2d 310, 313 (Mich. App. 1984) (Estrich notes that the "trial court sentenced the defendant, who pled no contest to first-degree criminal sexual conduct with his fourteen-year-old stepdaughter, to probation, and to treatment with Depo-Provera; the sentence was reversed on appeal"); MacKinnon, *Feminism, Marxism, Method, and the State*, at p. 646; Ellen Goodman, *Punishing the Rapists*, BOST. GLOBE, Dec. 1, 1983; Susan Brownmiller, AGAINST OUR WILL: MEN, WOMEN, AND RAPE (New York: Simon & Schuster, 1975) ("describing rape in riots, wars, and pogroms," Estrich notes); NOTE, *Forcible and Statutory Rape: An Exploration of the Operation and Objectives of the Consent Standard*, 62 YALE L.J. at p. 66 (1952); *People v. Thompson*, 324 N.W.2d 22, 24 (Mich. App. 1982); *People v. Burnham*, 222 Cal. Rptr. 630 (Cal. App. 1986).

5   *See* Kathleen Barry, *Social Etiology of Crimes Against Women*, 10 VICTIMOLOGY at p. 164 (1985).

6   *See* Linda R. Hirshman & Jane E. Larson, HARD BARGAINS: THE POLITICS OF RAPE (New York:, Oxford University Press, 1998) at p. 268.

7   *See* Thornhill & Palmer, *supra* note 140, ENDNOTES FOR CHAPTER THIRTEEN, at p. 55. *See also* R.D. Alexander, DARWINISM AND HUMAN AFFAIRS (Seattle: University of Washington, 1979); R.D. Alexander, THE BIOLOGY OF MORAL SYSTEMS (Hawthorne, N.Y.: Aldine de Gruyter, 1987); J.M. Bailey, S. Gaulin, Y. Agyei & B.A. Gladue, *Effects of Gender and Sexual Orientation on Evolutionary Relevant Aspects of Human Mating*, 66 J. PERSONALITY & SOC. PSYCHOL. at pp. 1081–1093 (1994); R.G. Bringle, *Sexual Jealousy in the Relationships of Homosexual and Heterosexual Men: 1980 and 1992*, 2 PERS. RELATIONSHIPS at pp. 313–325 (1995); H. Claypool & V. Sheets, *Jealousy: Adaptive or Destructive?* (paper presented at the annual meeting of the Human Behavior and Evolutionary Society, Evanston, Ill., June 1996) (cited in David M. Buss, THE DANGEROUS PASSION: WHY JEALOUSY IS AS NECESSARY AS LOVE AND SEX (New York: The Free Press, 2000), at p. 241.)

8   *Id.*

9   *Id.* at 55 (quoting Theodosius Dozhansky).

10   *Id.* at 53.

11   *Id.*

12   *Id.* at 60.

13   *See* Kevin Flynn, *9 Officers Face Discipline Over Central Park Attacks*, N.Y. TIMES, July 4, 2000, at A14; For news accounts, *see* C.J. Chivers, *3 More Are Killed as Spate of Crimes Continue Through the Weekend*, N.Y. TIMES, June 12, 2000, at A36; C.J. Chivers, *Police Study Central Park Mob's 35-Minute Binge of Sexual Assault*, N.Y. TIMES, June 13, 2000, at A25; C.J. Chivers & William K. Rashbaum, *Inquiry Focuses on Officers' Responses to Park Violence*, N.Y. TIMES, June 14, 2000, at A27; William K. Rashbaum, *Five More Arrested in Sex Attacks in Park*, N.Y. TIMES, June 16, 2000, at A29; David Barstow and C.J. Chivers, *Elements of Trouble Gelled in Rampage in Central Park*, N.Y. TIMES, June 17, 2000, at A1.

14   *Id.* at A14.

15   *Id.* at A1.

16   *Id.* at A14.

17   For media of accounts, *see, e.g.*, Mark Singer, *Dirty Laundry*, NEW YORKER, April 9, 2001, at pp. 50, 51; *4th Complaint Made in Stripping Case*, N.Y. TIMES, Jan. 10, 2001, at A18 (reporting that a fourth woman reported to investigators that an officer allegedly made her expose herself during a traffic stop; three other women reported similar incidents); Tina Kelly, *Officer Accused of Sexually Assaulting a Woman While on Duty*, N.Y. TIMES, Jan. 27, 2001, at A11 (reporting that a Nassau County police officer was arrested and charged following allegations that he allegedly forced a woman to have oral sex with him while he was on duty); *Sex Charge Reprieve*, ASSOCIATED PRESS (reprinted on ABC NEWS.COM, May 7, 2001) (reporting that the Nassau County officer pled guilty to lesser charges in connection with the previously reported incident); *Officer's Charge Reduced*, N.Y. TIMES, Feb. 3, 2001, at A10.

18   *See* Paul Zielbauer, *State Rape Charges Are Added Against Jailed Waterbury Mayor*, N.Y. TIMES, Sept. 11, 2001, at A21. (According to Zeilbauer, on September 10, 2001, "[s]tate prosecutors…charged Philip A. Giordano, the imprisoned three-term mayor of Waterbury, [Conn.] with raping two young girls, ages 9 and 10, with whom he is accused of having repeated sexual encounters this year); *Waterbury Mayor Accused of Using Office for Sex with Girls*, N.Y. TIMES, Sept. 21, 2001, at A24 (reporting that "[a] 14-count federal indictment against Waterbury's mayor, Philip A. Girdano, was unsealed today, revealing allegations that he paid a prostitute to provide him with repeated sexual access to her young daughter and niece").

19   *See* U.S. DEP'T. OF JUSTICE, OFFICE OF JUSTICE PROGRAMS, BUREAU OF JUSTICE STATISTICS REPORT, *Sex Offenses and Offenders: An Analysis of Data on Rape and Sexual Assault* (1994).

20   *Id.*

21   *See* Jerry A. Coyne and Andrew Berry, *Rape as an Adaptation: Is This Contentious Hypothesis Advocacy, Not Science?*, NATURE, March 2000, at p. 121.

22   *Id.*

23   *Id.*

24 *Id.*

25 *Id.*

26 *Id.*

27 The public debate on "male rape" and the obligations of the state to prevent it in prisons has begun, for example, to burgeon. *See, e.g.,* Daniel Brook, *The Problem of Prison Rape,* LEGAL AFFAIRS, March-April 2004, at pp. 24–29; Vivian Berger, *Sentenced to Rape,* NAT'L L.J., Jan. 21, 2002, at A17: Deborah L. Rhode, *Indifference Rules,* NAT'L L.J., Oct. 29, 2001.

28 *See* Kathy Silberger, *Every Two Minutes a Woman is Raped,* MARIE CLAIRE, April 2000, at pp. 126–132.

29 *See* Melba Newsome, *What Were You Doing Last Friday?,* MARIE CLAIRE, Sept. 2001, at pp. 166–168.

30 *See* Craven, *supra* note 27, at p. 3. (The author uses the word "suggest" because the definition of rape and, therefore, the statistics of rape is currently being debated by feminists and legislators. To get a sense of the debate and the heat involved, *see The Rape Debate,* MS., March/April 1998, at pp. 7–8.)

31 *See* Lawrence A. Greenfeld, U.S. DEPARTMENT OF JUSTICE, OFFICE OF JUSTICE PROGRAMS, BUREAU OF JUSTICE STATISTICS REPORT, *Sex Offenses and Offenders: An Analysis of Data on Rape and Sexual Assault* (Feb. 1997, revised Feb. 2, 1997), at p. 3.

32 *See* Callie Marie Rennison, U.S. DEPARTMENT OF JUSTICE, BUREAU OF JUSTICE STATISTICS REPORT, *Criminal Victimizations 1988: Changes 1997–1998 with Trends 1993–1998* (August 31, 1999), at p. 15, Table 7 (showing that: in 1993, there were an estimated 2.5 rapes/sexual assaults per 1,000 persons; in 1994, an estimated 2.1 rapes/sexual assaults per 1,000 persons; in 1995, an estimated 1.7 rapes/sexual assaults per 1,000 persons; in 1996, an estimated 1.4 rapes/sexual assaults per 1,000 persons; in 1997, also an estimated 1.4 rapes/sexual assaults per 1,000 persons; and, in 1998, an estimated 1.5 rapes/sexual assaults per 1,000 persons).

33 *See* Greenfeld, *supra* note 31, at p. 3.

34 *See* Newsome, *supra* note 29, at p. 166.

35 *Id.* (This version of events came directly from Elster, who told her story to Newsome.)

36 *Id.*

37 *Id.*

38 *See* Linda Fairstein, SEXUAL VIOLENCE: OUR WAR AGAINST RAPE (New York: William Morrow, 1993).

39 *See* Greenfeld, *supra* note 31, at p. 7. (For example, according to the Justice Department, in 1993, an estimated 37.4 percent of rapes and/or sexual assaults took place in the victim's home; an estimated 19.2 percent took place at a friend, neighbor or relative's house; an estimated 10 percent took place "[o]n street away from home"; 7.3 percent took place in a parking lot or garage; and, an estimated 26.1 percent took place in "other locations.")

40 *Id.* at 5. (The authors of the Justice Department report explain that "the [National Crime Victimization Survey] begun in 1972, was designed to complement what is known about crimes reported to local law enforcement agencies under the FBI's annual compilation known as the Uniform Crime Reports (UCR)." Further, "[t]he NCVS gathers information about crime and its consequences from a nationally representative sample of U.S. residents age 12 or older about any crimes they may have experienced—whether or not the crime was reported to a law enforcement agency." The numbers are estimated from a sample of 50,000 households nationwide, and involving over 100,000 respondents, making it "the second largest ongoing household survey sponsored by the federal government.")

41 *Id.*

42 *Id.* (The authors note with regard to this definition that "[i]n the latter half of the 1980s, the Bureau of Justice Statistics (BJS), together with the Committee on Law and Justice of the American Statistical Association, sought to improve the survey components to enhance the measurement of rape, sexual assault, and domestic violence. The new NCVS questions broadened the scope of covered sexual incidents beyond the categories of rape and attempted rape to include sexual assaults and other unwanted sexual contacts. [¶] The new questions and revised procedures were phased in from January 1992 through June 1993, in half of the sampled households. Since July 1993, the redesigned methods have been used for the entire national sample. Based upon the half-sample, [Bureau of Justice Statistics] was able to determine that the new questionnaire would produce estimated rates of rape and sexual assault that were about 4 times higher than previously measured.")

43 *Id.* at 6. (According to the Justice Department, an estimated 43.4 percent of all rapes occur between 6 P.M. through midnight; 33 percent occur between 6 A.M. and 6 P.M.; and an estimated 23.6 percent of rapes and sexual assaults occur between midnight and 6 A.M.)

44 *Id.*

45 *Id.*

46 *Id.*

47   *Id.* The report provides the following figure:

FIGURE 4. RAPES AND SEXUAL ASSAULTS BY NUMBER OF OFFENDERS AND VICTIM-OFFENDER RELATIONSHIP, 1993

Violent victimizations	10,848,090
Rapes and sexual assaults	485,290
SINGLE OFFENDERS	91.1%
Strangers	17.6%
Nonstrangers	73.5%
MULTIPLE OFFENDERS	8.9%
Strangers	6.8%
Nonstrangers	2.1%

48   *Id.*
49   There is some research to suggest, however, that roughly 10 percent of rape victims who seek help at rape crisis centers are male. *See* Robin Warshaw, I NEVER CALLED IT RAPE: THE MS. REPORT ON RECOGNIZING, FIGHTING, AND SURVIVING DATE AND ACQUAINTANCE RAPE (New York: Harper & Row, 1988), at p. 98.
50   *See* Greenfeld, *supra* note 31, at p. 6.
51   *Id.* at p. 7. (By contrast, only 17.6 percent of reported rapes and/or sexual assaults involved strangers. In terms of specific findings, the Justice Department notes that "[t]hree out of four rape/sexual assault victimizations involved offenders (both single- and multiple-offender incidents) with whom the victim had a prior relationship as a family member, intimate, or acquaintance. Strangers accounted for nearly 20 percent of the victimizations involving a single offender but 76 percent of the victimizations involving multiple offenders. About 7 percent of all rape/sexual assault victimizations involve multiple offenders who were strangers to the victim.")
52   *Id.*
53   *Id.* at pp. 7–8. The report provides the following figure:

FIGURE 5. RAPES AND SEXUAL ASSAULTS BY NUMBER OF OFFENDERS AND THE AGE OF THE OFFENDERS, 1993

Violent victimizations	10,848,090
Rapes and sexual assaults	485,290
SINGLE OFFENDERS	91.1%
Younger than 18	10.9%
18–20	8.0%
21–29	31.2%
30 or older	40.9%
MULTIPLE OFFENDERS	8.9%
Younger than 18	4.4%
18–20	2.5%
21–29	.7%
30 or older	1.3%

54   *See Twins, 13, Are Arrested in Rape of a Woman*, 40, N.Y. TIMES, Oct. 17, 2000, at A26.
55   *See* Greenfeld, *supra* note 31, at p. 3.
56   *Id.* (The Justice Department notes that half of these defendants "had to post a financial bond." The median bond amount was $23,500.)
57   *Id.* at 4.
58   *Id.*
59   *See* Estrich, *supra* note 1, at p. 449.
60   Scholars note that the rationale behind the "fresh complaint" rule was that "outraged victims would be more likely to report attacks immediately (despite their likely fear or shame) and that lairs would be more likely to make up their stories at a distance. *See* DATE RAPE: FEMINISM, PHILOSOPHY, AND THE LAW (University Park, Penn.: Pennsylvania State University Press, 1996) (Leslie Francis, ed.), at p. ix.
61   *See* Estrich, *supra* note 1, at p. 449.
62   *Id.*
63   *Id. See also* Hirshman and Larson, *supra* note 6, at p. 269.
64   *See* Susan Griffin, *Rape: The All-American Crime*, included in SEX, VIOLENCE, WORK, AND REPRODUCTION (Philadelphia: Tempe University Press) (D. Kelly Weisberg, ed., 1996) (First printed in *Ramparts* Magazine, Vol. 10 (Sept. 1971), at 26–35)), at p. 429.
65   *See* Hirshman and Larson, *supra* note 6, at p. 269.
66   *Id.*
67   *See* Francis, *supra* note 60, at p. 1.
68   *Id.* at viii (citing Estrich, *supra* note 4, at 41ff).
69   *Id.* at ix.

70 For reading on the issues of rape, *see, e.g.*, Stephen J. Schulhofer, UNWANTED SEX: THE CULTURE OF INTIMIDATION AND THE FAILURE OF LAW (Cambridge, Mass.: Harvard University Press, 1998); Maria Bevacqua, RAPE ON THE PUBLIC AGENDA: FEMINISM AND THE POLITICS OF SEXUAL ASSAULT (Boston, Mass.: Northeastern University Press, 2000); Sue Bessmer, THE LAWS OF RAPE (New York: Praeger Publisher, 1984); Estrich, *supra* note 4; Estrich, *supra* note 1, at p. 449.

71 *See* Angela P. Harris & Lois Pineau, *A Dialogue on Evidence*, included by Francis in DATE RAPE, *supra* note 60, at p. 123.

72 *U.S. v. Saunders*, 943 F.2d 388 (4th Cir. 1991).

73 *Saunders*, 943 F.2d at 391 (citing *Doe*, 666 F.2d at 47, 48).

74 For an overview of the statistics, *see* Craven, *supra* note 91, ENDNOTES FOR CHAPTER THIRTEEN, at p. 2.

75 *See* Francis, *supra* note 60, at p. 1.

76 *See* Griffin, *supra* note 64, at p. 429.

77 *See* Brownmiller, *supra* note 4, at p. 15. (As Francis explains further, in AGAINST OUR WILL, Brownmiller details "the occurrence of rape during the Second World War, the struggle of Bangladesh for independence form Pakistan, and the war in Vietnam." Further, "[i]n American history, the rapes of Native American women by white men and of black women slaves by their white masters, are particular instances of dominance by means of sex." Francis adds to Brownmiller's assessment that "[t]he contemporary rapes of Muslim women in Bosnia, aimed at both humiliation and impregnation, add yet another sad chapter to the sexual oppression of women in war." *See* Brownmiller, *supra* note 4. This author notes that acts of this kind were held to be a "war crime" in 2001. *See* Jerome Socolovsky, *Sex Slavery is a War Crime*, CHI. SUN-TIMES, Feb. 23, 2001, at p. 33; Ian Fisher & Marlise Simons, *U.N. Details Vicious Acts Charges Against Milosevic*, N.Y. TIMES, Feb. 14, 2001, at A8.)

78 *See* Griffin, *supra* note 64, at p. 429. *See also* Sally Gold and Martha Wyatt, *The Rape System: Old Roles and New Times*, 27 CATH. U. L. REV. at pp. 696–700 (1978); NOTE *Forcible and Statutory Rape: An Exploration of the Operation and Objectives of the Consent Standard*, 62 YALE L.J. at pp. 72–73 (Dec. 1952).

79 *See* Angela Y. Davis, WOMEN, CULTURE & POLITICS (New York: Random House, 1989 (original copyright 1984)), at p. 47.

80 *See* Hirshman and Larson, *supra* note 6, at p. 268.

81 *See* Eldridge Cleaver, SOUL ON ICE (New York: McGraw Hill, 1968), at p. 14. (Everyday rape tends, however, to be intraracial. *See* Irene Sege, *Race, Violence Make Complex Picture*, BOSTON GLOBE, Jan. 31, 1990, (National News), at p. 1 (finding 70 percent of African American rape victims are raped by African American perpetrators and 78 percent of white rape victims are raped by white perpetrators); Jennifer Wriggins, *Rape, Racism, and the Law*, 6 HARV. WOMEN'S L.J. at p. 103 (1983); Lisa Crooms, *Speaking Partial Truths and Preserving Power: Deconstructing White Supremacy, Patriarchy, and the Rape Corroboration Rule in the Interest of Black Liberation*, 40 HOW. L.J. 459 (1997); Elisabeth M. Iglesias, *Rape, Race, and Representation: The Power of Discourse, Discourses of Power, and the Reconstruction of Heterosexuality*, 49 VAND. L. REV. 868 (1996); Darci E. Burrell, COMMENT, *Myth, Stereotype, and the Rape of Black Women*, 4 UCLA WOMEN'S L.J. 87 (1993).)

82 *See* Jerome Socolovsky, *Sex Slavery is a War Crime*, CHI. SUN-TIMES, Feb. 23, 2001, at 33; Ian Fisher & Marlise Simons, *U.N. Details Vicious Acts Charges Against Milosevic*, N.Y. TIMES, Feb. 14, 2001, at A8.

83 *See* Seth Mydans, *Sexual Violence as Tool of War: Pattern Emerging in East Timor*, N.Y. TIMES, March 1, 2001, at A1.

84 Hirshman and Larson note, for example, as have others before them that during the 1800s in America, "[w]ives, daughters, and female slaves in elite households...enjoyed strong, albeit secondhand, bargaining power in their sexual dealings with predatory males. This power was not an extension of the females' sexual will; to the contrary, patriarchs often used rape law to separate their women from desired sexual partners. But a woman under such a regime could at least deny sex to some men, even if she lacked the autonomy to grant access to others. This describes, for example, the white women in the antebellum South, whose sexual position was more secure and dignified than that of an enslaved women explicitly denied the protections of rape law, or even of a free black woman, who was regarded by social custom as simply 'unrapeable.'" *See* Hirshman and Larson, *supra* note 6, at p. 269.

85 *See* Vivian Berger, *Sentenced to Rape*, NAT'L L.J., Jan. 21, 2002, at A17; Deborah W. Denno, "Introduction," *Why Rape is Different*, 63 FORDHAM L. REV. 125, 127 (noting that it has been estimated that somewhere between 19 and 45 percent of men in prison have been raped).

86 *See, e.g.*, Madeline Morris, *By Force of Arms: Rape, War, and Military Culture*, 45 DUKE L.J. 651, 653 (1996) (According to Morris, "the ratio of military rape rates to civilian rape rates is substantially larger than the ratio of military rates to civilian rates of other violent crime").

87 *See* TRANSFORMING A RAPE CULTURE (Minneapolis, Minn.: Milkweed Editions, 1993) (Emilie Buchwald, Pamela Fletcher, Martha Roth, *eds.*)), at vii.

88 *See* Francis, *supra* note 60, at p. 1.

89 *Id.* (citing *Coker v. Georgia*, 433 U.S. 584 (1977)).

90   *Id.* (Francis explains that "[t]he term ['real rape'] comes from Susan Estrich, REAL RAPE (Cambridge: Harvard University Press, 1987)).

91   *Id.* (citing Brownmiller, *supra* note 4).

92   *See* Schulhofer, *supra* note 70, at p. 25. (Schulhofer, as others before him, explains that "[p]rosecutors and police often assumed that a woman was fabricating her rape accusation or blamed her for provoking the incident by her supposedly suggestive clothing or behavior"); Morrison Torrey, *When Will We Be Believed? Rape Myths and the Idea of a Fair Trial in Rape Prosecutions,* 24 U.C. DAVIS L. REV. at p. 1025 (1991); Estrich, *supra* note 4; Griffin, *supra* note 64; NOTE, *Police Discretion and the Judgment that a Crime Has Been Committed—Rape in Philadelphia,* 117 U. PA. L. REV. at p. 277 (1968).

93   According to *Ms.* magazine, the British Court of Appeals held that "the time has now arrived when the law should declare that a rapist remains a rapist irrespective of his relationship with his victim." *See* MS., June 1991, at p. 11.

94   For background, *see* Schulhofer, *supra* note 70, at p. 30 (citing Or. Rev. Stat. Sec. 163.305-475 (Repl. 1977); Leigh Bienen, *Rape III—National Developments in Rape Reform Legislation,* 6 WOMEN'S RTS. L. REP. at pp. 185–189 (1980)).

95   *Id.*

96   *See* Benedict, *supra* note 44, ENDNOTES FOR INTRODUCTION, at p. 44.

97   *See* Bevacqua, *supra* note 70, at p. 155, no. 1. (In a footnote, Bevacqua writes: "In RAPE ON TRIAL (1996), Lisa Cuklanz explores news coverage of several sensational rape trials, including that of John Rideout, and how such attention constructs the public's understanding of the issues involved. Rideout was not the first man to be tried for raping his non-estranged wife. In 1974, for example, a Missouri court convicted James Edward Drope for involvement in the gang rape of his wife (*citing* WASH. POST 1974). The *Drope* case received little publicity as compared to *Rideout.*")

98   *See* Benedict, *supra* note 96, at pp. 44–45.

99   *Id.*

100   *Id.* at 45. (According to Benedict, Greta told *Los Angeles Times* reporter Betty Liddick her reasons for accepting the proposal: "I was on welfare. I didn't have a car. It seemed exciting, flying to Ft. Stewart in Georgia to get married.")

101   *Id.*

102   *Id.*

103   *Id.*

104   *See* Schulhofer, *supra* note 70, at p. 29.

105   *Id.* (citing Jeanne C. Marsh, Alison Geist & Nathan Caplan, RAPE AND THE LIMITS OF LAW (Boston, Mass.: Auburn House, 1982).

106   *Id.* (citing Bienen, *supra* note 94, at pp. 170–171).

107   *See* Bevacqua, *supra* note 70, at p. 103.

108   *Id.* (citing *e.g.,* Laura Kiernan, *Rape Crisis Center Described,* WASH. POST, Oct. 12, 1974, at C4).

109   *Id.*

110   *Id.* at 103–104. (According to Bevacqua, "[t]he collective, in fact, became quite active in the local effort to reform rape laws. One NYWAR member, Emma, worked with NOW and other women's groups interested in forming a rape coalition, as recorded in meeting minutes on 8 June 1973 (NYWAR). On 26 June 1973, the Women's Anti-Rape Coalition (WARC), the resulting organization, held its first meeting, declaring as its purpose raising public awareness of rape and repealing the corroboration requirement (NYWAR records). At least five groups made up this coalition at its inception: NYWAR, NY-NOW, New York Radical Feminists, and the Manhattan Women's Political Caucus (a chapter of the National Women's Political Caucus). Two more feminist associations, the National Black Feminists Organization (NBFO) and the Coalition of 100 Black Women, joined within a year. The Women's Anti-Rape Coalition declared August Rape Prevention Month, engaged in a media campaign to call attention to rape, and successfully lobbied the legislature to repeal the corroboration requirement of New York's rape law. At WARC's 1975 conference, the various women's groups in attendance were united in their call for federal funding for feminist rape crisis centers, increased numbers of women officers in New York City's rape investigation units, and electing more women to the state legislature who would work for improved rape laws (NEW YORK TIMES 1975). It was clear that WARC viewed reforming the law and supporting crisis centers as complementary and compatible.")

111   *Id.* at 105. ("In Washington in 1973," Bevacqua reports, "a representative of the D.C. RCC served on the D.C. Task Force on Rape, organized by Councilman Tedson Meyers to investigate the legal and institutional response to rape victims there. Other members of the young collective testified during the task force's hearings before the Public Safety Committee, as reported in the Washington Post" (citing Kirk Scharfenberg, *D.C. Law on Rape Scored: More Evidence Needed Than in Murders,* WASH. POST, Sept. 21, 1973, at C1 and C4).)

112   *Id.* at 104. (According to Bevacqua, goals set forth by the Chicago Coalition Against Rape, "included investigating needed legal changes and how rape cases were handled by area hospitals, reported the Chicago Tribune" (citing Edward Schreiber, *In City Council Meeting: Rape Case Unit Proposed,* CHI. TRIB., April 18, 1974, Sec. 1, at p. 5).)

113 *Id.* at 100.
114 *Id.*
115 *Id.* (citing Bienen, *supra* note 94).
116 *People v. Bain,* 283 N.E.2d 701 (1972).
117 *Bain,* 283 N.E.2d at 702.
118 *Id.*
119 *Id.*
120 *Id.*
121 *Id.* (citing *People v. Szybeko,* 24 Ill.2d 335).
122 *Id.* at 703.
123 *Id.*
124 *See* Schulhofer, *supra* note 70, at p. 29.
125 *See* NOTE, *The Resistance Standard in Rape Legislation,* 18 STAN. L. REV. at p. 682 (Feb. 1966) (citing Gray and Mohr, FOLLOW-UP OF MALE SEXUAL OFFENDERS, SEXUAL BEHAVIOR AND THE LAW (Ralph Slovenko, *ed.*) (Springfield, Ill.: Charles C. Thomas, 1965), at pp. 742–746.
126 *See* Schulhofer, *supra* note 70, at p. 25.
127 *Id.* (citing NOTE, *Police Discretion and the Judgment That a Crime Has Been Committed—Rape in Philadelphia,* 117 U. PA. L. REV. at p. 277 (1968)).
128 *See* Hirshman and Larson, *supra* note 6, at p. 181.
129 *Id.* at 185.
130 As set forth above, Griffin argues that "…in the act of rape, the rage that one man may harbor toward another higher in the male hierarchy can be deflected toward a female scapegoat." *See* Griffin, *supra* note 64, at p. 429.
131 *See* Estrich, *supra* note 4, at p. 42.
132 *See* Schulhofer, *supra* note 70, at p. 20, n. 11. (According to Schulhofer, "[s]eventeen people served as reporters, associate reporters, or special consultants for the Model Penal Code project; none was a woman. Of the forty lawyers and professors who served on the institute's Criminal Law Advisory Committee, only one was a woman" (citing MPC COMMENTARIES at v–vii).)
133 *Id.*
134 *Id.* at 18, n. 1 (citing William Blackstone, 4 COMMENTARIES ON THE LAWS OF ENGLAND (1765) (Chicago: University of Chicago Press, 1979), at p. 210).
135 *Id.* n. 2 (citing 1 Matthew Hale, THE HISTORY OF THE PLEAS OF THE CROWN 629 (S. Emlyn ed., 1778). (Schulhofer notes that "[c]onversely, because of the notorious 'marital exemption,' rape did not include a man's conduct in compelling intercourse with his wife, even if he did use physical force. Between husband and wife, the law's conception of consent remained the one that the British Chief Justice Lord Hale had set forth in the seventeenth century: 'by their marital consent and contract, the wife hath given up herself in this kind unto her husband, which she cannot retract.'")
136 *People v. Abbott,* 19 Wend. 192 (N.Y. 1838).
137 *State v. Camp,* 3 Ga. 417 (1847).
138 For a modern contrast, *see, e.g., U.S. v. Saunders,* 736 F. Supp. 698 (E.D. Va. 1990), aff'd, 943 F.2d 388 (4th Cir. 1991), *cert. den.,* 112 S. Ct. 1199 (holding that even women of "easy virtue" can be victims of rape. Thus, they too are entitled to the full protection of the law).
139 *Titus v. State,* 7 Baxt. 132, 133–34 (Tenn. 1874) (holding that "[i]t would be absurd, and shock our sense of truth, for any man to affirm that there was not a much greater probability in favor of the proposition that a common prostitute had yielded her assent to sexual intercourse than in the case of the virgin of uncontaminated purity").
140 *People v. Jackson,* 15 N.Y. 391 (1857).
141 *See, e.g., State v. Rice,* 35 Fla. 236 (1895) (similarly allowing testimony of a woman's alleged "bad" reputation).
142 *Christian v. Commonwealth,* 64 Va. (23 Gratt.) 954 (1873).
143 The language of the court's reasoning in reversing the conviction was that "[t]he evidence indicated that [the defendant] had wooed her pretty roughly in a way that would have been horrible and a shocking outrage toward a woman of virtuous sensibilities, and should have subjected him to the severest punishment which the law would warrant. But how far it affected the sensibilities of the prosecutrix does not appear. It by no means appears, from the facts certified, that it was an attempt to ravish her, against her will, or that it was not only an attempt to work upon her passions, and overcome her virtue, which had yielded to others before—how often it does not appear . . . Without any interference, or any *outcry* on her part, together with his after conduct, show, we think, that his conduct, though extremely reprehensible, and deserving of punishment, does not involve him in the crime which this statute was designed to punish." 64 Va. (23 Gratt.) 959. (*Emphasis in original.*)
144 *Whittaker v. State,* 50 Wis. 519, 520, 522 (1880).
145 *But compare Commonwealth v. Hart,* 131 Va. 726 (1921) (holding the death penalty appropriate in the case of an attempted rape of a white woman—a "simple, good, unsophisticated country girl"—by a black man, because the "utmost exertion" was required to prevent such things, the Virginia court reasoned).

146　For a case in contrast, *see People v. Serrielle*, 354 Ill. 182 (1933).
147　*State v. Burgdorf*, 53 Mo. 65 (1873).
148　*People v. Dohring*, 59 N.Y. 374 (1874).
149　The specific facts of this case, as testified to by the 14-year-old victim in court were that "she was in the prisoner's [defendant's] barn throwing down some hay; her brother, twelve years old, and a sister, four years old, were with her; that the prisoner came in, sent the children home, and fastened the barn door; that he then called down to her, took hold of her and after a struggle threw her down; that she commenced to cry, when he said if she would consent he would buy her a new dress; she answered she did not wish a new dress; she tried to get up; he held her down and threw her clothes up over her head; she said he would get her in the family way; he said he was an old man, if he was [*sic*] young he might do so; that then the offence [*sic*] was committed; that she cried out and tried to get away but could not, as he held her down." *People v. Dohring*, 59 N.Y. at 375.
150　*Id.* at 384.
151　*Reynolds v. State*, 27 Neb. 90 (1889) (citing *Conners v. State*, 47 Wis. 523 (1879)).
152　*Id.* at 92 (*emphasis added*). (The defendant had asked for the following jury instructions: "You must find on the part of the woman, not merely a passive policy or equivocal submission to the defendant; such resistance will not do. Voluntary submission by the woman, while she has the power to resist, no matter how reluctantly yielded, removes from the act an essential element of the crime of rape. [¶] If the carnal knowledge was with the consent of the woman, no matter how tardily given, or how much force had theretofore been employed, it is not rape.")
153　*State v. Perez*, 94 S.W. 1036 (Tex. Crim. App. 1906).
154　*Brown v. State*, 127 Wis. 193 (1906).
155　*Brown*, 127 Wis. at 199.
156　*State v. Hoffman*, 280 N.W. 357 (Wis. 1938).
157　*State v. Prokop*, 148 Neb. 582 (1947).
158　*Prokop*, 148 Neb. at 587 (citing *State v. Cascio*, 147 Neb. 1075, 1078–79 (1947)).
159　*State v. Killingwoth*, 226 S.W.2d 456 (Tex. Crim. App. 1950).
160　*State v. Shields*, 45 Conn. 256 (1877).
161　*Bailey v. Commonwealth*, 82 Va. 107 (1886).
162　Specifically, the court asked: "Should *he* be permitted to shelter himself behind the circumstance that she made but little actual resistance, and no outcry, under circumstances, to her, so confusing and so intimidating? There he was, one in authority, standing over her. He had come stealthily back from his party on a predetermined errand. He had contrived to have her protectors (her mother and older sister were at the party), as against him, well out of the way, and was present announcing his lustful purpose, with full power to execute it against her will. [¶] That she *felt* herself in his power, and took too much counsel of her fears, and her helplessness, is a matter that he cannot plead in extenuation of his crime." 82 Va. at 113 (*emphasis in original*). *But compare State v. Lester*, 321 S.E.2d 166 (N.C. Ct. App. 1984) (holding that a stepfather who sexually abused three daughters could be prosecuted for the crime of incest, but not rape because there was no showing of force); *Commonwealth v. Biggs*, 467 A.2d 31, 32 (Pa. Super. Ct. 1983).
163　*See, e.g., State v. Lewis*, 154 Tex. Crim. 329 (1950).
164　*State v. Dusenberry*, 20 S.W. 461 (Mo. 1892).
165　*Commonwealth v. Hart*, 131 Va. 726 (1921).
166　*State v. Catron*, 296 S.W. 141 (Mo. 1927).
167　Although testimony offered at trial showed that the victim had lain down and submitted, crying all the while, the court chose to focus, instead, on fear. Specifically, the court noted that "…because of the age and weight of the girl, 18 years and 155 pounds respectively, and the age and weight of defendant, 19 years and 119 pounds respectively, rape was inconceivable. Where relevant facts justify it, this argument would probably have force, but, inasmuch as it casts aside the fear of harm engendered by the duress of abduction and threatened injury, it is impertinent to the facts here developed…. For a girl to be accosted on a road at 2:30 o'clock in the morning, taken from her companion at the point of a pistol, and carried away by ruffians she never knew existed, puts her in such fear, we will presume, as to overcome, and continue to overcome, her will…. That she was physically weak from fear and mental strain never tended to show reluctance and resistance to her utmost strength." *State v. Catron*, 296 S.W. at 143.
168　*State v. Esposito*, 191 A. 341 (Conn. 1937).
169　*Esposito*, 191 A. at 342 (citing *State v. Shields*, 45 Conn. at 256, 264).
170　*People v. Kinne*, 76 P.2d 714 (Cal. App. 1938).
171　*People v. Flores*, 62 Cal. App. 2d 700 (1944).
172　*Id.* at 703.
173　*People v. Cassandras*, 83 Cal. App. 2d 272 (1948).
174　*People v. Tollack*, 233 P.2d 121 (Cal. App. 1951).
175　*People v. Blankenship*, 225 P.2d 835 (Cal. App. 1951).
176　*People v. Harris*, 238 P.2d 158 (Cal. Dist. Ct. App. 1951).

177   Indeed, an apparently blushing court appears to have been horrified, detailing that the plaintiff, "[h]aving alighted from a streetcar about one o'clock in the morning, she walked along the sidewalk toward her home. While thus proceeding she observed appellant driving by her, return on the same street and, having again directed his automobile toward her, he stopped, stepped up beside the prosecutrix, and grabbed her by the neck and right arm. Undaunted after his modest approach, in language that would blush the cheeks of the hardened mistress of a brothel, appellant startled the young woman with the announcement that he desired to lick her private parts and then he would let her go. She 'struggled a little but then he forced me and dragged me into his car * * * we still argued a few minutes.'" *People v. Harris*, 238 P.2d at 159. Later, in the kind of language often clearly meant to convey implications, the court went even further. According to the court, "[n]ot only did [the defendant] declare his purpose but he lewdly and lasciviously 'placed his mouth on her private parts,' a felony. She was an utter stranger to him; but he was bent upon the consummation of his deliberate design to gratify his debased and depraved desires. The still hour of midnight, the solitude of the place, the loneliness of the prosecutrix, the brutal boldness of appellant, his vile and resolute purpose, and withal, his avowed, obscene desire—these omit nothing that was essential to the establishment of his guilt even though he had never spoken to the officers. But to them he confessed his criminal scheme and its achievement." *Id.* at 160.

178   *Harris*, 238 P.2d at 160 (*emphasis added*). *See also State v. Hinton*, 333 P.2d 822, 825 (Cal. App. 1959) (involving the rape and kidnapping of a white woman by three African American men with the court holding that "[c]onsent induced by fear is no consent at all").

179   *Satterwhite v. Commonwealth*, 201 Va. 478 (1960).

180   *Id.*

181   *State v. Hazel*, 221 Md. 464 (1960).

182   *State v. Dizon*, 390 P.2d 759 (Hawaii 1964).

183   *State v. Hunt*, 135 N.W.2d 475 (Neb. 1965).

184   *See, e.g., King v. State*, 210 Tenn. 150 (1962) (holding that in a rape case, women must undertake resistance and "in every way possible…continue[d] such resistance until she was overcome by force, was insensible through fright, or ceased resistance from exhaustion, fear of death, or great bodily harm"). *King v. State* represents a typical example of how the law of the time was applied.

185   *Commonwealth v. Childs*, 10 P.L. J. 209 (Allegheny County, Pa. 1863).

186   *Bedgood v. State*, 115 Ind. 275, 276–77 (1888).

187   *Roberts v. State*, 106 Neb. 362 (1921).

188   *Roberts*, 106 Neb. at 367. (According to the court, the defendant was accused of raping the girl not once, but twice on different nights.)

189   *State v. Connelly*, 57 Minn. 482, 484 (1894).

190   *State v. Anderson*, 272 Minn. 384 (1965).

191   *Territory v. Nishi*, 24 Hawaii 677 (1919).

192   *State v. Pitts*, 19 Ala. App. 564 (1923) (holding that a previous relationship between victim and defendant was enough to raise doubt as to whether "rape" really occurred).

193   *State v. Mosley*, 1 So.2d 593 (Ala. 1941).

194   *State v. Lewis*, 217 Miss. 488 (1953).

195   *Commonwealth v. Barker*, 95 S.E.2d 137 (Va. 1956).

196   *Shay v. State*, 299 Miss. 186 (1956).

197   *People v. Walker*, 150 Cal. App. 2d 594 (1957).

198   For other surprises, *see also, State v. Lefler*, 153 Ind. 82 (1899) (holding that carelessness is not a defense, because the law is meant to protect "those who cannot protect themselves"); *People v. Clarke*, 64 Colo. 164 (1918); *State v. Nash*, 110 Kan. 550 (1922); *R. v. Clarke*, [1949] 2 A11 E.R. 448.

199   *State v. Reynolds*, 27 Neb. 90 (1889).

200   *People v. Travis*, 246 Mich. 516 (1920).

201   *Packineau v. United States*, 202 F.2d 681 (8th Cir. 1953).

202   *Packineau*, 202 F.2d at 685–86, 688 (holding that "[t]o an ordinary person called on to make an appraisal of [the victim's accusation that one of the young men with whom she was out for dalliance on this night had raped her], the reaction would certainly be very different if it were known that she had been openly cohabiting with a young man only a few months before than it would be if she were the unsophisticated young lady she appeared to be." On the subject of one of the defendant's "good many" arrests, however, the court ruled that "[t]he prejudicial effect of such questioning of defendants concerning matters entirely irrelevant to the issues is apparent. Questioning [the defendant] about his illegitimate family, and multiplying questions to both defendants about their arrests from alleged disorderly conduct and petty misdemeanors necessarily prejudiced the jury against them. A conviction so obtained may not be sustained in this court").

203   *Stafford v. State*, 285 S.W.314 (Tex. Crim. App. 1926).

204   *Commonwealth v. Grigsby*, 187 S.W.2d 259 (Ky. 1945).

205   *State v. Frank*, 150 Neb. 745 (1949).

206   *Teague v. State*, 208 Ga. 459 (1951).

207   *People v. Collins*, 25 Ill.2d 605 (1962).

208   *See* Schulhofer, *supra* note 70, at p. 18, n. 4 (citing *United States v. Wiley*, 492 F.2d 547 (D.C. Cir. 1974)).

209 *Id.*

210 Early cases applying this rule were *State v. Richards,* 36 Neb. 17, 27 (1893) (with the court noting that "[t]he conduct of the prosecutrix is inexplicable on the theory that the act was accomplished by force and against her will. So far as appears there was no visible mark of violence noticeable on either her person or clothing. She does not seem to have been excited, nor was anything noticed out of the ordinary course"); *State v. Wheeler,* 116 Iowa 212 (1902) (holding that "...the existence of marks and bruises on the person [does] not alone even tend to point out the person who caused them; and while evidence of complaint by the prosecutrix, if recently made, has uniformly been received, it has never been regarded, unless forming part of the *res gestae,* as original or independent evidence"); *Stewart v. State,* 145 So. 162 (Ala. Ct. App. 1932) (the court noting that the "failure of the assaulted party to make complaint recently after the occurrence, opportunity offering itself, will cast suspicion on the bona fides of the charges") among others.

211 For a progression of case law, *see, e.g., People v. Deitsch,* 237 N.Y. 300 (App. Div. 1923) (reversing a conviction of rape for insufficiency of evidence after ruling that corroboration was improper); *State v. Power,* 43 Ariz. 329 (1934) (holding that "[i]f proof of opportunity to commit the crime were alone sufficient to sustain a conviction, no man would be safe"); *State v. Wulff,* 194 Minn. 271 (1935) (asserting that the corroboration rule was necessary to prevent "...errant young girls and women [from] coming before the court" and "... contriving false changes of sexual offences by men"); *Young v. Commonwealth,* 185 Va. 1032 (1947) (requiring corroboration of various claims regarding rape, i.e., penetration, force, resistance); *People v. Masse,* 5 N.Y.2d 217 (1959) (a modified standard of corroboration applied); and, *State v. Anderson,* 272 Minn. 384 (1965) (noting that corroboration in rape cases is required because "sexual cases are particularly subject to the danger of deliberately false charges, resulting from sexual neurosis, phantasy [*sic*], jealousy, spite, or simply a girl's refusal to admit that she consented to an act of which she is now ashamed"); *People v. Radunovic,* 287 N.Y.S.2d 33 (1967) (declaring the testimony of an obstetrician insufficient corroboration). *See also Walker v. United States,* 223 F.2d 613 (D.C. Cir. 1955); *United States v. Wiley,* 492 F.2d 547 (1973.)

212 *See* Hirshman and Larson, *supra* note 6, at p. 196.

213 *See* Estrich, *supra* note 4, at p. 42.

214 *See* Hirshman and Larson, *supra* note 6, at p. 196.

215 *Id.*

216 *Id.*

217 *Id.* (As set forth above, the drafters reportedly put a great deal in the writings of Morris Ploscowe. Thus, "[a]s Ploscowe had recommended, the Model Penal Code undermined the prohibitions against nonconsensual sex with significant defenses and barriers to prosecution. The comments identify the problems of proof in rape cases as especially severe, suggesting that women are likely to lie because of social pressures to recast a voluntary act as forced in order to preserve reputation, to revenge a failed relationship, to respond to an unwanted pregnancy, or as a means of requiring prompt complaint. The victim of sexual violence has no reason to delay reporting such a crime, the comments observe, and if she does delay, her motives are likely to be blackmail or her own 'psychopathy,' which makes corroboration imperative. No complainant can prove her case based on her testimony alone, and juries are to be instructed 'to evaluate the testimony of a victim or complaining witness with special care in view of the emotional involvement of the witness and the difficulty of determining the truth with respect to alleged sexual activities carried out in private.' Although the definition of felony rape mentions the victim's nonconsent the elements of the crime emphasize proof of objective acts and evidence (*e.g.,* presence of force, prompt complaint, and physical evidence.) Although proof of victim resistance is not required, the comments assert that the degree to which the victim fights back is relevant to her credibility. Prior promiscuity bars a complaint of gross sexual imposition or misdemeanor sexual assault. If a woman was drinking when raped, she must show that she was fully unconscious before any impairment of her capacity to consent to sex is recognized.")

218 *See* Schulhofer, *supra* note 70, at p. 20 (citing Peggy Reeves Sanday, *A Woman Scorned* (New York: Doubleday, 1996), at pp. 3–15, 28–49).

219 *Id.* at 21. (Schulhofer further explains that "[i]nterestingly, the code placed substance over legal form by extending the marital exemption to unmarried couples who were living together, but it placed form over substance by preserving the exemption for most legally married couples who were living apart. The consistent thread in both situations was that fear of false accusations and appreciation for a man's sexual needs prevailed over his partner's claim to determine for herself whether to permit sexual intimacy.")

220 *See* Hirshman and Larson, *supra* note 6, at p. 197.

221 *See* Francis, *supra* note 60, at p. x. (Explains Francis, "[i]n REAL RAPE, Susan Estrich argued that rapes committed by acquaintances are as real as the rapes inflicted by lurking strangers—even though they are often not recognized as such, either by formal definitions in the criminal law or by juries or judges applying these formal provisions. A number of jurisdictions have amended rape laws to include spousal rape, either in all cases or in situations in which the husband and wife have taken steps toward separation or divorce. Jurisdictions have also adopted statutes defining degrees

of sexual assault. Typical statutes graduate the offense by the kind and amount of force used, the age differential between the victim and the offender, the nature of the sexual acts committed, and the relationship between the victim and the offender." (citing Linda Brookover Bourque, DEFINING RAPE (Durham, N.C.: Duke University Press, 1989), at p. 111).)

222 *See* Hirshman and Larson, *supra* note 6, at p. 186.

223 *Id.*

224 *Id.*

225 *See* Schulhofer, *supra* note 70, at pp. 29–30.

226 For review of where "rape shield" law stands today, *see, e.g., Michigan v. Lucas,* 500 U.S. 145 (1991); *U.S. v. White Buffalo,* 84 F.3d 1052 (8th Cir. 1996); *U.S. v. Powers,* 59 F.3d 1460 (4th Cir. 1995), *cert. den.,* 116 S. Ct. 784; *Stephens v. Miller,* 13 F.3d 998 (7th Cir. 1994), *cert. den.,* 115 S. Ct. 57; *U.S. v. Jones,* 15 F.3d 740 (8th Cir. 1994); *Sandoval v. Acevedo,* 996 F.2d 145 (7th Cir. 1993); *Wood v. Alaska,* 957 F.2d 1544 (9th Cir. 1992); *U.S. v. Torres,* 937 F.2d 1469 (9th Cir. 1991); *U.S. v. Saunders,* 943 F.2d 388 (4th Cir. 1991); *U.S. v. Begay,* 937 F.2d 515 (10th Cir. 1991); *Cook v. Greyhound Lines, Inc.,* 847 F. Supp. 725 (Minn. Dist. Ct. 1994); *Carrigan v. Arvonio,* 871 F. Supp. 222 (Dist. Ct. N.J. 1994); *Roberts v. Singletary,* 794 F. Supp. 1106 (Fla. S.D. 1992), *aff'd,* 29 F.3d 1474; *U.S. v. Stamper,* 766 F. Supp. 1396 (N.C. W.D. 1991), *aff'd, In re One Female Juvenile Victim,* 959 F.2d 231; *Shaw v. U.S.,* 812 F. Supp. 154 (S.D. Dist. 1993), *aff'd,* 92 F.3d 1189; *Hoke v. Thompson,* 852 F. Supp. 1310 (E.D. Va. 1994); *Harris v. State,* 907 S.W.2d 729 (Ark.1995); *State v. Orantez,* 902 P.2d 824 (Ariz. 1995); *Davlin v. State,* 899 S.W. 2d 451 (Ark. 1995); *Byrum v. State,* 884 S.W.2d 248 (Ark. 1994); *Cupples v. State,* 883 S.W.2d 458 (Ark. 1994); *Evans v. State,* 878 S.W.2d 750 (Ark. 1994); *Drymon v. State,* 875 S.W.2d 73 (Ark. 1994); *Laughlin v. State,* 872 S.W.2d 848 (Ark. 1994); *Gaines v. State,* 855 S.W.2d 956 (Ark. 1993); *Slater v. State,* 832 S.W.2d 846 (Ark. 1992); *People v. Murphy,* 919 P.2d 191 (Colo. 1996); *State v. Kulmac,* 644 A.2d 887 (Conn. 1994); *State v. Christiano,* 637 A.2d 382 (Conn. 1994), *cert. den.,* 115 S. Ct. 83; *State v. Rinaldi,* 599 A.2d 1 (Conn. 1991); *Lewis v. State,* 591 So.2d 922 (Fla. 1991); *Jenkins v. State,* 627 N.E.2d 789 (Ind. 1993); *Thompson v. State,* 492 N.E.2d 410 (Iowa 1992); *State v. Jones,* 490 N.W.2d 787 (Iowa 1992); *State v. Lewis,* 847 P.2d 690 (Kan. 1993); *State v. Walker,* 845 P.2d 1 (Kan. 1993); *State v. Arrington,* 840 P.2d 477 (Kan. 1992); *Commonwealth v. Dunn,* 899 S.W.2d 492 (Ky. 1995); *Billings v. Commonwealth,* 843 S.W.2d 890 (Ky. 1992); *Barnett v. Commonwealth,* 828 S.W.2d 361 (Ky. 1992); *Gilbert v. Commnwealth,* 838 S.W.2d 376 (Ky. 1991); *State v. Sargent* 656 A.2d 1196 (Me. 1995); *State v. Hoffstadt,* 652 A.2d 93 (Me. 1995); *Shand v. State,* 672 A.2d 630 (Md. 1996); *Johnson v. State,* 632 A.2d 152 (Md. 1993); *White v. State,* 598 A.2d 187 (Md. 1991); *People v. Adair,* 550 N.W.2d 505 (Mich. 1996); *Peterson v. State,* 671 So.2d 647 (Miss. 1996); *Holland v. State,* 587 So.2d 848 (Miss. 1991); *State v. Weeks,* 891 P.2d 477 (Mont. 1995); *State v. Steffes,* 887 P.2d 1196 (Mont. 1994); *State v. Stuit,* 885 P.2d 1290 (Mont. 1994); *State v. Welch,* 490 N.W.2d 216 (Neb. 1992); *Drake v. State,* 836 P.2d 52 (Nev. 1992); *State v. Ellsworth,* 613 A.2d 473 (N.H. 1992); *State v. Budis,* 593 A.2d 784 (N.J. 1991); *State v. Sexton,* 444 S.E.2d 879 (N.C. 1994); *State v. Boggs,* 588 N.E.2d 813 (Ohio 1992); *State v. Lajole,* 849 P.2d 479 (Or. 1993); *Commonwealth v. Spiewak,* 617 A.2d 696 (Pa. 1992); *State v. DeNoyer,* 541 N.W.2d 725 (S.D. 1995); *Lykken v. Class,* 561 N.W.2d 302 (S.D. 1992); *State v. Leggett,* 664 A.2d 271 (Vt. 1995); *In Interest of Michael R.B.,* 499 N.W.2d 641 (Wis. 1993); *Kelly v. State,* 602 So.2d 473 (Ala. Crim. App. 1992); *Mitchell v. State,* 593 So.2d 176 (Ala. Crim. App. 1991); *Heath v. State,* 849 P.2d 786 (Ala. App. 1993); *Samples v. State,* 902 S.W.2d 257 (Ark. App. 1995); *People v. Franklin,* 30 Cal. Rptr. 2d 376 (Cal. App. 6 Dist. 1994); *People v. Murphy,* 899 P.2d 294 (Colo. App. 1994); *People v. Schmidt,* 885 P.2d 312 (Colo. App. 1994); *People v. Braley,* 879 P.2d 410 (Colo. App. 1993); *People v. Aldrich,* 849 P.2d 821 (Colo. App. 1992); *State v. Manini,* 659 A.2d 196 (Conn. App. 1995); *State v. Siering,* 644 A.2d 958 (Conn. App. 1994); *State v. Harrison,* 642 A.2d 36 (Conn. App. 1994); *State v. Kindrick,* 619 A.2d 1 (Conn. App. 1993); *Castro v. State,* 591 So.2d 1076 (Fla. App. 3 Dist. 1991); *Martin v. State,* 464 S.E.2d 872 (Ga. App. 1995); *Dunton v. State,* 453 S.E.2d 800 (Ga. App. 1995); *Logan v. State,* 442 S.E.2d 883 (Ga. App. 1994); *Brown v. State,* 448 S.E.2d 723 (Ga. App. 1994); *Humphrey v. State,* 428 S.E.2d 362 (Ga. App. 1993); *Lemacks v. State,* 427 S.E.2d 536 (Ga. App. 1993); *Hall v. State,* 419 S.E.2d 503 (Ga. App. 1992); *White v. State,* 410 S.E.2d 441 (Ga. App. 1991), *cert. granted, rev'd,* 412 S.E.2d 831; *In Interest of Doe,* 918 P.2d 254 (Hawaii App. 1996); *State v. Peite,* 839 P.2d 1223 (Idaho App. 1992); *People v. Weatherspoon,* 202 Ill.Dec. 112 (Ill. App. 1 Dist. 1994), *app. den.,* 205 Ill.Dec. 183; *People v. Jones,* 201 Ill.Dec. 172 (Ill. App. 1 Dist. 1993); *People v. Todd,* 181 Ill.Dec. 682 (Ill. App. 4 Dist. 1993); *People v. Sizemore,* 168 Ill. Dec. 883 (Ill. App. 4 Dist. 1992); *People v. Mason,* 161 Ill.Dec. 705 (Ill. App. 4 Dist. 1991); *Caley v. State,* 650 N.E.2d 54 (Ind. App. 5 Dist. 1995); *Little v. State,* 650 N.E.2d 343 (Ind. App. 1995); *Koo v. State,* 640 N.E.2d 95 (Ind. App. 5 Dist. 1994); *Steward v. State,* 636 N.E.2d 143 (Ind. App. 1 Dist. 1994); *Kielblock v. State,* 627 N.E.2d 816 (Ind. App. 1 Dist. 1994); *Posey v. State,* 624 N.E.2d 515 (Ind. App. 1 Dist. 1993); *Tyson v. State,* 619 N.E.2d 276 (Ind. App. 2 Dist. 1993), *aff'd in part,* 626 N.E.2d 482, *cert. den.,* 114 S. Ct. 1216; *Kelly v. State,* 586 N.E.2d 927 (Ind. App. 5 Dist. 1992); *State v. Lavery,* 877 P.2d 443 (Kan. App. 1993); *State v. Davis,* 664 So.2d 821 (La. App. 3 Cir. 1995); *State v. Billings,* 640 So.2d 500 (La. App. 3 Cir. 1994); *State v. Womack,* 592 So.2d 872 (La. App. 2 Cir. 1991); *State v. Trosclair,* 584 So.2d 270 (La. App. 1 Cir. 1991), *writ. den.,* 585 So.2d 575; *Shand v. State,* 653 A.2d 1000 (Md. App. 1995), *cert. granted, Allen v. State,* 661 A.2d 733; *Johnson v. State,* 613 A.2d 450 (Md. App. 1992); *Daven-*

port v. State, 598 A.2d 827 (Md. App. 1991); *Miles v. State*, 594 A.2d 634 (Md. App. 1991), *cert. den.*, 599 A.2d 634; *Commonwealth v. Hynes*, 664 N.E.2d 864 (Mass. App. Ct. 1996); *Commonwealth v. McGregor*, 655 N.E.2d 1278 (Mass. App. Ct. 1995); *Commonwealth v. Herrick*, 655 N.E.2d 637 (Mass. App. Ct. 1995); *Commonwealth v. Syrafos*, 646 N.E.2d 429 (Mass. App. Ct. 1995); *Commonwealth v. Costello*, 635 N.E.2d 255 (Mass. App. Ct. 1994); *Commonwealth v. Baxter*, 627 N.E.2d 487 (Mass. App. Ct. 1994); *Commonwealth v. Thevenin*, 603 N.E.2d 222 (Mass. App. Ct. 1992); *Commonwealth v. Fionda*, 599 N.E.2d 635 (Mass. App. Ct. 1992); *Commonwealth v. Gauthier*, 586 N.E.2d 34 (Mass. App. Ct. 1992); *People v. Mooney*, 549 N.W.2d 65 (Mich. App. 1996); *People v. Hurt*, 536 N.W.2d 227 (Mich. App. 1995); *People v. Adair*, 524 N.W.2d 256 (Mich. App. 1994); *People v. Powell*, 506 N.W.2d 894 (Mich. App. 1993); *People v. Lucas*, 484 N.W.2d 685 (Mich. App. 1992), *cert. den.*, *Lucas v. Michigan*, 115 S. Ct. 593; *People v. Wilhelm*, 476 N.W.2d 753 (Mich. App. 1991); *State v. Davis*, 546 N.W.2d 30 (Minn. App. 1996); *State v. Crims*, 540 N.W.2d 860 (Minn. App. 1995); *State v. Enger*, 539 N.W.2d 259 (Minn. App. 1995); *Amacker v. State*, 676 So.2d 909 (Miss. 1996); *State v. Hale*, 917 S.W.2d 219; *State v. Sloan*, 912 S.W.2d 592 (Mo. App. E.D. 1995); *State v. Danback*, 886 S.W.2d 204 (Mo. App. E.D. 1994); *State v. Nixon*, 858 S.W.2d 782 (Mo. App. E.D. 1993); *State v. Murray*, 842 S.W.2d 122 (Mo. App. E.D. 1991); *State v. Ramos*, 858 P.2d 94 (N.M. App. 1993); *People v. Becraft*, 604 N.Y.S.2d 437 (A.D. 4 Dept. 1993); *People v. Goodwin*, 579 N.Y.2d 805 (A.D. 4 Dept. 1992); *People v. Perryman*, 578 N.Y.S.2d 785 (A.D. 4 Dept. 1991); *State v. Ginyard*, 468 S.E.2d 525 (N.C. App. 1996); *State v. Graham*, 454 S.E.2d 878 (N.C. App. 1995); *State v. Jenkins*, 445 S.E.2d 622 (N.C. App. 1994); *State v. Mustafa*, 437 S.E.2d 906 (N.C. App. 1994); *State v. Black*, 432 S.E.2d 710 (N.C. App. 1993); *State v. McCarroll*, 428 S.E.2d 229 (N.C. App. 1993); *State v. Smelcer*, 623 N.E.2d 1219 (Ohio App. 1993); *State v. Guthrie*, 621 N.E.2d 551 (Ohio App. 12 Dist. 1993); *State v. Jones*, 615 N.E.2d 713 (Ohio App. 2 Dist. 1992); *State v. Cervantes*, 881 P.2d 151 (Or. App. 1994); *State v. Niles*, 817 P.2d 293 (Or. App. 1991); *Wofford v. State*, 903 S.W.2d 796 (Tex. App. Dallas 1995); *Neeley v. Commonwealth*, 437 S.E.2d 721 (Va. App. 1993); *Evans v. Commonwealth*, 415 S.E.2d 851 (Va. App. 1992); *State v. Gallegos*, 828 P.2d 37 (Wash. App. Div. 1 1992); *State v. Wirts*, 500 N.W.2d 317 (Wis. App. 1993); *State v. G.S.*, 650 A.2d 819 (N.J. Super. App. Div. 1994); *Commonwealth v. Widmer*, 667 A.2d 215 (Pa. Super. 1995); *Commonwealth v. Berkowitz*, 609 A.2d 1338 (Pa. Super. 1992); *Smith v. Penn. Bd. of Probation & Parole*, 636 A.2d 291 (Pa. Super. 1991); *Commonwealth v. Boyles*, 595 A.2d 1180 (Pa. Super. 1991). Though plentiful for an endnote, the above represent but a few of the cases decided by the courts on these issues.

227   *See* Schulhofer, *supra* note 70, at pp. 29–30. (And, indeed, as late as 1992, Illinois courts considering the validity of the marital exemption. *See, e.g., People v. M.D.*, 172 Ill.Dec. 341 (Ill. App. 2 Dist. 1992) (interpreting Illinois statute and United States Constitution).)

228   *R. v. Miller*, [1954] 1 A11 E.R. 529.

229   *See* Bevacqua, *supra* note 70, at p. 155, n. 1.

230   According to the National Clearinghouse on Marital and Date Rape in Berkeley, California, twenty-seven had passed laws foreclosing prosecution of a husband where only "simple force"—as opposed to a weapon—was used or where a wife was unable to consent due to mental or physical disability by 1991, and only four states—Missouri, North Carolina, Oklahoma, and South Carolina—held that a husband could not be prosecuted for raping his wife. For overview of this area of the law, *see* Sanford H. Kadish & Stephen J. Shulhofer, CRIMINAL LAW AND ITS PROCESSES (Boston: Little, Brown, 6th ed., 1995), at p. 368. For further background, *see also* Diana E. H. Russell, RAPE IN MARRIAGE (Bloomington: Indiana University Press, 2d ed. 1990), at pp. 375–382.

231   *Kizer v. Commonwealth*, 321 S.E.2d 291 (Va. 1984).

232   For further reading, *see* Russell, *supra* note 230, at pp. 375–382.

233   For background, *see* Carolyn Pesce, *Marital Rape: Verdict*, USA TODAY, April 21, 1992, at 3A; LARRY KING LIVE, *A Controversy Over Marital Rape*, CNN, airing May 15, 1992; DATELINE, NBC-TV, interviews with Mr. And Mrs. Crawford separately, airing June 2, 1992; SONYA LIVE, *Spousal Rape Laws*, CNN, July 31, 1992; Linda Goldstone, *California Moves to Strengthen Law for Prosecuting Spouse Rape*, HOUSTON CHRONICLE, Aug. 2, 1992, at A13.

234   *See supra* note 230.

235   *See, e.g., People v. Liberta*, 474 N.E.2d 567 (N.Y. 1984); *State v. Smith*, 426 A.2d 38 (N.J. 1981); *Warren v. State*, 336 S.E.2d 221 (Ga. 1985).

236   *See* National Clearinghouse on Marital and Date Rape.

237   For further reading of this issue, *see* Richard A. Posner and Katherine B. Silbaugh, A GUIDE TO AMERICA'S SEX LAWS (1996), at pp. 35–43; Robin West, *Equality Theory, Marital Rape, and the Promise of the Fourteenth Amendment*, 42 FLA. L. REV. at pp. 45–48 (1990).

238   *See* Schulhofer, *supra* note 70, at p. 43 (citing Russell, *supra* note 230, at pp. 375–382). (And sometimes the reforms coupled. For example, in 1992, an Illinois appellate court ruled that the past sexual history of a wife was shielded against admission by husband, even where a woman admitted her husband was the father of her two children. *See, e.g., People v. M.D.*, 172 Ill.Dec. 341 (Ill. App. 2 Dist. 1992) (interpreting Illinois statute and United States Constitution).)

239   *See* Bevacqua, *supra* note 70, at p. 100.

240   *See* Schulhofer, *supra* note 70, at p. 44. For a case example of this standard, *see, e.g., Morse v. Commonwealth*, 17 Va. App. 627 (1994).

241 *See, e.g., People v. Harris,* 238 P.2d 158 (Cal. App. 1951); *People v. Hinton,* 333 P.2d 822 (Cal. App. 1959).

242 *See* Schulhofer, *supra* note 70, at pp. 30, 44.

243 For review of rape laws and cases involving the issue of "resistance" and the conduct of the victim, *see, e.g., People v. Barnes,* 721 P.2d 110 (Cal. 1986); *State v. Kulmac,* 644 A.2d 887 (Conn. 1994), *aff'd,* 707 A.2d 1290; *State v. Mezrioui,* 602 A.2d 29 (Conn. App. 1992); *State v. Williams,* 546 A.2d 943 (Conn. App. 1988); *State v. Mackor,* 527 A.2d 710 (Conn. App. 1987); *Hall v. State,* 375 S.E.2d 460 (Ga. App. 1998); *People v. Stengel,* 155 Ill.Dec. 878 (Ill. App. 1 Dist. 1991), *app. den.,* 162 Ill.Dec. 504; *People v. Geneva,* 143 Ill.Dec. 621 (Ill. App. 1 Dist. 1990); *People v. Robinson,* 145 Ill.Dec. 302 (Ill. App. 1 Dist. 1989); *People v. Leonhardt,* 527 N.E.2d 562 (Ill. App. 1 Dist. 1988); *People v. Nelson,* 102 Ill.Dec. 275 (Ill. App. 2 Dist. 1986), *app. den.,* 106 Ill.Dec. 53; *People v. Gramc,* 130 Ill.Dec. 380 (Ill. App. 5 Dist. 1989), *app. den.,* 136 Ill.Dec. 596; *Gilliam v. State,* 509 N.E.2d 815 (Ind. 1987); *Smith v. State,* 500 N.E.2d 190 (Ind. 1986); *State v. Dee,* 752 S.W.2d 942 (Mo. App. 1988); *State v. RDG,* 733 S.W.2d 824 (Mo. App. 1987); *State v. Koonce,* 731 S.N.2d 431 (Mo. App. 1987); *State v. Hannett,* 713 S.W.2d 267 (Mo. App. 1986); *People v. Gregory ZZ.,* 521 N.Y.S.2d 873 (A.D. 3 Dept. 1987), *app. den.,* 527 N.Y.S.2d 1014; *People v. Rodriquez,* 509 N.Y.S.2d 227 (A.D. 4 Dept. 1986); *State v. Harrison,* 380 S.E.2d 608 (N.C. App. 1989); *Commonwealth v. Mlinarich,* 542 A.2d 1335 (Pa. 1988); *Hernandez v. State,* 804 S.W.2d 168 (Tex. App. Houston 1991); *Parrish v. Commonwealth,* 346 S.E.2d 736 (Va. App. 1986); *State v. McKnight,* 774 P.2d 532 (Wash. App. 1989); *Scadden v. State,* 732 P.2d 1036 (Wyo. 1987). For review of cases involving the issue of "force," *i.e.,* the legal requirement of conduct to prove the offense, *see, e.g., Rhoden v. Rowland,* 10 F.3d 1457 (9th Cir. 1993); *U.S. v. Fulton,* 987 F.2d 631 (9th Cir. 1993); *Stokes v. State,* 648 So.2d 1179 (Ala. Crim. App. 1994); *Sartin v. State,* 601 So.2d 1142 (Ala. Crim. App. 1992); *Smith v. State,* 601 So.2d 201 (Ala. Crim. App. 1992); *Cure v. State,* 600 So.2d 415 (Ala. Crim. App. 1992), *cert. den.,* 600 So.2d 421; *Ayers v. State,* 594 So.2d 719 (Ala. Crim. App. 1991); *Parks v. State,* 587 So.2d 1015 (Ala. Crim. App. 1991); *Lee v. State,* 586 So.2d 264 (Ala. Crim. App. 1991); *Hutchins v. State,* 568 So.2d 395 (Ala. Cr. App. 1990); *Smith v. State,* 545 So.2d 198 (Ala. Cr. App. 1989); *Lockett v. State,* 518 So.2d 877 (Ala. Cr. App. 1987); *Parrish v. State,* 494 So.2d 705 (Ala. Cr. App. 1985); *Mosley v. State,* 914 S.W.2d 731 (Ark. 1996); *Caldwell v. State,* 891 S.W.2d 42 (Ark. 1995); *Skiver v. State,* 826 S.W.2d 309 (Ark. App. 1992); *People v. Senior,* 5 Cal. Rptr. 2d 14 (Cal. App. 6 Dist. 1992); *People v. Young,* 235 Cal. Rptr. 361 (Cal. App. 5 Dist. 1987); *People v. Montero,* 229 Cal. Rptr. 750 (Cal. App. 4 Dist. 1986); *State v. Kumac,* 644 A.2d 887 (Conn. 1994); *State v. Jackson,* 620 A.2d 168 (Conn. App. 1993), *cert. den.,* 623 A.2d 1026; *State v. Butler,* 529 A.2d 219 (Conn. App. 1987), *cert. den.,* 531 A.2d 938; *State v. Sedia,* 614 So.2d 533 (Fla. App. 4 Dist. 1995); *Russell v. State,* 576 So.2d 389 (Fla. App. 1 Dist. 1991); *Edmondson v. State,* 464 S.E.2d 839 (Ga. App. 1995); *Callahan v. State,* 418 S.E.2d 157 (Ga. App. 1992); *Shelton v. State,* 395 S.E.2d 618 (Ga. App. 1990); *State v. Gossett,* 808 P.2d 1326 (Idaho App. 1991); *People v. Fryer,* 187 Ill.Dec. 786 (Ill. App. 1 Dist. 1993); *People v. Pearson,* 191 Ill.Dec. 305 (Ill. App. 2 Dist. 1993), *app. den.,* 197 Ill.Dec. 493; *People v. Bowen,* 182 Ill.Dec. 43 (Ill. App. 4 Dist. 1993), *cert. den., Bowen v. Illinois,* 114 S. Ct. 387; *People v. Smith,* 185 Ill.Dec. 641 (Ill. App. 5 Dist. 1993), *vac.,* 189 Ill.Dec. 449; *People v. Smith,* 185 Ill.Dec. 641 (Ill. App. 5 Dist. 1993); *People v. Washington,* 181 Ill.Dec. 473 (Ill. App. 1 Dist. 1992), *app. den.,* 183 Ill.Dec. 870; *People v. Singleton,* 160 Ill.Dec. 513 (Ill. App. 5 Dist. 1991), *app. den.,* 164 Ill.Dec. 925; *People v. Bolton,* 152 Ill.Dec. 661 (Ill. App. 1 Dist. 1990); *People v. Geneva,* 143 Ill.Dec. 621 (Ill. App. 1 Dist. 1990); *People v. Robinson,* 145 Ill.Dec. 302 (Ill. App. 1 Dist. 1989); *People v. Fosdick,* 116 Ill.Dec. 460 (Ill. App. 1 Dist. 1988); *People v. Jung Oh Kim,* 101 Ill.Dec. 53 (Ill. App. 1 Dist. 1986); *People v. Nelson,* 102 Ill.Dec. 275 (Ill. App. 2 Dist. 1986); *Tobias v. State,* 666 N.E.2d 68 (Ind. 1996); *Bryant v. State,* 644 N.E.2d 859 (Ind. 1994); *Bryant v. State,* 644 N.E.2d 859 (Ind. 1994); *Jones v. State,* 589 N.E.2d 241 (Ind. 1992); *Wesby v. State,* 550 N.E.2d 321 (Ind. 1990); *Gonzales v. State,* 532 N.E.2d 1167 (Ind. 1989); *Smith v. State,* 500 N.E.2d 190 (Ind. 1986); *Stewart v. State,* 601 N.E.2d 1 (Ind. App. 2 Dist. 1992); *Moore v. State,* 551 N.E.2d 459 (Ind. App. 3 Dist. 1990); *State v. Taylor,* 538 N.W.2d 314 (Iowa App. 1995); *State v. Borthwick,* 880 P.2d 1261 (Kan. 1994); *Yarnell v. Commonwealth,* 833 S.W.2d 834 (Ky. 1992); *State v. Martin,* 645 So.2d 190 (La. 1994), *cert. den.,* 115 S. Ct. 2252; *State v. Martin,* 645 So.2d 190 (La. 1994), *cert. den.,* 115 S. Ct. 2252; *State v. Porter,* 639 So.2d 1137 (La. 1994); *State v. Simmons,* 621 So.2d 1135 (La. App. 4 Cir. 1993); *State v. Montana,* 533 So.2d 983 (La. App. 1 Cir. 1988); *State v. Rosa,* 575 A.2d 727 (Me. 1990); *Commonwealth v. Caracciola,* 569 N.E.2d 774 (Mass. 1991); *People v. Brown,* 495 N.W.2d 812 (Mich. App. 1992); *People v. Kline,* 494 N.W.2d 756 (Mich. App. 1992); *State v. Hart,* 477 N.W.2d 732 (Minn. App. 1991); *State v. Nixon,* 858 S.W.2d 782; *State v. Davenport,* 839 S.W.2d 723 (Mo. App. S.D. 1992); *State v. Jones,* 809 S.W.2d 37 (Mo. App. 1991); *State v. Hannett,* 713 S.W.2d 267 (Mo. App. 1986); *State v. Johnson,* 547 A.2d 213 (N.H. 1988); *McNair v. State,* 825 P.2d 571 (Nev. 1992); *State v. Oliver,* 627 A.2d 144 (N.J. 1993); *State in Interest of M.T.S.,* 609 A.2d 1266 (N.J. 1992); *State in Interest of M.T.S.,* 588 A.2d 1282 (N.J. Super. A.D. 1991); *State v. Leiding,* 812 P.2d 797 (N.M. App. 1991); *People v. Roman,* 578 N.Y.S.2d 544 (A.D. 2 Dept. 1992), *app. den.,* 583 N.Y.S.2d 206; *People v. Kranz,* 604 N.Y.S.2d 225 (A.D. 2 Dept. 1993), *rev'd,* 620 N.Y.S.2d 821; *People v. Cook,* N.Y.S.2d 919 (A.D. 3 Dept. 1992), *app. den.,* 594 N.Y.S.2d 723; *People v. Howard,* 558 N.Y.S.2d 921 (A.D. 4 Dept. 1990); *People v. Gregory ZZ.,* 521 N.Y.S.2d 873 (A.D. 3 Dept. 1987); *State v. Penland,* 472 S.E.2d 734 (N.C. 1996), *cert. den.,* 117 S. Ct. 734, *reh'g den.,* 117 S. Ct. 1291; *State v. Moseley,* 449 S.E.2d 412 (N.C. 1994), *cert. den.,* 115 S. Ct. 1815; *State v. Lilly,* 450 S.E.2d 546 (N.C. App. 1994), *aff'd,* 464

S.E.2d 42; *State v. Black,* 432 S.E.2d 710 (N.C. App. 1993); *State v. Scott,* 372 S.E.2d 572 (N.C. 1988); *State v. Locklear,* 360 S.E.2d 682 (N.C. 1987); *State v. Moorman,* 358 S.E.2d 502 (N.C. 1987); *State v. Freeman,* 356 S.E.2d 765 (N.C. 1987); *State v. Etheridge,* 352 S.E.2d 673 (N.C. 1987); *State v. Strickland,* 351 S.E.2d 281 (N.C. 1987); *State v. Parks,* 386 S.E.2d 748 (N.C. App. 1989); *State v. Morrison,* 380 S.E.2d 608 (N.C. App. 1989); *State v. Dillard,* 368 S.E.2d 442 (N.C. App. 1988); *State v. Midyette,* 360 S.E.2d 507 (N.C. App. 1987), *aff'd,* 366 S.E.2d 440; *State v. Morrison,* 355 S.E.2d 182 (N.C. App. 1987); *State v. Eskridge,* 526 N.E.2d 304 (Ohio 1988); *State v. Fenton,* 588 N.E.2d 951 (Ohio App. 6 Dist. 1990); *State v. Ambrosia,* 587 N.E.2d 892 (Ohio App. 6 Dist. 1990), *dism'd,* 569 N.E.2d 504; *State v. Smelcer,* 623 N.E.2d 1219 (Ohio App. 8 Dist. 1993); *State v. Swift,* 621 N.E.2d 513 (Ohio App. 11 Dist. 1993); *State v. Soke,* 584 N.E.2d 1273 (Ohio App. 11 Dist. 1989); *State v. Fowler,* 500 N.E.2d 390 (Ohio App. 1985); *Commonwealth v. Berkowitz,* 641 A.2d 1161 (Pa. 1994); *Commonwealth v. Mlinarich,* 542 A.2d 1335 (Pa. 1988); *Commonwealth v. Jones,* 672 A.2d 1353 (Pa. Super. 1996); *Commonwealth v. Smolko,* 666 A.2d 672 (Pa. Super. 1995); *Commonwealth v. Riley,* 643 A.2d 1090 (Pa. Super. 1994); *Commonwealth v. Berkowitz,* 609 A.2d 1338 (Pa. Super. 1992), *aff'd in part, rev'd in part,* 641 A.2d 1161; *Commonwealth v. Ables,* 590 A.2d 334 (Pa. Super. 1991), *app. den.,* 597 A.2d 1150; *Commonwealth v. Ruppert,* 579 A.2d 966 (Pa. Super. 1990), *app. den.,* 588 A.2d 914; *Commonwealth v. Titus,* 556 A.2d 425 (Pa. Super. 1989); *Commonwealth v. Gabrielson,* 536 A.2d 401 (Pa. Super. 1988); *Commonwealth v. Stambaugh,* 512 A.2d 1216 (Pa. Super. 1986); *State v. Maggs,* 588 A.2d 601 (R.I. 1991); *State v. Jacques,* 536 A.2d 535 (R.I. 1988); *State v. Burks,* 521 A.2s 725 (R.I. 1987); *State v. Jones,* 521 N.W.2d 662 (S.D. 1994); *State v. McKnight,* 900 S.W.2d 36 (Tenn. Crim. App. 1994); *Suarez v. State,* 901 S.W.2d 712 (Tex. App. Corpus Christi 1995); *Clifton v. Commonwealth,* 468 S.E.2d 155 (Va. App. 1996); *Sprouse v. Commonwealth,* 453 S.E.2d 303 (Va. App. 1995); *Carter v. Commonwealth,* 428 S.E.2d 34 (Va. App. 1993); *State v. Ritola,* 817 P.2d 1390 (Wash. App. Div. 2 1991); *State v. George W.H.,* 439 S.E.2d 423 (W.Va. 1993); *State v. Bonds,* 469 N.W.2d 184 (Wis. App. 1991), *rev'd,* 477 N.W.2d 265.

244 *See, e.g., People v. Barnes,* 721 P.2d 110 (Cal. 1986) (interpreting an amendment to the law that eliminated the resistance requirement for victims); *State v. Kulmac,* 644 A.2d 887 (Conn. 1994) (holding that the focus of sexual assault prosecution is not the failure of resistance or the conduct of the victim, but rather the actions of the defendant); *State v. Mezrioui,* 602 A.2d 29 (Conn. App. 1992) (holding that it was not necessary that victim of unwanted sexual advances said "no" or "stop"); *State v. Williams,* 546 A.2d 943 (Conn. App. 1988) (holding that the state's rape statute does not require a showing that defendant overcame victim's resistance); *State v. Mackor,* 527 A.2d 710 (Conn. App. 1988) (holding that consent and resistance were not elements of the crime of sexual assault); *Hall v. State,* 375 S.E.2d 460 (Ga. App. 1988) (holding that a victim of rape did not consent by failing to resist with all her might and/or until her strength was completely gone); *People v. Smith,* 185 Ill.Dec. 641 (Ill. App. 5 Dist. 1993) (finding that a showing of resistance was not necessary where resistance would be futile, might endanger the life of the victim or where victim is overcome by fear or superior strength); *People v. Stengel,* 155 Ill.Dec. 878 (Ill. App. 1 Dist. 1991) (holding that failure to cry out and/or to resist did not establish consent where woman was threatened or in fear of being harmed), *app. den.,* 162 Ill.Dec. 504; *People v. Geneva,* 143 Ill.Dec. 621 (Ill. App. 1 Dist. 1990) (holding that although the facts of each case must be examined individually, in some instances, resistance is not essential where it could be futile, such as in the case where there is use of a deadly weapon); *People v. Robinson,* 145 Ill.Dec. 302 (Ill. App. 1 Dist. 1989) (holding that the law does not require a person to be "foolhardy" or to endanger her life to resist rape); *People v. Leonhardt,* 527 N.E.2d 562 (Ill.App. 1 Dist. 1988) (holding that a victim's failure to resist and disrobing of herself did not establish consent, given the circumstances); *People v. Nelson,* 102 Ill.Dec. 275 (Ill. App. 2 Dist. 1986) (holding that resistance not necessary where futile); *People v. Gramc,* 130 Ill.Dec. 380 (Ill. App. 5 Dist. 1989) (ruling conviction sound even though sexual assault victim did not try to escape where she was "restrained" by fear or it would have endangered her life to try); *Bryant v. State,* 644 N.E.2d 859 (Ind. 1994) (holding that state need only show that victim did not consent to sustain conviction for rape); *Gilliam v. State,* 509 N.E.2d 815 (Ind. 1987) (victim must resist sufficiently to show a lack of consent; but she is not obligated to do so where she fears great bodily harm); *Smith v. State,* 500 N.E.2d 190 (Ind. 1986) (though resistance of rape victim is one way to establish there was not consent, it is not an element of the crime; *State v. Borthwick,* 880 P.2d 1261 (Kan. 1994) (force required to resist rape and, therefore, to sustain a conviction, is not so great that victim risks becoming victim of another crime in the process); *State v. Martin,* 645 So.2d 190 (La. 1994) (distinction between aggravated and forcible rape involves analysis of degree of force by assailant and resistance by victim); *State v. Porter,* 639 So.2d 1137 (La. 1994) (consumption of alcohol may negate resistance requirement); *State v. Dee,* 752 S.W.2d 942 (Mo. App. 1988) (defendant may be guilty of rape even where victim offered no physical resistance); *State v. RDG,* 733 S.W.2d 824 (Mo. App. 1987) (utmost resistance not required where it would be futile); *State v. Koonce,* 731 S.W.2d 431 (Mo. App. 1987) (an army reservist was not required to use "combat methods" to resist rape); *State v. Hannett,* 713 S.W.2d 267 (Mo. App. 1986) (law does not require resistance where "not feasible" or otherwise futile); *People v. Gregory ZZ.,* 521 N.Y.S.2d 873 (A.D. 3 Dept. 1987) (earnest resistance not necessary to prove charge of rape); *People v. Rodriquez,* 509 N.Y.S.2d 227 (A.D. 4 Dept. 1986) (standard is reasonable resistance, not utmost resistance); *State v. Harrison,* 380 S.E.2d

608 (N.C. App. 1989) (physical resistance not necessary to show lack of consent); *Commonwealth v. Mlinarich*, 542 A.2d 1335 (Pa. 1988) (useless resistance not necessary); *State v. Jones*, 521 N.W.2d 662 (S.D. 1994) (resistance by victim not an element of rape); *Suarez v. State*, 901 S.W.2d 712 (Tex. App. Corpus Christi 1995) (to show that a victim was physically unable to resist, state must prove victim suffered an impairment such that it would make reasonable resistance impossible); *Hernandez v. State*, 804 S.W.2d 168 (Tex. App. Houston 1991) (victim not required by law to resist during sexual assault); *Clifton v. Commonwealth*, 468 S.E.2d 155 (Va. App. 1996) (alleged non-resistance does not establish consent); *Parrish v. Commonwealth*, 346 S.E.2d 736 (Va. App. 1986) (rape statute does not require physical resistance by victim); *State v. McKnight*, 774 P.2d 532 (Wash. App. 1989) (isolation in defendant's apartment and "physical weakness" of the 14-year-old victim could lead a reasonable jury to conclude that resistance was reasonable given the circumstances); *Scadden v. State*, 732 P.2d 1036 (Wyo. 1987) (manifested opposition to rape does not require a victim to do more than her abilities and strength allow).

245   *State v. Rusk*, 289 Md. 230 (1981).

246   *See* Estrich, *supra* note 4, at p. 63.

247   *Id.* at 62 (noting that "Rusk had been convicted of second-degree rape in violation of Maryland Code art. 27, sec 463(a)(1), which provides in part: "A person is guilty of rape in the second degree if the person engages in vaginal intercourse with another person: (1) By force or threat of force against the will and without the consent of the other person." ANNOTATED CODE OF THE PUBLIC GENERAL LAWS OF MARYLAND (Charlottesville, Va.: Michie, 1982), Vol. 3A, art. 27, Sec. 463(a)(1), at p. 455).

248   *State v. Rusk*, 43 Md. App. 476, 478–479.

249   *Rusk*, 289 Md. 230, 255 (Cole, J., dissenting).

250   *See* Estrich, *supra* note 4, at p. 65 (noting that "[t]his is exactly how Judge Wilner, the dissenting judge in the Court of Appeals, characterizes the majority's decision to reverse Rusk's conviction. *Rusk v. State*, 43 Md. App. at 498. The Supreme Court dissenters, for their part, attacked that majority for declaring her innocent: 'The law regards rape as a crime of violence. The majority today attenuates this proposition. It declares the innocence of an at best distraught women. It does not demonstrate the defendant's guilty of the crime of rape.' *State v. Rusk*, 289 Md. at 255–256 (Cole J., dissenting). The debate quite clearly is focused not so much on whether Rusk is a rapist but on whether [the woman] is a real victim").

251   *Rusk*, 289 Md. at 246–247.

252   *Goldberg v. Maryland*, 41 Md. App. 58 (1979) (involving an 18-year-old girl who thought she would be modeling, but was duped into going to a condominium with a man who would later allegedly rape her. At trial, the girl testified that she was afraid and that appellant said he would not hurt her. The girl testified that the man was bigger than she was and that, because there were no buildings near, she felt trapped. On cross-examination, the young woman testified that she thought she was "going to be killed." Despite this testimony, the Court of Special Appeals held that overall the evidence was not enough to sustain the jury's finding of guilt, because the young girl's testimony had not established that she had either exerted sufficient resistance and/or that she had failed to do so because she had a reasonable fear of bodily harm).

253   *People v. Warren*, 446 N.E.2d 591 (Ill. App. 1983).

254   *State v. Alston*, 312 S.E.2d 470 (1984).

255   *Alston*, 312 S.E.2d at 471.

256   *Id.* at 472–473.

257   *Id.* at 476.

258   *See People v. Howard*, 555 N.Y.S.2d 376, 377 (A.D. 1990).

259   *See, e.g., Commonwealth v. Titus*, 556 A.2d 1425 (Pa. Super. 1989); *State v. Schaim*, 600 N.E.2d 661 (Ohio 1992).

260   *See People v. Yeadon*, 548 N.Y.S.2d 468 (A.D. 1989).

261   *See, e.g., People v. Senior*, 2 Cal. App. 4th 765, 775 (1992); *People v. Hodges*, 612 N.Y.S.2d 420 (A.D. 1994); *Powe v State*, 597 So.2d 721 (Ala. 1991); *Caldwell v. State*, 891 S.W.2d 420 (Ark. 1995); *Commonwealth v. Dorman*, 547 A.2d 757 (Pa. Super. 1988); *State v. Eskridge*, 526 N.E.2d 304, 306 (Ohio 1988) (holding that a father may be convicted of raping a child, though the force he may use may "subtle and psychological" as opposed to physical).

262   *See, e.g., State v. Waites*, 1994 Ohio App. Lexis 3651, at * 15 (holding, in the case of a man posing as a doctor, which allowed him to fondle several girls and have sexual intercourse with at least one (a learning disabled child), that although "appellant's conduct was deceitful and reprehensible;...unlike [a situation involving] a parent, there is no implicit threat of punishment for not complying"). *Compare State v. Eskridge*, 526 N.E.2d 304, 306 (Ohio 1988).

263   *See* Schulhofer, *supra* note 70, at p. 46.

264   For review of the current state and application of "rape shield" law, *see supra* note 226.

265   *See* Bevacqua, *supra* note 70, at p. 96.

266   *See New Hampshire v. Colbath*, 130 N.H. 316 (1988).

267   *See* Francis, *supra* note 60, at p. 123.

268   *Doe v. United States*, 666 F.2d 43 (4th Cir. 1981).

269   See Francis, *supra* note 60, at p. 123.
270   *United States v. Saunders*, 938 F.2d 388 (4th Cir. 1991).
271   See *Saunders*, 943 F.2d at 390.
272   *Id.*
273   *Id.*
274   *Id.*
275   *Id.* at 391.
276   *Id.* (citing Spector & Foster, *Rule 412 and the Doe Case: The Fourth Circuit Turns Back the Clock*, 35 OKLA. L. REV. at pp. 96–97 (1982): [T]he court arrogated to itself the authority to declare that the categorical mandate expressed in the rule did not fully articulate Congress's intent. Furthermore, the court fashioned and propounded its own exception to the rule's explicit ban on previous sexual behavior, an exception unauthorized by legislative fiat that is of such magnitude that its very existence threatens to…vitiate the utility of Rule 412 as a means of implementing the federal legislative purposes motivating its enactment.") *But see* Galvin, *Shielding Rape Victims in the State and Federal Courts: A Proposal for the Second Decade*, 70 MINN. L. REV. 763 at pp. 890–93 (1986).
277   The federal law the Fourth Circuit cites is Title 18, Chapter 109A and 18 U.S.C. Sec. 2241, which the court deemed applicable in this case.
278   *Saunders*, 943 F.2d at 391 *(emphasis added)*.
279   *Id.* (citing *United States v. Torres*, 937 F.2d 1469, 1471 (9th Cir. 1991); *United States v. Duran*, 886 F.2d 167, 168 n. 3 (8th Cir. 1989)).
280   *Id.*
281   *Id.* at 392. *See also Chenowith v. State*, 905 S.W.2d 838 (Ark. 1995).
282   See, e.g., *People v. Verona*, 143 Cal. App. 3d 566 (Cal. App. 1983); *New York v. Doe*, 170 Misc.2d 762 (A.D. 1996); *New Mexico v. Johnson*, 121 N.M. 77 (N.M. App. 1995); *People v. Casas*, 181 Cal. App. 3d 889 (Cal. App. 1986). *See also* Tracy Wilkinson, *Victim of Alleged Rape May Have Fled Because of History as Prostitute*, L.A. TIMES, Nov. 17, 1990, at B3.
283   *Saunders*, 943 F.2d at 392.
284   *Id.*
285   See, e.g., *U.S. v. Norrquay*, 987 F.2d 475 (8th Cir. 1993), *app. after rem.*; *U.S. v. Schoenborn*, 19 F.3d 1438, *cert. den.*, 115 S. Ct. 284 (holding that a defendant's need to employ force generally will indicate a lack of consent); *State v. Jackson*, 620 A.2d 168 (Conn. 1993) (holding that the victim of a potential rape need not resist to the point of physical injury in order to establish that she did not consent to the acts); *State v. Mezriouri*, 602 A.2d 29 (Conn. App. 1992) (holding that a woman need not say no or physically resist); *State v. Sedia*, 614 So.2d 533 (Fla. App. 4 Dist. 1993) (holding that a where a physical therapy patient had no opportunity to communicate her unwillingness to have sex, she was "physically helpless to resist" the encounter within the meaning of Florida sexual abuse law); *State v. Simmons*, 621 So.2d 1135 (La. App. 4 Cir. 1993), *amended on reh'ring* (holding that as defined by law, the act of forcible rape occurs upon a victim "without consent; upon a victim who was prevented from resisting by force or threat of physical violence; and who reasonably believed that resistance would not prevent rape"); *State v. Gallen*, 613 So.2d 1145 (La. App. 5 Cir. 1993) (defining that the difference between aggravated and forcible rape is the degree of force used by the defendant and the amount of resistance attempted by the victim); *Commonwealth v. Price*, 616 A.2d 681 (Pa. Super. 1992) (clarifying that the subsection of the Pennsylvania criminal statutes proscribing intercourse with "unconscious" people was intended to protect persons not able to give or refuse consent to intercourse due to their unconscious state); *Commonwealth v. Berkowitz*, 641 A.2d 1161 (Pa. 1994) (holding that where there is a lack of consent, but no showing of either a threat or physical force, "forcible compulsion" requirement of the rape statute was not met); *State v. Jackson*, 679 A.2d 572 (N.H. 1996) (holding that "consent" issue involves objective manifestation of unwillingness).
286   See, e.g., *Portuondo v. Agard*, 529 U.S. 61 (2000), *rev'sing and rem'ding* 117 F.3d 696 (1998).
287   See Benedict, *supra* note 44, ENDNOTES FOR INTRODUCTION, at pp. 18–19.
288   See, e.g., *United States v. Galloway*, 937 F.2d 542 (10th Cir. 1991), *cert. den.*, 506 U.S. 957, 113 S. Ct. 418, 121 L. Ed. 2d 341 (1992) (holding that a complainant's use of contraceptives was inadmissible because it might be interpreted as a readiness for sexual activity); *United States v. One Feather*, 702 F.2d 736 (8th Cir. 1983) (holding that testimony regarding a complainant's "illegitimate" child was inadmissible); *State v. Carmichael*, 727 P.2d 918, 925 (Kan. 1986) (holding evidence of a venereal disease inadmissible). Some scholars note, however, that where the evidence of a complainant's past sexual history is a lack of sexual history, courts have seen no problem with admitting it. *See, e.g., People v. Johnson*, 671 P.2d 1017 (Colo. App. 1983) (holding that there was no error where a doctor was allowed to testify that a complainant was a virgin); *Forrester v. State*, 440 N.E.2d 475 (Ind. 1982) (holding that testimony regarding the recently injury to a complainant's hymen was appropriate given that the state rape shield statute was intended to protect the victim of rape, not the accused); *State v. Singleton*, 102 N.M. 66 (N.M. App. 1984) (holding that testimony of a complainant's pleas to defendant not to rape her because she was a virgin was properly admitted).

289 *See* PRIMETIME LIVE, ABC-TV, Sept. 26, 2002, (Cynthia McFadden reporting). (McFadden reported on an interview with convicted rapist and murderer Mathias Reyes, who confessed on camera to attacking the jogger. New York authorities were reportedly investigating the claim.)

290 *See New Hampshire v. Colbath*, 130 N.H. 316 (1988).

291 *See Portuondo v. Agard, supra* note 286.

292 *Id.* at 63.

293 *People v. Agard*, 199 A.D.2d 401 (2 Dept. 1993).

294 According to Justice Scalia, writing for the Court, "[d]uring summation, defense counsel charged [the two women involved] with lying. The prosecutor similarly focused on the credibility of the witnesses. She stressed respondent's interest in the outcome of the trial, his prior felony conviction, and his prior bad acts. She argued that respondent was a 'smooth slick character...who had an answer for everything,' and that 'part of his testimony sound[ed] rehearsed.' Finally, over defense objection, the prosecutor remarked: 'You know, ladies and gentlemen, unlike all the other witnesses in this case the defendant has a benefit and the benefit that he has, unlike all the other witnesses, is he gets to sit here and listen to the testimony of all the other witnesses before he testifies. * * * * That gives you a big advantage, doesn't it? You get to sit here and think what am I going to say and how am I going to say it? How am I going to fit it into the evidence? He's a smart man. I never said he was stupid.... He used everything to his advantage." *See Portuondo, supra* note 286, at p. 63–64.

295 *See People v. Agard*, 83 N.Y.2d 868 (1994).

296 *See Francis, supra* note 60, at p. 123.

297 This law is codified at 108 STAT. 1796, PUB. L. 103–322 (1994).

298 *See* 42 U.S.C. Sec. 13981(b).

299 *See* 42 U.S.C. Sec. 13981(a).

300 *Id.*

301 *See* Linda Greenhouse, *Justices Cool to Law Protecting Women*, N.Y. TIMES, Jan. 12, 2000, at A15.

302 The stated purpose of the Violence Against Women Act was "...to protect the civil rights of victims of gender-motivated violence and to promote public safety, health, and activities affecting interstate commerce by establishing a federal civil rights cause of action for victims of crimes of violence motivated by genders." 42 U.S.C. Sec. 13981(a). In addition, Sec. 13981(c) sets forth that "[a] person (including a person who acts under color of any stature, ordinance, regulation, custom, or usage of any state) who commits a crime of violence motivated by gender and thus deprives another of the right declared in subsection (b) of this section shall be liable to the party injured, in an action for the recovery of compensatory and punitive damages, injunctive and declaratory relief, and such other relief as a court may deem appropriate." The act defined a "crime of violence" as "...an act or series of acts that would constitute a felony." Further, Sec. 13981(e)(2) stated that "nothing in this section requires a prior criminal complaint, prosecution, or conviction to establish the elements of a cause of action under subsection (c) of this section."

303 *See* Linda Greenhouse, *Battle on Federalism*, N.Y. TIMES, May 17, 2000, at A16.

304 *See* 42 U.S.C. Sec. 13981(c).

305 *See* 42 U.S.C. Sec. 13981(d)(1).

306 *See* 42 U.S.C. Sec. 13981(d)(2).

307 *See* 42 U.S.C. Sec. 13981(e)(2).

308 *See* 42 U.S.C. Sec. 13981(e)(3).

309 *See* STAFF OF SENATE COMM. ON THE JUDICIARY, VAWA, S. REP. 138, 103D CONG., 2D SESS. (1994), at pp. 48–54.

310 *See* 42 U.S.C. Sec. 13981(a); *United States v. Morrison* and *Brzonkala v. Morrison*, 120 S. Ct. 1740 (2000).

311 *See* Linda Greenhouse, *Justices to Rule on Right of Women to Sue Their Attackers*, N.Y. TIMES, Sept. 29, 1999, at A21.

312 *Brzonkala v. Virginia Polytechnic and State University*, 132 F.3d 949 (4th Cir. 1997).

313 *United States v. Morrison*, 120 S. Ct. 1740 (2000).

314 *See Civil Rights Law on Rape Victims is Unconstitutional, Court Says*, ASSOCIATED PRESS, March 5, 1999 (reprinted N.Y. TIMES, March 6, 1999, at A8).

315 *See United States v. Morrison*, 120 S. Ct. 1740, 1476 (2000).

316 *See Brzonkala v. Virginia Polytechnic and State University*, 132 F.3d 950, 955 (4th Cir. 1997).

317 *See* 86 STAT. 373-375, 20 U.S.C. Sec. 1681–1688.

318 *See* Greenhouse, *supra* note 311, at A21.

319 *See* Greenhouse, *supra* note 301, at A15.

320 *See Brzonkala v. Virginia Polytechnic Institute and State University*, 935 F. Supp. at 772 (W.D. Va. 1996).

321 *Id.* at 779.

322 *See Brzonkala v. Virginia Polytechnic and State University*, 132 F.3d 949 (4th Cir. 1997).

323 *See Morrison, supra* note 315, at 1747, n. 2 (explaining that "[t]he *en banc* Court of Appeals affirmed the District Court's conclusion that Brzonkala failed to state a claim alleging disparate treatment under Title IX, but vacated the District Court's dismissal of her hostile environment claim and remanded with instructions for the District Court to hold the claim in abeyance pending this Court's decision in *Davis v. Monroe County Bd.*, 526 U.S. 629 (1999) (citing *Brzonkala v.*

Virginia Polytechnic and State University, 169 F.3d 820, 827, n. 2 (4th Cir. 1999). Our grant of *certiorari* did not encompass Brzonkala's Title IX claims, and we thus do not consider them in this opinion")).

324   *See Brzonkala v. Virginia Polytechnic and State University*, 169 F.3d 820 (4th Cir. 1999).
325   *See* Greenhouse, *supra* note 311, at A21.
326   *See Brzonkala v. Virginia Polytechnic and State University*, 169 F.3d 820 (4th Cir. 1999).
327   *See* Greenhouse, *supra* note 311, at A21.
328   *Id.*
329   *Id.*
330   *Id.*
331   *See* Greenhouse, *supra* note 303, at A16.
332   *Id.*
333   *Id.* at A21.
334   Among the federal courts to uphold the Violence Against Women Act was the Federal District Court for the Southern District of New York. *See Federal Gender Violence Law Upheld*, NAT'L L.J., April 26, 1999, at A6.
335   *See* Linda Greenhouse, *Justices, by a Narrow Margin, Void Women's Right to Sue Attackers in Federal Court*, N.Y. TIMES, May 16, 2002, at A14.
336   *See* Greenhouse, *supra* note 301, at A15.
337   *Id.*
338   *See* Marcia Coyle, *What's Left After "Morrison,"* NAT'L L.J., May 29, 2000, at A1, A11.
339   *Id.*
340   That year, the United States Supreme Court's term began on October 4, 1999, and ended on June 28, 2000.
341   *See* Linda Greenhouse, *The Court Rules, America Changes*, N.Y. TIMES, July 2, 2000, Sec. 4, at p. 1.
342   *See* Marcia Coyle, *An Activist Court Rules on Speech, Immigration and One Big Election*, NAT'L L.J., Aug. 6, 2001, at C3.
343   *See* Greenhouse, *supra* note 341, at p. 1.
344   *Id.*
345   *Id.*
346   *See* Coyle, *supra* note 342, at C3.
347   *Id.*
348   *Stenberg, et al. v. Carhart*, 120 S. Ct 865 (2000). (The Nebraska statute at issue provided that "[n]o partial birth abortion shall be performed in this state, unless such procedure is necessary to save the life of the mother whose life is endangered by a physical disorder, physical injury, including a life-endangering physical condition caused by or arising from the pregnancy itself." *See* Neb. Rev. Stat. Ann. Sec. 28-328(1) (Supp. 1999). But the Nebraska statute defined "partial-birth abortion" as "an abortion procedure in which the person performing the abortion partially delivers vaginally a living unborn child before killing the unborn child and completing the delivery." *See* Neb. Rev. Stat. Ann. Sec. 28-326(9). What was troubling for the Justices, however, was that the statute also defined "partially delivers vaginally a living unborn child before killing the unborn to" mean "deliberately and intentionally delivering into the vagina a living unborn child, or a substantial portion thereof, for the purpose of performing a procedure that the person performing such procedure knows will kill the unborn child and does kill the unborn child." *Id.* Violation of the Nebraska law was deemed a "Class III felony" carrying a possible prison sentence of up to 20 years, a $25,000 fine, and the automatic revocation of a doctor's license. *See* Neb. Rev. Stat. Ann. Sec. 28-328(4) The Nebraska statute, challenged before the court by Leroy Carhart, a Nebraska physician, was held unconstitutional by the United States Supreme Court.)
349   *See* Greenhouse, *supra* note 341, at p. 1.
350   *Id.* at 5.
351   *See* Coyle, *supra* note 342, at A1, A11.
352   *See* Greenhouse, *supra* note 311, at A21.
353   *See* Coyle, *supra* note 342, at A1, A11.
354   *Id.*
355   *Id.*
356   *See* Greenhouse, *supra* note 341, at p. 5.
357   *See Morrison*, *supra* note 315, at 1748 (quoting *Marbury v. Madison*, 1 Cranch 137, 175 (1803)).
358   *See* 42 U.S.C. Sec. 13981(a).
359   *See Morrison*, *supra* note 315, at 1748 (citing *United States v. Lopez*, 514 U.S. 549, 568, 577–578 (1995) (Kennedy J., concurring); *United States v. Harris*, 106 U.S. 629, 635 (1883)).
360   514 U.S. 549 (1995).
361   The syllabus of *United States v. Lopez*, 514 U.S. 549 (1995), notes that Chief Justice Rehnquist delivered the opinion for the Court with Justices O'Connor, Scalia, Kennedy, and Thomas joining. The syllabus in *United States v. Morrison*, 120 S. Ct. 1740 (2000), similarly notes that Chief Justice Rehnquist delivered the opinion for the Court with Justices O'Connor, Scalia, Kennedy, and Thomas joining.

362 301 U.S. 1 (1937).

363 In *Lopez*, the majority held that "...even [our] modern-era precedents which have expended congressional power under the Commerce Clause confirm that this power is subject to outer limits. In *Jones & Laughlin Steel*, the Court warned that the scope of the interstate commerce power 'must be considered in the light of our dual system of government and may not be extended so as to embrace effects upon interstate commerce so indirect and remote that to embrace them, in view of our complex society, would effectually obliterate the distinction between what is national and what is local and create a completely centralized government.'" *Lopez*, 514 U.S. at 556–557 (quoting *Jones & Laughlin Steel*, 301 U.S. at 37).

364 *See Lopez*, 514 U.S. at 558 (citing *Hodel v. Virginia Surface Mining & Reclamation Assn., Inc.*, 452 U.S. 264, 276–77 (1981); *Perez v. United States*, 402 U.S. 146, 150 (1971)).

365 *See Morrison*, supra note 315, at 1750 (citing *Heart of Atlanta Motel, Inc. v. United States*, 379 U.S. 241, 256 (1964); *United States v. Darby*, 312 U.S. 100, 114 (1941)).

366 *Id.* at 1749 (citing *Lopez*, 514 U.S. at 558; *Shreveport Rate Cases*, 234 U.S. 342 (1914); *Southern R.R. Co. v. United States*, 222 U.S. 20 (1911); *Perez*, supra note 364).

367 *Lopez*, 514 U.S. at 558–559 (citing *Jones & Laughlin Steel*, 301 U.S. at 37).

368 *See* Linda Greenhouse, *Women Lost Right to Sue Attackers in Federal Court*, N.Y. TIMES, May 16, 2000, at A1.

369 *See Morrison*, supra note 315, at 1749.

370 *Id.* (The majority noted that "[i]n *Lopez*, we held that the Gun-Free School Zones Act of 1990, 18 U.S.C. Sec. 922(q)(1)(A), which made it a federal crime to knowingly possess a firearm in a school zone, exceeded Congress's authority under the Commerce Clause." *Lopez*, 514 U.S. at 551. "Several significant considerations contributed to our decision. First, we observed that Sec. 922(q) was 'a criminal statute that by its terms has nothing to do with "commerce" or any sort of economic enterprise, however broadly one might define those terms.' *Id.* at 561. Reviewing our case law, we noted that 'we have upheld a wide variety of congressional Acts regulating intrastate economic activity where we have concluded that the activity substantially affected interstate commerce.' *Id.* at 559. Although we cited only a few examples, including *Wickard v. Filburn*, 317 U.S.111 (1942); *Hodel, supra*; *Perez supra*; *Katzenbach v. McClung*, 379 U.S. 294 (1964); *Heart of Atlanta Model, supra*, we stated that the pattern of analysis is clear. *Lopez*, 514 U.S., at 559–560. 'Where economic activity substantially affects interstate commerce, legislation regulating that activity will be sustained.'" *Id.* at 560.)

371 *Id.* at 1750 (citing *Lopez*, 514 U.S. at 551 (noting that "'[t]he Act [d]oes not] regulat[e] a commercial activity'), 560 ('Even *Wickard*, which is perhaps the most far reaching example of Commerce Clause authority over intrastate activity, involved economic activity in a way that the possession of a gun in a school zone does not'), 561 ('Section 922(q) is not an essential part of a larger regulation of economic activity'), 566 ('Admittedly, a determination whether an intrastate activity is commercial or noncommercial may in some cases result in legal uncertainty. But, so long as Congress's authority is limited to those powers enumerated in the Constitution, and so long as those enumerated powers are interpreted as having judicially enforceable outer limits, congressional legislation under the Commerce Clause always will engender legal uncertainty'), 567 ('The possession of a gun in a local school zone is in no sense an economic activity that might, through repetition elsewhere, substantially affect any sort of interstate commerce'); *see also id.* at 573–574 (Kennedy, J., concurring) (Stating that *Lopez* did not alter our 'practical conception of commercial regulation' and that Congress may 'regulate in the commercial sphere on the assumption that we have a single market and a unified purpose to build a stable national economy'), 577 ('Were the federal government to take over the regulation of entire areas of traditional state concern, areas having nothing to do with the regulation of commercial activities, the boundaries between the spheres of federal and state authority would blur'), 580 ('[U]nlike the earlier cases to come before the Court here neither the actors nor their conduct has a commercial character, and neither the purposes nor the design of the statute has an evident commercial nexus. The statute makes the simple possession of a gun within 1,000 feet of the grounds of the school a criminal offense. In a sense any conduct in this interdependent world of ours has an ultimate commercial origin or consequence, but we have not yet said the commerce power may reach so far' (citation omitted)). *Lopez*'s review of Commerce Clause case law demonstrates that in those cases where we have sustained federal regulation of intrastate activity based upon the activity's substantial effects on interstate commerce, the activity in question has been some sort of economic endeavor").

372 *Id.* at 1751 (citing *Lopez*, 514 U.S. at 562).

373 *Id.* (citing *Ibid.* quoting Brief for United States, O.T. 1994, No. 93-1260, at pp. 5–6).

374 *See Lopez*, 514 U.S. at 562 (citing *McClung*, 379 U.S. at 304; *Perez*, 402 U.S. at 156).

375 *Id.* at 563.

376 *See Morrison*, supra note 315, at 1751 (citing *Lopez*, 514 U.S. at 563–567, with the majority noting that "[t]he United States argued that the possession of guns may lead to violent crime, and that violent crime, 'can be expected to affect the functioning of the national economy in two ways. First, the costs of violent crime was substantial, and, through the mechanism of insurance, those costs are spread throughout the population. Second, violent crime reduces the willingness of individu-

als to travel to areas within the country that are perceived to be unsafe.' *Id.* at 563–564 (citation omitted). The Government also argued that the presence of guns at school poses a threat to the educational process, which in turn threatens to produce a less efficient and productive workforce, which will negatively affect national productivity and thus interstate commerce. *Id.*")

377   *See Morrison, supra* note 315 at 1752 (citing H.R. CONF. REP. NO. 103-711, p. 385 (1994); S. REP. NO. 103-138, p. 40 (1993); S. REP. NO. 101-545 (1990), at p. 33).

378   *See Morrison, supra* note 315, at 1761 (citing H.R. REP. NO. 103-395, at p. 25 (1993) (further citation omitted)).

379   *Id.* (citing S. REP. NO. 103-138, p. 38 (1993) (citing Surgeon General Antonio Novello, *From the Surgeon General, U.S. Public Health Services,* 267 JAMA at p. 3132 (1992))).

380   *Id.* at 1762 (citing S. REP. NO. 101-545, at 33 (further citation omitted)).

381   *Id.* (citing S. REP. NO. 101-545, at 31 (citing R. Warshaw, I NEVER CALLED IT RAPE 117 (1988)).

382   *Id.* (citing S. REP. NO. 101-545, at p. 43 (further citing the testimony of Dr. Mary Koss before the Senate Judiciary Committee, Aug. 29, 1990)).

383   *Id.* at 1752. (The majority noted further that "'[a]s we stated in *Lopez,* '[S]imply because Congress may conclude that a particular activity substantially affects interstate commerce does not necessarily make it so.'" 514 U.S. at 557, no. 2 (quoting *Hodel,* 452 U.S. at 311 (Rehnquist, J. concurring in judgment)). Rather, "[w]hether particular operations affect interstate commerce sufficiently to come under the constitutional power of Congress to regulate them is ultimately a judicial rather than a legislative question, and can be settled finally only by this Court." 514 U.S. at 557, no. 2 (quoting *Heart of Atlanta Motel,* 379 U.S. at 273) (Black, J., concurring).)

384   *Id.* at 1754.

385   *Id.* (citing *Lopez,* 514 U.S. at 568; *Jones & Laughlin Steel,* 301 U.S. at 30).

386   *Id.* (citing *Cohens v. Virginia,* 6 Wheat 264, 426, 428 (1821) (Marshall, C.J.,) (stating that Congress "has no general right to punish murder committed within any of the States," and that it is "clear…that [C]ongress cannot punish felonies generally").

387   *Id.* (citing *U.S. v. Lopez,* 514 U.S. at 566 ("The Constitution…withhold[s] from Congress a plenary police power") (Thomas, J., concurring) ("[W]e always have rejected readings of the Commerce Clause and the scope of federal power that would permit Congress to exercise a police power"); *U.S. v. Lopez,* 514 U.S. at 596–597, and n. 6 (noting that the first Congresses did not enact nationwide punishments for criminal conduct under the Commerce Clause).

388   *Id.* at 1758.

389   *Id.* (The majority offered that "[f]or example, in *Katzenbach v. Morgan,* 384 U.S. 641 (1966), Congress prohibited New York from imposing literary tests as a prerequisite for voting because it found that such a requirement disenfranchised thousands of Puerto Rican immigrants who has been educated in the Spanish language of their home territory. That law, which we upheld, was directed at New York officials who administered the State's election law and prohibited them from using a provision of that law. In *South Carolina v. Katzenbach,* 383 U.S. 301 (1966), Congress imposed voting rights requirement on states that, Congress found, had a history of discriminating against blacks in voting. The remedy was also directed at state officials in those states. Similarly, in *Ex parte Virginia,* 100 U.S. 339 (1880), Congress criminally punished state officials who intentionally discriminated in jury selection; again, the remedy was directed to the culpable state official.")

390   *Id.* at 1759.

391   *See* Coyle, *supra* note 342, at A1, A11.

392   *See* Greenhouse, *supra* note 303, at A16.

393   *Id.*

394   *Id.*

395   *Id.*

396   *Id.*

397   *See Morrison* (Souter, J., dissenting), *supra* note 315, at 1760 (citing *Wickard v. Filburn,* 31 U.S. 111, 124–128 (1942); *Hodel v. Virginia Surface Mining & Reclamation Assn.,* 452 U.S. 264, 277 (1981)).

398   *Id.*

399   *Id.* at 1761–63.

400   *Id.* at 1763.

401   *Id.* at 1764.

402   *See* Greenhouse, *supra* note 303, at A16.

403   *Id.*

404   *See* Greenhouse, *supra* note 335, at A14.

405   *Carter v. Carter Coal Co.,* 298 U.S. 238 (1936) (holding that the regulation of unfair labor practices in mining production was not "commerce").

406   *Schechter Poultry Corp. v. United States,* 295 U.S. 495 (1935) (holding invalid the regulation of activities that "indirectly" affected commerce).

407   *National League of Cities v. Usery,* 426 U.S. 883 (1976) (later overruled by *Garcia v. San Antonio Metropolitan Transit Authority,* 469 U.S. 528 (1985)).

408   *Redrup v. New York,* 386 U.S. 767 (1967) (*per curiam*).

409   *Miller v. California,* 413 U.S. 15 (1973).

410   *See Morrison* (Souter, J., dissenting), *supra* note 315, at 1773.
411   *Id*. at 1774 (citing O. Holmes, THE COMMON LAW 167 (Howe ed. 1963)).
412   *Id*.
413   *See* Coyle, *supra* note 342, at A1, A11.
414   *Id*.
415   528 U.S. 141 (2000).
416   *See* Coyle, *supra* note 342, at A1, A11.
417   *See* Greenhouse, *supra* note 335, at A14.
418   *Id*.
419   *Id*.
420   *Id*.
421   *See* Tony Mauro and Jonathan Ringel, *Women Can't Sue Under VAWA, Court Rules*, TEXAS LAWYER, May 22, 2000, at 2.
422   *See Judge Orders Rapist to Pay Victim $3 Million*, NAT'L L.J., August 13, 2001, at B3.
423   *See Bill Passed to Toughen Law on 'Date-Rape' Drug*, N.Y. TIMES, Feb. 2, 2000, at A20.
424   *See Protect Yourself: A New Way to Detect Date-Rape Drugs*, MARIE CLAIRE, July 2002, at 9. (The strips may be ordered at www.drinksafetech.com.)
425   *See* Bill Dedman, *A Rape Defendant with No Identity, But a DNA Profile*, N.Y. TIMES, Oct. 7, 1999, at A1.
426   *See* Newsome, *supra* note 29, at p. 168.
427   *Id. See also* C.J. Chivers, *Statutes of Limitations Under Fire as DNA Use in Rape Cases Grows*, N.Y. TIMES, Feb. 9, 2000, at A1.
428   *See* Newsome, *supra* note 29, at p. 168.
429   *See Why 500,000 Rape Cases Are Still Unsolved*, MARIE CLAIRE, August 2002, at p. 125.
430   *Id*.

CHAPTER FIFTEEN

The Private Story of Private Abuse

BATTERY BEGINS AT HOME:
Private Crimes or Public Health Problems

Former United States Attorney General Janet Reno characterized domestic violence as a "public health problem" during a speech before a Women Lawyers of Achievement award luncheon in August 1993. And she drew the ire of critics, journalist Barbara Victor and attorney Raoul Felder among them.

"Domestic violence is a crime," Victor and Felder argue, that "becomes a public health problem when physical injury and psychological trauma (if they don't result in death) are seen and treated by health care providers in hospitals and private offices."[1]

Victor and Felder concede that cooperation between members of the medical and legal professions makes a difference once a person enters the criminal justice system in terms of treatment, testimony, and prosecution. But domestic violence is a crime "that causes, just as stranger crime does, physical and emotional injuries," Victor and Felder argue.[2]

Few dispute that there is "a problem," though many may debate the name. In addition to Reno, Felder, and Victor, there are others who argue, for example, that the term "domestic violence" is itself misleading because it implies that the "problem" is smaller or less urgent than it actually is. But by either classification or any name, what is clear is about domestic violence in America is that it happens daily; its fallout is at times deadly; and its victims are overwhelmingly women who are being battered by "loved ones."

"Violence against women is primarily partner violence," according to a 1998 report issued by the United States Department of Justice, Bureau of Justice Statistics. Roughly 76 percent of the women 18 and older who reported rapes or physical assaults were raped or assaulted by "a current or former husband, cohabiting partner, or date, compared with 18 percent of men," according to the report.[3]

It is a trend in modern events that caselaw and media reports bear out. In February 1998, for example, former heavyweight boxing champion Riddick Bowe decided to get his estranged wife Judy back. The two had dated since they were 14 and had several children. But Judy left Bowe in April of 1997, after Bowe "knocked her unconscious," according to media reports.[4] "That was the first time he had ever knocked me out," Judy Bowe said in an interview. "I remember my youngest boy, Julius, telling the other kids when they came home that 'Daddy killed Mommy.' They had stopped noticing and stopped crying. They were getting used to it way too much."[5]

But that was ten months before the day that Bowe decided to get Judy back. During the intervening period, Bowe had "hung a portrait of her minister in his house and sent Judy a Mercedes truck"[6] in the hopes of regaining her affection. Nothing worked. So Bowe and his brother climbed into a Lincoln Navigator, drove to the town where Judy was staying and began "prowling" the streets. Then, at about 6:30 A.M., he spotted three of his children waiting at a bus stop. He told them to get into the car. They did, and soon afterwards they headed towards his wife's home.

When Bowe arrived, Judy was still in her pajamas. Bowe ordered her and the couple's two smaller children into the car as well and he began to drive. At some point during the "drive," Bowe reportedly "opened a bag filled with duct tape, a buck knife, and pepper spray and announced, 'I came prepared.'"[7] But as it would happen, a car full of children would prevail.

During a stop at a McDonald's, Judy Bowe went to the bathroom and called a friend on her cell phone. The friend notified the police. She also called a friend of Bowe's who promised to have Bowe admitted to a psychiatric hospital if she did not have him arrested. The police eventually pulled Bowe over and Judy and the children were taken home, while Riddick Bowe was driven by limousine to a hospital. But he was charged by federal authorities with interstate domestic violence, and in June 1998, Bowe pleaded guilty to the charges.[8]

It is possible that the public doesn't really expect much from the Riddick Bowes of the world outside of a boxing ring. Indeed, he may be—as this incident seems to suggest—more of a fighter than a lover. As a nation, America expects a great deal from sports figures on the court or rounding the bases on the field. But we have accepted less in their day-to-day lives. Like Bowe, boxer Sugar Ray Leonard had a few scrapes with the law revolving around the issue of domestic violence. And yet, the public still thinks of him as brilliant. One-time baseball hero Darryl Strawberry is understood today to be a "troubled" soul, but less for the incidents of domestic battery than for the drug addiction and other problems with the law that will keep him out of the Hall of Fame.[9]

There are other elite athletes in this less-than-elite club. Among them: "former University of Alabama basketball coach Wimp Sanderson; former heavyweight champ Mike Tyson, cited [for striking] then-wife Robin Givens and subsequently convicted of raping Miss Black Rhode Island; California Angels pitcher Donnie Moore, who shot and wounded his estranged wife, Tonya, before killing himself in 1989; and the Philadelphia Eagles defensive lineman Blenda Gay, stabbed to death in 1976 by his battered wife, Roxanne, who said she acted in self-defense," writer Ann Jones notes.[10]

Of course, the problem of domestic abuse is not limited to sports figures or the cold calculation of government statistics. Rather, as the Bowe incident suggests, news reports tend to tell the story as well. By some estimates, a woman is physically abused every nine to fifteen seconds in the United States.[11] Others suggest that the numbers may be closer to every 12 seconds.[12] Still others suggest that either or both of these numbers is too "high" and are the "exaggeration" of feminists. And yet, the slightest glimpse at the volume and variety of "domestic violence" claims heard by the courts each year suggest that the above numbers are in the ball park.

In February 1999, an elderly man in Nebraska shot his wife of 57 years to death.[13] In September 2001, a 23-year-old man shot and killed his girlfriend while she sat in a parked car outside his Long Island home. The man then killed himself. The woman's child sat in the backseat of the car the entire time.[14] In October 2001, a 49-year-man, described in media reports as a "successful businessman and a leader of the Washington Heights neighborhood in Manhattan" was found guilty of murdering his former girlfriend in a scene befitting of a tragic opera: he shot the woman on her wedding day as she stood—in her wedding dress—presenting bouquets to bridesmaids gathered in her living room before the ceremony.[15]

The day after Valentine's Day in February of 2000, the following item appears in *The New York Times*:

> They had little or nothing in common. And in the normal course of events, it is unlikely their worlds would ever have intersected.
>
> Kathleen A. Roskot, 19, the daughter of middle-class parents on Long Island, was a star athlete on the Columbia University lacrosse team. Marie Jean-Paul, 39, known to her friends as Carol, grew up in Haiti, and worked as a nurse's aide at a hospital in Brooklyn. Joy Thomas, 18, graduated from Mount Vernon High School in June and was studying to be a teacher at Westchester Community College.
>
> Yet in the course of 48 hours, the lives of these three women were abruptly and horribly linked together: they were, all three, the targets of homicidal attacks by men with whom they had had romantic relationships.[16]

Roskot's throat was reportedly cut by a Columbia student she had once dated. He used a kitchen knife. Jean-Paul's throat was also cut. But with a machete. And her estranged husband reportedly went the extra mile, dousing her body with a flammable liquid, then setting it on fire. Thomas was shot in the head. But she survived because the gun her former boyfriend held over her jammed. All three men later killed themselves.

Breaking up can be a deadly enterprise for women. And yet, staying in a relationship with a violent partner is not much safer. For example, among the "intimate partner" violence cases heard by the courts was *People v. M.D.*, an Illinois case involving charges of criminal sexual assault against a husband who thrust his fist—cradling an egg—into his wife's vagina. He was later convicted.[17]

In *People v. Vega*, a California Appellate Court affirmed a conviction for willingly "inflicting upon a person who was the mother of his child corporal injury resulting in traumatic condition."[18] According to court documents, Vega beat his on-again, off-again girlfriend until she had a "severely swollen face, a bloody lip, and left eye...almost swollen shut." During treatment at the hospital, the woman was "placed in a neck brace." Later, her left ear had to be drained of fluid.[19]

And in *People v. Ciccarello*, the Supreme Court of New York held that a "defendant's conviction for rape in the first degree was supported by legally sufficient evidence that the defendant broke into the home of his former girlfriend, held her captive for five hours, and subjected her to sexual intercourse by forcible compulsion."[20]

Studies suggest that spousal abuse is highest "among men with some high school education and then steadily decrease[s] at higher levels of education, with an overall trend showing violent men to be less educated than their nonabusive counterparts."[21] Still, partner violence runs through all racial and age groups and across economic lines.

A WOMAN'S PLACE IS IN THE HOSPITAL:
The Statistical Side of Domestic Violence and Murder

Domestic—or "intimate partner"—violence, as it is referred to in Justice Department reports, is among these categories of crime for which data is collected and compiled by federal officials. According to that data, in 1998 "women were victims in about 876,340" violent incidents, which is far more than men, who were "victims in about 157,330" violent incidents."[22]

In addition, though women have long been taught to fear dark alleys and lonely streets, women were more likely in 1998, and every other year, "to be victimized by nonstrangers, which includes a friend, family member, or intimate partner, while men were more likely to be victimized by a stranger," according to Justice Department figures. Although "intimate partner" violent crime rates fell nationwide for women from roughly 1.1 million in 1993 to 848,480 in 1997, intimate partner victimization rates fell similarly for men between 1993 and 1998.[23]

But women were still the victims of domestic or intimate partner violence far more often than men: 7.5 to 7.7 per every 1,000 women compared to 1.0 per 1,000 men that same year.[24] Women are also murdered more often than men in domestic "incidents," in sizable numbers.

According to the Justice Department, in 1998 "intimate partner homicides comprised about 33 percent of the murders of women but about 4 percent of the murders of men."[25] On a national level, "intimate partner homicides" accounted for a full 11 percent of all murders, with the victims overwhelmingly female. "Of the 1,830 persons murdered by intimates in 1998, 72 percent—or 1,320—were women," according to Justice Department statistics.[26]

WHO TAKES A BEATING:
A Socio-economic Portrait of "Intimate Partner" Violence

"[W]hen we think of domestic violence, we do not think about women of means," writes psychotherapist Dr. Susan Weitzman in *Not to People Like Us: Hidden Abuse in Upscale Marriage*. "Despite occasional sensational news stories of upscale or celebrity women falling prey to a maniacal mate—Tina Turner, for example, or Pamela Anderson—the public overwhelmingly assumes that domestic violence is confined to couples with little education and few resources. And unfortunately most statistics support this belief."[27]

Though studies of domestic violence have tended traditionally to focus on the problem among women in lower-income families—largely because they call police, notes Weitzman—these findings may have "skewed society's perception of who exactly becomes an 'abused wife.'"[28]

"Middle- and upper-class women—the wives and lovers of successful, even prominent men—have rarely been studied as victims of abuse," argues Weitzman.[29]

Further confusing the picture is the assumption that well-educated women who have money or careers have the means to extricate themselves from situations of violence. This belief, coupled by the fact that fear and shame keep wealthy or educated women from reporting incidents of domestic violence in much the same way that they keep poorer women away from authorities, often prevent upper-middle-class women from being counted.[30]

Social scientists suggest that in addition to the immediate danger of domestic violence and the lasting trauma of having been a battered spouse, there may be lasting effects of a different sort as well. As a child, author Marian Betancourt heard her parents fighting. Each time she prayed that her mother wouldn't hit her father back, because she feared he would kill her. Betancourt describes her father as a "white-collar" executive. After the devastation of her parents' marriage, Betancourt and her mother began a "hardscrabble" life. And still, Betancourt grew up to marry a man who would abuse her.[31] But that choice appears to be part of a pattern for some women.

"Increased risk of adult intimate partner violence is associated with exposure to violence between a person's parents while growing up. One-third of children who have been abused or exposed to parental violence become violent adults," note the authors of *Understanding Violence Against Women*, the collaborative effort of a National Research Council's Panel on Research on Violence Against Women.[32]

Specifically, the National Research Council found that "…based on a critical review of all 52 studies conducted in the prior 15 years (including comparison groups)[33] found that the only risk marker consistently associated with being a victim of physical abuse was having witnessed parental violence as a child."[34] In addition, "[s]ons of violent parents are more likely to abuse their intimate partners than boys from nonviolent homes."[35]

Marian Betancourt appears to be among the women who prove the rule: "The first time I was beaten for refusing to cook something the way he liked it," wrote Betancourt in the 1997 book *What to Do When Love Turns Violent*. "Another time, I was beaten for having a minor accident with the car. Once I was beaten for challenging his 'order' for me to take the children to Sunday school, even though he was the one who claimed to have religious faith."[36]

Accountant Carole Kasson stayed in a violent marriage for more than a decade and continued to fear her husband after she left until he committed suicide by shooting himself in the head. Kasson called his suicide a "gift." And yet, according to Kasson, the first few months of their relationship were romantic. But there came a day during that first year, when he "threw a bowl of lentil salad across the apartment because he got mad at me for something forgettable," Kasson wrote.[37] It was just the beginning.

That too may be part of a pattern.

"[I]n about two-thirds of violent homes, there are three phases the couple goes through over and over," writes Dawn Bradley Berry, author *of The Domestic Violence Sourcebook*.[38] "The aspects of the violence may vary from home to home, but the cycle almost always has these ongoing components. First, tension builds. The man becomes edgy, critical, irritable. The woman may go out of her way to try to keep the peace during this period, 'walking on eggshells' to try to pacify him. She avoids anything she fears may set him off on a tirade.

"Meanwhile, he becomes gradually more abusive, often with 'minor' incidents such as slapping, verbal abuse, and increased control techniques. The woman allows this behavior in a desperate attempt to keep the abuse from escalating. Yet docile behavior tends to legitimize his belief that he is all-powerful and has a right to be abusive. She continues to try to control the environment and the people around him, and her isolation increases as she tries to keep things on an even keel. This uncomfortable stage may last from a few days to a period of years. Usually, both can sense the impending loss of control [the final component] and become more desperate, which only fuels the tension," Berry explains.[39]

Sally's story was a bit like that. "Sally," as Weitzman describes her, is a "a pretty, educated, forty-eight-year-old homemaker" married to "Ray, a highly successful businessman."[40] In this life, "Sally" gave "elegant parties only to be brutally beaten afterwards for offering some of her husband's favorite dessert for admiring guests to take home…. 'This is not what Martha Stewart would have had in mind,'" Ray allegedly shouted during the attack.[41]

Dinner parties? White-collar jobs and educations to boast about? It would seem that the women above may be playing against type, but they are not. It is true that "[t]he assault rate of blue-collar husbands is 70 percent greater than the assault rate of the white-collar employed husbands," according to University of Pennsylvania and University of New Hampshire sociologists Richard Gelles and Murray Strauss. "If the combined income of the couple was $9,000 or less, the rate of assault by husbands on their wives was 368 percent higher than in families with a more adequate income."[42] By contrast, "percentages gathered in the *U.S. Department of Justice's Criminal Sourcebook* suggest that in only 8 percent of reported cases of domestic attacks by a spouse or romantic companion, the income level is greater than $75,000 per year."[43]

In other words, "[a]mong women, being black, young, divorced or separated, earning lower incomes, living in rental housing and urban areas were all associated with higher rates of intimate partner victimization between 1993 and 1998," Justice Department research suggests.[44] "Overall, blacks were victimized by intimate partners at significantly higher rates than persons of any other race between 1993 and 1998," according to the Bureau of Justice Statistics. In terms of specific numbers, "[b]lack females experienced intimate partner violence at a rate 35 percent higher than that of white females, and about 22 times the rate of women of other races."[45]

It should come as no surprise then, perhaps, that "[i]ntimate partner victimization rates were significantly higher for persons living in rental housing regardless of the victim's gender," government statistics suggest. And that generally means trouble for women. In terms of specific numbers, in 1998, for example, women "residing in rental housing were victimized by…intimate partner violence at more than three times the rate of women living in owned housing, and males residing in rental housing were victimized by an intimate partner at more than twice the rate of men living in purchased housing."[46]

In addition, "[w]omen in urban areas were victims of intimate partner violence at significantly higher rates than suburban women and at somewhat higher rates than rural women. Ten per 1,000 urban women were victims of intimate partner violence compared to 8 per 1,000 women in suburban and rural areas between 1993 and 1998," data shows.[47]

Age also appears to be a factor. Women in their twenties were more likely to be victimized than others, statistics suggest. "For both women and men, rates of violence by an intimate partner were below 3 victimizations per 1,000 for persons under age 16 or over age 50." But "[w]omen ages 20–24 were victimized by an intimate partner at the highest rate, 21 per 1,000 women. This rate was about eight times the peak rate for men," Justice Department researchers note.[48]

Being poor doesn't help. "Intimate partners victimized women living in households with the lowest annual household income at a rate nearly seven times that of women living in households with the highest annual household income," according to the Justice Department.[49] And women often get hurt during these incidents. "A full 50 percent of female victims of these attacks and/or 'intimate partner violence' in general reported being injured by partners,"[50] Bureau of Justice Statistics data show.[51] But there is an important note to that statement: most of the victims of these injuries do not voluntarily report them. Rather, they are reported by law enforcement officials or medical personnel,[52] which is where Reno's "public health problem" meets Felder and Victor's "crimes."

Finally, as set forth above, women estranged, separated, or attempting divorce are in the most dangerous position. Justice Department statistics suggest that in 1998, women who were "divorced or separated...were subjected to the highest rates of intimate partner victimization, followed by never-married persons."[53]

And there is another note here that tends to lend at least anecdotal support to Weitzman's arguments as it involves murder. In simplest terms, most of the people who are killed as a result of intimate partner violent are killed by spouses. These numbers have fallen, but not as sharply for women as in other areas. Between 1976 and 1993, the number of women killed by intimate partners fell by 23 percent, according to Justice Department data. And another 8 percent between 1997 and 1998."[54] By contrast, "[t]he number of men murdered by an intimate partner fell 60% from 1976 to 1998."[55]

But there is one segment of the population that did not experience a decline in the rate of homicide by intimate partners.

"White females represent the only category of victims from whom intimate partner homicide has not decreased substantially since 1976," according to the Justice Department. Indeed, the number of intimate partner homicides for all other racial and gender groups declined during the period—with the rate of intimate partner homicide among African American women falling 45 percent; the rate of intimate partner homicide among African American men falling 74 percent; and the rate of intimate partner homicide among white males falling 44 percent. By contrast, during this same period, the rate of intimate partner homicide among white women rose by 15 percent.[56]

VIOLENCE AND THE CONTEMPORARY LOVE AFFAIR:
Why Battery Prevails When All Else Fails

Researchers have long argued that a "vital part of understanding a social problem, and a precursor to preventing it, is an understanding of what causes it."[57] Thus, considerable effort has been spent examining those "causal factors" thought to trigger violence against women. The research in this area generally involves "joint consideration" of "two complementary processes: those that influence men to be aggressive and channel their expressions of violence toward women and those that position women for receipt of violence and operate to silence them afterwards," according to researchers.[58]

Some researchers have subdivided men who batter women into three major categories.[59] These categories include: (1) "psychopathic wife assaulters," *i.e.*, men who "show no remorse, exhibit little conscience, much less empathy for others,...usually have a criminal history" and are often diagnosed with some form of antisocial personality disorder;[60] (2) "over-controlled wife assaulters," *i.e.*, men who "dominate" or "distance" themselves from their partners and who tend to abuse partners "emotionally" but who may also "erupt with physical violence after a long period of built-up rage;"[61] and, (3) "cyclical/emotionally volatile wife abusers," *i.e.*, men who often exhibit "dual personalities"—loving, then violent, then remorseful—given a "deep need to control the level of intimacy in a relationship and are unable to express their feelings."[62]

In terms of research findings, a 1996 survey by the National Research Council found that recent efforts "have tested complex models of violence with multiple factors to explain battering, and to model the common roots of verbal, physical, and sexual coercion toward women."[63] And "[a]lthough current understanding suggests that violent behavior is not caused by any single factor, much of the research has focused on single cases."[64] Findings "...on general violence and...on violence against women suggest that violence arises from interactions among individual biological and psychological factors and social processes,[65] but it is not known how much overlap there is in the development of violent behavior against women and other violent behavior."[66]

In addition to attempts to determine the personality profile of male aggressors, "[r]esearch on the causes of violence against women has consisted of two lines of inquiry: examination of the characteristics that influence behavior of offenders and consideration of whether some women have a heightened vulnerability to victimization," National Research Council scientists offer.[67]

Among the possible influences examined are: "biologic factors;"[68] "evolutionary theories;"[69] "intrapsychic explanations;"[70] "social learning models that highlight the socialization experiences that shape individual men to be violent;"[71] "social information processing;"[72] "sociocultural analyses aimed at understanding the structural features of society at the level of the dyad, family, peer group, religion, media, and state that encourage males and maintain women as a vulnerable class of potential victims;"[73] and "feminist explanations stressing the gendered nature of violence against women and its roots in patriarchal social systems."[74]

VIOLENT FACTORS IN EVERYDAY LIFE:
The Power to Be a Reign of Terror

But how do all of these factors manifest themselves in real life? Is it, for example, a narcissistic personality disorder that allows a man to rationalize posting nude photos of female friends or even a women he does not know on the Internet?[75] To throw soup in a woman's face should she fail to warm it enough?[76] Or to install a global positioning device on his ex-wife's car so he may track her movements?[77]

Do these sociological questions matter in the legal context? In other words, how does "the law"—*i.e.*, judges, juries, and the courts—handle cases that would appear to tangle with several of the above factors? It might be easier to answer that question if one considers a case involving a tangle of "factors" and issues. *People v. Sowewimo*[78] involves just such a tangle.

The facts in *People v. Sowewimo* were that the defendant, Abiodun Sowewimo and the woman he would later terrify (identified in court documents only as P.S.) began dating in 1991. But by August 1992, the relationship was apparently on the rocks and Sowewimo was making excuses to keep P.S. near. On August 7, for example, P.S. agreed to let Sowewimo take her car on the belief that he would replace a lost key. But when she went to pick up the car at Sowewimo's home, he reportedly told her a friend was going to get the car and he "refused to let P.S. leave his bedroom for 30 minutes, running to the door when she tried to leave."[79]

"Jude, I'd rather be dead than be with you," P.S. responded.

In the face of such clear rejection, Sowewimo upped the ante. According to court documents he "picked up a switchblade" and put it to the throat of P.S., asking her, "What did you say? You would rather be *what* than be with me?"[80] Sowewimo then "forced" P.S. to remain at his home for five hours; at midnight he gave P.S. money and allowed her to take a taxi home. But it was not over.

At 5 A.M. the following morning, Sowewimo showed up at P.S.'s home and rang the doorbell until P.S. let him in. Sowewimo "appeared to be drunk," then passed out. P.S. found her car keys in his pocket and drove the car around for several hours while Sowewimo slept in her house. When P.S. returned home, she found Sowewimo on her bed naked. P.S. told him he was "disrespecting her" and that she did not want anything to do with him.[81] When Sowewimo tried to grab her arm, P.S. again left the apartment.

Once outside, P.S. called her sister and asked her sister to meet her at the apartment. By the time P.S. returned home again, Sowewimo was gone. But he began making repeated telephone calls to P.S.'s home. Most of these calls were answered by others. But P.S. answered one during which Sowewimo reportedly told her, "You better come back or I'm going to fuck you up."[82] In all, Sowewimo is estimated to have called between thirty and fifty times—five of which were answered by P.S., who later filed a report of threatening phone calls with police.

Later that night, at 10 P.M., P.S. returned home to find her back door broken in. Though nothing of major value was taken from the apartment, photos of P.S. and friends were torn, her answering machine was smashed, and her clothes were burned in the closet. A personal file containing her birth certificate and personal bills was taken. P.S. would later learn that her tires also had been slashed. P.S. called the police, who took a report. The next morning, P.S.'s sister found that her tires were slashed and a headlight on her car had been smashed out. The police were called again. They took another report.

Things would get worse.

On August 11, 1992, Sowewimo called P.S. at work to threaten her friends and family and warned that they should all get bodyguards. Then, at lunch time, Sowewimo showed up at P.S.'s job asking to see her. P.S. refused. A manager went to talk to Sowewimo instead and eventually the police were called. Sowewimo was arrested based upon a complaint by P.S. But he was soon released from custody and continued to call P.S. every day. P.S. filed another police report.

On August 12, P.S. appeared in court on her complaint against Sowewimo. Despite the clear escalation of events, Sowewimo was given probation and a verbal warning by a judge who told Sowewimo to stay away from P.S., her family, and her workplace. The judge also told Sowewimo not to call her. But Sowewimo continued to call P.S. every day until the night of September 24, 1992, when P.S. returned to her apartment to find several messages from Sowewimo. Sowewimo then called and when P.S. answered he asked her where she had been. When she answered, he accused her of lying and "playing games with him." Then, according to court records, Sowewimo told P.S., "I'm going to fuck you and your family up."

And the next morning, he tried to.

According to the Illinois Court of Appeals for the First District, on September 25, 1992, P.S. had an office meeting at 8:30 A.M. in the lunchroom of her place of employment when Sowewimo "walked into the lunchroom and pulled out a gun." Everybody in the room ran out except P.S. According to the court, Sowewimo then "grabbed P.S. by the hair and said, 'I told you, P., if you don't come back to me, I was going to come and get you.'"[83]

When one of P.S.'s colleagues attempted to intervene, asking Sowewimo to "[p]lease leave her alone. Let her go. This isn't the way to do this," Sowewimo responded by raising his arm and pointing the gun at the man.

"Who the fuck are you?" Sowewimo asked.

The man did not respond.

"What the fuck do you want?" Sowewimo asked.

Again the man did not respond.

"Get the fuck away from me," Sowewimo then said, turning toward P.S., but firing a shot in the man's direction.[84] Although the shot missed, Sowewimo apparently thought he had hit the man and became even more agitated, barricading the doors to the room and throwing P.S. on a couch. "This is the last time we're going to make love before you and I die," Sowewimo said, according to court testimony, before taking off her panty hose and ripping her underwear.

Sowewimo then had "sexual intercourse" with P.S.; got dressed; told P.S. they were going to be on CNN and A Current Affair; told the police through the door he had killed a man and was not going to jail; stuffed bullets and the victim's underwear down the drain and eventually surrendered to authorities after a four-hour hostage crisis.[85] He was later convicted of aggravated sexual assault, aggravated unlawful restraint, stalking, aggravated stalking, attempted first-degree murder, and aggravated discharge of a weapon.[86]

Defense attorneys and mental health professionals might ask whether Sowewimo was suffering a narcissistic personality disorder that compelled him to act out violently given his fear of abandonment when he attacked and held P.S. hostage. Was he psychopathic? Did he have an antisocial personality disorder? Or was he a cyclical/emotionally volatile abuser? A psychiatrist might be called as an expert witness to say whether organic brain disease or cerebral abnormalities were present and/or the cause.

But from a law enforcement perspective, these kinds of questions matter less than they once did. In recent years, as the nation has moved from a society with "rehabilitative" interests towards one of punitive goals, judges, juries, and lawmakers have begun to care less about the reasons a man may batter his wife or girlfriend and more about preventing the possibility of it happening again by incarcerating an offender for long periods of time. In addition, in response to pressure from women's groups and media reports of violent incidents, lawmakers and prosecutors have begun in recent years to take domestic violence as seriously as Victor and Felder urge, which raises a question: If Sowewimo had been given jail time instead of probation, might the September 25, incident not have happened? Recent developments in the law suggest that lawmakers have begun to ask that question of themselves.

MANDATORY ARRESTS:
The Heavy Hand of the Law

Progress has been made in the area of domestic violence law, though some would almost certainly argue that there is plenty of room for more. Advocates of women have long argued, for example, that while domestic violence laws exist, police officers responding to a call and prosecutors charged with the authority to take abusers to court have historically fallen down on the job. Thus, one of the most potentially significant developments in the past two decades has been passage of "mandatory arrest" laws that became standard practice, some argue, as a result of the infamous O.J. Simpson case.

"Nicole Brown Simpson's tragic death...brought domestic violence to the attention of the American public," suggests Chicago attorney Marion Wanless.[87]

By 1996, fifteen states and the District of Columbia had adopted "mandatory arrest" laws in cases of domestic violence.[88] These laws require law enforcement officers to arrest men—and women—when there is "probable cause" to believe domestic and/or intimate partner violence has occurred, even if the alleged victim declines to press charges. Proponents of mandatory arrest laws have suggested that such laws will create a new procedural template for handling incidents in cases of domestic violence. And the potential for good is enormous.

New York State passed a mandatory arrest law in 1994, for example, shortly after Governor George Pataki took office. The measure was widely heralded as one of those rare occasions when a law viewed overwhelmingly as "in the public good" received enthusiastic bipartisan support. Feminists and women's rights advocates applauded.

"Historically, arrest rates in domestic violence cases have been very low," says Wanless. "Police officers often employ irrelevant criteria such as the 'reason' for the abuse or the severity of the victim's injuries in making their decision to arrest. Police officers often discourage victims from pressing charges. Many describe the procedure for obtaining an arrest warrant as arduous and time-consuming or counsel victims that their desire to prosecute will probably change. They outline the impact of arrest on abusers—loss of wages, possible job loss, stigma of arrest—and insinuate that the victims do not want to be responsible for inflicting such hardship on their attackers."[89]

Mandatory arrest laws changed that. But they have proved controversial as well, largely because law enforcement officers are empowered—and indeed urged—to arrest possible offenders even where alleged victims do not want to press charges.[90] From a traditional perspective, prosecutors rarely brought cases against abusers unless the victims of their mistreatment testified as witnesses. "Also, prosecutors often acquiesce[d] quickly to a victim's request to have the charges against her batterer dropped."[91]

In addition, though lawmakers praised mandatory arrest laws, some law enforcement officials opposed them, arguing that they usurp an officer's on-the-scene discretion, threaten his control, and thus pose a greater risk by inflaming an often volatile scene.[92] Critics of such measures also note that although mandatory arrest laws have increased the number of arrests, prosecutions in domestic violence cases remain more the exception than the rule in practice.[93]

Perhaps even more troubling from a women's rights perspective is that although mandatory arrest laws were intended largely to protect women—as the overwhelming victims of domestic and intimate partner violence—mandatory arrest laws have increasingly been used *against women* by partners allegedly making "retaliatory charges" that often leave police officers responding to the call with no option but to arrest both partners involved in the incident, some reports suggest.[94] This appears to be a growing trend.

Nearly 35 percent of all domestic violence arrestees in Concord, New Hampshire, during 1999, for example, were women.[95] In 1993, that number was just 23 percent.[96] In Vermont, the percentage of women arrested in domestic violence incidents was also 23 percent in 1999, but that number was 16 percent in 1997.[97] Colorado has also seen a rise. But the pressure to find a "solution" remains the goal of politicians, largely because women's groups have worked hard to keep the issue in the public eye.

In the summer of 2002, for example, actress Salma Hayek—accompanied by hundreds of women in white wedding dresses—led a highly publicized march on Washington in honor of Gladys Ricart, the New Jersey woman killed on her wedding day by an ex-fiancé.[98] The pressure of litigation and multimillion-dollar lawsuits has also kept lawmakers and law enforcement officials on their toes.

At about the same time that women's groups were planning the march in Washington in 2002, supervisors in Sonoma County were agreeing to pay $1 million to the family of a woman killed by her estranged husband after sheriff's deputies failed to enforce a restraining order. In a case establishing legal precedent, a California court ruled in 2002 that the family of Maria Teresa Macias was entitled to try to prove sheriff's deputies had violated federal law by ignoring Macias's repeated complaints and requests for help prior to her death.[99]

Macias, a mother of three, was shot to death in April 1996, by Avelino Macias, who later killed himself. Maria Teresa Macias's family filed a $15 million lawsuit against the sheriff's department, alleging that department personnel ignored Maria Teresa Macias's repeated complaints because she was "a woman, a Hispanic, and a domestic violence victim." Though county supervisors agreed to the settlement, the accord did not require an admission of negligence or other wrongdoing on the part of sheriff's department personnel. And county officials have argued that they do not believe sheriff's deputies did anything wrong.[100] The case marked a turning point. Previous attempts based upon these and other constitutional standards were rejected.[101]

In addition, in a case that may represent a new approach to domestic violence/divorce litigation, a woman was awarded a $5.56 million settlement. According to media reports, a pregnant Darlina Brown was beaten by her husband with a bedpost. She managed to escape and call sheriff's deputies, and her husband was charged with aggravated assault. Brown filed for divorce. She also filed tort claims for assault, aggravated assault, and intentional infliction of emotional distress within the divorce petition.[102]

Brown's lawyer assumed either the defense or the court would move to separate the tort claims from the divorce action. But no one did. As a result, all of the tort claims remained part of the divorce petition and were heard during the divorce trial before a jury. Brown's husband, a renowned Houston-area hand surgeon, filed his own tort claims in response, alleging specifically that Darlina Brown had converted 28 items from his home. Among the items was a box containing $100,000, Michael Brown alleged.[103]

At trial Michael Brown argued that his wife had been the aggressor during the incident. In response, Darlina Brown's attorney introduced the 911 tape to the sheriff's department into evidence. On the tape Darlina Brown could reportedly be heard begging the police to "[g]et here, he's going to kill me." The presence of tort claims also allowed the jury to hear evidence of other "bad acts" that might ordinarily have been excluded from a divorce case.

On October 19, 2001, a Conroe, Texas, jury awarded Darlina Brown $3.56 million—$3 million of which was reportedly for "mental anguish." Another $355,000 was awarded as the value of a prenuptial agreement, and $2 million was awarded in punitive damages. The jury rejected Michael Brown's conversion claim on all items except a letter from his daughter. The jury held, however, that the letter was without monetary value.[104] Though it is not clear that such an approach would work in all cases, the Texas jury's somewhat novel approach to damages may offer victims of domestic violence a new avenue of recovery in the future.

Mandatory arrest laws and large jury awards aside, smaller steps have been taken as well by local authorities that may one day achieve what mandatory arrest laws aspired to. During the late 1990s, the City of Chicago instituted the Target Abusers Call (TAC) program, combining the joint efforts of police officers, social workers, civil attorneys, and investigators to get women through the traumatic ordeal of abuse and court proceedings.[105] The program has been celebrated on a national level.

In New York, while still mayor of the city, Rudolph Giuliani signed an ordinance prohibiting employers from firing or refusing to hire persons being or having been threatened, stalked, or attacked by current or former partners, spouses, roommates, or significant others.[106] As *People v. Sowewimo* suggests, intimate partner violence often spills into the workplace. Justice Department statistics show that each year there are between 30,000 and 40,000 incidents of on-the-job violence "in which victims know their attackers intimately."[107] Domestic and intimate partner violence has also been estimated to cost employers roughly $5 billion each year in lost days and reduced productivity.

These facts would appear to be the kind of sound and substantial arguments employers might use to defend not hiring a woman or man who has faced, or is facing, domestic violence. But that, of course, is the point of the law: though there may be good reasons for not hiring victims of domestic violence, the position of New York officials was clearly that victims of domestic violence are "victims" often terrorized and brutalized by loved ones. Thus, they should not be victimized twice for actions usually well beyond their control. Other jurisdictions are expected to follow.

In the fall of 2002, New York authorities also announced that police officers had begun taking digital photos during domestic violence calls to memorialize events. The practice has been thought by some to be inspired, given the traditional alternative of Polaroid shots, which tend to be blurry and less detailed. By contrast, digital photos are detailed enough to show finger-shaped bruises on skin and can be transmitted via computer immediately to prosecutors and judges handling arraignments or bail hearings.[108] Digital photography is also useful, law enforcement officials assert, in cases where victims decline to press charges, because even if the victim never speaks, officers may present detailed photos to show what they saw.

But there also have been setbacks. Critics of the current system argue that wealthy men rarely face arrest or prosecution.[109] In addition, "zero-tolerance" domestic violence policies meant to discourage "incidents" and protect women by mandating eviction of an entire household following an event have served at times to hurt women, and thus they have been challenged.[110] And though the United States military reportedly spends $115 million a year on family advocacy and counseling programs, domestic violence remains a serious—and, according to some—unchecked problem within the armed forced community. Between 1997 and 2002, for example, some 58,000 military spouses and partners were victims of domestic violence.[111] Critics argue that military authorities do little or nothing to prevent abuse or punish the assaulters.[112]

And finally, despite the efforts and apparent gains in other areas, women's rights groups note that one troubling fact still remains: women continue to die of gunshot wounds. Roughly 10 (sometimes slightly more) of the estimated 15,000 homicides committed across the United States each year are domestic or intimate partner homicides. And "[a]lmost all are women, and most are killed with firearms," according to the General Accounting Office.[113] But a strong gun lobby with considerable political clout has continued to help put guns in the hands of men who may not have the right to have them.

Between 1998 and 2001, nearly 3,000 domestic violence abusers were able to buy firearms, despite federal laws intended to prevent them from doing so, the General Accounting Office found. The reason for the failure was that the Federal Bureau of Investigation was not able to complete the necessary background checks prior to sales going through. "As a result, federal authorities are then forced to try to retrieve and recover guns from felons and criminals."[114]

ENDNOTES FOR CHAPTER FIFTEEN

1   See Raoul Felder and Barbara Victor, GETTING AWAY WITH MURDER: WEAPONS FOR THE WAR AGAINST DOMESTIC VIOLENCE (New York: Simon & Schuster, 1996), at p. 33. (In objecting to Reno's reported statements, Felder and Victor wrote: "On August 8, 1993, United States Attorney General Janet Reno spoke at the Women Lawyers of Achievement Awards Luncheon. Her speech began, 'There is a lot of discussion about whether domestic violence is a public health problem. There should be none. Of course it is. If doctors and lawyers work together, focusing on it as a true public health problem, [in] a criminal justice system that cares, we can make a difference.'")

2   Id.

3   See Tjaden, supra note 119, ENDNOTES FOR CHAPTER THIRTEEN, at p. 3.

4   See Stephen Rodrick, Can Riddick Bowe Answer the Bell?, N.Y. TIMES MAG., October 22, 2000, at pp. 58, 61.

5   Id.

6   Id.

7   Id.

8   Id.

9   See Ann Jones, Still Going on Out There: Women Beaten Senseless by Men, COSMOPOLITAN, Sept. 1, 1994, at p.18 (reprinted in VIOLENCE AGAINST WOMEN: CURRENT CONTROVERSIES (San Diego: Greenhaven Press, Inc. 1999) (James D. Torr, ed.)).

10 Id.

11 The Family Prevention Fund of the National Coalition Against Violence estimated in 1997 that a woman is assaulted somewhere in America every nine seconds. This number has often been quoted. See, e.g., Action Against Abuse, Ms., Aug.–Sept.1999, at p. 43.

12 See COMMONWEALTH FUND, First Comprehensive National Health Survey of American Women (1993); Jennifer Baumgardner, Every 12 Seconds A Woman is Beaten by Her Boyfriend or Husband, MARIE CLAIRE, March 2000, at p. 154.

13 See Autopsy Finds No Cancer in Woman Shot by Husband, ASSOCIATED PRESS, Feb. 8, 1999 (reprinted in N.Y. TIMES, Feb. 9, 1999).

14 See Police Report Murder-Suicide, N.Y. TIMES, Sept. 9, 2001, at A54.

15 See Verdict is Murder in a Wedding-Day Killing, N.Y. TIMES, Oct. 23, 2001, at A20.

16 See Erica Goode, When Women Find Love is Fatal, N.Y. TIMES, Feb. 15, 2000, at D1.

17 See People v. M.D., 231 Ill.App.3d 175 (1992).

18 See People v. Vega, 39 Cal. Rptr. 2d 479 (Cal. App. 5 Dist. 1995).

19 Id. at 481–482.

20 See People v. Ciccarello, 276 A.D.2d 637 (2000).

21 See Susan Weitzman, PhD, NOT TO PEOPLE LIKE US: HIDDEN ABUSE IN UPSCALE MARRIAGE (New York: Basic Books, 2000), at p. 5 (citing R.J. Gelles, THE VIOLENT HOME: A STUDY OF PHYSICAL AGGRESSION BETWEEN HUSBANDS AND WIVES (Beverly Hills, Calif.: Sage Publications, 1974)).

22 See Rennison, supra note 123, ENDNOTES FOR CHAPTER THIRTEEN, at p. 3.

23 Id.

24 Id.

25 Id.

26 Id.

27 See Weitzman, supra note 21, at p. 4.

28 Id. at 6.

29 Id.

30 Id. at 5–6.

31 Some researchers suggest that this is pattern. See, e.g., Jeanne McCauley, et al., Clinical Characteristics of Women with a History of Childhood Abuse, 277 JAMA 1362 (May 7, 1997); Daniel Brookoff et al., Characteristics of Participants in Domestic Violence, 277 JAMA 1369 (May 7, 1997); Frederick P. Rivara et al., Alcohol and Illicit Drug Abuse and the Risk of Violent Death in the Home, 278 JAMA

569 (Aug. 20, 1997); *The Cycle of Violence Revisited*, RESEARCH PREVIEW, NATIONAL INSTITUTE OF JUS-
TICE, Feb. 1996; *Early Childhood Victimization Among Incarcerated Adult Male Felons*, RESEARCH
PREVIEW, NATIONAL INSTITUTE OF JUSTICE, April 1998.

32 *See* UNDERSTANDING VIOLENCE AGAINST WOMEN, *supra* note 141, ENDNOTES FOR CHAPTER THIRTEEN,
    at p. 62 (citing C.S. Widom, *Does Violence Beget Violence? A Critical Examination of the Literature*,
    106 PSYCHOL. BULLETIN at pp. 3–28 (1989)).

33 *Id.* at 70 (citing G.T. Hotaling & D.B. Sugarman, *An Analysis of Risk Markers in Husband and Wife
    Violence: The Current State of Knowledge*, 1 VIOLENCE AND VICTIMS at pp. 101–124 (1986)).

34 *Id.* (The authors note further that "…this factor characterized not only the victimized women, but
    also their male assailants. Recent studies also found no specific personality and attitudinal charac-
    teristics that make certain women more vulnerable to battering. Although alcoholic women are
    more likely to report moderate to severe violence in their relationships than more moderate
    drinkers, the association disappears after controlling for alcohol problems in their partners. On the
    basis of findings such as these, several writers have concluded that the major risk factor for batter-
    ing is being a woman" (citing N.E. Pittman & R.G. Taylor, *MMPI Profiles of Partners of Incestuous
    Sexual Offenders and Partners of Alcoholics*, 2 FAMILY DYNAMICS OF ADDICTION QUARTERLY at pp.
    52–59 (1992); K.E. Leonard, *Drinking Patterns and Intoxication in Marital Violence: Review, Cri-
    tique, and Future Directions of Research*, in ALCOHOL AND INTERPERSONAL VIOLENCE, Research Mono-
    graph-24, NIH Publication No. 9303496 (Rockville, Md.: National Institute on Alcohol Abuse and
    Alcoholism, National Institutes of Health, U.S. Dep't of Health and Human Services (1993), at pp.
    253–280).)

35 *Id.* (citing M.A. Straus, R.J. Gelles & S. Steinmetz, BEHIND CLOSED DOORS: VIOLENCE IN THE AMERI-
    CAN FAMILY (Garden City, N.Y.: Anchor Press, 1980)).

36 *See* Marian Betancourt, WHAT TO DO WHEN LOVE TURNS VIOLENT (New York: Harper Perennial,
    1997), at xxii.

37 *See* Baumgardner, *supra* note 12, at p. 154.

38 *See* Dawn Bradley Berry, THE DOMESTIC VIOLENCE SOURCEBOOK (Los Angeles, Ca.: Lowell House,
    1995), at p. 31 (citing Lenore Walker, THE BATTERED WOMAN (New York: Harper & Row, 1982)).

39 *Id. See also* D. Brookoff *et al.*, *Characters of Participants in Domestic Violence*, 277 JAMA 1369
    (1997).

40 *See* Weitzman, *supra* note 21, at p. 3.

41 *Id.*

42 *Id.* at 5 (citing M.A. Straus & R.J. Gelles, PHYSICAL VIOLENCE IN AMERICAN FAMILIES: RISK FACTORS
    AND ADAPTATIONS TO VIOLENCE IN 8,145 FAMILIES (New Brunswick, N.Y.: Transaction Publisher,
    1990), at p. 196).

43 *Id.* (citing U.S. DEPARTMENT OF JUSTICE, THE SOURCEBOOK OF CRIMINAL JUSTICE STATISTICS (Wash-
    ington, D.C.: U.S. Department of Justice, 1997), at p. 1998).

44 *See* Rennison, *supra* note 22, at p. 4. (Justice Department research also suggests that "[m]en who
    were young, black, divorced or separated, or living in rented housing had significantly higher rates
    of intimate partner violence than other men.")

45 *Id.* By contrast, "[b]lack males experienced intimate partner violence at a rate [of] about 62 per-
    cent higher than that of white males and about 22 times the rate of men of other races."

46 *Id.*

47 *Id.* at 5.

48 *Id.* at 4.

49 *Id.* (Justice Department researchers note that there was "[n]o discernible relationship between male
    intimate partner violence and household income.")

50 *Id.* at 6. (This is as opposed to 32 percent of male victims.)

51 *Id.* ("About six in ten female and male victims of intimate partner violence were injured but not
    treated," according to Department of Justice estimates. "In general, injuries were minor, involving
    cuts and bruises. Most of those injured who were treated received care at home or at the scene of
    the victimization (17 percent of women and 24 percent of men).")

52 *Id.* ("About six in ten female and male victims of intimate partner violence were injured but not
    treated," according to Department of Justice estimates. "In general, injuries were minor, involving
    cuts and bruises. Most of those injured who were treated received care at home or at the scene of
    the victimization (17% of women and 24 percent of men).")

53 *Id.* (The authors of the report note that "[b]ecause [it] reflects a respondent's marital status at the
    time of the interview, it is not possible to determine whether a person was separated or divorced at
    the time of the victimization or whether separation or divorce followed the violence.") *Id.* at 5.

54 *See* Rennison, *supra* note 22, at p. 3.

55 *Id.*

56 *Id.* at 3–4.

57 *See* UNDERSTANDING VIOLENCE AGAINST WOMEN, *supra* note 32, at p. 49.

58 *Id.*

59 Among these researchers is Donald Dutton, author and director of the Assaultive Husbands Pro-
    gram in Vancouver, British Columbia.

60   *See* Weitzman, *supra* note 21, at p. 135 (citing D.G. Dutton, THE BATTERER (New York: BasicBooks, 1995), at p. 26). (These men, believed to represent 40 percent of "wife assaulters," have often also exhibited "flat brain stem activity, which is different from normal men," Weitzman and Dutton note.)

61   *Id.* (citing Dutton, *supra* note 60, at pp. 29–33). (These men are thought to represent about 30 percent of the "abuser" population.)

62   *Id.* at 136 (citing Dutton, supra note 60, at pp. 33–38). (As Weitzman interprets it, "Dutton concluded that the majority of batterers from the cyclical group probably suffer from Post Traumatic Stress Disorder (PTSD), which contributes greatly to their anger and mood swings. Themselves abused growing up and shamed by the rejection they felt as children, these men feel ambivalent about their ability and desire to attach to others. They are fearful of attachment and may bring anger to relationships.")

63   *See* UNDERSTANDING VIOLENCE AGAINST WOMEN, *supra* note 32, at p. 49 (citing N.M. Malamuth *et al.*, *Using the Confluence Model of Sexual Aggression to Predict Men's Conflict with Women: A Ten-Year Follow-Up Study*, 69 J. PERS. SOC. PSYCHOL. at 353–369 (1995)). The authors further note that "[a]lso new are integrative metatheories of intimate violence that consider the impact of historical, sociocultural, and social factors on people, including the processes whereby social influences are transmitted to and represented within individual psychological functioning, including cognition and motivation."

64   *Id.* at 51.

65   *Id.* (citing UNDERSTANDING AND PREVENTING VIOLENCE, *supra* note 9).

66   *Id.* at 50–51.

67   *Id.*

68   Among the "biologic factors" considered are androgenic hormonal influences. *Id.* at 49.

69   "Evolutionary theories" include considering whether "the goal of sexual behavior is to maximize the likelihood of passing on one's genes." *Id.* at 49–51.

70   "Intrapsychic explanations focused on mental disorder or personality traits and profiles," authors of UNDERSTANDING VIOLENCE AGAINST WOMEN, *supra* note 32, at p. 50.

71   *Id.*

72   "Social information processing theories" include examination of "cognitive processes that offenders engage in before, during, and after violence," the authors explain. *Id.*

73   *Id.*

74   *Id.* at 50.

75   *See Dirty Money*, 48 HOURS, CBS-TELEVISION, aired April 1, 1999; DATELINE, aired June 30, 1998.

76   *See* Betancourt, *supra* note 36, at xxii.

77   *See GPS-Using Ex-Husband Said to be Stalking Wife*, NAT'L L.J., July 29, 2002, at B4 (citing *People v. Sullivan*, 53 P.3d 1181 (Colo. App. 2002)). (The *National Law Journal* noted that after a Colorado woman filed for divorce, her soon-to-be ex-husband set fire to her clothes and installed a global positioning device in her car so that he can track her movements. He was convicted of second-degree arson and stalking.)

78   *People v. Sowewimo*, 657 N.E.2d 1047 (Ill. App. 1 Dist. 1995).

79   *Sowewimo*, 657 N.E.2d at 1049.

80   *Id.*

81   *Id.* at 1050.

82   *Id.*

83   *Id.*

84   *Id.* at 1051.

85   *Id.*

86   *Id.* at 1047.

87   *See* Marion Wanless, *Mandatory Arrest: A Step Toward Eradicating Domestic Violence, But Is it Enough?*, U. Ill. L. REV., Spring 1996 (reprinted in VIOLENCE AGAINST WOMEN: CURRENT CONTROVERSIES (San Diego, Calif., 1999) (James Torr, ed.), at p. 113).

88   *Id.*

89   *Id.* at 115.

90   For an overview of the issue, *see* Cheryl Hanna, *No Right to Choose: Mandated Victim Participation in Domestic Violence Prosecutions*, 109 HARV. L. REV. 1850 (1996); Eve S. Buzawa and Carl G. Buzawa, DOMESTIC VIOLENCE: THE CRIMINAL JUSTICE RESPONSE (2nd ed. 1996); Donna Mills, *Domestic Violence: The Case for Aggressive Prosecution*, 7 UCLA WOMEN'S LJ. 173–182 (1997); Cheryl Hanna, *The Paradox of Hope: The Crime and Punishment of Domestic Violence*, 39 WM. & MARY L. REV. 1505 (1998); Deborah Epstein, *Effective Intervention in Domestic Violence Cases: Rethinking the Roles of Prosecutors, Judges, and the Court System*, 11 YALE J. L. & FEM. at pp. 19–20 (1999).

91   *See* Wanless, *supra* note 87, at 119.

92   *Id.* at 115.

93   *Id.* at 118. (Wanless notes that "[h]istorically, prosecutors have been as guilty as the police of not taking domestic violence seriously and [of] trying to persuade victims to drop criminal charges. Lax prosecution practices undermine the effectiveness of mandatory arrest laws. Since Washington enacted a mandatory arrest law over a decade ago, arrests in domestic violence incidents have

soared, increasing six-fold. Prosecution of batters, however, remains the exception rather than the norm. Seattle police officers are frustrated that they repeatedly arrest the same batterers, but the men are seldom prosecuted and punished.")

94 *See, e.g.,* Somini Sengupta, *Wide Support for Renewing Law on Arrest for Abuse,* N.Y. TIMES, June 11, 2001, at A14.

95 *See* Carey Goldberg, *Crackdown on Abusive Spouses, Surprisingly, Nets Many Women,* N.Y. TIMES, Nov. 23, 1999, at A1.

96 *Id.*

97 *Id.*

98 *See Salma Hayek Makes a Vow to Stop Domestic Violence* (as told to Stacy Morrison), MARIE CLAIRE, Oct. 2002, at pp. 98–110.

99 *See* Justin Pritchard, *Family of Woman Killed Despite Restraining Order Gets $1M,* ASSOCIATED PRESS, June 19, 2002, (reprinted on LexisOne, at www.lexisone.com, June 23, 2002).

100 *Id.*

101 *See, e.g., Hynson v. City of Chester,* 864 F.2d 1026 (3rd Cir. 1988); *Brown v. Grabowski,* 922 F.2d 1097 (3rd Cir. 1990).

102 *See* Margaret Cronin Fisk, *In Divorce Case, Wife Files Tort Claim and Wins $5.56M,* NAT'L L.J., Nov. 5, 2001, Sect. B., at p. 1.

103 *Id.*

104 *Id.*

105 *See* Barbara Mahany, *Teaming Up on Domestic Violence,* CHI. TRIB., Oct. 30, 1998, Sec. 5, at p. 1.

106 *See* Tim Pareti, *Employer Awareness: Lawyers Can Help Ward Off Liability When Domestic Violence Spills Into Workplace,* A.B.A. J., May 2001, at p. 70.

107 *Id.*

108 *See* Sarah Kershaw, *Digital Photos Give the Police A New Edge in Abuse Cases,* N.Y. TIMES, Sept. 3, 2002, at A1.

109 *See* Weitzman, *supra* note 21, at pp. 155–156.

110 *See* Tamar Lewin, *Zero-Tolerance Policy is Challenged,* N.Y. TIMES, July 11, 2001, at A10.

111 *See The War at Home,* 60 MINUTES, CBS-TELEVISION, airing Sept. 1, 2002, (Ed Bradley reporting), at p. 8 (transcript available through Burrelle's).

112 *Id.* at 8–13.

113 *Id. See also Predicting Criminal Behavior Among Authorized Purchasers of Handguns,* NATIONAL INSTITUTE OF JUSTICE, CENTER FOR DISEASE CONTROL AND PREVENTION, U.S. DEP'T OF JUSTICE, OFFICE OF JUSTICE PROGRAMS, April 1998; Annys Shin, *Gun Bills Catch Women and Kids in the Crossfire,* MS., July/Aug., 1997, at p. 25.

114 *See* Dan Eggers, *Domestic Abusers Bought Guns,* WASH. POST, June 26, 2002, at A8.

Epilogue

I'm probably foolish to admit it, but I learned a lot while researching and writing this book. Among the larger lessons was the recognition of a trend toward determined ignorance where the law is concerned. I also learned—or perhaps more precisely, I finally understood—that some men (and it is still overwhelmingly men) will fight forever to limit the reproductive choices of women. Editorial writers have called efforts to preserve the precedent of *Roe v. Wade* and all that is supposed to go with it "the battle that never ends." And yet, in light of the current climate, statements of this sort are more hopeful than fact.

Gone in all but name today is the notion of respect for a woman as an individual—separate, complete, and autonomous from a developing fetus. Indeed, so far removed are we today from the time of the fetus, that "fetus" isn't even the word most often used these days, though it is still the language of Supreme Court law.

As part of this movement, politicians—at times bowing to the pressure of religious rights groups and other "political rights forces," or acting on their own personal feelings—have written and passed bill after bill into law declaring developing fetuses to be "unborn children." The result of so sustained a campaign of what might fairly be called "political tyranny" is that talk of "unborn children" has supplanted the terminology of the debate. Laws providing medical coverage for "unborn children," protecting "unborn children," and creating greater criminal penalties for persons who harm "unborn children," either by negligence or via abuse to the woman carrying the fetus, have been passed in recent years on the federal and state levels.

The significance of this change in language has been enormous. And calculatedly so, because *"killing unborn children"* is far less popular than "ending a pregnancy" or having tissue—even fetal tissue—removed. Thus, abortions—

and the women who have them—have become unpopular. So unpopular that even those representatives who say they consider themselves "pro-choice" have joined so-called "pro-life" forces in recent years in voting to outlaw certain procedures.

Senator Blanche Lincoln, a democrat from Arkansas, reportedly remarked after voting in favor of the controversial "partial-birth abortion" bill in October of 2003, that she is "about 99 percent pro-choice." It was that troubling one percent that led her to vote as she had, Lincoln argued. She was one of seventeen democratic senators to do so.[1] The bill was signed into law by President George W. Bush, an outspoken opponent of abortion, whose administration has drafted and engineered the passage of several antiabortion and anticontraceptive measures. In doing so, he became the first president ever to criminalize an abortion technique.

Of course, not everything is about reproductive rights. But if history is any indication, an awful lot is. Women bear children, anchoring them as the cornerstone of modern society. But women may also *carry* disease, and must therefore be punished for their wanton desires. Women conceive "unwanted children" who drain the welfare system, an offense that prompted editorial writers during the early 1990s to propose tying benefits to mandatory contraceptives even as lawmakers were finding new and creative ways to limit public funding for contraceptives and abortion.

So contradictory a plight led Katha Pollitt to comment in a 1996 article facetiously titled, *Devil Women*, that "[w]ith a little imagination, poor women can be blamed for just about everything" from emptying the national coffers, though "federal spending on Aid to Families with Dependant Children [which was] only 12 billion, 200 million dollars—one percent of federal spending" while "[p]ayments to corporations [were] a 167 billion dollars a year;" to lowering the IQs of their children a full twenty points by *refusing to work*.[2] And then there is the evil of the other choices they might make.

These are changing times for women as traditional supporters cross lines, legal precedents are ignored, and women are demonized for making choices they have a right to make as a matter of law. In an attempt to shine a light on some of this change, I have saved several articles for discussion in this Epilogue. These were articles chosen at times as much for their titles as for their content. But all are offered for what they tend to suggest about women, that other bad word—"feminism"—and the direction in which our society appears to be moving with regard to these issues.

The first of these articles was a column provocatively titled, "Are Men Obsolete?" published in the June 23, 2003, edition of *U.S.News & World Report*. I chose it because it *provocatively* opens the door to the discussion of a reality that once seemed impossible. Jodie Allen bases her remarks in economics, arguing specifically that "…at least for a few centuries, men have found productive niches in industrialized society, building roads, bridges, and communication networks, and founding (and periodically bilking) massive conglomerates, while contributing to the sciences, arts, and humanities. But even during these periods of industrial growth, the great majority of the male species contributed far more muscle than mind to the commonweal."[3]

In many ways the title could be the modern story of man and not just from the perspective of economics. It is true that "[w]omen are rapidly closing the M.D. and Ph.D. gap and make up almost half of all law students."[4] In addition, during the 1990s, women joined the national workforce in record numbers in a trend that began fifty years earlier, during World War II. And though women still tend to make less than men overall, the losses greeting men in other areas of the social and cultural landscape have created gains of a different sort for women.

Advances in medicine and assisted reproductive techniques, for example, have made men obsolete for many women. Their genetic material is still necessary at the moment to fertilize eggs. But relationships between men and women—long deemed the essence of the "family unit," especially where the woman voluntarily adopted the requisite submissive role—are no longer a requirement for "getting women in the family way," which, incidentally, is no longer the same today either.

"Families" are increasingly made up today of unmarried, mixed race, or same-sex couples. In addition, while perhaps the great social argument of the new millennium has revolved around the prospect of "gay marriage" and the projected demise of the "American family," as we know it, it might fairly be argued that a greater dismantling of that gracious institution began the day the first baby was conceived in a test tube. That singular advance, perhaps more than any other, spelled the end of the sexual intimacy once necessary to conceive a child.

Extending the reach of the reproductive rights decisions of the 1960s and '70s, assisted reproduction gave women a new array of choices, many of them exclusive of intimate male-female contact. And that has given women even greater freedom. Of course, that is the liberal feminist point of view, which brings us to the next issue: feminism and the dirty word it has become.

A friend's daughter, currently attending a college consistently ranked in the top ten small liberal arts institutions in the country, admitted to her mother that she did not get the "whole feminism thing." To her and to many young women her age "feminism" is about a lot of old noise left over from the '60s and "feminists" are radical, braless, angry women who refuse to shave and are against the application of makeup. I emailed her mom back to say (in typical feminist fashion) a few choice truisms about the young; among them that my brother—just seven years my junior, who is an electrical engineer—was shocked to learn of the depth of the Civil Rights struggle *from TV* after finding a copy of *Eyes on the Prize* in my video collection.

The revolutions of the 1960s and the cultural crises they would spark are clearly too far removed from the lives of young people today to mean more than an historic footnote. As the reference points of generations change, pivotal moments are often forgotten. Maybe it is the "failure of the American education system" as critics and politicians often accuse. Or maybe it simply has more to do with the fact that many of the teachers charged with educating young people today were born after the restoration of calm. And so my brother, who was born in 1970, doesn't have a memory of the violence it took to bring about significant change. In the same way, feminism has become "...a mood ring left over from the bell-bottom epoch."

"'Feminism' doesn't get much respect these days," writer Dorothy Wickenden notes. "But after a generation of struggle its results are everywhere; in jobs, from the precinct house to the Pentagon; in legal and reproductive rights; in politics, with women in noticeable numbers now being elected to the offices of mayor and governor; in the parade of firsts, among them Bishop Barbara Harris, Sally Ride, Geraldine Ferraro, and Sandra Day O'Connor. As a way of living, feminism is flourishing, even if lately it has had to travel under assumed names: in a recent Harris poll, although only half of the women questioned identified themselves as feminists, 71 percent said they support 'political, economic, and social equality for women.'"[5]

Like Wickenden, I consider myself a writer. But I wasn't anywhere near as eloquent in my answer to my friend's daughter. While I noted that I could understand her reluctance to embrace the feminist brand, given the negative taste it seems so often to leave in the mouths of young women today, I added—as a card-carrying feminist should—that young women still have a lot to be thankful for. "Do you play a sport, for example?" I asked.

Of course, the only reason that anyone's opinion of feminism matters is that the feminist movement has always been linked to the women's rights movement. It was the "feminists," after all—those radical, noisy women—who pushed the wagon of reform uphill and who are, therefore, directly responsible for the waves of "woman-friendly" legislation that swept the nation during the late 1960s and early '70s. These were—and are—laws that changed the lives of women and continue to direct positive change in the lives of girls, whether or not they realize it. These shifts were sometimes momentous; at other times, smaller. Laws requiring equal funding for male and female sports programs, for example, were the result of women's groups pushing an agenda of absolute equality. That is why I asked the sports question. Despite the law, I am part of that generation of women who were forced to play on boys teams throughout high school.

What I find interesting about the perceptual gaps between older and younger women is what they seem to suggest. Statements of the sort made by my friend's daughter are often viewed as a blanket rejection of the feminist movement by today's young women. But what may be closer to the truth is that they expose generational differences of opinion among women of different ages about what feminism *ought* to be today.

There are the "old arguments" made by the "old forces": that women are absolutely equal and should be treated as such (with no excuses); and that all women—young and old—owe the gender a measure of respect. But that's a hard sell for young girls who know little or nothing of the movement and who have come of age at a time when things are already "better" than they were and the freedom of sexual choice is the only reality they have ever known. It is a bit like my brother who never had to make a single choice of "race" on an application form, because by the time he graduated from high school, the world had begun to realize—officially—that people could be of more than one race. As a result, he doesn't really understand it when I say there was a time when we were only allowed to be "black" or "Afro-American."

From the things I've read, the current divide between women who proudly declare themselves "feminists" and those who do not, but who still believe in equality, sexual freedom, choice and other "feminist issues" revolves around the evolution in recent years of feminism's sexier other self. "Can You Dress Like a Porn Star and Still be a Feminist?" a recent article in *Elle* magazine asked, in detailing the rise of the so-called "do-me feminist" approach to gender economics. It is an approach, supporters say, that allows women to claim the power of their sexuality by "exploiting" it themselves—should they choose to do so— as opposed to letting men reap the rewards.[6]

Conventional wisdom tells us that "old-time" feminists would almost certainly cringe at the notion of the sexual exploitation of women—even if done by women. When confronted by today's feminists, who say it is a measure of the victories won that they *can* choose to exploit themselves, the old-time feminists would argue that these poor lost girls have been co-opted and do a disservice to women by lowering the overall rank of the gender. This clash of ideals appears, in fact, to be the essence of the problem in a nutshell.

The twenty- and even thirty-something women of today grew up in a time of forward-moving sexuality, when the sale of the female body in any number of forms built empires and when some women very publicly took the reigns of that male-driven chariot, riding insatiable waves of desire into mansions of their own. There are lots of reasons, of course, for this turn of events. The Internet and web-cam sites allow women to run their own businesses and offer up "the product" (usually themselves) with a minimum of overhead. In addition, traditional taboos have fallen as cultural lines blur.

Exotic dancers—once participants in an industry that was forbidden enough on its own—have begun to bump up appearance fees by doing a blue movie or two. And today, a previous life as a porn star or a history of "dirty pictures"—once so serious a moral lapse that it cost Miss America her crown—are no longer reasons to keep a girl out of prime time. On the contrary, the release of a sex video starring a hotel heiress before the debut of her reality show appears to have done little more than hype the show. And then there is the nudity.

Blame it on Madonna or call it the "Britney-ization" of America. By any name, the message in the time capsule of today is that sex sells. Magazines and movies are a given, of course. But in recent years traditional role models of all sorts—from rock stars to world-class athletes—have taken off their clothes in a very public fashion as well. Olympians—their celebrated physiques wrapped around the covers of sports magazines—have disrobed to make "feminist statements." It is an approach to the female body that will probably make some women as rich as the men who currently dominate the skin business.

This is the world of young women today. In the light of this everchanging reality, arguments that tend to suggest young women are foolish or part of male-driven conspiracies that lower the esteem of women seem not only to be the outdated view of has-been radicals, but perhaps even a bit paranoid. The women who make such arguments seem out of touch; their battles are the ghosts of a by-gone era. There is also resentment against the perceived conde-scension, because young women—as young people often do—see themselves as independent, intelligent, and capable of making informed choices. In that sense, the aggressive sexuality and nudity of the times, and their desire to be part of it, may simply be the long hair of today.

I am a feminist and a woman deeply concerned about the future of women's rights. As a result, I am both troubled and encouraged by what I have seen in the recent years of this debate. Troubled, because this may be the most serious divide women have faced in recent years. And encouraged, because it is rare today to see the word "feminism" mentioned in connection with anything remotely positive. For better or worse, "do-me feminism" has a growing band of supporters and has launched itself into the debate.

As a woman who grew up during the late 1970s and '80s, my feminist views tend to straddle the divide between "good" and "bad" feminists. I believe, for example, that a woman can dress like a porn star, or a nun, or Madonna, or a biker, and still be a feminist. And yet, like the "old-time" girls, the sexual exploitation of women (and anyone else, for that matter) troubles me. I find pornography particularly disturbing, especially some of the "world's biggest gang-bang" stuff being offered today (involving women who often claim, ironically, that "the choice" to have sex with upwards of 800 men at a time is *feminist*).

But I am also a realist who has gotten tired of seeing Hugh Hefner in a bathrobe and hearing about the millions of dollars men make off women's bodies. And so I reluctantly accept that there may be something to the notion of controlling (even for exploitative purposes) one's body and the profits to be made from it. I also understand on a personal level that it can be very empow-ering to feel that you have taken possession of your sexuality. The trouble for many feminists is that the means often used by young women to announce claim of this possession involves what hard-line feminists would call "exploita-tion." Thus, the differences of opinion reemerge and we are back at the starting point of this debate.

But where does that leave feminism and the women's rights movement?

In a morass, it seems. And yet, while the negative image of "feminists" might easily be repaired with greater tolerance and an inclusive outreach effort that seeks to embrace, rather than divide, women, the future of women's rights seems to be in far greater jeopardy. Critics have long argued that feminism is a middle-class movement, the pet project of elite women with grand ideas. And sadly, of late the movement toward protesting and preserving the rights of women—not to mention advancing the cause—has taken on the feel of a wealthy women's charity.

Genteel. Polite. With battles that are carefully chosen and calmly planned by a close circle of highly educated and roundly celebrated women who have tended to take the high road. All seem to agree that it is a nice way to handle it: not to stoop to the "their level." The problem with this approach, however, is that the high road is rapidly leading women to defeat. In the last year, despite the public pronouncements of women's rights groups to fight, women who care about reproductive freedoms have continued to lose ground as the leaders of once-celebrated women's groups—who seem thrown by the unrelenting guerrilla tactics of antiabortion groups and religious leaders—struggle to find their footing.

We are sliding. As a result, scarce have been the responses to assertions that women who have abortions kill "unborn children" and abstinence is the best way to prevent pregnancy. Focusing the issue on "unborn children" raises the stakes. And maybe that is the reason that so many middle-class women—many of them mothers themselves—have found it difficult to counter this assault directly. But there is an answer.

From 1988 through 1990, I lived in Pennsylvania. For those of you who don't remember, these were the lead-up years to 1992, the year the United States Supreme Court would issue the long-awaited decision in *Planned Parenthood of Southeastern Pennsylvania v. Casey*. Women in America were prickly with anticipation that the precedent of *Roe v. Wade* was about to fall. In anticipation of the Court's decision, local newspapers began running articles on the impact—pro and con—of a ruling that many feared would do away with the choice of abortion. One of the stories I read was by a police sergeant who began her story with six words I have never forgotten: *I am an illegal abortion orphan*, she wrote.

When I think of the current efforts to dismantle the gains made by women and the startling silence that has come from the leadership of women's groups, I wonder if perhaps they are as out of touch with the realities of this desperate war as young women—who simply expect that the privileges they currently enjoy will always be there—say they are. As I listen to religious leaders celebrate the latest victory, what frustrates me is this: Why don't we talk more about the women in the middle of this mess? Illegal abortion orphans are still a possibility, though you wouldn't know it from the lack of urgency the fighters on our side of the wall seem to be giving the issue. If we are going to preserve the rights we have, women have to start "rehumanizing" women as emotionally and completely as pro-life forces have created "children" out of "fetuses."

Obviously, I don't have a crystal ball. But from all I've read in creating this book, if I had to guess at the future for women I would say we stand to lose many more significant battles—and the rights that go with them—if our "leadership" doesn't begin to abandon the niceties of a comfortable life with educated opinions and start waging the kind of aggressive, no-holds-barred guerrilla war that antichoice groups have been riding to victory.

Kate Michelman, the soft-spoken head of NARAL Pro-Choice America, said recently in an interview that she intended to resign, which would give her time to campaign for a democratic nominee for president. But as the votes of Blanche Lincoln and her sixteen colleagues suggest, democrats—though traditionally supporters of women's issues—can't always be relied upon today to tow what was once the party line. The rules of the game are clearly new. And we—women and feminists—need a new game plan if we are going to win.

ENDNOTES FOR EPILOGUE

1 *See* Sheryl Gay Stolberg, *Abortion Vote Leaves Many in Senate Conflicted*, N.Y. TIMES, October 23, 2003, at A14.
2 *See* Katha Pollitt, *Devil Women*, THE NEW YORKER, Feb. 26 & March 4, 1996, pp. 58–64, at p. 58.
3 *See* Jodie T. Allen, *Are Men Obsolete?*, U.S.NEWS & WORLD REPORT, June 23, 2003, at p. 33.
4 *Id.*
5 *See* Dorothy Wickenden, *Sister Acts*, THE NEW YORKER, Feb. 26 & March 4, 1996, pp. 11–12.
6 *See* Virginia Vitzthum, *Stripped of Our Senses*, ELLE, Dec. 2003, pp. 186–188, 284.

INDEX

C

W

Y

Z

ABOUT THE AUTHOR

Debran Rowland is an attorney, a writer, and an artist who earned her law degree at Loyola University of Chicago School of Law. In addition, Ms. Rowland holds a degree in English from Carleton College and an M.A. in cultural anthropology from Columbia University in New York. She has studied at the Art Student's League of New York and her illustrations have been published in *Al Dia* newspaper in addition to other places.

Ms. Rowland has written for *The Korea Times, New York; The New Pittsburgh Courier; Pittsburgh Press*; the *Chicago Tribune*; and, the *Commercial Appeal*. Writing awards include Best News Feature, Chicago Association of Black Journalists, 1991, and the Robert L. Vann award for Best Print News Series, 1988.

Legal academic awards for Ms. Rowland include the American Jurisprudence and *Corpus Secundum* awards. Legal articles written by Ms. Rowland have been published in AMERICAN LAW REPORTS (5th Series); *Loyola University School of Law Public Interest Law Reporter*; and, the *Illinois Bar Examiner*.

She has lived in India, where she taught English to "untouchable" children in a slum, and in Australia, where she covered the Constitutional Convention in 1998. In addition to writing, Ms. Rowland is a volunteer with Chicago Volunteer Legal Services, where she handles civil rights-based immigration appeals in federal court.